SECOND EDITION

Programming Entity Framework

Julia Lerman

Beijing • Cambridge • Farnham • Köln • Sebastopol • Tokyo

Programming Entity Framework, Second Edition
by Julia Lerman

Printed in the United States of America.

Published by O'Reilly Media, Inc., 1005 Gravenstein Highway North, Sebastopol, CA 95472.

O'Reilly books may be purchased for educational, business, or sales promotional use. Online editions are also available for most titles (*http://my.safaribooksonline.com*). For more information, contact our corporate/institutional sales department: 800-998-9938 or *corporate@oreilly.com*.

Editors: Mike Hendrickson and Laurel Ruma
Production Editor: Loranah Dimant
Copyeditor: Audrey Doyle
Proofreader: Sada Preisch
Indexer: Ellen Troutman Zaig
Cover Designer: Karen Montgomery
Interior Designer: David Futato
Illustrator: Robert Romano

Printing History:

February 2009: First Edition.
August 2010: Second Edition.

ISBN: 978-0-596-80726-9

[LSI] [2011-08-12]

1312919683

Table of Contents

Foreword

I first met Julie Lerman (rhymes with "German") while she was visiting the Microsoft campus for a Software Design Review (SDR). An SDR is an event where we invite customers we trust to be representative of a much larger crowd. In this particular case, I was new to the SQL Server division and trying hard to catch up on the raft of technologies Microsoft shipped in the data space for developers. Julie, on the other hand, was a seasoned veteran and not only knew the answers to all of my Entity Framework questions but had already written a book on the topic. That book, *Programming Entity Framework*, was the first edition of the book you're now holding in your hands. Or, if you are a .NET programmer, you know it simply as "THE book on EF."

As the months went on, I ran into Julie more and more. She was researching the second edition of her famous EF book. And by "researching," I mean "pointing out our mistakes." Julie was not only invaluable for teaching customers the real-world ins and outs of EF, she had a way of asking questions about alphas and betas that made us rethink what we were doing in many cases to improve the version of EF that ships with .NET 4 as well as the supporting functionality in Visual Studio 2010. And she was so well respected because of her first EF book that anything she said received extra attention from the EF team in ways I don't see for many senior architects, let alone lowly program managers. Julie had become an ad hoc member of the EF team itself.

My most recent encounter with Julie was by far the most fun. At a talk at the 2010 TechEd in New Orleans, I had the privilege of being Julie's "code monkey," which meant mostly that I fetched her coffee, carried her bags, and wrote her code while she entertained and educated a packed room. In 60 minutes, she did a tour de force tour through nearly all the new features in EF 4.0, driving me through one complete demo every 4 minutes. Normally, this would make an audience's heads spin, but she has such a grasp of the material and such a clear way of presenting it that she had everyone's rapt attention.

It's this same completeness and clarity that you'll find in this book, in chapters ranging from the basics in the details you'll need to write actual applications for your actual business needs. If there is more material to lead you through the basics of the Entity Framework and to be a continuing reference, I don't know what it is.

During her presentation, Julie fielded questions on all manner of EF details and related topics, but the one that made me cringe under the weight of history is the one I always get, too: "Why should we use EF when Microsoft has already given us so many other data access technologies?" Julie's answer came without hesitation: "Because it's the best!"

Now, as a Microsoft employee sensitive to the needs of a wide-range of customers across a wide-range of needs, I have to say that officially you should use the technology that best fits your specific business problem. I can also say that the Entity Framework is the .NET technology against which we're placing all of our future bets and making all of our biggest investments, which means that it's the technology that we hope meets most of your needs now and will meet more of your needs in the future.

But, I have to say, I do like Julie's answer a great deal.

—Chris Sells, SQL Server division, Microsoft Corporation

Preface

In June 2006, I was invited to attend a meet-up for data geeks at Tech Ed North America. As the meet-up was early enough not to compete with the many fun evening parties at Tech Ed, I happily crossed the lovely bridge between the Convention Center and the hotel where the meeting was to take place.

Little did I know I was about to see a new technology from Microsoft's Data Programmability team that was going to be the focus of my attention for the next few years. In addition to other geeky discussions about data access, Pablo Castro, Mike Pizzo, and Britt Johnson (all from Microsoft) talked to us about a new technology that was coming in the next version of ADO.NET. It would allow developers to create their own views of their database and query against these views rather than against the database.

As usual, Tech Ed was overwhelming, so as interesting as this new way of working with data looked to me, I had to put it in a back corner of my mind and let it simmer for a few months. I finally downloaded the preview and began playing with it. What was most fun to me when I started exploring this technology, called Entity Framework, was the lack of serious documentation, which forced me to play with all of its knobs and dials to figure out what was in there and how it worked.

Unlike many in-development technologies from Microsoft, the Entity Framework did not start off with a cool name as did WCF (née Indigo) and ADO.NET Data Services (Astoria). Although it is often hard to give up these early technology nicknames for their final (and relatively boring) names, the Entity Framework has had its "grown-up name" since the beginning.

Over this time, it also became clear how important the Entity Framework and its underlying Entity Data Model are to Microsoft. They are a critical part of Microsoft's strategy for the data access that all of its products perform, whether this is the data that Reporting Services uses to enable us to build reports, the data that comprises Workflow, data in the cloud, or data that we developers want our .NET applications to access.

As the Entity Framework evolved and further CTPs were released, followed by betas, I became quite fond of working against a data model and no longer having to think about the structure of the database I was working against. I began to peel away the top layers of the Entity Framework and discovered that I could make it do nearly anything I wanted as I gained a better understanding of how it worked. When I hit a wall, I asked the Entity Framework team how to get past it, and if there wasn't a way to do so, I camped out on their virtual doorstep until they modified the framework or Designer to enable me to do what I wanted and what I knew other developers would need.

During this time, I was excited to share what I was learning with other developers through the MSDN forums, my blog, conference sessions, and articles. However, I constantly felt restrained by the time or space allotted to me. Conference sessions are generally 75–90 minutes long. Magazine articles tend to be 5–10 pages. I felt as though I was going to self-combust if I couldn't share all of this new information, and so I contacted O'Reilly to ask whether I could write a book about the Entity Framework. My editor on the first edition, John Osborn, was a bit taken aback because for years I had shunned publishers, saying I would have to have lost my mind to write a book. It's not a simple undertaking. But I knew that if I didn't write a book about ADO.NET Entity Framework, I certainly would lose my mind. The time had come. I was so excited, and of course, I had no idea what I was in for!

I spent almost a year writing the book that ended up at a little over 800 pages and more than two pounds on the scale. When the book was released in February 2009, Microsoft was already well underway on the next version of Entity Framework, which was going through major changes. After spending some time with the early releases of what was to become Entity Framework 4, and with some trepidation, I finally decided to revise the book. This was after having enlisted many friends to "please, just shoot me" if I ever talked about writing another book. Thankfully, nobody took me up on the request. They admitted it was because they wanted a new version of my book targeted at the new version of Entity Framework.

Once again, I had no idea what I was in for. This edition has been much more than a revision. I have had to rethink every sentence in the book, throw out entire chapters, add new chapters, rethink and rewrite most of the code samples, and of course, learn about a slew of major features that have been added to Entity Framework. I spent over nine months of constant effort writing this new edition, and now here it is.

Who This Book Is For

This book is written for developers who are familiar with .NET programming, whether they are entirely new to the Entity Framework or have been using it and want to solidify their current understanding as well as go deeper. Throughout the book, I highlight notable changes for developers who have been using the first version of Entity Framework. The first half of the book (Chapters 1–12) covers introductory topics, and the latter half (Chapters 13–27) dives under the covers to give you a deep understanding of what you'll find in the Entity Framework and how it works, as well as how to get the most out of it.

The early walkthroughs, which demonstrate the use of the Entity Framework in a variety of applications (Windows Forms, Windows Presentation Foundation, ASP.NET, WCF services, and WCF Data Services), are written so that you can follow them even if you have never created a particular application type before.

The goal of this book is to help developers not only get up and running with the Entity Framework, but also be empowered to gain granular control over the model and the objects that result through use of the core Entity Framework APIs. This second edition focuses on the version of Entity Framework in Visual Studio 2010 and .NET 4.

Although the book will provide some guidance for using the Entity Framework in your application architecture, it is not a book about architecture. Instead, the book attempts to provide you with the information and knowledge you need to use the Entity Framework to solve your specific domain problems.

Because of the vast scope of the Entity Framework, many topics on tools that leverage the Entity Framework, such as WCF RIA Services (a.k.a. Astoria) and SQL Modeling, are touched on but not covered in depth.

Some of the Entity Framework's features are comparable to LINQ to SQL and other object relational models such as NHibernate and LLBLGen Pro. Apart from a few paragraphs in Chapter 1, this book does not directly position the Entity Framework against these object relational models.

All of the code samples in *Programming Entity Framework*, Second Edition, are provided in C#. Where there are significant syntax differences, Visual Basic is included as well.

How This Book Is Organized

Programming Entity Framework, Second Edition, focuses on two ways for you to learn. If you learn best by example, you'll find many walkthroughs and code samples throughout the book; if you're always looking for the big picture, you'll also find chapters that dive deep into conceptual information. I have tried to balance the walkthroughs and conceptual information I provide so that you will never get too much of one at a time.

The first half of the book is introductory, and the second half digs much deeper. Following is a brief description of each chapter:

Chapter 1, *Introducing the ADO.NET Entity Framework*
: This chapter provides an overview of the ADO.NET Entity Framework—where it came from, what problems it attempts to solve, and the classic "10,000-foot view" of what it looks like. The chapter also addresses the most frequently asked

questions about the Entity Framework, such as how it fits into the .NET Framework, what databases it works with, what types of applications you can write with it, how it differs from object relational models, and how it works with the rest of ADO.NET.

Chapter 2, *Exploring the Entity Data Model*
: The Entity Data Model (EDM) lies at the core of the Entity Framework. This chapter explains what the EDM is, and teaches you how to create one using the EDM Wizard and then manipulate your model using the Designer. You will also get a walkthrough of the various parts of the EDM, viewing it through the Designer or through its raw XML.

Chapter 3, *Querying Entity Data Models*
: The Entity Framework provides a number of methods for querying against the EDM—LINQ to Entities, Entity SQL with `ObjectQuery`, `EntityClient`, and a few more. Each method has its own benefits. In this chapter, you will learn the basics for leveraging the various query modes by requesting the same data using each mechanism. You will also learn the pros and cons for choosing one method over another, as well as gain an understanding of what happens behind the scenes in between query execution and the creation of objects from the data that results.

Chapter 4, *Exploring LINQ to Entities in Greater Depth*
: With the query basics in hand, you can now learn how to perform different types of tricks with querying: projection, filtering, aggregates, and so forth. Because the objects you are querying are related, you can also query across these relationships. This chapter will walk you through a great variety of queries focusing on LINQ to Entities. This is by no means an exhaustive depiction of every type of query you can perform, but it will give you a huge head start.

Chapter 5, *Exploring Entity SQL in Greater Depth*
: This chapter revisits the LINQ to Entities queries from Chapter 4 and shows how to express the same types of queries using Entity SQL. You'll also learn some specific tips about working with Entity SQL in this chapter.

Chapter 6, *Modifying Entities and Saving Changes*
: This chapter presents a high-level view of how the Entity Framework tracks changes to entities, processes updates, and builds the final queries that are executed at the database. By having a better understanding of the Entity Framework's default functionality, you will be better prepared to address common concerns regarding security and performance. Additionally, understanding the default process will make the following chapter on stored procedures much more meaningful.

Chapter 7, *Using Stored Procedures with the EDM*
: This chapter is the first of two to dig into using stored procedures in the Entity Framework. The EDM Designer provides support for one set of scenarios, and that is what is covered in this chapter. Chapter 16 covers the set of scenarios that require more effort.

Chapter 8, *Implementing a More Real-World Model*
: Up to this point in the book, you will have been working with a very simplistic database and model so that you can focus on all of the new tools. This chapter introduces a larger model and database that support the fictitious travel adventure company BreakAway Geek Adventures and which you will use throughout the rest of the book. With this model, you will get a better understanding of building and customizing a model. Chapters 14 and 15 will go even further into customizing the model with advanced modeling and mappings.

Chapter 9, *Data Binding with Windows Forms and WPF Applications*
: This chapter provides two walkthroughs for using the Entity Framework to perform data binding in Windows Forms and Windows Presentation Foundation (WPF). In the course of these walkthroughs, you'll learn a lot of tips and tricks that are specific to doing data binding with Entity Framework objects, as well as expand your knowledge of the Entity Framework along the way.

Chapter 10, *Working with Object Services*
: The Entity Framework's Object Services API provides all of the functionality behind working with the objects that are realized from the data shaped by your Entity Data Model. Although the most critical of Object Services' features is its ability to keep track of changes to entity objects and manage relationships between them, it offers many additional features as well. This chapter provides an overview of all of Object Services' responsibilities, how it impacts most of the work you do with the Entity Framework, and how you can use these features directly to impact how the Entity Framework operates. Later chapters focus even more deeply on particular areas within Object Services.

Chapter 11, *Customizing Entities*
: So far, the objects you will have been working with are based on the default classes that the Entity Framework generates directly from the model, but you don't need to be limited to what's in the objects. There are plenty of opportunities for customizing the code-generated classes. This chapter walks you through how to take advantage of these extensibility points. It is also possible to completely avoid the generated classes and use your own custom classes, an option we will cover in Chapter 13.

Chapter 12, *Data Binding with RAD ASP.NET Applications*
: It's time to create another application with the Entity Framework. There are a lot of hurdles to overcome when using the Entity Framework in an ASP.NET application that allows users to edit data. The `EntityDataSource` control is part of the family of ASP.NET `DataSource` controls that you can configure in the UI and that will automate data access and updating for you. This chapter will show you how to use this control. You'll also get a chance to use ASP.NET Dynamic Data Controls in this chapter. Later chapters will teach you what you need to know to overcome these hurdles yourself, and Chapter 27 leverages this knowledge to address building layered ASP.NET applications rather than putting the logic in the UI.

Chapter 13, *Creating and Using POCO Entities*
: A critical advancement to Entity Framework in .NET 4 is its support for Plain Old CLR Objects (POCOs). The POCO support means that entity classes are not required to inherit from Entity Framework's `EntityObject` class. Building POCOs opens the door for a more agile architecture, unit testing, repositories, and persistence ignorance, all while continuing to benefit from the Entity Framework. This chapter provides an introduction to Entity Framework's POCO support. Later chapters will leverage POCOs to show alternative patterns, build repositories and tests, and consume the POCOs in a variety of application types.

Chapter 14, *Customizing Entity Data Models Using the EDM Designer*
: One of the most important features of the Entity Data Model is the ability to customize it to shape your data structure in a way that is more useful than working directly against the database schema. This chapter walks through many of the ways you can achieve this with the Designer, demonstrating how to implement a variety of inheritance mappings, create an entity that maps to multiple tables, build complex types, and more. If you are following along with the walkthroughs, most of the modifications you make to the sample model in this chapter you will use for applications you'll build in later chapters.

Chapter 15, *Defining EDM Mappings That Are Not Supported by the Designer*
: The Entity Framework model supports even more ways to map back to the database but, unfortunately, not all are supported by the Designer. In this chapter, you'll learn about the most common types of mappings that you might want to use but will have to open up the raw XML to implement. Among these are `DefiningQuery`, `QueryView`, and even nonexistent database views and stored procedures that you can define directly in the Entity Framework metadata.

Chapter 16, *Gaining Additional Stored Procedure and View Support in the Raw XML*
: Chapter 7 covers the stored procedure scenarios that the Designer supports, but you can achieve much more if you are willing to crack open the model's raw XML and perform additional customizations. This chapter will walk you through adding "virtual" store queries and stored procedures into the model, and taking advantage of other features that will make the model work for you, rather than being constrained by the Designer.

Chapter 17, *Using EntityObjects in WCF Services*
: Like ASP.NET, using the Entity Framework in web and WCF services provides a number of challenges. In this chapter, you will learn how to build and consume a WCF service that interacts solely with `EntityObjects`. If you have never created services before, have no fear. The walkthroughs will help you with step-by-step instructions. You will also create a WCF Data Service and get a quick look at WCF RIA Services. This chapter is the first of two that address building services.

Chapter 18, *Using POCOs and Self-Tracking Entities in WCF Services*
: The new POCO support in Entity Framework 4 makes building WCF Services a lot simpler. This chapter enhances the POCO entities you built in Chapter 13 and

uses them in a revised implementation of the WCF Services you created in Chapter 17. You'll also learn about some of the differences when building WCF Data Services and WCF RIA Services with POCOs.

The preceding chapters will have provided you with a solid base of understanding for working with the Entity Framework. Starting with Chapter 19, you will learn about the Entity Framework's advanced topics:

Chapter 19, *Working with Relationships and Associations*
: The Entity Data Model is based on Entity Relationship Modeling, which is about entities and relationships. Relationships are a critical part of the model and how the Entity Framework performs its functions. To really understand and control the Entity Framework and avoid hurting your head when the relationships don't behave the way you might expect, you will benefit from a deep comprehension of how relationships work in the model and your Entity Framework code. This chapter will provide you with that understanding.

Chapter 20, *Real World Apps: Connections, Transactions, Performance, and More*
: Up to this point, you have seen bits and pieces of code out of the context of real-world applications. But how does the Entity Framework fit in with the everyday concerns of software developers? This chapter will address some of the many questions developers ask after learning the basics about the Entity Framework. How do you control connections? Is there any connection pooling? Are database calls transactional? What about security? How's the performance?

Chapter 21, *Manipulating Entities with ObjectStateManager and MetadataWorkspace*
: This is another chapter where you get to dig even further into the APIs to interact with your objects in the same way that many of the internal functions do. With the two classes featured in this chapter, you can write code to generically work with entities or raw data whether you want to create reusable code for your apps or write utilities. There are some hefty samples in this chapter.

Chapter 22, *Handling Exceptions*
: Hard as we try to write perfect code, things can still go wrong in our applications, which is why we need exception handling. The Entity Framework provides a set of its own exceptions to help you deal with the unique problems that may occur when working with entities—poorly written queries, entities that are missing required related objects, or even a problem in the database.

Chapter 23, *Planning for Concurrency Problems*
: This chapter follows up what you learned about exception handling in Chapter 22 with details on a particular type of exception: the `OptimisticConcurrencyException`. In addition to typical coding problems, data access highlights another arena of issues regarding concurrency: when multiple people are editing and updating data. The Entity Framework supports optimistic concurrency and uses this exception to detect these problems. The chapter will show you how to prepare for concurrency issues and take advantage of this exception.

Chapter 24, *Building Persistent Ignorant, Testable Applications*
: Chapter 13 introduced you to Entity Framework's POCO support. Chapter 24 shows you where the POCO support really shines. Here you'll get a chance to use a pattern that leverages POCO support. You will create repositories and a Unit of Work and build unit tests against your Entity Framework code. You'll get to use the repository in some applications in later chapters.

Chapter 25, *Domain-Centric Modeling*
: You'll find more new .NET 4 and Visual Studio 2010 goodness in this chapter as well as a look to the future. You are no longer required to build database-first models. The EDM Designer in Visual Studio 2010 supports model-first design. Build your model in the Designer and then automatically create a database schema from the model. In this chapter, you'll learn a lot more about working with the Designer. This chapter also takes a look at two not-yet-released technologies: Entity Framework's code first and SQL Modeling's "M." Both of these technologies let you use Entity Framework without depending on a physical XML-based model.

At this point in the book, you will have learned quite a lot about how the Entity Framework functions and how to work with the objects and the model in a granular way. The final two chapters focus on challenges and solutions for using the Entity Framework in enterprise applications. The book concludes with three appendixes: one that serves as a guide to the assemblies and namespaces of the Entity Framework, another that highlights unexpected behaviors when data-binding complex types, and a third that looks more deeply into the XML of the model's metadata.

Chapter 26, *Using Entities in Layered Client-Side Applications*
: The earlier client application walkthroughs (Windows Forms and WPF) focused on simple architectures to get you started with data binding. Most medium to large applications are not written in this way, but rather separate their logic and data layers from the UI. This chapter will look at some of the specific features you can take advantage of and challenges you might face when architecting Windows and WPF applications to keep the data access and business logic out of the user interface. The chapter focuses on a sample WPF application using the repositories from Chapter 24.

Chapter 27, *Building Layered Web Applications*
: Chapter 12 focused on building RAD ASP.NET apps using the `EntityDataSource` control to avoid some of the issues with change tracking across tiers in the Entity Framework. Now that you have learned much more about working with entities, it is time to address these challenges head-on and learn how you can build ASP.NET application layers. This chapter begins by addressing the specific issues that the ASP.NET `Page` life cycle poses for entities, and then walks through two solutions that leverage the repositories from Chapter 24. The first is an ASP.NET Web Forms application that is built without the support of data source controls. The second is an ASP.NET MVC application that focuses on keeping data access code out of

the controller. The samples in this chapter provide a first step toward concepts that will help you architect applications to fit your own domain model.

Appendix A, *Entity Framework Assemblies and Namespaces*
: This appendix is a guide to the physical files that are part of the Entity Framework and each namespace in the programming model.

Appendix B, *Data-Binding with Complex Types*
: In Chapter 14, you learn how to create complex types in the model. Complex types have some interesting (and often unexpected) behavior in data-binding scenarios. This appendix will prepare you for what to expect.

Appendix C, *Additional Details About Entity Data Model Metadata*
: Chapter 2 goes into plenty of detail about the model's metadata, but if you are hardcore and want to dig a little further into the raw XML, this appendix should satisfy your cravings.

What You Need to Use This Book

This book focuses on the release of Entity Framework that is part of Microsoft Visual Studio 2010 and .NET 4. You can use any of the Visual Studio 2010 versions, from Express through Ultimate.

Although the Entity Framework can work with many database providers, the `SqlClient` provider is part of Visual Studio 2010, and therefore all of the samples here are based on SQL Server. You can use SQL Server Express or Standard, and although the Entity Framework runtime will recognize versions 2000, 2005, and 2008, the design tools will not work with SQL Server 2000. This book was written against SQL Server 2008 Standard.

Following is a specific list of system requirements:

- Windows XP with SP2, Windows Server 2003, Windows Vista and SP1, or Windows 7
- Microsoft SQL Server 2005, Microsoft SQL Server 2005 Express Edition, Microsoft SQL Server 2008, or Microsoft SQL Server 2008 Express Edition
- Microsoft Visual Studio 2010

This Book's Website

Visit *http://www.ProgrammingEntityFramework.com/* (also available at *http://www.LearnEntityFramework.com/*) for downloads, errata, links to resources, and other information. In the Downloads area, you will find:

- Scripts for creating the sample databases used in this book.
- The sample applications from the book. I will do my best to provide Visual Basic versions of many of the book's samples. Note that there are also hundreds of small code samples in the book. In general, you will not find these small examples replicated on the website, although I will provide some of them for varying reasons.

Conventions Used in This Book

The following typographical conventions are used in this book:

Italic
: Indicates new terms, URLs, email addresses, filenames, file extensions, pathnames, directories, and Unix utilities

`Constant width`
: Indicates commands, options, switches, variables, attributes, keys, functions, types, classes, namespaces, methods, modules, properties, parameters, values, objects, events, event handlers, XML tags, HTML tags, macros, the contents of files, or the output from commands

`Constant width bold`
: Shows commands or other text that should be typed literally by the user

`Constant width italic`
: Shows text that should be replaced with user-supplied values

This icon signifies a tip, suggestion, or general note.

This icon indicates a warning or caution.

VB
: This icon indicates a Visual Basic code sample.

C#
: This icon indicates a C# code sample.

Using Code Examples

This book is here to help you get your job done. In general, you may use the code in this book in your programs and documentation. You do not need to contact us for permission unless you're reproducing a significant portion of the code. For example, writing a program that uses several chunks of code from this book does not require permission. Selling or distributing a CD-ROM of examples from O'Reilly books *does* require permission. Answering a question by citing this book and quoting example code does not require permission. Incorporating a significant amount of example code from this book into your product's documentation *does* require permission.

We appreciate, but do not require, attribution. An attribution usually includes the title, author, publisher, and ISBN. For example: "*Programming Entity Framework*, Second Edition, by Julia Lerman. Copyright 2010 Julia Lerman, 978-0-596-80726-9."

If you feel your use of code examples falls outside fair use or the permission given here, feel free to contact us at *permissions@oreilly.com*.

Safari® Books Online

Safari Books Online is an on-demand digital library that lets you easily search over 7,500 technology and creative reference books and videos to find the answers you need quickly.

With a subscription, you can read any page and watch any video from our library online. Read books on your cell phone and mobile devices. Access new titles before they are available for print, and get exclusive access to manuscripts in development and post feedback for the authors. Copy and paste code samples, organize your favorites, download chapters, bookmark key sections, create notes, print out pages, and benefit from tons of other time-saving features.

O'Reilly Media has uploaded this book to the Safari Books Online service. To have full digital access to this book and others on similar topics from O'Reilly and other publishers, sign up for free at *http://my.safaribooksonline.com*.

Comments and Questions

Please address comments and questions concerning this book to the publisher:

O'Reilly Media, Inc.
1005 Gravenstein Highway North
Sebastopol, CA 95472
800-998-9938 (in the United States or Canada)
707-829-0515 (international or local)
707-829-0104 (fax)

We have a web page for this book, where we list errata, examples, and any additional information. You can access this page at:

http://www.oreilly.com/catalog/9780596807269

To comment or ask technical questions about this book, send email to:

bookquestions@oreilly.com

For more information about our books, conferences, Resource Centers, and the O'Reilly Network, see our website at:

http://www.oreilly.com/

Acknowledgments

And now for the most rewarding writing task after completing over 800 pages of technical writing—thanking the Academy. My academy is a host of bright, generous, and dedicated geeks (and a few nongeeks) who have helped make this book the best it can be.

First nods go to the technical reviewers. These are the folks who were willing to read the book in its roughest format and provide feedback to help me make it more useful and comprehensible to you, the readers of the final version. The award for helping to keep me from exposing myself to humiliation over my nascent C# skills goes to Wesley Bakker, a Dutch developer who does code reviews for a living. I learned a lot from Wes and am grateful for his patience and kid-glove handling of my poor ego. I also had a number of EF and EF 4 newbies on board to help ensure that I didn't make any leaps without bringing them along. You who are new to EF should thank them as well: Camey Combs, Suzanne Shushereba, Doug Holland, and John McConnell. Ward Bell's brilliant architectural mind was displayed in comments that nearly exceeded my own text. He kept me honest and kept me thinking. Everyone should email Ward and beg him to write a book. I don't care what the topic is. Ward has deep EF knowledge, as does Per Okvist, whose feedback was also invaluable. Two database gurus were enormously helpful: Bob Beauchemin and Anil Das. Their meticulous minds helped me in areas that reached much further than discussions about database specifics.

I also brought in some big guns to look at particular chapters in their area of expertise. Thanks so much to Greg Young, Bobby Johnson, Jarod Ferguson, and Mike Campbell for helping me with my education in persistence ignorance and related topics and for looking over the critical chapter on PI and testing to make sure that I had learned my lessons well. I was close, but they helped guide me where I had strayed. K. Scott Allen and Imar Spaanjaars, both ASP.NET gurus, provided some additional guidance and a read-through of a number of chapters.

And then there was the real editing—the organization and flow of the text. John Osborn, who was the editor on the first edition of this book, was engaged to edit this edition as well. It's hard for me to express my gratitude for the incredible dedication and expertise he provided. Even though I thought myself much more experienced this time around, John took every chapter and reorganized it, clarifying its focus and flow. He is an incredible editor and I was very lucky to have him work on my book again.

Along the way, of course, I had help from so many people at Microsoft on the Entity Framework team and beyond. There is no way I can list them all, but here's my best shot (not in any special order): Danny Simmons, Elisa Flasko, Noam Ben-Ami, Diego Vega, Kati Iceva, Srikanth Mandadi, Alex James, Jarek Kowalski, Jeff Derstadt, Rowan Miller, Craig Lee, David Annesley-DeWinter, Adi Unnithan, Andrew Peters, Shyam Pather, and Tim Laverty. Forgive me if I've neglected to mention someone.

You'll find that I have used (and recommended) a few additional tools throughout the book. The publishers generously provided me free licenses for which I'm grateful. The recommendations are because they are great tools, not because I didn't have to pay for them. The tools include LINQPad (*http://linqpad.net*), written by another O'Reilly author, Joseph Albahari; and ReSharper from JetBrains (*http://jetbrains.com*). ReSharper was my first line of defense for ensuring that my C# code wasn't an embarrassment, while Wesley Bakker was my second. I learned so much from both of them. Entity Framework Profiler (*http://EFProf.com*) is an awesome tool for keeping track of what's going on in your database when using Entity Framework. I also used two tools for producing images in this book. The first is Snagit from TechSmith (*http://techsmith.com*), which was completely invaluable for capturing and editing screenshots. The second is Balsamiq Mockups (*http://balsamiq.com*), which enabled me to have a little fun creating mock-ups of application UIs in a number of chapters. Finally, thanks to Red Gate (*http://red-gate.com*), a great company with many awesome tools. For this book, I used its .NET Reflector to inspect some assemblies, and I've used their SQL Packager for creating a simple-to-install version of the sample databases for you to use.

My publisher has, as usual, provided great support for me. I had not one, but two editors—this is not the job of editing the book, but of counseling me and holding my hand throughout the process. Thanks to Laurel Ruma (who moved on to become O'Reilly's über–Government 2.0 guru), and Mike Hendrickson who brings years of experience (not saying he's old) for keeping me focused and helping me avoid being taken away in a funny white coat. I was also lucky to have Audrey Doyle as my copy editor again. She did an amazing job on the first edition, so I begged O'Reilly to contract her again. Lucky me, they did. (She is going to hate that last nonsentence; I dare you to leave it in, Audrey.)

If you read the Preface of my first book, you'll be happy to know that this time around I have no heart-wrenching pet losses to report, so you can put away the tissues you may have prepared yourself with. In fact, we adopted a teenage Newfoundland dog named Sampson just as I began to write this edition. Thank goodness for his needed afternoon walks and his constantly entertaining personality, without which I'd have gone completely mad during the time I have been writing this book. You can meet this silly boy on my blog at *http://thedatafarm.com/blog/tags/Sampson*.

Somehow I have managed to retain my patient husband, Rich Flynn, to whom I promised "don't worry, never again" when I finished the first edition. He has just suffered through another year of spaghetti, dirty dishes, ravaged potato chip supplies, and having to cede a little more space in bed as my waistline expanded thanks to my life in the computer chair (and all those potato chips).

And finally, thanks to all of the incredible support that has come from the .NET community. I'm very proud of the first edition of the book, and each private "thank you" or complimentary public review on places like Amazon.com and your blogs has meant so much to me. This truly kept me going through what my Twitter followers know only too well was an arduous process in writing this second edition.

Oh, and to anyone who gave me chocolate...thanks!

Author Note for Third Printing, August 2011

In this new age of the e-book, I'm happy to see Programming Entity Framework, Second Edition, enter its third printing. There have been some changes to Entity Framework since this edition was first published in August 2011 which you should be aware of. As this is only a reprint, not a new edition, I'm unable to incorporate the updates into this book, but am able to provide this short overview for you.

Entity Framework 4.1 (Code First and DbContext) Has Released

Chapter 25 briefly discusses the Entity Framework Feature Community Technical Preview (CTP) which included the Code First modeling strategy and DbContext API. Code First and the DbContext API were wrapped into what is now known as Entity Framework 4.1 and were released in April 2011. You can learn much about using Code First and the other EF 4.1 features at *http://msdn.com/data/ef*. Watch my book blog, *learnentityframework.com*, for news about some upcoming projects I'm working on around Entity Framework 4.1.

In May 2011, Microsoft gave us a preview of updates to the EDM Designer called the EF Power Tools CTP1. The most interesting designer feature in this CTP allows developers to reverse engineer an existing database into Code First style classes and a DbContext. Some additional designer features were included as well. See the team blog post, EF Power Tools CTP1 Released, at *http://blogs.msdn.com/b/adonet/archive/2011/05/18/ef-power-tools-ctp1-released.aspx* for more information.

After the release of EF 4.1, the team also shared the work they are doing on Code First database migrations. See their blog post titled, Code First Migrations: August 2011 CTP Released, at *http://blogs.msdn.com/b/adonet/archive/2011/07/27/code-first-migrations-august-2011-ctp-released.aspx*.

Entity Framework June 2011 CTP

At the end of June 2011, the Entity Framework team released another CTP which incorporates things they are working on for an upcoming release (at this time, no dates have been announced) of Entity Framework. Much of what's in the June 2011 CTP fixes features that we have been requesting for a while. For example, the most requested Entity Framework feature on Microsoft's Connect site is enum support. Enum support is added in this CTP. But there's much more in the CTP as well. Some examples are: auto-compiled LINQ queries, support for spatial data types, multiple resultsets support for stored procedures. There have been many improvements to the designer including the ability to create multiple views of an Entity Data Model. The CTP was released alongside another CTP for WCF Data Services which included many improvements to that technology as well. Take a look at the EF team's blog post, Announcing the Microsoft Entity Framework June 2011 CTP, at *http://blogs.msdn.com/b/adonet/archive/2011/06/30/announcing-the-microsoft-entity-framework-june-2011-ctp.aspx* .

CHAPTER 1

Introducing the ADO.NET Entity Framework

At Microsoft's November 2009 Professional Developer Conference, the legendary Don Box, a Distinguished Engineer at Microsoft, said, "If you're a .NET developer Entity Framework is where we're going. We're there. Get on board, it's time."

Yes, it's time.

Developers spend far too much of their precious time worrying about their backend database, its tables and their relationships, the names and parameters of stored procedures and views, as well as the schema of the data that they return. For .NET developers, Microsoft's new Entity Framework changes the game so that you no longer have to be concerned with the details of the data store as you write applications. You can focus on the task of writing those applications, rather than accessing the data.

The ADO.NET Entity Framework has shifted into becoming Microsoft's core data access platform for building .NET applications. It was released in July 2008 as part of the Visual Studio 2008 Service Pack 1 and .NET 3.5 Service Pack 1, two years after Microsoft announced it at its TechEd 2006 Conference. As a version 1 product, Entity Framework was greeted at first with skepticism, and its adoption was far from sweeping. However, with the release of Visual Studio 2010 and .NET 4 in April 2010, a much improved Entity Framework finally got the attention and excited responses of many developers and .NET teams, who are now quickly jumping aboard.

Although ADO.NET retains its existing data access, as Microsoft's core data access strategy going forward the Entity Framework will receive the bulk of the innovation and resources from the Business Platform Division (which owns all of the data programmability tasks at Microsoft). It's an important technology for Microsoft, and one that you should not ignore. Entity Framework is also being integrated into many of Microsoft's products, whether the product uses Entity Framework to support its own features, such as with Commerce Server 2009's Multi-Channel Commerce

Foundation,[*] or whether the product has support for interacting with the Entity Framework, such as with SQL Server Modeling.

Why do we need a new data access technology? After forcing developers to switch from one data access technology to another—from DAO to RDO to ADO and then to ADO.NET—with ADO.NET Microsoft seemed to have finally settled on a single tool in which developers could invest. With each release of Visual Studio and the .NET Framework, ADO.NET has been enhanced and added to, but has remained backward compatible all along. Our investment has been safe.

And it remains safe, even though it will be stagnant. The Entity Framework is another enhancement to ADO.NET, giving developers an added mechanism for accessing data and working with the results in addition to `DataReaders` and `DataSets`.

But Microsoft went as far as it could with the `DataSet` paradigm. The next step was to enable developers to focus on a domain model while .NET would automate the redundant tasks of database interaction.

In this chapter, you will learn about the critical pieces of the Entity Framework, the Entity Data Model, entity classes, the core .NET APIs, and Visual Studio design tools. You will also learn about how Entity Framework fits in with ADO.NET's `DataSets` and LINQ to SQL. Finally, you will learn about many of the changes and additions to Entity Framework in Visual Studio 2010 and .NET 4, and how so many of the pain points in the first version have been eliminated.

The Entity Relationship Model: Programming Against a Model, Not the Database

A central benefit of the Entity Framework is that it frees you from being concerned with the structure of your database. All of your data access and storage is done against a conceptual data model that reflects your own business objects.

With ADO.NET `DataReaders` and many other data access technologies, you spend a lot of time writing code to get data from a database, read the results, pick out bits of data you want, and push them into your business classes. With the Entity Framework, you no longer query against the schema of a database, but rather against a schema that reflects your own business model. As data is retrieved, you are not forced to reason out columns and rows and push them into objects, because they are returned as objects. When it's time to save changes back to the database, you have to save only those objects. The Entity Framework does the necessary work of translating your objects back into the rows and columns of the relational store. The Entity Framework does this part of the job for you, similar to the way an Object Relational Mapping (ORM) tool works.

[*] See *http://msdn.microsoft.com/en-us/library/dd327929(v=CS.90).aspx*.

The Entity Framework uses a model called an Entity Data Model (EDM), which evolved from Entity Relationship Modeling (ERM), a concept that has been used in database development for many years.

The Entity Data Model's Roots

Microsoft's Entity Framework evolved from a methodology known as Entity Relationship Modeling (ERM), which has been trapped on whiteboards for more than 30 years. An ERM defines a schema of entities and their relationships with one another. Entities are not the same as objects. Entities define the schema of an object, but not its behavior. So, an entity is something like the schema of a table in your database, except that it describes the schema of your business objects. Developers have drawn ERMs for years to help us figure out how to transpose the structured tabular data of a database into business objects we can program against.

No mention of ERM is complete without a nod to Dr. Peter Chen, who is credited with the first definitive paper on ERM in 1976: "The Entity-Relationship Model—Toward a Unified View of Data" (*http://csc.lsu.edu/news/erd.pdf*).

With a host of database gurus in its ranks, Microsoft Research began to devise a way to automate the process of bridging a conceptual model and database schemas. And it needed to be a two-way street so that developers could retrieve data from the database, populate entities, and persist changes back into the database.

In June 2006, Microsoft Research published its first paper on the EDM, its answer to ERM. The paper's authors include database legend Jim Gray, who tragically disappeared while sailing off the coast of San Francisco Bay in 2007.

The Entity Data Model: A Client-Side Data Model

An Entity Data Model (EDM) is a client-side data model and it is the core of the Entity Framework. It is not the same as the database model, which belongs to the database. The data model in the application describes the structure of your business objects. It's as though you were given permission to restructure the database tables and views in your enterprise's database so that the tables and relationships look more like your business domain rather than the normalized schema that is designed by database administrators.

Figure 1-1 shows the schema of a typical set of tables in a database. `PersonalDetails` provides additional information about a `Person` that the database administrator has chosen to put into a separate table for the sake of scalability. `SalesPerson` is a table that is used to provide additional information for those who are salespeople.

Working with this data from an application requires queries that are full of inner joins and outer joins to access the additional data about `Person` records. Or you will access a variety of predefined stored procedures and views, which might each require a different set of parameters and return data that is shaped in a variety of ways.

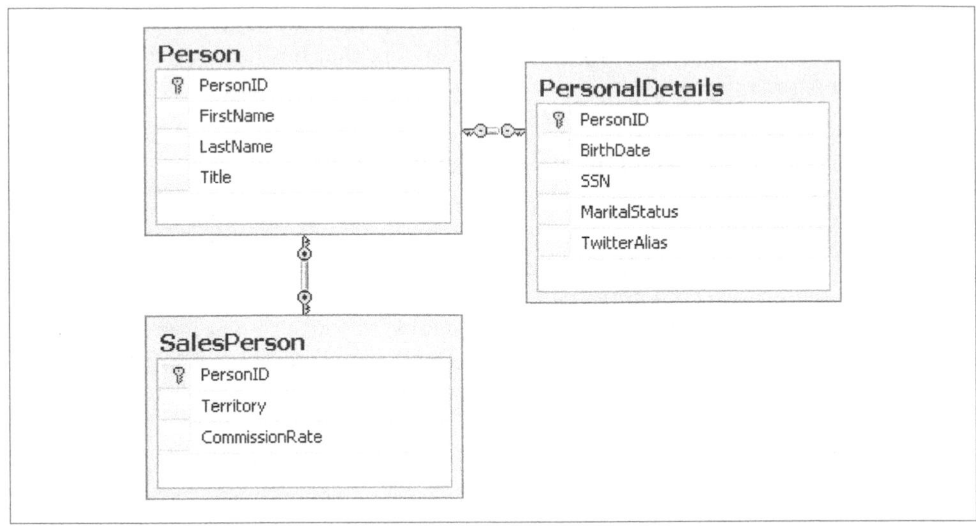

Figure 1-1. Schema of normalized database tables

A T-SQL query to retrieve a set of SalesPerson records along with their personal details might look something like this:

```
SELECT      SalesPerson.*, PersonalDetails.*, Person.*
FROM        Person
            INNER JOIN PersonalDetails
            ON Person.PersonID = PersonalDetails.PersonID
               INNER JOIN SalesPerson ON Person.PersonID = SalesPerson.PersonID
```

Imagine that a particular application could have its own view of what you wish the database looked like. Figure 1-2 reshapes the schema.

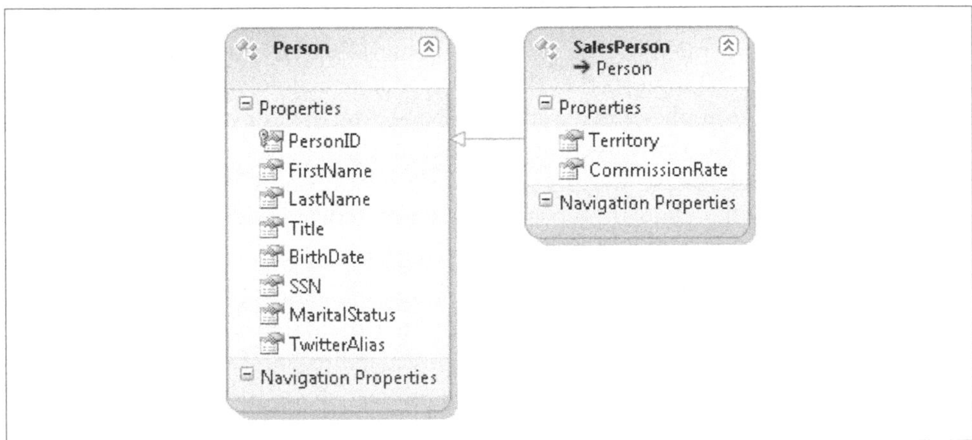

Figure 1-2. Person data shaped to match your business objects

All of the fields from `PersonalDetails` are now part of `Person`. And `SalesPerson` is doing something that is not even possible in a database: it is deriving from `Person`, just as you would in an object model.

Now imagine that you can write a LINQ query that looks like this:

```
from p in People.OfType<SalesPerson>() select p
```

In return, you will have a set of `SalesPerson` objects with all of the properties defined by this model (see Figure 1-3).

Person ID:	2
Commission Rate:	25
First Name:	Willy
Last Name:	Loman
Title:	Mr
Birth Date:	3/1/1920
Marital Status:	Married
SSN:	000-11-2222
Territory:	NYC
Twitter Alias:	WillyLoman

Figure 1-3. The SalesPerson object

LINQ exists only in the C# and Visual Basic languages. With the Entity Framework there is another way to express queries, which not only allows you to use other languages, but also provides additional benefits that you can take advantage of as necessary. It's called Entity SQL, and you will learn much more about it and LINQ to Entities in Chapters 3 through 5.

This is the crux of how the Entity Framework can remove the pain of having not only to interact with the database, but also to translate the tabular data into objects.

.NET is but one tool that uses an EDM. The next version of SQL Server will use an EDM for Reporting Services and you will soon begin to see other Microsoft applications that will adopt the EDM concept as well. In fact, you will find that model-driven development in general is getting more and more attention from Microsoft.

When working with the Entity Framework, you will implement an EDM that is particular to the Entity Framework. In the Entity Framework, an EDM is represented by a single XML file at design time that is split into a set of three XML files at runtime, only one of which represents a conceptual model. The other two provide metadata that enables Entity Framework to interact with a database. You'll learn much more about this metadata in Chapter 2.

Entities: Blueprints for Business Classes

The items described by an EDM are known as *entities*. Classes that are generated from the model entities, along with their instantiated object, are also referred to as entities but are often called *entity classes* or *entity objects*. The generated entity classes differ from typical business classes in that they have properties but no behavior apart from methods to enable change tracking.

Figure 1-4 shows the class diagram for the `Person` and `SalesPerson` classes that the model shown in Figure 1-2 would generate automatically. Each class has a factory method (e.g., CreatePerson) as well as methods used to notify the Entity Framework when a property changes.

With the classes the Entity Framework generates, you can add your own business logic, pull the results into business objects of your own, and even link your business objects to the EDM, replacing the generated classes. But by definition, the entity classes describe only their schema.

In addition to being able to reshape the entities in a data model as with the inheritance hierarchy shown in Figure 1-2, you can define relationships between entities. Figure 1-5 adds a `Customer` entity to the model which also derives from `Person` as well as an `Order` entity. Notice the relationship lines between `SalesPerson` and `Order`, showing a one-to-many relationship between them. There is also a one-to-many relationship between `Customer` and `Order`.

When you write queries against this version of the model, you don't need to use `JOIN`s. The model provides navigation between the entities.

The following LINQ to Entities query retrieves order information along with information about the customer. It navigates into the `Customer` property of the `Order` to get the `FirstName` and `LastName` of the `Customer`.

```
from o in context.Orders
select new {o.OrderID,o.OrderNumber,o.Customer.FirstName,o.Customer.LastName}
```

Once that data is in memory, you can navigate through each object and its properties, such as `myOrder.Customer.LastName`, just as readily.

The Entity Framework also lets you retrieve graphs, which means you can return shaped data such as a `Customer` with all of its `Order` details already attached.

These are some of the major benefits to querying against a data model, rather than directly against the database.

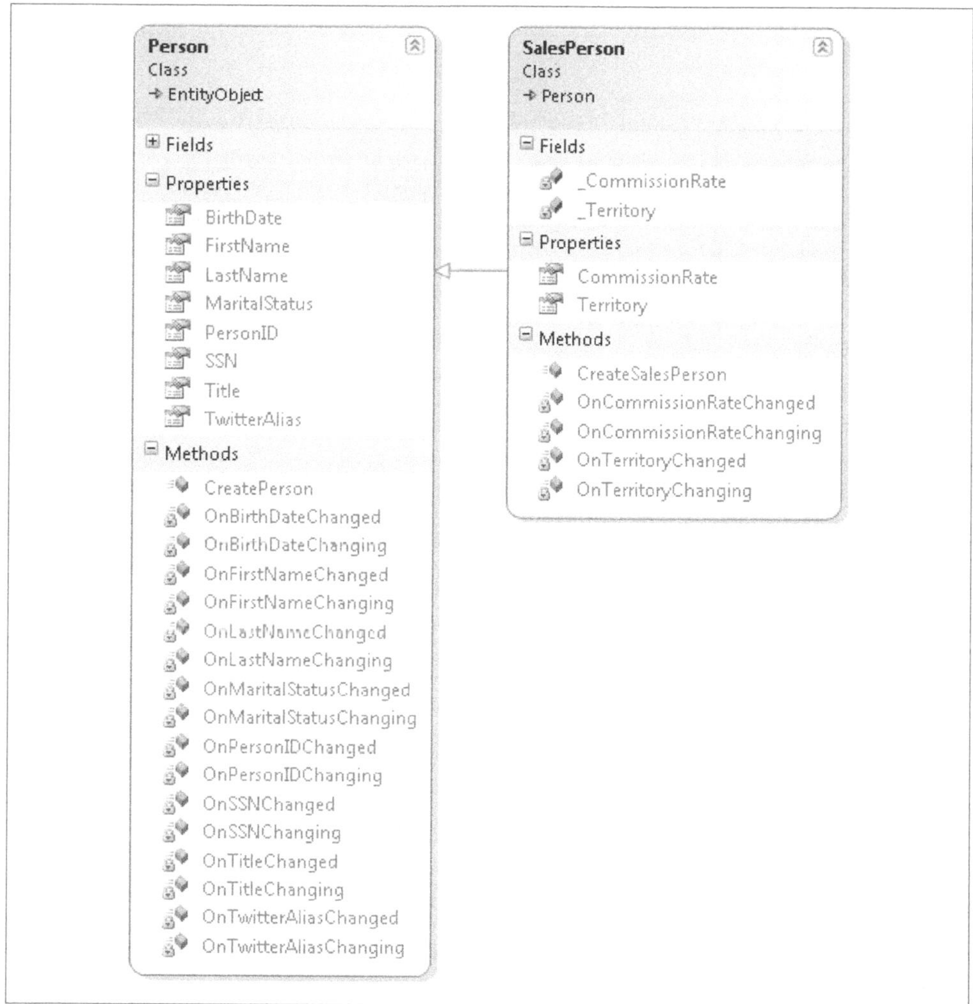

Figure 1-4. Class diagrams for the Person and SalesPerson entities

The Backend Database: Your Choice

You may have noticed that I have not mentioned the actual data store that owns the data being queried. The model doesn't have any knowledge of the data store—what type of database it is, much less what the schema is. And it doesn't need to.

The database you choose as your backend will have no impact on your model or your code.

The Entity Framework communicates with the same ADO.NET data providers that ADO.NET already uses, but with a caveat. The provider must be updated to support the Entity Framework. The provider participates in reshaping the Entity Framework's

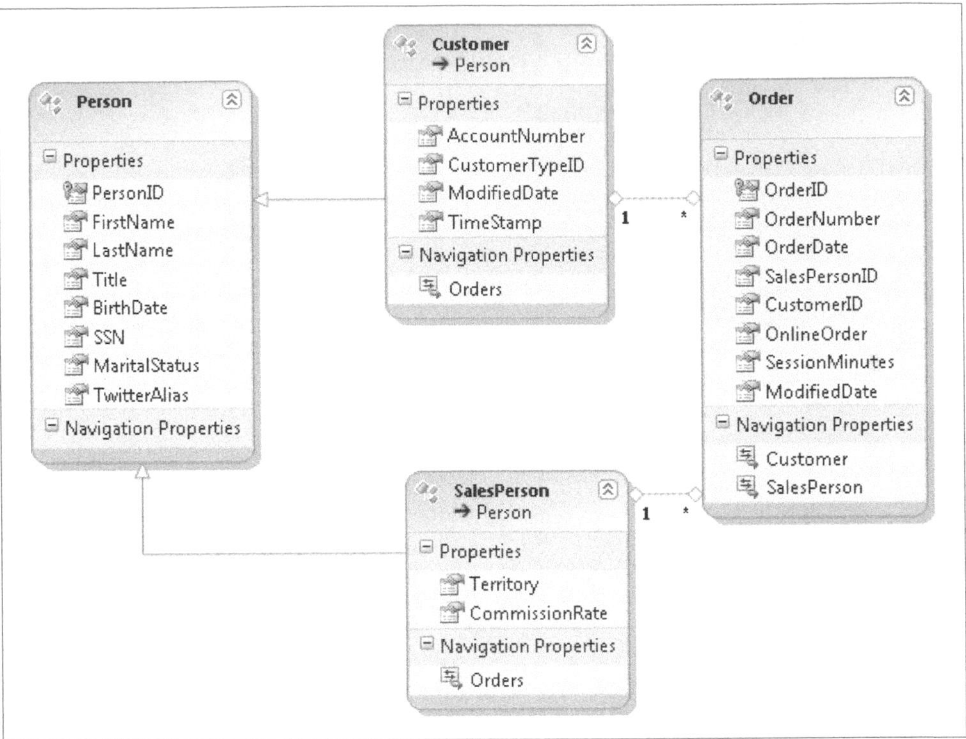

Figure 1-5. SalesPerson and Customer entities, each with a relationship to Order entities

queries and commands into native queries and commands. All you need to do is identify the provider and a database connection string so that the Entity Framework can get to the database.

This means that if you need to write applications against a number of different databases, you won't have to learn the ins and outs of each database. You can write queries with the Entity Framework's syntax (either LINQ to Entities or Entity SQL) and never have to worry about the differences between the databases. If you need to take advantage of functions or operators that are particular to a database, Entity SQL allows you to do that as well.

Database Providers

Microsoft's `SqlClient` APIs that are included with Visual Studio 2008 SP1 and Visual Studio 2010 support the Entity Framework. They will allow you to use SQL Server 2000, 2005, and 2008. You can use the full or Express version of SQL Server 2005 and 2008 and the full version of SQL Server 2000. Note that the Entity Data Model Designer cannot interact with SQL Server 2000. This is not a limitation of Entity Framework's design tools but Visual Studio 2010 itself. None of Visual Studio's tools recognizes SQL

Server 2000. However, the Entity Framework runtime can. SQL Server CE version 3.5 and 4 support the Entity Framework as well. Check out the July 7, 2010, blog post from the SQL Server CE team about SQL Server Compact 4 at *http://blogs.msdn.com/sqlservercompact*.

At the time of this writing, a host of other providers are available—and more are on the way—that will allow you to use Oracle, IBM databases, SQL Anywhere, MySQL, SQLite, VistaDB, and many other databases. The providers are being written by the database vendors as well as by third-party vendors. Many of these providers were written for .NET 3.5. There is only one critical feature that they will not support until they have been updated to .NET 4: a feature called *model first*, which you will learn about in Chapter 25.

Microsoft lists providers on the "ADO.NET Data Providers" page of the Data Developer Center at *http://msdn.microsoft.com/en-us/data/dd363565.aspx*.

Microsoft provides guidance for developers who want to build Entity Framework support into their database providers. I will not be covering this topic in this book. You can see EF team blog posts about writing providers at *http://blogs.msdn.com/b/adonet/archive/tags/sample+provider*.

Access and ODBC

A provider that supports the Entity Framework needs to have specific knowledge about the type of database it is connecting to. It needs to be aware of the available functions and operators for the database, as well as the proper syntax for native queries. Open Database Connectivity (ODBC) providers provide generic access to a variety of databases, including Access, and cannot furnish the necessary database particulars to act as a provider for the Entity Framework. Therefore, ODBC is not a valid provider for the Entity Framework. Unless someone creates a provider specifically for Access, you won't be able to use it with Entity Framework applications. Microsoft does not have plans to build an Access provider, because the demand is too low.

Entity Framework Features: APIs and Tools

In addition to the EDM, the Entity Framework provides a set of .NET runtime APIs that let you write .NET applications using the EDM. It also includes a set of design tools for designing the model. Following is a synopsis of the Entity Framework's key features.

Metadata

Although the Entity Framework is designed to let you work directly with the classes from the EDM, it still needs to interact with the database. The conceptual data model that the EDM describes is stored in an XML file whose schema identifies the entities and their properties. Behind the conceptual schema described in the EDM is another pair of XML files that map your data model back to the database. One is an XML file that describes your database and the other is a file that provides the mapping between your conceptual model and the database.

During query execution and command execution (for updates), the Entity Framework figures out how to turn a query or command that is expressed in terms of the data model into one that is expressed in terms of your database. It does this by reading the metadata.

When data is returned from the database, it uses the metadata to shape the database results into the entities and further materializes objects from those results.

Entity Framework acquires the ability to use an in-memory model with a feature called *code first* that is part of the Entity Framework Community Technical Preview (CTP). It is not yet part of Entity Framework and must be downloaded separately. Code first allows you to work solely with classes, and the necessary XML metadata is generated in memory on the fly at runtime. You'll learn more about this feature in Chapter 25, but be aware that at the time of this book's publication, code first is still a CTP and is not yet fully developed.

Entity Data Model Design Tools

The screenshots in Figures 1-2 and 1-3 are taken from the EDM Designer. It is part of Visual Studio and provides you with a way to work visually with the model rather than tangle with the XML. You will work with the Designer right away in Chapter 2, and you'll learn how to use it to do some more advanced modeling, such as inheritance, in Chapter 14 and "model-first" design in Chapter 25. You will also learn about the Designer's limitations, such as the fact that it does not support all of the features of the EDM. With some of the less frequently used EDM features, you'll have to work directly with the XML after all. In Chapter 2, you will get a look at the XML and how it relates to what you see in the Designer so that when it comes time to modify it in Chapter 15, you'll have some familiarity with the raw schema files.

In Visual Studio 2010, the Designer supports many more features than it did in Visual Studio 2008 SP1. However, as you will see in Chapters 14 and 15, there are still some things you will need to do manually.

The Designer also allows you to map stored procedures to entities, which you'll learn about in Chapter 6. If you are coming from Visual Studio 2008 SP1, you'll find that the Designer's stored procedure support has been greatly improved in Visual Studio 2010.

Another notable feature of the Designer is that it will let you update the model from the database to add additional database objects that you did not need earlier or that have been added to the database since you created the model.

Database-first design

One of the EDM design tools is the Entity Data Model Wizard. It allows you to point to an existing database and create a model directly from the database so that you don't have to start from scratch. Once you have this first pass at the model, you can begin to customize the model in the Designer.

Model-first design

Not every development project begins with a legacy database. One of the new features in Visual Studio 2010 is the ability to create a model directly in the Designer and then generate database schema based on that model. Although we'll focus on a model created using database-first design through most of this book, you'll get a chance to drill into model-first design, as well as some additional Designer features, in Chapter 25.

Code generation

Once you have a model to define your domain entities, you'll need classes to represent them at runtime. The Designer automatically generates those classes for you from the model. However, we've gained another critical feature in Visual Studio 2010. Rather than using the proprietary code generator that was written for Entity Framework in Visual Studio 2008 SP1, the classes are generated using Visual Studio's Text Template Transformation Toolkit (T4). Not only does this provide a more commonly known mechanism for code generation, but also you can much more easily customize the provided templates to define exactly how you would like classes to be generated from your model. You'll learn about the code generation capabilities beginning with Chapter 11 and work further with T4 customization in later chapters. There are some scenarios where you will be able to skip code generation completely and simply use your own classes.

Object Services

The Entity Framework runtime's most prominent feature set and that which you are likely to work with most often is referred to as Object Services. Object Services sits on top of the Entity Framework stack, as shown in Figure 1-6, and provides the functionality needed to work with objects that are based on your entities. Object Services provides a class called `EntityObject` and can easily manage any class that inherits from `EntityObject`. This includes materializing objects from the results of queries against the

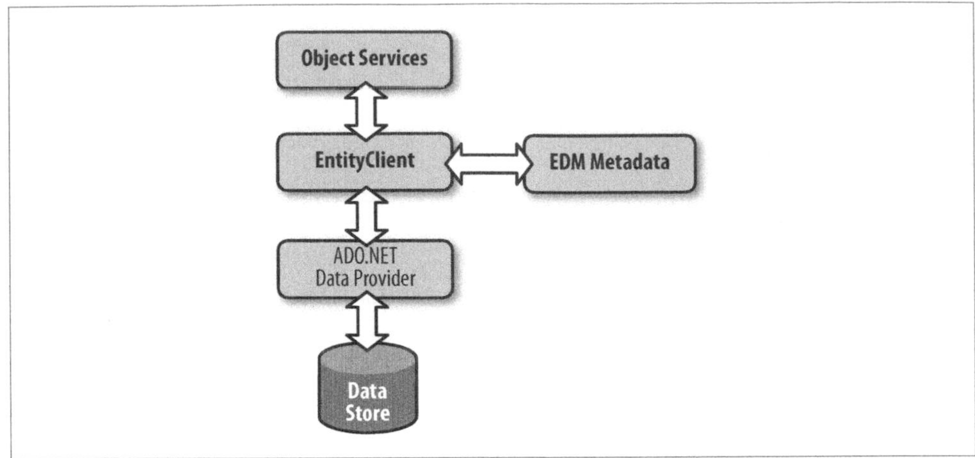

Figure 1-6. The Entity Framework stack

EDM, keeping track of changes to those objects, managing relationships between objects, and saving changes back to the database.

In between querying and updating, Object Services provides a host of capabilities to interact with entity objects, such as automatically working with a lower level of the Entity Framework to do all of the work necessary to make calls to the database and deal with the results. Object Services also provides serialization (both XML and binary).

POCO Support

One of the most important runtime enhancements in .NET 4 is the ability for the Entity Framework to manage entities that do not inherit from `EntityObject`. This is Entity Framework's new POCO (Plain Old CLR Objects) support, and you will learn much more about this feature beginning with Chapter 13. POCO support is critical to enable a variety of different programming styles. With POCO entities, developers can more easily build unit tests as well as persistent ignorant entity classes. These capabilities are crucial to developers who follow the coding patterns recommended by domain-driven and agile development. These same developers were unable to use the Entity Framework in .NET 3.5. Now Entity Framework embraces a wider population of the development community.

Change Tracking

Once an entity object has been instantiated, either as a result of data returned from a query or by instantiating a new object in code, Object Services can keep track of that object. This is the default for objects returned from queries. When Object Services manages an object, it can keep track of changes made to the object's properties or its relationships to other entity objects.

Object Services then uses the change-tracking information when it's time to update the data. It constructs `Insert`, `Update`, and `Delete` commands for each object that has been added, modified, or deleted by comparing the original values to the current values of the entity. If you are using stored procedures in conjunction with entities it will pass the current values (and any original values specifically identified) to those procedures.

Relationship Management and Foreign Keys

Relationships are a critical piece of the EDM; however, in .NET 4, an important new feature was added: foreign key support. In a classic Entity Relationship Model, foreign keys are not exposed in the conceptual model. Entity Framework followed this paradigm in .NET 3.5 SP1, but we developers still wanted access to those foreign key values for many reasons. In fact, in the first edition of this book, I showed a variety of ways to go "under the covers" to get and set foreign keys. Now Entity Framework supports having the foreign keys in the conceptual model. However, for backward compatibility, you can still use the former mechanism which, because of the lack of foreign keys, instantiates relationships as objects.

I will not spend a lot of time focusing on the older style of building relationships in this book as it is not the default and will be used minimally. If you need in-depth guidance on how to work with relationships when the foreign key is not available in the conceptual model, I recommend that you read the first edition of this book.

As you will find, especially in Chapter 19, which dives deep into relationships, even with foreign keys, you will need to have a very good understanding of how relationships work. Some of the rules of engagement when working with related data are not very intuitive, and you can write code that will raise plenty of exceptions, or worse, will return invalid results, if you break these rules. Chapter 19 will provide insight into relationships in the EDM so that you will be able to work with them in an expert manner.

Data Binding

You can use entities in many .NET data binding scenarios. In Windows Forms and WPF, you can use entities as a data source for data-bound controls or as the data source for `BindingSource` controls, which orchestrate the binding between objects and UI controls on the form. Chapter 9 provides a well-informed walkthrough for using entities with `BindingSource` controls to edit and update data. Chapter 26 focuses on separating the data access and other business logic from the user interface to provide better architecture for your applications.

Chapter 9 also provides a walkthrough for data-binding entities in Windows Presentation Foundation (WPF) applications. Visual Studio 2010 introduced a host of enhancements for data binding in WPF, and you'll benefit greatly from these when data-binding with entities.

For ASP.NET, there is a `DataSource` control called `EntityDataSource` that works in a similar way to the ASP.NET `SqlDataSource` and `LinqDataSource` controls, allowing you to declaratively bind entity objects to your user interface. Chapter 12 is all about using `EntityDataSource`. You'll also get a quick look at binding with ASP.NET Dynamic Data in that chapter.

n-Tier Development

Entity Framework made significant advancements for *n*-tier development in .NET 4. In .NET 3.5 SP1, it was just too hard; as such, in the previous edition of this book I devoted a lot of pages to hacks and workarounds. Now we can benefit greatly from not only the foreign keys but also a slew of state management methods that make working across processes much simpler. Additionally, POCOs make *n*-tier development easier to achieve as you'll see in the final chapters of this book.

For layered applications, Chapter 24 and Chapter 25 focus on pulling all of the data access tasks out of the ASP.NET user interface, and you'll see a WPF application, an ASP.NET Web Forms application, and an ASP.NET MVC application using various patterns to separate your logic.

EntityClient

`EntityClient` is the other major API in the Entity Framework, though one that you are less likely to work with directly. It provides the functionality necessary for working with the store queries and commands (in conjunction with the database provider) connecting to the database, executing the commands, retrieving the results from the store, and reshaping the results to match the EDM.

You can work with `EntityClient` directly or work with Object Services, which sits on top of `EntityClient`. Not only is `EntityClient` able to perform queries, but it does this on behalf of Object Services. The difference is that when you work directly with `EntityClient`, you will get tabular results (though the results can be shaped). If you are working with Object Services, it will transform the tabular data created by `EntityClient` into objects.

The tabular data returned by `EntityClient` is read-only. `EntityClient` is well suited for reporting and moving data from one persistence mechanism to another. Only Object Services provides change tracking and the ability to save changes back to the data store.

The Entity Framework and WCF Services

You can use the Entity Framework anywhere you can use ADO.NET, including web services and WCF services. Chapters 17 and 18 walk you through the process of providing services for `EntityObject` entities and POCO entities.

In these chapters, we'll also take a look at WCF Data Services, WCF RIA Services, and a specialized POCO template called Self-Tracking Entities, which provides client-side change-tracking capabilities to entities, thereby allowing a simpler way to send changes to WCF services and then persist them to the database.

What About ADO.NET DataSets and LINQ to SQL?

The Entity Framework is only the latest addition to the ADO.NET stack. How does that impact existing code that uses `DataSets` and `DataReaders` or LINQ to SQL? Can you continue to write new code using these technologies?

DataSets

`DataSets` and `DataReaders` are not going away. All of your existing investment will continue to function and you can continue to use this methodology of retrieving data and interacting with it. The Entity Framework provides a completely different way to retrieve and work with data. You would not integrate the two technologies—for example, using the Entity Framework to query some data, and then pushing it into a DataSet; there would be no point. You should use one or the other. As you learn about the Entity Framework, you will find that it provides a very different paradigm for accessing data. You may find that the Entity Framework fits for some projects, but not others, where you may want to stick with `DataSets`.

The Entity Framework uses `DataReaders` as well in the form of an `EntityDataReader`, which inherits the same `DbDataReader` as `SqlDataReader`. This is what a query with `EntityClient` returns. In fact, you'll find that the code querying the EDM with `EntityClient` looks very similar to the code that you use to query the database directly with ADO.NET. It uses connections, commands, and command parameters, and returns a `DbDataReader` that you can read as you would any other `DataReader`, such as `SqlDataReader`.

Some ADO.NET tools that are not available with the Entity Framework are query notification and ASP.NET's `SqlCacheDependency`. Additionally, ADO.NET's `SqlBulkCopy` requires a `DataReader` or `DataSet` to stream data into the database; therefore, you cannot do client-side bulk loading with the Entity Framework. The Entity Framework does not have an equivalent to ADO.NET's `DataAdapter.BatchUpdate`. Therefore, when the Entity Framework saves changes to the database, it can send only one command at a time.

LINQ to SQL

LINQ to SQL and the Entity Framework look similar on the surface. They both provide LINQ querying against a database using a data model.

A frequently asked question is: why did Microsoft create two similar technologies? LINQ to SQL evolved from the LINQ project, which came out of team working with language development. The Entity Framework was a project of the Data Programmability team and was focused on the Entity SQL language. By the time each technology had come along far enough that it was being shown to other teams at Microsoft, it was clear that Microsoft had two great new technologies that could target different scenarios. The Entity Framework team adapted LINQ to work with entities, which confused developers even more because LINQ to Entities and LINQ to SQL look so much alike.

LINQ to SQL eventually was brought into Microsoft's Data Programmability team, and in November 2008 the team announced that because the technologies target the same problems, going forward they would focus on developing the Entity Framework, which supports multiple databases and aligns with many of Microsoft's upcoming technologies through its use of an Entity Data Model. However, they will continue to maintain and tweak LINQ to SQL. This is not a happy situation for many developers who have made an investment in LINQ to SQL. Microsoft is committed to maintaining LINQ to SQL in ADO.NET and has made no statements regarding deprecating it. It has also promised to provide a migration path from LINQ to SQL to the Entity Framework and will recommend the Entity Framework over LINQ to SQL in future programmer guidelines.

Entity Framework Pain Points Are Fading Away

In the first edition of this book, Chapter 1 listed two pages of pain points. Their section titles were "The Entity Framework Designer" (which focused on the lack of support for stored procedures and other EDM features), "Challenges with Change Tracking Distributed Applications," "Domain-Driven Development," and "Unit Testing." I'm very happy to have removed every one of these sections thanks to the great improvements that have been made in .NET 4 and Visual Studio 2010.

There are still definitely a lot of nits to pick, however. The model would benefit from support for things such as unique foreign keys, table-valued functions, enhanced many-to-many relationships, and a problem that is much more than a nit: support for very large models.

Entity Framework's state management and relationship management still have a lot of behavior that is not intuitive and will certainly bite you if you don't study up on it. Take a look at Chapter 19 for a good study guide.

This book spends plenty of time looking into the depths of the Entity Framework runtime to show you how to get around some of these limitations, and attempts to point out potholes, hiccups, and omissions.

Users of more mature ORM tools continue to have complaints about Entity Framework as well, such as the difficulty of providing internal transactions (database transactions, however, are supported). But if you look around the marketplace, even Entity Framework's staunchest competitors are getting on board and leveraging their experience to provide advanced tools for working with Entity Framework. The principal player, NHibernate, created a wonderful database profiling tool for Entity Framework (*http://www.efprof.com/*), and LLBLGen Pro has built a powerful designer for Entity Framework that takes a very different approach for managing an Entity Framework EDM and its metadata (*http://www.llblgen.com*).

Programming the Entity Framework

As you read through this book, you will gain experience in designing EDMs and using the Entity Framework to write applications, as well as dig deep into the APIs to learn how to manipulate entity objects and have granular control over much of their behavior. A lot of functionality is very accessible, and there's a lot of hidden power. You will learn what's under the covers so that you can realize the true benefits of the Entity Framework.

Even as I wrap up this edition of *Programming Entity Framework*, I look forward to future versions of the framework as it continues to evolve.

CHAPTER 2

Exploring the Entity Data Model

An Entity Data Model (EDM) is the bridge between your application and your data store. An EDM provides you with the ability to work with a conceptual view of your data rather than the actual database schema. .NET APIs provided by the Entity Framework use an EDM for every interaction with the data store, whether it is to retrieve or to save data. The Entity Framework tools generate classes from this model that enable you to work with objects described by the EDM.

In this chapter, you will create a simple EDM using the Entity Data Model Wizard, and then you will inspect the model both in the Designer and by looking at its raw XML. This chapter will stick to the basics of the model so that you can become familiar with how an EDM is structured and how the most common elements relate to one another, to your code, and to the database.

In Chapter 14, you will begin to explore the more complex aspects of the EDM, such as its different inheritance capabilities and how to customize models so that they can better reflect your business logic.

Why Use an Entity Data Model?

Well-designed databases can pose a problem for developers.

In the data world, a database is designed for maintainability, security, efficiency, and scalability. Its data is organized in a way that satisfies the demands of good database design, yet provides challenges for the developer who needs to access that data.

Entity Data Model is a concept. The Entity Framework has a particular implementation that is realized as the EDMX file at design time. At runtime, the EDMX file is broken up into three separate XML files. For the sake of clarity, this book will simply refer to the EDM or Entity Data Model (or simply "the model") when discussing the Entity Framework's implementation. But keep in mind that the EDM literally refers to the concept of using some type of model to represent your entities in an application.

The EDM follows the concept of Entity Relationship Modeling discussed in Chapter 1, but in the Entity Framework, it moves the model into XML files that are used by the Entity Framework runtime.

With an EDM in place, developers can focus on their business objects even when retrieving data from the database or persisting it back to the database. You, the developer, will not have to worry about the structure of the database, the names of the tables or views, or the names of stored procedures or their required parameters. Nor will you have to create the objects necessary for making connections to the database, or be concerned with the schema of the returned data and then transform the results into objects to use in your code.

You will simply work against your conceptual model and the classes that represent the model's entities. And when you do so within the scope of the Entity Framework, the Entity Framework runtime will handle database connections, database command generation, query execution, object materialization, and the details of persisting changes back to the database.

The EDM Within the Entity Framework

In the Entity Framework's implementation of the EDM, the primary XML file represents the conceptual model, which is the actual EDM. A second XML file represents the database schema, and a third represents the mapping between the first two. At design time, all three files are bundled into a single EDMX file. The build process splits the EDMX out into the three metadata files that are used at runtime. The Entity Framework then provides a framework that allows developers to write .NET applications based on this model.

In Chapter 25, you will learn about alternatives to the XML schema that are included in future technologies coming from Microsoft that will enhance the Entity Framework.

As long as the EDM provides the conceptual schema, a representation of the database, a mapping file, and access to an Entity Framework-aware ADO.NET provider for the target database, the Entity Framework doesn't care what database is being targeted. It provides a common means of interacting with the database, common query syntax, and a common method for sending changes back to the database.

Although the Entity Framework provides a very rich set of features for developers, its most important capabilities are the following:

- By default, it automatically generates classes from the model and updates those classes dynamically anytime the model changes.
- It takes care of all of the database connectivity so that developers are not burdened by having to write lots of code for interacting with the database.
- It provides common query syntax for querying the model, not the database, and then translates these queries into queries that the database can understand.
- It provides a mechanism for tracking changes to the model's objects as they are being used in applications, and handles the updates to the database.

In addition, because the model's classes are dynamically generated, minor changes to the model need not have a major impact on your application. Furthermore, modifying the model is much simpler than modifying your objects and the data access code on which they rely.

All of the work you will do in this book will depend on an EDM, so in preparation for this, we'll create a simple model and then put it under a microscope so that you'll have a thorough comprehension of what the Entity Framework is working with.

Walkthrough: Building Your First EDM

Let's start by creating a model from the sample database, ProgrammingEFDB1. This is a simple database with only two tables, one view, and some stored procedures, and therefore it's a great place to begin. With an EDM in hand, you'll be able to explore its elements and their relationships, which we'll do later in this chapter.

This walkthrough will use a custom SQL Server database, ProgrammingEFDB1, which you can download from the book's website at *http://www.learnentityframework.com*. Visual Studio 2010 provides Entity Framework connectivity to SQL Server. As mentioned in Chapter 1, you can install additional providers to connect to other databases, such as SQL Server CE, MySQL, Oracle, and VistaDB.

1. Create a new Console Application project by choosing the Console Application project template (see Figure 2-1). I've named mine Chapter2ConsoleApp.

Be sure that the project is a .NET Framework 4 project. You can see the filter option at the top of the New Project window. Many of the features throughout this book are not available in .NET 3.5 and you will find yourself very confused!

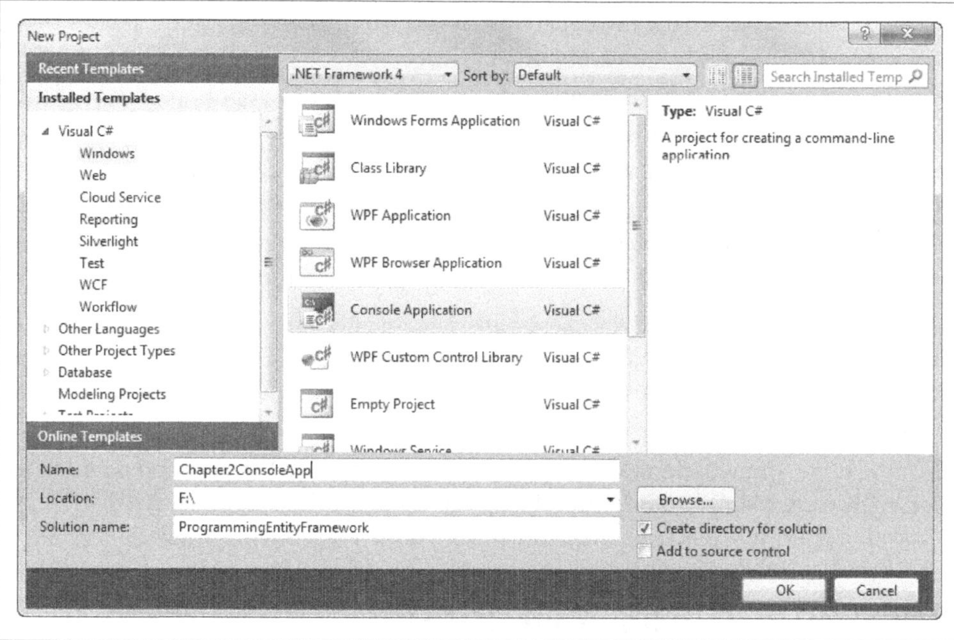

Figure 2-1. Creating a new Console Application project

2. Add a new item to the project by right-clicking on Chapter2ConsoleApp in the Solution Explorer, clicking Add, and then clicking New Item.
3. Select ADO.NET Entity Data Model from the Templates list and click Add (see Figure 2-2).
4. On the Choose Model Contents page, select the Generate from Database option and click Next.
5. On the Choose Your Data Connection page, select ProgrammingEFDB1 from the drop-down list of available connections.

If you do not have ProgrammingEFDB1 set up as a database connection in Visual Studio, click New Connection to open the Connection Properties dialog and create a new connection to the database.

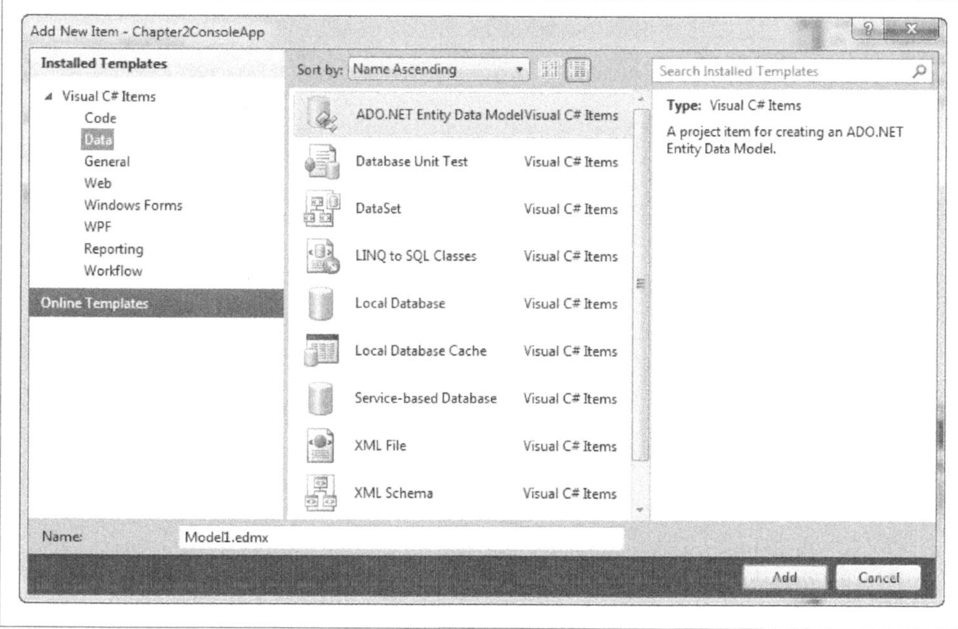

Figure 2-2. Selecting ADO.NET Entity Data Model on the Add New Item page to create an EDM

6. At the bottom of this page, change the connection settings name from the lengthy default of "ProgrammingEFDB1Entities" to "SampleEntities" and then click Next.
7. On the Choose Your Database Objects page, check the Tables and Views nodes.

   This will select all of the tables and views in the database. Alternatively, you can expand any of the nodes and select the specific objects you want. This database has two tables (`Contact` and `Address`), one view (`vOfficeAddresses`), and six stored procedures. For this demo, you'll want only the tables and the view.

We are skipping over the Stored Procedures checkbox for now; we'll come back to stored procedures in Chapter 7.

8. At the bottom of this page, change the Model Namespace from its default to "SampleModel" to align with the connection settings name.
9. Click Finish.

   The new model will be displayed in the Designer window, and its file, *Model1.edmx*, will appear in the Solution Explorer (see Figure 2-3).

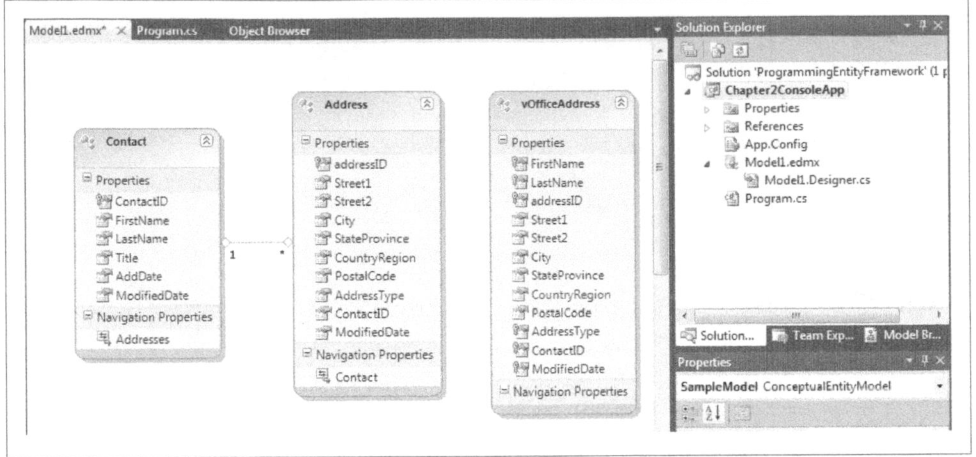

Figure 2-3. Model1.edmx added to the project, and the model automatically opened in the Designer

Beginning with Visual Studio 2010, the Entity Framework also supports *model-first design*, whereby you can build a model from scratch and then create a database based on the model. We'll cover model-first design in Chapter 25.

Inspecting the EDM in the Designer Window

The Entity Designer window is useful for viewing a graphical representation of an EDM and its members. Otherwise, you would have to dizzy yourself with lots of raw XML, which you'll get an opportunity to do later in this chapter, after you have had your graphical introduction.

After you generate the model from the wizard, the model will be open in the Designer view. If you have closed it, you can double-click on the EDMX file in the Solution Explorer to reopen it. The designer view is the default view for an EDMX file.

The Designer display of *Model1.edmx* shown in Figure 2-3 depicts an EDM that consists of three entities: a `Contact` entity, an `Address` entity, and a `vOfficeAddress` entity. The first two came from the tables in the database and the third came from the view. The Designer also displays a line connecting `Contact` and `Address` that represents a one-to-many relationship between them. Each entity has a number of scalar properties, and the entities with relationships additionally have navigation properties.

Scalar properties are properties whose values are literally contained in the entity. For example, the `Contact` entity is described by such things as `ContactID`, `FirstName`, `LastName`, and `Title`. These correspond with the table columns.

Navigation properties are pointers to related entities. The Contact entity has an Addresses property that will enable the application to *navigate* from a Contact to a set of Addresses related to that Contact. The Address entity has a Contact property that allows you to navigate from an Address to the single Contact associated with the Address entity.

The lines that connect the related entities represent *associations*, which are the relationships between the entities. Be aware that the position of the association ends, which in Figure 2-3 are nearest to Contact.LastName and Address.StateProvince, has no specific meaning. The association is only connecting the entities and is not implicating any particular properties.

Navigations and Associations: What to What?

The two ends of a relationship are often described with shortcut syntax that defines how many entities can be on each end. This is referred to as describing the *multiplicity* of the end. Multiplicity is also known as *relationship cardinality*, though you won't see this term used much within the Entity Framework.

The multiplicity options are:

- 1 (One)
- * (Many)
- 0..1 (Zero or One)

The two ends are then combined to describe the relationship.

For example, "1:*" means "One to Many." A canonical example of this is one order and its many line items.

"0..1:*" means "'Zero or One' to Many." An example of this is a relationship between shippers and orders. One shipper may ship many orders, but only one shipper can be related to an order. However, it's possible that the shipper was not assigned to the order at first; therefore, it can be zero or one on the shipper end of the relationship.

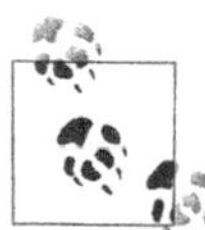

Notice that the Address entity has both a scalar property for the ContactID as well as a navigation property to the Contact entity referenced by the ContactID. If you have been working with the previous version of Entity Framework, the presence of the foreign key (ContactID) is new. It is optional, but it is there by default. You'll read more about this later in the chapter.

When working in the Entity Designer, you can see more information about the container, each entity, and each entity property in the Visual Studio IDE's Properties window.

Entity Container Properties

The logical group of entities in a model is called an *entity container*.

Figure 2-4 shows the Properties window for the entity container with some of the sections collapsed. Here you can modify the names of the container and its namespace, define the model's pluralization rules, and more.

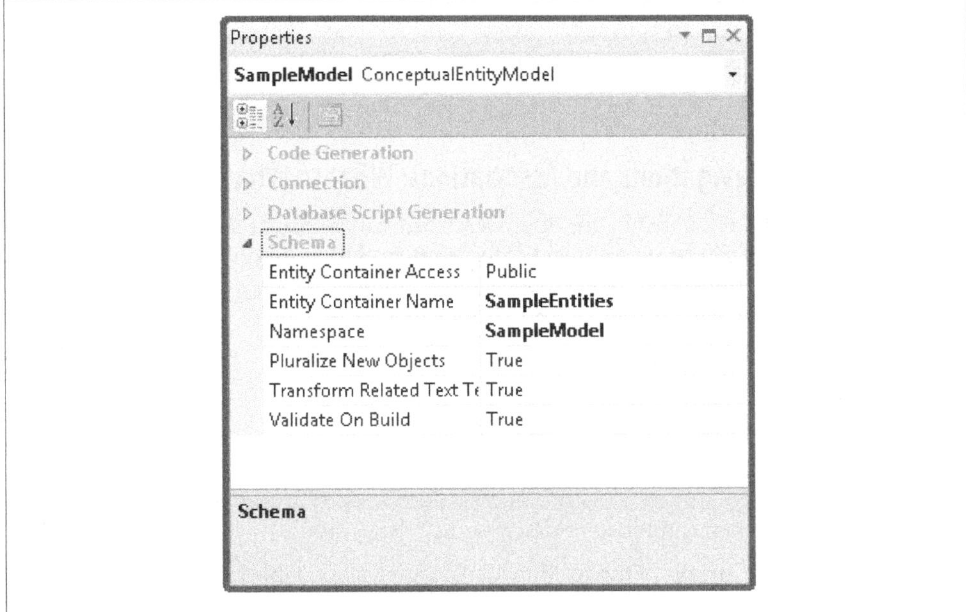

Figure 2-4. The Properties window for the entity container

Entity Properties

Each entity and each association of an EDM, as well as the model itself, has properties. Let's look at some properties of the `Contact` entity in the model that you've created.

Select the `Contact` entity to view its Properties window (see Figure 2-5).

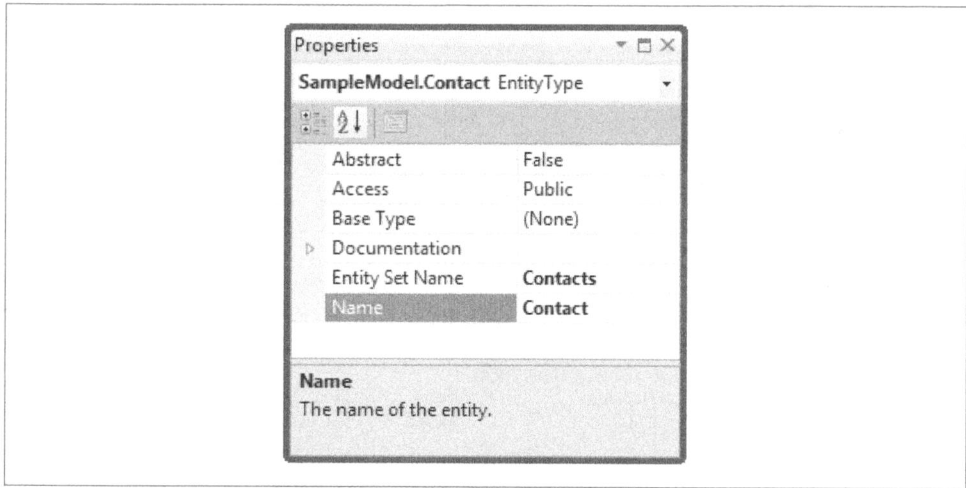

Figure 2-5. Viewing the Properties window for the Contact entity

In the Properties window, you can see that the entity not only has the name "Contact," which it derived from the table name in the database, but also has an `Entity Set Name` property. If the table name in the database had been plural, e.g., Contacts, the wizard would have still named the entity Contact because an entity name should be singular.

An *entity set* is a container for a collection of entities of a single type. Therefore, the entity set named "Contacts" will contain a collection of `Contact` entities. By default, the wizard pluralized the entity name when creating the entity set name. You can change this behavior by unchecking the "Pluralize or singularize generated object names" checkbox in the Entity Data Model Wizard.

Entity Property Properties

Figure 2-6 displays the properties of the `Contact`'s `FirstName` property. You can see, for example, that `FirstName` is a string (`Type` is `String`) that is not nullable (`Nullable` is `False`).

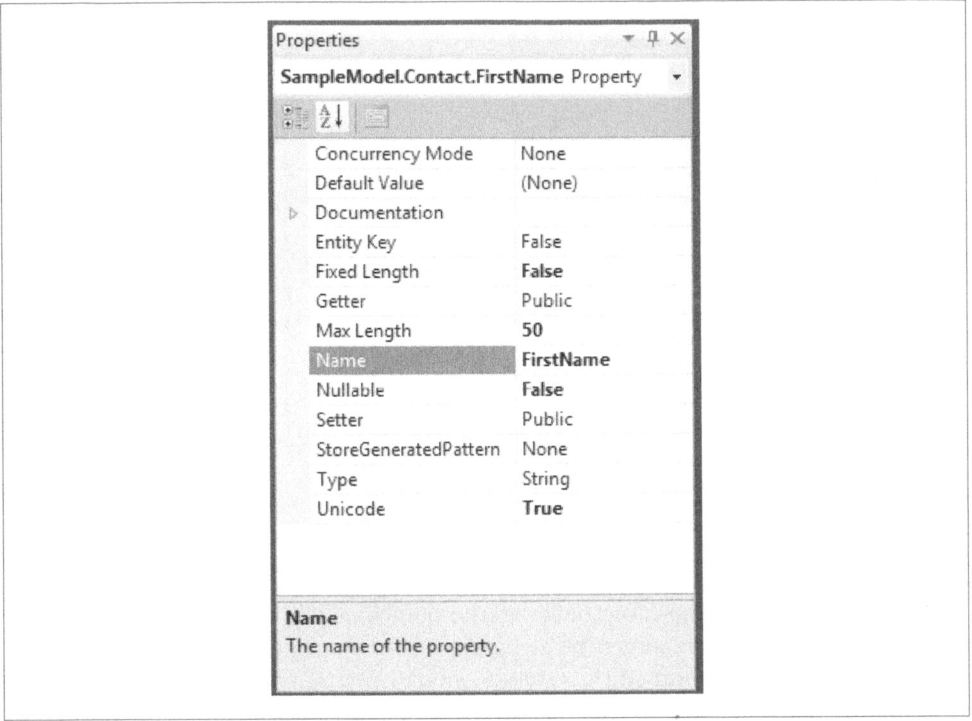

Figure 2-6. The properties of the FirstName property

Properties that describe the schema of an entity property, such as `Fixed Length`, are also known as *attributes*. Because it can be confusing to discuss "the properties of the properties," I will frequently refer to them as attributes.

The `Unicode`, `Max Length`, and `Fixed Length` properties are ignored by the Entity Framework runtime. Do not expect the Entity Framework to automatically perform validation based on these properties. These attributes are used by other consumers of the EDM, such as ASP.NET MVC 2.0 and ASP.NET Dynamic Data Controls, and, as you will learn in Chapter 25, for generating database scripts along with the `StoreGeneratedPattern` property. You can use them yourself when working at a lower level with Entity Framework; e.g., with `MetadataWorkspace`, which you will learn about in Chapter 21.

Although you can do much more with the Designer, it is time to open the model in its raw format. You will find additional discussion of the raw XML in Appendix C. Be sure to save all of your work before moving on.

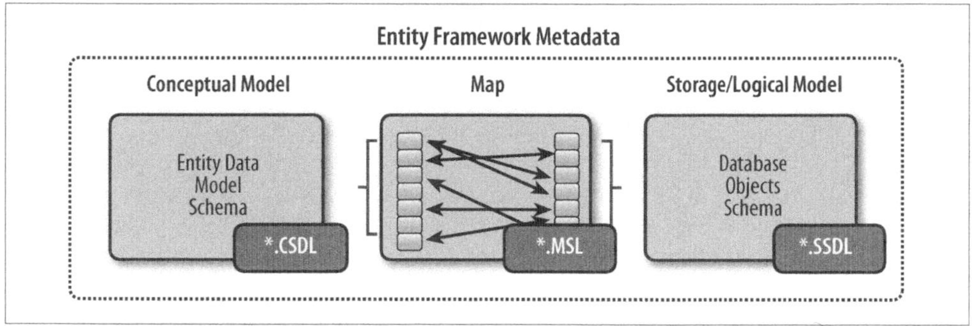

Figure 2-7. The components of the Entity Framework's model metadata

When building a model from scratch in the Designer in Chapter 25, you will learn more about various features of working with entities, their properties, associations, and more.

The Model's Supporting Metadata

So far in the Designer you have seen only the conceptual portion of the model, but there are more critical sections of the EDMX: `StorageModels` and `Mappings`.

There are, in fact, four sections in the EDMX file, but one of those four contains instructions to the Designer for object placement. I'll be ignoring that section in this discussion.

These additional parts of the metadata enable the Entity Framework APIs to translate between the conceptual model and the actual data store. The `StorageModels` represent the schema of the database objects that you selected for inclusion, and the `Mappings` describe how to get from the entities and properties of the conceptual model to the tables and columns described in the storage model (see Figure 2-7).

Why use the storage layer to represent the data store when you have the actual data store to work with? There are a number of reasons to use this piece of the model. The most important reason is that this provides loose coupling to the database; not every object in the database needs to be in the model, and as you will learn in Chapter 16, it is possible to customize even the storage layer to suit the needs of the model.

Although the entire model is contained in a single file at design time, when the project is compiled it will create three separate files—one for each of these sections. The conceptual layer is saved to a file with a *.csdl* extension, which stands for Conceptual Schema Definition Language. The storage layer is saved to a file with an *.ssdl* extension (which stands for Store Schema Definition Language) and the mapping layer is saved to a file with an *.msl* extension (which stands for Mapping Specification Language).

These files are used at runtime, which is why they are contained in a section called `edmx:Runtime` in the model.

By default, you will never see these physical files because they are embedded into the project assembly when the project is compiled. This is convenient for a lot of scenarios, though it is possible to change the model's `Metadata Artifact Processing` property to read "Copy to Output Directory."

A Schema by Any Other Name: Nicknames

The three parts of the model have a variety of descriptions that you will see used in documentation, articles, training, and even this book. Here is a list of the various "nicknames":

Conceptual Schema Definition Language (CSDL)

- Conceptual layer
- Conceptual schema
- Conceptual model
- C-side

Store Schema Definition Language (SSDL)

- Store/storage layer
- Store/storage schema
- Store/storage model
- Store/storage metadata
- Store/storage metadata schema
- S-side

Mapping Specification Language (MSL)

- Mapping layer
- Mapping specification
- C-S mapping (referring to "conceptual to store")

Each section is controlled by its own XML Schema Definition (XSD) file that lives deep within the .NET Framework files. One schema file defines what the structure of the CSDL should be, another defines the MSL, and yet another defines the SSDL. Visual Studio's IntelliSense uses these schema files to help you as you're working directly with the XML, pointing out errors and presenting you with options. Compiler errors will also be displayed if the files don't fall in line with their schema rules.

Schemas for the Schemas

If you're among the very curious you can take a look at the schema files that drive the rules for the CSDL, SSDL, and MSL sections in the model. The schema files for Visual Studio 2010 are located in *C:\Program Files\Microsoft Visual Studio 10.0\xml\Schemas*. If you are running a 64-bit O/S, check in the Program Files (x86) path instead. The three files to look for are:

- *System.Data.Resources.CSDLSchema_2.xsd*
- *System.Data.Resources.CSMSL_2.xsd*
- *System.Data.Resources.SSDLSchema_2.xsd*

If you open these in Visual Studio, you will see that they are formatted as XML files and are easy to navigate.

Viewing the Model in the Model Browser

The Entity Data Model Designer also provides another view of the metadata with the Model Browser. You can access the Model Browser from the context menu of the model's design surface.

Figure 2-8 shows the Model Browser with a number of items expanded. The Model Browser lets you see an overview of the CSDL and SSDL items. From here you can access the property window of various entities and properties. You can also navigate to a particular entity or property by right-clicking and selecting Show in the Designer. As your model gets more complex, the Model Browser is a convenient way to see an organized view of the metadata.

Viewing the Model's Raw XML

Now it's time to get down and dirty with the EDM. Only a portion of the model is visible in the Designer, which means you can learn a lot more by looking at it in its raw format. In places where the model has a counterpart in the Designer, you'll see both views.

By default, the file will open in the Designer; therefore, you need to use a different method to open it in its raw format. In the Solution Explorer, right-click the *Model1.edmx* file. From the context menu that opens, select Open With, and then choose XML Editor and click OK.

Visual Studio cannot display the model in Design view and in XML at the same time, so you will see a message asking whether it's OK to close the Design view of the model. Click Yes.

Model Browser
Type here to search
Model1.edmx
SampleModel
Entity Types
Address
Contact
ContactID
AddDate
FirstName
LastName
ModifiedDate
Title
Addresses
vOfficeAddress
Complex Types
Associations
FK_Address_Contact
EntityContainer: SampleEntities
SampleModel.Store
Tables / Views
Address
Contact
ContactID
AddDate
FirstName
LastName
ModifiedDate
Title
vOfficeAddresses
Stored Procedures
Constraints

Figure 2-8. The Model Browser

For those who have the common *Fear-of-XML* syndrome, this may look at little daunting at first. Have no fear and just follow along. We won't go too deep, but if you are interested in the real plumbing, you'll find more details about the raw metadata in Appendix C.

Later in this book, you will be working directly in the XML to make some model customizations that are not supported by the Designer. Additionally, you will write some code that interacts directly with the raw model. When performing these tasks, you will benefit from having had the interaction with the XML in the following pages and continued in Appendix C.

The EDMX file is composed of two main sections: the runtime information and the Designer information. The runtime section comprises three additional sections: one each for storage models, conceptual models, and mappings. The Designer section specifies where the various model elements should be placed visually in the Designer.

Collapse all of the main sections of the model. You can do this quickly by right-clicking in the XML and choosing Outlining, then Toggle All Outlining. Now you will see only the main node—`edmx:Edmx`. You can expand that until your view matches Figure 2-9.

```
Model1.edmx
<?xml version="1.0" encoding="utf-8"?>
<edmx:Edmx Version="2.0" xmlns:edmx="http://schemas.microsoft.com/ado/2008/10/edmx">
  <!-- EF Runtime content -->
  <edmx:Runtime>
    <!-- SSDL content -->
    <edmx:StorageModels>...</edmx:StorageModels>

    <!-- CSDL content -->
    <edmx:ConceptualModels>...</edmx:ConceptualModels>

    <!-- C-S mapping content -->
    <edmx:Mappings>...</edmx:Mappings>

  </edmx:Runtime>
  <!-- EF Designer content (DO NOT EDIT MANUALLY BELOW HERE) -->
  <Designer xmlns="http://schemas.">...</Designer>

</edmx:Edmx>
100 %
```

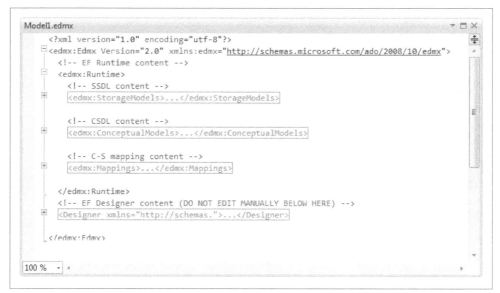

Figure 2-9. The main sections of the model

Now you can see the main sections of the model. The `Designer` element is metadata that tells the Designer how to position the entities. Feel free to explore that at a later time. The critical sections of the model are the runtime `ConceptualModels`, `StorageModels`, and `Mappings`.

CSDL: The Conceptual Schema

Let's begin by taking a closer look at the CSDL, the conceptual schema for the EDM.

In the XML, use the + icons to expand the `ConceptualModels` section until you have exposed the `Schema` and the `EntityContainer`, as shown in Figure 2-10.

Sometimes the XML formatting is affected and a particular section might lose all of its hard returns, resulting in one very long line of code that is hard to decipher. To fix this, highlight the line and then, from the Visual Studio menu, select Edit→Advanced→Format Selection. This will make the XML formatting much more palatable.

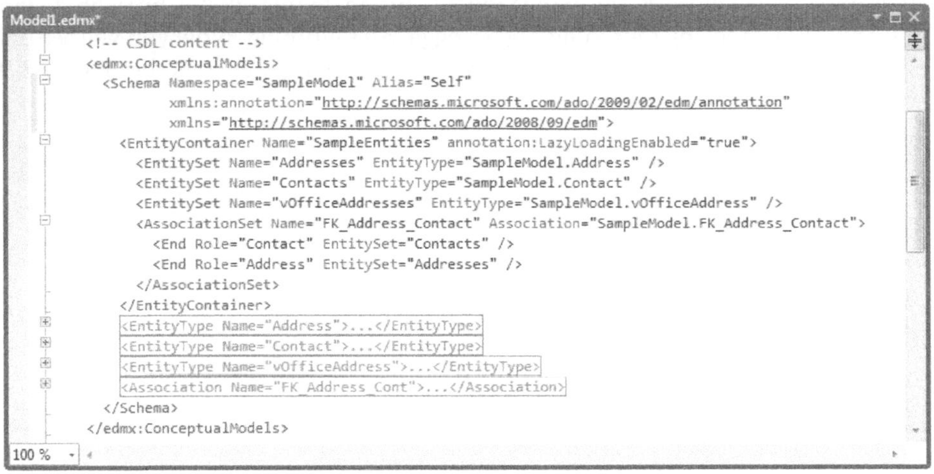

```
<!-- CSDL content -->
<edmx:ConceptualModels>
  <Schema Namespace="SampleModel" Alias="Self"
          xmlns:annotation="http://schemas.microsoft.com/ado/2009/02/edm/annotation"
          xmlns="http://schemas.microsoft.com/ado/2008/09/edm">
    <EntityContainer Name="SampleEntities" annotation:LazyLoadingEnabled="true">
      <EntitySet Name="Addresses" EntityType="SampleModel.Address" />
      <EntitySet Name="Contacts" EntityType="SampleModel.Contact" />
      <EntitySet Name="vOfficeAddresses" EntityType="SampleModel.vOfficeAddress" />
      <AssociationSet Name="FK_Address_Contact" Association="SampleModel.FK_Address_Contact">
        <End Role="Contact" EntitySet="Contacts" />
        <End Role="Address" EntitySet="Addresses" />
      </AssociationSet>
    </EntityContainer>
    <EntityType Name="Address">...</EntityType>
    <EntityType Name="Contact">...</EntityType>
    <EntityType Name="vOfficeAddress">...</EntityType>
    <Association Name="FK_Address_Cont">...</Association>
  </Schema>
</edmx:ConceptualModels>
```

Figure 2-10. Expanding the conceptual model, its schema, and the EntityContainer inside the schema

Here you can see how the `EntityContainer`, `EntitySets`, and various `EntityTypes` that we looked at previously in the Designer are defined in the metadata and contain the various `EntitySets`.

Now we will take advantage of the structured XML to learn more about the different elements of an Entity Data Model.

EntityContainer

Within the schema is an `EntityContainer` named `SampleEntities` (by default). Like the namespace, this is the pattern for the default `EntityContainer` name using the database name plus the word *Entities*. You can view and change this name in the model's Properties window when you have the model open in the Designer.

The `EntityContainer` is a wrapper for `EntitySets` and `AssociationSets`. You may recognize the `Contacts EntitySet` from the Properties window in Figure 2-5. `Association Sets` reference the associations between the entities. We'll come back to `Association Sets` after we've discussed the `Association` elements.

As shown in Figure 2-11, the `EntityContainer` is the critical entry point for querying the model. It exposes the `EntitySets`, and it is the `EntitySets` against which you will write your queries. The `EntitySets`, in turn, give you access to their entities.

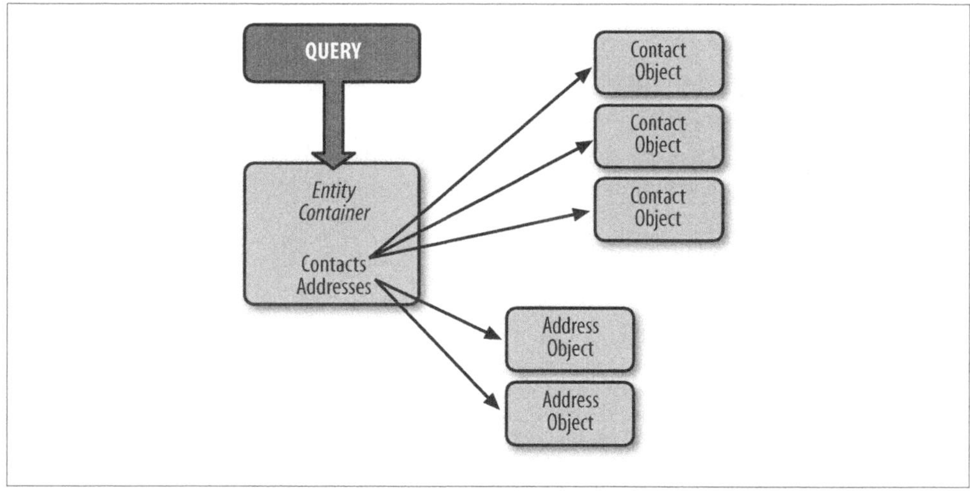

Figure 2-11. The relationship of the EntityContainer to its EntitySets and Entity objects

`EntityContainer` has an attribute: `annotation:LazyLoadingEnabled="true"`. Annotations exist only in the EDMX file, and are directions for the generation of code based on the model and have nothing to do with the model itself. This setting is also available in the model's Properties window.

EntitySet

An `EntitySet` is a container for a type of entity. Its two attributes are `Name` and `EntityType`. `EntityType` defines which entity the set contains using its strongly typed name. The entity's strongly typed name includes the model's namespace, as shown in the following code snippet:

```
<EntitySet Name="Addresses"
           EntityType="SampleModel.Address" />
<EntitySet Name="Contacts"
           EntityType="SampleModel.Contact" />
```

It is through the `EntitySet` that you have access to the individual entities when querying against the model. When you begin to query in the next chapter, you will see that you use code that translates to "find some entities in the `Addresses EntitySet`." The model instructs your query to return `Address` entity types.

As you will learn later in the book, the Entity Data Model allows for inherited types. Therefore, your model may have a `Contact` entity and a `Customer` entity, where the customer is a type of `Contact`. In this case, the `Contacts EntitySet` will serve as a wrapper for both the `Contact` entities and the `Customer` entities.

EntityType

An EntityType is a data type in the model. You have already seen a Contact entity type and an Address entity type.

In the XML schema, expand the Address entity type, which will look like Example 2-1, to get a closer look at it. It contains a Key element and a list of Property elements.

Example 2-1. The Address entity's XML

```
<EntityType Name="Address">
  <Key>
    <PropertyRef Name="addressID" />
  </Key>
  <Property Name="addressID" Type="Int32" Nullable="false"
            annotation:StoreGeneratedPattern="Identity" />
  <Property Name="Street1" Type="String" MaxLength="50"
            Unicode="true" FixedLength="true" />
  <Property Name="Street2" Type="String" MaxLength="50"
            Unicode="true" FixedLength="true" />
  <Property Name="City" Type="String" MaxLength="50"
            Unicode="true" FixedLength="true" />
  <Property Name="StateProvince" Type="String" MaxLength="50"
            Unicode="true" FixedLength="true" />
  <Property Name="CountryRegion" Type="String" MaxLength="50"
            Unicode="true" FixedLength="true" />
  <Property Name="PostalCode" Type="String" MaxLength="20"
            Unicode="true" FixedLength="true" />
  <Property Name="AddressType" Type="String" Nullable="false"
            MaxLength="10" Unicode="true" FixedLength="true" />
  <Property Name="ContactID" Type="Int32" Nullable="false" />
  <Property Name="ModifiedDate" Type="DateTime" Nullable="false" />

  <NavigationProperty Name="Contact"
            Relationship="SampleModel.FK_Address_Contact"
            FromRole="Address" ToRole="Contact" />

</EntityType>
```

The Key element

The Key element defines which properties comprise the identity key for the entity. In the Designer and at runtime you will see this represented as an EntityKey.The entity's key plays a critical role in the life cycle of an entity, enabling your application to keep track of an entity, perform database updates and refreshes, and more. You will learn more about this in Chapter 10. In the Designer, you can specify the key in the Properties window of the entity.

The key for the Address entity uses only a single property, addressID. It is possible to have keys composed of multiple properties. These are called *composite entity keys* and are similar to composite keys in databases. You'll learn more about composite keys in Chapter 10.

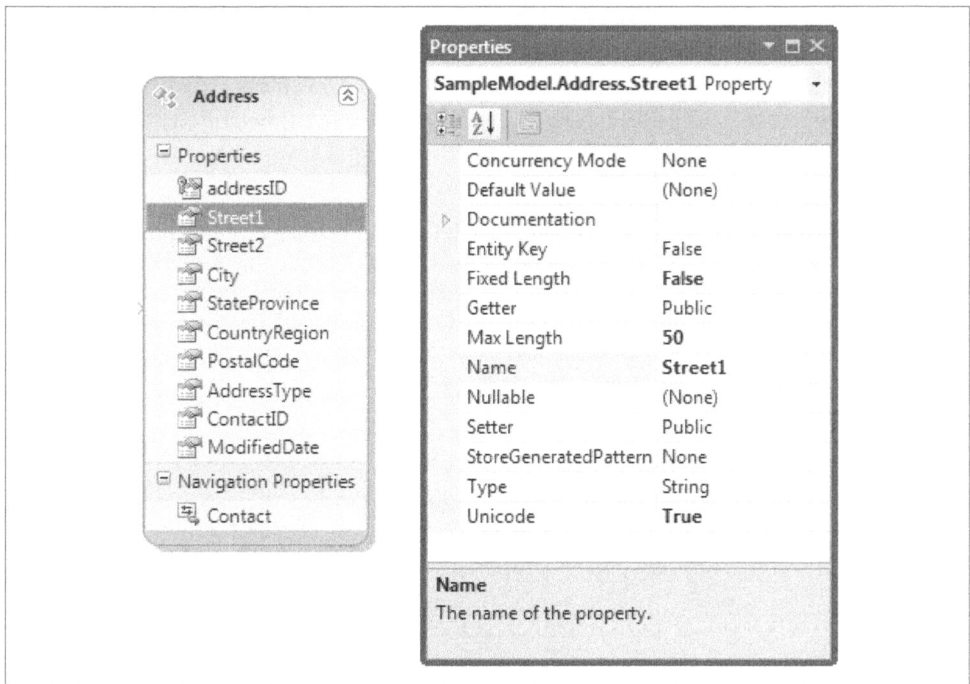

Figure 2-12. The Address entity with its Street1 property selected and the Street1 details shown in the Properties window

The Property elements

Not only do the `Property` elements have names, but they are additionally defined by their data type and a variety of "facets" that further describe them.

The data types that define these properties are called *simple types*. These are primitive types in the Entity Framework object model that closely line up with the data types in the .NET Framework. The Entity Framework's primitive types, however, are used only to define the entity property. They do not have their own properties. They are truly simple.

You can view and edit most of this information in the Properties window, as shown in Figure 2-12.

You can also see properties in the Properties window that are not shown in the XML.

You cannot have both the XML and the Designer open at the same time. To return to the Designer, close the XML view of the model and then double-click on the EDMX file.

Properties that are set to their default values are not explicitly written out in the XML. This is the case for a number of the properties of `Address.Street1`, including `ConcurrencyMode`, `Default Value`, `Getter`, and `Setter`. The `EntityKey` property is not a facet of `Street1` but is used to create the `EntityKey` element described earlier. If you look at the properties of `addressID`, you'll see that its `EntityKey` property is `True`.

The `Getter` and `Setter` properties define the accessibility of each property in the class that is generated from the model's entity. By default, all of the properties are public, allowing anyone to read or write to them. Changing the values of `Getter` and `Setter` will impact the property declarations. Chapter 23 digs further into concurrency, and there you will learn about the `ConcurrencyMode` property.

The navigation properties

The navigation properties of the entities are tightly bound to the associations that are represented by the lines between the entities, as you saw earlier in Figure 2-3. We'll dig further into the subject of navigation properties after we discuss associations.

Associations

Associations define the relationships between entity types. The association doesn't define the relationship completely, however. It defines the endpoints (i.e., the entities that are involved in the relationship) and their multiplicity.

In the example model, there is only one association, which is between the `Contact` entity type and the `Address` entity type, telling us that there is a relationship between the two. The name of this association was taken from the predefined relationship in the database when the wizard first created the model. Like any other element in the model, you can edit the name of the association if you prefer more readable names, or if you have naming conventions that you need to follow.

Let's first look at the association's properties in the Design view. If you are following along, close the XML and open the model in the Designer and click on the association. Figure 2-13 shows the Properties window for the association between `Contact` and `Address`.

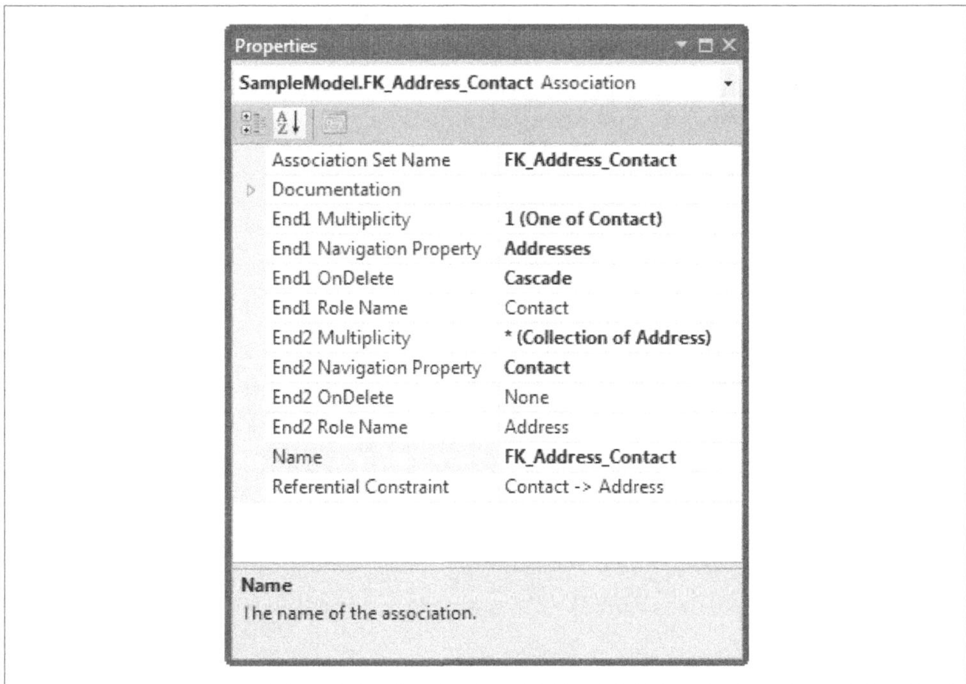

Figure 2-13. Association properties

The association lists both ends. `End1` is the `Contact` entity type. It is assigned a role called "Contact," which acts as the name of `End1` so that elements elsewhere in the model can point to it. Additional `End1` properties tell us more about this end of the association. `Multiplicity` specifies that there will be only one contact in a relationship between `Contact` and `Address`. `Navigation Property` shows that the `Addresses` property in the `Contact` type leads us to the other end of the association. `OnDelete`, whose options are `Cascade` and `None`, lets us know if any related `Address` entities in memory will be deleted when the `Contact` entity is deleted.

The second end will be an `Address` entity type, and there can be many addresses in this relationship. After "reading" the association, you can see that there is a one-to-many relationship between `Contact` and `Address`. A single contact might have a home address, a work address, and even other addresses. However, an address will only ever be associated with a single contact. In the real world, it is possible for an address to be associated with multiple people—for example, family members or roommates or employees at a single organization. That would involve a many-to-many relationship, which we will explore in Chapter 8.

As with entities, an association defines the name of the `AssociationSet` that contains this type of association. By default, it matches the name of the association. You could also make this name plural, but doing so is not as critical as having plural `EntitySet` names because you won't be interacting with the `AssociationSets` in code.

Learn more about `AssociationSet` in Appendix C.

Finally, make note of the `Referential Constraint` property. In a model that contains foreign keys in the entities, such as the `ContactID` property of `Address` shown in Figure 2-14, the `Referential Constraint` is critical. It defines any dependency between the related entities.

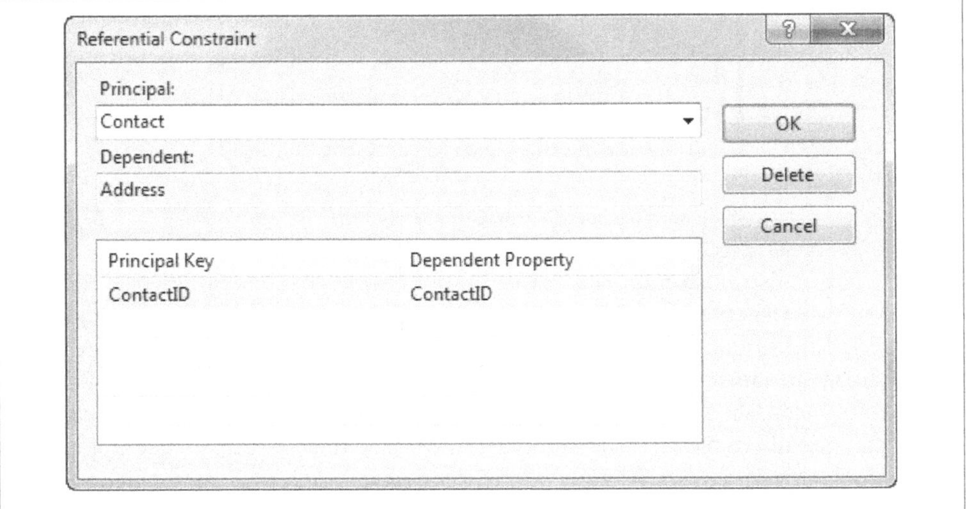

Figure 2-14. Referential Constraint details

Every `Address` entity must point to a `Contact`. Referential constraints are checked when you attempt to store data in the database.

For backward compatibility with version 1 models, it is still possible to define the constraints with association mappings (more on these shortly) when you have a relationship between two primary keys.

Including foreign key properties is the default mode for creating an Entity Data Model. You can build models following the version 1 approach whereby entities do not include the foreign key. In this case, the `Referential Constraint` would not be used and the dependency between the `Contact` and `Address` would be defined in the association's mappings. You will learn more about this alternative use in Chapter 19. The associations in this type of model are referred to as *independent associations*, whereas those in a model using foreign keys are called *foreign key associations*.

We will discuss associations in more detail later in this chapter, and in even greater detail in Chapter 19, which focuses on relationships and associations.

Navigation Property

Finally, we can look at the navigation properties in the `Address` and `Contact` entity types. Now that I've explained associations, navigation properties should be much easier to comprehend.

Although it is easily possible for entities to have more than one navigation property, in this particular model we have only one in each entity type. Figure 2-15 shows the Properties window for the `Contact` navigation property of the `Address` entity.

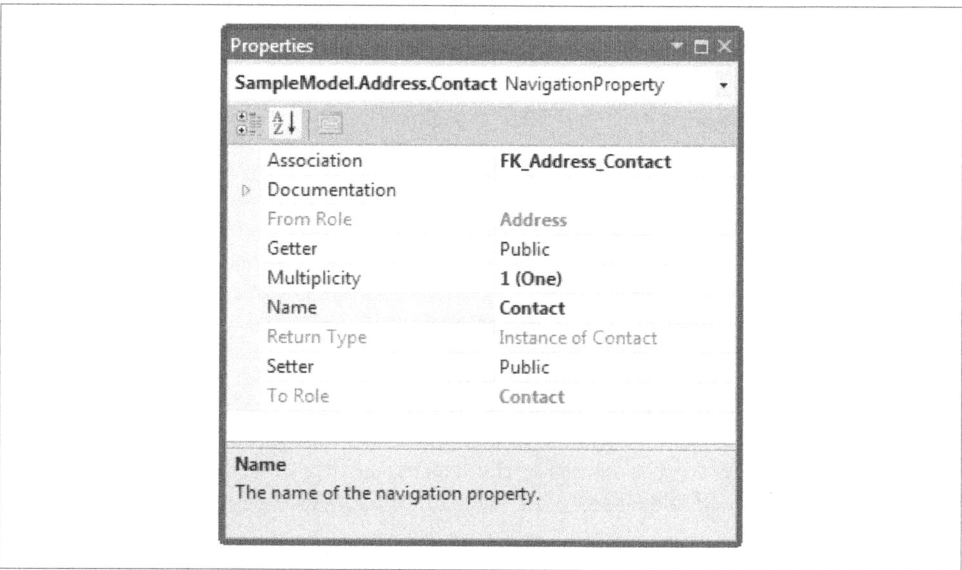

Figure 2-15. The Contact navigation property of the Address entity

When you're working with the `Address` in code, the `Contact` navigation property will appear as just another property. Although the other properties are referred to as *scalar* properties, meaning that they are values, the navigation property describes how to navigate to a related entity.

A critical property of the navigation is its association. This tells the navigation property which association in the model contains information regarding how to navigate to the related entity (or entities in the case of `Contact.Addresses`).

As I explained earlier, that association defines the relationship between the `Address` and `Contact` entity types. The `FromRole` and `ToRole` attributes tell the Entity Framework that when it looks at this association, it needs to navigate *from* the endpoint named `Address` *to* the endpoint called `Contact`. This, in turn, will allow you to navigate from the `Address` entity type to its associated `Contact` entity type in your code.

As with entities, the Designer shows some properties that are used for code generation: `Getter`, `Setter`, and `Documentation`. Additionally, `Multiplicity` is linked to the multiplicity of that same end in the association. You can change it in the Navigation Property properties or in the Association properties. The `Contact`'s multiplicity is "1 (One)," telling you that when you navigate to `Address.Contact`, you will get an instance of a contact (a single contact object). A navigation property that returns a single object is referred to as a *navigation reference*. `Return Type` is a read-only property that is located in the Designer's Properties window to help you to better understand the navigation.

When looking at this same navigation property in the XML you will not see these last two properties, and because the `Setter`, `Getter`, and `Documentation` properties are using the defaults, they are not listed either, as shown in the following code snippet:

```
<NavigationProperty Name="Contact"
            Relationship="SampleModel.FK_Address_Contact"
            FromRole="Address"
            ToRole="Contact" />
```

Navigation Properties That Return Collections

The `Contact` property of an `Address` entity returns a single instance of a contact. What about the `Addresses` property of a `Contact` entity? Figure 2-16 shows the `Addresses` property.

When navigating from `Contact` to `Addresses`, the `Addresses` endpoint defined in the `FK_Address_Contact` association has a multiplicity of * (Many). Therefore, the Entity Framework expects a collection inside the `Addresses` property. In the Designer, the `Return Type` property of `Addresses` is a collection of `Address` types.

This type of navigation property is called a *navigation collection*.

In code, the `Contact.Addresses` property will return a collection of `Address` entities, even if there is only one address in the collection. If there are no addresses for a particular person, the collection will be empty.

The collection that is exposed in the `Addresses` navigation property is not a collection from the `System.Collections` namespace, but rather an `EntityCollection`. The `EntityCollection` is a completely unique class in the Entity Framework. So, although it is simpler to say "a collection of addresses," it is important to pay attention when

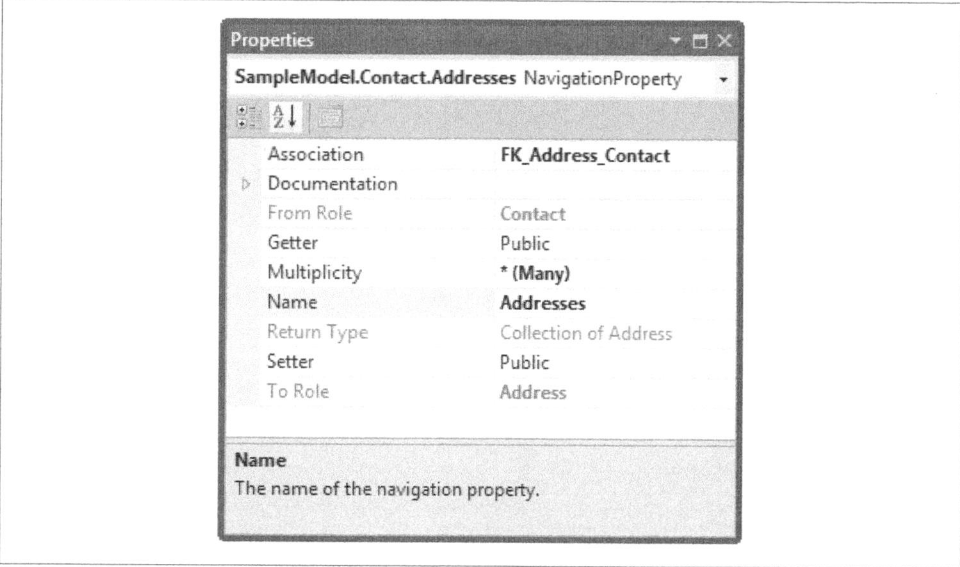

Figure 2-16. The Addresses navigation property

you are working with an `EntityCollection` versus a type that implements `System.Collections.ICollection`, as they are not interchangeable.

It is important to note that in this simple model, the conceptual layer has not been customized. It mirrors the schema of the database, which is a very good place to begin to learn about the EDM. Later in the book, you will learn about customized models and begin to leverage the real power of the EDM.

SSDL: The Store Schema

Continuing with our simple model, it's time to look at another piece, the SSDL, which you will need to understand before we discuss the MSL.

The `StorageModels` section of an EDMX file is a schematic representation of its associated data store. The elements of this file are similar to those of the CSDL file. Figure 2-17 shows the complete SSDL from the EDMX file, although not every section is expanded.

The EDM design tools include a feature that allows you to update the model from the database. It is available in the context menu that you get when you right-click in the EDM Designer. You'll work with this feature in Chapter 7 to bring a database's stored procedures into the model.

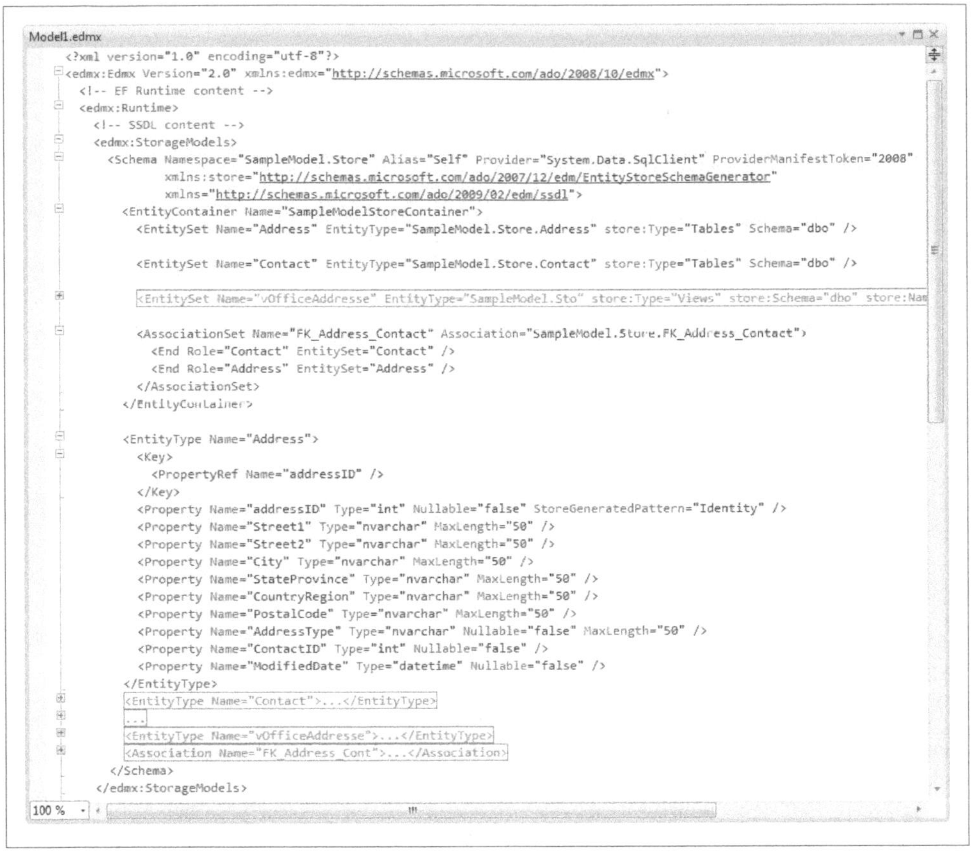

```
Model1.edmx
<?xml version="1.0" encoding="utf-8"?>
<edmx:Edmx Version="2.0" xmlns:edmx="http://schemas.microsoft.com/ado/2008/10/edmx">
  <!-- EF Runtime content -->
  <edmx:Runtime>
    <!-- SSDL content -->
    <edmx:StorageModels>
      <Schema Namespace="SampleModel.Store" Alias="Self" Provider="System.Data.SqlClient" ProviderManifestToken="2008"
            xmlns:store="http://schemas.microsoft.com/ado/2007/12/edm/EntityStoreSchemaGenerator"
            xmlns="http://schemas.microsoft.com/ado/2009/02/edm/ssdl">
        <EntityContainer Name="SampleModelStoreContainer">
          <EntitySet Name="Address" EntityType="SampleModel.Store.Address" store:Type="Tables" Schema="dbo" />

          <EntitySet Name="Contact" EntityType="SampleModel.Store.Contact" store:Type="Tables" Schema="dbo" />

          <EntitySet Name="vOfficeAddresse" EntityType="SampleModel.Sto" store:Type="Views" store:Schema="dbo" store:Nam

          <AssociationSet Name="FK_Address_Contact" Association="SampleModel.Store.FK_Address_Contact">
            <End Role="Contact" EntitySet="Contact" />
            <End Role="Address" EntitySet="Address" />
          </AssociationSet>
        </EntityContainer>

        <EntityType Name="Address">
          <Key>
            <PropertyRef Name="addressID" />
          </Key>
          <Property Name="addressID" Type="int" Nullable="false" StoreGeneratedPattern="Identity" />
          <Property Name="Street1" Type="nvarchar" MaxLength="50" />
          <Property Name="Street2" Type="nvarchar" MaxLength="50" />
          <Property Name="City" Type="nvarchar" MaxLength="50" />
          <Property Name="StateProvince" Type="nvarchar" MaxLength="50" />
          <Property Name="CountryRegion" Type="nvarchar" MaxLength="50" />
          <Property Name="PostalCode" Type="nvarchar" MaxLength="50" />
          <Property Name="AddressType" Type="nvarchar" Nullable="false" MaxLength="50" />
          <Property Name="ContactID" Type="int" Nullable="false" />
          <Property Name="ModifiedDate" Type="datetime" Nullable="false" />
        </EntityType>
        <EntityType Name="Contact">...</EntityType>
        ...
        <EntityType Name="vOfficeAddresse">...</EntityType>
        <Association Name="FK_Address_Cont">...</Association>
      </Schema>
    </edmx:StorageModels>
100 %
```

Figure 2-17. Expanded StorageModels section to explore the store layer of the model

For consistency, the tables and columns are called `EntityType` and `Property`. Frequently, you will see these referred to in documentation as tables and columns, and even as such in the visual tools.

Note the following ways in which the SSDL differs from the CSDL:

- Schema element:
  - —The namespace has ".Store" appended to it so that it's clear that this schema is for the data store, not the conceptual layer of the model.
  - —There is a `ProviderManifestToken` attribute. The value in the example represents the simple expression of the version of SQL Server—for example, `2008`—which is the database being used for this model. The true version number of SQL Server 2008 is 10.0.1600.22. The Entity Framework relies on this bit of information, so it is required. The values are determined by the provider that you are using (in this case, `SqlClient`) and what values it exposes for the token.

—The `xmlns` namespace indicates the namespace used for this section of the XML file. Again, this particular parameter is static.

- Entity container:

  —The name of the `EntityContainer` is "SampleModelStoreContainer," which was derived from the database name.

- Entity type:

  —The entity type names are the actual names of the tables in the database.

  —The property types are the data store data types—in this case, SQL Server data types.

  —The identity columns are attributed with `StoreGeneratedPattern="Identity"`, meaning that the value will be generated (e.g., by the database) when the row is inserted and will not otherwise change. The other options are `"Computed"`, which specifies that the value will be generated on inserts and updates, and `"None"`, which is the default.

In Chapter 16, you will have an opportunity to work directly with the SSDL metadata. You can find additional details about the SSDL metadata in Appendix C.

Pay attention to the database version specified in the `ProviderManifestToken`. If you are moving from one version of SQL Server to another (e.g., your development machine uses SQL Server 2008 but a client that you work with uses SQL Server 2005), you will need to modify that value manually in the XML.

MSL: The Mappings

The last section of the EDMX file to look at is the `Mappings` section. In the Entity Framework metadata, the mapping layer sits between the conceptual and store layers and not only provides the map from the entity properties back to the tables and columns in the data store, but also enables further customization of the model.

You can view the mappings in the Designer's Mapping Details window. To follow along, close the XML view of the model and open the model in the Designer by double-clicking the model's EDMX file in the Solution Explorer.

To see the Mapping Details window, right-click the `Contact` entity and select Table Mapping from the menu. The `Contact`'s mapping information will be displayed in the Mapping Details window, as shown in Figure 2-18.

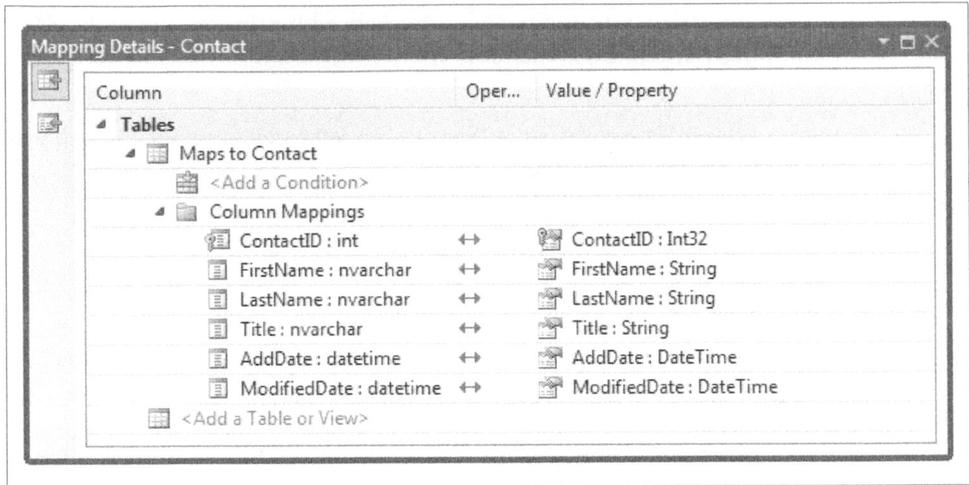

Figure 2-18. The Contact's mapping information as displayed in the Mapping Details window

Figure 2-18 shows visually how the `Contact` entity maps to the `Contact` table in the store layer. This is defined by "Maps to Contact," which refers to the table name in the SSDL. In other words, the `Contact` entity maps to the `Contact` table. Because the `Contact` entity has not been customized, the mapping is straightforward—there is a one-to-one mapping between the conceptual layer and the store layer.

Beneath the table selection for the `Contact` table, you can see that the columns from the table (on the left) are mapped to the entity's properties on the right. When you are creating the mappings yourself rather than relying on the wizard, the Designer, by default, will match identical names to each other, which is a great help.

You can also see that the columns include the provider type (`int`, `nchar`, and `datetime` from SQL Server), whereas the properties include the Entity Framework's primitive types (`Int32`, `String`, and `DateTime`).

You can use the "Add a Condition" and "Add a Table or View" placeholders to further customize the model. We will cover this subject in Chapter 14.

Appendix C explores the XML representation of this entity mapping.

There's more to come on associations and mappings in Chapter 19.

Database Views in the EDM

Something we haven't yet explored in the EDM is the database view from the sample database. The wizard pulled one view into the model and this resulted in the `vOfficeAddress` entity. Database views are handled by the Entity Framework in essentially the same way it handles tables.

If you were to dig through the model, you would find that something in the SSDL, called a `DefiningQuery`, contains the T-SQL from the database that defines the view.

When you originally built the model with the EDM Wizard, you may have seen some warnings in the Error List window about this view. The wizard will discover that there is no primary key for the view and will infer an entity key from any non-nullable properties in the entity. The warning message informs you of this and the same message is embedded into the EDMX file.

The wizard cannot create an entity with no `EntityKey`. Therefore, if there are no non-nullable values in the view, or in a table, for that matter, it will completely skip entity creation for that object.

Chapter 16 will dig deeper into `DefiningQuery`. For now, remember that the view comes into the model as an entity and if the view is not updatable, you can update it by tying it to stored procedures, a feature called *function mapping*. You will learn about function mapping in Chapter 7.

Keep in mind that any changes to the database tables, views, or other objects will not automatically be updated in the model. You'll learn about updating the model in Chapter 7.

Summary

This chapter introduced you to the Entity Data Model and to a bit of the functionality of the design tools. You created your first EDM and looked under the covers to gain an understanding of its most common components. You explored the mappings in the Designer and in the raw XML.

As explained previously, the EDM shines when you can begin to take advantage of the fact that it is highly customizable. Now that you have a solid understanding of the EDM, you are prepared to learn about advanced mappings and customization, which we will explore in Chapters 14 through 16. But for now, this model provides enough to get started with querying, which you will begin in the very next chapter.

CHAPTER 3

Querying Entity Data Models

You can query Entity Data Models in a variety of ways. Some ways you will choose for personal preference and others you will choose so that you can leverage particular benefits. You have likely heard of LINQ to Entities and Entity SQL. You can also use special methods (some based on LINQ and others based on the Entity Framework's `ObjectQuery` class) to express queries. Each of these query styles will result in materialized objects. There is a lesser-known means of querying using Entity Framework's `EntityClient` API, which allows you to stream raw data back to your applications.

In this chapter, you will get a chance to try out all of these different styles of querying. You will repeat a few simple queries using the various mechanisms and look at the results so you can see how the different query methods relate to one other.

By the end of this chapter, you will have gained a high-level understanding of all of the query options and their basic uses. In further chapters, you will write more complex queries; the foundation you will receive from this chapter will make that task much easier. In addition, at the end of this chapter you'll find a critical lesson on query execution.

Although the query examples in this chapter are presented within a console application, you can use LINQPad to test the queries and see the results. Some of the guidance in this chapter will also inspect the debugger, which you will not be able to do in LINQPad. See the sidebar "LINQPad" on page 56 for more information about this tool.

Query the Model, Not the Database

In this chapter, you will learn how to construct queries against the EDM that you created in Chapter 2, and you will learn to let the Entity Framework take it from there. Here is where you will experience the difference between writing queries against a data model and writing queries against the database. The Entity Framework will process your queries and will leverage the ADO.NET provider (in this case, `System.Data.SqlClient`) to turn the EDM query into a query the target database will comprehend. After the database has executed the query, the results will be turned into objects that are based on the entities in the model.

These returned objects are an important piece of the querying process, but surely you want to start querying, so first we'll query and then we'll take a peek under the covers.

Your First EDM Query

In Chapter 2, you created an EDM inside a console application. Here you'll create your first queries against that EDM. You can use that same project, so if you've closed it, open it and let's get started. The code in this section will execute the simplest form of a query, which will return every `Contact` entity from the database, and then display the results in a console window.

1. Open the *Program.cs* file.
2. Add the method in Example 3-1 beneath the `Main` method. IntelliSense will assist you as you type. After you've written a few basic queries, you'll make the code a little more efficient.

   Example 3-1. Querying Contacts and writing out their names

   ```
   private static void QueryContacts()
   {
     using (var context = new SampleEntities())
     {
       var contacts = context.Contacts;
       foreach (var contact in contacts)
       {
         Console.WriteLine("{0} {1}",
                           contact.FirstName.Trim(),
                           contact.LastName);
       }
     }
     Console.Write("Press Enter...");
     Console.ReadLine();
   }
   ```

3. Add the following code into the `Main` method:

   ```
   QueryContacts();
   ```

4. Press F5 to run this bit of code. When the code hits the `ReadLine()` method, all of the names are listed in the console window.

   You have just executed your first query against an EDM and seen the objects that result.

5. Press the Enter key to finish running the app.

Now you'll run the query again, but this time you'll look at some of what's going on:

1. Set a breakpoint at the end of the `foreach` block, which is at the closing brace (}).

2. Press F5 to run the code again.
3. When the debugger reaches the breakpoint, hover your mouse pointer over the `contact` variable in the `foreach` statement and you will see that it is a `Contact` entity type (see Figure 3-1).

Figure 3-1. The query results returning Contact entities at runtime

4. Next, hover your mouse pointer over the `contacts` variable in that same statement and you'll see that its type is a `System.Data.Objects.ObjectSet` of `Contact` types.

   `System.Data.Objects` is the Entity Framework's API for creating and managing entity objects. The `ObjectSet` is what the Entity Framework returns when you make a call to an `EntitySet` (e.g., `Contacts`). It derives from another important class called `ObjectQuery`, which is used to construct and execute queries that will return objects. Once the `ObjectQuery` has been executed, it contains results, which were all of the contacts you saw listed in the console. The context took the data that was returned and used it to create these `Contact` objects on your behalf.

   Because you asked only for the `Contacts` and did not request any filtering, all of the contacts were retrieved from the database when the query was executed.

   Although this doesn't really look like a query, it is a query—albeit a very simple one. You'll take a closer look at this after the next query.
5. You can continue the application or stop it by pressing Shift-F5.

Now that you know this query returns an `ObjectSet` you can rewrite the code that uses implicit typing with the `var` keyword to explicitly declare the type. This way, you can specify the type when the code (e.g., `context.Contacts`) does not make it obvious what will be returned, which will make it easier for you or others to understand your code at a later time.

```
ObjectSet<Contact> contacts = context.Contacts;
```

`ObjectSet` is in the `System.Data.Objects` namespace. Either specify that in the code line or add the namespace to the beginning of the code file (using `System.Data.Objects;` or for VB, `Imports System.Data.Objects`).

Where Did the Context and Classes Come From?

Since you just dove right into the code, you might have a few questions. For instance, where did the `Contact` type come from? How did you go from an XML file (the EDMX file) to strongly typed .NET objects? Why is `context.Contacts` a query unto itself, and what is that context anyway?

One of the features of the EDM design tools is that the Designer automatically performs code generation based on the model. The model's *Designer.cs* file is attached to the model in the Solution Explorer, as shown in Figure 3-2.

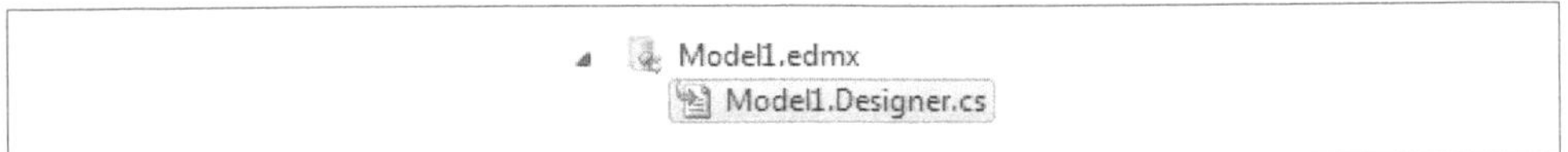

Figure 3-2. The automatically generated code file attached to the model in Solution Explorer

Expand the *.edmx* file in the Solution Explorer to see the generated code file. Open the file to see what's in there.

Because the file is generated automatically, you don't want to edit it directly. You'll learn how to customize the classes in this file in Chapter 11.

The generator reads the conceptual layer of the model and creates from it an `ObjectContext` class based on the `EntityContainer`, and then one entity class for each entity in the model (see Figure 3-3).

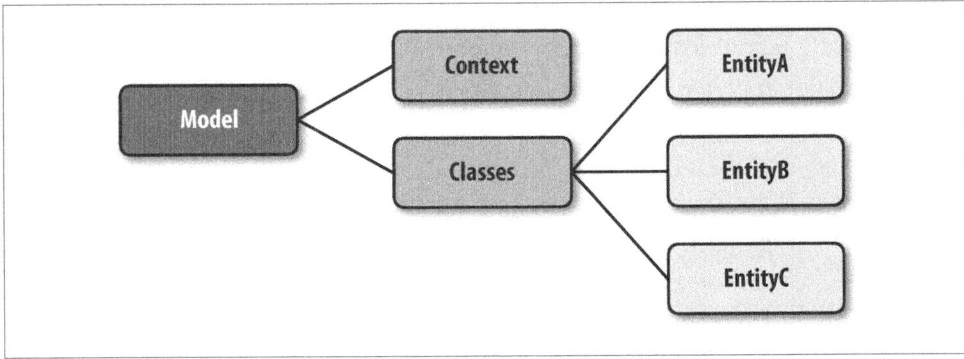

Figure 3-3. Generated ObjectContext and Entity classes based on the conceptual model

The generated code file contains four classes. Figure 3-4 shows these classes in Visual Studio's Class Designer view. You can open a class in the Class Designer by right-clicking on the class in the Solution Explorer and then choosing View Class Diagram.

The first class (which I've expanded from its default view by clicking on the arrows in the upper-right corner) is `SampleEntities`. This class has taken the model's `EntityContainer` name. The others are for each entity—`Address`, `Contact`, and `vOfficeAddresses`.

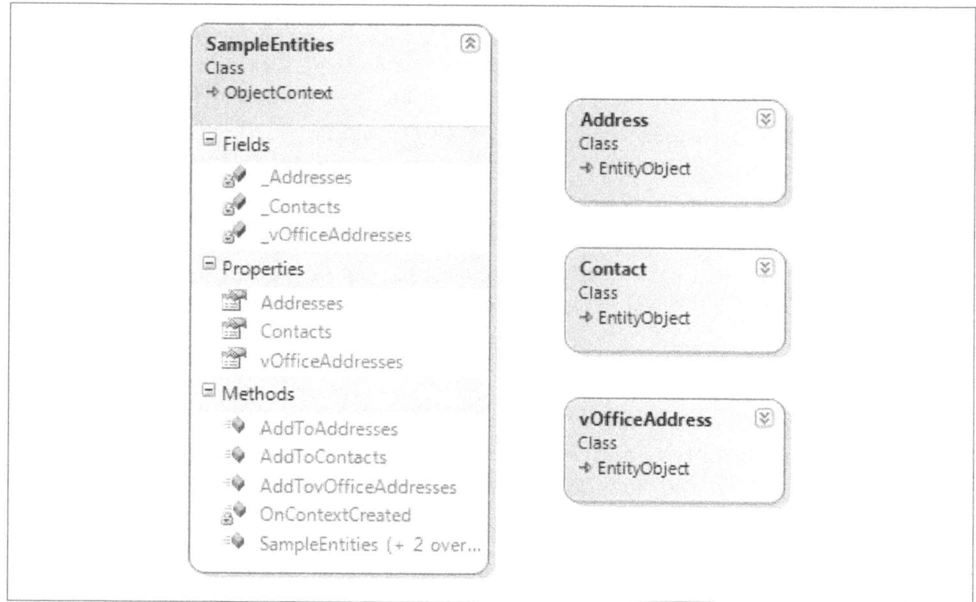

Figure 3-4. The four classes in Visual Studio's Class Designer view

The ObjectContext class, SampleEntities

When you looked at the XML view of the model in Chapter 2, you saw an `EntityContainer` that contained the `EntitySets` and `AssociationSets`.

The `SampleEntities` class represents that `EntityContainer` and inherits from an Entity Framework type called `ObjectContext`. This is why `context` is used for the variable in the example. `SampleEntities` has three properties—`Addresses`, `Contacts`, and `vOfficeAddresses`—which are the `EntitySets` defined in the model. The three `AddTo` methods were created by the code generator to provide a means of adding new object instances to the context, which will then be able to insert those into the database. These `AddTo` methods exist for backward compatibility with the .NET 3.5 version of Entity Framework. In .NET 4, you should take advantage of the `Add` method provided by `ObjectSet`, which you will learn about in later chapters.

My convention when coding Entity Framework is to always use "context" as the variable name for `ObjectContext` instances.

Looking more closely at the `Contacts` property, you can see that it returns an `ObjectSet` of `Contact` types:

```
public ObjectSet<Contact> Contacts
```

For VB developers: if you are unfamiliar with the syntax for generics, C# expresses the type in angle brackets, whereas VB uses parentheses plus the keyword `Of`. The preceding code in VB would be as follows:

```
Public Property Contacts As ObjectSet(Of Contact)
```

An `ObjectSet` is the basis for our queries, whether you want the entire set of `Contact` entities, as you requested in Example 3-1, or you request a subset, which you will do in Example 3-2. You will write entity queries against the `ObjectSet` in much the same way that you would write a database query against a database table.

The entity classes

The three entities defined in the model are the source for the three entity classes. Each class inherits from the Entity Framework's `EntityObject` class and has properties based on the properties defined in the model, including the `Contact.Addresses` and `Address.Contact` navigation properties where necessary (see Figure 3-5).

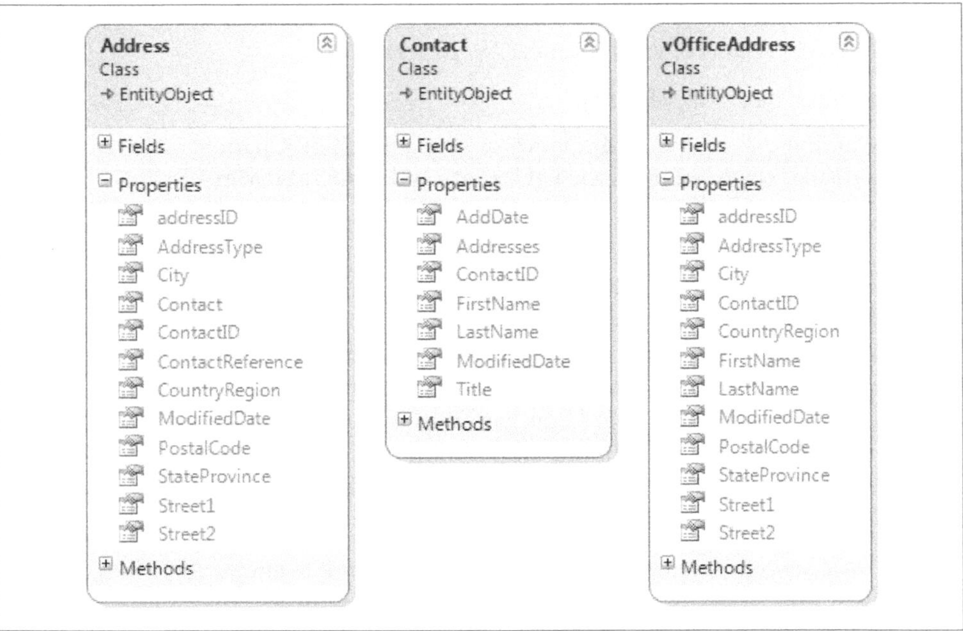

Figure 3-5. The entity classes in the Class Designer

But there's something new in the `Address` class: `ContactReference`, which is another way to access the `Contact` property. You'll learn about `EntityReference` properties in detail in Chapter 19. These classes have more members, but as they are not relevant to the querying you'll do in this chapter, we will dissect them later in the book.

Dig deeper: don't be afraid to poke around in the generated code file, but remember that any changes you make will be overwritten anytime the model is modified and saved.

Querying with LINQ to Entities

The LINQ to Entities query syntax is easier to learn and to use than Entity SQL, and it's possibly already familiar to you if you have been using LINQ elsewhere. LINQ to Entities will very likely cover a large portion of your query needs.

LINQ is a language enhancement that was added to Visual Basic and C# in .NET 3.5. LINQ stands for *Language INtegrated Query*, and LINQ to Entities is one of its implementations.

Although F# does not natively support LINQ, the F# Power Pack (*http://fsharppowerpack.codeplex.com*), created by the F# team, provides LINQ querying.

LINQ was originally written to provide an independent query language that could be used across all CLR objects. There are now many implementations of it. You just used an implementation created to work with entity objects. Visual Studio and the .NET runtime also include LINQ to SQL, an implementation that queries directly against SQL Server databases. Many third parties are also writing LINQ providers.

It is possible to get very creative with LINQ queries, and you will easily find a number of books devoted entirely to LINQ. When you're starting out it's helpful to understand the basic structure.

Writing Your First LINQ to Entities Query

The preceding query used a shortcut that produced a query for you. But it didn't really feel like a query. Now you'll write a LINQ to Entities query using LINQ operators.

Remove the breakpoint that you set in the previous steps. In the line of code that created the `contacts` memory variable, replace `context.Contacts` with the query in Example 3-2, which retrieves a subset of the contacts.

Example 3-2. A LINQ to Entities query in VB and C#

VB
```
Dim contacts=From c In context.Contacts
             Where c.FirstName = "Robert"
```

C#
```
var contacts = from c in context.Contacts
               where c.FirstName == "Robert"
               select c;
```

You'll find many differences between VB and C# syntax when writing LINQ queries. Besides the casing, notice that VB does not require that you explicitly use the `Select` operator, whereas C# does.

Run the application again and you will see that only a small number of contacts are listed and they all have Robert as their first name.

The most obvious sign of integration in LINQ queries is that as you typed your query, you had the benefit of IntelliSense assisting you—for example, providing `FirstName` as an option for the `c` variable. That was because when you identified `Contacts` at the beginning of the query, the compiler was able to determine that the items in that collection are `Contact` items. When you typed `c` later in the query in the `SELECT` and `WHERE` clauses, IntelliSense was able to present a list of `Contact` properties in the IntelliSense suggestions.

Why Does LINQ Start with FROM?

LINQ queries begin with the `FROM` clause, rather than the `SELECT` clause that most of us are familiar with in other query languages. When LINQ was being created, query statements did begin with `SELECT`. However, the developers at Microsoft quickly realized that identifying the type that is being used up front enabled IntelliSense to provide meaningful suggestions as the rest of the query was constructed.

According to Microsoft's Y. Alan Griver, who was very involved with the LINQ project during its early stages, the Microsoft developers jokingly referred to this syntax as "Yoda speak" when they altered the syntax for the sake of IntelliSense.

In the query, `c` is just an arbitrary variable name that lets you reference the *thing* you are working with further on in the query. It's referred to as a *control variable*. The control variable provides another means by which IntelliSense and the compiler are able to make LINQ more productive for developers.

LINQPad

LINQPad is a wonderful tool written by fellow O'Reilly author, Joseph Albahari (*LINQ Pocket Reference* [*http://oreilly.com/catalog/9780596519254/*], *C# 4.0 in a Nutshell* [*http://oreilly.com/catalog/9780596800963/*], and more). It was originally written to be used with LINQ to Objects, but over time, Joseph added support for LINQ to SQL and Entity Framework (Entity SQL as well as LINQ to Entities). It is a great way of testing your queries outside your application.

You can download LINQPad for free at *http://www.linqpad.net*. There's an inexpensive (and well worth the nominal fee) upgrade to enable IntelliSense in the tool. On the LINQPad website and in the download, you will find lots of great tutorial instruction on how to use LINQPad and how to use it with the Entity Framework.

Many of the examples in this chapter focus on only the query. These are great queries to test in LINQPad. Other examples involve additional tasks beyond the queries and you may want to perform these in a console application as instructed.

Querying with Object Services and Entity SQL

Another way to create a query, instead of LINQ to Entities, is by using the Entity Framework's Object Services (in the `System.Data.Objects` namespace) directly. You can create an `ObjectQuery` directly combined with the Entity Framework's T-SQL-like query language, called Entity SQL, to build the query expression.

To see how this works, modify your example with the following steps:

1. Replace (or comment out) the line of code containing the LINQ to Entities query with the code in Example 3-3.

   Example 3-3. Querying with Entity SQL

   ```
   var queryString = "SELECT VALUE c " +
                     "FROM SampleEntities.Contacts AS c " +
                     "WHERE c.FirstName='Robert'";
   ObjectQuery<Contact> contacts = context.CreateQuery<Contact>(queryString);
   ```

2. Run the app again, and the results will be the same as before.

In the first line of code, you created an Entity SQL expression. In the second, you created an `ObjectQuery`, passing in the expression that the query should use. The existing code in your example then executes the query and returns results. If you have constructed SQL queries before, the Entity SQL syntax you used in Example 3-3 looks familiar but not quite right.

The return type of this query at design time is an `ObjectQuery <Contact>`, which implements `IQueryable`. But as you will learn later in this book, it is possible to cast the LINQ to Entities `IQueryable` to an `ObjectQuery` and then access those properties and methods. This means that even if you choose to use LINQ to Entities, you will still get to benefit from these properties and methods.

Why Another Way to Query?

Why would you need another means of querying the EDM in addition to LINQ to Entities? Microsoft did not plan in advance to confuse you with these two options. In fact, Entity SQL was being created before LINQ existed, but now each serves its own purpose. LINQ is obviously much easier to use because it is a query language you can use throughout .NET, not just in Entity Framework, and its strong typing makes it fairly easy to construct the queries. However, LINQ can't be used for every scenario. It is part of C# and Visual Basic but is not built into the other .NET languages. Additionally, you'll learn later about streaming query results in `DataReaders` when you don't need to materialize objects. This can be done only with Entity SQL expressions. As you will see in Chapter 5 and later chapters, there are also some scenarios where being able to build Entity SQL strings is advantageous. Therefore, although you will most likely do the bulk of your querying with LINQ to Entities, when you do encounter these less common cases, you'll be prepared.

Entity SQL

Entity SQL (ESQL) was actually the first syntax devised for querying entities. LINQ was being developed as a language extension by the VB and C# language teams, and eventually it became obvious that LINQ would be a fabulous addition to the Entity Framework, which is how LINQ to Entities came to be.

Entity SQL has its roots in SQL because it makes sense to start with something that is well known. However, because entities are different from relational data, Entity SQL deviates from SQL to provide the necessary capabilities for querying the EDM.

How Is Entity SQL Different from T-SQL?

The Entity Framework documentation has a topic called "How Entity SQL Differs from Transact-SQL." It provides a list of differences with an extended explanation for each difference. For example, Entity SQL supports the inheritance and relationships found in an EDM, whereas in T-SQL you must use joins to work with relationships. Relational databases do not even have the concept of inheritance; therefore, T-SQL doesn't support that either.

Looking more closely at the Entity SQL query string you built earlier, you'll notice that, like LINQ to Entities, it defines a variable for use in the query: `c`. In LINQ this is referred to as a *control variable*, but in Entity SQL it is just called a *variable*.

Figure 3-6 deconstructs the query string without the `WHERE` clause. The variable is defined using the `AS` keyword and is referenced in the `SELECT` clause. The `VALUE` keyword specifies that you want to return a collection of single items; in this case, it will be `Contact` entities.

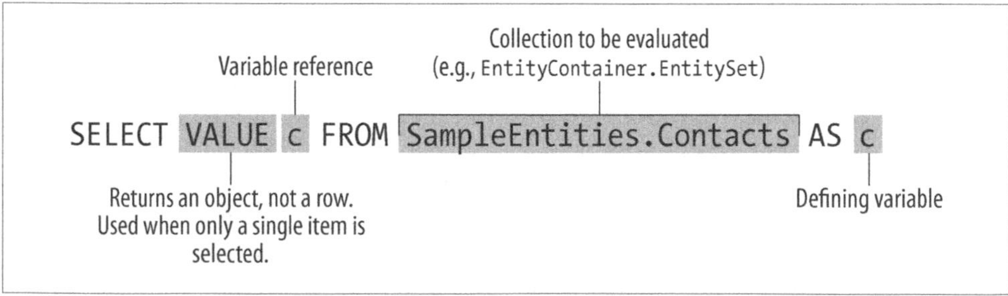

Figure 3-6. Deconstructing a simple Entity SQL query

The VALUE clause is needed if you are selecting a single type, which can be an entity, a single property, or even an entity collection, and that you want to return strongly typed objects. This is shown in the following code snippet:

```
SELECT VALUE c FROM SampleEntities.Contacts ...
SELECT VALUE c.FirstName FROM SampleEntities.Contacts ...
SELECT VALUE c.Addresses FROM SampleEntities.Contacts ...
```

If you are selecting multiple items, you cannot use VALUE, as shown here:

```
SELECT c, c.Addresses FROM SampleEntities.Contacts ....
SELECT c.LastName,c.Title FROM SampleEntities.Contacts ...
```

If you forget to use VALUE, the strongly typed objects will be inside a wrapper, which we will discuss in more detail momentarily. You will need to explicitly cast the results back to the desired type or you could encounter an InvalidOperationException at runtime.

If you include VALUE with multiple items, an EntitySqlException will be thrown that specifically tells you the following:

```
"SELECT VALUE can have only one expression in the projection list."
```

It will even tell you the line number and column number of the problem. But unfortunately, because the Entity SQL string is not compiled until runtime, you won't be aware of this problem until then.

Chapter 22 delves deeper into Entity Framework exceptions.

Without the VALUE clause, the results will be wrapped in tabular rows and you will have to dig into the rows and columns to get at the data. Similar to the LINQ query, you are selecting FROM a collection. In this query, that collection is the entity set, Contacts, but it is necessary in Entity SQL to specify the EntityContainer as well. Again, c is a random variable name I used in the query used to represent contact items within the Contacts entity set.

The WHERE clause in Entity SQL uses SQL-like syntax, as in the following:

```
WHERE c.FirstName='Robert'
```

Entity SQL canonical functions

The Entity SQL language is very robust and offers a lot of functionality. Although it would be impossible to cover all of the operators and functions the language supports, you will see many of them used throughout this book and you can get the full list by looking at the Entity SQL documentation in the MSDN Library.

Entity SQL supports a large set of *canonical functions*, which are functions that all data providers are required to support. It also enables data providers to include their own specific functions. The .NET Framework provider for SQL Server, written by Microsoft, offers approximately 75 specific functions that you can use in Entity SQL queries when the target database is SQL Server; some of these overlap with the canonical functions. The provider additionally offers the provider-specific primitive types and their facets as well as the internal logic for mapping between the EDM and SQL Server. Other providers that are written for the EDM will have their own lists of additional functions and features that are supported.

Remember that one of the great benefits of querying in Entity Framework is that it is database-agnostic. Therefore, you should be considerate before adopting provider-specific elements in your Entity SQL queries.

If you are familiar with T-SQL, you'll be happy to know that one of the canonical functions is `Trim()`, which means you won't have to use the silly `LTRIM(RTRIM())` combo anymore.

The Parameterized ObjectQuery

`ObjectQuery` allows you to create parameterized queries. Similar to some other query languages, you use an `@` placeholder in the string, and then define its value in a parameter.

To use a parameterized query, you can add parameters to an `ObjectQuery` created with the `CreateQuery` method of the `ObjectContext` or to one that you have instantiated explicitly, as shown in Example 3-4. You also need to pass the `ObjectContext` as a parameter when you instantiate an `ObjectQuery`.

You then add parameters to the `ObjectQuery` prior to execution. To see how this works, you can rewrite the query you've been working with to enable dynamic changes to the query, as in Example 3-4.

Example 3-4. Adding an ObjectParameter to an ObjectQuery

```
qStr = "SELECT VALUE c FROM SampleEntities.Contacts AS c " +
       "WHERE c.firstname=@firstName";

ObjectQuery<Contact> contacts = new ObjectQuery<Contact>(qStr, context);
contacts.Parameters.Add(new ObjectParameter("firstName", "Robert"));
```

The namespaces in many of the examples are not spelled out along with the classes. Be sure to reference the appropriate namespaces at the top of your code files with `Imports` for Visual Basic and `using` for C#. For example, for the `ObjectQuery` class you'll need the `System.Data.Objects` namespace.

Although it may seem tempting, you cannot use parameters to replace property names in the query string. In other words, if you tried to create the Entity SQL string `SELECT @myproperty FROM SampleEntities.Contacts AS c` and you created a parameter that set `@myproperty` to `c.LastName`, the ESQL that results would look like this:

```
"SELECT 'c.LastName' FROM SampleEntities.Contacts AS c"
```

This is invalid ESQL and will throw an error. You would need to use string concatenation with variables to build the ESQL:

```
"SELECT " + _propName + " FROM SampleEntities.Contacts AS c"
```

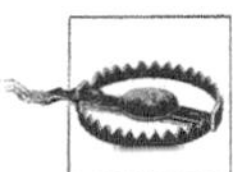

Because of security concerns, you should be extremely careful about where the property names come from. You should not concatenate from user input. Imagine someone enabling a query such as "Select Login, Password from Contacts".

Querying with Methods

So far, the LINQ to Entities and Object Services queries you have seen have been written as standard query expressions. Both LINQ to Entities and Object Services provide a way to write queries as methods, rather than as operators and functions (as in LINQ) or as a string (as in Entity SQL).

Both query languages have a method syntax that you can use, but each exists for opposite reasons. The C# and Visual Basic implementations of LINQ sit on top of query methods. Your LINQ expressions are translated into these query methods, but you can use them directly if you like.

The Entity Framework processes Entity SQL directly; however, a method-based syntax is available that will construct Entity SQL expressions for you.

Querying with LINQ Methods

Although Visual Basic and C# understand LINQ syntax, the CLR does not. One of the first things to happen when the compiler compiles LINQ queries is that it translates the query into a set of method calls on the collection being queried. All of the standard query operators (`WHERE`, `SELECT`, `JOIN`, etc.) have associated methods in .NET.

You can write your queries using the method syntax directly, if you prefer. Many developers do happen to prefer this, although many others would rather use the query expression syntax. The MSDN documentation says, "In general, we recommend query syntax because it is usually simpler and more readable; however, there is no semantic difference between method syntax and query syntax."* Therefore, using one over the other is a matter of style and personal choice.

MSDN provides a list of LINQ methods and whether they are supported by LINQ to Entities. The topic title is "Supported and Unsupported LINQ Methods (LINQ to Entities)" and its URL is *http://msdn.microsoft.com/en-us/library/bb738550.aspx*.

To write method-based queries, you will need to leverage a feature introduced in .NET 3.5, called *lambdas*. Lambdas are inline methods with a very specific syntax. If you are new to LINQ and lambdas and have never used anonymous delegates, this will make more sense after you've seen some examples.

Let's use the `Where` clause to explore working with a method rather than an operator. A standard `Where` clause is written as `where LastName=="Hesse"`. The `Where()` method requires the condition `LastName=='Hesse'` as a parameter. You will write this lambda very differently in C# and Visual Basic.

Wrapping Your Head Around Lambdas

There's no question that lambda expressions are a little confusing at first; but once you get the hang of them, they make perfect sense and can help you write some very efficient code. Admittedly, my Visual Basic background prepared me a little less for lambdas than if I had been programming in C++ or more frequently in C#. Some great articles are available that can help you learn more about lambda expressions. For C# developers, the excellent *MSDN Magazine* article by Anson Horton, "The Evolution of LINQ and Its Impact on the Design of C#" (*http://msdn.microsoft.com/en-us/magazine/cc163400.aspx*), has a great explanation of lambdas. For VB developers, the great *MSDN Magazine* article by Timothy Ng, "Basic Instincts: Lambda Expressions" (*http://msdn.microsoft.com/en-us/magazine/cc163362.aspx*), puts lambdas into perspective.

Here we'll take a look at the query you used in the previous examples, now written using method-based queries. In Visual Basic, the expression begins with `Function`, to indicate that you are performing a function on a control variable; then it states the condition. The control variable, `c` in this example, is named on the fly:

```
Dim contacts = context.Contacts _
               .Where(Function(c) c.FirstName="Robert")
```

* LINQ Query Syntax versus Method Syntax (C#): *http://msdn.microsoft.com/en-us/library/bb397947.aspx*.

The C# LINQ to Entities query using the method-based syntax looks very different:

```
var contacts = context.Contacts
               .Where(c => c.FirstName=="Robert");
```

C# lambda expressions begin by identifying the control variable, followed by `=>` (the lambda) and then the expression, `[controlVariable].FirstName=="Robert"`.

When using LINQ methods in C#, you are not required to use a `Select` command as you are with LINQ query operators.

In the `Where` clauses, the expression that returns a Boolean is called a *predicate*. The query will return all of the contacts for which the expression evaluates to `True`.

Try it out:

1. Replace your existing query with one of the method queries. You will see that IntelliSense is helpful when writing the lambdas.
2. Press F5 to run the application. The results will be the same as before.

Chaining methods

You can combine LINQ query methods to build more useful expressions. This is referred to as *chaining*. To try this, add an `OrderBy` method to the previous query. Notice that the lambda expression for `OrderBy` does not need to evaluate a condition to see whether it is true or false, as does the `Where` method. It only needs to return a property, as in Example 3-5.

Example 3-5. Chaining LINQ methods

```
var contacts = context.Contacts
               .Where((c) => c.FirstName == "Robert")
               .OrderBy((foo) => foo.LastName);
```

When a method's signature requests a predicate, as is the case with the `Where` method, it is asking for an expression that returns a Boolean. Otherwise, the lambda only needs to be a function, as in the `OrderBy` method. You'll see that in Visual Basic, the signatures of all methods refer to this as a function. The C# methods specifically refer to predicates in the methods that require an expression that returns a Boolean. You can view the signatures of the various LINQ to Entities methods in the MSDN documentation topic, "Supported and Unsupported Methods (LINQ to Entities)."

Although you can easily use the same variable name throughout compound methods, the variables don't represent the same instance. In the preceding LINQ query, I named the variables differently to highlight how the compiler evaluates the query.

LINQ actually evaluates the query one method at a time. First it evaluates `context.Contacts`. Then it applies the `Where` method to those results. Finally, it applies the `OrderBy` method to the results of the `Where` method. The `c` in the `Where` method refers to the items returned by `context.Contacts`. The `foo` in the `OrderBy` method refers to the `IQueryable` that is returned by `context.Contacts.Where(....)`.

Evaluating one method at a time does not mean executing one query at a time. LINQ to Entities will evaluate this query one method at a time and then will create a SQL query based on the complete method, unless you are also using methods that must be performed on the client side. It does not execute each method separately.

Here is the T-SQL that results from the preceding query:

```
SELECT
[Extent1].[ContactID] AS [ContactID],
[Extent1].[FirstName] AS [FirstName],
[Extent1].[LastName] AS [LastName],
[Extent1].[Title] AS [Title],
[Extent1].[AddDate] AS [AddDate],
[Extent1].[ModifiedDate] AS [ModifiedDate]
FROM [dbo].[Contact] AS [Extent1]
WHERE N'Robert' = [Extent1].[FirstName]
ORDER BY [Extent1].[LastName] ASC
```

Querying with Query Builder Methods and Entity SQL

It's possible to use Entity SQL with method syntax as well, although a limited number of methods are available: 13, in fact, including `Where` and `Select`. These methods are called *query builder methods*. Query builder methods will do as their name suggests: build an `ObjectQuery` with the correct Entity SQL expression for you.

Although the query builder methods may look like some of the LINQ methods, they are definitely different. The compiler can tell when you are using a query builder method based on the parameter expression, which will contain either a lambda expression for LINQ queries or an Entity SQL expression.

Since you have explored only `WHERE` and `SELECT` so far while learning about the different ways to query, we'll hold off on listing methods and operators until the following chapter, which has many queries.

Example 3-6 shows the latest query using Entity SQL as the method parameters.

Example 3-6. Entity SQL query builder method

```
var contacts = context.Contacts
               .Where("it.FirstName = 'Robert'")
               .OrderBy("it.LastName");
```

The most common question regarding these expressions is "Where did `it` come from?" `it` is the default alias for the control variable. There is no opportunity to define the control variable as you have had to do with all of the other queries we have looked at so far, though it is possible to define your own for nested queries, as you'll see in Example 3-8.

When debugging, you can inspect the `CommandText` property of the `contacts` `ObjectQuery` to see that the query builder did indeed build the Entity SQL for you as shown in Example 3-7. It's a little more complex than what you might have written yourself. This is a result of the query builder's need to be flexible. Additionally, it does not specify the `EntityContainer` name in the expression, something that you can't get away with when building the Entity SQL yourself.

Example 3-7. The Entity SQL built by the query builder methods

```
SELECT VALUE it
FROM (SELECT VALUE it
      FROM ([Contacts]) AS it
      WHERE it.FirstName = 'Robert')
AS it
ORDER BY it.LastName
```

An interesting difference between query builder methods with Entity SQL and LINQ methods with lambdas is that the Entity SQL expressions remove the need to worry about any syntax differences between Visual Basic and C#.

Whether you use LINQ predicates or Entity SQL predicates, at compile time the Entity Framework will be able to determine which query compilation path to choose by looking at the predicate.

Specifying the control variable

As you can see in Example 3-8, you also can combine query builder methods. The Entity SQL control variable is always `it` by default for all new `ObjectQuery` instances. Once you have an `ObjectQuery` instance, however, you can change the control variable name by setting the name property. From there you could continue composing the query as shown in Example 3-8.

Example 3-8. Naming a control variable

```
var contactsQuery = context.Contacts;
contactsQuery.Name = "con";
var contacts = contactsQuery.Where("con.FirstName = 'Robert'");
```

The preceding example demonstrated an additional feature, called *composable queries*. A query was defined (`contactsQuery`) and then another query was written against it. The first query is not executed separately. It is compiled into the second query, `contacts`. When the `contacts` query is finally executed, the composed query is compiled by Entity Framework and sent to the database.

LINQ to Entities queries are composable as well.

The Shortest Query

Remember the first query in this chapter?

```
ObjectSet<Contact> contacts = context.Contacts;
```

In this case, `context.Contacts` refers to the `Contacts` property of the `SampleEntities`.

If you look back at the code generated from the model, you can see that `context.Contacts` returns the following query:

```
_Contacts = base.CreateObjectSet<Contact>("Contacts");
```

This is an `ObjectSet` of `Contact` types. When you pass in only the name of the `EntitySet`, the Entity Framework will do the rest of the work. You can use this shortcut yourself as well, but it is no different from calling `context.Contacts`; it's just longer.

Combining LINQ Methods and Query Builder Methods

Because their methods are evaluated incrementally, it is possible to combine LINQ query methods and the query builder methods. Then you can get the variety of methods, strong typing, and IntelliSense provided by LINQ, plus the ability to build dynamic expressions and use provider functions, among other benefits of Entity SQL. However, there's a catch. You can add LINQ methods to an `ObjectQuery` or to query builder methods, but the only query builder method that you can add to a LINQ expression is `Include`.

ObjectQuery, ObjectSet, and LINQ to Entities

Simply requesting and then executing `context.Contacts` without building a query is enough to allow the context to construct and execute a query to return the `Contact` entities. You saw that effect in Example 3-1. That is possible because `ObjectSet` is a type of `ObjectQuery`. `ObjectQuery` is the class that provides all of the information the context needs to execute the query. In addition to being a type of `ObjectQuery`, `ObjectSet` also implements the `IObjectSet` interface, which provides collection-like functionality. This allows us to manipulate an `ObjectSet` (e.g., adding and removing entities).

Example 3-9 shows the class declaration for `ObjectSet` with the base class and interfaces that give `ObjectSet` its core functionality.

Example 3-9. ObjectSet declaration in VB and C#

VB
```
Public Class ObjectSet(Of TEntity As Class)
    Inherits ObjectQuery(Of TEntity)
    Implements IObjectSet(Of TEntity), IQueryable(Of TEntity), IEnumerable(Of
TEntity), IQueryable, IEnumerable
```

C#
```
public class ObjectSet<TEntity> : ObjectQuery<TEntity>, IObjectSet<TEntity>,
IQueryable<TEntity>, IEnumerable<TEntity>, IQueryable, IEnumerable where TEntity :
class
```

It's important to recognize that an `ObjectSet` is not a LINQ to Entities query. LINQ to Entities comes into play when you write LINQ queries against this `ObjectSet`.

However, as shown in Figure 3-7, `IObjectSet` extends `IQueryable and ObjectQuery` actually implements `IQueryable` (as well as other interfaces), which is a LINQ query type. `IQueryable` contains metadata about the query, such as the query expression and the provider being used. `ObjectQuery` is an `IQueryable` with additional query details that are specific to Entity Framework queries. By inheriting from `ObjectQuery`, `ObjectSet` gains the Entity Framework-specific attributes as well.

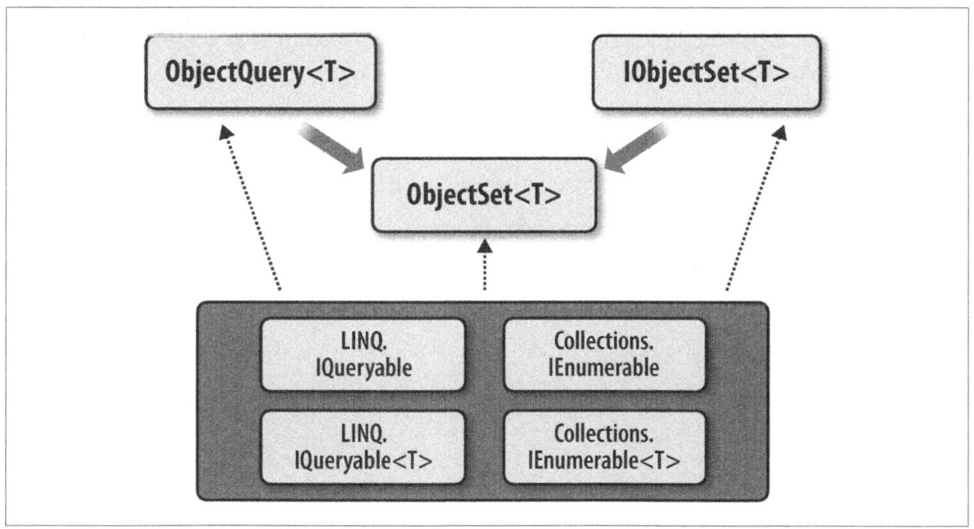

Figure 3-7. ObjectSet deriving much of its functionality from ObjectQuery, IObjectSet, and various IQueryable and IEnumerable interfaces

`IQueryable` is a common link between `ObjectSet`/`ObjectQuery` and LINQ to Entities queries because a LINQ to Entities query is also an `IQueryable`.

Once a query has been executed, `IQueryable` exposes its query metadata as well as the new query results.

The query results inside `IQueryable` are described as an "enumerable type," based on .NET's `IEnumerable` interface. An `IEnumerable` allows you to enumerate or iterate through each item in the collection as you did in the `foreach` code block in Example 3-1. An `ICollection` is an enhanced `IEnumerable`. Whereas an `IEnumerable` is read-only, the more familiar `Collection` class allows you to perform additional actions, such as adding or removing items from the group.

Terminology: IQueryable and IEnumerable

It is important to be familiar with the terms *IQueryable* and *IEnumerable* because they are used frequently when discussing LINQ (not just LINQ to Entities) and Entity Framework queries. Although the phrase "this query returns a collection" is easier for developers to understand, the phrase "this query returns an `IQueryable/IEnumerable`" is more technically correct.

Querying with EntityClient to Return Streamed Data

There is still one additional way to query the EDM: via `EntityClient`. `EntityClient` differs from LINQ to Entities and Object Services because it does not materialize objects. Instead, it streams data back to the requesting application as rows and columns in an `EntityDataReader`, which inherits from `DbDataReader`.

If you have experience with ADO.NET, `EntityClient` is comparable to `SqlClient`, `OracleClient`, and other client providers; these clients return `SqlDataReader`, `OracleDataReader`, and so forth, which also inherit from `DbDataReader`.

A data reader represents data in rows and columns. With the familiar `DataReaders`, each "cell" contains a scalar value—in other words, a primitive type such as a string or an integer. For example:

	Column 1	Column 2	Column 3
Row 1	1	John	Doe
Row 2	2	Jessica	Rabbit
Row 3	3	Cecil	De Mille

`EntityDataReaders` are designed to represent the entities and relationships that exist in an EDM; therefore, scalar data is not enough. An `EntityDataReader` has the ability to return data as shaped results. In an `EntityDataReader`, the cells in the preceding example could contain not only scalar values, but also an entire `DbDataReader`, a `DbDataRecord` (a single row from a `DbDataReader`), or even an `EntityKey` object. You saw `EntityKey` as a property of an entity in the EDM you built in Chapter 2; the `EntityKey` class is a full class implementation based on that property, which you will learn more about in Chapter 10.

EntityClient uses Entity SQL for its query syntax and contains methods and properties that will be familiar if you have worked with ADO.NET previously, including connections, commands, parameters, and transactions.

The next example will give you a chance to work with EntityClient. Following the example is an explanation of the code.

1. Add the following namespace declarations to the beginning of the code file:

```
using System.Data;
using System.Data.EntityClient;
```

2. Add the method in Example 3-10 to your existing code to perform the same query you wrote earlier with LINQ to Entities and Object Services. This time you will be using the EntityClient provider.

Example 3-10. Querying with EntityClient

```
static void EntityClientQueryContacts()
{
 using (EntityConnection conn = new
  EntityConnection("name=SampleEntities"))
 {
   conn.Open();

   var queryString = "SELECT VALUE c " +
       "FROM SampleEntities.Contacts  AS c " +
       "WHERE c.FirstName='Robert'";

   EntityCommand cmd = conn.CreateCommand();
   cmd.CommandText = queryString;
   using (EntityDataReader rdr =
    cmd.ExecuteReader(CommandBehavior.SequentialAccess |
                      CommandBehavior.CloseConnection))
   {
     while (rdr.Read())
     {
       var firstname = rdr.GetString(1);
       var lastname = rdr.GetString(2);
       var title = rdr.GetString(3);
       Console.WriteLine("{0} {1} {2}",
             title.Trim(), firstname.Trim(), lastname);
     }
   }
   Console.Write("Press Enter...");
   Console.ReadLine();
 }
}
```

3. Call this new method from the Main method.

You may want to comment out the call to QueryContacts so that only the new method is run.

4. Press F5 to test the new method.

The result will be similar to the previous two queries.

There is a bit to explain regarding the code for calling the `EntityCommand`.

EntityConnection and the Connection String

With other client providers, the connection connects directly to the data store. However, the `EntityConnection` provides a connection to the EDM. When you created the model with the ADO.NET Entity Data Model Wizard, you may remember seeing the odd connection string in the wizard's page where you selected the connection. An `EntityConnection` string consists of pointers to the EDM XML metadata files as well as a database connection string.

The wizard wrote the `EntityConnection` string into the *app.config* file. You can open this file from the Solution Explorer and see that the `ConnectionString` named `SampleEntities` is composed of three parts: the metadata, provider, and provider connection string.

The metadata contains file path pointers to the three files that are created from the model when the project is built. The data provider refers to the `SqlClient` provider that is being used to connect to the SQL Server database in this example. And finally, the provider connection string is a standard database connection string:

```
metadata=res://*/Model1.csdl|res://*/Model1.ssdl|res://*/Model1.msl;
provider=System.Data.SqlClient;
provider connection string=
 "Data Source=MyServer;
  Initial Catalog=ProgrammingEFDB1;
  Integrated Security=True;
  MultipleActiveResultSets=True"
```

The `res://*` in the metadata indicates that the files are embedded into the assembly file of the project that contains the model and its classes. This is the default, although you can specify that the files be saved to the filesystem. You'll learn more about this in Chapter 8.

`EntityConnection` provides an easy way to reference the connection string in the *app.config* file, which is to set a `name` property to the same name of the connection string: for example, `"name=SampleEntities"`. As you saw in Example 3-10, the quotes are required.

EntityCommand

Creating the `EntityCommand` is no different from creating any other provider command and setting its `CommandText`. The `CommandText` here is the Entity SQL expression defined in the variable, `queryString`.

ExecuteReader

With `EntityClient`, the `SequentialAccess CommandBehavior` is required for the `ExecuteReader` method. With other `DbDataReader`s, rows must be accessed sequentially, but the columns within the rows need not be. This rule exists to control memory consumption. You can combine the `SequentialAccess` behavior with `CommandBehavior.CloseConnection`. `CloseConnection` is a commonly used (and highly recommended) behavior to use with ADO.NET `dbCommand` as another assurance that an unused connection does not inadvertently remain in memory.

Forward-Only Access to the Fields

`DbDataReader`s are streams of data and are, by definition, forward-only. This also means that the columns must be read in this way, which made the code in Example 3-10 a little cumbersome.

In the string concatenation, you want to combine the fields to read `Title FirstName LastName`. But this is not the order of the fields returned in the `DataReader`. `Title` is the fourth column in the row, whereas `FirstName` is the second column and `LastName` is the third; therefore, you cannot read the `Title` data first, and instead must read the fields in the order in which they are streaming.

That is why this method creates the variables prior to building the string—so the data can be extracted in sequential order. Once the variables exist, you can build the string. This is an important lesson to remember, regardless of how you plan to use the streamed data returned by the `EntityClient`.

Translating Entity Queries to Database Queries

Although we will explore query processing in detail later in the book, you may already be wondering what kind of query the Entity Framework is sending to your database.

The Entity Framework will break down the LINQ or Entity SQL query into a *command tree* and, with the help of the EDM and the database provider, will create another command tree that is specific to the database.

Command trees will be familiar to hardcore database geeks and computer science majors. If you don't fit into either group, MSDN defines it's DbCommandTree class as "an abstract class that is used to represent queries, Data Manipulation Language (DML) operations and function/procedure invocations."

You can imagine how flexible the API needs to be to pull this off no matter what query you write. Although the examples so far have been simplistic, it is possible to write very complex LINQ to Entities or Entity SQL queries. The Entity Framework needs to be able to deal with anything you throw at it. Therefore, the resulting store queries may not look exactly the same as you might write them directly in your database's query syntax, because they are being constructed in a somewhat formulaic manner.

Sometimes the queries may look more complex but have no negative impact whatsoever on performance. But don't expect this to always be the case.

Here is the T-SQL rendered from the LINQ to Entities and Entity SQL queries that returned `Contacts` named `Robert`:

```
SELECT
[Extent1].[ContactID] AS [ContactID],
[Extent1].[FirstName] AS [FirstName],
[Extent1].[LastName] AS [LastName],
[Extent1].[Title] AS [Title],
[Extent1].[AddDate] AS [AddDate],
[Extent1].[ModifiedDate] AS [ModifiedDate]
FROM [dbo].[Contact] AS [Extent1]
WHERE [Extent1].[FirstName] = 'Robert'
```

Both queries result in the same T-SQL because they are fairly simple queries.

Pay Attention to the .NET Method's Impact on Generated SQL

In the end it is the actual ADO.NET provider—for example, `System.Data.SqlClient` or perhaps a third-party provider such as `FirebirdSql.Data.FirebirdClient`—that builds the actual query string to be executed by the database. The Entity Framework team put a great deal of effort into improving the SQL generated from the .NET 4 version of this product. If you are using the `SqlClient` provider that is part of .NET 4, it has been enhanced to produce more efficient T-SQL.

A key improvement to look for in the T-SQL generated by `System.Data.SqlClient` is smarter translation of queries that use `StartsWith` or `Contains`. In .NET 3.5, `Contains` was not even supported. However, if you used `StartsWith` in a query—for example, `Contacts.Where(c=>c.LastName.StartsWith("T"))`—the database query that resulted performed poorly in the database. Now `StartsWith` and its newly supported siblings, `EndsWith` and `Contains`, all result in queries that leverage T-SQL's `LIKE` operator, which takes advantage of indexing in SQL Server.

The previous version of Entity Framework generated queries that forced the database to perform a full table scan, which brought pain to the hearts of many database developers. The use of the `LIKE` operator in .NET 4 will be a relief to many database professionals.

Entity Framework also has many opportunities to tune the performance of a query as it moves along the query pipeline to the ADO.NET provider. Improvements in the query pipeline benefit all of the database providers that support Entity Framework.

The August 5, 2009, ADO.NET Team blog titled "Improvements to the Generated SQL in .NET 4.0 Beta1" lists the Beta 1 improvements and discusses changes that appeared in the Beta 2 version of Visual Studio 2010. All of these changes are in the final release. The URL for this post is *http://blogs.msdn.com/adonet/archive/2009/08/05/improvements-to-the-generated-sql-in-net-4-0-beta1.aspx*.

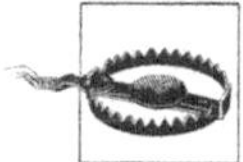

The MSDN blogs were revamped in 2010. The original URLs should automatically resolve to the new URLs. However, if you do have a problem getting to this or any other MSDN blog posts pointed to throughout this book, you can specify the new locations by adding a "b/" to the path between msdn.com/ and the specific blog. For example, if the pointer is to *http://blogs.msdn.com/adonet*, you would change that to *http://blogs.msdn.com/b/adonet*.

It's wonderful that the improvements have been made, but this doesn't mean you are off the hook. You should always pay attention to what's happening in your applications and in your database regardless of what tool or framework you are using for data access.

You have a number of options for watching the queries hit your database.

An Entity Framework method called `ToTraceString` allows you to look at some queries at runtime. With `ToTraceString`, you can inspect some, but not all, queries and you cannot see updates. You will learn more about `ToTraceString` in Chapter 10.

If you are using SQL Server (Developer or higher version), you can watch SQL Profiler. Visual Studio 2010 Ultimate's new IntelliTrace feature will expose the queries and updates to the database. However, IntelliTrace will not display parameter values. There are also third party tools such as EFProf (*http://www.efprof.com*) from Hibernating Rhinos and the Query Profiler (*http://huagati.com/L2SProfiler/*) from Huagati.

A Bit of Entity Framework Profiler History

I was elated that Oren Eini (a.k.a. Ayende Rahien), the author of NHProf and LINQ to SQL Prof, wanted to create a version for Entity Framework, and I spent a bit of time helping him out—but not in an office. The collaboration began at an after-conference party at the Øredev Conference in Malmö, Sweden, then continued later that evening in the back corner of a local bar. For the curious, some evidence of that is captured on Steve Bohlen's blog at *http://unhandled-exceptions.com/blog/index.php/2009/11/10/travelogue-oredev-2009-wrap-up/*. I merely played the muse (and guide through the Entity Framework APIs) to Oren's genius as he hammered out his solution.

What About SQL Injection Attacks?

SQL injection attacks can be used to insert commands into your queries that can display data or impact your database by leveraging your connection to the database and any permission your connection may have.

This is a common threat to database applications, and you can find plenty of information in books and on the Web about how to avoid it.

Anytime a variable is used in a LINQ to Entities query, the generated store query will be parameterized, thus avoiding SQL injection. In Entity SQL, most SQL injections won't even evaluate as correct Entity SQL syntax, and therefore they cannot be executed. However, someone could attempt to inject Entity SQL. `ObjectParameters` can help avoid this problem. Chapter 20 addresses security in the Entity Framework, and you can read more about this topic there.

Avoiding Inadvertent Query Execution

You may have noticed when debugging some of the queries in this chapter that next to the `Results` property it says "Expanding the Results View will enumerate the IEnumerable." This is a very important behavior to be aware of and it impacts all LINQ queries (including in-memory queries and LINQ to SQL) as well as `ObjectQuery` queries. Whether you do it in debug mode or in code, every time you do anything to force the enumeration or execution of a query, the query will be executed on the database again.

In the Entity Framework, this means that even if you have already done something to enumerate the query (e.g., bound it to a control, run it through a `foreach` iteration, called `ToList()` on the query, etc.), anytime you repeat one of these methods that forces execution it will go back to the database, run the query again, bring back the results again, and then merge the results into the cache that's in memory.

Once you have executed a query, you will most likely want to work with the results and no longer the actual query.

When querying for sets of data, I recommend calling `ToList()` to force query execution and provide a variable to work with. That variable will be a `System.Collections.Generic.List<T>` (`List(Of T)` in VB) of whatever type the query returns. You can also use `ToArray()` if that better suits your needs. When returning a single result, you should consider using the `Single()` or `SingleOrDefault()` method. `First()` and `FirstOrDefault()` can also be used, but will additionally work when the query might return multiple results but you wish for only the first one. We'll look at the `Single` and `First` methods in a little more detail in Chapter 4.

Another method to be aware of is `ObjectQuery.Execute`, which will also force execution. `Execute` returns a `System.Data.Objects.ObjectResult<T>`. `ObjectResult` has some special functionality that makes it the right choice for data-binding scenarios; you'll see `ObjectResult` in later chapters where you will be doing data binding in various applications. `Execute` takes a `MergeOption` parameter that specifies how the query results should be merged into existing entities; you'll learn more about `MergeOption` in Chapter 10. But the `ObjectResult` from `Execute` is forward-only. You'll learn more about the limitations this creates in Chapter 9.

I use `ToList` and other methods throughout this book to avoid accidentally repeating query execution. This is my practice in production applications as well.

Summary

In this chapter, you learned about the many different ways to query an EDM using LINQ to Entities, the `ObjectQuery` with Entity SQL, LINQ methods, query builder methods, and streaming data with `EntityClient`. Along the way, you learned about many of the fundamentals that will make it easier for you to construct intelligent queries.

In Chapter 10, you will spend some time comparing how these queries are processed so that you can see the different paths the various query methods embark on as they are resolved. Chapter 20 will cover the performance differences between the various query methods and will demonstrate ways to affect performance directly.

Although this chapter focused on a single simple query with a twist here and there, the next two chapters will delve more deeply into querying, demonstrating ways to retrieve more complex data using all of the methods you are now familiar with.

CHAPTER 4

Exploring LINQ to Entities in Greater Depth

In Chapter 3, you wrote the same basic query over and over and over again. I hope you'll agree that this was a great way to get exposure to the many different ways of writing queries against the Entity Data Model.

There is a lot more to querying an EDM, however. You'll need to learn about the flexibility you have for expressing complex queries, projecting data, combining and nesting queries, and writing parameterized queries. There are also nuances regarding what type of data is returned based on how you construct your queries. Sometimes you will get objects, as you saw in the examples in Chapter 3, but other times you will get unknown objects (*anonymous types*). It is also possible for Object Services queries to return rows and columns. You'll need to know when to expect these varied forms of data to be returned.

Covering all of this exhaustively would require hundreds of pages. Therefore, the goal of these next two chapters on LINQ to Entities and Entity SQL is to teach you the critical features and many of the possibilities, focusing on the most typically needed query features. You will learn how to project specific values (rather than entire objects) in queries, how to query across relationships, how to write nested queries and joins, and how to control when trips are made to the database. Along the way, I will introduce and explain additional new concepts to help you truly understand the workings of the Entity Framework.

This chapter will focus on LINQ to Entities and introducing new concepts. The queries you build here will be demonstrated using Entity SQL in Chapter 5.

Throughout the rest of the book, you will see variations on queries that take advantage of even more techniques as we use queries in real-world examples.

A number of resources provide many specific examples of queries. Here you will learn some of the more common query tasks so that you will know enough to write queries without constantly having to search online for the perfect example of what you are trying to accomplish. It is also useful to check out resources such as the 101 LINQ Examples on MSDN (for VB and for C#), the number of great books dedicated to LINQ, and the Entity Framework Samples, which provide a great variety of query examples with helpful commentary.

Due to some syntax differences between VB and C# when creating LINQ expressions, you will see a number of Visual Basic examples in this chapter along with the C# versions when the difference is significant.

Getting Ready with Some New Lingo

Here is a list of terms used in this chapter (and throughout the book) that may be new to you:

Projection
: Selecting specific properties or expressions in a query, rather than the entity being queried. For example: `from c in context.contacts select c.firstname + c.lastname, c.contactID`.

Eager loading
: Requesting that related data be returned along with query results from the database. For example: when querying contacts, eager-load their addresses. The contacts and their addresses will be retrieved in a single query.

Deferred loading
: Delaying the loading of related data until you specifically request it. For example: when working with query results for a particular contact, you can make a request to retrieve that contact's addresses from the database. When deferred loading happens automatically (implicitly), it is called *lazy loading*.

Navigating
: Moving from an entity to its related data. For example: navigate from a contact to its addresses using the `contact.Addresses` property.

Projections in Queries

So far, the queries you have seen return an entire object, comparable to writing a `SELECT` SQL query requesting every column in a table. By returning an entire object in your query, you will get all of the benefits associated with the entity classes—the most important of which is the ability to keep track of changes to an entity class for database updates.

Often in SQL, you will select particular columns to return from a table (`SELECT Firstname, Lastname FROM Contact`) or from a set of joined tables. This is referred to as *projection*. With LINQ or Entity SQL queries you can shape your results by picking particular properties or expressions rather than entities. You can also select properties from related data.

In the Chapter 3 queries, you returned an entire object but used only the `Title`, `FirstName`, and `LastName` properties. You can rewrite those queries to return only these three properties. As long as you won't need to modify and update these results, a projection will suffice.

Projections in LINQ to Entities

To see how projections work, you can continue modifying the `QueryContacts` method that you worked on in Chapter 3. Replace the latest version of the query with the query in Example 4-1. The difference from earlier LINQ queries is that rather than ending with `select c` to select the entire contact, you are selecting only a few properties.

Example 4-1. Simple LINQ to Entities query with projection in VB and C#

VB
```
Dim contacts = From c In context.Contacts
               Where c.FirstName= "Robert" _
               Select New With {c.Title, c.LastName, c.FirstName}
```

C#
```
var contacts = from c in context.Contacts
               where c.FirstName=="Robert"
               select new { c.Title, c.FirstName, c.LastName };
```

Why are we back to using `Dim` and `var` again? You'll see the reason shortly in the section titled "Implicitly typed local variables" on page 81.

VB and C# Syntax Differences

You may have noticed the syntax differences between VB and C# projections. This is not particular to LINQ to Entities, but it is common for all implementations of LINQ.

C# requires that you use `select new {...}` when projecting. Visual Basic is more lenient. The most explicit syntax for VB is `Select New With {...}` as in Example 4-1, though you could write the Visual Basic query in this simpler format:

```
From c In context.Contacts _
          Where c.FirstName= "Robert" _
          Select c.Title, c.LastName, c.FirstName
```

There are plenty of other nuances to LINQ projections in both languages. For example, you can project into predefined types. In addition, C# projections always create immutable (read-only) results, whereas VB allows the creation of immutable and mutable results. You can learn more about projecting with LINQ in the MSDN Library and from the many great resources that focus on LINQ.

LINQ Projections and Special Language Features

A number of language and compiler features that were added to Visual Basic and C# (in the VB 9 and C# 3.0 versions that were released along with Visual Studio 2008 and .NET 3.5) have made it easier for developers to implement LINQ projections. We'll examine several of these in this section, including anonymous types and implicitly typed local variables.

If you hover your mouse pointer over the `contacts` variable, when the code is not running, the DataTip will show you what the query returns. It's an `IQueryable` of an "anonymous type," rather than an `IQueryable` of contact types. The anonymous type is a result of the projection in your query, which returned results that don't match a defined type. The DataTips and debuggers in Visual Basic and C# often show different information. In this case, the difference is interesting, as you can see in Figures 4-1 and 4-2.

```
Dim contacts = From c In context.Contacts
  Dim contacts As System.Linq.IQueryable(Of <anonymous type>)
               Select New With {c.Title, c.FirstName, c.LastName}
```

Figure 4-1. The DataTip in Visual Basic, which shows the new contacts variable to be an IQueryable(Of <anonymous type>)

```
foreach (var contact in contacts)
{                           (local variable) IQueryable<'a> contacts
  Console.WriteLine("{0}
                       cont Anonymous Types:
                       cont     'a is new { string Title, string FirstName, string LastName }
}
```

Figure 4-2. The DataTip in C#, which shows even more details regarding the anonymous type

Anonymous types

What is this *anonymous type* that the LINQ to Entities projection is returning?

The anonymous type is a language enhancement that was introduced in Visual Basic 9 and C# 3.0 that allows compilers to work with types that were not previously defined. Anonymous types are generally used for on-the-fly types that won't be used elsewhere in the application. You cannot even pass them from one method to another. Anonymous types relieve you from having to define a class for every type, even if the type is to be used only briefly. Yet an anonymous type returned by the query is still strongly typed, which means you can easily interact with it in the code following its creation.

The sidebar "Wrapping Your Head Around Lambdas" on page 62 includes a link to an article by Anson Horton. The article contains a great introduction to anonymous types. Anonymous types are a powerful feature that you can use throughout .NET, but they have special importance for LINQ queries because of their ability to allow projections that can return anything a developer can dream up.

So, the query in Example 4-1 returned an anonymous type that doesn't have a name, but has the properties Title, FirstName, and LastName. If you are still modifying the earlier query method, you can see a bit of .NET magic by removing the Console.WriteLine method and retyping it. The anonymous type is strongly typed and recognized by IntelliSense. Pretty cool!

> **Anonymous Types and Updates**
>
> Although later chapters will introduce the concepts of tracking changes to entities and performing updates to the database, it is important to keep in mind that this takes place only with entities defined in your model. Anonymous types do not participate in change tracking or updates. With any projections, it's important to know whether the operation returns entities or anonymous types, because the result determines how the object can be used.

Implicitly typed local variables

Another new compiler trick that you have been taking advantage of in some of the code samples so far is the use of implicitly typed local variables. In C# you use them with a new keyword, var, and in VB you use them with the existing Dim keyword. It is possible to declare variables without identifying their types. They will infer the type based on the value that is being set.

Hasn't it always seemed redundant to say something like Dim str as String="this is some text" or int MyInt=123? With implicitly typed local variables, Dim str="this is some text" and var MyInt=123 are enough. In the case of replacing int with var the benefit is not very obvious. Had that type been MyCustomType<Myothercustomtype<T>>, suddenly var would look pretty convenient.

> This shortcut is not always a good thing, as it removes some of the explicitness of your code. I wrote a blog post on DevSource.com titled "How Visual Studio 2008 made me even lazier" (*http://blogs.devsource.com/devlife/content/net_general/how_visual_studio_2008_made_me_even_lazier.html*). There is an interesting discussion in the comments about the pros and cons of implicit typing. Throughout the book, I will attempt to declare types explicitly for the sake of clarity. However, in cases where the type name is quite long, you may find a var in its place.

Where implicitly typed local variables really shine, however, is with LINQ query projections, because there's no way to say "Dim contacts as a thing with a Title, a FirstName, and a LastName." Instead, you can write "Dim contacts (and just look at the other side of the equals sign to figure out what this is)." In this context, `Dim` in VB and `var` in C# essentially translate to "thing," or for some readers, "whatever."

Run the application and you'll see that, once again, the results are the same as they were previously. You can modify the `Console.WriteLine` command to include the `Title` property that is in the newest query.

In Chapter 10, you will learn more about Object Services and all of the functionality it provides to objects returned by queries against the EDM. This will help you better understand the significance of returning anonymous types rather than entire entity objects defined by the EDM.

Implicit and explicit anonymous type creation

You can project into anonymous types in a number of ways. For instance, it is possible to give a name to the returned variable, such as `ContactName` in Example 4-2.

Example 4-2. Naming a projected anonymous type in LINQ in VB and C#

VB

```
From c In context.Contacts _
Where c.FirstName = "Robert" _
Select ContactName = New With {c.Title, c.LastName, c.FirstName}
```

C#

```
from c in context.Contacts
where c.FirstName == "Robert"
let ContactName = new {c.Title, c.LastName, c.FirstName}
select ContactName
```

C# does not allow naming in the `SELECT` statement; it has another operator, `LET`, that can be used for this purpose.

There are so many ways to do projection and use anonymous types in LINQ queries. Here you are seeing just a small slice of what you can achieve, so be sure to look to the dedicated LINQ resources to expand your understanding.

Naming the anonymous type is more useful if this new type is a property of the projected results. In Example 4-3, a projection is used to project much more than some strings. It creates a new type with another anonymous type as the first property and the addresses of the contact as the second.

I'm projecting the `Addresses` property here to highlight the projection. You'll learn more about working with related data later in this chapter.

When you name the anonymous type, the property that results will have the name specified in the query. Notice that the property name is used later in the query for the `Order By` operator and when working with the results.

Example 4-3. Anonymous types as properties

```
var contacts =
      from c in context.Contacts
      where c.FirstName == "Robert"
      let foo= new {
                    ContactName = new {c.Title, c.LastName, c.FirstName},
                    c.Addresses
                    }
      orderby foo.ContactName.LastName
      select foo;

foreach (var contact in contacts)
{
  var name = contact.ContactName;
  Console.WriteLine("{0} {1} {2}: # Addresses {3}",
                    name.Title.Trim(), name.FirstName.Trim(),
                    name.LastName.Trim(),contact.Addresses.Count());
}
```

Figure 4-3 shows the shape of the new range variable, `foo`. The first property is the `ContactName` anonymous type.

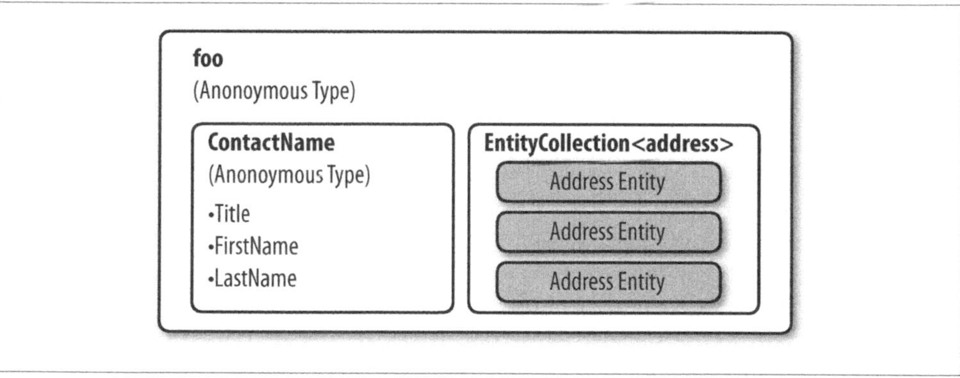

Figure 4-3. A named anonymous type with a named anonymous type property

Unlike the `ContactName` anonymous type in this query, the `Address` entities that this query returns will participate in the change tracking and database updates.

Projections with LINQ Query Methods

To project using LINQ's method-based query syntax, you would use the `Select` method and then identify the properties you want in its parameter. The method-based query syntax requires the syntax for creating an anonymous type in the lambda (see Example 4-4).

Example 4-4. Projecting using LINQ's method-based syntax

```
context.Contacts
.Where(c => c.FirstName == "Robert")
.Select(c => new {c.Title, c.LastName, c.FirstName})
```

Using Navigations in Queries

One of the big benefits that the EDM lends to querying is that the relationships are built into the model and you won't have to construct joins very often to access related data. Additionally, when using LINQ for the queries, the related data is presented via IntelliSense, which makes it very discoverable.

Using the model, let's take a look at some more queries, this time digging into associations.

The model has only one association, that which lies between `Contact` and `Address`. The association provides two navigations—one from `Contact` to all of its related addresses and one from `Address` to its related contact.

You can easily do projection, drilling into related entities, although drilling into a collection is different from drilling into a reference entity. For example, you can't request `Contact.Addresses.Street` in a query. `Contact` to `Addresses` is a one-to-many relationship and `Addresses` is a collection of `Address` entities, not a single entity. `Street` is not a property of the `Addresses EntityCollection`. However, you could select `Address.Contact.LastName`, because you would be navigating to a single entity. There is only one contact per address; therefore, there is no question regarding from which entity the query should retrieve the `LastName`.

Navigating to an EntityReference

Recall that navigating to the "one" end of a one-to-one or many-to-one relationship is referred to as a *navigation reference*. The entity you are pointing to is referred to as an `EntityReference`, sometimes called an *EntityRef*.

Chapter 19 will drill further into `EntityReferences` and `EntityCollections`, and how they are surfaced as navigation properties.

The LINQ query in Example 4-5 returns an anonymous type containing an address and its related contact.

Example 4-5. Projecting into an EntityRef with LINQ to Entities

```
var addresses = from a in context.Addresses
                where a.CountryRegion == "UK"
                select new { a, a.Contact };
```

Figure 4-4 displays the anonymous type that results in the debugger, where you can see that one property is the address record and the other is the contact.

```
foreach (var newtype in newTypes)
{
    newtype {a = {ProgrammingEntityFramework.Chapter4.Address}, Contact = {ProgrammingEntityFramework.Chapter4.Contact} }
      a        {ProgrammingEntityFramework.Chapter4.Address}
      Contact  {ProgrammingEntityFramework.Chapter4.Contact}
```

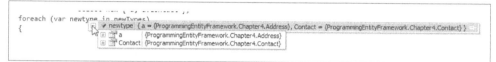

Figure 4-4. The query results, which contain a new type with the address and its contact

When working with the results, you'll have to drill into the new type's properties (the `Address` and the `Contact`) and from there you'll have to drill into their properties, as shown in Example 4-6.

Example 4-6. Accessing the properties of an anonymous type

```
foreach (var address in addresses)
{
  Console.WriteLine("{0} {1} {2}",
                    address.Contact.LastName, address.a.Street1,
                    address.a.City);
}
```

The first property is named `a` because it is using the variable name given in the query. If you want to be sure the property is called `Address` you can use that instead of the simpler `a`, or use LINQ syntax to rename the property:

VB

```
Select New With {.Address = a, a.Contact}
```

C#

```
select new {Address= a, a.Contact };
```

Then you can work with `address.Address` in the data which results.

Although this may suit many scenarios in your applications, you may prefer to project individual properties from the reference navigation. Example 4-7 shows such a query using LINQ to Entities. This projection returns a new type with three properties. The first is an `Address` entity; the second and third are strings. Again, the property names are based on the query defaults—`a`, `FirstName`, and `LastName`.

Example 4-7. Combining properties from related entities

```
var addresses = from a in context.Addresses
                where a.CountryRegion == "UK"
                select new { a, a.Contact.FirstName,
                             a.Contact.LastName };

foreach (var address in addresses)
{
  Console.WriteLine("{0} {1} {2} {3}",
                    address.FirstName, address.LastName,
                    address.a.Street1, address.a.City);
}
```

Filtering and Sorting with an EntityReference

You can filter and sort based on a property of an `EntityReference` whether or not you are selecting the related data.

For example, you can select all addresses for contacts with a particular last name. The LINQ to Entities query in Example 4-8 sorts by `Contact.LastName` and filters on the `Contact.AddDate` field even though `AddDate` is not part of the results.

Example 4-8. Filtering and sorting on reference properties

```
from a in context.Addresses
where a.Contact.AddDate > new System.DateTime(2009, 1, 1)
orderby a.Contact.LastName
select new {a, a.Contact.LastName};
```

Navigating to Entity Collections

Querying with related data is straightforward when the related data is a single entity, but what about when the navigation property is an `EntityCollection` such as `Contact.Addresses`?

Let's start with a simple scenario that you have seen a few times already in this chapter: returning a contact and its collection of addresses. To highlight the difference between the original properties and the results, the `EntityCollection` in the new type is given a random name, as shown in Example 4-9.

Example 4-9. Projecting an EntityCollection with LINQ

```
var contacts =  from c in context.Contacts
                select new {c, Foos = c.Addresses};
```

This query creates a new anonymous type with two properties. The first is the `Contact` and the second is Foos, which is the `EntityCollection` of `Addresses` related to that `Contact`.

You can enumerate through the results, and then, for each result, enumerate through the collection of the `Foos` property, as shown in Example 4-10.

Example 4-10. Enumerating over shaped data that includes an EntityCollection

```
foreach (var contact in contacts)
{
  Console.WriteLine("{0}: Address Count {1} ",
                    contact.c.LastName.Trim(), contact.Foos.Count);
  foreach (var foo in contact.Foos)
  {
    Console.WriteLine("   City= {0}", foo.City);
  }
}
```

Projecting Properties from EntityCollection Entities

If you wanted to select particular properties such as `Street` and `City` from each `Address` of each `Contact`, the method you should use to build the query depends on what shape you want the results to be.

Shaped results

You could shape the data similar to the previous example, but instead of a set of complete address entities as the `Foos` property, you can project some of the address properties. This would result in a set of anonymous types, named `StreetsCities` instead of `Foos`, in the second property.

You can achieve this with a nested query, a feature we'll look at more closely later in the chapter. For now, you can see in the query in Example 4-11 that the third property, `StreetsCities`, contains the results of querying the `Contact`'s `Addresses`.

Example 4-11. Projecting values from an EntityCollection

```
from c in context.Contacts
select new {c.FirstName, c.LastName,
            StreetsCities = from a in c.Addresses
                            select new { a.Street1, a.City }
           }
```

The anonymous type that is returned has the properties `FirstName` and `LastName`, along with a collection of anonymous types with `Street1` and `City` properties. The debugger screenshot in Figure 4-5 displays the new type.

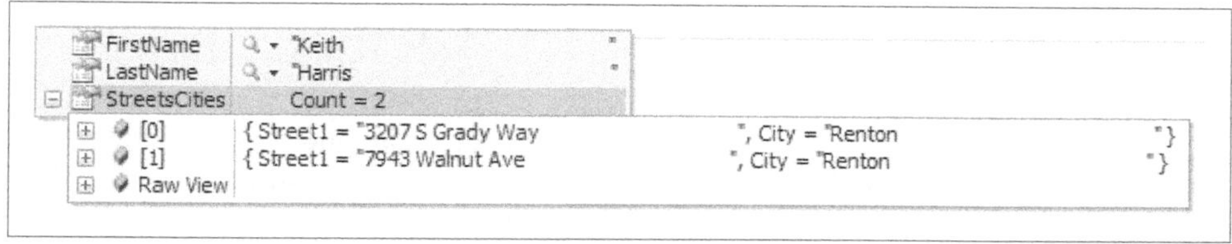

Figure 4-5. The newly shaped anonymous type

Flattened results

Another way to project into the addresses is to merely turn the query around. That is, query the addresses and their contact data to flatten the results, as shown in Example 4-12, so that the data is no longer shaped.

Example 4-12. Flattening the related data

```
var contacts =
from a in context.Addresses
orderby a.Contact.LastName
select new {a.Contact.LastName, a.Contact.FirstName, a.Street1, a.City};
```

This will result in a single type with four properties, but contacts with multiple addresses will appear multiple times, as you can see in this section of the results. For instance, Katherine Harding and Keith Harris each have two results:

```
Hanson, John: 825 W 500 S, Bountiful
Harding, Katherine: 52560 Free Street, Toronto
Harding, Katherine: 25   Flatiron Blvd., Vancouver
Harrington, Lucy: 482505   Warm Springs Blvd., Fremont
Harris, Keith: 3207 S Grady Way, Renton
Harris, Keith: 7943   Walnut Ave., Renton
Harui, Roger: 9927 N.   Main St., Tooele
Hass, Ann: Medford Outlet  Center, Medford
```

Filtering and Sorting with EntityCollections

Although you can easily use related data in projections or for filtering, sorting, and other operations, it is important to keep in mind that when the related data is in a collection, you need to leverage operations that can be performed on a set of data. For example, if you want to find contacts with addresses in the United Kingdom (represented as UK in the database), you can use the `ANY` method in LINQ to Entities (see Example 4-13) or the `EXISTS` operator in Entity SQL (which you'll see in the next chapter) to search the contact's addresses. The LINQ query uses a predicate to provide the condition for `ANY`.

Example 4-13. Filter condition provided by an EntityCollection with LINQ

```
from c in context.Contacts
where c.Addresses.Any(a => a.CountryRegion == "UK")
select c;
```

Aggregates with EntityCollections

Aggregates perform calculations on a series of data. Aggregate methods include `Count`, `Sum`, `Average`, `Min`, and `Max`. You may not want the entire collection of addresses, but rather some aggregated information about that collection.

Aggregates in LINQ to Entities

Aggregating data with LINQ is easyusing one of the aggregate methods such as `Count`; simply append the method to the collection name. The `Count` method will return the count of the items in the collection (see Example 4-14).

Example 4-14. Using the Count aggregate method in LINQ to Entities

```
from c in context.Contacts select new {c.LastName, c.Addresses.Count};
```

Other types of aggregates, such as `Max`, require a specific value to aggregate. You can supply that value using a lambda expression, as shown in Example 4-15.

Example 4-15. Using an aggregate method with a lambda in LINQ

```
from c in context.Contacts
select new { c.LastName, MaxPC = c.Addresses.Max(a => a.PostalCode)};
```

It's important to name the property returned by the aggregate function, because LINQ is unable to derive one based on the method. If you forget to do this, both VB and C# will give a compiler error explaining the problem.

Visual Basic has an `Aggregate` operator for LINQ that you can use in place of `FROM` in your LINQ queries. Check the MSDN Library topic "Aggregate Clause (Visual Basic)" for more information.

Aggregates in LINQ Methods

The LINQ aggregates are methods, not query operators. Therefore, they work very naturally with the LINQ query methods. Example 4-16 uses the `Max` aggregate as one of two projected values to be returned.

Example 4-16. A LINQ method syntax query using an aggregate

```
context.Contacts
  .Select((c) => new { c.LastName,
             MaxCode = c.Addresses.Max(a => a.PostalCode) });
```

This query does two interesting things with the lambdas. First it uses a lambda expression to specify what values should be projected: `LastName` and `MaxCode`. Once the variable, `c`, has been declared, the function projects an anonymous type consisting of `LastName` as the first property and `MaxCode` as the second. `MaxCode` is defined by using the `Max` aggregate on the `Addresses` collection of the contact.

Joins and Nested Queries

Although associations in the EDM minimize the need for joins in queries, sometimes a relationship may exist but there is no association to represent the relationship. In these and other cases, you can use nested queries or joins to bring the data together.

> **From the Source: Should You Even Use Joins?**
>
> Zlatko Michailov, former Entity SQL program manager at Microsoft, writes in his blog: "A well defined query against a well defined entity data model does not need JOIN. Navigation properties in combination with nesting sub-queries should be used instead. These latter constructs represent task requirements much more closely than JOIN does."*
>
> You may not always have the opportunity to define a model the way you'd like, because of limitations in the database or your domain. What you should take away from Zlatko's quote is that using `JOIN`s should not be your first stab at expressing a query. I've seen clients using `JOIN`s in queries simply because they don't understand yet how to take advantage of navigation properties in their queries.

LINQ to Entities provides a `JOIN` operator as well as `GROUPJOIN`. Entity SQL provides a variety of options in the `JOIN FROM` clause, including inner joins, as well as left, right, and full outer joins. It also enables joining multiple collections separated by commas.

Joins

The `vOfficeAddresses` entity in the current model has all of the contact properties except for the contact's `Title`. Because there is no association between `vOfficeAddresses` and `Contact`, you will need to use `JOIN` to combine the `vOfficeAddresses` entity properties with the `Title` property.

You could, of course, add the association to the model in this case, but then there would be no lesson here, would there?

Example 4-17 shows the syntax of a LINQ `JOIN`.

Example 4-17. JOIN syntax for LINQ

```
FROM [variableA] IN collectionA
JOIN [variableB] IN collection
ON variableA.commonproperty EQUALS variableB.commonProperty
SELECT .....
```

* *http://blogs.msdn.com/esql/* (November 1, 2007).

Example 4-18 shows how to combine data from `Contact` entities and `vOfficeAddresses` entities using the `JOIN`.

Example 4-18. A LINQ to Entities query using a JOIN

```
from c in context.Contacts
join oa in context.vOfficeAddresses on c.ContactID equals oa.ContactID
select new { oa.FirstName, oa.LastName, c.Title, oa.Street1, oa.City,
             oa.StateProvince };
```

This provides an inner join where only entities with matching `ContactID`s are returned. Any contacts with no match in the `vOfficeAddresses` will not be returned. `vOfficeAddresses` with no match in `Contacts` will not be returned either.

Nested Queries

Both LINQ and Entity SQL provide the ability to nest queries, and you have already seen some examples of this. When you write a query, anywhere a value is expected you can use another query in its place, as long as that query returns an acceptable type. You can use a nested query in place of an expression or a collection, as you will see in the following examples.

The goal of the previous `JOIN` queries was to return properties from a `Contact` entity combined with properties from the `vOfficeAddresses` entities where the `ContactID` matches.

Using a nested LINQ query as a projection

Example 4-19 shows how to express the previous query in LINQ using a nested query instead of a `JOIN`. The query uses a nested query (highlighted) combined with the `FirstOrDefault` method in place of a projected value to return results from `vOfficeAddresses`.

Example 4-19. Nested query in place of a SELECT expression in LINQ

```
from oa in context.vOfficeAddresses
select new { oa.FirstName,  oa.LastName,
             Title = (from c in context.Contacts
                      where c.ContactID == oa.ContactID
                      select c.Title).FirstOrDefault(),
             oa.Street1, oa.City, oa.StateProvince
};
```

There are a few notable twists to this query. The first should be familiar: an anonymous type is not able to automatically name the return from the nested query. Therefore, it is given the name "Title". The second twist is that the subquery returns an `IQueryable` of `String`, not just a string, which is why the `FirstOrDefault` method is appended to the query.

Using a nested LINQ query as the collection to be queried

You can also use the nested query in place of the collection being queried. The nested query merely returns another collection to be queried.

Let's start with a basic example. Rather than querying all `vOfficeAddresses`, you could create a subquery that returns only `vOfficeAddresses` in Ontario and then query against that. Example 4-20 is simplistic and could easily be expressed without the nested query. The technique can be useful when you are attempting to express queries that are much more complex.

Example 4-20. Nested query in place of a target collection in LINQ

```
var contacts = from add in
                 (from oa in context.vOfficeAddresses
                  where oa.StateProvince == "Ontario" select oa)
               select ...
```

You can benefit from using nested queries to help with complicated queries by separating the nested query from the main query.

On its own, this particular example doesn't seem very useful, but imagine being able to use subqueries to redefine the universe of `vOfficeAddresses` from which to query, and then passing that into different methods which will perform additional queries on that subset.

Example 4-21 ties a subquery to a variable and then uses that variable in another query. The second query is complex enough, using another nested query to join `vOfficeAddresses` back to `Contact`. Breaking up the query makes the code much more readable. When the query is executed, the Entity Framework will create a single query from the combined expressions.

Don't forget the importance of knowing what is going on at the database level by using some type of profiler, as suggested in Chapter 3.

Example 4-21. Breaking a nested query out of the main query in LINQ

```
var universe = from oa in context.vOfficeAddresses
               where oa.StateProvince == "Ontario"
               select oa;

var query = from oa in universe
               select new
               {
                 oa,
                 contact = (from c in context.Contacts
                            where c.ContactID == oa.ContactID
                            select c)
```

```
            };
var AddressesWithContacts = query.ToList();
```

You can't separate out a nested query that's inside a projection, as in Example 4-21, because its filter condition is dependent on the main query.

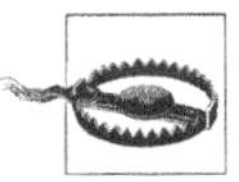

An Order operator in a subquery will be ignored. The main query controls ordering.

Grouping

Both LINQ and Entity SQL provide operations for grouping data. You can use grouping in connection with aggregates or to shape data.

LINQ to Entities has a Group operator (literally Group By in Visual Basic and Group in C#) and a GroupBy method (with eight overloads). Entity SQL provides a GROUP BY operator and a GroupBy query builder method.

The results of the grouping can use automatic naming, and in other cases can be explicitly named. In addition, an INTO GROUP clause is required in Visual Basic. C# has an optional INTO clause.

The constructs for VB and C# are quite different and it's easiest to explain them with examples. Example 4-22 shows the simplest form of grouping in LINQ for both Visual Basic and C#.

Example 4-22. Simple grouping in LINQ to Entities in VB and C#

VB
```
From c In context.Contacts Group By c.Title Into Group
```

C#
```
from c in context.Contacts group c by c.Title into mygroup select mygroup
```

The result of this query is an IQueryable of an Entity Framework class called Grouping; more specifically, System.Data.Objects.ELinq.InitializerMetadata.Grouping<K,T>. In our example, it's a Grouping<string,Contact>. This is something like a key/value pair where the key is K (the string in our example) and the value is an IEnumerable of T (e.g., the group of Contact types).

The results, therefore, are a set of these key/value pairs. If we select one of the groupings, as you can see in Figure 4-6, VB automatically names the property containing the title as "Title".

(5)	Title="Sr.
Group	Count = 3
(0)	{VBModelSamplePEF.Contact}
(1)	{VBModelSamplePEF.Contact}
(2)	{VBModelSamplePEF.Contact}
Title	"Sr.

Figure 4-6. The VB result, which contains a Title property and a Group property that contains three contacts

By default, C# uses the word *Key* as the name for the key of the grouping and doesn't name the property that contains the grouped records, as you can see in Figure 4-7.

Key	"Ms.
Results View	Expanding the Results View will enumerate the IEnumerable
[0]	{ProgrammingEntityFramework.Chapter4.Contact}
[1]	{ProgrammingEntityFramework.Chapter4.Contact}
[2]	{ProgrammingEntityFramework.Chapter4.Contact}
[3]	{ProgrammingEntityFramework.Chapter4.Contact}
[4]	{ProgrammingEntityFramework.Chapter4.Contact}

Figure 4-7. Default C# grouping

VB allows you to specify the property name rather than use the default. In Visual Basic, to change the `Title` property of the preceding query to `MyTitle`, you would use the syntax `Group By MyTitle=c.Title`.

In VB, the `Group` property is available to access the group. You can rename this as well. For example, `Into MyGroup = Group` renames the property to `MyGroup`.

Naming Properties When Grouping

The optional `INTO` clause in C# allows you to specify a group name, but this is not exposed as a property. You specify the name with `INTO` so that you can perform further functions on the group. Note that in C#, using the `INTO` clause requires that you also use the `SELECT` clause. The `Key` property is then accessible as a property of the group.

With the group specified, it is now possible to explicitly name the properties in C#. LINQ queries in Visual Basic will imply a `SELECT` statement if it is not used. In this case, the query will still return `Title` and `MyGroup` by default without specifying `SELECT`. Of course, you can shape the data further by specifying your own output with an explicit `SELECT` operator.

Example 4-23 demonstrates these changes to the previous queries.

Example 4-23. LINQ Group By with explicitly named groups and targets in VB and C#

VB
```
From c In context.Contacts _
Group By c.Title Into MyGroup = Group
```

C#
```
from c in context.Contacts
group c by c.Title into MyGroup
orderby MyGroup.Key
select new {MyTitle = MyGroup.Key, MyGroup};
```

Chaining Aggregates

Visual Basic provides a simple way to use aggregates in grouping queries, by specifying one or more aggregates in the `INTO` clause separated by commas. In Example 4-24, your result will contain the properties `Max` and `Count`.

Example 4-24. Chained aggregates in VB LINQ

VB
```
From c In context.Contacts _
Group By c.Title Into MyGroup = Group, _
Max(c.AddDate), Count()
```

In C#, you need to explicitly project these properties in the `Select` clause using methods and predicates, as shown in Example 4-25.

Example 4-25. Combining aggregates in C# LINQ

C#
```
from c in context.Contacts
group c by c.Title into MyGroup
orderby MyGroup.Key
select new {MyTitle = MyGroup.Key, MyGroup,
            Max = MyGroup.Max(c => c.AddDate),
            Count = MyGroup.Count()}
```

Filtering on Group Conditions

There is so much more that you can do with grouping in LINQ. For now, we'll take a look at one more variation: filtering on the grouping condition.

The `Title` fields in the sample data contain Mr., Mrs., Ms., Sr., and a few other titles. Also, some contacts have no title. Perhaps you would like to group on title, but exclude empty titles. To filter what is being grouped, such as "only group contacts with something in the `Title` field," you can apply the filter to the control variable, `Title`, to make sure it contains a value.

You may, however, want to filter on a property of the `Group`. With LINQ you can continue to use the `WHERE` operator, as shown in Example 4-26.

Example 4-26. Filtering on a Group property with LINQ

```
From c In context.Contacts _
Group By c.Title Into MyGroup = Group, Count() _
Where (MyGroup.Count() > 150)
```

```
from c in context.Contacts
group c by c.Title into MyGroup
where MyGroup.Count() > 150
select new { MyTitle = MyGroup.Key,
             MyGroup,
             Count = MyGroup.Count()};
```

In LINQ, you will also need to be aware of variables going out of scope, as in the Visual Basic query shown in Example 4-27, which won't compile. The `a` in `Group by a.CountryRegion` is out of scope because by this point in the query, you are working with the anonymous type returned by the `Select` statement. And the `Select` does need to go before the `Group By`.

Example 4-27. An out-of-scope variable preventing this query from compiling

```
From a In context.Addresses _
Select a.Contact.FirstName, a.Contact.LastName, a.CountryRegion _
Group By a.CountryRegion Into MyGroup = Group, Count() _
Where (MyGroup.Count() > 150)
```

You can avoid this problem by naming the anonymous type, and then grouping by a field within the name, as shown in Example 4-28.

Example 4-28. Naming variables to keep them from going out of scope

```
From a In context.Addresses _
Select c = New With {a.Contact.FirstName,
                     a.Contact.LastName, _
                     a.CountryRegion} _
Group By c.CountryRegion Into MyGroup = Group
```

```
from a in context.Addresses
let c= new {a.Contact.FirstName, a.Contact.LastName,
           a.CountryRegion} group c by c.CountryRegion
           into MyGroup where (MyGroup.Count() > 150)
           select MyGroup;
```

Both the Visual Studio documentation and the ADO.NET Entity Framework documentation and samples can provide you with an astounding array of data shaping that you can perform with `Group By`/`groupby` in LINQ, and even then there are still many more.

See "Finding More Query Samples" on page 109 for links to these resources.

Like everything else this chapter has covered so far, we have only skimmed the surface of `GROUP BY` in Entity Framework queries. You will see more uses throughout this book and can find more details (and plenty of rules) in the documentation. The rest of this chapter will explain some important concepts that have been exposed by the queries you've seen so far.

LINQ Compiled Queries and Entity SQL Cached Queries

One of the expensive processes of executing queries is in the query compilation. This is when the query is transformed into the proper query to be sent along to the database. LINQ to Entities has a feature called *precompilation* whereby you can compile a query in advance and access that compiled version as needed. Even if some of the query parameters change, such as searching for `LastName="Smith"` and then searching for `LastName="Holbert"`, the precompiled query will be used. This has a huge impact on performance, and Microsoft recommends that you use precompilation for any queries that might be called repeatedly.

Entity SQL has the ability to cache its queries, and does this by default. The performance benefit is similar to that of using precompiled LINQ queries.

Chapter 20 explores both of these features.

Shaping Data Returned by Queries

Whether you write a query that returns entities, anonymous types, `DbDataRecords`, or `DbDataReaders`, you can return shaped data. You've seen this in several of the previous queries, with a variety of shaped results. How you use this data depends on how the data is shaped. Let's take a further look at the results of some of the earlier queries.

The LINQ and Object Services queries that returned entities defined in the model are not shaped. They are purely a collection of individual entities.

For instance, Example 4-13 returned an `IQueryable` of `Contact` objects. Example 4-9, however, returned an anonymous type with two properties. The first property was a `Contact` entity and the second was a collection of `Address` entities related to that `Contact`. The code in Example 4-10 enumerated over that data, albeit in a somewhat boring way, to demonstrate what the data looked like. It showed the contacts and the addresses but did not truly demonstrate the relationship between the two.

Example 4-29 executes the same query and then enumerates through the anonymous types that result. This time, however, the code accesses the `Addresses` as a navigation property of the `Contact`.

`LazyLoadingEnabled` is set to `false` to ensure that the `Count` method does not impact the results.

Example 4-29. LINQ query creating shaped results

```
context.ContextOptions.LazyLoadingEnabled=false;
var addressGraphs = from a in context.Addresses
                    where a.CountryRegion == "Canada"
                    select new { a, a.Contact };

foreach (var ag in addressGraphs)
{
  Console.WriteLine("LastName: {0} # Addresses: {1} ",
    ag.Contact.LastName.Trim(), ag.Contact.Addresses.Count());

  foreach (Address address in ag.Contact.Addresses)
  {
    Console.WriteLine(".....{0}", address.City);
  }

  Console.WriteLine();
}
```

There's a simpler way to express this particular query with the `Include` method, which you will see next. But what differentiates this from `Include` is that with it you can take the projection in Example 4-29 a step further in a direction that you won't be able to do with `Include`. I'll discuss this after we look at the results of this example.

Let's turn the query around a bit to see how this can work. Imagine you are querying contacts and want to also return their addresses.

The `WriteLine` method doesn't access the `a` property of the anonymous type, but instead navigates to the addresses through the `Contact` property of the anonymous type.

As the `Contact` and `Address` entities are materialized, the Entity Framework recognizes that they are related to each other and wires them up so that you can navigate between them. The `Address` objects have a `Contact` object in their `Contact` property and the `Contact` objects have `Address` objects in their `Addresses` property. This is a very high-level explanation of an important function of the Entity Framework's Object Services API, which you will learn plenty about throughout the book.

There is an interesting thing to be aware of with respect to how the Entity Framework connects the related entities in the scenario laid out in Example 4-29. If you look at the following sample of the output, you can see that two addresses belong to the contact "Harding." One is in Toronto and the other is in Vancouver. But the first instance says that Harding has only one address. Not until the code has reached the second address is the contact aware that two addresses exist in its `Addresses` navigation collection.

```
LastName: Garza # Addresses: 1
....Burnaby

LastName: Harding # Addresses: 1
....Toronto
```

```
LastName: Harding # Addresses: 2
....Toronto
....Vancouver

LastName: Caprio # Addresses: 1
....Toronto

LastName: Blackwell # Addresses: 1
....Toronto

LastName: Hamilton # Addresses: 1
....Chalk Riber
```

The second address isn't recognized initially because it hasn't been materialized as an object yet. As the code enumerates through the query results for the first time, the objects are created from the query results as each contact or address is reached. Once the second address is encountered and turned into an object, its relationship to the contact is identified.

I had you disable lazy loading in order to see this because when you requested `Addresses.Count`, lazy loading would have kicked in and gone to the database to retrieve the contact's complete `Addresses` collection. For the sake of the demo, I did not want this behavior. You'll learn more about lazy loading further on in this chapter, and later in the book as well.

We will explore the object life cycle more deeply in a later chapter, but this should give you some idea for now about what's going on in this example.

Limiting Which Related Data Is Returned

At the end of the previous example, I mentioned that projections will allow something that the upcoming `Include` method won't allow. That is the ability to filter which related data is returned.

If you were querying for contacts with their addresses, a projection would look like this:

```
var contactGraphs = from c in context.Contacts
                    select new { c, c.Addresses };
```

You can modify the query to load all of the contacts, but only a subset of their addresses, as in Example 4-30.

Example 4-30. Filtering related data in a query using projections

```
var contactGraphs = from c in context.Contacts
                    select new { c, MyAddresses = c.Addresses.Where(a=>a.CountryRegion="UK")};
```

I'll refer back to this example as we look at other means of loading related data.

Loading Related Data

So far, all of the queries that involved returning related data have explicitly asked for that data in the query itself. The Entity Framework will only return data that you explicitly ask for. If your query asks only for contacts, the Entity Framework will not make an assumption that just because contacts have addresses, it should return the addresses anytime you query for contacts. Consider a typical model for sales information. A contact is related to a customer; a customer has sales orders; each sales order has line items; each line item relates to a product; each product comes from a vendor and is also related to a category. Can you imagine if you queried for contacts, and without expecting it, the entire contents of the database were returned—because it was all related?

It is possible to get related data after the fact. For example, if you queried for a selection of contacts, as you work with those contacts in code you can request the contacts' addresses without performing another complete query.

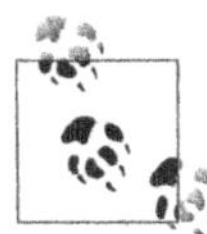

For developers coming from the first version of Entity Framework, there is a big change to be aware of here. The implicit, automatic loading of related data, controlled by the `ObjectContext.ContextOptions.LazyLoadingEnabled` property, is a new option in the Entity Framework. It is enabled (i.e., set to `true`) by default, for newly created models. The property will be `false` on existing models pulled into .NET 4 to prevent breaking changes in your existing code.

This is referred to as *deferred loading* or *implicit deferred loading*, and is most commonly known as *lazy loading*.

As of .NET 4, Entity Framework performs lazy loading by default.

The LINQ to Entities query in Example 4-31 returns an `ObjectSet` of `Contact` entities. As the code enumerates through the results, it also asks for information about the related `Addresses`. But the `Addresses` were not returned with the original query.

Example 4-31. Implicitly loading related data after the fact

```
var contacts= from c in context.Contacts select c;
foreach (var contact in contacts)
{
  Console.WriteLine("{0} #Addresses: {1}",
                   contact.LastName,contact.Addresses.Count());
}
```

Unlike the filtered projection in Example 4-30, lazy loading has no means of filtering the data being loaded.

However, each time the code hits a request for the address count of the current contact, a new query will be executed on the server to retrieve the addresses for the current contact. You should understand that this means that if there were 10 contacts in the original result, there will be 10 additional trips to the database as you iterate through the 10 contacts.

Controlling Lazy Loading

Lazy loading is surely convenient, but if you are not paying attention, you could be abusing your server resources by unknowingly or even unnecessarily causing repeated trips to the database. You can disable (and reenable) lazy loading as needed in code or modify the default behavior for the context. There are other ways to load related data when you need it even if you are not depending on lazy loading.

Disabling and enabling lazy loading programmatically

Lazy loading can be controlled through the `ObjectContext`'s `ContextOptions.LazyLoadingEnabled` property:

```
var context = new SampleEntities();
context.ContextOptions.LazyLoadingEnabled = false;
```

Once it is disabled, you can still explicitly load related data on demand if needed, or even load the data along with the initial query. These two methods are covered in the next few pages.

Changing the default behavior for lazy loading

In the default generated classes, the constructors for the `ObjectContext` (e.g., `SampleEntities`) set `LazyLoadingEnabled` based on an annotation in the EDMX. The XML annotation was pointed out in the CSDL `EntityContainer` section of Chapter 2.

Models that are created in Visual Studio 2010 have this annotation with the value set to `true`. Models that were created in Visual Studio 2008 SP1 do not have the annotation, and therefore, if you are using an older model, by default, lazy loading will not be enabled.

The Lazy Loading Enabled setting is exposed in the model's Properties window in the Designer, in the Code Generation section, where you can change the default behavior for a particular model.

Explicitly Loading Entity Collections and Entity References

Let's return to the query in Example 4-31:

```
var contacts= from c in context.Contacts select c;
```

When lazy loading is disabled, because the query does not explicitly request the addresses, the `Addresses.Count` for every single contact will be zero.

But you can explicitly tell the Entity Framework to get the addresses for the current contact, as shown in the Example 4-32.

Example 4-32. Explicitly loading related data with the Load method

```
foreach (var contact in contacts)
{
  contact.Addresses.Load();
  Console.WriteLine(contact.Addresses.Count);
}
```

When `Load` is called, Object Services will execute a query to retrieve all of the addresses for that contact. In the preceding example, after `Load` is called, the value of `Count` will be correct and all of the `Address` entities for that contact will be available.

Using `Load` is another case where you cannot filter the related data being loaded as you can with the projection in Example 4-30.

In .NET 4, a new method was introduced to load from the context, not from the navigation property. The method is `ObjectContext.LoadProperty` and it was created as part of the support for classes that do not inherit from `EntityObject`. You'll learn about `LoadProperty` in Chapter 11.

Loading the EntityReference

You can also perform deferred loading for `EntityReference` navigation properties—for example, `Address.Contact`. However, rather than load from the `Contact` property, you must load from the additional property that was created by the code generation: `ContactReference`. The Entity Framework sees `Address.Contact` as merely a `Contact` entity, and the `Contact` class does not have the `Load` method. It is the `ContactReference` property that has the knowledge of how to load the related information. Each `EntityReference` navigation property will have a related property with the word *Reference* appended to its name.

Example 4-33 shows how to load `Contact` data for particular addresses after the addresses have already been queried.

Example 4-33. Loading the Contact using ContactReference.Load

```
var addresses = from a in context.Addresses select a ;
foreach (var address in addresses)
{
  if (address.CountryRegion != null)
  {
    if (address.CountryRegion.Trim() == "UK")
    {
      address.ContactReference.Load();
    }
  }
}
```

Performance considerations with deferred loading

There is a big performance consideration here. Whether you are lazy-loading or explicitly loading the related data for each contact, the code is forcing an extra round trip to the database, something many developers won't realize unless they are profiling the database activity. This can be extremely inefficient and might also get you into big trouble with the IT pros in your company. With lazy loading disabled, you can have some control over when the extra trip is made.

`Load` is a great choice in cases where you want to inspect the contacts and then load addresses for only particular contacts. Perhaps you want to list all contacts, but for contacts that were added after a particular date you need to see how many addresses are in the database. The code in Example 4-34 demonstrates this scenario, where you may determine it is more efficient to make a small number of database trips rather than preloading addresses for every contact.

Example 4-34. Loading addresses for some of the contacts

```
foreach (Contact contact in contacts)
{
  Console.WriteLine(contact.LastName);
  if (contact.AddDate > System.Convert.ToDateTime("1/1/2008"))
  {
    contact.Addresses.Load();
  }
}
```

With lazy loading enabled, this kind of granular control is a bit more difficult to achieve.

The benefit of having lazy loading enabled is that you won't have to worry about reporting that there are no addresses for a contact when in fact there are a number of them in the database because you forgot to, or didn't know that you needed to, explicitly load those related addresses.

Using the Include Method to Eager-Load

In cases where you know you will need all of the addresses up front, it may be more efficient to retrieve them as part of the original query. Although you have seen how to do this with projection by including the addresses in the `SELECT` clause, the `Include` method is another way to achieve this and may be preferable for a variety of reasons. The most notable reason is that the resultant objects will be your entities, rather than anonymous types with entities as their properties. However, `Include` does not allow you to filter the related data as you can with a projection.

`Include` is a query builder method and you can apply it to an `ObjectQuery` or `ObjectSet` (which, as you may recall, derives from `ObjectQuery`). Because `context.Contacts` is an `ObjectSet`, you can use `Include` even within a LINQ query, as shown in Example 4-35.

Example 4-35. The Include method in a LINQ to Entities query

```
from c in context.Contacts.Include("Addresses")
where c.LastName.StartsWith("J")
select c
```

The argument for `Include` is a string that is the name (or names) of the navigation properties to bring back along with the contacts. This is referred to as *eager loading* or *eager fetching*.

You can use `Include` only when returning an `ObjectQuery` or `ObjectSet` of a single entity type. You cannot use it with projections, and if you do project, `Include` will be ignored.

In the sample model, there is only one navigation property for `contact`, which is `Addresses`. Imagine a sales model with a number of entities and a variety of navigations. You could query customers and eager-load the orders and all of the orders' details by querying `Customers.Include("Orders.OrderDetails")`. The string is called a *query path* because it defines the path that the query should navigate through the model. This will bring in both the `Orders` and `OrderDetails`. Additionally, you could eager-load the orders and the customers' addresses by chaining the `Include` methods like this:

```
Customers.Include("Orders.OrderDetails").Include("Addresses")
```

How is the data shaped with Include?

Data shaping is one of the interesting benefits of `Include`. The previous `Contacts.Include("Addresses")` query returns a set of `Contact` entities. This does not have the same effect as projection, which would have to return `DbDataRecords`.

Figure 4-8 shows the query results in the debugger's QuickWatch window. You can see that the results are strictly a set of `Contact` entities. Where are the addresses?

Figure 4-9 drills into one of the contacts, and you can see that both of this contact's addresses are there. The `Include` brings in the related data, and unlike the issue you saw in the results of Example 4-29 (not all addresses were being attached to Ms. Harding from Toronto until the addresses had been enumerated), all of these addresses are present as soon as you get to the contact.

> Lazy loading will still be active when you are inspecting data in debug windows such as the QuickWatch window in Figure 4-9. I disabled lazy loading for the context prior to opening the QuickWatch window. You can also watch a database profiler to ensure that the `Addresses` count you are looking at is truly a result of eager loading and is not being provided by way of lazy loading and an extra hit to the database.

QuickWatch

Expression:

contacts, results

Value:

Name	Value
Results View	Expanding the Results View will enumerate the IEnumer
[0]	{ProgrammingEntityFramework.Chapter4.Contact}
[1]	{ProgrammingEntityFramework.Chapter4.Contact}
[2]	{ProgrammingEntityFramework.Chapter4.Contact}
[3]	{ProgrammingEntityFramework.Chapter4.Contact}
[4]	{ProgrammingEntityFramework.Chapter4.Contact}
[5]	{ProgrammingEntityFramework.Chapter4.Contact}
[6]	{ProgrammingEntityFramework.Chapter4.Contact}
[7]	{ProgrammingEntityFramework.Chapter4.Contact}
[8]	{ProgrammingEntityFramework.Chapter4.Contact}
[9]	{ProgrammingEntityFramework.Chapter4.Contact}
[10]	{ProgrammingEntityFramework.Chapter4.Contact}
[11]	{ProgrammingEntityFramework.Chapter4.Contact}
[12]	{ProgrammingEntityFramework.Chapter4.Contact}
[13]	{ProgrammingEntityFramework.Chapter4.Contact}
[14]	{ProgrammingEntityFramework.Chapter4.Contact}
[15]	{ProgrammingEntityFramework.Chapter4.Contact}

Figure 4-8. The result of the Include with no projections, which returns only the primary entity of the query

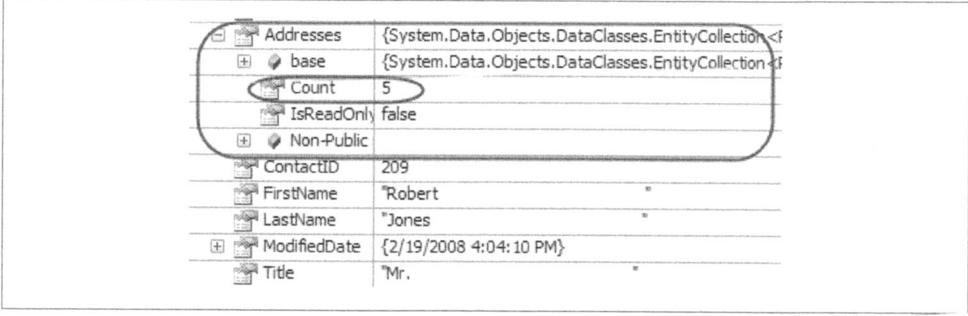

Figure 4-9. The result of the Include with projections, with lazy loading disabled, which returns the contact's related Addresses in the query

Accessing properties from an Include in the query

You can use the properties of the `Include` entities in many of the same ways you can use properties of any related data when querying.

Example 4-36 uses the `CountryRegion` field of `Address` to limit which contacts are retrieved. But be sure you are clear on the results. This will return contacts that happen to have any of their addresses in the United Kingdom. If a contact has multiple addresses and only one of them is in the United Kingdom, you will still get all of those addresses.

Example 4-36. Limiting which contacts are retrieved

```
from c in context.Contacts.Include("Addresses")
where c.Addresses.Any((a) => a.CountryRegion == "UK")
select c
```

Although you can use the properties of the included data in your query, you cannot filter or sort the included data. There's no way to say "when you return the addresses along with the contacts, please sort the addresses by city." Additionally, as mentioned before, you can't filter the included data either.

Pros and Cons of Load and Include

You have some things to consider when choosing between the `Load` and `Include` methods. Although the `Load` method may require additional round trips to the server, the `Include` method may result in a large amount of data being streamed back to the client application and then processed as the data is materialized into objects. This would be especially problematic if you are doing all of this work to retrieve related data that may never be used. As is true with many choices in programming, this is a balancing act that you need to work out based on your particular scenario.

The documentation also warns that using query paths with `Include` could result in very complex queries at the data store because of the possible need to use numerous joins. As the model becomes more complex, the potential for trouble increases.

You could certainly balance the pros and cons by combining the two methods. For example, you can load the customers and orders with `Include` and then pull in the order details on an as-needed basis with `Load`.

The correct choice, or combination, will most likely change on a case-by-case basis.

Retrieving a Single Entity

All of the queries so far have returned sets of data. What if you wanted to retrieve a single entity or a single result? The queries return IQueryables or ObjectQuerys and you need to dig into those to get at the actual data, which might be entities, anonymous types, or DbDataRecords.

This is reasonable if you are returning multiple items, but what about cases where you query for one particular item—for example, the contact whose ContactID is 63—and you don't want to have an IQueryable returned, but just the item?

LINQ to Entities has a pair of methods, First and FirstOrDefault, which will return the first item in the result set. Additionally, Single and SingleOrDefault are useful when you are expecting only one item in the result set—for example, if you are querying for a single contact. These methods are not specific to LINQ to Entities, but come from LINQ and may be familiar to you already.

Example 4-37 shows two techniques for using these methods. In the first technique, a query is defined and then the Single method is called. This will cause the query to be executed and the contact entity to be returned. The second technique appends the Single method directly to the query. Even though Single is a LINQ method, you can combine it with the query operator syntax by wrapping the query in parentheses. In this case, the query is executed immediately and the contact is returned.

Example 4-37. Querying with the Single method

```
IQueryable<Contact> contacts = from c in context.Contacts
                               where c.ContactID == 1
                               select c;
Contact contact = contacts.Single();
Console.WriteLine(contact.LastName);
Contact singleContact = (from c in context.Contacts
                         where c.ContactID == 2
                         select c).Single();
Console.WriteLine(singleContact.LastName);
```

There's a potential problem here. If there are no items, First and Single will throw an InvalidOperationException with the message "Sequence contains no elements." FirstOrDefault and SingleOrDefault protect you from the exception by returning the default, which is generally a null (Nothing in VB). Additionally, if you use Single or SingleOrDefault but the result set contains more than one item, an exception will be thrown. In that case, you should be using First or FirstOrDefault.

In Example 4-38, `SingleOrDefault` is used to avoid an exception being thrown. `Contact` in this case will be `Nothing/null` after the query is executed.

Example 4-38. Using SingleOrDefault to avoid an exception

```
var contact = (from c in context.Contacts
               where c.ContactID == 7654321
               select c).SingleOrDefault();
```

Another way to use these methods is to pass the predicate directly to them, rather than using a `where` operator.

For example:

```
var contact = context.Contacts.Single(c => c.ContactID == 1);
```

Retrieving a Single Entity with GetObjectByKey

The `ObjectContext.GetObjectByKey` method and its counterpart, `TryGetObjectByKey`, provide a way to query for an object without having to construct and execute a query. However, this has a notable twist. The runtime will first look in the existing instantiated objects to see whether the object has already been retrieved. If it is found, this is what will be returned. If not, the query to the data store will be executed automatically and the object will be returned.

`GetObjectByKey` takes an `EntityKey` type that defines what object to retrieve based on its `EntitySet`, its key property name, and the value of that property. For example, `EntityKey("SampleEntities.Contacts","ContactID",5)` defines an object in the `Contacts EntitySet` with a `ContactID` value of `5`. Once the `EntityKey` has been created, `GetObjectByKey(myEntityKey)` will return the object either from memory or from the database.

`TryGetObjectByKey` uses the .NET `Try` pattern to avoid returning an exception if the object is not found in memory or in the database.

You will see both of these used many times in later chapters, and you will learn all about the `EntityKey` class in Chapter 10.

There is also a method for retrieving an entity by only looking in memory and not checking the database, called `GetObjectStateEntry`. You'll learn about this method in Chapter 10.

Finding More Query Samples

This chapter is filled with many queries, but there are so many possibilities for querying with LINQ or Entity SQL that you will certainly benefit from checking these other great resources:

MSDN's 101 C# LINQ Samples
: *http://msdn.microsoft.com/en-us/vcsharp/aa336746.aspx*

MSDN's 101 Visual Basic LINQ Samples
: *http://msdn.microsoft.com/en-us/vbasic/bb688088.aspx*

MSDN's Entity Framework Query Samples
: *http://code.msdn.microsoft.com/EFQuerySamples*

There are also a number of excellent books that are focused on LINQ or that contain LINQ content. Some that I recommend are *LINQ Pocket Reference (http://oreilly.com/catalog/9780596519254/)* by Joseph Albahari and Ben Albahari (O'Reilly), *LINQ in Action* by Fabrice Marguerie et al. (Manning Press), and *Essential LINQ* by Charlie Calvert and Dinesh Kulkarni (Addison-Wesley).

Summary

In this chapter, you have learned a variety of ways to use LINQ to Entities to express more complicated queries. You have used projections, queried across navigations, and learned how to group. You have also learned about various ways to load related data, whether through returning shaped results with the `Include` method, retrieving related data after the fact with lazy loading or explicitly calling a `Load` method. With LINQ to Entities, Entity SQL, Object Services, and `EntityClient`, the Entity Framework provides myriad possibilities for querying data and shaping results. In the next chapter you will see how many of the queries written in this chapter can be written with Entity SQL.

Although it would take a few hundred more pages to ensure that you have seen an example of almost any type of query you may want to write, these past two chapters should leave you very prepared to venture forth.

In Chapter 6, you will learn about updating the data you have queried and taking advantage of stored procedures. Then, beginning with Chapter 9, you will start to write some small applications and be able to leverage many of these types of queries.

CHAPTER 5

Exploring Entity SQL in Greater Depth

Chapter 4 introduced you to a number of new querying concepts and how to express those queries with LINQ to Entities. LINQ to Entities will most likely be the more common form of querying in your applications. But there are still many scenarios where you may find that Entity SQL gives you an advantage, such as with complex dynamic query building. Outside of the MSDN documentation, you will find that the resources for learning Entity SQL are few and far between. Therefore, in this chapter, we will run through the same types of queries explored in Chapter 4 and I will demonstrate how to express them using Entity SQL. But we'll begin with a look at some nuances for expressing Entity SQL that don't exist with LINQ to Entities.

Literals in Entity SQL

When writing queries in LINQ to Entities, you don't have to be too concerned about the data types that you are using for projections or filtering, but in Entity SQL there are rules about including many of the types you may want in your query. As an example, you must use special syntax with date types. Many SQL syntaxes require special handling for date types. T-SQL is very forgiving, as it simply requires that you express the date as a string.

Entity SQL, however, has specialized formatting for a number of literals. There is an MSDN topic called "Literals (Entity SQL)" (*http://msdn.microsoft.com/en-us/library/bb399176.aspx*) that drills into these, but unfortunately it is very easy to miss the critical information in the document. I've done it myself, and so have many people who have emailed me with questions about Entity SQL.

Therefore, I will highlight a few of these literals here. I won't cover every literal type, but once you have the hang of it, you can refer back to the MSDN topic for the other types.

Without the specific syntax, in some cases you will get an error message, in others it won't pose a problem, but in others still you will simply get inaccurate results.

Because you'll be writing a lot of Entity SQL expressions in this chapter, I am using a shorter container name, `PEF` (an abbreviation of Programming Entity Framework), rather than `SampleEntities`. See the sidebar "Simplifying the Container Name for Our Examples" on page 113 for steps to do this yourself.

Expressing a DateTime Literal

To express a `DateTime` in Entity SQL, the value must be formatted minimally as `DATETIME'YYYY-MM-DD HH:MM'`, as shown here:

```
SELECT c FROM PEF.Contacts as c
WHERE c.ModifiedDate>DATETIME'2009-01-01 00:00'
```

Even if you are using a SQL Server 2008 `Date` type, you need the `DATETIME` keyword. You must also include the hours and minutes, but you can go further with seconds and beyond if you like. Incorrect syntax with dates will generally cause an exception to be thrown.

Expressing a Decimal Literal

Decimals are trickier. The following expression queries a model based on Microsoft's AdventureWorksLT sample database:

```
SELECT p FROM AdventureWorksEntities.Products as p
WHERE p.ListPrice=133
```

The `ListPrice` column in the database table is defined as a `Decimal` data type. The expression uses an `Integer` (133) as a filtering value against this column, and the query will return the expected results.

However, if you wanted to express a `Decimal` value and simply used `WHERE p.listprice=133.34`, you would get an `EntitySQLException` stating "The argument types 'Edm.Decimal' and 'Edm.Double' are incompatible for this operation."

The documentation tells you to follow the value with an uppercase *M*.

Here is the correct syntax for this query:

```
select p from AdventureWorksEntities.Products as p
WHERE p.listprice=133.34M
```

Using Additional Literal Types

There are a number of different value modifiers depending on the type. Single types must be followed by a lowercase *f*; an Int64 (bigint) is followed by an uppercase *L*. Examples of other types that use literal keywords in Entity SQL are `Time`, `GUID`, `BINARY`, and `DATETIMEOFFSET`.

Pay attention to these syntax requirements when constructing Entity SQL.

> **Simplifying the Container Name for Our Examples**
>
> Since you will be writing a lot more Entity SQL expressions in this chapter, you may want to modify the `EntityContainer` name so that you have something even simpler to type. The Designer makes this easy to do.
>
> Open the model in the Designer and click the background of the model. This will cause the model's properties to show up in the Properties window. Change the `Entity Container Name` to `PEF`, the acronym of this book's title.
>
> This change will have an impact in three places in your application:
>
> - `PEF` will be the new `EntityContainer` name for the model.
> - `PEF` will be the new name of the `EntityContainer` class that you will instantiate to perform queries.
> - `PEF` will be the new name of the connection string in the *app.config* file.
>
> You should double-check that the change was made in all three locations.
>
> You will also need to change any existing code references that use this model from the longer name to the new short name. If you are using Find & Replace, I recommend using the Current Document option.
>
> This new name is not a recommended naming convention, but a convenience for the sake of writing numerous Entity SQL queries in this chapter.

Projecting in Entity SQL

You can use projections with Entity SQL queries in both Object Services and `EntityClient` queries. Only LINQ queries can return anonymous types as you saw in Chapter 4. This is not a concern with `EntityClient` queries as `EntityClient` does not attempt to materialize objects from the results.

When projecting with Entity SQL and Object Services, the query will return data records. These are the same `System.Data.Common.DbDataRecords` returned by `Entity Client` queries, which you saw in Chapter 3.

First look at the code in Example 5-1 and then at the query results. I've added `System.Data.Common` to the `using` statements at the beginning of the class file.

Example 5-1. Projection with Entity SQL

```
String query = "SELECT c.FirstName,c.LastName, c.Title " +
               "FROM   PEF.Contacts AS c " +
               "WHERE c.FirstName='Robert'";
ObjectQuery<DbDataRecord> contacts = context.CreateQuery<DbDataRecord>(query);
```

Notice that in the Entity SQL string, the keyword VALUE is gone. That's because the projection is selecting multiple values. Also, note that the type being passed into the CreateQuery method is now a DbDataRecord.

In the introduction to EntityClient in Chapter 3, you learned that a DbDataRecord represents a single item in a DbDataReader. Therefore, you will need to interact with these results in the same way you did when using the EntityClient example.

There is one very nice difference, however. The results are not being streamed; they have been materialized into the DbDataRecord. Therefore, you can access the column data in any order you want. To highlight this, the query string selected FirstName, LastName, and then Title. When you build the code to display the results, shown in Example 5-2, you'll see that it's OK to use Title first.

Example 5-2. Enumerating through the DbDataRecord returned by an Entity SQL projection

```
foreach (DbDataRecord record in contacts)
{
  Console.WriteLine("{0} {1} {2}",
                    record["Title"].ToString().Trim(),
                    record["FirstName"].ToString().Trim(),
                    record["LastName"].ToString().Trim());
}
```

In Example 5-2, I used an alternative way of pulling data from a DbDataRecord. Item takes a string parameter (the column name) or an integer (the column position), whereas the GetString, GetInt, and other related methods take only an integer as a parameter. I've used the string here for clarity; however, be aware that there is a slight performance penalty for using the string instead of the integer.

DbDataRecords and Nonscalar Properties

Most of these examples project strings, though you saw one example with LINQ for Entities where an anonymous type and an EntityCollection of Address types were projected. How would you interact with a DbDataRecord that contains an entity or another object in its columns? The Entity SQL expression in Example 5-3 selects the entire Contact entity as the first property of the results and the contact's addresses as the second property.

Example 5-3. Projecting objects with Entity SQL

```
String query = "SELECT c, c.Addresses " +
               "FROM PEF.Contacts AS c " +
               "WHERE c.FirstName='Robert'";
ObjectQuery<DbDataRecord> contacts = context.CreateQuery<DbDataRecord>(query);

foreach (DbDataRecord c in contacts)
{
  var contact = c[0] as Contact;
```

```
    Console.WriteLine("{0} {1} {2}",
                              contact.Title.Trim(),
                              contact.FirstName.Trim(),
                              contact.LastName);
    foreach(var a in contact.Addresses)
    {
      Console.WriteLine("    {0}, {1}",
                                   a.Street1.Trim(), a.City);
    }
  }
```

Remember, `DbDataRecord` is in the `System.Data.Common` namespace. You'll need that in a `using`/`Imports` statement in your code file.

In Example 5-2, you had to explicitly cast the items of the results to `String` types. In this case, because you know the first item will contain a `Contact` type, you can cast the column to `Contact` and then work directly with that strongly typed object. You can do the same with the collection of `Address` types in the second column.

Projecting with Query Builder Methods

Example 5-4 shows an example of using a query builder method to do projection. In the projection, you use the `it` alias to access the properties.

Example 5-4. Using query builder methods to project data

```
ObjectQuery<DbDataRecord> contacts = context.Contacts
                                         .Where("it.FirstName='Robert'")
                                         .Select("it.Title, it.FirstName,
                                                  it.LastName");
```

Projection with query builder methods also returns `DbDataRecord`s. You'll need to access the results through the data record's items, as with Example 4-6 in Chapter 4.

Using Navigation in Entity SQL Queries

In Chapter 4, you saw LINQ to Entities queries that leveraged navigation properties whether for projecting, filtering, or performing other query tasks. Here we will look at how to use navigations in Entity SQL.

Navigating to an EntityReference

Recall that navigating to the "one" end of a one-to-one or many-to-one relationship is referred to as a navigation reference. The entity you are pointing to is an `EntityReference`.

Chapter 19 will drill further into `EntityReferences` and `EntityCollections`, and how they are surfaced as navigation properties.

Example 5-5 demonstrates how to query for a type (`Address`) along with an `EntityReference` navigation property (`Address.Contact`) using Entity SQL.

Example 5-5. Projecting into an EntityRef with Entity SQL

```
SELECT a,a.Contact
FROM PEF.Addresses AS a
WHERE a.CountryRegion='UK'
```

This will return `DbDataRecord` objects. When working with these results you can cast the data in the first position to an `Address` and the data in the second position to a `Contact`, as you did in Example 4-7 in Chapter 4.

Filtering and Sorting with an EntityReference

You can filter and sort based on a property of an `EntityReference` even if you are not selecting the related data.

The Entity SQL query in Example 5-6 sorts by `Contact.LastName` and filters on the `Contact.AddDate` field even though `AddDate` is not part of the results.

Example 5-6. Filtering and sorting on reference properties

```
SELECT a,a.Contact.LastName
FROM PEF.Addresses AS a
WHERE a.Contact.AddDate>DATETIME'2009-01-1 00:00'
ORDER BY a.Contact.LastName
```

Filtering and Sorting with EntityCollections

In Chapter 4, we used the LINQ `Any` method to filter based on an object's `EntityCollection` navigation property. The relevant Entity SQL `EXISTS` operator is not as facile as the `ANY` method. You'll need to pass a subquery into `EXISTS` so that it knows what to search. Look closely at the subquery in Example 5-7. It is querying `c.Addresses`, which is the collection of addresses that belongs to the value being returned in the main query. The subquery is able to take advantage of the navigation from a contact to its addresses.

Example 5-7. Filtering across a navigation with Entity SQL

```
Select VALUE c
FROM PEF.Contacts as c
WHERE EXISTS(SELECT a from c.Addresses as a
          WHERE a.CountryRegion='UK')
```

Aggregating with EntityCollections

Working with aggregates in Entity SQL is not as simple as it is in LINQ to Entities. For example, LINQ is able to count the elements in a collection and doesn't care whether the collection contains values or objects. But Entity SQL can perform aggregates on only a set of values, and even then on only certain types of values. This behavior mirrors how SQL Server uses aggregates. Therefore, with Entity SQL you can't write `Count(c.Addresses)`, but rather you need to pass a value, such as `AddressID`, in to the `Count` function. To do this, you can use a subquery against `c.Addresses` that returns a collection of `AddressIDs`. You can then `COUNT` the results of that query, as shown in Example 5-8.

Example 5-8. Using the Count aggregate function in Entity SQL

```
Select c, COUNT(Select VALUE a.AddressID FROM c.Addresses as a)
FROM PEF.Contacts as c
```

The other aggregates work in the same way. Example 5-9 shows the `MAX` query written with Entity SQL.

Example 5-9. Using the MAX aggregate function in Entity SQL

```
SELECT c.LastName,
       MAX(SELECT VALUE a.PostalCode FROM c.Addresses AS a)
FROM PEF.Contacts AS c
```

You can even use an aggregate in a subquery, as in Example 5-10.

Example 5-10. An aggregate in a subquery

```
SELECT c.LastName,
      (SELECT VALUE MAX(a.PostalCode) FROM c.Addresses as a)
FROM PEF.Contacts AS c
```

In this example, the second column of the query results does not contain the string value of the `PostalCode`. It contains the results of a query, and therefore it is a collection of string values. If you want to read the `PostalCodes`, you can iterate through the collection or use a `SET` operator.

Using Entity SQL SET Operators

Like aggregates, `SET` operators work with a set of values. The `ANYELEMENT` operator is a `SET` operator that will randomly pick an element from a collection. As shown in Example 5-11, you can even use this with collections that contain only one element, such as the `MAX PostalCode` column.

Example 5-11. Using the ANYELEMENT operator against a set of data

```
SELECT c.LastName,
       ANYELEMENT(SELECT VALUE max(a.PostalCode)
                  FROM c.Addresses AS a) AS MaxPostal
FROM PEF.Contacts AS c
```

The results of this query will now contain a string in the second position, not a collection.

The `SET` operators in Entity SQL are `ANYELEMENT`, `EXCEPT`, `FLATTEN`, `INTERSECT`, `EXISTS` and `NOT EXISTS`, `IN` and `NOT IN`, `OVERLAPS`, `SET`, and `UNION`. There is also an `ELEMENT` operator that has not yet been implemented but is reserved. If you attempt to use it in the first version of the Entity Framework, you will get an exception that explains that `ELEMENT` cannot be used yet.

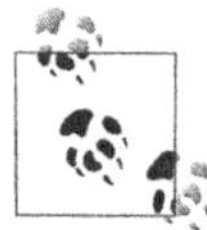

Take some time to explore these operators in the documentation and in code to get a feel for where and when you might want to use them.

Aggregating with Query Builder Methods

The Entity SQL query builder methods do not provide aggregate methods. However, you can use an Entity SQL query as the argument of the `SELECT` query builder method to perform the aggregate.

Remember that the collection being queried in the subquery is based on the main query's control variable, referred to with the `it` alias by default.

Example 5-12 uses the `MAX` aggregate as one of two projected values to be returned.

Example 5-12. An Entity SQL query builder method using an aggregate

```
context.Contacts
  .Select("it.LastName, " +
        "( MAX(SELECT VALUE a.PostalCode FROM it.Addresses AS a))");
```

Using Joins

Example 5-13 shows the syntax of an Entity SQL `JOIN`.

Example 5-13. JOIN syntax for Entity SQL

```
SELECT variableA, variableB
FROM collection as variableA
JOIN Collection as variableB
ON Property = Property
```

Entity SQL has the ability to do cross joins. You can express them explicitly; however, a `JOIN` without an `ON` clause will implicitly become a cross join, pairing every entity in the first collection with every entity in the second collection. So, watch out!

Example 5-14 demonstrates a `JOIN` query expressed in Entity SQL.

Example 5-14. An Entity SQL query using JOIN

```
SELECT c.Title,oa.FirstName, oa.LastName,
       oa.Street1, oa.City, oa.StateProvince
FROM PEF.Contacts as c
JOIN PEF.vOfficeAddresses as oa
ON c.ContactID = oa.ContactID
```

Nesting Queries

Both LINQ and Entity SQL provide the ability to nest queries, and you have already seen some examples of this. When you write a query, anywhere a value is expected you can use another query in its place, as long as that query returns an acceptable type. You can use a nested query in place of an expression or a collection, as you will see in the following examples.

The goal of the previous `JOIN` queries was to return properties from a `Contact` entity combined with properties from the `vOfficeAddresses` entities where the `ContactID` matches.

With Entity SQL, the nested query works in the same manner as with LINQ to Entities, using the query in place of an actual value, though there's no need to name the property it represents (see Example 5-15). Here you will also see the Entity SQL `TRIM` function in effect.

Example 5-15. Nested query in place of a SELECT expression in Entity SQL

```
SELECT TRIM(oa.FirstName), oa.LastName,
ANYELEMENT(SELECT VALUE c.Title
          FROM PEF.Contacts as c
          WHERE c.ContactID=oa.ContactID),
oa.Street1, oa.City, oa.StateProvince
FROM PEF.vOfficeAddresses as oa
```

The query in Example 5-16 demonstrates replacing the queried collection with a nested query.

Example 5-16. Nested query in place of a FROM expression in Entity SQL

```
SELECT TRIM(oa.FirstName), oa.LastName
FROM (SELECT VALUE oa
      FROM PEF.vOfficeAddresses  AS oa
      WHERE oa.StateProvince='Ontario')
AS oa
```

You can easily break this up for readability, because you are merely building strings, and you can concatenate the queries, as shown in Example 5-17.

Example 5-17. Breaking up a nested query in Entity SQL

```
string subQuery = "SELECT VALUE oa " +
             "FROM PEF.vOfficeAddresses  AS oa " +
             "WHERE oa.StateProvince='Ontario'";
String queryString = _
  "SELECT add.FirstName, add.LastName FROM (" + subQuery + ") as add";
```

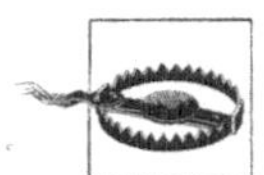

Remember that an `Order` operator in a subquery will be ignored. The main query controls ordering.

Grouping in Entity SQL

LINQ will spoil you with its grouping capabilities. Like SQL, Entity SQL comes with a lot of rules so that you can convert queries into a command tree and then into the provider's query syntax.

For example, in SQL the most commonly encountered rule is that every expression in the `SELECT` must either be accounted for in the `GROUP BY` clause or be wrapped in an aggregate. The same is true in Entity SQL, which prevents you from being able to select entire objects in the `SELECT` clause. However, it is still possible to return entire objects and shape data in Entity SQL by putting the `GROUP BY` operator into a nested query. First take a look at Example 5-18, which shows some simple grouping in Entity SQL.

Example 5-18. A simple GROUP BY example in Entity SQL

```
SELECT c.Title, COUNT(c.Title)
FROM PEF.Contacts as c
GROUP BY c.Title
```

The two projected expressions in the `SELECT` are covered by either the `GROUP BY` or an aggregate (`COUNT`). The query returns the following:

```
[blank]   6
Mr.     255
Ms.     177
Sr.       3
Sra.      2
```

To group on an expression that is evaluated, such as `"Title" + c.Title`, the grouping must be explicitly named and that name needs to be used as a projected expression.

Example 5-19 shows the Entity SQL syntax for creating an expression and grouping on it in the same query. The expression, `EvalTitle`, is built in the `GROUP BY` clause and is used by name in the `SELECT`.

Example 5-19. Grouping by a calculated expression

```
SELECT evalTitle,count(c.Title)
FROM PEF.Contacts as c
GROUP BY "Title: " +c.Title as EvalTitle
```

Returning Entities from an Entity SQL GROUP BY Query

Now, let's take a look at how you can return full objects from Entity SQL when using `GROUP BY`. The trick is in using nested queries.

To reproduce the LINQ query that grouped by `Title` and returned each title with its collection of contacts, you can use a nested query as an expression in the `SELECT` statement, as shown in Example 5-20. It seems as though the query does not have to follow the rule of being part of the `GROUP BY` clause or the target of an aggregate.

Example 5-20. An Entity SQL GROUP BY query that returns entities

```
SELECT groupCon.Title,
 (SELECT c FROM PEF.Contacts as c
           WHERE c.Title= groupCon.Title)
FROM PEF.Contacts as groupCon
GROUP BY groupCon.title
```

The nested query returns a collection of contacts whose `Title` property equals the current title being returned by the group. Although this looks like it might do some scary things on the server with respect to the generated SQL, the SQL is similar to the SQL created as a result of the first LINQ query in this section on grouping.

Filtering Based on Group Properties

You saw that LINQ uses the `WHERE` clause to filter within a group. In Entity SQL, you can use the `HAVING` clause for this purpose, as shown in Example 5-21.

Example 5-21. Entity SQL's HAVING clause, which helps with filtering

```
SELECT groupCon.Title,count(groupCon.ContactID)
FROM PEF.Contacts as groupCon
GROUP BY groupCon.title
HAVING count(groupCon.ContactID)>150
```

This returns only the title groups that contain more than 150 contacts. The results will be as follows:

```
Mr.  255
Ms.  177
```

Shaping Data with Entity SQL

As you've seen already, projections in Object Services result in `DbDataRecords`, as opposed to the anonymous types that LINQ returns. However, even in these `DbDataRecords`, you can still find complete entities and navigate through their associations.

The query shown in Example 5-22 results in an `ObjectQuery` of `DbDataRecords` that are structured as rows and columns. Each row in this result has two columns (also called *fields*). An `Address` entity is contained in the first field and a `Contact` entity is contained in the second field.

Example 5-22. Entity SQL resulting in addresses with their contacts

```
SELECT a,a.Contact
FROM PEF.Addresses AS a
WHERE a.CountryRegion='Canada'
```

Figure 5-1 shows the first column of one of the `DbDataRecords` in the results. The item is an `Address` entity. The second column contains a `Contact` entity. So, even though it is a `DbDataRecord`, it still can contain known objects.

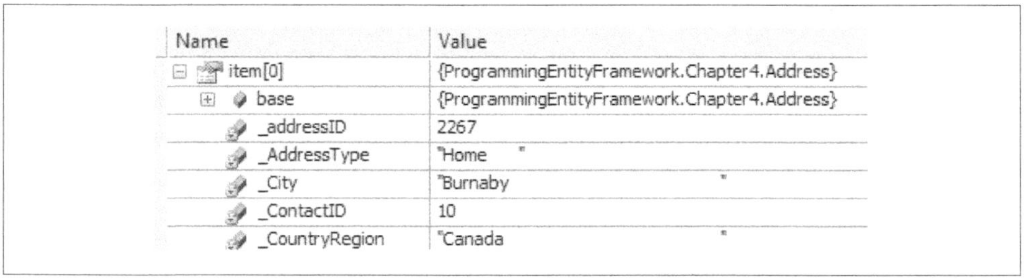

Name	Value
item[0]	{ProgrammingEntityFramework.Chapter4.Address}
base	{ProgrammingEntityFramework.Chapter4.Address}
_addressID	2267
_AddressType	"Home "
_City	"Burnaby "
_ContactID	10
_CountryRegion	"Canada "

Figure 5-1. The first column of each DbDataRecord result, which contains an Address entity

The code in Example 5-23 inspects the `Address` entity in the first field and the `Contact` entity in the second field. As with the earlier LINQ example, the contacts will not be aware of all of the related addresses until each address has been enumerated over. With the strongly typed variables and the IntelliSense that results, it is easy to work with the objects.

Example 5-23. Enumerating through and reading the shaped data from an ObjectQuery

```
foreach (DbDataRecord item in addresses)
{
```

```
    var con = (Contact)item["Contact"]; //cast to Contact type
    Console.WriteLine("LastName: {0} #Addresses: {1}",
                      con.LastName.Trim(), con.Addresses.Count());
    foreach (Address a in con.Addresses)
    {
      Console.WriteLine("....." + a.City);
    }
    Console.WriteLine();
  }
```

Using Include with an ObjectQuery and Entity SQL

How would you apply `Include` when creating an `ObjectQuery` directly rather than using LINQ to Entities?

`Include` is a query builder method and you can use it in the same manner as other query builder methods. You can add it to `ObjectSets`, `CreateQuery` methods, or to an `ObjectQuery` returned by a `CreateQuery`. Example 5-24 shows how to apply `Include` when using `CreateQuery`.

Example 5-24. The Include method in an Object Services query with Entity SQL

```
String query = "SELECT VALUE c " +
               "FROM PEF.Contacts AS c ";
ObjectQuery<Contact> contacts = context.CreateQuery<Contact>(query)
                                 .Include("Addresses");
```

The same rule applies for projections when using Entity SQL with `Include`. If you project in your query, `Include` will be ignored. It is able to work only when complete entities are involved.

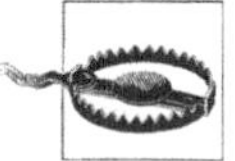

Pay attention to `JOIN` queries. If you use `Include` in a query that also has a `JOIN`, the `Include` will be discarded—no warnings, no compiler errors. Try a nested query instead, but validate your results.

When using the `Include` method to eager-load entity references, use the navigation property for that property name (`Contact`), not the `EntityReference` property (`ContactReference`), as with the `ObjectQuery` in Example 5-25.

Example 5-25. Eager loading an entity reference with an ObjectQuery

```
String query = "SELECT VALUE add "  +
               "FROM PEF.Addresses AS add";
ObjectQuery<Address> addresses = context.CreateQuery<Address>(query)
                                  .Include("Contact")
```

Just as you saw when using `Include` to load entity collections, an entity object will be returned, not a `DbDataRecord`, and the entity reference data is loaded.

Understanding Entity SQL's Wrapped and Unwrapped Results

There is one last concept to highlight before finishing this chapter and moving on: understanding when Entity SQL queries will return rows containing values, or just values.

By default, queries using Entity SQL (`ObjectQuery` and `EntityClient` queries) return rows. The rows are contained in the `ObjectQuery` results, or in the `EntityClient`'s `DbDataReader`. When the data is pulled out of the row as part of the query process, this is referred to as *unwrapping*. Then, rather than a row, the `ObjectQuery` and `DbDataReader` will contain the returned value.

Near the end of Chapter 4, you saw the `First` and `FirstorDefault` methods used to return a single object, rather than an `IQueryable`, which would then need to be enumerated through to get at the object. Conceptually, Entity SQL queries that unwrap results are doing the same.

Unwrapping is possible only when a single value is returned in the `ObjectQuery` or `DbDataReader`. An Entity SQL query will return rows with the same number of columns as items listed in the projection, regardless of what type the item is—a string, an entity, or even a collection. Take, for example, a simple projection of names as shown in Table 5-1, or a projection that returns shaped data. Table 5-2 shows rows, each containing three strings and an `EntityCollection`. Each row in the results of Table 5-3 contains an entity and an `EntityCollection`. Note that the rows in the tables represent a `DbDataRecord` type.

Table 5-1. A simple projection of names

	Column 1	Column 2	Column 3
Row 1	Mr.	John	Doe
Row 2	Sr.	Pablo	Rojas
Row 3	Mrs.	Olga	Kolnik

Table 5-2. Rows containing three strings and an EntityCollection

	Column 1	Column 2	Column 3	Column 4
Row 1	Mr.	John	Doe	`Address` entity
				`Address` entity
Row 2	Sr.	Pablo	Rojas	`Address` entity
				`Address` entity
Row 3	Mrs.	Olga	Kolnik	`Address` entity
				`Address` entity

Table 5-3. Rows containing an entity and an EntityCollection

	Column 1	Column 2
Row 1	`Contact` entity	`Address` entity
		`Address` entity
Row 2	`Contact` entity	`Address` entity
		`Address` entity
Row 3	`Contact` entity	`Address` entity
		`Address` entity

Because neither Object Services nor `EntityClient` can return anonymous types, the only way to return these multicolumn rows is to wrap them in rows where the values are contained in columns. Once you have the result set in memory, you can extract the entities or values programmatically and interact with them as you have done in this chapter and the previous chapter.

However, consider a query with only one value being returned in each row. By default, you will still get a `DbDataRecord`, and that value will be the first and only column of the row (see Table 5-4).

Table 5-4. Contact entities that are contained within rows

	Column 1
Row 1	`Contact` entity
Row 2	`Contact` entity
Row 3	`Contact` entity

By adding the `VALUE` keyword (`SELECT VALUE ...`), you're signaling that you want the value to be unwrapped. With Object Services, this will result in an `ObjectQuery` of `Contact` entities. As you have seen, you must specify the proper type for the `ObjectQuery`. This could be one of the `EntityObject` types defined in your model, or some other type, such as a string or an integer. Look at the difference in how you need to work with the results when the contact is wrapped (Example 5-26) and unwrapped (Example 5-27). When it's wrapped you still need to cast the value in the first column (`Item(0)`) to a contact before you can work with the contact, even though it's the only value in the result.

Example 5-26. Wrapped Contact needs to be cast

```
String esql =
 "SELECT c FROM PEF.Contacts  AS c WHERE c.FirstName='Robert'";
var wrappedContacts = context.CreateQuery<DbDataRecord>(esql);
foreach (DbDataRecord record in wrappedContacts)
{
```

```
  Contact contact = (Contact)(record[0]);
  Console.WriteLine(contact.LastName);
```

Example 5-27. Unwrapped Contact does not need to be cast

```
String esql =
 "SELECT VALUE c FROM PEF.Contacts AS c WHERE c.FirstName='Robert'";
var unwrappedContacts = context.CreateQuery<Contact>(esql);
foreach (Contact contact in unwrappedContacts)
  Console.WriteLine(contact.LastName);
}
```

Entity SQL Rules for Wrapped and Unwrapped Results

Here are some rules to remember for Entity SQL queries:

- Use `SELECT` when projecting more than one type Do not include the `VALUE` keyword.
- When querying with `SELECT` (without the `VALUE` keyword) the `ObjectQuery` type must be a `DbDataRecord`.
- You can use `SELECT VALUE` when projecting a single value or entity.
- When querying with `SELECT VALUE`, the `ObjectQuery` type must be the same type as the value being returned.

Breaking any of these rules will result in a runtime exception when the Entity Framework attempts to generate the store's SQL from the Entity SQL or when the data is returned and the Entity Framework is trying to align the returned type with the type defined for the `ObjectQuery`.

Digging a Little Deeper into EntityClient's Results

Because `EntityClient` streams results and does not materialize records, you won't get entity objects. However, the data that results will be shaped based on the entity shape, and therefore, as you saw in some of the earlier examples, you can cast the results back to the appropriate entity. You can force the results to be wrapped or unwrapped.

Remember that `DbDataRecords` can contain nested `DbDataRecords`, or even nested `DbDataReaders`, which is how it's possible to shape the results.

Here are a variety of different queries and the results to expect in `EntityClient`:

- Query projecting two simple types:

  ```
  SELECT c.FirstName,c.LastName FROM PEF.Contacts AS c
  ```

  Each row of the `DataReader` that results is a `DbDataRecord` *with two columns*. Each column contains a string.
- Query projecting a single value that is an entity without using the `VALUE` keyword:

  ```
  SELECT c FROM PEF.Contacts  AS c
  ```

Each row of the DataReader that results is a DbDataRecord *with one column*. The column contains an IExtendedDataRecord, which is a type of a DbDataRecord. The DbDataRecord contains one column for every property in a Contact entity, filled with the relevant values.

- Complex query projecting an entity and a collection of entities:

```
SELECT  c, c.Addresses FROM PEF.Contacts AS c
```

Each row of the DataReader that results is a DbDataRecord. There are two columns: the first contains an IExtendedDataRecord with one column for each property of the Contact entity, and the second contains a whole DbDataReader that implements IExtendedDataRecord. This allows the data to be cast to an EntityCollection of address types.

- Query projecting a single entity using SELECT VALUE:

```
SELECT VALUE c FROM PEF.Contacts  AS c
```

Each row of the DataReader that results is an IExtendedDataRecord. There is one column for every property of the Contact entity, filled with the relevant data.

- Query projecting a single simple type using SELECT VALUE:

```
SELECT VALUE c.LastName FROM PEF.Contacts AS c
```

Each row of the DataReader that results is a string.

The ADO.NET documentation has a great example of reading a DbDataReader and handling any of these data types as you hit them. Look for the MSDN Library topic "How to: Execute an Entity SQL Query Using EntityCommand (Entity Framework)."

Summary

In this chapter, you learned a variety of ways to express more complex queries in Entity SQL and how to read the query results. You've also learned some of the nuances of using Entity SQL.

Entity SQL is certainly the underdog for querying in Entity Framework. Although most scenarios will be satisfied by LINQ to Entities queries, there will still be times when Entity SQL will come to the rescue. The most obvious scenario is when you simply want to stream data without materializing objects—for example, when writing reports. In this case, EntityClient with Entity SQL expressions is the most favorable solution.

I have clients who need to build very complex queries dynamically. These are cases where their users have many fields and a variety of options for constructing a search, and in code, we need to build a query. Although LINQ to Entities is composable and very flexible, there may be a point at which you begin to hit walls. Reverting to the simpler task of building and concatenating string-based expressions (addressing any possible security concerns) has solved this problem many times. There's also another option to consider: a `PredicateBuilder` class created by Joseph Albahari at *http://www.albahari.com/nutshell/predicatebuilder.aspx*.

CHAPTER 6

Modifying Entities and Saving Changes

So far, we have focused on the many ways to query an EDM to retrieve data from the database. This is only part of the Entity Framework story and the beginning of the life cycle of an entity. Once you have retrieved entities you can modify them, delete them, or even add new ones and then save all of these changes back to the database. In this chapter, we'll take a high-level look at the way in which the Entity Framework is able to track these changes and get the necessary data back to the database. Then we'll watch updates, inserts, and deletions in action, not only in code samples, but also in terms of what happens in the database in response.

Later chapters will focus on modifying the default behavior.

Keeping Track of Entities

In the previous chapters, you used an `ObjectContext`, the `SampleEntities` class (renamed "PEF" in Chapter 5), which inherits from `ObjectContext`, to create and execute queries. You also worked with the objects that were returned by those queries, whether they were entities, anonymous types, or objects within a `DbDataRecord`. The nature of this interaction was to iterate through the objects and extract a few properties to display in a console window.

The context can also keep track of these entities once they've been returned by a query. As your application logic modifies the objects, the context is notified and makes note of changes. The context is responsible for managing the state of its entities, including those that you create in memory.

Entity Framework takes a snapshot of an entity's values when the `ObjectContext` first becomes aware of the entity. This will happen by default when query results are being materialized into objects. The context stores two sets of these values. The first set represents the original values and remains static. The second set represents the entity's current values, and these will change in response to edits being performed to the entity properties.

Managing an Entity's State

By default, as each entity is materialized from the query results, the `ObjectContext` creates an extra object behind the scenes, called an `ObjectStateEntry`. This is where the snapshot—that is, the two copies of the object's values—is stored.

Think of the `ObjectStateEntry` as the hidden twin of its companion `EntityObject`. Entity Framework uses each `ObjectStateEntry` to keep track of any changes made to its relevant entity. If you execute an additional query using the same context, Entity Framework will create more `ObjectStateEntry` objects. The context will manage all of these as well for as long as their related entity remains in memory, unless you indicate in your code using the `Detach` method that you would like the context to stop tracking the changes. You'll learn more about detached entities in Chapter 10.

The `ObjectContext` can track only entities. It cannot keep track of anonymous types or nonentity data that is returned in a `DbDataRecord`.

`ObjectStateEntry` also has a `State` property whose value reflects the state of the entity (`Unchanged`, `Modified`, `Added`, or `Deleted`). As the user modifies the objects, the `ObjectContext` updates the current values of the related `ObjectStateEntry` as well as its `State`. As you learn more about the Entity Framework, you'll discover how to locate and inspect the details of an `ObjectStateEntry`.

The object itself also has an `EntityState` property, which it inherits from `EntityObject`. As long as the object is being managed by the context, its `EntityState` will always match the `State` of the `ObjectStateEntry`. If the object is not being managed by the context, there is no `ObjectStateEntry` and the entity's state is `Detached`.

Entities have three different types of properties: scalar properties, complex properties (which contain more scalar properties), and navigation properties. `ObjectStateEntry` keeps track of only the scalar values (including those inside the complex properties) of its related entity.

You'll learn more about complex types and complex properties in Chapter 15.

The navigations are tracked in a very different way that is out of scope for this overview but that you will learn a lot about in Chapter 10 as well as in Chapter 19, which focuses on relationships and associations.

If you have been using version 1 of Entity Framework, you'll be happy to know that having the foreign key value as a scalar value in the entity will make change tracking of relationships enormously simpler in Entity Framework 4. You'll see more about this in Chapter 19.

As the scalar properties are changed—for example, Contact.LastName—the new value of LastName is stored in the ObjectStateEntry's set of current values for that contact, and if the ObjectStateEntry.State value was Unchanged at the time of the modification, its value will be set to Modified.

Saving Changes Back to the Database

ObjectContext has a single method, SaveChanges, which persists back to the database all of the changes made to the entities. A call to SaveChanges will check for any ObjectStateEntry objects being managed by that context whose State is not Unchanged, and then will use its details to build separate Insert, Update, and Delete commands to send to the database. We'll start by focusing on entities that have come into the context as a result of queries and have been modified.

Example 6-1 shows a simple ObjectQuery to retrieve the first contact from the Contacts EntitySet. Remember from Chapter 3 that context.Contacts is a method that will return an ObjectSet of Contact types. The example then uses the LINQ extension method First to pull back only the first result.

The FirstName and ModifiedDate properties are given new values, and then SaveChanges is called.

Example 6-1. Querying for a contact, editing, and then saving back to the database

```
using (PEF context = new PEF())
{
  var contact = context.Contacts.First();
  contact.FirstName = "Julia";
  contact.ModifiedDate = DateTime.Now;
  context.SaveChanges();
}
```

Looking at the SQL Profiler, you can see the following parameterized Update command, which was sent to the SQL Server database when SaveChanges was called:

```
exec sp_executesql N'update [dbo].[Contact]
set [FirstName] = @0, [ModifiedDate] = @1
where ([ContactID] = @2)
',N'@0 nvarchar(50),@1 datetime2(7),@2 int',@0=N'Julia',
@1='2009-11-30 09:27:20.3335098',@2=1
```

This command updates the Contact table, setting the FirstName and ModifiedDate properties for the Contact whose ContactID is 1. The values are passed in via parameters, and the last parameter, @2, shows the value used for the ContactID.

If the FirstName column in the database was a char or nchar rather than nvarchar, Entity Framework would have padded the incoming value (Julia) with enough spaces to match the length of the field. Using nvarchar not only is more efficient in the database, but also results in more efficient messages to the server.

When the context was notified of a property change, not only did it modify the current value in the ObjectStateEntry, but it also set another tracking value that indicates that the property was changed. During SaveChanges, the context then looks for those tracking values to determine which fields were changed. In our sample, the FirstName and ModifiedDate properties had changed, and therefore those are the only values that it sends into the command. It uses the value of the property that is marked as the EntityKey, ContactID, to identify which row to update.

Even if the property was modified using the same value as the original value, the context will use that value in the update. It's not comparing the original and current values, but is depending on the knowledge that the property was modified, regardless of what the modification was.

Let's see what happens when we have more than one entity.

Example 6-2 queries for all contacts named Robert, along with their addresses, then returns a List of the entity graphs: Contacts with Addresses. The example then randomly selects one of these contacts and changes its FirstName to Bobby. Another contact is selected and the Street property of the first Address is edited. Finally, SaveChanges is called.

Example 6-2. Editing various entities and calling SaveChanges

```
var contacts = context.Contacts.Include("Addresses")
                      .Where(c =>c.FirstName=="Robert").ToList();
var contact = contacts[3];
contact.FirstName = "Bobby";
contact = contacts[5];
var address = contact.Addresses.ToList()[0];
address.Street1 = "One Main Street";
context.SaveChanges();
```

Initially, 12 contacts and 13 addresses were retrieved. Let's look at the SQL commands sent to the database when SaveChanges is called:

```
exec sp_executesql N'update [dbo].[Address]
set [Street1] = @0
where ([addressID] = @1)
',N'@0 nvarchar(50),@1 int',@0=N'One  Main Street',@1=2424

exec sp_executesql N'update [dbo].[Contact]
set [FirstName] = @0
```

```
where ([ContactID] = @1)
',N'@0 nvarchar(50),@1 int',@0=N'Bobby',@1=298
```

The first command sent to the database updates the single `Address` that was modified, and only its `Street` value and identity, `AddressID`, are included. Next, the command to update the contact was sent. None of the other entities was modified, so the `ObjectContext` doesn't bother to construct or send any commands for those entities. The call to `SaveChanges` is very efficient in this aspect.

`ObjectContext` learned everything it needed to know to create these commands, not by looking at the `Contact` and `Address` objects that it was managing but by looking at the `ObjectStateEntry` objects that it was maintaining for each of the 12 `Contact` and 13 `Address` entities. `ObjectContext` first checked the `State` to see whether anything needed to be processed. Because the `State` for the untouched entities was `Unchanged`, it ignored them. For the two that were `Modified`, it checked its internal list of modified properties to determine what properties needed to be included in the `Update` command.

When the update completes, the modified `Contact` and `Address` entities will be refreshed so that their `EntityState` is `Unchanged`, and the original values will be set to match the current values.

You'll learn about alternatives to using `SaveChanges`' default behavior in Chapters 10 and 11.

From Entity Framework Command to Native Command

In between the call to `SaveChanges` and the execution of SQL commands in the database, the Entity Framework did a lot of work under the covers to construct the command. The process is similar to how the commands and queries are compiled and converted into store queries.

As noted earlier, the first step in the process is to inspect all of the `ObjectStateEntry` objects for the entities that the context is managing. Those that have a `State` of `Unchanged` are ignored. The `Modified` entities that you worked with earlier, as well as any that are `Added` or `Deleted`, are processed by the context. As the commands are built, the model's metadata (conceptual, store, and mapping layers) is read and the mapping information is used to translate the entities and their properties into table and column names. The mappings also provide the knowledge to move from model relationships to database foreign keys. The ADO.NET provider, such as `SqlClient`, does the final job of constructing the appropriate native command.

You'll look more closely at this process in later chapters.

Inserting New Objects

Now that you have an idea of how edits are handled, let's look at how to insert data.

In Example 6-3, a new address is created in memory. Rather than use `Address.CreateAddress`, this code instantiates a new `Address` directly, because even if I had used the factory method, I still would have to set all of the string scalars. Then, after attaching the address to a contact that was queried from the database, `SaveChanges` is called.

There are many different ways to link entities to one another based on particular scenarios. You will learn about this in Chapter 19.

Example 6-3. Creating a new address in memory

```
var contact = context.Contacts.Where(c => c.FirstName == "Robert").First();
var address = new Address();
address.Street1 = "One Main Street";
address.City = "Burlington";
address.StateProvince = "VT";
address.AddressType = "Business";
address.ModifiedDate = DateTime.Now;
//join the new address to the contact
address.Contact = contact;
context.SaveChanges();
```

When the newly created address is joined with the contact, because `ObjectContext` is managing the contact the context will recognize that it needs to create a new `ObjectStateEntry` for the `Address`. Its `State` will be set to `Added`. When `SaveChanges` is called, because the `State` is `Added` an `Insert` command is constructed and sent to the database. Here is that command:

```
exec sp_executesql N'insert [dbo].[Address]([Street1], [Street2], [City],
 [StateProvince], [CountryRegion], [PostalCode], [AddressType],
 [ContactID], [ModifiedDate])
values (@0, null, @1, @2, null, null, @3, @4, @5)
select [addressID]
from [dbo].[Address]
where @@ROWCOUNT > 0 and [addressID] = scope_identity()',
N'@0 nvarchar(50),@1 nvarchar(50),@2 nvarchar(50),@3 nvarchar(50),
@4 int,@5 datetime2(7)',
@0=N'One Main Street',@1=N'Burlington',@2=N'VT',@3=N'Business',
@4=209,@5='2009-11-30 09:20:50.2291578'
```

This SQL command sent to the database by Entity Framework performs a number of notable actions.

First, it has an `Insert` command that inserts a new address using the values of each property of the entity. Notice that even though the code did not set all of the properties, the command uses all of the properties and inserts defaults, in this case `null`, where the properties weren't explicitly set in the code.

The fifth line down is the beginning of a `Select` command. In addition to inserting the new address, the command will return to the application the primary key value that the database generated for the new address. As part of the call to `SaveChanges`, the new address in the application memory will receive its `AddressID` from the database so that you can continue working with it in code if you wish.

When the insert completes, not only will the address in memory have its new `AddressID` value, but like the update in the preceding section, the entity will be refreshed and its `EntityState` will be set to `Unchanged`.

You may have noticed that sometimes I use `State`, while others I use `EntityState`. That's because the `ObjectStateEntry` property for tracking state is `State`, while the `EntityObject` property is named `EntityState`.

Inserting New Parents and Children

The preceding example inserted a new address to an existing contact. What if you wanted to create a new contact with a new address? In typical data access scenarios, you would have to first insert the new contact, retrieve its `ContactID`, and then use that to insert the new address. `SaveChanges` does all of this for you when it sees that both are new and that they are related. It also uses the model's mappings to figure out which is the dependent entity (in this case, `Address`) and needs the foreign key (`ContactID`). With this information, it executes the database inserts in the correct order.

The code in Example 6-4 creates a new contact on the fly using the `Contact` class's `CreateContact` factory method.

Recall that the model's default code generator creates a factory method for every `EntityObject`. The method uses all of the non-nullable properties as its arguments. I'm using an example of this, `CreateContact`, in Example 6-4. In Chapter 10, we'll create an overload to allow you to pass in a more logical set of parameters. The method exists only for our own use and is not used internally by Entity Framework.

The example then creates a new address in the same manner as with Example 6-4. Next, it joins the new contact to the new address. At this point, the context has no knowledge of these new entities; therefore, they need to be added to the context. Because the entities are joined, you can add either entity, and it will bring along the rest of the graph. So, in this case, the contact is added explicitly and the address is pulled into the context along with the contact.

ObjectQuery has an AddObject method that is inherited by ObjectSet. It's easiest to use the ObjectSet.AddObject method (as in Example 6-4) as it requires fewer parameters. You'll learn more about adding and attaching entities to the context and to each other in Chapter 19. You will also see a variety of examples of these methods in many of the samples throughout the book.

Finally, SaveChanges is called.

Example 6-4. Inserting a new contact with a new address

```
var contact = Contact.CreateContact
              (0, "Camey", "Combs", DateTime.Now, DateTime.Now);
var address = new Address();
address.Street1 = "One Main Street";
address.City = "Olympia";
address.StateProvince = "WA";
address.AddressType = "Business";
address.ModifiedDate = DateTime.Now;
//join the new address to the contact
address.Contact = contact;
//add the new graph to the context
context.Contacts.AddObject(contact);
context.SaveChanges();
```

As the entities are added to the context, the context creates a new ObjectStateEntry for each one and sets their State to Added. SaveChanges handles these as it did with the previous insert, except that it also takes care of using the contact's new ContactID when inserting the address.

The following SQL is the result of the call to SaveChanges. There are two commands. The first command inserts the new contact and performs a Select to return the new contact's ContactID.

The second command inserts the new address, and as you can see in the last line, the @4 parameter has a value of 714. This is the new ContactID. This command also selects the new address's AddressID value to return to the application.

```
exec sp_executesql N'insert [dbo].[Contact]([FirstName], [LastName], [Title],
 [AddDate], [ModifiedDate])
values (@0, @1, null, @2, @3)
select [ContactID]
from [dbo].[Contact]
where @@ROWCOUNT > 0 and [ContactID] = scope_identity()',
N'@0 nvarchar(50),@1 nvarchar(50),@2 datetime2(7),@3 datetime2(7)',
@0=N'Camey',@1=N'Combs',@2='2009-08-30 09:27:31.7449098',
@3='2009-11-30 09:27:31.7449098'

exec sp_executesql N'insert [dbo].[Address]([Street1], [Street2], [City],
 [StateProvince], [CountryRegion], [PostalCode], [AddressType],
 [ContactID], [ModifiedDate])
values (@0, null, @1, @2, null, null, @3, @4, @5)
```

```
select [addressID]
from [dbo].[Address]
where @@ROWCOUNT > 0 and [addressID] = scope_identity()',
N'@0 nvarchar(50),@1 nvarchar(50),@2 nvarchar(50),@3 nvarchar(50),
@4 int,@5 datetime2(7)',
@0=N'One Main Street',@1=N'Olympia',@2=N'WA',@3=N'Business',
@4=714,@5='2009-11-30 09:27:31.7449098'
```

As you build more complex models later in the book, you will see how the insert can handle various types of entities with data that is related through navigation properties. In addition, with other types of mappings, such as inheritance, you will see entities that map back to multiple database tables and even entities in a many-to-many relationship.

Deleting Entities

The last type of modification to look at is deleting entities. The Entity Framework has a very specific requirement for deleting data: it must have an entity in hand in order to delete it from the database. `ObjectContext` has a `DeleteObject` method that takes an `EntityObject` as a parameter—for example, an instance of a `Contact`. When `DeleteObject` is called, the context sets the `State` of that object's `ObjectStateEntry` to `Deleted`. To be explicit, it does not delete the entity, but marks it as "to be deleted from the database. " When `SaveChanges` is called, the context notes the `Deleted State` and constructs a `Delete` command to send to the database.

If the entity has already been retrieved from the database, this will not pose a problem. But sometimes you might want to delete data from the database that has not been queried. Entity Framework does not provide a way to delete data in the database directly; however, as you will learn in Chapter 16, it is possible to pass commands directly to the database with the `ExecuteStoreCommand` method. You could use that to send a delete command.

Example 6-5 demonstrates the scenario where the contact to be deleted has not yet been retrieved. It uses the `GetObjectByKey` method described in Chapter 4 to retrieve the contact.

Here you can also see how an `EntityKey` is constructed on the fly using the strongly typed `EntitySet` name (which includes the name of the `EntityContainer`, `PEF`), the name of the property that is the `EntityKey`, and the value of the key. Therefore, the `EntityKey` is for a `Contact` whose `ContactID` is `438`.

The `EntityKey`, which is in the `System.Data` namespace, is passed into the `GetObjectByKey` method, which will first inspect the existing `EntityObjects` being managed by the context to see whether that contact has already been retrieved. If it is not found there, the context will create and execute a query to retrieve that contact from the data store.

The `GetObjectByKey` method returns an `Object`. If you wanted a `Contact` type, you would have to explicitly cast the `Object` to `Contact`. But in this case, it is not necessary to cast that to a Contact type, which is why a contact variable is declared with var in Example 6-5.

Once the object is in hand, it is passed into the DeleteObject method, which marks it for deletion by setting the EntityState to Deleted.

Example 6-5. Retrieving and deleting a contact entity

```
System.Data.EntityKey contactKey =
  new System.Data.EntityKey("PEF.Contacts", "ContactID", 438);
var contact = context.GetObjectByKey(contactKey);
context.DeleteObject(contact);
context.SaveChanges();
```

Here is the Store command that GetObjectByKey executed, as well as the Delete command that was executed as a result of the call to SaveChanges:

```
exec sp_executesql N'SELECT
[Extent1].[ContactID] AS [ContactID],
[Extent1].[FirstName] AS [FirstName],
[Extent1].[LastName] AS [LastName],
[Extent1].[Title] AS [Title],
[Extent1].[AddDate] AS [AddDate],
[Extent1].[ModifiedDate] AS [ModifiedDate]
FROM [dbo].[Contact] AS [Extent1]
WHERE [Extent1].[ContactID] = @p0',N'@p0 int',@p0=438

exec sp_executesql N'delete [dbo].[Contact]
where ([ContactID] = @0)',N'@0 int',@0=438
```

The Delete command simply passes in the ContactID to delete the appropriate data.

If you don't already happen to have the object in memory and don't want to retrieve it from the database just for the sake of deleting it, there are some alternatives. One is to use a stored procedure that allows you to pass in the ContactID and then performs the delete on your behalf. Another is to use Entity Framework's new ExecuteStoreCommand method. You will learn how to use both of these methods in Chapter 16.

An additional possibility, which is a bit of a hack, is to create an entity in memory to delete. But you need to be careful not to indicate that it is a new entity or Entity Framework will attempt to insert it into the database. Alex James, from the Entity Framework team, discusses pros and cons of this method in Tip 9 of his excellent blog series: *http://blogs.msdn.com/alexj/archive/2009/03/27/tip-9-deleting-an-object-without-retrieving-it.aspx*.

The sample database has a constraint defined for the `Address` table's `ContactID` column, called a *cascading delete*. This tells the database that when the contact with the matching `ContactID` is deleted from the `Contacts` table, it should delete any `Addresses` that have the same `ContactID` value. You'll learn more about cascading deletes in the database and the model in Chapter 19.

Summary

In this chapter you saw how the Entity Framework creates the necessary `Insert`, `Update`, and `Delete` commands to store your changes to the database with a single call to `SaveChanges`. This is the default behavior of the Entity Framework and one of its core features.

However, you are not bound by this default behavior. It is possible to override this mechanism to leverage your own stored procedures. The Entity Framework has a number of ways to use stored procedures. The next chapter will introduce you to overriding the dynamic generation of `Insert`, `Update`, and `Delete` commands with your own stored procedures, and show you how to use stored procedures to query data. You also can work with stored procedures that the Designer does not support as easily. We will cover these more advanced techniques in Chapter 16.

You will learn even more about object materialization, `ObjectStateEntry`, change tracking, and other subjects in great detail in Chapter 10. There are additional functions of database updates that are critical, such as transactions and concurrency. These are advanced topics that we will cover in later chapters.

CHAPTER 7

Using Stored Procedures with the EDM

Many databases use stored procedures to perform predefined logic on database tables, and many organizations have policies in place that require the use of these stored procedures. Although one of the key features of the Entity Framework is its ability to automatically build native commands based on your LINQ to Entities or Entity SQL queries, as well as build the commands for inserting, updating, or deleting data, you may want to override these steps and use your own predefined stored procedures. Although the dynamically built commands are secure, efficient, and generally as good as or better than those you may write yourself, there are many cases where stored procedures already exist and your company practices may restrict direct use of the tables. Alternatively, you may just want to have explicit control over what is executed on the store and prefer to create stored procedures.

The sample database includes six stored procedures that we skipped in our discussion of model creation in Chapter 2. In this chapter, you will update the model, pulling in those six stored procedures, implementing them in the model, and interacting with them in some code.

In this chapter, you will override the Entity Framework's command generation feature for a particular entity and direct it to use your stored procedures instead when `SaveChanges` is called. You'll also learn how to incorporate and use procedures that return data. The chapter will also address the concept of combining entities that map to database views with stored procedures to provide fully functional entities that completely avoid direct table access. See the sidebar "Protecting Tables by Using Views and Stored Procedures" on page 147.

This chapter will focus on the stored procedures functionality that the Entity Data Model (EDM) Designer readily supports. In Chapter 16, you'll work with stored procedures that are not so easily implemented.

Updating the Model from a Database

When we originally created this model in Chapter 2, we brought in only the tables and view, and skipped over the stored procedures in the database. Now we will bring those into our model.

The EDM tools provide a feature called Update Model from Database, which is available from the Designer context menu. You can use it to add previously skipped database objects or those that have been added to the database since the time you originally created the model. Update Model from Database can also recognize new fields added to tables that have already been mapped in the database.

To bring these stored procedures into the model, start by right-clicking anywhere in the Model Browser or the Designer and selecting Update Model from Database. This will open the Update Wizard, which instructs you to Choose Your Database Objects. In this case, you can expand only the Stored Procedures node because there are no tables or views in the database that aren't already in your model. The list of database objects available in this view is not based on which entities you have created, but on which tables, views, and other objects are represented in the Store Schema Definition Layer (SSDL) portion of the model. Because you did not include the stored procedures when you first built the model, they are not part of the SSDL, and therefore the Update Model from Database tool sees them as being new.

If you had added new tables and views to the database, you would see them listed here as well.

The Stored Procedures node will display user-defined stored procedures as well as user-defined scalar-valued functions in the database.

Checking the Stored Procedures checkbox will automatically select all of the available procedures. You can expand the node to see what's there or to individually select the objects you want to use. For this example, you'll want all six procedures: `AddressCountForContact`, `AddressTypeCount`, `ContactsbyState`, `DeleteContact`, `InsertContact`, and `UpdateContact`, as shown in Figure 7-1.

The wizard has two additional tabs that are read-only: Refresh and Delete. These tabs will display which existing items in the model will be refreshed and which will be deleted (if the tables they map to have been deleted from the database).

Click Finish to add the stored procedures to the model. When the update is complete, the model will not look any different when viewed in the Designer. Stored procedures are not automatically added to the conceptual layer of the model. Instead, they have been represented in the SSDL as function elements. It will be your job to define how these functions should be implemented in the conceptual model using mapping.

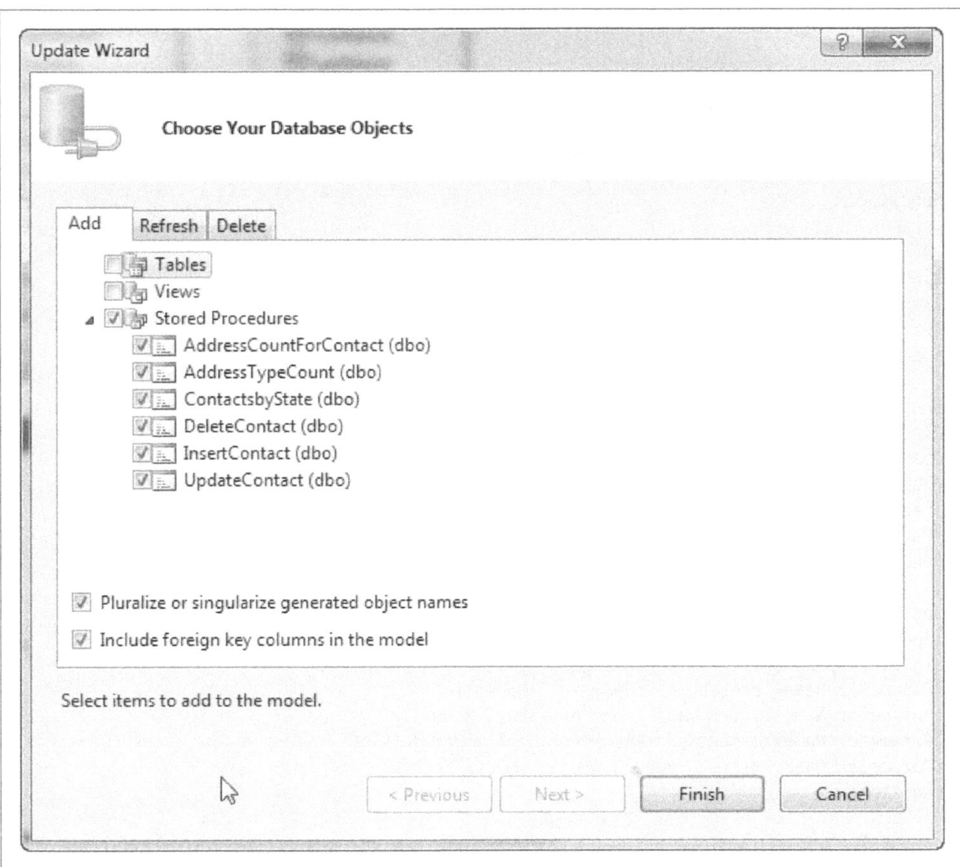

Figure 7-1. Selecting database objects that aren't already contained in your model

Working with Functions

Stored procedures and user-defined functions (UDFs) in the database are represented in the metadata as *functions*. Example 7-1 lists the six functions that were created in the SSDL to represent the six stored procedures you just brought in from the sample database.

Example 7-1. Functions created in the SSDL

```
<Function Name="AddressCountForContact" Aggregate="false" BuiltIn="false"
 NiladicFunction="false" IsComposable="false"
 ParameterTypeSemantics="AllowImplicitConversion" Schema="dbo">
  <Parameter Name="contactID" Type="int" Mode="In" />
</Function>

<Function Name="AddressTypeCount" Aggregate="false" BuiltIn="false"
 NiladicFunction="false" IsComposable="false"
 ParameterTypeSemantics="AllowImplicitConversion" Schema="dbo">
```

```
  <Parameter Name="AddressType" Type="nvarchar" Mode="In" />
</Function>

Function Name="ContactsbyState" Aggregate="false" BuiltIn="false"
 NiladicFunction="false" IsComposable="false"
 ParameterTypeSemantics="AllowImplicitConversion" Schema="dbo">
  <Parameter Name="state" Type="nvarchar" Mode="In" />
</Function>

<Function Name="DeleteContact" Aggregate="false" BuiltIn="false"
 NiladicFunction="false" IsComposable="false"
 ParameterTypeSemantics="AllowImplicitConversion" Schema="dbo">
  <Parameter Name="contactid" Type="int" Mode="In" />
</Function>

<Function Name="InsertContact" Aggregate="false" BuiltIn="false"
 NiladicFunction="false" IsComposable="false"
 ParameterTypeSemantics="AllowImplicitConversion" Schema="dbo">
  <Parameter Name="firstname" Type="nvarchar" Mode="In" />
  <Parameter Name="lastname" Type="nvarchar" Mode="In" />
  <Parameter Name="title" Type="nvarchar" Mode="In" />
</Function>

<Function Name="UpdateContact" Aggregate="false" BuiltIn="false"
 NiladicFunction="false" IsComposable="false"
 ParameterTypeSemantics="AllowImplicitConversion" Schema="dbo">
  <Parameter Name="contactid" Type="int" Mode="In" />
  <Parameter Name="firstname" Type="nvarchar" Mode="In" />
  <Parameter Name="lastname" Type="nvarchar" Mode="In" />
  <Parameter Name="title" Type="nvarchar" Mode="In" />
</Function>
```

Each of these six functions represents a different stored procedure in the database. The first three return query results. The last three—the `Insert`, `Update`, and `Delete` procedures—perform the changes you would expect to the database.

Function Attributes

Most of the function attributes align with attributes that are common to database procedures. Because the SSDL is describing the data store, these attributes are applied in the model so that the Entity Framework API will have a thorough description of the procedures.

`Aggregate`, `BuiltIn`, and `NiladicFunction` are attributes that apply to UDFs, not stored procedures. For stored procedures, they will always be `false`. Because these are optional and `false` by default, they are not even required here. If you were adding functions to the SSDL manually for stored procedures, you wouldn't even need to use these, but the wizard inserts them.

What the heck does *niladic* mean anyway? Niladic is a mathematical term meaning that the function takes no input parameters. SQL Server's `GetDate()` is an example of a niladic function.

`IsComposable` refers to whether you can use the results of the function in another query. This must always be `false` for stored procedures. You'll learn more about this in the section "Avoiding Inadvertent Client-Side Processing" on page 159.

The `ParameterTypeSemantics` attribute refers to the input parameter, such as `State` in the `ContactsbyState` function. The `AllowImplicitConversion` enum (which is the default) merely means that the data type input can be converted implicitly to a store provider data type if necessary. For example, if an integer is passed into this parameter, the Entity Framework will just go ahead and convert it to a char when creating the command to execute the stored procedure.

The `Parameter` element describes any input or output parameters. In the case of the `ContactsbyState` function, there is only an input parameter, specified by `Mode="In"`. Additional mode options are `InOut` and `Out`. All three align with the stored procedures flags to define parameters that are being sent to the procedure. Here is a description of each mode option:

`In`
: `In` parameters are read by the stored procedure.

`Out`
: `Out` parameters are populated by the procedure and returned.

`InOut`
: `InOut` parameters are read by the stored procedure and returned. The procedure may or may not update this parameter before returning it.

You'll notice that the parameter in the SSDL is `nvarchar`, whereas the parameter in the database's procedure is more explicit: `nvarchar(50)`. Neither Entity Framework nor SQL Server will complain if you pass in more than 50 characters; SQL Server simply truncates the extra characters. The other `Function` attributes are explained in the documentation.

Notice that for this query function, the SSDL defines only what is necessary to call the function. There is no indication of returned data. You'll learn more about how stored procedures are implemented from the SSDL back to the Conceptual Schema Definition Layer (CSDL) later in this chapter.

Now let's take a look at a more complex function, `UpdateContact`. Here is the actual stored procedure:

```
PROCEDURE UpdateContact
@contactid INT,
@firstname NVARCHAR(50),
@lastname NVARCHAR(50),
@title NVARCHAR(50)
AS
UPDATE Contact
SET [FirstName]=@firstname,[LastName]=@lastname,[Title]=@title,
[ModifiedDate]=GETDATE()
WHERE [ContactID]=@contactid
```

The `UpdateContact` function in the SSDL has the same attributes as the `ContactsbyState` function, as well as parameter elements to represent the input parameters. You will see later in this chapter how you can use mappings to easily leverage the `Update`, `Insert`, and `Delete` stored procedures when coding against the EDM. You'll also see how the query stored procedures are handled differently than the Data Manipulation Language (DML) functions that modify the database.

DML, CRUD, and CUD

DML is a frequently used acronym that stands for Data Manipulation Language, and it most often refers to the three types of functions a data access technology must provide to manipulate data: `Insert`, `Update`, and `Delete`. Some interpretations include `Select`. You will also frequently see the term *CRUD* used, which stands for Create, Read, Update, and Delete (*Create* is used rather than *Insert* since CRUD sounds much better than IRUD). Lastly, some people use the term *CUD* to refer to the same three DML operations (`Create`, `Update`, and `Delete`). Unfortunately, CUD has a different meaning for people who live in cow country, which may cause some developers to prefer DML instead.

Mapping Functions to Entities

As you saw in Chapter 6, the default behavior of the Entity Framework is to construct the necessary `Insert`, `Update`, and `Delete` commands on the fly when you call `SaveChanges`.

You can override this behavior for specific entities by using the SSDL functions (based on the database stored procedures) instead. You can map these functions to specific entities. Then, when `SaveChanges` is called, the Entity Framework will use the designated stored procedures rather than generate commands. For entities that have no function mappings, the Entity Framework will perform the default behavior of generating the commands dynamically.

The `ContactsbyState`, `AddressCountForContact`, and `AddressTypeCount` stored procedures are for reading data, not updating. You can link functions for "read" stored procedures to entities that match what the procedure returns, to a scalar value, or to a special type, called `ComplexType`, when the procedure returns a unique set of columns.

You can use these functions in the EDM in other ways, but the Designer supports only these scenarios and these are the scenarios we will cover in this chapter. A later chapter will dig into working with store commands that are not as simple to implement.

You will find the terms *stored procedures* and *functions* used interchangeably throughout the metadata and the Designer. The model consistently refers to *functions*, whereas the Designer, in an effort to use familiar terminology, uses *stored procedures* in a number of places.

The single mapping rule that remains in place is that every input parameter of a function must match a property in the entity. You can't substitute your own data to use as an input parameter. You only can use one of the entity's properties.

If you have moved from Entity Framework version 1, you'll be happy to know that many of the former mapping function rules have been relaxed. You are no longer required to map all three functions and you no longer need to provide foreign key parameters for entity references when mapping. The latter was an aggravating rule, because it meant you needed to provide a foreign key for delete functions.

There is a known behavior with respect to the mapping function feature. If you map an update function but no delete function, you will get an error when attempting to delete these entities. Therefore, even though the schema does not require that you map both, if you want users to be able to delete a particular entity type and you are mapping its update function, you should also map its delete function.

Protecting Tables by Using Views and Stored Procedures

There's another great benefit to mapping the `Insert`, `Update`, and `Delete` functions, and that is security.

If you are reluctant to expose your database tables for querying, you don't have to. Earlier in this book, I discussed database views in the model. Views come into the model as entities, but because views are read-only, Entity Framework is not able to construct commands to persist data back to the database when you call `SaveChanges`. That makes sense because you don't persist back to the views; you need to send the data to tables. However, these entities still participate in change tracking just like any other entities (with a caveat about `EntityKeys` that I'll discuss momentarily). You can then map stored procedures to these view-based entities in order to persist their data when `SaveChanges` is called. This gives you a complete round trip to query and update data without exposing your database tables.

The caveat with view-based entities is that views do not have primary keys. The Entity Data Model Wizard relies on primary keys to create `EntityKeys`, and `EntityKeys`, in turn, are relied on for change tracking. When the wizard cannot find a primary key it constructs a composite `EntityKey` from all of the non-nullable values in the entity. You may want to modify the defined `EntityKey`, removing all of the properties that you don't want included.

Mapping Insert, Update, and Delete Functions to an Entity

If you look more closely at the Mapping Details window, you will notice two icons in the upper-left corner. Select the `Contact` entity in the Designer to display its mappings. The icons will become active. Clicking the top icon causes the Mapping Details window to display the table mappings. The lower icon is for displaying function, a.k.a. stored procedure, mappings. You can also display function mappings by right-clicking an entity and choosing Stored Procedure Mapping.

In the Mapping Details window, you will see three placeholders for selecting an `Insert` function, an `Update` function, and a `Delete` function, as shown in Figure 7-2.

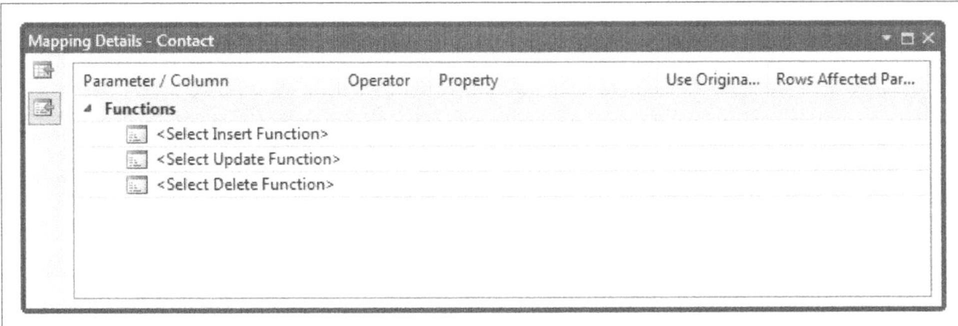

Figure 7-2. The function or stored procedures view of the Mapping Details window

Click the first item, Select Insert Function, which will display an arrow to the right that represents a drop-down list. Click the drop-down arrow to see your options. The Designer will identify all of the functions in the store layer and present them in the drop-down list. Select the `InsertContact` function. The Designer will discover the parameters that are defined in the SSDL and will automatically map them to properties in the `Contact` entity that have matching names. In this example, everything lines up perfectly, as you can see in Figure 7-3.

The `InsertContact` stored procedure happens to return the new `ContactID` that was generated when the contact was inserted:

```
ALTER PROCEDURE [dbo].[InsertContact]
@FirstName NVARCHAR(50),
@LastName NVARCHAR(50),
@Title NVARCHAR(50)
AS
```

```
INSERT INTO [Contact]
          ([FirstName]
          ,[LastName]
          ,[Title]
          ,[AddDate]
          ,[ModifiedDate])
     VALUES
          (@Firstname,@Lastname,@Title,GETDATE(),GETDATE())

SELECT SCOPE_IDENTITY() AS NewContactID WHERE @@ROWCOUNT > 0
```

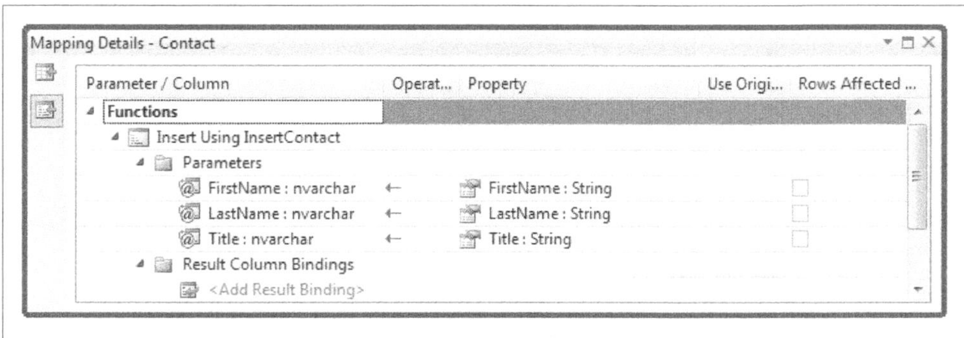

Figure 7-3. The InsertContact function mapped to the Contact entity

You may recall from Chapter 6 that when the Entity Framework constructs its own `Insert` command, it selects the new identity value and automatically pushes it into the entity object that was inserted. You can achieve the same effect by mapping the returned `NewContactID` value directly to the entity's `ContactID` property. That will mean it will not be necessary to requery the database to acquire the `ContactID` for an inserted contact.

To map the returned value, type **`NewContactID`** over the text "<Add ResultBinding>". The `ContactID` will be automatically chosen as the property to map to because it is the `EntityKey` for `Contact`, and therefore it is a very good first guess for the Designer to make for you. Output parameters are supported, but not for `EntityKey` properties. See the note about this in the following section, "Concurrency checking with Use Original Value and Rows Affected Parameter options".

Select the `DeleteContact` and `UpdateContact` functions to map to the other two functions. Notice that the `contactid` parameter in `DeleteContact` does not automatically map to the `ContactID` property. That's because the automatic mapping is case-sensitive. Map this parameter yourself. There are no other return values, so you will not need to apply a Result Column Binding for the update (see Figure 7-4).

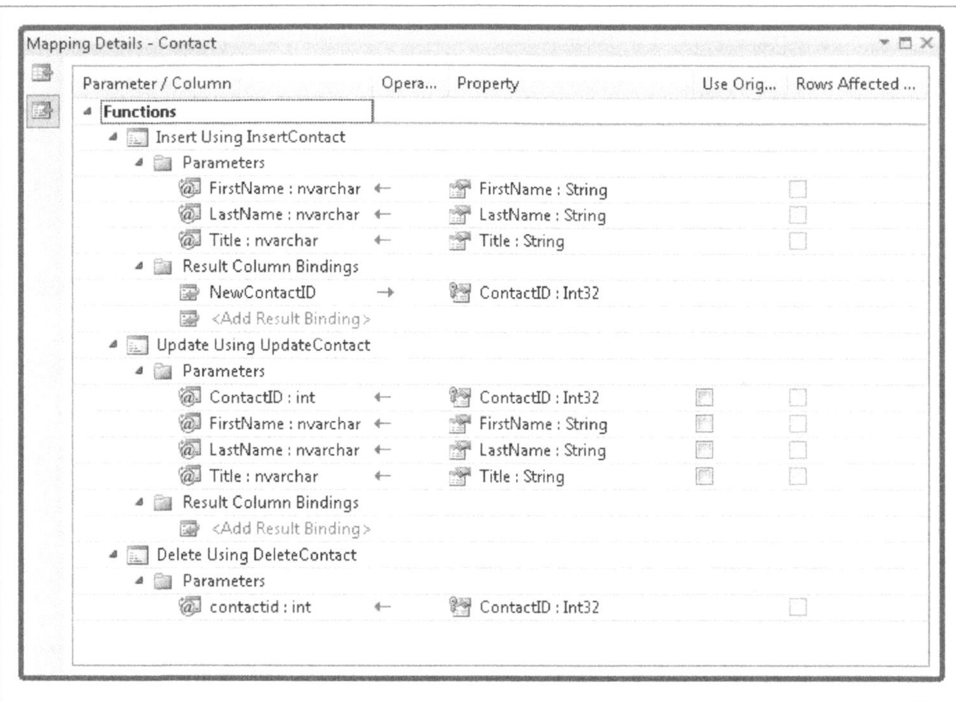

Figure 7-4. The function mappings for Contact after you've finished mapping the stored procedures functions

Concurrency checking with Use Original Value and Rows Affected Parameter options

There are two additional options to point out in the function mappings. The first is the Use Original Value checkbox for the `Update` function. As you learned in Chapter 6, an entity will have an original value and a current value stored in its `ObjectStateEntry`. If the entity has been modified, the current value will be used for the update by default. Here you have the ability to modify that behavior by forcing the original value to be used as a parameter for the function. This is useful in scenarios where you want to leverage particular fields to identify concurrency issues in the database. The original property value will be compared to the current database value. If the values do not match, an `OptimisticConcurrencyException` will be thrown. Figure 7-5 shows a timeline with two users editing the same piece of information and how using the `rowversion` (`timestamp` in SQL Server 2005 and earlier) for concurrency checking causes a concurrency exception when the second update occurs. In SQL Server, `rowversion` types are binary data. The figure uses simple strings for demonstration only.

For example, you may be using a SQL Server `rowversion` type to identify that a row has been modified. Each time a row is modified, the `rowversion` field is automatically updated. If a user pulls data from the database and edits it, it's possible that someone else edited the same database row before the user called `SaveChanges`. In that case, the `rowversion` value in the user's entity will be different from the `rowversion` in the

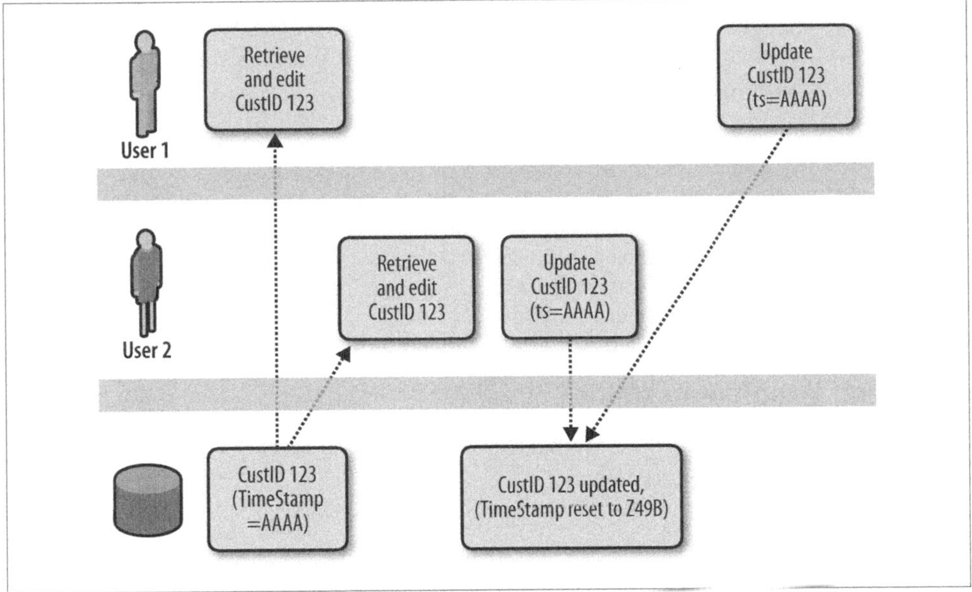

Figure 7-5. Using a timestamp/rowversion to check for concurrency conflicts when multiple users edit the same record

database. This is a convenient way of identifying that data is being edited concurrently, and you might want to act on that knowledge—for example, alert the user and ask if he wants to overwrite the changes the other user made. If the update stored procedure requests the `rowversion` as a parameter, you can force the original value to be used by checking the Use Original Value option. That way, you don't have to worry if the code changed the `rowversion` (which it shouldn't have done).

You will learn much more about concurrency with function mapping and in other scenarios, as well as handling the `OptimisticConcurrencyException`, in Chapter 23.

The Rows Affected Parameter option will be enabled for any parameters that are defined as `OUTPUT` parameters in the stored procedure, and will return an integer. Your job will be to know whether the stored procedure uses that output value to return a number indicating how many rows were affected by the command. If this is the case, you should check the Rows Affected Parameter option to let the Entity Framework know it should use that return value to determine whether any rows were affected by the command. If the number "0" is returned, that will indicate that no rows were affected, with the assumption that this is unexpected and, therefore, an `OptimisticConcurrencyException`.

An output parameter must be mapped to something. If it is not mapped to an entity's property through the Result Column Binding, the model will expect the parameter to be marked as a Rows Affected Parameter. Otherwise, you will get an error when the model is being validated.

You cannot map an `EntityKey` property to a stored procedure's output parameter. If, for example, your procedure uses an output parameter to return the identity value of a newly inserted entity (e.g., `ContactID`), you won't be able to map it to the `ContactID` property of the `Contact` entity. The Designer will allow the mapping, as will the compiler. You will only discover the problem at runtime.

Inspecting Mappings in XML

Now it's time to see how these mappings affect the Mapping Schema Layer (MSL) section of the model in the raw XML.

Remember that you can get to the XML view of the metadata by right-clicking on the EDMX file in the Solution Explorer, choosing Open With, and then selecting XML Editor.

A second `EntityTypeMapping` section has been added within the `EntitySetMapping` section for the `Contacts EntitySet`. The first is the one that defines the scalar property mappings for `Contact`. The new `EntityTypeMapping` contains an inner element called `ModificationFunctionMappings`. Within this element the three functions are mapped out, as shown in Example 7-2.

Example 7-2. Contacts EntitySetMapping with function mappings added

```
<EntitySetMapping Name="Contacts">

<!--PROPERTY MAPPINGS-->
  <EntityTypeMapping TypeName="SampleModel.Contact">
    <MappingFragment StoreEntitySet="Contact">
      <ScalarProperty Name="ContactID" ColumnName="ContactID" />
      <ScalarProperty Name="ModifiedDate" ColumnName="ModifiedDate" />
      <ScalarProperty Name="AddDate" ColumnName="AddDate" />
      <ScalarProperty Name="Title" ColumnName="Title" />
      <ScalarProperty Name="LastName" ColumnName="LastName" />
      <ScalarProperty Name="FirstName" ColumnName="FirstName" />
    </MappingFragment>
  </EntityTypeMapping>

<!--FUNCTION MAPPINGS-->
  <EntityTypeMapping TypeName="SampleModel.Contact">
    <ModificationFunctionMapping>
```

```
      <DeleteFunction FunctionName="ProgrammingEFDB1Model.Store.DeleteContact">
        <ScalarProperty Name="ContactID" ParameterName="contactid" />
      </DeleteFunction>

      <InsertFunction FunctionName="ProgrammingEFDB1Model.Store.InsertContact">
        <ScalarProperty Name="Title" ParameterName="title" />
        <ScalarProperty Name="LastName" ParameterName="lastname" />
        <ScalarProperty Name="FirstName" ParameterName="firstname" />
        <ResultBinding Name="ContactID" ColumnName="NewContactID" />
      </InsertFunction>

      <UpdateFunction FunctionName="ProgrammingEFDB1Model.Store.UpdateContact">
        <ScalarProperty Name="Title" ParameterName="title"
                        Version="Current" />
        <ScalarProperty Name="LastName" ParameterName="lastname"
                        Version="Current" />
        <ScalarProperty Name="FirstName" ParameterName="firstname"
                        Version="Current" />
        <ScalarProperty Name="ContactID" ParameterName="contactid"
                        Version="Current" />
      </UpdateFunction>

    </ModificationFunctionMapping>
  </EntityTypeMapping>
</EntitySetMapping>
```

In Example 7-2, you can see that a second `EntityTypeMapping` element has been added to the `Contacts EntitySetMapping`. Each function is listed within this new section, and based on everything you have already learned about reading this file, the elements should be familiar and the mappings should be logical. Notice in `UpdateContact` that each `ScalarProperty` has a `Version` attribute. That is the notation that ties back to the Use Original Version checkboxes, which are unchecked, therefore indicating that the version is `Current`.

Using Mapped Functions

Once you've mapped the functions to entities, when you call `SaveChanges` the Entity Framework will automatically use the functions to handle any entities that need to be persisted to the database anytime you call `SaveChanges`. It does this only for the entities to which you have mapped the functions. Other entities will be dependent on their own function mappings, otherwise they will be persisted using EF-generated commands. That's all there is to it. You won't call these functions directly in your code.

If you have mapped only `Insert`, and not `Update` or `Delete`, Entity Framework will use it where available but will revert to the default pattern of building commands on the fly for the `Update` and `Delete`, which are not mapped.

You can use one of the database profiling tools mentioned in Chapter 3 to verify that stored procedures are being called for operations that you have indicated with the mappings.

Example 7-3 shows a method that retrieves an address and a contact, edits both of them, and then saves them back to the database with SaveChanges.

Example 7-3. Testing the function mapping

```
private static void FunctionOverride()
{
  using (PEF context = new PEF())
  {
    var contact = context.Contacts.Include("Addresses")
                  .Where(c => c.Addresses.Any()).First();
   //make a change to contact
    contact.LastName = contact.LastName.Trim() + "-Jones";
   //make a change to the address
    var address = contact.Addresses.First();
    address.Street2 = "Apartment 42";
   //call SaveChanges
    context.SaveChanges();
  }
}
```

When the SaveChanges method is called, the required updates are sent to the database. Because you mapped the functions to the Contact entity, the change to this contact object is manifested in the following command, which executes the UpdateContact stored procedure:

```
exec [dbo].[UpdateContact]
 @contactid=3,
 @firstname=N'Donna                                          ',
 @lastname=N'Carreras-Jones',
 @title=N'Ms.                                          '
```

Notice that some of the parameter values are padded to 50 characters. They are the properties that have not been edited since they arrived in the query results. Even though the parameters for the char values are all nvarchar both in the definition of the table and in the stored procedure parameters, the original values are sent in their full field length.

The Address entity has no mapped functions; therefore, Object Services constructed this Update command, which was sent to the database:

```
exec sp_executesql N'update [dbo].[Address]
set [Street2] = @0
where ([addressID] = @1)',
N'@0 nvarchar(50),@1 int',@0=N'Apartment 42',@1=2260
```

The first line of the command contains the `Update` command. The second line defines the parameters for the command while the third provides the filter. The last line passes in the parameter values. `'Apartment 42'` is the new value of `Street2` and `2260` is the `addressID` of the address to update.

You will learn a lot more about how the Entity Framework performs saves and how you can impact them as you read through the book. For now, let's continue to focus on stored procedures.

Using the EDM Designer Model Browser to Import Additional Functions into Your Model

The Entity Data Model Designer has a feature that we have not yet used: the Model Browser. The Model Browser helps you navigate the objects in the conceptual layer (entities, properties, and associations). The lower portion allows you to navigate the items in the SSDL. Notice that in the Model Browser, these are referred to as Tables, Views, and Stored Procedures and not by their SSDL schema names of Entity and Function.

To access the Model Browser, you need to right-click in the background of the model in the Designer, and then select Model Browser from its context menu.

In Figure 7-6, a number of the model's objects have been expanded. This view of the model gives you a great way to see the overall picture of the conceptual layer and the store layer without all of the nitty-gritty XML.

Many of the features of the Designer are available in the context menu of the Model Browser as well, such as validating the model or view mappings, and updating the model from the database.

The Model Browser also provides a means for mapping the functions from the SSDL. Although you can also map some of these from an entity's Mapping Details window, you can map functions that are for reading data from the store only from the Model Browser.

Take a few minutes to explore the other capabilities of the Model Browser that are displayed in the context menu.

Figure 7-6. Viewing the CSDL and SSDL in the Model Browser

Mapping the First of the Read Stored Procedures: ContactsbyState

In addition to the stored procedures that insert, update, and delete data, you also pulled a few stored procedures into the metadata that read data from the database. Here we'll map the first of the read stored procedures, `ContactsbyState`.

1. Right-click the `ContactsbyState` stored procedure in the Model Browser and choose Add Function Import from its context menu.

   The Add Function Import dialog box will let you name the function import and map it to an existing entity, scalar type (e.g., an integer, string, etc.), or complex type; see Figure 7-7.

2. Change the Function Import Name to GetContactsbyState. By default, the function name will be the same as the stored procedure. This is a nice advantage of the loose

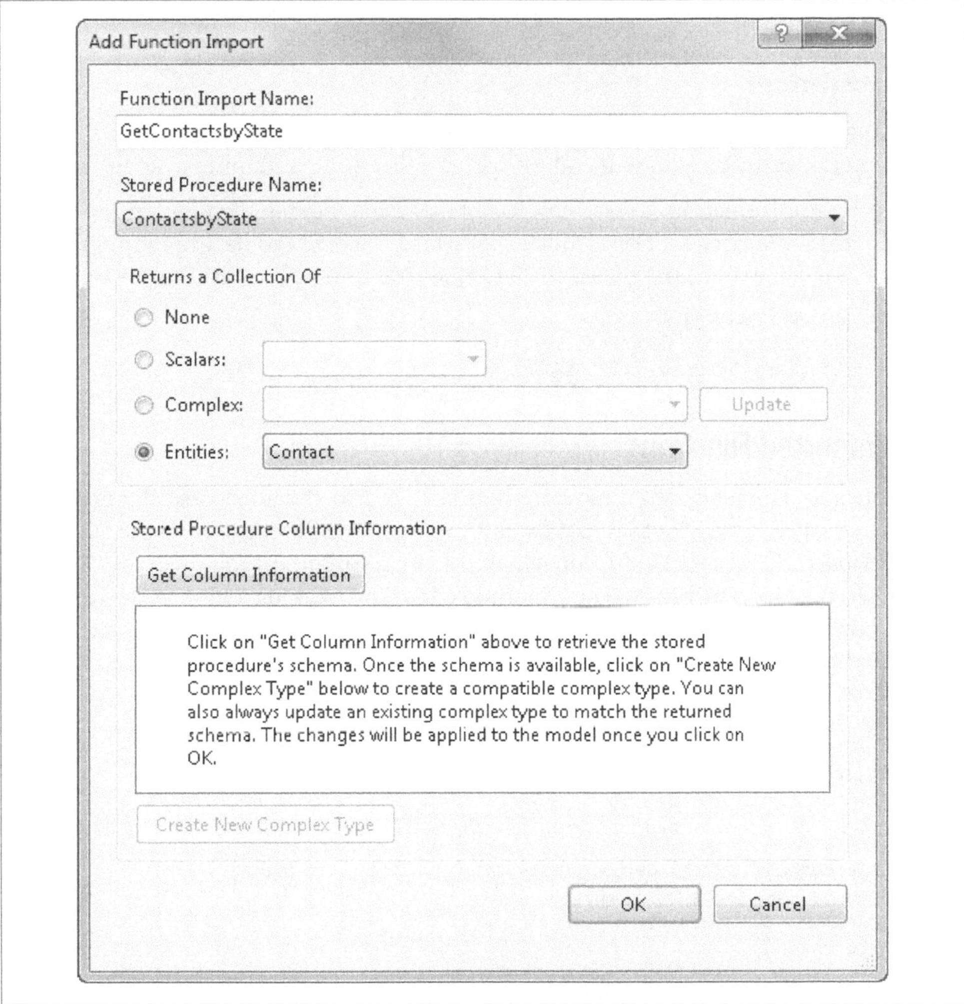

Figure 7-7. Mapping a stored procedure to an entity that will return a Contact entity

coupling between the model and the database. I can name the function in a way that makes sense to my domain.

3. Click the Entities option, which will enable the Entities drop-down list. Select Contact from that list and then click OK.

The new function import will not be displayed in the model in the Designer, but you can see it in the Model Browser if you open the first node (`SampleModel`) and drill first into EntityContainer and then into Function Imports.

In the XML, you will find the following additions to the CSDL section inside the `EntityContainer` element:

```
<FunctionImport Name="GetContactsbyState" EntitySet="Contacts"
                ReturnType="Collection(SampleModel.Contact)">
  <Parameter Name="state" Mode="In" Type="String" />
</FunctionImport>
```

Notice that the return type is not a single contact, but a collection of contacts. If only one contact is returned, you will end up with a collection containing a single item.

The mapping information is in a new FunctionImportMapping element in the MSL's EntityContainerMapping section. Unlike the Update, Insert, and Delete mappings, this is not included as part of the contact's EntitySet mappings, but rather stands alone:

```
<FunctionImportMapping
   FunctionImportName="GetContactsbyState"
   FunctionName="ProgrammingEFDB1Model.Store.ContactsbyState" />
```

Using Imported Functions

After you map the function, a new method is added to the automatically generated context class, PEF, called ContactsbyState. If you open the file containing the generated classes (*Model1.Designer.cs/.vb*), you will find a Function Import region in the PEF class, which contains not one, but two new methods. It's worth taking a look at the function, which, unlike the other context methods you've seen so far, returns a System.Data.Objects.ObjectResult. ObjectResult implements IEnumerable, but not IQueryable.

The method is a wrapper for a call to ObjectContext.ExecuteFunction, which you could call directly if you prefer (see Example 7-4).

Example 7-4. One of the two methods created for the GetContactsbyState function import

```
public ObjectResult<Contact> GetContactsbyState(global::System.String state)
{
  ObjectParameter stateParameter;
  if (state != null)
  {
   stateParameter = new ObjectParameter("state", state);
  }
  else
  {
    stateParameter = new ObjectParameter("state",
                          typeof(global::System.String));
  }
  return base.ExecuteFunction<Contact>("GetContactsbyState", stateParameter);
}
```

The second method (not listed in the example) overloads the first with something called a MergeOption which prescribes what to do when duplicate entities are being returned from the database. You'll learn more about MergeOption in Chapter 10.

You can call the method directly in your code using an instantiated context, as shown in Example 7-5.

Example 7-5. Testing the function mapping

```
ObjectResult<Contact> results= context.GetContactsbyState("Washington");
```

This is not the same as creating and executing a query. The function will be executed immediately when the function is called in code. The execution will not be deferred. The return type will be a `System.Data.Objects.ObjectResult<Contact>` (in VB, an `ObjectResult(Of Contact)`), which you can enumerate through or bind to data controls.

You could also use one of the LINQ conversion methods to return a more common type of `IEnumerable`. For example, you could return a list of `Contact` objects rather than the `ObjectResult`, using the following code:

```
context.GetContactsbyState("Washington").ToList()
```

Avoiding Inadvertent Client-Side Processing

Because the function returns an `IEnumerable` (the `ObjectResult`), it is *technically* possible to use the function in a query, as shown in the following code:

```
var results =
    from c in context.GetContactsbyState("Washington")
    where c.LastName.StartsWith("S")
    select c;
```

However, this is not a LINQ to Entities query, but a LINQ to Objects query—the query will be performed on the results of the function. That means the function will be executed on the server side and then the results will be filtered further in memory.

For example, if there are hundreds of contacts in Washington but only a small number of them have last names that begin with *S*, every contact will be returned from the database into your application memory and then LINQ will pull out the small number that you were really looking for.

Databases do not support the use of stored procedures as subqueries, which is why it is not possible to compose a LINQ to Entities query using these functions. .NET and the Entity Framework coordinate to break up the query into a function call and a separate LINQ to Objects query.

Therefore, you'll want to avoid writing queries against these functions. There will be no warnings or exceptions, but perhaps instead, you'll receive a phone call from the performance testers on your team.

Mapping a Function to a Scalar Type

Entities from your model are only one of the types that can be mapped to data returned from a stored procedure. Now we will work with a stored procedure that returns scalar types, `AddressTypeCount`. This takes a `ContactID` as a parameter and returns an `int`. You saw in Example 7-1 that the function contains a `Parameter` element.

Follow the same steps as you did before, except this time, map to the Scalars option (indicating that each row in the result set contains only a single unit of data) rather than an entity. In the case of this function, the result set will contain only one row and that will contain a single piece of data. After you select the Scalars option, the Scalars drop-down list will be enabled so that you can define the type of the value. Select Int32 from the drop-down list.

If you do not know the schema of the results returned by a function, you can use the Get Column Information button to display the schema of the results. You'll learn more about this and the other button in the Function Imports Wizard in the next section of this chapter.

The new `AddressTypeCount` method will be added to the Function Imports section of the context class. You will find only one method. There is no need for the `MergeOption` overload because the method returns a scalar value, not an entity.

The signature of the new method is notable:

```
public ObjectResult<Nullable<global::System.Int32>>
  AddressTypeCount(global::System.String addressType)
```

Rather than simply returning an `Int32`, it returns a `Nullable` version of `Int32`. This accounts for the possibility of the database returning nulls. You'll need to honor the `Nullable` when working with this function, as shown in Example 7-6.

Example 7-6. Testing the function mapping for a scalar result

```
ObjectResult<int?> results = context.AddressTypeCount("Home");
int? HomeAddressCount = results.FirstOrDefault();
```

Here I'm pushing it to another `Nullable<int>` using the C# shortcut `int?` to define the type. If you want to use a regular `int`, you'll need to test that the result has a value (`results.FirstOrDefault().HasValue`) and then get the value (`results.FirstOrDefault.Value`).

Coming from Entity Framework version 1? Note that you can now call the method directly from the context. Previously, the only way to execute this function was to use `EntityClient`.

Mapping a Function to a Complex Type

Entity Framework 4 supports a new function import mapping: mapping the results to complex types.

Toward that end, the last stored procedure we'll work with is `AddressCountForContact`, which returns data whose schema does not match an existing entity or a known scalar type. There is another type in the Entity Data Model that we haven't explored yet, called a `ComplexType`. A `ComplexType` has properties but does not have an `EntityKey` and therefore cannot be managed by an `ObjectContext`. Complex types do not display in the model designer view, but you can see and create them in the Model Browser. There are a few uses for complex types. Here we will focus on using them to capture the results of stored procedures. But another very important function of the complex type is to encapsulate fields in an entity. You will learn more about this latter purpose in Chapter 14.

Coming from Entity Framework version 1? Mapping to a complex type using the Designer is one of the new features that I hinted at earlier in the chapter.

When the EDM Wizard pulled this stored procedure into the metadata of the model, it was only able to discover the procedure's required parameters. However, in order to capture the results of the procedure, we'll need to define some type. This seems like a possible opportunity for an anonymous type, but a complex type is more advantageous. It provides consistency. Not only it is part of the model, but because it is really a type, you can pass it between methods—something you can't do with an anonymous type.

The Function Import Wizard will help with this. Let's see how it works.

Once again, right-click the `AddressCountForContact` procedure in the Model Browser to activate the Function Import Wizard. Then follow these steps:

1. Rename the function to `GetAddressCountForContact`.
2. In the wizard, select Complex as the return type.
3. On the lower part of the window, the Get Column Information button is enabled. Click that button to force the wizard to determine the schema of the results of this stored procedure.

The Get Column Information feature accesses the database to get the needed information.

4. Once the box below the button is populated with the column information, click the Create New Complex Type button to create a complex type with the schema of the discovered columns.

   A new type will automatically be created and named using the name of the Function Import with "_Result" appended to it, in this case `GetAddressCountForContact_Result`. This type will also be automatically selected as the return type for the function. You can rename the type to something more meaningful, which I have done, as show in Figure 7-8. My new `ComplexType` will be named `ContactAddressCount`.

Because the returned columns become properties of the new complex type, I cannot use either of those names for the name of the complex type.

5. Click OK to finish.

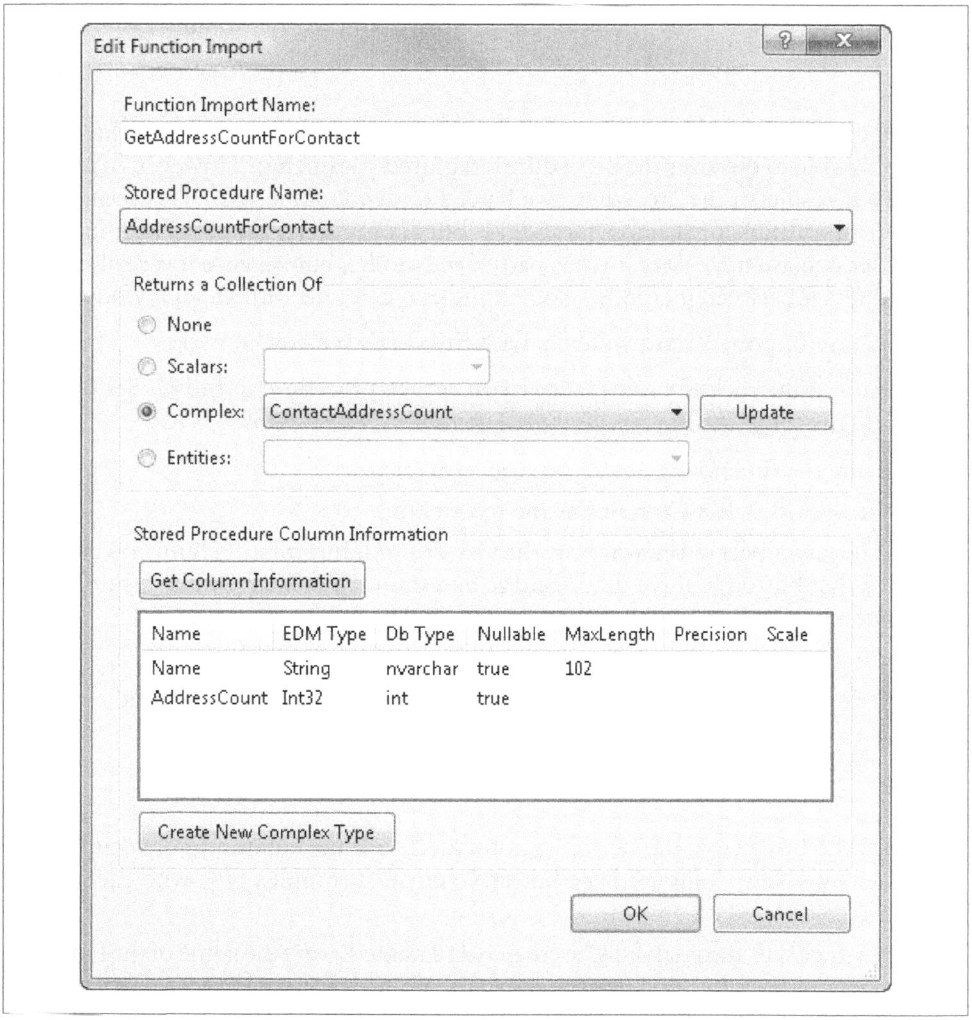

Figure 7-8. Creating a complex type on the fly from a stored procedure

Once you have finished, you will see the new function in the Model Browser as well as in the SampleEntities class.

Because the complex type does not have an EntityKey, there is no need for the MergeOption overload. Therefore, you will see only one method for GetAddressCountForContact with the following method signature:

```
public ObjectResult<ContactAddressCount >
 GetAddressCountForContact(Nullable<global::System.Int32> contactID)
```

This feature is a huge improvement over the cumbersome means of incorporating this type of stored procedure into the EDM in the first version of the Entity Framework. There are still a few steps you need to execute for each procedure, and it would be nice if these steps could be executed automatically in a batch. But I'll take this behavior over what was available in the earlier version of Entity Framework.

Summary

Many database administrators rely (and insist) on stored procedures for a variety of reasons, including consistency, security, and reliability, although many are starting to gain confidence in ORMs. You also may already have a big investment in stored procedures that you don't want to give up. Even though the Entity Framework composes queries and commands automatically, you can override this default behavior by implementing your own stored procedures in the model.

This chapter highlighted functionality that the Designer readily supports: mapping procedures to entities when the procedure's input parameters and results line up with existing entities and their properties, and mapping read queries to scalar or complex types.

If you have been working with the first version of Entity Framework, you have seen some significant improvements for stored procedure support.

Chapter 16 will dig further into additional ways to implement database stored procedures, and even to define commands and views directly in the model when they do not exist in the data store.

CHAPTER 8

Implementing a More Real-World Model

In the previous chapters, we discussed the core concepts of the Entity Framework, including the Entity Data Model (EDM), querying, and other straightforward operations. We used a simple database and console application to illustrate key points and keep you focused on the lessons. Now it's time to look at some more real-world scenarios.

In this chapter, we'll create a more realistic EDM based on a database of the kind you're more likely to encounter in your work. The model is based on a more complex sdatabase—the BreakAway database—designed to support a fictional travel agency. With a more complex database, you must typically tweak the EDM you create to resolve naming conflicts and other issues. More complex databases are also likely to contain many-to-many relationships and additional stored procedures, both of which you'll learn how to handle in this and later chapters.

We'll build the model using the database-first approach as we did with the sample model in Chapter 2.

Chapter 25 will teach you how to do *model-first* design, where you define an Entity Data Model from scratch and build a database from that model, and *code-first* design, which leverages the Entity Framework without using a designer-based model.

Finally, the model will be contained in its own assembly so that you can reuse it. We'll use the model and add to it throughout the rest of the book.

The model you will build here, though more realistic than the sample model of earlier chapters, is still smaller than a typical enterprise model. This is intentional in order to prevent you from getting distracted from the various tasks at hand. You'll find a brief discussion of larger models at the end of Chapter 14.

Introducing the BreakAway Geek Adventures Business Model and Legacy Database

The company for which we will be writing software is a fictional business named BreakAway Geek Adventures. This small company arranges adventure vacations for hard-working programmers who need a break. Examples of vacations that can be booked through BreakAway Geek Adventures include whitewater rafting in Belize and bicycling in Ireland. The company has been in business for a number of years and has an old application that uses a SQL Server database for its data store. Now it's time to write shiny new applications for this venerable firm in .NET, leveraging the Entity Framework.

You can download a script for creating this database from the book's website, *http://learnentityframework.com*. Look for the database named BreakAway. The script will work for both SQL Server 2005 and SQL Server 2008.

Figure 8-1 shows the BreakAway database schema.

This example database was designed with two goals in mind. First, it's structured in a way that allows you to explore various features of modeling in this chapter and later in Chapters 14 and 15. Second, the tables in this database track minimal information in an attempt to be a little less distracting from the main tasks throughout the book. For example, you won't find details such as email addresses or phone numbers for the contacts.

Some contacts are customers. Customers make reservations for particular trips; however, the database doesn't account for the possibility of a customer wanting to make a reservation for multiple people—for example, family members or friends.

The database revolves around two core tables. The first is `Contacts`, which could be anyone from a vendor to a potential customer to an actual customer. Contacts who are customers have an additional record in the `Customers` table that includes information such as their favorite two destinations and their favorite two activities.

The second core table is `Events`. Events (a.k.a. trips) are what the company sells. A trip has a start date, end date, and price and it links to other tables that identify the trip destination, a list of one or more activities, and lodging associated with that particular trip.

Customers make reservations for trips. Then they can make one or more payments to pay for the reservation.

The schema allows us to perform a variety of modeling tasks as well as to create small applications to enable employees of the company to perform some of their tasks (defining trips, taking reservations, browsing customer information) as well as a few tasks

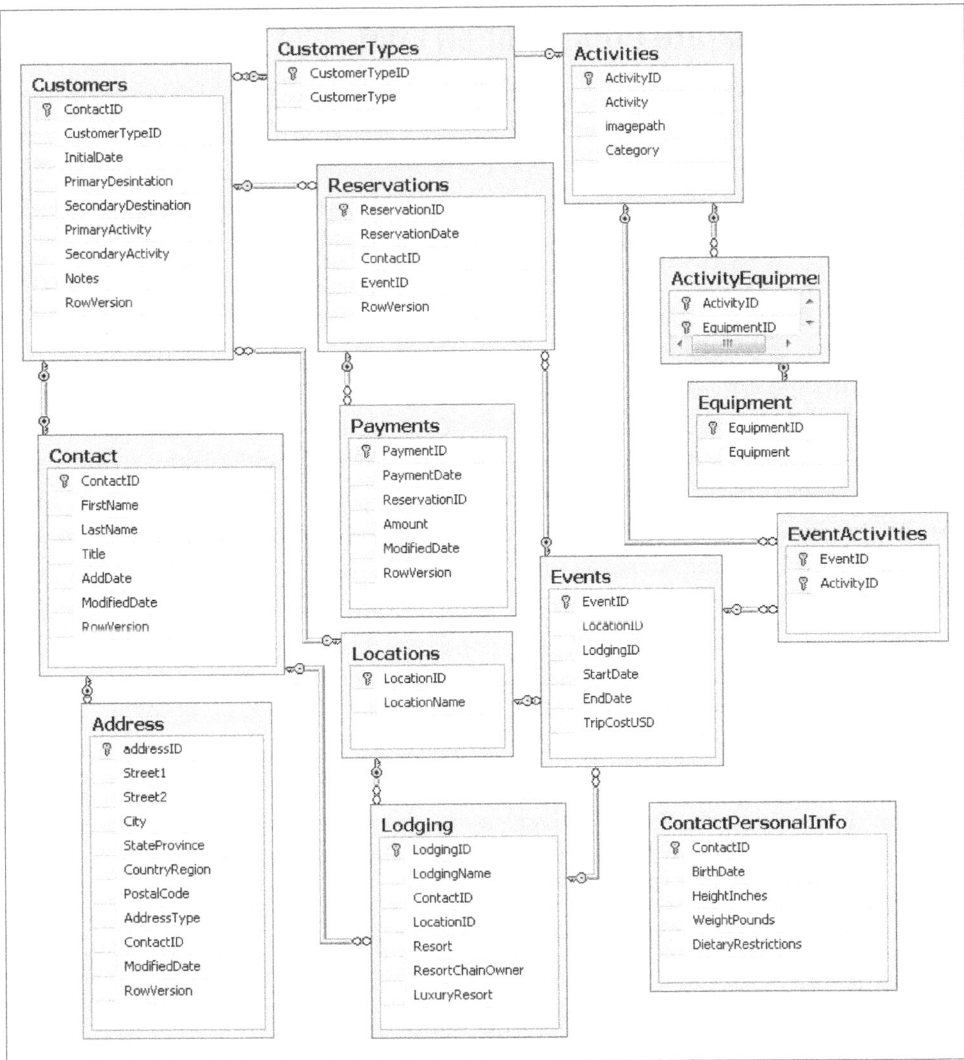

Figure 8-1. The BreakAway database schema

that are targeted to customers, such as a web app where they can look up their trip history and edit their addresses.

With this in mind, let's begin building the BreakAway model that you will use going forward.

Creating a Separate Project for an EDM

The first step is to create the new model. Rather than create the EDM directly in an application, you will create a separate project for the EDM. This is a good start on your way to planning for larger applications and being able to reuse the model.

1. In Visual Studio, create a new Class Library project named BreakAwayModel.
2. Delete the *Class1* file that was automatically created.
3. Add a new ADO.NET Entity Data Model to the project. Change the default name (*Model1.edmx*) to *BAModel.edmx*.
4. On the Choose Model Contents page, choose Generate from Database and then select the BreakAway Data Connection if it has already been added to Visual Studio. If it hasn't been added, create it on the fly using the New Connection button. Leave the default connection settings name, BreakAwayEntities, alone for now and go to the next page of the wizard.
5. On the Choose Your Database Objects page, check all three objects: Tables, Views, and Stored Procedures.

If you have created any diagrams of your SQL Server database, there will be an extra table and a number of stored procedures and functions that you'll want to keep out of your model. When the database contains a diagram, the table that controls the diagram is listed (`sysdiagrams`). Creating the diagram in SQL Server Management Studio also results in seven stored procedures and one function being added for the sake of diagramming. Their names begin with either *fn_* or *sp_* and contain the word *diagram*. They won't interfere with your model, but you may prefer not to have them in there.

6. Leave the default model namespace intact. You'll get a chance to change that shortly.
7. Wrap up model creation by clicking the Finish button.

The newly created model will open in the Designer window and should look something like Figure 8-2.

Inspecting and Cleaning Up a New EDM

The first thing you should always do with a newly generated model is make sure the `Entity` names and `EntitySet` names make sense. Thanks to the wizard's pluralization and singularization capabilities (added as of Visual Studio 2010), this chore has been reduced immensely.

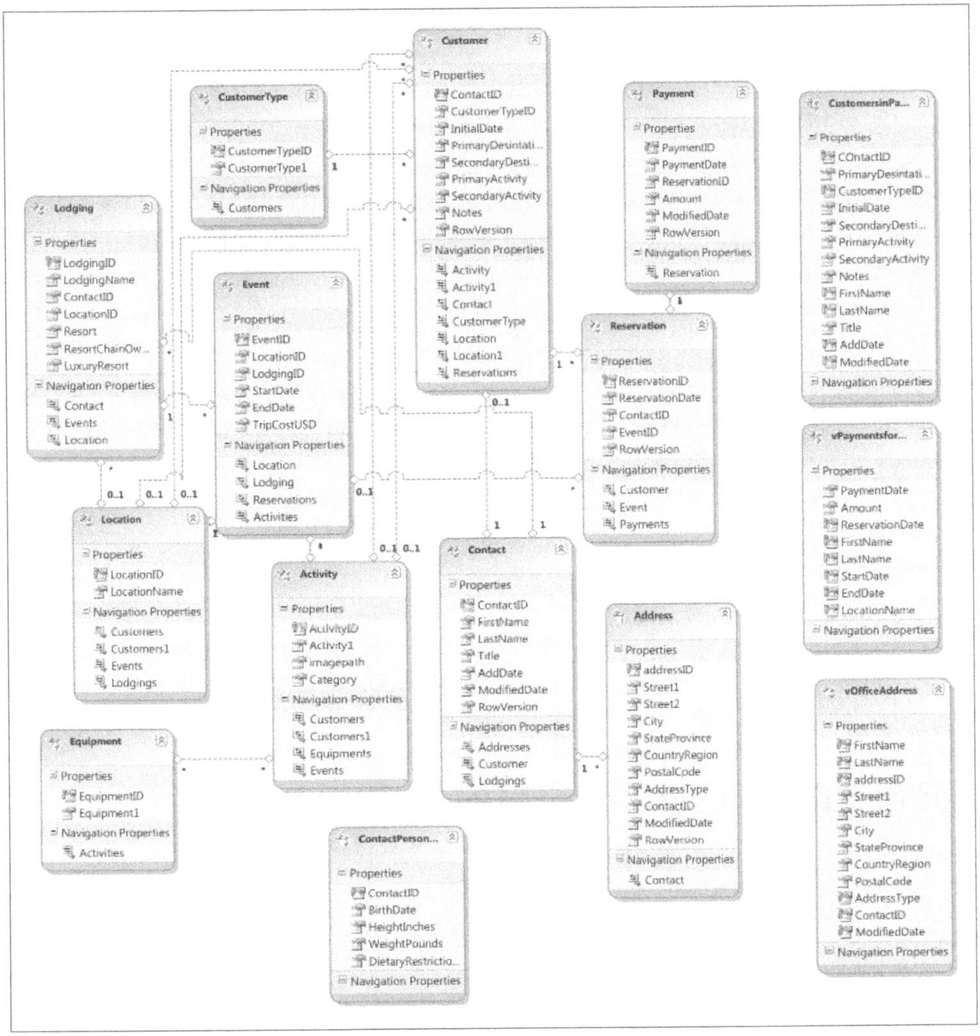

Figure 8-2. The initial model created from the BreakAway database

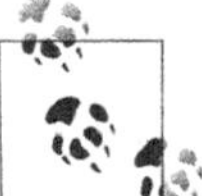

The Entity Data Model Wizard's ability to correctly singularize and pluralize entity names, entity set names, and navigation property names is limited to English words.

The `Entity` names should be singular (`Contact`, `Address`, `Customer`, etc.) and the `EntitySet` names should be the plural form of the `Entity` names (`Contacts`, `Addresses`, `Customers`, etc.).

However, there are a few table names that pose a challenge to the wizard and you should manually fix these after the model has been created. For instance, the word *equipment* poses a challenge since the singular and plural versions are the same. The wizard made the entity set name `Equipments`, which has a bitter taste to me. Let's change it.

If you look in the Properties window of the model, you will see there is a Boolean property called `Pluralize New Objects`. If you created the model with the Pluralization/Singularization settings checked, this was set to `True` when the model was created. As you create new entities in the Designer, each entity's `EntitySet` name will automatically be created as a plural of the `Entity` name. If the entity name is plural, it will not be made singular. If this property is set to `False`, the `EntitySet` name will consist of the `Entity` name with the word *Set* appended to it. We'll follow the latter convention and use `EquipmentSet` in this model. Although you can edit the `Entity` names right in the Designer, you can edit the `EntitySet` names only in the Properties window. You may find it more efficient to edit both in the Properties window.

There are three ways to get an entity's properties to display in the Properties window:

- Select the entity in the Designer.
- Select the entity in the Model Browser.
- Select the entity from the drop-down list of objects in the Properties window.

Modifying the Names of Entities and Properties

The database has a table named `Events` that refers to the trips that BreakAway schedules. The original name of this table was an unfortunate choice because the .NET word *Event* is a reserved keyword in both VB and C#. This normally isn't a problem, but if you were to use *Event* as the entity name, the `EntityObject` named `Event` would create a conflict. With the EDM, you can rename the entity without having to rename the database table. The term *Trip* makes more sense anyway, so renaming this will be a bonus. As you fix the names of the `Entity` objects and `EntitySets`, rename the `Events` entity to `Trip`. The entity will still map back to the `Events` table, so everything will stay in sync.

When you make this change, the `EntitySet` name will automatically change to `Trips`.

You should also change the `EventID` property name to `TripID` so that as you are working with objects, you won't be confused by an entity whose ID property doesn't match the name of the entity. Now you have a domino effect. `EventID` is also a foreign key in the `Reservation` table. So, change that one as well, to `TripID`.

Do the same for the entity named `Location`, changing it to `Destination`. You'll need to change the `LocationID` and `LocationName` properties as well, to `DestinationID` and `Name`. Don't forget the foreign keys.

Table 8-1 provides a recap of these changes.

Table 8-1. Entity, EntitySet, and Property name changes in the model

	Old name	New name
Entity	`Event`	`Trip`
Entity set	`Events`	`Trips`
Entity set	`Equipments`	`EquipmentSet`
Property	`Trip.EventID`	`Trip.TripID`
Property	`Trip.LocationID`	`Trip.DestinationID`
Foreign key	`Reservation.EventID`	`Reservation.TripID`
Entity	`Location`	`Destination`
Entity set	`Locations`	`Destinations`
Property	`Location.LocationID`	`Destination.DestinationID`
Property	`Location.LocationName`	`Destination.Name`
Navigation property	`Destination.Events`	`Destination.Trips`
Property	`Lodging.LocationID`	`Lodging.DestinationID`

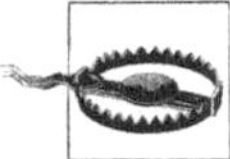

If you completely delete and reenter the name of an entity, the entity set name will not change. However, if you simply modify an entity name—for example, change `Equipment` to `EquipmentXYZ`—the Designer will automatically rename the `EntitySet` using the pluralization feature. You can turn off the pluralization by changing the `Pluralize New Objects` property of the model to `False`.

There are some other properties that should be attended to. Some of the foreign key properties in the database were poorly named and it's difficult to identify them as foreign keys. Fix them up in the model using the changes listed in Table 8-2.

Table 8-2. Fixing foreign key property names

Old property name	New property name
`Customer.PrimaryDesintation`	`Customer.PrimaryDestinationID`
`Customer.SecondaryDestination`	`Customer.SecondaryDestinationID`
`Customer.PrimaryActivity`	`Customer.PrimaryActivityID`
`Customer.SecondaryActivity`	`Customer.SecondaryActivityID`

Did you notice that the PrimaryDestination column was misspelled in the database? In the previous application, the developers had to constantly tangle with this field name. But with the EDM it will no longer be a problem. Though a small detail, this is a really nice benefit of using the data model. Changing the field name in the database could have a big impact in the database schema, especially if that field name is used in views, functions, or stored procedures. In the model, you can change the property to whatever name you like without impacting the database.

Resolving Collisions Between Property Names and Entity Names

The wizard identified a conflict when it was building two of the entities from the database. An entity cannot contain any properties that have the same name as the entity. In the case of three entities, the wizard dealt with this conflict by appending the number "1" to the property name. Check CustomerType, Equipment, and Activity. They contain the properties CustomerType1, Equipment1, and Activity1. Modify the property names as shown in Table 8-3.

Table 8-3. Property name changes to be made

Old property name	New property name
CustomerType.CustomerType1	CustomerType.Type
Activity.Activity1	Activity.Name
Equipment.Equipment1	Equipment.Name

You may have other renaming preferences, but for the sake of aligning with examples throughout the book, you'll want to be sure that your model matches mine.

Cleaning Up Navigation Property Names

There is still a bit of cleaning up to do. Although the wizard properly named most of the navigation properties (singular when pointing to an entity reference and plural when pointing to an entity collection), there are some other navigations that confused the wizard. These are navigations from an entity with multiple relationships to a single entity.

Take a look at the Customer entity. It has those two funny pairs of navigation properties: Activity and Activity1, and Location and Location1. These property pairs will make more sense if you check the Customers table in the database, shown in Figure 8-3. BreakAway keeps track of each customer's first and second preferences for destination and activity. This is not an uncommon database scenario, but the wizard will always create the names in this way, so let's see how to add clarity to these names.

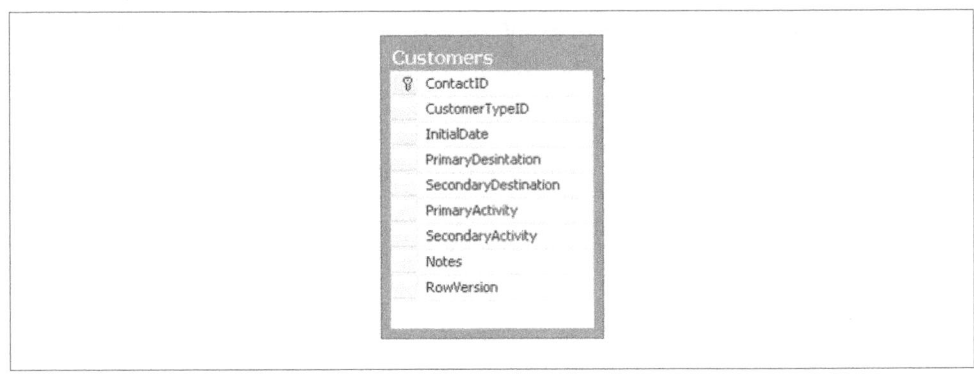

Figure 8-3. The Customers table in the database, with two columns that relate to the Destination table (PrimaryDesintation—a database typo that BreakAway developers have had to live with for years—and SecondaryDestination) and two columns that point to the Activities table

The navigation property names are derived simply from the name of the table on the other end of the relationship. Since there are two associations to one entity, the wizard appended a "1" to the second navigation property.

Before you can rename these navigation properties, you'll need to figure out which foreign key fields the navigation properties belong to. For example, does `Customer.Activity` refer to the `PrimaryActivity` or the `SecondaryActivity`?

You can do this by looking at the properties of each navigation property and seeing which association it is bound to, and then looking at that association and seeing which field is involved.

Let's start with `Activity`. Click the `Activity` navigation property in the `Customer` entity. In its Properties window, `BreakAway.FK_Customers_Activities` is the `Association` property.

Use the Properties window drop-down (near the top of the Properties window) to select that association. You can also get to the correct association by right-clicking the `Navigation` property and choosing Select Association from the context menu.

There are a number of ways to select an association in the model. The Properties window drop-down is one way to select the association. You can also select it in the Model Browser. An additional method is to right-click a navigation property and to choose Select Association from its context menu. Any of these methods will cause the association to be highlighted in the Designer and its properties to display in the Properties window.

In a model that uses foreign key associations, the actual properties are used by the referential constraints.

Click the ellipses next to the `Referential Constraint` property to see the details. It is the `PrimaryActivityID`. Now you can rename the `Activity` navigation property to `PrimaryActivity` and, by process of elimination, the `Activity1` navigation property to `SecondaryActivity`.

You can do the same detective work for the `Location` and `Location1` navigation properties to see which one should be named `PrimaryDestination` and which one should be named `SecondaryDestination`.

You need to fix the other ends of these associations as well. The `Activity` entity has two navigations back to the `Customer` entity. Going in this direction, the navigations represent "Customers who have listed this activity as their primary activity" and "Customers who have listed this activity as their secondary activity." Rename `Customers` to `PrimaryPrefCustomers` and `Customers1` to `SecondaryPrefCustomers`. Make the same changes to the `Customers` and `Customers1` navigation properties in the `Destination` entity.

Because we changed the entity name of `Event` to `Trip` and of `Location` to `Destination`, you'll want to modify the navigation properties that reference these entities, as shown in Table 8-4.

Table 8-4. Fixing navigation property names related to Trip

Navigation property	New property name
`Reservation.Event`	`Reservation.Trip`
`Destination.Events`	`Destination.Trips`
`Lodging.Events`	`Lodging.Trips`
`Lodging.Location`	`Lodging.Destination`
`Trip.Location`	`Trip.Destination`
`Activity.Events`	`Activity.Trips`

Setting Default Values

The Entity Data Model allows you to set default values on scalar properties. This means you can set a default `CustomerType` for customers. BreakAway customers can be Standard, Silver, or Gold. In the database, Standard is equal to 1. Modify the `Customer.CustomerTypeID` foreign key property of the `Customer` entity by setting its `Default Value` to `1`. You'll see the effect of this in the next chapter.

If you are moving from version 1 of Entity Framework, you might be overjoyed at the ability to do this in the new version. Although you could set defaults on scalars in the first version, because the foreign keys were not exposed as scalar values, setting foreign key values was not simple or obvious. It was certainly possible, but setting default foreign keys meant even more work. Now it is this simple.

Unfortunately, you can't easily set default date values. Although it is possible to enter a specific date as a default value on a date property, there is no way in the model to specify something akin to `DateTime.Now`. You will see ways to customize the classes further on in the book, including enabling the class to take care of injecting the current date and time.

You can also set default values in your database, so why define defaults directly in the model? The `CustomerTypeID` property is non-nullable. Not only is this defined in the database, but it is also defined in the conceptual model. Because it's non-nullable in the conceptual model, you must provide a value for this property; otherwise, when you call `SaveChanges`, a runtime exception will be thrown. Therefore, setting the default in the model ensures that some value is provided even when the developer doesn't specifically assign the property value.

Mapping Stored Procedures

The BreakAway database has a number of stored procedures, as is the case with most legacy enterprise databases. For now, we'll use function mapping to map the `InsertPayment`, `UpdatePayment`, and `DeletePayment` stored procedures to the `Payment` entity using the same technique you learned in Chapter 7. We'll deal with other stored procedures in this database in later chapters.

Open the Stored Procedure Mappings window for the `Payment` entity and select the appropriate functions for insert, update, and delete.

As a reminder, you can right-click on the `Payment` entity in the Designer and select Stored Procedure Mapping.

When parameter names don't match the property names of the entity because of the casing you will need to manually map the properties.

Notice that the `InsertPayment` function needs to know the `ReservationID`. Because our model uses foreign keys, this is not a problem. If you were using a model without foreign keys, you would have access to the navigation property in the mapping window, so you can select `Reservation.ReservationID` to map to the required parameter.

The date parameter of the stored procedure is for the `PaymentDate`. The procedure itself will apply the `ModifiedDate` when it inserts the new payment.

The `InsertPayment` function returns a newly generated `PaymentID` called `NewPaymentID`. Be sure to map that to the Result Column Bindings item, as you did for the `InsertContact` function in the preceding chapter. The insert mapping should look the same as in Figure 8-4.

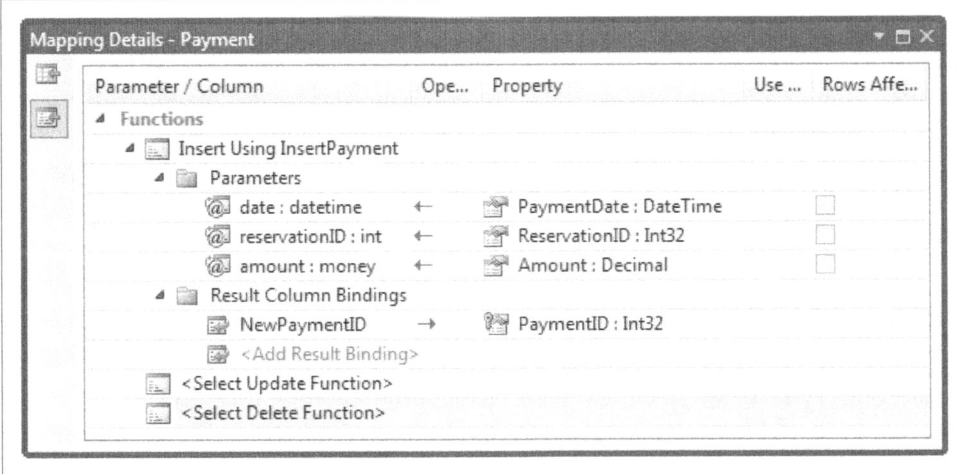

Figure 8-4. Mapping the input parameters and the results of the InsertPayment stored procedure to properties in the Payment entity

Map the `UpdatePayment` stored procedure to the `Update` function. Again, you will need to manually map the `date` parameter to the `PaymentDate` property.

Using the Use Original Value Checkbox in Update Mappings

Because of the way this stored procedure works, you can take advantage of the special Use Original Value column that exists only for the update functions. The `UpdatePayment` stored procedure performs a concurrency check against the `RowVersion` field. When a payment is updated, SQL Server automatically updates the `RowVersion` field. If anyone edited the record in between the time the user retrieved the record and when he attempted to save changes, `RowVersion` won't match, the order won't be updated, and an `OptimisticConcurrencyException` will be thrown. You'll learn more about working with concurrency in Chapter 23.

SQL Server Confusion: timestamp or rowversion?

SQL Server's `timestamp` type is the same as the ISO standard `rowversion` type and its name is a bit confusing. Microsoft changed the name of this type to `rowversion` in SQL Server 2008, but SQL Server Management Studio and Visual Studio 2010 still use `timestamp` in the design tools. You will rarely see the `rowversion` type when working with your databases, which makes the terminology confusing.

Here is the official statement in the MSDN documentation (*http://msdn.microsoft.com/en-us/library/ms182776.aspx*):

"The timestamp syntax is deprecated. This feature will be removed in a future version of Microsoft SQL Server. Avoid using this feature in new development work, and plan to modify applications that currently use this feature."

In the BreakAway database, the columns that contain the `timestamp`/`rowversion` types are named `RowVersion`, and I will refer to the `rowversion` type with an occasional nod to the former type name, `timestamp`.

When a payment is updated, the database will automatically update the `RowVersion` field. The `UpdatePayment` procedure returns the new value. Map that return value as shown in Figure 8-5.

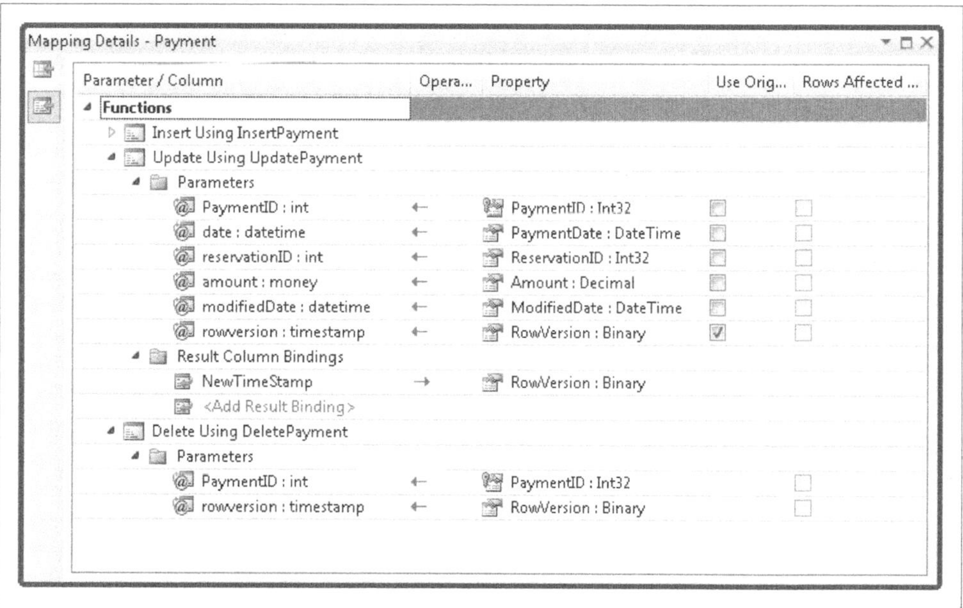

Figure 8-5. The UpdatePayment and DeletePayment function mappings

Mapping the `delete` function is straightforward. Select the `DeletePayment` function; the single parameter, `PaymentID`, will automatically align with the `PaymentID` property.

Moving from Entity Framework version 1? There is a significant improvement in this mapping. Previously, the schema required that you map all foreign keys. This meant you needed to have a `ReservationID` parameter in both the `Update` and `Delete` stored procedures to map to the `ReservationID` foreign key. In most cases, it makes no sense for the `Delete` procedure to have this parameter, and it was aggravating to have to add it. Thankfully, this restriction has been eliminated.

Since you have already done so much work on this model, we will leave the task of performing more advanced customizations to Chapters 14 and 15.

Working with Many-to-Many Relationships

There is one more thing to point out about this model: the two many-to-many relationships. BreakAway Adventures' database keeps track of which type of equipment is needed for which activities. It also tracks which activities will be available on which events ("trips" in the model). To accomplish this, an `ActivityEquipment` join table between `Equipment` and `Activities` defines many-to-many relationships between equipment and activities, and an `EventActivities` join table between `Activities` and `Events` defines many-to-many relationships between activities and events, as shown in Figure 8-6.

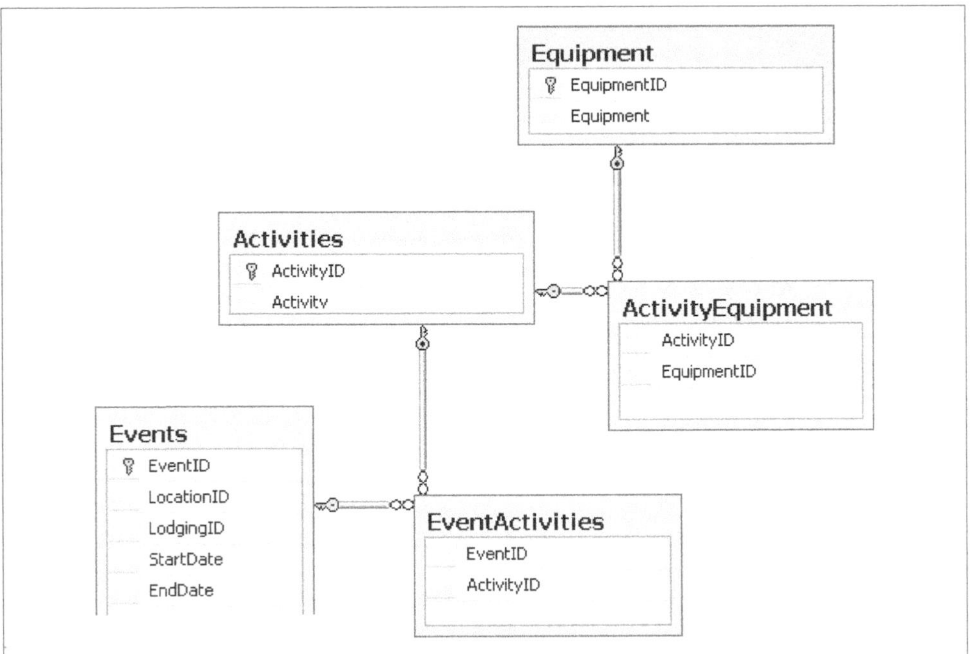

Figure 8-6. The database join tables, EventActivities and ActivityEquipment

These tables did not appear in the model as entities. The EDM has the ability to represent many-to-many relationships while hiding the join in the mappings. But it can do this only when the join table has just the relevant keys and no additional fields. These two tables meet that criterion, as they have only the IDs of the items they are joining. If the join tables had additional properties, such as `DateCreated`, the EDM would have created entities for them.

> **Many-to-Many or Joins?**
>
> The criterion for the conceptual model to display many-to-many relationships by linking the relationship ends together directly (as shown in Figure 8-7) is very limited. As explained in this chapter, the database table that joins to two ends must contain *only* the primary keys of the tables being joined. This does result in a very convenient relationship in the model, and with this type of many-to-many relationship, querying and coding against the relationship is fairly simple.
>
> However, it is more likely that your database join table does have additional fields and you will end up with an extra entity (a.k.a. a *join entity*), a need to use "join" in your queries, and somewhat more complicated coding with the related objects.

Instead, the joins are controlled in mappings; in the conceptual layer the relationships are expressed as navigation properties. Example 8-1 shows the mapping for the `EventActivities` association in the XML file. The mapping identifies the `EventActivities` table as the target of the mapping, and then shows its `ActivityID` field wired up to the `ActivityID` field of the `EventActivities` table. Meanwhile, its `EventID` field is wired up to the `EventID` field of the `Events` table.

Example 8-1. Many-to-many association mapping

```
<AssociationSetMapping Name="EventActivities"
                       TypeName="BreakAwayModel.EventActivities"
                       StoreEntitySet="EventActivities">
  <EndProperty Name="Activities">
    <ScalarProperty Name="ActivityID" ColumnName="ActivityID" />
  </EndProperty>
  <EndProperty Name="Events">
    <ScalarProperty Name="EventID" ColumnName="EventID" />
  </EndProperty>
</AssociationSetMapping>
```

As you can see in Figure 8-7, `Activity` and `Equipment` are joined in a many-to-many relationship. Each piece of equipment has activities and each activity has a collection of equipment. `Trip` and `Activity` also have a many-to-many relationship.

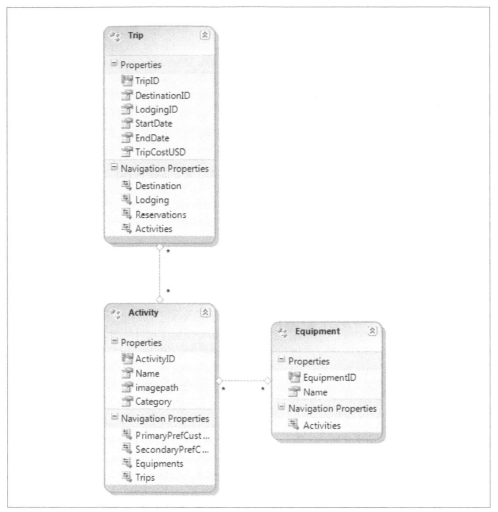

Figure 8-7. Activity and Equipment joined in a many-to-many relationship

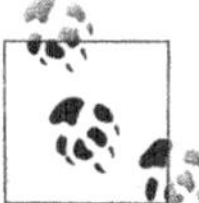

If you were expecting to see foreign key properties in the `Activity` or `Trip` entity keep in mind that the foreign keys don't exist in their tables, but instead exist in the join table, which is not mapped to either entity.

There is also a many-to-many relationship between `Activity` and `Trip`.

It will be very convenient not to have to construct joins when traversing these relationships in queries. Because the join tables contain only the keys involved, the EDM can easily represent the relationship without the aid of a join entity.

This mapping not only enables a convenient association directly between the two entities, but also manages querying, inserts, and updates across this join. You'll see this in action as you move through the book.

Inspecting the Completed BreakAway Model

Figure 8-8 shows the BreakAway model after all of the changes have been made. The few entities that are based on views are not shown in this screenshot.

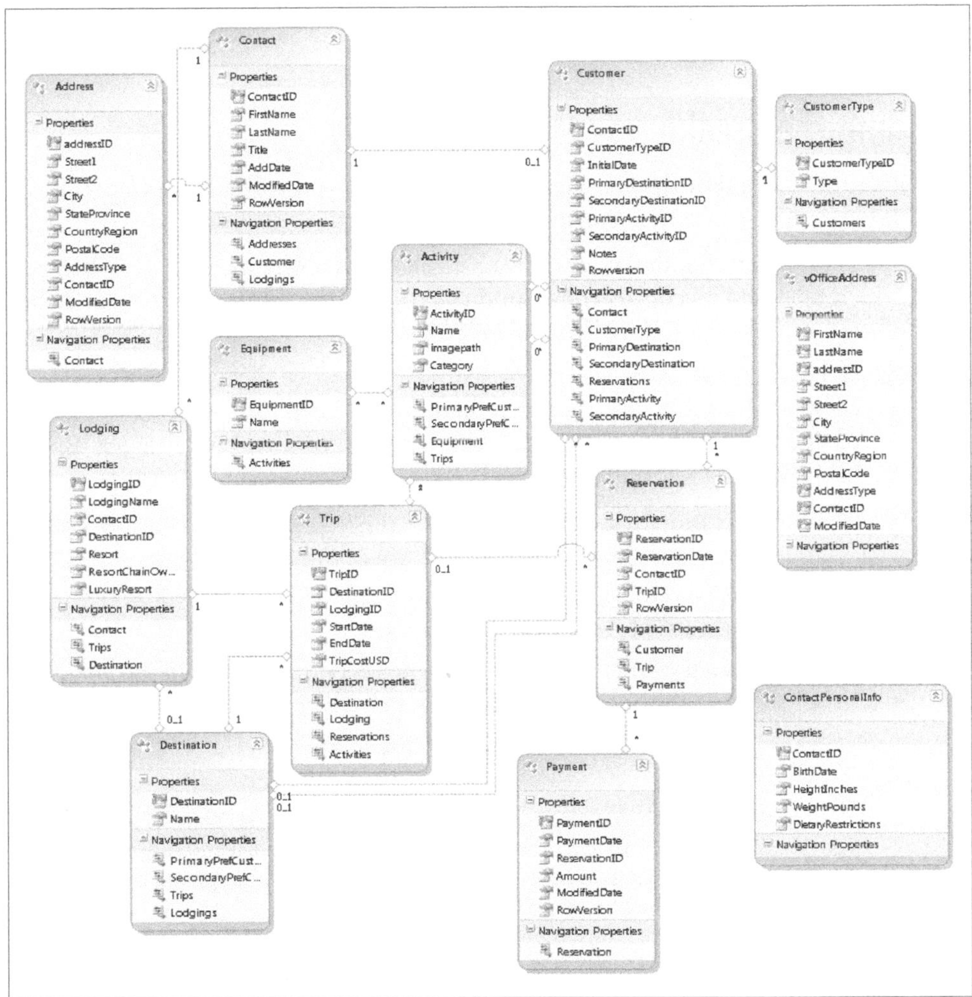

Figure 8-8. The BreakAway model that you will use in chapters that follow

I've ignored an entity in this discussion, and it is called `ContactPersonalInfo`. Although it has a `ContactID`, the database does not define a primary key/foreign key constraint between this table and the `Contact` table. As a result, the wizard did not create an association between them.

However, I have more interesting plans for the `ContactPersonalInfo` table. In Chapter 14, you will learn about a model customization referred to as *entity splitting*. We will use this feature to combine the `Contact` table fields and the `ContactPersonalInfo` table fields into a single entity. The result will be that the `Contact` entity will contain fields from both tables.

Building the BreakAway Model Assembly

Now it's time to build the model into an assembly that you will be able to use in the many projects you will be building in upcoming chapters.

Before you compile the model, you will want to change a few names so that when you access the model and its classes from another project, you won't have to work with cumbersome names.

You will have to make references to the assembly namespace throughout the code of your other applications that are using that namespace. Therefore, it will be handy to have a nice, short name for the namespace. The acronym for BreakAway Geek Adventures is BAGA, which is a good option.

1. Open the project's Properties window, and on the first page, Application, change the "Default namespace" (C#) / "Root namespace" (VB) to BAGA.

   When you created the model with the Entity Data Model Wizard, you left the default name for the `EntityContainer` as `BreakAway`.

2. Change that `EntityContainer` name to `BAEntities`. You can do this in the Designer. Clicking anywhere in the background of the model will open the Properties window for the model itself. Here you can change the entity container name.

   When you change this name and save the model, the `Connection String` name in the *app.config* file should change to `BAEntities` as well. It's not a bad idea to double-check that this happened by looking in the *app.config* file.

   Changing this name will make typing Entity SQL expressions easier, as you will have to include this container name in every Entity SQL expression.

3. Change the model's namespace so that it's consistent with the container name, in this case to `BAModel`.

Looking at the Compiled Assembly

When a project containing an EDMX is compiled, the compiler extracts the `StorageModels`, `ConceptualModels`, and `Mappings` sections of the EDMX file and creates individual schema files from them. In this case, the files are *BAModel.ssdl*, *BAModel.csdl*, and *BAModel.msl*. By default, these files are embedded into the assembly that is built from the project.

Figure 8-9 shows the compiled assembly in Red Gate's .NET Reflector tool, with the embedded files listed under Resources.

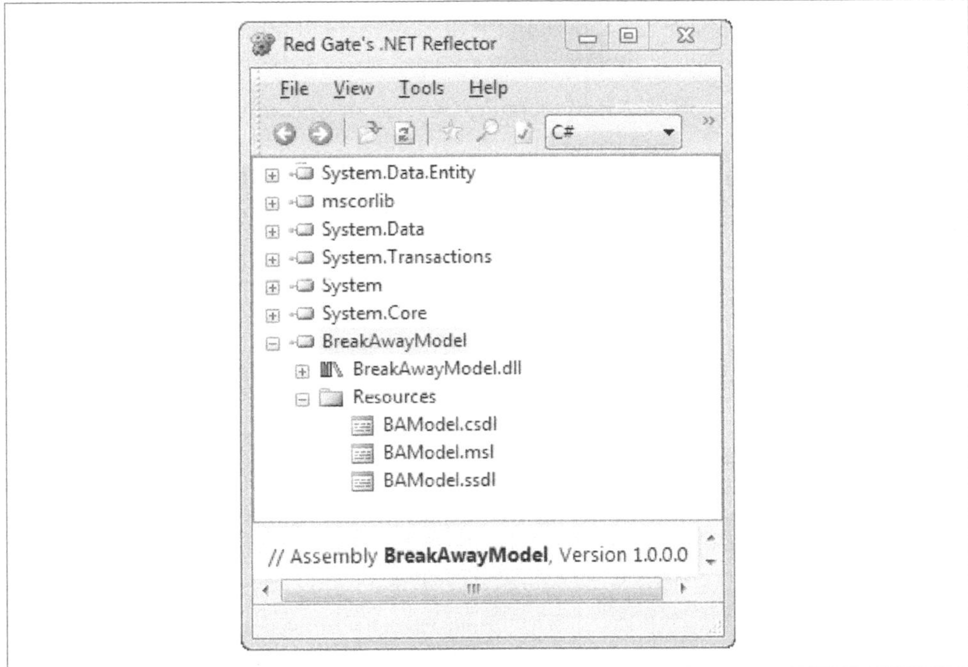

Figure 8-9. The schema files embedded in the assembly by default

If you look at the metadata portion of the `EntityConnection` string that the Entity Data Model Wizard inserted into the *app.config* file, you'll see the following notation:

```
res://*/BAModel.csdl|res://*/BAModel.ssdl|res://*/BAModel.msl
```

Much of the functionality in the Entity Framework depends on its ability to read the schema files. The * in the metadata of the connection string indicates that you can find the files in an assembly. Entity Framework will search all loaded assemblies until it finds the one with these embedded files.

Splitting Out the Model's Metadata Files

Having the model in the assembly is convenient when you don't expect the model to change often after it has been deployed. However, you may want to take advantage of the model's loose coupling at some point. For example, you or your database administrator might modify the database in a way that changes the schema, but introduces nothing new that would impact the objects in the application. In this case, you would need to update the metadata so that the database changes are reflected in the SSDL schema. Then, because of this change, you would need to adjust some of the mappings to be sure that the entities are mapped correctly to the SSDL. So, in this scenario, the SSDL and MSL layers change, but no change is made to the conceptual layer.

You may not want to have to rebuild and redeploy the assembly. Doing so may also affect the versioning of your application.

Although the files are embedded by default, there is an option to have the files exist outside the assembly. The model has a property called `Metadata Artifact Processing`. The property is available in the model's Properties window, as shown in Figure 8-10.

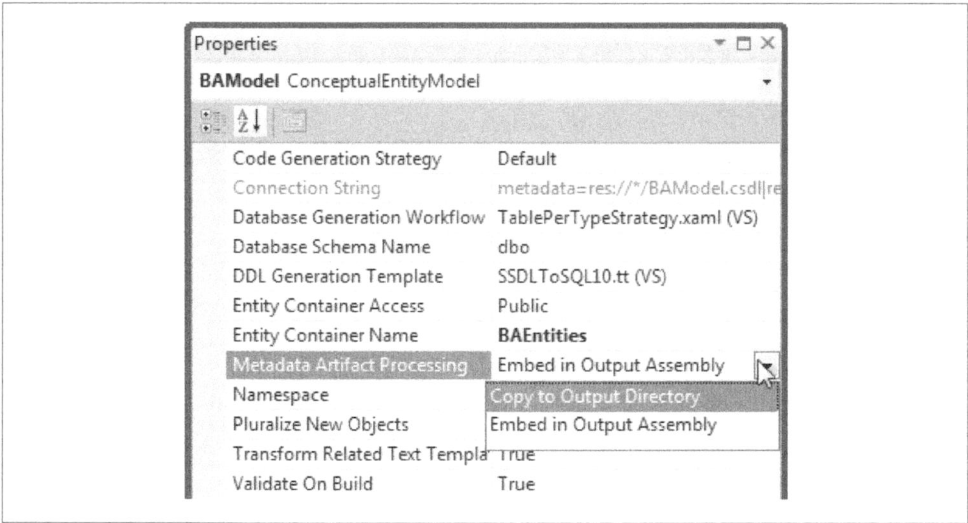

Figure 8-10. Changing how the model's metadata files are deployed during the build process

You can test the impact of changing this setting. Set the value to Copy to Output Directory and then rebuild the project.

Notice that the connection string has changed. The metadata no longer has a * to indicate that the files are embedded. Instead, it shows the relative path of the files. You will find them in the project's output directory, which by default is in either the *bin\debug* or the *bin\release* folder in the project folder.

If you have performed this test, be sure to set the value back to Embed in Output Assembly and rebuild the project again.

> **What's an Artifact?**
>
> The property that determines whether the runtime metadata files should be embedded into the assembly or spit out as independent files is called `Metadata Artifact Processing`. The term *artifact* comes from the Unified Modeling Language. An artifact is a piece of data (e.g., a file) that is created as a stepping-stone or a final product of a particular process. So, the artifacts in this case are the three XML files (*CSDL.xml*, *MSL.xml*, and *SSDL.xml*) that are extracted from the EDMX file when the project is built.

Moving the schema files

If you do choose to use the metadata artifact files separately rather than embedding them into the assembly, you can put them anywhere you want. However, you will need to be sure that the connection string points to the correct path. If, for example, you place the files in *C:\EDMS*, you'll need to modify the `metadata` attribute to the following:

```
metadata=C:\EDMS\BAModel.csdl| C:\EDMS\BAModel.ssdl| C:\EDMS\BAModel.msl
```

Although this chapter covered creating a model in a separate assembly, it's useful to be aware of a special case for the `metadata` attribute. If you create an EDM inside an ASP.NET Web Site Project, because of the way in which Web Site Projects are compiled, the path will be affected. The entire metadata attribute will be `metadata=res://*`. This does not happen with Web Application Projects.

You can learn more about the `EntityConnection`'s `metadata` attribute in the MSDN Library documentation.

Summary

In this chapter, you went through the steps of creating an EDM from a more realistic database, which you will be using throughout the rest of this book. Then you spent some time cleaning up many of the automatically created entity and property names so that they will be more logical when it comes time to use the model in your applications.

You have now prepared an assembly that can easily be referenced from a variety of projects and used in other applications. Because the runtime schema files are embedded into the assembly, it will be even simpler to reuse and share the model.

In the next chapter, you will write your first Windows applications using this model.

CHAPTER 9

Data Binding with Windows Forms and WPF Applications

So far, you've seen how to interact directly with an EDM using snippets of code in a console application. Although there is much more to learn about the Entity Framework, at this point it's time to see how you can use the Entity Framework as part of your applications.

In this chapter, you will explore basic data-binding scenarios in Windows Forms and Windows Presentation Foundation (WPF). You'll see how the Entity Framework objects work with Visual Studio's data-binding features in much the same way that `DataTables` and `DataSets` do, without having to explicitly set and retrieve the values of each control. The data binding's change notification mechanism works automatically with the Entity Framework's change tracking, so editing data that was queried through the Entity Data Model does not require a lot of extra coding. In the examples here, you'll bind directly to the results of Entity Framework queries as you learn the concepts. In Chapter 26, after you have learned much more about the Entity Framework, I will address *n*-tier applications and more robust patterns for enterprise applications.

The chapter will begin with data binding in Windows Forms and will then move on to the WPF techniques.

Data Binding with Windows Forms Applications

To demonstrate data binding of an EDM in a Windows form, let's build a small application to let you view customers and their reservations as well as edit the customers and add new reservations. Figure 9-1 shows a mock-up of this form, which uses a `BindingSource` and a navigation toolbar. As noted in the acknowledgments in the book's preface, this mock-up was created using Balsamiq Mockups.

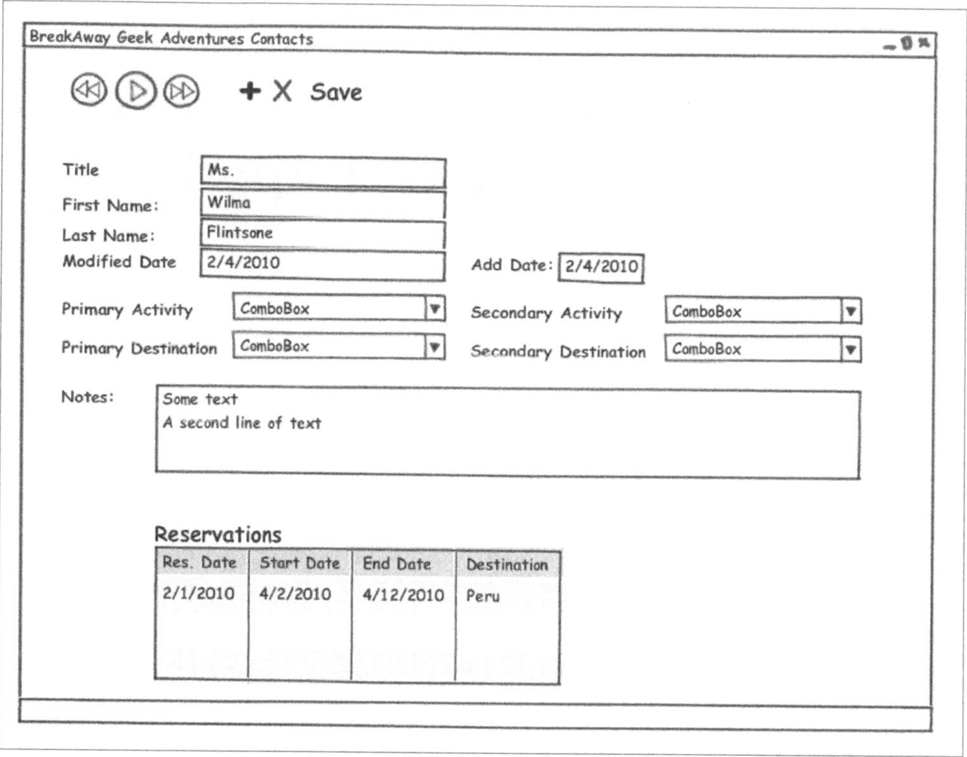

Figure 9-1. The Windows Forms application you'll be building

This chapter does not presume that you are familiar with Windows Forms or with WPF data-binding techniques in the IDE. So, you'll get a step-by-step walkthrough to be sure that the UI tasks don't trip you up.

You'll be building the form in stages, adding a little more functionality in each stage and then testing what you've built so far.

Creating a Windows Forms Application

The first task is to create a Windows Forms project. In our example, we'll use the BreakAwayModel project you created in Chapter 8. You should add this new Windows Forms project into the same solution that contains the BreakAwayModel project. In that way, you can easily reference the model and make changes to it as needed.

If you did not follow the walkthroughs in Chapter 8, you can download the completed BreakAwayModel project from the Downloads page of the book's website (*http://learnentityframework.com*). Both C# and Visual Basic versions are available, as well as the C# and VB versions of the applications built in this chapter. As with previous examples, VB is shown if the code difference is significant.

1. Add a new Windows Forms Application project to the solution and give it the name BreakAwayWinForms.

The next three steps will be common for any application that needs to use an EDM that is in a separate assembly.

2. Add a reference to the BreakAwayModel project. To do this, right-click the BreakAwayWinForms project in the Solution Explorer and select Add Reference. In the Add Reference dialog, select the Projects tab, then select BreakAwayModel and click OK. This will allow the new application to use everything in the model as well as the generated entity classes.
3. Add a reference to `System.Data.Entity`, which is under the .NET tab of Add References.

   When you created the model, the Entity Data Model Wizard automatically pulled in the necessary references to the Entity Framework APIs. Your new project will need this particular reference as well, which is why you need to add it manually.
4. Copy the *app.config* file from the BreakAwayModel project into the new Windows Forms project. Overwrite the existing *app.config* if necessary.

You only need to copy the `BAEntities` connection string element from the model's *app.config* to this project's *app.config*. In this case, since the new project's *app.config* has only minimal settings, you can cheat by just copying the whole file.

Using Windows Forms Data Sources

Data sources have been a feature of Windows Forms since Visual Studio 2005 and are a very convenient way to perform data binding. They provide a bridge between your data and the controls to which you are binding your data. There are three types of data sources: those that bind directly to a database, those that bind to a service, and those that bind to objects.

In this application, you will be creating data sources that bind to objects—specifically, to the entity classes that were dynamically generated from your EDM. An Object data source won't bind to the entire `EntityContainer`; it will bind to only one individual class. Additionally, although a data source that is derived directly from a database (an option you may have used in the past) will trigger the interaction with the database, an Object data source will not. It provides the schema of the classes to the controls to which you are binding data, and it provides the ability to interact with the objects. You will still have to write the actual code that populates the data source at runtime.

Using data sources is a great example of how the EDM and the Entity Framework work seamlessly with existing tools in Visual Studio.

This is not to say that the Entity Framework works with all of the existing features of Visual Studio. You will find that some gaps still exist, such as the inability of the Microsoft `Report` control to work with hierarchical data that comes from the EDM.

Creating an Object Data Source for a Customer Entity

In the following walkthrough you will create an Object data source that binds to the `Customer` entity. Then, using the properties that are exposed through the Data Sources window, you will add controls to the form so that the controls are automatically bound to these properties. After adding a simple query to the form's code, you will be able to run the application and scroll through the customer data. With a few more minor changes to the form, you will also be able to edit the data.

The first step is to create the data source that will help you to create the data-bound controls on the form. The Object data source you will need is for the `Customer` class. Here's how to create it:

1. From the Visual Studio menu, select the Data menu item, and then select Show Data Sources from that menu's drop-down, to open the Data Sources window (see Figure 9-2).
2. Click the Add New Data Source hyperlink to open the Data Source Configuration Wizard.
3. Select Object in the Choose Data Source Type window, and then click Next.
4. The next window will present you with the available assemblies in the current solution. Expand the `BreakAwayModel` assembly to reveal the `BAGA` namespace, and then expand that to reveal the entity classes, as shown in Figure 9-3.
5. Select Customer and then click Finish.

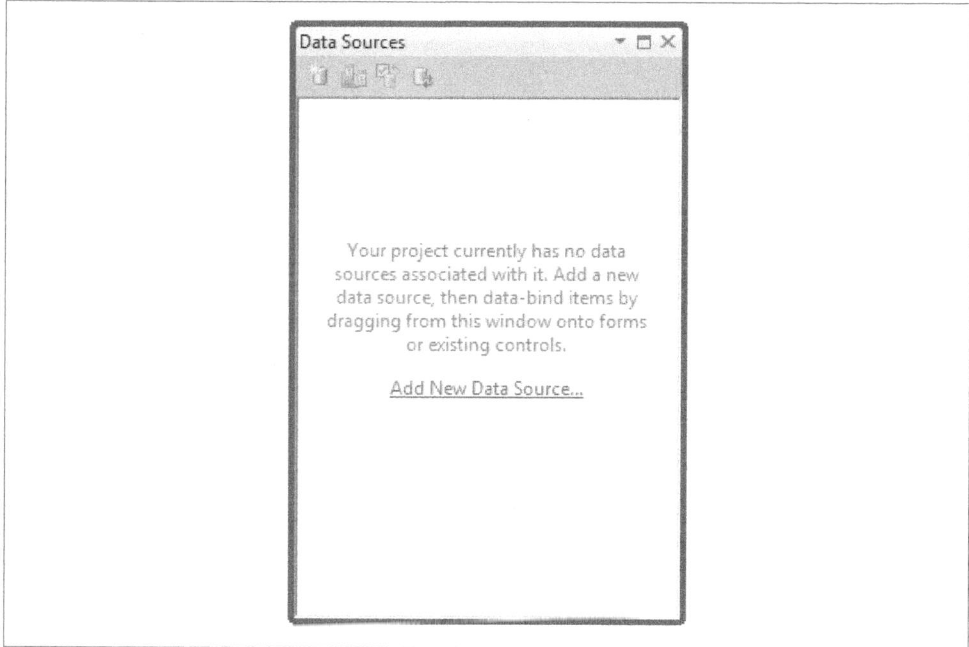

Figure 9-2. The Data Sources window before the new data source has been created

If you do not see the `BreakAwayModel` assembly listed when you get to Step 5, be sure to build the project so that it knows to display the referenced assembly.

The Customer data source will now display in the Data Sources window. Expand the Customer data source to see its properties. Notice that the navigation properties are there, including `Reservations` with its properties, as shown in Figure 9-4. Entity Framework classes are built to expose their navigation properties for data binding.

What's interesting about the `Customer` entity and class is that the most critical information—the customer's name, address, reservations, and preferences—is not available in its scalar properties. You need to navigate to other entities to get this data. Although the `Customer` entity represents contacts who are customers, it depends on the related `Contact` entity to provide name information and to give you access to the contact's addresses. `Customer` relies on its relationship to `Reservations` to supply details about what makes each customer a customer—all of the trips they have taken or are planning to take. Even their `Activity` and `Destination` preferences are navigation properties.

If you were to create a `DataGridView` from the Customer data source, the only properties that would display by default are the scalar properties. Instead, you'll need to leverage the related contact and reservations details to build a more useful form.

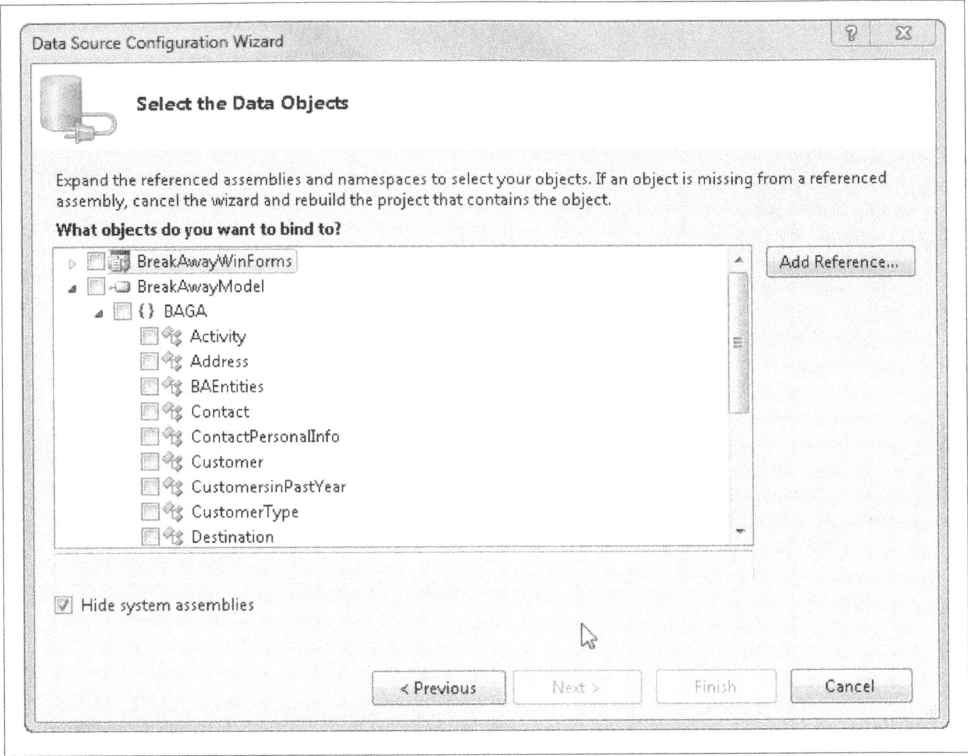

Figure 9-3. The classes from your model, available for creating a data source

Getting an Entity's Details onto a Form

Data sources allow for some very convenient drag-and-drop operations that make it easy to specify which properties of an object are displayed on a form. You don't want to drag the entire `Customer` object, because, by default, that will result in a `DataGridView` with the scalar properties and the IDs of the entity reference properties. You could change the default control used or drag the individual properties onto the form. But let's look at this from a different perspective.

Later in this chapter, you'll see the problem of the default `DataGridView` when you data-bind to the `EntityCollection`. But if you are curious now, nothing is stopping you from dragging the entire `Customer` object onto the form so that you can see the effect.

In this example, we'll want most of the customer's contact details on the form, so let's use that rather than the `Customer` itself. You can select `Contact` from inside Customer in the Data Sources window and drag it onto the form. Contact's default control should be a Details view as you can see by the icon next to Contact in Figure 9-4 . Because

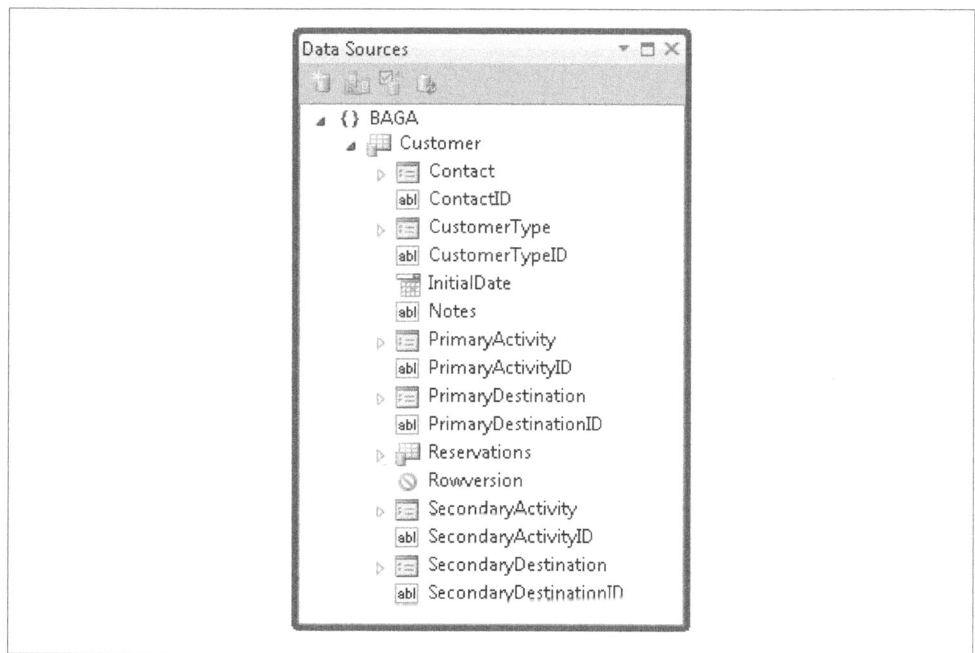

Figure 9-4. The Customer data source, which includes its navigation properties

`Contact` is a class unto itself, all of its details will come over to the form at once. The impact of dragging the properties onto the form is that a new navigation toolbar will be created, as well as the appropriate controls for the various properties—`TextBox` controls for the integers and strings, and `DateTimePicker` controls for the date properties. Additionally, on the perimeter of the design window, you'll see that a `CustomerBinding Source` and a `CustomerBindingNavigator` were added. These are components that work hand in hand with the data sources in Windows Forms. The `BindingSource` will coordinate the form fields with the data. The `BindingNavigator` coordinates the actions of the toolbar (navigation, inserts, deletes, and updates) with the `BindingSource`. Remember that these are not Entity Framework features, but standard functionality in Windows Forms.

You will also see, on the lower half of the form, fields representing all the scalar values of the `Customer` entity on the form. This is standard behavior when working with graphs in Windows Forms data sources. Visual Studio infers the scalars of the parent data source on the form. Delete all of the ID values from the lower part of the form, but you can leave the `InitialDate` and `Notes` intact. `InitialDate` represents the first date the contact became a customer, which is useful in case the person was on a mailing list for a while before finally becoming a customer.

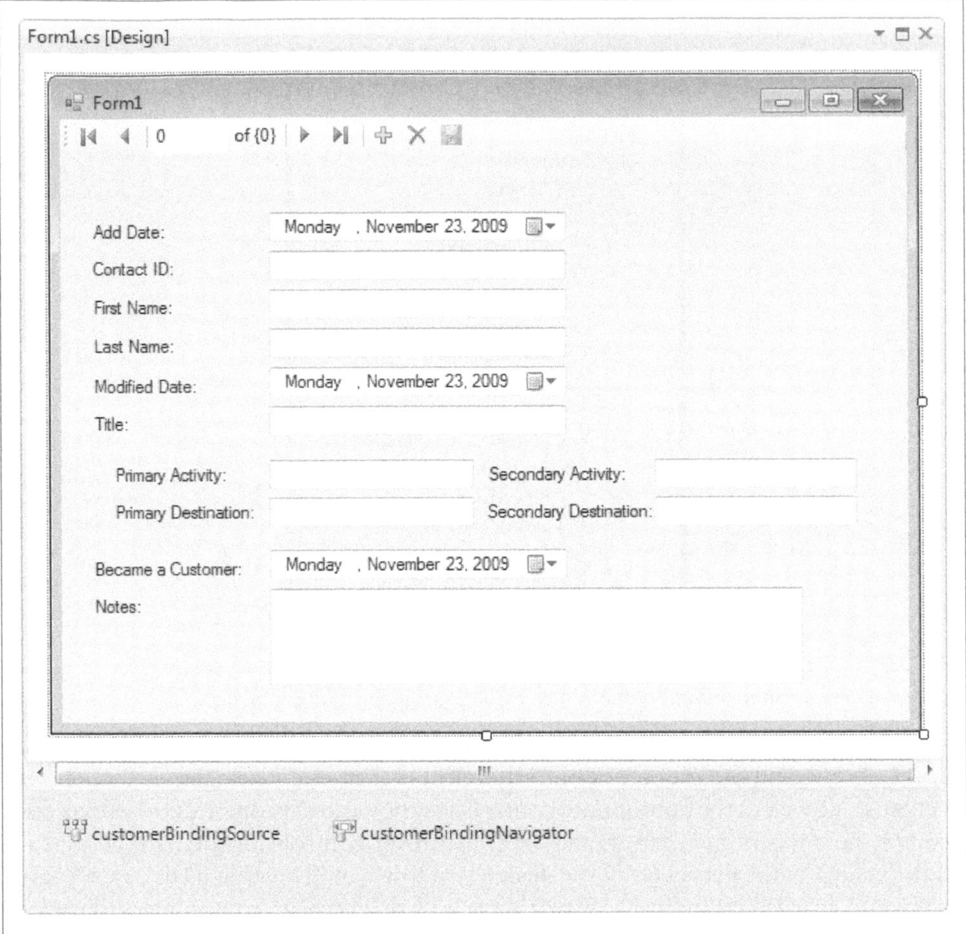

Figure 9-5. The form with the first bits of data binding

Next, expand the `PrimaryActivity` property and drag its `Name` to the form. You'll need to modify the label so that it reads "Primary Activity". Do the same for the other preferences.

If you care to line up and organize the fields on the form, your form will look something like Figure 9-5 after you have added these fields.

Adding Code to Query an EDM When a Form Loads

You'll need to execute a query when the form loads to retrieve the customers along with their related data from the database. You will bind these query results with the `BindingSourceControl` that was created for the Customer data source.

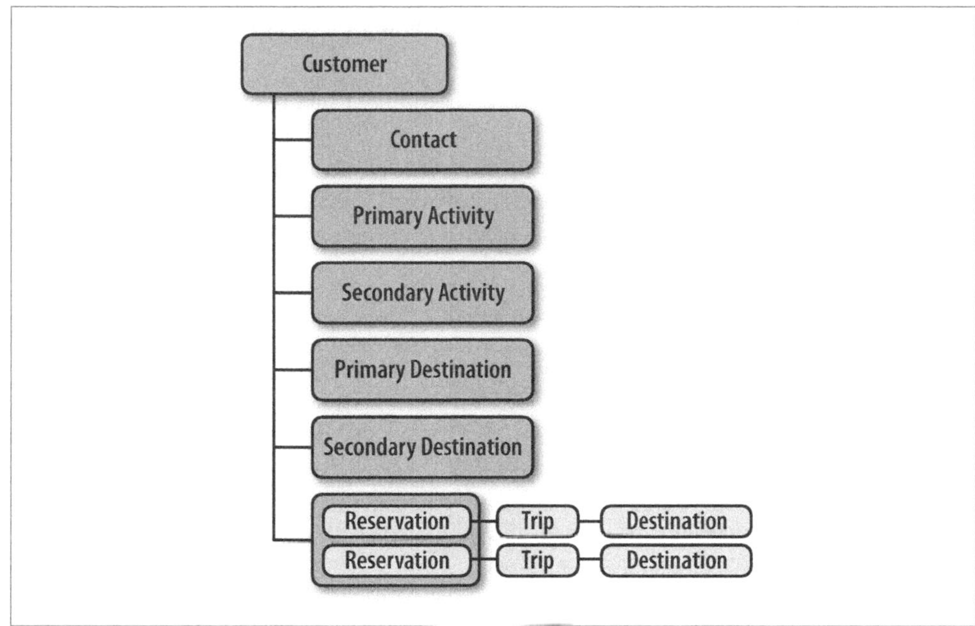

Figure 9-6. The customer graph

You'll get to take advantage of eager loading, which you learned about in Chapter 4, by using a number of `Include` methods in this query. This is because the form relies on five navigation properties.

In the form's `Load` event, add the code from Example 9-1.

Example 9-1. Querying for customers in the form load

```
var context = new BAGA.BAEntities();
List<BAGA.Customer> customers=
    context.Customers.Include("Contact")
    .Include("PrimaryActivity")
    .Include("SecondaryActivity")
    .Include("PrimaryDestination")
    .Include("SecondaryDestination")
    .Include("Reservations.Trip.Destination")
    .ToList();
customerBindingSource.DataSource = customers;
```

The query is written to ensure that all of the necessary related information is retrieved from the data store. Each `Customer` in the results will be a graph shaped as shown in Figure 9-6.

This particular query is not designed for efficiency, but rather to give you an idea of how the `Include` method works and how the data binding implements related data. Notice that the query does not even bother to filter the data. The SQL query that results and the amount of data returned may make you gasp. So, although it's very important to be aware that this is not a best practice, it's a handy query for this lesson based on what you've learned so far.

Most of the related entities are small. `Activity` and `Destination` have only an `ID` field and a `Name` field. `Reservations` and `Trip` don't have a lot of fields, either. But a lot of redundant data will be sent back to the application. For example, each customer who has Madagascar selected as her primary or secondary destination will cause that row of data to be transmitted back to the application. If 100 people favor that locale, 100 copies of that row will be returned.

As Object Services materializes objects from those rows, it will recognize the redundancy and will not create multiple copies of that particular object in memory, so on the application side the query results will be efficient.

Later in this chapter, we'll look at more efficient ways to return the related data without this redundancy.

Go ahead and run what you've built so far. As you use the navigation toolbar to move from one customer to another, you'll be able to see that all of the navigation properties automatically change as well (see Figure 9-7).

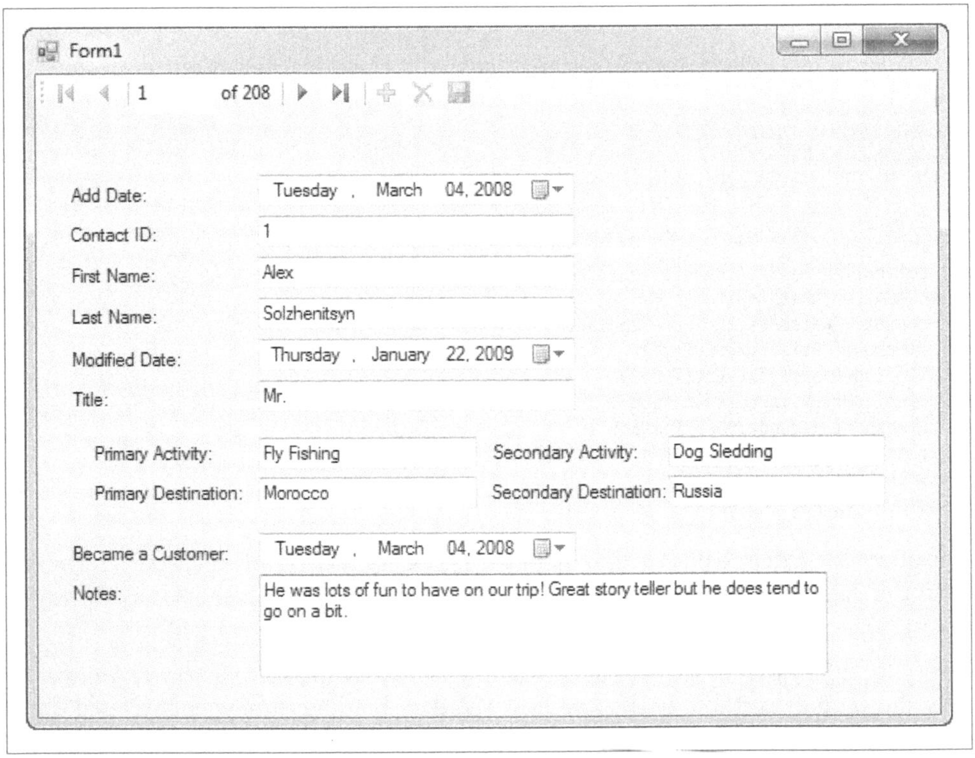

Figure 9-7. A customer's details on display

Binding Without a BindingSource

When you bind query results to a BindingSource, the BindingSource will act as an agent to coordinate the entities, the fields, and the navigation toolbar. The BindingSource will update the entities when a change is made in the form's fields. In this example, when it's time to have the Entity Framework send the entity changes to the data store, all of the change information will be available.

As you have seen so far, I prefer to force query execution and work with the results of the query, not the query itself. This allows me to depend on explicit behavior. Therefore, in Example 9-1, I am binding a List<Customer>, not the query, to the binding source.

There is another route to binding. I introduced the Execute method in Chapter 3, with a teaser about using it in data binding. Execute returns an Entity Framework IEnumerable type called ObjectResult<T>. If I were to use it in this example, it would return an ObjectResult<Customer>.

Feel free to experiment with the Execute method in your Windows Form, but I won't be providing a walkthrough for testing it out.

Rather than binding directly to the query, you can use the Execute method on the query to push results into an ObjectResult, and bind to that instead. ObjectResult is a stream that can be read through only once. ObjectResult contains a dbDataReader, so this is where it gets it's forward-only streaming behavior. This is quite different from getting a List, which allows you to move back and forth, iterating, identifying specific objects with an indexer, and so forth.

Another big difference between List<T> and ObjectResult<T> is that ObjectResult inherits IListSource. IListSource provides the same data-binding and change-tracking benefits without relying on the UI BindingSource component.

You can also combine it with the UI BindingSource as follows:

```
CustomerBindingSource.DataSource=context.Customers.Execute(MergeOption.AppendOnly)
```

But more importantly, you can bind the ObjectResult (or any IListSource) directly to a data-bound control such as a DataGridView without losing the change-tracking benefits. You can't do this with List<Customer> because List does not implement IListSource and you would no longer have any coordination between the context and the control. If you edited something in a control, the context would not be aware of it.

Therefore, if you are binding directly to controls without using a BindingSourceControl in between, and you do not want to have to be responsible for the code that ensures that changes to controls are tracked by the context, or if programmatic changes to your objects are surfaced in the controls, you should use a type that inherits from IList

`Source` (with the caveat about binding directly to an `ObjectQuery`, which also inherits from `IListSource`, because of the repeated execution).

Microsoft's Dinesh Chandnani wrote an informative blog post titled "BindingSource – A Closer Look." You can find it at *http://blogs.msdn.com/dchandnani/archive/2005/03/15/396387.aspx*. Be aware that it is dated, but the explanations are enlightening.

Diego Vega, from the Entity Framework team, wrote an in-depth post on data binding with entities at *http://blogs.msdn.com/diego/archive/2008/10/09/quick-tips-for-entity-framework-databinding.aspx*.

`Execute` takes a `MergeOption` parameter. `MergeOption` specifies what to do if the query results already exist in the context. It's possible to execute many queries against the same context (or even to execute one query multiple times). If duplicate data is pulled down from the data store, you can control how those duplicates are handled. In this case, the `AppendOnly` option (the default for queries that don't use this method) tells the context to only add entities that don't already exist in the context. In this way, you won't have to worry about overwriting changes you have made. You'll learn more about `MergeOption` in Chapter 10.

Adding an EntityCollection to the Form

Now it's time to get the reservations onto the form. The `Reservation` entity presents the same problem as the `Customer` entity in that the majority of the most useful information is in its navigation property, `Trip`, and the `Trip`'s navigation property, `Destination`.

Start by dragging the `Reservations` property onto the form. Along with the new grid Visual Studio will add a `ReservationsBindingSource` to the form. The default control, `DataGridView`, will display the reservations as shown in Figure 9-8 when the application is run. This creates the same problem that I alluded to earlier regarding dragging the entire `Customer` object onto the form. The control is not able to work out the navigations to the `Reservation`'s `Customer` and `Trip` references, and therefore displays only the type name for each. Even if you edit the `DataPropertyName` property of the `Trip` column to be `Trip.StartDate`, Windows Forms will not be able to navigate into `Trip` to find its `StartDate`. This problem is not specific to the Entity Framework, but a result of how the `DataGridView` functions.

	ReservationID	ReservationDate	ContactID	TripID	Customer	Trip	Payments
▶	244	1/22/2007 9:24 ...	1	17	BAGA.Customer	BAGA.Trip	
	277	1/22/2007 9:24 ...	1	68	BAGA.Customer	BAGA.Trip	
	336	9/23/2009 3:47 ...	1	34	BAGA.Customer	BAGA.Trip	
*							

Figure 9-8. Default grid for the Reservations navigation property

By default, the `Timestamp` column is included, but it causes a `DataGridView` error to be thrown as each row is rendered, because the grid is unable to figure out how to display the binary data. So, I have already removed that column from the grid.

Displaying the Properties of Related Data in the Grid

There is a way to display properties of related objects in `DataGridView`, and you can take advantage of that here. The grid will be useful if it displays the reservation date, the start and end dates of the trip, and the destination of the trip. `Destination` comes from a navigation property of the `Trip` entity, so first we'll need to modify the columns in the grid.

Edit the grid's columns by making the following changes:

1. Make the `ReservationID`'s `Visible` property `false`.
2. Remove the `TimeStamp`, `Customer`, `Trip`, and `Payments` columns.
3. Remove the foreign key columns, `ContactID` and `TripID`, as well.
4. Add three new unbound `DataGridViewTextBoxColumn` columns named `tripStartColumn`, `tripEndColumn`, and `destinationColumn`. Make sure their `ReadOnly` property is `True`.

The trick to displaying the navigation properties is in the code. You must override the individual cells as the grid is being rendered for display. A useful event for doing this is the `DataGridView.DataBindingComplete` event. Example 9-2 shows how to do this.

In the previous edition of this book, I used the `RowPrePaint` event, but have since discovered that this event is hit a great number of times while the form is active.

In C#, you can access the `DataGridView.DataBindingComplete` event from the Events page of the grid's Properties window. In VB, you can do the same or access the event in the code window by choosing `ReservationsDataGridView` from the Class Name drop-down and then `DataBindingComplete` from the Method Name drop-down.

Example 9-2. Forcing the DataGridView to display navigation properties

```
private void reservationsDataGridView_DataBindingComplete
  (object sender, DataGridViewBindingCompleteEventArgs e)
{
  var gridView = (DataGridView)sender;
  foreach (DataGridViewRow row in gridView.Rows)
  {
    if (!row.IsNewRow)
    {
      var reservation = (BAGA.Reservation)(row.DataBoundItem);
      var trip = reservation.Trip;

      row.Cells[tripStartColumn.Index].Value = trip.StartDate.ToShortDateString();
      row.Cells[tripEndColumn.Index].Value = trip.EndDate.ToShortDateString();
      row.Cells[destinationColumn.Index].Value = trip.Destination.Name;
    }
  }
}
```

The trick shown in Example 9-2 is required because we are binding directly to the `EntityObjects`. In a more highly architected application, you would likely be using patterns that would not force you to perform this type of logic.

Now, run the application again and take a look at the result. Notice that you don't have to add any additional querying or binding code into the form's `Load` event. The fact that you have already bound the customers to the `BindingSource` is enough. The two `BindingSource` controls will work out all of the relationships. In the form, as you navigate from one customer to the next, that customer's reservations will be displayed in the grid (see Figure 9-9).

	ReservationDate	Start	End	Destination
▶	1/5/2005	4/15/2006	4/22/2006	Costa Rica
	11/16/2005	11/27/2006	12/4/2006	India

Figure 9-9. The formatted reservations grid

The trip start and end dates were formatted in the `DataBindingComplete` event using `ToShortDateString`. The `ReservationDate` was formatted using the Designer. I have demonstrated both ways simply so that you can see each of them, but in a production app, you'll want to pick a single pattern for formatting your data. See the MSDN topic "How to: Set Default Cell Styles and Data Formats for the Windows Forms DataGridView Control Using the Designer," at *http://msdn.microsoft.com/en-us/library/95y5fz2x(VS.100).aspx*.

Because of the convenient but inefficient query, all of the `Customer` objects with all of their reservations and related trip data are in memory. So, in this example, the application does not need to return to the database to retrieve additional data as you move from one customer to the next. In a properly designed application, you will need to be more diligent about retrieving only the data the user will need, and you'll want to be considerate about balancing the client-side resources with the trips to the server and the amount of data being transmitted based on your scenario.

Allowing Users to Edit Data

So far, you have been using the form to view data. What about editing or adding data? `BindingSource` supports editing, but you'll need to make a few small modifications to the form and the code to get this functionality. We'll start with editing, and in the next section we'll enable adding.

By default, the navigation toolbar disables the Save button when the toolbar is first created. Right-click the button and check the Enabled property in the context menu.

Before you can add the method to save data, you have to make an important change in the existing code. Currently, you are instantiating the `BAEntities ObjectContext` in the form's `Load` event. This prevents the context from being available outside that particular event.

As you saw in Chapter 6, when you query data with the context, by default the entities that result are managed by the context that keeps track of changes made to those entities. You can then use the `ObjectContext.SaveChanges` method to save those changes back to the data store. Although you will learn much more about this later in the book, here you'll need to be aware of the fact that only the context that is tracking the changes is able to save them. You can't instantiate a new context and expect it to save changes to the entities that you're working with in the form. It won't know anything about them.

Therefore, it is important to be sure that when you call `SaveChanges`, you are working with the *same* context you used to retrieve the data.

To do this in the form, you need to declare the context in the form declarations, not within a method. In this way, all of the form's methods can work with the same context and you will be able to call `SaveChanges` in the `Click` event of the Save button.

Just beneath the line of code that declares the form, add the following code to declare the context, so that the code now looks like this:

```
public partial class Form1 : Form
{
  BAGA.BAEntities _context;
```

Since I'm changing the context variable to a form variable, I've renamed it `_context` to follow good coding practices. Be sure to fix up any use of the variable accordingly.

In the form's `Load` event, change the code that declared and instantiated the context so that it instantiates the already declared context, as shown in the following code snippet:

```
_context = new BAGA.BAEntities();
```

Back in the form's Design view, double-click the Save button to get to its `Click` event handler. Then add the `SaveChanges` code into the `Click` event, as shown in the following code:

```
_context.SaveChanges();
```

That is the complete code for saving all of the entity changes! There is no connection code, no need to build commands, and no need to worry about what entities are being saved or what types of changes are being made. Object Services reads all of the change information that it has kept track of for the entities that it is managing, works out the proper commands (`Insert`, `Update`, or `Delete`), and then executes them.

If the model had any stored procedure mappings, Object Services would use stored procedures to perform the changes on the entities that have functions mapped to them.

In its current state, you can test-edit a customer. Another tweak is necessary before you can edit the navigation properties, though, and yet another before you can add a new customer. So for now, try editing and saving the name fields of a customer.

Editing Navigation Properties (and Shrinking the Query)

The next stage of building up the functionality in this form is to make it possible to edit the other navigation properties.

You are already able to edit the `Contact` navigation property because it has a relationship with the customer. It is essentially an extension of the customer. The preference properties—`PrimaryActivity`, among others—are values selected from a list of possible items. You'll need two things to be able to change the selections. First, you will need access to a complete list of the items (activities and destinations). Therefore, you'll need queries in the code to retrieve these lists. Second, you'll need some type of selection control, for example, a drop-down list, on the form to display the lists and allow the user to choose from them.

Activities and destinations are reference data. Each is a short list of options shared by everyone. You'll need the full lists in order to allow users to select different activity or destination options. Rather than retrieve them as part of the customer query, we'll write two independent queries to retrieve all of the activities and all of the destinations.

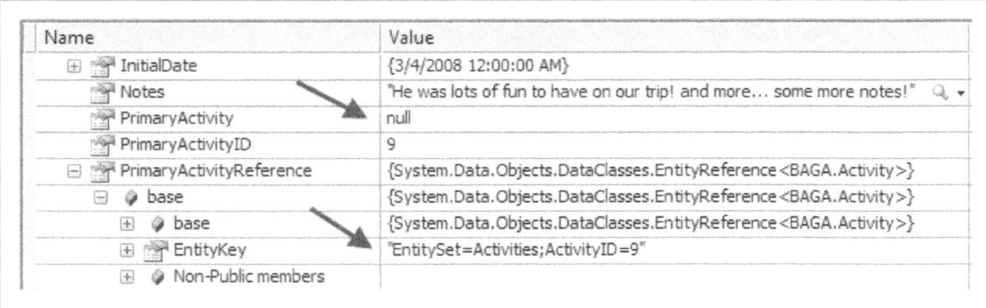

Name	Value
InitialDate	{3/4/2008 12:00:00 AM}
Notes	"He was lots of fun to have on our trip! and more... some more notes!"
PrimaryActivity	null
PrimaryActivityID	9
PrimaryActivityReference	{System.Data.Objects.DataClasses.EntityReference<BAGA.Activity>}
base	{System.Data.Objects.DataClasses.EntityReference<BAGA.Activity>}
base	{System.Data.Objects.DataClasses.EntityReference<BAGA.Activity>}
EntityKey	"EntitySet=Activities;ActivityID=9"
Non-Public members	

Figure 9-10. PrimaryActivity and PrimaryActivityReference properties of a Customer that was queried without any of its related data

Providing independent lists will add a big performance benefit to the application. When the activities and destinations are queried, you'll store their objects in memory. More specifically, they will be managed by the `ObjectContext`.

It won't be necessary to include the activity and destination data in the `Customers` query; they'll already be in memory. The queried customers have the `Activity` and `Destination` reference `EntityKey`s inside them; that will be all they need to acquire the related `Activity` and `Destination` entities when we need them.

Figure 9-10 shows the `PrimaryActivity` and `PrimaryActivityReference` properties of a `Customer` that was queried without any of its related data. When the context creates the `Customer` object, if the `Activity` object with that same `EntityKey` is already in the context, the two will be hooked up. The same happens if you were to query the customers first and then the activities.

As a reminder, an `EntityReference` property is generated from the model as a supplement to any navigation property that points to an entity. `PrimaryActivityReference` is the `EntityReference` property that supplements the `PrimaryActivity` property of `Customer`. The `PrimaryActivityID` property will be populated only if the database column is not null.

In order to get the true state of the entity in the debugger, I temporarily set `LazyLoadingEnabled=false`. Otherwise, even the debugger would cause the lazy load on the navigation properties in the visualizer. In order to see these properties, I've debugged into the `customers` variable (a `List<Customer>`) in `Form1_Load`.

So, now you can add the two new reference data queries and remove the corresponding `Include`s in the `Customers` query so that it doesn't pull all of that extra data out of the database and over to the application.

At the same time, you'll create two new form-level variables to contain the activities and destinations.

Add the new `_activities` and `_destinations` variables to the form declarations, as shown in Example 9-3.

Example 9-3. Adding two new variables, _activities and _destinations, to hold the new lists

```
public partial class Form1 : Form
{
  BAGA.BAEntities _context;
  List<BAGA.Activity> _activities;
  List<BAGA.Destination> _destinations;
```

Next, as shown in Example 9-4, add the new queries into the `Form1_Load` and modify the existing `Customers` query to remove the extraneous navigations. Notice that `Destination` is also removed from the `Reservations.Trip` navigation path. `Trip` will also be able to find its related destinations in the context after they are retrieved by the `Destinations` query.

Example 9-4. Querying for the list data

```
private void Form1_Load(object sender, EventArgs e)
{
  _context = new BAGA.BAEntities();
  _activities = _context.Activities
              .OrderBy(a => a.Name).ToList();
  _destinations = _context.Destinations
                .OrderBy(d => d.Name).ToList();
  var customers = _context.Customers.Include("Contact")
                .Include("Reservations.Trip")
                .ToList();
```

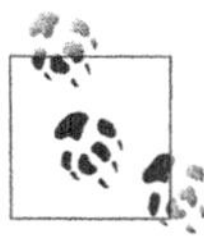

You can run the application again if you want to see that all of the reference properties are still intact.

Even if you were binding directly to the UI controls, `ToList` would be sufficient for executing the queries and binding their results, rather than using `Execute`. The activities and destinations will be used only for pick lists and will not be edited directly, so you don't have to worry about an `IListSource` failing to pass along change information for activities and destinations to the context.

Replacing the Navigation Property TextBoxes with ComboBoxes

Now that the data for the lists exists, you can change the controls for `PrimaryActivity` and the other navigation properties to ComboBoxes so that it will be possible to edit a customer's preferences.

You can bind the ComboBox controls in code or in the UI. Since there are four properties to change, I'll have you use both methods so that you can learn each one.

Replace the TextBox controls for the PrimaryActivity and PrimaryDestination target properties with ComboBox controls, giving them names to help you differentiate them. The FillCombos method in Example 9-5 performs the standard bindings for a ComboBox and additionally binds them to the Customer's PrimaryActivity and Primary Destination navigation properties. Notice that the first argument for the new binding is SelectedItem. You may be more familiar with using Text in that argument. SelectedItem will cause the control to read the entire Activity object attached to the Customer and will work out how to match it up with the items in the ComboBox.

Example 9-5. Code for filling two of the ComboBoxes

```
private void FillCombos()
{
  activity1Combo.DisplayMember = "Name";
  activity1Combo.ValueMember = "ActivityID";
  activity1Combo.DataSource = _activities;
  activity1Combo.DataBindings.Add
   (new Binding("SelectedItem",customerBindingSource,
              "PrimaryActivity", true));

  dest1Combo.DisplayMember = "Name";
  dest1Combo.ValueMember = "DestinationID";
  dest1Combo.DataSource = _destinations;
  dest1Combo.DataBindings.Add
   (new Binding("SelectedItem",customerBindingSource,
              "PrimaryDestination", true));
}
```

Insert a call to the FillCombos method into the form's Load event. You can put this line at the end of the existing code. Run the application again if you want to see how the ComboBoxes have been populated so far.

The other ComboBoxes will be bound in the UI. To do this, you will need to create one new Object data source for the BAGA.Activity class and one for the BAGA.Destination class. To create these, use the same steps as you did to add the Customer data source at the beginning of this chapter. These new data source objects default as DataGrid Views. Change them to ComboBox controls:

1. Open the form in Design view.
2. Click Destination in the Data Sources window.
3. Click its drop-down arrow.
4. Click Customize from the list.
5. Choose ComboBox from the Associated controls.
6. Click OK.
7. Drag Destination onto the form.

8. Click Activity.
9. Select ComboBox from its drop-down list.
10. Drag Activity onto the form.

You will now have two new `ComboBox` and `BindingSource` controls.

In the form load, add the following code to bind the new `BindingSources` to the list variables, as shown in the following code:

```
activityBindingSource.DataSource = _activities;
destinationBindingSource.DataSource = _destinations;
```

The order of the method calls in `Form.Load` will impact the UI. If you perform this binding at the end of the `Form.Load`, the very first record will not display the correct items until you move to another record and back again in the UI. However, if you place these two lines of code prior to the query that retrieves the `Contact` data, the combo boxes will be correct right away.

Using the ComboBox Tasks window, you can see that three of the four properties for each `ComboBox` were filled by the drag-and-drop operation. Because our model uses foreign keys, you can set the selected value to point to the `CustomerBindingSource.SecondaryActivityItemID`, as shown in Figure 9-11.

Because the Tasks window cannot be expanded, you cannot see the complete property name displayed in the screenshot.

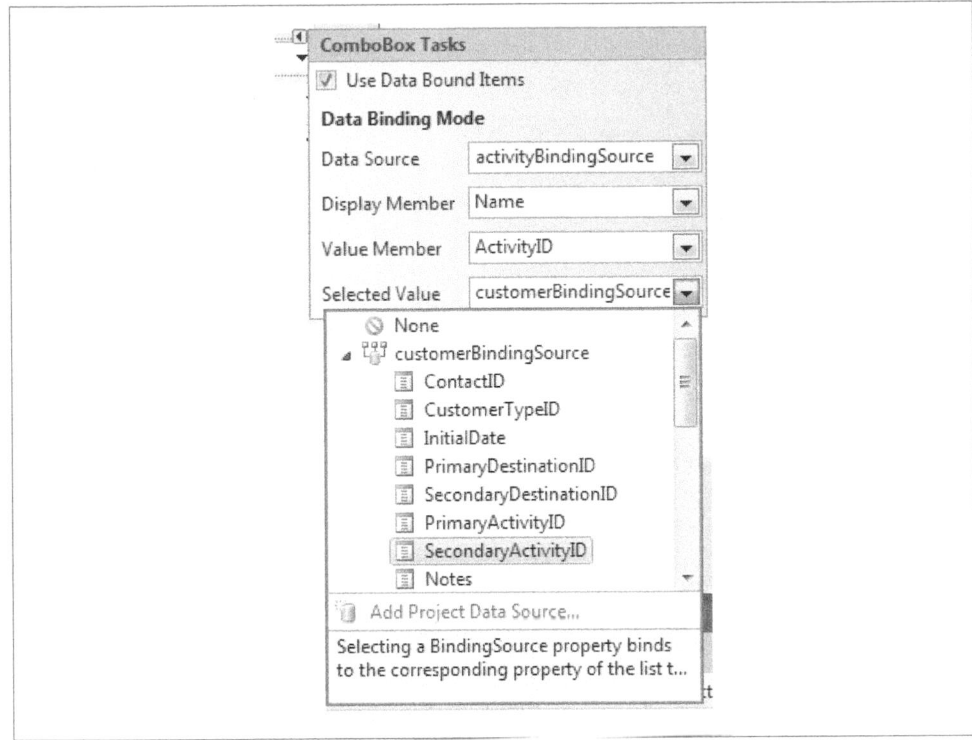

Figure 9-11. Binding properties through the ComboBox Tasks window

You also have the option of binding directly to the `SecondaryActivity` navigation property, which you would be forced to do if you weren't using foreign keys. If you want to go this route, you can set the property in the Properties window, as shown in Figure 9-12.

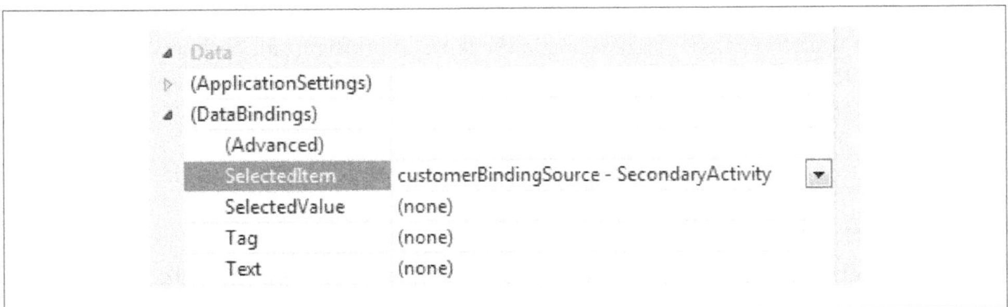

Figure 9-12. Alternatively, binding the ComboBox selection using SelectedItem, which is available in the ComboBox Properties window

Now you can view, edit, and save these properties along with the rest of the customer data, as shown in Figure 9-13.

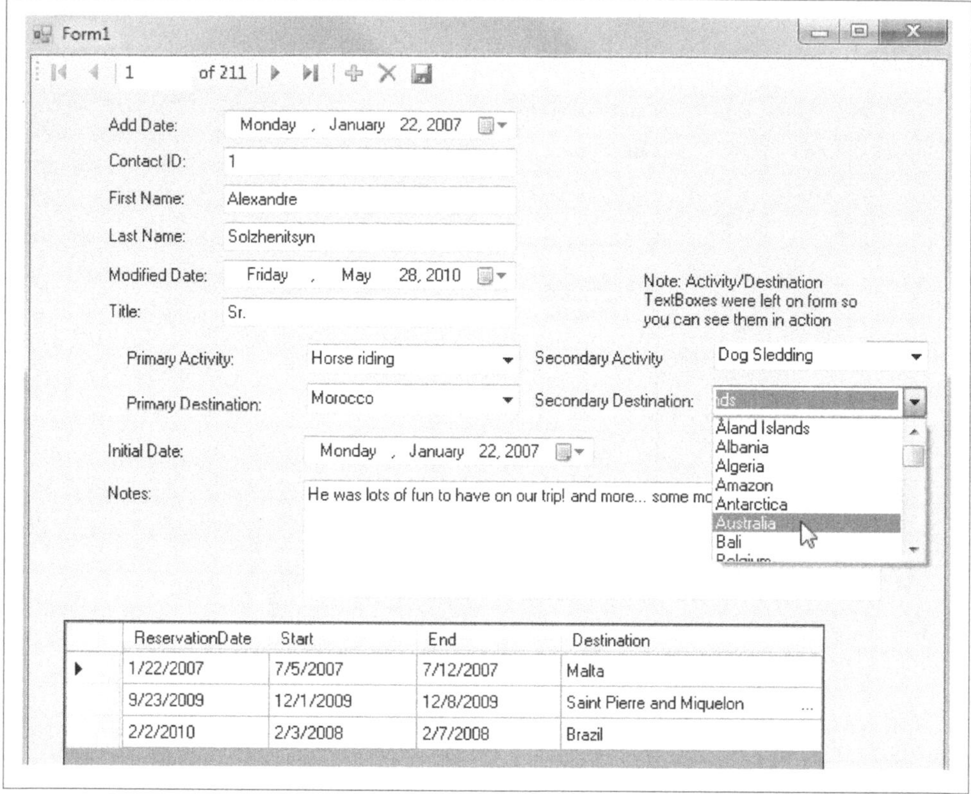

Figure 9-13. Editing the navigation properties with pick lists

If you are not familiar with Windows Forms data binding, it may be helpful to understand that changes to a control's value are not registered until the user moves away from the control and selects another control. Therefore, after you have made the last edit on the form, click any of the other controls before you click the Save button. In a production app, you would need to ensure that the user is not susceptible to this default behavior.

Adding New Customers

We'll take on one last task in this Windows form before moving on: adding new customers.

The data sources don't handle the related entities quite as seamlessly when adding as they do when editing, so we'll have to add a little bit of code to make this work.

When you click the plus sign icon to add a new customer, a new customer is added to the `CustomerBindingSource`. But because of the constraints of the model, you also need a new `Contact` entity to be created at the same time. Remember that a `Customer` entity merely extends a `Contact`. The `BindingSource` has an `AddingNew` event, but this occurs before the new entity is created. The next event to fire is `CurrentChanged` as the `BindingSource` moves its pointer to the newly created `Customer`. In the `CurrentChanged` event, you can add the new contact and set any other properties that are necessary.

Here you will have your first opportunity to see how to create new entities in code, to create a relationship, and to be sure the new entity is being managed by the context.

We've established that clicking the plus sign icon adds a new `Customer` to the `BindingSource`, and that the `CurrentChanged` event is your first opportunity to work with the new `Customer` entity. But the `CurrentChanged` event is hit anytime the `BindingSource` points to a different `Customer`. You'll need a way to discern the newly added `Customer` from those that already existed in the `BindingSource`.

One way might be to check the `Customer`'s `ContactID`, because it will not have been created yet. But if the user has added a number of customers prior to saving, `ContactID=0` will not necessarily mean that the user just clicked the Add New icon.

Until you have more tools in your Entity Framework tool belt, the best way to determine a newly added `Customer` at this point is to use a flag to identify that a new `Customer` is being added to the `BindingSource`. We'll employ a Boolean variable named `adding` for the flag.

Once that is in place, you will need to do the following for new customers:

1. Create a new contact object.
2. Add the contact to the new customer.
3. Set necessary defaults on the contact.
4. Set necessary defaults on the customer.
5. Set the `adding` flag to `false`.

Let's see how to implement these steps.

In Chapter 11, you will learn how to add business logic to entities and these types of steps won't be necessary, especially not in the user interface.

First we'll add the code to ensure that new customers are created properly.

Add the Boolean variable in Example 9-6 to the form's declarations.

Example 9-6. Placing the adding variable into the form's declarations

```
public partial class Form1 : Form
{
  BAGA.BAEntities _context;
  List<BAGA.Activity> _activities;
```

```
List<BAGA.Destination> _destinations;
bool _adding;
```

Using the Events view of the Properties window for the CustomerBindingSource control, create new methods to respond to the AddingNew event and the CurrentChanged event.

Then, in the code view, fill out the new methods as described in the next two examples.

In the CustomerBindingSource.AddingNew event, set the adding flag to true, as shown in Example 9-7.

Example 9-7. Setting the adding flag to true

```
private void customerBindingSource_AddingNew
 (object sender, AddingNewEventArgs e)
{
  _adding = true;
}
```

In the CurrentChanged event, you will check the adding flag, as shown in Example 9-8. If it is true, the code should perform the steps outlined earlier on the new Customer. If adding is false, this logic will be skipped. In this example, CustomerBindingSource.EndEdit is called prior to adding the related entities to the Customer. This method will trigger the BAEntities context to recognize the new Customer, and therefore the context will also manage the new Contact entity properly. Without this method call here, you may experience problems when it comes time to call SaveChanges.

Example 9-8. Filling out the defaults for a new Customer

```
private void customerBindingSource_CurrentChanged
 (object sender, EventArgs e)
{
  if (_adding)
  {
    customerBindingSource.EndEdit();
    //TODO: Move "create new customer" logic out of the UI code
    var newCust = (BAGA.Customer)customerBindingSource.Current;
    if (newCust.Contact == null)
    {
      newCust.Contact = new BAGA.Contact();
      newCust.Contact.ModifiedDate = DateTime.Now;
      newCust.Contact.AddDate = DateTime.Now;
    }
    newCust.InitialDate = DateTime.Now;
    _adding = false;
  }
}
```

In the previous chapter, you were instructed to set a default value for the CustomerTypeID in the model. If you hadn't done that, you would need to set it in the CurrentChanged method since it is a non-nullable property.

You'll need one last line of code for saving newly added customers. It's not uncommon for the BindingSource to leave its current item in the "edit state." With entities, this means that the changes in the UI won't be pushed into the entities, and therefore SaveChanges will not see the need to do any updates to the database. BindingSource.EndEdit will ensure that the UI changes are registered with the entities.

Add the method shown in Example 9-9 to the Save Item button's Click event, just before SaveChanges is called.

Example 9-9. Using EndEdit to ensure that BindingSource completes the current edit process

```
private void customerBindingNavigatorSaveItem_Click
 (object sender, EventArgs e)
{
  customerBindingSource.EndEdit();
  _context.SaveChanges();
}
```

EndEdit has been something of an enigma in Windows Forms data binding. In some apps you'll never need to use it; in others it solves some strange problems related to updates and persisting to the database. This has nothing to with Entity Framework.

Run the form again and add a new customer.

You'll be able to enter name and preference information and save the record. You should see a new value pop into the ContactID field when you save. That's a pretty good indication that the insert was performed in the database because this is the new value returned by the insert operation.

Because the context is keeping track of additions and edits, it is possible to make changes to multiple records before clicking the Save button. When you do, all of the changes you have made to the list of customers, whether they were additions or edits, will be sent to the database. The best way to ensure that the code is working is to stop the application after you have saved your changes, and then start it again. This will force it to requery the database, and you can verify that the changes were definitely persisted to the store.

Deleting Reservations

If you are new to data binding, it is essential to understand an important concept about working with "child" data, such as the reservations in a grid control. The grid control has the ability to allow users to remove rows. This requires that you check Enable Deleting in the grid's Task window, or set the AllowUserToDeleteRows property to True in the Properties window. With this enabled, a user can highlight a row, hit the Delete key on his keyboard, and the row will disappear.

However, the term *delete* is misleading. In the case of this child data, the row is removed, but that piece of data will not be deleted from the database when a save is made. This is not specific to Entity Framework. You'll experience this with DataSets and custom objects as well.

What happens is that the data is removed from the collection that contains it. In the case of the reservations, the "deleted" reservation is removed from the Reservations EntityCollection of the current customer. Now that Reservation has no Customer, when you call SaveChanges you will get an exception because a constraint was defined by the one-to-many relationship between the two (every reservation must have a Customer). The save will fail.

It is best to handle the user action more explicitly rather than rely on the data binding. If you truly want users to be able to delete a reservation by removing the row, you'll need to handle that event and ensure that the reservation is marked for database deletion.

The grid has a UserDeletingRow event and a UserDeletedRow event. In the first event, you need to identify which reservation was just removed. In the second, you can delete the reservation from the context. You can't delete from the context in the first event because the grid will get confused and remove the next item from the collection.

This two-step process requires that you first declare a class-level variable in the form declarations, such as:

```
Reservation resToDelete;
```

Next, add the two events for the reservationsGridView and fill out their logic as follows:

```
private void reservationsDataGridView_UserDeletingRow
 (object sender, DataGridViewRowCancelEventArgs e)
{
  resToDelete = reservationsBindingSource.Current as BAGA.Reservation;
}

private void reservationsDataGridView_UserDeletedRow
 (object sender, DataGridViewRowEventArgs e)
{
  if (resToDelete != null)
  {
    _context.DeleteObject(resToDelete);
    resToDelete = null;
  }
}
```

Be aware that this particular example is not completely fleshed out. A Reservation might have related Payments and you should take those into account when deleting a reservation.

Not all of the form features will work. For instance, you will run into problems if you attempt to delete a customer or a customer's reservation because of constraints in the database that we have not yet addressed. In upcoming chapters, you will learn how to perform this and other types of functions with your entities, how to add business logic, how to write layered applications, and more.

You could add plenty of features to this form to make it even more functional, but it's time to move on to a different type of client-side data binding: data binding in WPF.

Data Binding and Separation of Concerns

The data binding that you have seen so far and the example you will build in the next part of the chapter work directly with the `ObjectContext` in the user interface. If you are building small applications, this is a sufficient pattern. However, for enterprise applications, there are well-known patterns for keeping this type of logic out of the user interface. The focus of many of these patterns is that UI code should be related to work in the UI, not code that interacts with a database or performs business logic on objects. Using the context directly in your UI for queries and calling `SaveChanges` is an example of code that interacts, albeit indirectly, with the database. It has nothing to do with the UI itself. Applying default values to a newly created entity is also unrelated to the user interface.

Data Binding with WPF Applications

For the WPF data-binding example in this section, you'll focus on interacting with trips and their details: destination, lodging, and activities. You will also get a chance to see how many-to-many relationships work both for data retrieval and for updates.

We will continue providing our data in the form's code, but read the "Data Binding and Separation of Concerns" sidebar on this page for a short discussion of why this is acceptable for small applications, but not for large applications. Further on in the book you will learn how to take these next steps with the Entity Framework. However, as you work through the WPF example, bear in mind that the lesson is not about application architecture, but about how data binding functions with WPF and Entity Framework.

If you've never created a WPF application before, this will be a useful, albeit simple, introduction. It will be a bit of a dive into the not-so-shallow end of the WPF pool, but the code samples should provide sufficient buoyancy. If you are looking for tips on how to make WPF perform its many shiny tricks, a data access book is not the place to look.

Quite a number of wonderful WPF books, articles, and other resources are available—too many to list here. For a good first look at WPF, I recommend MSDN's "How Do I?" videos, at *http://msdn.microsoft.com/en-us/bb629407.aspx#wpf/*.

You may be happy to learn that data-binding controls for WPF were introduced in Visual Studio 2010, which makes this example much simpler to achieve than in the previous version.

Creating the WPF Form

The purpose of this form will be to edit trips that exist in the BreakAway catalog. Trips are defined by a destination, a start and end date, a price, lodging, and a list of activities. Figure 9-14 shows a mock-up of the form you will build.

A slew of controls are involved in this form. You'll learn how to bind `ListBoxes` and `TextBoxes` and how to have them interact with one another, as well as some tricks that you'll need to know for doing all of this with the Entity Framework.

WPF data binding has had some wonderful improvements in Visual Studio 2010. This impacts binding to Entity Framework objects as well as other data sources. In this example, you'll do some of the binding manually and let the Designer handle some of it for you.

Creating the WPF Project

We'll begin by creating a new WPF project, adding the references to use the model, and getting all of the controls onto the form:

1. Create a new WPF project in the same solution where you created the model and the Windows Forms application.
2. Add a reference to the BreakAwayModel project and to `System.Data.Entity` as you did for the previous application.
3. Copy the *app.config* file from the Windows Forms project into this project.

   Remember, this is just a cheat to quickly get the `ConnectionString` into the current application.

Adding the Necessary Data Source Objects

To begin, this form will need to use `Trips`, `Destinations`, and `Lodgings` as data sources.

1. Using the same method you did with the Windows Forms example, create three new Object data sources—one for the `Destination` class, one for `Lodging`, and one for `Trip`.

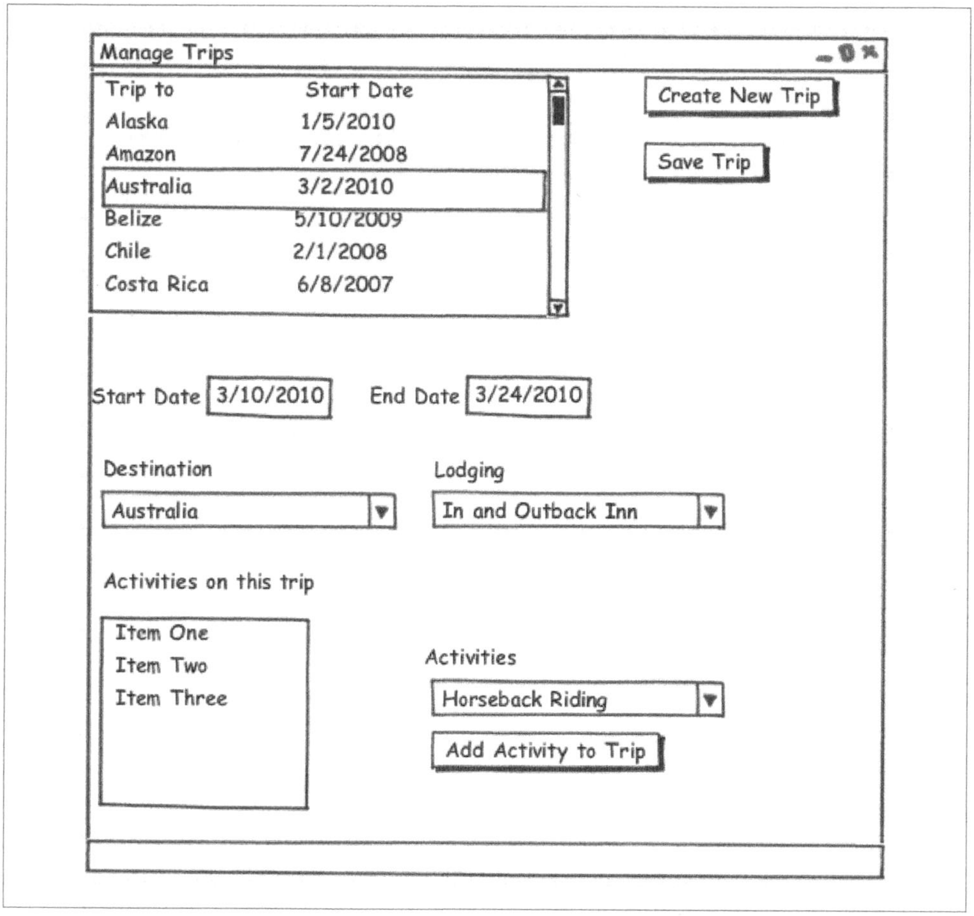

Figure 9-14. Mock-up of a WPF form for managing BreakAway's Trips catalog

If your EDM were in the same project as the WPF window, the EDM classes would automatically be available as data sources. You wouldn't have to explicitly add them. This is really handy for building rapid applications.

The new data sources will have a `DataGrid` as the default control binding.

2. Change the control binding for `Destination` and `Lodging` to `ComboBox`, and then change the control binding for `Trip` to `ListBox`. The WPF designer window needs to be open in order to do this.

   You will need to use the `Customize` option to add the `ComboBox` and `ListBox` to the drop-down choices.

3. Drag `Destination` onto the window's design surface and then `Lodging` and `Trip`. In a few more steps, I'll explain why it was important to drag `Destination` first.

They will be named `destinationComboBox`, `lodgingComboBox`, and `tripListBox`. Visual Basic will capitalize the first letters of the control names.

If you haven't used WPF before, you might appreciate that the `Name` property is at the top of the control's Properties window.

You'll be customizing these controls, but first we'll look at how these data sources appear in the window's XAML and then we'll write some code to get data that will populate the controls.

Inspecting the XAML and Code Generated by the Automated Data Binding

In addition to creating the controls, there are other notable changes that the data binding made to the XAML and to the code for this window. None of this is specific to the fact that you are binding to `Entity` objects. This is the common behavior for WPF data binding.

XAML data-binding elements

In the XAML, a new element was added, called Windows Resources. This element contains three new `CollectionViewSource` elements, one for each object being used in the window. These are comparable to the `BindingSource` used in Windows Forms. They will act as the conduit between your data and the controls.

Look farther down at the `Grid` that wraps the three controls. The `Grid` defined a `DataContext` that points to the `CollectionViewSource` of the first object you dropped onto the screen. Because you dropped the Destination data source first, the context will be named `destinationViewSource`:

```
<Grid DataContext="{StaticResource destinationViewSource}">
```

The `destinationComboBox` will then default to the binding of its parent (the grid) using the `ItemsSource` attribute. To do so, the `ItemsSource` says to use the `Binding` with no additional details:

```
ItemsSource="{Binding}"
```

What about the other two controls? How do they bind to their `CollectionViewSources`? The `Lodging` and `Trip` controls have additional information in the `ItemsSource Binding` property, referring back to the `CollectionViewSources` that are defined in the `Windows.Resources` element:

```
ItemsSource="{Binding Source={StaticResource tripViewSource}}"
```

This is the default behavior of the WPF Designer. You do not need to use `Resources` and can bind directly in code. However, leveraging XAML's composability is a good and recommended practice. Additionally, if you plan to reuse a resource within a window, there is a performance gain at compile time. Again, this example is not meant to be a primer on how to use WPF, so refer to more focused learning resources for further details.

In the code-behind for the window, you will find two new lines of code for each `CollectionViewSource` that was added to the XAML. The first is to create a class instance of these elements and the second is to bind some data to them. This latter line is commented out. If the model had been inside the WPF project, you'd see a lot more code. Check the sidebar "WPF and EDM: So RAD Together" on page 217 for more information about this.

Let's create some data sources to hook up to these view sources.

Adding Code to Query the EDM When the Window Loads

Adding events to WPF is the same as for Windows Forms. In C#, you can use the Events page of the Properties windows. In VB, you can do the same or use the Class Name and Method Name drop downs in the Code window.

We'll start by declaring variables for the form. As in the previous application, you'll need a context and some variables to contain the selection lists. You can add an `Imports` or `using` statement for the `BAGA` namespace so that you don't have to type it repeatedly. While you're at it, add the `System.Data.Objects` namespace as well. This will reduce the amount of typing you need to do later on. (See Example 9-10.)

WPF and EDM: So RAD Together

An earlier note mentioned that if the EDM was in the same project as the WPF window, the data sources would have automatically been created. Another RAD feature that you would see if your EDM was in the same project is that after dragging the data sources onto the window, Visual Studio would have created code to declare and instantiate a context, defined and execute a query and bind the results to the control's binding source. The result is that simply by dragging and dropping the data source on to the form you would have a form that would run and display data without having to write a single line of code. You can see a demonstration of this in a video I created that is on the MSDN Data Development Center as part of a series of EF4 Introductory videos at *http://msdn.com/data/videos*. The particular video is number 11 in the series: Data-Binding with WPF and the Entity Framework.

Example 9-10. Adding the necessary namespaces and variables for the form

```
using BAGA;
using System.Data.Objects;
using System.Collections.ObjectModel;
```

```
namespace Chapter_9_WPF
{
  public partial class MainWindow : Window
  {
    private BAEntities _context;
    private List<Activity> _activities;
    private List<Destination> _destinations;
    private List<Lodging> _lodgings;
    private List<Trip> _trips;
```

In the `Window_Loaded` event handler, add the code for retrieving the trips as well as the related selection lists (see Example 9-11).

Later on in the book, you'll learn how to create a generic method that you can use to query for any reference lists so that it won't be necessary to have separate queries for selection lists such as Destinations, Lodgings, and Activities.

Example 9-11. Querying for lists that will be needed by the form

```
private void Window_Loaded(object sender,RoutedEventArgs e)
{
  _context = new BAEntities();
  _activities = _context.Activities
               .OrderBy(a => a.Name).ToList();
  _destinations = _context.Destinations
                 .OrderBy(d => d.Name).ToList();
  _lodgings = _context.Lodgings
            .OrderBy(l => l.LodgingName).ToList();
  _trips = _context.Trips
            .OrderBy(t => t.Destination.Name).ToList()
}
```

Now that you have some data, you can bind it to the view sources, which, in turn, will feed the data to the controls.

1. Return to the code that was inserted when you dragged the controls onto the form, and define instances for the three `CollectionViewSource` elements.
2. Uncomment each line that defines a data source.
3. Modify the code to apply the lists you created earlier to these view sources as follows:

```
tripViewSource.Source = _trips;
destinationViewSource.Source = _destinations;
lodgingViewSource.Source = _lodgings;
```

If you were to run this application at this point, you'd see that the form is now able to display data, though it's not quite ready for prime time. You'll have to give the XAML a bit more information regarding what to display.

Customizing the Display of the Controls

When the controls were created on the page, Visual Studio did its best job of defining what to display in the controls. Each control displays the values of the first scalar property listed in the object and displays the property's value using the `DisplayMemberPath` attribute.

Now you will modify this to display the correct information.

In the `ListBox`, we want to display the name of the destination along with the date the trip starts. `DisplayMemberPath` allows only a single value, so you'll replace that with a new element, an `ItemTemplate` that contains additional WPF controls.

Modify the ListBox so that it matches the XAML in Example 9-12. The changes you need to make are:

1. Delete the attribute `DisplayMemberPath="DestinationID"` from the `ListBox` element.
2. Remove the closing slash from the end of the `ListBox` element and add a closing tag to the `ListBox`.

   This will change from `Width="120" />` to `Width="120" > </ListBox>`.
3. Add the `ItemTemplate` element shown in Example 9-12.

Example 9-12. The ListBox and its ItemTemplate

```
<ListBox Height="136" HorizontalAlignment="Left" Margin="73,32,0,0"
         Name= "tripListBox" VerticalAlignment="Top" Width="406"
         ItemsSource="{Binding Source={StaticResource tripViewSource} }">
  <ListBox.ItemTemplate>
    <DataTemplate >
      <StackPanel Orientation="Horizontal">
        <TextBlock Width="200" Text="{Binding Path=Destination.Name}"/>
        <TextBlock Text="{Binding Path=StartDate, StringFormat=MM/dd/yyyy}"/>
      </StackPanel>
    </DataTemplate>
  </ListBox.ItemTemplate>
 </ListBox>
```

The margins and other position settings that you see in the examples are what happened to be set by the Designer as I was creating my own WPF window for these samples, and are not necessarily values that you will need to use.

You've got enough to see some action already. Run the form to see the trip destinations and start dates listed in the `ListBox`.

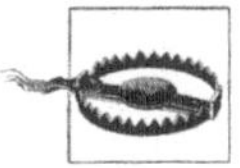

The typing you've done in the XAML may result in some typos. Although the consequences of some typos will be exceptions thrown at runtime, often you won't see the results you expect even if there are no typos highlighted by IntelliSense in the code. If you're testing the code, and controls are empty when they shouldn't be, ensure that you typed in the correct control names and property names.

Selecting an Entity and Viewing Its Details

The next step is to view the trip details. On the form shown in Figure 9-15, you can see that the start and end dates appear in the (new to Visual Studio 2010) `DatePicker` controls on the form. The destination and lodging information is displayed in the combo boxes that are already on the form. Eventually, you will use combo boxes for editing trips as well.

WPF's binding goes far beyond binding data to controls. You can also bind controls to each other, creating dependencies between them. We'll use this feature to link the `DatePicker` and `ComboBox` controls to the `ListBox`. The controls will obtain their values from the `ListBox`'s selected trip.

Let's start with the `ComboBox` controls that are already on the form. They already are bound to the lists that populate them, but now you want to ensure that they display the information from whatever trip is currently selected in the `ListBox`.

As noted before, the `destinationComboBox` by default is using the `DisplayMemberPath` attribute to display the `DestinationID`.

First, change the `DisplayMemberPath` target from `DestinationID` to `Name`.

The `DisplayMemberPath` and `SelectedValuePath` attributes refer to the properties of the list of Destinations to which you bound the `ComboBox` in code. `SelectedValue` gets the `DestinationId` from the currently selected trip in the `ListBox`.

Now add a `SelectedValue` attribute that binds the `ComboBox` to the currently selected item in the `tripListBox`. Example 9-13 shows the final XAML for the `destinationComboBox`, which binds to the foreign key property, `DestinationID`, of the selected trip.

The `ItemsPanel` element was added by the Designer when you originally created the control. It contains a `VirtualizingStackPanel`, which is there to help with UI performance.

Example 9-13. XAML for displaying the destination of the selected trip

```
<ComboBox DisplayMemberPath="Name" Height="23" HorizontalAlignment="Left"
          ItemsSource="{Binding Source={StaticResource destinationViewSource}}"
          Margin="89,238,0,0" Name="destinationComboBox"
          SelectedValuePath="DestinationID"
          SelectedValue="{Binding ElementName=tripListBox,
```

```
                Path=SelectedItem.DestinationID}"
        VerticalAlignment="Top" Width="120">
  <ComboBox.ItemsPanel>
    <ItemsPanelTemplate>
      <VirtualizingStackPanel />
    </ItemsPanelTemplate>
  </ComboBox.ItemsPanel>
</ComboBox>
```

You should make similar modifications to the lodgingComboBox. Change the DisplayMemberPath of the lodgingComboBox to LodgingName. Then add a SelectedValue attribute to the ComboBox in order to bind the control to the tripListBox.

Example 9-14 shows the critical portion of the lodgingComboBox after these changes have been made.

Example 9-14. XAML for displaying the lodging of the selected trip

```
<ComboBox DisplayMemberPath="LodgingName" Height="23" HorizontalAlignment="Left"
          ItemsSource="{Binding Source={StaticResource lodgingViewSource}}"
          Margin="254,238,0,0" Name="lodgingComboBox" SelectedValuePath="LodgingID"
          SelectedValue="{Binding ElementName=tripListBox,
                         Path=SelectedItem.LodgingID}"
          VerticalAlignment="Top" Width="120">
```

Now you should be able to witness the interaction between the controls. Run the app, and as you select different trips from the ListBox notice that the combo boxes update accordingly. You can also see that the combo boxes are populated with the appropriate lists if you open them.

Next, you'll add the trip dates to the form and bind them to the tripListBox as well.

From the Data Sources window, drag the StartDate and EndDate properties from the Trip data source onto the form.

The default control binding for date types is the DatePicker control. The Designer will create a small grid that contains the label and the DatePicker.

Because you are using properties, not entire classes, the Designer will not create new view sources. The controls will be dependent on the existing TripViewSource for their data.

If the Trip data source is the first one you added to the control, the parent grid is bound to the tripViewSource through its DataContext attribute. In this case, you will not need to modify the DataContext of the DatePicker controls. By default, they will depend on the parent's DataContext using the syntax DataContext="{Binding}".

However, if the Grid's DataContext is set to one of the other view sources, you will need to specify the Binding as you have done previously.

Modify the DataContext attribute of the startDateDatePicker to match that in Example 9-15.

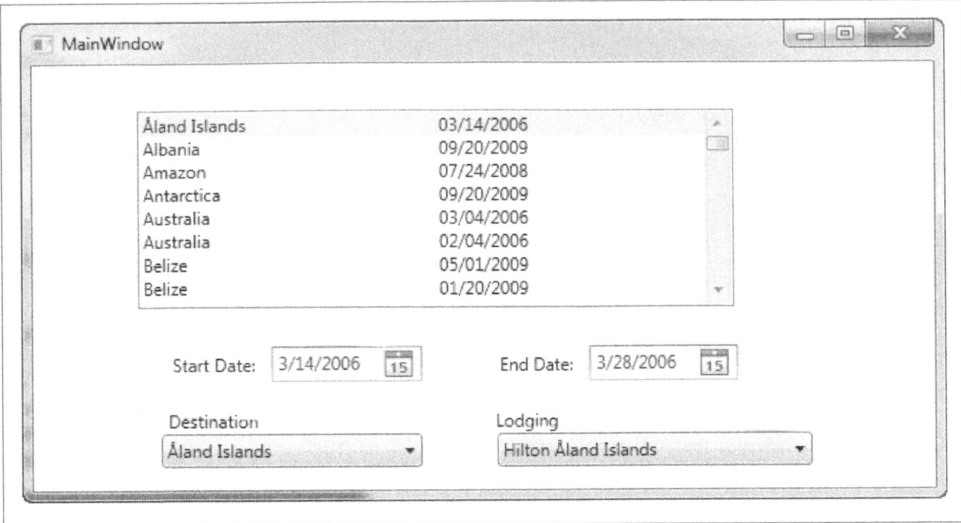

Figure 9-15. The window with the selection functionality enabled

Example 9-15. XAML for displaying the destination of the selected trip

```
<DatePicker Grid.Column="1" Grid.Row="0" HorizontalAlignment="Left" Margin="3"
           Name="startDateDatePicker"
           SelectedDate="{Binding Path=StartDate}"
           VerticalAlignment="Center"
           DataContext="{Binding Source={StaticResource tripViewSource}}">
</DatePicker>
```

Now modify the `DataContext` attribute of the `endDateTimePicker` to also point to the same binding source as `startDateTimePicker`.

Notice that I've set the `SelectedDate` binding differently than I did for the `SelectedValue` in Example 9-14. In Example 9-15, I'm reading the `StartDate` value directly from the `tripViewSource`. In Example 9-14, I'm reading the `LodgingID` value from within the `tripListBox` control, which is why I use the `ElementName` attribute. I could have used the same pattern for the date control, reading from the `tripListBox` control's `SelectedItem` when looking for the `StartDate` value. Both binding methods are valid. A more targeted WPF resource could provide guidance on when to use one pattern over the other.

Now your form is starting to get interesting. When you run the application, the Start Date and End Date text boxes and the Destination and Lodging combo boxes should sync up to whatever trip is selected in the `ListBox`, as shown in Figure 9-15.

You still have three more tasks to complete: viewing the activities for a trip, editing trip details, and adding new trips.

Adding Another EntityCollection to the Mix

The `Activities` property is an `EntityCollection` and you need to display it in a control that can display sets. For that, we'll use another `ListBox`.

Working with a many-to-many relationship

Activities and trips are joined in a many-to-many relationship. Although the Entity Framework can query across this type of relationship and coordinate inserts, updates, and deletes without you having to work directly with the `Join` table, there is one thing that the Entity Framework is unable to do with this type of relationship, which is explained in the following paragraphs.

In previous examples, you saw how Object Services can automatically wire up related objects that are in the context. It will find entities that are related and build graphs between them. You took advantage of this in the Windows Forms application earlier. Because the activities and destinations were being returned in their own queries, you were able to remove the `Include` paths to the `Customer` preference properties.

In the `Window.Loaded` event for this WPF form, you have a query that returns a list of activities. You will use this as a pick list when you create a new trip. So, since those activities are already in the cache, it would make sense that they will automatically be wired up to the existing trips. But they aren't, and that's because of the many-to-many relationship. This is expected behavior and you'll need to either load the related data with `Include` or `Load`, or manually attach the entities. In this example, you will use an `Include`. You'll learn more about this in Chapter 15.

Object Services can automatically wire related entities only when one of the ends of the relationship has an `EntityReference` property that points to the other end of the relationship. Because both the `Activities` property of `Trip` and the `Trips` property of `Activity` are `EntityCollection`s, the relationship information that is needed to bind them doesn't exist within either entity. That is why you need to explicitly create the graph with one of the Object Services methods for joining related entities.

Modifying the code to eager-load the related activities

The bottom line is that you need to change the `Trip` query in the `Window.Loaded` event. To do this, add an `Include` method to pull in the activities, as shown in the following code:

```
_trips = _context.Trips.Include("Activities")
                 .OrderBy("it.Destination.Name")
                 .ToList()
```

Adding the Activities ListBox and binding it to the Trips ListBox

The next step is to change the binding control for the `Activities` property of the Trip data source to be a `ListBox`. To do this, drag the `Activities` property onto the form. Then change the new `ListBox` control's default `DisplayMemberPath` from `ActivityID` to `Name`.

Example 9-16 shows the modified `ListBox` with all of the data-binding attributes in place. Notice that the `Binding Source` was properly defined. You shouldn't have to edit it.

Example 9-16. The modified ListBox

```
<ListBox DisplayMemberPath="Name" Height="100" HorizontalAlignment="Left"
         ItemsSource="{Binding Source={StaticResource tripActivitiesViewSource}}"
         Margin="50,271,0,0" Name="activitiesListBox"
         SelectedValuePath="ActivityID"
         VerticalAlignment="Top" Width="227" />
```

Although we are depending on the Designer to automate this data binding, don't forget that you can set some of these values in the Properties window for the control. Since the goal here is to see the Entity Framework objects in action with WPF, not to become a WPF guru, I will not delve into the many variations that WPF provides.

Testing the application again

Once you have the `ListBox` control configured, you should be able to see the effect of having each trip's activities displayed in this `ListBox` as you select different trips from the main `ListBox`. Figure 9-16 shows the application performing its newest trick.

Editing Entities and Their Related Data

Now it's time for some editing.

In the Windows Forms application, the `BindingSource` coordinated user actions with entities. If a user edited data on the form, the `BindingSource` automatically pushed that change into the entity, even for the related entities.

WPF's `CollectionViewSource` performs the same task. Therefore, as you make changes in these controls that are wired up, the changes will be tracked all the way back to the entity. Add a new button to the form and change its `Content` property to `Save`. Next, double-click the button to get to the `Click` event handler, the button's default event. Finally, add a call to `SaveChanges` in the event handler, as shown in Example 9-17.

Example 9-17. Enabling saves

```
private void button1_Click(object sender, System.Windows.RoutedEventArgs e)
{
  _context.SaveChanges();
}
```

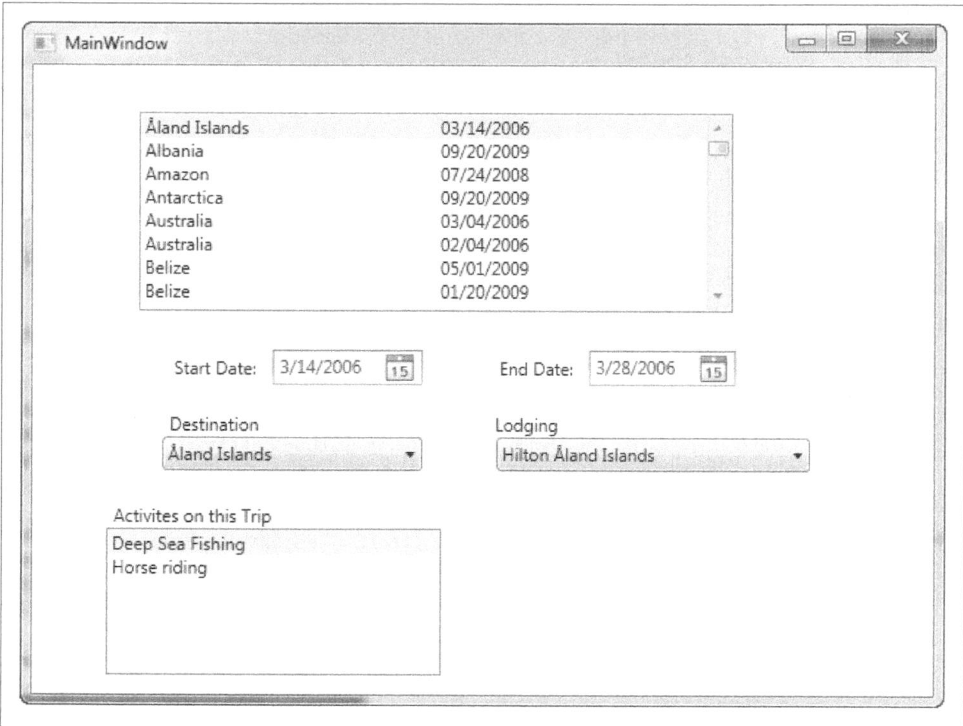

Figure 9-16. The WPF window with the Activities ListBox displaying an EntityCollection

Run the form and edit one of the trips, changing a date and the lodging, then click the new Save button. Close the form and then run it again. Thanks to the new data-binding features added in Visual Studio 2010, the edits were successfully saved.

If you followed the WPF example in the prior edition of this book using Visual Studio 2008, you were required to do a lot more work to get this sample to run.

Using SortDescriptions to Keep Sorting in Sync with Data Modifications

You might prevent destinations from being edited on existing trips, but you'll still need to use that `ComboBox` for new trips. If the user changes the trip's destination, you won't see the change on the `ListBox`.

WPF provides a way to sort the items in a `CollectionViewSource` with a `SortDescriptions` collection. If you re-sort the list after the user selects a destination from the combo box, the list will be refreshed, the new destination name will appear, and the item will be properly sorted using the new name.

WPF's sorting features are very different from what you may be used to. You can read more about `SortDescriptions` in the MSDN documentation.

Although you can define `SortDescriptions` in XAML, you will do it in code in response to a selection from the `destinationComboBox`. Not only will you sort by the trip's destination name, but then any trips to a common destination will be sorted by their start date. I suggest putting `SortDescriptions` into the control's `DropDownClosed` event so that it gets hit only when the user changes the selection.

1. Add `System.ComponentModel` to the `Imports/using` statements to use this feature.
2. Add a `DropDownClosed` event for the `destinationComboBox`.
3. Add the code from Example 9-18 into the `DropDownClosed` event.

Example 9-18. Allowing the List to be sorted

```
tripListBox.Items.SortDescriptions.Add(new SortDescription("Destination.Name",
                                           ListSortDirection.Ascending));
tripListBox.Items.SortDescriptions.Add(new SortDescription("StartDate",
                                           ListSortDirection.Descending));
```

In order to make the sorting work even as a user is modifying data, you need to add the `SortDescription` each time. Unfortunately, this means compounding the number of `SortDescription` objects in the collection. You'll see in the downloaded code example for this chapter the additional logic that I added into this solution to avoid this problem. This extra code is not included here as it is a bit out of scope and requires a number of extra steps that detract from the focus of the sample.

Adding Items to the Child EntityCollection

Next, we'll provide the ability to add activities to a trip. To do this, you'll need a way to select a new activity to add. Since you won't need two-way binding, we'll do the data binding in code this time.

Start by adding a new `ComboBox` to the form with the name `activityComboBox`. In the `Window.Loaded` event, you have already queried for the list of activities. Now you need to bind those results to this new `ComboBox`. Therefore, add the following binding code to the end of the `Window.Loaded` event:

```
activityComboBox.ItemsSource = _activities;
```

The `ComboBox` needs to know which property to display and which to use as the value. So, in the Properties window for the `ComboBox`, set `SelectedValuePath` to `ActivityID` and `DisplayMemberPath` to `Name`.

The ComboBox has a SelectionChanged event, but it's not useful for reacting to a user selection because it is also hit when other code changes the selection. Instead, add a button to the form so that the user can explicitly add the selected activity. Name the button btnAddActivity.

All that's left to do is to wire up the button's Click event to read the selected item in the activityComboBox and add it to the current trip's Activities EntityCollection. The ListBox that shows the activities will update automatically because of its bindings. Add the code in Example 9-19 to the new button's Click event.

Example 9-19. Adding Activities to the selected trip entity

```
private void btnAddActivity_Click
 (object sender, System.Windows.RoutedEventArgs e)
{
  Activity selectedActivity = activityComboBox.SelectedItem as Activity;
  if (selectedActivity != null)
  {
    var selectedTrip = tripListBox.SelectedItem as Trip;
    if (selectedTrip != null)
    {
      selectedTrip.Activities.Add(selectedActivity);
    }
  }
}
```

This code ensures that an activity and a trip are selected before it tries to perform the main task. Notice how the new activity is added to the trip's Activities collection with the Add method. You will likely use the EntityCollection.Add method quite a lot in your Entity Framework–based applications. Chapter 19 drills into this functionality in detail.

Testing the new feature for adding activities

Run the application, select a trip, and add some activities. You'll see the Activities ListBox react. You can save the changes with your Save button. Note that since the data is not refreshed, again you may want to stop and start the application for proof that the change was saved.

The Last Task: Adding New Trips to the Catalog

Adding new trips will take a bit more code to implement. Not only will you need to set some defaults on the new trip entity, but you'll also have to use a few tricks to make the user interface flow properly.

Start by adding a new button to the form that will be the user's New Trip button. That's all you need to do in the UI. In the button's Click event, you'll create a new trip and set some defaults.

A few WPF tricks for a more interactive ListBox

Before modifying the new button's `Click` event, you'll need to make two changes that are related to WPF's data binding and are not specifically related to the Entity Framework.

WPF's data source controls can inform a class of changes to its properties, however, it cannot inform a regular collection such as a List when items have been added or removed from a bound control. Instead, you'll need to use a different type of .NET collection called `ObservableCollection`. Without getting too sidetracked, if you use an `ObservableCollection` of trips as the source for the `Trip ListBox` control, as you add and remove items from this collection the `ListBox` will respond by adding or removing the items from the display.

It's worth the effort to use this rather than a `List` so that you won't have to write the extra code to stuff your new trip into the `ListBox`.

To pull this off, we can change the `_trips` variable from a `List` to an `ObservableType`, as shown in the following code:

```
//private List<Trip> _trips;
private ObservableCollection<Trip> _trips;
```

Add the `Collections.ObjectModel` namespace to the `Imports/using` statements to use this feature.

In the `Window.Loaded` event, modify the `Trips` query to return an `ObservableCollection` rather than a `List`:

```
//_trips = _context.Trips.Include("Activities")
//              .OrderBy("it.Destination.Name").ToList();
_trips = new ObservableCollection<Trip>(
        _context.Trips.Include("Activities")
                     .OrderBy("it.Destination.Name"));
```

Now when you add new trips to the collection, they will automatically pop into the `ListBox`. But they'll be at the bottom and will remain there until you run the application again. That's no good. You can copy the sorting code from the `Destination ComboBox`'s `DropDownClosed` event into the `Window.Loaded` event to benefit from the sorting early on. In this way, if you add a new trip before you hit the other location where the sort is applied, the new trip will drop into the correct position in the `ListBox`. With the `ListBox` controlling the sort, you can remove the `OrderBy` method in the `Trips` query.

You'll still need the sorting code in the `ComboBox` to trigger the refresh. There may be a better way to trigger a refresh in the `ListBox` than adding the `SortDescription` again. But this little trick will suffice for now.

Coding the Add New Trip feature

With that functionality in place, you can now add a new trip and have the form respond in an expected manner.

The `Click` event of the New Trip button will add a new trip, set some default values, and add the trip into the `ListBox`'s items (see Example 9-20).

Example 9-20. The Click event of the New Trip button

```
private void btnNewTrip_Click
 (object sender, System.Windows.RoutedEventArgs e)
{
 //create a new Trip object with default System.DateTime values
  var newTrip = new Trip();
  newTrip.StartDate = DateTime.Today;
  newTrip.EndDate = DateTime.Today;

 //add a default destination. Sorting will fail if Destination == @null
  newTrip.Destination = _destinations[0];

 //add the trip to the context so that its changes will get tracked;
  _context.AddToTrips(newTrip);

  //add the new trip to the bound collection
   _trips.Add(newTrip);
  //select the new trip so that the bound controls will be tied to it
   tripListBox.SelectedItem = newTrip;
}
```

Testing the final version of the WPF demo

Run the demo again and check out the new features. When you add a new trip, watch how smoothly the bound `Trip ListBox` displays the new trip at the top of the `ListBox`. When you change the default destination, the trip will reappear alphabetically sorted in the `ListBox`, but still selected. Add some activities to the new trip. Save your changes and restart the application to prove that it all really worked (see Figure 9-17).

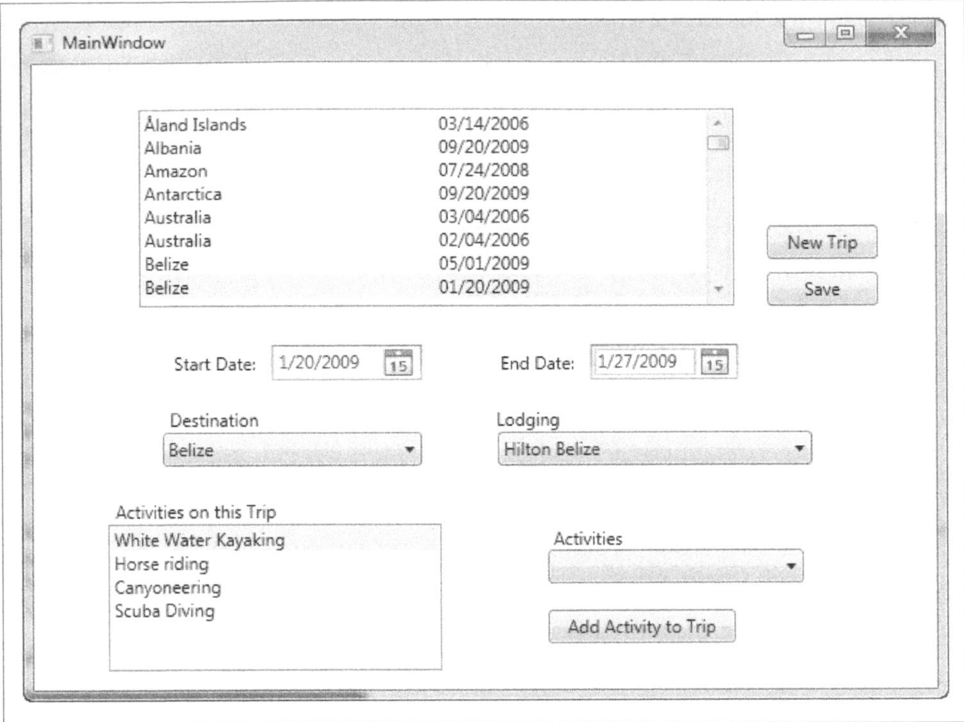

Figure 9-17. The final WPF window with all of its features in place

Summary

The Entity Framework has a number of levels of entry. In this chapter, you got a chance to apply much of what you learned in previous chapters in creating two starter client-side applications. The Windows Forms application leaned heavily on drag-and-drop data binding, whereas the WPF application let you get your hands a little dirtier as you interacted with the entities in code.

You learned a variety of ways to provide related data to the forms and allow users to make changes. You worked with Lists, learned about `ObjectResult`, and worked with the `ObservableCollection`, which is a critical class for WPF data binding.

Although not highly architected, the applications in this chapter went beyond typical "Hello World" introductory demos and gave you an opportunity to learn some of the nuances of data binding with entity objects. At the same time, you learned how to perform some good data-binding tricks in Windows Forms and WPF that will make life with entities a little easier.

This is a good start for data binding and a great way to whip together small applications.

In the next chapter, you will dive into a little more theory as we go into much more detail regarding how Object Services manages entity objects.

CHAPTER 10

Working with Object Services

Most of the work that you will do in the Entity Framework will involve the objects that are based on the entities in your Entity Data Model (EDM). Object Services is the part of the framework that creates and manages these objects. Although you have worked with Object Services in earlier chapters, you haven't yet seen the big picture. The API has a lot of tools that you can access directly to take charge of your entity objects.

This chapter is devoted to giving you a better understanding of the Object Services API: what it's responsible for, what it does under the covers, and some of the ways that you can take advantage of it. In this chapter, you'll also get a closer look at the `ObjectContext`, the most important Object Services class.

You will learn about how queries are processed and turned into objects, how these objects are managed during their life cycle, and how Object Services is responsible for the way entities are related to each other. You will see how the `ObjectQuery` and the new `ObjectSet` work and how they relate to LINQ to Entities queries under the covers. This chapter will also give you a better understanding of how Object Services manages an entity's state, beyond what you learned in Chapter 6.

As you become more familiar with the purpose, features, and implementation of Object Services, you will be better prepared to solve some of the challenges you will face as you move from using the "drag-and-drop" application-building features that Visual Studio provides to building enterprise applications where you need to have much more control over how all of the pieces of the application interact with one another.

Where Does Object Services Fit into the Framework?

Object Services is at the top of the Entity Framework stack, and as the name suggests, it works directly with instantiated objects. The namespace for this API is `System.Data.Objects`, and it provides all of the necessary functionality for generating and interacting with the objects that are shaped by the conceptual layer and are populated from a data store.

As shown in Figure 10-1, Object Services processes your LINQ to Entities and `ObjectQuery` queries, and materializes the query results as objects. Through its core `ObjectContext` class, Object Services also keeps track of the state of those returned objects and their relationships, maintains the metadata needed to compose queries on their properties, acts as a caching coordinator for those that are in-memory, and more.

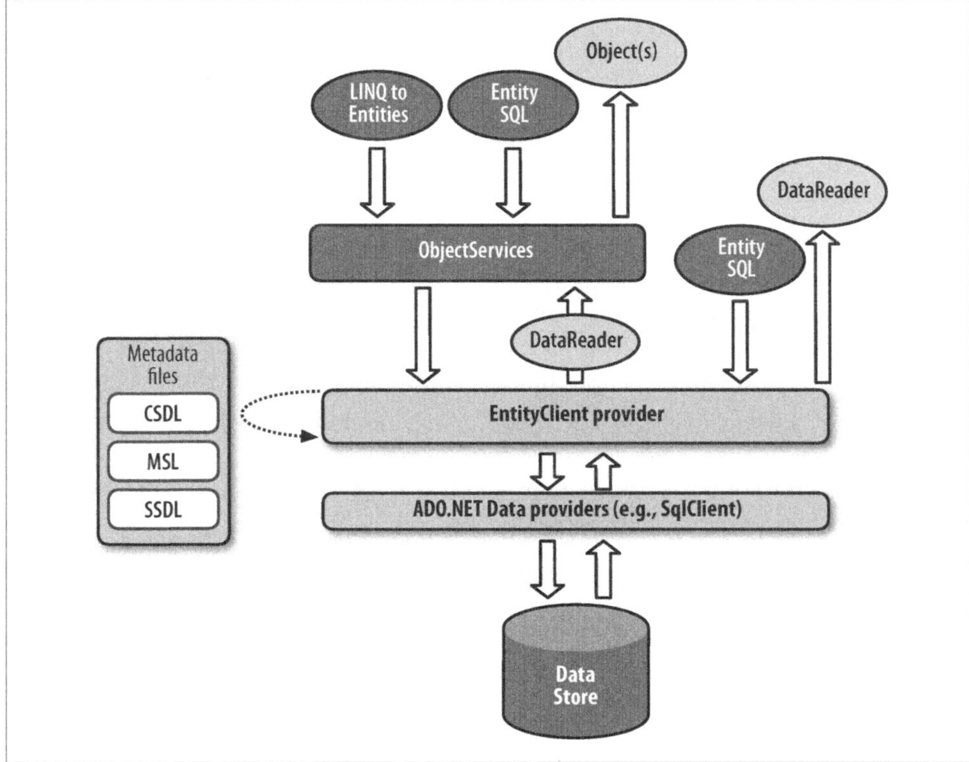

Figure 10-1. Object Services as it relates to the rest of the Entity Framework stack

One way to approach Object Services is to examine in turn each specific role it performs on behalf of the Entity Framework and your applications. These fall roughly into the following seven categories:

- Processing queries
- Materializing objects
- Managing objects
- Managing object relationships
- Managing object state
- Sending changes back to the database
- Implementing serialization, data binding, and other services

Processing Queries

Processing queries is arguably Object Services' most visible role. As you've seen, there are many ways to query data in the Entity Framework. All of Entity Framework's query mechanisms use Object Services except `EntityClient`, which is part of a lower-level API. Object Services uses `EntityClient`'s functionality on your behalf.

At a high level, query processing in the Entity Framework involves translating LINQ to Entities or Entity SQL queries into SQL queries that a data store can execute. At a lower level, Object Services first parses your query into a command tree of LINQ or Entity SQL query operators and functions, combined with the necessary entities and properties of your model. The command tree is a format the various providers that have been designed to work with the Entity Framework will be expecting. Next, the provider API (implemented over Oracle, SQL Server, MySQL, and other databases) transforms this tree into a new expression tree composed of the provider's SQL-specific dialect, operators, and functions, as well as the database's tables and columns, and then works out the specific query expression that will be recognized by the database.

Figure 10-2 shows the steps these queries take to get to the data store; a description of this process follows.

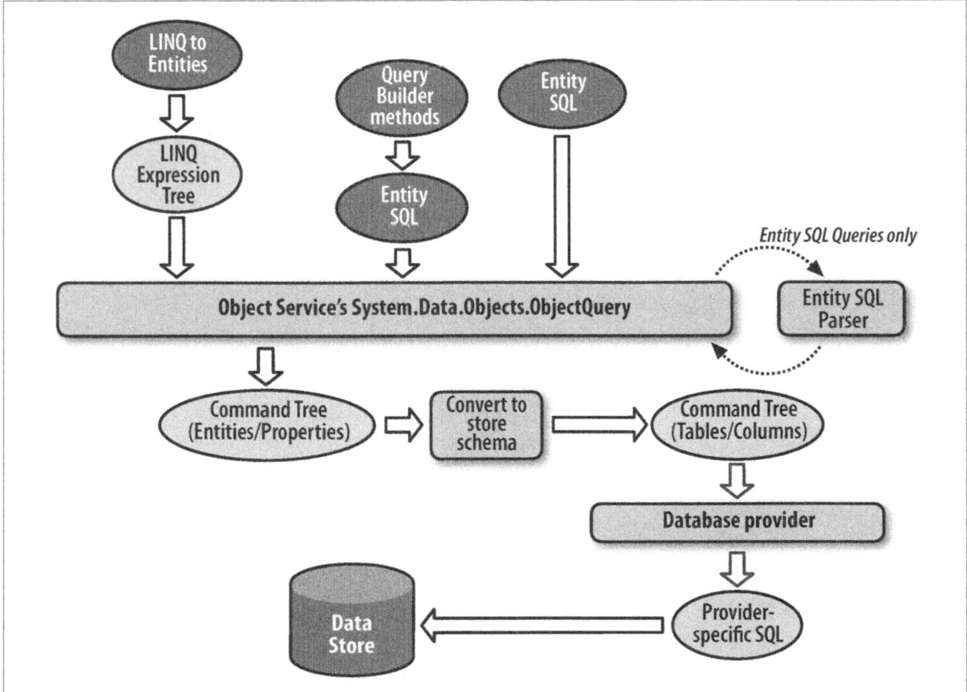

Figure 10-2. How the various query styles get to the data store

Parsing Queries: From Query to Command Tree to SQL

LINQ to Entities leverages the LINQ parser to begin processing the query, whereas `ObjectQuery` uses the Entity SQL parser. After each has gone through its first transition, they both follow the same path. Let's take a look at how each query is turned into the data store command.

Store command or *native command* refers to the command that the data store uses—for example, a T-SQL command for SQL Server.

From a LINQ to Entities query to a command tree
: LINQ to Entities starts its journey in the LINQ APIs and is then passed to the Object Services API. When you create a LINQ to Entities query, you are using syntax that is built into Visual Basic and C# that has enhancements added by the Entity Framework. LINQ converts this query into a LINQ expression tree, which deconstructs the query into its common operators and functions. The LINQ expression tree is then passed to Object Services, which converts the expression tree to a command tree.

From Entity SQL and query builder methods to a command tree
: The `ObjectQuery` class and the query builder methods that you've been using are part of Object Services. When building a query with `ObjectQuery`, you provide an Entity SQL string to express the query. If you use query builder methods, those methods will build an Entity SQL expression and an `ObjectQuery` for you. The `ObjectQuery` then passes the Entity SQL string to the entity client's parser, and this parser creates a command tree.

Whether a query began as a LINQ to Entities query or as an `ObjectQuery` with Entity SQL, the command trees are the same. From this point on, both types of queries follow the same processing path.

For the sake of comparison, when you query using `EntityClient`, its Entity SQL expression is also parsed into a command tree, enters the query path at this stage of the process, and is treated the same as the command trees that were created from LINQ to Entities and `ObjectQuery` queries.

From command trees to data store commands
: The newly created command tree is still expressed in terms of the entities in the model's conceptual layer. So at this point, the processor uses EDM mappings to transform the terms of the command tree into the tables, columns, and other objects of the database. This process might run through the command tree a number of times to simplify the demands made in the query before it comes up with an

equivalent of the database's tables and columns. Once this new version of the tree has been created, it is sent to the store provider (e.g., `SqlClient`), which will know how to convert the command tree into its native command text.

Entity Framework provider writers use the common schema of a command tree to create their functionality for generating SQL from the command tree. For example, the `SqlClient` provider will transform the tree into T-SQL that SQL Server can execute; an Oracle provider will transform the tree into a proper PL/SQL command.

Expression Trees and Command Trees

Expression tree and *command tree* are terms you will see when discussing LINQ and the Entity Framework. An expression tree is a way to represent code in a data structure. This is not limited to LINQ, but by creating an expression tree from a LINQ query, your application can identify particular elements of the query and process them accordingly. A command tree is a form of an expression tree that is used in the Entity Framework. It has a particular structure that can be depended on by the ADO.NET providers, which will need to read that command tree in order to translate the command into their native command syntax. If you'd like to learn more, see the MSDN documentation on expression trees at *http://msdn.microsoft.com/en-us/library/bb397951.aspx* and on command trees at *http://msdn.microsoft.com/en-us/library/ms689768(v=VS.85).aspx*.

Understanding Query Builder Methods

Writing Entity SQL is not always simple. Although the process is familiar to those who already write store commands, it is different enough that it will probably take some time before the syntax rolls naturally from your fingertips. Query builder methods can be quite useful, as the methods are discoverable through IntelliSense and take away some of the pain of remembering the exact syntax.

In Chapter 3, you built a variety of queries using the `CreateQuery` method with an Entity SQL expression as its parameter. You also used query builder methods. Take a look at Examples 10-1 and 10-2 to refresh your memory.

Example 10-1. CreateQuery with Entity SQL

```
var queryStr = "SELECT VALUE c " +
               "FROM PEF.Contacts AS c " +
               "WHERE c.FirstName='Robert'";
var contacts = context.CreateQuery<Contact>(queryStr);
```

Example 10-2. Query builder method with Entity SQL parameters

```
var contacts = context.Contacts
               .Where("it.FirstName = 'Robert'")
```

Both of the preceding examples define the same ObjectQuery (contacts), which searches for contacts whose first name is Robert. Neither will actually return results until something forces the query to be executed.

The query builder methods may still require that you write part of the expression, such as the Where predicate it.FirstName='Robert' in Example 10-2, but they are still a great deal easier than using the CreateQuery method. More importantly, they can help steer you away from some of the possible security pitfalls you might encounter when building Entity SQL. You'll learn more about security concerns in Chapter 20.

Query builder methods and EntitySets

Query builder methods are methods of ObjectQuery. How is it, then, that these methods are available from context.Contacts? The classes generated from the model reveal the answer to this question. The preceding queries are based on the first model you built and used in Chapters 3 and 5. context is a variable that represents the PEF ObjectContext, which is the wrapper class that serves up the EntitySets of the various classes in the model. (In Chapter 3 this was called SampleEntities, but in Chapter 5 we simplified it to PEF.) Example 10-3 shows the declaration of this class in the classes generated from the model.

Example 10-3. Declaration of the ObjectContext class

VB
```
Public Partial Class PEF
    Inherits ObjectContext
```

C#
```
public partial class PEF : ObjectContext
```

This class has a property for each EntitySet—for example, Contacts. Each of these properties returns an ObjectSet(Of T)/ObjectSet<T> of the entity type it wraps. ObjectSet is a new type in Entity Framework and can be thought of as a strongly typed EntitySet, which provides collection-like capabilities such as Add and Remove. The Contacts property returns an ObjectSet of Contact entities, as shown in Example 10-4.

Example 10-4. The ObjectContext.Contacts property

VB
```
Public ReadOnly Property Contacts() As ObjectSet(Of Contact)
  Get
    If (_Contacts Is Nothing) Then
      _Contacts = MyBase.CreateObjectSet(Of Contact)("Contacts")
    End If
    Return _Contacts
  End Get
End Property
```

C#
```
public ObjectSet<Contact> Contacts
{
  get
  {
    if ((_Contacts == null))
    {
```

```
            _Contacts = base.CreateObjectSet<Contact>("Contacts");
        }
        return _Contacts;
    }
}
```

As I mentioned in an earlier chapter, `ObjectSet` inherits `ObjectQuery`, and therefore it has the methods and properties of an `ObjectQuery`, including the query builder methods: `Select`, `Where`, `GroupBy`, and so forth.

Even as you build LINQ queries, you are querying against these `ObjectSet`s. Therefore, you are able to leverage the `ObjectQuery` method, `Include`, within a LINQ to Entities query. `ObjectQuery`, and therefore `ObjectSet`, also implements `IEnumerable`, which is why you can append LINQ methods to it as well.

From query builder methods to Entity SQL expressions

Object Services uses the query builder methods and any expressions, such as what is contained in a `Where` clause, to build an Entity SQL expression. The result is the same as what you'd get had you explicitly created an `ObjectQuery` and typed in the Entity SQL yourself. You can then use the expression to create an `ObjectQuery` in the same way you would use a `CreateQuery` method.

> **How Can You Tell the Difference Between LINQ Methods and Query Builder Methods?**
>
> LINQ's method syntax looks very similar to the query builder methods, except for one big difference: the parameters. The parameters of a LINQ method are lambda expressions, whereas the parameters of the query builder methods are Entity SQL string expressions. A number of methods have the same name: `Where`, `OrderBy`, `Select`, and others. The compiler uses the parameters to determine which path to go down, in much the same way that the .NET compiler handles overloaded methods anywhere else.

Combining LINQ methods and query builder methods

Query builder methods return an `ObjectQuery`. You can use a LINQ to Entities method on an `ObjectQuery`. Therefore, it's possible to compose a query such as the following:

```
context.Contacts.Where("it.FirstName='Robert'").Take(10)
```

The first part, `context.Contacts.Where("it.FirstName='Robert'")`, returns an `ObjectQuery`. Then, LINQ's `Take` method is appended to that. `Take` returns an `IQueryable`. The type of the query that results will be a `System.LINQ.IQueryable`—in other words, a LINQ to Entities query.

You can't go the other way, though, adding query builder methods to a LINQ method. For instance, `context.Contacts.Take(10)` returns a `System.LINQ.IQueryable`. You can use query builder methods only on an `ObjectQuery`. If you wanted to append a query builder method to this `IQueryable`, you would first have to cast the LINQ query to an `ObjectQuery` and then append the method. Casting a LINQ to Entities query to `ObjectQuery` is possible because `ObjectQuery` implements `IQueryable`, which is beneficial in a number of scenarios, as you'll see as you move forward in this chapter.

`ObjectQuery` implements more than just `IQueryable`. It also implements `IOrderedQueryable`, `IEnumerable`, and `IListSource`.

Analyzing a Query with ObjectQuery Methods and Properties

You have already seen some of the members of `ObjectQuery`, such as the query builder methods and the `Include` method. Additional methods and properties are available that will help you better understand the role of `ObjectQuery`. Here are some that you can see when inspecting an `ObjectQuery` in the debugger.

Figure 10-3 shows an `ObjectQuery` in debug mode with its properties and the Results View. Figure 10-4 shows a LINQ to Entities query in the debugger; as you can see, LINQ to Entities exposes the results directly, but also contains an `ObjectQuery`. The only obvious evidence that it is a LINQ to Entities query is in the Type column (circled).

Name	Value
contactsOQ	{System.Data.Objects.ObjectQuery<BAGA.Contact>}
base	{System.Data.Objects.ObjectQuery<BAGA.Contact>}
CommandText	"SELECT VALUE it\r\nFROM (\r\n[BAEntities].[Contacts]\r\n)
Context	{BAGA.BAEntities}
EnablePlanCaching	true
MergeOption	AppendOnly
Parameters	{System.Data.Objects.ObjectParameterCollection}
Non-Public members	
Results View	Expanding the Results View will enumerate the IEnumerable
Name	"it"
Static members	
Non-Public members	
Results View	Expanding the Results View will enumerate the IEnumerable

Figure 10-3. The various properties of ObjectQuery as seen in debug mode

Name	Value	Type
contactsL2E	{System.Data.Objects.ObjectQuery<BAGA.Contact>}	System.Linq.IQueryable<BAGA.Contact> {System.Data.Obje
base	{System.Data.Objects.ObjectQuery<BAGA.Contact>}	System.Data.Objects.ObjectQuery {System.Data.Objects.Ob
CommandText	""	string
Context	{BAGA.BAEntities}	System.Data.Objects.ObjectContext {BAGA.BAEntities}
EnablePlanCaching	true	bool
MergeOption	AppendOnly	System.Data.Objects.MergeOption
Parameters	{System.Data.Objects.ObjectParameterCollection}	System.Data.Objects.ObjectParameterCollection
Non-Public members		
Results View	Expanding the Results View will enumerate the IEnumerab	
Name	"it"	string
Non-Public members		
Results View	Expanding the Results View will enumerate the IEnumerab	

Figure 10-4. The circled IQueryable type, which tells us that this is a LINQ to Entities query

Remember that if you want to get to `ObjectQuery` properties and methods from a LINQ to Entities query, you can cast the LINQ to Entities query to `ObjectQuery`.

Let's take a closer look at four especially helpful `ObjectQuery` methods.

ObjectQuery.ToTraceString

`ToTraceString` displays the native store command that will be created from your query. Figure 10-5 shows some code that calls `ToTraceString` and the value the method returns at runtime.

Example 10-5 demonstrates casting a LINQ to Entities query to an `ObjectQuery` in order to call the `ToTraceString` method.

Example 10-5. Casting a LINQ to Entities query to use ObjectQuery methods such as ToTraceString

VB
```
Dim contacts = From c In context.Contacts
               Where c.FirstName = "Robert"
Dim str = CType(contacts,ObjectQuery).ToTraceString
```

C#
```
var contacts = from c in context.Contacts
               where c.FirstName == "Robert"
               select c;
var str = ((ObjectQuery)contacts).ToTraceString();
```

If your query expression includes an executing method such as First or Single, these won't be included in the `ToTraceString` result but rest assured, they will be part of the query executed on the server.

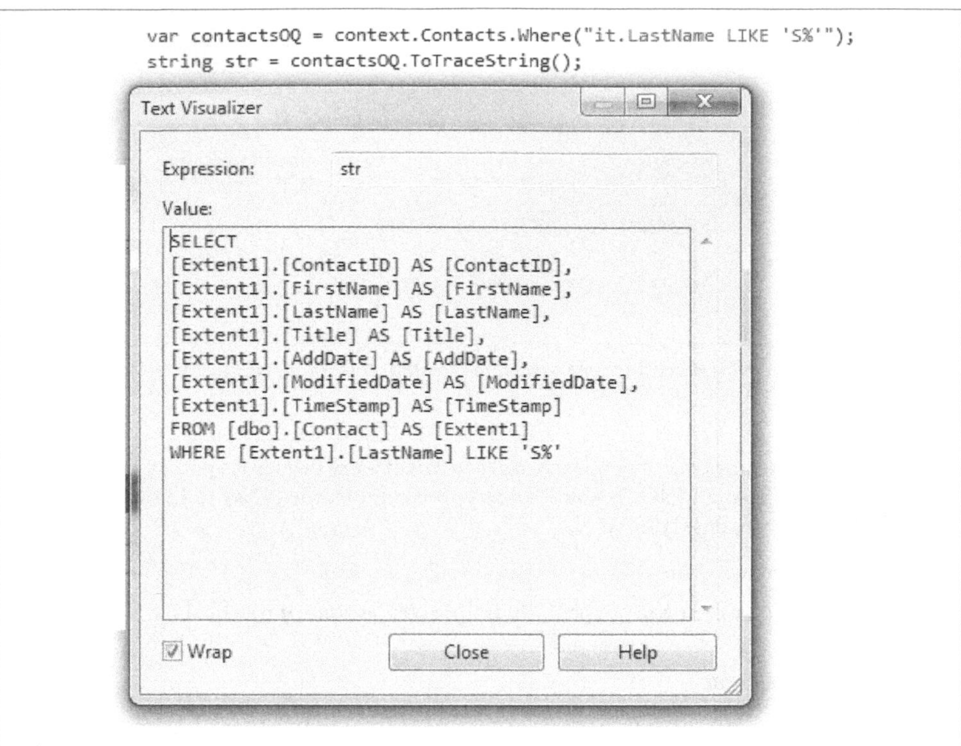
var contactsOQ = context.Contacts.Where("it.LastName LIKE 'S%'");
string str = contactsOQ.ToTraceString();
Text Visualizer
Expression:
str
Value:
SELECT
[Extent1].[ContactID] AS [ContactID],
[Extent1].[FirstName] AS [FirstName],
[Extent1].[LastName] AS [LastName],
[Extent1].[Title] AS [Title],
[Extent1].[AddDate] AS [AddDate],
[Extent1].[ModifiedDate] AS [ModifiedDate],
[Extent1].[TimeStamp] AS [TimeStamp]
FROM [dbo].[Contact] AS [Extent1]
WHERE [Extent1].[LastName] LIKE 'S%'
Wrap
Close
Help

Figure 10-5. Viewing the native command that will be generated from an ObjectQuery using the ToTraceString method while debugging

ObjectQuery.CommandText

As with ADO.NET, `CommandText` refers to the query string being passed in for execution. Because of the different ways in which you can build queries with the Entity Framework, `CommandText` is represented in a variety of ways, as shown in Table 10-1.

Table 10-1. CommandText values of various types of queries

Query method	Query	ObjectQuery.CommandText
`ObjectQuery`/`ObjectSet`	`Context.Contacts`	`[Contacts]`

`ObjectQuery` with Entity SQL	`context.CreateQuery<Contact>`
	`("SELECT VALUE c`
	`FROM PEF.Contacts AS c`
	`WHERE`
	`c.FirstName='Robert'")`
		`SELECT VALUE c`
		`FROM PEF.Contacts AS c`
		`WHERE`
		`c.FirstName='Robert'`

Query builder	`context.Contacts`
	`.Where("it.FirstName =`
	`'Robert'")`
	`.OrderBy("it.LastName")`
		`SELECT VALUE it`
		`FROM (`
		`SELECT VALUE it`
		`FROM (`
		`[Contacts]`
		`) AS it`
		`WHERE`
		`it.FirstName = 'Robert'`

Query method	Query	ObjectQuery.CommandText
		`) AS it ORDER BY it.LastName`
LINQ to Entities	`from c in context.Contacts where c.FirstName == "Robert" select c`	(empty)

ObjectQuery.Parameters

In Chapter 3, you saw how to build a parameterized query. Any parameters that you created then will be listed in the `ObjectQuery`'s `Parameters` property.

ObjectQuery.Context

The `Context` property refers to the instantiated `ObjectContext` from which the `ObjectQuery` is being run. The `ObjectContext` not only coordinates the execution of queries and provides the mechanism for `SavingChanges` back to the data store, but it also plays a much bigger role as the manager of objects in memory.

Executing Queries with ToList, ToArray, First or Single

So far, the query has been defined but no data retrieval has actually occurred. Query execution occurs when the Entity Framework retrieves the data from the store. Queries can be executed implicitly or explicitly.

In previous chapters, you enumerated over the results of a query (using VB's `For Each` or C#'s `foreach`). Enumerating over a query will force a query to execute implicitly. You don't need to specifically say "go get the data." The fact that you are attempting to work with the query results will cause the Entity Framework to do that for you.

Another way to force execution is to append the `ToList` or `ToArray` LINQ method to a query. Example 10-6 appends `ToList` to the `CreateQuery` method to execute the query immediately and return a list of `Contact` entities.

Example 10-6. Executing a query with ToList

```
List<Contact> contacts = context.CreateQuery<Contact>(queryStr).ToList();
```

A big difference between using `ToList` or `ToArray` rather than enumerating is that these methods will force the complete results to be returned all at once. When enumerating, depending on what you are doing with each result as you get to it, it may take awhile before you get to the end of the results. Until that time, the database connection will remain open.

Like the `ToList` and ToArray methods, the `Single` and `First` methods will also force a query to execute. Their counterparts, `SingleOrDefault` and `FirstOrDefault`, also cause execution. You learned about the differences between these four methods in Chapter 4.

Executing Queries with the Execute Method

As you learned in Chapter 9, `ObjectQuery` has an `Execute` method, which you can also use to force execution, but it requires a parameter to define `MergeOptions` for the objects that result, as shown in the following code:

```
var contacts = context.Contacts.Execute(MergeOption.AppendOnly);
```

`MergeOption` is also a property of the `ObjectQuery`, so you can set the value directly even when you're not using the `Execute` method.

Four merge options influence how newly returned objects impact objects that may already exist in memory and be tracked by the context.

`AppendOnly` is the default, and it will be used when you don't set the option directly while executing queries *without* the `Execute` method. However, with `Execute`, you must set this parameter, even if you just want the `AppendOnly` default.

You'll see shortly how to use `MergeOptions` when you are executing queries without using the `Execute` method.

`Execute` returns a type called `ObjectResult`. The `ObjectResult` streams the results to whatever is consuming it. Using `Execute` is beneficial in some scenarios, but in others, its limitations, such as the fact that you can enumerate over `ObjectResults` only once because it is a stream, might be a problem.

Because `MergeOption` impacts what happens with the returned data, its purpose will make more sense after we have discussed some additional topics. We'll return to `MergeOption` in more detail later in this chapter.

Overriding a Default Connection with ObjectContext.Connection

By default, `ObjectContext` will use the `EntityConnectionString` defined in the application's *app.config* file that has the same name as the name of the context's `EntityContainer`. For example, when the `EntityContainer` name is `BAEntities`, Object Services will search for a connection string named `BAEntities` in the *app.config* file. If no matching connection string is found and no override is provided, an exception will be thrown at runtime. The exception reads, "The specified named connection is either not found in the configuration, not intended to be used with the EntityClient provider, or not valid."

The default generated context (BAEntities, in your case) has four constructor overloads so you can designate a connection in a variety of ways. One way to override the default is to supply a different connection string name in the constructor of the `ObjectContext`. This string needs to be available in the *app.config* file as well. Example 10-7 uses the name of the connection string named `connStringName` to create an `ObjectContext`.

Example 10-7. Specifying which EntityConnection string to use for a context

```
var context = new BAEntities("Name=connStringName");
```

You can't use the connection string, nor can you use the connection string name on its own. You must include `"Name="` with the connection string name in the parameter.

Another way to override the default is to supply an `EntityConnection` object instead. This is the same `EntityConnection` that is used with the `EntityClient` provider. By creating an explicit `EntityConnection`, you can manipulate that `EntityConnection` prior to instantiating a context with it. Example 10-8 creates the `EntityConnection` but does not do anything special with it. You will learn a lot more about manipulating an `EntityConnection` in Chapter 16.

Example 10-8. Explicitly creating a new EntityConnection to use with a context

```
var econn = new EntityConnection("name=connStringName");
var context = new BAEntities(econn);
```

The `EntityConnection` gives `ObjectContext` three important pieces of information: the model metadata location, database connection information, and the name of the ADO.NET data provider. Example 10-9 shows the `EntityConnection` string for the BreakAway model used in the preceding chapter.

Example 10-9. The EntityConnection string in app.config for the BreakAway model

```
<add name="BAEntities" connectionString=
"metadata=res://*/BAModel.csdl|res://*/BAModel.ssdl|res://*/BAModel.msl;
 provider=System.Data.SqlClient;
 provider connection string=&quot;Data Source=.;Initial Catalog=BreakAway;
                                    Integrated Security=True;
                                    MultipleActiveResultSets=True&quot;"
 providerName="System.Data.EntityClient" />
```

Following are descriptions of each of the `EntityConnection` string attributes:

`metadata`
: The `metadata` attribute, which points to the Conceptual Schema Definition Layer (CSDL), Store Schema Definition Layer (SSDL), and Mapping Schema Layer (MSL) files, tells the context where to find these files. They can be embedded into an

assembly (the default), or you can place them somewhere in the filesystem. The context needs access to the metadata files to begin the process of transforming the query into the store command.

`provider`
: The `provider` element of an `EntityConnection` string is the name of the data provider (e.g., `System.Data.SqlClient`). This tells the Entity Framework to which data provider to send the command tree to assist with query processing.

`provider connection string`
: This is the database connection string. `ObjectContext` will pass this database connection string onto the `EntityClient` layer so that it will be able to connect to the database and execute the command.

`ProviderName`
: `ProviderName` is not part of the `EntityConnectionString`, but rather is metadata for the connection. By default, Entity Framework will use its own `EntityClient` API to build the store queries and interact with the database. However, you can override this with your own API by defining it dynamically in the connection metadata.

The `ProviderName` attribute is a useful extensibility point in the Entity Framework. Jaroslaw Kowalski has a great blog post on this advanced topic. The blog post also points to some fantastic samples on creating a server-side tracing and caching provider on Microsoft's Code Gallery (see *http://blogs.msdn.com/jkowalski/archive/2009/06/11/tracing-and-caching-in-entity-framework-available-on-msdn-code-gallery.aspx*).

Handling Command Execution with EntityClient

So, what's next? You've got your `ObjectQuery` all set. You know the `ObjectQuery` will do all of the work to create a command tree. Somehow the command tree gets handed off to the `EntityClient` provider along with the database connection string provided by the `ObjectContext`. If you dig into the Entity Framework assemblies using a tool such as Red Gate's .NET Reflector, you will find that the `ObjectContext` calls on `EntityClient` to do the job of creating the connection and executing the command on the data store.

As you saw with the `EntityClient` queries in Chapter 3, `EntityClient` returns an `EntityDataReader`, not objects.

Materializing Objects

After `EntityClient` retrieves the database results into an `EntityDataReader`, it passes the `EntityDataReader` back up the stack to Object Services, which transforms, or *materializes*, the results into entity objects. The data in `EntityDataReader` is already structured to match the conceptual layer, so it's just a matter of those contents being cast to objects.

If the query used a projection and there is no matching entity, the results are materialized into DbDataRecords (or anonymous types when a LINQ to Entities query was used) instead of entity objects, as you saw in many of the queries you wrote earlier.

Most of what happens here goes on- under the covers, and therefore there is not much to see. There is a single event, introduced in .NET 4, called ObjectContext.ObjectMaterialized. This event gives you access to each entity just after it has been created from the query results. You'll learn about this event when customizing the entity classes in Chapter 11.

Figure 10-6 demonstrates the path a query takes from the command tree to the database and then back to Object Services to be materialized into objects.

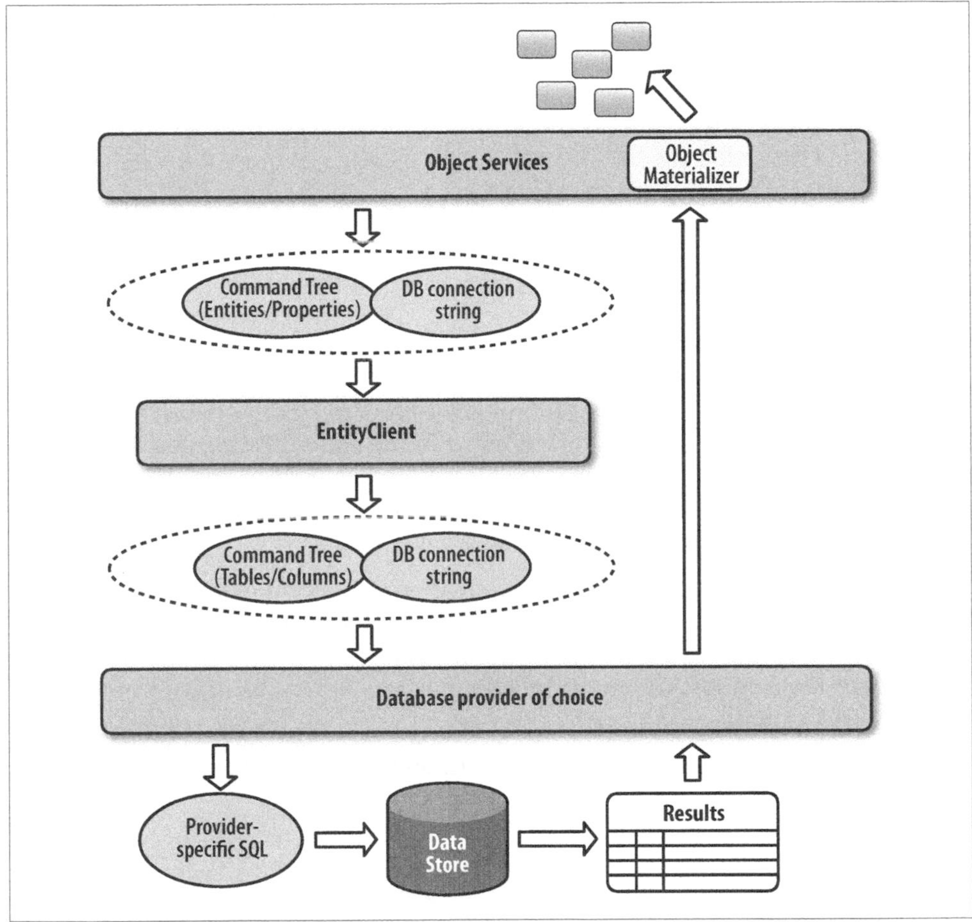

Figure 10-6. The EntityClient providing the command execution functions for an ObjectQuery

Managing Object State

In Chapter 6, you learned that `ObjectContext` manages the state information for each of its objects. You were also introduced to the `ObjectStateEntry` classes that `ObjectContext` maintains—one for each entity in its cache. When your associations are defined without the benefit of foreign key scalar properties, Entity Framework reverts to the .NET 3.5 way of defining associations and in that case it creates `ObjectStateEntries` to represent relationships as well.

When objects are returned from queries, `ObjectContext` creates these `ObjectStateEntry` objects, in effect, caching references to the entities. In these state entries, `ObjectContext` not only keeps track of all of these entities, but also keeps track of other information regarding those entities, including their state, their original and current values, and their relationships to one another.

This section focuses on the default behavior of the `ObjectContext`. In the section "Taking Control of ObjectState" on page 259, you will learn how to override this default behavior.

Using EntityKey to Manage Objects

The context uses the `EntityKey` as its link between the `ObjectStateEntry` and the entity.

`EntityKey` is a critical class for keeping track of individual entities. It contains the entity's identity information, which could be from a single property, such as `ContactID`, or could be a composite key that depends on a number of the entity's properties. Figure 10-7 shows an `EntityKey` for a BreakAway `Contact`. It says that this entity belongs to the `BAEntities` container and to the `Contacts` `EntitySet`, and that its key property is composed of only one property, `ContactID`, whose value is `1`.

The `ObjectContext` reads the `EntityKey` information to perform many of its functions. For example, it is used when the context merges objects, locates entities in the cache, or creates `EntityReference` values. The type information, e.g., Contact, is not included in the `EntityKey`. Instead, the `EntitySetName` indicates to which `EntitySet` the object with this key belongs, e.g., Contacts.

This little class is one of the most important classes in the Entity Framework. It acts as an object's passport throughout the application's runtime.

⊟ EntityKey	"EntitySet=Contacts;ContactID=6"
EntityContainerName	"BAEntities"
⊟ EntityKeyValues	{System.Data.EntityKeyMember[1]}
⊟ [0]	{[ContactID, 6]}
Key	"ContactID"
Value	6
⊞ Non-Public members	
EntitySetName	"Contacts"
IsTemporary	false
⊞ Static members	
⊞ Non-Public members	
EntityState	Unchanged

Figure 10-7. An object's EntityKey, which includes critical identity information for each object

Merging Results into the Cache with MergeOptions

By default, anytime the `ObjectContext` performs a query, if any of the returned objects already exist in the cache the newly returned copies of those objects are ignored. The `EntityKeys` are instrumental in enabling this to happen. The `EntityKeys` of the objects returned from a query are checked, and if an object with the same `EntityKey` (within the same `EntitySet`; e.g., `Contacts`) already exists in the cache, the existing object is left untouched. You can control this using an `ObjectQuery` property called `MergeOption`, which was introduced briefly earlier in this chapter. The four possibilities for `MergeOption` are as follows:

`AppendOnly` *(default)*
: Add only new entities to the cache. Existing entities are not refreshed with the data returned by the query.

`OverwriteChanges`
: Replace the current values of existing entities with values coming from the store, even if the in-memory entity has been edited.

`PreserveChanges`
: Replace original values of existing entities with values coming from the store. The current values of existing entities are not refreshed from the database, and therefore any changes the user makes will remain intact. This will make more sense after we discuss state management later in this chapter. If you use it without fully comprehending its behavior, this option could have some subtle, but unwelcome, effects on how updates are reasoned about when it is time to save changes to the database.

`NoTracking`
: Objects returned by the query will not be managed by the context, will not have their changes tracked, and will not be involved in `SaveChanges`. Again, this will make more sense after we discuss state management.

There are two ways to define MergeOptions. The first is to use the MergeOption method of ObjectQuery, as shown in the following code:

```
var contactsQuery = context.CreateQuery<Contact>(queryString);
contactsQuery.MergeOption = MergeOption.PreserveChanges;
```

The second way to define a MergeOption is as a parameter of ObjectQuery.Execute, as you saw earlier in this chapter.

Developers often ask if the query takes into account the objects that are already in memory. The answer is no. What this means is that if you execute a query that returns 100 Contacts and then execute another query that returns the same 100 contacts, Entity Framework will indeed execute the query, pull back all of the results into an EntityDataReader, and then decide whether or not to materialize the objects as it reads through them and determines their EntityKeys. If the MergeOption is AppendOnly, that's a big waste of resources. You should be aware of this as you are designing your applications and be considerate of how and when queries are executed.

Remember that you can cast a LINQ to Entities query to an ObjectQuery and use ObjectQuery methods, including MergeOption, as you did with ToTraceString earlier in this chapter:

```
var contactsQuery = context.Contacts.Where(c => c.FirstName == "Robert");
((ObjectQuery)contactsQuery).MergeOption = MergeOption.PreserveChanges;
var results = contactsQuery.ToList();
```

The context maintains ObjectStateEntry objects whether your entity is one that inherits from EntityObject or one that is a simpler class that does not inherit from EntityObject. You'll learn more about how Entity Framework supports classes that do not inherit from EntityObject in Chapter 13, which covers Plain Old CLR Objects (POCO) support.

Inspecting ObjectStateEntry

Let's look more closely at the ObjectStateEntry classes that track the entity objects.

You can retrieve an ObjectStateEntry by passing an entity (again, this works with a POCO object as well as with an EntityObject) or its EntityKey to the ObjectContext.ObjectStateManager.GetObjectStateEntry method.

GetObjectStateEntry has a sibling method, TryGetObjectStateEntry. In this chapter, you will get a high-level look at the ObjectStateManager and ObjectStateEntry classes. Chapter 21 will dig much deeper into these classes.

Debugging the `ObjectStateEntry` won't give you much insight into the object, however, the C# debugger does allow you to look at many more of the private members of `ObjectStateEntry` than does the VB debugger. Figure 10-8 shows the watch window for the `Contact` whose `ContactID` is `6`.

Name	Value
ose	{System.Data.Objects.EntityEntry}
[System.Data.Objects.EntityEntry]	{System.Data.Objects.EntityEntry}
Entity	{BAGA.Contact}
EntityKey	"EntitySet=Contacts;ContactID=6"
EntitySet	{Contacts}
IsRelationship	false
ObjectStateManager	{System.Data.Objects.ObjectStateManager}
RelationshipManager	{System.Data.Objects.DataClasses.RelationshipManager}
State	Unchanged
Non-Public members	

Figure 10-8. The ObjectStateEntry for a Contact whose ContactID is 6

The more interesting information is returned from some of the methods of the entry: `CurrentValues` and `OriginalValues`. These methods return an array of the values for each scalar property. If you want to get a particular value, you will need to know the index position of the property you are seeking; for example, you can return the original value of `FirstName` by calling `contactEntry.OriginalValues(1)` in VB or `contactEntry.OriginalValues[1]` in C#. The value will come back as an object; so, depending on your goal, you may want to cast the return value to the desired type.

Metadata about the type is available from the `ObjectStateEntry`, so it is possible to find values by using the property names. This will take a bit more effort, and you'll learn about navigating around these entries in Chapter 21.

Figures 10-9 and 10-10 use a custom utility to show the `ObjectStateEntry` information for an entity before and after some changes have been made. I call the utility the ObjectStateEntry Visualizer and you will be writing it yourself in Chapter 21.

What is most important to understand right now is that `CurrentValues` and `OriginalValues` are tracked, but it is the `ObjectContext`, not the entity, which maintains this information.

Maintaining EntityState

In the preceding three figures, you may have noticed that the state of the entity was displayed. In Figure 10-8, you can see the `ObjectStateEntry`'s `State` property in the debug view. In the custom viewer shown in Figures 10-9 and 10-10, the contact's current state is displayed. It begins as `Unchanged`, and then, after the contact has been edited, the state is `Modified`.

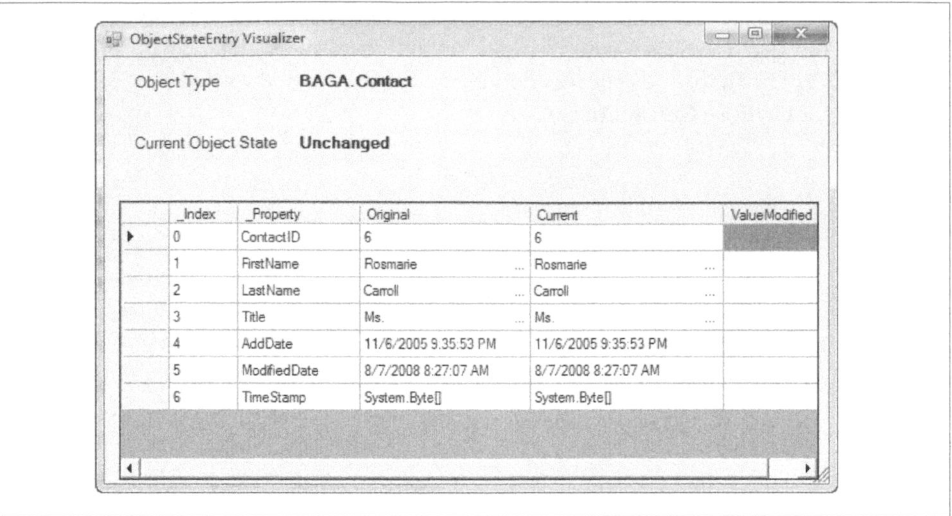

Figure 10-9. Inspecting information from an unchanged entity's ObjectStateEntry

There are five `EntityState` enums that define the possible state of an entity:

`Added`
: An entity that was (most likely) created at runtime was added to the context. When `SaveChanges` is called, Object Services will create an `Insert` command for this entity.

`Deleted`
: An entity managed by the cache and has been marked for deletion. When `SaveChanges` is called, Object Services will create a `Delete` command for this entity.

`Detached`
: The `ObjectContext` is not tracking the entity.

`Modified`
: The entity has been changed since it was attached to the context.

`Unchanged`
: No changes have been made to the entity since it was attached to the context.

The `ObjectContext` changes the value of `ObjectStateEntry.State` based on notifications from `EntityObject`. When we look at POCOs in Chapter 13, you'll learn that the context has a way to discover information about entities that do have the ability to send notifications. For now, we'll focus on the `EntityObject` entities that you have been using thus far.

`EntityObject` implements the `IEntityWithChangeTracker` interface, so the default entities that you are currently working with also implement this interface. As you will see in Chapter 11, the `PropertyChanging` and `PropertyChanged`events in the generated model classes represent part of the change-tracking functionality. When an object's property is changed, the `IEntityWithChangeTracker` interface reports this change to the designa-

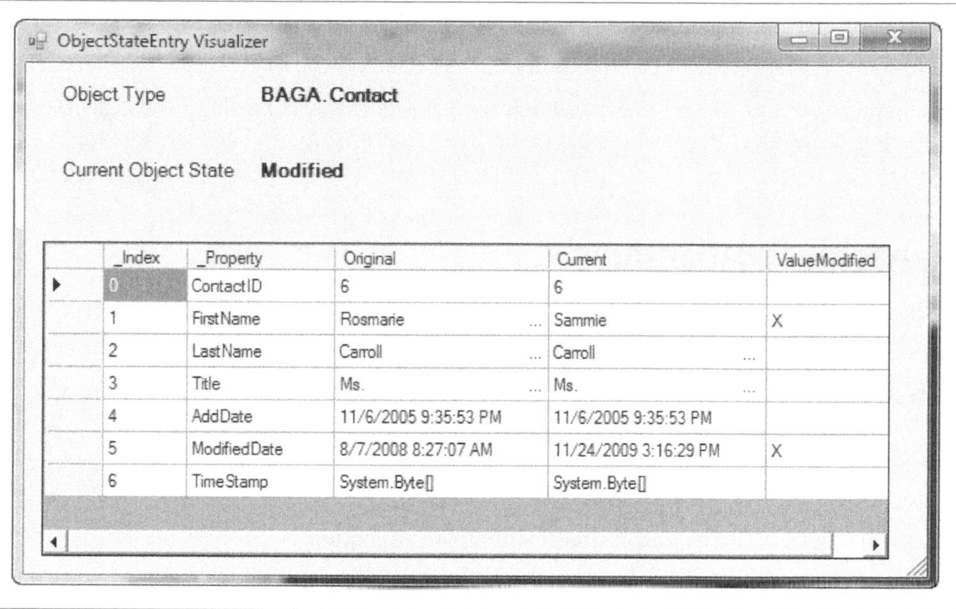

Figure 10-10. The ObjectStateEntry of the same object shown in Figure 10-9 after changes have been made to the entity

ted `ChangeTracker`—that is, the current `ObjectContext`, which updates the appropriate Current value of that object's `ObjectStateEntry`. For this to work, the object implements internal functions from `IEntityWithChangeTracker`.

Objects Are Not Required to Be in the ObjectContext Cache

Objects can be in memory without being managed by the `ObjectContext`. That means that although the object instance exists, the `ObjectContext` is not aware of the object. You can have an `EntityObject` in application memory that is not being tracked by the context, by doing any one of the following:

- Explicitly instruct the `ObjectQuery` to return objects without attaching them to the cache. You can do this by setting `ObjectQuery.MergeOption` to the `NoTracking` option.
- Use the `ObjectContext.Detach` method to explicitly detach an object from the `ObjectContext`.
- Create a new object in memory. Unless or until you explicitly attach or add the object to the `ObjectContext` or to an object that is already in the cache (e.g., adding a `Reservation` to a `Customer`'s `Reservation EntityCollection` property or adding a `Customer` as a `Reservation`'s `CustomerReference`), it is not part of the cache.
- Deserialize entities that were serialized. Although the act of serializing an entity or entities does not detach entities from their `ObjectContext`, the entities that are in

the serialized package will not be attached to an `ObjectContext` when they are deserialized.

The `EntityState` of an object that is not in the cache is always `Detached`.

Chapters 19 and 21 will provide much more insight into controlling the `ObjectContext` and the effect that caching has on entities' relationships and change tracking.

Managing Relationships

Although objects know how to traverse from one to another, it is the `ObjectContext` that binds related objects together.

This may not be evident, even if you perform a query that explicitly retrieves a graph, such as in the following:

```
context.Customers.Include("Reservations.Trip")
                 .Include("Reservations.Payments")
```

Figure 10-11 depicts the graph that results from this query.

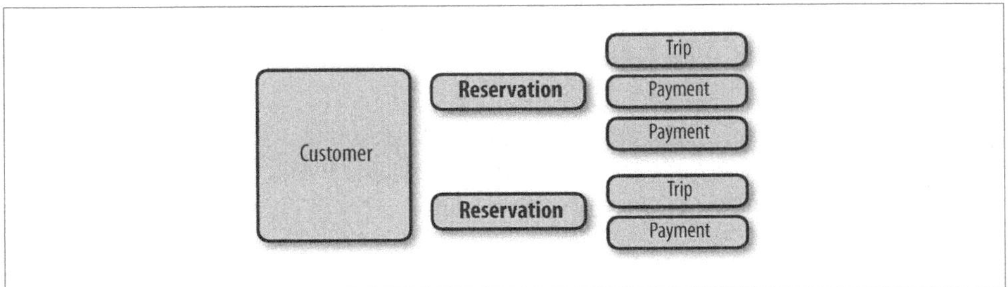

Figure 10-11. A Customer graph including Reservations and other related objects

In fact, although it may look like your query is shaping the returned data, the object graph is shaped by the `ObjectContext` after the objects have been materialized and attached to the context. The `ObjectContext`'s ability to identify and implicitly join related entities is referred to as its *relationship span*.

This chapter aims to give you a high-level understanding of relationships. We will cover them much more thoroughly in Chapter 19.

You can explicitly combine related entities in code. Here's an example of code that creates a new `Reservation` object and then adds it to a `Customer`'s `Reservations` property. The `Reservations` property is an `EntityCollection`, so this code adds the new `Reservation` not to the `Customer`, but to the collection:

```
var reservation = new BAGA.Reservation
   { ReservationDate = System.DateTime.Today,
     TripID = 132 };
cust.Reservations.Add(reservation);
```

However, if you were to perform queries that returned `Customers` and `Reservations` separately, the `ObjectContext` would identify those that are related and make it possible for you to traverse through `Customer.Reservations` or `Reservation.Customer` with no effort. The `ObjectContext` takes care of that for you through its relationship span capability.

`EntityCollection` properties, such as `Addresses` and `Reservations`, are essentially read-only. Because of the way `ObjectContext` works, you can't attach an `EntityCollection` directly to an entity. In other words, if you had a collection of `Addresses` that belong to a contact, you can't just call `Contact.Addresses=myAddressCollection`. Instead, you must add the `Address` entities to the `Contact.Addresses` entity collection one at a time using `context.Addresses.Add(myAddress)`.

The compiler will allow you to set an `EntityCollection` value; however, at runtime, an exception will be thrown.

Chapter 19 is devoted to the ins and outs of relationships in the Entity Framework.

Attaching and Detaching Objects from the ObjectContext

I have mentioned the topic of attaching and detaching objects a number of times in this chapter. Objects whose changes and relationships are being managed by the context are considered to be *attached* to the context. `EntityObject` instances that are in memory but are not being managed by the context are considered to be *detached*, and their `EntityState` value is `Detached`.

Attaching and detaching can happen implicitly thanks to the internal functionality of the Entity Framework, or explicitly by calling methods to add, attach, or detach in your code.

You have seen that an object that is attached to an `ObjectContext` has its state and its relationships managed by that context. You also know that an object that is detached has no state. And you have dealt with many objects in the coding samples that were automatically attached to the `ObjectContext` as the result of executing a query; you even added an object or two using the `Add` and `Attach` methods. Now you will look a little more closely at explicitly attaching and detaching objects.

ObjectContext.AddObject and ObjectSet.AddObject

Use the `AddObject` method to add newly created objects that do not exist in the store. The entity will get an automatically generated temporary `EntityKey` and its

EntityState will be set to Added. Therefore, when SaveChanges is called, it will be clear to the Entity Framework that this entity needs to be inserted into the database.

The preferred method is to use ObjectSet.AddObject, which is new to .NET 4. The context needs to know which EntitySet the object belongs to. Since the ObjectSet is an instance of the EntitySet, the necessary information is available.

```
context.Contacts.AddObject(contact);
```

ObjectContext.AddObject was the only option in .NET 3.5 and it exists mostly for backward compatibility. It requires that you pass in the EntitySet name as a string because there is no other way to determine which EntitySet the object belongs to:

```
var contact = new Contact();
contact.LastName = "Lerman";
context.AddObject("Contacts",contact);
```

If you add an object which has an EntityKey, the context will set EntityKeyValues of the EntityKey to null. This is different from the first version of Entity Framework, which would throw an exception at runtime when you attempted to add an object with an EntityKey. This change is part of enhancements that simplify working with *n*-tier architectures.

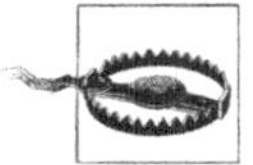

Beware of added entities that are joined to other objects. Object Services will attempt to add the related objects to the database as well. You'll learn more about this, and see an example of how to deal with this behavior when building WCF Services with EntityObjects, in Chapter 17.

ObjectContext.Attach and ObjectSet.Attach

Attach is used for entities that already exist in the database. Rather than setting the EntityState to Added, which tells SaveChanges to create an insert command, Attach results in an Unchanged EntityState—that is, it has not changed since it was attached to the context. Objects that you are attaching are assumed to exist in the data store. If you modify the objects after they've been attached, when you call SaveChanges the value of the EntityKey is used to update (or delete) the appropriate row by finding its matching ID (most often a primary key) in the appropriate table.

To attach an object to a context, use either the ObjectContext.Attach method or the ObjectSet.Attach method. For example, in the following two lines of code, context.Attach is used to attach a contact object and then the Attach method of the Contacts ObjectSet, context.Contacts, is used for the same purpose:

```
context.Attach(contact);

context.Contacts.Attach(contact);
```

Similar to AddObject, when you use ObjectContext.Attach (which exists for backward compatibility), if the object does not have an existing EntityKey, an exception will be thrown since the context cannot work out with which EntitySet to associate the object.

ObjectSet.Attach handles keyless entities differently. It will create an EntityKey dynamically when it attaches the entity. The values from the properties flagged as EntityKey properties will be used to construct the EntityKey, even if the value is 0.

An object will have an EntityKey if it has come from the data store or if you explicitly create the key.

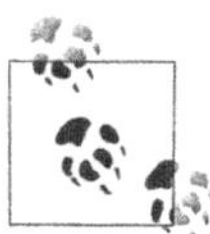

Creating an EntityKey dynamically is new in Entity Framework 4. Previously, if there was no EntityKey, an exception would be thrown.

When you Attach to a context, a brand-new ObjectStateEntry is created. The property values for the incoming object are used to populate the OriginalValues and CurrentValues arrays of the ObjectStateEntry.

So, what becomes of an attached entity that you modified, then detached, and then attached again? As I stated earlier, the newly attached entity will be Unchanged and all of the change tracking (including original values) will be lost. In fact, the original values are lost the moment you detach the entity. This is expected behavior for the Entity Framework, but to many developers who are new to working with the Entity Framework, it is surprising behavior.

Remember that the object doesn't own its state information; the ObjectContext does. If you have an object that is being tracked and has changes, but then you detach the object, the ObjectStateEntry for that object is removed from the context. All of the state is gone, including the original values. Poof!

ObjectContext.AttachTo

AttachTo is a method from the first version of Entity Framework that you shouldn't need to use thanks to the introduction of ObjectSet. With AttachTo, if an EntityKey does not exist, you can specify the EntitySet, just as you do with ObjectContext.AddObject. An object needs an EntityKey to be change-tracked and to be involved in relationships. If you need to attach an object that does not have an EntityKey, you can use the AttachTo method, which also requires that you indicate to which EntitySet the object belongs. With the name of the EntitySet, the Context can dynamically create an EntityKey for the object. The following code shows how to use the AttachTo method, where myContact is an already instantiated Contact entity object:

```
context.AttachTo("Contacts",contact);
```

In some cases, an object may not have an EntityKey. For example, an EntityKey is generally an indication that the object has come from the data store and has some type of a primary key field. Newly added objects are given temporary EntityKeys. But what if you want to work with an object whose data exists in the data store, but you are creating that object on the fly in memory without actually retrieving it first? In this case, this object will not have an EntityKey by default, and you'll need to create one yourself.

However, it is much simpler and safer to use the ObjectSet.Attach rather than using a string.

Creating EntityKeys On the Fly

With the introduction of foreign key support in the model and enhancements to AddObject and Attach in .NET 4, you should find fewer scenarios where you might want or need to create an EntityKey on the fly. When working with graphs and relationships, Entity Framework still relies on the EntityKey of a reference entity even if the foreign key exists as a scalar property. However, the ObjectContext will keep the EntityKey of a ReferenceEntity in sync with the scalar property which maps to the relevant foreign key, as well as with the navigation property.

If you are not using the foreign key scalars in your model, you will have more scenarios where you may want to construct EntityKeys. Additionally, as you take advantage of some of the more complex features of the Entity Framework, you will find instances where creating an EntityKey on the fly will be helpful.

The simplest constructor for an EntityKey takes a qualified EntitySet name (the EntityContainer name plus the EntitySet name), the name of the property that holds the key, and the value. Example 10-10 shows a new EntityKey being created for a CustomerType that is wrapped by the CustomerType EntitySet.

Example 10-10. Creating a new EntityKey

```
var entityKey = new EntityKey("BAEntities.CustomerTypes",
                              "CustomerTypeID", 1);
```

When your EntityKey is composed of more than one property, you need to create a KeyValuePair and then use that to build the key. There are no entities in the BreakAway model that have composite keys, but Example 10-11 shows an example of such a key.

Example 10-11. Creating a composite EntityKey

```
var eKeyValues =
   new KeyValuePair<string, object>[] {
       new KeyValuePair<string, object>("PropertyA", 12),
       new KeyValuePair<string, object>("PropertyB", 103)
   };
EntityKey ekey = new EntityKey("BAEntities.EntitySetName", eKeyValues);
```

There is also another option to be aware of: ObjectContext has a CreateEntityKey method. Here is an example of using this method while at the same time, using the CreateObjectSet method to return the EntitySet name, rather than using a string as in Example 10-10:

```
var destinationEntityKey =
_context.CreateEntityKey
(_context.CreateObjectSet<Destination>
().Name, dest);
```

Taking Control of ObjectState

With .NET 4, Entity Framework provides you with many more capabilities to impact entity state than were available in the first version of Entity Framework. For now, let's take a quick look at the methods. As you dig further into Object Services later in the book and then begin working with services and other disconnected applications, you will see how valuable these methods can be.

ObjectContext Methods

Here is a list of the `ObjectContext` methods that allow you to directly impact the state of entities:

`ApplyCurrentValues<TEntity>`
: This is the renamed method that was `ApplyPropertyChanges` in .NET 3.5. It will take the values of the provided detached entity and use its `EntityKey` to locate the same entity in the context. Then it will replace the attached entity's current scalar values with the property values from the detached entity. The method requires you to supply a string identifying the entity set that the entity belongs to. See the `ObjectSet` and `ObjectStateEntry` variations on this method for cleaner usage.

```
context.ApplyCurrentValues<Contact>("Contacts", myDetachedContact)
```

`ApplyOriginalValues`
: This method is similar to `ApplyCurrentValues`, except that it replaces the attached entity's original values with the values from the detached entity.

`AcceptAllChanges`
: `AcceptAllChanges` is not a new method. By default, the `SaveChanges` method calls this method after it has performed the database modifications. `AcceptAllChanges` pushes the current values of every attached entity into the original values and then changes their `EntityState` to `Unchanged`. After this, the entities will appear as though they had just been retrieved from the data store. If you are used to working with ADO.NET, this is similar to the `DataSet.AcceptChanges` method.

ObjectStateManager Methods

Here is a list of the `ObjectStateManager` methods that allow you to directly impact the state of entities:

`ChangeObjectState`
: `ChangeObjectState` will allow you to change an entity's state to `Added`, `Deleted`, `Modifed`, or `Unchanged`. This is an extremely powerful feature, but you should understand the impact of calling this. Not only will the `EntityState` change, but the original and current values of the properties will be affected as well. We'll take a closer look at `ChangeObjectState` later in this chapter.

`ChangeRelationshipState` *and* `ChangeRelationshipState<TEntity>`
: This pair of methods will be especially critical for working with *n*-tier applications when you don't have the benefit of foreign key scalar values in your model. As you have learned, the context owns all of the change-tracking information. Therefore, when an entity or a graph is detached from one context and then attached to another context, only the current state of the entities and relationships will be known in the new context. As an example, you may have added a reservation for a customer or changed which trip a particular reservation is for. The new context will not detect that these are modifications and database changes need to be made. Although you will be dependent on some other mechanism to discover the original state, you can use `ChangeRelationshipState` to align the existing relationships in such a way that the proper action is taken during `SaveChanges`.

  The method signature needs to know which entities are involved (you can pass in an object or just its `EntityKey`), which navigation property defines the relationship to be changed, and what the new state should be. Here is an example of the method in use:

```
context.ObjectStateManager.ChangeRelationshipState<Reservation>
   (customer, reservation, c => c.Reservation, EntityState.Added);
```

ObjectStateEntry State Methods for Managing State

Many of the methods of the `ObjectStateEntry` class are the same as `ObjectStateManager` methods. This gives you the flexibility to change state more simply if you are already working with an `ObjectStateEntry`.

`AcceptChanges`
: This method is similar to `ObjectContext.AcceptAllChanges`, except that it will impact only the specific entity. It is not new to .NET 4.

`ApplyCurrentValues`
: If you are working with the `ObjectStateEntry` of the entity you wish to update, you can use this version of the method, which does not require you to specify the type or the `EntitySet`:

```
contactOSE.ApplyCurrentValues(myDetachedContact)
```

`ApplyOriginalValues`
: This is a the same as `ObjectStateManager.ApplyOriginalValues`, but you can call it directly when you are working with an `ObjectStateEntry`.

`ChangeState`
: As with the other `ObjectStateEntry` methods, when you already have your hands on the `ObjectStateEntry`, this is a simpler way to impact the state compared to `ObjectContext.ChangeObjectState`. It performs the same function as the `ObjectContext` method.

`DetectChanges`
: This is used to force the context to inspect the entities and update their state. It is not necessary when using `EntityObjects`, because they automatically notify the context of changes. However, you will learn about POCO entities in Chapter 13, which, by default, do not notify the context. In that case, you can force the context to update the change-tracking information by calling `DetectChanges`.

ObjectSet State Methods

You can also impact the state of objects directly from an `ObjectSet`. Here are the state methods for `ObjectSet`:

`ApplyCurrentValues`
: This method emulates the `ApplyCurrentValues` method of the context, except that you do not need to define the generic type or the entity set:

```
context.Contacts.ApplyCurrentValues(myDetachedContact);
```

`ApplyOriginalValues`
: As with the `ApplyCurrentValues` method, this is a simpler variation on `ObjectContext.ApplyOriginalValues`.

Sending Changes Back to the Database

Not only is Object Services focused on getting data from the database and managing those objects, but it also manages the full life cycle of the objects, including persisting changes back to the database.

ObjectContext.SaveChanges

You spent a good deal of time learning about the `ObjectContext.SaveChanges` method in action in Chapter 6. This is an important function of Object Services. Here we'll take a look at a few more features of `SaveChanges`.

SaveChanges returns an integer

A little-known fact about the `SaveChanges` method is that it returns an integer representing the number of `ObjectContext` objects that were affected.

SaveChanges refreshes the state of tracked entities

After a successful `SaveChanges` call, all of the changes will be accepted in the `ObjectContext` and every object's `EntityState` will become `Unchanged`. This is done, as you learned earlier, because the `SaveChanges` method calls the `AcceptAllChanges` method and this is the default behavior. So, whether that object is new, is deleted, has a scalar value change, or has a relationship change, it will be counted in the number returned by `SaveChanges`.

Chapter 21 focuses on exception handling with Entity Framework. There you will learn about what happens and what you can do when `SaveChanges` fails.

> ### Can Updates, Inserts, and Deletes Be Handled in Bulk?
>
> As you saw in Chapter 6, each command generated by `SaveChanges` is sent to the database one at a time to be executed. Unfortunately, bulk processing of commands is not something that the Entity Framework is able to perform intrinsically. However, Alex James, a program manager on the Entity Framework team, has written a series of blog posts about how to pull this off with the Entity Framework. See *http://blogs.msdn.com/alexj/* for more information.

Affecting SaveChanges Default Behavior

As I stated earlier, `SaveChanges` calls `AcceptAllChanges` as well as `DetectChanges` (for POCO classes, which you will learn about in Chapter 13). There are a number of ways to modify the default behavior. In Chapter 20, you will learn to take control of the transaction surrounding `SaveChanges`, and when you use your own transaction neither `AcceptAllChanges` nor `DetectChanges` will be automatically called. You will be responsible for it yourself.

When you call `SaveChanges` with no parameters, the following method overload is executed:

```
public int SaveChanges()
{
  return this.SaveChanges
   (SaveOptions.DetectChangesBeforeSave | SaveOptions.AcceptAllChangesAfterSave);
}
```

Notice that the method calls the core `SaveChanges` method which takes `SaveOptions` enums. The three options are `DetectChangesBeforeSave`, `AcceptAllChangesAfterSave`, and `None`. The first option will cause the `DetectChanges` method to be called. The second option will cause `AcceptAllChanges` to be called. If you pass in `None`, even combined with one of the other enums, neither of those methods will be called.

`DetectChangesBeforeSave` is useful when you are using your own classes with Entity Framework, rather than the automatically generated classes. You'll learn more about this in Chapter 13.

Overriding SaveChanges Completely

As of .NET 4, the `SaveChanges` method is virtual (*overridable* in Visual Basic), which means that you can completely override its internal logic when you have advanced scenarios to implement. You could add logic, such as validation logic, to `SaveChanges` and then call `base.SaveChanges` so that Entity Framework will perform its normal saving routine.

Or you could completely avoid the `base.SaveChanges` logic and take total control over what happens when `SaveChanges` is called. You would have to have deep knowledge of the Entity Framework to do this successfully. I recommend starting with a look at the internal code in the `SaveChanges` method, which you can do with Visual Studio's Source Server support or a tool such as Red Gate's .NET Reflector.

Data Validation with the SavingChanges Event

`ObjectContext` has two public events: `ObjectMaterialized` (mentioned earlier) and `SavingChanges`. The latter occurs when `SaveChanges` is called. You can place validation logic here as an alternative to placing it in the virtual `SaveChanges` method.

The code you insert into `SavingChanges` will run before the API performs the actual `SaveChanges` method.

In this single location, you can perform validation on any of the entities that the `ObjectContext` is managing.

You'll learn how to implement `SavingChanges` and perform validation directly in that method in Chapter 11, and then in later chapters you'll learn how to use `SavingChanges` to trigger class-level validation code.

The difference between using the `SavingChanges` method and overriding `SaveChanges` is that the former will continue on to the `base.SaveChanges`, while the latter gives you the option to call `base.SaveChanges` or avoid it completely, either to abort the save or to use your own saving logic.

Concurrency Management

Data concurrency is the bane of any data access developer trying to answer the question "What happens if more than one person is editing the same data at the same time?"

The more fortunate among us deal with business rules that say "no problem, last one in wins." In this case, concurrency is not an issue.

More likely, it's not as simple as that, and there is no silver bullet to solve every scenario at once.

By default, the Entity Framework will take the path of "last one in wins," meaning that the latest update is applied even if someone else updated the data between the time the user retrieved the data and the time he saved it. You can customize the behavior using a combination of attributes in the EDM and methods from Object Services.

Chapter 23 will deal with this topic in depth, but here is a brief overview of the functionality provided.

Optimistic concurrency

The Entity Framework uses an optimistic concurrency model. Optimistic concurrency is a fairly complex topic, but the essence is that you will not get record locking in the database. This makes it possible for others to read and write data in between a user's retrieval and update.

ConcurrencyMode

In the EDM, the scalar properties of an entity have an attribute called `ConcurrencyMode`. By default, this is set to `None`. In a typical data application, a single field, such as a `rowversion` field (which we covered in previous chapters), is used to identify that a database row has been modified. When you set the `ConcurrencyMode` of a particular property (e.g., `Contact.RowVersion`) to `Fixed`, Object Services will use the value of that property to alert you to concurrency conflicts in the database.

OptimisticConcurrencyException

When `SaveChanges` is called, if any of the flagged values in the database differ from the corresponding original values in the entities, an `OptimisticConcurrency` exception will be thrown. Chapter 22 will go into great detail about handling these exceptions.

Transaction Support

Object Services operations performed against the data store, such as queries or the `SaveChanges` method, are transactional by default. You can override the default behavior using `System.Transaction.TransactionScope`, `EntityTransaction`, or one of the other `System.Data.Common.DbTransaction` classes, such as `SqlClient.SqlTransaction`. `EntityTransaction` inherits from `DbTransaction` as well.

Entity Framework's transaction support works only with operations against the store, not with operations against entity objects.

By default, the last step of SaveChanges is to call AcceptAllChanges, as we discussed earlier. This is especially important with respect to values that are generated on the server, such as incremented primary keys or timestamps (a.k.a. rowversion). AcceptAllChanges will use those returned values as well.

However, when SaveChanges is inside your own transaction, the changes don't come back from the server until you call DbTransaction.Commit or TransactionScope.Complete. Because of this, you need to explicitly set AcceptChangesDuringSave, the SaveChanges argument, to False. Additionally, after the Commit or Complete is called, you will need to manually call ObjectContext.AcceptAllChanges.

You'll find more information on transactions in Chapter 20.

Implementing Serialization, Data Binding, and More

Object Services' core features revolve around query processing and managing objects, as you have seen. However, Object Services works with entity objects in other ways as well. We'll look at some of the more important of these features.

Object Services Supports XML and Binary Serialization

Data is serialized in order for it to be transmitted across boundaries and processes, most commonly with remote or message-based services.

Entity classes generated from the EDM are decorated with the Serializable and DataContractAttribute attributes, as shown in the following code:

```
[EdmEntityTypeAttribute(NamespaceName="BAModel", Name="Contact")]
[Serializable()]
[DataContractAttribute(IsReference=true)]
public partial class Contact : EntityObject
{}
```

System.Serializable enables the object to be binary-serialized and XML-serialized. Binary serialization is used implicitly in ASP.NET, though in some scenarios you may want to explicitly code the serialization to persist or stream data. XML serialization is most commonly used to send messages to and from web services. The DataContractAttribute enables serialization for exchanging data with Windows Communication Foundation (WCF) services.

In addition, EntityKeys are serialized along with the object. This means the object can be transmitted between applications and services, in some cases with very little effort on the part of the developer.

ObjectContext, ObjectStateManager, and ObjectStateEntry are not serializable

It is very important to keep in mind that ObjectContext, ObjectStateEntry, and ObjectStateManager are not serializable. This is one of the reasons I have emphasized the fact that objects do not retain their own state information. Without writing your own custom code, you cannot serialize or transport the change-tracking or state information of your objects. There is a new feature in Entity Framework 4, called self-tracking entities, which provides a big boost toward overcoming this limitation. You will learn more about this, and how to handle state when crossing process boundaries, first in Chapters 17 and 18, and later in Chapter 27. These chapters deal with WCF services and ASP.NET applications.

Automatic serialization

Anytime you pass an object or a set of objects as a parameter to a web or WCF service operation, the object will automatically be serialized as it is sent to the service. When it receives the serialized data, the service will automatically deserialize the object(s) and be able to work with it right away.

XML and DataContract serialization. XML serialization is used for ASMX Web Services and can also be used with WCF. WCF more commonly uses data contract serialization, which does serialize into XML, but differently than XML serialization.

Aaron Skonnard compares the two in the *MSDN Magazine* article "Serialization in Windows Communication Foundation" (*http://msdn.microsoft.com/en-us/magazine/cc163569.aspx*).

Whether you are using an ASMX Web Service or WCF, your entities are automatically serialized into XML when they are transmitted between a service operation and a client application.

You are getting only a quick overview of building and consuming web services and WCF services here. Chapters 17 and 18 provide detailed walkthroughs of these processes.

In the following example of a WCF service contract, the `GetContact` operation signature indicates that a `ContactID` must be sent from the client and that a `Contact` entity is returned to the client:

```
[OperationContract()]
 Contact GetContact(int contactID );
```

In the next code snippet, the function queries the EDM to retrieve the data, and then returns the `Contact`:

```
using (var context = new BAEntities())
{
  var cust = from c in context.Contacts.Include("Customer")
             where c.ContactID == contactID
             select c;
```

```
        return cust.FirstOrDefault();
    }
```

There is no code here for serialization. The act of serialization is an inherent function of the service.

On the client side, again, no explicit deserialization is occurring. .NET knows the payload is serialized and will automatically deserialize it to a `Customer` object:

```
    private void GetCustFromService()
    {
      var proxy = new BreakAwayCommonService.BreakAwayCommonServiceClient();
      var cust = proxy.GetCustomer(21);
      Console.WriteLine("{0} {1}", cust.FirstName.Trim(), cust.LastName.Trim());
    }
```

In Chapters 17 and 18, you will build WCF clients and services and see more regarding how this works. You'll also learn about the conflict between lazy loading and serialization in that chapter.

Binary serialization

In an ASP.NET website, ASP.NET uses binary serialization to store information in the session cache or in the page's `ViewState`. You can place objects directly into these caches, and extract them without having to explicitly serialize them since Object Services handles the serialization automatically.

Serialization and object state

Since you are serializing only the objects and not the context, the state data stored in the `ObjectStateEntry` is not included. The `EntityState` of the objects in the serialized form is `Detached`; when you deserialize the objects they remain in a `Detached` state. If you attach them to an `ObjectContext`, whether it's a new `ObjectContext` or the same one to which they were previously attached, their state will become `Unchanged`. Your starting point with those objects is a snapshot of the values when the data was serialized.

Explicit serialization

You can also use methods in the `System.Runtime.Serialization` namespace to serialize your objects explicitly. The Entity Framework documentation has a great sample of serializing objects to a binary stream and then deserializing them again. This works no differently than serializing any other types of objects, and therefore it is not specific to the Entity Framework. Look for the topic titled "How To: Serialize and Deserialize Objects" in the Entity Framework MSDN documentation for more information.

Object Services Supports Data Binding

`EntityCollection` and `ObjectQuery` both implement `IListSource`, which enables them to bind to data-bound controls. Because the objects implement `INotifyProperty`

Changed, you can use them in two-way binding, which means that updates made in the control can be sent back to the objects automatically.

In Chapter 9, you wrote a Windows Forms application that bound data to a BindingSource that in turn tied the data to various binding controls. You also performed data binding with WPF objects. In both applications, when updating the form's controls those changes were automatically made in the objects. This occurred thanks to the IListSource.

ASP.NET data-bound and list controls also support data binding. Because of the nature of web pages, however, you'll need to pay attention to postbacks and their impact on change tracking. You can bind directly to the DataSource properties of the controls, or use a client-side EntityDataSource control. Although LINQDataSource does support read-only use of LINQ to Entities queries, it is more closely focused on LINQ to SQL and doesn't support everything in LINQ to Entities. Therefore, it's best to use EntityDataSource instead in cases where the client-side data binding is sufficient for your application's architecture.

In the next chapter, you will focus on using the ASP.NET EntityDataSource to build data-bound web pages. Some of the chapters appearing later in the book will demonstrate how to use business layers with Windows Forms and ASP.NET applications.

Summary

In this chapter, you got an overview of the Object Services features. You've seen how queries are processed, how the results are materialized into objects, and how Object Services keeps track of those objects until it's time to save any changes back to the database. Object Services plays a critical role in getting those changes to the database. The ObjectContext is the key agent in the Object Services API. You have already worked with the context directly, but should now have a much better understanding of what it has been doing in response to your actions.

Except for working with EntityClient, nearly everything you will learn in the rest of this book will be dependent on Object Services. As I noted throughout this chapter, many of the later chapters in this book will more thoroughly cover the individual topics highlighted here.

It's been many pages of theory, so now, with the next chapter, you can get back to coding as you learn various ways to customize entities.

CHAPTER 11
Customizing Entities

In previous chapters, we worked with entity classes and the context class that were generated from the model. The methods and events available to you for these classes were limited to the methods and events derived from their base classes: `EntityObject` and `ObjectContext`, as well as those inserted by the code generation.

Because the purpose of entities is to provide data schema, they contain little in the way of business logic. This is great for getting started, but many applications will need more.

The extensibility of the Entity Framework provides a number of ways to not only add your own logic, but also use your own classes and plug them into an `ObjectContext`.

In this chapter, you'll learn how to use partial classes to add new logic to entities or override their existing logic. You will also learn how to change the rules for code generation and in doing so create classes from the model that are more to your liking.

In Chapter 13, you will learn how you can use your own custom classes in the Entity Framework.

Partial Classes

All of the classes that are generated from an Entity Data Model (EDM)—the class that inherits from `ObjectContext` as well as the entities themselves—are partial classes. Partial classes allow you to break a class into multiple code files, and they are especially valuable when you want to make changes to generated code. Without partial classes, modifications to generated code will be lost whenever the generation is performed again. Rather than making your changes directly in the generated code, you can make them in a separate file that will not be touched when the code generator performs its magic. As long as your class is declared a partial class, another class with the same name will not cause a conflict. During compilation, .NET merges the separate files into one class.

For a great introduction to partial classes, the article "Implications and Repercussions of Partial Classes in the .NET Framework 2.0" (*http://www.code-magazine.com/article.aspx?quickid=0503021*) by Dino Esposito is very informative.

For example, a quick look at the code that is generated for the BreakAway application described in previous chapters reveals that the `ObjectContext` class and the application entities are marked as partial classes, as shown in Example 11-1.

Example 11-1. The ObjectContext and entities marked as partial classes

VB
```
Public Partial Class BAEntities
    Inherits ObjectContext

Public Partial Class Trip
    Inherits EntityObject
```

C#
```
public partial class BAEntities : ObjectContext

public partial class Trip : EntityObject
```

To add to any of these classes all you need to do is to create another file and declare the same class, which you will see in the upcoming examples. There are a few rules for implementing partial classes: you don't need to repeat inheritance or interface implementations; all of the partial classes for a particular class need to be in the same assembly; and you must not repeat any attributes. With regard to that last point, if you try to state the attributes more than once, you will get a compiler error letting you know that this is a problem.

Creating and Naming Files That Contain Partial Classes

How you organize partial classes is a matter of coding style, and you or your development team may already have a practice that you use for partial classes.

My pattern is to create a separate code file for each partial class that I implement. Therefore, I have an *Entities.vb/.cs* file for all of the additions to the class that implements the `ObjectContext` (e.g., `BAEntities`), as well as individual files for each entity—*Customer.vb/.cs*, *Trip.vb/.cs*, and so on.

You must always create these new files in the same assembly as the files that contain the generated classes.

Visual Basic infers the assembly namespace when creating additional parts of a partial class, whereas C# requires the namespace to be specified, as shown in Example 11-2.

Example 11-2. Declaring additions to the partial classes

VB
```
Public Class BAEntities

End Class
```

C#
```
namespace BAGA  //assembly namespace is required for C# partial classes
{
  public class BAEntities
  {
  }
}
```

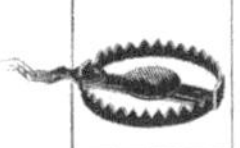

If you create a separate folder to contain the partial classes, as I do, pay attention to a C# feature which will create a namespace based on the folder name for classes created inside this folder. In my case, the folder was named *Partial Classes*. When I create new classes in there, they are wrapped in a namespace called `BAGA.Partial_Classes`. Because of the different namespace, these won't find their matching partial classes. Be sure to edit the namespace so that it matches that of the other partial classes, which in this example is simply `BAGA`.

Using Partial Methods

In addition to being able to split classes into multiple files, partial classes allow you to split methods across the files as well, using a technique called *partial methods*. The Entity Framework creates a few partial methods for its code-generated classes. These methods are declared but not implemented in the generated class. You can then add the method's implementation in your partial class. These generated partial methods include one that is called when an `ObjectContext` is instantiated, named `OnContextCreated`, and a pair of methods, `Changed` and `Changing`, for every property of every entity. In the following sections we'll look at each in more detail.

The OnContextCreated Method

The first partial method, `ObjectContext.OnContextCreated`, lets you add custom code that will be executed at the time the context is instantiated. Here is how that is implemented in the generated code.

At compile time, if the partial method is not implemented, it is not included in the compiled assembly, which is a nice form of optimization.

The method is defined in the class that derives from `ObjectContext` (e.g., `BAEntities`). As you can see in Example 11-3, VB and C# differ in their syntax.

Example 11-3. The generated OnContextCreated partial method declarations

VB
```
Partial Private Sub OnContextCreated()
End Sub
```

C#
```
partial void OnContextCreated();
```

`OnContextCreated` is called by the context object's constructor and the constructor overloads, as shown in Example 11-4.

Example 11-4. OnContextCreated being called in the generated context constructors

VB
```
Public Sub New()
  MyBase.New("name=BAEntities", "BAEntities")
  MyBase.ContextOptions.LazyLoadingEnabled = true
  OnContextCreated
End Sub

Public Sub New(ByVal connectionString As String)
  MyBase.New(connectionString, "BAEntities")
  MyBase.ContextOptions.LazyLoadingEnabled = true
  OnContextCreated
End Sub

Public Sub New(ByVal connection As EntityConnection)
  MyBase.New(connection, "BAEntities")
  MyBase.ContextOptions.LazyLoadingEnabled = true
  OnContextCreated
End Sub
```

C#
```
public BAEntities() : base("name=BAEntities", "BAEntities")
{
  this.ContextOptions.LazyLoadingEnabled = true;
  OnContextCreated();
}

public BAEntities(string connectionString) : base(connectionString, "BAEntities")
{
  this.ContextOptions.LazyLoadingEnabled = true;
  OnContextCreated();
}

public BAEntities(EntityConnection connection) : base(connection, "BAEntities")
{
  this.ContextOptions.LazyLoadingEnabled = true;
  OnContextCreated();
}
```

By default, the `OnContextCreated` partial method contains no code, because in the generated classes, the partial methods are only being declared. In the partial class that you write, you can add your own code to the method.

To add code that you want to run when a context is instantiated, add the `OnContextCreated()` method to the partial class for the `ObjectContext`.

Visual Basic has properties, events, and methods available in drop-down boxes at the top of the code window. Select BAEntities in the Class Name drop down on the left, and then select OnContextCreated from the Method Name drop down on the right. This will automatically create the VB code shown in Example 11-5, which you could also just type in manually; in C#, you *must* type the method in manually.

Example 11-5. The custom OnContextCreated method in your custom context class

VB
```
Private Sub OnContextCreated()
  'add logic here
End Sub
```

C#
```
partial void OnContextCreated()
{
  //add logic here
}
```

Now you can add whatever logic you might want to execute anytime the `ObjectContext` is instantiated.

The On[Property]Changed and On[Property]Changing Methods

Every scalar property of every entity has its own version of `PropertyChanging` and `PropertyChanged`—for example, `FirstNameChanged` and `FirstNameChanging`. Like `OnContextCreated`, there is no default implementation for `PropertyChanging` and `PropertyChanged`; only a declaration. This provides you the opportunity to execute custom logic as the property is about to change (`PropertyChanging`) as well as just after the property value has changed (`PropertyChanged`).

In the generated code, the methods are declared and then called in each property's setter. The following examples show what this looks like for the `Name` property of the `Activity` entity in the generated code. First the two partial methods are declared (see Example 11-6).

Example 11-6. The generated property Changing and Changed method declarations

```
partial void OnNameChanging(string value);
partial void OnNameChanged();
```

Then the `Name` property calls those methods just before and after the value is changed (see Example 11-7).

Example 11-7. The generated class calling the Changing and Changed methods

```
public global::System.String Name
{
  get
  {
    return _Name;
  }
  set
```

```
    {
      OnNameChanging(value);
      ReportPropertyChanging("Name");
      _Name = StructuralObject.SetValidValue(value, true);
      ReportPropertyChanged("Name");
      OnNameChanged();
    }
}
```

To implement the PropertyChanged and PropertyChanging methods, create a new code file to contain custom code for the Activity entity, and name the file *Activity.vb* or *Activity.cs*. In the file, add the code shown in Example 11-8. Remember to fix the default namespace in the C# file, removing the folder name.

Example 11-8. Defining a partial class for an entity

```
public partial class Activity
{
}
```

Visual Basic's event drop downs make the next steps a little simpler than in C#.

In VB, select Address from the Class Name drop down; this will cause the Method Name drop down to populate with all of the property-changing methods. Choose OnNameChanging and OnNameChanged, which will stub out the event handler methods for you automatically.

In C#, IntelliSense will help you as you type the methods into your code, shown in Example 11-9.

The value parameter of the Changing method is the value that is about to be applied to the property.

In this method, we'll supplement the Activity to restrict the length of the Activity Name field in the OnNameChanging method.

Example 11-9. The partial method implementations

```
partial void OnNameChanging (string value)
{
  if ((value.Length) > 50)
    throw new ArgumentException
     ("Activity Name must be no longer than 50 characters", "value");
}
partial void OnNameChanged()
{}
```

If you look at the signatures of the Changed and Changing methods for the individual properties, you'll see that the Changed method has no parameters at all and the Changing method receives the new value. Because you are coding within the entity's class, you have access to the entity, its properties and methods, and its related data. This means you can interact with properties of the Activity entity in this business logic.

Using PropertyChanged to Calculate Database-Computed Columns Locally

Here's an example of taking advantage of these methods. Many databases use computed columns to perform calculations on the fly. An example of this is in Microsoft's sample database, AdventureWorksLT. The `LineTotal` column of the `SalesOrderDetail` table is a computed column. Figure 11-1 shows the column properties in the database. You can see that the Computed Column Specification property formula calculates the `LineTotal` based on the `UnitPrice`, `UnitPriceDiscount`, and `OrderQty` columns.

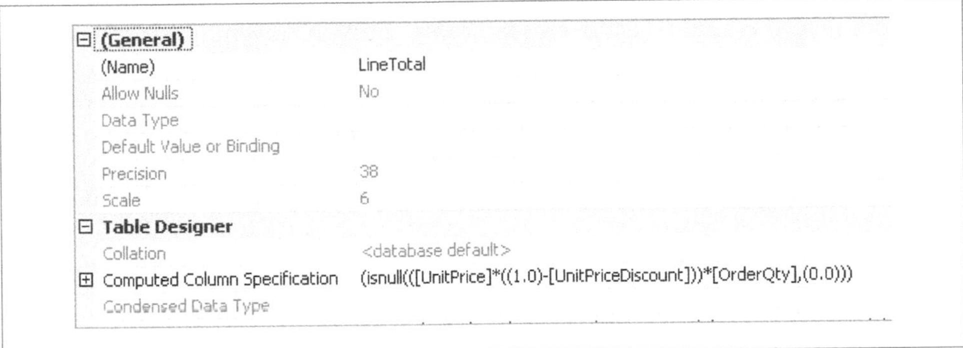

Figure 11-1. The LineTotal column, a computed column in the AdventureWorksLT SalesOrderDetail table

You would likely want to know this value in your application as the order is being created or modified, without depending on a trip to the database to get the `LineTotal`. Instead, you can create a method or read-only property in the partial class to compute the `LineTotal` locally, and then call that method anytime the `UnitPrice`, `UnitPriceDiscount`, or `OrderQty` column is changed.

Using Microsoft's sample AdventureWorksLT database for this example is simply a convenience. No other demos in the book rely on it. I mention it because I have had emails requesting the database. If you wish, you can download it from *http://msftdbprodsamples.codeplex.com/*.

Because `LineTotal` is a computed column in the database, the value created on the client side will not be sent to the server upon calling `SaveChanges`. Thanks to the default dynamic command generation capability, that `LineTotal` value will be replaced by the value computed by the database when you call `SaveChanges`.

Computed columns are marked as `StoreGeneratedValue` in the model, just as an identity column is. Therefore, `SaveChanges` will construct the command to send the updates and return any properties that are `StoreGeneratedValues`.

The custom method or property gives you the ability to calculate that property locally as needed and not relying on the database.

Although this computed property works very well for formulas in which the required values are contained within the same entity, you have to be careful if you are calculating data from related entities. The `SalesOrderHeader` entity in AdventureWorksLT has a `SubTotal` property that could be populated by summing up the `LineTotal` properties of all related `SalesOrderDetails`. But this assumes that all of the related details have been retrieved, and it may require a quick trip to the database to ensure that this is so. Depending on your application's architecture this could be a bad assumption to make, so this is something to consider before depending on this type of calculation on the client side.

`EntityObject` also has `PropertyChanged` and `PropertyChanging` events. These are true events, unlike the partial methods. So, although you can insert logic based on a specific property changing with the partial methods, you can also have logic that runs regardless of which property is changed. We will discuss these events in the following section.

Extensibility Points

Suppose you want to do something whenever any property changes—without having to write a partial method for each property individually. For this, Entity Framework offers some "life cycle events." Although `EntityObject` and `ObjectContext` expose some partial methods, which let you jump in and add your own logic, it would be nice to insert custom logic in a lot of other places as well. Later in this chapter, you'll get an introduction to Entity Framework's use of T4 code generation. This template-driven approach to building classes based on the model's XML provides you with great flexibility to inject your own custom methods and other logic, as you'll see in the sample provided along with that discussion.

Subscribing to Event Handlers

You can subscribe to only a few Entity Framework events in your applications:

- `ObjectContext.ObjectMaterialized`
- `ObjectContext.SavingChanges`

- `EntityObject.PropertyChanging`
- `EntityObject.PropertyChanged`
- `RelatedEnd.AssociationChanged`

The ObjectContext.ObjectMaterialized Event

The `ObjectMaterialized` event is raised anytime data is returned from a query (whether it's one that you executed explicitly or one that is executed behind the scenes, as is the case with lazy loading) as the context is creating the entity objects from that data. The event is raised just after the values are applied to scalar properties and reference properties, but prior to the `EntityCollections` being created.

`ObjectMaterialized` is new to Entity Framework 4.

This event is useful when you want to apply logic to any of the entity objects in your model or perform a particular action anytime objects are materialized.

If you set property values in this event, they will override values that came from the database.

If you have some logic that pertains to only a particular class, you should consider executing that logic when the class is being instantiated, which you'll see further on in this chapter. The caveat to this is that when you insert values in the class constructor, any properties which map back to the database will get overwritten during object materialization. Therefore, you'll be better off performing some of these tasks in the `ObjectMaterialized` event handler.

If you want to apply common logic that pertains to any and every class, or even for a group of classes, this is the place to do it.

To override the event, in VB you can implement the event using the class and event drop downs in the editing window. In C#, you need to wire up the event handler in the `OnContextCreated` method and then define the method elsewhere in the class, as shown in Example 11-10.

Example 11-10. Handling the ObjectMaterialized event in VB and C#

VB
```
Private Sub BAEntities_ObjectMaterialized
 (ByVal sender As Object,
  ByVal e As System.Data.Objects.ObjectMaterializedEventArgs)
 Handles Me. ObjectMaterialized
```

```
    'apply logic here
  End Sub
```

```
partial void OnContextCreated()
{
  ObjectMaterialized += BAEntities_ObjectMaterialized;
}
public void BAEntities_ObjectMaterialized(object sender,
                                          ObjectMaterializedEventArgs e)
{
  //apply logic here
}
```

Later on in this chapter, you will see `ObjectMaterialized` in action in combination with creating custom properties for entities.

The ObjectContext.SavingChanges Event

As I mentioned in the preceding chapter, `SavingChanges` provides an opportunity to validate or affect data before it is persisted to the database. `SavingChanges` executes just prior to when the `SaveChanges` method builds the database `Insert`, `Update`, and `Delete` commands. You'll want to consider how you organize these validations.

You can perform them per entity type, or per `EntityState`.

You can build the validators into partial classes for the various entities, and call those from `ObjectContext.SavingChanges`. You'll see some additional ways of organizing validation logic later in this book, and your own coding practices might suggest others yet.

Remember that you also have the option of overriding `SaveChanges` for any logic you want to execute prior to (or instead of) the base `SaveChanges` method being executed.

GetObjectStateEntries: A critical method when validating entities from the context

There's a method that you haven't seen yet that is frequently used when handling the `SavingChanges` event or overriding `SaveChanges`. `GetObjectStateEntries` is a method of `ObjectContext.ObjectStateManager` that allows you to extract the `ObjectStateEntry` objects managed by the context so that you can perform logic such as validation on the entities. You'll be spending more time with the `ObjectStateManager` in Chapter 21. `GetObjectStateEntries` is the only way to access the entities in `SavingChanges` or `SaveChanges`. This method returns an `IEnumerable<ObjectStateEntry>` of entries managed by the context by filtering on a particular `EntityState`.

Once you have the `ObjectStateEntry` objects in hand, you can navigate from them to the actual entity objects, as you will see in the code sample in Example 11-11.

You can pass in one or more `EntityState` enumerations (separated by VB's `Or` or C#'s `|`) to determine which group or groups of entities you want to work with. For instance, `GetObjectStateEntries(EntityState.Added)` returns all of the new entities in the context; GetObjectStateEntries(EntityState.Added | EntityState.Modified) returns all of the new entities as well as any that have been modified.

The only downside to this is that if you want to explore the entries in any way, not just by EntityState, GetObjectStateEntries still requires that you use the enums. For example, if you wanted to find all of the Trip entries in the ObjectStateManager, regardless of their state, you would need to pass in all of the possible EntityState options—Added, Deleted, Modified, and Unchanged.

In Chapter 21, you will see some overloads that I've created to make it simpler to work with the GetObjectStateEntries method.

Then you can filter on the type of the entity referenced by these ObjectStateEntries, as shown in Example 11-11, which uses LINQ to Objects to query the ObjectStateEntries.

Example 11-11. Retrieving ObjectStateEntry objects from the context in VB and C#

VB
```
Dim TripEntries As List(Of ObjectStateEntry) TripEntries = _
    From entry In ObjectStateManager.GetObjectStateEntries _
        (EntityState.Added Or EntityState.Deleted _
         Or EntityState.Modified Or EntityState.Unchanged) _
    Where TypeOf entry.Entity Is Trip
```

C#
```
List<ObjectStateEntry> tripEntities =
    from entry in ObjectStateManager.GetObjectStateEntries
        (EntityState.Added | EntityState.Deleted |
         EntityState.Modified | EntityState.Unchanged)
     where entry.Entity is Trip
     select entry;
```

There is one more EntityState enum that the preceding discussion has ignored: Detached. Detached entities don't exist in the ObjectContext, so there's no reason to look for them here.

Implementing SavingChanges

Before you add an event handler to the SavingChanges event, you'll need to extend the partial class for the ObjectContext if you didn't do so during the discussion of OnContextCreated. You can do this in the *Entities.vb* or *Entities.cs* code file.

Example 11-12 and Example 11-13 demonstrate subscribing to the SavingChanges event in the BreakAway context. The handler updates the ModifiedDate property for every contact that is new or modified. The example first grabs every ObjectStateEntry that is either Modified or Added. Then, it identifies any entries that represent Contact entities and updates the ModifiedDate field. Visual Basic is included in the example to demonstrate its particular syntax. In both examples, both the System.Data and System.Data.Objects namespaces are added to the directives at the top of each code file.

Example 11-12. Setting default values in SavingChanges in VB

```
Private Sub BAEntities_SavingChanges _
 (ByVal sender As Object, ByVal e As System.EventArgs) _
 Handles Me.SavingChanges

  Dim osm = ObjectStateManager
 'get Added or Modified entries
  For Each entry In osm.GetObjectStateEntries
                  (EntityState.Added Or EntityState.Modified)
    If TypeOf entry.Entity Is Contact Then
      Dim con = CType(entry.Entity, Contact)
      con.ModifiedDate = Now
    End If
  Next
End Sub
```

As with the `ObjectMaterialized` event, in C# you have to perform an extra step to wire up the `SavingChanges` event handler. You can do this in the `OnContextCreated` partial method, as shown in Example 11-13.

Example 11-13. Setting default values in SavingChanges in C#

```
partial void OnContextCreated()
{
  ObjectMaterialized +=  BAEntities_ObjectMaterialized;
  SavingChanges += BAEntities_SavingChanges;
}
public void BAEntities_SavingChanges (object sender, System.EventArgs e)
{
  var osm =ObjectStateManager;
 //get Added | Modified entries;
  foreach (var entry in osm.GetObjectStateEntries
                      (EntityState.Added | EntityState.Modified))
  {
    if (entry.Entity is Contact)
    {
      var con = (Contact)entry.Entity;
      con.ModifiedDate = DateTime.Now;
    }
  }
}
```

If the `ModifiedDate` field in the database table was automatically updated with a database trigger, you could simply mark the `ModifiedDate` property as a computed column (by setting the `StoreGeneratedPattern` attribute to `Computed`), and therefore eliminate any need to update this field manually.

Setting default foreign keys in SavingChanges when no foreign key scalar property exists

The first version of Entity Framework did not support foreign keys in the model. You can continue to create models without foreign keys or you may be working with a legacy model. If you are using a model without foreign keys as entity properties, you will have to deal with any foreign keys that are non-nullable and may not have been set elsewhere in your code. A good example would be the `CustomerType` of a `Customer`. In our model, we set the `CustomerTypeID` foreign key value to have a default of `1`, representing Standard customers. But what if you had only the `CustomerType` navigation property and the `CustomerTypeReference` to work with? You can't set defaults for those in the model.

In this case, there are two possible places to set the default foreign key reference: in the constructor of the `Contact` entity (discussed shortly) or during `SavingChanges`. Otherwise, if you leave that value unassigned, you will get an `UpdateEntityException` when you attempt to save.

Taking care of this constraint during `SavingChanges` by providing a default for the entities so that the value is not null is a convenient way to solve the problem. Otherwise, if the `CustomerTypeID` had been left empty, an exception would be thrown.

Adding the logic shown in Example 11-14 to the enumeration through `Modified` and `Added` entities would take care of this during `SavingChanges`.

Example 11-14. Setting foreign keys when there are no foreign key properties

VB
```
If TypeOf entry.Entity Is Customer Then
  Dim cust = CType(entry.Entity, Customer)
  With cust
    If cust.CustomerTypeReference.EntityKey Is Nothing Then
      cust.CustomerTypeReference.EntityKey = _
      New EntityKey("BAEntities.CustomerTypes", "CustomerTypeID", 1)
    End If
  End With
End If
```

C#
```
if (entry.Entity is Customer)
{
  var cust = (Customer)entry.Entity;
  if (cust.CustomerTypeReference.EntityKey == null)
  {
    cust.CustomerTypeReference.EntityKey =
     new EntityKey("BAEntities.CustomerTypes", "CustomerTypeID", 1);
  }
}
```

Enums Not Supported in Entity Framework

You'll notice in Example 11-14 that an integer is assigned to the `EntityKey` value. This is a case where it might make more sense to predefine a set of enums that might be identified as `CustType.Standard`, `CustType.Silver`, and `CustType.Gold`. In this way, there would be no need for the developer to remember the actual value, `1`, for the Standard customer. Unfortunately, if you were to use an enum when building the `EntityKey`, for example:

```
New EntityKey("BAEntities.CustomerTypes",
              "CustomerTypeID", CustType.Standard)
```

an exception would be thrown indicating that the constructor requires an integer. That is because the Entity Framework does not support enums as of .NET 4. Alternatively, you could use constants, which are preferable to a number or string. I've used the integer in Example 11-14 in order to highlight this problem.

The EntityObject.PropertyChanging and EntityObject.PropertyChanged Events

In addition to the `Changing` and `Changed` methods for the individual properties of a class, `EntityObject` has class-level `PropertyChanged` and `PropertyChanging` methods as well. These two events are raised anytime any property in a particular entity class changes.

The order of the Changing/Changed events

If you subscribe to the class-level events as well as any of the specific property methods, both the method and the event will be hit when the particular property is modified. Here is the order in which the events are hit:

1. Property-level `On[Property]Changing` method
2. Class-level `PropertyChanging` event
3. Class-level `PropertyChanged` event
4. Property-level `On[Property]Changed` method

PropertyChanged and PropertyChanging Events and Methods Fire During Object Materialization

You may build the event handlers and methods we've discussed in this chapter with the idea of using them whenever your custom code impacts the data in your entities. But be aware that all of these methods and events will also be hit when an entity is being populated from a query. So, if you are querying for addresses, these events will be raised over and over again as each address is materialized. This may or may not be desirable.

Unfortunately, there is no built-in way to discern whether you are in the process of materializing objects. However, you could set up a global Boolean variable that is set to true just before you execute a query, check its value in the PropertyChanged/PropertyChanging events, and then set it to false when the query is complete. You can find another workaround by searching the MSDN forums for a thread titled "PropertyChanged during ObjectMaterialization" (which I started, as a matter of fact). As a response to my question, Matthieu Mezil proposed a solution that reads the stack trace.

So, although there is always a way to solve these types of problems, the key is to be aware of what your code is doing and what impact it may have on your application or resources.

Event parameters

The Sender parameter of the PropertyChanged and PropertyChanging events contains the entity in its current state. You'll have to cast Sender back to the actual type to access these values. The EventArgs for both events have a PropertyChanged property that is a string that defines the name of the changing/changed property. Example 11-14 and Example 11-15 (in the following subsection) demonstrate accessing that property. Unlike the property-level method (e.g., AddressPropertyChanging), the PropertyChanging event does not provide the new value.

Subscribing to the class-level PropertyChanging and PropertyChanged events

Once again, the place to subscribe to the PropertyChanging and PropertyChanged events is in an entity's partial class.

Using the Address class as an example again, in the Address partial class, select Address Events from the Class Name drop-down and then select OnPropertyChanged and On-PropertyChanging from the Method Name drop down. The event handlers shown in Example 11-15 will automatically be created.

Example 11-15. Implementing PropertyChanged and PropertyChanging in VB

VB
```
Private Sub Address_PropertyChanged(ByVal sender As Object, _
  ByVal e As System.ComponentModel.PropertyChangedEventArgs) _
  Handles Me.PropertyChanged
   Dim propBeingChanged As String = e.PropertyName
   'add your logic here
End Sub

Private Sub Address_PropertyChanging(ByVal sender As Object, _
  ByVal e As System.ComponentModel.PropertyChangingEventArgs) _
  Handles Me.PropertyChanging

  Dim propBeingChanged As String = e.PropertyName
  'add your logic here
End Sub
```

In C#, you'll need to manually subscribe to the event handlers as you did for the previous event overrides. You can do this by adding a constructor to the partial class, as shown in Example 11-16. The PropertyChanged and PropertyChanging events expect your handlers to have the same signature as the PropertyChangedEventHandler delegate from a different .NET namespace: System.ComponentModel, rather than that of the System.EventHandler which you used for SavingChanges.

Example 11-16. Implementing PropertyChanged and PropertyChanging in C#

```
public partial class Address
{
 //subscribe to the events inside the Address class constructor
  public Address()
  {
    PropertyChanged += Address_PropertyChanged;
    PropertyChanging += Address_PropertyChanging;
  }

 //create the methods that will be used to handle the events
  private void Address_PropertyChanged(object sender,
   System.ComponentModel.PropertyChangedEventArgs e)
  {
    string propBeingChanged = e.PropertyName;
    //add your logic here
  }
  private void Address_PropertyChanging(object sender,
   System.ComponentModel.PropertyChangingEventArgs e)
  {
    string propBeingChanged = e.PropertyName;
    //add your logic here
  }
}
```

The AssociationChanged Event

With foreign keys in the model—for example, Address.ContactID—you could leverage the OnContactIDChanging and OnContactIDChanged methods when that relationship changes (e.g., the address is associated with a different contact).

If you don't have foreign keys (e.g., you are using a model created in Visual Studio 2008 SP1 and don't want to shift that or your code to using foreign keys), you still have an option. An AssociationChanged event will be raised for Address.ContactReference after a change has been made to the EntityReference or the entity itself (Address.Contact).

Even if you have foreign keys, a change to an entity's EntityCollection (e.g., Contact.Addresses) will not trigger an event. That's because EntityCollection does not implement INotifyCollectionChanged. You can use an AssociationChanged event on Contact.Addresses to execute logic in this scenario.

With the foreign key property methods you get both changed and changing notifications and you are able to navigate to the related entity or collection. The AssociationChanged event does not have the partner event (AssociationChanging), but, unlike the foreign key method, you do have the ability to place an event handler in the Contact class. If you need to impact the Contact or the entire collection of Addresses for that contact, you can do that from the Address class, but placing code related to the Contact in the Address class may convolute your business logic. You will need to assess the options based on your needs, your application domain, and your coding practices and then choose your weapon.

You can create an AssociationChanged event handler for any navigation property of an entity. There is no way to subscribe to an overall event to capture all association changes in an ObjectContext.

You'll need to wire this up manually in VB and C#. Example 11-17 demonstrates creating an AssociationChanged event handler for the ContactReference property of the Address. In the partial class for the Address, create a method (in the example it's called ContactRef_AssociationChanged) to execute the desired logic; then in the class constructor, add code to wire up the event handler to this method.

The implementation is the same for EntityReferences as it is for EntityCollection.

Event arguments

Both the EntityReference and EntityCollection implementations have CollectionChangeEventArgs in their parameters. This argument contains two properties: Action and Element.

The Action property can be one of the CollectionChangeAction enums: Add, Refresh, or Remove.

The Element property returns an object that is the entity on the other end of the relationship being changed. You can cast it back to the appropriate entity type if you want to work with that entity.

Example 11-17 shows an AssociationChanged event handler for the CustomerReference of the Address, followed by the opposite—an AssociationChanged handler for the Addresses property of the Customer. Each method demonstrates how to access the related end in the association.

Example 11-17. Implementing the AssociationChanged event

```
using System.ComponentModel;
namespace BAEntities
{
  public partial class Address
  {
    public Address()
```

```
    {
      ContactReference.AssociationChanged +=  Add_CustRefChanged;
    }
    private void Add_CustRefChanged(object sender,CollectionChangeEventArgs e)
    {
      CollectionChangeAction act  = e.Action;
      var custOnOtherEnd = (Contact)e.Element;
      //add your logic here
    }
  }

  public partial class Contact
  {
    public Contact ()
    {
      Addresses.AssociationChanged += Addresses_AssociationChanged;
    }
    private void Addresses_AssociationChanged
       (object sender, CollectionChangeEventArgs e)
    {
      CollectionChangeAction act  = e.Action;
      var addOnOtherEnd = (Address)e.Element;
      //add your logic here
    }
  }
}
```

Creating Your Own Partial Methods and Properties

With partial classes, you can do more than extend existing methods and handle events. You can also create your own methods or properties.

Overriding the Object Constructor

You may have noticed in the generated classes that there is no constructor for the entity classes. In other words, there is no specific code for when an entity is being instantiated. This provides a great opportunity for you to implement custom logic for an entity's constructor. This constructor will impact entities that are newly created in memory as well as entities that are being materialized as a result of a query.

With regard to the latter, be aware that the constructor is hit before the object materialization applies the resultant values. By default, you wouldn't use this to set property values that you do not want to be overwritten by object materialization. You could, however, take advantage of the `ObjectContext.ObjectMaterialized` event to avoid overwriting.

However, the benefit of this is that you can set property values for new objects without affecting the values of queried objects.

For example, the Contact entity has an AddDate property to indicate when the entity was created. The database does not automatically populate this value; therefore, it is up to your application to do so. You can use the Contact's constructor to insert the current date and time when a new Contact is created.

To see how this works, create a new partial class for Contact. Remember in the C# class to fix the namespace as you have done with the previous partial classes. Then, add a class constructor with the code to affect AddDate, as shown in Example 11-18.

Example 11-18. Overriding the constructor in VB and C#

VB
```
Public Sub New()
  AddDate = DateTime.Now
End Sub
```

C#
```
public Contact()
{
 AddDate = DateTime.Now;
}
```

In Chapter 17, you'll learn about another new feature of Entity Framework, called *self-tracking entities*. These entities benefit from the ObjectMaterialized event as can other Plain Old CLR Objects (POCO) entities that you may create.

Overriding ObjectContext.SaveChanges

A new feature in Entity Framework 4 that I've mentioned a few times already is the ability to override ObjectContext.SaveChanges, because it is now a virtual method. The term *virtual* in C# is the same as *overridable* in Visual Basic. It allows you to replace the base method with your own in a class that derives (a.k.a. inherits) from another. BAEntities inherits ObjectContext. By default, when you call BAEntities.SaveChanges you will execute the ObjectContext.SaveChanges method. However, you can override the logic of SaveChanges in the BAEntities partial class.

Here is the signature of SaveChanges:

```
public virtual int SaveChanges(SaveOptions options)
```

In the Entities.cs or Entities.vb class you can add the following methods which will override the inherent SaveChanges method:

VB
```
Public Overrides Function SaveChanges _
 (ByVal options As System.Data.Objects.SaveOptions) As Integer
   Return MyBase.SaveChanges(options)
End Function
```

C#
```
public override int SaveChanges(System.Data.Objects.SaveOptions options)
{
  return base.SaveChanges(options);
}
```

In these examples, although the code overrides the base `SaveChanges`, it still calls `base.SaveChanges`, that is, the actual `ObjectContext.SaveChanges` method. You can add logic to execute before or after `base.SaveChanges` is called, or even completely redefine the logic for `SaveChanges` by eliminating the call to `base.SaveChanges`. You may also have logic that determines whether or not to call `base.SaveChanges`. These are things you can't achieve in the `SavingChanges` handler.

You will want to have a deeper understanding of Entity Framework than you do at this point before you start messing around with this method, especially if you are considering a complete replacement of the existing logic.

The impact of being able to override `SaveChanges` increases dramatically as you get into more advanced features of Entity Framework, such as implementing POCO classes. You'll learn more about this in Chapter 13.

Creating Custom Properties

Custom properties are a way to provide computed properties (e.g., a `FullName` property based on an existing `FirstName` and `LastName`) to entities.

Custom properties don't necessarily need to be calculated from other existing properties. For example, you may have an investment application that would need to leverage real-time stock prices. Rather than build a `CurrentPrice` property in the model, which would be required to map back to the data store, you could create the property in the partial class and then populate it during object materialization or on demand if you don't believe that every entity object will need to provide that information.

Another example would be to access some cached data. The BreakAway application has a utility that grabs the next day's forecast at each of the lodgings in the database. This happens once per day and the results are stored in a local XML file.

My blog post, "Building an XML file with Google's Weather and LINQ to XML," shows you how you can build the same type of file that is accessed by the code in Example 11-19. You can find the post at *http://blogs.devsource.com/devlife/content/net_general/building_an_xml_file_with_googles_weather_and_linq_to_xml.html*.

Using Example 11-19, you can create a new `TomorrowForecast` custom property and populate it with the data in that local XML file (which has been loaded into memory) after each `Lodging` entity has been materialized.

Precalculating the custom property for every entity being materialized is useful when you know that the value will be accessed for all (or at least most) of the entities being materialized. Otherwise, you should consider calculating the property only as needed and not during object materialization.

The logic for populating the forecast property is placed in the `Lodging` partial class as an `internal` (`Friend`, in Visual Basic) method. This prevents developers from calling the method. Only other classes in the model assembly are able to call it and that is what the `ObjectMaterialized` method does in Example 11-19.

Example 11-19. Populating a custom property with ObjectContext.ObjectMaterialized

```
//custom property in Lodging.cs
public string TomorrowForecast { get; set; }

//custom method in Lodging.cs
internal void Materialized()
{
   if (_foreCastsXml == null)
      {
        if (System.IO.File.Exists("LodgingForecasts.XML"))
        {
          //read the file with xelement - move code to application logic
          _foreCastsXml = XElement.Load("LodgingForecasts.XML",
                                        LoadOptions.None);
        }
        else
        {
          throw new System.IO.FileNotFoundException
            ("The LodgingForecasts.XML file was not found");
        }
      }
    //LINQ to XML query of the file
    string f = (from item in file.Elements("Lodging")
                where item.Attribute("ID").Value == LodgingID.ToString()
                select item.Attribute("forecast").Value).FirstOrDefault();
    if (f != null)
      TomorrowForecast = f;
    else
      TomorrowForecast = "";
  }

//ObjectMaterialized method in Entities.cs
void BAEntities_ObjectMaterialized(object sender, ObjectMaterializedEventArgs args)
{
  if (args.Entity is Lodging)
  {
    Lodging lodging = (Lodging)args.Entity;
    lodging.Materialized();
  }
}
```

You cannot use these custom properties in LINQ to Entities or Entity SQL queries, but you can use them in client-side queries, which are just LINQ to Objects queries.

Custom properties can also be useful when you want to define a function that relies on CLR methods that are not available in the model. Example 11-19 leverages the `System.String.Format` method to create some properties that you will be able to use in a number of samples as the book progresses. These properties display the details of a `Reservation`. The `Reservation` entity does not contain much interesting information in its scalar properties. The useful details are in the `Trip` navigation property (start and end dates, trip cost) and in the `Destination` property of the `Trip` (the destination name).

Rather than reconstruct this information over and over again (as you did in Chapter 8), you can create a property of `Reservation` that will give this to you already concatenated. The same information is convenient to concatenate from the `Trip` entity. After adding a `TripDetails` property to the `Trip` entity, you can then add a `TripDetails` property to `Reservation` that reads the `Trip.TripDetails`.

Later in the book, you will learn how to create model-defined functions directly in the EDM. Model-defined functions do not provide you with entity properties at runtime, but one of their benefits over custom properties, however, is that they can be used in queries where properties cannot.

The `Trip.TripDetails` property in Example 11-20 won't presume you are using lazy loading to ensure that the destination information has been loaded, and therefore tests for nulls.

Example 11-20. A custom property to provide a commonly needed concatenation in the BreakAway application

```
using System;
namespace BAGA
{
  public partial class Trip
  {
    public string TripDetails
    {
      get
      {
        string tripCost = "";
        string dates = "";
        if (StartDate > DateTime.MinValue && EndDate > DateTime.MinValue)
        {
          dates = " (" + StartDate.ToShortDateString() + "-" +
                    EndDate.ToShortDateString() + ")";
        }
```

```
            if (TripCostUSD.HasValue)
            { tripCost = string.Format(" ({0:C})", TripCostUSD.Value); }

            if (Destination != null)
            {
              return Destination.Name.Trim() + dates + tripCost;
            }

            return "n/a";
          }
        }
      }
      public partial class Reservation
      {
        public string TripDetails
        {
          get
          {
            return Trip.TripDetails;
          }
        }
      }
    }
```

It's possible to have custom properties with setters. As an example, perhaps your database actually stores full names as "LastName, FirstName". But you want to provide a first and last name in your data entry forms to ensure that the first and last names go into the database in the correct order without depending on the user to enter them properly. You could create custom properties, `FirstName` and `LastName`. The getters for these properties would return the relevant part from the `Name` property. In the setters, you could update the `Name` property based on the incoming part. When `SaveChanges` is called, the value of the `Name` property will get sent to the database in an update.

Using custom properties to perform calculations on child collections

In the BreakAway model, you could create custom read-only properties in the `Reservation` entity for `TotalPaid` and `PaidinFull` that would be calculated based on the sum of the payments for that reservation. As I mentioned earlier in the discussion of computed columns, the data would be valid only if you could ensure that all of the payments are accounted for. If there is a chance that some of the payments have not been retrieved from the database, you shouldn't depend on this.

Overloading Entity Creation Methods

The default code generation template creates a *factory method*[*] for each entity. The methods—which are `static` (`Shared` in VB)—all begin with the word *Create* and let

[*] *http://en.wikipedia.org/wiki/Factory_method_pattern*

you quickly create a new entity. The parameter list for these factory methods consists of all of the non-nullable properties in the class.

The entire set of non-nullable properties isn't always the most desirable list of fields to populate when creating a new class. For example, in the BreakAway model classes, the `Contact.CreateContact` factory method has the signature shown in Example 11-21.

Example 11-21. Signature of the Contact.CreateContact factory method

```
public static Contact CreateContact
(int contactID, string firstName, string lastName,
 global::System.DateTime addDate, global::System.DateTime modifiedDate)
```

In most cases, the `ContactID` will be `0`, and in this case `AddDate` and `ModifiedDate` would most likely be the current date. Why be forced to enter them when you create a new `Contact`? You may also have some of the other values available, which means that after calling `CreateContact`, you still have to set more properties.

Creating an overload of the method would be very convenient. You can request the nonobvious values, such as `FirstName` and `LastName`, and then delegate out to the generated factory method to fill in the rest of the non-nullable values. You can place the new version of the method in the `Contact`'s partial class. Example 11-22 shows a more useful `CreateContact` method.

Example 11-22. Overriding the Create factory method

```
public static Contact CreateContact(string firstName, string lastName)
{
  var contact = CreateContact(0, firstName, lastName,
                              DateTime.Now, DateTime.Now, new Byte[]{0});
  return contact;
}
```

When you call the `CreateContact` method, two signatures will be available, as shown in Figure 11-2.

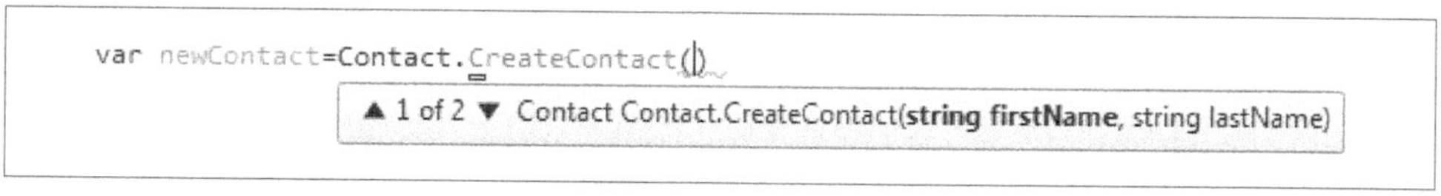

```
var newContact=Contact.CreateContact(
    ▲ 1 of 2 ▼ Contact Contact.CreateContact(string firstName, string lastName)
```

Figure 11-2. The new CreateContact overload as shown by IntelliSense

As you use the different methods that the entities inherit from `EntityObject` or `ObjectContext`, keep your mind open to the idea of being able to enhance them to suit your purposes.

Using Partial Classes for More Than Just Overriding Methods and Events

You can, of course, create all kinds of new logic in partial classes, whether the logic pertains to properties or to methods.

For example, perhaps you want to perform some validation logic without saving changes, such as supplying default values for entities. You could place methods for this within an entity's partial class and then call that method as needed. If you like the idea of having validation performed on a number of entities at once, or even on a variety of entity types (as `SaveChanges` can do), you could place the method in the `ObjectContext`'s partial class. Keep in mind that only attached entities will be available at that point.

Other than creating your own classes, the partial classes are the primary mechanism in the Entity Framework for adding business logic to entities.

Overriding Default Code Generation

In the first version of Entity Framework, it was possible to override EDM code generation completely so that you can define what the generated classes look like. The code generator was based on the `System.Data.Entity.Design` API, which you could use directly. However, it was a proprietary code generator written by the Entity Framework team, was a lot of work, and required developers to learn yet another API.

In Visual Studio 2010, the Entity Framework now uses a code generator that was already a part of Visual Studio, known as Textual Transformation Template Toolkit or T4. T4 was added to one of the Domain Specific Language (DSL) tools that appeared in Visual Studio 2008. The essential function of T4 is to create a code file by transforming a text file (e.g., your EDMX file) into another file (e.g., a class) using rules that you write in yet another file (a template file) with the T4 syntax. The beauty of using T4 to generate classes from the EDMX is that T4 is a common tool that you can use for many other code generation tasks. This way, you can use something you may already be familiar with, or at least you will be using a transferable skill.

T4 can be used to generate code in whatever language you want. Entity Framework provides templates to output C# and Visual Basic code files.

The default code generation that you have been taking advantage of thus far in this book uses a T4 template file. If you want to change how the classes are generated you can start with a copy of the default template and edit it. The default template is buried deep within the file path of the Visual Studio 2010 installation. But the Designer can easily make a copy for you that you can customize and use in your projects. Microsoft provides a few templates for transforming EDMX files, and you will also find that there are templates others have created as well. For your first stab at customizing the classes, we'll start by modifying the default template.

Visual Studio 2010 does not have a T4 editor to help you with things such as syntax highlighting, formatting, or IntelliSense. When you open a T4 file in Visual Studio it will look like a simple text file. There are third-party tools that you can use, such as Visual T4 from Clarius Consulting (*http://www.visualT4.com*) and T4 Editor from Tangible Engineering (*http://www.tangible.de*).

Visual Studio 2010 has a built-in Extension Manager that lets you easily install extensions. See my blog post on using this feature to download and install T4 Editor (*http://blogs.devsource.com/devlife/content/net_general/vs2010_vsx_and_t4_editor.html*).

Switching to a Template

Rather than customizing the default, the Entity Framework Designer will make a copy of the default for you to work with and place that in your project. Let's see how that works.

1. Open the Entity Data Model in the Designer.
2. Right-click in the Designer background.
3. From the context menu, choose Add Code Generation Item.

   The Add New Item window will open displaying all available templates. You will most likely have only the default template, ADO.NET EntityObject Generator, and the ADO.NET Self-Tracking Entity Generator templates to begin with.
4. Select the ADO.NET EntityObject Generator template.
5. Change the default template name from *Model1.tt* to *BreakAway.tt*.

Now look in the Solution Explorer. You will notice a number of changes to the project:

- The code file attached to the EDMX is still there, but it contains nothing more than a note indicating that the default code generation has been disabled.
- There is a new file, *BreakAway.tt*, in the project. This is the template that is now being used to generate the classes from the EDMX.
- The *BreakAway.tt* file has an attached code file, *BreakAway.cs* (or *.vb*). This is the new version of the generated file. If you open this file, you will see that it is exactly the same as the previously generated class files. That's because your current template file is the same as the default.

The *BreakAway.tt* file is now responsible for generating the classes based on the model.

Reading the Template

Before editing the code, let's take a quick look at a bit of the template syntax.

Open the BreakAway template file, *BreakAway.tt*.

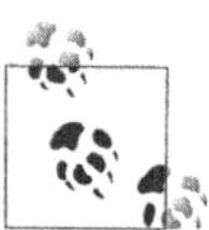

Don't miss the helpful notes that the Entity Framework team embedded into the first 20 or so lines of the file.

Do a search for the word *ObjectContext*. The first instance of the word will be in a comment. The second one will be in this line of code at about line 110:

```
<#=Accessibility.ForType(container)#>
   partial class <#=code.Escape(container)#> : ObjectContext
```

The line is not wrapped in the *.tt* file. It is wrapped here only to accommodate the margins of this book's pages.

Code that is surrounded by `<#= ...... #>` directives is processing instructions. Everything else is text that will go directly into the code file. Therefore, this particular line says to execute a processing method which will read the `EntityContainer`'s `Accessibility` (defined by Entity Container Access in the EDMX) and output the value (`Public` or `Internal`). Then it will directly write out the words *partial class*. Next, there is another processing directive, `code.Escape(container)`, which is another internal T4 method. This outputs the name of the `EntityContainer`. Finally, some more text is output: ": `ObjectContext`"<# #>, enclosing processing instructions in templates.

When T4 processes this line of code against *BreakAway.EDMX*, it will output the following:

```
public partial class BAEntities : ObjectContext
```

Modifying the Template

Let's make some minor changes to the template so that you can get a feel for using T4 and taking ownership of the generated classes.

Earlier in this chapter, you added the `ObjectMaterialized` event in the `Entities` partial class and then a `Materialized` method, to be called by `ObjectMaterialized`, in the `Lodging` partial class. Now you will use T4 to inject the `Materialized` partial method into each entity class

When planning a template customization, be careful not to insert actual business logic into the template. During code generation, you do not know what logic you want to be executed in `ObjectMaterialized`, so you don't want to write that into the generated class. You can at least provide a partial `Materialized` method for each entity class. This way, the developer implementing the custom logic will use the common method name.

Inserting the Managed partial method in each entity class

Search for the term *SummaryComment(entity)* to find the beginning of the section which creates the entity class code. This section is executed for every entity discovered in the model.

Approximately 15 lines farther down you'll see a declaration that begins with `if (!entity.Abstract)`.

Just above the opening tag (`<#`) add the first three lines of code shown in Example 11-23. The rest of the code, shown in bold in the example, is there to help clarify the position of the new code.

Example 11-23. Overriding the Create factory method

```
    #region <#=GetResourceString("Template_RegionPartialMethods")#>

    partial void Materialized();

    #endregion

<#
        if (!entity.Abstract)
        {
            WriteFactoryMethod(entity, code);
        }
```

When you save the file, the BreakAway class file will be regenerated. If you check the generated classes you'll see that the partial method is now declared in each class. The beginning of the `Address` partial class is shown in Example 11-24.

Example 11-24. Overriding the Create factory method

```
public partial class Address : EntityObject
{
  #region Partial Methods

  partial void Materialized();

  #endregion
```

This particular modification doesn't relieve you of the steps for adding the `ObjectMaterialized` event handler and its method, or for creating the `Materialized` method in the `Lodging` class. But it will help developers on your team by providing the proper common method for them to implement in the class logic.

Other ways to create common methods or properties for all entities

In addition to customizing the code generation to add a common method or property to entities, there are a few other ways you can get the same effect:

- Place the method into the `ObjectContext`'s partial class and pass the entity in as a parameter. This will work only for entities that are attached to the `ObjectContext`.
- Create an extension method for `EntityObject`. This will then be an available method for any class that inherits from `EntityObject`.

Customizing a Template for Major Class Modifications

The preceding example demonstrated a small change to the generated class. Many developers will want to modify the template to remove their class's dependency on the Entity Framework APIs. The default template forces each entity to inherit from `EntityObject`. The new support for POCOs will enable developers to remove that inheritance. The first step is to remove the template code which adds in the inheritance. Rather than directly writing out `EntityObject`, you'll find that the inheritance is created with the following syntax:

VB
```
Inherits <#=BaseTypeName(entity, code)#>
```

C#
```
: <#=BaseTypeName(entity, code)#>
```

Removing this simple bit of code will have a major impact on the classes, since you will now lose the functionality provided by the `EntityObject` class. In Chapter 13, you will learn about POCO classes, which are much lighter in weight than the generated `EntityObject` classes. There is a Microsoft-provided T4 template for creating POCO classes. Even if the provided template isn't exactly what you need, it will likely be a much better starting point for generating your own simple classes than trying to whittle down the default template.

One other T4 template is available in Visual Studio 2010 for Entity Framework: the Self-Tracking Entities template. You will learn about self-tracking entities in Chapter 17.

Switching Between the Default Template and a Custom Template

If you open the EDMX in the Designer after switching to your own code generation template, you will find that the model's `Code Generation` property in the Properties window is `None`. The options, provided by a drop down, are `Default` and `None`. `Default` will use the default template to generate the entity classes directly from the model. When you created the custom template this value was switched to `None`. As a result, you may recall that the class file attached to the model contains nothing but some comments.

If you set the property back to `Default`, you can regenerate the classes from the model itself by saving the model, or by forcing the default generation by right-clicking on the EDMX file and choosing Run Custom Tool.

However, this will create a conflict, because the classes already exist in the file created from the template. If, for some reason, you want to revert to the default `EntityObject` template, you need to prevent the custom template from generating classes. You can do that by removing the template's `Custom Tool` property. The name of the tool which processes the template is `TextTemplatingFileGenerator`. When you delete the `Custom Tool`'s property value, *BreakAway.tt*'s attached class file will disappear.

Therefore, if you have the need, it is indeed possible to switch back and forth between generating classes from the model to generating them from a custom template.

Look at how the T4 template handles the `LazyLoadingEnabled` annotation in the CSD's `EntityContainer` element for inspiration on how you can add your own annotation into the EDMX's XML, and then use T4 to generate code based on those annotations. I won't be writing about this in this book.

Summary

In this chapter, you learned how to use partial classes generated by the Entity Framework to insert your own business logic into entity classes and to the class that serves as your context. You can subscribe to events, add code to partial methods, and even add completely new methods and properties to the generated classes.

Although there are a lot of opportunities for customizing entities and the `ObjectContext`, sometimes you will find that these are not enough. The `EntityObjects` are designed to encapsulate schema and relationships, not behavior. The lack of an opportunity to tap into `AssociationChanging` when you do have access to `AssociationChanged` is an obvious example.

If you still want more out of these classes, you should consider using POCO classes instead, which we will cover in Chapter 13.

The next chapter, however, will give you a chance to build another application—this time, a Rapid Application Development (RAD) ASP.NET application.

CHAPTER 12

Data Binding with RAD ASP.NET Applications

With the Entity Framework you can build both Rapid Application Development (RAD) applications and highly architected applications. On the RAD end, the ASP.NET `EntityDataSource` control enables quick declarative data binding that you can use in a number of scenarios. Dynamic Data controls and templates build on the `EntityDataSource` to make RAD sites with Entity Framework even easier to create.

Using entities in web applications can be challenging because the `ObjectContext` does not survive postbacks, and therefore cannot do its job of keeping track of changes to your entities. The `EntityDataSource` control helps you resolve many of the challenges in scenarios where you do not need to use a business or data access layer. Later in the book, after you have learned about the Entity Framework in more detail, you will learn about building layered ASP.NET applications.

In this chapter, you will build four RAD ASP.NET web applications using entities that make use of the `EntityDataSource` control. The first application, Hello Entities, will introduce you to the `EntityDataSource`. The second will add some more complexity by working with entity reference data. The third example features hierarchical data as well as greater interaction between the controls. After you build the examples, the chapter will bring you on a tour of some of the more interesting features of the `EntityDataSource` control. Finally, you'll build a quick ASP.NET Dynamic Data website so that you can see how Dynamic Data simplifies some of the manual tasks you have to perform when using the `EntityDataSource` directly. Both the `EntityDataSource` and Dynamic Data templates are highly customizable. This chapter won't delve too deeply into this area, as you can learn much more about these in many ASP.NET resources.

Using the EntityDataSource Control to Access Flat Data

Although you can bind query results directly to any data-binding or list control in a web application, updating entities is challenging due to the life cycle of an ASP.NET `Page` class. As you expand your knowledge of the Entity Framework, you will be better prepared to address these challenges, and you'll leverage this understanding to build two more web applications, in Chapter 27. In that chapter, we will also look closely at the life cycle of the ASP.NET `Page` class so that you understand why it presents such difficulties for change tracking.

For now, it helps to know that there's an easy way to use entities in web applications when you are looking for a quick solution. The Entity Framework adds a new control to the set of existing (and possibly familiar) ASP.NET `DataSource` controls (`SqlDataSource`, `LinqDataSource`, etc.), which simplifies data binding for read/write functionality. You can configure the `EntityDataSource` control in the UI and it will handle all of the grunt work for retrieving, inserting, updating, and deleting entities on your behalf. Once you've defined an `EntityDataSource` control, you can bind it to any web control that supports data binding.

Let's start with a small and simple Hello Entities application so that you can get a feel for how the control works. The following pages will walk you through the steps for displaying and editing contacts from the BreakAway model. This will be flat data—no related data will be used in the creation of this simple web page.

Creating the Hello Entities Project

You'll begin by creating a new ASP.NET Web Application project for this example:

1. In the same solution you have been working with in previous chapters, create a new Empty ASP.NET Web Application project.

There are two templates in Visual Studio 2010 for ASP.NET Web Applications. The default creates a predesigned site, while the other is an empty site.

2. Add a reference to the BreakAwayModel project and `System.Data.Entity`.
3. Copy the `connectionStrings` section from the BreakAwayModel project's *app.config* file into the web application's *web.config* file.
4. Save and build the application. This is an important step that allows the Entity Data Source Wizard that you'll be using to find the connection string information in the *web.config* file.
5. Add a new web form to the project and open it in Design mode to begin adding controls.

Creating a GridView and an EntityDataSource Concurrently

Although you can create the `EntityDataSource` control first and then create the binding control and link them up, ASP.NET also lets you create an `EntityDataSource` control in the wizard of the binding control that will consume the data, in this case a `GridView`. We'll use this latter method.

1. Drag a `GridView` from the `Data` section of the Toolbox onto the web page.
2. From the GridView Tasks window, choose <New data source> from the Choose Data Source drop-down list (see Figure 12-1).
3. In the Data Source Configuration Wizard that appears, select Entity from the Choose a Data Source Type page, as shown in Figure 12-2, and click OK.

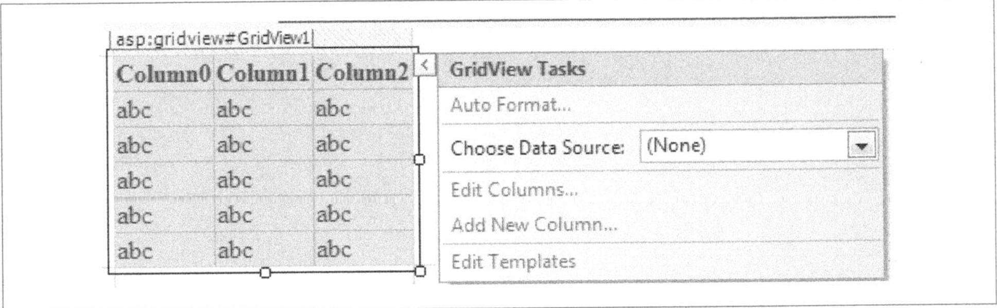

Figure 12-1. The GridView Tasks window

Configuring an EntityDataSource with Its Wizard

The `EntityDataSource` will need to know where its entity comes from. The wizard will walk you through the critical properties that need to be configured.

You can configure many more properties of the `EntityDataSource` through its Properties window or directly in its markup. You will work with these additional properties further on in the chapter.

The first page of the Data Source Configuration Wizard will allow you to select a named connection from the connections that the wizard finds in the *web.config* file:

1. Select BAEntities in the Named Connection drop down.

   The wizard finds the container name by looking in the Conceptual Schema Definition Layer (CSDL) file listed in the connection string you selected in the first drop down. This should automatically be populated with `BAEntities`.
2. Click Next.

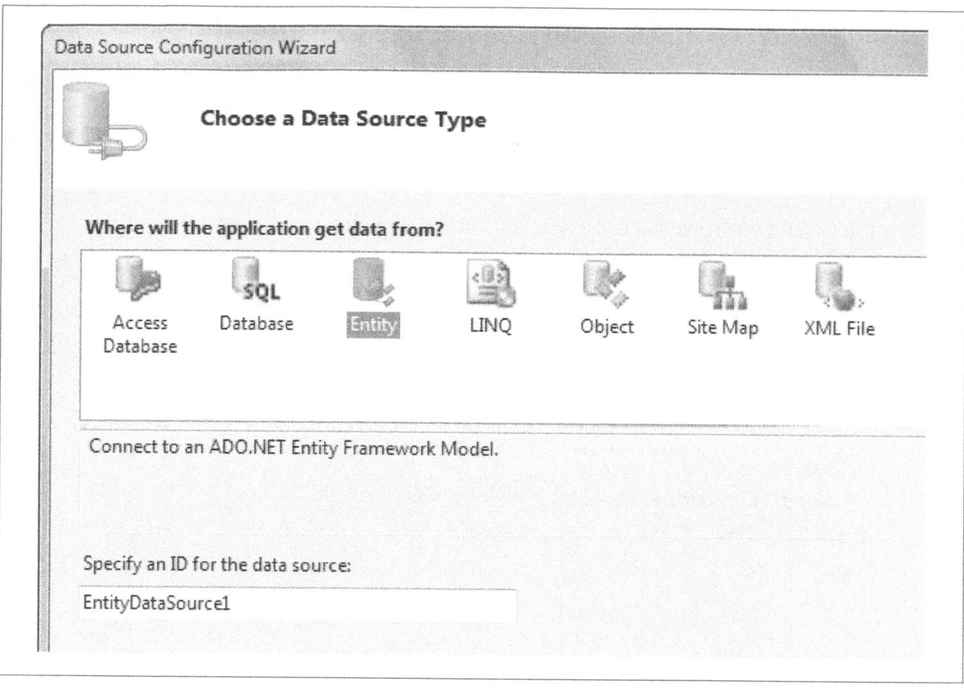

Figure 12-2. Defining the data source to be an EntityDataSource

3. On the Configure Data Selection page, choose Contacts from the EntitySetName drop down.

   Again, the wizard has inspected the model to discover the available `EntitySets`.

4. Leave Select All (Entity Value) checked.

   By default, all of the properties will be used. If you choose specific properties, you won't get an entity object back. Instead, you will get a `DbDataRecord`, which cannot be change-tracked, and therefore cannot be updated. Because of this, if you check any of the properties, you will notice that the checkboxes for enabling automatic inserts, updates, and deletes will be disabled.

5. Check the three boxes for enabling automatic inserts, updates, and deletes so that you will be able to conduct a test edit with the `EntityDataSource` control. When you're finished, the page should look like Figure 12-3.

6. Click Finish.

Figure 12-4 shows the grid and `EntityDataSource` control as they are displayed on the page after you finish configuring the `EntityDataSource`. The `EntityDataSource` control will not be displayed on the page at runtime.

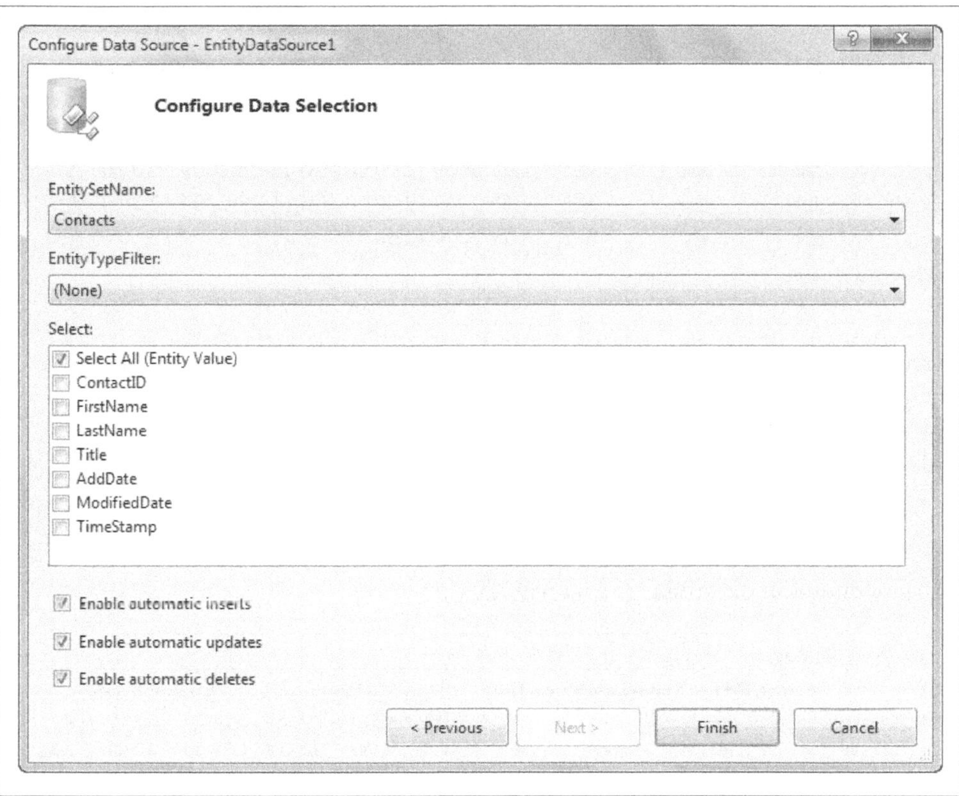

Figure 12-3. Configuring the EntityDataSource to use the Customer entity type, and selecting all properties so that you can perform inserts, updates, and deletes

Formatting the GridView

Even though you configured the `EntityDataSource` control to support inserts, updates, and deletes, you'll need to specifically enable the `GridView` to allow the same functionality.

The `EntityDataSource` control also supports dynamic sorting and paging, but again, you need to enable the features in the grid so that you can take advantage of them:

1. Select the GridView's Smart Tag to open its Tasks window again.

   A control's Smart Tag becomes visible when the control is selected. You can see the grid's Smart Tag attached to the upper-right corner of the selected grid in Figure 12-5.

2. Check the Enable Paging, Enable Sorting, Enable Editing, and Enable Deleting checkboxes.

body

ContactID	FirstName	LastName	Title	AddDate	ModifiedDate
0	abc	abc	abc	11/28/2009 12:00:00 AM	11/28/2009 12:00:00 AM
1	abc	abc	abc	11/28/2009 12:00:00 AM	11/28/2009 12:00:00 AM
2	abc	abc	abc	11/28/2009 12:00:00 AM	11/28/2009 12:00:00 AM
3	abc	abc	abc	11/28/2009 12:00:00 AM	11/28/2009 12:00:00 AM
4	abc	abc	abc	11/28/2009 12:00:00 AM	11/28/2009 12:00:00 AM

EntityDataSource - EntityDataSource1

Figure 12-4. The design-time GridView after it has been hooked up to the EntityDataSource

The ASP.NET `GridView` control does not support insertion even though the `EntityDataSource` control does. There are ways around this, but a solution is not something to get into in a Hello Entities demonstration. We'll discuss inserting in the next example.

The grid should look similar to Figure 12-5.

asp:gridview#GridView1

	ContactID	FirstName	LastName	Title	AddDate	ModifiedDate
Edit Delete	0	abc	abc	abc	11/28/2009 12:00:00 AM	11/28/2009 12:00:00 AM
Edit Delete	1	abc	abc	abc	11/28/2009 12:00:00 AM	11/28/2009 12:00:00 AM
Edit Delete	2	abc	abc	abc	11/28/2009 12:00:00 AM	11/28/2009 12:00:00 AM
Edit Delete	3	abc	abc	abc	11/28/2009 12:00:00 AM	11/28/2009 12:00:00 AM
Edit Delete	4	abc	abc	abc	11/28/2009 12:00:00 AM	11/28/2009 12:00:00 AM
Edit Delete	5	abc	abc	abc	11/28/2009 12:00:00 AM	11/28/2009 12:00:00 AM
Edit Delete	6	abc	abc	abc	11/28/2009 12:00:00 AM	11/28/2009 12:00:00 AM
Edit Delete	7	abc	abc	abc	11/28/2009 12:00:00 AM	11/28/2009 12:00:00 AM
Edit Delete	8	abc	abc	abc	11/28/2009 12:00:00 AM	11/28/2009 12:00:00 AM
Edit Delete	9	abc	abc	abc	11/28/2009 12:00:00 AM	11/28/2009 12:00:00 AM
1 2						

EntityDataSource - EntityDataSource1

Figure 12-5. The GridView with editing, deleting, sorting, and paging enabled

> ### Dynamic Paging and Entity Framework Queries
>
> ASP.NET data sources support server-side paging. Although the `GridView` controls the actual paging settings, the `DataSource` needs to have its `AutoPage` property set to `True` to support the feature (`AutoPage` is `True` by default).
>
> With paging, rather than downloading and viewing all of the rows at once, the `DataSource` can query for only a certain number of rows at a time to be displayed in the `GridView`, and then can make another call to the database to get another subset of data as needed. The default number of rows it can query is 10.
>
> Depending on your application scenario, more calls to the database with less data to manage may be preferable to fewer calls to the database and more data to manage.
>
> See the "GridView Web Server Control Overview" topic in the MSDN documentation for more information on working with `GridViews` and paging.

Testing the Web Application

There's a lot more you will want to do to make this a nicely usable grid, such as hiding the `ContactID`, formatting the date columns, and so forth. These are not Entity Framework-specific tasks, so let's just jump ahead to see the `EntityDataSource` in action. Set the new web form as the Start page and run the application to test the paging, sorting, and editing features, as shown in Figure 12-6.

	ContactID	FirstName	LastName	Title	AddDate	ModifiedDate
Edit Delete	1	Alex	Solzhenitsyn	Mr.	1/8/2009 11:41:45 AM	1/22/2009 3:43:24 PM
Edit Delete	2	Keith	Harris	Mr.	2/13/2003 8:23:01 PM	8/7/2008 8:27:07 AM
Edit Delete	3	Donna	Carreras	Ms.	3/23/2008 5:51:55 PM	8/7/2008 8:27:07 AM
Edit Delete	4	Janet	Gates	Mrs.	6/11/2004 3:10:10 PM	8/7/2008 8:27:07 AM
Edit Delete	5	Lucy	Harrington	Mr.	9/16/2005 11:29:12 PM	8/7/2008 8:27:07 AM
Update Cancel	6	Rosmarie	Carroll	Ms.	11/6/2005 9:35:53 PM	8/7/2008 8:27:07 AM
Edit Delete	7	Dominic	Gash	Mr.	11/10/2005 6:13:49 PM	8/7/2008 8:27:07 AM
Edit Delete	10	Kathleen	Garza	Ms.	9/26/2006 2:57:45 AM	8/7/2008 8:27:07 AM
Edit Delete	11	Katherine	Harding	Ms.	3/9/2004 1:12:57 PM	8/7/2008 8:27:07 AM
Edit Delete	12	Johnny	Caprio	Mr.	2/15/2003 7:49:09 AM	8/7/2008 8:27:07 AM
12345678910...						

Figure 12-6. Editing a contact at runtime

If you attempt to delete a contact that has related data (addresses or a customer record), you'll get a Reference Constraint error. We're not going to worry about this in the Hello Entities application.

Understanding How the EntityDataSource Retrieves and Updates Your Data

As you saw in the preceding example, the grid was populated by the `EntityDataSource` without the need for you to write any code to define and execute a query. And it seemed to magically handle the update for you. How did the data get to the form? How did the changes get back to the database?

EntityDataSource and Its Query

At runtime, when the `EntityDataSource` needs to populate itself, it begins by reading the `EntityConnectionString`, `EntityContainer`, and `EntitySet` properties you defined. It then creates a new `ObjectContext` using the `EntityConnectionString` name, and an `ObjectQuery` using the `EntitySet`. If you had chosen individual entity properties, such as `FirstName` and `LastName`, it would build an Entity SQL string using the `EntityContainer` name and the names of the selected properties. The query is built dynamically based on the properties of the `EntityDataSource`.

The wizard that you walked through configured only the most elemental properties of the `EntityDataSource`, but the control has many more properties, and some of those allow you to further define the query. A subset of these additional `EntityDataSource` properties mimic query builder methods: `Where`, `GroupBy`, `Select`, and `OrderBy`. At runtime, the same query pipeline that creates a query from the query builder methods creates a query based on these `EntityDataSource` properties. In fact, the `EntityDataSource`'s internal method uses the Entity SQL query builder methods to build its queries.

The `EntityDataSource` control also has an `Include` property that emulates the `ObjectQuery.Include` method. There's an `EntityTypeFilter` property that internally leverages Entity SQL's `OFTYPE ONLY` operator to work with inherited entity types. You will learn more about inheritance in the Entity Data Model in the next chapter.

By assigning values to the `EntityDataSource` properties, you can achieve the same results as though you had built a query using query builder methods. For example, an `EntityDataSource` with the property settings shown in Table 12-1 is equivalent to the `ObjectQuery` created by the following query builder methods:

```
context.Contacts.Include("Addresses")
       .Where("it.FirstName='Robert'").OrderBy("it.LastName")
```

Table 12-1. EntityDataSource property settings to create the query

Property	Value
`EntitySet`	`Contacts`
`Include`	`Addresses`
`Where`	`it.FirstName='Robert'`
`OrderBy`	`it.LastName`

You'll learn more about these various properties as you read through this chapter.

EntityDataSource and Its ObjectContext

In the previous example, you had a single `EntityDataSource` on the page to manage `Contact` entities. As you'll see later in the chapter, you can have multiple `EntityDataSource` controls on a page. By default, each `EntityDataSource` on a page creates its own `ObjectContext`. If you have more than one `EntityDataSource`, you will get multiple `ObjectContext` objects and multiple connections to the database.

Every time a page posts back, the contexts that were created are dropped. When the page is re-created, the `EntityDataSource` creates a new `ObjectContext` for itself. Because the previous context is no longer being used, .NET's garbage collector will eventually remove it. Like any `ObjectContext` object, the `EntityDataSource`'s context does not hold on to connections to the database once it has executed its command and retrieved the requested data, so this is not something to worry about, yet it's good to be aware of if you are focused on resource usage.

Using your own context

You can override the creation of individual contexts and thereby have more control over the entities.

One way to do this is to instantiate your own context in the form, and force the `EntityDataSource` to use that. The `EntityDataSource` has a `ContextCreating` event, which fires just as the `DataSource` is about to create its own context. The signature of the event has a parameter that passes in the `EntityDataSourceEventArgs`, as shown in the following code:

```
EntityDataSource.ContextCreating(object sender,
 System.Web.UI.WebControls.EntityDataSourceContextCreatingEventArgs e)
```

The `EventArgs` has a `context` property that represents the context for the data source.

When you set that context to your own context, your context becomes responsible for the `DataSource` and the entities it returns. The following code sample assumes that the context, `myContext`, has been instantiated elsewhere in the form and is declared as a class-level variable:

```
protected void EDS_ContextCreating(object sender,
 System.Web.UI.WebControls.EntityDataSourceContextCreatingEventArgs e)
{
  e.Context=myContext;
}
```

Why use a single context for your `EntityDataSource` controls? Creating your own context has many benefits. When you have multiple `EntityDataSource` controls with objects that are related to one another, those objects are never connected, so you can't build a graph or update a graph. By creating a single context to manage multiple `EntityData`

Source controls, you would be able to work with graphs comprising the entities in the various EntityDataSource controls.

Relationships among entities will not be recognized unless the same ObjectContext is managing the entities. Otherwise, even if you have customers and reservations that do belong to one another, if separate contexts are managing them you will not be able to traverse from customers to reservations or from reservations to customers. In other words, Customer.Reservations would result in zero reservations and Reservation.Customer would return null or nothing.

Although you gain a resource usage advantage by sharing a context, the gain won't necessarily be large. The ability to control which ObjectContext is managing your entities, however, is very powerful.

EntityDataSource Context Events

A number of events are related to the context for the EntityDataSource. Each event offers an opportunity to have more control over the default context the data source uses. Here are some of the more interesting details exposed during these events:

ContextCreating
: e.Context provides a hook to the context before it even exists. As you saw earlier, this is where you can tell the data source to use another context instead of creating its own.

  There is no Cancel argument in this event. There would be no point to canceling the creation of a context for the data source as it would not function at all.

ContextCreated
: The EventArgs of this event also returns the EntityDataSource's context, whether this is the default context or one that you substituted in the ContextCreating event. You have an opportunity to work directly with this context in the page's code-behind.

ContextDisposing
: e.Cancel allows you to stop the context from being disposed. You may need to use this if you are managing the context and know it will need to do more work before page creation is complete.

  e.Context returns the context.

EntityDataSource and ViewState

Although there is an ObjectContext for creating and executing queries and for saving changes to the database, an instantiated ObjectContext does not live across the many postbacks your page will perform. Therefore, the context itself is not able to track the changes to the objects. So, how does the ObjectDataSource control manage to send your changes to the database?

Chapter 27 will provide an in-depth look at how the life cycle of an ASP.NET page impacts `ObjectContext` as you prepare to build a layered web application with entities. `EntityDataSource` hides all of those concerns from you.

The `EntityDataSource` control not only maintains the current values of its data, but also (by default) keeps track of the original values as they were retrieved from the data store. This is necessary for performing the updates to any modified data so that the `DataSource` knows exactly which fields were modified, as well as whether any of the properties in the model have been flagged for concurrency checks. The original values are critical.

The `EntityDataSource` maintains the state information by keeping the original and current values, as well as any other critical values such as those that are being used for concurrency checking, in the `ControlState` of the ASP.NET page. `ControlState` is a special subset of `ViewState` that you cannot disable. The values are retained across postbacks and are then available when it is time to perform an update.

You can modify this behavior with two properties of the `EntityDataSource`: `EnableViewState` and `StoreOriginalValuesinViewState`. Both properties are `True` by default. If you are new to ASP.NET, you can learn more about `ViewState` in the MSDN documentation as well as a variety of other resources.

As you will see shortly, even if you choose not to retain the original values in `ViewState`, you have opportunities to define original values prior to data updates in the `EntityDataSource.Updating` event.

Taking Stock of the EntityDataSource's Database Hits

`EntityDataSource` is a very convenient control. Because it is completely declarative, you, the programmer, need to make only a small investment in providing data to your website. But you should be aware of what it's doing in the background.

The `EntityDataSource` makes a lot of hits to the database. If you have one `EntityDataSource` that retrieves contacts and you edit the contacts in a `GridView`, here is a rundown of the events that will occur when you use the default settings:

Page load
: A single query is run to retrieve the set of entities required for the control. If it is a `GridView` that uses paging, the query will retrieve the number of records defined by the page count. If it is a `DetailsView` or `FormView`, it will retrieve a single entity.

  If the binding control does any type of paging at all, including `DetailsView` and `FormView`, a query is run in advance that gets a count of how many records satisfy the query before the paging records are selected.

  This means that for most controls, two queries are run every time the page loads.

User clicks Edit

This causes a page refresh. The initial query (or queries) is run again. If you are binding to another `DataSource`—for example, the `Activity EntityDataSource` to populate the drop-down list—its query is run as well. The queries are run separately so that there will be a number of hits to the database.

A query is run against the database to retrieve a fresh copy of the entity to be edited.

User clicks Cancel

This causes the page to refresh again so that the initial query (or queries) is run again.

User clicks Update

The page is refreshed. An `Update` command is sent to the database, and then the initial query (or queries) is run again.

This does not represent every action on the page, but it should give you an idea of what's happening on the server side.

Accessing Foreign Keys When There Is No Foreign Key Property

When foreign keys are used in the model, those scalar properties will be included in the `EntityDataSource`, but the navigation property is not. In other words, when you build a data source from `Customer`, the `PrimaryActivityID` and other foreign key scalar properties will be part of the data source, but the actual navigation entity, `PrimaryActivity`, will not be there.

Most of this book focuses on using a model that includes foreign keys and foreign key associations. The first edition of this book was focused on models without foreign keys in the entities. In that version there was no foreign key support, and the associations were defined in the mappings section of the metadata. These are called *independent associations* and were the only option.

Because you can continue to use independent associations with Entity Framework, it will be useful to point out a new property in the `EntityDatasource` control: `EnableFlattening`, which is `True` by default.

When you create an `EntityDataSource` for an entity that has entity references—for example, `Reservation` has `Customer` and `Trip`—the `EntityDataSource` is not able to represent those entities. Therefore, its default behavior is to "flatten" the relationship by drilling into the navigation's entity key.

Figure 12-7 shows flattened navigations for a `Reservation` that depends on independent associations. If `EnableFlattening` were set to `false`, the two navigation fields would not be surfaced by the `EntityDataSource`. You would have only the `ReservationID` and `ReservationDate` fields.

ReservationID	ReservationDate	Customer.ContactID	Trip.TripID
0	11/30/2009 12:00:00 AM	0	0
1	11/30/2009 12:00:00 AM	1	1
2	11/30/2009 12:00:00 AM	2	2
3	11/30/2009 12:00:00 AM	3	3
4	11/30/2009 12:00:00 AM	4	4

EntityDataSource - EntityDataSource1

Figure 12-7. Flattened navigation properties where foreign keys are unavailable

There is one exception to the rule that the `EntityDataSource` uses for flattening relationships. If the reference key is also a property of the entity and a member of the entity's `EntityKey` (when an `EntityKey` is a composite key), it won't be flattened.

You can see an example of this scenario if you create a model from the AdventureWorksLT database. The `SalesOrderID` foreign key of the `SalesOrderDetail` table is part of the table's primary key, and in the model, the `SalesOrderID` is a scalar property of `SalesOrderDetail` and part of its composite `EntityKey`.

Working with Related EntityReference Data

The Hello Entities sample uses a single entity: `Contact`. What if you want to work with `Customers` instead? As you have seen in some of the book's earlier examples, most of the customers' relevant information lies in related `EntityReference` data: `FirstName` and `LastName` are in `Customer.Contact`, and preferences are in `Customer.PrimaryActivity` and the other preference properties.

You can access all of this information with a single `EntityDataSource` control, but you'll have to do some additional work to bring back the data related to a customer and to be able to view and edit that data on the form.

Using EntityDataSource.Include to Get Related Data

The `EntityDataSource.Include` property, which you learned about earlier in this chapter, works the same way as the `ObjectQuery.Include` method. Although `EntityDataSource` works most easily with the individual object you return, you can manually code some of the markup and work directly in the code-behind to exert more control over how the `EntityDataSource` functions, including how it handles the related data returned by the `Include` property. There are some limitations to how this related data is realized and what you can do with it, however.

You can eager-load related data using the Include property of the EntityDataSource. This will add an Include method to the query that results, along with whatever navigation path you define in the property.

If you set Include to PrimaryActivity, the related entity for each contact will be included in the returned data. But it will not automatically be bound to the data grid.

Once you have loaded related data, much of the work you will do in markup is similar to that which is necessary for any type of related objects and is not specific to Entity Framework.

Include is very handy for displaying read-only data with the EntityDataSource control. As you move through this chapter, you'll find that editing related data will most often require the use of additional EntityDataSource controls.

Displaying Data That Comes from EntityReference Navigation Properties

By default, the individual columns in a GridView contain <asp:BoundField> controls. However, you cannot access properties from the related entity with these BoundFields, even if the related entity has been loaded. Instead, you need to use <asp:TemplateField> controls, which provide you with more flexibility. You can easily convert BoundField controls to TemplateField controls in the UI if you don't want to build the markup by hand:

1. Set the Include property of the EntityDataSource control to PrimaryActivity. You can do this by simply typing **PrimaryActivity** into the property value; no quotes are necessary.
2. Change the EntityDataSource EntitySet Name property to Customers.
3. Refresh the EntityDataSource to reflect the Customers EntitySet by clicking the Refresh Schema item in the EntityDataSource Tasks window.
4. Click Yes to answer the question about refreshing the grid layout.
5. Open the GridView Tasks window and select Edit Columns.
6. In the Available Fields listbox, expand the Bound Field node and double-click PrimaryActivity so that it moves to the Selected Fields list.
7. Move the field up so that it is positioned just after the PrimaryActivity.ActivityID field.
8. Edit the new field's DataField property to read PrimaryActivity.Name.

If you attempted to run the form now, you would get an error because the BoundData control is unable to resolve the PrimaryActivity.Name property.

9. Change the `PrimaryActivity`'s `ReadOnly` property to `True`.

   This is an important step. Otherwise, the `EntityDataSource` will not be able to update the related entity properties and will throw an error.
10. Click the "Convert this field into a TemplateField" hyperlink.
11. Click OK.

You can see the `TemplateField` in the markup that's generated, as shown in Example 12-1.

Example 12-1. The new TemplateField as seen in the page's markup

```
<asp:TemplateField HeaderText="PrimaryActivity"
                   SortExpression="PrimaryActivity">
  <EditItemTemplate>
    <asp:Label ID="Label1" runat="server"
              Text='<%# Eval("PrimaryActivity.Name") %>'>
    </asp:Label>
  </EditItemTemplate>
  <ItemTemplate>
    <asp:Label ID="Label2" runat="server"
              Text='<%# Bind("PrimaryActivity.Name") %>'>
    </asp:Label>
  </ItemTemplate>
</asp:TemplateField>
```

Notice that because you changed the `ReadOnly` property to `True` before converting, the `EditItemTemplate` is a `Label`, not a `TextBox`, and it won't be editable.

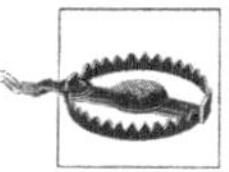

When the wizard converted the bound field to a template, it may have named both of the new labels "Label1", which will cause a compile-time error because they are not unique. You can edit the markup directly to give those labels appropriate names.

When you run the application, you'll see that the `Activity.Name` is displayed but is not editable when you edit a row, and therefore will be blank. You'll need to provide a drop-down list containing all of the possible activities in order to edit the `PrimaryActivity` property.

You may have noticed the `TemplateField`'s automatically generated `SortExpression` property in Example 12-1. When binding to an `EntityDataSource`, you can override this by specifying an Entity SQL expression such as `it.PrimaryActivity.Name` to control how the data is sorted. This will also impact the `Eval` expressions in the individual templates.

Why Do You Need to Use Include When LazyLoadingEnabled Is True?

The EntityDataSource control automatically disables lazy loading on the ObjectContext, forcing you to use the Include property. Although this happens quietly in the background and you may be surprised by the behavior, it is to your benefit. If you didn't use Include, simply populating the grid would cause numerous hits to the database in order to display the related data. That is in the case of accessing the related data during page rendering. After the page has rendered, there's no way to lazy load data from the browser anyway so it's best to just have it disabled and not be lulled into mistakenly expecting it to work from the client side.

Using a New EntityDataSource Control to Enable Editing of EntityReference Navigation Properties

To edit the PrimaryActivity fields you will need two elements. The first is a new EntityDataSource control to provide a list of activities. The second is an <asp:DropDownList> control in the grid.

1. Add a new EntityDataSource control named ActivityDataSource to the form.
2. Rebuild this project so that the new data source will recognize the model.
3. Configure it to use BAEntities as its ConnectionString and EntityContainer.
4. Choose Activities for the EntitySetName. Leave Select All checked in the properties box. Do not check the checkboxes for enabling inserts, updates, or deletes because this will be used only for selection.
5. Complete the Data Source Wizard.

The Activity pick list will be more useful if it's sorted. You can use the OrderBy property of the EntityDataSource control to sort the data. Remember that you will need to use the same Entity SQL syntax you used with the query builder methods:

6. Change the OrderBy property to it.Name.

   The property uses the same Entity SQL syntax that you use with query builder methods, which is why you use the it reference variable. This task is not specific to the EntityDataSource control, but rather is one that you would have to perform regardless of the data source.

You can define the DropDownList in the Design view, but you need to handle some of the binding in the Source view. You'll begin by replacing the asp:Label inside the EditItemTemplate tags with an asp:DropDownList. You'll see the effect of this in Example 12-2.

The DataSourceID binds the DropDownList to the new ActivityDataSource, and the DataTextField and DataValueField define which Activity fields to use for the display and value. The `SelectedValue` property gives you two-way data binding back to the `PrimaryActivityID` property of `Customer`, as shown in Example 12-2.

Example 12-2. The modified EditItemTemplate now with a DropDownList

```
<EditItemTemplate>
  <asp:DropDownList runat="server" ID="act1DDL"
                    DataSourceID="ActivityDataSource"
                    DataTextField="Name"
                    DataValueField="ActivityID"
                    SelectedValue=
                     '<%# Bind("PrimaryActivityID") %>'>
  </asp:DropDownList>
</EditItemTemplate>
```

The Web Designer in Visual Studio makes navigating to markup easy. In Design view, select the control whose markup you want to see. Then click Source at the bottom of the Designer window. The Source view will open and the markup for the control you selected in the Designer will be automatically selected in the source.

Now you can edit a customer, select a new `PrimaryActivity`, and then update with ease.

You will find that some of the `PrimaryActivity` selections for customers are null. This will cause a page error to be thrown when you attempt to edit those customers. There's a simple way to avoid the problem. Add the `AppendDataBoundItems=True` parameter to the drop-down list and an `asp:ListItem` as a child, as shown here:

```
<asp:DropDownList runat="server" id="act1DDL"
     DataSourceID="ActivityDataSource"
     DataTextField="Name"
     DataValueField="ActivityID"
     AppendDataBoundItems="True"
     SelectedValue=
       '<%# Bind("PrimaryActivityID") %>'>
   <asp:ListItem Value="">Select...</asp:ListItem>
</asp:DropDownList>
```

Editing EntityReferences That Cannot Be Satisfied with a Drop-Down List

The preference properties that you can now edit directly in the grid are not the only flavor of `EntityReference` that a `Customer` entity points to. `Customer` has a relationship to `Contact`, which supplies properties such as `FirstName` and `LastName`, as well as accesses other data that is related to `Contact`.

The `BoundField` control binding does not support navigating to or editing the `Contact` properties either. But neither does the solution you used for the preference properties, which was to embed a `DropDownList` into the grid.

You can view the related Contact data in the same way you were able to view the Name—by adding Contact to the Include property so that the property now reads as PrimaryActivity,Contact. Then you can create TemplateFields bound to Contact.LastName and Contact.FirstName. You can also make this column read-only by using a label in the EditTemplate as you saw with the initial rendering of the Activity's Name column.

But what about editing?

An EntityDataSource will update only the specific entity to which it is bound. If you use Include to bring the additional Contact entity back from the database, it will be ignored during updates. Instead, you'll have to edit the Contact by creating an EntityDataSource specifically for contacts and binding that EntityDataSource to the selected item of the grid that displays the customers.

If you are following along in Visual Studio and have added Contact to the Include property of the CustomerDataSource, remove Contact from the Include property before performing the following walkthrough.

Binding an EntityDataSource to Another Control with WhereParameters

The WhereParameters element is not the same as the Where clause in a query. It's a feature common to ASP.NET DataSource controls that enables filtering based on the values of other controls. This will help solve the problem of editing Customer.Contact entities. You'll create an EntityDataSource for Contacts and filter it based on the ContactID of the currently selected Customer in Customers.

You enter WhereParameters directly in the markup and it requires that the EntityDataSource.AutoGenerateWhereClause property be True. This will tell the EntityDataSource to generate the query's Where clause from WhereParameters. You can change this latter property in the Properties window or directly in the markup:

1. Create a new EntityDataSource named ContactDataSource.
2. Change the AutoGenerateWhereClause property to True.
3. Modify the source of the control, adding WhereParameters, so that the markup now looks like Example 12-3.

Example 12-3. The WhereParameters element used to bind the EntityDataSource to a GridView's SelectedValue

```
<asp:EntityDataSource ID="ContactDataSource" runat="server"
  ConnectionString="name=BAEntities"
  DefaultContainerName="BAEntities" EnableUpdate="True"
  EntitySetName="Contacts"
  AutoGenerateWhereClause="True">
  <WhereParameters>
    <asp:ControlParameter
        ControlID="GridView1"
```

```
            Name="ContactID"
            PropertyName="SelectedValue"
            DbType="Int32" />
    </WhereParameters>
</asp:EntityDataSource>
```

`WhereParameters` is instructing the control to modify the query to look for `Contacts` with a `ContactID` equal to `GridView1.SelectedValue`. However, the grid is not able to provide a `SelectedValue` until you have specified which column should be used. Additionally, you need to enable selection on the grid.

4. In the Properties window for `GridView1`, change the `DataKeyNames` property to `ContactID`.
5. Using the GridView Tasks window, check Enable Selection.

Because most of the data-binding controls return their `SelectedValue` as a string, the additional `DbType` attribute in `WhereParameters` ensures that this is passed in as an integer. This filter becomes part of the Entity SQL query that is translated and sent to the database each time a new selection is made in the `GridView`.

So far, you have performed setup tasks. We still haven't created a way to display or edit the contact names. That comes next.

If you forget to set the `AutoGenerateWhereClause` to `True`, you will get an exception message that says you can't have `WhereParameters` when the `AutoGenerateWhereClause=False`. Remember that `AutoGenerateWhereClause=True` plus the `WhereParameters` is an alternative to using the `Where` property of the `EntityDataSource`.

Setting EntityDataSource Properties Programmatically

All of the values you have set through the `EntityDataSource`'s wizard or the Properties window are parameters of the control that you can also set directly in markup or programmatically.

Here is what the control currently looks like in the Source view of the web page:

```
<asp:EntityDataSource ID="ContactDataSource" runat="server"
     ConnectionString="name=BAEntities"
     DefaultContainerName="BAEntities"
     EnableUpdate="True"
     EntitySetName="Contacts"
     AutoGenerateWhereClause="True"
     >
</asp:EntityDataSource>
```

You can make changes directly in the markup and even use expressions to populate the values as you can with any other ASP.NET or HTML control.

If you want the option to set any of the parameters at runtime, you can set them in the code-behind as well. For example:

```
ContactDataSource.EntitySetName="Contacts"
```

This enables you to change any of the parameters dynamically if you won't know the values until runtime.

Editing Related Data Concurrently with Multiple EntityDataSource Controls

Editing customers in the `GridView` and editing a customer's contact information will occur as separate actions. This is just the nature of the ASP.NET `DataSource` controls. In the case of the `EntityDataSource`, this means it can create insert, update, and delete commands for only a single entity, not for graphs.

There is just one more step to finish off this part of the example:

1. Drag a `DetailsView` onto the form and bind it to the `ContactDataSource`.

Run the form and you will see that as you select different customers, the contact details change to reflect the contact information of the selected customer. You can edit the contact information if you like.

This example demonstrated how data binding works between `EntityDataSources` and data-binding controls. You can clean up the `GridView` and `DetailsView` by formatting the columns, but more important to keep in mind about this example is that separation of the customer's information in the `GridView` and `DetailsView` is not a user-friendly design. As long as `Contact` and `Customer` are in two separate entities, you won't be able to edit them as a single unit using the `EntityDataSource` control.

It's still possible to make a logical UI, however. In the page shown in Figure 12-8, I've reversed the `EntityDataSources` so that the `Customer`'s `WhereParameters` defines a dependency on the `ContactDataSource`. The `DetailsView` that is bound to the `Contacts` has paging and is used for navigation. As the user navigates from one contact to another, the contact's customer data, if any, is displayed in the second `DetailsView`. Given the particular scenario, this makes more sense visually than using a `GridView`.

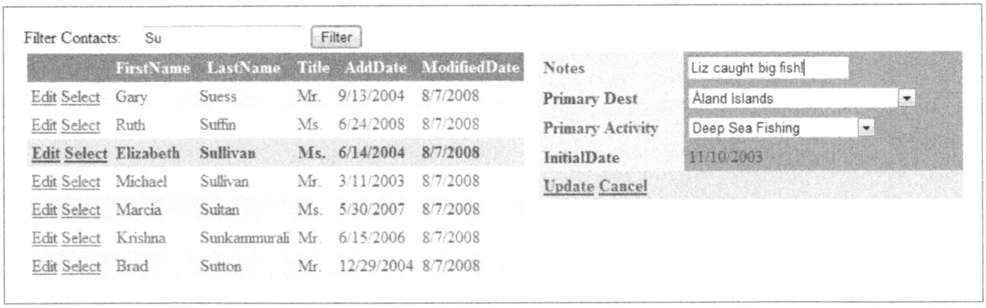

Figure 12-8. A data-driven form that is defined declaratively with EntityDataSource and DetailsView controls—not a single line of code

The screenshot also shows ASP.NET 4's new `QueryExtender` control in action. The filtering on the page is done declaratively along with the rest of the data access; in other words, still there is not one line of code in the example. `QueryExtender` works with `EntityDataSource` and `LINQDataSource`. The sample used for the screenshot is available on the book's download page, and you can read more about `QueryExtender` in the MSDN documentation at *http://msdn.microsoft.com/en-us/library/dd537669(VS.100).aspx*.

In the next chapter, you'll learn how to build inheritance into the model to make `Customer` and `Contact` blend into a single entity. However, modifying your model is not the solution to making it easier to build your UI. `EntityDataSource` is not going to be the solution for every scenario. If you were using a business layer, as you'll learn to do in Chapter 27, you won't be tied down to the rules of the `EntityDataSource` and you will have more flexibility in building your UI.

Working with Hierarchical Data in a Master/Detail Form

Many data-focused applications are used to present hierarchical data, so this next example will focus on parent/child/grandchild data using `EntityDataSource` controls. As the previous example allowed you to work with related `EntityReference` data, this example will give you an opportunity to use `EntityDataSource` controls to work with related child entities.

In this example, you will use a variety of methods to populate controls on a web form and take advantage of the `EntityDataSource`'s editing capabilities. This form, shown in Figure 12-9, will let BreakAway employees view customers and their reservations as well as add payments. You will get a chance to work with a variety of relationships and binding scenarios. And in the course of doing this, you will hit a few speed bumps and learn how to get around them.

The form will use `EntityDataSource` controls; in addition, you will do some direct data binding to query results.

Setting Up the Web Application

Now that you have an idea of the tasks that this application will teach you, let's start building it:

1. Add a new web form, named `HierarchicalEDS`, to the current Web Application project that you are working with.
2. Add a reference to `System.Data.Entity`.
3. Build the project so that the `EntityDataSource` controls will be able to find the entity connection string in the *web.config* file.

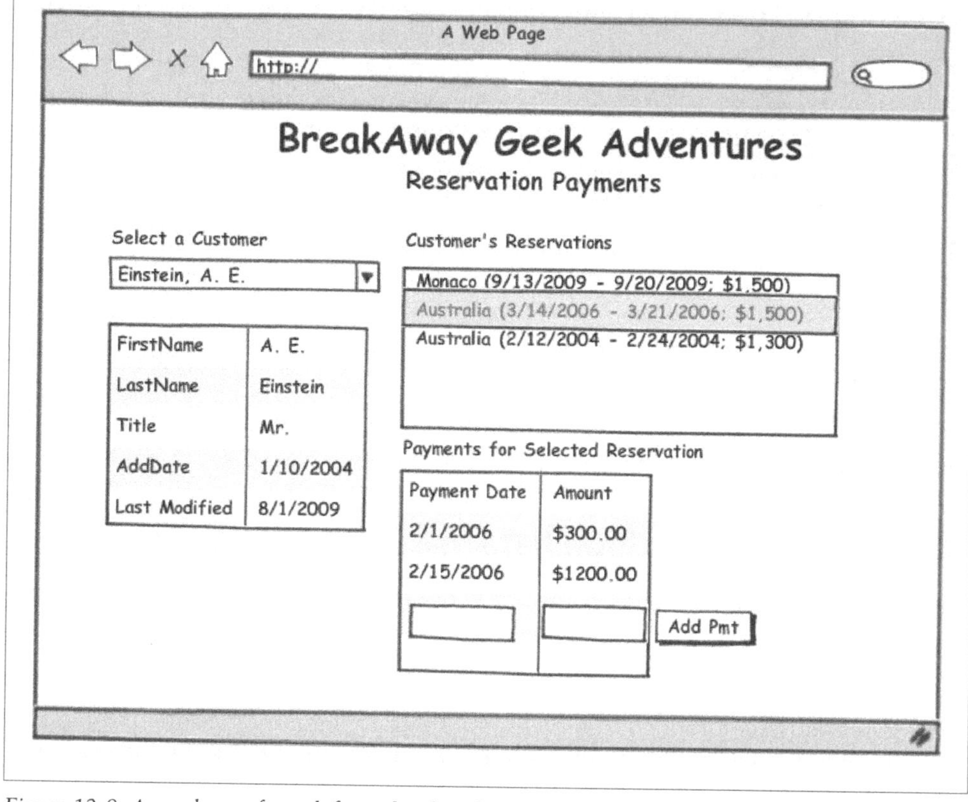

Figure 12-9. A mock-up of a web form that lets the user interact with hierarchical data

4. Drag a `DropDownList` onto the web form.
5. In the `DropDownList`'s `TaskList`, check the Enable AutoPostBack checkbox. This will ensure the correct behavior each time the user selects an item from the list.
6. Create a new `EntityDataSource` named `ContactNamesDataSource` using `BAEntities` and the `Contacts EntitySet`.

Specifying Your Own Entity SQL Query Expression for an EntityDataSource

The Entity Data Source Wizard only allows you to select entire entities or properties from those entities. However, for this `DropDownList` you want to combine the `LastName` and `FirstName` properties.

It's possible to do this by using your own Entity SQL string, rather than letting the query builder methods construct the string based on the various properties of the `EntityDataSource`.

Keep in mind that the results of these custom queries will be read-only.

The Entity SQL string shown here will return a `ContactID` field and a `Name` field that you can bind to the drop-down list. It also returns only those contacts that have a `Customer` record; therefore, you can be sure you'll be working only with customers, as noncustomer contacts do not have reservations, destination or activity preferences, or other properties specific to a customer.

```
SELECT  c.contactid, TRIM(c.lastname) + ", " + c.firstname AS Name
FROM BAEntities.Contacts  AS c
WHERE c.Customer IS NOT NULL
ORDER BY Name
```

Using `IS NULL` or `IS NOT NULL` is useful for testing for the existence of an `EntityReference`. To do this with an `EntityCollection`, you would use `EXISTS` or `NOT EXISTS`, with a subquery into the collection to see whether there are any items in the collection.

1. Enter the Entity SQL query into the `CommandText` property of the `EntityDataSource`.

   `EntityDataSource` cannot have an `EntitySet` designated if you want to override the query using the `CommandText` property. You selected it in the wizard because the Finish button is inactive until you select something.
2. Remove `Contacts` from the `EntitySet` property.

If you forget to do this, an exception will be thrown that specifically says you cannot have an `EntitySet` value if you also have a `CommandText` value.

Binding a DropDownList to an EntityDataSource Control

The last task for the first pass at this web page is to wire up the new `EntityDataSource` to the `DropDownList` that you already added to the page, and then to check your progress by running the application.

You might consider a few options for populating the drop-down list. What's useful to realize is that, by default, the `DropDownList` will use `ViewState` to retain the values and display text for the items in the list. If you use an `EntityDataSource` to populate this drop-down list, you won't have to worry about that query being called every time the page is refreshed.

1. In the DropDownList's Tasks window, select the Choose Data Source option.
2. Be sure its data source is pointing to the new ContactNamesDataSource you created.
3. In the combo box that says "Select a data field to display in the DropDownList," enter **Name**, and in the box that says "Select a data field for the value of the DropDownList," enter **ContactID**.

   Because the properties are coming from the Entity SQL expression, the wizard will not be able to detect the property names, and therefore they won't be available in the drop downs. Just type them in directly.
4. Run the application to test that the drop-down list works.

Creating a Parent EntityDataSource That Is Controlled by the DropDownList and Provides Data to a DetailsView

The next step is to create a DetailsView that is dependent on the selection of the DropDownList. A new EntityDataSource will use the WhereParameters to bind to the SelectedValue of the DropDownList.

1. Drag a DetailsView onto the form.
2. Use its Tasks window to create a new EntityDataSource control named ContactDataSource.
3. Set the EntityDataSource's ConnectionString and EntityContainer to BAEntities.
4. Select Contacts as the EntitySet.

   When you complete the Entity Data Source Wizard, the DetailsView should automatically populate with the Contact properties.
5. In the Source view of the page, add the WhereParameters directly into the markup to bind the new EntityDataSource control to the SelectedValue of the DropDownList, as shown in Example 12-4.

Don't forget to set the AutoGenerateWhereClause to True.

Example 12-4. Defining the WhereParameters for an EntityDataSource

```
<asp:EntityDataSource ID="ContactDataSource" runat="server"
                      ConnectionString="name=BAEntities"
                      DefaultContainerName="BAEntities"
                      EntitySetName="Contacts"
                      AutoGenerateWhereClause="True">
  <WhereParameters>
    <asp:ControlParameter ControlID="DropDownList1" Name="ContactID"
        PropertyName="SelectedValue" DbType="Int32" />
```

```
  </WhereParameters>
</asp:EntityDataSource>
```

Now the `DetailsView` will update every time an item is selected in the `DropDownList`. In Figure 12-10 a bit of formatting has been applied. Most notably, the `DataFormatString` for the two date fields in the `DetailsView` was changed to `{0:d}` to affect the default display of the date values.

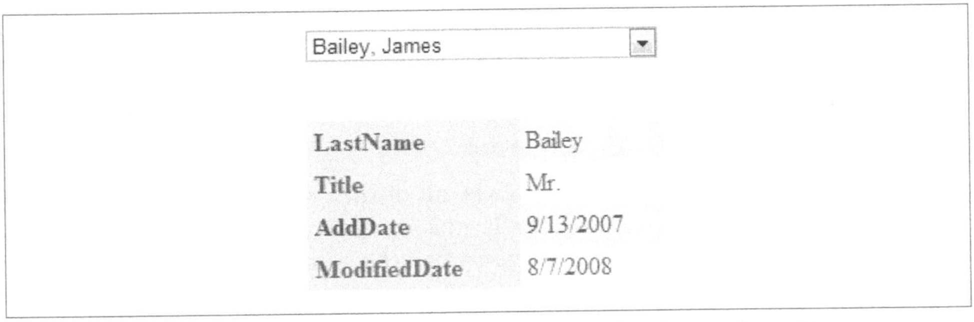

Figure 12-10. The DetailsView displaying the customer selected in the DropDownList

Using the EntityDataSource.Where Property to Filter Query Results

Currently, we're using the `CommandText` property of the `ContactNamesDataSource` to project and to filter contacts to return only customers. There's another way to filter that you should be aware of. Similar to the `OrderBy` property, which you used in the Hello Entities demo earlier, the `Where` parameter allows you to insert query logic that will become part of the actual query the `EntityDataSource` builds. The value needs to be in the Entity SQL format that you would use with query builder method parameters.

For example, if you wanted to start with the query that is called in the form load that filters only on customers and then enhance it to return only those customers who have reservations, you would first need to translate the query into a query builder method using Entity SQL syntax:

```
BAEntities.Contacts.OfType<Customer>
.Where("it.Customer IS NOT NULL")
```

The `where` clause for this query is `it.Customer IS NOT NULL`. If you were using the `Where` property to filter, that is the expression you would put into the value of the `Where` property in the `EntityDataSource` Properties window.

Displaying Read-Only Child Data Through the Parent EntityDataSource

In this form, the user will be viewing, but not editing, reservations. Therefore, you can take advantage of the `Include` property of the `Contact DataSource` and you won't need a separate `EntityDataSource` for the `Reservation` entities.

We'll use a `ListBox` to display the reservations:

1. Drag a `ListBox` control onto the form.
2. In the `ListBox`'s properties window, set the `DataTextField` property to `TripDetails` and the `DataValueField` property to `ReservationID`.

   The model allows for navigation from `Contact` to `Customer` to `Reservations` to `Trip`, and then to `Destination`. All of these relationships will make it possible to display the detailed reservation information for each contact who is a customer. Recall that we added the `TripDetails` custom property to `Reservation` in the previous chapter.
3. Add the following to the `Include` property of the `ContactDataSource` control:

   ```
   Customer.Reservations.Trip.Destination
   ```

Because the `ContactDataSource` uses `Include`, all of the entities listed in the `Include` path—the reservations, the trip, and the destination associated with the selected customer—will be retrieved from the database when the contact query is executed. But you still need to push the details into the `ListBox`, which you'll need to do in code.

The `EntityDataSource` control's `Selected` event is just the place to do this. The `Selected` event provides an `EntityDataSourceEventArgs` object as the parameter, `e`. This, in turn, provides you with a `Results` property that returns an object—in this case, a `Contact` entity. By casting that result to a `Contact` type, you can navigate to the customer's reservations, trip, and destination details.

From the Events list in the `ContactDataSource` Properties window, double-click the `Selected` event. Because it is possible to select multiple items, the `e.Results` from the `EntityDataSourceSelectedEventArgs` contains an `IEnumerable` of objects. To get the selected contact, you'll need to cast that collection to the correct entity type using the LINQ `Cast` method and then extract the first item in the collection.

Once you've done that, you can use the `TripDetails` property you created in the preceding chapter to display useful information about the reservations. If you didn't have that already, you would be able to write a LINQ to Objects query against the reservations and shape the data as you want to display it in the `ListBox`.

Add the code shown in Example 12-5 to the `Selected` event method.

Example 12-5. Using the EntityDataSource.Selected event to populate a listbox control

```
protected void ContactDataSource_Selected
 (object sender, EntityDataSourceSelectedEventArgs e)
{
  var contact = e.Results.Cast<BAGA.Contact>();
  var res=contact.First().Customer.Reservations;
  if (res.Count > 0)
  {
    ListBox1.DataSource = res.ToList();
    ListBox1.DataBind();
    ListBox1.SelectedIndex=0;
```

```
    }
    else
    {
      ListBox1.DataSource = res.ToList();
      ListBox1.DataBind();
    }
}
```

Now, each time a customer is selected, the `ListBox` will update with a list of that customer's reservations. If the customer has no reservations, the list will be empty thanks to the code in the `else` clause.

Using a New EntityDataSource to Add a Third Level of Hierarchical Data to the Master/Detail Form

When a customer is selected and her reservations are displayed, the user's next step is to select a reservation and view its payments. You can enable this by combining a new `ListView` with yet another `EntityDataSource`. The user will also be allowed to enter new payments; that's why the new `EntityDataSource` is necessary. We're using the `ListView` in this example because unlike the `GridView`, the `ListView` control allows easy insertion. The new `EntityDataSource` will use `WhereParameters` to create a dependency on the selected reservation from the `ListBox`.

1. Set `Enable AutoPostBack` on the `ListBox` that displays reservations.

   This will force the page to respond to a user selecting an item in the `ListBox`.
2. Add a `ListView` to the form.
3. From the ListView Tasks window, create a new `EntityDataSource` control and name it `PaymentDataSource`.
4. Set the `EntityDataSource`'s `Connection` and `EntityContainer` to `BAEntities`.
5. Set the `EntityDataSource`'s `EntitySetName` to `Payments`.
6. Check Enable Automatic Inserts.

   The `ListView` will look much better if you do some formatting. If you haven't used a `ListView` before, you might be surprised that most of its formatting is performed in the markup.

   The `ListView` creates templates for Select, Insert, Edit, Alternate, and Empty views. As you will need only Select and Insert views, you can delete the other sections.

   Example 12-6 shows the markup for the `ListView` after it has been trimmed down.

   Example 12-6. Formatted ListView after deleting much of the default markup

   ```
   <asp:ListView ID="ListView1" runat="server" DataKeyNames="PaymentID"
                 DataSourceID="PaymentDataSource"
                 InsertItemPosition="LastItem" Style="font-size: small">
     <ItemTemplate>
       <tr style="">
   ```

```
        <td></td>
        <td>
          <asp:Label ID="PaymentDateLabel" runat="server"
                     Text='<%# Eval("PaymentDate","{0:d}") %>' />
        </td>
        <td>
          <asp:Label ID="AmountLabel" runat="server"
                     Text='<%# Eval("Amount","{0:c}") %>' />
        </td>
      </tr>
    </ItemTemplate>
    <InsertItemTemplate>
      <tr style="">
        <td>
          <asp:TextBox ID="PaymentDateTextBox" runat="server"
                       Text='<%# Bind("PaymentDate") %>' />
        </td>
        <td>
          <asp:TextBox ID="AmountTextBox" runat="server"
                       Text='<%# Bind("Amount") %>' />
        </td>
        <td>
          <asp:Button ID="InsertButton" runat="server"
                      CommandName="Insert" Text="Insert" />
          <asp:Button ID="CancelButton" runat="server" />
        </td>

      </tr>
    </InsertItemTemplate>
    <LayoutTemplate>
      <table runat="server">
        <tr runat="server">
          <td runat="server">
            <table id="itemPlaceholderContainer" runat="server"
                   border="0" style="">
              <tr runat="server" style="">
                <th runat="server">PaymentDate</th>
                <th runat="server">Amount</th>
                <th runat="server"></th>
              </tr>
              <tr id="itemPlaceholder" runat="server"></tr>
            </table>
          </td>
        </tr>
        <tr runat="server">
          <td runat="server" style=""></td>
        </tr>
      </table>
    </LayoutTemplate>
  </asp:ListView>
```

Notice the formatting that's been added to the `ReservationDate` property. Date and currency formatting is controlled by culture info settings, which you can control programmatically or in your application's *web.config* file. Look for globalization topics in the MSDN documentation for more information on this.

7. Click the `Payments EntityDataSource` the wizard created.
8. Set the `AutoGenerateWhereClause` property to `True`.
9. Add the following `WhereParameters` to the `Payments EntityDataSource` markup in the source of the page. This wires the data source up to the reservations listbox.

```
<WhereParameters>
  <asp:ControlParameter Name="ReservationID"
    ControlID="ListBox1" PropertyName="SelectedValue"
    DbType="Int32"
    DefaultValue="0" />
</WhereParameters>
```

The `DefaultValue` is set to `0` because even if there are no reservations, the `Payments` query will run. Without the default, all of the payments in the database will be returned. The default forces the query to search for payments whose `ReservationID=0`, which will return no data.

Check the previous section on `WhereParameters` if you need a reminder of exactly where this needs to be placed in the markup of the data source.

Using the EntityDataSource.Inserting Event to Help with Newly Added Entities

The `ListView` has built-in functionality for inserting items, but one thing is missing. You will need to manually add the `ReservationID` because the `PaymentDataSource` doesn't automatically know which `Reservation` is selected.

`EntityDataSource` has a number of events that you can take advantage of. The `Inserting` event gives you an opportunity to impact the entity that is about to be inserted into the database. Here is where you can add the `ReservationID` to the new payment before it goes to the database.

The `EntityDataSourceChangingEventArgs` exposed by the `Inserting` event (as well as many of the control's events) has an `Entity` property. In the `Inserting` event, the `Entity` property refers to the entity that is about to be sent to the database.

Example 12-7 shows the `Payment.ReservationID` being set. The value comes from the selected item in the `ListBox`.

Example 12-7. Defining the payment's ReservationReference in the Inserting event

```
protected void PaymentsDataSource_Inserting
 (object sender, EntityDataSourceChangingEventArgs e)
{
  var newPmnt = (BAGA.Payment)e.Entity;
  newPmnt.ReservationID= Convert.ToInt32(ListBox1.SelectedValue);
}
```

Look how easy it is to assign the payment's `ReservationID` now that foreign keys are available in the model. In the first edition of this book, I had to do a lot of work to perform this same task!

Testing the Application

Finally, it is time to test your handiwork. Press F5 to run the application, which should look something like Figure 12-11. Select various customers and reservations. You can see how the hierarchical data is automatically presented as you change selections—and all with a minimum of code, highlighting the RAD capabilities of the Entity Framework.

Figure 12-11. Parent, child, and grandchild hierarchical data being served up by EntityDataSource controls

In Chapter 8, you mapped `Insert`, `Update`, and `Delete` functions to the `Payment` entity.

Now, every time you create a new payment, the `InsertPayment` stored procedure is executed in the database. If you were to look in SQL Server Profiler, you would see the following command:

```
exec [dbo].[InsertPayment]
@date='2006-02-01 00:00:00:000',
@reservationID=90,@amount=250.0000
```

There is some fine-tuning to be done with respect to the data-binding actions that is not specific to Entity Framework. A more complete sample is available for download on the book's website.

Exploring EntityDataSource Events

`EntityDataSource` is a control that is packed with events you can use to exert granular control over its behavior as well as its interactions with other entities in the application. You have used only a few in this chapter, but here is an overview of the events that you can take advantage of as you build your own applications with the `EntityDataSource` control.

When a page with an `EntityDataSource` starts up, here is the order in which the `EntityDataSource` and `Page` events fire:

1. `Page BeginLoad`
2. `EntityDataSource Load`
3. `Page BeginPreRender`
4. `EntityDataSource.ContextCreating`
5. `EntityDataSource.ContextCreated`
6. `Page EndPreRender`
7. `EntityDataSource ContextDisposing`
8. `Page Unload`

A number of additional events are related to data modification:

- `Deleting` and `Deleted`
- `Inserting` and `Inserted`
- `Updating` and `Updated`
- `Selecting` and `Selected`

All of these events represent opportunities to customize your control's behavior. For instance, in the preceding example you trapped the `Inserting` event to add an additional value to an entity that was about to be inserted. Additionally, you used the `Selected` event to determine which entity had been selected and then populated a `ListBox` with its related data.

Each of these events provides relevant information through its `EventArgs` variable, `e`. Here are the ones that are of the greatest interest:

`Inserting`
: `e.Entity` returns the entity that is being inserted. If you want to work with this entity, you will need to cast it to its proper type as you did in the sample you just built.

`e.Cancel` gives you an opportunity to cancel the insert. You would do this by setting the value of `e.Cancel` to `True`.

`Inserted`
: This event fires after the item was inserted into the data store.

  `e.Entity` returns the entity that was just inserted. This includes the new `EntityKey` because the data store returned the necessary value.

  Remember that if you are letting the Entity Framework generate the commands, it will get the new key by default. If you are using your own stored procedure, as we did for the payments, this value will be returned only if the procedure sends it back and if you have wired it up in the mappings, which you did at the beginning of the chapter.

  `e.Context` gives you access to the context.

  `e.Exception` and `e.ExceptionHandled` give you an opportunity to trap any problems that may have occurred either by constraints in the model or by constraints in the database.

`Updating`
: `e.Entity` returns the entity in its current state. You will need to cast the `NewEntity` to the correct entity type to interact with it in detail.

  `e.Cancel`, `e.Exception`, and `e.ExceptionHandled` are available in this event.

`Updated`
: The `EventArgs` provides the same properties as with `Updating`.

`Selecting`
: `e.DataSource` provides a reference to the `EntityDataSource` and its properties so that you can affect them at runtime if necessary. By changing the properties in the `Selecting` event, you can redefine the `DataSource` prior to the retrieval of data from the store. The properties you can access or change during this event are `CommandParameters`, `CommandText`, `OrderBy`, `OrderByParameters`, `Where`, and `WhereParameters`.

  `e.SelectArguments` provides you with an opportunity to tweak the properties of the `EntityDataSource` control, including properties that define its query. It also exposes some of the properties from the data-bound control (e.g., `GridView`) that the `EntityDataSource` is bound to, such as `MaximumRows`, `RetrieveTotalRowCount`, `SortExpression`, `StartRowIndex`, and `TotalRowCount`.

  You can cancel this event with `e.Cancel` if you need to.

`Selected`
: `e.Results` provides an array of entities. You worked with this property in the second example.

  This event also provides access to the context, any exceptions that were thrown, and `SelectArguments`.

`Deleting`
: `e.Cancel` gives you an opportunity to cancel the delete. You would do this by setting the value of `e.Cancel` to `True`.

  `Context.Entity` and `Exceptions` are available in this event.

`Deleted`
: This provides access to the context, the entity, and any exceptions.

Building Dynamic Data Websites

ASP.NET Dynamic Data is ASP.NET's highly effective RAD offering for data-driven websites. At a high level, you can just point this framework to a data model and it will automatically create a website. The premise, made famous with Ruby on Rails, is that there are a lot of assumptions that can be made about what a website should contain based on its data. This is referred to as *convention*. If you start with these assumptions and then tweak the results to better meet your needs, this follows a design pattern called *convention over configuration*. That's what Dynamic Data relies on.

By convention, you an create a new website with a Dynamic Data project template by pointing it to an existing Entity Data Model or LINQ to SQL model. The project template leverages lots of page and control templates. When you go the path of Entity Framework, one of the critical pieces of the template is that it uses `EntityDataSource` controls for all of the data binding.

To you, this means all of that extra configuration you had to do when building pages with `EntityDataSource` is taken care of for you.

Given a `Customer`, for example, a dynamic website will display an editable list of customers with links to drill into the customer's related data. The default site will have one page per entity type. So, if you begin with a customer, you could then click a link and navigate to a page that lists that customer's `Reservations`. You could navigate back to the customer or farther in to another page with the customer's payments. The site emulates the navigation between entities in your Entity Data Model. You do not need to expose the entire model, either. Through configuration, you can specify which entities in the model should be exposed through the website.

There are so many introductory demos on using Dynamic Data that it may not make sense to add yet another one to this book which is not about ASP.NET. However, one of the new ASP.NET 4 Dynamic Data features works so beautifully with the Entity Data Model's many-to-many relationships that it's worth spending a few minutes walking through the following scenario.

Dynamic Data Videos and Demos Galore

Check out the official ASP.NET Dynamic Data website at *http://www.asp.net/dynamicdata/*, where you'll find tons of information not only on getting started with Dynamic Data, but also on configuring your way to very customized sites with all of the data pain taken away.

1. Start by creating a new Dynamic Data Entities Web Application project in your existing solution.
2. Add a reference to the BreakAwayModel project and add the connection string from that project into the new project's *web.config* file.
3. After adding the reference, build the new project.

A critical step in creating a Dynamic Data application is to point to the data source, which will be the Entity Data Model and classes provided in the BreakAway model. This is done in the *Global.asax* file, which is opened by default after you create the new project. *Global.asax* contains a lot of notes and instructions because much of the site configuration happens in this file.

4. In the middle of the first section of comments, find the commented line that begins with "DefaultModel.RegisterContext" and uncomment it.
5. Modify the code line to point to the `BAEntities` class in the BreakAway model assembly, replacing "YourDataContextType".
6. Change the value of `ScaffoldAllTables` to `true`:

   ```
   DefaultModel.RegisterContext(typeof(BAGA.BAEntities),
      new ContextConfiguration() { ScaffoldAllTables = true });
   ```

   This last change will cause the website to expose every entity in the model. This is not what you would do in production code. You can leave the value as `false` and set an attribute on only those classes which you want to be used in the site. For this quick walkthrough, we're taking a few shortcuts and will make no more changes to the site. We have enough in order to see how the site treats many-to-many relationships.
7. Run the new web application.

   You'll see a list of all of the possible classes to view similar to Figure 12-12.
8. Select Trips.

Each page is built on the fly, dynamically, at runtime based on the site configuration. There is no Trips page defined in the website solution.

There is a many-to-many relationship between `Trip` and `Activity` in the model.

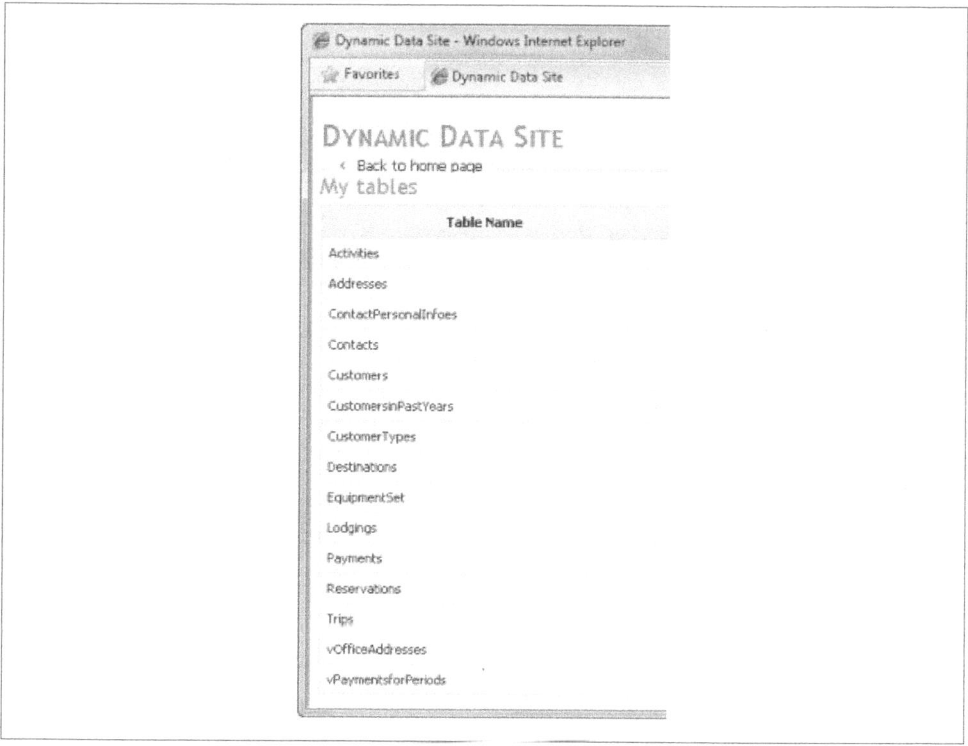

Figure 12-12. Default page of Dynamic Data site displaying all BreakAway classes

Check out the last column, Activities, in the grid that lists the trips. Rather than use a separate list to display the activities for each trip, as we did for customers and reservations in the previous sample, the framework has worked out a list of linked activities within the column! For example, in Figure 12-13, you can see that the first trip in the grid has three different activities listed.

And to make this even sweeter, each related activity is a hyperlink that allows you to drill into its own edit page. That is not something I would have wanted to take the time to code!

9. Now pick one of the trips and click its Edit link.

Figure 12-14 shows the default page for editing a `Trip` with the multiple option selection list generated by the Dynamic Data templates. And with no code at all, the framework took care of the many-to-many relationship between trips and activities. Seeing this definitely improved my perception of Rapid Application Development.

Because of the work that you did to create the drop-down lists earlier in this chapter, there is one more thing to point out in this website before wrapping up this chapter. Notice the Destination and Lodging drop-down controls on the page, again dynamically created.

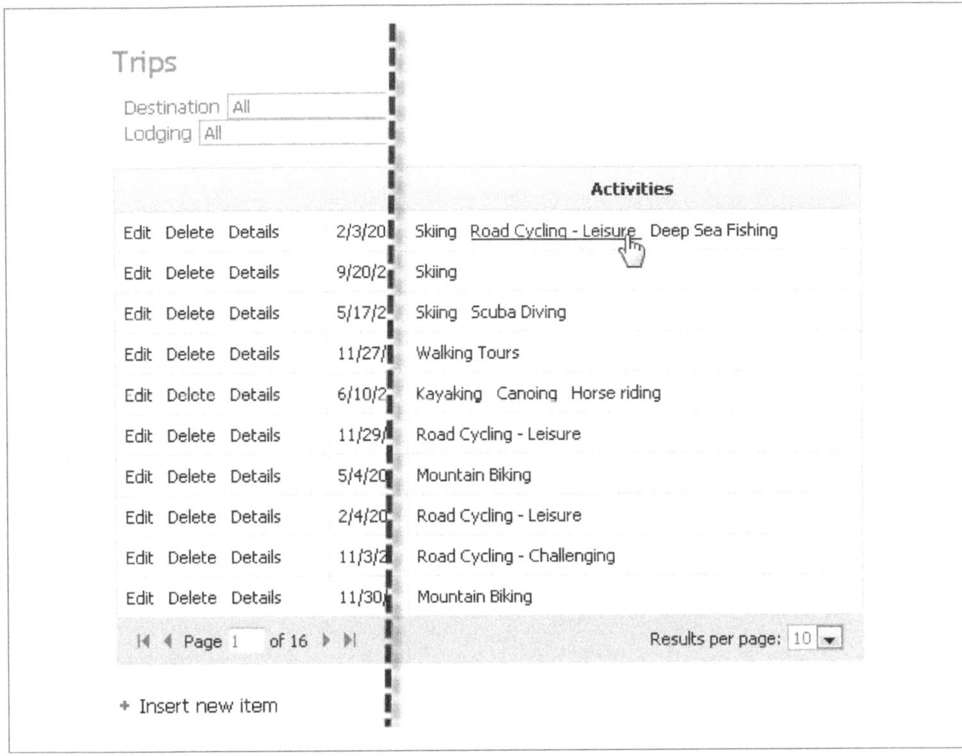

Figure 12-13. Multiple, linked activities displayed for each Trip in the Trips detail page

This is not to say that you should forget working with the `EntityDataSource` manually. There are different levels of RAD design, and in some cases Dynamic Data will suit your needs, whereas in others the more granular control of working with the `EntityDataSource` directly will be appropriate.

Summary

In this chapter, you built three small applications using the `EntityDataSource` control, which gave you a hands-on opportunity to see how you can use entities and query results in some simple web application scenarios. Then you let the Dynamic Data templates create another application for you that relies on `EntityDataSource` controls.

The `EntityDataSource` control, used alone or within a Dynamic Data application, is perfect for Rapid Application Development, and if you take advantage of its properties and events, it provides you with a lot of control over its functionality.

`EntityDataSource` offers a convenient way to build quick web applications against an Entity Data Model. Although it's convenient, its use incurs some resource overhead that you may not want. For more complex applications, which typically require

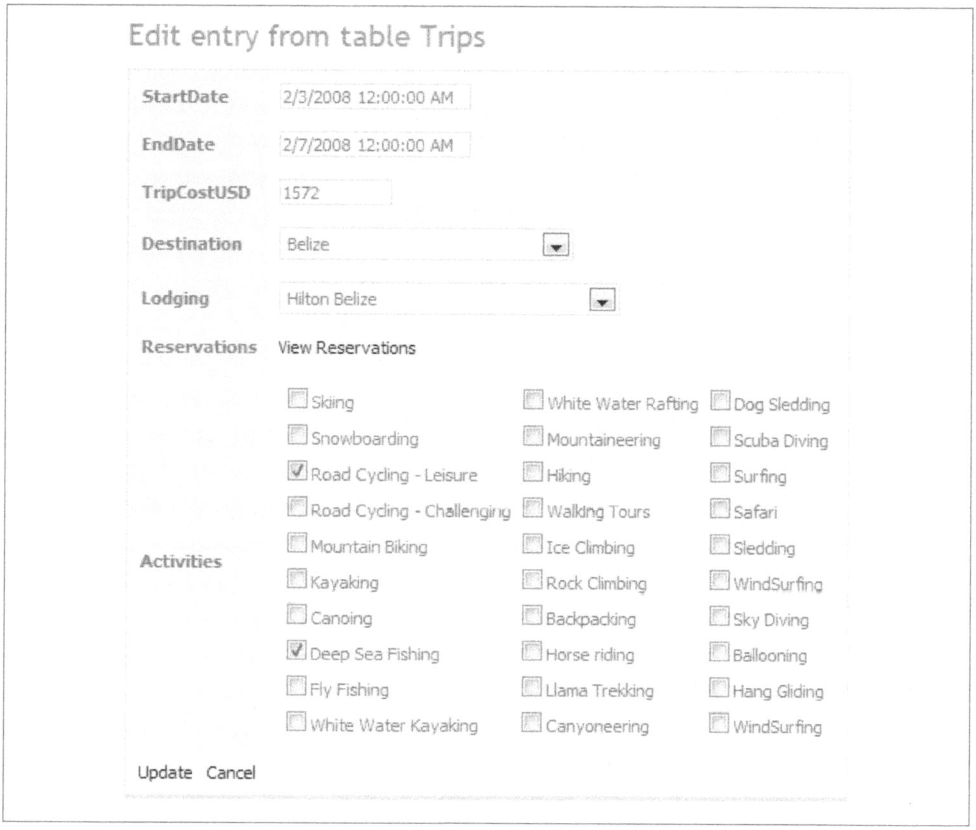

Figure 12-14. *Editing a many-to-many relationship with Dynamic Data templates*

business layers, defining their data in the UI might not even be an option. In the second half of this book, you'll learn how to build ASP.NET sites that use business layers.

Before we embark on building any more applications, it's time to learn about the Plain Old CLR Objects (POCO) support in Entity Framework that I've been tempting you with in many of the previous chapters. The next chapter will focus on POCOs, which will allow you to use POCO entities in the upcoming sample applications as well as `EntityObjects`.

CHAPTER 13

Creating and Using POCO Entities

When it was first released, Entity Framework was roundly criticized by agile developers. These developers hold the tenets of domain-driven development and testability very high. The classes generated from the Entity Data Model (EDM) are very tightly bound to the Entity Framework APIs by either inheriting from the `EntityObject` or implement interfaces that allow the classes to participate in change tracking and relationship management.

The problem with this is that it is extremely difficult to separate the concerns of your application into smaller pieces of logic to make it more maintainable. Additionally, it is difficult to write unit tests with `EntityObjects`. Many of the methods that need to be tested perform some type of interaction with the database. In unit testing, you need to emulate this persistence. In other words, instead of literally querying the database, a test might supply some fake data to a class, or instead of sending data to the data store, a test might say "OK, let's pretend that part just happened and we'll move on now."

In addition to the problems the dependent classes create for separation of concerns and for testing, it also makes it difficult for developers to change their backend infrastructure if needed. For example, an application might be written using another object relational mapping tool, such as NHibernate. If a developer wanted to switch to the Entity Framework, version 1 made it very difficult to just take the existing classes and put Entity Framework behind. The developer would be required to make some major changes to the classes, binding them tightly to Entity Framework.

The Entity Framework team listened to and learned from the agile community and added a number of new mechanisms for supporting agile development.

One of these is support for Plain Old CLR Objects (POCO). POCOs are classes that remain free from a backing infrastructure, such as Entity Framework. A POCO class would not inherit from Entity Framework's `EntityObject`. But as you've seen, the `EntityObject` performs all of the important work for providing relationship and change tracking information to the context. In order to remove the dependency on `EntityObject`, the Entity Framework gained some new functionality that allows the `ObjectContext` to acquire relationship and change tracking information from classes that do not inherit from `EntityObject`. In fact, as you'll see, it can do so with classes that have no knowledge at all about the Entity Framework.

In addition to POCO support, the team added two other important features for developers who do not want to be tied up with the concerns of the database. One is support for *model-first development*, which allows developers to begin a project with a model and use that model to create a database. The other is called *code-first development*. You'll learn more about model first and code first, as they are called, in Chapter 25. Do be aware that code first is still a work in progress and is available as part of a separate download called the Entity Framework CTP.

In this chapter, you'll learn the basics of how to create and work with POCOs in Entity Framework. There are two avenues to the POCO support. You'll begin with the simplest form, which requires a bit of extra work on the part of the `ObjectContext`. Then you'll learn about another form of POCO support that let's the POCOs behave similarly to `EntityObjects` at runtime. Later chapters in the book will leverage POCOs as well as classes that inherit directly from `EntityObject`. Chapter 24 is devoted to using Entity Framework POCO classes in a more flexible architecture using repositories and unit testing.

Creating POCO Classes

POCO classes work in conjunction with a model in that they must mirror the entities in the model.

To begin this discussion, we'll return to `SampleModel`, the very simple model and database that you used in the first few chapters of the book. Let's create the model and then the classes, as it will be helpful to point out how they relate to one another. It is just as likely that you will create the classes first or even that they will pre-exist.

Start by creating a new Console Application project. Then add a new Entity Data Model based on ProgrammingEntityFrameworkDB1. Name the `EntityContainer` `POCOEntities` and select all tables. Now you are back to your simple model.

There are a few rules that you need to follow when creating classes that will interact with Entity Framework. One is that the class and property names should align with the model. Another is that *every* property in the model entity must be represented in the class, this includes scalar properties and navigation properties. For this example, we'll just follow the existing model to determine the names and structure of the classes.

Add two new class files to the project, called *Contact.cs* and *Address.cs*. Next, add properties to the `Contact` class for every property in the `Contact` entity.

Be sure to mimic the names as well as the types, with one caveat. The `Addresses` navigation property returns an `EntityCollection`, which is a very constrained type. In your class, use an `ICollection` to return the related collection. An `ICollection` will give you ultimate flexibility when you consume the class.

Figure 13-1 serves as a reminder of what the entities look like in the model.

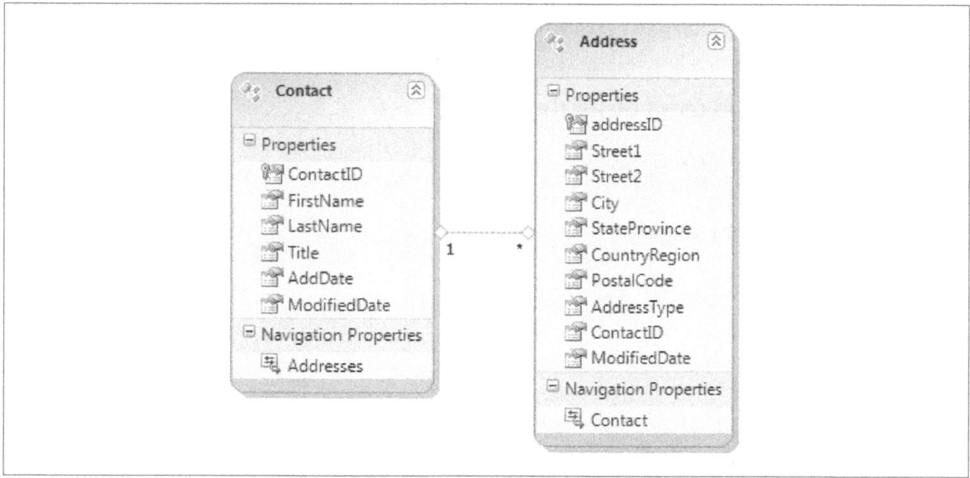

Figure 13-1. The simple model that we'll use in the following examples

Building POCOs by Hand Versus Generating with a T4 Template

The POCO and related classes created in this chapter are built manually. If you are starting with a model, it makes much more sense to use a T4 template to generate the POCO classes from the model. You'll get a chance to generate POCOs from a T4 template later in this chapter.

Example 13-1 displays the code listing for the `Contact` class. Notice that it uses auto-implemented properties, which don't require a backing variable to retain their values.

Example 13-1. A simple Contact class

```
using System;
using System.Collections.Generic;
using System.Linq;
using System.Text;

namespace Chapter13SimplePOCO
{
  public class Contact
  {
    public int ContactID { get; set; }
    public string FirstName { get; set; }
    public string LastName { get; set; }
    public string Title { get; set; }
    public System.DateTime AddDate { get; set; }
    public System.DateTime ModifiedDate { get; set; }
    public ICollection<Address> Addresses { get; set; }
```

```
    }
}
```

Add properties to the Address class for every property in the Address entity. Again, be sure to mimic the names as well as the types.

Example 13-2 displays the code for the Address class.

Example 13-2. A simple Address class

```
using System;
using System.Collections.Generic;
using System.Linq;
using System.Text;

namespace Chapter13SimplePOCO
{
  public class Address
  {
    public int addressID { get; set; }
    public string Street1 { get; set; }
    public string Street2 { get; set; }
    public string City { get; set; }
    public string StateProvince { get; set; }
    public string CountryRegion { get; set; }
    public string PostalCode { get; set; }
    public string AddressType { get; set; }
    public System.DateTime ModifiedDate { get; set; }

    #region FKs and Reference properties/value objects
    public int ContactID { get; set; }
    public Contact Contact { get; set; }
    #endregion
  }
}
```

For the purpose of introducing POCO classes into the Entity Framework, let's leave these classes as they are now without adding any additional business logic.

It is perfectly acceptable to have additional properties and methods in the POCO classes. As long as you minimally include the entity properties, the classes will work within the Entity Framework.

Now that you have your own classes, there is no need for the model to generate classes. You can turn off the code generation.

Open the model in the Designer. In the Properties window for the model, change the Code Generation Strategy property from Default to None. As you learned in the previous chapter, the class file attached to the model will still exist but will contain only a comment as a reminder that the code generation from the model has been disabled.

Because the class and property names align exactly with the entity and property names, Entity Framework will be able to work out the mapping between the classes and the entities, but you're not done yet.

Since these classes will not be able to rely on the `EntityObject` to communicate back to an `ObjectContext`, or even know that there is such a thing as an `ObjectContext`, the context will need another way to manage these classes so that it can perform its job of executing queries, returning objects, persisting changes to the database, and so forth.

Creating an ObjectContext Class to Manage the POCOs

The `Contact` and `Address` classes have no knowledge at all about the Entity Framework. This is a good thing, as it is the desired effect. However, we need to let the Entity Framework be aware of the classes.

Recall that the default code generator not only created the entity classes, but also created a class that inherited from `ObjectContext`. We don't have one of those yet. The next step is to create your own class that inherits from `ObjectContext` and let it know about your custom classes. Once you have done this, the `ObjectContext` will do its job of querying, materializing, and managing the custom classes.

For the sake of this simple demo, I am having you put everything into a single project. This is not the proper way to architect this type of solution, but is a simpler way to be introduced to the basic concepts. We'll separate things out properly in the next example.

Create a new class called `Entities` and add the code in Example 13-3, which emulates what you've seen in previous `ObjectContext` classes.

Example 13-3. An ObjectContext class that works with the Contact and Address classes

```
using System;
using System.Collections.Generic;
using System.Linq;
using System.Text;
using System.Data.Objects;

namespace Chapter13SimplePOCO
{
  class Entities : ObjectContext
  {
    private ObjectSet<Contact> _contacts;
    private ObjectSet<Address> _addresses;

    public Entities()
      : base("name=POCOEntities", "POCOEntities")
    {
      _contacts = CreateObjectSet<Contact>();
      _addresses = CreateObjectSet<Address>();
```

```
    }
    public ObjectSet<Contact> Contacts
    {
      get
      {
        return _contacts;
      }
    }
    public ObjectSet<Address> Addresses
    {
      get
      {
        return _addresses;
      }
    }
  }
}
```

The `Entities` class inherits from `ObjectContext` just as the other `Entities` classes you have seen thus far. The class constructor uses the signature of `ObjectContext`, which takes in the name of the `EntityConnection` string in the *app.config* file as well as the name of the `EntityContainer` in the model. As with the other `Entities` classes, this class contains read-only properties that return an `ObjectSet` of each type that you want to work with. The fields for these `ObjectSet` properties are instantiated in the class constructor. Remember, this only defines the `ObjectSet` but does not execute a query.

Verifying the POCOs with a query

Now you can write your first queries to see how this all fits together.

In the application's main module, add the code in Example 13-4, which will instantiate your new `ObjectContext`, query for all of the contacts, eager-load their addresses, and then look at the addresses for a single contact.

Example 13-4. Verifying that a query returns your POCOs

```
static void Main(string[] args)
{
  using (Entities context = new Entities())
  {
    var query = from c in context.Contacts.Include("Addresses") select c;
    var contactList = query.ToList();
    int contactCount = contactList.Count;
    Contact firstContact = contactList.Where(c => c.Addresses.Any()).First();
    int addressCount = firstContact.Addresses.Count;
  }
}
```

If you debug through this you'll see that all of the contacts are returned to `contactList` and that the first contact has one address in its collection.

Change Tracking with POCOs

There are a number of things to be aware of when you create your own POCO entities rather than using `EntityObjects`.

Keep in mind that there are two ways to use POCOs. You are starting here with the simplest form. Later in the chapter, you'll see another that has a very different way of interacting with the `ObjectContext`.

When you perform a query that results in POCO entities, the `ObjectContext` creates `ObjectStateEntry` objects for each result just as it does with an `EntityObject`. However, classes that inherit from `EntityObject` interact continuously with the `ObjectContext`, and therefore the context is able to keep track of the state of the classes as well as their relationships to one another.

POCOs do not communicate back to the context. Therefore, the context needs at some point to take a look at the POCOs and synchronize their data with the `ObjectStateEntry` objects that represent them. The `ObjectContext` class has a method called `DetectChanges` that satisfies this purpose.

Understanding the Importance of DetectChanges

It is important to instruct the context to detect changes prior to constructing the various `SaveChanges` commands when you want to send any changes made to your POCOs to the database. Otherwise, the `ObjectStateEntry` objects that the context is managing will not reflect the changes and no insert, update, or delete commands will be sent to the data store.

You may recall from Chapter 6 that one of the `SaveOptions` parameters for `SaveChanges` is `DetectAllChanges`. That option will force the context to call `DetectChanges` prior to the save logic. The default behavior for `SaveChanges` is that it will call `DetectChanges`, so you do not need to explicitly call the method or set the `SaveOptions` enum.

Loading Related Data with POCOs

In previous chapters, you have loaded related data explicitly with the `EntityCollection.Load` method or the `EntityReference.Load` method or taken advantage of lazy loading to bring in related data without creating a new query. You won't be able to do that with the POCOs you have just built. The navigation properties are no longer `EntityCollections` or `EntityReferences` so the `Load` method is unavailable. It is also the `EntityCollection` and `EntityReference` class that provides Entity Framework with its lazy loading capabilities. Without these types in your classes, you'll need another mechanism for loading data after the fact.

Loading from the Context

As mentioned earlier, much of Entity Framework's POCO support is based on new capabilities of `ObjectContext`. In .NET 4, `ObjectContext` has a new method called LoadProperty and this is how you can explicitly load data with your POCOs.

Rather than call Load on a navigation property (e.g., contact.Address.Load), you can let the context perform the load with the following syntax:

```
_context.LoadProperty<Contact>(myContact, c => c.Addresses)
```

This overload uses generics to specify the type that will be loaded from (`<Contact>`) so that you can benefit from strong typing to use the lambda to specify which property should be loaded (`c.Addresses`). Because of the strong typing, Intellisense will help you build the lambda expression. There are a few other overloads for this method which you can find at *http://msdn.microsoft.com/en-us/library/dd382880.aspx*. However, I prefer using the lambda.

Lazy Loading from a Dynamic Proxy

If you want to get lazy loading behavior for your POCO, you'll need to leverage a trick provided by the Entity Framework runtime. By marking a navigation property as `virtual` (`Overridable` in Visual Basic), at runtime, Entity Framework will create a wrapper around that property that will turn it into either an EntityCollection or EntityReference (as appropriate). Therefore, if you have lazy loading enabled, it will simply work as expected. This topic will be covered in more depth in the section "Lazy Loading by Proxy" on page 348.

Exploring and Correcting POCOs' Impact on Two-Way Relationships

In addition to syncing up the `ObjectStateEntry` objects, the context will force `EntityObject` classes to be aware of any two-way relationships. With an `EntityObject` class, if you add an address to the `contact.Addresses EntityCollection`, not only does that impact the `Addresses` property, but you also automatically get the two-way relationship fix-up. As a result, `Address.Contact` is also populated. The two-way relationship also works in the other direction. If you assign a contact instance to `Address.Contact`, that contact also recognizes that address in its `Addresses EntityCollection`.

However, this doesn't automatically happen with the POCOs.

Let's modify the earlier code to see what happens when you build relationships with POCOs. Add the code in Example 13-5 below the last line of code in Example 13-4. That line is included here for placement reference.

Example 13-5. Experimenting with two-way relationships

```
  int addressCount = firstContact.Addresses.Count();
  //new code begins here
  Address newAddress = new Address
  {
    Street1 = "1   Main Street",
    City = "Mainville",
    StateProvince = "Maine",
    ModifiedDate = DateTime.Now
  };
  firstContact.Addresses.Add(newAddress);
  addressCount = firstContact.Addresses.Count;
  Contact newAddressContact = newAddress.Contact;
  //new code ends here
}
```

If you run the code now, you will find that `newAddressContact` is null because the POCO classes don't comprehend the two-way relationship. You added the address to the contact's collection of addresses, but you did not add the contact to the address.

There are three ways to solve this problem. The first relies on the `ObjectContext` to fix the relationship using the `ObjectContext.DetectChanges` method. The second is to give the classes themselves the intelligence to automatically assign the alternate relationship at the time that you modify the property. The last involves virtual (overridable in VB) properties and proxies, which will be explained on the following pages.

It's possible that you do not want two-way relationships. In fact, you may not want to be able to navigate from address to contact. You can easily control this with the existence or accessibility of the setters and getters in the POCO classes. For this example, you will support the two-way relationship and automatic fix-up.

Using the DetectChanges Method to Fix Relationships

Modify the example by adding the following code just before the code line that assigns `newAddressContact`:

```
context.DetectChanges();
```

Run the code again and you should see that the address is now aware of its contact.

Be careful how you use this method. You do not want to automatically call `DetectChanges` anytime you assign a relationship, because it will process every entity that is being tracked by the context. Implement it explicitly if you really need to be aware of the two-way relationship anytime prior to saving changes.

You may prefer to put the onus on the classes themselves to do the fix-up.

Enabling Classes to Fix Their Own Relationships

The other fix-up path lets the classes be responsible for fixing their relationships.

There are varying definitions surrounding the purity of POCO classes. Some developers would find it undesirable to have one POCO class affect the properties of another, and therefore would not approve of this method.

First we'll attack the `Contact` class's `Addresses` property. Unless you want to create a new type of collection class, the simplest thing to do is to create an explicit method in the `Contact` class, which you can call `AddAddress`.

Example 13-6 displays the pattern for this method. First you'll need to instantiate the `Addresses` property if it has not yet been instantiated. Then you can add the new address after verifying that it does not already exist in the collection. So far, this only adds the address to the `Contact`'s collection. Finally, it is time to "fix up" the relationship by ensuring that the address will also know about its contact. The code comment about the circular reference will make more sense after you modify the `Contact` class.

Example 13-6. The Contact.AddAddress method to fix up a two-way relationship

```
public void AddAddress(Address address)
{
  //instantiate Addresses if necessary
  if (Addresses == null)
  {
    Addresses=new List<Address>();
  }
  //add the address if it is not already in the list
  if (!Addresses.Contains(address))
  {
    Addresses.Add(address);
  }
  //set the contact property, but protect from circular reference
  if (address.Contact != this)
  {
    address.Contact = this;
  }
}
```

Next, you can modify the `Address` class so that it will also provide two-way relationship fix-ups.

The current `Contact` property of the `Address` class uses an auto-implementer. Replace that with the code in Example 13-7.

Example 13-7. The modified Address.Contact property to fix up the two-way relationship

```
private Contact _contact;
public Contact Contact
```

```
{
  get { return _contact;}
  set {
    _contact = value;
    //explicit relationship fixup
    _contact.AddAddress(this);
  }
}
```

Notice that the property provides the alternate relationship by calling the AddAddress method of the contact. This is why the AddAddress method checks the value of the Address.Contact prior to setting the value; otherwise, you will trigger an infinite loop.

Now, back in the Main method, comment out the call to DetectChanges that you added earlier, and run the application again. You'll see that the newAddressContact does get populated.

Finally, you can check the other direction of the relationship. Replace the line of code that reads firstContact.Addresses.Add(newAddress); again, this time with newAddress.Contact=firstContact;. Now you are only setting the contact property of addresses. The address class will provide the fix-up for the other direction. You should find that this has caused the firstContact.Addresses.Count() to increase.

Using Proxies to Enable Change Notification, Lazy Loading, and Relationship Fix-Up

As you read earlier, DetectChanges also forces the context to update the ObjectStateEntry objects that it uses for change tracking. When you call DetectChanges, the context takes a snapshot of the current state of the entities.

It is possible to force the entities to notify the context of changes so that you don't have to wait until you (or the SaveChanges method) call DetectChanges.

You can do this by using a special feature of Entity Framework that enables classes to be wrapped by a special proxy class at runtime. To use this, you must mark every property in the class as virtual. In VB, this is Overridable. At runtime, Entity Framework uses reflection to discover that you have marked the properties as virtual and it will create a DynamicProxy class on the fly, then force it to inherit from your entity. This proxy will add functionality to the runtime POCO class that has many of the same features as an EntityObject. But as you'll see further on, it is not an EntityObject. It is something completely different.

Using proxies will automatically provide your classes with automatic relationship fix-up. At the same time, you also gain (or regain, as it were) many of the same behaviors provided by EntityObject, such as change notification and lazy loading.

Change Notification by Proxy

As you learned previously, the `EntityObject` notifies the `ObjectContext` when a scalar property has changed, enabling the context to keep track of the entity's state.

When you make properties virtual, anytime you inspect the `ObjectStateEntry` objects that the context is maintaining they will be current and there will be no need to call `DetectChanges`.

Every scalar and navigation property in the class must be marked as virtual for this to work. Example 13-8 shows a few of the scalar properties with the `virtual/Overridable` keyword.

Example 13-8. Enabling POCO classes to use a proxy for change tracking

VB
```
Public Overridable Property FirstName As String
Public Overridable Property LastName As String
```

C#
```
public virtual string FirstName {get; set;}
public virtual string LastName {get;set;}
```

Lazy Loading by Proxy

Entity Framework's `ObjectContext` can perform lazy loading on any navigation properties that are virtual. If you have marked all of the properties as virtual in order to get change tracking, you will also get lazy-loading behavior when the context has lazy loading enabled. However, as mentioned earlier, you can get lazy loading on navigation properties even if you do not set up the class to enable change tracking.

If you are not marking every single property as virtual in order to get the runtime change notification and relationship fixup, you can pick and choose which navigation properties support lazy loading. You can do this by marking just those navigation properties that should lazy load as virtual properties.

There is one more rule for enabling lazy loading on the navigation properties. Navigation properties that point to collections must be an `ICollection<T>`. The `ObjectContext` will take care of the rest of the work for you but only if the context's ContextOptions.LazyLoadingEnabled property is set to True. While Microsoft's code generation template will do this for you (as you saw in Example 11-3), if you are constructing the ObjectContext manually, you will need to set this property yourself. You could also set this property on the fly, as you'll see in Example 13-9.

Example 13-9 shows the `Addresses` navigation property of the `Contact` class as a virtual property.

Example 13-9. Enabling POCO classes to use a proxy for lazy loading

VB
```
Public Overridable Property Addresses() As ICollection(Of Address)
```

C#
```
public virtual ICollection<Address> Addresses {get; set;}
```

Example 13-10 displays a method you can add to your console app to check three things for you. First, it verifies that the context recognizes you have modified the contact using the `ObjectStateManager`. Next, it will automatically load the `Addresses`. Finally, it saves your changes to the POCO `Contact` back to the database.

Example 13-10. Verifying change tracking

```
private static void VerifyVirtualChangeTracking()
{
  using (Entities context = new Entities())
  {
    var contact = context.Contacts.First();
    contact.LastName = "Zappos";
    contact.FirstName = "Zelly";
    int modifiedEntities = context.ObjectStateManager.
      GetObjectStateEntries(System.Data.EntityState.Modified).Count();
    context.ContextOptions.LazyLoadingEnabled = true;
    ICollection<Address> addresses = contact.Addresses;
    //break to verify that modifiedEntities is 1 and that addresses is not null
    context.SaveChanges();
  }
}
```

You can put a breakpoint on the last line of code (`context.SaveChanges();`); when it breaks, you can check in the debugger to see what's in `modifiedEntities` and `addresses` just before `SaveChanges` is called, as noted in the comment.

Exploring the Proxy Classes

When debugging code that uses these new classes, it is eye-opening to take a closer look at the classes.

Figure 13-2 shows the `Contact` that you queried and edited in Example 13-10.

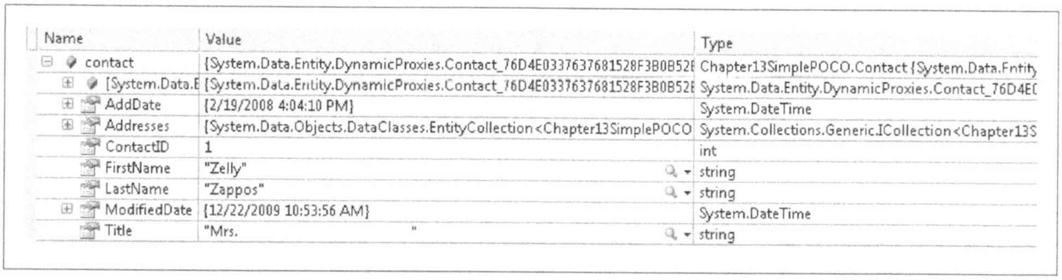

Name	Value	Type
contact	{System.Data.Entity.DynamicProxies.Contact_76D4E0337637681528F3B0B52E	Chapter13SimplePOCO.Contact {System.Data.Entity
[System.Data.E	{System.Data.Entity.DynamicProxies.Contact_76D4E0337637681528F3B0B52E	System.Data.Entity.DynamicProxies.Contact_76D4EC
AddDate	{2/19/2008 4:04:10 PM}	System.DateTime
Addresses	{System.Data.Objects.DataClasses.EntityCollection<Chapter13SimplePOCO	System.Collections.Generic.ICollection<Chapter13S
ContactID	1	int
FirstName	"Zelly"	string
LastName	"Zappos"	string
ModifiedDate	{12/22/2009 10:53:56 AM}	System.DateTime
Title	"Mrs. "	string

Figure 13-2. A high-level view of the proxy class at runtime

The first thing you should notice is that `contact` is not simply a `Contact` type. The Value column tells us that it is a dynamically created type within the `System.Data.Entity.DynamicProxies` namespace. The type name is a combination of the simple type and a hash of the metadata type:

```
System.Data.Entity.DynamicProxies.Contact_
 76D4E0337637681528F3B0B52EC17A15AA07781EFC8A3CF472468413B5BB6966
```

In the Type column, the type is listed as:

```
Chapter13SimplePOCO.Contact {System.Data.Entity.DynamicProxies.Contact_
 76D4E0337637681528F3B0B52EC17A15AA07781EFC8A3CF472468413B5BB6966}
```

One other notable listing in Figure 13-2 is the type of the `Addresses` property. Rather than the `ICollection` that is defined in the class, it has become an `EntityCollection`. Because it is an `EntityCollection`, it will be able to perform the automatic two-way relationship fix-up that we're used to seeing in `EntityObject` entities.

Let's look at the dynamic proxy's impact on the `Contact` entity a bit more closely in Figure 13-3.

Name	Value
⊟ contact	{System.Data.Entity.DynamicProxies.Contact_76D4E0337637681528F3B0B52EC17A
⊟ [System.Data.Entity.DynamicProxies.Contact_76	{System.Data.Entity.DynamicProxies.Contact_76D4E0337637681528F3B0B52EC17A
⊟ base	{System.Data.Entity.DynamicProxies.Contact_76D4E0337637681528F3B0B52EC17A
⊞ AddDate	{2/19/2008 4:04:10 PM}
⊞ Addresses	{System.Data.Objects.DataClasses.EntityCollection<Chapter13SimplePOCO.Addre
ContactID	1
FirstName	"Zelly"
LastName	"Zappos"
⊞ ModifiedDate	{12/22/2009 10:53:56 AM}
Title	"Mrs. "
⊟ _entityWrapper	{System.Data.Objects.Internal.EntityWrapperWithRelationships<System.Data.Entity
⊟ base	{System.Data.Objects.Internal.EntityWrapperWithRelationships<System.Data.Entity
⊞ base	{System.Data.Objects.Internal.EntityWrapperWithRelationships<System.Data.Entity
⊞ Entity	{System.Data.Entity.DynamicProxies.Contact_76D4E0337637681528F3B0B52EC17A
⊞ EntityKey	"EntitySet=Contacts;ContactID=1"
RequiresAnyChangeTracking	true
RequiresComplexChangeTracking	true
RequiresScalarChangeTracking	false
⊞ TypedEntity	{System.Data.Entity.DynamicProxies.Contact_76D4E0337637681528F3B0B52EC17A
⊞ Static members	
⊞ Non-Public members	
OwnsRelationshipManager	true
RequiresRelationshipChangeTracking	false

Figure 13-3. A closer inspection of the dynamic proxy

The key to the dynamic proxy is the `EntityWrapper`. This is where the change tracking and relationship management features are provided to your POCO class. These are the same features that allow an `EntityObject` to do its job. A dynamic proxy is able to tap into the same set of services that the `EntityObject` has access to. The POCO class now has access to these services and can therefore interact with the `ObjectContext` in a similar fashion to the `EntityObject`.

Synchronizing Relationships by Proxy

Finally, we can return to the third method of fixing up two-way relationships. With proxies, this also benefits classes with both a foreign key and related navigation property instance (e.g., `Address.ContactID` and `Address.Contact`) because the proxy will synchronize them. You may recall seeing `EntityObjects` do this in Chapter 10.

First let's look at a scenario where you are linking two existing entities. The following code queries for a random `Contact` and an `Address` and then joins them:

```
var address = context.Addresses.
                Where(a=>a.City=="Winnipeg").FirstOrDefault();
var contact = context.Contacts.FirstOrDefault();
contact.Addresses.Add(address);
```

If you are not using the proxy behavior (i.e., the properties are not marked as virtual), then after this code is run, `address.Contact` and `address.ContactID` will be null.

If you have enabled the proxy to work, `address.Contact` will point to the contact and `address.ContactID` will have the correct value.

If you are creating new objects and you want the relationships to be fixed up there is another important rule to know about.

You might just create a new address by instantiating it:

```
var address = new Address();
```

The context will have absolutely no clue about this address, and if you added it to `contact.Addresses`, you would not get the fix-up behavior.

You need to let the context instantiate the object for you:

```
var address = context.CreateObject<Address>();
```

Then when you add this address to the collection, or set `address.Contact` to the existing contact, the relationship and foreign key will be automatically fixed.

If you are joining two new objects that were created with `CreateObject`, you will still get the fix-up behavior, but remember that the foreign key value (e.g., `ContactID`) will be `0` since it is unassigned. But that is still different from `null`, which is what you would get when the fix-up is not occurring at all.

The Critical Rules for Getting Proxy Behavior with POCOs

I pointed out three critical rules in the previous text that are worthy of highlighting along with some others that are equally important.

Rule 1: To get the proxy behavior for a POCO, every single property (scalar and navigation properties) must be made virtual and public using the C# `virtual` keyword or the VB `Overridable` keyword.

Rule 2: To enable lazy loading on a navigation property to an `EntityReference`, the property must be marked as virtual.

Rule 3: To enable lazy loading on a navigation that is pointing to a dependent collection, it must marked as virtual and be of the type `ICollection<T>`.

Rule 4: When instantiating new POCOs that you want to participate in the proxy behavior (change notification, relationship fix-up, etc.) you must use `ObjectContext.CreateObject<T>` to create the object rather than simply creating a new instance.

Rule 5: The class cannot be sealed.

Rule 6: The class cannot be abstract.

Rule 7: The class must have a constructor that takes zero parameters. By default, a class with no explicit constructors already follows this rule. But if you create a constructor that has a parameter, you must also provide one that takes no parameters.

Rule 8: The navigation properties must not be sealed.

Using T4 to Generate POCO Classes

So far in this chapter you manually built POCO classes. Don't forget about the T4 templates you learned about in Chapter 11. It's a lot of work to strip down the default T4 template to force it to create simple objects. If you enjoy visiting the dentist, you might be interested in doing this work yourself. However, Microsoft has created templates that build Entity Framework POCOs from the EDMX. You could start with one of those and then tweak the template further to make it create classes that follow your desired pattern.

Unfortunately, the POCO templates are not "in the box" when you install Visual Studio 2010 RTM, but they are extremely easy to add in. Microsoft has created two pairs of POCO templates that are available from the Visual Studio 2010 Extension Manager. If you search for POCO in the Extension Manager, the first pair "Microsoft ADO.NET C# POCO Entity Generator" and "Microsoft ADO.NET VB POCO Entity Generator" are the most commonly used. The second pair is specifically for websites and I won't be focusing on those. You can also go directly to *http://www.visualstudiogallery.com/* to download Visual Studio extensions.

After you have installed a POCO Entity Generator extension, the ADO.NET POCO Entity Generator template will be an option when you choose to Add a Code Generation Item to your model. Selecting this template will, in fact, add two templates to your project. One template, with the extension *BreakAway.Context.tt*, is specifically for generating the `ObjectContext` class. The other, *BreakAway.tt*, will generate the entity classes. Figure 13-4 shows the two new templates in the Solution Explorer along with their automatically generated entity classes.

Figure 13-4. The two templates added by the ADO.NET POCO Entity Generator and their generated classes

You'll notice that both the context and the entity template are in the model project. If you are architecting to separate your application concerns, you probably do not want the entity classes in the same project with the model and persistence layer. In Chapter 24, you'll learn how to get the *BreakAway.tt* template into its own project that has no ties whatsoever to the Entity Framework.

The POCO template creates fairly simple classes with all of their properties marked as virtual, forcing them to use the `DynamicProxy` classes at runtime. Additionally, it adds code to ensure that any foreign keys stay in sync with their related navigation property. And finally, there is code in there to maintain two-way relationship fix-ups similar to what you saw earlier in the chapter, although they use a class called `FixUpCollection`, which you'll find in *BreakAway.cs*.

Example 13-11 shows the complete listing for the generated `Payment` class. Notice the code in `ReservationID` that keeps the `Reservation` property in sync with the `ReservationID` foreign key. Additionally, you can see the fix-up code that adds or removes the `Payment` to the `Reservation.Payments` collection as necessary.

Example 13-11. The Payment POCO class generated using the POCO T4 template

```
//------------------------------------------------------------------------------
// <auto-generated>
//     This code was generated from a template.
```

```
//
//     Changes to this file may cause incorrect behavior and will be lost if
//     the code is regenerated.
// </auto-generated>
//------------------------------------------------------------------------------

using System;
using System.Collections;
using System.Collections.Generic;
using System.Collections.ObjectModel;
using System.Collections.Specialized;

namespace BAGA
{
  public partial class Payment
  {
    #region Primitive Properties

    public virtual int PaymentID
    {
      get;
      set;
    }

    public virtual Nullable<System.DateTime> PaymentDate
    {
      get;
      set;
    }

    public virtual int ReservationID
    {
      get { return _reservationID; }
      set
      {
        if (_reservationID != value)
        {
          if (Reservation != null && Reservation.ReservationID != value)
          {
            Reservation = null;
          }
          _reservationID = value;
        }
      }
    }
    private int _reservationID;

    public virtual Nullable<decimal> Amount
    {
      get;
      set;
    }

    public virtual System.DateTime ModifiedDate
    {
```

```
    get;
    set;
  }

  public virtual byte[] TimeStamp
  {
    get;
    set;
  }

  public virtual Nullable<int> ContactID
  {
    get;
    set;
  }

  #endregion
  #region Navigation Properties

  public virtual Reservation Reservation
  {
    get { return _reservation; }
    set
    {
      if (!ReferenceEquals(_reservation, value))
      {
        var previousValue = _reservation;
        _reservation = value;
        FixupReservation(previousValue);
      }
    }
  }
  private Reservation _reservation;

  #endregion
  #region Association Fixup

  private void FixupReservation(Reservation previousValue)
  {
    if (previousValue != null && previousValue.Payments.Contains(this))
    {
      previousValue.Payments.Remove(this);
    }

    if (Reservation != null)
    {
      if (!Reservation.Payments.Contains(this))
      {
        Reservation.Payments.Add(this);
      }
      if (ReservationID != Reservation.ReservationID)
      {
        ReservationID = Reservation.ReservationID;
      }
    }
```

```
        }

        #endregion
    }
}
```

Taking a quick peek into the generated Customer class, you'll find that the template also read the default value setting for CustomerID and applied it:

```
private int _customerTypeID = 1;
```

Modifying the POCO Template

Although this template is Microsoft's default for creating a POCO class it doesn't mean it's perfectly suited to your domain.

Following are two examples of modifying this template.

The first targets scenarios where you do not want the dynamic proxies. In that case, you can modify the template to remove its insertion of virtual in front of properties. If you do a quick search on the word *virtual* you can find the method that inserts that keyword. The method appends virtual to only nonprivate properties.

```
string PropertyVirtualModifier(string accessibility)
{
    return accessibility + (accessibility != "private" ? " virtual" : "");
}
```

These are called when the properties are being created.

Here is the VirtualModifier being used as each primitive type is being declared:

```
<#=PropertyVirtualModifier(Accessibility.ForProperty(edmProperty))#>
  <#=code.Escape(edmProperty.TypeUsage)#> <#=code.Escape(edmProperty)#>
```

The method is responsible for applying the accessibility (e.g., public or private) as well as the virtual keyword. Remove the PropertyVirtualModifier function that surrounds the Accessibility.ForProperty method to insert only the accessibility and not the virtual keyword:

```
<#=Accessibility.ForProperty(edmProperty)#>
```

In Chapter 11, we modified the Activity class so that it will validate the length of the ActvityName field. We did this by manually adding code, along with the desired maximum length, in a partial class.

What's frustrating is that the maximum length is defined in the database and available in the SSDL, and in most cases (except when running the Update Model Wizard), the property was brought forward to the conceptual model as well. But Entity Framework doesn't automatically validate against that property. You can modify the template to read the Max Length attribute of String properties and build validation code when the code is generated.

You can accomplish this with the addition of some new processor methods and then calling those in during the code generation.

You can find the section of the template that contains the processing method near the bottom of the template file. It is introduced by a set of comments surrounded by `<auto-generated>` tags.

I prefer to insert my custom processing methods before this first method so that I can easily find them.

The two methods to include are the ones that get an attribute value given the name of the attribute. For example, if you pass in `Max Length` it will read the metadata for that property and return the value (say, `50`) of the `Max Length` property.

The first method builds a setter for the given property that includes code to perform validation on the length of the field. It calls the second method, which takes an attribute name (such as `MaxLength`) and reads the metadata to return the value of that attribute (for example, `50`) so that the setter can build the proper validation code as well as a helpful error message.

Some of the code uses .NET Reflection, but some of it uses features of Entity Framework's `MetadataWorkspace`, which knows how to read the metadata files.

You will learn much more about the `MetadataWorkspace` in Chapter 21.

For example, the code to return the `attrib` value uses the `MetadataWorkspace` `TypeUsage` method to find the `MaxLength` attribute. If the `MaxLength` attribute is found, the code first checks for three possible problems. If the `MaxLength` is empty, is set to SQL Server's "Max" (e.g., `varchar(Max)`), or is a binary (`Byte`) field, the validation code is not written. Otherwise, the method builds up a string that will test the value of the property being set against the maximum length value. If the validation fails, an `ArgumentException` is thrown with a specific description of the problem. If `MaxLength` is not found, an empty string is returned.

Example 13-12 shows the template function that will generate the validation code for you.

Example 13-12. The T4 template code for generating MaxLength validation

```
string MaxLengthValidation(EdmProperty prop)
{
  var attrib=prop.TypeUsage.Facets.FirstOrDefault(p=>p.Name=="MaxLength");
  if (attrib != null)
  {
    string aVal=GetAttributeValue(attrib);
    if (aVal == "Max" | aVal=="" | prop.TypeUsage.EdmType.Name == "Binary")
```

```
        return "";
      else
      {
        return  System.Environment.NewLine +
                "if (value.Length > " + aVal + ") " + System.Environment.NewLine +
                new ArgumentException(\"" + prop.Name +
                " must be less than " + aVal +" characters\");" +
                System.Environment.NewLine +
                "       else";
      }
    }
    else
      {
        return "";
      }
}

string GetAttributeValue(Facet attrib)
{
  var aVal=attrib.Value;
  return Convert.ToString(aVal);
}
```

The next step is to modify the template itself, and the first task is to ensure that the property you are working with does, indeed, have a `MaxLength` attribute.

Locate the code near the beginning of the template that begins the iteration through the properties. It should begin on or near line 34. Example 13-13 shows the section of code to look for.

Example 13-13. Section of T4 template where you will be inserting code

```
foreach (EdmProperty edmProperty in entity.Properties.
  Where(p => p.TypeUsage.EdmType is PrimitiveType && p.DeclaringType == entity))
{
  bool isForeignKey =
   entity.NavigationProperties.Any(np=>np.GetDependentProperties()
        .Contains(edmProperty));
  bool isDefaultValueDefinedInModel = (edmProperty.DefaultValue != null);
  bool generateAutomaticProperty = false;
```

You'll need to add one more `bool` to this set of code. This also uses the `MetadataWorkspace` to read the metadata to discover whether there is a `MaxLength` attribute.

```
bool hasMaxLengthAttrib=
 (edmProperty.TypeUsage.Facets.FirstOrDefault(p=>p.Name=="MaxLength") != null);
```

Finally, the meat of the code goes in the place where the setter is defined. In the code for the property, you'll find nearly 100 lines devoted to foreign key properties. On or near line 145 will be the getter and setter for nonforeign key properties. Here is the section of code you should look for:

```
else
{
   generateAutomaticProperty = true;
```

```
#>
<#=code.SpaceAfter(Accessibility.ForGetter(edmProperty))#>get{return <#=code.FieldName(edmProperty)#>;
<#=code.SpaceAfter(Accessibility.ForSetter(edmProperty))#>set;<#}#>
```

Insert the code in Example 13-14 in between the line that injects the `get` and the line that injects the `set`. Those two preexisting lines of code are included in the example and highlighted in bold for clarity.

Example 13-14. Template code to add validation logic

```
<#=code.SpaceAfter(Accessibility.ForGetter(edmProperty))#>get;

<#if (hasMaxLengthAttrib)
 {
#>
<#=code.SpaceAfter(Accessibility.ForSetter(edmProperty))#>
set
{<#=MaxLengthValidation(edmProperty)#>
  { <#=code.FieldName(edmProperty)#> = value;}
}
<#  }
   else
{

<#=code.SpaceAfter(Accessibility.ForSetter(edmProperty))#>set;<#}#>
```

When T4 generates the new classes, if it determines that the `MaxLength` is needed, it will write out a setter that includes the `MaxLength` validation; otherwise, the original setter will be called. You'll also need to make a small change a few lines lower, to ensure that the field required by the validation is created—an `if` statement that already tests for `generateAutomaticProperty` also must test `hasMaxLengthAttrib`.

Figure 13-5 shows the relevant section of the template after the changes from Example 13-14 have been made as well as the change to check the value of `hasMaxLengthAttrib`.

Once you have the new code in place, the validation will automatically be part of your generated class. Example 13-15 shows the `addressID` and `Street1` properties of the `Address` class using the modified template. The `addressID` property was not impacted because it does not have a `MaxLength` attribute, but the `Street1` property now has validation code using the `MaxLength` value, `50`, found in the metadata.

Example 13-15. The validation for Address.Street1 as generated from the modified template

```
public int addressID
{
  get;
  set;
}

public string Street1
{
  get;
```

```
  set
  {
    if (value.Length > 50)
      {new ArgumentException("Street1 must be less than 50 characters");}
    else
    { _street1 = value;}
  }
}
```

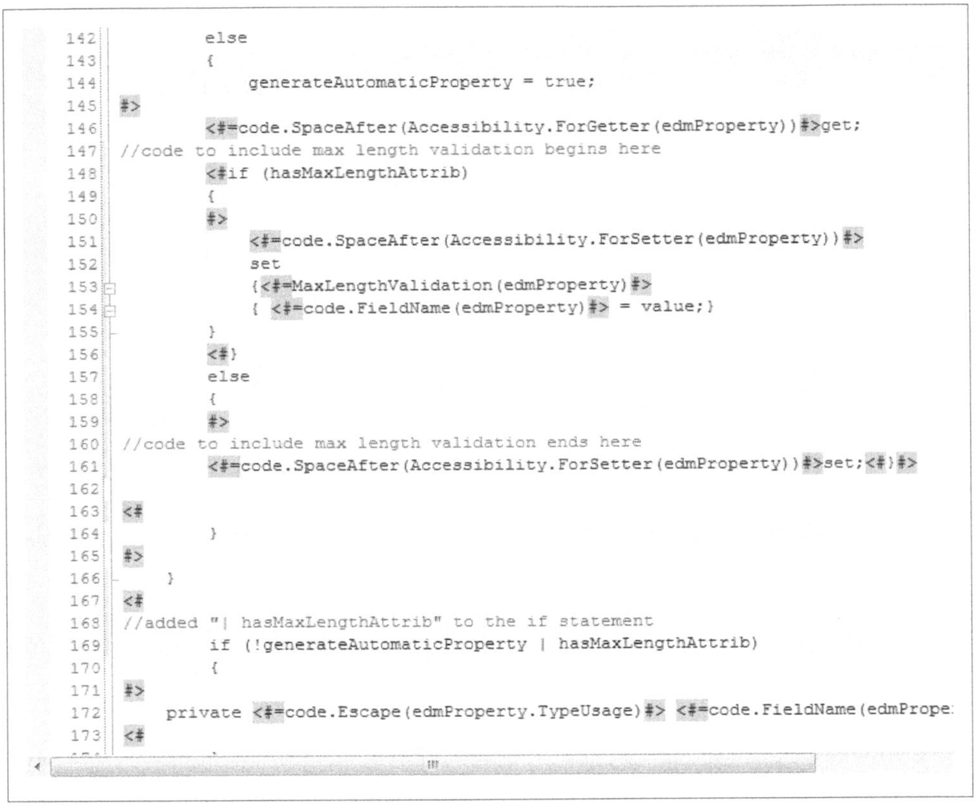

```
            else
            {
                generateAutomaticProperty = true;
#>
            <#=code.SpaceAfter(Accessibility.ForGetter(edmProperty))#>get;
//code to include max length validation begins here
            <#if (hasMaxLengthAttrib)
            {
            #>
                <#=code.SpaceAfter(Accessibility.ForSetter(edmProperty))#>
                set
                {<#=MaxLengthValidation(edmProperty)#>
                { <#=code.FieldName(edmProperty)#> = value;}
            }
            <#}
            else
            {
            #>
//code to include max length validation ends here
            <#=code.SpaceAfter(Accessibility.ForSetter(edmProperty))#>set;<#}#>

<#
            }
#>
        }
<#
//added "| hasMaxLengthAttrib" to the if statement
            if (!generateAutomaticProperty | hasMaxLengthAttrib)
            {
#>
        private <#=code.Escape(edmProperty.TypeUsage)#> <#=code.FieldName(edmPrope
<#
```

Figure 13-5. Placement of template modifications for MaxLength validation

Using these patterns you can add validation for other property attributes in your model as well. This is a much more convenient solution than manually creating predictable, repetitive logic in partial classes.

Creating a Model That Works with Preexisting Classes

Many developers may be moving existing applications to the Entity Framework. If that is your scenario, you may already have classes that you want to use in the new solution. Along with existing classes, there's also a good chance that you have an existing database from which to generate a model.

After you create the model (using the EDM Wizard to reverse-engineer the database), the entities in the model will probably not match up with your classes in a way that allows the Entity Framework's POCO support to work.

When you built the BreakAway model in Chapter 8, you made a number of simple modifications to the names of entities and properties. In that chapter, we discussed only some of the many possible ways in which you can customize a model once it has been created by the wizard. The Entity Data Model and the Designer support a variety of scenarios, including various types of inheritance, combining tables into a single entity, splitting tables into multiple entities, abstract entities, and more.

In Chapter 14, you will learn how to customize models without impacting their ability to work with your database. Then you will see that it is possible to reshape the entities and the model to match your classes. You still may have to do a little bit of work on your classes to get the proper alignment, but this is a strategy that you should consider when migrating applications.

Code First: Using Entity Framework with No Model at All

The Entity Framework supports one additional scenario, and that is one that relies solely on classes and doesn't include the Entity Framework metadata. There is no EDMX file at design time, and there are no physical CSDL, MSL, or SSL files to work with at runtime. This feature is called code-first development. It is not included in .NET 4 and Visual Studio 2010, but it is part of the Entity Framework Feature CTP that is currently released as an "out of band" addition to Entity Framework. Chapter 25 contains a preview of using code first for your Entity Framework-based applications.

Summary

In this chapter, you learned about one of the most important features added to Entity Framework in .NET 4: support for classes that do not inherit from the `EntityObject` class. You learned how to create simple classes that will still benefit from the Entity Framework's modeling, querying, change tracking, and relationship management features. The `ObjectContext` can manage these classes by taking snapshots of their current state or by using proxy dynamic proxies to provide change notification and relationship management on the fly. In later chapters, you will see POCO classes used in application solutions. You will also see how they fit into more agile software architectures and can be part of good testing practices.

CHAPTER 14

Customizing Entity Data Models Using the EDM Designer

So far in this book, you have worked with models that closely match the database. You also have made some simple changes to the names of entities and properties.

The Entity Data Model (EDM) offers enormous flexibility when it comes to customizing models so that they are more than mere reflections of your database. This capability is one of the main reasons many developers choose to use the Entity Framework.

In this chapter, you will learn about some of the many ways in which you can customize an EDM, the benefits of these customizations, and when you would want to take advantage of them. Although most customization occurs in the Conceptual Schema Definition Layer (CSDL), you can use additional mappings and even storage schema modifications to create a model that truly describes your data in a way that fits well with your vision of how the data should look.

Most customizations that are created in the conceptual layer are dependent on their mappings back to the database to function properly. Because of this, the customizations are more often referred to as *mappings*, as you will see throughout this chapter.

You will also learn how to build queries using the new mappings and interact with the objects that are based on the various entities.

The great array of mapping capabilities is instrumental in setting the Entity Framework apart from other ORMs. There are so many, in fact, that all of them are not covered in this chapter. Chapter 15 shows you how to apply mappings that are not supported by the EDM Designer. You will spend much of your time in that chapter working directly with the XML. In addition, many more modeling techniques are related to stored procedures and views. Chapter 16 will be devoted to that set of mappings.

Samples used throughout the rest of this book will be dependent on most of the model changes that the mapping walkthroughs in this chapter describe. If you are following the examples, be sure to perform the steps described in this chapter. A few of the walkthroughs at the end of the chapter are not used by later examples (these are noted).

Mapping Table per Type Inheritance for Tables That Describe Derived Types

The BreakAway business has a number of different types of contacts. The `Contact` table keeps track of the common information for all contacts, such as `FirstName` and `LastName`. Some of those contacts are customers, and a separate table keeps track of the additional information about these types of contacts—their preferences, notes, and the date they first became customers. In the past few chapters, when working with customers you have had to constantly go back to the `Contacts` entity to get the customers' names.

In object-oriented programming, when one object is a type of another object you can use inheritance to share properties so that the properties of a base type (e.g., `Contact`) are exposed directly in a derived type (e.g., `Customer`). The EDM supports inheritance as well. The inheritance mapping used to allow `Customer` to derive from `Contact` and absorb `Contact`'s properties is called *Table per Type inheritance*. Let's investigate this one first, and modify the model to simplify working with customers.

Table per Type (TPT) inheritance defines an inheritance that is described in the database with separate tables where one table provides additional details that describe a new type based on another table. Figure 14-1 depicts the concept of TPT inheritance.

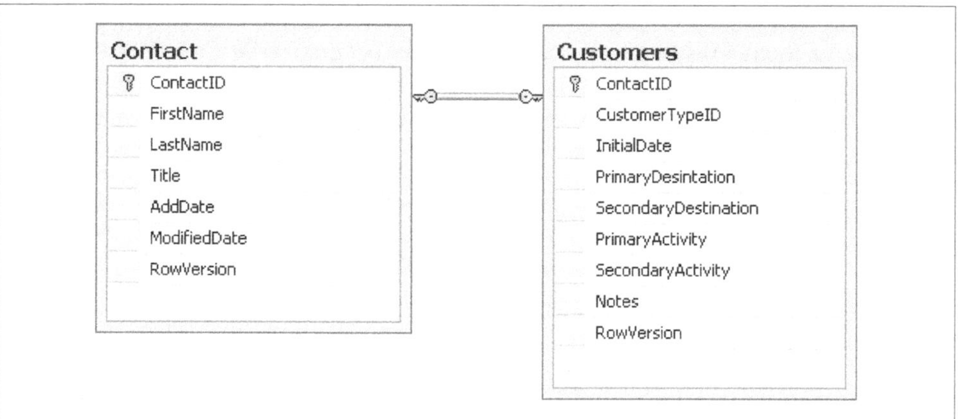

Figure 14-1. Database tables that can be used for TPT inheritance

Figure 14-1 shows a 1:0..1 (One to Zero or One) relationship between `Contact` and `Customer` in the database. This means a `Contact` could have a related `Customer` entity, but it's not required. It also means a `Contact` cannot have more than one related `Customer` entity. The `Customer` table provides additional information about a subset of the contacts.

Mapping TPT Inheritance

Let's replace the navigation that the Entity Data Model Wizard created between `Contact` and `Customer` with an inheritance hierarchy that maps back to the database tables.

1. Delete the association between `Contact` and `Customer` that the EDM Wizard created when you originally created the model in Chapter 8.

   You can do this by selecting the line that represents the association and deleting it. Notice that when you do this, the navigation properties that used the association are automatically removed.

   The Designer provides two ways to add inheritance. You can select an inheritance object from the Toolbox, click on the entity that is to serve as the base, and then click on the entity that will be derived from the base. Alternatively, you can add it from an entity's context menu. Let's use the context menu method.
2. Right-click the `Contact` entity. Choose Add and then Inheritance from the context menu.
3. In the Add Inheritance window, select Contact as the base entity and Customer as the derived entity, as show in Figure 14-2. `Customer` will inherit properties from `Contact`.
4. Delete the `EntityKey` (`ContactID`) from the derived type (`Customer`). `Customer` will now inherit its `EntityKey` from `Contact`. You can do this be clicking the property and hitting the delete key on your keyboard.
5. Change the name of the `Customer`'s `RowVersion` property to `CustomerRowVersion`.
6. Change the `CustomerRowVersion`'s `ConcurrencyMode` property to `None`.
7. Open the Mapping Details window for `Customer`.
8. Map the `Customer`'s new `ContactID` property (which now comes from the `Contact` entity) to the `ContactID` column in the `Customers` table.

When the inheritance is set up, the `Customer` entity will have an arrow glyph at the top that indicates it is inheriting from `Contact`. There is an inheritance line between the two entities as well, with the arrow pointing to the base entity (see Figure 14-3).

Handling duplicate names and concurrency properties in an inheritance hierarchy

In the preceding steps, you made two changes to the `Customer`'s `RowVersion` property. The first was to change its name. You can't have properties in an inheritance hierarchy with matching names. Since `Contact` already has a `RowVersion` property, `Customer` cannot.

Derived entities cannot support concurrency checking; therefore, you don't truly need to have this property in `Customer`. If you define any concurrency for the base entity, `Contact`, the concurrency checking will now include the `Customer` entity, or more

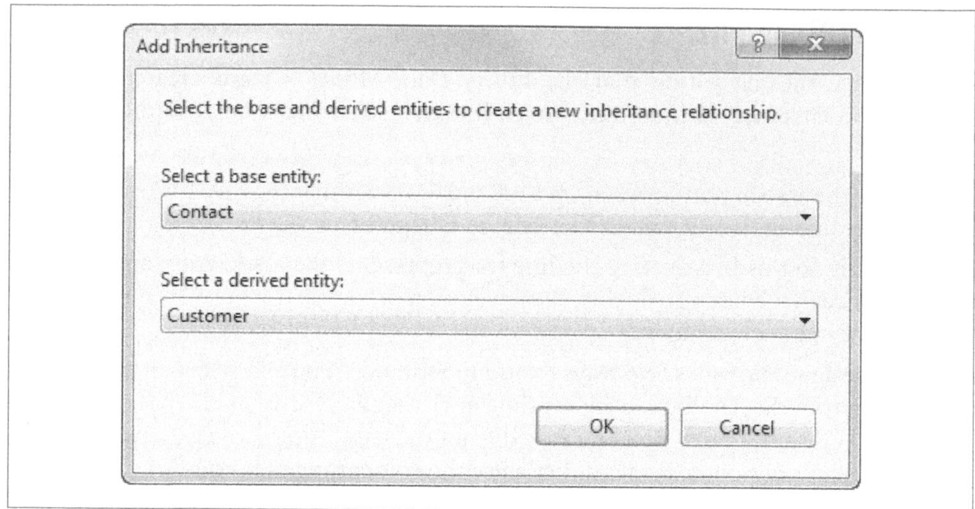

Figure 14-2. Defining an inheritance between Contact and Customer

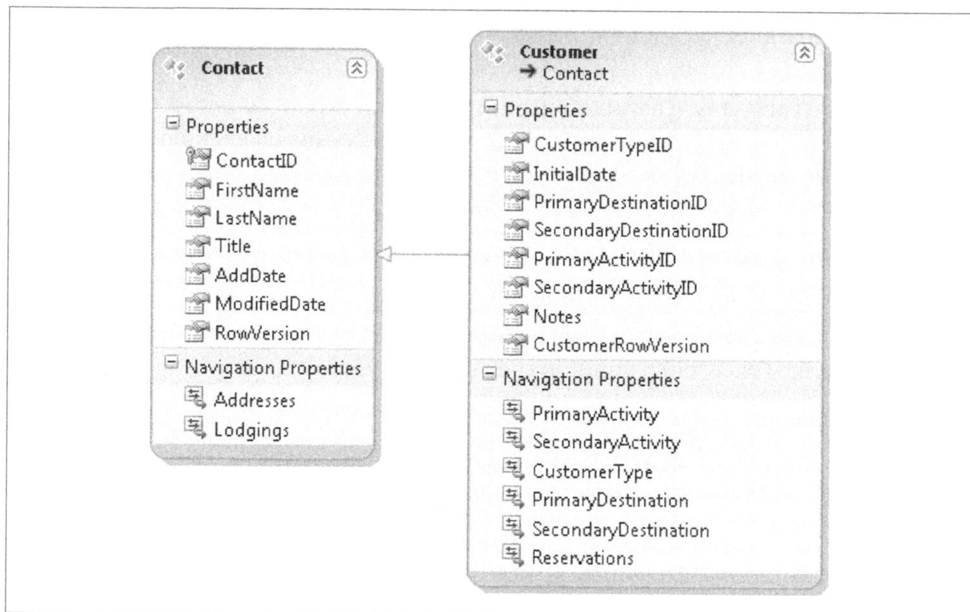

Figure 14-3. The new inheritance displayed in the model

specifically, the table that the `Customer` entity maps to—`Customers`—as well. You'll learn more about concurrency in Chapter 23.

You could, in fact, simply delete the `CustomerRowVersion` property since in this hierarchy, Entity Framework has no use for it. If you have plans to use the field for other purposes, then by all means, leave it in.

Fixing a potential constraint problem

Because the Customer's ContactID was deleted so that it can now inherit from Contact, I have seen occasions when the associations involving Customer.ContactID were broken. Compile the model to verify that it validates.

If it doesn't, you may need to make the following fix.

Look for two errors listed for *BAModel.edmx*. The first complains about the Principal in a constraint:

```
The element 'Principal' in namespace
'http://schemas.microsoft.com/ado/2008/09/edm'
has incomplete content.
List of possible elements expected: 'PropertyRef' in namespace
'http://schemas.microsoft.com/ado/2008/09/edm'.
```

The second error is almost the same, except that its complaint is about a dependent.

The problem is in the association between Customer and Reservation, since Reservation has a foreign key that points to Customer.ContactID. When you deleted the ContactID from Customer, the reference to ContactID was removed from the constraint. You need to add it back in.

To fix the constraint problem:

1. Click the association line between Customer and Reservation.
2. In the Properties window, select Referential Constraint and then click the ellipses to open the Referential Constraint dialog.

   You'll see that the Dependent Property is missing.
3. Change the Dependent Property to ContactID, as shown in Figure 14-4.
4. Rebuild the model's project, and the errors in the Error List should go away.

Querying Inherited Types

As a result of the inheritance, the Customer object now inherits the Contact properties. You no longer need to navigate to Contact to get the Customer's LastName, FirstName, or other Contact properties. You can also navigate directly to the Addresses EntityCollection through the Customer.Addresses property.

In the model, this also means the Customers EntitySet is now gone and its strongly typed ObjectSet will no longer be among the properties of BAEntities. Customer is now served up from the Contacts EntitySet. When you request Contacts, those Contacts that have a Customer entity will be returned as Customer types.

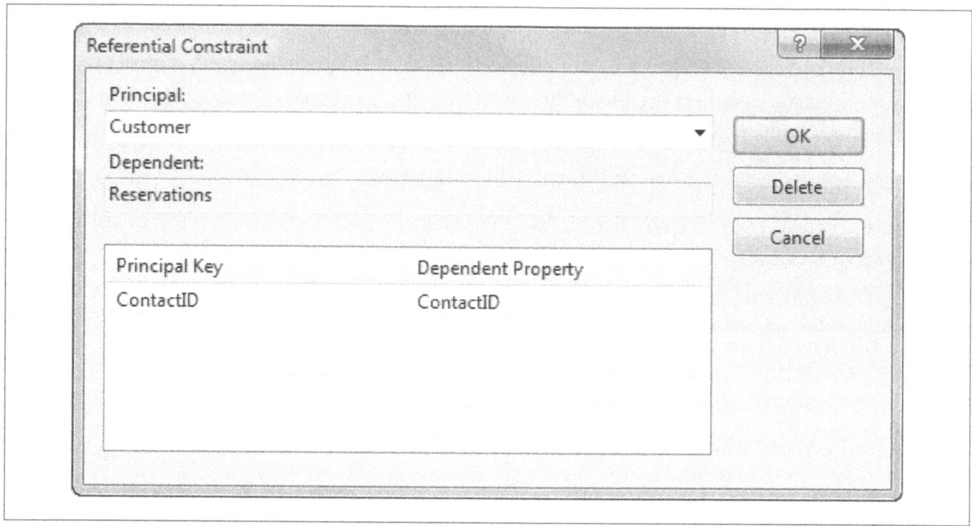

Figure 14-4. Fixing the referential constraint between Customer and Reservations

To query for customers specifically, you will need to use the `OfType` method to specify which type of contact you are seeking, as shown in the following code:

VB
```
From c in Contacts.OfType(Of Customer) Select c
```

C#
```
from c in Contacts.OfType<Customer> select c;
```

You'll see many more examples of querying types in an inheritance hierarchy throughout this chapter and the rest of the book.

POCO Classes and Inherited Objects

If you are using the Microsoft-supplied T4 template to generate POCOs from your Entity Data Model, the inheritance will be recognized and reflected in the generated classes.

The `Customer` class inherits from `Contact`:

```
public partial class Customer : Contact
```

The `Contact` properties such as `FirstName` and `LastName` are available directly from the `Customer` class.

Inserting TPT Inherited Types

To test this new TPT inheritance, as well as the various customizations you will be creating further on in this chapter, create a new Console Application project and then follow these steps:

1. Set up the Console Application project to use the model, as you did with the previous projects:
   a. Add references to `System.Data.Entity` and to the BreakAwayModel project.
   b. Copy the *app.config* file from the model's project into the new console application project.
2. Open the project's main code file (*Module1.vb* or *program.cs*).
3. Import the model's namespace, `BAGA`, at the top of the code file.
4. Add the method in Example 14-1 to the module. This will query for contacts who are customers.

Example 14-1. Querying a derived type

```
private static void TPTMap()
{
  using (var context = new BAEntities())
  {
    var query =
        from c in context.Contacts.OfType<Customer>()
        select c;
    Console.WriteLine("Customers: " + query.Count().ToString());

    //query all Contacts
    Console.WriteLine("All Contacts: " +
                      context.Contacts.Count().ToString());

    Customer newCust = new Customer();
    newCust.FirstName = "Noam";
    newCust.LastName = "Ben-Ami";
    context.Contacts.AddObject(newCust);

    context.SaveChanges();
  }
}
```

If you did not implement the constructor in Example 11-18, which sets the `Contact.AddDate` property, you will get an exception when running the `TPTMap` method. Alternatively you can explicitly set `newCust.AddDate=DateTime.Now` in `TPTMap`.

5. Call the `TPTMap` method from the module's `Main` method.
6. Set a breakpoint at the line that instantiates `newCust`.
7. Run the application.

When debugging the `Customer` results, you can see that the `Customer` has inherited the `LastName` and `FirstName` properties of `Contact`. When debugging the `Contact` results, you can see that only the `Contact` properties are there, even for contacts who are Customers.

Finally, looking at the counts displayed in the output, you'll find that the number of queried customers is much smaller than the number of contacts, and is, in fact, a subset of contacts.

SaveChanges and newly added derived types

In Example 14-1, a `Customer` was created in memory, added to the context, and then saved to the database with `context.SaveChanges`. When `SaveChanges` is called, the Entity Framework constructs commands to first create a new `Contact` record, and then, based on the newly generated ID returned from the database, to create the `Customer` record.

Example 14-2 shows the two commands executed on the database as a result of the code in Example 14-1. The first inserts a contact and does a `SELECT` to return the new `ContactID` and `RowVersion`. The second inserts a new `Customer` using the new `ContactID`, 735.

Example 14-2. T-SQL commands created based on the new Customer created in the previous example

```
exec sp_executesql
N'insert [dbo].[Contact]([FirstName], [LastName], [Title], [ModifiedDate])
values (@0, @1, null, @2)
select [ContactID], [AddDate], [RowVersion]
from [dbo].[Contact]
where @@ROWCOUNT > 0 and [ContactID] = scope_identity()',
N'@0 nvarchar(50),@1 nvarchar(50),@2 datetime2(7)',@0=N'Noam',
@1=N'Ben-Ami',@2='2009-14-10 19:57:31.7540626'

exec sp_executesql
 N'insert [dbo].[Customers]([ContactID], [CustomerTypeID], [InitialDate],
 [PrimaryDesintation], [SecondaryDestination], [PrimaryActivity],
 [SecondaryActivity], [Notes])
values (@0, @1, null, null, null, null, null, null)
select [RowVersion]
from [dbo].[Customers]
where @@ROWCOUNT > 0 and [ContactID] = @0',
N'@0 int,@1 int',@0=735,@1=1
```

As a reminder, the `Contact` insert is returning the new `ContactID` as well as the two computed columns, `AddDate` and `RowVersion`, to be pushed into the object. The `Customer` insert has a value for `CustomerTypeID`. That's coming from the default value that you defined in the model for the `CustomerTypeID` property in Chapter 8.

The new `Customer` record is seen as both a `Contact` type and a `Customer` type. Therefore, as `SavingChanges` tested for the entity type and populated values based on that, the new `Customer` entity got the required values for `Contact` and for `Customer`.

Specifying or Excluding Derived Types in Queries

You can explicitly query for different types within an inheritance structure. To specify a derived type of an ObjectSet, you can append the OfType method to the ObjectSet being queried:

VB
```
context.Contacts.OfType(Of Customer)
```

C#
```
context.Contacts.OfType<Customer>()
```

You can use OfType when building LINQ queries against the ObjectSet. But there are other ways to filter by type in LINQ as well.

In Visual Basic, you can use the TypeOf operator for type filtering:

VB
```
From c In context.Contacts _
Where TypeOf c Is Customer Select c

From c In context.Contacts _
Where Not TypeOf c Is Customer Select c
```

In C#, you can do direct type comparison:

C#
```
from c in context.Contacts where c is Customer select c;

from c in context.Contacts where !(c is Customer) select c;
```

Entity SQL also has operators for working with types, and in fact, it can filter out types in a way that is not possible with LINQ to Entities.

The type operators you will use most commonly in Entity SQL are OFTYPE and IS [NOT] OF. The following code snippets represent examples of how you could rewrite the preceding queries with Entity SQL. Note that you could do this by using query builder methods, as well.

To return only Customer types:

```
SELECT VALUE c
FROM OFTYPE(BAEntities.Contacts, BAModel.Customer)
AS c
```

To return Contacts that are not Customer types:

```
SELECT VALUE c
FROM BAEntities.Contacts
AS c
where c IS NOT OF(BAModel.Customer)
```

There is an additional Entity SQL operator called TREAT AS that allows you to do type casting directly in the Entity SQL expression.

The preceding two Entity SQL expressions will return results that are still shaped like Contacts. To ensure that the results are shaped like the types that you are seeking, you'll need to use TREAT AS. As with the OFTYPE operator, be sure to use the assembly namespace in the full name of the type you are casting to.

To return only Customer types that are type-cast as Customer types:

```
SELECT VALUE TREAT(c AS BAModel.Customer)
FROM OFTYPE(BAEntities.Contacts, BAModel.Customer)
AS c
```

As you can see, you can also use Object Services and EntityClient with Entity SQL to build more complex queries around types.

In LINQ, the safest way to do type filtering is to use the OfType method, because the rest of the query will know you are working with Customer and not Contact, allowing you to do any further filtering or projection based on Customer properties.

When you place the type filter in the Where clause, the rest of the query is still based on the type being queried—in the preceding example, Contact. You won't be able to do projection or filtering on Customer properties.

Creating New Derived Entities When the Base Entity Already Exists

What if you have a contact that becomes a customer? This is an important business rule for BreakAway Geek Adventures, and one that TPT inheritance doesn't readily support. This isn't to say that the Entity Framework doesn't support this scenario, but TPT by definition doesn't support it.

Let's look at what may seem like logical options using the Entity Framework, and why they won't work. The counterpoints provide a lot of insight into the workings of Object Services.

Add a new Customer *object*
: As you have seen, adding a new Customer object will cause a new Contact to be created in the database. Therefore, you can't just add a new customer for an existing contact.

Create a new Customer *and populate its* ContactID *with the* ContactID *of the* Contact
: If the Contact is not being managed by the context, the Entity Framework will still see this as a new Customer and will try to add the Contact to the database.

Get the Contact *into the context and add a new* Customer *with the same* ContactID
: Both the Contact and the Customer are members of the Contacts entity set. You will not be able to add the Customer to the context because a member of the Contacts entity set with the same EntityKey already exists in the context.

Detach the Contact *from the context, set* Customer.EntityKey=Contact.EntityKey *and* Customer.ContactID=Contact.ContactID, *and then call* SaveChanges
: You would be getting closer to a solution with this. However, the Customer will be seen as having no changes, and therefore nothing will happen when SaveChanges is called. If you do something to make the Customer "modified," the database command that results will be to update a nonexistent Customer record, and that too would fail. In addition, that is a lot of steps to solve a simple problem.

Delete the `Contact` *and create a new customer (which in turn will create the Contact row in the database)*

This would mean that the new `Contact` would get a new `ContactID`, breaking any relationships to other entities, such as `Addresses`.

Use Entity SQL's `TREAT` *operator to "upcast" the* `Contact` *to a* `Customer` *type*

Unfortunately, this won't work either. The Entity Framework cannot cast from one type to another.

Although you may want to continue banging your head against the wall with creative hacks, the reality is that the inheritance does not support this scenario, and even with all of the other benefits that came along with having `Customer` inherit from `Contact`, this is a big problem.

Locked into a Corner with Inheritance?

Early in the classic programming book *Design Patterns* (Addison-Wesley Professional), authors Erich Gamma, Richard Helm, Ralph Johnson, and John Vlissides discuss inheritance versus composition and conclude that one should "favor composition over inheritance." Composition uses building blocks. This would mean changing the model so that the `FirstName` and `LastName` properties of `Contact` would be accessed from the `Customer` type using `Customer.Contact.FirstName`. Inheritance is definitely more convenient for many reasons, but it also has its drawbacks. As you can see with TPT inheritance, the derived type is completely bound to the base type and there is no way to separate the two. One example of a drawback is the inability to delete a `Customer` entity without also deleting its `Contact`. In the BreakAway business, it could be necessary to be able to do that.

Having `Customer` inherit from `Contact` is something you should consider prior to designing your EDM. TPT inheritance may be perfect for your business model; it may create some rare annoyances; or it may not be the right way to go at all. These are decisions you'll need to make.

Given the existing model, the best way to create a `Customer` for an existing `Contact` is to use a stored procedure—not a stored procedure that is wired up to the `Customer` entity through mappings, but a separate one that can be called explicitly from code. This will allow you to have your cake (the convenience of the derived type) and eat it too (perform functions that TPT inheritance does not support). We will discuss stored procedures in Chapter 16, and at that time you'll see how to leverage the EDM's flexibility to solve this problem and how this stored procedure can be called as a method of the `BAEntities` class.

TPT with Abstract Types

In the current inheritance model, the base type, `Contact`, is instantiated for some entities, and `Customer` is instantiated for others. It is possible to have base types that are *abstract*, which means they are there to help define the structure of entities that derive from them, but they will never be instantiated.

If you turned `Contact` into an abstract type, however, a few hundred contacts (those that are not customers) will never appear in your application because they won't have an instantiated type to map to. You would have no way to access contacts who are not customers.

To solve this you need to create derived entities to represent other types of contacts.

What would a derived type that accesses the noncustomer contacts look like? Let's modify the model to see:

1. Open the model in the Designer and select the `Contact` entity.
2. In the Properties window, change the value of its `Abstract` property to `true`.

   Now `Contact` is an abstract type.
3. Run the `TPTMap` method again.
4. When the breakpoint is hit, debug the results of the `Contact` query and you will see that only customers are returned. The entire set of data for contacts who are not customers is missing.

Now it's time to create the new derived type:

1. In the EDM Designer, create a new entity and name it `NonCustomer`.

   You can create a new entity by right-clicking in the design window and selecting Add and then Entity, or by dragging an `Entity` from the Toolbox.
2. Select Contact from the "Base type" drop-down list. The other fields in the Add Entity window will become disabled since they don't pertain to a derived type.
3. Click OK.

   That's it. Because there are no additional fields in this new entity, there's no need to do any mapping.

Unfortunately, there is a bug in the EDM Designer that will cause it to report that `NonCustomer` is not mapped. This will show up as an Error in the Visual Studio IDE. Normally, errors prevent applications from compiling, but not this one. You'll simply have to ignore it; it will have no impact on your application.

If you were to look in the raw XML of the EDMX file, the only instance of `NonCustomer` you will find in the XML (other than the Designer information) is this element in the CSDL:

```
<EntityType Name="NonCustomer" BaseType="BAModel.Contact" >
</EntityType>
```

If any fields in the `Contact` entity were relevant to a `NonCustomer` but were not relevant to a `Customer`, you could move them over to the new entity. That scenario would require additional mapping. But in this case, everything you need for `NonCustomer` is already provided by the `Contact` abstract type.

4. Run the application again and check out the `Contact` query results in the debugger when you hit the breakpoint. All of the additional contacts are back as `NonCustomer` types.

Because `Contact` is now abstract, the custom `CreateContact` method added to the `Contact` partial class in Chapter 11 is no longer valid because you cannot instantiate a contact. You'll need to delete or comment out that method so that the model project will compile.

I cover additional types of inheritance that the EDM supports later in this chapter.

Mapping Unique Foreign Keys

Often, a foreign key in a database relationship must be unique. There is no such example in the BreakAway database, but I'll use the relationship between `Contact` and `Address` to explain. Currently `Contact` has a one-to-many relationship with `Address`. `Address` has a primary key of `addresssID` and another field, `ContactID`, which is a foreign key in this relationship. A contact can have many addresses. You could enforce a rule in the database that a contact can have only one address. In SQL Server Management Studio, you can do this by creating a unique index on the Address table as shown in Figure 14-5.

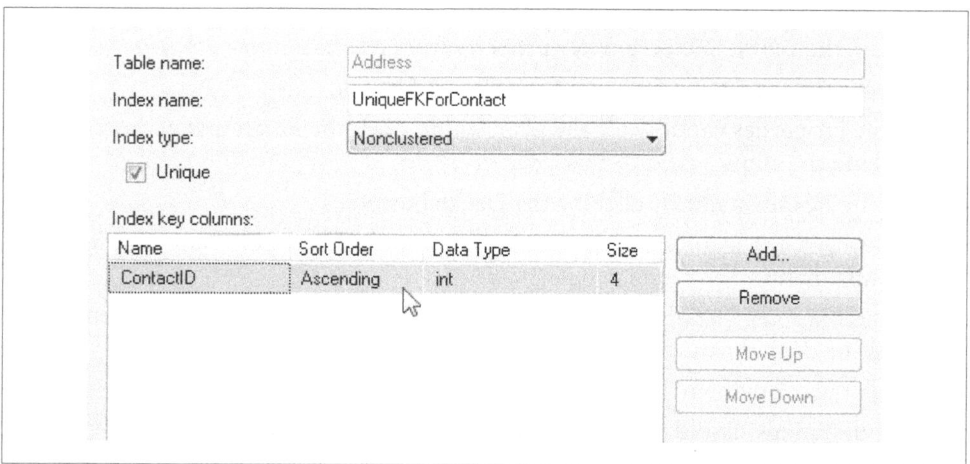

Figure 14-5. Defining a unique index on a foreign key in SQL Server Management Studio

Now the challenge is to reflect this unique constraint in the model.

What seems to be the obvious solution is to change the 1:* association between `Contact` and `Address` in the EDM into a 1:1 association. However, the mapping will not validate when you have a foreign key association between the two entities as in the BreakAway model. The only way to map a unique foreign key association is by using an independent association. This is the same type of association that you may be familiar with from using Entity Framework in .NET 3.5, where foreign keys were not supported.

To turn the foreign key association into an independent association would mean removing the `ContactID` foreign key from the `Address` entity and recreating the association through mappings. When encountering this problem in your production applications, you'll have to decide which is more important to your model and your application logic: the foreign key scalar (e.g., `Address.ContactID`) or being able to define a 1:1 association between one entity (`Contact`) and another (`Address`) when they are joined through a foreign key (ContactID).

If you are using WCF RIA Services (see Chapter 17), be aware that they do not support independent associations; they support only relationships that are defined on scalar foreign key properties.

To make the change to the association, you'll need to do the following:

If you practice these steps on the BreakAway model, please be sure to revert to the original, foreign key association.

1. Delete the `ContactID` foreign key property from `Address` entity.
2. Select the `Association` between `Contact` and `Address`.
3. In the Properties window for the association, open the Referential Constraints by clicking the ellipses next to that property.
4. Delete the constraint by clicking the Delete button.
5. Right-click the association in the Designer and select Table Mapping from the context menu.
6. In the Mapping Details window, click the <Add a Table or View> element to expose the drop-down.
7. From the drop-down, select `Address`.

   The mappings should populate automatically as shown in Figure 14-6.
8. Return to the Properties window for the association.

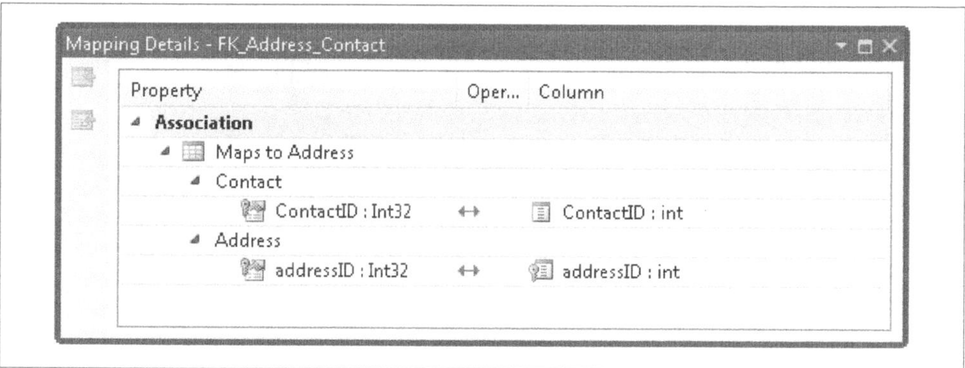

Figure 14-6. Association mapping between Contact and Address

9. For the property called "End2 Multiplicity," which currently has the value `* Collection of Addresses`, change that property to `1` (One of Address) using its drop-down list.
10. Validate the model by right-clicking the design surface and choosing Validate. You should not see any error messages related to this mapping.

Now you have defined a unique foreign key relationship between `Contact` and `Address` in the model.

If you followed these steps, please remember to revert to the foreign key association that was originally defined between these two entities.

Mapping an Entity to More Than One Table

Entity splitting, also referred to as *vertical splitting*, allows you to map a single entity to more than one table. You can use entity splitting when tables share a common key, for example, when a contact's personal and business information is stored in separate tables. You can use entity splitting as long as the primary keys in the database tables match.

The BreakAway model contains an entity that we have thus far ignored: `ContactPersonalInfo`, which has a `ContactID` property (see Figure 14-7 for the database representation and Figure 14-8 for the entity). The purpose of the database table from which the entity was created is to provide additional information about customers that might be useful for BreakAway employees to be aware of when these customers participate in trips. This table is the victim of poor database design. There is no primary key/foreign key constraint between it and `Contact` or `Customer`.

One way in which you can link this new entity to a customer is to create a 1:1 association between `Customer` and `ContactPersonalInfo` using `ContactID`. That would make `Customer` a navigation property of `ContactPersonalInfo` and vice versa. However, this

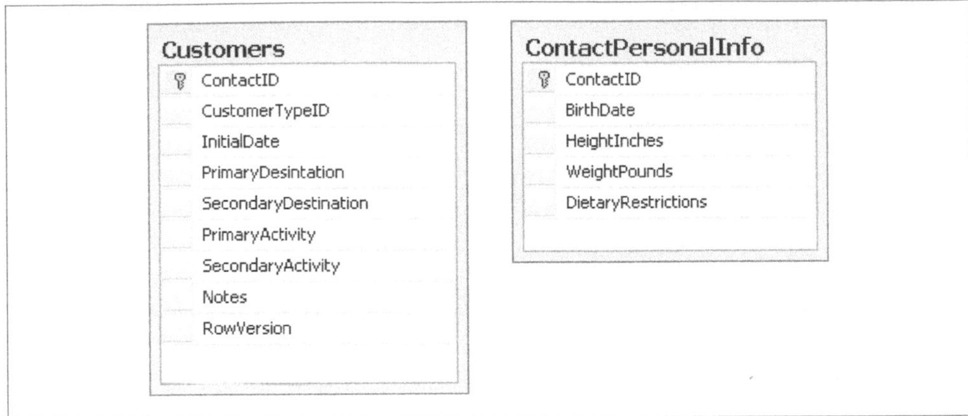

Figure 14-7. Two database tables that share a primary key and can be represented as a single entity

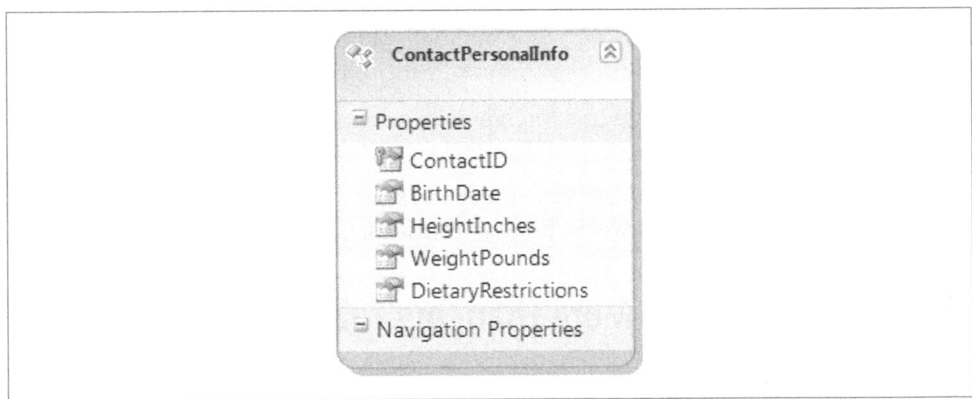

Figure 14-8. The ContactPersonalInfo entity

wouldn't be very convenient, as you would always have to traverse the navigation to get to the properties—for example, `Customer.ContactPersonalInfo.BirthDate`.

Wouldn't it be nice to just call `Customer.BirthDate`? Entity splitting can solve this problem very easily, by mapping both the `Customer` table and the `ContactPersonalInfo` table to the `Customer` entity.

Merging Multiple Entities into One

Thanks to the Designer's copy-and-paste functionality, you can easily copy the `ContactPersonalInfo` properties into the `Customer` entity. Once you have done that, all that's left is to map the `Customer` entity's new properties back to the appropriate table.

1. Copy and paste all but the `ContactID` properties from `ContactPersonalInfo` into the `Customer` entity.

2. Delete the `ContactPersonalInfo` entity from the model.

   Since you will still need the table schema information, answer No to the dialog that asks if you want to delete the table from the store model. See the sidebar "Adding and Deleting Entities from the Model" on page 380 for more information about this step.

3. Open the table mappings for the `Customer` entity.
4. At the bottom of the property mappings, select Add a Table or View, which will cause a drop-down arrow to display to the right of the column.
5. Click the drop-down arrow and choose ContactPersonalInfo from the list of available tables in the Store schema.

   All of the column mappings should populate automatically, as shown in Figure 14-9.
6. Save the model.

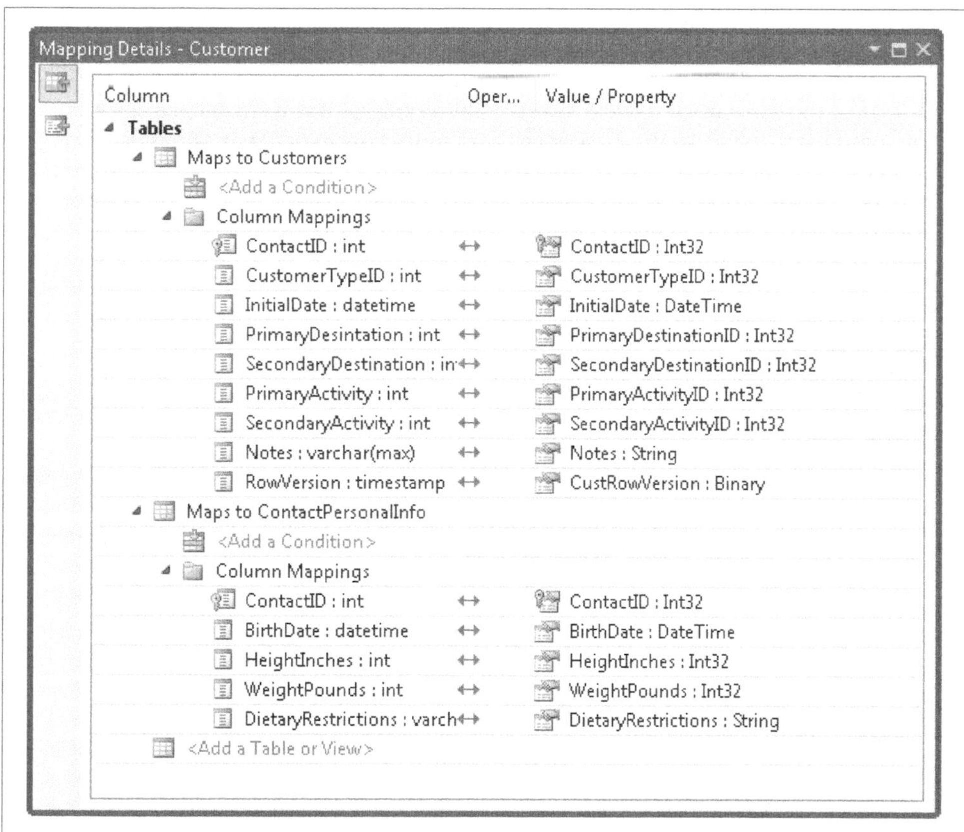

Figure 14-9. Mapping an entity to multiple tables

Adding and Deleting Entities from the Model

In Chapter 6, you used the Update Model Wizard to pull in the stored procedures from the database. As the current discussion is about modifying models, this is a good time to revisit the Update Model Wizard and some related features of the Designer.

Although you used the wizard to add database objects that you skipped over when first creating the previous model, you can also use the wizard to add objects that were created in the database after you originally built the model.

For example, if a new table has been added to the database, the Update Model Wizard will discover that the table is not already listed in the Store Schema Definition Layer (SSDL) of the model and will display it in the Add page of the wizard. If you select this new table, the wizard will add the table to the model and will create a new entity for it. This is the same way that the Entity Data Model Wizard works when you are creating new models.

The Update Model Wizard does not allow you to specify changes to existing objects—for example, tables that were included in the model but have since been modified in the database. The wizard will automatically apply those changes. If you have added new columns to an existing table for which an entity exists in the model, those fields will come into the model and will be added to the entity automatically. Not all changes will affect the conceptual model, however. For example, if you change the spelling of a column name in the database, the wizard will not know to line it up with the existing entity property and instead will create a new property. In this case, you would need to remove the new property and modify the entity mappings so that the existing property points to the correct column.

One Designer feature that you should pay attention to is what happens when you delete entities from the design surface. The Designer asks a question that, at a quick glance, might appear to be a simple confirmation: for example, "Are you sure you want to delete the entity?" But if you look more carefully at the dialog, as shown in Figure 14-10, you'll see that the question is more involved than this and you might want to think a moment before responding.

If you select Yes, the SSDL representation of the table will be removed. That means if you run the wizard again, you will have a chance to add the entity back into the model. If you choose No, the SSDL definition will remain in place and the entity will not show up the next time you run the Update Model Wizard.

This confirmation when deleting entities is new to the EDM Designer in Visual Studio 2010. Previously, when you deleted an entity the SSDL representation was left intact, which made it difficult to reintroduce a particular table into the model. This was a source of confusion for many developers.

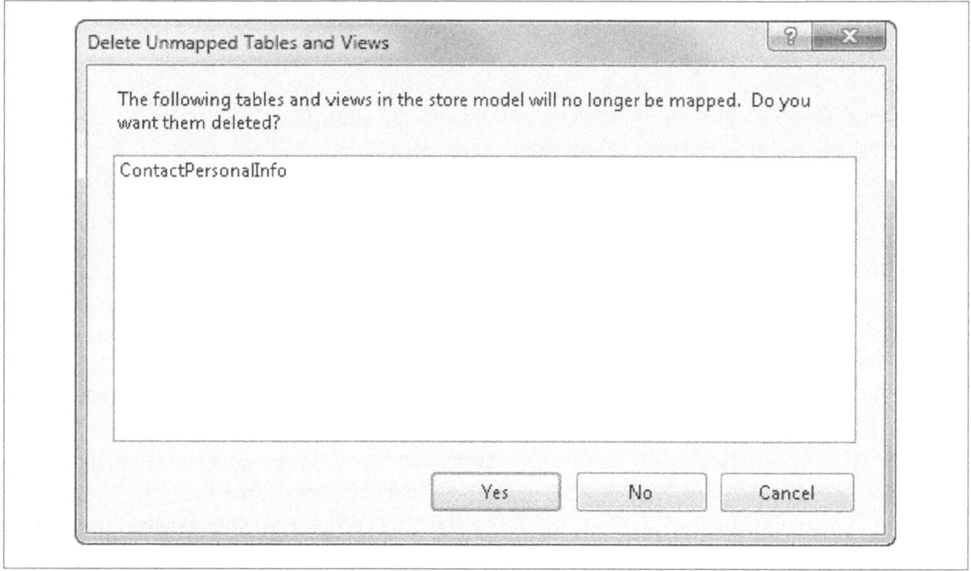

Figure 14-10. The confirmation dialog when deleting entities from the model

Querying, Editing, and Saving a Split Entity

Now you can test the revised entity. In the following exercise, you'll query the new entity, modify the returned object, create a new entity, and then save your changes. These actions will allow you to see how the Entity Framework handles an update and an insert involving multiple tables.

1. Add the method in Example 14-3 to the project's main code file.

Example 14-3. Querying for and modifying a type that maps to multiple tables

```
private static void EntitySplit()
{
  using (var context = new BAEntities())
  {
    //query for a customer and modify a new property
    var firstCust = (from c in context.Contacts.OfType<Customer>()
                     select c)
                    .First();
    firstCust.BirthDate = new System.DateTime(1981, 1, 26);
    var newCust = new Customer
   {
    FirstName = "Nola",
    LastName = "Claire",
    HeightInches = 68,
    WeightPounds = 138,
    DietaryRestrictions = "Vegetarian"
  };
```

```
        context.AddToContacts(newCust);
        //save modified customer and new customer to db
        context.SaveChanges();
    }
}
```

2. Add code to call `EntitySplit` in the `Main` method.
3. If you are interested in seeing the results in the database and are using SQL Profiler, start a new trace.
4. Run the project.

A quick check in SQL Profiler shows that when querying for the first customer, an inner join was used to include the values from the `ContactPersonalInfo` table.

The SQL Profiler screenshot in Figure 14-11 shows the commands that are executed when editing a `Customer` and when adding a new `Customer`. The first two commands update the `ModifiedDate` field in `Contact` and the `BirthDate` field in `ContactPersonalInfo` for the first `Customer` that was queried and edited. The newly added `Customer` results in the creation of a `Contact`, a `ContactPersonalInfo` record, and finally, a new row in the `Customers` table.

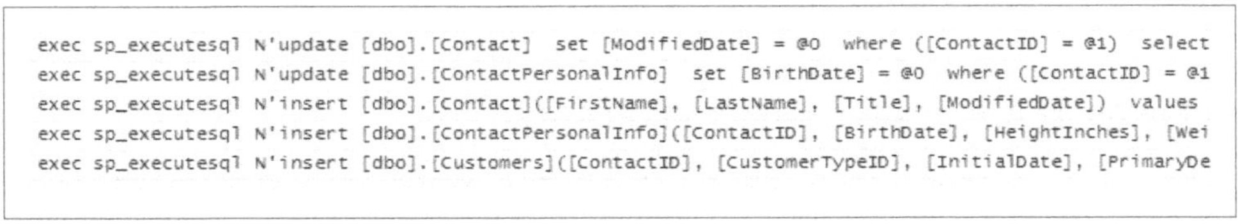

```
exec sp_executesql N'update [dbo].[Contact]  set [ModifiedDate] = @0  where ([ContactID] = @1)  select
exec sp_executesql N'update [dbo].[ContactPersonalInfo]  set [BirthDate] = @0  where ([ContactID] = @1
exec sp_executesql N'insert [dbo].[Contact]([FirstName], [LastName], [Title], [ModifiedDate])  values
exec sp_executesql N'insert [dbo].[ContactPersonalInfo]([ContactID], [BirthDate], [HeightInches], [Wei
exec sp_executesql N'insert [dbo].[Customers]([ContactID], [CustomerTypeID], [InitialDate], [PrimaryDe
```

Figure 14-11. A screenshot from SQL Profiler showing the commands that are executed when editing a Customer and adding a new Customer

The first insertion occurs because of the inheritance you created between `Customer` and `Contact`, but the insertion to the `ContactPersonalInfo` table occurs thanks to the entity splitting you just defined in the model. The Entity Framework is able to work out this customization in the model and translate it into the correct commands in the database without the developer having to worry about modification operations or about the fact that a number of tables are involved in the query.

Mapping Stored Procedures to Split Tables and More

The BreakAway database has a stored procedure called `UpdateCustomerWithMapping`, which updates values in `Customers`, `Contact`, and `ContactPersonalInfo`. Now that the `Customer` maps to columns in all three tables you could map this stored procedure to the `Customer` entity. Figure 14-12 shows the mapped function.

This function mapping is just a sample to help you understand that it is still possible to map stored procedures to complicated entities. However, it is not designed to be a permanent part of the BreakAway model. If you do follow the step of mapping this function, please remove it before moving on with this chapter.

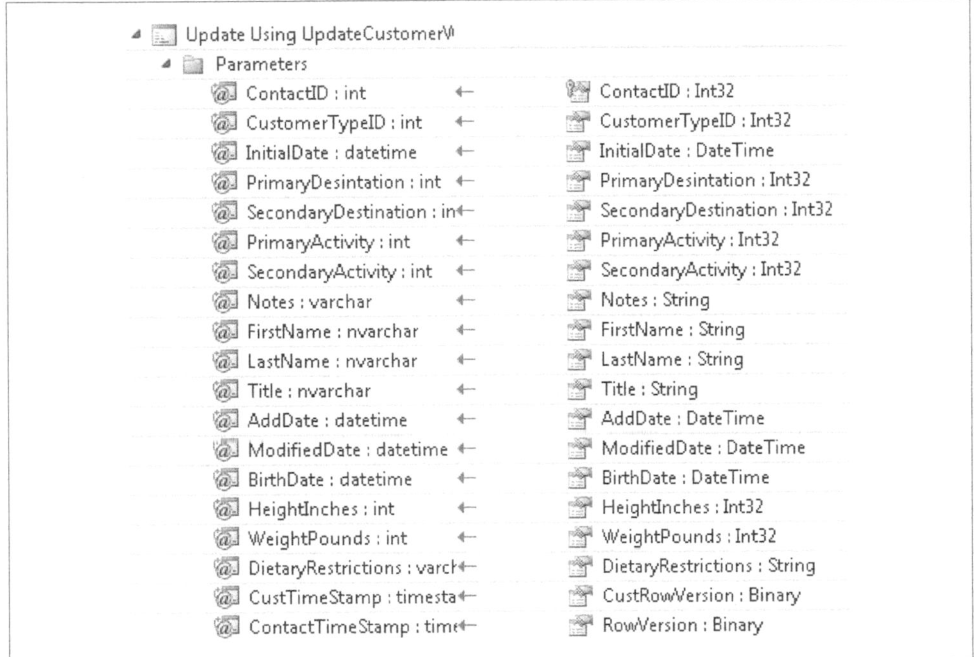

Figure 14-12. Mapping a stored procedure to an entity that is derived from one entity and points to multiple tables

Chapter 16 provides some additional information about mapping stored procedures in an inheritance hierarchy. See the section titled "What If Stored Procedures Affect Multiple Entities in an Inheritance Structure?" on page 447.

Splitting a Single Table into Multiple Entities

Table splitting (a.k.a. *horizontal splitting*) allows you to create multiple entities from the properties of a single table. This is convenient for tables that have many columns where some of those columns might not be needed as frequently as others.

A great use case for this is a scenario in which you want to load some properties for an entity but defer loading other properties. Splitting the entity into one or more related entities will allow you to do this. Lazy loading makes this even more interesting because you will, in reality, be lazy loading select columns of your database table.

Consider entities that have fields containing large amounts of data, such as a blob or an image. Loading these columns is expensive. By mapping to that column from a separate, related entity, you can defer loading it until you explicitly need it.

The BreakAway model doesn't present a great use case for table splitting, but I will use the `Address` entity to demonstrate the technique. However, I will not save these changes to the `Address` entity since I want it to remain in its current state.

We'll split the `Address` entity into two entities, creating a separate entity for the `StateProvince`, `CountryRegion`, and `PostalCode` properties. As I said, there's no real use case with this entity, but it's good enough to show how it's done.

1. Copy and paste the `Address` entity to create a duplicate entity that, by default, is called `Address1`.
2. Rename this new entity `AddressExtra`.
3. Delete the three target fields (`StateProvince`, `CountryRegion`, and `PostalCode`) from the `Address` entity.
4. Delete all but the `addressID` and three target fields from the `AddressExtra` entity.

   The new entity did not retain its mappings when you created it.
5. Open the Mapping Details window for `AddressExtra`.
6. Map it to the `Address` table, as shown in Figure 14-13.

   Next, create an association between the two entities.
7. Right-click on `Address` and choose Add Association.
8. Set up a 1:1 association between `Address` and `AddressExtra`, as shown in Figure 14-14. Be sure to uncheck the option to add a foreign key property since you already have a matching key.

   The next step is the secret sauce! Create a referential constraint between the two entities.
9. Open the Properties window for the association and click on Referential Constraint.
10. Click the ellipses for the Referential Constraint property and create the constraint as displayed in Figure 14-15.

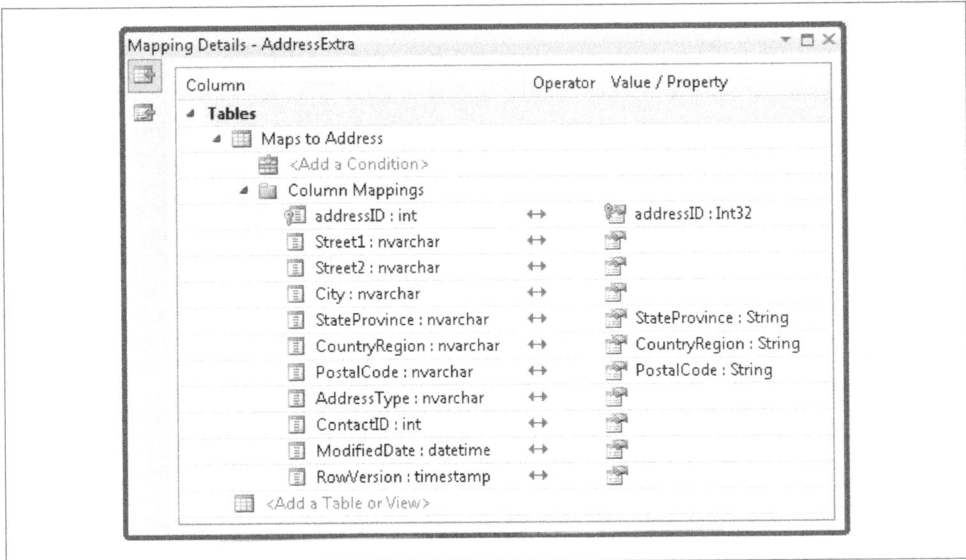

Figure 14-13. Mapping the new entity

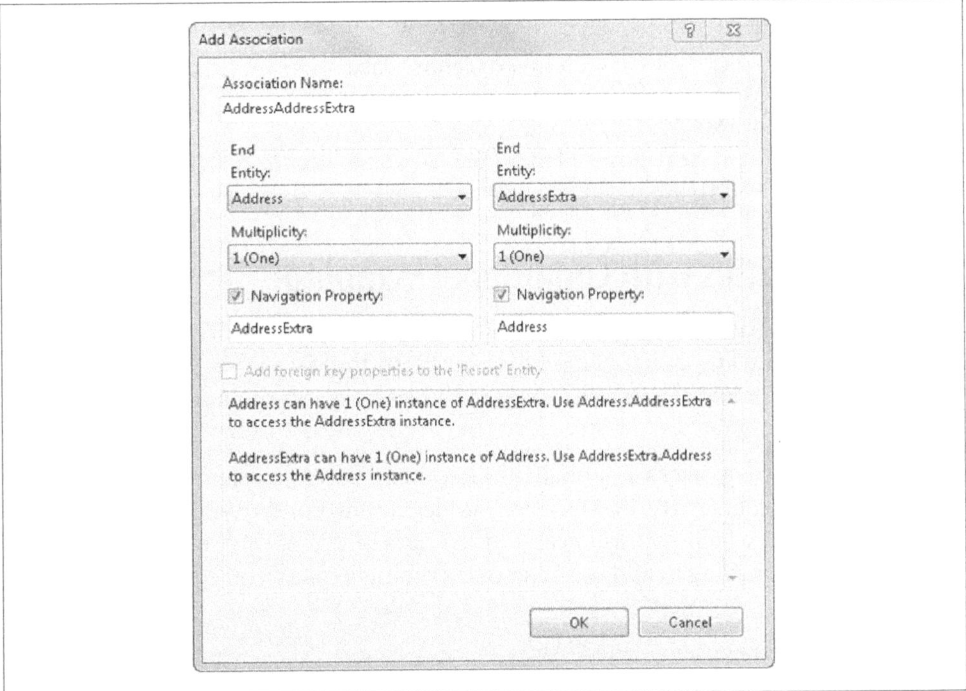

Figure 14-14. Defining an association

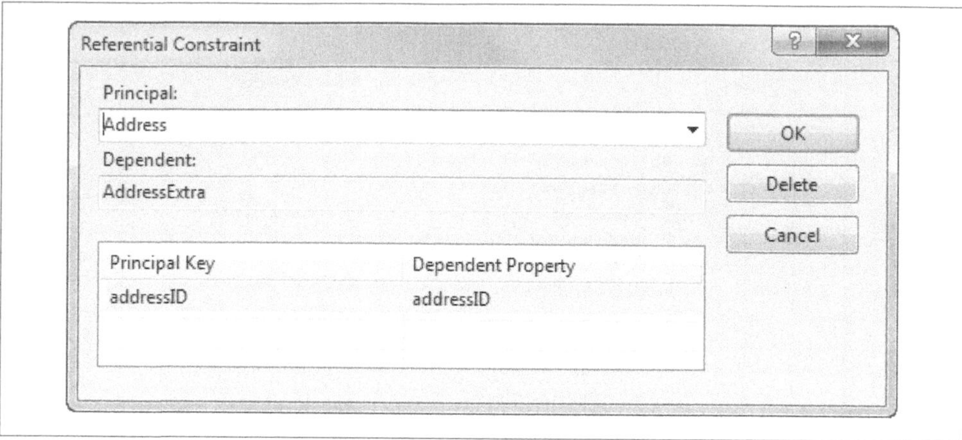

Figure 14-15. Creating a referential constraint

Now that you have split the `Address` table across multiple entities, you can interact with them separately. You can work with `AddressExtra` directly without needing an `Address` type and vice versa.

Remember to undo this change in order to move forward with this book. You can easily reset the `Address` entity with the following steps:

1. Delete both the `Address` and `AddressExtra` entities from the model. When asked if you want to delete the tables from the store model, answer Yes.
2. Run the Update Model from Database Wizard and add the `Address` table back into the model.

Filtering Entities with Conditional Mapping

The next area of customization to cover is conditional mapping. You can use conditional mapping directly when mapping an entity to the data store, or in inheritance scenarios. We'll look at the first mapping in this section and the inheritance use later in the chapter.

Conditional mapping places a permanent filter on an entity by defining that an entity will be mapped to data in the database only under certain conditions. Therefore, if you have a scenario in which you will need to filter data 100% of the time on a particular value, rather than having to add this filter to every single query you can define it as part of the mapping.

As an example, imagine that BreakAway Geek Adventures' owner decides that from now on she will provide only water-related activities. However, she does not want to delete historical data from the database. The model can use conditional mapping to ensure that any time activities are requested, only water-related activities are brought into the application, and that anytime a new activity is created it will automatically be defined as a water activity.

As another example, rather than filtering by activity type, you can introduce a Boolean field named `Discontinued` into the `Activities` table in the database. Then in the conditional mapping, you can create a filter that allows only activities to be returned from the database when `Discontinued=0` or `False`.

It is possible to use conditional mapping in the following ways:

`[value] Is Null`
`[value] Is Not Null`
`[integer value]` (e.g., `1`)
`[string value]` (e.g., `Water`)

The Designer supports conditional mapping, but in the Designer, you do not use the quotations around the integer or the string. In the XML, those values will be surrounded by quotations.

The `Activity` entity contains a `Category` property that is a string. In the following section, we will walk through the first scenario: working solely with activities whose category is "Water".

Single Mappings Only, Please

With one exception, you can map a field in a table only once. Therefore, you can have either a mapping to a property or a conditional mapping, but not both. The exception is for conditions you set to `Is NotNull`. In that case, you must also map the column. The model validation will be happy to let you know when you have broken these rules.

Creating a Conditional Mapping for the Activity Entity

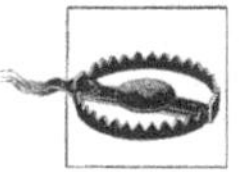

The changes made to the model in this walkthrough will not be used going forward. At the end of the walkthrough, you will be instructed to undo this mapping.

Because you can map a database column only once, you must remove from the entity's scalar properties whatever property you will be using for a conditional mapping:

1. Select the `Activity` entity.
2. Delete the `Category` property from the entity.
3. Open its Mapping Details window.
4. Click <Add a Condition>, and then click the drop-down arrow that appears.
5. Select Category from the drop-down list.

6. In this mapping, use the default operator (=) for the value comparison.
7. Under Value/Property, type **Water**. Figure 14-16 shows what the settings should look like when you are finished.

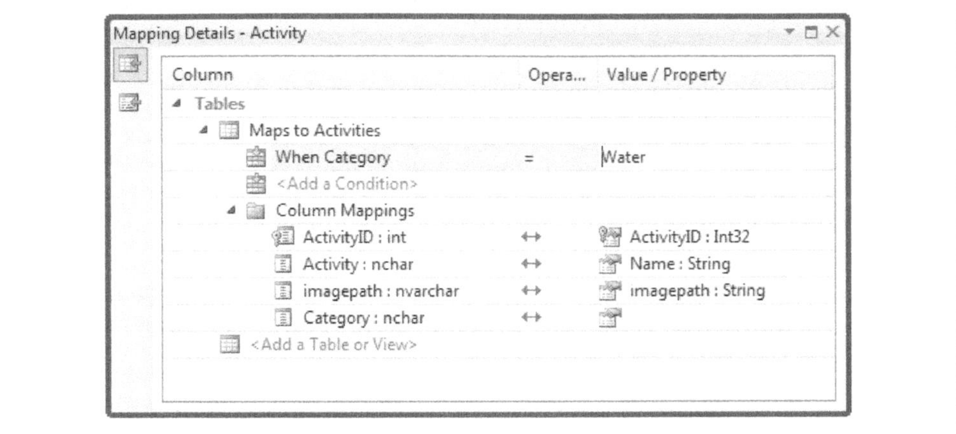

Figure 14-16. Adding a conditional mapping to the Activity entry indicating that only rows whose Category value is equal to Water should be returned when querying against this entity

The Is Null/Is Not Null Conditions

If you wanted the condition to test for null values, you can change the operator by using the drop down and selecting Is. When you set the operator to Is, Value/Property becomes a drop down with the options Null and Not Null, as shown in Figure 14-17.

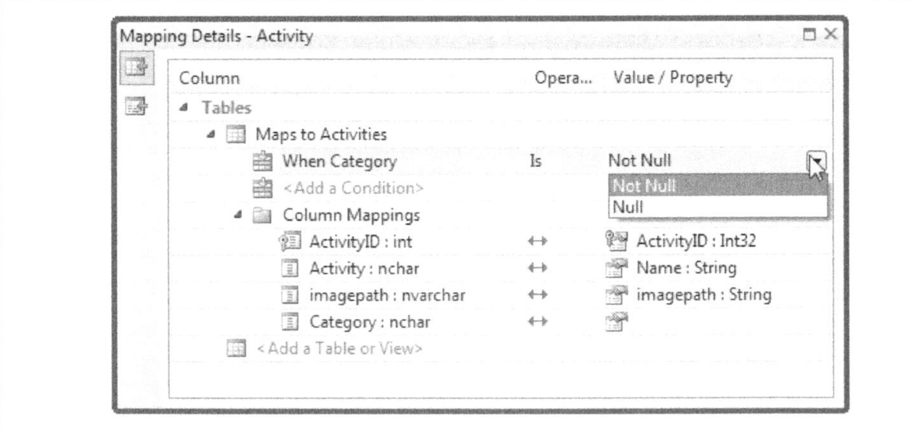

Figure 14-17. Changing the condition operator to Is, which turns Value/Property into a drop-down list with the options Not Null and Null

Querying, Inserting, and Saving with Conditional Mappings

You'll see with the following exercise that the condition not only filters data coming from the database, but also impacts data going into the database. This tests the Category = Water condition in your mapping.

1. Add to the test module the method shown in Example 14-4.

Example 14-4. Querying, creating, and saving conditionally mapped entities

```
private static void ConditionalMap()
{
  using (var context = new BAEntities())
  {
    var query =
        from a in context.Activities
        select a;
    var activities = query.ToList();

    var newAct = new Activity();
    newAct.Name = "WindSurfing";
    context.Activities.AddObject(newAct);
    context.SaveChanges();
  }
}
```

2. Call the `ConditionalMap` method from the module's `Main` method.
3. You might want to comment out the previous method calls from `Main`.
4. Set a breakpoint on the code after `query.ToList` is called.
5. Run the application.

When you hit the breakpoint, look at the `activities` variable in the QuickWatch window. You will see that only activities in the Water category were retrieved.

The insert is even more interesting. Although the only property you set in code was the `ActivityName`, look at the T-SQL that was generated and you will see that `Water` was inserted into the `Category` field:

```
exec sp_executesql N'insert [dbo].[Activities]([Activity], [imagepath], [Category])
values (@0, null, @1)
select [ActivityID]
from [dbo].[Activities]
where @@ROWCOUNT > 0 and [ActivityID] = scope_identity()',
N'@0 nvarchar(50),@1 nvarchar(50)',@0=N'WindSurfing',@1=N'Water'
```

The condition was automatically used in the insert. The condition that all `Activity` entities should have a category of "Water" also means that any newly created `Activity` entities will also have a category of "Water".

Filtering on Other Types of Conditions

What if you wanted to include any activity except water-related activities? Unfortunately, it is not possible to map this directly in the model. There is no operator for "not equals" because the mapping tool won't be able to automatically assign a value to the database column. It is not possible to map a table column more than once except in one case. See the sidebar "Single Mappings Only, Please" on page 387 for more details on that.

What you see in the Designer—an equals sign combined with an integer or string, `Is Null`, and `Is Not Null`—is the full extent of what the model is capable of. This also means that in conditional mapping, you can't use operators such as greater than (>) or less than (<), or filter on other types such as a date. However, deeper in the model there is still a way to achieve this, using a mapping element called `QueryView`. We will discuss `QueryView` in detail in the next chapter.

If it's an option, you may need to resort to adding a new column, such as `WaterActivity` or `DiscontinuedActivity`, into the database table. Then you can easily create a conditional mapping on the Boolean field. Yet another option is to create a view in the database and use that rather than the activity table along with stored procedures for inserting, updating, and deleting.

Removing the Conditional Mapping from Activity and Re-creating the Category Property

You may not want to have this conditional mapping in place going forward, so feel free to remove it. A bunch of Undos might do the trick. You could even delete `Activity` from the model (allowing the wizard to delete the table and two related join tables from the store schema), and then run the Update Model from Database Wizard to bring it and the join tables back in.

Otherwise, you'll need to manually add the `Category` property back into the `Activity` entity and map it to the `Category` field in the `Activities` table.

1. Click the When Category mapping in the Mapping Details window.
2. Select <Delete> from its drop-down list.
3. Right-click the `Activity` entity in the Designer, and choose Add and then Scalar Property from the context menu.
4. Fix up its properties: Name = Category, Type = String, Nullable = False, Fixed Length = False, MaxLength = 50, and Unicode = False.
5. Return to the Mapping Details window and map the `Category` field of the `Activities` table to the `Category` property.

I like to either validate the model (from the Designer's context menu) or rebuild its project whenever I've made modifications in case I've done something wrong and have broken the model.

Implementing Table per Hierarchy Inheritance for Tables That Contain Multiple Types

Another type of inheritance that the EDM supports is Table per Hierarchy (TPH). TPH inheritance depends on conditional mapping. Rather than including only records that match the condition, the condition is used to define records as different types.

Figure 14-18 displays the `Lodging` entity with the `Resort` Boolean to define lodgings that are resorts. You can use this Boolean to create a new type in your model: `Resort`, which will inherit from `Lodging`. This is very different from the tables that provided for TPT inheritance where the properties of the derived type were defined in a separate table.

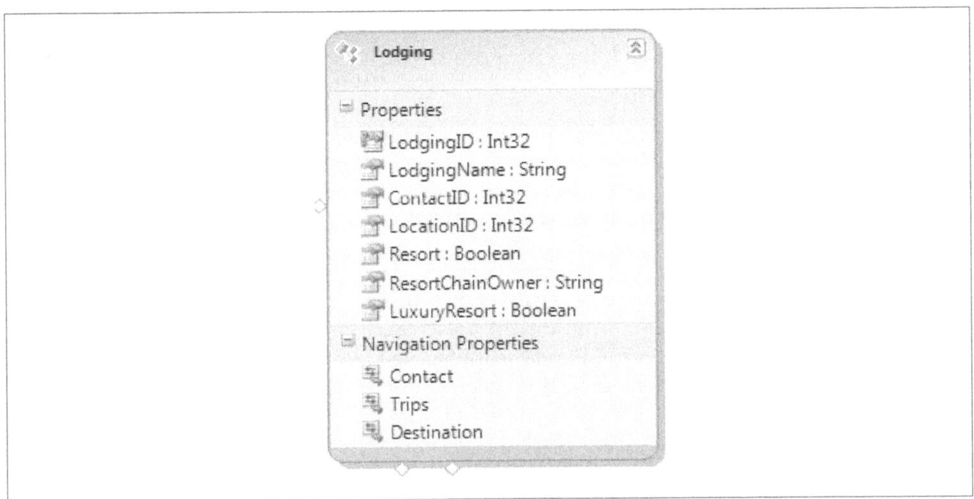

Figure 14-18. The Resort property of the Lodging entity, which suggests a new inherited type, Resort

By default, the EDM Designer shows only the names of scalar properties. However, the Designer context menu option, Scalar Property Format, allows you to display property names along with their type, as you see in Figure 14-18. Right-click in the Designer background to find the Scalar Property Format setting.

As you'll see in the following walkthrough, TPH mapping uses conditional mapping to help determine which data describes a lodging that is not a resort and which data describes a resort.

Creating the Resort Derived Type

The BreakAway `Lodging` entity has a Boolean property called `Resort`. Let's use this property to define `Resort` as a new type of lodging:

1. Right-click the background of the Designer.
2. From the context menu, choose Add and then Entity.
3. Change the entity name to Resort.
4. Select Lodging from the "Base type" drop down.

Notice that the `EntitySet` automatically becomes `Lodgings` and is disabled so that you cannot modify it. Since `Resort` will inherit from `Lodging`, it will be part of the `Lodgings EntitySet`.

Notice also that the section for the `Key` property has become disabled. The `Lodging` entity will still control the entity key, even for derived types.

Now that you have the new type defined, how will the Entity Framework decide which `Lodging` records go into the `Lodging` entity and which go into the `Resort` entity? The answer is conditional mapping.

First, we'll use conditional mapping to filter `Lodging` records into the base or derived type:

1. Delete the `Resort` property from the `Lodging` entity.

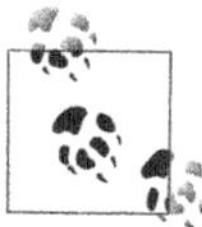

As you learned when creating the conditional mapping earlier, you can't map a table column more than once. Since you will be using the `Resort` property for conditional mapping, you can't use it in the property mapping. Therefore, there is no need for the `Resort` property.

2. Open the Mapping Details window for the `Lodging` entity and click <Add a Condition>.
3. Select Resort from the Condition drop down and change the condition value to 0. This condition states that records that are filtered into the `Lodging` entity will be records whose `Resort` property equals `0` or `False`.
4. Select the `Resort` entity and open its Mapping Details window.
5. Map the entity to the `Lodging` table. Then create a condition for `Resort = 1` (or `True`).

Next, we'll move resort-specific properties to the `Resort` entity type:

6. The `ResortChainOwner` and `LuxuryResort` properties don't make sense in the `Lodging` entity. They belong in the `Resort` entity. So, cut and paste these two properties from the `Lodging` entity into the `Resort` entity.

7. Open the Mapping Details window for `Resort`, and map the `ResortChainOwner` and `LuxuryResort` properties to the appropriate columns in the `Lodging` table.

When you're done, the `Lodging` and `Resort` types should look as they do in Figure 14-19.

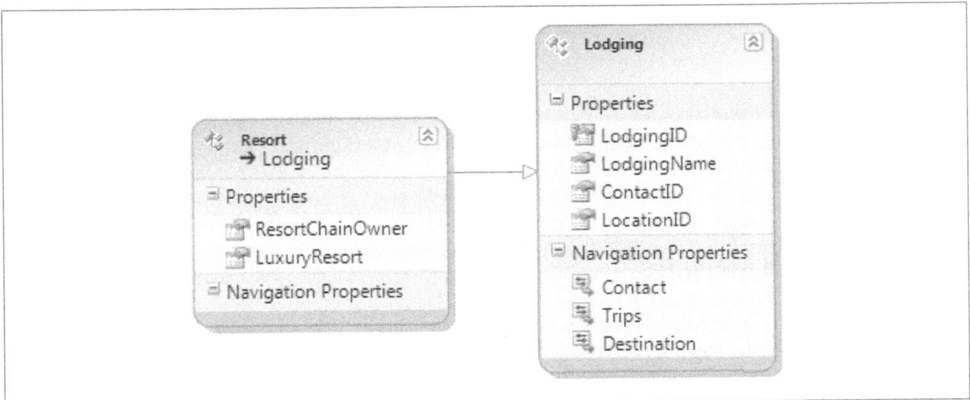

Figure 14-19. Resort now inheriting from Lodging based on a conditional mapping

Setting a Default (Computed) Value on the Table Schema

If you try to run any code against `Lodging` at this point, you will encounter a problem. The `LuxuryResort` field is a Boolean field. In the database, the field is non-nullable and has a default value of 0. The EDM Wizard does not bring default values over to the model's SSDL. This creates a problem for the `Lodging` entity. The `Lodging` entity maps to the `Lodging` table but does not map the `LuxuryResort` or `ResortChainOwner` column because we removed the properties from the `Lodging` entity. Only the `Resort` entity maps those fields. Because `Lodging` does not map those fields, the model will throw a runtime exception telling you that `Lodging` doesn't know how to deal with `LuxuryResort` because it is non-nullable and has no default value. Therefore, the Entity Framework runtime wants to populate this field, but because the properties don't exist in `Lodging`, the field is not mapped, and therefore the `Lodging` entity is unable to modify the value.

There are two ways to correct this. Neither is pretty. Both solutions require that you manually edit the SSDL's XML. The first way to correct this is to use the `StoreGeneratedPattern` attribute to let the Entity Framework know that the database will take care of this value. You can do this by setting `StoreGeneratedPattern` to `Computed`:

```
<Property Name="LuxuryResort" Type="bit" Nullable="false"
          StoreGeneratedPattern="Computed" />
```

Alternatively, you can set the column's `DefaultValue` to `false`:

```
<Property Name="LuxuryResort" Type="bit" Nullable="false"
          DefaultValue="false"
```

There is a `StoreGeneratedPattern` attribute available in the Properties window for entity properties. This will not apply the setting in your SSDL. This is used for model-first development (Chapter 25). You'll also see there is a Default Value property. This is only to define defaults in the conceptual model and won't impact the SSDL. You really must edit the SSDL manually to affect either of these settings for this mapping.

Remember that if you run the Update Wizard, manual changes to the SSDL will be overwritten and need to be made again.

Testing the TPH Mapping

The following method will help you see the effect of the TPH mapping. You can query for all lodgings, including any derived types, or for a specific derived type. This is similar to the tests you did against the TPT mapping. It's a little trickier to query for a subset that is not a derived type.

The following queries are executed in unique contexts so that entities that are a result of one query do not merge with entities of another query. In this way, you can more easily see the full impact of each of the various queries.

1. Add the method in Example 14-5 to the test module.

Example 14-5. Querying types in a TPH mapping

```
private static void TPHMap()
{
  using (var context = new BAEntities())
  {
    var query =
        from lodge in context.Lodgings
        select lodge;
    Console.WriteLine("All Lodgings: " + query.Count().ToString());
  }
  using (var context = new BAEntities())
  {
    var query =
        from lodge in context.Lodgings.OfType<Lodging>()
        select lodge;
    Console.WriteLine("NonResort Results: " + query.Count().ToString());
  }
  using (var context = new BAEntities())
  {
    var query =
        from lodge in context.Lodgings.OfType<Resort>()
        select lodge;
    Console.WriteLine("Resort Results: " + query.Count().ToString());
  }
}
```

2. Call the TPHMap method from the module's Main method.
3. Run the application.

When you see the output of the console window, you may be surprised that the second query, which you may have expected to return only NonResort lodgings, returned all of the lodgings, regardless of the Resort filter:

```
All Lodgings Results: 101
NonResort Type Only Results: 101
Resort Type Only Results: 10
```

Why is this?

Even though you put a condition on Lodging that states Resort=0 (false), Lodging is a base type. No matter what, Lodging will return itself and all types that derive from it. With a simple query it is not easy to say "give me the base type but none of its derived types." So, even though the condition is there, you'll continue to receive all of the Lodgings, even with Resort=1.

If you want an easy way to retrieve non-resort lodgings, you can create a second derived type that inherits from Lodging to retrieve all of the Lodging entities that are not resorts. In this case, the actual Lodging entity would become an abstract type because it will never be instantiated. The Lodging entity itself cannot be instantiated and will never return Lodging entities. Instead, the Lodgings EntitySet will return only those entities that come from its derived types: Resort and NonResort.

To do this, follow the same steps that you did to turn Contact into an abstract type and create the NonCustomer entity to represent all of the contacts who are not customers.

Choosing to Turn a Base Class into an Abstract Class

You've just seen a demonstration of how TPH inheritance works. If your business rules define that you would never want to get the entire set of types (e.g., all of the lodgings at once), it makes sense to have the abstract class in the model and to use the derived types to interact with the objects. If your business rules define that in many cases you will want to work with all lodgings, regardless of type, using the base type without defining it as an abstract class may be preferable.

Creating Complex Types to Encapsulate Sets of Properties

Complex types are a convenient way to encapsulate a set of properties. You may want to do this when you have properties that are common among entities (e.g., different entities that have properties to contain addresses). You may just want to use a complex type to create a better structure in your entity. Imagine that your model has a Customer entity that contains address properties. You may prefer to navigate through the contact with the address fields tucked inside a complex type.

Therefore, rather than having all of this to deal with when programming:

```
Customer
  FirstName
  LastName
  Street
  City
  State
  Zip
  Phone
```

you could encapsulate those properties related to the address into a complex type called `Address`, and then insert `Address` as a property into the `Customer` type:

```
Customer
  FirstName
  LastName
  Address
  Phone
```

Then, to get at the address information, you can drill further:

```
Customer.Address.City
Customer.Address.State
```

What's really nice is that the complex types are still types, so you can instantiate them and use them outside their parent entity. However, complex types are not `EntityObjects`, but `ComplexObjects`. They don't have `EntityKeys` and are not contained in their own `EntitySet`; therefore, they cannot be queried directly or persisted into the database on their own. As part of an entity object, you get all of the benefits—change tracking, updates, and so forth—of the entity.

Defining a Complex Type

The EDM Designer provides a few ways to create complex types. We'll focus for now on the method that fits the scenario of encapsulating entity properties.

We'll use the `Address` entity again as our guinea pig and then unwind the changes going forward. We'll encapsulate a piece of the address into a new complex type called `Mail`.

1. In the Designer, select the following properties from the `Address` entity: `Street1`, `Street2`, `City`, and `StateProvince`.
2. Right-click on one of them and choose Refactor into New Complex Type from the context menu, as shown in Figure 14-20.

   As a result, the Model Browser will open with the new complex type highlighted. Its default name is ComplexType1.
3. Rename this to `Mail`, as shown in Figure 14-21.

   In the entity, the four properties have been replaced by a new property named `ComplexProperty`. Its type, as shown in Figure 14-22, is the new `Mail` type.
4. Rename the property to `Mail`.

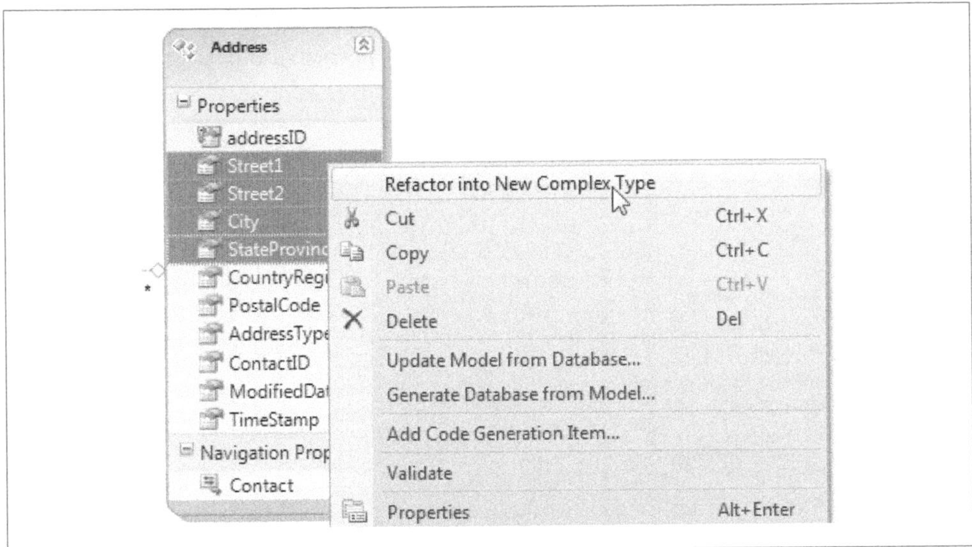

Figure 14-20. Creating a complex type from selected properties

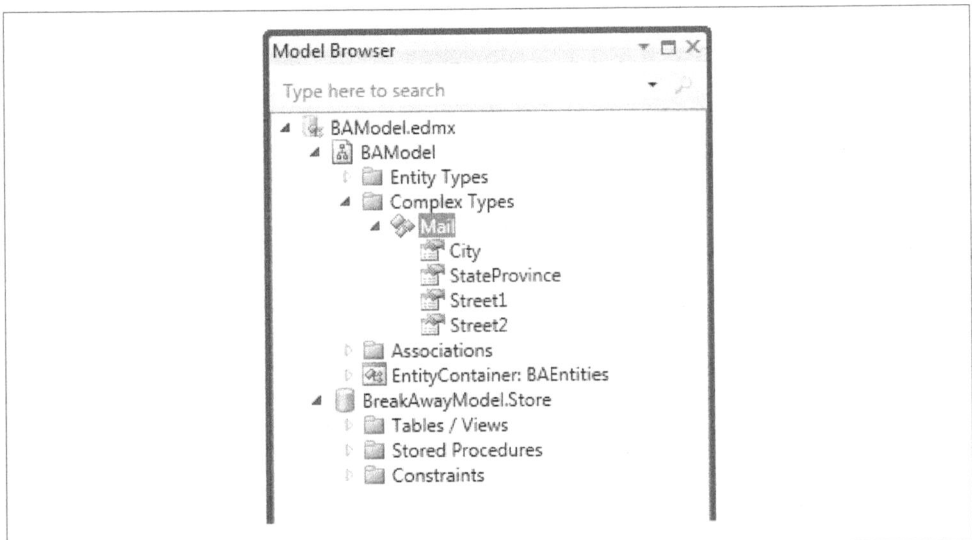

Figure 14-21. The renamed complex type in the Model Browser

Unfortunately, you can't open the `Mail` subproperties in the `Address` entity in the Designer. You can see them only in the Model Browser.

In Figure 14-23, you will notice that there is no `Nullable` property in the `ComplexProperty`'s Properties window. That's because complex types cannot be nullable.

If you look at the mapping details for `Address`, shown in Figure 14-23, you can see that the wizard changed the mappings to point to the properties of the `Mail` complex type.

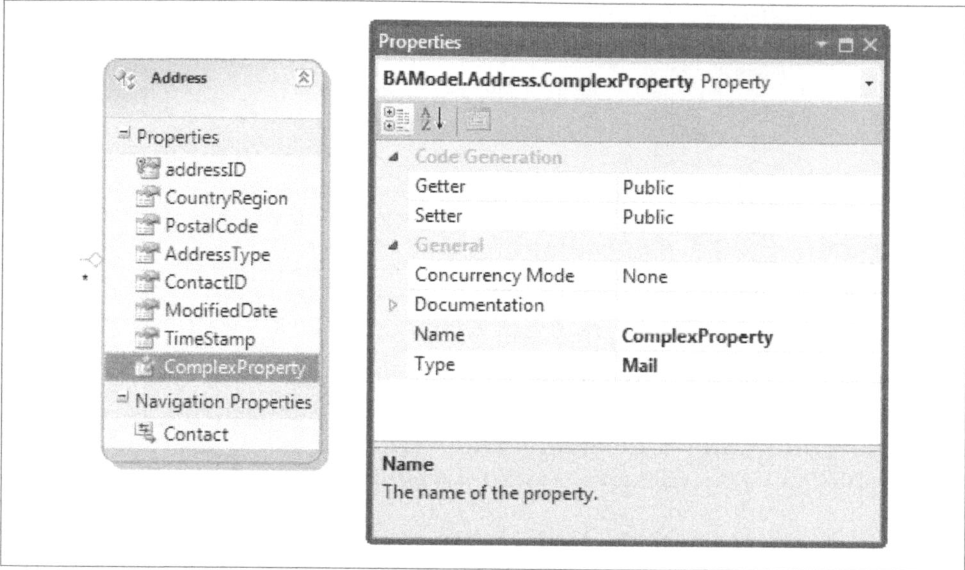

Figure 14-22. The property that houses the new complex type before it has been renamed

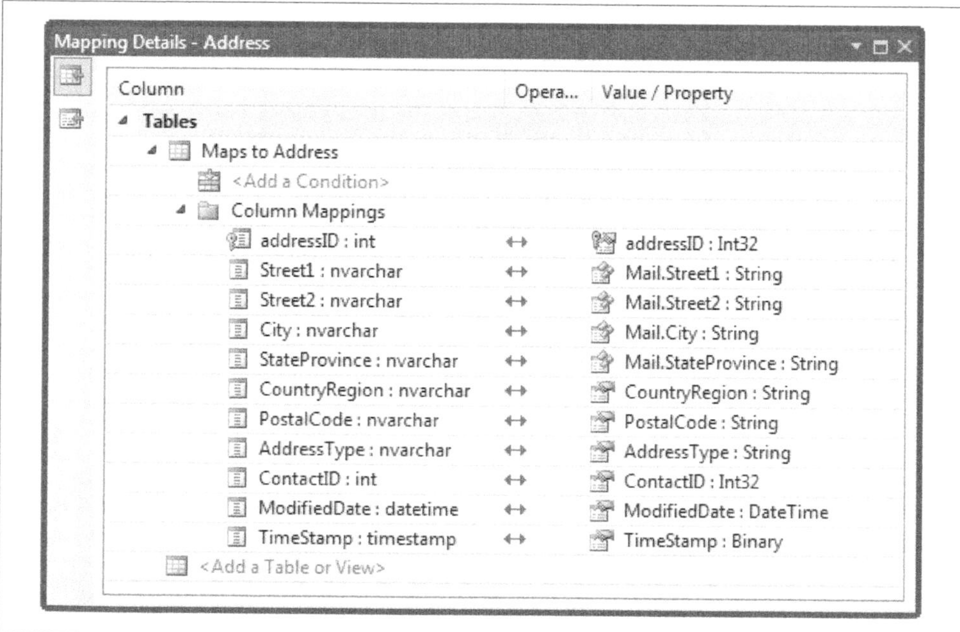

Figure 14-23. Table columns mapped to complex type properties

Reusing Complex Types

Once you've created a complex type, you can use the same type in other entities that have the same sets of fields. For example, in addition to the imaginary `Customer` entity described at the beginning of this section, you might have another entity, such as `Vendor`, in that same model that also contains `Street`, `City`, `State`, and `Zip` properties. You could reuse the `Address` complex type that was created to encapsulate the `Customer`'s address fields in the `Vendor` entity. The `Vendor` entity's mappings for the complex type fields would point back to `Vendor.Street1`, `Vendor.Street2`, and so forth in the database.

> **Complex Types Are Not EntityObjects**
>
> Looking at the generated class for `AddressDetail` you will see that it is not an `EntityObject`, but rather a `ComplexObject`:
>
> ```
> public partial class Mail : ComplexObject
> ```
>
> Although you can instantiate and use these types directly in code, they do not have `EntityKeys`, cannot be queried directly, and cannot be persisted to the database.
>
> `ComplexObject` does allow the properties of the `ComplexType` to be change-tracked along with the other properties of its parent entity, though. You can look further at the generated class and even drill into the `System.Data.Objects.DataClasses.ComplexObject` class in Visual Studio's Object Browser or in another tool such as Reflector.

> **Complex Types in POCO Classes**
>
> Just as you don't want your entities to inherit from `EntityObject` in a POCO class, neither do you want a `ComplexType` to inherit from `ComplexObject`. To leverage a model's `ComplexType` types with POCO classes, simply create a class to represent the type. There are two important rules for enabling the class to map with the `ComplexType`. The first is that you must use a class to define a type—you cannot use a struct. The second is that you cannot use inheritance with the complex type classes.

Querying, Creating, and Saving Entities That Contain Complex Types

The method in Example 14-6 shows the `ComplexType` in action where data is queried, modified, and persisted back to the database. The mappings take care of retrieving and updating the values of the complex type properties.

Example 14-6. Querying, creating, and saving entities that contain a complex type

```
private static void ComplexType()
{
  using (var context = new BAEntities())
  {
```

```
            Contact contact = (from c in context.Contacts.Include("Addresses")
                               where c.Addresses.Any()
                               select c).First();

            Address firstAddress = contact.Addresses.First();

            Mail currentMail = firstAddress.Mail;
            Console.WriteLine("Street: {0}, City: {1}, State: {2}",
                               currentMail.Street1, currentMail.City,
                               currentMail.StateProvince);

            Mail newMail = new Mail();
            newMail.Street1 = "1 Rue Cardinale";
            newMail.City = "Montreal";
            newMail.StateProvince = "Quebec";
            firstAddress.Mail=newMail;

            context.SaveChanges();
        }
    }
```

This method first queries the model for a single `Contact` entity, along with its addresses.

It then extracts the `Mail` from the first address and displays some of its properties, demonstrating that you can create an instance of the complex type. Next, it instantiates a new `Mail` type, and sets that instance as the `Mail` property of the first address. Finally, `SaveChanges` is called, which updates the address information for the contact.

Here is the T-SQL that was executed on the server. You can see that the change tracking does take into account the property values of the complex type:

```
exec sp_executesql N'update [dbo].[Address]
set [Street1] = @0, [Street2] = null, [City] = @1, [StateProvince] = @2
where ([addressID] = @3)
select [TimeStamp]
from [dbo].[Address]
where @@ROWCOUNT > 0 and [addressID] = @3',
N'@0 nvarchar(50),@1 nvarchar(50),@2 nvarchar(50),@3 int',
@0=N'1 Rue Cardinale',@1=N'Montreal',@2=N'Quebec',@3=2513
```

Complex types do not always behave the way you might expect them to in data-binding scenarios. See Appendix B to learn about the behavior of complex types when data-binding with Windows Forms Data Source controls, the ASP.NET `EntityDataSource` control, ASP.NET Dynamic Data, and more.

Removing the Complex Types from the Model

If you have followed along and modified the model, you may want to undo these changes so that you'll be able to use the model while working through more sample code in this book: there's nothing wrong with the complex type technically, but this particular one is not a strong use case.

You can use the same method that you used to refresh the `Address` entity at the end of the table-splitting example. Alternatively, you could delete the `Mail` property and re-create the four properties (`Street1`, `Street2`, `City`, and `StateProvince`) in the `Address` entity and remap them.

Using Additional Customization Options

There are yet more ways to customize the EDM. This section details some interesting ones to be aware of. In addition, the Entity Framework team created a tool called the Entity Framework Mapping Helper, which is on their Code Gallery site at MSDN. It can give you a good view of the various mappings. See *http://code.msdn.microsoft.com/EFMappingHelper/*.

Using GUIDs for EntityKeys

In .NET 4, the Entity Framework supports using GUIDs as `EntityKey`. There are a few nuances you should be aware of. If your GUID is store generated, unfortunately, the Entity Data Model Wizard neglects to note that when buildling the SSDL. You will need to manually edit the SSDL section of the EDMX file and set that property's `StoreGeneratedPattern` to `Identity`. This is a bug with the Designer. You can learn more about dealing with the problem in a blog post by Lee Dumond who learned it the hard way: *http://leedumond.com/blog/using-a-guid-as-an-entitykey-in-entity-framework-4*.

If you do not need store generated keys, it will be up to you to ensure that your code provides new GUIDs before inserting new entities.

The Entity Framework team has a helpful blog post about using GUIDs as Entity Keys, performance issues to be aware of and even some plans for the future. See this post at *http://blogs.msdn.com/b/adonet/archive/2010/06/28/performance-impact-of-server-side-generated-guids-in-ef.aspx*.

Mapping Stored Procedures

In addition to the function mapping you used earlier in the book, you can map stored procedures manually using a number of other methods. This includes mapping those that are already in your database and those that you can create directly in the model. We'll cover these in Chapter 16.

Mapping Multiple Entity Sets per Type

Multiple Entity Sets per Type (MEST) allows you to contain a single entity in different types, which could allow you to have different views of the same type without using an inheritance model. However, MEST gets tricky pretty quickly when you start to introduce entities that have relationships with other entities. Alex James from the Entity Framework team provides useful information about MEST and its gotchas in his May 16, 2008, blog post, "MEST—What is it and how does it work?" (*http://blogs.msdn.com/alexj/archive/2008/05/16/mest-what-is-it-and-how-does-it-work.aspx*).

Mapping Self-Referencing Associations

You can find a great example of self-referencing associations when building a model against Microsoft's sample Northwind database, where employees and their supervisors (who are also employees) are contained in the same table. A field called `ReportsTo` points back to other employees in the table. When you use the EDM Wizard to create a model from Northwind, you will see that an association has been created that links the `ReportsTo` property back to the `EmployeeID` in the same table. By default, the two relevant navigation properties were named `Employees` and `Employees1`. Figure 14-24 shows this association along with the details of the referential constraint behind the association.

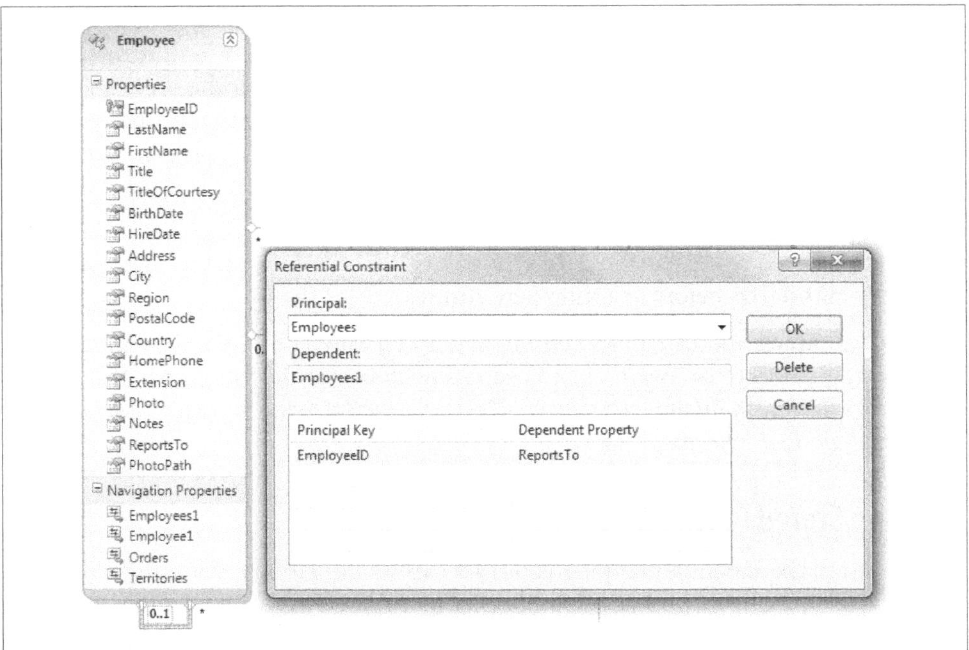

Figure 14-24. An example of a self-referencing association in the Employee entity, which is created from the Employees table in the Northwind database

Modeling Large Databases

Developers often ask what to do about large legacy databases. The Designer does not handily support huge databases, for a few reasons. Most importantly, large models are much too unwieldy and difficult to navigate around. There is no way to visually group entities onto different design surfaces or even by color.

Some third-party tools are exploring better ways to handle large models. Developer Matthieu Mezil has some experiments along these lines on his blog (*http://msmvps.com/blogs/matthieu*), and LLBLGen Pro v3.0 (*http://www.llblgen.com*) has an Entity Framework designer that takes a different approach to the model design that enables working with large models in great detail.

Additionally, there is a performance issue at design time with very large models, as the Designer chugs away trying to represent the entire thing visually.

But the real question concerns not Designer support, but practicality. Do you really want all of those entities in a single model?

My recommendation is to break the model into smaller logical models. Foreign key support makes it even easier to leap from one model to another in your applications. Remember that you must use separate contexts in your application when working with entities from separate models.

I have clients who are successfully following this path with both Visual Studio 2008 SP1 and Visual Studio 2010.

Diving into this discussion would extend the chapter enormously. Ward Bell, from IdeaBlade, the company behind DevForceEF, has written a fantastic thesis on dealing with large models. Ward reaches the same conclusion about breaking up the model as I have. He also has created a video and sample application demonstrating this practice, which I have recommended to many clients. You can find this content under the section "Break Up Large Models" at "Ward's Corner" on the IdeaBlade site: *http://ideablade.com/WardsCorner/WardsCorner_home.aspx*.

Summary

The real power of the EDM lies in its ability to go beyond the simplistic representation of the database, providing you myriad ways to shape your data model so that it is much better suited to your business and your applications. This chapter showed you how to achieve and leverage many of the mapping capabilities: TPT and TPH inheritance, conditional mapping, entity splitting and table splitting, complex types, and more.

You can take advantage of these features in far more ways than I discussed here, so don't stop with this book. Keep your eyes open for blog posts and articles by the many people who are learning more and more about the Entity Framework to expand your understanding.

Although the Designer supports some of these advanced techniques, you can achieve even more by working directly with the EDMX's XML, which you will do in the next chapter.

CHAPTER 15

Defining EDM Mappings That Are Not Supported by the Designer

In Chapter 14, you learned many ways to customize the conceptual model using the Entity Model Designer (EDM). The model's schema supports even more mappings beyond those which you can achieve with the Designer.

In this chapter, you'll learn how to modify the XML manually to benefit from the more commonly useful of these additional features of Entity Framework: model-defined functions, table per concrete type inheritance, and QueryView. How this impacts your work depends on which unsupported customization you are using. Unsupported features can affect the use of the Designer in the following ways:

- The feature does not appear in the Designer. This is the most common.
- The Designer goes into Safe Mode when you attempt to open the model in the Designer. Safe Mode presents a message that indicates the model cannot be opened in the Designer, and displays a link to open the model in XML view.
- The Mapping Designer goes into Safe Mode, but the CSDL Designer displays.

As we walk through the following mappings, I will indicate how each mapping is handled (or not handled) by the Designer.

Using Model-Defined Functions

Model-defined functions are new to Entity Framework 4. In the previous version of Entity Framework, you could create a new property based on other properties in a model only if you created that new property as a class property. In Chapter 11, you created custom properties. Although they are convenient, they have two downsides. The first is that class properties cannot be used in a LINQ to Entities query or an Entity SQL expression. The second is that if you want to share the model and you also want those custom properties to be shared, you'll have to share class files in addition to the metadata.

Now it is possible to define functions directly in the conceptual model, although it's important to keep in mind that these are functions, not entity properties. You can benefit by combining the functions with properties, as you'll see in this section.

It is also possible (and was in the previous version of Entity Framework) to use user-defined functions from the database. That's a different topic, and we'll look at it at the end of Chapter 16.

The basic mechanism for creating model-defined functions is to write Entity SQL in a function element in the conceptual model. It's fairly simple to use these functions in Entity SQL query expressions, but for LINQ to Entities, a few extra steps are necessary.

Let's start with a simple function, one that I wanted to create the first time I started playing with Entity Data Models a number of years ago: `FullName`.

Most databases give us `FirstName` and `LastName`. You always have to concatenate them into a full name—for instance, sometimes into a reverse name such as Lerman, Julie or sometimes just as Julie Lerman.

With the custom properties, you can create a full name property and easily access that property when working with the instantiated object, but you can't use it in a query such as:

```
from p in context.Person orderby p.FullName select p;
```

Entity Framework can build only store expressions from elements in the model. In this case, you would still always have to use `orderby p.LastName + p.firstName`.

Now you can create a function in the model to accomplish this.

Because the Designer does not support model-defined functions, you need to do this work directly in the XML.

The Entity SQL expression to create a `Lastname, Firstname` result is:

```
SELECT Trim(c.LastName) + ", " + c.FirstName FROM BAEntities.Contacts AS c
```

To build a function in the model, you embed the part of the expression that returns the value (`Trim(c.LastName) + ", " + c.FirstName`) in a new CSDL element called `DefiningExpression`. `DefiningExpression` is a child of `Function`. Therefore, you need to first create a `Function` element and place the `DefiningExpression` within it.

Model-defined functions are part of the conceptual model. Therefore, the function goes in the Conceptual Schema Definition Language (CSDL) section of the XML file. The function must be a sibling of the `EntityTypes`. I place my functions below the last `EntityType` in the XML:

```
<!-- CSDL content -->
    <edmx:ConceptualModels>
      <Schema...>
        <EntityContainers> . . . </EntityContainers>
```

```
<EntityType> . . . </EntityType>
<EntityType> . . . </EntityType>
<EntityType> . . . </EntityType>
<Function>
  <DefiningExpression>
    Trim(c.LastName) + ", " + Trim(c.FirstName)
  </DefiningExpression>
</Function>
```

There's more to the function. You'll need to provide some attributes for it, such as `Name`, but more importantly, you have to pass in a parameter on which to perform the expression. In this case, the parameter will be a `Contact` type; more specifically, a `BAModel.Contact`. We'll name it "c" to stay in line with the expression.

Example 15-1 shows the complete function.

Example 15-1. A simple function defined in the conceptual model

```
<Function Name="FullNameReverse" ReturnType="Edm.String" >
  <Parameter Name="c" Type="BAModel.Contact"/>
  <DefiningExpression>
    Trim(c.LastName) + ", " + Trim(c.FirstName)
  </DefiningExpression>
</Function>
```

Now you can call this from an Entity SQL expression. Unfortunately, you need to call the function by its full name, using the namespace of the model.

```
SELECT c FROM BAEntities.Contacts  AS c ORDERBY BAModel.FullNameReverse(c)
```

You could also use the function to return results:

```
SELECT c.ContactID, BAModel.FullNameReverse(c) FROM BAEntities.Contacts AS c
```

If you already have a custom property in the `Contact` entity for `FullNameReverse`, it is still useful to use the function in a projection in cases where you do not need to return a complete entity or when you are using `EntityClient` to stream back data without materializing objects. Remember that you can't use the custom properties in queries, but you can use the model-defined functions.

As I mentioned, calling the function from LINQ to Entities is a bit trickier. By default, the function is not built into the generated classes, and therefore LINQ to Entities won't have access to it. The function needs to be in a static class. I created a `Functions` class and placed it in the solution where the model is because model-defined functions rely on the Entity Framework.

The trick to the function is that it uses an attribute (new to .NET 4) that ties it back to the model namespace and function. As shown in Example 15-2, there is no implementation in the method. In fact, to prevent developers from using the method directly in code, it throws an exception. You'll need the `System.Data.Objects.DataClasses` namespace for access to the `EdmFunction` attribute. Don't confuse that with the `EdmFunction` class in `System.Data.Metadata.Edm`.

Notice that this is an extension method, as I have the keyword `this` as the first parameter.

Example 15-2. Exposing a model-defined function for LINQ to Entities queries

```
namespace BAGA
{
  public static class Functions
  {
    [EdmFunction("BAModel", "FullNameReverse")]
    public static string FullNameReverse(this Contact c)
    {
      throw new NotSupportedException
                ("This function can only be used in a query");
    }
  }
}
```

Here's a great example of how you might want to modify the T4 template even if you are not creating POCO classes. You could instruct the template to spit out these functions for you.

Now you can use the function within a LINQ to Entities query in projections, operators, or methods:

```
from c in context.Contacts orderby c.FullNameReverse() select c
```

or:

```
from c in context.Contacts orderby c.FullNameReverse
select c.ContactID, c.FullNameReverse
```

or:

```
context.Contacts.Select(c =>c.FullNameReverse)
```

If you hadn't declared `FullNameReverse` as an extension method, but simply a method, you would have had to use the function in this much less discoverable way:

```
from c in context.Contacts orderby Functions.FullNameReverse(c) select c
```

In the first of these queries, `FullNameReverse` was used for sorting, but the query returned `Contact` entities. Once you have a `Contact` entity in hand, you can then use its custom `FullName` property in your application. You cannot access the `FullNameReverse` function from the entity. It is only available as part of a query.

Using Model-Defined Functions to Return More Complex Results

FullNameReverse is a simple example of a model-defined function that returns only a string.

Model-defined functions can return more complex types than just a scalar value. You can return entities, other types, and even collections from one of these functions. The most challenging part is to understand Entity SQL in order to pull it off.

I'll demonstrate defining a type in Entity SQL and then using a DefiningExpression to return it.

What if we wanted to calculate a few different properties from Customer and return them as a single type? For example, in addition to FullNameReverse (which we can also build from Customer because it inherits Contact), say we'd like to calculate the person's age on the fly.

Example 15-3 displays a function that defines a type and then returns that type from the DefiningExpression.

Example 15-3. A model-defined function that returns a new type

```
<Function Name="CalculatedDetails">
  <ReturnType>
    <RowType>
      <Property Name="Age" Type="Double" />
      <Property Name="FullName" Type="String"/>
    </RowType>
  </ReturnType>
  <Parameter Name="c" Type="BAModel.Customer" />
  <DefiningExpression>
     Row(
          DiffDays(c.BirthDate,CurrentDateTime())/365.255,
          Trim(c.FirstName) + " " + c.LastName
        )
  </DefiningExpression>
</Function>
```

In the function displayed in Example 15-1, one of the Function attributes was ReturnType. In Example 15-3, ReturnType is now in its own element so that you can define the type to be returned, in this case a RowType. But what is RowType?

If you think back to the lessons in Chapter 5 about wrapped and unwrapped entities, it may help you understand the concept of an Entity SQL RowType. When results are wrapped, they are contained in what is essentially a row. Therefore, in order to define a type that can be returned as results, the type must be wrapped in a row— each property is an item in the row. A type that is a row is represented in Entity SQL as a RowType.

Within the RowType you can then define properties.

Like the FullNameReverse function, CalculatedDetails expects a parameter. This time it's a BAModel.Customer. And finally, the DefiningExpression calculates both the age and the full name, and then returns those in a Row.

Consuming the Complex Results

Again, using the function in Entity SQL is not terribly challenging.

Because the function can work only on contacts of type Customer, we just need to be careful to construct a query that returns only customers. You saw queries like this in Chapter 14, in the section on TPH inheritance. Example 15-4 shows that using the more complex function is no different from calling the simpler FullNameReverse function.

Example 15-4. Using the new function in an Entity SQL expression

```
String esql= "SELECT VALUE BAModel.CalculatedDetails(c) " +
             "FROM OFTYPE(BAEntities.Contacts, BAModel.Customer) " +
             "AS c"
ObjectQuery<DbDataRecord> detailsQuery = context.CreateQuery<DbDataRecord>(esql);
var detailsList = detailsQuery.ToList();
```

Reading the Results from a Complex Function

The results will be DbDataRecords, just as any other nonentity result set. You did a lot of this in Chapters 3 and 5.

Figure 15-1 shows the results of the query expression in Example 15-4 displayed in LINQPad.

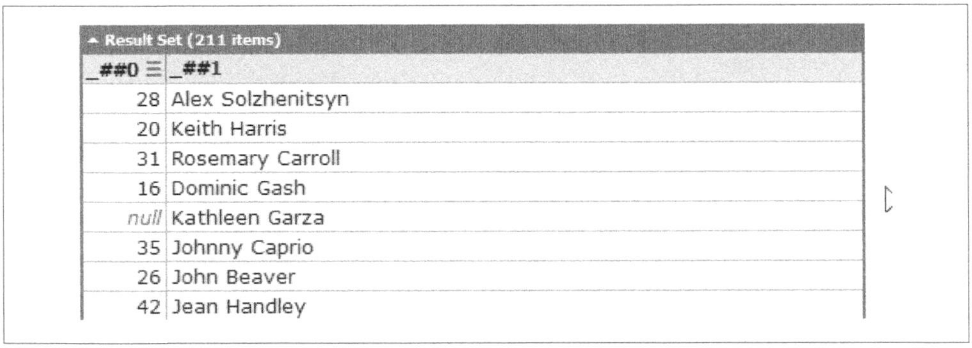

Result Set (211 items)

_##0	_##1
28	Alex Solzhenitsyn
20	Keith Harris
31	Rosemary Carroll
16	Dominic Gash
null	Kathleen Garza
35	Johnny Caprio
26	John Beaver
42	Jean Handley

Figure 15-1. LINQPad displaying the results of a query that uses the complex function

If you want to read the contents of detailsList, you have to drill into each item of each result. To access the Age item in the results, you would ask for detailsList[0][0]. For the name of the Age item, you would ask for detailsList[0][1].

Even if you created a function that is accessible from a LINQ query, the function must return a dbDataRecord, as shown in Example 15-5.

Example 15-5. Exposing a complex function for use in LINQ to Entities queries

```
[EdmFunction("BAModel", "CalculatedDetails")]
public static DbDataRecord CalculatedDetails(this Customer c)
{
  throw new NotSupportedException
          ("This function can only be used in a query");
}
```

When I first attempted to write this function, even with my experience with Entity SQL and Entity Framework, use of RowType and Row was not intuitive to me. It took me a few hours to realize that I needed to wrap the results of the calculations in a Row. Hopefully, these concepts will help you go further and create even more complex functions if and when the need arises.

As with so many other concepts, this is just the tip of the iceberg in terms of how you can extend your model with model-defined functions. For some additional ideas, check out my June 2009 blog post on this topic at *http://thedatafarm.com/blog/data-access/ef4-model-defined-functions-level-1-amp-2/*, as well as the Entity Framework team's January 2009 blog post at *http://blogs.msdn.com/efdesign/archive/2009/01/07/model-defined-functions.aspx*.

Mapping Table per Concrete (TPC) Type Inheritance for Tables with Overlapping Fields

Another scenario where you can use inheritance mapping is when you have database tables with overlapping fields. A classic example of this appears in Figure 15-2, where a copy of the Reservations table was created to store old reservations that are rarely accessed.

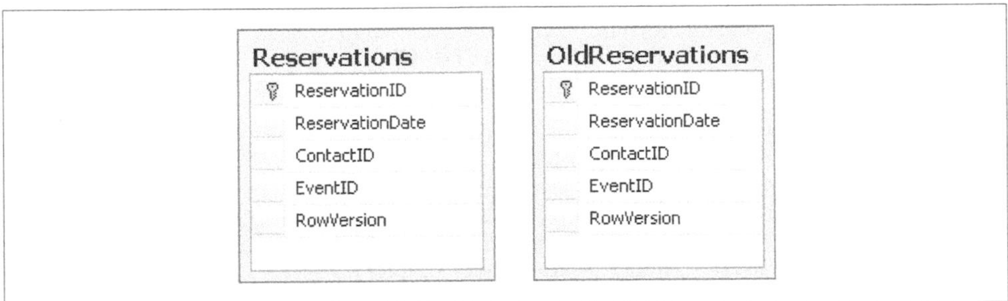

Figure 15-2. Reservations split into two tables in the database

The inheritance implementation used for this mapping is called *Table per Concrete Type* or *TPC* inheritance. You can define the inheritance between the two in the Designer, but you will have to manually map the `OldReservations` entity to its table in the XML.

To create the inheritance, you need to remove all of the overlapping properties from the derived entity. In this case, that means every property. Figure 15-3 displays what the inheritance looks like in the EDM Designer.

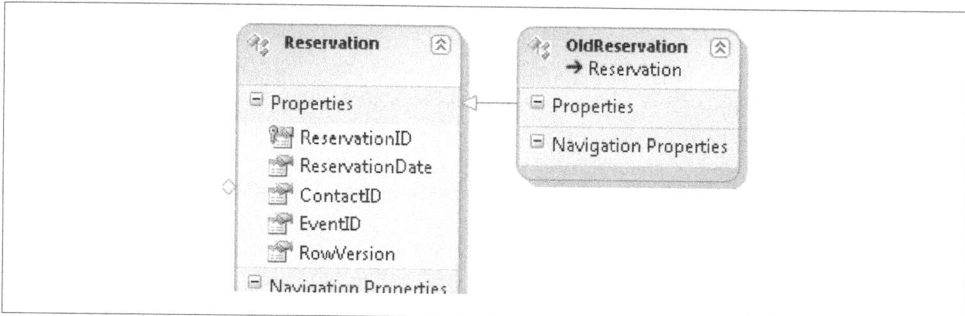

Figure 15-3. Base and derived entities in TPC inheritance mapping

You'll find that none of the `OldReservations` table fields were mapped after you made these modifications. You can map the `ReservationID` field to the `ReservationID` property, but the rest must be mapped in the XML of the EDMX file.

Example 15-6 shows the mapping. The `Reservation EntityTypeMapping` contains one mapping for the `Reservation` entity and another mapping for the derived `OldReservation` entity.

Example 15-6. TPC mapping

```
<EntitySetMapping Name="ReservationSet">
  <EntityTypeMapping TypeName=" BAModel.Reservation">
    <MappingFragment StoreEntitySet="Reservations">
      <ScalarProperty Name="ReservationID" ColumnName="ReservationID" />
      <ScalarProperty Name="ReservationDate" ColumnName="ReservationDate" />
      <ScalarProperty Name="ContactID" ColumnName="ContactID" />
      <ScalarProperty Name="EventID" ColumnName="EventID" />
      <ScalarProperty Name="RowVersion" ColumnName="RowVersion" />
    </MappingFragment>
  </EntityTypeMapping>
  <EntityTypeMapping TypeName="BAModel.OldReservation">
    <MappingFragment StoreEntitySet="OldReservations">
      <ScalarProperty Name="ReservationID" ColumnName="ReservationID" />
      <ScalarProperty Name="ReservationDate" ColumnName="ReservationDate" />
      <ScalarProperty Name="ContactID" ColumnName="ContactID" />
      <ScalarProperty Name="EventID" ColumnName="EventID" />
      <ScalarProperty Name="RowVersion" ColumnName="RowVersion" />
    </MappingFragment>
```

```
  </EntityTypeMapping>
</EntitySetMapping>
```

With this mapping, you will be able to work with the `OldReservations` table when you need to. Also with this mapping, you will get the `OldReservations` anytime you query for `Reservation` without specifically excluding them. Therefore, you may want to consider turning `Reservation` into an abstract type and creating another entity to represent current reservations as you did to solve a similar problem with `Lodging` entities that are not resorts in Chapter 14.

Although you can't see the mapping in the Designer, you will still be able to use the model in the Designer when TPC is implemented.

You won't be doing anything further with `OldReservations` in the book samples, so feel free to remove it and its mapping if you have followed the steps in this section.

Using QueryView to Create Read-Only Entities and Other Specialized Mappings

`QueryView` is a mapping that allows you to override the default mapping for an entity set and return read-only data. `QueryView` is something you need to enter manually in the XML, and it belongs in the mapping layer.

A `QueryView` is a query that is expressed using Entity SQL syntax. However, rather than creating the Entity SQL expression against the conceptual layer of the model as you are accustomed to, the target of the expression is the store (SSDL) layer. In other words, when you construct the Entity SQL for a `QueryView`, the query is written against the elements of the SSDL.

Entities from QueryViews Don't Have to Be Read-Only

`QueryView` returns entities that are considered to be read-only. But they aren't truly read-only because they are still change-tracked by the `ObjectContext`. They are considered read-only because the Entity Framework is not able to automatically generate `Insert`, `Update`, and `Delete` commands for these entities. Instead, you can always create function mappings, as you did for the `Payment` entity. Then the entity that came from a `QueryView` will be persisted back to the data store by a call to `SaveChanges`.

In addition to returning read-only entities, another benefit of `QueryView` is that you can overcome the limitations of conditional mapping. As you saw earlier, conditional mapping lets you filter using `=`, `Is Null`, and `Is Not Null`. Using a `QueryView` you can filter with a much wider variety of operators, including `>` and `<`.

> **QueryView: All or Nothing?**
>
> As you can see in the list following this sidebar, there are a lot of caveats to using `QueryView`. Essentially it can turn into an all-or-nothing mapping choice in your model because of the requirement to use `QueryView` to map any entity that is related to another entity that is mapped with `QueryView`. In a typical model most entities are related to at least one other entity, so you will end up needing `QueryView` for a good percentage of the entities in your model. This is something you will want to plan for in advance. You'll learn in the next chapter how to build model-based views with a `DefiningQuery` that pulls data directly from the database, rather than creating a view over the store metadata as `QueryView` does.

Before using `QueryView`, you should be aware of the following:

- `QueryView` is another mapping that the Designer does not support. The lack of support in this case means you can only design the query view directly in the XML of the model.
- If an `EntitySet` is being mapped with a `QueryView`, all related `EntitySets` and `AssociationSets` must be mapped with `QueryViews` as well.

  This could get a little tricky in the BreakAway model, as every entity is related to at least one other entity through associations. So, you need to plan ahead if you want to take advantage of `QueryViews`.

  For a nice example of adding `QueryViews` to a model with TPH inheritance, see the blog post by Danny Simmons, of the Entity Framework team, titled "Mapping Read-only Entities" (*http://blogs.msdn.com/dsimmons/archive/2007/11/08/mapping-read-only-entities.aspx*).
- As you've seen already, entities returned by `QueryView` are read-only. If you want the entities that result to be updatable, you can use function mappings to map stored procedures to the entity, as you did earlier in this book with the `Payment` entity.
- In the `EntitySetMapping`, you need to remove the `StorageSetName` as well as the property mappings.
- `QueryViews` impact other types of mappings in the model. As per the MSDN documentation, you need to pay attention to these scenarios as well:

  —Many-to-many associations

  —Inheritance hierarchies
- The syntax for writing a `QueryView` is a subset of the Entity SQL language. Functions are not allowed, which means you can't do something like create a `FullName` property by concatenating `FirstName` and `LastName`. Of course, that was the first thing I tried.

  Here are the operators you can use with `QueryView`:

Cast, Case, Not, Or, And, IsNull, Equals, NotEquals, LessThan, LessThanOrEquals, GreaterThan, GreaterThanOrEquals, Project, NewInstance, Filter, Ref, Union, UnionAll, Scan, FullOuterJoin, LeftOuterJoin, InnerJoin, EntityRef

Finding a Common Use Case for QueryView

As you can see, `QueryView` comes with a host of caveats. The scenario that makes `QueryViews` the most daunting is when they are used for entities that have some type of relationship to any other entity, whether that is through an association or within a hierarchy.

Using `QueryView` in a scenario where you must change the mappings for most of your model's entities to `QueryViews` is somewhat of an edge case. If you do want to see how to deal with this situation, look for a download on the book's website that contains a short article and a walkthrough that comes from the first edition of this book.

For now, let's focus on a use for `QueryView` that you can leverage in later chapters in this book. Because an entity that comes from a `QueryView` is inherently read-only, this is a great way to create new entities that are shaped for views of your data that can be used for selection lists in your applications.

For example, a common need throughout the enterprise is to provide a list of customer names and IDs. This can be used for customer selection elements, such as a drop-down list, in your apps.

Of course, you can use projections to create this list, but then you will be dealing with anonymous types, which you can't pass around from one method to another, or `DbDataRecords`, which are not always easy to work with.

With a `QueryView`, you can get the benefit of a projection, but return an entity. Not only does this give you a result that is easy to work with, but the entity will be a known type in your model and your generated classes. The biggest benefit is that the entity can be isolated from other entities in the model—no associations and no inheritance. Therefore, you won't have to worry about modifying related entities to map to `QueryViews` as well.

Creating a CustomerNameAndID Entity

Before creating the `QueryView`, you'll want an entity in the model that will encapsulate the results of the `QueryView`.

1. Create a new entity in the model.
2. In the Add Entity dialog, name the new entity `CustomerNameAndID` and leave the default Key Property settings intact.

3. Add two scalar properties to the new entity: `FirstName` and `LastName`. By default, new scalar properties are of type `String` and are not nullable. You can leave the default attributes for these new properties.

Having to use two properties in this new entity is a huge frustration for me. I really want to expose only `FullName`. But as you'll see, `QueryView` does not allow the use of any type of function, including concatenation. In fact, I have made a suggestion to the team to add this support in a future version on Microsoft's Connect website (*https://connect.microsoft.com/data/feedback/details/557121/allow-esql-functions-when-defining-queryview*).

Creating a QueryView Mapping for CustomerNameAndID

You'll have to define the `QueryView` manually in the mapping layer in the XML of the model file.

If the entity was mapped to something in the SSDL, there would already be an `EntitySetMapping` element for the `CustomerNameAndIDs EntitySet`. But in this case, nothing is in the mapping layer for the new entity. You'll need to create it manually.

1. Close the Designer and open the model in the XML editor.
2. Scroll down to the `<edmx:Mappings>` section.
3. Add a new `EntitySetMapping` for the `CustomerNameAndIDs` element above the `EntitySetMapping` for Activities.

   Example 15-7 shows what the beginning of the mapping section looks like with the new `EntitySetMapping` element inserted. I've used comments to highlight the new element.

   Example 15-7. Inserting a new EntitySetMapping

```
<!-- C-S mapping content -->
<edmx:Mappings>
  <Mapping Space="C-S" xmlns="http://schemas.microsoft.com/ado/2008/09/mapping/cs">
    <EntityContainerMapping StorageEntityContainer="BreakAwayModelStoreContainer"
                            CdmEntityContainer="BAEntities">
     <!-- New Mapping -->
      <EntitySetMapping Name="CustomerNameAndIDs">

      </EntitySetMapping>
     <!-- End of New Mapping -->

<EntitySetMapping Name="Activities">
```

4. Inside the `EntitySetMapping` tags, insert the `QueryView` so that the `EntitySetMapping` looks like Example 15-8.

Example 15-8. The mapping with a QueryView

```
<EntitySetMapping Name="CustomerNameAndIDs">
  <QueryView>
    SELECT VALUE BAModel.CustomerNameAndID(c.ContactID, c.FirstName,c.LastName)
    FROM BreakAwayModelStoreContainer.Contact  AS c
    JOIN BreakAwayModelStoreContainer.Customers  AS cu
    ON c.ContactID=cu.ContactID
  </QueryView>
</EntitySetMapping>
```

Compare this `EntitySetMapping` to the one for `Activities` just below it, which maps entity properties to database table columns.

`BreakAwayModelStoreContainer` is the SSDL's `EntityContainer` name that the wizard generated automatically. Just as you need to use the model's `EntityContainer` name when constructing regular Entity SQL queries, you need to use the store's `EntityContainer` name with the Entity SQL expressions you create for `QueryViews`.

The query joins `Contact` and `Customers` because it needs the name fields from the `Contact` table but needs to limit the results to only those contacts that are in the `Customers` table.

What's really nice here is that the Designer is able to validate the syntax of the query, something you can't get when you write Entity SQL strings in your application.

5. To test the EDMX validation, remove `AS c` from the end of the query and build the project.

   The entire `EntitySetMapping` section will be underlined and in the Error List you will see the following error:

   ```
   Error 2068: The query view specified for the EntitySet 'CustomerNameAndIDs'
   is not valid. The query parser threw the following error :
   'c.ContactID' could not be resolved in the current scope or context.
   Make sure that all referenced variables are in scope, that required schemas
   are loaded, and that namespaces are referenced correctly.
   Near member access expression, line 1, column 41
   ```

   The cause of the error is that the `c` in `c.ContactID` can't be resolved because you removed the definition of `c`.

In some cases, you may have to open the model in the Designer to highlight the `QueryView` errors.

6. Replace the `as c` and rebuild the project. The error message will go away.

Testing the QueryView

You can test the QueryView in LINQPad or in your program module.

Since you are querying entities, you can sort, filter, or use other methods to compose queries against the CustomerNameAndID entities. For example:

```
context.CustomerNameAndIDs.OrderBy(c => c.LastName + c.FirstName)
                          .Take(30).ToList()
```

You can also do projections; however, that will defeat the benefit of returning a known type that can be passed around.

Deconstructing the QueryView

The order of the projected columns in the preceding example is not random. Since you no longer have any property mappings, the Entity Framework relies on the QueryView to provide the values (more specifically, the correct types) in the order in which the entity expects.

The following expression is different from those that you have written against the conceptual layer:

```
SELECT VALUE BAModel.CustomerNameAndID(c.ContactID,c.FirstName,c.LastName)
FROM BreakAwayModelStoreContainer.Contact  AS c
```

Using VALUE designates that you will be returning an object, as you have seen before. Following that is a type constructor, similar to what you would use in .NET code.

In fact, you can see this in action if you return to the XML and modify the query. Moving the ContactId to the last position in the list will throw a mapping exception when you build the project that reads, in part, as follows:

```
Error 2068: The query view specified for the EntitySet 'CustomerNameAndIDs'
is not valid. The query parser threw the following error : The argument type
'Edm.String(Nullable=True,DefaultValue=,MaxLength=50,Unicode=True,
FixedLength=False)' is not compatible with the property 'Id' of formal type
'Edm.Int32(Nullable=False,DefaultValue=)'.
```

Entity Framework expected an Int32 in the first position but found a String instead.

We'll take advantage of this new QueryView in an application example in Chapter 17 and elsewhere in the book.

Summary

Although the Entity Framework's modeling capabilities are very sophisticated, unfortunately the Designer still has some catching up to do. Though these additional mappings are not supported by the Designer, they are very useful and certainly worth the effort of cracking open the EDMX in its raw form and applying these mappings when they will benefit your model.

Keep in mind that what you've seen in this chapter is not an exhaustive list of the mapping possibilities. There are even more, though not commonly used, mappings you can achieve. For additional ideas, including how to combine different types of inheritance, explore the EF Mapping Helper listed on the Entity Framework team's page on the MSDN Code Gallery at *http://code.msdn.com/adonetefx*. The EF Mapping Helper is listed under the section titled "Entity Framework Learning Tools."

I look forward to seeing more innovation by developers to take advantage of the flexibility offered by the new model-defined functions in Entity Framework. While many people are daunted by the `QueryView`'s use of Entity SQL and its potential to force you to use `QueryViews` for more entities than you intended, it is another mapping that offers advanced flexibility so that you can solve more and more of your modeling quandaries.

The next chapter takes another perspective on working with the model by exploring the many ways to use stored procedures in your model beyond the function mappings and function imports that you created in Chapter 8.

CHAPTER 16

Gaining Additional Stored Procedure and View Support in the Raw XML

In Chapter 7, you learned about function mapping and function imports to map stored procedures in the Entity Data Model (EDM). Mapping read, insert, update, and delete stored procedures to entities is the simplest way to use stored procedures in the EDM. Thanks to new Designer features that you worked with in that chapter, it is also now fairly easy to work with stored procedures that return results that don't map to an entity—by returning complex types instead. There are still a number of scenarios involving stored procedures that haven't been addressed yet—those that require working directly in the XML of the EDMX file.

This chapter will cover ways to implement stored procedures beyond the function mapping you already performed in the Designer. These additional implementations will create functions that you can call directly in your code.

In addition to implementing stored procedures from your database, you'll also learn how to create native functions and views directly in your model.

The first part of the chapter will focus on stored procedures that are used for querying the database. The latter part of the chapter will address stored procedures for performing inserts, updates, and deletes in your database. You'll also learn a few more tricks with respect to database views and user-defined functions along the way.

Reviewing Procedures, Views, and UDFs in the EDM

As you have learned in earlier parts of the book, the Entity Framework supports tables, stored procedures, database views, and user-defined functions (UDFs). Stored procedures and UDFs are realized in the SSDL as functions that you have to import into your conceptual model, while views are surfaced in the conceptual model as entities that can be updated through the use of function mapping.

You can map stored procedures to entities, as you have seen in previous chapters. Most stored procedures can't be mapped to entities, but they can be mapped to scalar values or complex types. You use these stored procedures by calling their functions directly as methods of the `ObjectContext`, as you saw in Chapter 7.

You can define UDFs in the store layer of your EDM, and the Entity Data Model Wizard and Update Model Wizard will pick them up. We'll look at UDFs at the end of this chapter.

Working with Stored Procedures That Return Data

In Chapter 7, you learned that the Entity Data Model Designer supports a number of scenarios for "read" stored procedures—that is, those that return data. You can use the Function Import Wizard to map read stored procedures to entities, complex types, or primitive types. The result of this mapping is a function in the CSDL that can also be realized as a method of your generated `ObjectContext`, which you will get when using the default code generation template.

These functions have some nuances that you should be aware of, and I'll cover them in this section.

Are Stored Procedures Second-Class Citizens in the Entity Framework?

It's important to not lose sight of the EDM and the Entity Framework's bigger benefits when thinking about stored procedures. Two of the Entity Framework's core features are the ability it gives you to compose queries, and the command generation it can perform for queries and updates. This is especially useful if you lack an experienced SQL developer on your team and would otherwise be writing queries that start with something such as `SELECT * FROM`. Admittedly, a code generator will not be as good at composing commands as a seasoned developer. But the Entity Framework is good at both tasks, regardless of your backend database. Another benefit, of course, is that it lets you use an EDM to describe your data.

Yet stored procedures are a critical part of many organizations' databases. Although the Entity Framework supports the use of stored procedures in the EDM and API, those stored procedures are treated as functions. As you have learned in earlier chapters, some of these functions can be mapped to entities and used to override the `SaveChanges` behavior, while others can be called directly in your code.

Using Functions That Match an Entity Whose Property Names Have Been Changed

As you learned in Chapter 7, if the schema of the return type matches up exactly with an existing type in your model, you are a few clicks away from mapping the function. However, there is one caveat to this. The function truly expects an exact match. If you have changed property names in entities and they do not match column names being returned, the function will fail.

One function in the model that demonstrates this problem is `ActivitiesOnATrip`. Example 16-1 shows the database procedure for this function. The procedure returns all of the columns from `Activities`.

Example 16-1. The select statement in the ActivitiesOnATrip stored procedure

```
SELECT  Activities.ActivityID,
        Activities.Activity,
        Activities.imagepath,
        Activities.Category
FROM    dbo.Activities
WHERE   Activities.activityid IN (
        SELECT  EventActivities.ActivityID
        FROM    dbo.EventActivities
        WHERE   EventActivities.eventid = @tripid )
```

In the model, the `Activity` entity has a direct mapping to the `Activities` table, so the fields and properties line up exactly. The `Activity` entity has the same fields—or does it? The field names in the `Activities` table are `ActivityID`, `Activity`, `imagepath`, and `Category`. You may recall that when changing the original entity name from `Activities` to `Activity`, there was a conflict with the property named `Activity`, so you changed the property name to `Name`. Even this minor change causes the function to fail when it attempts to match up the results of the returned data with the `Activity` entity.

You'll be allowed to implement the mapping function in the model, but when you try to execute the function you will get this error:

```
The data reader is incompatible with the specified 'BAModel.Activity'. A member of
the type, 'Name', does not have a corresponding column in the data reader
with the same name.
```

Because neither the model nor the Designer gives you an opportunity to define the mapping between the results and `Activity`, you can't provide the necessary information to make this work.

One possible solution to this problem is to create a `ComplexType` for the function and then coerce the results into `Activity` entities.

You could also leverage a `DefiningQuery`, which you will learn about a bit later in this chapter.

Query Stored Procedures and Inherited Types

What about inherited types? If you have a procedure whose results match up with a derived type, such as `Customer` is now, you can map the function in the Designer with no problem. The `CustomersWhoTravelledinDateRange` stored procedure returns all of the appropriate fields to match up with the `Customer` type. This includes fields from the

Customer table, fields from the Contact table, and fields from the ContactPersonalInfo table.

You will see the originally misspelled Customer table column, PrimaryDesintation, in the stored procedure as a nice reminder that you don't have to live with these problems in your EDM.

```
PROCEDURE  CustomersWhoTravelledinDateRange
--returns customer records with contact info for customers
@startdate DATETIME,
@enddate datetime

AS

SELECT Customers.ContactID, Customers.PrimaryDesintation as PrimaryDestinationID,
       Customers.CustomerTypeID, Customers.InitialDate,
       Customers.SecondaryDestination as SecondaryDestinationID,
       Customers.PrimaryActivity as PrimaryActivityID,
       Customers.SecondaryActivity as SecondaryActivityID,
       Customers.Notes, Contact.FirstName,
       Contact.LastName, Contact.Title, Contact.AddDate,
       Contact.ModifiedDate, ContactPersonalInfo.BirthDate,
       ContactPersonalInfo.HeightInches,
       ContactPersonalInfo.WeightPounds,
       ContactPersonalInfo.DietaryRestrictions,
       Contact.TimeStamp as ContactTimeStamp
FROM   Customers INNER JOIN Contact
       ON Customers.ContactID = Contact.ContactID
       INNER JOIN ContactPersonalInfo
       ON Customers.ContactID = ContactPersonalInfo.ContactID
WHERE customers.contactid IN
 (SELECT Customers.ContactID
  FROM Customers INNER JOIN Reservations
       ON Customers.ContactID = Reservations.ContactID
       INNER JOIN Events ON Reservations.EventID = Events.EventID
  WHERE events.startdate>=@startdate AND events.startdate<=@enddate
  GROUP BY Customers.contactid)
```

You can use the Model Browser to create a function import for this stored procedure and point the return type to the Customer entity. You can test the function with the code in Example 16-2.

Example 16-2. Calling a function that returns a derived type

```
using (var context = new BAEntities())
{
  var customers = context.CustomersWhoTravelledinDateRange
   (new DateTime(2006, 1, 1), new DateTime(2006, 12, 31));
}
```

Composing Queries Against Functions

You can include functions in queries; however, only the UDFs are truly composable. When the function is from a stored procedure only the procedure itself will be processed on the server side. The rest of the query is processed on the client side in memory. This is because in most databases, stored procedures are not composable.

For example, if you have a stored procedure that returns all orders for a particular company, and you write a LINQ to Entities query adding an additional filter to it, such as the following:

```
from o in context.OrdersForACustomer(12345)
where o.Total>10000 select o
```

the stored procedure will execute on the database, returning all orders for the customer; then, in memory, LINQ will query all of those orders and return only the subset. This is not a limitation of the Entity Framework, but the nature of stored procedures.

UDFs are composable, and therefore their EDM functions are composable as well.

Replacing Stored Procedures with Views for Composability

In the previous version of Entity Framework, there was no support in the model for read stored procedures that returned randomly shaped results. A nice trick for getting around that was to create a view in the database that returns data of the same structure as the stored procedure, and then to use the view in place of the stored procedure.

Even though this is no longer necessary because the stored procedures can now be returned into complex types, the trick is still quite useful.

The benefit is that a database view is composable, whereas the function derived from the stored procedure is not. You can write queries against the view and those queries will become native store commands, executed on the server. When using the function, though, you can call the function and you can even use it in a query; however, the function itself, as you saw in Chapter 7, will execute the stored procedure on the server, and then the results will be further manipulated on the client side by the rest of the query operators. This could result in very inefficient queries if your stored procedure returns many more entities than your query specifies.

If you have `Insert`, `Update`, and `Delete` procedures that align with the results of that view, you can map them back to that new entity using function mapping and use it as your object. If you do this, you'll want to remove the entity that this is replacing so that you don't have update collisions.

An additional benefit of using the view to create an entity for capturing the results of the stored procedure is that you will receive an object that can be change-tracked and that will have its relationships managed by the `ObjectContext`.

Queries That Return Multiple Result Sets

The Entity Framework does not directly support queries that return multiple result sets. However, Colin Meek, one of the members of the Entity Framework team, created a project called EFExtensions that contains a method for using stored procedures that return multiple result sets. The extensions were originally written for Entity Framework's .NET 3.5 version and have been updated for EF4. In its current iteration, each result set can match up with an existing entity. You can find EFExtensions on the MSDN Code Gallery at *http://code.msdn.microsoft.com/EFExtensions/*. Colin wrote an in-depth explanation of how these extensions work, along with a walkthrough of his sample application, on his blog, at *http://blogs.msdn.com/meek/archive/2008/03/26/ado-entity-framework-stored-procedure-customization.aspx*.

Executing Queries on Demand with ExecuteStoreQuery

`ObjectContext.ExecuteStoreQuery` is a handy addition to this new version of Entity Framework that allows developers to create and execute store queries on the fly.

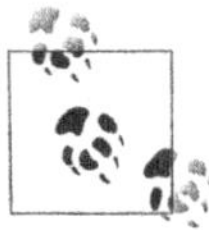

`ExecuteStoreQuery` has a counterpart, `ExecuteStoreCommand`, which will be discussed later in the chapter.

You can use `ExecuteStoreQuery` to return data into objects or entities. If you return entities you can force those entities to participate in change tracking.

Since LINQ to Entities doesn't readily support many `datetime` functions, let's look at this method to leverage a store's `datetime` function. In this case, I'll be using T-SQL against my database, which is SQL Server.

For example, this LINQ query will compile, but it will fail at runtime because Entity Framework is unable to translate the `DateTime` calculations into store functions:

```
var q=context.Contacts.OfType<Customer>().
      Select(c=>new {c.FirstName,c.LastName,
            Age=(c.BirthDate-DateTime.Today)/365.255});
```

You could write an Entity SQL statement, but many developers prefer not to mix Entity SQL into their applications. And as you saw in Chapter 15, you could create a model-defined function to calculate age. But this might not be part of your model.

Querying to a Class That Is Not an Entity

You could create the T-SQL on the fly and execute it with the `ExecuteStoreQuery` function. This query, listed in Example 16-3, returns data into a class whose definition is also in the code listing.

Example 16-3. Using ExecuteStoreQuery

```
string tsql =
  "SELECT  FirstName, LastName, " +
  "        DATEDIFF(Day,ContactPersonalInfo.BirthDate,GETDATE())/365.255 AS Age " +
  "FROM    Contact,ContactPersonalInfo " +
  "WHERE Contact.ContactID=ContactPersonalInfo.ContactID";

List<MyClass> results=context.ExecuteStoreQuery<MyClass>(tsql).ToList();

class MyClass
{
  public string FirstName { get; set; }
  public string LastName { get; set; }
  public int? Age { get; set; }
}
```

Like the `ExecuteFunction` method that you saw in Chapter 7, `ExecuteStoreQuery` returns a `System.Data.Objects.ObjectResult`—in this case, an `ObjectResult<MyClass>`, which I have converted to `List<MyClass>`.

Querying into an Entity

You can also return results into an entity. Example 16-4 shows a T-SQL query that does another `datetime` calculation that you cannot perform in LINQ to Entities. It returns all of the contacts who have made reservations less than 30 days prior to the start date of a trip. Recall that in the database what we know as "Trips" is contained in the table named "Events".

Example 16-4. Performing a datetime calculation in T-SQL

```
SELECT   Locations.LocationID as DestinationID, MAX(Locations.LocationName)as Name
FROM     Locations,
         Events,
         Reservations
WHERE    Locations.LocationID = Events.LocationID
         AND Reservations.EventID = Events.EventID
         AND DATEDIFF(DAY, StartDate, ReservationDate) <= 10
GROUP BY Locations.LocationID
```

If you assign this query to a string, you can use it with `ExecuteStoreQuery` to return the `Destination` entities defined in the model.

When creating the string to pass in as the query, you'll need to take into account the actual field names of the target entity since the context will match the names of the incoming results to the names of the entity properties in order to materialize the property.

By default, the entities returned will not be attached to the context and will not be change-tracked. If you want these to participate in change tracking, you'll need to use the overload for `ExecuteStoreQuery`, supplying the name of the `EntitySet` and the desired MergeOption value. For this example, I'll use the PreserveChanges option, which will prevent any preexisting entities that have been modified from being overwritten.

```
List<Destination> results = context.ExecuteStoreQuery<Destination>
(tsql,"Destinations",MergeOption.PreserveChanges).ToList();
```

You can additionally pass in parameters, which is described further in the reference documentation for ExecuteStoreQuery.

What you won't see in the reference documentation is the host of caveats for returning entities from this method. However, in the MSDN forums there is a great thread titled "My discoveries with ExecuteStoreQuery," begun by Zeeshan Hirani with follow-up from Entity Framework team member Diego Vega, which drills into additional details about the method. The URL for this thread is *http://social.msdn.microsoft.com/Forums/en-US/adonetefx/thread/44cf5582-63f8-4f81-8029-7b43469c028d*.

Adding Native Queries to the Model

In addition to defining native queries on the fly in code, you can add native queries directly into the model using the Function element. The store query text is embedded in Function's CommandText element.

As an example, it would be very convenient to query payments for a particular contact rather than all contacts in a date range.

You can do this directly in the SSDL without adding a new stored procedure to the database.

Remember that manual additions to the SSDL will be destroyed if you run the Update Model Database Wizard.

If the procedure existed in the database, the following function would represent it in the model:

```
<Function Name="PaymentsForContact" IsComposable="false">
  <Parameter Name="ContactID" Type="int" Mode="In"/>
</Function>
```

The Function element has a child element called CommandText. You can enter native store commands, such as a SQL Server T-SQL query, directly into the CommandText element. Therefore, you can add the new query directly into the SSDL of the model.

The entire function would now look like Example 16-5.

Example 16-5. A custom query manually embedded into the SSDL

```
<Function Name="PaymentsForContact" IsComposable="false">
  <CommandText>
    SELECT   Payments.PaymentDate, Payments.Amount,
             Reservations.ReservationDate, Contact.FirstName,
             Contact.LastName, Events.StartDate, Events.EndDate,
             Locations.LocationName
    FROM     Payments INNER JOIN
             Reservations ON Payments.ReservationID =
             Reservations.ReservationID INNER JOIN
             Contact ON Reservations.ContactID = Contact.ContactID
             INNER JOIN Events ON Reservations.EventID = Events.EventID
             INNER JOIN Locations ON Events.LocationID =
             Locations.LocationID
    WHERE Contact.ContactID=@ContactID
  </CommandText>
  <Parameter Name="ContactID" Type="int" Mode="In"/>
</Function>
```

If you have any less-than (<) signs in your query, you'll need to either use the escaped notation (`<`) or surround the entire command with a `CDATA` directive so that there is no conflict with the XML, which interprets < as the beginning of a node. You'll see both solutions in action in "Implementing a DefiningQuery" on page 435.

In Chapter 6, you learned about the Function Import Wizard and its ability to create complex types on the fly for stored procedures. The wizard is able to do this with stored procedures in the database, but unfortunately not with commands defined directly in the SSDL functions. In this scenario, you would need to manually define the complex type. Previously you created complex types either by building them from entity properties or by using the Function Import Wizard. You can also use the Model Browser to manually define complex types. Here is a quick walkthrough to build the type that will satisfy the results of `PaymentsForContact`, something you have not done yet.

Defining a Complex Type in the Model Browser

The query returns four `datetime` values, three `char` values, and one decimal. Let's build a complex type to match.

1. Open the Model Browser.
2. Under `BAModel`, right-click Complex Types and select Create Complex Type from the menu.

   A new complex type will appear in the Complex Types node.
3. Rename `ComplexType1` to `TripPayment`.
4. Right-click `TripPayment` and choose Add, then Scalar Property, and then DateTime, as shown in Figure 16-1.

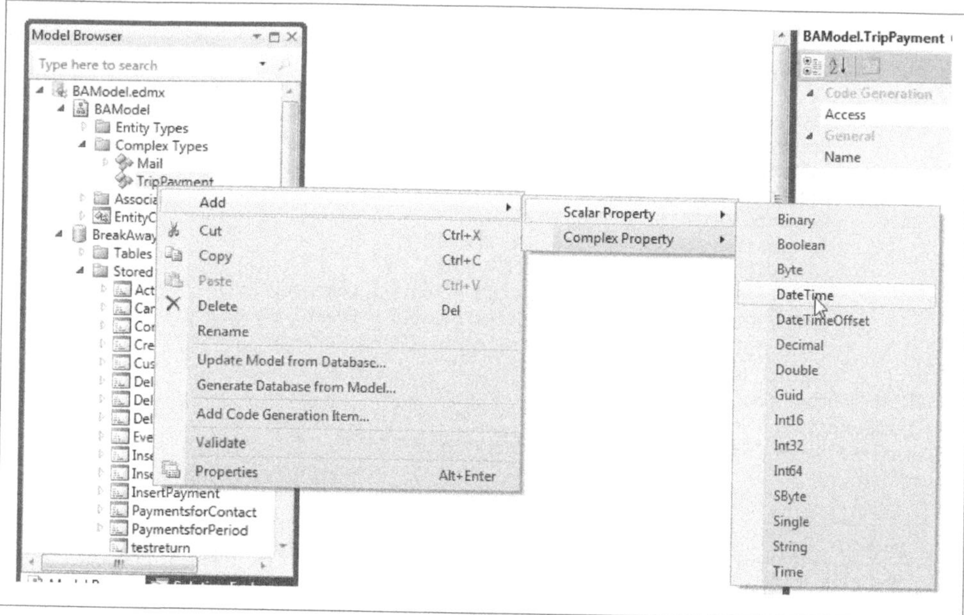

Figure 16-1. Adding a scalar property to a complex type

5. Rename the newly created property `PaymentDate`.

   Leave all of the other attributes set to the defaults, but note that you can define the attributes just as you can for entity types.

6. Create a new scalar property, this time a `Decimal`, and rename it `Amount`.
7. Create scalar properties for the other return values projected in the earlier query.

In the end, you should have the following properties:

- `PaymentDate (DateTime)`
- `Amount (Decimal)`
- `ReservationDate (DateTime)`
- `FirstName (String)`
- `LastName (String)`
- `StartDate (DateTime)`
- `EndDate (DateTime)`
- `LocationName (String)`

For a shortcut, you can copy and paste the properties and then just rename the new ones. Just be careful to use the correct types.

Now you can use the Function Import Wizard that you learned about in Chapter 7 to map the `PaymentsForContact` function to the `TripPayment` complex type. If you are using the default code generation template, PaymentsForContact will be a method of the BAEntities ObjectContext.

```
List<TripPayment> payments = context.PaymentsForContact(569).ToList();
```

You may recall from Chapter 6 that the generated method uses the ObjectContext.ExecuteFunction. If you are not using the default generation template and don't have a PaymentsForContact method, you can use the ExecuteFunction method directly, as shown in Example 16-6. Note that the method takes an ObjectParameter.

Example 16-6. Using ExecuteFunction

```
var contactIDParameter = new ObjectParameter("ContactID", 569);
ObjectResult<TripPayment> payments=
  context.ExecuteFunction<TripPayment>("PaymentsForContact", contactIDParameter);
```

Now that you have learned how to create complex types in the Model Browser, I'll let you in on a secret. There is a view in the database that is represented in the model as vPaymentsForPeriod. The schema of this view is the same as the PaymentsForContact procedure. Rather than creating the complex type, you can map the function to the vPaymentsForPeriod entity. The advantage of mapping to the view is that the data can be change-tracked and updated with stored procedures if necessary.

Adding Native Views to the Model

In addition to being able to add your own stored procedures to the model, you can also add views that don't exist in the database. However, rather than using a function, you use an element called DefiningQuery.

DefiningQuery Is Already in Your Model

A DefiningQuery is comparable to a database view. Like a view, a DefiningQuery cannot take parameters or return multiple result sets, as a stored procedure can.

However, because a DefiningQuery is a virtual table, when you write LINQ or Entity SQL queries against these views, query operators such as WHERE filters will be processed on the server side. This is quite different from working with functions that are embedded in the model. Queries written against functions will have filters performed on the client side, which could be a problem for unsuspecting developers.

Native Objects in the Store Layer

One of the interesting features of the SSDL is that it does not have to be a perfect reflection of your database. You can add objects into the SSDL that don't exist in the database; such objects are referred to as *virtual*.

When working with the `DefiningQuery` in this chapter you will create a virtual table in the SSDL that does not exist in the database. You'll do this because the `DefiningQuery` will actually perform the query in the database and return data. The data must be returned to an entity. That's not a problem, since you can create that entity in the conceptual layer of the model. However, the EDM has a rule that every entity in the Conceptual Schema Definition Layer (CSDL) must map to something in the SSDL.

The solution to this is to create a fake table in the SSDL to map to. The fake table must have an `EntitySet`, so you will also create a virtual `EntitySet`. None of these things actually exist in the database, and the model doesn't care about that. The only problem is that the current version of the Designer will overwrite any customizations of the SSDL if you run the Update Model Wizard. So, keep a copy of these changes in a separate file in case you need to re-create them.

You'll get a step-by-step walkthrough for creating virtual tables later in this chapter.

If you open the BreakAway model in the XML Editor, you will find that you already have three `DefiningQuery` elements. The EDM Wizard turned all of the database views into `DefiningQuery` elements in the SSDL.

The first one is for `vOfficeAddresses` and contains a T-SQL query against the database's `vOfficeAddresses` view:

```
<EntitySet Name="vOfficeAddresses"
 EntityType="BreakAwayModel.Store.vOfficeAddresses" store:Type="Views"
 store:Schema="dbo" store:Name="vOfficeAddresses">
   <DefiningQuery>
     SELECT
      [vOfficeAddresses].[FirstName] AS [FirstName],
      [vOfficeAddresses].[LastName] AS [LastName],
      [vOfficeAddresses].[addressID] AS [addressID],
      [vOfficeAddresses].[Street1] AS [Street1],
      [vOfficeAddresses].[Street2] AS [Street2],
      [vOfficeAddresses].[City] AS [City],
      [vOfficeAddresses].[StateProvince] AS [StateProvince],
      [vOfficeAddresses].[CountryRegion] AS [CountryRegion],
      [vOfficeAddresses].[PostalCode] AS [PostalCode],
      [vOfficeAddresses].[AddressType] AS [AddressType],
      [vOfficeAddresses].[ContactID] AS [ContactID],
      [vOfficeAddresses].[ModifiedDate] AS [ModifiedDate]
     FROM [dbo].[vOfficeAddresses] AS [vOfficeAddresses]
   </DefiningQuery>
</EntitySet>
```

The `EntitySet` attributes are different from standard `EntitySet` definitions in the store layer. For the sake of comparison, here is the `EntitySet` for the `Payments` table:

```
<EntitySet Name="Payments" EntityType="BreakAwayModel.Store.Payments"
 store:Type="Tables" />
```

The `DefiningQuery` in the `vOfficeAddresses EntitySet` surfaces the results of the `vOfficeAddresses` view as a `SELECT` query. Rather than just duplicating the SQL of the existing view, it does a `SELECT` against the existing view. Since database views are most often read-only, using this `SELECT` explicitly restricts the Entity Framework from attempting to perform inserts, updates, or deletes against the view.

Because a database view has no primary key, the wizard infers an `EntityKey` by combining the non-nullable fields of the view. In the SSDL, the wizard also inserts a comment indicating this action:

```
<!--Errors Found During Generation:
warning 6002: The table/view BreakAway.dbo.vOfficeAddresses'
does not have a primary key defined. The key has been inferred and the
definition was created as a read-only table/view.
-->
<EntityType Name="vOfficeAddresses">
  <Key>
    <PropertyRef Name="FirstName" />
    <PropertyRef Name="LastName" />
    <PropertyRef Name="addressID" />
    <PropertyRef Name="AddressType" />
    <PropertyRef Name="ContactID" />
    <PropertyRef Name="ModifiedDate" />
  </Key>
  <-- Property Elements -->
</EntityType>
```

The fact that the `EntitySet` is defined with a `DefiningQuery` has no other impact on the entity in the CSDL or the mappings. Figure 16-2 shows the entity in the model and its mappings back to the entity defined in the SSDL. The only difference from table-based entities is the inability to persist changes to the database from the view-based entities without using stored procedures for updating.

Using DefiningQuery to Create Your Own Views

> DefiningQuery provides an ultimate escape hatch for cases where the mapping is too complex to define in MSL.
>
> —Mike Pizzo, principal architect on the Data Programmability team at Microsoft, in the MSDN forums for the Entity Framework

`DefiningQuery` really is the ultimate escape hatch. Even with the incredible flexibility that the model's various mapping capabilities provide, there still may be some things that you just cannot manage to pull off.

A `DefiningQuery` lets you add queries using the store's native language—for example, T-SQL or PL/SQL—directly to the store layer of the model. It's the last step before swallowing your modeling wizardry pride and asking the person in charge of your

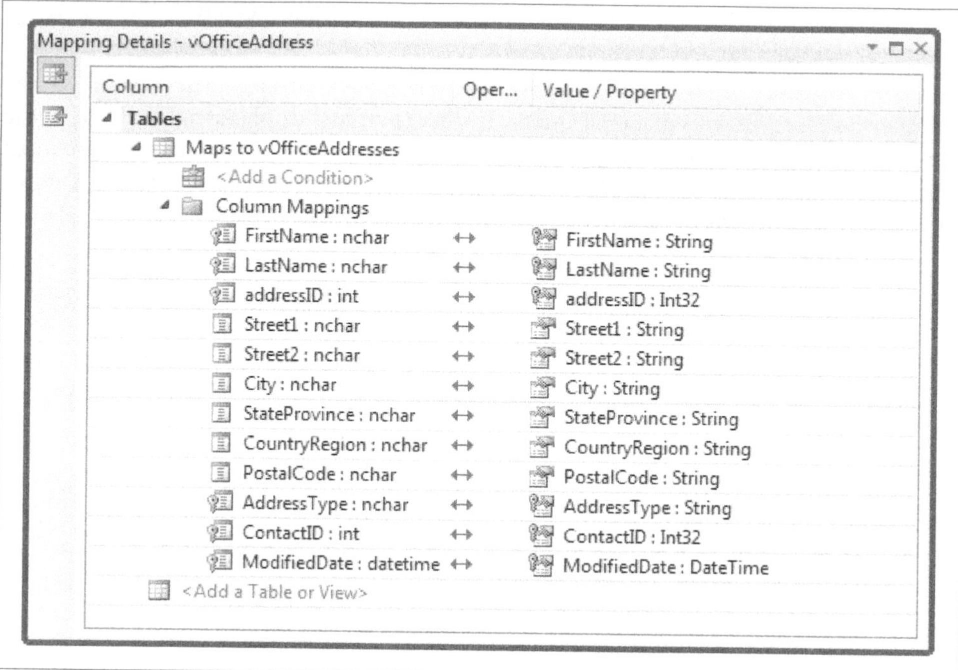

Figure 16-2. The mappings for the view-based entity, which are the same as any other entity's mappings

database to add another view or stored procedure to the database; or in cases where modifying the database is not a possibility.

In addition to creating completely new database views with a `DefiningQuery`, there are other uses for `DefiningQuery`. One example is to write a `DefiningQuery` that returns an entity with properties that don't exist in the database tables. While you can use model-defined functions to create calculated entity properties, a `DefiningQuery` would give you access to database operators and functions.

Be warned that when you create your own `DefiningQuery`, if the model does not already have an entity that lines up with its results, you will have to create all of the model elements yourself: the `Entity` and `EntitySet` in the CSDL, the `Entity` and `EntitySet` in the SSDL, and the mappings. In the next walkthrough, along with creating a `DefiningQuery`, you will see how to implement these additional necessary elements manually in the model.

A view that would be very useful for BreakAway's team to have is one that returns information about customers whose trips are starting within the next week.

Another option might be to create a `QueryView`, as you learned in the previous chapter. There are pros and cons to choosing `DefiningQuery` over `QueryView`. One advantage is that when you are writing the query with the native syntax, you can have more control over how the query is executed on the database. Another is that if you want to create a relationship between the results of a QueryView and another entity, you fall into the trap of having to create QueryViews for every related entity. Additionally, there may be queries you would like to express that use native SQL that has no equivalent in Entity SQL. A DefiningQuery allows you to access the database features directly by embedding a native query into your model.

Alex James, of the Entity Framework team, wrote a great blog post comparing QueryView and DefiningQuery. You can find it at *http://blogs.msdn.com/alexj/archive/2008/12/19/definingquery-versus-queryview.aspx*.

Implementing a DefiningQuery

To create the DefiningQuery you'll need the following elements in your model:

1. The native command to express the query defined in the SSDL
2. An Entity, and an EntitySet in the CSDL
3. A virtual table in the SSDL in the form of an Entity
4. An EntitySet in the SSDL to contain the DefiningQuery
5. A mapping between the entity and the virtual table

You can create items 2 and 5 in the preceding list using the Designer, whereas you must create the others using the XML Editor.

If the store query simply returned results that match an existing view or table and can map to an existing entity, you would not have to create all of these elements in the metadata. However, I have chosen this particular use case in order to provide instruction on what to do when you aren't so fortunate as to have the existing objects.

The first step to implementing the DefiningQuery, which I'll call TimeToFirstReservation, is to work out the native database query. For SQL Server, that would look like Example 16-7.

Example 16-7. T-SQL query to calculate TimeToFirstReservation

```
SELECT  Contact.ContactID,
        Events.EventID AS TripID,
        RTrim(Contact.LastName) + ', ' + Contact.FirstName AS Name,
        Events.StartDate,
        Locations.LocationName as Destination
FROM    Reservations
        INNER JOIN Events ON Reservations.EventID = Events.EventID
                          AND Reservations.EventID = Events.EventID
        INNER JOIN Locations ON Events.LocationID = Locations.LocationID
```

```
        INNER JOIN Contact ON Reservations.ContactID = Contact.ContactID
WHERE   DATEDIFF(Day, Events.StartDate, GETDATE()) <= 7
```

It's quite possible that when you run this example query, the `Trip` data in the sample database will be for dates too far in the past and you will not get any results. Feel free to modify the `DATEDIFF` function if you want to return data.

DefiningQuery Versus Stored Procedure

A `DefiningQuery` is comparable to a view in the database in that it does not take parameters. However, like other views in the model, you can query against the entity that is mapped to a `DefiningQuery` and add additional filters that become part of the query sent to the store. Additionally, since you are working with the resultant entity, you can perform eager-loading or deferred loading with related data.

A stored procedure, on the other hand, is seen as a function, not an entity. You cannot query a function. Also, a stored procedure is executed immediately; it is not deferred. From a maintenance perspective, when using a stored procedure or view directly, the database administrator can maintain the object in the database, and as long as the parameters and result schema of the procedure don't change, you're good to go. Changes to a view that is part of the model will be accounted for when you update the model.

This `DefiningQuery` will be a permanent addition to the BreakAway model, not the test model you used for `QueryViews`. Be sure to switch back to the BreakAway model when making these changes.

1. Create a new entity in the Designer, named `UpcomingTripParticipant`, and name its `EntitySet UpcomingTripParticipants`.
2. Add the following scalar properties, which match the result set of the query:
   - `ContactID` (`Type=Int32`, `Nullable=false`, `EntityKey=true`)
   - `TripID` (`Type=Int32`, `Nullable=false`, `EntityKey=true`)
   - `StartDate` (`DateTime`, `Nullable=false`)
   - `Name` (`String`, `Nullable=false`)
   - `Destination` (`String`, `Nullable=false`)

   Figure 16-3 displays the entity.

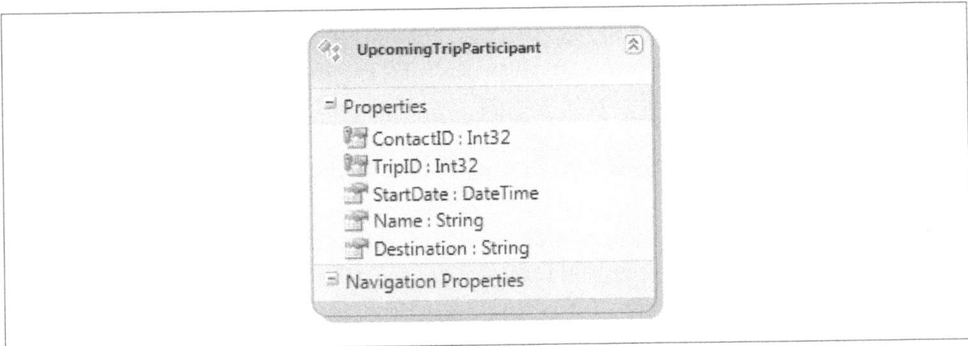

Figure 16-3. The manually created entity

3. Open the model in the XML Editor and scroll down to the `EntityContainer` element of the SSDL section. This is where you will add the `EntitySet` with the `DefiningQuery`.
4. Add the `EntitySet` and `DefiningQuery` element into the SSDL section:

```
<EntitySet Name="UpcomingTripParticipants" store:Type="Views"
                 EntityType="BreakAwayModel.Store.UpcomingTripParticipant">
  <DefiningQuery>
  </DefiningQuery>
</EntitySet>
```

The additional attributes that the `vOfficeAddress EntitySet` uses (i.e., `store:Schema` and `store:Name`) are not used here. Those attributes are necessary so that when the Update Model Wizard is called, the Designer knows how to resolve the views properly. Because the `EntitySet` you are creating does not exist in the database, those attributes are not required.

5. Within the `DefiningQuery` tags, enter the stored procedure listed in Example 16-7, with one exception. The XML will be confused by the `<`, so you will need to replace that character with an HTML-encoded version, `<` as shown here:

```
WHERE DATEDIFF(Day,Events.StartDate,GETDATE())&lt;=7
```

Alternatively, you can use a cleaner and more readable approach, which is to surround the entire command with a `CDATA` directive, as shown here:

```
<DefiningQuery>
  <![CDATA[
  SELECT  Contact.ContactID,
  Events.EventID AS TripID,
  RTrim(Contact.LastName) + ', ' + Contact.FirstName AS Name,
  Events.StartDate,
  Locations.LocationName as Destination
  FROM    Reservations
  INNER JOIN Events ON Reservations.EventID = Events.EventID
  AND Reservations.EventID = Events.EventID
```

```
    INNER JOIN Locations ON Events.LocationID = Locations.LocationID
    INNER JOIN Contact ON Reservations.ContactID = Contact.ContactID
    WHERE DATEDIFF(Day,Events.StartDate,GETDATE())<=7
    ]]>
  </DefiningQuery>
```

Next, you'll need to create the virtual table to which the `UpcomingTripParticipant` entity will map.

6. In the section where `EntityType` elements are defined within the SSDL, add the `UpcomingTripParticipant` virtual table:

```
<EntityType Name="UpcomingTripParticipant">
  <Key>
    <PropertyRef Name="ContactID"/>
  </Key>
  <Property Type="int" Name="ContactID" Nullable="false" />
  <Property Type="int" Name="TripID" Nullable="false" />
  <Property Type="datetime" Name="StartDate" Nullable="false" />
  <Property Type="char" Name="Name" Nullable="false" />
  <Property Type="char" Name="Destination" Nullable="false" />
</EntityType>
```

7. Save and close the model, and then open it in the Designer so that you can map the entity to the virtual table you just created. The mapping should look like Figure 16-4.

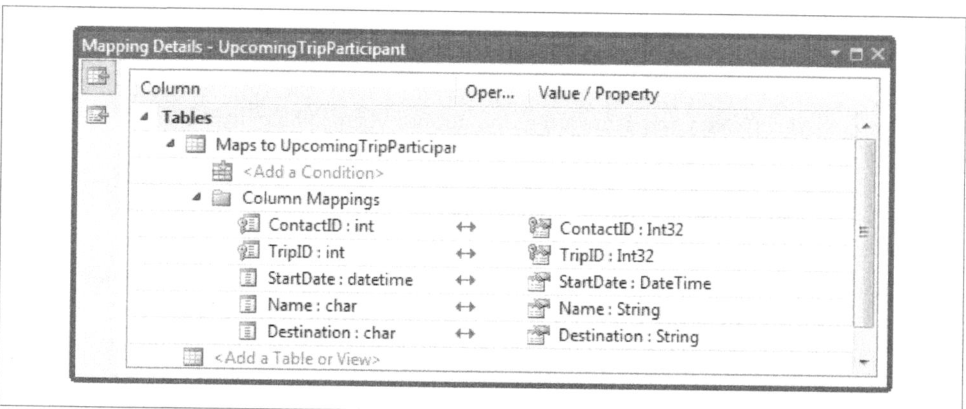

Figure 16-4. Mapping the new entity to the new virtual table

Now you can use the new `UpcomingTripParticipant` entity and `UpcomingTripParticipants` entity set as you would any others. Here, for example, is a LINQ to Entities query:

```
from p in context.UpcomingTripParticipants orderby p.Destination select p
```

On the server, the following command will be executed:

```
SELECT
[Extent1].[ContactID] AS [ContactID],
[Extent1].[TripID] AS [TripID],
[Extent1].[StartDate] AS [StartDate],
```

```
[Extent1].[Name] AS [Name],
[Extent1].[Destination] AS [Destination]
FROM (
              SELECT  Contact.ContactID,
              Events.EventID AS TripID,
              ( Contact.LastName ) + ', ' + Contact.FirstName AS Name,
              Events.StartDate,
              Locations.LocationName as Destination
              FROM    Reservations
              INNER JOIN Events ON Reservations.EventID = Events.EventID
              AND Reservations.EventID = Events.EventID
              INNER JOIN Locations ON Events.LocationID = Locations.LocationID
              INNER JOIN Contact ON Reservations.ContactID = Contact.ContactID
              WHERE   DATEDIFF(Day, Events.StartDate, GETDATE()) <= 7
            ) AS [Extent1]
ORDER BY [Extent1].[Destination] ASC
```

Creating Associations with the New Entity

Now that you have the entity in the model, you can create an association back to the `Contact` or `Trip` entity and tie right into the model and all of the other relationships. This will be a great benefit because you will be able to provide additional details from queries against `UpcomingTripParticipant`.

Although we know the relationship to be a One to Zero or One relationship, where there may be an `UpcomingTripParticipant` entity for a particular `Contact` or `Trip` but never more than one, you should not define the association as a 1:0..1. This "virtual" entity will create a problem when you attempt to delete a related entity. The model constraints will expect you to delete an `UpcomingTripParticipant` as well. With entities that are mapped to database tables, this is not a problem. In this case you can avoid this problem by defining a one-to-many relationship between `Contact` or `Trip` and `UpcomingTripParticipant`.

I'll create a 1:* relationship from `Customer` to the new entity. Notice in Figure 16-5 that I eliminated the navigation from `Customer` to `UpcomingTripParticipant` and unchecked the "Add foreign key" option.

It makes sense to navigate to `Customer` but not from `Customer`, and the foreign key is unnecessary since I already have `ContactID`.

Finally, add a referential constraint to the association between the two entities (see Figure 16-6).

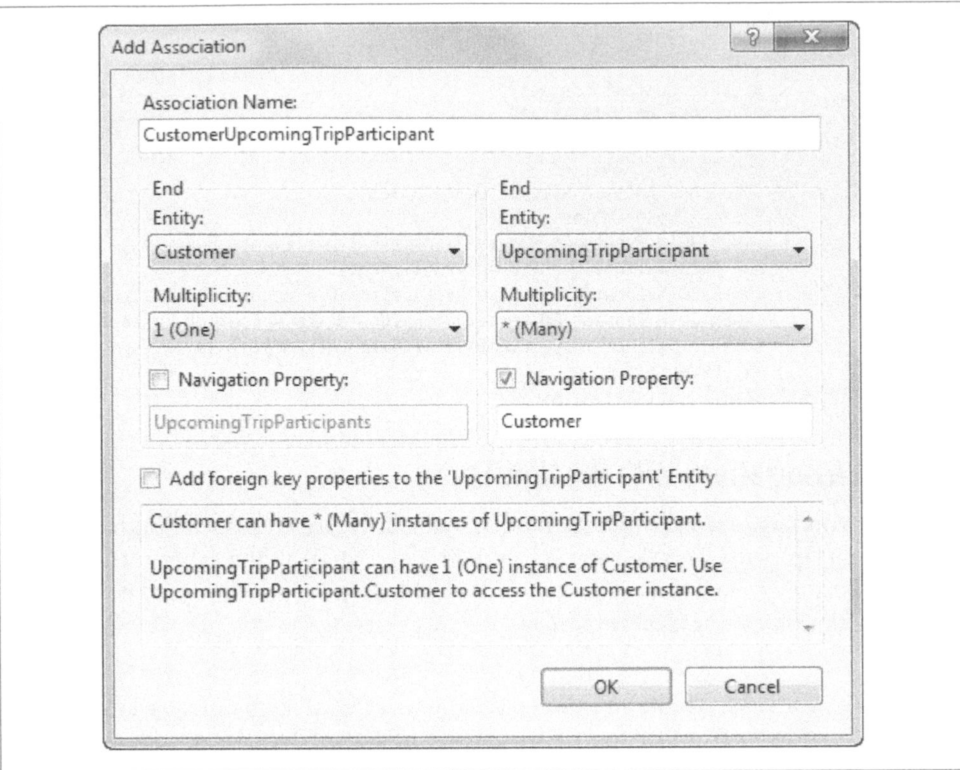

Figure 16-5. The association settings for relating the new entity to Customer

Testing the DefiningQuery in an association

Figure 16-7 shows a simple query of `UpcomingTripParticipants`, which eager-loads the related `Customer` entities. After executing the query and selecting one entity, you can see, via IntelliSense, that the `Customer` and all of its related entities are available as well. This makes `UpcomingTripParticipant` much more meaningful.

Don't forget that SSDL modifications are overwritten by the Update Model from Database Wizard. It's a harsh reality that you need to be prepared for. You might want to copy the SSDL modifications into a separate file so that you can push them back in quickly if you do overwrite the new elements.

Using DefiningQuery to Solve More Complex Problems

`DefiningQuery` also allows you to solve more complex problems. Here is another quote from Mike Pizzo, taken from the MSDN forums, describing the ability to create mappings that you cannot create with entities that map directly to tables:

> ...with DefiningQuery, you can map multiple entities to the same table outside of a type hierarchy, or a single entity to multiple rows within a single table (I did a demo at TechEd where I mapped an "Activity" Entity to a Sharepoint schema in which the properties of the Activity were actually mapped to different rows within a single "universal" table according to a row ordinal). The list goes on... In fact, every time I think I've found a mapping scenario that we don't support in Entity Framework 1.0, I find a way to do it using DefiningQuery.

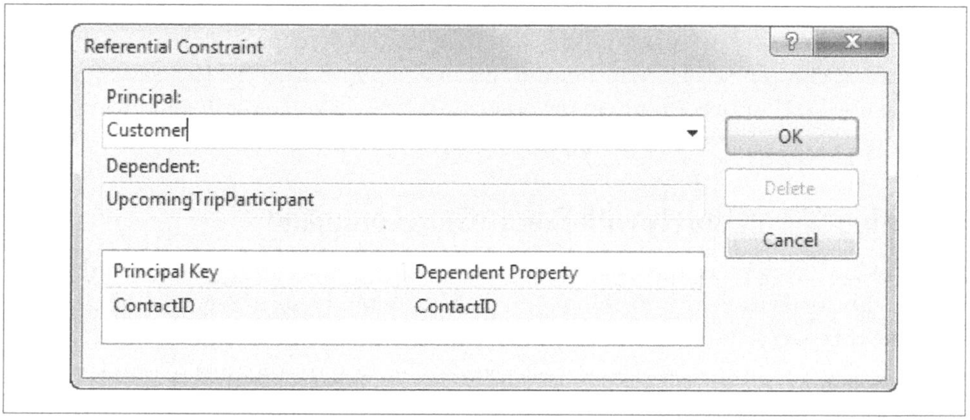

Figure 16-6. The referential constraint for the new association

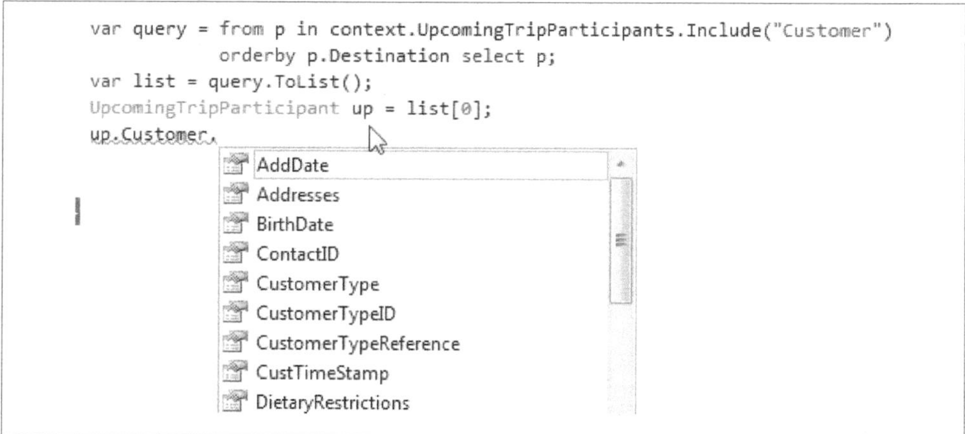

Figure 16-7. Navigating from the results of a DefiningQuery into other entities

Keep `DefiningQuery` in mind as a possible way to solve problems down the road that you might not even be dreaming of right now.

Using Commands That Affect the Database

So far, this chapter has focused on retrieving data from the database. In addition to the many views and stored procedures for read operations that have been implemented for your databases, you also probably have many Database Manipulation Language (DML) procedures for performing updates, inserts, and deletes.

In Chapter 7, you learned how to use the simplest form of these in the model, by performing function mapping for the `Insert`, `Update`, and `Delete` functions of particular entities and creating a function import to map read stored procedures to a entities, scalars, and complex types. You also did this in Chapter 8 with the `Payment` entity. Yet you can use DML procedures in many other scenarios. Leveraging them in your model and using them with the Entity Framework is possible, if not always pretty.

Executing SQL on the Fly with ExecuteStoreCommand

`ExecuteStoreCommand` is the last of the set of direct execution methods that are new to Entity Framework in .NET 4. You have already seen `ExecuteFunction` and `ExecuteStoreQuery`.

In Chapter 6, you learned how to use `ObjectContext.DeleteObject` to delete data from the database. The downside to this method is that it requires the entity to be in memory. This means that if you simply wish to delete data in the database, you first need to query that data, and then delete it and save the changes back to the database. At that time, I hinted at a simpler way to do this, and I was talking about `ExecuteStoreCommand`.

With `ExecuteStoreCommand` you could send a store delete command directly to the database and have it executed immediately.

You'll want to prevent possible SQL injection attacks, so always use parameters. There are two ways to send parameters along with your commands. The first is to use the substitution pattern that you may be familiar with for formatting strings:

```
context.ExecuteStoreCommand
  ("DELETE FROM ContactPersonalInfo WHERE ContactID={0}",contactid);
```

The second is to use `DbParameters`, such as `System.Data.SqlClient.SqlParameter`:

```
var param = new SqlParameter { ParameterName = "p0", Value = contactid };
context.ExecuteStoreCommand
  ("DELETE FROM ContactPersonalInfo WHERE ContactID=@p0", param);
```

Be mindful of the fact that if you use a specific provider's parameter, such as `SqlClient.SqlParameter`, your code will work only with that provider. If you want to be more generic in case you switch databases, consider using ADO.NET's `DbProviderFactory`, which you can learn about at *http://msdn.microsoft.com/en-us/library/wda6c36e.aspx*.

Both will result in the same parameterized store query, where the value of `ContactID` was `241`:

```
exec sp_executesql
N'DELETE FROM ContactPersonalInfo
WHERE ContactID=@p0',N'@p0 int',
@p0=241
```

Using Functions to Manipulate Data in the Database

With a function you can inject a simple command, perhaps a delete command that you would like to be part of the model, or even complex commands, such as ones that modify data in the database and also return data.

The BreakAway database has a stored procedure called `CreateCustomerfromContact`. This is an important function for BreakAway's business model. The company has many contacts who are potential customers, yet they are not officially customers until they book their first trip. That's when BreakAway begins to track more details regarding the customer with a row in the `Customers` table. Sometimes the company needs to create a new `Customer` that does not already have a `Contact` record in the database, and the inheritance in the model takes care of that.

But if the `Contact` record already exists and you want to create a new `Customer` record to tie back to that `Contact`, inserting a `Customer` entity won't work, because that will attempt to insert a new `Contact` as well.

`CreateCustomerfromContact` solves this problem, and not only extends the `Contact` to be a `Customer` but also passes back the newly created `Customer` so that it can be used immediately. It takes a `ContactID` as a parameter, inserts a new row into the `Customer` table using that `ContactID`, and then returns a complete `Customer`. Here is the T-SQL for the procedure:

```
INSERT INTO customers (ContactID,customers.[InitialDate])
VALUES (@contactid,GETDATE())

INSERT INTO ContactPersonalInfo (ContactID) VALUES (@contactid)

SELECT Customers.*,
 Contact.FirstName, Contact.LastName, Contact.Title, Contact.AddDate,
 Contact.ModifiedDate, CPI.BirthDate,  CPI.HeightInches,
 CPI.WeightPounds, CPI.DietaryRestrictions
FROM Customers INNER JOIN
  Contact ON Customers.ContactID = Contact.ContactID INNER JOIN
  ContactPersonalInfo CPI ON Customers.ContactID = CPI.ContactID
  WHERE Customers.ContactID=@contactID
```

The results map directly back to a `Customer` entity—almost. Unfortunately, we've changed some of the property names in the entity and they don't match up with the column names of the `Customers` table in the database. If they did, you could simply create the `FunctionImport`, map it back to the `Customer` entity, and then go ahead and execute the method from the `BAEntities` context, as shown in Example 16-8.

Example 16-8. Calling function that updates the database and returns data

```
Customer newCust=context.CreateCustomerfromContact(contactID).SingleOrDefault();
```

But since the results don't line up with the `Customer` entity, you'll have a few options to choose from. One is to modify the stored procedure in the database. The next option is to create a complex type that matches the return of this procedure, but that would mean the results would not be a customer unless you take the results and push them into a customer.

A third option is to leverage the `CommandText` element of the existing `Function` element that you learned about earlier in this chapter. You can embed your own version of the command into the `Function` element, which the wizard created for this procedure, and override the use of the stored procedure in the database.

Here is what the function looks like as defined by the wizard:

```
<Function Name="CreateCustomerfromContact" Aggregate="false" BuiltIn="false"
          NiladicFunction="false" IsComposable="false"
          ParameterTypeSemantics="AllowImplicitConversion" Schema="dbo">
  <Parameter Name="contactID" Type="int" Mode="In" />
</Function>
```

After you have modified the command to rename the columns so that they match the `Customer` entity, Example 16-9 is what the function looks like with the new `CommandText` element.

Example 16-9. Defining a complex command in the SSDL

```
<Function Name="CreateCustomerfromContact" Aggregate="false" BuiltIn="false"
          NiladicFunction="false" IsComposable="false"
          ParameterTypeSemantics="AllowImplicitConversion" Schema="dbo">
  <CommandText>
    INSERT  INTO customers( ContactID, customers.[InitialDate] )
    VALUES  ( @contactid, GETDATE() )

    INSERT  INTO ContactPersonalInfo ( ContactID )
    VALUES  ( @contactid )

    SELECT  Customers.ContactID,CustomerTypeID,InitialDate,
    PrimaryDesintation AS PrimaryDestinationID,
    SecondaryDestination AS SecondaryDestinationID,
    PrimaryActivity AS PrimaryActivityID,
    SecondaryActivity AS SecondaryActivityID,
    Notes,Customers.RowVersion AS CustRowVersion,
    Contact.FirstName, Contact.LastName, Contact.Title, Contact.AddDate,
    Contact.ModifiedDate, Contact.RowVersion, CPI.BirthDate, CPI.HeightInches,
    CPI.WeightPounds,CPI.DietaryRestrictions
    FROM    Customers
    INNER JOIN Contact ON Customers.ContactID = Contact.ContactID
    INNER JOIN ContactPersonalInfo CPI ON Customers.ContactID = CPI.ContactID
```

```
    WHERE   Customers.ContactID = @contactid
  </CommandText>
  <Parameter Name="contactID" Type="int" Mode="In" />
</Function>
```

Now you can create a `FunctionImport` for this new function and set its return type to `Customer`. Then you can call the function as shown earlier in Example 16-8.

You can also import functions for stored procedures that impact the database and do not return any data. In the Function Import dialog, select None as the return type for the function.

Changing from one derived type to another

There are a few things to consider when calling this method.

The first is to know whether the contact is already a customer. The stored procedure could be modified to handle that logic. Currently, it is written with the assumption that you are already confident that the incoming ID is for a contact who is not yet a customer. That would require that your code has logic to verify the contact's status prior to calling the function. If the contact is in memory, you can check its type easily enough. If it is not in memory, you'll have to query for it. It might be a lot easier just to have the stored procedure deal with the validation and return the already existing `Customer` record if necessary.

The second consideration is if the contact that you are converting is in memory. If it is in memory, you would have a conflict when the new customer is returned. That's because the original contact would be a `NonCustomer` type of `Contact`. When you call the function and it attempts to return a `Contact` with the same `ContactID` but of a different type, you will get an exception. The `Customer` will have been created; the problem is just a conflict when an attempt is made to add the newly returned `Customer` into the context.

Both of these considerations require that you check the existing context for the `Contact` to be converted.

The second consideration then requires that if the `Contact` is indeed in memory, you should remove it before doing the conversion. You can do this by first detaching the `Contact` from the context (which rids the context of the relevant `ObjectStateEntry`) and then setting the `Contact` to `null`, which removes it from memory completely.

Example 16-10 shows a method that does a few more checks and balances and retrieves the newly created customer.

When you are creating the function import, you can use the Get Column Information feature to check the schema of the results, even though you won't be creating a complex type from that information.

Before the method executes the function, it first tests to ensure that the contact already exists in the database and that it is not already a customer.

Example 16-10. Using a function to turn an existing contact into a customer

```
public static Customer ConvertContacttoCustomer(int contactID, BAEntities context)
{
  ObjectStateEntry contactStub;
  bool inMemory =
  context.ObjectStateManager.TryGetObjectStateEntry
    (new System.Data.EntityKey("BAEntities.Contacts", "ContactID", contactID),
     out contactStub);

  if (inMemory)
  {
    //remove contact from the context and then from memory
    Contact inMemContact = (Contact)contactStub.Entity;
    context.Detach(inMemContact);
    inMemContact = null;
  }
  //call the function which returns a customer
  return context.CreateCustomerfromContact(contactID).SingleOrDefault();
}
```

Mapping Insert/Update/Delete to Types Within an Inheritance Structure

One more rule regarding stored procedures in the EDM may come as a surprise, whether you are using the Designer or implementing the stored procedures by hand.

When mapping stored procedures to base or derived types, you are also required to map the stored procedures to any other type within the inheritance structure. Therefore, if you map a function to a base type, you must also map a function to its derived types. Conversely, mapping to a derived type, such as `Customer`, requires that you also map functions to the base type (`Contact`) and any other derived types (`NonCustomer`). If you forget this rule, the compiler will happily remind you with an error message. The following error message, which results when you have mapped to the `Customer` entity but not the `Contact`, is an example:

```
If an EntitySet mapping includes a function binding, function bindings
must be included for all types. The following types do not have function
bindings: BreakAwayModel.Contact.
```

Default Command Generation Versus Stored Procedures for Inherited Types

When SaveChanges performs insert and delete operations on a Customer in the BreakAway model, it will create and execute three separate commands: one for the Contact table, one for the Customer table, and one for the ContactPersonalInfo table. The command(s) created for an update depend on which properties have been modified. Using a stored procedure, which internalizes the work on these three tables, you can reduce Customer modifications to a single call to the database. For example, a single insert stored procedure could contain the three Insert commands to insert into the three relevant tables. That would mean one trip to the database instead of three.

On the other hand, an update stored procedure predefines which properties are passed to the database for an update, regardless of which properties have changed. When the Entity Framework creates the commands, the commands are more efficient because only the modified properties are sent as parameters. Depending on how your stored procedure is written, this could be seen as a benefit of using the Entity Framework's default query and command processing over stored procedures.

What If Stored Procedures Affect Multiple Entities in an Inheritance Structure?

You can take a few approaches when working with stored procedures. The procedures in the BreakAway database take the more standard route, which is to simply perform the tasks at hand. The database contains stored procedures for performing inserts, updates, and deletes on customers as well as contacts. InsertCustomer, UpdateCustomer, and DeleteCustomer interact with the Customer, Contact, and ContactPersonalInfo tables, and InsertContact, UpdateContact, and DeleteContact interact with only the Contact table.

When the Entity Framework uses these stored procedures it will not overlap them. When saving changes to Customers it will call only the Customer entity's functions. When saving changes to Contacts it will call only the Contact entity's functions.

You can try to map these functions, or just be prepared for when you are defining your own model with inherited entities and stored procedures.

Implementing and Querying with User-Defined Functions (UDFs)

Many databases allow you to create your own functions, called user-defined functions, or UDFs. In SQL Server, these can be table-valued functions, scalar functions, or array functions. The Entity Framework's EDM supports UDFs, with the exception of table-valued functions.

The EDM Wizard and the Update Model Wizard list UDFs along with stored procedures in the Stored Procedures node. Like stored procedures, UDFs are resolved as functions in the store layer of your model.

In the BreakAway database, because a customer's weight is stored in U.S. pounds, a function is defined to convert pounds into kilograms. It's called `ufnLBtoKG`. If you were to select this UDF in either of the wizards, you would find the following function in the SSDL section of the EDMX file:

```
<Function Name="ufnLBtoKG" ReturnType="nvarchar" Aggregate="false"
          BuiltIn="false" NiladicFunction="false" IsComposable="true"
          ParameterTypeSemantics="AllowImplicitConversion" Schema="dbo">
  <Parameter Name="Pounds" Type="int" Mode="In" />
</Function>
```

Notice that the `IsComposable` attribute is `true`. This is different from the stored procedures whose `IsComposable` attribute must be `false`. You can use UDFs as parts of queries.

Another big difference between UDFs and stored procedures is that you call UDFs directly from the store layer rather than doing function mapping and calling them from the conceptual model.

This means that by default the functions are not available in LINQ. You can access them easily in Entity SQL statements, which you can then use with `ObjectQuery` or with `EntityClient`. If you think back to how you created a LINQ query function for the model-defined function in Chapter 15, you will discover that you can use the same `EDMFunction` attribute to allow using UDF functions in LINQ queries.

Example 16-11 uses the `ufnLBtoKG` function with Entity SQL. You will find that there is a surprising difference between this expression and those you wrote earlier. This is because the function is only in the store.

The example will return a list of customer names, their weight in pounds, and their weight in kilograms.

Because `Customer` is a derived type, you will need to use the `TREAT AS` Entity SQL operator that you learned about in Chapter 14. Remember that Entity SQL points back to the assembly namespace, not the model namespace, when casting to derived types.

Example 16-11. Querying with a UDF

```
var esql = "select TREAT(c as BAGA.Customer).WeightPounds," +
           "BreakAwayModel.Store" +
           ".ufnLBtoKG(TREAT(c as BAGA.Customer).WeightPounds) " +
           "from BAEntities.Contacts AS c where c is of(BAGA.Customer)";
var query = context.CreateQuery<DbDataRecord>(esql);
var weightList = query.ToList();
```

Remember that `DbDataRecord` is in the `System.Data.Common` namespace. You'll need a `using` or `Imports` statement for the namespace at the beginning of your code file.

Notice how the function is called: `BreakAwayModel.Store.ufnLBtoKG`. It is using the full name of the function in the store layer, not the CSDL.

In fact, if you use function mapping to map this function back to the conceptual layer, at runtime you will get the following error when executing a query that uses the function:

```
"A FunctionImport is mapped to a storage function 'BreakAwayModel.Store.ufnLBtoKG'
that can be composed. Only stored procedure functions may be mapped."
```

The reason is that Entity Framework does not currently support mapping UDFs into the model. This is why you must access it directly from the SSDL.

Summary

As you learned in this chapter, the Entity Framework supports stored procedures in many more ways than the Designer-supported function mappings. And there's not much that you can't pull off. You've seen how to execute stored procedures on the fly, build them directly into the model, work with queries that return data or persist data to the database, and so much more. The only drawback is that in some cases, much more manual effort may be involved than you might want to employ.

For some *read* stored procedures, you may find that it is easier to create a view that returns a similarly shaped result and implement that in your model instead of the stored procedure. You can also define native stored procedures directly in your model for reading or writing to the database. Some of the functions that result from stored procedures can be called as a method of the `ObjectContext`, whereas others must be called from `EntityConnection`.

For organizations that have an investment in stored procedures but want to leverage the model and the change tracking of the Entity Framework, additional effort will be required to get the best of both worlds.

CHAPTER 17

Using EntityObjects in WCF Services

Services are a critical part of today's (and tomorrow's) application environments. You can use entities in service applications, and depending on your needs you can approach the task of using the Entity Framework with services in a number of ways. You can build your own Entity Framework logic into a Windows Communication Foundation (WCF) service, or use a framework that leverages it, such as WCF Data Services or WCF Rich Internet Applications (RIA) Data Services.

It is also possible to use entities in Active Server Method (ASMX) web services, which are still supported in Visual Studio 2010. You can download the ASMX sample created in the first edition of this book from the downloads page of the book's website (*http://www.learnentityframework.com*). Note, however, that the sample does not benefit from any of the new features of Entity Framework, such as foreign keys or POCO support.

In this chapter, we'll take a look at all three scenarios. First, you will write a WCF service that makes use of `EntityObject`-based entities and learn about some of the complications that arise (and their solutions) while you work across the tiers of a distributed application. Even if you don't plan to write your services with `EntityObjects`, you will find a lot of useful information in this chapter. We'll also take a quick look at WCF Data Services and WCF RIA Services in order to get an understanding of how they relate to the Entity Framework.

WCF Data Services and WCF RIA Services are Microsoft's solutions for encapsulating much of the logic that you would otherwise have to code manually (as you'll be doing in the next two chapters). Data Services provides the raw data from the model through a queryable URL, while RIA Services is more familiar, providing service operations. With RIA Services, much of the change tracking, authorization, and authentication are handled automatically. If you do not need ultimate control over your service operations, you should definitely consider both of these technologies. Although digging deep into these topics is out of scope for this book, you'll get a quick look at them in the next two chapters and can find myriad resources to continue your education.

In the next chapter, you'll get a chance to use POCOs in services as well as Entity Framework's new self-tracking entities, a specially designed set of POCO classes and other supporting classes that were designed specifically for using entities in WCF.

Services are much easier to write using POCO classes, but because `EntityObject` is inherited by the default classes generated from an Entity Framework Entity Data Model, many developers will want to know how to work with `EntityObjects` in their services.

In addition to building services in this chapter, you'll create a simple console application to consume the `EntityObject`-based service and then reuse it for the WCF data service later in the chapter.

If you have never built a WCF service before, have no fear. The walk-throughs will provide you with step-by-step details.

Planning for an Entity Framework–Agnostic Client

In this chapter, the samples depend on the Entity Framework on the server side only. The clients that consume the services use a simplified version of the classes that the services provide. The client will not perform any database connections, change tracking, relationship management, or anything else that depends on Object Services. This means not only that your client does not have to install the Entity Framework APIs—or your own model, for that matter—but also that you can build clients that are not even written in .NET, as long as they follow the services' rules. Figure 17-1 displays how the client application interacts only with the service.

You will use a .NET client in this chapter so that you can get some hands-on experience manipulating the objects returned by these services as well as interacting with the services themselves.

Unless you want to take advantage of Object Services on the client side, for the sake of either change tracking or relationship management, there's no reason to reference your model assembly or the Entity Framework in the client at all. As you learned in Chapter 10, the `ObjectContext` along with any `ObjectStateEntry` objects do not get serialized when your entities move from a service to a client or from a client to a service. Even if you had Entity Framework on the client side to handle change tracking, you would still lose any changes you make on the client when you send the objects back to the service.

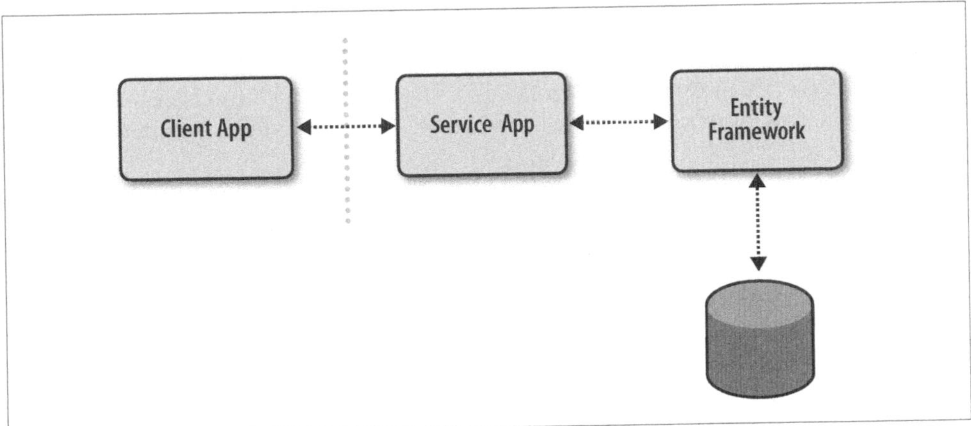

Figure 17-1. Client application consuming a WCF Service without a need for direct interaction with the Entity Framework

Assessing the Pros and Cons of an Entity Framework–Agnostic Consumer

Without the Entity Framework APIs in the client application, you will be faced with a few additional challenges that you should have some experience handling. You'll find in this chapter's WCF example that the lack of references to the model and `System.Data.Entity` is noticeable and educational.

For one thing, `EntityCollections` won't exist on the client, as they are a class in the `System.Data.Entity` assembly. As a result, the children of an object are contained in a `List` rather than an `EntityCollection`. You'll see how it is necessary to explicitly instantiate the `Reservations` property of a new customer by calling `Customer.Reservations = new List<Reservations>`.

Another example is that you don't automatically get two-way relationship navigation. If you add a `Reservation` to a `Customer`, you will find that `Reservation` in `Customer.Reservations`, but `Reservation.Customer` will return null. If you needed to navigate in both directions, you would have to explicitly bind them in both ways (e.g., additionally calling `Reservation.Customer=myCustomer`). This is similar to the explicit two-way navigation fix-up you looked at in Chapter 13 when building POCO classes.

This is not to say that excluding the references in the model assembly and `System.Data.Entity` is a bad thing. In many scenarios your business rules may prevent you from having the client depend on these things, so it's very useful to see how to build clients in this way. On the other hand, those references can be a welcome inclusion in some situations. The relationship management will be simpler, and although you will get change tracking on the client, keep in mind that the changes stored in the `ObjectStateEntry` objects will be lost when transferring the objects back to the service. Although you already learned about the `ObjectStateEntry` objects, you will learn more about this problem, and solutions for it, in later chapters. My personal preference is to keep the Entity Framework APIs out of the client.

Returning EntityObjects from a Service: Good or Bad?

If you are using the default code generator for your model, your entity classes all inherit from `EntityObject`. Creating service operations that return and receive `EntityObject` classes makes for simple programming, but is it recommended?

There's an age-old debate along these lines about transmitting ADO.NET `DataSets` or `DataTables` in services as well. The biggest reason not to send `DataSets` or `DataTables` is because it makes your service difficult to consume by non-.NET clients.

I prefer not to pass `EntityObjects` between my service and client. As the needs of my service or consumers of my service get more complex, it becomes more difficult to work around the boundaries of `EntityObjects`.

With the advent of Entity Framework's POCO support in .NET 4, I recommend to my clients to use POCO classes for their WCF services rather than `EntityObject` classes.

As you work through the sample in this chapter where `EntityObjects` are used in the service, and then samples in the next chapter where you'll use POCO classes in WCF services, you'll see how the POCO classes simplify many of the tasks that become chores with `EntityObjects`.

Serialized `EntityObjects` are also very fat. They have a lot of `EntityObject`- and Entity Framework-specific schema information in them that you will have no use for on the client side.

This is not to say that you should never use the `EntityObject` classes in services. It is certainly supported and your needs may be satisfied with the `EntityObjects`. As you'll see in the first example, the most obvious use case would be if your service does not need to support updates or at least updates that involve graphs.

If you are building a consumer in .NET, the Visual Studio proxy generator (result of using the Add Service Reference feature) makes it simple to use the classes that are being returned from the service, even if the client is not using Entity Framework.

But in the end, when you want to have more control over the classes that are sent to your client, you will find that using POCO classes is much simpler. You can construct your own POCO classes, use the POCO template provided ADO.NET POCO Entity Generator extensions for Visual Studio 2010, or use the template that builds the self-tracking entities (which are also POCOs) and their supporting classes. The next chapter will be entirely devoted to POCOs in services.

Building a Simple WCF Service with EntityObjects

The WCF sample you'll build in this section will work with graphs and deal with the challenges introduced by performing updates on graphs that have come across a tier. As your first foray into WCF with Entity Framework, this will be a simple CRUD service with explicit operations exposed for read, insert, update, and delete for a single type,

`Customer`. However, within the operations, you will be dealing with a `Customer` graph that contains `Reservations` and `Trip` details.

With the other options available for creating services in Entity Framework 4 (POCOs or even self-tracking entities) you may never choose `EntityObjects` for your service. As stated earlier, it is not my personal preference, but you still may find it beneficial to see what it takes to implement a service in this way. There will be scenarios where you simply want to use the out-of-the-box default classes, and therefore you may be going this route with your service. If nothing more, it will give you an appreciation for the simplicity of using POCOs or self-tracking entities.

Creating a WCF service begins with defining a set of interfaces that represent contracts for the necessary operations. Then you will implement those interfaces as methods in a separate code file.

The goal of this service will be to allow the consuming application to create new reservations for existing customers. It will need to have the following capabilities:

- Provide a list of customers for the end user to choose from.
- Provide a customer record for a single customer.
- Provide the existing reservations along with trip details for a single customer.
- Provide a list of upcoming trips so that new reservations can be created.
- Delete existing reservations.
- Update changes to the customer details.

Creating the Service

We'll start by creating a WCF Service Application project:

1. Add a new WCF Service Application project from the Web tab of the Add New Project dialog into the solution you've been working with. I've named mine CustomerWCFServiceApp.

   Don't forget to be sure you are targeting .NET Framework 4.0 when creating new projects in this chapter.

   Note that the project has one file named *IService1* and another named *Service1*. Notice that *Service1* is not a *.vb* or *.cs* file, but an *.svc* file. That is a pointer to the actual service that your consuming application will interact with.

2. Rename *Service1.svc* to *CustomerService.svc*.

3. Rename *IService1.cs/.vb* to *ICustomerService.cs/.vb*.

   You will use `ICustomerService` to describe what the service will do. It contains a list of the operations, but doesn't have the code for implementing them. This type of file is referred to as an *interface*, which is a very common programming construct. In WCF, this interface acts as a "contract," or a promise, regarding what to expect of the service. Also in this file, you can define additional data types that can be used to send data to or from the service. These are referred to as *data contracts*.

4. Open the *ICustomerService* file and rename the `IService1` interface to `ICustomerService`. Be sure to follow the instructions in the comment at the top of the file for renaming because Visual Studio needs to change the name in a number of places for you. In Visual Studio 2010, renaming WCF interfaces and classes does a more thorough job than previously.

5. Open the *CustomerService* file. You'll see that the `Service1` class now implements the renamed `ICustomerService` interface. Rename the `Service1` class to `CustomerService`.

6. Add project references to `System.Data.Entity` and to the BreakAwayModel project.

7. Copy the `ConnectionStrings` section from the BreakAwayModel project's *app.config* file to the *web.config* file.

Defining the Service Operations

Operation contracts are defined in the interface, `ICustomerService`. Each method has an `OperationContract` attribute to indicate that it is an operation that is part of the contract for your service.

1. Open the *ICustomerService* file.
2. Delete the default (example) operations for `GetData` and `GetDataUsingDataContract`.
3. Add an `Imports` or `using` statement to the class for `BAGA`.
4. Add the `OperationContract` methods in Example 17-1 into the `ICustomerService` interface.

Example 17-1. Defining the service operation contracts

```
[OperationContract]
List<CustomerNameAndID> GetCustomerPickList();

[OperationContract]
List<Trip> GetUpcomingTrips();

[OperationContract]
Customer GetCustomer(int customerId);

[OperationContract]
string UpdateCustomer(Customer customer);

[OperationContract]
```

```
string InsertCustomer(Customer customer);

[OperationContract]
string DeleteCustomer(int customerId);
```

Visual Basic attributes are contained in angle brackets, not square brackets. The first method would look like this:

```
<OperationContract>
Function GetCustomerPickList As String
```

Defining Extra Service Classes

While most of the operations work with entity types (`Customer`, `CustomerNameandID`, and `Trip`), there is one method that will need a special type. The `UpdateCustomer` method currently expects a `Customer` to be returned. Since this service will be working with `Customer` graphs that include `Reservations`, there is a special scenario that will require `UpdateCustomer` to expect additional information.

WCF services allow you to define types that are particular to the service. As each expected operation is referred to as an `OperationContract`, each special type is called a `DataContract` and is defined by a `DataContract` attribute.

With a `DataContract`, the contract will say, "Not only will I provide this set of operations, but I also will send and receive data that has the following schema." By creating classes that are `DataContracts`, the service can provide this information in the commonly understood description of the service supplied by a *Web Service Description Language* (WSDL) file, and both the service and the client can use it easily. Each property you need to serialize is flagged as a `DataMember`.

Now to the special case. While we have an operation to delete a customer, what about the scenario where an end user has deleted a `Reservation` from an existing customer? That reservation to be deleted would need to be marked on the client side as "to be deleted" and then returned as part of the `Customer` graph. That will take a bit of extra coding in the consumer app. Instead, the service will allow the consumer to simply return a list of `ReservationIDs` to be deleted along with the `Customer` graph that is returned to the `UpdateCustomer` operation. That means we'll need to create a type that accepts a `Customer` graph and a list of integers to represent the `ReservationID` targeted for deletion.

We'll create a new type called `CustomerUpdate` with two properties to represent this data. The first property will encapsulate the `Customer` object (which will be a graph including the customer's reservations and the trip details for each reservation). The second property, `ReservationsToDelete`, is a `List` of integers.

Add the class in Example 17-2 to the *ICustomerService* file below the interface. There is a default `CompositeType` class that you can delete.

Example 17-2. Creating the DataContract class

```
[DataContract()]
public class CustomerUpdate
{
  [DataMember()]
  public BAGA.Customer Customer  {get; set;}

  [DataMember()]
  public List<int> ReservationsToDelete{get; set;}
}
```

Modify the `UpdateCustomer` operation so that it takes a `CustomerUpdate` type, as shown in Example 17-3. I've also changed the variable name to `customerUpdate`.

Example 17-3. Fixing the UpdateCustomer operation signature

```
[OperationContract]
string UpdateCustomer(CustomerUpdate customerUpdate);
```

Entity or DataContract? Leveraging the QueryView-based Entity from Chapter 15

In Chapter 15, you created a new entity, `CustomerNameandID`, which was populated by a `QueryView` in the mapping layer. The `GetCustomerPickList` operation will return a list of this special type to be used by the consuming application as a pick list. If the type did not exist in the model, you could have created an additional `DataContract` type in the service contract to represent this view of the `Customer`. Because it is in the model, that isn't necessary. But you'll see another case later in the chapter where the additional `DataContract` is not an option and the fact that the entity is in the model is even more beneficial.

Exposing Custom Properties

Although the code-generated entity classes and their properties are marked with `DataContract` and `DataMember` attributes by default, the custom properties that you have created in earlier chapters are not. The service will be more useful if it can provide the `TripDetail` property that you added to the `Trip` and `Reservation` classes in Chapter 11. To make this property available as part of the WCF service payload, you'll need to add the `DataMember` attribute.

When doing so, you have one more serialization rule to satisfy. `DataMembers` must have both a getter and a setter to be serializable. Otherwise, you will get an error in the service that is using the class.

Open the `Trip`'s partial class in the model project and modify the `TripDetails` property by adding the `DataMember` attribute and the `set` clause, as shown in Example 17-4.

Example 17-4. Modifying the Trip in the partial class of the EDM

```
[System.Runtime.Serialization.DataMember]
public string TripDetails
{
  get
  {
    //existing code
  }
  set{}
}
```

Do the same for the `TripDetails` property of the `Reservation` partial class so that you can use `Reservation.TripDetails` on the client side.

Implementing the Service Interface

Now it's time to add some logic to the operations that are based on the interface. You'll do this in the `CustomerService` class.

1. Remove the default methods (`GetData` and `GetDataUsingDataContract`).
2. Import the `BAGA` namespace into the class with `using` or `Imports`.
3. Implement the `ICustomerService` interface.

   You'll do this differently in VB and C#. In VB, place your cursor at the end of the `Implements ICustomerService` line of code and press the Enter key. In C#, right-click on `ICustomerService` in the class declaration, select Implement Interface from the context menu, and select Implement Interface from that context menu's submenu. All of the methods defined in the interface will be stubbed out for you.
4. Add the code for `GetCustomerPickList` shown in Example 17-5. It will be up to consumers how to combine the `FirstName` and `LastName` properties in their logic and UI.

   Example 17-5. Filling in the logic for the GetCustomerPickList method

   ```
   public List<BAGA.CustomerNameAndID> GetCustomerPickList()
   {
     using (var context = new BAEntities())
     {
       return context.CustomerNameAndIDs
                     .OrderBy(c => c.LastName + c.FirstName).ToList();
     }
   }
   ```

   Notice that the code in this method creates a new context and disposes it within the scope of the method. This is the pattern you should always use for service operations. See the following sidebar "Services Demand Short-Lived ObjectContext" to understand why.

Services Demand Short-Lived ObjectContext

When executing queries in the web service, you want your context and connection to be as short-lived as possible. You should create the context, execute the query (causing the context to open the connection and then close it when the data has been retrieved), and then get rid of the context immediately. With the possibility that many clients will make many calls to your services, you don't want to have any of those contexts or connections hanging around in memory or they could cause unexpected results. Imagine one user calling an update operation that calls `SaveChanges` on a context being used by many users.

Therefore, each operation that needs a context should instantiate and dispose a new context.

5. Supply the logic for the `GetUpcomingTrips` operation:

```
public List<Trip> GetUpcomingTrips()
{
  using (var context = new BAEntities())
  {
    //Serialization will attempt to load navigation properties
    // if lazy loading is enabled.
    context.ContextOptions.LazyLoadingEnabled = false;
    return context.Trips.Where(t => t.StartDate > DateTime.Today).ToList();
  }
}
```

It is very important to disable lazy loading for services before returning the resultant data. If lazy loading is on, while WCF is serializing the results it will attempt to load every navigation property in each entity in the result set. For example, a reservation will load its customer, and the customer will load its preferences. The reservation will also load its trip, the trip its destination, and so forth. If the context is unavailable to execute the lazy loading (which it should be at the point the data is being serialized) the serialization will fail. If you have allowed the context to remain in scope by not disposing it, the lazy loading will occur but it will be performed first for related entities, and then for their relationships, and then for the relationships' relationships, and so on.

6. Add the code for `GetCustomer` (see Example 17-6).

   Here we return a `Customer` graph that includes the customer's reservations, the trip information for the reservations, and the location information for the trips. This will satisfy the requirement for the consuming application to be able to view a customer and the customer's existing reservations.

Example 17-6. Logic for the GetCustomer method

```
public Customer GetCustomer(int custID)
{
```

```
    using (var context = new BAEntities())
    {
      context.ContextOptions.LazyLoadingEnabled = false;
      var cust =
          from c in context.Contacts.OfType<Customer>()
            .Include("Reservations.Trip.Destination")
          where c.ContactID == custID
          select c;
      return cust.Single();
    }
  }
```

7. Add the code in Example 17-7 to the `InsertCustomer` method.

Example 17-7. Code for the InsertCustomer method

```
public string InsertCustomer(BAGA.Customer cust)
{
   if (cust.CustomerTypeID==0)
     { cust.CustomerTypeID = 1; }
  try
  {
    using (var context = new BAEntities())
    {
      RemoveTripsFromGraph(cust);
      context.Contacts.AddObject(cust);
      context.SaveChanges();
    }
    return cust.ContactID.ToString();
  }
  catch (Exception ex)
  {
    string errorMessage="";
    //TODO: construct a message to return to the client
    return errorMessage;
  }
}
```

There are a number of things to note about inserting new customers.

The first is that default values defined in the model for scalar properties are not serialized with `EntityObjects`. Therefore, you will not get the default value you defined for the foreign key, `CustomerTypeID`. This property is non-nullable and required.

The next is the `RemoveTripsFromGraph` method. Thanks to the way the `ObjectContext` works with related objects, adding the new `Customer` to the context also adds any reservations that are attached to it. However, if there are `Trips` attached to those `Reservations`, `AddObject` will fail because the `Trip` object will have a `TripID` but the `Trip`'s `EntityKey` will be null. If the consumer has defined the relationship by setting the `Reservation.Trip` property rather than `Reservation.TripID`, you'll also find that `Reservation.TripID` is null. The helper method, `RemoveTripsFromGraph`, which you'll see shortly, will fix this problem for us. This is another example of the type of problem you will run into when depending on the `EntityObjects` generated by the default template.

Testing the WCF Services and Operations, and Viewing the Payload

You can verify that the service runs by viewing it in the browser. Although the .NET SDK provides a WCFTestClient utility for testing operations without having to write a consumer, it is unable to display responses that contain `EntityObjects`. Using Visual Studio's Unit Testing feature is complicated with WCF services. The console app that I'll use to interact with the services is the simplest way to go.

Another benefit of the WCFTestClient is that it displays the payload (the results) of the operations that are sending data back to the caller. Without the WCFTestClient, you can still see the payload by using WCF message logging. Be sure to set `LogMessagesAtServiceLevel` to `true` so that you can see the unencrypted response. To learn how to use WCF message logging, see the MSDN documentation for the Configuration Editor tool at *http://msdn.microsoft.com/en-us/library/ms732009.aspx*.

You'll see an example of the unencrypted response further on in this chapter as you consume this first service.

Adding Graphs to ObjectContext

The concept of relationship spanning and its rules may make it easy to add a graph to a context, yet it has a limitation. Because you are adding the new `Customer`, everything in the graph will be treated as something to be added. That's very handy for `Reservations`, but what about `Reservation.Trip`? `Reservation.Trip` will also be treated as a new object. Entity Framework will not make any assumptions about the state of the entity based on existing properties (e.g., an identity key). This will cause the `Add` to fail because the `Trip` entity came from the database and has an `EntityKey`. When the context attempts to add the trip, an exception will be thrown. The fact that it has an `EntityKey` tells the context that it is not a new `Trip`, and therefore cannot be added.

How do you add some things from a graph and not others? You need to disassemble part of the graph before it is added to the context, which is not an obvious task.

The best option is to simply set the `TripID` of the reservation. The reservation may come back from the client with an attached `Trip` or with the `TripID` populated or both. The helper method assures that the `TripID` is set and that there is no `Trip` entity attached.

Add the `RemoveTripsFromGraph` method to the `CustomerService` class, as shown in the following code:

```
private void RemoveTripsFromGraph(Customer customer)
{
  var query = from reservation in customer.Reservations
           .Where(r=> r.Trip != null && r.TripID == null)
           select reservation;

  foreach (var reservation in query)
  {
    reservation.TripID = reservation.Trip.TripID;
```

```
            reservation.Trip = null;
        }
    }
```

With a few checks and balances, the method ensures that there is no `Trip` attached and that the `TripID` is populated if it wasn't.

Deleting Objects

Deleting the `Customer` requires another involved piece of logic, as deleting the `Customer` means deleting the `Customer`'s `Reservations`. A referential constraint in the BreakAway database says that every `Reservation` must be related to a `Customer`. If you attempt to delete a customer that has reservations, the database will throw an error because it won't allow orphaned reservations.

In the meantime, the `DeleteCustomer` routine will need to explicitly delete all of the related `Reservations` for the `Customer` object. Don't forget that the `Customer` is derived from a contact. The `Customer` record is only an extension of a `Contact` record. Therefore, a business decision is involved here: will the `Contact` record be deleted? In the case of BreakAway Geek Adventures, the rule is not to delete customers and reservation history, but for the sake of your education, we have permission to circumvent this rule in this service.

You have a decision to make about the operation, since there are a number of ways to define it.

1. You can receive the entity to be deleted and use the `DeleteObject` method. Remember that to call the `DeleteObject` method of `ObjectContext`, the object to be deleted must be in the cache. So, the incoming object would first need to be attached to the context and then be deleted before calling `SaveChanges`.
2. Another option is to send up only the identity key of the `Customer`, in which case you could query for the `Customer` and its `Reservations` and then iteratively call `DeleteObject` on each of these entities.
3. Yet another option is to send the `Customer`'s identity key and then use `ExecuteCommand` to delete the `Customer` directly from the database. This still leaves the reservations to be dealt with if you do not have cascading deletes defined.

I've chosen to use the second option. I will send only the `ContactID` to the service. This minimizes the amount of data being sent from the client to the server. Then I will do a quick query to grab the customer and reservations and delete them all using `DeleteObject`, and then call `SaveChanges`. In a highly concurrent system (many users, many possible conflicts) the cascade delete would be the most efficient and reliable method. In the BreakAway enterprise the chance of a new reservation being made in between the time of the query and the call to `SaveChanges` is so small that this method will be sufficient.

Add the code in Example 17-8 to the `DeleteCustomer` method.

Example 17-8. Code for the DeleteCustomer method

```
public string DeleteCustomer(int customerId)
{
  try
  {
    using (BAEntities context = new BAEntities())
    {
        var customerToDelete = (from cust in context.Contacts.OfType<Customer>()
                                .Include("Reservations")
                                where cust.ContactID == customerId
                                select cust).Single();

        var reservationsToDelete = customerToDelete.Reservations.ToList();

        foreach (Reservation r in reservationsToDelete)
        {
            context.DeleteObject(r);
        }

        context.DeleteObject(customerToDelete);
        context.SaveChanges();
        return "Success";
    }
  }
  catch (Exception ex)
  {
    string errorMessage = "";
    //TODO: construct a message to return to the client
    return errorMessage;
  }
}
```

What Exactly Is Being Deleted When You Delete Inherited Objects?

Although customers are in a separate database table from contacts, because they derive from contacts in the model, when the Entity Framework sees an instruction to delete a `Customer` it will delete the `Contact` record as well, even though this doesn't make sense in the database schema or even in the business logic—it would be handy to remove a customer but to leave the contact information intact. If you did want to perform this action, your best bet would be to use a function backed by a stored procedure, an `ExecuteCommand`, or methods that you learned about in Chapter 16.

Updating the Object Graph

The last method to fill out is the `UpdateCustomer` method. Updating just the `Customer` entity is simple. But this is not a single object; it is a graph. Not only will you need to update the customer, but you will also need to deal with its reservations. The reservations might be modified, new, or even deleted. So, although you are updating the `Customer` overall, you have a lot more logic to consider in this method.

Client Rules for Identifying Changes in an EntityCollection

The possible states for the reservations that need to be dealt with are newly added reservations, preexisting reservations that have been modified, and reservations that need to be deleted. However, the `Reservation` objects coming from the client will have no idea about their state, which means the service will need to determine the state of the `Reservations` based on a number of assumptions. These assumptions will require that the consuming client follow some rules to ensure that the service will come up with the correct conclusions about the state of each `Reservation`.

New `Reservations` do not need to be too challenging, as you can identify them by the fact that their `ReservationID` has not been created yet, and therefore is equal to 0. As long as the client does not populate the ID or does not remove the ID value from preexisting reservations, this assumption will work.

`Reservations` with a `ReservationID` value that is greater than 0 should be those that preexisted. These will be either modified or unchanged.

The service won't need to do anything with unchanged reservations, so the client could remove these before returning the graph to the service, thereby reducing the amount of data sent over the wire.

If a reservation is deleted, it will not be returned to the service and will therefore be ignored. In this service, we will attack the deleted object problem by requiring that the client send back a list of the IDs of objects that should be deleted. That is the purpose of the `ReservationsToDelete` property of the `CustomerUpdate` class you defined in the service interface.

The UpdateCustomer Method

We have two paths to choose from when updating a customer and any preexisting reservations. The first involves querying for a fresh set of data and using the data from the client to update those objects and then call `SaveChanges`. The second skips the additional trip to the database and simply uses the `ChangeState` method to render the `Customer` object that came from the client application as `Modified`. While the second path will mean a less efficient update command (every field will be sent in the update), it can still be better than the extra round trip to the database.

I have struggled with this choice—extra round trip to the database or extra fields in the update command—since the first version of Entity Framework. In the first edition of this book, I chose the extra database trip. The method you choose depends on your understanding of the performance consequences in your particular scenario. For some, just choosing the simpler coding method is the way to go.

The UpdateCustomer first extracts the Customer object from the incoming CustomerUpdate type into the customer variable. Before you attach the graph, you need to call the RemoveTripsFromGraph method that you created earlier. If you have any preexisting trips attached to a new reservation, this conflicts with a referential constraint defined in the model, and the attach will fail.

Having access to the foreign keys can make this referential constraint a nonissue. This is another great benefit of the foreign key support introduced in .NET 4. As with the insert, if you can be absolutely positive that the consuming application will simply assign the TripID rather than the entire Trip entity to the Reservation, life gets much simpler. The problem arises when you don't have control over what happens on the client side. Certainly, you can make developers of your consuming applications agree to a "contract" of rules that will enable them to successfully interact with your service, but it's still not a bad idea to have additional protections, such as the RemoveTripsFromGraph method, to help ensure success.

Enter the code in Example 17-9 into the UpdateCustomer method.

Example 17-9. Code for the UpdateCustomer method, with placeholders

```
public string UpdateCustomer(CustomerUpdate customerUpdate)
{
  try
  {
    var customer = CustomerUpdate.Customer;
    using (var context = new BAEntities())
    {
      RemoveTripsFromGraph(customer);
      context.Contacts.Attach(customer);
      context.ObjectStateManager.ChangeObjectState(customer,EntityState.Modified);
      //Code for Existing and New Reservations will go here;
      //Code for Deleted Reservations will go here;
      context.SaveChanges();
    }
    return "Success";
  }
  catch (Exception ex)
  {
    string errorMessage = "";
    //TODO: construct a message to return to the client
    return errorMessage;
  }
}
```

EntityState depends on the System.Data namespace being declared at the top of the code file.

Handling New and Existing Reservations

The first placeholder is for adding and updating reservations. When you attached the customer, that included the entire graph (i.e., the reservations got attached as well). But, when you called `ChangeObjectState` on the customer, it affected only the scalar values. You will need to update any related data explicitly.

We'll use `ChangeObjectState` to fix the attached `Reservations`.

Replace the "Existing and New Reservations" placeholder with the code in Example 17-10.

Example 17-10. Existing Reservations logic for the UpdateCustomer method

```
context.ContextOptions.LazyLoadingEnabled = false;
foreach (var res in customer.Reservations)
{
  if (res.ReservationID > 0)
  { context.ObjectStateManager.ChangeObjectState(res, EntityState.Modified); }
  else
  {context.ObjectStateManager.ChangeObjectState(res, EntityState.Added); }
}
```

The preceding code iterates through all reservations coming in from the client and marks them as either modified or added depending on the `ReservationID`. If you take a look at `customer.Reservations` in debug mode, you'll see that its `IsLoaded` property is `false`. That will cause lazy loading to attempt to load the `Reservations` from the database rather than just looking at what's in memory. That's why I've explicitly disabled lazy loading.

It is possible that the consuming application did not filter out any reservations that need to be deleted or those that were unchanged. In that case, wasted commands will be sent to the database. Unchanged data will still get updated (using original values). In the next step, we'll be sure to remove any reservations that the user marked for deletion. That way, no unnecessary update commands for those `Reservations` will be sent to the database.

This is another reason I may consider doing the entire `UpdateCustomer` method based on fresh data from the database, as I'm constantly evaluating whether it's better to make the up-front trip or not. If you want to see how that path works out, take a look at the code sample from the first edition of the book, which is available on this book's website.

Deleting Reservations

The last piece of the `UpdateCustomer` method deals with reservations the user deleted. The client application must send a list of `ReservationID`s that need to be deleted. The list is contained in the `ReservationsToDelete` property of the `CustomerUpdate` type.

We've got a number of what-ifs to consider with the delete:

What if the reservation was in the graph?
If so, it's been marked as `Modified` and we simply need to change its state to `Deleted`.

What if the reservation was not in the graph?
We could simply call `ExecuteCommand` along with a delete command since we have the ID; however, that will not be in the same transaction as `SaveChanges`, and this could cause problems (There's more on transactions in Chapter 20.)

What if payments are attached to the reservation?
In this case, we cannot delete the reservation or the customer. The database will cause `SaveChanges` to fail; the entire transaction (all of the other updates and inserts) will be rolled back. It would be good to clear this up before calling `SaveChanges`. That means a well-spent trip to the database.

The `TryGetObjectByKey` method helps us with the first two points. It will first look in the context for the reservation, and if it is not found it will get it from the database.

Then we'll leverage lazy loading to check for the existence of any payments for each reservation before deleting it.

I've encapsulated the logic for deleting reservations into a separate method, shown in Example 17-11.

Example 17-11. The DeleteReservations method

```
private static void DeleteReservations(BAEntities context,
                                       List<int> reservationsToDelete)
{
  var query = from reservation in context.Reservations
              join reservationId in reservationsToDelete
              on reservation.ReservationID equals reservationId
              where reservation.Payments.Count == 0
              select reservation;

  foreach (var reservation in query)
  {
    if (reservationsToDelete == null) return;
    context.DeleteObject(reservation);
  }
}
```

Now you can replace the `DeleteReservations` placeholder with the code in Example 17-12.

Example 17-12. Calling DeleteReservations in the UpdateCustomer method

```
List<int> deleteResIDs = customerUpdate.ReservationsToDelete;
DeleteReservations(context, deleteResIDs);
```

Once you've done that, we'll build the client so that you can test the functionality of this WCF service.

Forcing the WCF Service to Stay on the Same Port

If you are using Visual Studio's default web development server to host the service, you might want to prevent it from changing the port number that it lives on. Otherwise, the consuming app might have a hard time finding it during testing if the port number changes. You can do this in the project properties.

1. Open the properties of the WCF service.
2. Select the Web tab.
3. Under the Servers section of the Web page, click the option for "Specific port."

Building a Simple Console App to Consume an EntityObject Service

In order to interact with the service, we'll build a simple console app and debug it to see what's going on.

1. Create a new Console Application project. I've called mine Chapter17ConsoleApp.

   The console app needs only a reference to the service, but it's a special type of reference.
2. Right-click the new project and select Add Service Reference from the menu.
3. Click the Discover button, which will discover all services in your solution, in this case the `CustomerService`.
4. Rename the namespace as shown in Figure 17-2.
5. Click the Advanced button.
6. Change the Collection type from System.Array to Generic List.

   This will ensure that any collections returned by the service are returned as List<type>.
7. Click OK and then click OK again to close the dialog.

The result of this is that Visual Studio will create locally accessible classes representing all of the exposed classes in the service. These are referred to as *proxy classes* as they act as proxies to the classes in the service. Not only will the `CustomerService` class and its methods be available, but you'll also find the `CustomerUpdate` class and all of the model classes that the service accesses through its reference to the BreakAwayModel project.

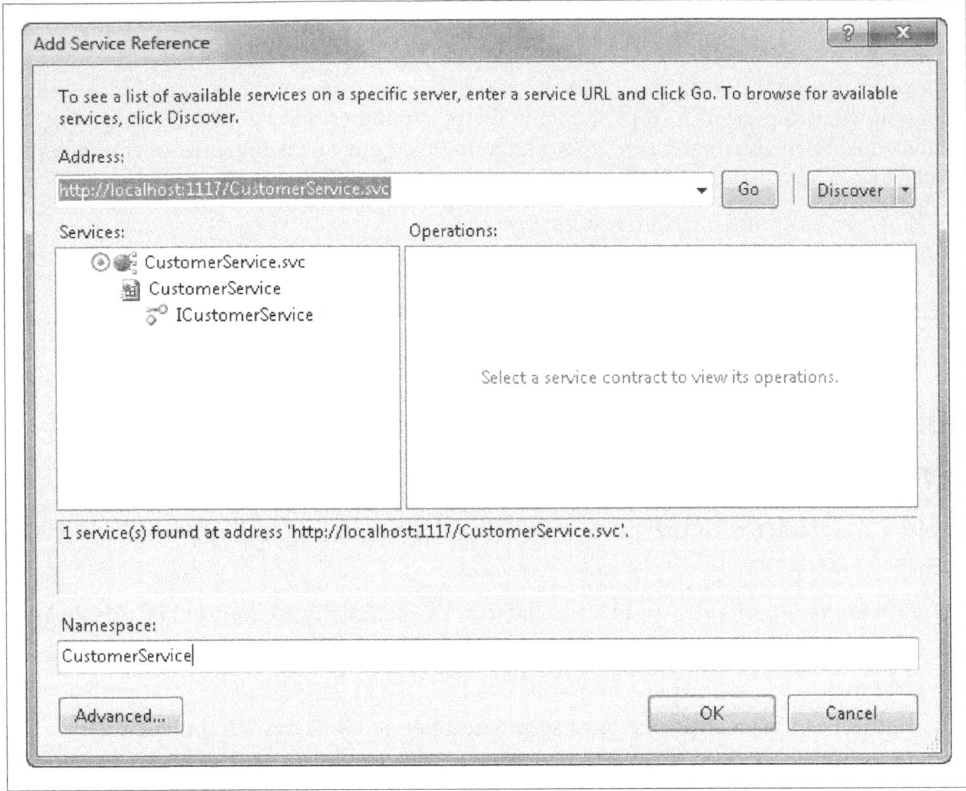

Figure 17-2. Adding a reference to the CustomerService

Enabling the Client Application to Receive Large Messages from the Service

There's one last task to perform with respect to the service reference. The WCF service has a lot of specialized configuration in its *web.config* file. The consuming application inherited some client-side configuration information for interacting with the service, which was automatically inserted into its *app.config* file when you added the service reference. One of the options specifies the maximum size of messages that the client app will accept from the service. Some of these operations will hit that boundary quickly, so you'll need to increase it.

There is a WCF Configuration tool that you can use, but we'll just go right to the source and edit the config file manually.

1. Double-click the *app.config* file in the Solution Explorer to open it.
2. In the binding element, look for the attribute called `MaxReceivedMessageSize`.
3. Increase its value by adding a 0 to the end.
4. Do the same to the `MaxBufferSize`.

Both MaxReceivedMessageSize and MaxBufferSize need to be the same value as the default configuration.

Creating Methods to Test the Service Operations

Now you can write code against the service. We'll create and debug a few methods in the console application's main module.

1. In the class file for the main module, add a reference to the CustomerService namespace. The namespace will begin with the namespace of the console application followed by the namespace you gave the service reference. For me that's:

    ```
    using Chapter17ConsoleApp.CustomerService;
    ```

2. Add the first test method, to check out the GetUpcomingTrips operation shown in Example 17-13.

    Example 17-13. Testing the service's GetUpcomingTrips operation

    ```
    private static void GetUpcomingTrips()
    {
      using (CustomerServiceClient proxy = new CustomerServiceClient())
      {
        List<CustomerService.Trip> results = proxy.GetUpcomingTrips();
      }
    }
    ```

    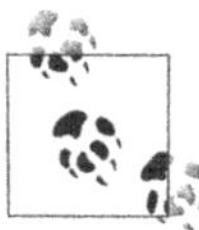

    You don't need to use the fully qualified name of the Trip type. I did so only to demonstrate where it's coming from.

3. Call GetUpcomingTrips from the Main method. If you set a breakpoint, you can debug and step through the method and the service operation to watch things work.

The results should contain a set of Trip objects.

As noted in earlier chapters, the sample data may be out of date by the time you are building these samples, and in this case, no trips will be returned. You might want to manually modify some of the data in the BreakAway example database.

Each Trip has an EntityKey property and the scalar, navigation, and reference properties so that it resembles the EntityObject class on which it's based. Figure 17-3 shows one of these objects in a debug window. TripID, StartDate, and EndDate are the scalar properties. Each of these is represented twice. Then, for the navigation properties that are reference properties, you have the foreign key value (e.g., DestinationID), the entity value (e.g., Destination), and the EntityReference (e.g., DestinationReference).

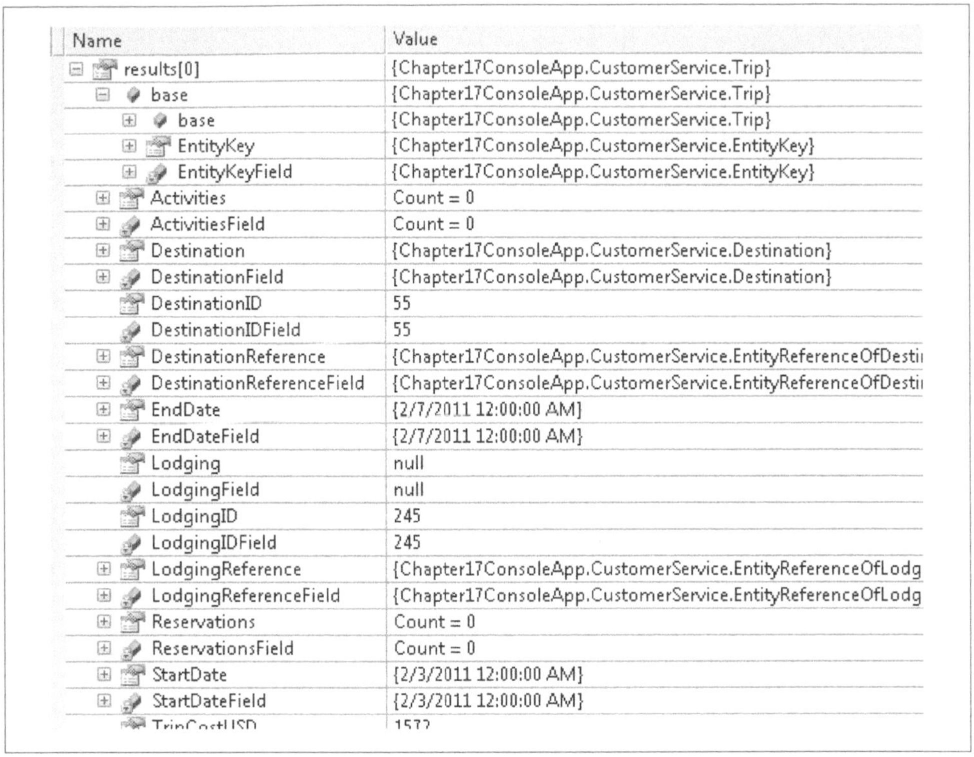

Name	Value
results[0]	{Chapter17ConsoleApp.CustomerService.Trip}
base	{Chapter17ConsoleApp.CustomerService.Trip}
base	{Chapter17ConsoleApp.CustomerService.Trip}
EntityKey	{Chapter17ConsoleApp.CustomerService.EntityKey}
EntityKeyField	{Chapter17ConsoleApp.CustomerService.EntityKey}
Activities	Count = 0
ActivitiesField	Count = 0
Destination	{Chapter17ConsoleApp.CustomerService.Destination}
DestinationField	{Chapter17ConsoleApp.CustomerService.Destination}
DestinationID	55
DestinationIDField	55
DestinationReference	{Chapter17ConsoleApp.CustomerService.EntityReferenceOfDesti
DestinationReferenceField	{Chapter17ConsoleApp.CustomerService.EntityReferenceOfDesti
EndDate	{2/7/2011 12:00:00 AM}
EndDateField	{2/7/2011 12:00:00 AM}
Lodging	null
LodgingField	null
LodgingID	245
LodgingIDField	245
LodgingReference	{Chapter17ConsoleApp.CustomerService.EntityReferenceOfLodg
LodgingReferenceField	{Chapter17ConsoleApp.CustomerService.EntityReferenceOfLodg
Reservations	Count = 0
ReservationsField	Count = 0
StartDate	{2/3/2011 12:00:00 AM}
StartDateField	{2/3/2011 12:00:00 AM}

Figure 17-3. A client-side Trip object in debug view

Another interesting piece of information to look at is the unencrypted XML that came over the wire. Example 17-14 shows the XML for one of the trips that was sent across in the response. Keep this in mind when you're looking at the response that contains POCOs in the next chapter.

Example 17-14. The XML for a single Trip EntityObject returned by the service

```
<d4p1:Trip z:Id="" xmlns:z="http://schemas.microsoft.com/2003/10/Serialization/">
  - <EntityKey xmlns:d6p1="http://schemas.datacontract.org/2004/07/System.Data"
              z:Id="" xmlns="http://schemas.datacontract.org/2004/07/
                                    System.Data.Objects.DataClasses">
    <d6p1:EntityContainerName>BAEntities</d6p1:EntityContainerName>
    - <d6p1:EntityKeyValues>
      - <d6p1:EntityKeyMember>
        <d6p1:Key>TripID</d6p1:Key>
        <d6p1:Value xmlns:d9p1="http://www.w3.org/2001/XMLSchema"
                              i:type="d9p1:int">78</d6p1:Value>
      </d6p1:EntityKeyMember>
    </d6p1:EntityKeyValues>
    <d6p1:EntitySetName>Trips</d6p1:EntitySetName>
    i2
  </EntityKey>
```

```
<d4p1:Activities />
- <d4p1:Destination z:Id="">
  - <EntityKey xmlns:d7p1="http://schemas.datacontract.org/2004/07/System.Data"
              z:Id="" xmlns="http://schemas.datacontract.org/2004/07/
                                         System.Data.Objects.DataClasses">
    <d7p1:EntityContainerName>BAEntities</d7p1:EntityContainerName>
    - <d7p1:EntityKeyValues>
      - <d7p1:EntityKeyMember>
        <d7p1:Key>DestinationID</d7p1:Key>
        <d7p1:Value xmlns:d10p1="http://www.w3.org/2001/XMLSchema"
                              i:type="d10p1:int">55</d7p1:Value>
      </d7p1:EntityKeyMember>
    </d7p1:EntityKeyValues>
    <d7p1:EntitySetName>Destinations</d7p1:EntitySetName>
    i4
  </EntityKey>
  <d4p1:DestinationID>55</d4p1:DestinationID>
  <d4p1:Lodgings />
  <d4p1:Name>Belize</d4p1:Name>
  <d4p1:PrimaryPrefCustomers />
  <d4p1:SecondaryPrefCustomers />
  - <d4p1:Trips>
    <d4p1:Trip z:Ref="">i1</d4p1:Trip>
  </d4p1:Trips>
  i3
</d4p1:Destination>
<d4p1:DestinationID>55</d4p1:DestinationID>
- <d4p1:DestinationReference xmlns:d6p1="http://schemas.datacontract.org/2004/07/
                                                    System.Data.Objects.DataClasses">
  <d6p1:EntityKey xmlns:d7p1="http://schemas.datacontract.org/
            2004/07/System.Data" z:Ref="">i4</d6p1:EntityKey>
</d4p1:DestinationReference>
<d4p1:EndDate>2011-02-07T00:00:00</d4p1:EndDate>
<d4p1:Lodging i:nil="true" />
<d4p1:LodgingID>245</d4p1:LodgingID>
- <d4p1:LodgingReference xmlns:d6p1="http://schemas.datacontract.org/
                                            2004/07/System.Data.Objects.DataClasses">
  - <d6p1:EntityKey xmlns:d7p1="http://schemas.datacontract.org/
                                          2004/07/System.Data" z:Id="">
    <d7p1:EntityContainerName>BAEntities</d7p1:EntityContainerName>
    - <d7p1:EntityKeyValues>
      - <d7p1:EntityKeyMember>
        <d7p1:Key>LodgingID</d7p1:Key>
        <d7p1:Value xmlns:d10p1="http://www.w3.org/2001/XMLSchema"
                i:type="d10p1:int">245</d7p1:Value>
      </d7p1:EntityKeyMember>
    </d7p1:EntityKeyValues>
    <d7p1:EntitySetName>Lodgings</d7p1:EntitySetName>
    i5
  </d6p1:EntityKey>
</d4p1:LodgingReference>
<d4p1:Reservations />
<d4p1:StartDate>2011-02-03T00:00:00</d4p1:StartDate>
<d4p1:TripCostUSD>1572</d4p1:TripCostUSD>
<d4p1:TripDetails>Belize (2/3/2011-2/7/2011; $1,572.00)</d4p1:TripDetails>
```

```
  <d4p1:TripID>78</d4p1:TripID>
  i1
</d4p1:Trip>
```

In addition to providing the data for the `Trip`, the proxy has type definitions for things such as `EntityKey`, `EntityObject`, and many other types that the client will need to be aware of. Overall, a lot of extra work is being done just because we are serializing the `EntityObjects` rather than simple types.

Let's test some of the other functionality in the service. Rather than hit the operations one at a time, we'll build a small workflow in a single method in the console application. The code in Example 17-15 will emulate how the service might be used.

For the sake of seeing all of the code together, I haven't encapsulated or separated any of the logic as you might in a production application. I'll walk through the code after the listing.

Example 17-15. A client-side method to test various service operations

```
private static void GetandUpdateCustomer()
{
  using (var proxy =
      new CustomerServiceClient())
  {
    var custList= proxy.GetCustomerPickList();
    int randomCustomerID = custList[7].Id;
    var customer = proxy.GetCustomer(randomCustomerID);

    //edit the customer
     customer.Notes += ", new notes";

    //retrieve a list of trips
    List<Trip> trips = proxy.GetUpcomingTrips();

    //create a new reservation
    var newRes = new Reservation();
    newRes.ReservationDate = DateTime.Now;
    //emulate selection of a trip
    newRes.Trip = trips[8];
    newRes.RowVersion = System.Text.Encoding.Default.GetBytes("0x123");

   //instantiate Reservations list if necessary & add new reservation
    if (customer.Reservations == null)
    {
      customer.Reservations = new List<Reservation>();
    }
    else
    {
      customer.Reservations.Clear();
    }
    customer.Reservations.Add(newRes);
```

```
        //build CustomerUpdate to return to service
        var customerUpdate = new CustomerUpdate
                             { Customer = customer,
                               ReservationsToDelete = null };

        newRes.ContactID = customer.ContactID;
        string status=proxy.UpdateCustomer(customerUpdate);
    }
}
```

Analyzing the GetAndUpdateCustomer Method

Here's what the test does. First, it retrieves a list of names and IDs and then emulates the following user actions. The user selects a customer and requests `GetCustomer` using the ID of the selected customer. The user makes an edit to the customer's `Notes` field. In order to add a new reservation, you'll need a list of the upcoming trips, so that request is made. Then a new `Reservation` is created using a randomly selected trip. The `RowVersion` field must be set because XML serialization requires that binary fields are not null.

The proxy classes do not understand two-way relationships. If you set the `Reservation`'s `Customer` property to the `Customer` object and then pass the `Customer` object back to the service, it will not know about the reservation. Therefore, you need to add the reservation to the customer's `Reservations` property. If there were no reservations for this customer when it was retrieved from the service, this will be null and it will need to be instantiated before you can add the reservation. Since this code is not editing any existing reservations, there's no reason to send them back up to the service; that's why they've been cleared from the list.

Finally, it's time to update the customer. Remember that `UpdateCustomer` takes a `CustomerUpdate` object. So, you must first create a `CustomerUpdate` and feed it the customer. Since this example hasn't deleted any reservations, the `ReservationsToDelete` property will simply be null.

Now you can run the console app. You'll probably want to set a breakpoint near the beginning to step through all of the code in the console application and the service.

In addition to watching what's happening in the debugger, you might find what's happening in the database interesting as well.

Figure 17-4 shows all of the commands executed in the database as a result of this method.

```
SELECT    [Project1].[ContactID] AS [ContactID],    [Project1].[FirstName] AS [FirstName],    [Project1].[LastName] AS
exec sp_executesql N'SELECT   [Project2].[ContactID1] AS [ContactID],   [Project2].[ContactID2] AS [ContactID1],
exec sp_executesql N'SELECT   [Extent1].[EventID] AS [EventID],   [Extent1].[LocationID] AS [LocationID],   [Extent
exec sp_executesql N'update [dbo].[Contact]  set [FirstName] = @0, [LastName] = @1, [Title] = null, [AddDate] = @2,
exec sp_executesql N'update [dbo].[ContactPersonalInfo]  set [BirthDate] = null, [HeightInches] = null, [WeightPoun
exec sp_executesql N'update [dbo].[Customers]  set [CustomerTypeID] = @0, [InitialDate] = @1, [PrimaryDesintation]
exec sp_executesql N'insert [dbo].[Reservations]([ReservationDate], [ContactID], [EventID])  values (@0, @1, @2)  s
```

Figure 17-4. Commands sent to the database from the service

Testing Out the Other Service Operations

You can write additional console methods to test out the other operations in the service, or download sample code for this chapter from the book's website to see them in action. But now we'll move on to some other types of services.

Creating WCF Data Services with Entities

While most services provide service operations for consumers to request, WCF Data Services literally exposes data. Additionally, WCF Data Services is provided directly through HTTP—in other words, through a URL. You can use HTTP requests such as `GET` (to retrieve data), `POST` (to insert), `PUT` (to update), and `DELETE` (yes, to delete). Going directly through HTTP is referred to as a REST (Representational State Transfer) architecture. You can even browse data in a web browser. A typical service serves operations, but a data service literally serves data.

WCF Data Services is also known by its early code name, Astoria (my favorite, still), and by its .NET 3.5 name, ADO.NET Data Services.

You can create a WCF Data Service based on your Entity Framework model and, with or without the addition of authentication and authorization to protect your data, allow end users to query and even update the data directly through HTTP.

You can also create WCF Data Services based on LINQ to SQL classes or custom classes that expose `IQueryables`.

Putting WCF Data Services in Perspective

WCF Data Services is a big topic that deserves its own book, and there are a number of such books. Here I'll provide a short overview and point you to some great resources to learn more about it.

In addition to its RESTful capabilities, another benefit of WCF Data Services is that it provides data based on a specification called OData* (Open Data Protocol). The name for the specification is fairly new, though the results schema is the same one that has been used for the data services since their first release. Having a common expectation of how data will be provided simplifies the work for those who are consuming the service. Every WCF data service will provide data in the same format, which is based on a specification called AtomPub (Atom Publishing Protocol).

For the .NET developer, creating and consuming WCF Data Services is made easy with tools in Visual Studio. There is a Data Service item template for creating services and for building client applications, and there are two client .NET APIs that let you work fairly easily with WCF Data Services. One is for standard .NET clients such as Windows Forms or ASP.NET and the other is specifically for Silverlight clients. There are also APIs for PHP, Java, and Ajax. But you don't need a client API to interact with data services. You can use any programming language that allows you to make HTTP requests and receive HTTP responses to talk to these data services.

Microsoft is making a big investment in OData. Many products are being modified to easily consume data supplied by WCF Data Services. SharePoint 2010 and Excel 2010 can import AtomPub, and therefore OData. OData is also recognized by Windows Azure Table Storage. More integration is coming with Microsoft products. And it's not just Microsoft. IBM has a product called WebSphere eXtreme Scale REST Data Service that implements WCF Data Services and more are coming.

Creating a WCF Data Service

In the following walkthrough, you'll create a simple service from entities in the BreakAway model, access it directly through a browser, and then tweak the service to see how it impacts the available data. I will not provide examples of using the various client APIs to access the services, as that would take us a bit off track.

Your service needs to be hosted in some type of project. I generally start with an ASP.NET Empty Web Application, so create a new ASP.NET Empty Web Application. I've named mine Chapter17DataService.

As you've done with the other applications that consume the Entity Data Model, add a reference to the BreakAway model project and copy the `ConnectionStrings` section from that project into the *web.config* file. Add a WCF data service to the project. You'll find this item template under the Web templates in the Add New Item dialog. I'm leaving the default name, *WcfDataService1.svc*, for mine.

The code view of the service will open as a result of creating the service, and you'll find two different TODO items in the comments. The first is to let the service know what

* *http://www.odata.org*

data the service will be exposing. That is provided through the generated EntityContainer, BAGA.BAEntities.

Replace the following line of code:

```
DataService< /* TODO: put your data source class name here */ >
```

with DataService<BAGA.BAEntities>.

The second TODO is related to security. If there was no security in the services, anybody with network access to the endpoint would be able to read and write to your data through the model.

An important concept to understand is that the service is not a direct pointer to your database. Only that data that is exposed through your model is available to the service. The consumers will see the entities as we've defined them, not the database tables.

By default, the service is completely locked down. Nobody will have access to read or modify any data.

The second TODO lets you configure which entities (more specifically, which Entity Sets) users have access to and what they can do to them (e.g., read, write, create, etc.) using the SetEntitySetAccessRule setting.

For the sake of this demo, let's start by opening all of the entities for read access.

Uncomment the following line:

```
// config.SetEntitySetAccessRule("MyEntityset", EntitySetRights.AllRead);
```

In the MyEntityset placeholder you can specify individual EntitySets. For example, you can create a rule just for the Contacts or one just for the Trips. You might want users to view and edit Customers but only view Trips. You would set a different access rule for each EntitySet. Here we will grant AllRead rights for the Contacts set by replacing MyEntityset with Contacts.

```
config.SetEntitySetAccessRule("Contacts", EntitySetRights.AllRead);
```

That is the only configuration we'll do for now.

The service is now ready to be consumed. So, save and build the project, then right-click on the service (e.g., WcfDataService1.svc) in the Solution Explorer, and select View in Browser.

Figure 17-5 shows the results of browsing the service, which is essentially a list of all of the entity sets that are available—in this case, only Contacts. The URL points to an ASP.NET web development server on a random port of my computer.

Now here is the fun part. It's nice to know that there are Contacts in the service, but that's not data. Let's look at the actual data.

In the browser's address bar, change the URL to *http://localhost:1179/WcfDataService1.svc/Contacts* so that you tell the service to expose the Contacts. (Presuming your

```
http://localhost:1179/WcfDataService1.svc/

<?xml version="1.0" encoding="utf-8" standalone="yes" ?>
- <service xml:base="http://localhost:1179/WcfDataService1.svc/"
    xmlns:atom="http://www.w3.org/2005/Atom"
    xmlns:app="http://www.w3.org/2007/app"
    xmlns="http://www.w3.org/2007/app">
  - <workspace>
      <atom:title>Default</atom:title>
    - <collection href="Contacts">
        <atom:title>Contacts</atom:title>
      </collection>
    </workspace>
  </service>
```

Figure 17-5. The response to the service request

computer has selected a different port than mine, you'll want to use the correct port number, not 1179.)

Be sure that your browser is not configured to display RSS Feeds in feed-reading view or you won't see the raw response. For example, in Internet Explorer 8, go to Tools→Internet Options→Content→Feeds and Web Slices to change the setting.

The result will be a display of every contact exposed by your model, and since your model doesn't filter the contacts, this happens to be every contact in the database. Figure 17-6 shows the beginning of this response.

The base format that you are looking at is *AtomPub*, a protocol that has been around since 2003. It made sense to Microsoft to use a recognized format rather than invent a new one. AtomPub has its roots in blogging, which is why each item is called an entry and the details of that item are stored in a content tag. Within the content tag, you are seeing schema that is specific to the OData specification—`m:` for metadata, `d:` for data, and so forth.

Notice also in the screenshot that the very first contact displayed happens to be a `Customer`. WCF Data Services understands that we've built inheritance in our model. All of the properties of the `Customer` type are included.

In the same listing, a `NonCustomer` entity, which also inherits from `Contact`, is displayed along with its properties, as shown in Figure 17-7.

Notice that the entry has an `id` element that contains a URL, *http://localhost:1179/WcfDataService1.svc/Contacts(92)*. While that URL isn't a hyperlink, it is the proper URL for specifically accessing the data for that single `Contact`. You could copy and paste that URL into the browser address bar and retrieve that single piece of data.

http://localhost:1179/WcfDataService1.svc/Conta...
Page ▾ Safety
http://localhost:1179/WcfDataService1.svc/Contacts
<?xml version="1.0" encoding="utf-8" standalone="yes" ?>
- <feed xml:base="http://localhost:1179/WcfDataService1.svc/"
xmlns:d="http://schemas.microsoft.com/ado/2007/08/dataservices"
xmlns:m="http://schemas.microsoft.com/ado/2007/08/dataservices/metadata"
xmlns="http://www.w3.org/2005/Atom">
<title type="text">Contacts</title>
<id>http://localhost:1179/WcfDataService1.svc/Contacts</id>
<updated>2010-01-19T20:22:48Z</updated>
<link rel="self" title="Contacts" href="Contacts" />
- <entry>
<id>http://localhost:1179/WcfDataService1.svc/Contacts(1)</id>
<title type="text" />
<updated>2010-01-19T20:22:48Z</updated>
- <author>
<name />
</author>
<link rel="edit" title="Contact" href="Contacts(1)" />
<category term="BAModel.Customer"
scheme="http://schemas.microsoft.com/ado/2007/08/dataservices/scheme" />
- <content type="application/xml">
- <m:properties>
<d:ContactID m:type="Edm.Int32">1</d:ContactID>
<d:FirstName xml:space="preserve">Alex</d:FirstName>
<d:LastName xml:space="preserve">Solzhenitsyn</d:LastName>
<d:Title xml:space="preserve">Mr.</d:Title>
<d:AddDate m:type="Edm.DateTime">2009-01-07T11:41:45</d:AddDate>
<d:ModifiedDate m:type="Edm.DateTime">2009-12-02T19:59:37.723</d:ModifiedDate>
<d:CustomerTypeID m:type="Edm.Int32">1</d:CustomerTypeID>
<d:InitialDate m:type="Edm.DateTime">2008-03-04T00:00:00</d:InitialDate>
<d:PrimaryDestinationID m:type="Edm.Int32">5</d:PrimaryDestinationID>
<d:SecondaryDestinationID m:type="Edm.Int32">25</d:SecondaryDestinationID>
<d:PrimaryActivityID m:type="Edm.Int32">18</d:PrimaryActivityID>
<d:SecondaryActivityID m:type="Edm.Int32">21</d:SecondaryActivityID>
<d:Notes>He was lots of fun to have on our trip!</d:Notes>
<d:BirthDate m:type="Edm.DateTime">1981-01-26T00:00:00</d:BirthDate>
<d:HeightInches m:type="Edm.Int32">69</d:HeightInches>
<d:WeightPounds m:type="Edm.Int32">125</d:WeightPounds>
<d:DietaryRestrictions xml:space="preserve"></d:DietaryRestrictions>
<d:CustTimeStamp m:type="Edm.Binary">AAAAAAAAUgk=</d:CustTimeStamp>
</m:properties>
</content>
</entry>
- <entry>
<id>http://localhost:1179/WcfDataService1.svc/Contacts(2)</id>

Figure 17-6. The beginning of the response to requesting Contacts

In fact, there is an extensive URI syntax for querying the data exposed by the service. The MSDN white paper titled "Using ADO.NET Data Services" contains a listing of the various querying capabilities including filtering, sorting, and eager-loading of related data. With the newer version of the data services, more capabilities, such as projection, were added; however, be aware that at the time of this writing the paper had not been updated to reflect the .NET 4 version.

```xml
- <entry>
    <id>http://localhost:1179/WcfDataService1.svc/Contacts(92)</id>
    <title type="text" />
    <updated>2010-01-19T20:22:48Z</updated>
  - <author>
      <name />
    </author>
    <link rel="edit" title="Contact" href="Contacts(92)" />
    <category term="BAModel.NonCustomer"
      scheme="http://schemas.microsoft.com/ado/2007/08/dataservices/scheme" />
  - <content type="application/xml">
    - <m:properties>
        <d:ContactID m:type="Edm.Int32">92</d:ContactID>
        <d:FirstName xml:space="preserve">Jovita</d:FirstName>
        <d:LastName xml:space="preserve">Carmody</d:LastName>
        <d:Title xml:space="preserve">Ms.</d:Title>
        <d:AddDate m:type="Edm.DateTime">2007-01-21T20:35:35.95</d:AddDate>
        <d:ModifiedDate m:type="Edm.DateTime">2008-08-07T08:27:07.033</d:ModifiedDate>
        <d:TimeStamp m:type="Edm.Binary">AAAAAAAAK0E=</d:TimeStamp>
      </m:properties>
    </content>
  </entry>
```

Figure 17-7. A NonCustomer returned by WCF Data Services

This simple filter limits the results to contacts with the first name "George":

```
http://localhost:1179/WcfDataService1.svc/Contacts?$filter=FirstName eq 'George'
```

While the syntax is rich, considering that it can be used in a URI, it is certainly not as rich as what you can do with LINQ and other functionality in .NET. And this creates a problem for .NET developers using the .NET Client APIs for WCF Data Services. The Client API allows you to write LINQ queries against the proxy classes that represent the data in the service. These LINQ queries are then transposed into the appropriate URI so that the service can be called in the only way it understands: through HTTP. So, it's not uncommon to find that your very clever query throws an exception because it is not supported by the URI syntax.

Because of this, you should further consider what the service is exposing to the client. For example, you might only ever want the consumers of the service to access `Customers`. You can configure this in the service itself without impacting the model.

Filtering at the Service Level Using QueryInterceptor

You can do a lot more in the data service's code than specify `EntitySet` permissions. It is possible to intercept requests, both for queries and for updates.

The `QueryInterceptor` attribute allows you to capture incoming requests to the service and filter the results. The `QueryInterceptor` returns a lambda expression that will be used in a `Where` clause when retrieving the requested data, as shown in Example 17-16.

Example 17-16. Using a QueryInterceptor to filter all Contact queries

```
[QueryInterceptor("Contacts")]
public Expression<Func<Contact, bool>> OnQueryContacts()
{
  return c => c is Customer;
}
```

The name of the method is not important; however, `OnQueryContacts` follows the pattern that Microsoft has provided in all of its examples. This `QueryInterceptor` forces all requests for `Contacts` to return only `Customers`. No matter what the incoming query looks like, the service will append `.Where(c=>c is Customer)` to it.

`QueryInterceptor` is more commonly used for authorizing user access.

Example 17-17 shows an example where only authenticated users can access the `Contacts`.

Example 17-17. Filtering based on authentication in a QueryInterceptor

```
[System.Data.Services.QueryInterceptor("Contacts")]
public Expression<Func<Contact, bool>> OnQueryContacts()
{
  if (HttpContext.Current.User.Identity.IsAuthenticated == false)
  {
    throw new DataServiceException
      (400, "Not authorized to access Contact information");
  }
  else
  {
    return c => true;
  }
}
```

There is also a `ChangeInterceptor` attribute, which I'll discuss along with WCF Data Services' update features later in this section.

Anticipating Exceptions

If something goes wrong in your WCF data service, it is can be very difficult to discover the reason. There's a config setting that will show you the errors, and it's a good idea to have it in your code when debugging.

In the service code's `InitializeService` method, add the following:

```
config.UseVerboseErrors=true;
```

Exposing Related Data Through the Service

Let's add a few more `EntitySets` to the service. Add the following to the `InitializeService` method:

```
config.SetEntitySetAccessRule("Reservations", EntitySetRights.AllRead);
config.SetEntitySetAccessRule("Trips", EntitySetRights.AllRead);
```

Now take a look at the first `Reservation` in Figure 17-8. Be sure to replace my port number, 1179, with the one your service assigned:

```
http://localhost:1179/WcfDataService1.svc/Reservations?$top=1
```


```
- <entry>
    <id>http://localhost:1179/WcfDataService1.svc/Reservations(2)</id>
    <title type="text" />
    <updated>2010-01-20T14:23:14Z</updated>
  - <author>
      <name />
    </author>
    <link rel="edit" title="Reservation" href="Reservations(2)" />
    <link rel="http://schemas.microsoft.com/ado/2007/08/dataservices/related/Customer"
      type="application/atom+xml;type=entry" title="Customer" href="Reservations
      (2)/Customer" />
    <link rel="http://schemas.microsoft.com/ado/2007/08/dataservices/related/Trip"
      type="application/atom+xml;type=entry" title="Trip" href="Reservations(2)/Trip" />
    <category term="BAModel.Reservation"
      scheme="http://schemas.microsoft.com/ado/2007/08/dataservices/scheme" />
  - <content type="application/xml">
    - <m:properties>
        <d:ReservationID m:type="Edm.Int32">2</d:ReservationID>
        <d:ReservationDate m:type="Edm.DateTime">2006-09-
          02T16:00:13.513</d:ReservationDate>
        <d:ContactID m:type="Edm.Int32">607</d:ContactID>
        <d:TripID m:type="Edm.Int32">40</d:TripID>
        <d:TimeStamp m:type="Edm.Binary">AAAAAAAADCI=</d:TimeStamp>
      </m:properties>
    </content>
  </entry>
```


Figure 17-8. Returning a single Reservation through WCF Data Services

Notice the `<link>` tags in this response. In addition to the one that describes how to get directly to this reservation (`Reservations(2)`), there are two others. One indicates that there is a `Customer` attached and that you can get to that customer by navigating further into the `Reservation` (`Reservations(2)/Customer`). It's similar to navigating through the data structure in code. Additionally, there's a link for `Trip`. Considering the model, we know that there is also a `Payments` navigation property for `Reservation`. And if you look back at the response for the earlier customer, it's curious why there were no navigation property links there.

The reason some navigation properties are displayed and others aren't has to do with which `EntitySets` you are exposing from the service. When you queried the `Contacts` earlier, the `Reservations` and `Trips` weren't included in the service. So they didn't show up. The `Reservation` in Figure 17-8 is showing `Customer` and `Trip` because their `EntitySet`s are exposed by the services, while `Payments` is not.

In addition to navigating to the related entity, you can also eager-load it, similar to using the `Include` method in a query. The term in the URI syntax is `expand`.

Try to include the trip with:

```
http://localhost:1179/WcfDataService1.svc/Reservations?$top=1&$expand=Trip
```

Figure 17-9 shows the results.


```
- <link rel="http://schemas.microsoft.com/ado/2007/08/dataservices/related/Trip"
    type="application/atom+xml;type=entry" title="Trip" href="Reservations(2)/Trip">
  - <m:inline>
    - <entry>
        <id>http://localhost:1179/WcfDataService1.svc/Trips(40)</id>
        <title type="text" />
        <updated>2010-01-20T14:36:54Z</updated>
      - <author>
          <name />
        </author>
        <link rel="edit" title="Trip" href="Trips(40)" />
        <link
          rel="http://schemas.microsoft.com/ado/2007/08/dataservices/related/Reservations"
          type="application/atom+xml;type=feed" title="Reservations" href="Trips
          (40)/Reservations" />
        <category term="BAModel.Trip"
          scheme="http://schemas.microsoft.com/ado/2007/08/dataservices/scheme" />
      - <content type="application/xml">
        - <m:properties>
            <d:TripID m:type="Edm.Int32">40</d:TripID>
            <d:DestinationID m:type="Edm.Int32">72</d:DestinationID>
            <d:LodgingID m:type="Edm.Int32">262</d:LodgingID>
            <d:StartDate m:type="Edm.DateTime">2009-09-
              13T00:00:00</d:StartDate>
            <d:EndDate m:type="Edm.DateTime">2009-09-20T00:00:00</d:EndDate>
            <d:TripCostUSD m:type="Edm.Int32">1500</d:TripCostUSD>
          </m:properties>
        </content>
      </entry>
    </m:inline>
  </link>
```

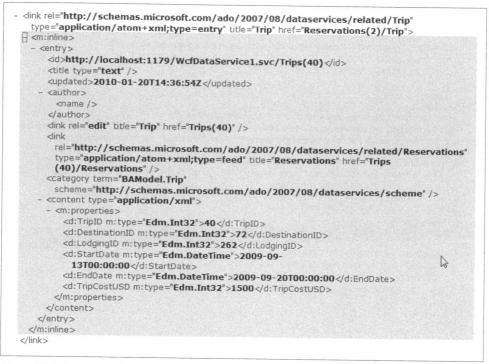

Figure 17-9. Returning shaped data using expand

The entire `Trip` was included inside its link tag. And the trip has a link back to the related `Reservations`. You could expand the trip to show all of its related `Reservations`.

The `Trip` data highlights an important concept. In an earlier chapter, you added a custom property to `Trip` called `TripDetails`, but that is not listed in the properties of the `Trip` in Figure 17-9. WCF Data Services is reading the XML metadata and not your code when it is using your entities in the background. It still leverages your classes for some of its operations—for example, when dealing with navigation properties.

This will be evident when exposing models that are rendered as Entity Framework POCO classes. We'll take a quick look at this in the next chapter.

Preparing for WCF Data Services' Limitations

Be aware that WCF Data Services is not yet able to reflect your model as you are used to seeing it in a regular application. For example, your model contains something that is not supported by WCF Data Services. Now that we have the `Reservations` `EntitySet` in the service, let's go back to the customer we looked at earlier and see what happens (Figure 17-10) when we try to retrieve that `Customer` again (`Contacts(1)`).

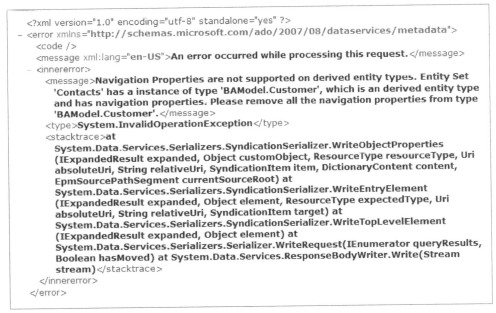

```
 <?xml version="1.0" encoding="utf-8" standalone="yes" ?>
- <error xmlns="http://schemas.microsoft.com/ado/2007/08/dataservices/metadata">
   <code />
   <message xml:lang="en-US">An error occurred while processing this request.</message>
 - <innererror>
     <message>Navigation Properties are not supported on derived entity types. Entity Set
       'Contacts' has a instance of type 'BAModel.Customer', which is an derived entity type
       and has navigation properties. Please remove all the navigation properties from type
       'BAModel.Customer'.</message>
     <type>System.InvalidOperationException</type>
     <stacktrace>at
       System.Data.Services.Serializers.SyndicationSerializer.WriteObjectProperties
       (IExpandedResult expanded, Object customObject, ResourceType resourceType, Uri
       absoluteUri, String relativeUri, SyndicationItem item, DictionaryContent content,
       EpmSourcePathSegment currentSourceRoot) at
       System.Data.Services.Serializers.SyndicationSerializer.WriteEntryElement
       (IExpandedResult expanded, Object element, ResourceType expectedType, Uri
       absoluteUri, String relativeUri, SyndicationItem target) at
       System.Data.Services.Serializers.SyndicationSerializer.WriteTopLevelElement
       (IExpandedResult expanded, Object element) at
       System.Data.Services.Serializers.Serializer.WriteRequest(IEnumerator queryResults,
       Boolean hasMoved) at System.Data.Services.ResponseBodyWriter.Write(Stream
       stream)</stacktrace>
   </innererror>
 </error>
```

Figure 17-10. WCF Data Services error

If you hadn't set `config.UserVerboseErrors` to `true`, this error would only say "An error occurred while processing this request." No amount of message logging, tracing, or inspection with a tool such as Fiddler would enlighten you as to the cause of the problem.

In your model, Customer derives from Contact, and Customer has navigation properties. This was not a problem when we were coding inside .NET, but, as you can see, it is a big problem for WCF Data Services. We didn't even attempt to expand any of the navigation properties. In this case, only the Reservations navigation property is available because its EntitySet is part of the service. Just the fact that the navigation property exists in the service causes the failure.

The suggestion made in the error is to completely remove the reservations. That would make it possible to query the Contacts again. But there will be no Reservations in the service. Depending on the goal of your service, this may not be an acceptable compromise.

There's no trick to fool WCF into accepting the inheritance/navigation in your model at this level. You would literally have to modify your model (or create a separate model just for the data service) to avoid the problem.

Modifying Data Through a Service

As a RESTful service, WCF Data Services allows other HTTP verbs (i.e., commands) besides GET. PUT, POST, and DELETE are the most typical ones to be used besides GET.

If you were interacting with the service directly (e.g., through JavaScript), you would need to know how to use these calls directly. Luckily, the client APIs hide the raw HTTP calls behind an object model.

For example, the .NET Client API provides a DataServiceContext, which is similar to the ObjectContext you have been working with. Using this special context, you can query the service with LINQ and insert, update, and delete data that's attached to the context with a SaveChanges method.

In the service, you can expose or limit access to editing EntitySet data with the SetEntitySetAccessRule configuration. EntitySetRights has the following enums: None, ReadSingle, ReadMultiple, AllRead, WriteAppend, WriteReplace, WriteDelete, WriteMerge, AllWrite, and All. You can combine rights to enable just the interaction you desire on a specific EntitySet by setting the rights individually, as in Example 17-18.

Example 17-18. Setting multiple access rules on a single EntitySet

```
config.SetEntitySetAccessRule("Contacts",EntitySetRights.AllRead);
config.SetEntitySetAccessRule("Contacts",EntitySetRights.WriteAppend);
config.SetEntitySetAccessRule("Contacts",EntitySetRights.WriteMerge);
```

You can further restrict updates using the ChangeInterceptor attribute similar to the QueryInterceptor, as shown in Example 17-19.

Example 17-19. Affecting updates to Contacts in a ChangeInterceptor

```
[ChangeInterceptor("Contacts")]
public void OnChangeContacts(Contact contact, UpdateOperations operations)
{
```

```
    if (operations == UpdateOperations.Change
        & HttpContext.Current.User.Identity.IsAuthenticated == false)
      {
        throw new DataServiceException
         (400, "Unauthenticated users may not update contact information");
      }
}
```

A ChangeInterceptor has the item to be changed and the type of change operation (Add, Change, Delete, or None) being requested. As with an ObjectContext.SaveChanges, each item to be persisted to the database is handled one at a time. This interceptor checks for any Change operations being performed by an unauthenticated user. In that case, an error is thrown since only authenticated users can edit data.

Notice that you can't prevent consumers of the service from coding the unauthorized calls. You can only stop the call from being processed through either the SetEntitySetAccessRules or the interceptors.

Learning More About Creating and Consuming WCF Data Services

These pages on WCF Data Services served merely as an introduction so that you can see how important these data services are to Microsoft, and how entities fit into the services. You can learn much more about WCF Data Services by starting at the MSDN Developer Center for WCF Data Services (*http://msdn.microsoft.com/en-us/data/bb931106.aspx*).

Understanding How WCF RIA Services Relates to the Entity Framework

WCF Data Services is a great way to make your data easily available to consumers. However, for many enterprise applications, you need much more control over access to the data and inside the service. You may not want to expose data, and instead provide operations like other services, but without the effort that was required in the first part of this chapter.

WCF RIA Services is another type of WCF service implementation from Microsoft. While this technology was originally created to simplify providing CRUD data operations for Silverlight, it can be used as the middle tier for other types of client applications as well, such as ASP.NET MVC applications.

RIA is a WCF-based service and leverages SOAP just as WCF does. It is not a RESTful service like WCF Data Services. The RIA SDK and toolkit provide a set of APIs and templates for you to create your services; and as long as you stick close to the prescribed guidance, they can provide a nice, simplified solution for dealing with CRUD at the middle tier.

WCF RIA Services for Visual Studio 2010 requires that your model exposes foreign keys. If you do not want to have foreign keys in your model, you have to customize the domain service and expose the foreign keys from the `EntityReference.EntityKey`, as you have seen in previous chapters.

While RIA Services doesn't depend on Entity Framework as its data layer, it has special templates and tooling specifically for consuming an Entity Framework model. You can also use LINQ to SQL or your own classes as the data layer.

RIA Services is not part of Visual Studio 2010, but was released in May 2010. It can be used with Visual Studio 2008 or Visual Studio 2010. The Visual Studio toolkit includes a project template and item templates. The project template ensures that your project is set up properly with the correct APIs and follows other guidelines for creating a RIA service. The templates create classes that follow the guidelines as well.

And finally, Visual Studio will create proxies to use on the client side that make it simple to call the service operations.

While the service class has explicit query, update, insert, and delete methods, it exposes operations and data contracts in such a way that data sent to the client contains properties to provide behind-the-scenes change tracking. One call to `Submit` from the client side will execute all of your explicit and easily customizable insert, update, and delete methods as necessary.

When you use an Entity Framework model as the data layer, RIA Services will use some special classes and interfaces that can leverage Entity Framework's functionality, and the classes created by the templates will do this as well. Example 17-20 shows a domain service created from the `Trip` entity using Visual Studio's Domain Service Class item template.

Example 17-20. A Domain Service class created from an Entity Data Model

```
[EnableClientAccess()]
public class DomainService1 : LinqToEntitiesDomainService<BAEntities>
{
  public IQueryable<Trip> GetTrips()
  {
    return this.ObjectContext.Trips;
  }

  public void InsertTrip(Trip trip)
  {
    if ((trip.EntityState != EntityState.Detached))
    {
      this.ObjectContext.ObjectStateManager
                    .ChangeObjectState(trip, EntityState.Added);
    }
    else
    {
```

```
      this.ObjectContext.Trips.AddObject(trip);
    }
  }

  public void UpdateTrip(Trip currentTrip)
  {
    this.ObjectContext.Trips.AttachAsModified
       (currentTrip, this.ChangeSet.GetOriginal(currentTrip));
  }

  public void DeleteTrip(Trip trip)
  {
    if ((trip.EntityState == EntityState.Detached))
    {
      this.ObjectContext.Trips.Attach(trip);
    }
    this.ObjectContext.Trips.DeleteObject(trip);
  }
}
```

The `DomainService` class, in this case the specialized `LinqToEntitiesDomainService` class, provides the operations, methods, and logic that the consuming client will use, such as `Submit`, which in turn calls the `InsertTrip`, `UpdateTrip`, and `DeleteTrip` methods as needed. The `GetTrips` method is one that you would call directly from the client. You are encouraged to customize the methods or even provide new query methods that better suit your domain. You can also modify the `Insert`, `Update`, and `Delete` methods as needed.

This template is a simple starting point. Many developers are injecting even more sophisticated architecture into the domain services—for example, to return classes that are designed for the UI rather than simply the entities that are created as a result of the queries.

WCF RIA Services does not recognize many-to-many relationships in an Entity Framework model. Additionally, only foreign key associations in your model are recognized. Independent associations are ignored.

The WCF RIA Services landing page on the official Silverlight website (*http://www.silverlight.net/getstarted/riaservices*) is a great place to get started with this technology.

Summary

The most daunting challenges you'll face when you work across tiers of a distributed application is that although `EntityObjects` are serialized, the `ObjectStateEntry` objects that contain the change tracking information are not. This leaves you with no state information when your object reaches its destination. In the WCF service example in this chapter, you solved this problem by explicitly changing the `EntityState` of objects prior to calling `SaveChanges`. This is one pattern for overcoming this problem, and you will learn more in later chapters.

WCF Data Services was built on top of Entity Framework and it provides a smooth, though sometimes simplistic, way to expose your data directly for consumption through HTTP. It certainly reduces the challenge for consumers who want to work with your data, but it may not be the answer for big enterprise applications. WCF RIA Services, which began as an attempt to make data consumption simpler in Silverlight applications, provides a different perspective on simplifying the creation and consumption of WCF services in .NET and it has great support for Entity Framework as a data layer.

In the next chapter, we'll look at using POCOs in services, which changes the game significantly for creating services using the Entity Framework. Some developers will prefer leveraging the default `EntityObjects` in their applications, while others will prefer the simpler objects. Either way, when it comes to developing custom WCF services you will find that some of the challenges we faced earlier in this chapter are greatly reduced when using POCOs.

Web services and WCF are big topics unto themselves, and wonderful books are devoted solely to these technologies. The samples in this chapter provided some patterns that will be great for many scenarios, but not all. Later in this book you will learn more patterns, but more importantly, throughout the book you will gain the knowledge to achieve whatever architecture you choose for your service-based applications.

CHAPTER 18

Using POCOs and Self-Tracking Entities in WCF Services

In Chapter 17, you built a custom WCF service using entities that inherit from `EntityObjects`. While some of the new Entity Framework features introduced in .NET 4, such as foreign key support and methods to change entity state, have made this much easier to do than in the previous version of Entity Framework, it is still challenging and requires that you know a lot about manipulating entities.

Removing `EntityObjects` from the payload removes some of these challenges. In the previous edition of this book, I demonstrated a common approach to building services in .NET 3.5, which was to use Data Transfer Objects (DTOs) to carry the object's data between the client and the service. But the most time-consuming part of this task was converting the `EntityObjects` to DTOs and back again. The DTOs, however, provided two key benefits. The first was that they greatly reduced the complexity of the payload. The second was that they enabled you to inject state properties directly into the classes so that when the data came back to the service, you didn't have to use extra logic to determine what was inserted, updated, deleted, or left untouched.

Now that Entity Framework supports POCO classes, the need for using DTOs is greatly reduced. You can do away with them completely if you want, although your architecture may require them for different reasons unrelated to the Entity Framework, or simply because your architecture is designed to keep everything related to the Entity Framework, including its classes, in a data access layer. Without the `EntityObject`, the message is much smaller and much less complex and you can use your code generation template to inject state properties into your classes.

In addition to using your own POCO classes in WCF services, Microsoft provides a specialized POCO template that creates what are called *self-tracking entities*. This template creates enhanced POCOs, which include state properties and some other specialized interfaces and functionality that allow state information to easily move between the client and the server without the author of either the service or the client application having to work out the logic of maintaining state information.

Self-tracking entities are an important addition to the available options in Entity Framework. With little effort, you can easily use entities in services. If you are looking for an out-of-the-box solution, don't have specialized needs for your entities, and know that the client applications are .NET, self-tracking entities could very well be the only form of entity that you'll need.

In this chapter, you'll begin by creating POCO classes based on the latest version of the BreakAway model. The new POCO classes will reflect all of the modifications you made in Chapters 14 through 16. Then you'll apply some enhancements to these POCO classes to make them friendlier for use in WCF services. You'll then build a service that makes use of these POCO classes, and finally you'll build a service that uses self-tracking entities. I'll also discuss the impact of using POCO entities in WCF Data Services and WCF RIA Services instead of `EntityObjects`, as you learned in the preceding chapter.

Creating WCF-Friendly POCO Classes

Before creating the services, you'll need an appropriate set of POCO classes to work with. Therefore, in this section you will walk through the following tasks:

- Using the T4 POCO template, you'll update your POCOs to reflect all of the changes made to the model in recent chapters.
- You'll move the generated POCO classes into their own project and allow them to be free of any dependency on the Entity Framework.
- You'll create a simple base class to provide state information to the entities and modify the template so that the entities automatically inherit from that class.
- You'll modify the template one more time to remove the `virtual` keywords from the generated entity properties. This will prevent the Entity Framework from creating dynamic proxies at runtime, helping you to avoid problems as entities are being sent from the service to the client.

Updating the POCO Classes Based on the Current BreakAway Model

The last time you worked with the POCO classes was prior to the many changes you made to the model in Chapters 14 through 16. You'll need to re-create the POCO classes based on the current version of the model. You have a few paths to choose from to accomplish this.

- If you have been using the same model from chapter to chapter, and your current BreakAwayModel project still has the T4 POCO template that you created in Chapter 13, just be sure you are letting the template generate your classes rather than having them generate from the model:

- Ensure that the Code Generation attribute in the model's Properties window is set to `None`. This prevents the model from using the default code generator, which creates `EntityObject` classes.
- Verify that both of the template files (*BreakAway.Context.tt* and *BreakAway.tt*) in your project have their `Custom Tool` property set to `TextTemplatingFileGenerator`.

- If your newest model is in a project that has no POCO template in it, do the following:
  - Add a new Code Generation Item to the model, selecting either the Microsoft ADO.NET C# POCO Entity Generator or the Microsoft ADO.NET VB POCO Entity Generator. Refer back to Chapter 13 to refresh your memory on how to do this.
- You may prefer to have a fresh project to work with:
  - Create a new Class Library project and copy your latest *BreakAway.EDMX* file into the project.
  - Add a reference to `System.Data.Entity`.
  - Copy the *app.config* from the model's project into this new project. If you have no intention of running the Update Model from Database Wizard, you can skip this step.
  - Add a new Code Generation Item to the model, selecting either the Microsoft ADO.NET C# POCO Entity Generator or the Microsoft ADO.NET VB POCO Entity Generator. Refer back to Chapter 13 to refresh your memory on how to do this.

Isolating the POCO Entities in Their Own Project

Placing the entities into their own project is a great first step for using POCO entities in WCF, but it is also a good practice for any solutions where you are using the POCO entities. By isolating the entity classes, you will ensure that they have absolutely no dependency on the Entity Framework. Separating your logic into different projects also sets you in the right direction for a cleaner application architecture and easier maintenance. There are two ways to achieve this. You'll walk through one method and then I'll provide you with a link to the other method. Here's how to do that with the entity template and its generated entity classes.

Further on in the book you will continue to benefit from this isolation in other scenarios that do not involve WCF.

1. Create a new Class Library project for the entity classes. I've called mine BreakAway Entities.
2. Move the *BreakAway.tt* template file that you created in Chapter 13 from its project into the new project.

   Because the generated classes are bound to the template, they will automatically come along with the template file.

   You'll also want the partial classes that go with the entities.
3. Create a folder in the new project, and name it *Partial Classes*.
4. Using the cut and paste feature in the Solution Explorer, move the partial classes from the BreakAwayModel project's *Partial Classes* folder that you first created in Chapter 11 into the new *Partial Classes* folder.

   Leave the *Entities.cs* partial class file and the *Functions.cs* file in the model project. Those are dependent on the context and the Entity Framework APIs.

Directing a template back to a model

In the template that builds the entity classes, there is a path setting to the model file. Now that the template and the model are in different locations, you'll need to change that path setting so that the template can find the model.

Open the template and locate the path for the model, which should be near the beginning of the file:

```
string inputFile = @"BAModel.edmx";
```

Unless you specifically created the BreakAway Entities project in a different folder, its folder should be contained in the same solution folder as the model's project. Therefore, you can use a relative path to the model's folder and file.

Modify the path to the model file using the relative path shown here. Your folder name may be different.

```
string inputFile = @"..\BreakAwayModel\BAModel.edmx";
```

Specifying the namespace of entity classes

By default, the template will use the namespace of the current project as the namespace for the generated entities. I want my entities to continue to be in the `BAGA` namespace. The T4 template properties allow you to specify a namespace.

Open the Properties window for the *BreakAway.tt* file, and set its `Custom Tool Namespace` property to `BAGA`.

Since you haven't edited the template file, you need to force the code generation to run again. So, rebuild the BreakAway Entities project.

You might want to verify the code generation. Open one of the generated files. Its namespace should be `BAGA`.

An alternate way to generate the POCOs inside their own project is to use a Visual Studio feature called *linking*. In the MSDN topic Walkthrough: Serialize Self-Tracking Entities (Entity Framework) (*http://msdn.microsoft.com/en-us/library/ee789839.aspx*), the step titled "To create the class library project that links to the self-tracking types template" describes how to link the template. You can use the same steps with the POCO template in your solution here.

Providing the ObjectContext with a reference to the entities

Remember that the `ObjectContext`, `BAEntities`, needs access to the classes. In the model project, add a reference to the BreakAway Entities project. Then rebuild the solution. Everything should build correctly.

Also remember that we have not added a reference to `System.Data.Entity` in the new project. By moving the classes into their own project you have created a clear separation between these classes and the Entity Framework.

Adding Custom Logic to the POCO Entities with a Base Class

The next step for preparing your entities for WCF involves providing them with some critical functionality. One of the biggest challenges when working with entities across processes is the loss of state information. In Chapter 17, you created explicit operations for inserting, updating, and deleting customers. For handling the reservations attached to a customer, you had to make assumptions regarding each reservation's state by checking if the `ReservationID` was equal to 0 (new) or was greater than 0 (existing). Then, to handle deleted reservations, you created a somewhat kludgey solution by forcing the consumer to pass in a collection of the `ReservationID` values of each reservation to be deleted.

With the simple addition of a new state property to the entities themselves, all of this unsettling code can be avoided. This new state property will have no dependence on the state information that is managed by the context. You'll have access to it in the client application and have total control over its value.

Although we could modify the template yet again to insert the new property, a more flexible solution is to create a class with state information that the entities can inherit from. If you need to add additional logic in the future, you can simply add it to this base class and it will be inherited by the entities.

Creating your own base classes to provide additional logic to your POCO classes remains in line with the goal of ensuring that your classes are not tightly bound to or dependent on the Entity Framework.

The StateObject class provides a State property that each entity will inherit. I've chosen to handcode this class, but you could add code into your T4 template (or create an additional template) to have it automatically generated. The DataContract and DataMember attributes allow the object and property to be serialized by WCF.

I've created a separate project to contain the StateObject class so that I can reuse it in other applications.

Example 18-1 shows the class, which you'll enhance further in a few pages.

Example 18-1. A simple class for providing state to POCO entities

```
using System.Runtime.Serialization;

namespace POCO.State
{
  [DataContract(IsReference = true)]
  public class StateObject
  {
    [DataMember]
    public State State { get; set; }
  }

  public enum State
  {
      Added, Unchanged, Modified,Deleted
  }
}
```

Modifying the template to apply the inheritance

Currently the entities generated from the model inherit from other entities only if that inheritance is defined in the model. For example, Customer inherits from Contact.

Example 18-2 shows the template code, which uses an existing method in the template, StringBefore, to add inheritance to entities when they inherit from another entity in the model.

Example 18-2. The code that the POCO template uses to inject inheritance into an entity

```
<#=code.Escape(entity)#><#=code.StringBefore(" : ", code.Escape(entity.BaseType))#>
```

This ensures that the Customer class inherits from Contact, or that any derived entity inherits from its base, in the generated code.

But we now want to have every entity inherit from the new StateObject class unless the entities are already deriving from another base entity. In other words, Contact should inherit directly from StateObject, while Customer continues to inherit from Contact (and therefore indirectly inherits StateObject). To our good fortune, the EntityObject template uses similar logic to have entities inherit either from EntityObject or from a base entity. You can borrow from that template to get similar logic into our POCO template.

First, you'll need to add the method, `BaseTypeName`, shown in Example 18-3, into the custom methods section of the template where you inserted the `MaxLengthValidation` method in Example 13-12. This method came from the EntityObject template but has been modified to insert an inheritance to `StateObject`.

Example 18-3. The BaseTypeName method to be used in the POCO template

```
string BaseTypeName(EntityType entity, CodeGenerationTools code)
{
  return entity.BaseType == null ? "POCO.State.StateObject" :
     code.Escape(entity.BaseType);
}
```

Now you can modify the code shown in Example 18-2, where the entity declaration is made to call the `BaseTypeName` method. Instead, the entity will inherit from either `StateObject` or its base type as defined in the model.

```
<#=code.Escape(entity)#> : <#=BaseTypeName(entity, code)#>
```

Finally, if you placed the `StateObject` class in a separate project (as I did), you'll need to be sure the entities can find the `StateObject` class. In the Entities project, add a reference to the new project.

When all of these modifications have been applied to the template, the generated entity classes that do not inherit from another entity should now inherit from the `StateObject`, as shown here with the `Activity` class:

```
public partial class Activity : POCO.State.StateObject
```

Following WCF Collection Rules

The POCO template uses `ICollection<T>` to expose navigation properties that are collections (e.g., the `Reservations` for a `Customer` is an `ICollection<Reservation>`). This allows the consuming application the flexibility to choose what variety of an `ICollection` it would like to use. However, data contract serialization will coerce the `ICollection` into a type that is not an interface and you cannot control the type that is chosen.

See the MSDN document "Collection Types in Data Contracts" at *http://msdn.microsoft.com/en-us/library/aa347850.aspx* for more details on collection serialization.

On the client, you can force the collection to become a generic `List<T>` when creating the proxy using the Advanced configuration settings. However, when the data is coming back to the service, you cannot control how the collection is deserialized. I have encountered scenarios where it is deserialized as an array that is immutable, and exceptions are thrown anytime my code attempts to add or remove items.

To avoid this problem, you should specify the collection type for these navigation properties. The POCO template creates and uses a class called `FixupCollection`, so you can use this type. Here's how to make that change.

In the template, there are two instances where `ICollection` is used. The first is to declare the navigation property and the second is to define the field used by the navigation property. Search the template for `ICollection` and replace it with `FixupCollection`.

When you're done, the property declaration should look like this:

```
[DataMember]
<#=Accessibility.ForReadOnlyProperty(navProperty)#>
   FixupCollection<<#=code.Escape(navProperty.ToEndMember.GetEntityType())#>>
   <#=code.Escape(navProperty)#>
```

The field declaration should look like this:

```
private FixupCollection<<#=code.Escape(navProperty.ToEndMember.GetEntityType())#>>
 <#=code.FieldName(navProperty)#>;
```

Preventing Properties from Being Marked As Virtual

There is one last item to take care of in the template. By default, the template will mark all properties with the `virtual` keyword to force the use of the dynamic proxies at runtime. This creates problems for serialization, and we don't need the benefits of dynamic proxies—features such as lazy loading and change notification—in the service.

The `virtual` keyword is applied using a template method called `PropertyVirtualModifier`. It is used when the properties are being declared. It is used in three instances in the template and we need to remove them.

The first two occur when defining primitive (a.k.a. scalar) and `ComplexType` properties:

```
<#=PropertyVirtualModifier(Accessibility.ForProperty(edmProperty))#>
```

The third occurs when we define the navigation properties:

```
<#=PropertyVirtualModifier(Accessibility.ForReadOnlyProperty(navProperty))#>
```

Remove the `PropertyVirtualModifier` function that wraps the `Accessibility` function in all three cases. Don't forget to also remove its closing parenthesis. The two function calls should now look like this:

```
<#= Accessibility.ForProperty(edmProperty)#>
<#= Accessibility.ForReadOnlyProperty(navProperty)#>
```

Don't hesitate to save copies of the T4 templates as you modify them. You may have a variety of templates that you'll want to pick and choose from depending on your needs.

The code generation will automatically be performed when you save the changes to your template. Take a look at the generated code to admire your new classes.

Building a WCF Service That Uses POCO Classes

In Chapter 17, you built a WCF service to allow consuming applications to interact with `Customers`, `Trips`, and `Reservations`. Here we'll build a service that satisfies the same needs as the previous service, although we will design it to use the POCO entities you just created. By rebuilding the service, you will be able to see the direct impact of using the POCOs instead of the `EntityObjects`.

Begin by creating a new WCF Service Application project as you did in Chapter 17, and rename the service interface to `ICustomerService` and the service class to `CustomerService`.

In the previous service, you had explicit operations for update, insert, and delete to specify the required action. Now that your entities contain a `State` property, all of the guesswork for the required action has been removed. You can now use a single `SaveCustomer` operation that will take a `Customer` type whether it is a sole entity or a graph that includes `Reservations` and more.

Example 18-4 lists the operations for the new `ICustomerService`.

Example 18-4. ICustomerService OperationContracts

```
[OperationContract]
List<CustomerNameAndID> GetCustomerPickList();

[OperationContract]
List<Trip> GetUpcomingTrips();

[OperationContract]
Customer GetCustomer(int customerId);

[OperationContract]
string SaveCustomer(Customer customer);
```

A big benefit is that you no longer need the complex `CustomerUpdate` type that you had to use previously in order to keep track of deleted `Reservations`. The `SaveCustomer` operation simply takes a `Customer` now.

Implementing the Interface

Now you can implement this interface in the `CustomerService` class. Begin by using the Visual Studio editor's interface generation capability that allows you to automatically create the various methods defined in the interface.

Check step 3 in the section titled "Implementing the Service Interface" on page 459 in Chapter 17 if you need a refresher on how to do that.

At this point, you can fill in the logic for the various methods.

Example 18-5 lists the three query operations—`GetCustomerPickList`, `GetUpcomingTrips`, and `GetCustomer`—with their logic added. Because you are no longer using the dynamic proxies with your entities (because you prevented the template from making the properties virtual), there is no need to disable lazy loading as you did in Chapter 17. Lazy loading works only when the navigation properties are virtual.

Example 18-5. The service query operations

```
public List<CustomerNameAndID> GetCustomerPickList()
{
  using (var context = new BAEntities())
  {
    return context.CustomerNameAndIDs
                  .OrderBy(c => c.LastName + c.FirstName).ToList();
  }
}
public List<Trip> GetUpcomingTrips()
{
  using (var context = new BAEntities())
  {
    return context.Trips.Include("Destination")
      .Where(t => t.StartDate > DateTime.Today).ToList();
  }
}

public Customer GetCustomer(int customerId)
{
  using (var context = new BAEntities())
  {
    var cust =
        from c in context.Contacts.OfType<Customer>()
          .Include("Reservations.Trip.Destination")
        where c.ContactID == customerID
        select c;
    return cust.Single();
  }
}
```

Now you can add code to the `SaveCustomer` method. Let's first take a look at what needs to go in the method.

Although each entity will have its `State` field populated by the consuming app, that property will not allow `SaveChanges` to build the appropriate database commands. You will need to add the incoming entity to the context and then set the `EntityState` property to the correct state in order for `SaveChanges` to do its work.

An explicit approach would be to use a `switch` statement to modify the `EntityState` based on `State`:

```
switch (customer.State)
{
  case State.Modified:
    context.ObjectStateManager.
      ChangeObjectState(customer,System.Data.EntityState.Modified);
  ...
}
```

A nicer approach was used by Rowan Miller, from the Entity Framework team, in his June 2009 blog post (*http://romillerblog.wordpress.com/2009/06/26/ntier-with-ef4-beta-1/*), where he encapsulates the `switch` statement into a `StateObject` helper method within a static class, as shown in Example 18-6.

Example 18-6. A method for replacing the POCO entity's State property with the relevant EntityState

```
public static class StateHelpers
{
  public static EntityState GetEquivalentEntityState(State state)
  {
    switch (state)
    {
      case State.Added:
        return EntityState.Added;
      case State.Modified:
        return EntityState.Modified;
      case State.Deleted:
        return EntityState.Deleted;
      default:
        return EntityState.Unchanged;
    }
  }
}
```

I've added this `StateHelpers` class to the project that contains the `StateObject` and I suggest that you do the same. This lets you keep the state logic code out of your service and simply call the method like this:

```
context.ObjectStateManager.ChangeObjectState(customer,
  StateHelpers.GetEquivalentEntityState(customer.State));
```

In the `SaveCustomer` method, when iterating through the `Reservations`, remember that they will already be attached to the context because you have attached the customer graph of which they are a part. But you'll still need to change the `EntityState` of each `Reservation` based on its `State` property.

Example 18-7 lists the `SaveCustomer` method in its entirety.

Example 18-7. The SaveCustomer method

```
public string SaveCustomer(Customer customer)
{
```

```
    try
    {
      using (var context = new BAEntities())
      {

        context.Contacts.Attach(customer);

        context.ObjectStateManager.ChangeObjectState(customer,
          StateHelpers.GetEquivalentEntityState(customer.State));

        foreach (var reservation in customer.Reservations.ToList())
        {
          context.ObjectStateManager.ChangeObjectState(reservation,
            StateHelpers.GetEquivalentEntityState(reservation.State));
        }
        context.SaveChanges();
        return "";
      }
    }
    catch (Exception ex)
    {
      return ex.Message;
    }
  }
```

Compare this to the code you wrote in Chapter 17 to add, delete, and save customers and the additional logic required to handle reservations in their various states. This is much simpler and the logic is far more comprehensible thanks mostly to the addition of the state properties.

There is a possibility that a reservation being deleted might have payments in the database, which you may not want to lose. In a production app, you'll likely want some additional code to ensure that reservations with payments are handled according to your business rules when the client has requested that they be deleted.

Using the Service

As you did in Chapter 17, you'll use a simple console application to hit the service and test out its various operations. In fact, you can use the same console application from Chapter 17, with some modifications to perform this test.

The following steps are based on altering the existing application. If you want to create a new project, you can copy the code from Example 17-5 into the new project's main module.

Begin by adding a reference to the new service. Your existing application already has a reference to the service you built in Chapter 17. There's no problem with adding more than one service reference to an application.

Using the steps from the section "Building a Simple Console App to Consume an EntityObject Service" on page 469, add a service reference to the new WCF service, giving it the name `POCOCustomerService`.

The modified version of the code will need a `using` statement pointing to the new proxy. Replace the original with:

```
using Chapter17ConsoleApp.POCOCustomerService;
```

Example 18-8 lists the new version of the `GetandUpdateCustomer` method. There are only a few changes to note. The first is that you will explicitly set the `State` property of entities that you're interacting with. The second is that if there are any existing reservations, you'll modify the first and delete the last. Finally, calling the `SaveCustomer` method is simpler than the previous `UpdateCustomer`. Just pass in the customer graph, rather than having to create the complex type and pass in the `ReservationIDs` for deleted `Reservations`.

Example 18-8. Testing out the POCO service

```
private static void GetandUpdateCustomer()
{
  try
  {
    using (var proxy = new CustomerServiceClient())
    {
      var custList = proxy.GetCustomerPickList();

      int randomCustomerId = custList[8].Id;
      var customer = proxy.GetCustomer(randomCustomerId);

      customer.Notes += ", new notes";
      customer.State = State.Modified;

      List<Trip> trips = proxy.GetUpcomingTrips();

      var newReservation = new Reservation();
      newReservation.ReservationDate = DateTime.Now;
      //emulate selection of trip from list of trips
      newReservation.TripID = trips[12].TripID;
      //create a default value for binary field
      newReservation.RowVersion = System.Text.Encoding.Default.GetBytes("0x123");

      if (customer.Reservations == null)
      {
        customer.Reservations = new List<Reservation>();
      }
      else
      {
        customer.Reservations[0].State = State.Modified;
```

```
          if (customer.Reservations.Count > 1)
          {
            customer.Reservations[customer.Reservations.Count - 1].State
             = State.Deleted;
          }
        }
        customer.Reservations.Add(newRes);
        newRes.ContactID = customer.ContactID;
        newRes.State = State.Added;
        string status = proxy.SaveCustomer(customer);
        Console.WriteLine("Status of SaveCustomer operation: " + status);
      }
    }
    catch (Exception ex)
    {
      Console.WriteLine(ex.Message);
    }
  }
```

The interesting events happen in the service's `SaveCustomer` method. When you debug through that you can watch the `EntityState` of the objects being modified, and finally, when profiling the database you can see the activity when `SaveChanges` is called.

In Figure 18-1, you can see that three update commands are related to the modification of the customer. Why three? Recall that in Chapter 10, you learned that changing the object's `EntityState` to `Modified` renders every property as modified. The `Customer` inherits from `Contact` and maps to `Customer` and `ContactPersonalInfo`. Entity Framework is updating all properties in all three tables.

```
exec sp_executesql N'update [dbo].[Contact]  set [FirstName] = @0...
exec sp_executesql N'update [dbo].[ContactPersonalInfo]  set [Bir...
exec sp_executesql N'update [dbo].[Customers]  set [CustomerTypeI...
exec sp_executesql N'update [dbo].[Reservations]  set [Reservatio...
exec sp_executesql N'delete [dbo].[Reservations]  where ([Reserva...
exec sp_executesql N'insert [dbo].[Reservations]([ReservationDate...
```

Figure 18-1. Database commands generated by the SaveCustomer method

The next `Update` command is updating the reservation that was marked as `Modified`. Then you see the delete command being executed for the reservation we marked as `Deleted`. Then finally the new reservation is added.

All of the modifications we made in the client application were easily identified thanks to the simplicity of including a `State` property in our classes.

Additionally, the performance over the wire is greatly improved thanks to the minimized payloads of serializing, transmitting, and deserializing data that is much smaller because we are using POCO classes and not `EntityObjects`. Another benefit is realized by consuming applications that are not using .NET. These developers will be much happier to work with the simple data structures than to have to comb through the payload generated by an `EntityObject`.

Using the Self-Tracking Entities Template for WCF Services

Microsoft has provided a specialized template that attempts to handle change tracking for WCF services and their clients for the most typical scenarios. This Self-Tracking Entities template creates POCO classes that encapsulate change tracking and notification without leaning on the Entity Framework APIs.

This template is included in the Visual Studio 2010 installation, so you will not need to download it as you did for the POCO template.

In addition to creating the classes, the template generates logic that you can use in the service to update the state of every entity in a graph without having to specifically walk through it as we did in the previous example, first updating the customer and then iterating through its `Reservations` collection.

The self-tracking entities are designed specifically for use with custom WCF services. They are not meant for other types of applications or for use in combination with other types of services, such as WCF Data Services or WCF RIA Services, unless you customize the provided templates.

Let's regenerate the entity classes using this template.

To avoid confusion, I've created a new solution using a new project that contains a copy of my current model. Then I removed artifacts of the previous use of the model by doing the following:

1. Remove the existing template (*BreakAway.Context.tt*) from the project.
2. Remove the references to BreakAwayEntities and POCOState projects.

Creating and Exploring the Self-Tracking Entities

With the new model project in hand, you can generate the new classes. Open the model in the Designer and add a code generation item from its context menu. This time, select ADO.NET Self-Tracking Entity Generator from the template list.

As a result, two templates will be added to your project, just as they were for the POCO template: one template for the context and another for the entities.

Rather than looking at the templates, you'll learn more by inspecting the generated classes. First look at what is created from the entities template.

The interesting logic in the generated entities falls into two categories. One is related to WCF's data contract serialization and the other is related to change tracking.

On the change tracking side, each entity implements a pair of interfaces: `IObjectWithChangeTracker` and `INotifyPropertyChanged`.

```
public partial class Reservation: IObjectWithChangeTracker, INotifyPropertyChanged
```

These are not Entity Framework interfaces. The first, `IObjectWithChangeTracker`, was created by the template in the generated class that was given the same name as the template. In my case, I did not rename the default template, so it is called *Model1.tt*. There is a class called `Model1.cs` that is among the entity classes generated by the model. It contains a lot of specialized logic that the self-tracking entities depend on, including `IObjectWithChangeTracker`.

The second interface, `INotifyPropertyChanged`, is part of `System.ComponentModel` and is frequently used for change notification behavior through .NET classes and in our own custom classes.

Like the classes that inherit from `EntityObject` (created by the default template) each property calls a local `OnPropertyChanged` method in its setter, as shown in Example 18-9.

Example 18-9. A self-tracking entity property

```
[DataMember]
public string LastName
{
  get { return _lastName; }
  set
  {
    if (_lastName != value)
    {
      _lastName = value;
      OnPropertyChanged("LastName");
    }
  }
}
```

Each class has its own `OnPropertyChanged` method as well as an `OnNavigationPropertyChanged` method.

The `IObjectWithChangeTracker` interface provides an `ObjectChangeTracker` property to each entity. This property ties back to a class that is also defined in the `Model1` class that has members such as `State`, `OriginalValues`, and `ChangeTrackingEnabled` properties.

The entity then adopts these same properties. For example, each entity will now have an `ObjectChangeTracker` property that gives you access to its `State` property. To get the `State` of `Contact`, you would call `Contact.ObjectChangeTracker.State`. The `Original`

Values property is even more interesting, as it allows the entity to store its original values and carry them back and forth between the client and the service.

A lot of backing code is generated by the template to enable the entities to retain their state and their original properties, and I will not walk you through the generated classes in detail. The meat of the self-tracking entities is in their change notification features which can automatically impact these properties that will make it easy to get changes made on the client back to the service. Additionally, as you'll see shortly, self-tracking entities nearly eliminate any effort needed in the service to persist those changes back to the client.

Putting the Change-Tracking Logic Where It's Needed

In the WCF service solutions you've already built, the client application was responsible for providing the state information to the service. When it didn't, the service had to make its best guess as to the entity's state, for example, by checking for an existing ContactID. If the ID was 0, it must be new.

This responsibility doesn't change. But to reap the full benefits of self-tracking entities, you must include them in the client applications. If you rely solely on the data contract serialization to provide the entities to the client application, you will get the properties—even, for example, Contact.ObjectChangeTracker.State—but you will not get the events and methods that provide all of the automated notification features. Instead, the developer of the client application would need to set the State property manually and push values into the ObjectChangeTracker.OriginalValues dictionary manually. Even if you chose this path, in the service you would still benefit from a special method generated by the Self-Tracking Entities template, the ApplyChanges extension method.

Interoperability with Self-Tracking Entities?

Self-tracking entities are a great solution for .NET 4 clients, but they are not so great for consuming applications that are not using .NET. Why? All of the built-in change-tracking and notification functionality requires that the generated classes be part of the client solution. The change tracking makes use of the NotifyCollectionChangedEventArgs class, which, in .NET 4, physically lives in *System.dll*, whereas in earlier versions of .NET it is in *WindowsBase.dll*. You would need to create a reference to that *WindowsBase.dll* assembly in your client app instead. You could not, however, target .NET 2.0, since the class doesn't exist anywhere in that version of the framework.

Without the entity classes, the developer of the client application will have to manually set the object state, original values, and other important relationship change-tracking information on the client side for the changes to be sent back to the service. This is certainly possible to do. The entities will have access to State and OriginalValues properties and the service can still reap the benefit of the ApplyChanges method extension if the consuming application follows the rules carefully. But if you are building a service that must be interoperable, you will probably be better off using simpler POCO classes that you can customize similarly to the example in the first part of this chapter.

In order to share the classes with the client, the classes need to be in a separate project so that you can compile them into their own assembly and provide that assembly to the consuming applications. You can follow the same steps as you did in "Isolating the POCO Entities in Their Own Project." There is one additional step, which is to add a reference to `System.Runtime.Serialization` to the new project so that the serialization logic in the entities will be recognized.

Now you will be able to add a reference to this new project to the client application when it's time to build it. But first we will need to build the service and, when doing that, we'll also take a look at some of the special logic created in the generated context class and its extensions.

Creating a WCF Service That Uses Self-Tracking Entities

The new service will have a lot in common with the one you created for the POCO entities. It differs only in how `SaveCustomer` is handled.

1. Create a new WCF Service application with references to both the model project and the new entities project.
2. As with all of your previous services, copy the `ConnectionStrings` section from the model project's *app.config* file into the service project's *web.config* file.

   The service interface will define the same `OperationContract` methods as the previous service.
3. Add the `OperationContract` methods as listed in Example 18-4 to the service contract interface.
4. Implement the three query methods exactly as you did in the previous service. Refer to Example 18-5 for these implementations.

The `SaveCustomer` method will be quite different from before. There is a lot less code. A method specific to the Self-Tracking Entities, ApplyChanges, makes all the difference. Create the `SaveCustomer` method as listed in Example 18-10.

Example 18-10. The SaveCustomer service method for self-tracking entities

```
public string SaveCustomer(Customer cust)
{
  try
  {
    using (BAPOCOs context = new BAPOCOs())
    {
      context.Contacts.ApplyChanges(cust);
      context.SaveChanges();
      return "";
    }
```

```
    }
    catch (Exception ex)
    {
      return ex.Message;
    }
  }
```

After running some client code against the service, you'll learn more about this special method and others that the Self-Tracking Entities templates has created in the context.

Watching Self-Tracking Entities Under the Covers

The most interesting part of implementing self-tracking entities is to watch them at work. Let's run some code and see what happens on the client side and then what happens on the service side during the update.

I'm going to use a console app with logic that is almost identical to that in Example 18-8. To follow along, you can create a new console app and copy the `GetAndEditCustomer` method from the previous example, or you can edit the code in the existing console application.

The changes to the code are as follows.

Remove the code that explicitly sets the customer's `State` property:

```
//customer.State = State.Modified;
```

Self-tracking entities have an impact on the collection type returned by collection navigation properties such as **`customer.Reservations`**. This collection is specifically a `TrackableCollection<T>`, which is another custom class generated by the template. Change the call to instantiate `Reservations` as follows:

```
//customer.Reservations = new List<Reservation>();
  customer.Reservations = new TrackableCollection<Reservation>();
```

Replace the line of code that simply marks a `Reservation` as modified with code that makes an actual modification:

```
//customer.Reservations[0].State = State.Modified;
  customer.Reservations[0].ReservationDate =
     customer.Reservations[0].ReservationDate.AddDays(1);
```

Remove the code that sets the new reservation's `State`:

```
//newRes.State = State.Added;
```

One of the methods provided in the specialized change-tracking functionality of the self-tracking entities is the `MarkAsDeleted` property. This is simpler than explicitly changing the `State`.

```
//customer.Reservations[customer.Reservations.Count - 1].State = State.Deleted;
  customer.Reservations[customer.Reservations.Count - 1].MarkAsDeleted();
```

Self-tracking entities also have `MarkAsAdded`, `MarkAsModified`, and `MarkAsUnchanged` methods so that you can impact state directly if you want without having to use the `State` property.

Debugging the client application

Now as the code executes, it is interesting to take a look at the effect on the `State` properties and the `OriginalValue` properties of the entities being impacted.

After the `customer.Notes` field has been changed, take a look at the customer's `ChangeTracker` property in the debugger shown in Figure 18-2. Remember that the `ChangeTracker` property exposes an `ObjectChangeTracker` object that is bound to that particular entity instance.

The next stop in the debugger is after modifying an existing reservation's `Reservation Date`. Its `State` property becomes `Modified`. Nothing else interesting is happening there, so let's move on.

Name	Value
customer	{BAGA.Customer}
base	{BAGA.Customer}
_addDate	{11/20/2004 11:10:27 PM}
_addresses	Count = 0
_changeTracker	{BAGA.ObjectChangeTracker}
_changeTrackingEnabled	true
_extendedProperties	Count = 0
_isDeserializing	false
_objectsAddedToCollections	Count = 0
_objectsRemovedFromCollections	Count = 0
_objectState	Modified
_originalValues	Count = 0

Figure 18-2. The modified customer's ChangeTracker

Notice that the `_objectState` field (which is exposed as the `State` property) is now `Modified`, but that no other metadata has been altered, not even `OriginalValues`.

Self-tracking entities do not store the original values of every changed property. Instead, they store only the original values of properties critical to performing database modifications as follows:

- Properties that are part of the entity's `EntityKey`
- Foreign key properties
- Any properties that you have marked in the model as `ConcurrencyMode=Fixed`

You can verify this by checking the generated entity classes, where you will find a call to `ChangeTracker.RecordOriginalValue` in the setter of these types of properties, but not in any of the other scalar properties.

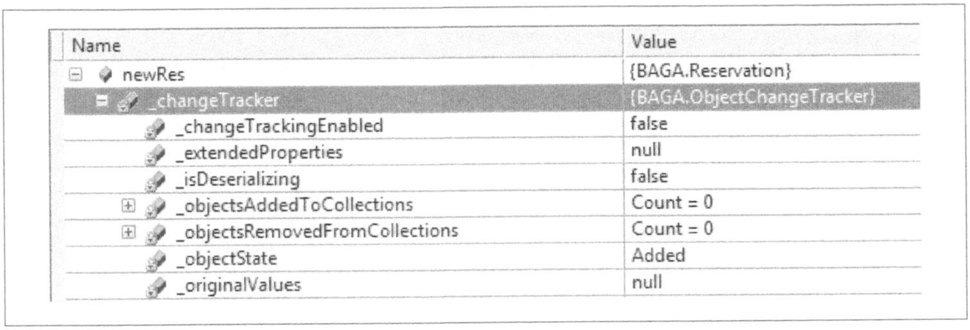

Name	Value
⊟ newRes	{BAGA.Reservation}
⊟ _changeTracker	{BAGA.ObjectChangeTracker}
_changeTrackingEnabled	false
_extendedProperties	null
_isDeserializing	false
⊞ _objectsAddedToCollections	Count = 0
⊞ _objectsRemovedFromCollections	Count = 0
_objectState	Added
_originalValues	null

Figure 18-3. The new reservation's ChangeTracker

While this makes the message sent back to the service more efficient, it does have an impact on the commands sent to the database, as you'll see when we get back to the service.

The next stop in the debugger is after the new `Reservation` has been instantiated. You will find that its `ChangeTracker` is not instantiated until a property is set. In our case we are setting a foreign key value first, but the impact would be the same even if it were a simpler scalar value such as `ReservationDate`. But the `ChangeTracker` is set up a bit differently than the `Customer`'s `ChangeTracker`. Compare the `newRes.ChangeTracker` displayed in Figure 18-3 to the `customer.ChangeTracker` earlier.

The `State` property (`_objectState` field in the screenshot) was set to `Added`, but more interestingly, `changeTrackingEnabled` is set to `false`. That is so as properties continue to be set or changed in this new `Reservation`, the change-tracking logic does not automatically set the `State` to `Modified`.

Notice also that the `_originalValues` and `_extendedProperties` fields are null.

After hitting the next line of code, where the `TripID` foreign key is given a value, you'll find that these two fields change to `Count=0`. That's the result of executing the `RecordOriginalValue` method, which was triggered by the change to the foreign key. However, there are still no items (e.g., no values in the `_originalValues` collection) because an `Added` entity does not have original values.

The next point of interest is when a `Reservation` is deleted. Because the `Reservation` is part of a collection it is removed from that collection. `Customer.Reservations` will have one less item in it. The `Reservation` is still in memory, and if you created a variable pointing to it before deleting, for example:

```
var resDelete = customer.Reservations[customer.Reservations.Count - 1];
resDelete.MarkAsDeleted();
```

you can take a look at the instance in debug mode. Figure 18-4 shows the deleted `Reservation`'s `ChangeTracker` in a watch window.

Name	Value
⊟ resDelete	{BAGA.Reservation}
⊟ _changeTracker	{BAGA.ObjectChangeTracker}
_changeTrackingEnabled	true
⊞ _extendedProperties	Count = 0
_isDeserializing	false
⊞ _objectsAddedToCollections	Count = 0
⊞ _objectsRemovedFromCollections	Count = 0
_objectState	Deleted
⊟ _originalValues	Count = 3
⊞ [0]	{[Customer, BAGA.Customer]}
⊞ [1]	{[TripID, 65]}
⊞ [2]	{[Trip, BAGA.Trip]}
⊞ Raw View	

Figure 18-4. A deleted Reservation's ChangeTracker

As expected, the `_objectState` field is now `Deleted`. But you can finally see some original values. The entity doesn't simply store the ID, but has stored away entire related entities representing the relationships that are impacted at the same time the `Reservation` is being deleted. This information will be used by the `ApplyChanges` method in the service.

What would happen if you had deleted the customer? `Customer` differs from `Reservation` in two significant ways. It's not a member of an entity collection for any of the in-memory entities, and it has properties that contain collections. Figure 18-5 shows the `ChangeTracker` of the customer after it's been marked as deleted.

Name	Value
⊟ _changeTracker	{BAGA.ObjectChangeTracker}
_changeTrackingEnabled	true
⊞ _extendedProperties	Count = 0
_isDeserializing	false
⊞ _objectsAddedToCollections	Count = 0
⊟ _objectsRemovedFromCollections	Count = 1
⊟ [0]	{[Reservations, BAGA.ObjectList]}
Key	"Reservations"
key	"Reservations"
⊟ Value	Count = 2
⊞ [0]	{BAGA.Reservation}
⊞ [1]	{BAGA.Reservation}
⊞ Raw View	
⊞ value	Count = 2
⊞ Raw View	
_objectState	Deleted
⊞ _originalValues	Count = 0

Figure 18-5. A deleted Customer's ChangeTracker property

Notice that `_originalValues` contains no items, but there is a property we haven't looked at before—`_objectsRemovedFromCollections`—that contains information. When I deleted the `Reservation` earlier, entities that were related were stored in `_originalValues`. But with `Customer`, related entities that are part of a collection are stored in `_objectsRemovedFromCollections`. Again, `ApplyChanges` will look at this information when fixing up the states of everything in the graph.

If you really did delete the `Customer`, you would need to attend to the related reservations as well. As it stands, you will get an exception when calling `SaveChanges` if you don't delete the reservations or attach them to another customer. Even then there is still the slim chance that there are more reservations in the database for this customer. The same issue arises when deleting a `Reservation` without considering its `Payments`.

This problem is not particular to self-tracking entities, but a general concern with Entity Data Models. In Chapter 21, you'll learn about deleting related entities as well as model-defined and database-defined cascading deletes.

Debugging the SaveCustomer service method

Now it's time to look at what happens when this graph transfers back to the service's `SaveCustomer` method.

The message that is sent from the client back to the server has a lot of information in it. It is too long to display here, as it would be nearly four pages. But its size is 7 KB and it contains 191 lines because of the inclusion of the change-tracking information. You can view the message from the book's downloads page at *http://www.learnentityframework.com/downloads* or go directly to *http://learnentityframework.com/downloadfiles/savecustomermessage.xml*.

The `ApplyChanges` method fires off a lot of activity. It painstakingly adds all of the entities into the context, managing the relationships and states of each entity by reading through their `ChangeTracker` details. If you are interested in the process, you can debug through all of the steps as they are executed.

Let's take a look at some of the entities after `ApplyChanges` has finished its work.

First, you can see what's in the `ObjectStateManager` using C#'s unique debugger view of fields such as `_addedEntityStore`. Otherwise, you'd have to look at `GetObjectStateEntries` for all of the `EntityState` enums. Figure 18-6 shows the debug view with the nonessential information grayed out.

The context identifies one `Added` entity, one `Deleted` entity, two `Modified` entities, and four `Unchanged` entities. That coincides with the modifications we made on the client. The `Unchanged` entities are the `Trip` and `Destination` entities that are attached to reservations from the original graph. The client could remove unmodified entities from the graph prior to returning it to the service for a more efficient message.

`DanglingForeignKeys` is interesting. It represents foreign keys that don't have a coinciding entity in memory. In this case, the keys are the various foreign keys in the graph (e.g., the customer's `PrimaryActivityID`).

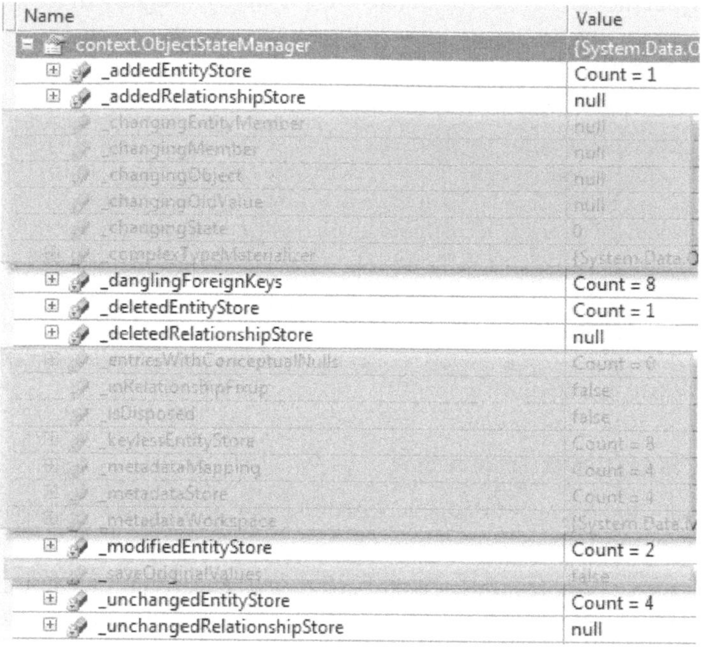

Figure 18-6. Looking at the critical entity state fields of the ObjectStateManager

Using the `ObjectStateEntry Visualizer` that was introduced in Chapter 10, Figure 18-7 displays the state of the `Customer` entity after `ApplyChanges` was called. As hinted at earlier, because `ApplyChanges` relies on the entity's state (`Modified`) rather than the actual original values, it changes the entire object to `Modified`, rendering every single property as a modified property. Notice that the original and current values of the `Notes` property are the same. The context doesn't know that we edited the `Notes` property or what its original value is.

And recall that the `Customer` is bound to not only the `Customer` table, but also the `Contact` and `ContactPersonalInfo` tables. Every field in all three of these tables will be updated when `SaveChanges` is called. But as discussed previously when considering the options for persisting changes to the database, in many cases this is still the most efficient method when balancing the service message size, the amount of coding, and the size and number of commands sent to the database.

As you can see, the self-tracking entities combined with the special context logic generated from the template makes the task of getting change information from a client back to a WCF service very simple. On the service side, all of the hard work of preparing those entities to be persisted to the database is handled by one method, `ApplyChanges`.

Self-tracking entities are a great solution when you want to reap the benefits of change tracking in WCF services with minimal investment. But keep in mind that the client

	Index	Property	Original	Current	ValueModified
▶	0	ContactID	360	360	X
	1	FirstName	Ramona ...	Ramona ...	X
	2	LastName	Antrim ...	Antrim ...	X
	3	Title	Mrs. ...	Mrs. ...	X
	4	AddDate	11/20/2004 11:1...	11/20/2004 11:1...	X
	5	ModifiedDate	2/5/2010 3:03:1...	2/5/2010 3:03:1...	X
	6	RowVersion	System.Byte[]	System.Byte[]	X
	7	CustomerTypeID	2	2	X
	8	InitialDate	5/25/2008 6:58:...	5/25/2008 6:58:...	X
	9	PrimaryDestinationID	54	54	X
	10	SecondaryDestinationID	57	57	X
	11	PrimaryActivityID	18	18	X
	12	SecondaryActivityID	21	21	X
	13	Notes	new notes 2:32 PM	new notes 2:32 PM	X
	14	BirthDate	9/27/1967 12:00	9/27/1967 12:00	X

Figure 18-7. The state of the Customer entity after ApplyChanges is called

must be .NET 3.5 or 4, the messages transferred across the wire are relatively large, and modified entities will push every property back to the database for an update.

Regarding this last point, I have taken the same path of changing object state to modified and letting all of the properties get persisted to the database whether they've been modified or not. However, in other solutions, you do have the option of using other mechanisms, such as pulling fresh data from the data store, updating only the modified values and letting `SaveChanges` build more efficient update commands.

Inspecting the Generated Context Class and Extensions

For a better understanding of how the self-tracking entities were able to do their job, you may be interested in taking a closer look at the classes and extension methods that were generated from the Self-Tracking Entities template.

The context template generated two files: the base context file, *Model1.Context.cs*, and a file containing extension methods, *Model1.Context.Extensions.cs*.The base context file is similar to the one generated from the POCO template but for two exceptions. The first is that it permanently turns off the creation of dynamic proxies, although it doesn't accomplish this by removing the `virtual` keyword from the properties as we did in the previous example. Instead, in the context's `Initialize` method, `ObjectContext.ContextOptions.ProxyCreationEnabled` is set to `false`. Additionally in the `Initialize` method, the code wires up the `ObjectMaterialized` event, which you learned about in Chapter 11, to a custom method, `HandleObjectMaterialized`.

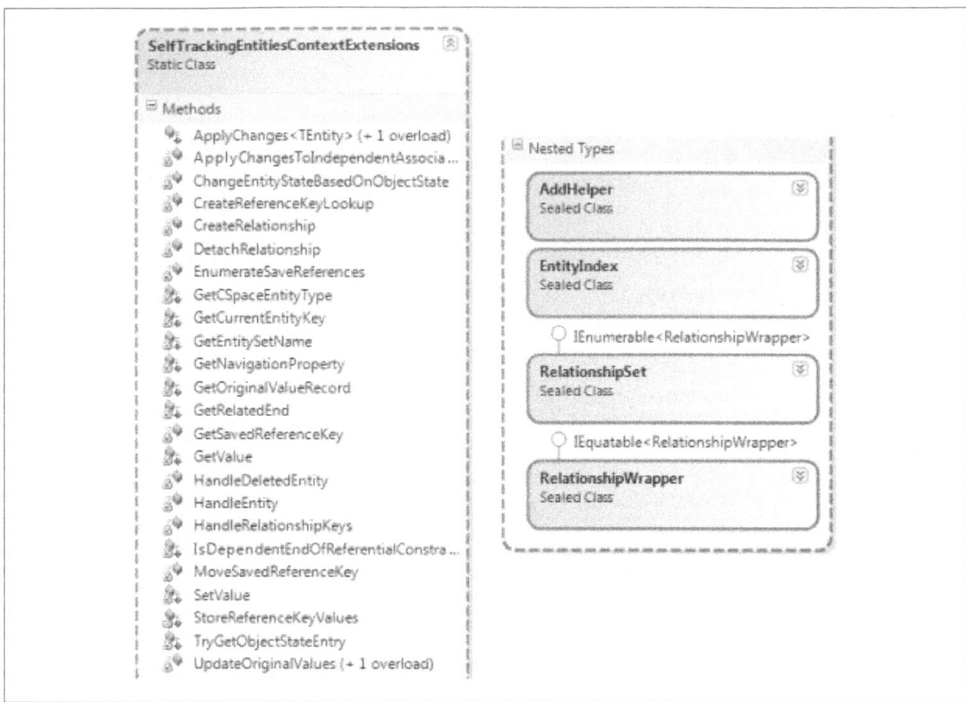

Figure 18-8. Class designer view of the specialized class generated by the Self-Tracking Entities template

This method performs three tasks to each entity being materialized during query execution. First, it ensures that the self-contained `State` property is set to `Unchanged`. Next, it enables the entity to participate in change tracking, and finally, it stores any key values, which, as you have seen throughout this book, are critical for change tracking as well as relationships.

Other than these method calls in the `Initialize` method, the context class is the same as the one generated from the POCO template.

The *Context.Extensions* file is where the bulk of the critical logic exists, with five classes and many methods, as shown in Figure 18-8.

There are more than 1,200 lines of code in this file, giving the `ObjectContext` the ability to work with the entities and graphs generically. The most important method for your code is the `ApplyChanges` method. But `ApplyChanges` has the ability to fix up state and relationships for any graph that you pass to it, as long as that graph contains self-tracking entities. This is a very difficult feat to pull off, which is why there is so much code in there.

If you think back to the `SaveCustomer` method in the POCO service and the `UpdateCustomer` method from the service in the previous chapter, these methods expected a specific type (`Customer`) and then worked explicitly with its related objects.

You iterated through the `Customer`'s `Reservations` collection. These methods depend on our prior knowledge of the exact shape of the graph that will be returned from the client. Therefore, you must write explicit update logic for every different graph that your service accepts from the client. If the customer graph also contained payment entities for each reservation, you would need additional code to explicitly work with each payment.

Alternatively, the `ApplyChanges` method is completely generic and can be used for any graph. This essentially makes it a universal method and the most valuable piece of logic created by the template.

Thanks to `ApplyChanges`, the new `SaveCustomer` method becomes much simpler because you no longer have to fix the `EntityState` or explicitly walk through the graph to fix the state of each related entity.

Using POCO Entities with WCF Data and RIA Services

You can certainly use your POCO entities behind WCF Data Services and WCF RIA Services. But there are a few things to be aware of.

First, I will repeat that self-tracking entities are not meant to be used with these technologies. They are for writing your own custom services. WCF Data Services and WCF RIA Services have their own change-tracking mechanisms. Using self-tracking entities will only weigh down the payloads and in some cases completely break the intended functionality.

Preparing for WCF Data Services

If you want to create a WCF data service from the model, context, and entities you created at the beginning of this chapter, there are some extra steps you'll need to take. First, your service project will need references not only to the project containing the model and context, but also to the project containing the entities. If you placed the `StateObject` into a separate assembly, as I recommended earlier, you'll need a reference to that as well.

Dealing with entities that live in a separate assembly

Having the entities in a separate assembly creates a problem for the service when it is trying to read the metadata that describes your model. The problem isn't about finding the metadata files, since you will have copied the connection string into the service's *web.config*. The issue is about finding the metadata in memory. You will learn more about metadata getting loaded into memory in Chapter 21, so for now I will show you how to get around the problem without providing a thorough explanation.

The problem will occur before the data service's `Initialize` method is even hit, so you can't even debug into the problem. Unless you have configured the service to set its

IncludeExceptionDetailInFaults to true, you will only get an error message saying "The server encountered an error processing the request. See server logs for more details." The more detailed error will tell you that a null value was encountered, and some further digging will let you know that this happened related to metadata.

To force all of the necessary metadata to be loaded into memory, you can override the service's CreateDataSource method. In your method, you can create the DataSource yourself (the ObjectContext) and then force the metadata to load using a trick—calling ToTraceString on a query. Example 18-11 shows the method that you should add to your service code.

Example 18-11. Overriding CreateDataSource in a WCF data service

```
protected override BAPOCOs CreateDataSource()
{
  var context = new BAPOCOs();
  var workspace = context.MetadataWorkspace;
  var tracestring = context.CreateQuery<Contact>("BAPOCOs.Contacts")
                           .ToTraceString();
  return context;
}
```

ToTraceString will force the context to work out the store query, and in order to do that, it needs to have the CSDL, MSL, and SSDL metadata in memory. It will load the metadata into memory as needed.

Once the metadata is loaded into memory, it stays there for the lifetime of the application process. However, WCF Data Services must explicitly unload the metadata from memory, because each time CreateDataSource is run, the metadata is no longer available. That is why the example code does not test to see if the metadata is loaded before calling ToTraceString.

Alternatively, you can use the MetadataWorkspace.LoadFromAssembly method, which you'll see in Chapter 21. LoadFromAssembly is more complicated; however, it will give you better performance than the ToTraceString method because it won't have to compile the query.

Avoiding problems caused by dynamic proxies

In the self-tracking entities discussion earlier, I pointed out that the context generated by the template sets the context's ContextOptions.ProxyCreationEnabled property to false. The self-tracking entities are set up to create dynamic proxies at runtime because each of their properties is marked as virtual. The entities take advantage of some of the benefits of the virtual properties, but the dynamic proxies create problems with serialization, so that functionality is turned off with the setting.

In the POCO entities you created at the beginning of the chapter, you explicitly removed the generation of the `virtual` keyword from the template. Those entities will not use proxies and you did not need to worry about the proxy-related serialization issue.

If you use the entities you generated in the early part of this chapter, or others that do not create proxies, you will not have any issues with WCF Data Services.

However, if your entities are set up to create proxies, you'll need to ensure that they do not get created as the entities are being serialized when being returned from the service.

The place to do this is in the same method used in Example 18-11, the `CreateDataSource` override. After you instantiate the context, you can disable the proxy creation, as shown in Example 18-12.

Example 18-12. Ensuring that entities with virtual properties do not create dynamic proxies in the data service

```
protected override BAPOCOs CreateDataSource()
{
  var context = new BAPOCOs();
  context.ContextOptions.ProxyCreationEnabled = false;
  return context;
}
```

Take note that if you create any other methods in your service that depend on proxy generation, such as a method that leverages lazy loading, you'll need to enable the proxy creation in that method but then disable it again at the end of the method.

Using POCO Entities in WCF RIA Services

When creating a domain service in WCF RIA Services, the template can create either a simple `DomainService` class or one that inherits either from `LinqToEntitiesDomainService` or from `LinqToSqlDomainService`. If the wizard sees that the classes your service is consuming are being controlled by an `ObjectContext`, it will implement the specialized template that includes the `LinqToEntitiesDomainService`. Similar logic will apply to drive the selection of the template for LINQ to SQL classes.

In Example 17-20 in Chapter 17, you saw the default methods `GetTrips`, `InsertTrip`, `UpdateTrip`, and `DeleteTrip` created by the Data Services Class Wizard for the `EntityObject`. Most of the logic in these methods is written so that it will work either with an `EntityObject` or with an entity that does not derive from `EntityObject`. For example, in `InsertTrip`, `this.ObjectContext.Trips.AddObject` can take an `EntityObject` or a POCO class as its parameter.

However, both `InsertTrip` and `UpdateTrip` do rely on an `EntityObject` property, `EntityState`. `EntityObject.EntityState` is formulated internally by reading the `ObjectStateEntry.State` property of the related tracking object being maintained by the `ObjectContext`.

Because the POCO entities do not inherit from `EntityObject`, they do not have this property. Additionally, because the POCO entities are not aware of the context, they do not have a way to get that information anyway.

In the data service class, however, you do have access to the context, so my solution is to replace those two requests to the `EntityState` property with a custom method called `GetEntityState`, added to the data service (see Example 18-13).

Example 18-13. The custom method, GetEntityState, added to the domain service

```
private EntityState GetEntityState(object entity)
{
  System.Data.Objects.ObjectStateEntry ose;
  if (this.ObjectContext.ObjectStateManager
                        .TryGetObjectStateEntry(entity, out ose))
    return ose.State;
  else
    return EntityState.Detached;
}
```

Typically, your WCF RIA Services application will have a number of domain service classes, so rather than adding the method repeatedly to each class, you should encapsulate it into another shared class where each domain service class can benefit from it.

Now you'll need to replace the use of `trip.EntityState` in the domain service with a call to the new method, `GetEntityState(trip)`. Example 18-14 does this to the two methods originally shown in Example 17-20 in Chapter 17.

Example 18-14. Using the GetEntityState method to determine an entity's state

```
public void InsertTrip(Trip trip)
 {
   if ((GetEntityState(trip) != EntityState.Detached))
   {
     this.ObjectContext.ObjectStateManager
                      .ChangeObjectState(trip, EntityState.Added);
   }
   else
   {
     this.ObjectContext.Trips.AddObject(trip);
   }
 }

 public void DeleteTrip(Trip trip)
 {
   if ((GetEntityState(trip)== EntityState.Detached))
   {
     this.ObjectContext.Trips.Attach(trip);
   }
   this.ObjectContext.Trips.DeleteObject(trip);
```

```
    }
}
```

At the time of this writing, WCF RIA Services was in a "Release Candidate" stage and was not yet fully released. It is possible that the problem I've described will be corrected prior to its release, and in that case, the custom method would not be required.

Sorting Out the Many Options for Creating Services

In the preceding two chapters, you were presented with an array of options for building services. Each option serves a different purpose. Now that you have worked with the various options, let's step back a bit and look at them from the perspective of which solution(s) applies to your needs.

POCO entities or `EntityObjects`*?*
: `EntityObjects` are the "out of the box" class that your entities are based on. While they provide a lot of useful automated change tracking and relationship management, it is challenging to work with services that depend on `EntityObjects` and transfer them across the wire. As you've seen, POCO entities remove many layers of pain, especially concerning state management, when you are creating services and making them easy for end users to consume.

Custom service, data service, or RIA service?
: There are three paths to choose for WCF services.

  The first is to write your own service. This is where you have ultimate control over the service operations and the other logic that they leverage, including handling features such as security.

  WCF Data Services is a more lightweight solution and allows you to provide your data to a wide range of consumers. Unlike WCF services, which use SOAP to move data across the wire, WCF Data Services exposes your data for access through URIs over REST (i.e., directly through HTTP). There are also convenient client APIs for .NET, Silverlight, PHP, AJAX, and other consumers. Many developers equate this to putting your database on the Internet, which is not the case. What is exposed is first defined by your model and further refined by settings in your service. You do have some control over securing the data, but it is not the same control you can exercise with your custom services.

  WCF RIA Services attempts to bridge the gap between roll-your-own services and WCF Data Services. Even though WCF RIA Services was originally designed to help with the complexities of getting data into and out of Silverlight applications, you can also consume RIA services from other applications as well, because in the end, unlike WCF Data Services, WCF RIA Services is still a WCF service. RIA services encapsulate some of the most common desired CRUD functionality and use templates and runtime generation to make it simple to build and consume the services. Again, if you want the ultimate in control, this may not be for you. But if you want to leverage a "canned" solution that is still highly customizable, you should take a look at WCF RIA Services.

Self-tracking entities?

Self-tracking entities are essentially a replacement for using ADO.NET `DataSets` in WCF services. They are not lightweight, and to get their true benefits, the consuming application must be a .NET 3.5 or 4 app that contains self-tracking entities. Self-tracking entities are your simplest path to using entities in WCF services.

Do not mistake self-tracking entities as a great solution for all of your applications. They are written specifically to be used with custom WCF services. They will not work with WCF Data Services or WCF RIA Services, nor can you use them to solve *n*-tier issues in other applications, such as ASP.NET. You do have the option of customizing the self-tracking entities templates, however, to make them suitable for other uses. Keep an eye on the ADO.NET team blog where you may find some guidance about this in the future.

Self-tracking entities are very different from other POCO classes, whether your POCO classes are generated from the provided template, a customized version of that template, or your own template.

Summary

WCF's various flavors of services are an increasingly critical element in many solution architectures. POCO entities, while not the default classes created by the Entity Framework tools, provide greater flexibility, simplicity, and control for using entities in WCF services.

The Microsoft-provided POCO template is not quite suited either for serialization or for use in services, but with a few minor customizations, you can make it work very nicely in your services.

For developers who are mourning the loss of the simplicity of using `DataSets`, self-tracking entities provide an easy-to-use, comparable solution in your custom WCF services.

You'll also need to keep in mind some of the nuances of WCF Data Services and WCF RIA Services when using your POCO entities in combination with these technologies.

Most importantly, understand what the different options are so that you can make the right choice when exposing your entities through WCF.

CHAPTER 19

Working with Relationships and Associations

At this point in the book, you have worked extensively with entities that are related to one another. You have also experienced a number of scenarios where it was necessary to do extra work to an object because of its associations. You learned that if an `EntitySet` is mapped using a `QueryView`, every other related entity also needs to be mapped using a `QueryView`. In building a WCF service in Chapter 17, you had to do a little extra work to make sure that when inserting new `Reservations`, the context did not also attempt to add a new `Trip` entity.

So much happens behind the scenes as the Entity Framework manages entities and their relationships that unexpected behaviors and seemingly strange errors can sometimes result, unless you follow the rules designed to maintain these relationships.

In this chapter, you'll learn how relationships and associations fit into the EDM and how they work both inside and outside the `ObjectContext`. With this knowledge, you will be better prepared to manipulate relationships between entities, adding or removing relationships between objects in the way that the Entity Framework expects; you will be able to solve problems that arise because of relationships; you will even enhance your ability to build more meaningful Entity Data Models. All the while, you'll be able to perform these tasks in the manner that Entity Framework expects. And if you happen to break an Entity Framework rule, hopefully this knowledge will help you to quickly see where you went wrong. You will also see this knowledge of working with relationships pay off in a big way when you build *n*-tier applications.

The chapter will focus on foreign key associations, which are the default in .NET 4. If you are not using foreign keys and need more information on independent associations, read the sidebar "Understanding Independent Associations" on page 524.

The behaviors outlined in this chapter pertain to `EntityObjects` and POCOs that create dynamic proxies. Otherwise, your POCOs will be dependent on whatever code you included to handle their relationships.

The chapter is divided into two parts. The first part is devoted to teaching you how relationships and associations work in the Entity Framework, from the EDM to the `EntityObjects`. The second part will teach you how to perform a number of critical tasks relating to entity graphs as you work with sets of related entities.

> **Understanding Independent Associations**
>
> The introduction of foreign keys into the model in .NET 4 has removed many layers of pain around relationships. While foreign key associations between entities are now the default when creating models, you may be using independent associations where mappings defined the relationships because no foreign key is available. The previous edition of this book covered independent associations in depth. You can find a copy of the relevant chapter from the first edition, Chapter 9, on the book's website at *http://www.learnentityframework.com/downloads*.

Deconstructing Relationships in the Entity Data Model

Many developers new to the Entity Framework have a lot of questions about relationships as they attempt to build Entity Data Models and write code to interact with entities. Having a better understanding of the fundamentals of these associations and how they work will allow you to create more powerful applications and better comprehend the Entity Framework's behavior. First we'll look at the model and then at Object Services.

In the Designer, `Associations` are represented as lines between related entities. The Designer displays the *multiplicity* between the entities. Multiplicity defines how many items a particular end can have. The multiplicity of an end can be defined in one of three ways:

One
: The end must have one item, no less and no more. This is quite often what we think of as a parent in a parent–child relationship.

Many
: The end can have many items. This is often a collection of children in a parent–child relationship. It's possible that no items (zero) exist in this collection.

Zero or One
: The end can have either zero items or one item but no more than one. Many of the entity references you have worked with in the BreakAway model have Zero or One ends. For example, the `Customer.PrimaryDestination` field may not have a destination defined, and therefore there will be zero items at that end. If a destination is defined, there can be no more than one.

As you learned in Chapter 2, the common notations for these are 1 (One), * (Many), and 0..1 (Zero or One). The EDM Designer displays the relationships with this notation.

When you hover your mouse pointer over a line representing an `Association`, you can see some additional details of the `Association`, as shown in Figure 19-1.

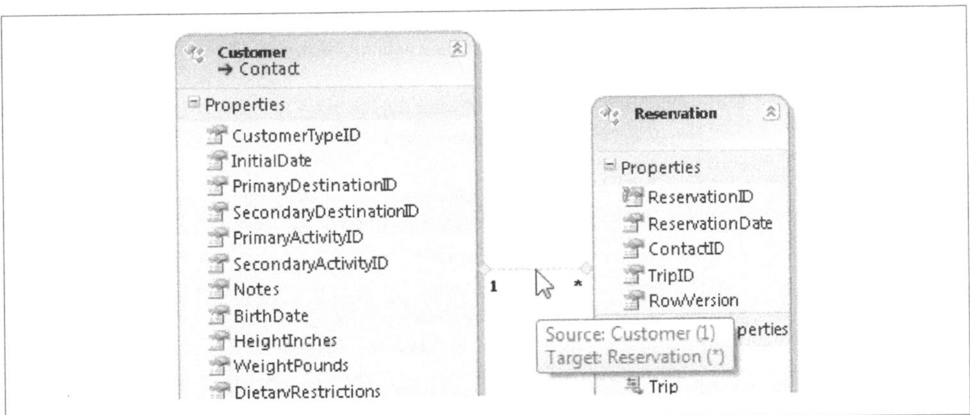

Figure 19-1. An association represented in the Designer

In the Properties window of the `Association`, shown in Figure 19-2, you can see even more details and make modifications if necessary.

By default, the `AssociationSet` has the same name as the `Association`. You may find it helpful to change the name of the `AssociationSet`, as shown in Figure 19-2, so that when you're looking at the EDMX in the XML Editor, it will be obvious whether you are looking at the `Association` or the `AssociationSet`. It is not common, however, to work with the `AssociationSet` directly in code, and therefore this is not a change that I have ever made when customizing my own EDMs.

Understanding How the Entity Data Model Wizard Creates the Association

The EDM Wizard created the `FK_Reservations_Customers` association shown in Figure 19-1 when it read the BreakAway database.

Figure 19-3 shows a portion of the database diagram for the BreakAway database. The diagram shows the `Customers` and `Reservations` tables as well as a visual representation of the 1:* (One to Many) relationship between `Customers` and `Reservations`. On the `Contact` side, the symbol for primary key is used because the primary key, `ContactID`, is used in the definition of the relationship.

The `ContactID` field in the `Reservations` table is a foreign key. The relationship is known as a *primary key/foreign key relationship*, which is often described and represented as

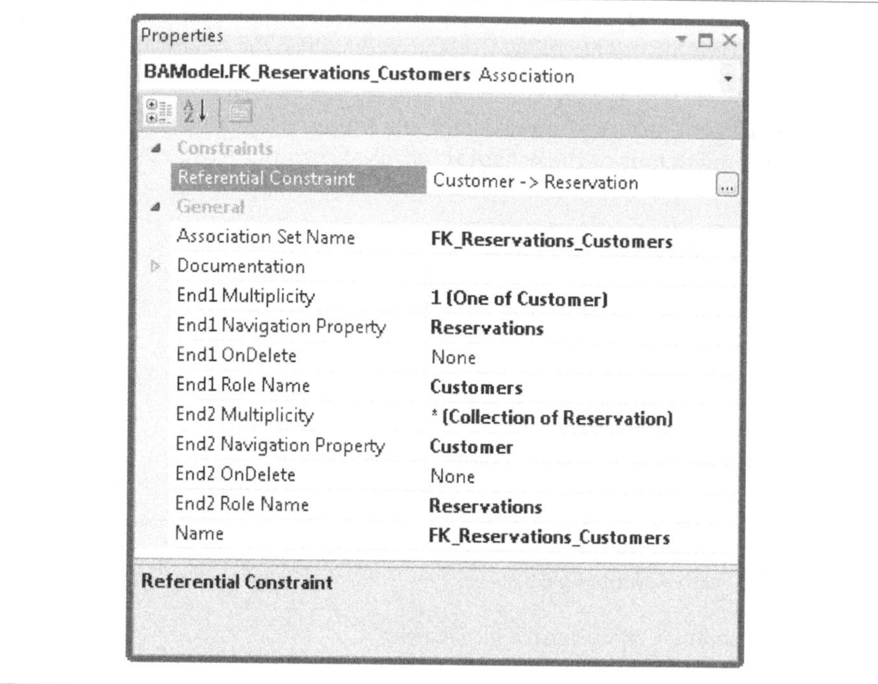

Figure 19-2. The Association's Properties window

PK/FK. This relationship is defined in a foreign key relationship of the `Reservations` table named `FK_Reservations_Customers`, as shown in Figure 19-4.

The `Customers` table has no knowledge of this relationship; the relationship and all of its rules (known as *constraints*) are contained in the `FK_Reservations_Customers` key. Figure 19-5 shows the details of this foreign key.

Although a *cascading delete rule* is not being used in this case, you could define such a rule so that anytime a contact is deleted all of its related `Reservations` records will be deleted automatically. You might expect this to be defined in the `Customers` table, but instead it is defined in the `Reservations` table's foreign key. To use a cascading delete rule in this case, you would change the Delete Rule in Figure 19-5 from No Action to Cascade.

Watch for a discussion later in this chapter about database-defined cascade deletes and their relationship to model-defined cascade deletes.

The EDM Wizard reads all of this information, creates the `FK_Reservations_Customers` association, and wires it up to the relevant items in the model.

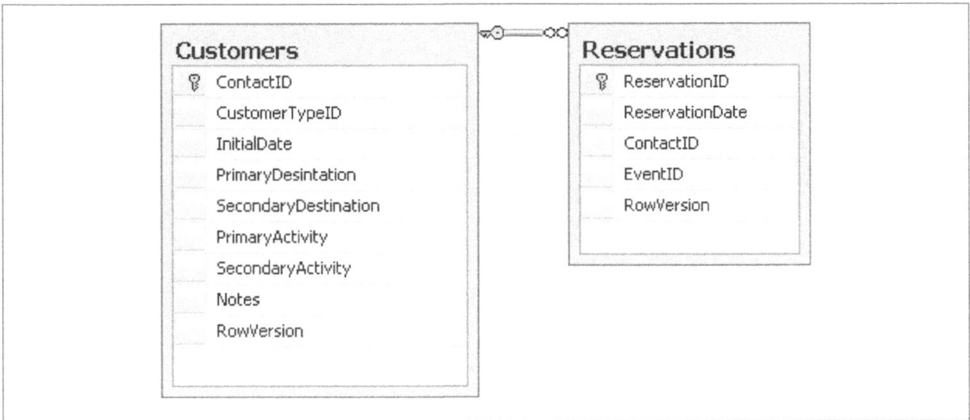

Figure 19-3. A primary key/foreign key relationship defined between the Customers and Reservations tables in the database

Figure 19-4. The relationship defined by the table that contains the foreign key

Understanding Additional Relationship Items

In addition to the association, a number of other items are created in the model as a result of this relationship:

Navigation properties

Navigation properties are the most visible properties that result from the relationship, and you have used them extensively in this book already.

The navigation property itself doesn't contain very much information, but it does have a pointer back to the association, which enables the navigation property to return the related entity or collection of entities.

`AssociationSets`

An `AssociationSet` is prominent when you are using independent associations. Like an `EntitySet`, an `AssociationSet` acts as a container for independent associations that have been instantiated as `ObjectStateEntry` types at runtime. If you have three contacts in the `ObjectContext` along with one or more addresses for those contacts, three instances of the `FK_Reservations_Customers` association will be in the context as well.

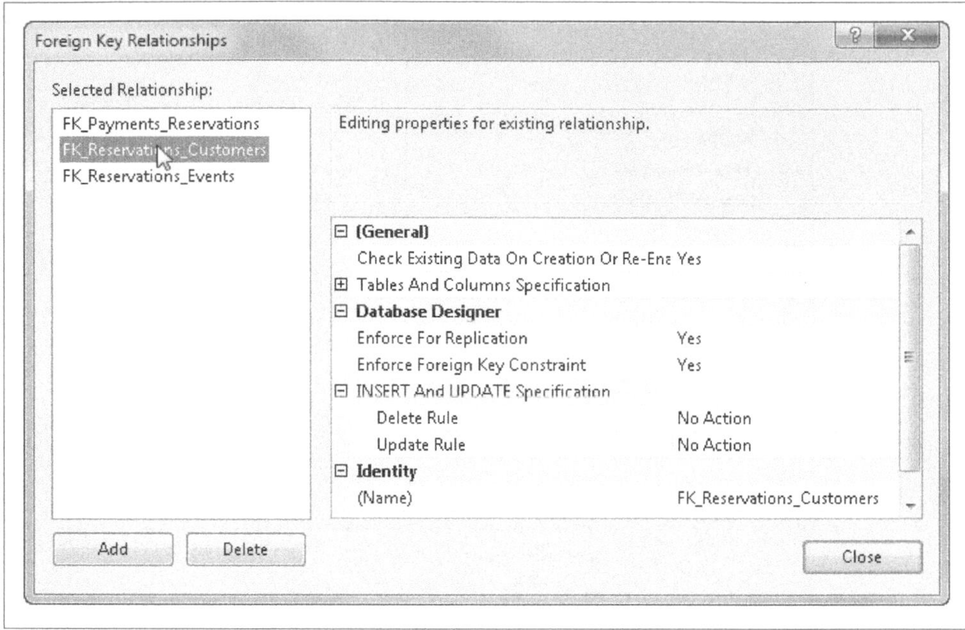

Figure 19-5. SQL Server Management Studio's property editor for defining a relationship between tables

When using foreign key association, no `ObjectStateEntry` types are created for relationships.

`AssociationSet` *mappings*

`AssociationSet` mappings are used only for independent associations. Foreign key associations are defined as referential constraints in the conceptual model. In the case of independent associations, the `EntitySetMapping` element in the model contains no information about navigations or associations, a fact you can confirm by viewing it. Only the scalar properties are mapped. All the relationship information is contained in the `AssociationSetMapping` element for the association that is bound to the entity. You have also seen that you can create or view these mappings in the Designer.

Handling Nonessential Navigation Properties

Although an association is always bidirectional, navigating with properties doesn't necessarily have to be. An interesting twist on relationships is that you are not required to have a navigation property in your model for every endpoint of a relationship.

As an example, the business logic of your application may define that you will frequently need to navigate from a contact to its reservation, but that you will never have to navigate from a reservation back to the contact, meaning `Reservation.Customer` will never be required, but `Customer.Reservations` will be useful.

In this case, you could simply delete the `Customer` navigation property from the `Reservation` entity in the model designer. This won't impact the association between the two entities, and in an edge case you can always dig into the `ObjectStateManager` to get from the `Reservation` to the `Customer`. In fact, you could delete both navigation properties from the related entities and leave the association intact. The plus side is that when you're coding or debugging, you won't have the unnecessary `Customer` and `CustomerReference` properties constantly in your face.

Understanding the Major Differences Between Foreign Key Associations and Independent Associations

Foreign keys in the model have simplified so much with regards to relationships. If you are moving from the .NET 3.5 SP1 version of Entity Framework to .NET 4, it will be useful to understand how they differ at a high level.

Remember that foreign key scalar properties and entity references are not mutually exclusive. By default, you will have both the scalar and navigation properties in the model. In the generated class when you are inheriting from `EntityObject`, you will have the scalar property, the navigation property, and the `EntityReference` property. With POCO classes, if you are enabling proxy generation, you'll get the `EntityReference` at runtime.

Updating .NET 3.5 Models to Get .NET 4 Foreign Keys and Their Associations

If you have a .NET 3.5 EDM (with no foreign keys) and you want to benefit from the foreign key support, the most pragmatic way to update the model is to recreate it from scratch.

Of course, this really depends on how complex your model is. If you have not performed a lot of customization on the conceptual model, recreating it with the VS2010 designer (and targeting .NET 4) should not be very painful.

The reason that updating the model won't work is that the foreign keys are already represented in the SSDL. Therefore, when you update the model even if you select the "Include foreign keys" option, the wizard will not rediscover the foreign keys from the database and bring them into the model as scalars.

You could still recreate the association manually in the designer. I think the easiest path is as follows. For each existing independent association:

1. Delete the association. This also deletes the association mapping, which you can't use with a foreign key association.
2. Recreate the association and allow the Add Association wizard to create a new foreign key scalar property.

3. Fix the name of the new scalar property if necessary.
4. In the table mappings window, map the new foreign key property back to the database table's foreign key property.
5. Verify that the Referential Constraint is set up correctly for the new association.

If you have lots of associations in your model, this one-time effort of manually recreating the associations will be worth it if you have a significant amount of model customization that you don't want to recreate.

Whichever method of updating you use, you should be sure to verify that all of your code with respect to relationships still works. In fact, you may very well find areas in your application where you can simplify code using the new foreign keys. I certainly have!

Defining Associations in Metadata

Foreign key associations are defined in the conceptual model using a referential constraint that links the primary property of the principal entity (e.g., `Customer.ContactID`) to the foreign key property of the dependent entity (e.g., `Reservation.ContactID`).

Independent associations are defined in the mapping layer. Since the foreign key is not exposed in the conceptual layer, the mapping layer hooks up the principal entity's primary key property with the foreign key in the store entity (e.g., the database table) that the dependent entity is mapped to.

Detecting Associations at Runtime

At runtime, the context is able to work out foreign key relationships by using the foreign key properties of the entity.

When you have independent relationships and no foreign key property, Entity Framework creates an object instance, specifically an `ObjectStateEntry` whose `IsRelationship` property is `true`, which can hold the necessary values defining the relationship.

Why Foreign Keys Were Brought into Entity Framework in .NET 4

Maintaining the independent association relationship objects created a lot of confusion for developers in the first version of the Entity Framework. It is the reason behind introducing foreign keys into the model in .NET 4 even though doing so caused the model to step away from its origins in Entity Relationship Modeling.

While it is still possible to use independent associations and have to work with and understand the relationship objects in .NET 4, it will be a much less common scenario.

Deconstructing Relationships Between Instantiated Entities

When instantiated objects are joined together in a relationship they are referred to as a *graph*, or an *entity graph*. The Entity Framework has some important rules about how graphs are maintained.

Relationship Span

The term *relationship span* is not an official term. You may not even find it in the EF documentation. But it is often used to describe the rules by which the Entity Framework handles related entities under the covers. When you create a query that traverses relationships, the Entity Framework will know not only how to construct the query, but also how to materialize the related objects. The relationship span defines that the `ObjectContext` will automatically attach an entity when you have joined it to another attached entity.

The fact that the context manages the relationships mandates that an object graph must be completely in or completely out of the `ObjectContext`. For example, if you have a customer graph that consists of a `Customer` with `Orders` and `OrderDetails` and for some reason you detach the `Customer` from the `ObjectContext`, the `Customer` will be disconnected from the rest of the entities in the graph. Because the relationship objects that involved that `Customer` were destroyed along with the `ObjectStateEntry` for that object, this means you can no longer traverse from the customer, which is not in the context, to the orders, which are in the context.

Conversely, if you have an entity that is not in the `ObjectContext` and you join it to an entity that is in the `ObjectContext`, to follow the rule that the entire graph must be either in or out of the context the detached entity will automatically be attached to the context in order to be part of the graph.

You will see this behavior repeated throughout this chapter as you look at the features and functionality regarding relationships.

Unmanaged Entities and Lazy Loading

When the context manages entities, it can ensure that the same entity is not duplicated in the context. However, if an entity is in memory but is detached, not only can you have multiple detached instances of the same entity, but also you can bring another instance into the context, through either a query, explicit loading, or lazy loading. You can use this to your advantage as easily as you can be surprised by finding multiple instances of your object hanging around in memory.

Understanding Relationship Manager and the IRelatedEnd Interface

Along with `ObjectStateManager`, Object Services provides a *relationship manager* to perform the tasks pertaining to relationships between entities being managed by the context. The relationship manager keeps track of how entities attached to the `ObjectContext` are related to each other. It's able to do this with the methods and properties that `EntityCollection` and `EntityReference` share through the `IRelatedEnd` interface, which they both implement. `IRelatedEnd`'s methods include `Add`, `Attach`, and `Load`, among others. When these methods are called, or when one entity is simply set to another entity's navigation property (e.g., `myAddress.Contact=myContact`), the relationship manager kicks in.

This may sound complex, but it is necessary so that Object Services has a dependable way to manage the many relationships that could exist at any given time. As you create and delete entities, attach and detach entities, and modify relationships, the relationship manager is able to keep track of all of this activity. When it comes time to call `SaveChanges`, the relationship manager plays a role that is just as important as that of `ObjectStateManager`. All of those updates you witnessed, in which related objects were taken care of automatically, were handled by the relationship manager. To have the flexibility that the Entity Framework provides at the coding level, it is necessary to have this complexity at lower levels.

With an understanding of how things are working at the lower levels, interaction with related objects should become much easier to comprehend, anticipate, and implement.

Remember that when you were working with the simpler POCOs in Chapter 13 (those that did not acquire dynamic proxies at runtime), this behavior didn't happen automatically. It was up to you to leverage some of the new methods in `ObjectContext`, which would then be able to detect what was going on in the classes with respect to properties and relationships.

Late-Binding Relationships

One of the jobs of the relationship manager is to "serve up" related entities when they are attached to the `ObjectContext`. When you navigate to a related entity—for example, by requesting `myAddress.Contact`—the relationship manager will identify the existing relationship between the `Address` and `Contact` entities, find the correct `Contact` entity in the `ObjectContext`, and return it.

A related object that the `ObjectContext` is not managing is seen as any other property in .NET. A call to `myAddress.Contact` when `myAddress` and its `Contact` are not attached to the context will merely return the `Contact` as a property. This contact will not interact with the `ObjectContext`.

Each ObjectStateEntry has a RelationshipManager property, which provides that particular entity access to the entities with which it has relationships.

Figure 19-6 shows the RelationshipManager of the ObjectStateEntry for a Reservation. The RelationshipManager identifies three relationships. The first two are for EntityReference properties that have not yet been loaded. The third is for an EntityCollection<Payment> that has been loaded. If you were to expand that node, you would be able to find references to each instantiated Payment entity belonging to this Reservation.

Name	Value
RelationshipManager	{System.Data.Objects.DataClasses.RelationshipManager}
Non-Public members	
_nodeVisited	false
_owner	{BAGA.Reservation}
_relationships	Count = 3
[0]	{System.Data.Objects.DataClasses.EntityReference<BAGA.Customer>}
[1]	{System.Data.Objects.DataClasses.EntityReference<BAGA.Trip>}
[2]	{System.Data.Objects.DataClasses.EntityCollection<BAGA.Payment>}
Raw View	
_wrappedOwner	{System.Data.Objects.Internal.LightweightEntityWrapper<BAGA.Reservation>}
HasRelationships	true
NodeVisited	false
Relationships	Count = 3
WrappedOwner	{System.Data.Objects.Internal.LightweightEntityWrapper<BAGA.Reservation>}

Figure 19-6. An ObjectStateEntry.RelationshipManager property

The Entity Framework uses an entity's ObjectStateEntry.RelationshipManager to supply values to the navigation properties when you request them in your query or in your code—for example, myReservationInstance.Payments. You can get the RelationshipManager in code by passing the object whose relationship manager you'd like to ObjectContext.GetRelationshipManager(Object).

Opening the relationships even further would reveal an internally managed property called IsLoaded. You'll see further on in this chapter how the context uses this property when deciding to lazy-load related data.

Taking a Peek Under the Covers: How Entity Framework Manages Relationships

Here's a geeky test that you can perform to see how some of the plumbing works. Looking at this in detail will give you a better understanding of how the Entity Framework manages relationships and why some of the rules that might not otherwise make sense exist. In order to see what's truly happening, you'll need to disable lazy loading; otherwise, it will automatically load related entities as you are inspecting results in the debugger.

Perform a query against the model that retrieves a single `Reservation` and then get a reference to all of the newly retrieved (`Unchanged`) `ObjectStateEntry` objects from the context, as shown in Example 19-1.

Example 19-1. Retrieving a single entity

```
using (var context = new BAGA.BAEntities())
{
  context.ContextOptions.LazyLoadingEnabled = false;
  var res = context.Reservations.FirstOrDefault();
  res.CustomerReference.Load();
}
```

Set a breakpoint on the last line of code that calls the `Load`. In debug mode, you'll take a look at the `ObjectStateManager` before and after loading the `Customer`.

When the `Reservation` is first loaded, the context is aware that the `Reservation` has foreign keys (`ContactID` and `TripID`) that can be represented by entities but that those entities are not yet known by the context. It creates `EntityKey`s for these two entities and stores them in the private property `_danglingForeignKeys`, shown in Figure 19-7.

Name	Value
context.ObjectStateManager	{System.Data.Objects.ObjectStateManager}
MetadataWorkspace	{System.Data.Metadata.Edm.MetadataWorkspace}
Static members	
Non-Public members	
[illegible]	null
_danglingForeignKeys	Count = 2
[0]	{[System.Data.EntityKey, System.Collections.Generic.HashSet`1[System.Data.Objects.EntityEntry]]}
[1]	{[System.Data.EntityKey, System.Collections.Generic.HashSet`1[System.Data.Objects.EntityEntry]]}
Raw View	
Comparer	{System.Collections.Generic.GenericEqualityComparer<System.Data.EntityKey>}
Count	2
Keys	Count = 2
[0]	"EntitySet=Contacts;ContactID=607"
[1]	"EntitySet=Trips;TripID=40"
Raw View	
Values	Count = 2
Static members	
Non-Public members	
_saveOriginalValues	false
_unchangedEntityStore	Count = 1
_unchangedRelationshipStore	null

Figure 19-7. Dangling foreign keys as placeholders for related data that is not yet loaded

When `CustomerReference.Load` is called, a SQL query, shown in Example 19-2, is executed in the database to retrieve that customer data.

Example 19-2. SQL executed by Entity Framework in response to calling Load

```
exec sp_executesql N'SELECT
''0X0X'' AS [C1],
[Extent1].[ContactID] AS [ContactID],
[Extent2].[FirstName] AS [FirstName],
[Extent2].[LastName] AS [LastName],
[Extent2].[Title] AS [Title],
[Extent2].[AddDate] AS [AddDate],
```

```
[Extent2].[ModifiedDate] AS [ModifiedDate],
[Extent2].[RowVersion] AS [RowVersion],
[Extent3].[CustomerTypeID] AS [CustomerTypeID],
[Extent3].[InitialDate] AS [InitialDate],
[Extent3].[PrimaryDesintation] AS [PrimaryDesintation],
[Extent3].[SecondaryDestination] AS [SecondaryDestination],
[Extent3].[PrimaryActivity] AS [PrimaryActivity],
[Extent3].[SecondaryActivity] AS [SecondaryActivity],
[Extent3].[Notes] AS [Notes],
[Extent1].[BirthDate] AS [BirthDate],
[Extent1].[HeightInches] AS [HeightInches],
[Extent1].[WeightPounds] AS [WeightPounds],
[Extent1].[DietaryRestrictions] AS [DietaryRestrictions],
[Extent3].[RowVersion] AS [RowVersion1]
FROM   [dbo].[ContactPersonalInfo] AS [Extent1]
INNER JOIN [dbo].[Contact] AS [Extent2]
 ON [Extent1].[ContactID] = [Extent2].[ContactID]
INNER JOIN [dbo].[Customers] AS [Extent3]
 ON [Extent1].[ContactID] = [Extent3].[ContactID]
WHERE [Extent1].[ContactID] = @EntityKeyValue1',
N'@EntityKeyValue1 int',@EntityKeyValue1=607
```

Figure 19-8 shows the `ObjectStateManager` after the last line of code is called, which explicitly loads the related customer. There are now six `danglingForeignKeys` but the one for the customer is gone. It is no longer "dangling" because the `Customer` entity and its `ObjectStateEntry` now exist. The `EntityKey` for the related `Trip` is still in the array of `danglingForeignKeys` as well as five new `EntityKeys` that are related to the `Customer` that was just loaded. The `EntityKey` that had been there for the customer is now part of an actual instantiated `Customer` entity.

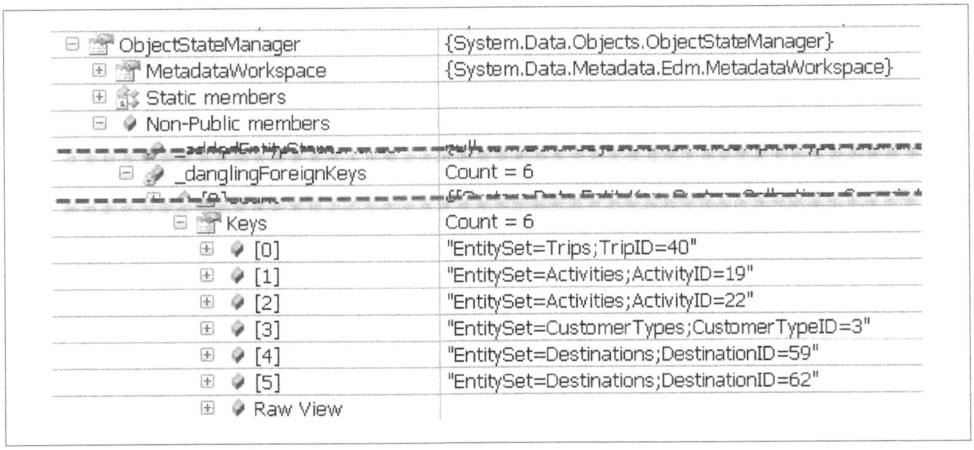

ObjectStateManager	{System.Data.Objects.ObjectStateManager}
MetadataWorkspace	{System.Data.Metadata.Edm.MetadataWorkspace}
Static members	
Non-Public members	
_danglingForeignKeys	Count = 6
Keys	Count = 6
[0]	"EntitySet=Trips;TripID=40"
[1]	"EntitySet=Activities;ActivityID=19"
[2]	"EntitySet=Activities;ActivityID=22"
[3]	"EntitySet=CustomerTypes;CustomerTypeID=3"
[4]	"EntitySet=Destinations;DestinationID=59"
[5]	"EntitySet=Destinations;DestinationID=62"
Raw View	

Figure 19-8. Dangling foreign keys for unloaded related data and keys for loaded related data

Even if a related entity doesn't exist in memory, the `ObjectContext` needs to be aware of any relationships that an existing entity (the `Reservation`) might have. That's because of the rule (created to cover all scenarios) that states that when a reservation is deleted, the relationship to its contact must also be deleted. This makes sense when both entities have been pulled into the `ObjectContext`, but not when only the reservation is in there.

While designing the Entity Framework, its creators decided it was safer to have an all-encompassing rule so that unexpected edge cases wouldn't result in errors. However, to satisfy the rule that the relationship must be deleted, the relationship must first exist. The pseudoentities hiding in the `_danglingForeignKeys` field were created during the query so that the relationships could be created without developers having to pull down additional data to satisfy the rule.

As you read through this chapter, this knowledge will help you better understand some of the rules and behavior surrounding relationships.

Understanding Navigation Properties

On their own, navigation properties are almost meaningless. They are completely dependent on an association to provide access to related data. The navigation property does nothing more than define which association endpoint defines the start of the navigation and which defines the end.

A navigation property is not concerned with whether the property leads to an entity or an `EntityCollection`. The multiplicity in the association determines that, and the results are visible in the object instances where the navigation property is resolved. The property is resolved either as an entity plus an `EntityReference`, as with the `Contact` and `ContactReference` properties of the `Address` entity in Figure 19-9, or as an `EntityCollection`, as with the `Addresses` property of the `Contact` entity. You can also see this by looking in the generated classes for the model. The Entity Framework still needs to make this determination as it is materializing objects from query results, and then populate the objects correctly.

EntityReference properties

Navigation properties that return `Entity` and `EntityReference` properties need to be addressed together because they come as a pair, even though both may not be populated. When the navigation property points to the "one" or "zero or one" side of a relationship, that property is resolved as two public properties. One property contains the actual entity, and the other property contains a reference to the entity. This reference contains the related entity's `EntityKey`, which is comparable to a foreign key in a database. The `EntityKey` provides just enough information about that entity to be able to identify it when necessary. When you execute a query that returns addresses, the `ContactID` from the `Addresse` table is used to construct the `EntityKey` for `ContactReference`. Even if the contact does not exist in memory, the `ContactReference` property provides the minimal information about the `Contact` that is related to the `Address`.

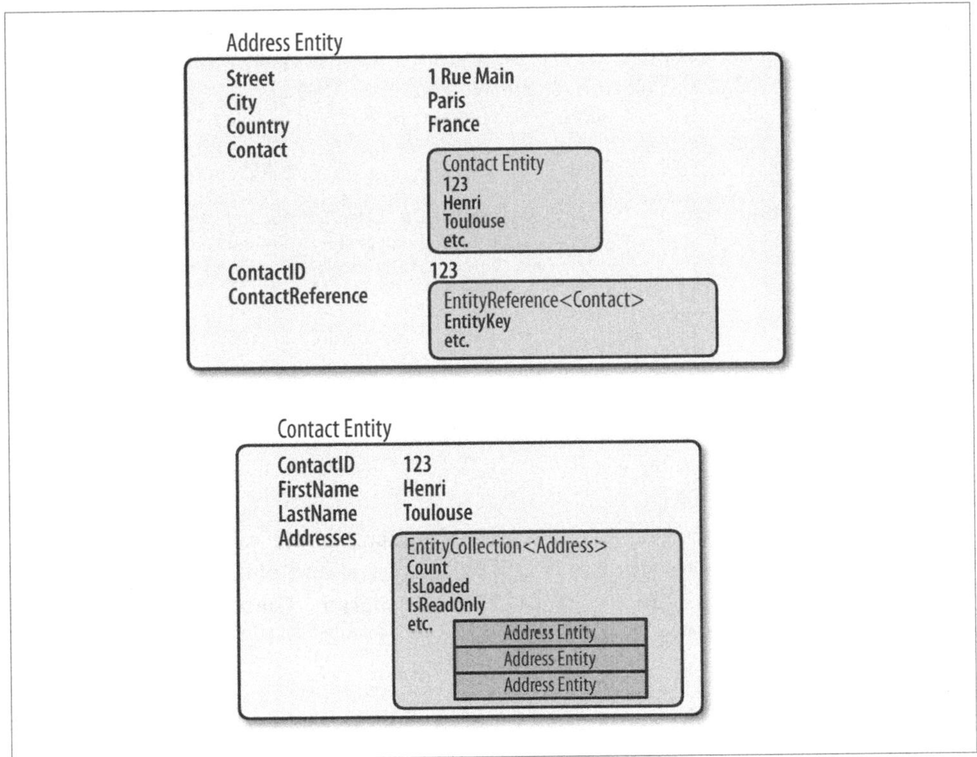

Figure 19-9. Resolving navigation properties as entities, EntityReferences, and EntityCollections

EntityReference.Value. The value object of an `EntityReference` shows up in two places. The first is the navigation property (`Address.Contact`) and the second is within the `EntityReference` property (`Address.ContactReference`). You can see this in Figure 19-10, where the `Contact` is loaded into the `ObjectContext` and therefore is hooked up with the `Address` entity.

⊞ Contact	{BAGA.Customer} ←
ContactID	570
⊟ ContactReference	{System.Data.Objects.DataClasses.EntityReference<BAGA.Contact>}
⊞ base	{System.Data.Objects.DataClasses.EntityReference<BAGA.Contact>}
⊞ Value	{BAGA.Customer} ←

Figure 19-10. The Contact property (which is a Customer derived from Contact) of the Address entity as the actual property and as the value of the EntityReference property, ContactReference

What if there is no EntityReference. In many scenarios, the "one" side of a relationship is required, such as the constraint in the BreakAway model that says a reservation can't exist without a related customer. However, in some relationships the target is 0..1, meaning the related end isn't required (e.g., if a customer's preferred activity does not need to be specified). In the case where there is nothing on that end, the navigation property (`Customer.PrimaryActivity`) will be null. The `EntityReference` will exist, but its `EntityKey` and `Value` will be null, as shown in Figure 19-11.

PrimaryActivity	null
PrimaryActivityID	null
⊟ PrimaryActivityReference	{System.Data.Objects.DataClasses.EntityReference<BAGA.Activity>}
⊟ base	{System.Data.Objects.DataClasses.EntityReference<BAGA.Activity>}
⊞ base	{System.Data.Objects.DataClasses.EntityReference<BAGA.Activity>}
⊞ EntityKey	null
⊞ Non-Public members	
Value	null

Figure 19-11. An unpopulated EntityReference, which will have no EntityKey and Value

EntityCollection properties

The other type of `IRelatedEnd` is an `EntityCollection`. `EntityCollection` is a generic class that is a container for entities of a particular type and is used by a navigation property to point to the "many" end of an association. `Contact.Addresses` is an `EntityCollection` of `Address` types.

`EntityCollection` is not based on other `Collection` classes in .NET. In fact, it implements an Entity Framework interface in the `System.Data.Objects.DataClasses` namespace, called `IRelatedEnd`.

You have worked with `EntityCollections` in many of the examples in this book already. Although you'll probably work with `EntityCollection` most frequently through a navigation property, it is also possible to instantiate an `EntityCollection` in memory and work with it directly.

You cannot attach an `EntityCollection` to an entity through its navigation property—for example, with:

```
MyContact.Addresses=myAddressEntityCollection
```

The `EntityCollection` *is* the navigation property (when the target is the "many" side of an association).

Unfortunately, the compiler will allow you to set a collection property; you will get no warnings. However, at runtime an exception will be thrown.

You need to insert items into the collection itself, which you can do explicitly or by setting the `EntityReference` on the child object, which you'll see next. You can also remove items from the collection as needed.

> ### Relationship Management in POCO Entities
>
> Entity Framework will provide the same relationship behavior for dynamic proxies as it does for `EntityObjects`. Therefore, when using POCO entities that are set up for runtime proxy generation, everything I've described thus far will essentially be the same.
>
> However, there are a few differences for entities that rely on the runtime dynamic proxies. The `EntityReference` properties that are generated for `EntityObject` classes will not exist in the POCO entities unless you specifically add code into your T4 template to create these properties, which would be an unusual thing to do.
>
> `Attach` and `Load`, which are discussed later in this chapter, are methods of `IRelatedEnd`; only `EntityReference` and `EntityCollection` derive from `IRelatedEnd` and only the `EntityObject` classes will have properties that are based on these types. Therefore, you won't be able to use these methods with POCO entities.
>
> POCO entities that are not virtualized will not have any of the automated relationship management. None of the `RelationshipManager` infrastructure will exist. Whatever logic you have defined for relationship fix-up in your classes is what your objects will follow.

Understanding Referential Integrity and Constraints

It is possible to place constraints in both the database and the EDM to ensure the integrity of the data. The point at which these constraints are checked in the pipeline varies.

Many developers approach the Entity Framework with the assumption that these constraints will be checked when their code is manipulating the entities. For example, if you delete an order, when you call `ObjectContext.DeleteObject` it would be nice to have the Entity Framework tell you, "Hey, there are still line items for this order. You can't do that."

Constraints that are not checked until they hit the database

Many constraint checks must be deferred to the database, because it is common for some dependent data not to be loaded into your application. Even if the Entity Framework did alert you to those details and you removed them as well, what if the database contains more order detail data that you hadn't loaded for some reason? This would make you feel uncomfortable deleting the order and sending that instruction to the database, which would throw an error anyway because of the other details that are still present.

Other constraint checks that, for the same reason, can't be made on the client side are for uniqueness, primary keys, and foreign keys. An `EntityReference` might contain a key value for data that is not loaded into the `ObjectContext` but that does exist in the database, so only the database can provide that check.

In Appendix C, you can see how database constraints were specified in the SSDL portion of the model, which only declares the existence of the constraints in the database. It is also possible to define constraints on the CSDL side. But even a referential constraint defined in the model (as you first saw in Chapter 2) is not checked at the object level. If you need the constraints to be checked while you are interacting with the objects, you will have to build your own validation logic to do so.

"Then why," you may ask, "did I bother defining constraints in the conceptual model?" In the conceptual model, the constraints exist to map the relationships. Without them you wouldn't be able to have associations and navigation properties to work with in queries or code.

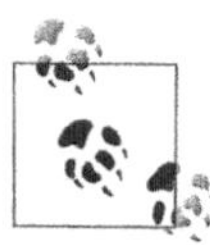

We'll look closely at Entity Framework exception handling in Chapter 22.

Checking for missing entity references with and without foreign keys

In the first version of Entity Framework, and when using independent associations in .NET 4 (rather than foreign keys), `SaveChanges` was able to detect a missing (and required) `EntityReference`.

For example, the 1:* relationship between `Contact` and `Address` means you can have one and only one `Contact` related to an `Address`—not five and not zero.

It is possible to create a new `Address` in code without assigning a `Contact`, `ContactID`, or `ContactReference`, as shown in Example 19-3. When you add the `Address` to the context, the Entity Framework can't possibly know whether you plan to create a relationship, so it's not going to complain at that point.

Example 19-3. Code that will not incur a constraint check

```
var address = new Address
                {
                  Street1 = "1 Main Street",
                  City = "Burlington",
                  StateProvince = "VT",
                  AddressType = "Business",
                  ModifiedDate = DateTime.Now
                };
context.Addresses.AddObject(address);
```

But when it comes time to call `SaveChanges`, after any custom `SavingChanges` logic has been implemented, it's pretty obvious that if there is no relationship by now, there never will be.

If you are using independent associations, Entity Framework will validate this constraint for you. That's when an UpdateException is thrown before the command is even created to send to the database. The UpdateException provides the following explicit message, which is great for debugging and for logging:

```
Entities in 'BAEntities.Addresses' participate in the 'FK_Address_ContactSet'
relationship.
0 related 'Contact' were found. 1 'Contact' is expected.
```

You should be able to catch a scenario like this before your code goes into production. Otherwise, you'll either want to check for this constraint yourself in business rules (e.g., in SavingChanges) or, as a last resort, catch the exception and either deal with the orphaned address or ask the user to do something about it.

However, with foreign key associations, the Entity Framework may not catch what you know to be missing references, even though they are defined in the referential constraints. In the previous code example, even though the Contact was not assigned, Address has a ContactID property. ContactID is a non-nullable integer that, because integer is a value type, will have a default value of 0 if you have not explicitly defined a default value.

When SaveChanges is called, because the foreign key is populated (with 0), that is enough for the constraint check to pass. There's a value that can be used to identify the Contact. Entity Framework cannot assume that 0 is an invalid value for the ContactID. It will send the insert command to the database, which will return an error because (presumably) there is no Contact in the Contacts table with a ContactID of 0 and the database will throw a foreign key constraint conflict error.

When using foreign key associations, it is your responsibility to validate foreign key constraints that the runtime will not properly detect if you do not want to make an unnecessary database call. Additionally, you can define checks and balances in your database to sort out what is and isn't valid incoming data.

Where should you validate? For the same reasons used with the independent association constraint validation, you'll want to validate just prior to saving changes to the database. If you are using EntityObjects and you don't want to modify the template, you can add validation code in SavingChanges or the SaveChanges override that you added in Chapter 10. You might also want to consider letting each entity type provide its own presaving validation logic. For example, in the partial class for Address you could have a method that updates the ModifiedDate property, forces something into the non-nullable AddressType property, and then checks to ensure that a Contact has been identified.

Such a method's signature could look something like this:

```
internal bool ValidateAddress(out string invalidReason)
```

After fixing up the `ModifiedDate` and `AddressType`, if the `Contact` validates, the method would return `true` and `invalidReason` would be empty.

If there is no `Contact` or `ContactID` assigned, you would return `false` and populate `invalidReason` with text such as "Contact not assigned".

Making this `internal` (or `Friend` in Visual Basic) means it can only be called from within the same assembly. Because this is the default generated code, the `ObjectContext` class is in the same assembly and you can add the code in Example 19-4 to the `SavingChanges` method. In the method you created in Chapter 10, there is a `foreach` clause that iterates over `ObjectStateEntries` that are `Added` or `Modified`. You'll want to apply your own rules to determine what you want to do if the address is, indeed, invalid.

Example 19-4. Adding Address self-validation into the SavingChanges override

```
public void BAEntities_SavingChanges(object sender, System.EventArgs e)
{
  var osm =ObjectStateManager;
  foreach (var entry in osm.GetObjectStateEntries
                      (EntityState.Added | EntityState.Modified))
  {
    if (entry.Entity is Contact)
    {
      var con = (Contact)entry.Entity;
      con.ModifiedDate = DateTime.Now; //replace with a db trigger?
      if (con.AddDate == DateTime.MinValue)
      { con.AddDate = DateTime.Now; }
    }
    if (entry.Entity is Address)
    {
      string invalidReason;
      if (((Address)entry.Entity).ValidateAddress(out invalidReason)==false)
      {
        //address is invalid, reason is contained in invalidReason
      }
    }
  }
}
```

It would make sense to do the same for `Contact`: move it's validation and other related logic, such as setting defaults, into the `Contact` class.

If you are using a T4 template to create POCO entities, you might consider creating a generic method that tests for `0` in any foreign key property that is non-nullable. We'll look at more validation logic for POCO entities in Chapter 24.

Implementing Deletes and Cascading Deletes

Most databases support cascading deletes, which are used to automatically (and unquestionably) delete all of the children of a parent when that parent record is deleted. Cascading deletes are supported in the Entity Framework as well, but with caveats.

The biggest caveat is that the Entity Framework can perform cascading deletes only on objects that are in memory, more specifically, objects that are in memory and being managed by an `ObjectContext`. This could cause problems if a database constraint is enforcing referential integrity, and if the database does not also have a cascading delete set up on the same set of data. In this case, if the database still contains children, an error will be thrown when Entity Framework sends a command to delete the principal.

Cascading deletes in the database

Referring back to Figure 19-5, a cascading delete in the database is defined in the `Key` definitions of the "child" or dependent table. If data in the related table is deleted, all of the related rows of the dependent table will be automatically deleted.

The EDM Wizard can identify cascading deletes in a database. Microsoft's sample database, AdventureWorksLT, defines cascading deletes in many relationships, including the relationship between `SalesOrderDetails` and its "parent," `SalesOrderHeaders`. The wizard recognizes and includes that cascading delete in the `Association` definition, as shown in Example 19-5.

Example 19-5. An Association's OnDelete action set to Cascade as defined in the CSDL

```
<Association Name="FK_SalesOrderDetail_SalesOrderHeader_SalesOrderID">
  <End Role="SalesOrderHeader"
       Type="AdventureWorksLTModel.SalesOrderHeader" Multiplicity="1">
    <OnDelete Action="Cascade" />
  </End>
  <End Role="SalesOrderDetail"
       Type="AdventureWorksLTModel.SalesOrderDetail" Multiplicity="*"/>
  <ReferentialConstraint>
    <Principal Role="SalesOrderHeader">
      <PropertyRef Name="SalesOrderID" />
    </Principal>
    <Dependent Role="SalesOrderDetail">
      <PropertyRef Name="SalesOrderID" />
    </Dependent>
  </ReferentialConstraint>
</Association>
```

The wizard will automatically apply the same Cascade Delete rule to the association's `SalesOrderDetails` end (`End1 OnDelete`) in the conceptual model, as shown in Figure 19-12.

Anytime your code calls `ObjectContext.DeleteObject` on a `SalesOrderHeader` entity, any related `SalesOrderDetail` entities being managed by the context will also be deleted with `DeleteObject`. When `SaveChanges` is called, the delete commands for the `SalesOrderDetail` entities will be sent to the database first, followed by the command to delete the `SalesOrderHeader`. This database cascade delete rule will ensure that any other `SalesOrderDetails` related to the order that are in the database are also deleted.

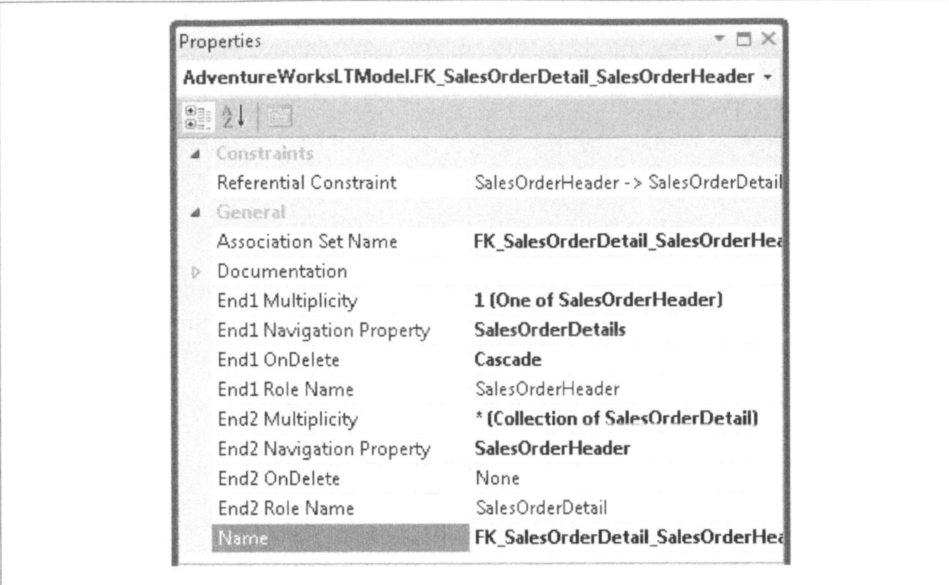

Figure 19-12. Cascade Delete in the conceptual model

Sending the related entity delete commands first prevents a conflict. If the order was deleted first, the database would automatically delete all of the detail records and the following delete commands for the detail entities would fail because those records would already have been removed from the database.

Recommendation: Cascade in both the model and the database, or in neither

Although you can define a cascade delete action to a model's association when the cascade is not defined in the database, this is not recommended. Doing so will create incorrect expectations on the part of the developer, and unpredictable results. The recommendation is to use the `OnDelete` action in the model as a reflection of its definition in the database. If it exists in the database, it should exist in the model. If it does not exist in the database, it should not exist in the model. You can, of course, ignore the recommendations as long as your code is prepared for the possible repercussions.

Defining Relationships Between Entities

Now that you have had a tour through the plumbing of how relationships work in the Entity Data Model and in instantiated objects, it's time to see how you can impact relationships in your code.

Anytime you set one entity as the property of another (e.g., `Reservation.Customer=aCustomer`) or add an entity to an `EntityCollection` property of an entity (e.g.,

`Reservations.Payments.Add(aNewPayment)`) you are defining a relationship. The relationship will be noted in the `RelationshipManager` of each entity involved in the relationship.

You can create relationships between entities in a number of ways. You have seen several of them in the applications you built in previous chapters.

The CLR Way: Setting a Navigation Property to an Entity

The simplest way to create relationships between entities is to create the relationship the CLR way—by setting one entity as the property of another entity:

```
MyAddress.Contact = myContact
```

If you are starting with the child entity (e.g., `MyAddress`), this is pretty obvious. But if you are starting with the contact and you want to add the address to its collection, there's no reason not to switch your perspective and simply set the address's `Contact` property. It's simpler and has the same effect.

This covers the most common scenarios, though you should be aware of the following subtleties:

- If both objects are detached, the `ObjectContext` will not be involved at all. You are simply setting a property the CLR way.
- If both objects are attached, the relationship manager will create the necessary `EntityCollection` or `EntityReference`.
- If only one of the objects is attached, the other will become attached (thanks to relationship span) and the `EntityCollections` and/or `EntityReferences` will be created by the `RelationshipManager`. If that detached object is new, when it is attached to the context its `EntityState` will be `Added`.
- As described in earlier chapters, the relevant foreign key property and `EntityReference.EntityKey` will be updated to synchronize with the newly related entity.

Setting a Foreign Key Property

If you have access to the value of the related entity but not the entity itself, you can simply set the foreign key property (e.g., `Reservation.TripID=3`). The `EntityReference.EntityKey` will be synchronized, and if the related entity is in the context's cache, the entity navigation property will also be synchronized. If the related entity is not in the cache, setting the foreign key scalar property will *not* trigger a lazy load from the database.

Using Foreign Key Properties from Reference List Entities

It is possible that the foreign key points to an entity that is in memory but is not being change-tracked. For example, you may have a list of `Trip` entities that you queried using the NoTracking MergeOption because the trips will only be used as a reference list and are not being edited. When creating a new reservation, if you set the Reservation.Trip navigation property to the desired Trip entity, relationship span will cause that Trip entity to be pulled into the context and be change-tracked. Because the Reservation is new, the Trip's EntityState will be Added and give you extra work to do to fix up the entity state before saving.

On the other hand, if you simply use the TripID of the selected Trip to set the new Reservation's TripID property, you won't have to worry about the Trip entity being managed by the context.

If you do not have a foreign key property, you can set the EntityReference.EntityKey and still avoid forcing the related entity into the context.

Setting an EntityReference Using an EntityKey

If the relationship you are building is based on an independent association and no foreign key property is available, you can create the EntityReference using only an EntityKey. This requires that you know the key value of the related entity.

This allows you to create a foreign key for an entity without having the related data in memory. Example 19-6 shows how to create and set the EntityKey when the key contains only a single property.

Example 19-6. Defining an EntityReference with an EntityKey

```
var singleKey= new EntityKey("BAEntities.CustomerTypes", "CustomerTypeID", 1);
cust.CustomerTypeReference.EntityKey = singleKey;
```

Example 19-7 shows how to define an EntityKey that comprises multiple values using an entity created from the SalesOrderDetail table in the AdventureWorksLT database. The table has a composite primary key that results in the SalesOrderDetail entity having an entity key comprising two properties, SalesOrderID and SalesOrderDetailID.

Example 19-7. Defining a composite EntityKey

```
var compositeKeyValues =
  new[] {
       new KeyValuePair<string, object>("SalesOrderDetailID", 12),
       new KeyValuePair<string, object>("SalesOrderID", 103)
       };
var key = new EntityKey("AdventureWorksLTEntities.SalesOrderDetails",
compositeKeyValues);
```

Loading, Adding, and Attaching Navigation Properties

There are a number of ways to populate navigation properties using methods provided by the IRelatedEnd interface, which EntityCollection and EntityReference implement. Depending on the type (collection or reference) from which you call the methods, the

Entity Framework performs slightly different methods in the background to achieve the goal.

As discussed in the sidebar "Relationship Management in POCO Entities" on page 539, `EntityCollection` and `EntityReference` are specific to `EntityObject` types. These methods will not be available for POCO entities and you will need to depend on setting navigation properties in the manner of standard CLR properties (e.g., `myReservation.Trip=myTrip`).

Lazy Loading

You first learned about lazy loading in Chapter 4, but here is a quick overview. Lazy loading causes related data to be retrieved from the database on demand. No query is necessary. If you have a `Customer` instance that is being managed by the context, but no `Reservations`, any reference to that `Customer`'s `Reservations` (e.g., `myCust.Reservations`) will force a behind-the-scenes query to the database.

Lazy loading will always load the entire navigation property, regardless of any filtering you may be applying. For example, if you called `myCust.Reservations.FirstOrDefault()`, the `Reservations` property will be loaded (retrieved from the database) and then the `FirstOrDefault` method will be applied locally to return the first of those reservations.

Lazy loading depends on the `IsLoaded` property of `IRelatedEnd` to determine if it should perform the lazy load or not. You used the `IsLoaded` property in the WCF service in Chapter 17.

When `IsLoaded` is `false`, this indicates to the context that the related data has not been loaded and the context will execute the lazy load. If `IsLoaded` is `true`, the context will not perform the implicit loading.

The following events make `IsLoaded true`:

- Eager loading with `Include`
- Lazy loading
- Explicit loading with `Load`

When you load related data in a query projection, that related data will not be seen as `IsLoaded`.

For example, the following query returns reservations and their payments. But the reservations' payments are returned separately.

```
from r in context.Reservations
          where r.Payments.Any()
          select new {r, pmts=r.Payments}
```

Even though the context recognizes the relationship and you can navigate from the reservation to those payments and from the payments to their reservations, `Reservation.Payments.IsLoaded` is `false`.

The same is true when loading related data by performing a separate query.

If you queried for reservations and then executed a separate query for payments, reservations and payments that are related will be hooked up through their navigation properties, but `Reservation.Payments.IsLoaded` will be `false` and `Payment.Reservation.IsLoaded` will also be `false`.

This is an example where lazy-loading support will cause unnecessary trips to the database, and it's another reason you should pay close attention to how and when you are using this feature.

Remember that with POCO entities, navigation properties must be marked as `virtual` for lazy loading to occur. Even if you aren't marking every property as `virtual`, you can still benefit from marking the navigation properties as `virtual` to get the lazy loading.

A side benefit to specifying virtual navigation properties in entities that depend on snapshot notification (when POCO entities do not use dynamic proxies) is that you are able to control which navigation properties will lazy-load and which will not. Entity Framework defines lazy loading at the context level. When using `EntityObjects` or dynamic proxies, you don't have control over which navigation properties are lazy-loaded in the way that many other ORMs define this feature. But with POCO entities, when you can pick and choose which navigation properties are lazy-loaded you can emulate this practice.

EntityReference.Load and EntityCollection.Load

Examples:

```
Contact.Addresses.Load
Address.ContactReference.Load
```

Although I discussed the `Load` method earlier in the book, here I will dig even deeper.

You can call `Load` from entities that are attached to the `ObjectContext`. Calling `Load` will cause a query to be created and executed to retrieve the related data that `Load` requested. As with the lazy loading, when loading a navigation that is a collection, the collection cannot be filtered. If you have a `Contact` and call `Contact.Addresses.Load`, every address belonging to that contact will be retrieved from the database.

`Load` has one overload. You can provide a `MergeOption` to control how the loaded data is handled during object materialization.

Remember that simple POCO entities whose navigation properties are not virtual will not benefit from lazy loading. Use the `ObjectContext.LoadProperty` method as discussed in Chapter 13.

Loading from Detached Entities: Lazy and Explicit

One condition allows you to load related data from detached entities whether you let lazy loading or the `Load` method do the job: when the entity was created as a result of a `NoTracking` query. Example 19-8 calls `Load` on a `Detached` entity.

Example 19-8. Calling Load on a detached entity

```
ObjectSet<Reservation> query = context.Reservations;
query.MergeOption= System.Data.Objects.MergeOption.NoTracking;
Reservation reservation - query.First();
reservation.CustomerReference.Load(); //<--succeeds
```

However, if you detach an entity from the context, calling `Load` will cause an exception to be thrown, as shown in Example 19-9.

Example 19-9. A failed attempt to call Load on a detached entity

```
ObjectSet<Reservation> query = context.Reservations;
Reservation reservation = query.First();
context.Detach(reservation);
reservation.CustomerReference.Load();  //<--InvalidOperationException
```

Frankly, I'm not sure why the "untracked" reservation is able to load when the detached reservation is not. In both cases, all of the relationships are intact when drilling into the reservation's `RelationshipManager`. But this anomaly has existed since the first version of Entity Framework, and disassembling the methods reveals explicit code that checks to see if an entity was loaded using `NoTracking` prior to executing the load query.

Using EntityCollection.Add

Example:

```
Contact.Addresses.Add(myNewAddress)
```

You use Add to add items to an EntityCollection. You can use Add only on EntityCollection. It isn't valid (or really necessary) with EntityReference, as you can set an EntityReference using its navigation property.

Again, depending on the state of an entity, you can use Add in one of several different ways, as discussed in the following subsections.

Adding new entities that are detached

You can use Add to add a new entity that is not yet attached to the ObjectContext. Add will first add the entity to the ObjectContext and will then add it to the EntityCollection of the calling entity. This requires that the entity have no EntityKey; otherwise, it will throw an exception. Any entity with an EntityKey is presumed to have come from the data store, and therefore it can't be treated as a new record.

For instance, the code in Example 19-10 queries for a Customer from the database, creates a new Address in memory, and then adds the Address to the Customer's Addresses collection.

Example 19-10. Adding a new, detached entity to another entity

```
using (var context = new BAEntities())
{
  var contact = (from c in context.Contacts.Include("Addresses") select c)
           .First();
  var address = new Address
                {
                  Street1 = "1 Main",
                  City = "Hamburg",
                  StateProvince = "NY"
                };
  contact.Addresses.Add(address);
}
```

When this is complete, not only is the address part of the Addresses collection, but also address's ContactID and Contact properties are populated and address.ContactReference is populated with an EntityKey and the Value. The address object instance is attached to the context with a temporary EntityKey and an EntityState of Added.

Adding existing entities that are detached

If a detached entity originally came from the database, has its EntityKey properties (e.g., Contact.ContactID), and even has an EntityKey that is populated (for EntityObjects), using Add to link it to another entity will change its EntityState to Added. Even though it is a preexisting entity, SaveChanges will create an insert command for this entity.

Adding new or existing entities that are attached

You can use Add to add entities that are already attached to the ObjectContext, regardless of whether they are new. The EntityState of the entity being added will not be affected.

If you add a managed `Address` whose current `EntityState` is `Unchanged`, it will remain `Unchanged` after calling `Add`. It is only the `Detached` entities that you need to be diligent about when using `Add` or `Attach`.

Adding entities to the EntityCollection of a detached object

If the calling entity is detached from the context, `Add` will be treated as a CLR method, as shown in Example 19-11.

Example 19-11. Adding to the EntityCollection of a detached entity

```
var reservation = context.Reservations.First();
context.Detach(reservation);
var payment = new Payment();
payment.Amount = 100;
reservation.Payments.Add(payment);
```

In this case, the `payment` entity will be added to the `Payments` collection and you'll be able to navigate from the `Payment` to the `Reservation` (`newPayment.Reservation`). In the case of `EntityObjects`, because the `ObjectContext` is not involved, no relationships are created, and therefore `payment.ReservationReference.EntityKey` will be null.

If you are using POCO entities, any fix-up logic that has been built into your entities will drive whether the relationship is one-way or two-way.

Using Attach and Remove

Examples:

```
Contact.Addresses.Attach(myAddress)
Address.ContactReference.Attach(contact)
```

In addition to `ObjectContext.Attach`, an `Attach` method exists for `IRelatedEnd`, which you can use for `EntityCollections` and `EntityReferences`.

Using the `Attach` method, you can define relationships between entities that already exist in the `ObjectContext` but that have not been connected automatically.

`EntityCollection.Remove` is used to remove an entity from a collection. It will continue to be managed by the `ObjectContext`, but will no longer be related to a parent in that particular association. There is no `Remove` method for `EntityReference`.

When removing entities from an `EntityCollection`, be careful not to orphan entities. If you leave a child entity without a required parent, you will get an `EntityReferenceException` when you call `SaveChanges`.

> **Cases Where You Cannot Use Attach**
>
> You'll encounter a lot of rules if you try to use `Attach` where it doesn't belong. Here are a few places where you might think you want to use `Attach`, but you will run into trouble. Most of these problems occur when you are not following the main purpose of `Attach`, which is to connect entities that are already attached to the `ObjectContext` and are not new.
>
> - You cannot use `Attach` to attach another `EntityCollection`; however, it is possible to attach an `IEnumerable` (discussed shortly). Otherwise, you need to attach one entity at a time.
> - You cannot use `Attach` when the `EntityState` of either end is `Detached`. `ObjectContext` is required to work out the relationship. Do an `ObjectContext.Attach` first.
> - You cannot use `Attach` when the ends are in different contexts.
> - You cannot use `Attach` to attach entities whose `EntityState` is `Added`. You'll want to use `Add` in this case.
> - You cannot use `Attach` to attach entities whose `EntityState` is `Deleted`. It's not possible to create an `IRelatedEnd` for a deleted entity.
> - You cannot use `Attach` to reassign entities to another graph.

Moving an Entity to a New Graph

Often you will want to move an entity from one graph to another, perhaps for the simple reason that an end user applied a payment to the wrong reservation.

In such a case, you can simply reassign the `Reservation` property:

```
myPayment.Reservation=myReservation
```

or add the payment to the `Payments EntityCollection` of the new reservation:

```
myReservation.Payments.Add(myPayment)
```

The `ObjectContext` will resolve the existing relationship, and the foreign key property, entity, and reference will all be synchronized. The change to the foreign key property will force the `EntityState` to become `Modified`.

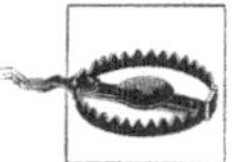

Remember that `Attach` will not work here. `Attach` is for creating a relationship in the context to reflect a relationship that already exists in the database.

Learning a Few Last Tricks to Make You a Relationship Pro

If you spend any amount of time in the MSDN Forums for the Entity Framework, you may recognize two questions that are asked frequently. The first is "How can I filter the children that are returned when I use `Load`?" and the second is "How can I get the foreign key value of a navigation property?" Thankfully, Microsoft solved the latter issue by introducing foreign key support in .NET 4. However, if you are not using foreign keys in your model, it's a handy trick to have up your sleeve.

Now that you have learned so much about relationships in the Entity Framework, you will be able to understand the solutions to both of these FAQs.

The first is solved with a little-known method called `CreateSourceQuery`. The second is solved by digging down into the `EntityReference` to get at its properties. Here is how to perform both tricks.

Using CreateSourceQuery to Enhance Deferred Loading

Not only can you attach an entity to an `IRelatedEnd`, but you can also attach an `IEnumerable` when you are calling `EntityCollection.Attach`. An `EntityCollection` is not an `IEnumerable`, which is why you can't just attach another `EntityCollection`. But if you want to attach a number of entities at once, you can wrap them in something as simple as a list or the results of another query.

Additionally, you can use this as an alternative to `EntityCollection.Load` because it will give you some flexibility regarding what you are loading. You can use `CreateSourceQuery` to create queries on the fly for an `Attach` method, though you'll use it a bit differently for `EntityCollection.Attach` and `EntityReference.Attach`.

The most efficient way to create an `IEnumerable` for attaching or loading entities into an `EntityCollection` is to use the `CreateSourceQuery` method. Like the `Load` method, `CreateSourceQuery` will take care of the query creation and execution for you, leveraging the existing `ObjectContext`.

As an example, if you have a customer in the `ObjectContext` and you want to get that customer's reservations, you could call the following:

```
myCust.Reservations.Load()
```

This would load all of the reservations for that customer.

However, if you want to filter those reservations, you can use `CreateSourceQuery` instead, as shown in the following code:

```
var customer=context.Contacts.OfType<Customer>().First();
var sourceQuery = customer.Reservations.CreateSourceQuery()
                  .Where(r => r.ReservationDate > new DateTime(2008, 1, 1));
customer.Reservations.Attach(sourceQuery);
```

The query will execute when the `Attach` method is called. Now only the subset of reservations for that customer will be retrieved from the database and materialized as objects.

You can also use `CreateSourceQuery` to filter on types. In the following code, `Attach` is being used with an `EntityReference`, which will not take `IQueryable`. Instead, you need to pass in an object, which you can get using the `FirstOrDefault` query method. Since

Attach will throw an exception if you attempt to pass in a null, you need to test for null before calling Attach:

```
var addresses = context.Addresses.Take(5);
foreach (var a in addresses)
{
  var sq = a.ContactReference.CreateSourceQuery()
           .OfType<Customer>().FirstOrDefault();
  if (sq != null)
    a.ContactReference.Attach(sq);
}
```

With this code, only customers will be loaded.

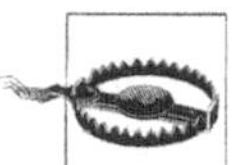

Watch those resources. Just like Load, the preceding query will be run whether the contact is a customer or not, so you may end up with a lot of wasted trips to the database. Consider your data, your resources, and your application's needs. In some scenarios, you may find yourself better off making one big query for customers and not doing this explicit lazy loading.

Getting a Foreign Key Value in an Independent Association

With models created in Visual Studio 2008 or new models that do not use foreign keys, you have only the navigation property to rely on to get to the foreign key value. Because you can traverse relationships in the EDM without having to perform JOINs, the need for foreign keys is greatly reduced. However, at times you may want to have access to a foreign key value such as Address.ContactID.

Although the value is not exposed directly, if you have the entity or the EntityReference, you can get to that value. For example, if the Address.Contact property is populated, you can simply request Address.Contact.ContactID.

If the ContactReference property is populated, you could drill into the EntityKey and extract the value. Don't forget that an EntityKey is composed of a collection of key/value pairs. Although a Contact entity may have only one key property (ContactID), in plenty of cases multiple properties are combined to make an EntityKey, just as you can use multiple fields in a database table to create a primary key.

Example 19-12 shows how to retrieve the ContactID from an Address entity.

Example 19-12. Retrieving the ContactID from an Address entity

```
var contactId=address.ContactReference.EntityKey.EntityKeyValues
              .Where(k=> k.Key == "ContactID")
```

You could encapsulate this logic in the Address's partial class, providing a ContactID property.

You can find examples of this in the previous edition of this book, as well as in my August 2008 blog post "More on Foreign Keys in EF" (*http://thedatafarm.com/blog/data-access/more-on-foreign-keys-in-ef*).

An extension method that can return a foreign key value for any `EntityReference` would be handy here. A simple approach requires that the developer knows about the `EntityReference`, and this particular method will presumptuously return the value of the first key, as shown in Example 19-13.

Example 19-13. Returning the foreign key value from an EntityReference property

```
public static class extension
{
  public static int ForeignKey(this EntityReference entRef)
  {
    return (int)entRef.EntityKey.EntityKeyValues[0].Value
  }
}
```

Now you can call the extension method like so:

```
address.ContactReference.ForeignKey()
```

Summary

Relationships are central to the EDM and to how the Entity Framework functions. There are a lot of subtleties to understand, and some rules are critical. Having foreign keys available as of .NET 4 removes a lot of pain, but there are still behaviors to be aware of.

`EntityObject` and dynamic proxies for entities will automate much of the relationship management and two-way fix-up for you.

The most important lesson is that you need to be watchful of how entity state is affected by relationships. As you saw in Chapters 17 and 18, you can use the new `ChangeState` and `ChangeObjectState` methods to remedy this impact.

You will continue to encounter complexities in your code where relationships are involved—unexpected rules regarding attaching entities to the context or other entities, unexpected changes to state when relating entities, and having the onus of constraint checking put on your code even though constraints are defined in the model. Having this deep understanding of how relationships work and how they relate to the rest of the Entity Framework means you have a lot of problem-solving tools at your disposal. We will continue to cover relationships, and how to solve other challenges that occur in various scenarios, throughout the remainder of the book.

CHAPTER 20

Real World Apps: Connections, Transactions, Performance, and More

By now, you must be wondering how the Entity Framework addresses the everyday concerns of software developers who must build real-world applications. How do you control connections? Is there any connection pooling? Are database calls transactional? What about security? How's the performance? This chapter will address these and many of the additional questions developers ask after learning the basics of the Entity Framework.

You'll learn more about working with entity connections and the database connections that they create for you, and how to explicitly open and control those connections, even when interleaving read and write operations to the database. You'll also learn how transactions work by default, as well as how to replace the default database transactions that Entity Framework uses with .NET's `TransactionScope`. For the security-minded, I'll show you where you should be taking extra cautions and where you might be able to worry a little less. You'll find a slew of ways you can improve performance in Entity Framework, as well as the results of some performance comparisons I've done. Finally, you'll get to take a look at how to use Entity Framework in a few multithreading scenarios.

Entity Framework and Connections

A benefit of using the Entity Framework is that it takes care of writing the code to set up a database connection. Given a connection string typically defined in the `EntityConnection` defined in a *.config* file, the Entity Framework will automatically set up, open, and close the database connection for you. Compared to typical ADO.NET code, which requires you to instantiate, define, and in many cases explicitly open a connection; define, instantiate, and execute a command; and then explicitly close the connection, letting the `ObjectContext` handle all of this in the background is certainly convenient. But sometimes, as you'll see shortly, you'll want more control over how and when connections are being made. To be able to do that, you first need to understand how `EntityConnection` and `DbConnection` work together so that you can force them to work the way you want when their default behavior doesn't meet your needs.

Overriding EntityConnection Defaults

An `EntityConnection` is not a connection to a database. And `EntityConnection` does include a database connection, but additionally it controls access to the model's metadata as well as access to the specific ADO.NET provider used by the application. This can be a big point of confusion. When you explicitly or implicitly open and close an `EntityConnection`, it is the `EntityConnection` that in turn opens and closes a connection to the database. Whether you use `EntityClient` directly or you let Object Services execute your commands and queries for you, the `EntityConnection` is just a path to the database connection.

An `EntityConnection` consists of four parts:

Metadata
: The pointer to the metadata files (CSDL, MSL, and SSDL).

Provider connection
: The database connection string.

Provider name
: The namespace of the database provider. This is the API that you will use to allow Entity Framework to communicate with your database—for example, `System.Data.SqlClient` to work with SQL Server.

Name
: The name of the connection string.

You can define the `EntityConnection` declaratively in the *.config* file. Example 20-1 lists the name of the connection string and then the `EntityConnection` string itself. Within the connection string, you can see the metadata parameter, the provider connection parameter, and the provider name.

See Microsoft's ADO.NET Providers page (*http://msdn.microsoft.com/en-us/data/dd363565.aspx*) for an updated list of database provider APIs that support Entity Framework.

When the EDM Wizard builds this string for you, it replaces the quotes around the provider connection string with an escaped quote (`"`), which is the XML encoding for a quote. For readability, you can replace the escaped quotes with single quotes, as in Example 20-1.

Example 20-1. The EntityConnection string in an app.config or web.config file

```
<connectionStrings>
<add
 name="BAEntities"
 connectionString=
   "metadata=res://*/BAModel.csdl|res://*/BAModel.ssdl|res://*/BAModel.msl;
    provider=System.Data.SqlClient;
    provider connection string='Data Source=.;
                               Initial Catalog=BreakAway;
                               Integrated Security=True;
                               MultipleActiveResultSets=True'"
    providerName="System.Data.EntityClient"
 />
</connectionStrings>
```

By default, an `ObjectContext` will use the connection string from the *.config* file that matches the `EntityContainer` name within your model. You have taken advantage of this in almost every code sample so far in the book, which is why you have not yet had to work explicitly with connection strings.

The database connection string that is embedded into the `EntityConnection` string is passed along to the database provider that eventually makes the actual connection to the database.

> **Moving from a Development Database to a Production Database**
>
> When you're moving from a development environment to a production environment, pointing to a new database can be as simple as changing the provider connection string parameter of the appropriate connection string in the *.config* file. You can also programmatically change the database connection string or modify connection strings on the fly.

Working with Connection Strings Programmatically

`EntityConnection` is a class within the `EntityClient` namespace. In Chapter 3, you worked directly with this class when you used `EntityClient` for your queries. In the following code, the name of the connection string in the *.config* file is passed as a parameter (along with the parameter key `name=`) in the `EntityConnection` constructor. The connection in this case will be created from the details provided in the connection string.

```
var conn = new EntityConnection("name=BAEntities");
```

You can use the preceding method to explicitly select a particular connection string from the *.config* file when instantiating an `ObjectContext`, as shown in the code that follows:

```
var context = new BAEntities("name=MyOtherConnectionString");
```

Yes, it's true. My development computer name is "honker64." Sometimes I do hardcode that into my database connection strings, although more often I use the "." shortcut.

If you inspect the `EntityConnection` in the debugger after it has been instantiated, you'll see that although the database connection object has been pulled into the `StoreConnection` property, the other parameters of the `EntityConnectionString` are nowhere to be found, as shown in Figure 20-1.

Name	Value
conn	{System.Data.EntityClient.EntityConnection}
base	{System.Data.EntityClient.EntityConnection}
ConnectionString	"name=BAEntities"
ConnectionTimeout	15
Database	""
DataSource	"honker64"
ServerVersion	'conn.ServerVersion' threw an exception of type 'System.Inva
State	Closed
StoreConnection	{System.Data.SqlClient.SqlConnection}
Static members	
Non-Public members	

Figure 20-1. The EntityConnection object with no properties for the metadata or provider namespace attributes

The metadata and provider namespace parameters are not displayed as properties of the `EntityConnection` class, and they won't be accessed until the point in the query pipeline when `EntityClient` needs to read metadata, and then again to determine which provider (e.g., `System.Data.SqlClient`) to pass the request to for further processing.

If you do want to read the full connection string from the configuration file, you can use one of the .NET methods, such as `System.Configuration.ConfigurationManager`.

Constructing connection strings on the fly with the EntityConnectionStringBuilder class

Frequently, developers want to avoid embedding the connection string in the *.config* file. Or they want more flexibility in pointing to databases or metadata that resides in different locations.

You can programmatically construct an `EntityConnectionString` with the `EntityConnectionStringBuilder`, which inherits from `DbConnectionStringBuilder`. For example, you might want to store the location of your metadata files (*.csdl*, *.msl*, *.ssdl*) in a resource file and wish to programmatically change the `EntityConnectionString` to point to this location. Or you may want to programmatically change the ADO.NET `DataProvider` (e.g., `System.Data.SqlClient`) on the fly.

The code in Example 20-2 reads the connection string from the configuration file into a string, creates an `EntityConnectionStringBuilder` from that string, modifies the `Metadata` property, instantiates an `ObjectContext` with the newly configured `EntityConnectionString`, and then executes a query against that context.

For this example, a string for the path to the metadata files has been stored in the project's settings as `MetadataFilePath`. Its value is:

```
F:\Models\BAModel.csdl|F:\Models\BAModel.ssdl|F:\Models\BAModel.msl
```

The files were created by setting the model's Metadata Artifact Processing property to Copy to Output Directory and then copying the output files into the *C:\Models* folder.

Example 20-2. Programmatically modifying an EntityConnectionString

```
var connectionString = ConfigurationManager
          .ConnectionStrings["BAEntities"].ConnectionString;
var connectionStringBuilder= new EntityConnectionStringBuilder(connectionString);
connectionStringBuilder.Metadata = Properties.Settings.Default.MetadataFilePath;
var context = new BAEntities(connectionStringBuilder.ConnectionString);
var query =
    from  c in context.Contacts
    where c.Addresses.Any(a => a.City == "Seattle")
    select c;
var contacts = query.ToList();
```

The `ConfigurationManager` class can be tricky to find. You need to reference the `System.Configuration` namespace in your project; then you can get to `System.Configuration.ConfigurationManager`.

Unfortunately, the `Metadata` parameter is a string, so there's no strongly typed way to construct it. Instead, you can use one of the common `DbConnectionStringBuilder` classes, such as `SqlConnectionStringBuilder`, to programmatically construct the provider connection string (`StoreConnection`) of the `EntityConnectionString`.

Choosing and loading a model programmatically. One of the overloads for the `EntityConnection` constructor allows you to pass in a model that is in memory along with a database connection. This allows you to work with models that may not be stored in a particular file. For example, if you were to define different models and store those in a database, at runtime the code would determine which model to work with. You could then load the model's XML from the database into memory—for example, into an `XmlReader`—and then create an `EntityConnection` with the `XmlReader`. Once this connection has been instantiated, you can use it with an `ObjectContext` to query that model.

The code-first design that is provided in the Entity Framework Feature CTP takes advantage of using in-memory metadata. This will allow you to use Entity Framework without having to create a model in advance. We'll take a look at code-first design in Chapter 25.

More is involved in this scenario because you will also need to have code that can determine what is in the model at runtime. The Entity Framework's `MetadataWorkspace` allows you to do this, and as such create a completely dynamic application. See Chapter 21 for more about `MetadataWorkspace`.

Opening and Closing Connections

If they have not yet been loaded, `EntityConnection.Open` loads the model's metadata files (*.csdl*, *.msl*, and *.ssdl*) into the application memory. This method calls the database provider's `Connection.Open` as well. `EntityConnection.Close` will, in turn, call the database connection's close method.

When an `ObjectContext` executes a query internally it creates an `EntityConnection` and an `EntityCommand`, and then executes the command. As soon as the data has been consumed, whether you call a method such as `ToList` to read all of the data at once or you iterate through the data and come to the end, the context will close the `EntityConnection`, which in turn closes the database connection.

Opening and closing connections to the database is something that many developers fret about because we want to make the most efficient use of available resources. You may want to control when the open and close happen so that you can control how resources are used.

Understanding the default connection usage

When working with `EntityClient` directly, you need to explicitly create and open an `EntityConnection` before you can have your query executed.

When working with the `ObjectContext`, the default behavior is that the `ObjectContext` opens and closes connections as needed and does so as efficiently as possible. It is possible, however, to override that behavior and explicitly control when `EntityConnection` is opened and closed.

You have a few options here. You can manually open the connection and let it be closed implicitly when the context is disposed, or you can manually open it and manually close it.

One of the advantages of opening and closing the connection yourself is that you can prevent the connection from being opened and closed numerous times when you are making a bunch of rapid-fire queries or performing a query followed by deferred loading.

You can see the difference in the following examples.

Default behavior 1: Many calls on a single connection. Example 20-3 performs a single query, iterates through the results, and calls `Load` and `EntityCollection` for some of the results. Each call to `Load` hits the database on the same connection because the context hasn't finished reading through the query results.

Example 20-3. The initial query and subsequent loads executed on the same connection

```
using (var context = new BAEntities())
{
  var query =
      from c in context.Contacts
      where c.FirstName == "Jose"
      select c;
  foreach (var contact in query
              .Where(contact => contact.AddDate <
                    new System.DateTime(2007, 1, 1)))
  {
    contact.Addresses.Load();
  }
}
```

Only a single connection is used in this case because a connection is not closed until the results have been consumed. Therefore, because you are iterating through the resultant contacts, the connection remains open until you have reached the first contact. In the meantime, the additional calls to the database to load the addresses use that same connection. The `MultipleActiveResultSets` setting in the connection string allows multiple streams to be read on the same connection.

> `MultipleActiveResultSets`, also known as MARS, was introduced in ADO.NET 2.0 and is specific to SQL Server. Unlike many other databases, SQL Server does not support streaming multiple result sets on a single connection by default. But MARS allows it to do this.

Default behavior 2: Multiple connections. The set of queries in Example 20-4 opens and closes a connection twice. It closes the first connection when `contacts.ToList` is called, because this forces the entire set of results to be consumed at once. Recall that a connection is disposed when its results have been fully consumed. Therefore, a new connection needs to be created for the second query.

Example 20-4. Two queries, each getting its own connection

```
using (var context = new BAEntities())
{
  var contacts = (from c in context.Contacts
                  where c.FirstName == "Jose"
                  select c).ToList();
  var allCustomers = context.Contacts.OfType<Customer>().ToList();
}
```

Forcing an explicit connection

To change the default behavior that happens in Example 20-4., you can force the connection to be reused by manually opening the connection, as shown in Example 20-5. Then you can either explicitly close it or let the context automatically close it when the context goes out of scope, or let the garbage collector dispose it when the time comes.

Example 20-5. Forcing queries to use the same connection

```
using (var context = new BAEntities())
{
  context.Connection.Open();
  var contacts = (from c in context.Contacts
            where c.FirstName == "Jose"
            select c).ToList();
  var allCustomers = context.Contacts.OfType<Customer>().ToList();
  context.Connection.Close();
}
```

Getting the Store Connection from EntityConnection

Although `ObjectContext.Connection` returns the `EntityConnection`, you can drill deeper, as you saw in Figure 20-1, and get the actual database connection using `EntityConnection`'s `StoreConnection` property.

If for some reason you want to have very granular control over the database connection—for example, by specifying a longer `ConnectionTimeout` to accommodate a slow network—you can do so by working directly with the `StoreConnection`.

Disposing Connections

As with any data access performed in .NET, it's important that you dispose database connections. A database connection is not a managed .NET resource and the garbage collector will not clean it up. Lingering database connections are a common cause of excessive memory consumption. Again, when you rely on the Entity Framework's default behavior, the database connection will be properly disposed. Disposing an `ObjectContext` automatically closes the `EntityConnection` and will close and dispose the database connection as well. You can either explicitly dispose the `ObjectContext` or wait for the garbage collector to do the job. However, in the latter scenario, that means the database connection is still hanging around until that time.

In common usage scenarios with the Entity Framework, the worst offense (holding a database connection open) should not be an issue, because as you have seen, the connection will be closed automatically. But if one of the triggers for closing a database connection has not been executed—completing the consumption of query results, calling `EntityConnection.Close`, or disposing the `ObjectContext`—you could unwittingly be consuming extra resources.

`ObjectContext`'s `Dispose` method calls `EntityConnection.Dispose` if `ObjectContext` created the connection. In turn, `EntityConnection.Dispose` will call the `Dispose` method on the `StoreConnection`. The code behind `ObjectContext.Dispose` is shown in Example 20-6 so that you can see just how it works.

Example 20-6. The ObjectContext.Dispose method

```
protected virtual void Dispose(bool disposing)
{
  if (disposing)
  {
    if (this._createdConnection && (this._connection != null))
    {
      this._connection.Dispose();
    }
    this._connection = null;
    this._adapter = null;
  }
}
```

An age-old debate in ADO.NET concerns whether you should close or dispose database connections. In fact, `DbConnection.Close` calls `Dispose` and `DbConnection.Dispose` calls `Close`. The methods make these calls using logic that avoids an infinite loop. `Close` takes care of the critical connection resources, but the connection object itself is still there.

So, if you are using the defaults with LINQ to Entities or an `ObjectQuery`, the connection will be disposed. If you want to be sure the connection is disposed right away, you need to either explicitly make that call or be sure the `ObjectContext` is explicitly disposed. If you have created the `EntityConnection` explicitly, you have to either dispose it explicitly or wait for the garbage collector to dispose it; again, this in turn will dispose the database connection.

Pooling Connections

Spinning up a database connection is expensive in terms of resources. When a connection is closed, it can be left in memory to be reused the next time a connection is required, eliminating the cost of creating a new connection. This is called *connection pooling*.

Developers often ask whether the Entity Framework does connection pooling. Because connection pooling is controlled by the database provider, the Entity Framework does not explicitly impact or interact with how connection pooling works. Instead, it relies on the provider's connection pooling. For more information on connection pooling in ADO.NET, a good starting point is the "SQL Server Connection Pooling (ADO.NET)" topic in the MSDN documentation.

Fine-Tuning Transactions

Another question that is frequently asked about the Entity Framework is whether it uses transactions. The simple answer is "yes," but, naturally, there's more to this answer.

A *transaction* defines a unit of work that can contain a number of actions, such as database updates. When all of the actions have completed successfully, the transaction is committed. If any of the actions fail, the transaction is "rolled back," which causes all of the actions to roll back. Therefore, if you have actions that depend on each other and one action fails, you don't have to manually undo those that have already occurred.

Resources that provide the capability to process transactions, such as databases, can have their transactions be enlisted—in other words, called into action—by .NET. Whether you have a number of updates on a single database connection within a single transaction, or you have a few of them combined with interactions on another database and possibly combined with work in message queuing, you can coordinate all of those individual transaction resource managers in a single transaction.

When performing a `SaveChanges` operation, the Entity Framework implicitly wraps all of the commands in a database transaction such as `SqlTransaction`; however, you can take control of transactions as well.

Why Use Your Own Transaction?

By default, Entity Framework uses `DbTransaction` (the base class for provider-based transactions such as `SqlTransaction` and `OracleTransaction`) to take care of operations on a single instance of a database connection.

There is another type of transaction in .NET. The `System.Transactions.Transaction Scope` class can coordinate operations across a variety of processes that use resource managers. Therefore, within a single transaction you could make calls to a database, to the Message Queue (MSMQ), or even to another database using ADO.NET. If one of those fails, `System.Transaction` will allow all of them to be rolled back together. `System.Transaction` leverages the Windows Distributed Transaction Coordinator (DTC) to make this happen, albeit with more overhead than a simple database transaction. But what is great about `System.Transaction` is that it will decide whether your actions need only the individual transaction (such as `SqlTransaction`), or whether they need to escalate to a DTC so that multiple transactions can be orchestrated. In that way, you don't needlessly waste resources with the DTC, but you also don't have to explicitly control it.

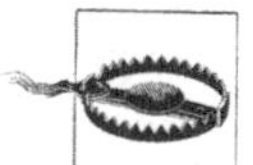

It's important to understand that the Entity Framework can only leverage transactions with database interaction. You cannot use transactions to control and roll back modifications to the `ObjectContext` itself—not even the creation of entities when performing a query.

Understanding Implicit Entity Framework Transactions

The database constraint between Contact and Address in the BreakAway database makes a good test case for demonstrating the implicit transactions in the Entity Framework. An address cannot exist without a contact, yet no cascading delete is defined in the database to delete related addresses when a contact is deleted. Therefore, an attempt to delete a Contact entity without deleting its related addresses in code will cause the database to throw an error when SaveChanges is called. Let's take advantage of that and write some code to see the transaction in action.

The code in Example 20-7 queries for a particular contact, deletes it from the ObjectContext, and then calls SaveChanges. To add a twist, the code also creates a new payment for a reservation. Remember that when you attach the payment to the reservation in the context, SaveChanges automatically pulls the payment into the context and inserts it into the database.

Example 20-7. An implicit transaction that will roll back

```
using (var context = new BAEntities())
{
  var contact = context.Contacts.Where(c => c.ContactID == 5)
                  .FirstOrDefault();
  context.DeleteObject(contact);
  var reservation = context.Reservations.FirstOrDefault;
  var payment = new Payment();
  payment.Amount = "500";
  payment.PaymentDate = System.DateTime.Now;
  payment.Reservation = reservation;
  context.SaveChanges();
}
```

The attempt to delete the contact from the database will fail because of the referential constraint. Figure 20-2, a screenshot from SQL Profiler, shows what happens when SaveChanges is called.

```
BEGIN TRANSACTION
exec sp_executesql N'delete [dbo].[Contact]  where ([Conta...
ROLLBACK TRANSACTION
```

Figure 20-2. The Entity Framework automatically forcing a rollback if any of the commands to the database fail

A transaction was created, and because the delete failed, the transaction is rolled back and the insert for the payment is not even bothered with.

On the client side, an exception is thrown containing the error from the database, which offers a very clear description of the problem:

```
"The DELETE statement conflicted with the REFERENCE constraint
"FK_Address_Contact". The conflict occurred in database "BreakAway", table
"dbo.Address", column 'ContactID'. The statement has been terminated."
```

This highlights a good reason to be sure to include exception handling around `SaveChanges` in cases where any constraints in the database are not constrained in advance in the model or in the application. Exception handling will be the focus of the next chapter.

In this example, `SaveChanges` was attempting to execute two database commands—the delete and the update. Even if `SaveChanges` created only one command, it would still be wrapped in a database transaction.

Where did the transaction come from? A `DbTransaction` is created within the `SaveChanges` method. If no exceptions are thrown during the actual command execution, `DbTransaction.Commit` is called.

Understanding SaveOptions and AcceptAllChanges in a transaction

`ObjectContext.AcceptAllChanges` updates the object state of all of the entities being change-tracked. This will set the `OriginalValues` to whatever the current values are and it will change the object's `EntityState` to `Unchanged`.

During the `SaveChanges` process and after the default transaction has been committed, `AcceptAllChanges` is automatically called, causing the `ObjectContext` to be up-to-date and its entities to match the data in the database. You may recall that `DetectChanges` is also called to accommodate for POCO entities that do not notify the context of their changes.

As you learned in Chapter 11, you can override the behavior by passing in a `SaveOptions` enum when you call `SaveChanges`. This is especially useful when you're using your own transaction, since you may want to retry the save or just call `AcceptAllChanges` even when the transaction did not complete. Calling `AcceptAllChanges` in this case would make the in-memory objects out of sync with the database. So, you should do this only if you have specific logic that behaves accordingly.

If you are overriding the default transaction that is used inside the `SaveChanges` method, you will most likely want to defer the `AcceptAllChanges` call until your own transaction has completed, as you will see in the next example.

Specifying Your Own Read/Write Transactions

Just as you can override the default behavior with connections, you can also override the default behavior of transactions. If you explicitly create your own transaction, `SaveChanges` will not create a `DbTransaction`. But when overriding the default transaction, you won't create a `System.Common.DbTransaction`. Instead, you need to use a `System.Transaction.TransactionScope` object.

You can use a transaction for read and write activities in the database, which means that this will work with both ObjectContext and EntityClient.

Remember that if you are using LINQ to Entities and you want to take advantage of ObjectQuery behavior, you can cast the LINQ to Entities query to an ObjectQuery, as you learned in Chapter 10.

Example 20-8 uses an explicit transaction to save a new customer to a database and, if the call to SaveChanges is successful, to add the customer's name to a completely separate database. The application has references to two different projects with EDMs. If something goes wrong with either database update, the TransactionScope will not be completed and both updates will be rolled back.

You'll need to add a reference in your project to System.Transactions and add a C# using or VB Imports statement for this namespace at the beginning of your code file.

Example 20-8. Creating your own System.Transaction for SaveChanges

```
using (var context = new BAEntities())
{
  var customer = new Customer
  { FirstName = "George",
    LastName = "Jetson",
    Notes = "A real space cadet",
    BirthDate = new DateTime(1962, 1, 1)
  };

  context.Contacts.AddObject(customer);
  using (var transactionScope = new TransactionScope())
  {
    try
    {
      context.SaveChanges(SaveOptions.None);
      var altContext = new AltDbEntities();
      var contact = new Contact
                  {Name = customer.LastName.Trim() + ", " + customer.FirstName};
      altContext.Contacts.AddObject(contact);
      altContext.SaveChanges();
      transactionScope.Complete();
      context.AcceptAllChanges();
      altContext.AcceptAllChanges();
    }
    catch Exception ex
    {
      //TODO: handle database or Entity Framework exceptions
      throw(ex);  //TODO: remove this after proper handling is added
    }
```

```
    }
}
```

You can watch the transaction being promoted from a local transaction to a distributed transaction in a few ways. For example, in SQL Profiler, you can see that `System.Transaction` starts out by using a simple database transaction, but as soon as it hits the call to `SaveChanges` to a different database, the transaction is promoted (see Figure 20-3).

```
Audit Login                     -- network protocol: LPC  set quote...
TM: Begin Tran starting         BEGIN TRANSACTION
TM: Begin Tran completed        BEGIN TRANSACTION
RPC:Completed                   exec sp_executesql N'insert [dbo].[...
RPC:Completed                   exec sp_executesql N'insert [dbo].[...
RPC:Completed                   exec sp_executesql N'insert [dbo].[...
Audit Login                     -- network protocol: TCP/IP  set qu...
TM: Promote Tran starting
TM: Promote Tran completed
RPC:Completed                   exec sp_executesql N'insert [dbo].[...
TM: Commit Tran starting        COMMIT TRANSACTION
TM: Commit Tran completed       COMMIT TRANSACTION
Audit Logout
```

Figure 20-3. SQL Profiler showing that a database transaction is used at first, but is then promoted when another database connection is made within the scope of a System.Transactions.TransactionScope

You can also add a variety of performance counters into the Windows Performance Monitor that tracks the DTC, and you can see whether a transaction was created, completed, or even rolled back.

If you are testing on a development machine, you may not have the DTC service started. When the code reaches the second `SaveChanges` and .NET attempts to promote the transaction to use the DTC, if the DTC is not started you will receive an exception telling you that the DTC has not started on the system. One of the ways you can start this service is through the Computer Management console in Windows.

The last way you can prove this is working is to force one of the updates to fail. You can see the rollback in the Profiler, or even just look in the database to verify that the changes have not been made.

The MSDN documentation has a nice example of combining SaveChanges with a message queue within a TransactionScope. You can find this example at *http://msdn.microsoft.com/en-us/library/bb738523(VS.100).aspx*.

Specifying Your Own Read-Only Transactions

It is also possible to use a transaction on a read-only query using System.Transaction or EntityClient.EntityTransaction. An EntityTransaction is merely a wrapper for the database provider's transaction, and calls EntityConnection.BeginTransaction to create it, as shown in Example 20-9.

Example 20-9. Using a transaction on a read to control whether the read will read data that is in the process of being modified in the database

```
using (var connection = new EntityConnection("name=BAEntities"))
{
  connection.Open();
  EntityTransaction transaction =
    connection.BeginTransaction(IsolationLevel.ReadUncommitted);
  var command = connection.CreateCommand();
  command.CommandText = "SELECT c.contactID FROM BAEntities.Contacts AS c";
  var dataReader = command.ExecuteReader
   (CommandBehavior.SequentialAccess | CommandBehavior.CloseConnection);
  while (dataReader.Read())
  {
     //do something with the data;
  }
  transaction.Commit();
}
```

At first glance, it may not make sense to have a transaction on a read, since you can't roll back a read. The purpose of performing a read within a transaction is to control how to read data in the database that may be involved in another transaction at the same time. Notice the IsolationLevel.ReadUncommitted parameter being passed in. IsolationLevel lets you determine how your query should read data that some other person or process is currently updating. The ReadUncommitted enum says that it is OK for this query to read data that is being modified, even if it has not yet been committed in the other transaction. The other possibilities are Serializable, RepeatableRead, ReadCommitted, Snapshot, Chaos, and Unspecified. IsolationLevel support is dependent on which database you are using and is not specific to Entity Framework. You can check the docs to learn more about these IsolationLevels.

Because the operation in Example 20-9 is a read operation, you could get away without calling `transaction.Commit` because of the `IsolationLevel` that is specified—`ReadUncommitted`. Additionally, if you were not using pooled connections, it would also be OK to neglect the `Commit`. However, there's no harm in calling it, and it's simply a good idea in general to always call `Commit`. If you were using different `IsolationLevels` in that transaction and didn't call `Commit` (because you were only doing a read anyway), you could actually get undesirable behavior.

Although you can use `EntityTransaction` directly, it is recommended that you use `System.Transaction.Transaction` or `TransactionScope`, where you can also set the `IsolationLevel`. For example, you could wrap the query (`EntityClient`, LINQ to Entities, or `ObjectQuery`) within a `TransactionScope`, just as in the previous example, which used `TransactionScope` for `SaveChanges`.

Distributed transactions are more expensive to process, and often the events that cause a transaction to be promoted do not really require the extra cost of the DTC. Improvements were made in `SqlClient` so that transactions are escalated more wisely when using SQL Server 2008. Prior to SQL Server 2008, it helps to explicitly open the connection after creating the transaction. To read more about this, see the ADO.NET Team blog post, "Extending Lightweight Transactions in SqlClient," at *http://blogs.msdn.com/adonet/archive/2008/03/26/extending-lightweight-transactions-in-sqlclient.aspx*.

Rolling Back Transactions

People often ask about the ability to roll back changes to entities in the context. Unfortunately, Object Services does not have a mechanism to achieve this. If you want to roll all the way back to the server values, you can use `ObjectContext.Refresh` to reset specific entities or a collection of entities, but you cannot do a thorough refresh of everything in the context. You'll learn more about refreshing in Chapter 23. Alternatively, you can dispose the context, create a new one, and requery the data. But still, this is not the same as rolling back to a previous state of the entities; all you're doing is getting fresh data from the store.

If you want to persist the state of your entities at any given point in time and then restore them into the context, you'll need a better understanding of the `ObjectStateManager`, which we will cover in detail in Chapter 21.

For now, I would recommend taking a good look at a caching provider written by Jaroslaw Kowalski, a member of the Entity Framework team. You can find the provider at *http://code.msdn.microsoft.com/EFProviderWrappers*.

Understanding Security

Security is an important issue to be concerned with, and it is the subject of frequently asked questions regarding the Entity Framework, mostly due to database access.

If you were to look at the security topic in the MSDN documentation (see the topic "Security Considerations [Entity Framework]"), you might find the lengthy list of items covered to be daunting. But on more careful inspection, you would see that most of the points are generic to programming or to data access, with only a few items pertaining specifically to the Entity Framework.

The most frequently asked security topic in the Entity Framework concerns SQL injection. Another security issue of interest is the fact that developers can piggyback onto the Entity Framework's database connections. I will discuss these two scenarios in this chapter. Check the aforementioned MSDN topic for additional security topics.

Guarding Against SQL Injection

SQL injection attacks are one of the most worrisome problems for data developers. An injection occurs when an end user is able to append actual query syntax in data entry form fields that can damage your data (e.g., `delete table x`) or access information by piggybacking on the executed command.

Wikipedia has a handy tutorial on SQL injection if you want to learn more. See *http://en.wikipedia.org/wiki/SQL_injection*.

SQL injection can occur when you build queries dynamically in your code. For example:

```
QueryString="select * from users where username='" & TextBox.Text & "'"
```

Therefore, it is always recommended that programmers avoid building dynamic queries. Instead, we use parameterized queries or leverage stored procedures in our data access code.

Because we have been trained to have an inherent fear of dynamic queries, on the surface the fact that the Entity Framework (and LINQ to SQL, for that matter) builds queries for us raises a big red flag.

Taking precautions with dynamic queries

You can relax when using LINQ to Entities (or LINQ to SQL). When you use variables in your LINQ queries, the store queries that eventually land in your data store for execution are parameterized queries, not dynamic ones. You've seen that throughout this book.

And of course, you can always use stored procedures, which are the ultimate way to avoid SQL injection attacks, presuming that those procedures themselves don't allow for dynamic SQL.

You'll need to be much more careful with Entity SQL. Entity SQL is broken down differently than LINQ to Entities, and the queries that result are composed differently.

Let's look at the difference between a few queries in which it might be possible to inject some debilitating SQL by way of a text box in a data entry form.

Here is a LINQ to Entities query:

```
from loc in context.Locations where loc.LocationName === textBox.Text
```

When the text box is populated with `Norway`, the T-SQL that results is parameterized:

```
SELECT
[Extent1].[LocationID] AS [LocationID],
[Extent1].[LocationName] AS [LocationName]
FROM [dbo].[Locations] AS [Extent1]
WHERE [Extent1].[LocationName] = @p__linq__1

@p__linq__1='Norway'
```

Similarly, when the text box contains `a' OR 't'='t` (a classic injection attack), the native query still puts this "value" into a single parameter, and the injection is unsuccessful:

```
SELECT
[Extent1].[LocationID] AS [LocationID],
[Extent1].[LocationName] AS [LocationName]
FROM [dbo].[Locations] AS [Extent1]
WHERE [Extent1].[LocationName] = @p__linq__1

@p__linq__1='a'' OR ''t''=''t'
```

However, the same query in Entity SQL looks like this:

```
SELECT VALUE loc FROM BreakAwayEntities.Locations  AS loc
WHERE loc.LocationName='" & city & "'"
```

With `Norway`, the T-SQL is benign:

```
SELECT
[Extent1].[LocationID] AS [LocationID],
[Extent1].[LocationName] AS [LocationName]
FROM [dbo].[Locations] AS [Extent1]
WHERE [Extent1].[LocationName] = 'Norway'
```

but the injection succeeds. Here is the T-SQL:

```
SELECT
[Extent1].[LocationID] AS [LocationID],
[Extent1].[LocationName] AS [LocationName]
FROM [dbo].[Locations] AS [Extent1]
WHERE ([Extent1].[LocationName] = 'a') OR ('t' = 't')
```

Getting a list of all of the cities is still somewhat benign, but the point is that you have just lost control of your query.

These types of attacks are not as easy to pull off with Entity SQL as they are when composing native queries in ADO.NET, because the injection needs to be valid Entity SQL syntax and valid native SQL syntax at the same time. Therefore, an attack using this method:

```
"a' ; SELECT * FROM LOGINS"
```

or even this one:

```
"a' UNION ALL (SELECT value log from entities.logins as log)"
```

will fail because the Entity SQL command text will be invalid in both cases.

Entity SQL injection

Injecting SQL that goes to the store is one problem. What about injecting Entity SQL into an Entity SQL string? Again, this is possible. Imagine appending a `JOIN` clause to your Entity SQL, followed by an Entity SQL expression that selects logins and passwords. The user only needs access to your EDM files to know the structure of the model and to figure out what your queries might look like to append the right string to get at the data she is looking for.

It may not sound very easy to do, but some people spend a lot of time figuring out how to crack into our applications, and that is who you need to worry about.

Therefore, as with any other data access that is dependent on user input, you need to validate all user input before inserting it into your queries; and you need to be very thoughtful regarding where and when you concatenate strings to build Entity SQL queries.

Remember that when using `ObjectQuery`, you can create `ObjectParameters`. And don't forget about the Entity SQL query builder methods, which provide the safest way to create Entity SQL.

Guarding Against Connection Piggybacks

Although your model might limit what parts of your database a user has access to, it does make a connection to the database, providing an open door to users who might not otherwise have access to the database.

As you saw in "Getting the Store Connection from EntityConnection" on page 564, it is possible to get at the database connection through an `EntityConnection`; therefore, a rogue developer writing queries against the model could easily execute his own commands by using the existing connection. If the database has not been properly secured, this could enable him to access data that is not even part of the model.

Consider the code in Example 20-10 where the developer uses the connection from the context to return the employee data from the database.

Example 20-10. Using the EntityConnection to make an ADO.NET call to the database

```
using (var context = new BAEntities())
{
  var query = context.Contacts.Take(10);
  var conn = context.Connection as EntityConnection;
  var dbconn = conn.StoreConnection;
  dbconn.Open();
  var sqlcmd = new SqlCommand("Select * from HR.Employees",
                              dbconn as SqlConnection);
  SqlDataReader dr = sqlcmd.ExecuteReader();
  while (dr.Read())
  {
    Console.WriteLine(dr["SocialSecurityNumber"]);
  }
}
```

Even worse, with the connection string, any type of command against the database can be executed (as long as the identity has permissions), not just queries.

Although the developer may not necessarily have access to the connection string being used for the EDM queries—for example, the connection string may be encrypted—he can use this connection and any of the permissions associated with the login.

This type of abuse is not particular to the Entity Framework, but it's important to be aware that the Entity Framework doesn't prevent it. As with any data access scenario, applying permissions carefully in your database can help you avoid this situation.

Fine-Tuning Performance

"What about performance?" is another question asked by developers, and is a completely valid concern.

There's no question that when you introduce layers into your application, performance will be impacted. Using ADO.NET to stream data directly from the database into your hands is certainly going to be faster than having a query interpreted and transformed and then having the returned data transformed again. And not only does Entity Framework materialize objects, but as you saw in the previous chapter, it does a lot of work setting up relationships and additional infrastructure so that as you work with the instantiated object, everything "just works."

When comparing query performance to a `DataReader`, keep in mind that while you pay a little extra in performance up front (during query and materialization), you reap a huge benefit for the rest of the process of working with and then persisting the data back to the database.

You can do some things to help, and they can be hugely beneficial, but compared to "classic" ADO.NET queries or even LINQ to SQL, you are definitely paying a price for the benefits you gain when you use Entity Framework.

Measuring Query Performance

Following are some tests to give you a feel for the difference in performance (speed) between the Entity Framework, classic ADO.NET, and LINQ to SQL, because that's an important comparison as well.

Backyard benchmarks is my own term for identifying that these are simple tests that I conducted on my computer and that do not represent any official benchmarks from Microsoft or follow any type of official testing guideline, if any even exists. The numbers are meant only to provide some relative comparisons between the Entity Framework, ADO.NET, and LINQ to SQL.

Here are the specs of the computer used for these tests:

- Intel Core 2 Duo CPU, E4600 at 2.4 GHz
- 6 GB of RAM
- Windows 7 Ultimate 64-bit operating system

Each test presents the time it takes to run the following steps 100 times: execute a simple query of the AdventureWorksLT `Customer` table and create objects from its results. The tests are designed so that the processes will be comparable. For example, with the `DataReader` test, the code performs 100 individual queries using a single open connection. In the LINQ to Entities and `ObjectContext` tests, the sample instantiates a new context and performs 100 queries on that context. I've used `MergeOption.OverwriteChanges` to ensure that the objects are materialized with each query to emulate the object creation in the `DataReader` test. The fourth test performs the same query using LINQ to SQL. I am using long-lived contexts for the Entity Framework and LINQ to SQL queries.

In each test, the loop of 101 queries runs twice. The first time is to "prime the pump" so that any performance advantages provided by repeated queries are evened out between the various tests. The second set of 101 tests is used to gather the timings. Then the first test is removed, leaving 100 results to analyze. In each test, the results are iterated through completely. The time quoted is not the time it took to perform a single query. It is the time it took to perform 100 queries, opening and closing the connection 100 times.

Because working with `DataReaders` is so different from working with Entity Framework or LINQ to SQL, you'll never achieve a totally fair performance comparison, so it's important that you look at these tests with an understanding that their purpose is to give you a general idea of the differences. And keep in mind that there are many ways to impact the Entity Framework queries, which you'll see shortly.

Table 20-1 compares the relative times for the different methods of querying. In the following section, I interpret the results as well as list the code used to generate the results.

Table 20-1. Comparison of relative times for different methods of querying with Entity Framework queries

Access type	100 queries	Diff from base
`DataReader` (populate field)	234 ms	–43%
`DataReader` (populate object)	407 ms	---
LINQ to Entities (short- running context)	1,044 ms	+156%
LINQ to Entities (long-running context)	972 ms	+139%
Precompiled LINQ to Entities (long-running context)	104 ms	–74%
`ObjectQuery` (short- running context)	791 ms	+94%
`ObjectQuery` (long-running context)	102 ms	–75%
LINQ to SQL	415 ms	+ 3%

It makes sense that the `DataReader` would be the fastest, as it has direct access to the database. It reads data directly from the database and streams it out to the client application. However, to make a fair comparison, the test with the `DataReader` reads through the results and materializes objects. This is comparable to what happens internally in the other tests.

LINQ to Entities goes through a number of transformations prior to hitting the database, and the returned results need to be materialized along with their relationship information (when the entity is being tracked), so this requires extra work. Table 20-1 shows the difference between querying with a context that is instantiated specifically to run the query, as in websites and services and queries that share a long-running context, as you've used in client applications such as Windows Forms and WPF.

I've included the very performant precompiled LINQ to Entities query measurement, which you will learn about further on in the chapter.

A query written in Entity SQL has one less transformation to go through before hitting the database, and you can see this in the shortened execution time, but whether you start with LINQ to Entities or an `ObjectQuery`, a number of expensive tasks need to be performed. The object materialization of the results incurs the same cost as using LINQ to Entities. But there is something else at play here. Notice the long-running context is only 102 ms. The query compilation is getting a built-in advantage from Entity SQL's query plan caching, which you will read about in the next section.

Finally, LINQ to SQL is added to the mix because it is another Microsoft ORM and it is not uncommon to wonder how it compares to Entity Framework on various levels. LINQ to SQL maps directly to the database, so the query generation is much less expensive. For the same reason, part of the process of materializing objects is quicker because there is no mapping to work out. And finally, LINQ to SQL handles relationships much differently than Entity Framework, so much of the expense that you have in Entity Framework to create the relationship information does not exist.

The code used for these performance tests is shown in Example 20-11.

Example 20-11. Comparing query performance

```
private static void DataReaderTest(string connstring)
{
  decimal testresults = 0;
  var resultList = new List<decimal>();
  string cmdText = "select CustomerID, NameStyle, Title, FirstName," +
                   "MiddleName, LastName,Suffix,CompanyName, " +
                   "SalesPerson, EmailAddress,Phone,PasswordHash, " +
                   "PasswordSalt, rowguid, ModifiedDate " +
                   "FROM SalesLT.Customer";
  // start the timer
  var sw = new System.Diagnostics.Stopwatch();
  for (int i = 0; i < 2; i++)
  {
    // testresults.Clear();
    var sqlCon = new SqlConnection(connstring);
    sqlCon.Open();
    resultList.Clear();
    for (int j = 0; j < 101; j++)
    {

      sw.Reset();
      sw.Start();

      var cmd = new SqlCommand(cmdText, sqlCon);
      var reader = cmd.ExecuteReader();
      while (reader.Read())
      {
        //var lastItem = reader[14];
        var cust = new Customer
                   {
                     CustomerID = (int)reader["CustomerID"],
                     NameStyle = (bool)reader["NameStyle"],
                     Title = (reader.IsDBNull(2) ? "" : (string)reader["Title"]),
                     FirstName = (string)reader["FirstName"],
                     MiddleName =
                      (reader.IsDBNull(4) ? "" : (string)reader["MiddleName"]),
                     LastName = (string)reader["LastName"],
                     Suffix = (reader.IsDBNull(6) ? "" : (string)reader["Suffix"]),
                     CompanyName = (string)reader["CompanyName"],
                     SalesPerson = (string)reader["SalesPerson"],
                     EmailAddress = (string)reader["EmailAddress"],
                     Phone = (string)reader["Phone"],
```

```
                    PasswordHash = (string)reader["PasswordHash"],
                    PasswordSalt = (string)reader["PasswordSalt"],
                    rowguid = (Guid)reader["rowguid"],
                    ModifiedDate = (DateTime)reader["ModifiedDate"]
                  };
      }

      resultList.Add(sw.ElapsedMilliseconds);
      reader.Close();
      sw.Stop();
    }
    sqlCon.Close();
  }
  Console.WriteLine("DataReader query 1:{0}", resultList[0]);
  Console.WriteLine("DataReader query 2:{0}", resultList[1]);
  Console.WriteLine("DataReader query 3:{0}", resultList[2]);
  resultList.RemoveAt(0);
  Console.WriteLine("count: {0}", resultList.Count());
  Console.WriteLine("Total last 100 queries: {0}", resultList.Sum());
  Console.WriteLine("Avg last 100 queries: {0}", resultList.Average());
  Console.WriteLine();
}

private static void EF_L2S_Tests(QueryType qType)
{
  var sw = new System.Diagnostics.Stopwatch();
  var resultList = new List<decimal>();

  //do two loops for each query
  for (int i = 0; i < 2; i++)
  {
    resultList = new List<decimal>();
    switch (qType)
    {
      case QueryType.L2E:
       ExecuteQueryLoop(new AWEntities(), null, resultList, QueryType.L2E,101);
       break;
      case QueryType.EntityObject:
           ExecuteQueryLoop(new AWEntities(),
                            null,resultList,QueryType.EntityObject,101);
       break;
      case QueryType.L2S:
       ExecuteQueryLoop(null, new AWL2SDataContext(),
                        resultList, QueryType.L2S,101);
       break;
    }

    testresults = sw.ElapsedMilliseconds;
  }
  Console.WriteLine("{0} query 1:{1}", qType.ToString(), resultList[0]);
  Console.WriteLine("{0} query 2:{1}", qType.ToString(), resultList[1]);
  Console.WriteLine("{0} query 3:{1}", qType.ToString(), resultList[2]);
  resultList.RemoveAt(0);
  Console.WriteLine("Total last 100 queries: {0}", resultList.Sum());
  Console.WriteLine("Avg last 100 queries: {0}", resultList.Average());
```

```
    Console.WriteLine();
}

private static void ExecuteQueryLoop
  (AWEntities oContext, AWL2SDataContext dContext,
   List<decimal> resultList, QueryType qType, int LoopCount)
{
  for (int j = 0; j < LoopCount; j++)
  {
    var sw = new System.Diagnostics.Stopwatch();
    sw.Start();
    switch (qType)
    {
      case QueryType.L2E:

        oContext.Customers.MergeOption = MergeOption.OverwriteChanges;
        var customers = (from c in oContext.Customers select c).ToList();
        break;
      case QueryType.EntityObject:
        oContext.Customers.MergeOption = MergeOption.OverwriteChanges;
        var oqCusts = oContext.CreateQuery<Customer>("Customers").ToList();
        break;
      case QueryType.L2S:
        var l2SCusts = (from c in dContext.L2SCustomers select c).ToList();
        break;
    }
    sw.Stop();
    resultList.Add(sw2.ElapsedMilliseconds);
  }
}
```

Measuring Startup Performance

Table 20-2 shows a comparison of LINQ to Entities and `ObjectQuery` queries. Each is run in its own application; therefore, each will instantiate an `ObjectContext` and load the metadata on the first query. In the previous tests, we avoided this expense by pre-instantiating the `ObjectContext` and timing queries that used metadata already loaded into memory.

Table 20-2. A new set of tests comparing only the EDM queries

Access type	First EDM query in application
LINQ to Entities	2,426 ms
Entity SQL with `ObjectQuery`	3,114 ms

Why did these queries take so long?

In both queries, a lot of up-front expense occurs in query compilation—getting from the original query to the native query.

The first is something that happens only once during the lifetime of an application—loading the EDM metadata into application process memory. Subsequent queries throughout the application do not have to load the metadata again. Because each of these tests is the first query in a newly running application instance, each of them incurs the cost of loading the metadata.

Additionally, with LINQ to Entities and `ObjectQuery`, other operations occur, such as the creation of `ObjectStateEntries` for entities and their relationship information. As objects are being materialized, the context must again read the metadata to map the streamed data to the appropriate entities and properties. Even without the expense of creating a context or loading the metadata, the query processing, state management, and object materialization are investments that you benefit from as you interact with the resultant data.

Reducing the Cost of Query Compilation

In an early 2008 blog post titled "Exploring the Performance of the ADO.NET Entity Framework—Part 1" (*http://blogs.msdn.com/adonet/archive/2008/02/04/exploring-the-performance-of-the-ado-net-entity-framework-part-1.aspx*), Brian Dawson of the Entity Framework team breaks down query time by task. In his tests, 56% of the total time for processing a query is devoted to "view generation." *View generation* refers to the process of creating the native command from an Entity SQL `ObjectQuery` or a call to `SaveChanges`. Fifty-six percent!

Here's a quick refresher on what's going on during this process. The Entity SQL is broken down into a command tree comprising Entity SQL operators and functions with entity names, properties, and relationships. This command tree is sent to the data provider, which translates the Entity SQL operators and functions to native operators and functions and uses the EDM to translate the entities and properties to tables and columns. Because the original query might be too complex for the native query, a series of simplifications is also performed on the tree. Finally, this newly created command tree is sent to the database.

This is a lot of work. But it doesn't necessarily need to happen on the fly at runtime. Given the queries and the EDM, the native queries can be precompiled. You can take advantage of query precompilation in two ways: precompiled views and precompiled LINQ to Entities queries.

Caching for Entity SQL Queries

By default, compiled Entity SQL queries are stored in an application domain cache for `EntityClient` queries and `ObjectQuery` queries as well as `ObjectSets`. As part of the query pipeline, the cache will be checked for a matching Entity SQL query (parameters are taken into account), and if a precompiled version of that query is available, it will be used.

ObjectQuery.EnablePlanCaching is the property for enabling or disabling query plan caching for ObjectQuery queries. You can set the Boolean EntityCommand.EnablePlan Caching to true or false to enable or disable caching for EntityClient.

Given the previous advice about avoiding SQL injection attacks with dynamic Entity SQL, Microsoft recommends that you disable query plan caching if you are building Entity SQL expressions dynamically. However, as discussed in the security section earlier, the best defense is to simply avoid building dynamic queries.

The stored queries are case-sensitive, so if you have a query in which you type "select value c ..." in one method and "SELECT VALUE c ..." in another, they won't be considered matching queries, and not only will you lose the benefit of the cached query, but the size of the cache will increase as a result of extra queries being stored.

Using tests similar to the previous performance tests, you can see the difference in query processing time when caching is enabled or disabled, as shown in the following code and in Table 20-3:

```
SELECT VALUE c from AWLTEntities.EFCustomers  AS c
```

Table 20-3. Comparing average query times for materialized entities versus streamed data

Query plan caching state	Enabled	Disabled
Entity SQL with Object Services	1.1 ms	3.23 ms
Entity SQL with EntityClient	4.1 ms	6.38 ms

Again, in this case the time for the cached query is significantly less than the noncached query.

This caching is why the second ObjectQuery in Table 20-1 was so fast. The query was only compiled on the first execution, and on the subsequent 100 queries, the store query was pulled directly from the cache and no compilation was necessary.

Comparing EntityClient to Object Services

Although the difference between querying with and without the cache may not be surprising, the difference between querying with Object Services and EntityClient might be.

When running the test with a query that returns data of a more complex shape, the difference shifts, as you can see in the following code and in Table 20-4:

```
SELECT c.CompanyName,c.SalesOrderHeader,
    (SELECT VALUE order.SalesOrderDetail
     FROM c.SalesOrderHeader AS order)
FROM AWEntities.Customers  AS c
```

Table 20-4. Average query times for shaped results

Query plan caching state	Enabled	Disabled
Entity SQL with Object Services	21.28 ms	42.51 ms
Entity SQL with `EntityClient`	17.05 ms	32.15 ms

Now the `EntityClient` and Object Services queries are more on par—with the `EntityClient` being about 15% faster. Because `EntityClient` does not materialize the objects, you would expect it to have some advantages. But why is the query itself impacting the difference between the two methods of querying?

Although object materialization takes some time, so does the task of shaping the `EntityDataReader` and then pushing in the results. In the case of the simple query, object materialization is very efficient in creating a `Customer` entity from data that maps exactly to the entity.

With the more complexly shaped data returned by the second query, once the `EntityDataReader` is created the cost of pushing the data into that `DataReader` is a lot less than the cost of materializing a lot of complexly shaped objects.

Precompiling Views for Performance

The EDM Generator, a command-line tool (*EDMGen.exe*), allows you to perform many of the same tasks that the EDM Wizard performs, as well as some others.

The EDM Generator has five `mode` command-line switches to determine which type of generation to perform:

`/mode:FromSSDLGeneration`
: Generates CSDL and MSL EDM files from an existing SSDL file

`/mode:EntityClassGeneration`
: Generates classes from a CSDL file

`/mode:ValidateArtifacts`
: Validates an EDM

`/mode:ViewGeneration`
: Precompiles queries from a specified project into a source code file

`/mode:FullGeneration`
: Creates CSDL, MSL, and SSDL files from a database, and generates the object classes and precompiled queries for each entity and relationship

Additionally, there are numerous other switches to specify metadata filenames, target projects, whether to use pluralization or foreign keys when generating a model, and more.

Try out `FullGeneration` on a database so that you can see what the output looks like. It's quick and painless. All you need to pass in is a connection string and the project parameter to give it a name that will be used for all of the created files:

```
C:\Program Files\Microsoft Visual Studio 9.0\VC>
  edmgen /mode:FullGeneration
   /c:"Data Source=127.0.0.1;
       Initial Catalog=AdventureWorksLT;
       Integrated Security=True"
   /p:AWEDMGenTest
```

You can add other parameters, such as a `Language` parameter, to create Visual Basic files.

Here are the files that result:

- *AWEDMGenTest.csdl*
- *AWEDMGenTest.ssdl*
- *AWEDMGenTest.msl*
- *AWEDMGenTest.ObjectLayer.cs*
- *AWEDMGenTest.Views.cs*

Pregenerating views for performance

Using the ViewGeneration mode to pregenerate model views impacts the performance of the very first query run during the application process. Once the first query is executed, all of the pregenerated views are loaded into memory and are used by the query plan caching mechanism described earlier.

The runtime view generation in .NET 4 has seen many improvements over its predecessor. Therefore, the pregenerated views will only give you a real advantage in cases where your model is very large and has a lot of mappings (e.g., inheritance, table splitting, relationships) to deal with.

Pregenerating views in the full generation will create views for each `EntitySet` and association. For example, the `Views` class for the `FullGeneration` example in the previous note will create a view for `dbo.Customers` that will be used anytime a query is made that involves customers. `FK_SalesOrderHeader_Customer_CustomerID` association also has a view that will be used anytime that association is required. It contains the necessary joins between the `Customer` table and the `SalesOrderHeader` table.

Example 20-12 shows a slice of a generated view file. The method constructs the store command for the `Customer` `EntitySet` so that the runtime `ObjectContext` doesn't have to go through this part of the process.

Example 20-12. Some of the pregenerated view code

```
viewString.Append(@"
  SELECT VALUE -- Constructing Customer
   [AWModel.Store.Customer](T1.Customer_CustomerID, T1.Customer_NameStyle,
    T1.Customer_Title, T1.Customer_FirstName, T1.Customer_MiddleName,
    T1.Customer_LastName, T1.Customer_Suffix, T1.Customer_CompanyName,
    T1.Customer_SalesPerson, T1.Customer_EmailAddress, T1.Customer_Phone,
    T1.Customer_PasswordHash, T1.Customer_PasswordSalt, T1.Customer_rowguid,
    T1.Customer_ModifiedDate)
    FROM (
        SELECT
            T.CustomerID AS Customer_CustomerID,
            T.NameStyle AS Customer_NameStyle,
            T.Title AS Customer_Title,
            T.FirstName AS Customer_FirstName,
            T.MiddleName AS Customer_MiddleName,
            T.LastName AS Customer_LastName,
            T.Suffix AS Customer_Suffix,
            T.CompanyName AS Customer_CompanyName,
            T.SalesPerson AS Customer_SalesPerson,
            T.EmailAddress AS Customer_EmailAddress,
            T.Phone AS Customer_Phone,
            T.PasswordHash AS Customer_PasswordHash,
            T.PasswordSalt AS Customer_PasswordSalt,
            T.rowguid AS Customer_rowguid,
            T.ModifiedDate AS Customer_ModifiedDate,
            True AS _from0
        FROM AWEntities.AWCustomers  AS T
  ) AS T1");
```

QueryViews will not be included in the generated views, and the *edmgen* command-line tool will list a warning to let you know if it encountered any QueryViews. The generation will succeed, but will simply skip generating views for any QueryViews.

Pregenerating views into an existing project

You can also target a project when pregenerating views. However, be aware that *edmgen* will not pregenerate any queries that are in the project. Only the model's EntitySets get compiled. The purpose of targeting a project when pregenerating views is so that the project's namespace gets used in the generated code.

To generate the views into an existing project, you'll need to select one of your projects that uses the BreakAway model.

The ViewGeneration option requires *.ssdl*, *.msl*, and *.csdl* files that you don't currently have because you have been embedding them into the compiled assemblies. So, you'll need to go back to the BreakAwayModel project and generate these files:

1. Open the BreakAwayModel project if it's not already open.
2. Open the EDMX file in the Designer.

3. Click the background of the model to open the model's Properties window.
4. Change the Metadata Artifact Processing property to Copy to Output Directory.
5. Save the project. This will create the files.
6. Open the project's output directory in Windows Explorer.

   You can do this directly from the Solution Explorer by right-clicking the project and choosing Open Folder in Windows Explorer, then navigating to the output folder.
7. Copy the CSDL, SSDL, and MSL files from the *bin* folder to another location (e.g., *c:\EDMs*).

   When you change the Metadata Artifact Processing property back to Embed in Output Assembly, the files will be removed from the output directory.

Now you can generate the view file. Note in Example 20-13 that the quotes around the project are there only because of a space in the file path.

Example 20-13. Using the EDM Generator command-line tool

```
C:\Program Files\Microsoft Visual Studio 9.0\VC>
edmgen /mode:ViewGeneration
 /inssdl:c:\efmodels\BAModel.ssdl
 /incsdl:c:\efModels\BAModel.csdl
 /inmsl:c:\efmodels\BAModel.msl
 /p: "F:\PEFBookSamples\Chapter20\Chapter20Samples.csproj"
```

The output code will be C# by default. You can specify VB with the additional switch, `/language:VB`.

You'll find the newly generated file in the folder designated in the `p` (path) parameter. Be sure to include the file in the project in the Solution Explorer. Again, it contains all the views that are represented in the model files. Now when you run this project, the runtime will be able to skip the bulk of the query compilation tasks.

At TechEd North America 2010, Diego Vega and Tim Laverty said in their session (*http://www.msteched.com/2010/NorthAmerica/DEV305*) that the EF team was working on a T4 template for view pre-generation for a future version of EF.

Precompiling LINQ to Entities Queries for Performance

Although the view generation feature lets you create the native SQL for all of the model's `EntitySets` and associations, there's also a way to precompile the actual queries that you create in your application and it has a much bigger impact on performance at runtime. For LINQ to Entities queries, you can explicitly precompile your queries in code using the `CompiledQuery.Compile` method.

CompiledQuery.Compile allows you to compile a particular query, even one that takes parameters, at runtime. Then, anytime you need to use that query, you can point to the compiled version.

Query compilation is also available in LINQ to SQL, though the syntax is a bit different.

Compiled queries can make a valuable performance improvement for queries that are used repeatedly in an application. You will still pay the compilation cost the first time the query is used, but subsequent uses of the query will avoid that part of the process.

The Entity Framework has a System.Data.Objects.CompiledQuery class, which lets you precompile a query into a CompiledQuery object and then reuse that object. CompiledQuery.Compile takes two parameters and a query in the form of a delegate:

```
Compile(args, ReturnType) (Delegate Query)
```

The first parameter is args and it is used to pass in any arguments. You'll want to pass in an instance of an ObjectContext and then any other variables that are used in the query. For example, your query may perform filtering on an integer, so you'll need to have an integer variable as one of the arguments.

The second parameter is ReturnType—for example, an entity or an IEnumerable of a particular type. The last, Delegate, will be a lambda expression whose function is a LINQ to Entities query.

Example 20-14 is an example of a query that might be used a number of times during an application's lifetime; it finds customers who have gone to a particular adventure location.

Example 20-14. A frequently used query that is a good candidate for precompilation

```
from Customer c in context.Contacts.OfType<Customer>()
where c.Reservations.FirstOrDefault().Trip.Destination.Name==dest
select c
```

To turn this into a compiled query, you will need a variable to represent the object context, such as ctx. You will also need a variable for the location name. Construct a lambda expression that processes these two variables in a LINQ to Entities query, as shown in Example 20-15. VB examples are included where the syntax differences may be confusing.

Example 20-15. A lambda expression of the query to be precompiled

VB
```
Function(ctx As BAEntities, dest As String) _
  From cust In ctx.Contacts.OfType(Of Customer)() _
  Where cust.Reservations.FirstOrDefault.Trip.Destination.Name = dest
```

C#
```
(BAEntities ctx,string dest) =>
  from cust in ctx.Contacts.OfType<Customer>()
  where cust.Reservations.FirstOrDefault().Trip.Destination.Name== dest
  select cust
```

This lambda expression is used as a parameter of `CompiledQuery.Compile`.

Example 20-16 shows the `CompiledQuery`, which will take a `BAEntities` object and a string when it's called, and will return an `IQueryable<Customer>`. Those are passed into the `Compile` generic method. Then the lambda expression follows, inside parentheses. The query passes these parameters into the lambda expression.

Example 20-16. The compiled LINQ to Entities query

VB
```
Dim compQuery = CompiledQuery.Compile(Of BAEntities, String,
                                      IQueryable(Of Customer))
(Function(ctx As BAEntities, dest As String) _
  From cust In ctx.Contacts.OfType(Of Customer)() _
  Where cust.Reservations.FirstOrDefault.Trip.Destination.Name = dest
)
```

C#
```
var compQuery = CompiledQuery.Compile<BAEntities, string, IQueryable<Customer>>
  ((BAEntities ctx, string dest) =>
   from Customer c in ctx.Contacts.OfType<Customer>()
   where c.Reservations.FirstOrDefault().Trip.Destination.Name == dest
   select c);
```

If you are creating the `func` as a class-level variable, it is important to make the variable `static` (`Shared` in VB) so that it will remain in memory. If you use the compiled query in a web application or service where the variable will get reinstantiated frequently, the query would get recompiled each time, causing you to lose the benefit of the precompilation. By marking the variable `static`, you can avoid unnecessary recompilation. For more information and an example of how to use the precompiled query in this scenario, see my March 2009 blog post titled "Using Pre-Compiled LINQ to Entities Queries in Web Apps and Services" (*http://thedatafarm.com/blog/data-access/using-pre-compiled-linq-to-entities-queries-in-web-apps-and-services*).

Once the `CompiledQuery` has been created, you can use it anytime you want to use the query by implementing its `Invoke` method, as demonstrated in Example 20-17. Because you have a parameter for this query, you can change the value of the parameter anytime you use the query, which makes the compiled query pretty flexible.

Example 20-17. Using the compiled LINQ to Entities query

```
var context = new BAEntities();
var loc = "Malta";
IQueryable<Customer> custs = compQuery.Invoke(context, loc);
var custlist = custs.ToList();
```

Now you can use the code in Example 20-18 to test the performance of the compiled query. The first query loads the metadata files into the application memory so that the time for that task is not counted in the first run of the compiled query. You'll learn more about metadata files in Chapter 21. Subsequent queries (the example lists only some of them) will not require query compilation and will be faster.

Example 20-18. A performance test of the compiled query

```
using (var context = new BAEntities ())
{
  var cust = context.Contacts.FirstOrDefault();
}
using (var context = new BAEntities ())
{
  string destination = "Malta";
  var custQuery = compQuery.Invoke(context, destination);
  var custlist = custQuery.ToList();
}
using (BreakAwayEntities context = new BAEntities ())
{
  string destination = "Bulgaria";
  var custQuery = compQuery.Invoke(context, destination);
  var custlist = custQuery.ToList();
}
```

Notice that for each timed test, a completely new context is created that also creates a new connection. The times shown in Table 20-5 are compared to performing the same test without using compiled queries. The times were collected by inserting a `StopWatch` object into code in Example 20-18 and capturing the elapsed time.

Table 20-5. Performance comparisons between compiled and noncompiled LINQ to Entities queries

	Query 1	Query 2	Query 3
Using a compiled query	68 ms	6 ms	5 ms
Using a standard query	71 ms	17 ms	32 ms

You can see that once the query has been compiled, query processing takes only a portion of the time it takes when repeating that particular task without the advantage of precompilation.

Not every query will benefit from being turned into a precompiled query. If you care about application performance, you should use a profiler to discover where it makes sense to apply performance tuning in your applications. Visual Studio 2010 Ultimate and Premium versions have built-in performance tools, and there are great third-party tools as well, such as Red Gate's ANTS Performance Profiler.

Fine-Tuning Updates for Performance?

Performance concerns with data access generally focus on querying because that is typically the bulk of the data interaction that an application performs. However, it's worth taking a quick look at update performance.

Again, the Entity Framework will need to generate commands and transform the entity structure into the database structure; thus, compared to working with ADO.NET, where you would be working directly against the database, there will be a performance hit.

In talking with one of the folks who focuses on performance for the Data Programmability team, I learned that the performance for updating data in the Entity Framework is very impressive when compared to other technologies. Although that was proof enough for me, I still had to see the performance benefits for myself!

For the following tests, I modified the previous tests to include updates and inserts, and because this is much more intensive and time-consuming than just querying data, there are only 10 iterations of the tests, not 100. Each test queries for the entire set of customers (approximately 450), iterates through those customers, and modifies a single field in each one. Once those modifications are made, 10 new customers are added. Finally, the appropriate update method is called (`DataAdapter.Update`, `DataContext.SubmitChanges`, or `ObjectContext.SaveChanges`).

To be fair, there are two tests for `DataSet`. The first uses the default `Update`, which sends one command at a time to the database. The second leverages `UpdateBatch` and sets the batch to 100 commands at a time. The final times represent the average of performing this entire operation 10 times.

Remember that these tests are meant only to be relative to one another. I conducted them on my computer, which might not be as tricked out as the average server. The tests are not meant to indicate the actual potential of any of the tested technologies' performance overall.

The results are interesting. The Entity Framework is faster than `DataAdapter` and LINQ to SQL, as you can see in Table 20-6.

Table 20-6. Comparing DataAdapter UpdateBatch to Entity Framework and LINQ to SQL

Method	Average time
`DataAdapter` with `UpdateBatch=1`	289 ms
`DataAdapter` with `UpdateBatch=100`	233 ms
Entity Framework Object Services	97 ms
LINQ to SQL	987 ms

You can perform updates with "classic ADO.NET" in a variety of ways, and you may achieve different results relative to the two newer technologies. But this at least gives you an idea that something very smart is happening under the covers of the Entity Framework when `SaveChanges` is called.

If you plan to do tests like these, don't forget to turn off Visual Studio 2010's IntelliTrace feature!

Lacking Support for Full Text Searches

Developers often ask about taking advantage of SQL Server 2008 and other databases' full text searching capabilities. Entity Framework does not support full text searches. The recommendation from Microsoft is to use stored procedures.

From the Horse's Mouth: Performance Tuning Guidance for Entity Framework

Danny Simmons, who is an architect on the Entity Framework team, gave this great advice on a Channel 9 MSDN podcast he and I participated in together as we were interviewed by Microsoft Sweden's Dag Konig (*http://channel9.msdn.com/posts/buzzfrog/MSDN-Radio-31-Maj--Entity-Framework*):

> I give the same recommendation about performance optimization with Entity Framework that I give with any code. Which is: write your code the simplest, easiest to maintain, most efficient possible way. And then profile it; find where the problems are and start applying optimizations.
>
> And when you do that, you typically will find that there are a set of things you can do to improve performance still using the Entity Framework, and eventually some very small set of cases you may find that the performance is very critical and even after you apply your tricks with entity framework, you need to do something faster than that. And then you can go to some of the extensibility mechanisms, like writing a stored procedure with hand written sql or those kinds of things to really optimize those few cases. And that mix allows you to have very rapid development,

easy to maintain code using the entity framework and then in a very few places have very highly tuned code.

Exploiting Multithreaded Applications

Like much of .NET, the Entity Framework is not thread-safe. Developers often treat this as though it was a major detriment, but as it is pretty common for .NET, this doesn't highlight some horrible deficiency for Entity Framework. This means that to use the Entity Framework in multithreaded environments, you need to either explicitly keep individual `ObjectContexts` in separate threads, or be very conscientious about locking threads so that you don't get collisions.

Straight from the source (MSDN docs): "ObjectContext only supports Single-Threaded scenarios."

You should also be aware of the new parallel support in .NET 4, which will reduce the number of scenarios where you will need to manually interact with threads. The next section will address .NET 4's parallel support as it is relevant to the Entity Framework.

Here are some examples of a few ways to use `ObjectContext` in separate threads.

Forcing an ObjectContext to Use Its Own Thread

Example 20-19 uses a separate class for managing the `ObjectContext` and performing the database interaction. The main program then creates a separate thread when it needs the `ObjectContext` to do something. Delegates and callbacks are used so that it's possible for entities to be returned from the separate thread.

Notice that every time the `ObjectContext` is about to be impacted, a lock is placed on it.

If you are unfamiliar with threading and delegates, you are not alone. It's an advanced topic, and lots of resources are available to help you get up and running on threading if you need to use it explicitly. The one area where it is useful to understand, even if you have no plans to perform advanced threading work, is in keeping your UI responsive while performing tasks such as making a call to the database, which might take some time. Look for topics on the `BackgroundWorker` component, which you can use in both Windows Forms and Windows Presentation Foundation (WPF), and the Asynchronous Page features in ASP.NET.

Example 20-19. Forcing an ObjectContext to use its own thread

```
using System;
using System.Collections.Generic;
using System.Linq;
using System.Threading;
using BAGA;

namespace Chapter20Console
{
  public class MyThreading
  {
    // Delegate that defines the signature for the callback method.
    public delegate void ContextCallback(List<Contact> contactList);
    private static List<Contact> _contacts;

    public static void Main()
    {
      var occ =
         new ObjectContextClass(new ContextCallback(ResultCallback));
      var t = new Thread(occ.GetCustomers);
      t.Start();
      t.Join();
      Console.WriteLine("Retrieved: " + _contacts.Count.ToString());
      Console.WriteLine(_contacts[0].LastName + _contacts[0].ModifiedDate);
      _contacts[0].ModifiedDate = DateTime.Now;
      Console.WriteLine(_contacts[0].LastName + _contacts[0].ModifiedDate);
      t = new Thread(occ.SaveChanges);
      t.Start();
    }

    public static void ResultCallback(List<Contact> contactList)
    {
      _contacts = contactList;
    }
  }

  public class ObjectContextClass
  {
    private BAEntities _context;
    private List<Contact> _conList;
    // Delegate used to execute the callback method when the task is done.
    private readonly MyThreading.ContextCallback _callback;
    // The callback delegate is passed in to the constructor
    public ObjectContextClass(MyThreading.ContextCallback callbackDelegate)
    {
      _callback = callbackDelegate;
    }

    public void GetCustomers()
    {
      if (_context == null)
      {
        _context = new BAEntities();
      }
      //put a lock on the context during this operation;
```

```
        lock (_context)
        {
          var contactquery = from c in _context.Contacts
                             where c.LastName.StartsWith("S")
                             select c;
          _conList = contactquery.ToList();
        }
        if (_callback != null)
          _callback(_conList);
      }

      public void SaveChanges()
      {
        lock (_context)
        {
          _context.SaveChanges();
        }
      }
    }
  }
```

It's important to call out the locking of the context. Because of the way the `ObjectContext` manages state and relationships, and because of the merge possibilities when new data is brought in, you need to be very careful so that two separate threads do not affect the context at the same time. You should consider this use as an edge case, and you should be sure that you really understand threading before you start spinning your own threads and working with classes that are not thread-safe.

It's much safer (though less practical in many cases) to keep individual `ObjectContext`s on completely separate threads so that you don't have to worry about this as much.

The `BackgroundWorker` component, introduced in .NET 2.0, does alleviate some of the complexities of working with multiple threads, but still, the Entity Framework does not have any inherent features that make it easy to use in multithreaded applications. Hopefully, future versions of the Entity Framework will make threading and asynchronous programming simpler to work with.

Implementing Concurrent Thread Processing

Example 20-19 used a separate thread to host the `ObjectContext`. Example 20-20 shows another way to use worker threads to perform some concurrent processing on entities. Because this example only performs reads on the entities, the concerns of Example 20-19 are not present. This example sends entities off to a variety of methods that will merely read information from the entities and possibly send a form letter or email. In this case, the code is writing some text out to the console only to demonstrate the concept.

The query pulls back customers along with their reservation and trip information. Then, based on the reservation status, the `Customer` entity is sent to a different method to create the email. Because the process is being performed in different threads, the emails can be written concurrently and there is no need in this case to wait for any type of result.

When the text is written out to the console, the example also displays the ID of the thread so that you can verify that different threads are being used.

Example 20-20. Managing threads to get concurrent processing

```
using System;
using System.Linq;
using BAGA;
using System.Threading;

namespace Chapter20Console
{
  class EmailThreads
  {
    public static void Main()
    {
      var emailThread = new EmailThreadClass();
      using (var context = new BAEntities())
      {
        var custs =
            from cust in context.Contacts.OfType<Customer>()
             .Include("Reservations.Trip.Destination")
            select cust;
        foreach (var cust in custs)
        {
          if (cust.Reservations
              .Any(r => r.Trip.StartDate > DateTime.Today.AddDays(6)))
          {
            //new thread for upcoming trip emails
            var workerThread =
               new Thread(emailThread.UpcomingTripEmails);
            workerThread.Start(cust);
          }
          else if (cust.Reservations
            .Any(r => r.Trip.StartDate > DateTime.Today
                 & r.Trip.StartDate <= DateTime.Today.AddDays(6)))
          {
            //new thread for very soon trip emails
            var workerThread = new Thread(emailThread.NextWeek);
            workerThread.Start(cust);
          }
          else //no future trips
          {
            //new thread for no upcmoing trips emails
            var workerThread =
               new Thread(emailThread.ComeBackEmails);
            workerThread.Start(cust);
          }
```

```
            }
            Console.ReadKey();
          }
        }
      }

      public class EmailThreadClass
      {
        public void UpcomingTripEmails(object customer)
        {
          var cust = (Customer)customer;
          var anytrip = cust.Reservations
           .Where(r => r.Trip.StartDate > DateTime.Today.AddDays(6))
           .First().Trip;

          Console.WriteLine("Thread " + Thread.CurrentThread.ManagedThreadId);
          Console.WriteLine("            Dear " + cust.FirstName.Trim() +
             ", Your trip to " + anytrip.Destination.Name.Trim() +
            " begins on " + anytrip.StartDate +
             ". We look forward to seeing you soon.");
          Console.WriteLine();
        }

        public void NextWeek(object customer)
        {
          var cust = (Customer)customer;
          var anytrip = cust.Reservations
           .Where(r => r.Trip.StartDate <= DateTime.Today.AddDays(6))
          .First().Trip;

          Console.WriteLine("Thread " + Thread.CurrentThread.ManagedThreadId);
          Console.WriteLine("            Dear " + cust.FirstName.Trim() +
            ",  Your trip to " + anytrip.Destination.Name.Trim() +
            " begins in only a few days. Please let us know if " +
            " you have any last minute questions.");
          Console.WriteLine();
        }

        public void ComeBackEmails(object customer)
        {
          var cust = (Customer)customer;

          Console.WriteLine("Thread " + Thread.CurrentThread.ManagedThreadId);
          Console.WriteLine("            Dear " + cust.FirstName.Trim() +
            ", We haven't seen you in a while. We hope you'll consider" +
            "  BreakAway Geek Adventures for your next vacation.");
          Console.WriteLine();
        }
      }
    }
```

Exploiting .NET 4 Parallel Computing

.NET 4 brought a major advancement for parallel computing with API-level support for parallel operations so that your applications can intelligently take advantage of multicore processors on your machine. The threading examples in this chapter will use threads only on the main core. If you want to leverage multiple cores, you should take a look at features in the `Task` class in the new `System.Threading.Tasks` namespace (*http://msdn.microsoft.com/en-us/library/system.threading.tasks(VS.100).aspx*).

An additional feature of the parallel support is called Parallel LINQ (PLINQ), which enables LINQ to split query processing across the cores by using a class called `ParallelEnumerable`. It is important to be aware that a query to a database cannot be broken up, and therefore LINQ to Entities and LINQ to SQL do not support PLINQ. Fortunately, if you do specifically use PLINQ with a LINQ to Entities or LINQ to SQL query, even if you explicitly tell it to use more than one core, PLINQ will recognize that this can't be done and will simply force the query to run on a single core. No exception will be thrown and your query will just run on the single core without notifying you that you are not getting the advantage of the multicore support.

Summary

This chapter looked at several important concerns of developers who are building real-world applications—connections, transactions, security, performance, and threading. You learned how these features are used by Entity Framework. You also learned many ways you can change the default behaviors to your benefit—for example, ways to control when database connections are opened and closed and numerous ways to fine-tune performance. You should now have a good understanding of not only how things work under the covers, but also how you can take advantage of the Entity Framework's flexibility to maintain control over your application.

There are many more angles you can look at with respect to performance and improving it, whether it is specific to Entity Framework or even to the database you are connecting. For example, Bob Beauchemin's August 2009 *MSDN Magazine* article, "How Data Access Code Affects Database Performance" (*http://msdn.microsoft.com/en-us/magazine/ee236412.aspx*), provides some additional insights.

The topics covered in this chapter will enable you to write enterprise-level applications while benefiting from using an EDM.

CHAPTER 21
Manipulating Entities with ObjectStateManager and MetadataWorkspace

It's time to delve deeper into the Entity Framework and work directly with its core components: the `ObjectStateManager` and `MetadataWorkspace` APIs.

These are truly the two workhorses of the Entity Framework. Under the covers, Object Services uses the classes in these two APIs extensively to interact with objects at a granular level. Most of the classes and methods are public, so you can use `ObjectStateManager` and `MetadataWorkspace` in your own applications to control and manipulate entity objects.

Separately or together, these two classes not only allow you to manipulate entities, but also enable you to write generic methods that you can use on various Entity Framework object types, as well as dynamically create objects at runtime without depending on the generated entity classes.

Along with learning the concepts of `ObjectStateManager` and `MetadataWorkspace`, you will find many code samples in this chapter that you can use in your applications. For example, you will find a set of extension methods to overload the `GetObjectStateEntries` method and a utility for inspecting in-memory entities at runtime.

You will learn how to interact with entities and entity state through the `ObjectStateManager` and build the State Entry Visualizer that you saw in Chapter 10. Then you will learn about interacting with the raw metadata using the `MetadataWorkspace`.

Later in the chapter, you will build more samples that will give you great hands-on experience working at this level. You will also get some ideas of what you can achieve with `ObjectStateManager` and `MetadataWorkspace`. In fact, most of the object interaction under the covers occurs using `ObjectStateEntries` and `MetadataWorkspace`. You have direct access to the same capabilities.

There are many benefits to writing generic code for entity objects. With generic code you can create reusable code that is able to work with any entity type—whether the code is a method for validating entities prior to a database save, a utility to return selection lists, or even, as you'll see in this chapter, logic to dynamically create and edit entities.

Manipulating Entities and Their State with ObjectStateManager

In Chapter 10, you got an introduction to `ObjectStateEntry` objects, which contain the value and state information for every object in the cache being managed by the context. The context begins managing entities in two distinct ways: as the result of a query or as the result of an explicit code instruction to add or attach an entity that is already in memory.

Anytime an entity begins being managed, the `ObjectStateManager` creates a state information object called an `ObjectStateEntry` for that object, as shown in Figure 21-1.

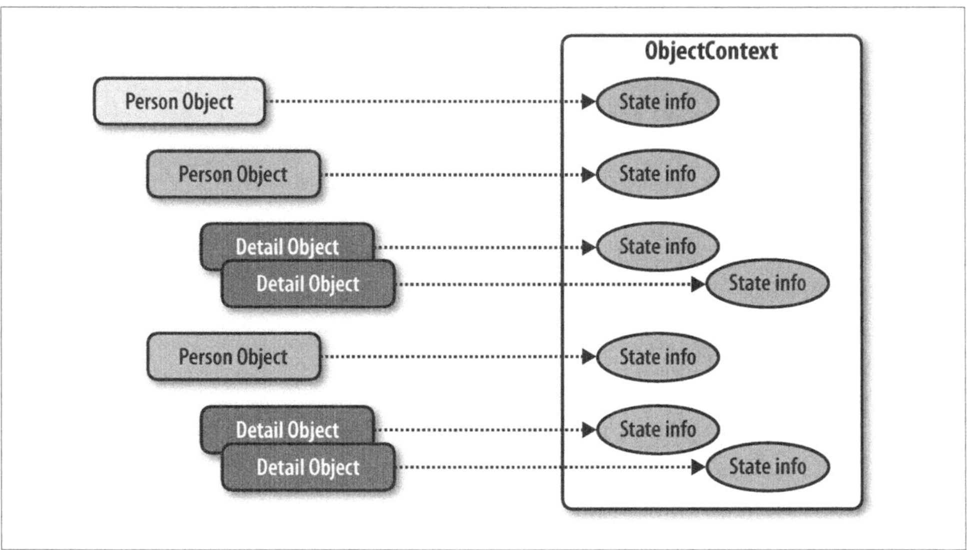

Figure 21-1. State information stored in ObjectStateEntries created by the ObjectContext for each entity it is managing

Anytime an entity leaves the context cache, its `ObjectStateEntry` is automatically destroyed as well as any `RelationshipEntry` objects that are bound to that entity.

Refreshing Your High-Level Understanding of ObjectStateEntry

Because `ObjectStateEntry` is critical to most of what you will be learning in this chapter, it might be helpful to have a quick refresher on this class.

The information that an entity's `ObjectStateEntry` exposes includes the following:

- An array of original values (the values when the entity was attached to the context)
- An array of current values
- An array of names of properties that have been modified
- A pointer back to the entity
- `EntityKey`
- `State`
- The `EntitySet` name
- `ObjectStateManager`

`ObjectStateEntry` also has an `IsRelationship` property to determine whether it's an `EntityEntry` or a `RelationshipEntry`.

Most of the `ObjectStateEntry` properties are null when the entry is a `RelationshipEntry`. However, these properties are still relevant and will be populated:

- `State`
- `EntitySet`
- `ObjectStateManager`

The pointer back to the `EntitySet` is important because the `EntitySet` itself provides all of the information regarding the two ends of the relationship.

You may recall that the debugger doesn't show all of the `ObjectStateEntry` information. You can access some of it only at runtime by calling properties that are not exposed in the debugger.

After you spend a bit of time learning how to get your hands on the `ObjectStateEntry` instances, you'll get a chance to dig more deeply into what is exposed through this type.

Getting an ObjectStateManager and Its Entries

Every `ObjectContext` has its own `ObjectStateManager`, which you can access using the `ObjectContext.ObjectStateManager` property.

The `ObjectStateManager` itself doesn't have properties. It only manages the `ObjectStateEntry` objects; therefore, it has methods to return those entries.

Getting groups of entries with GetObjectStateEntries

`ObjectStateManager.GetObjectStateEntries` returns an `IEnumerable` collection of entries. As you learned in the brief introduction to `GetObjectStateEntries` in Chapter 10, you must specify one or more `EntityState` enums to determine which types of entities to return. It won't just return all entries by default.

For example, to get all `Unchanged` entries that are currently in the context, you can use the code in Example 21-1.

Example 21-1. Retrieving Unchanged ObjectStateEntry entries

```
context.ObjectStateManager.GetObjectStateEntries(EntityState.Unchanged)
```

You can specify multiple states by separating the enums with the or (|) operator, as shown in Example 21-2.

Example 21-2. Specifying more than one EntityState for GetObjectStateEntries

```
context.ObjectStateManager.GetObjectStateEntries
  (EntityState.Added | EntityState.Unchanged)
```

Building Extension Methods to Overload GetObjectStateEntries

If you use `GetObjectStateEntries` frequently, you are sure to find the use of the `EntityState` parameters annoying. Sometimes you'll want all of the entries and you'll need to type in each `EntityState` over and over. Other times you'll want to find entries of a certain type.

.NET's *extension methods* allow you to add functionality to internal classes. You can take advantage of this in many places with the Entity Framework. If you want to learn more about extension methods, check the MSDN topics for C# (*http://msdn.microsoft.com/en-us/library/bb383977.aspx*) and for Visual Basic (*http://msdn.microsoft.com/en-us/library/bb384936.aspx*).

The following examples represent a set of three extension methods to make the use of `GetObjectStateEntries` more convenient. The extension method in Example 21-3 takes no parameters, and returns all of the entries regardless of `EntityState`.

In VB, extension methods are housed in modules and must have the `Extension` attribute. The first parameter defines the class that the method will extend. C# requires that the methods be static and be in a static class. The extended class parameter is preceded with `this`.

Example 21-3. GetObjectStateEntries overload to return all entries regardless of their EntityState

VB
```
<Extension()> _
Public Function GetObjectStateEntries _
     (ByVal osm As Objects.ObjectStateManager) _
      As IEnumerable(Of Objects.ObjectStateEntry)
  Return osm.GetObjectStateEntries(EntityState.Added Or EntityState.Deleted
                                   Or EntityState.Modified
                                   Or EntityState.Unchanged)
End Function
```

C#
```
public static IEnumerable<ObjectStateEntry>
 GetObjectStateEntries(this ObjectStateManager osm)
{
  return osm.GetObjectStateEntries(EntityState.Added | EntityState.Deleted
                                 | EntityState.Modified | EntityState.Unchanged);
}
```

This definitely beats having to specify four entity state enums in the frequent cases where you'll want to do that.

The extension method in Example 21-4 returns all objects of a particular type by taking advantage of generics. It uses the overload from Example 21-3 to return all `EntityState`s and then filters those results further.

Example 21-4. GetObjectStateEntries overload to return all entries of a particular entity type

VB
```
<Extension()> _
Public Function GetObjectStateEntries(Of TEntity) _
   (ByVal osm As Objects.ObjectStateManager) _
    As IEnumerable(Of Objects.ObjectStateEntry)

   Return osm.GetObjectStateEntries()
            .Where(Function (entry) entry.Entity Is TEntity)
End Function
```

C#
```
public static IEnumerable<ObjectStateEntry>
 GetObjectStateEntries<TEntity>(this ObjectStateManager osm)
{
   return osm.GetObjectStateEntries().Where(entry => entry.Entity is TEntity);
}
```

Now you can get all entities of a particular type without having to build a LINQ query. The following code demonstrates how to call the overload:

```
myObjectStateManager.GetObjectStateEntries<Customer>();
```

The extension method in Example 21-5 takes the `EntityState` parameters and filters on a particular type using generics again.

Example 21-5. GetObjectStateEntries overload to return all entries of a particular entity type and EntityState

VB
```
<Extension()> _
Public Function GetObjectStateEntries(Of TEntity) _
   (ByVal osm As Objects.ObjectStateManager, _
```

```
        ByVal state As EntityState) _
        As IEnumerable(Of Objects.ObjectStateEntry)

      Return osm.GetObjectStateEntries(state)
                .Where(Function(entry) entry.Entity Is TEntity)
    End Function
```

```
public static IEnumerable<ObjectStateEntry>  GetObjectStateEntries<TEntity>
 (this ObjectStateManager osm, EntityState state)
{
  return osm.GetObjectStateEntries(state).Where(entry => entry.Entity is TEntity);
}
```

The code in Example 21-6 calls each new `GetObjectStateEntries` overload.

Example 21-6. Calling all three GetObjectStateEntries overloads

```
//query for some contacts
var contacts = context.Contacts
                      .Where(c => c.Addresses.Any(a => a.CountryRegion == "UK"))
                      .ToList();
//Get all entries in the context
var allOses = context.ObjectStateManager.GetObjectStateEntries().ToList();
//Get all Customer entries
var custOses = context.ObjectStateManager
   .GetObjectStateEntries<Customer>().ToList();
//Get only Modified Customer entries
var modifiedCustomerOses = context.ObjectStateManager
  .GetObjectStateEntries<Customer>(EntityState.Modified)
  .ToList();
```

Building a Method to Return Managed Entities

Building these extensions led me to create a method that I now use frequently in my applications, a generic `ManagedEntries<T>` method. I commonly want to work with entities that are being managed by the context and I prefer using a higher-level method.

The `ObjectStateEntry.Entity` property points back to the entity that the entry represents. Therefore, I can return a collection of entities rather than the `ObjectStateEntry` types. This is convenient when you want to validate certain types during a call to `SaveChanges`.

Example 21-7 shows this method as an extension method of the `ObjectContext` class. This method uses the extension method created in Example 21-4.

Example 21-7. Returning entity objects that are managed by the context

```
public static IEnumerable<TEntity> ManagedEntities<TEntity>
  (this ObjectContext context)
{
  return context.ObjectStateManager.GetObjectStateEntries<TEntity>()
                                   .Select(entry => (TEntity) entry.Entity);
}
```

Now when I want to work with a particular set of entities, such as all of the `Customer` objects that are managed by the context, I can easily grab them by calling `context.ManagedEntities<Customer>().ToList()`.

Using GetObjectStateEntry and TryGetObjectStateEntry

You can also retrieve a single entry from the `ObjectStateManager` using either `GetObjectStateEntry` or its counterpart, `TryGetObjectStateEntry`. These methods will look in the context to return an entry. They each have two overloads that let you use either an entity or an `EntityKey` as a parameter. If you pass in the entire entity, the method will extract its `EntityKey` and use that to find the entry. Example 21-8 uses an entity to find its related `ObjectStateEntry`, whereas Example 21-9 uses an `EntityKey` (created on the fly) to find an `ObjectStateEntry`.

Example 21-8. Using an entity to find its related ObjectStateEntry

```
GetObjectStateEntry(myReservation)
```

Example 21-9. Using an EntityKey to find an ObjectStateEntry

```
GetObjectStateEntry(new EntityKey("BAEntities.Reservations","ReservationID",10)
```

If the entry cannot be found (meaning that the object doesn't exist in the context), an `InvalidOperationException` will be thrown.

`TryGetObjectStateEntry` is safer than `GetObjectStateEntry`. `TryGetObjectStateEntry` emulates the `TryParse` and `TryCast` methods in the .NET Framework. Rather than throwing an exception, it will return a Boolean if the entry is not found. You need to create a variable in advance for the entry and pass that into the method to be populated. Again, you can pass in either the entity or the `EntityKey`. You can then use the Boolean to determine whether the operation succeeded or failed, and have your code smoothly handle a failure, as shown in Example 21-10.

Example 21-10. Using TryGetObjectStateEntry to avoid an exception

```
if (context.ObjectStateManager.TryGetObjectStateEntry(myReservation,out ose))
 {// success logic
 }
else
 {// failure logic
 }
```

> **GetObjectStateEntry Versus GetObjectByKey**
>
> You may recall the `ObjectContext.GetObjectByKey` and `TryGetObjectByKey` methods from Chapter 4. If you were to dig into these methods in Reflector, you would discover that they actually use the `GetObjectStateEntry` method to find the object. However, there are two big differences between the `GetObjectByKey` methods and the `GetObjectStateEntry` methods. First, `GetObjectByKey` returns an entity object, whereas `GetObjectStateEntry` returns an `ObjectStateEntry`. More importantly, `GetObjectByKey` queries the database if it is unable to find the object in the context, whereas `GetObjectStateEntry` only looks in the context for existing entries. It will not make a trip to the database. Many times you only want to work with what is already in memory and you do not want to bring additional data back from the database.

Mining Entity Details from ObjectStateEntry

Digging around in the `ObjectStateManager`, reading entity information, and tracking down the related entities is a lot of work. Many developers won't have a reason to go to this trouble. But the fact that all of this information is exposed means you can create very dynamic features in your application, or even create dynamic applications, whereby you can pass any Entity Data Model (EDM) and create objects and graphs on the fly. Even if you are not building third-party tools, you can use the power of this functionality to encapsulate a lot of reusable and generic functionality within and across your applications.

.NET developers have been performing such tasks using reflection since .NET 1.0. Although you can also use reflection to work with entity types, using the `ObjectStateManager` results in much better performance. When you add in the `MetadataWorkspace` and reading the model, you can go even further with these capabilities.

Once you have an `ObjectStateEntry` for an entity in hand, you can view some of its details in the debugger watch window. However, the debug view doesn't show much more than what you can already get from the entity itself (see Figure 21-2).

The real information comes through the methods and properties that are not exposed in the debugger, although C#'s debugger does expose much more information than VB's debugger does.

Once you know what the methods and properties are, you can type them directly into the debugger to see their results.

Reading and writing values

The `CurrentValues` property returns a `CurrentValueRecord` (an enhanced version of a `DbDataRecord`), which is an `ObjectStateEntryDbUpdatableDataRecord`, and it contains three members:

[1]	{System.Data.Objects.EntityEntry}
[System.Data.Objects.EntityEntry]	{System.Data.Objects.EntityEntry}
_cache	{System.Data.Objects.ObjectStateManager}
_entitySet	{Reservations}
_state	Unchanged
Entity	{BAGA.Reservation}
EntityKey	"EntitySet=Reservations;ReservationID=2"
EntitySet	{Reservations}
IsKeyEntry	false
IsRelationship	false
ModifiedProperties	null
ObjectStateManager	{System.Data.Objects.ObjectStateManager}
RelationshipManager	{System.Data.Objects.DataClasses.RelationshipManager}
State	Unchanged
System.Data.IEntityStateEntry.IsKeyEntry	false
System.Data.IEntityStateEntry.ModifiedProperties	null
System.Data.IEntityStateEntry.StateManager	{System.Data.Objects.ObjectStateManager}
System.Data.Objects.DataClasses.IEntityChangeTracker.EntityState	Unchanged

Figure 21-2. An ObjectStateEntry for a Reservation in debug view

- An array of the property values for the entity
- A `FieldCount` property
- A `DataRecordInfo` object containing the metadata about the entity, such as the name and type of each property

It is possible not only to read the current values of the object, but to write to them as well using a method such as `SetValue`, `SetString`, or `SetDateTime`. You will see `SetDateTime` in use in Example 21-12.

The `OriginalValues` property returns a `DbDataRecord` that contains the array of original property values and a `FieldCount` property. It does not include a `DataRecordInfo` object. Under the covers, this is an `ObjectStateEntryDbDataRecord`. Notice that the word *Updatable* is missing from this type. You cannot write to the original values, only to the current values.

Entities in the `Added` state do not have any original values. In fact, calling `OriginalValues` will throw an exception.

The value array contains scalar property values of the entity. If the property is a complex type, the value is a nested `DbDataRecord`.

Remember that the `ObjectContext` has a different definition of *original* than you may have. Although the original values are typically the database values, they are reset using the current values anytime you attach the entity to the `ObjectContext`. So, if you have detached and reattached an entity, there's no longer a guarantee that the values are what originally came from the database.

The way to access the values is through the Item property or one of the many casting methods such as GetString or GetByte. You can't expand the array in the debugger, and no property returns the entire array. If you are familiar with working with DbDataReaders, the properties are exposed in the same way.

The code in Example 21-11 grabs an entry for a Customer that is in the context and displays its property values.

Example 21-11. Reading the CurrentValues of an ObjectStateEntry

```
var objectStateEntry = osm.GetObjectStateEntry(customer.EntityKey);
var currentValues = objectStateEntry.CurrentValues;
for (var i = 0; i < currentValues.FieldCount; i++)
{
  Console.WriteLine("Field {0}: {1}", i, currentValues[i]);
}
```

The example code returns the following:

```
Field 0: 1
Field 1: Alex
Field 2: Solzhenitsyn
Field 3: Mr.
Field 4: 1/7/2009 11:41:45 AM
Field 5: 2/27/2010 2:39:10 PM
Field 6: System.Byte[]
Field 7: 1
Field 8: 3/4/2008 12:00:00 AM
Field 9: 5
Field 10: 25
Field 11: 18
Field 12: 21
Field 13: He was lots of fun to have on our trip!
Field 14: 1/26/1981 12:00:00 AM
Field 15: 69
Field 16: 125
Field 17:
Field 18: System.Byte[]
```

Even if the reservations or other related data for the customer was in the context, it won't be listed here. No navigation properties are retained in an ObjectStateEntry for an entity. However, it is possible to use the RelationshipManager for this entry, and from there you can locate the related entities. In this way, you can identify or interact with the graph, if you need to do so from this direction.

If this customer's reservations are loaded, you can see them through the ObjectStateEntry.RelationshipManager. Figure 21-3 shows the Reservations EntityCollection exposed through the RelationshipManager property of the customer's ObjectStateEntry.

Since you can just get those reservations through the entry itself, this is interesting only when you are writing dynamic code and do not have access to the strongly typed navigation properties. We'll be doing this further on in the chapter.

Name	Value
ModifiedProperties	null
ObjectStateManager	{System.Data.Objects.ObjectStateManager}
RelationshipManager	{System.Data.Objects.DataClasses.RelationshipManager}
_nodeVisited	false
_owner	{BAGA.Customer}
_relationships	Count = 6
[5]	{System.Data.Objects.DataClasses.EntityCollection<BAGA.Reservation>}
[System.Data.Objects.DataClasses.En	{System.Data.Objects.DataClasses.EntityCollection<BAGA.Reservation>}
base	{System.Data.Objects.DataClasses.EntityCollection<BAGA.Reservation>}
_onAssociationChangedforObjectVi	null
_relatedEntities	null
_wrappedRelatedEntities	null
Count	5
CountInternal	5
IsReadOnly	false
System.ComponentModel.IListSour	false
WrappedRelatedEntities	Count = 5
[0]	{[BAGA.Reservation, System.Data.Objects.Internal.LightweightEntityWrapper`1
Key	{BAGA.Reservation}
key	{BAGA.Reservation}
Value	{System.Data.Objects.Internal.LightweightEntityWrapper<BAGA.Reservation>}
[System.Data.Objects.Inte	{System.Data.Objects.Internal.LightweightEntityWrapper<BAGA.Reservation>}
Context	{BAGA.BAEntities}
Entity	{BAGA.Reservation}
EntityKey	"EntitySet=Reservations;ReservationID=244"

Figure 21-3. Finding an EntityCollection through an ObjectStateEntry

The `ObjectStateEntry` Visualizer extension method you looked at briefly in Chapter 10 takes advantage of inspecting an entity in a generic way using information from the `ObjectStateEntry`. Although it doesn't inspect relationships, it does use an important feature of `ObjectStateEntry`, so let's look at that before looking at the method extension.

Accessing object metadata with CurrentValueRecord.DataRecordInfo

The `DataRecordInfo` that is returned by `CurrentValues` provides two important functions. The first is that it enables you to access the metadata about the entity: property names, EDM types, and more. Additionally, it allows you "back-door" access to edit the entity objects. This is especially useful in scenarios where you don't have specific references to entities that are being managed by the context. You can grab an `ObjectStateEntry` from the context and then get the entity from there. This allows you to work directly with the entity after all.

`OriginalValues` does not expose a `DataRecordInfo` property. You can see `OriginalValues.DataRecordInfo` in the debugger, but you can't access it in code. If you need the metadata information, use `CurrentValues` to get the `DataRecordInfo`. Also, it's not possible to update the original values. The only time you would explicitly impact the original values is if you call `AcceptAllChanges` on the `ObjectContext`, forcing the original values to be updated with the current values.

Figure 21-4 displays the debug window for the `CurrentValueRecord` of a `Reservation` entity. In Example 21-11, the values were retrieved by reading the `CurrentValues`. The `FieldMetadata` lists details for each field. The first is expanded a bit and highlighted.

Name	Value
((System.Data.Objects.DbUpdatableDataRecord)(context.Object	{System.Data.Common.EntityRecordInfo}
[System.Data.Common.EntityRecordInfo]	{System.Data.Common.EntityRecordInfo}
_fieldMetadata	Count = 5
[0]	{System.Data.Common.FieldMetadata}
_fieldType	{ReservationID}
_ordinal	0
FieldType	{ReservationID}
[System.Data.Metadata.Edm.EdmProperty]	{ReservationID}
base	{ReservationID}
_memberGetter	null
_memberSetter	null
BuiltInTypeKind	EdmProperty
DefaultValue	null
EntityDeclaringType	{System.RuntimeTypeHandle}
Nullable	false
PropertyGetterHandle	{System.RuntimeMethodHandle}
PropertySetterHandle	{System.RuntimeMethodHandle}
ValueGetter	null
ValueSetter	null
base	{ReservationID}
_declaringType	{BAPOCOModel.Reservation}
_name	"ReservationID"
_typeUsage	EdmType={Edm.Int32}, Facets.Count=2
DeclaringType	{BAPOCOModel.Reservation}
Identity	"ReservationID"
IsStoreGeneratedComputed	false
IsStoreGeneratedIdentity	false
Name	"ReservationID"
TypeUsage	EdmType={Edm.Int32}, Facets.Count=2
Ordinal	0
[1]	{System.Data.Common.FieldMetadata}
[2]	{System.Data.Common.FieldMetadata}
[3]	{System.Data.Common.FieldMetadata}
[4]	{System.Data.Common.FieldMetadata}

Figure 21-4. The FieldMetadata value of CurrentValues, which lets you discover plenty of information about each property

Notice that you can see the property name, `ReservationID`, here. Now you have a way to align the value of the first item with the property name of the first field, and you can conclude that `ReservationID=1` rather than just "the first field=1".

The properties and methods of `ObjectStateEntry` give you direct access to some of the metadata without having to use the `MetadataWorkspace`. This is the tip of the iceberg in terms of what you can achieve when coding directly with the `MetadataWorkspace`.

Getting started with the FieldMetadata hierarchy

The metadata hierarchy goes even deeper, and as you will see in some of the following examples, it can definitely be a worthwhile effort to uncover that data. Everything that's described in the model's metadata is accessible programmatically. But knowing where the information is and how to access it is definitely a challenge. In the MSDN documentation, a topic called "Metadata Type Hierarchy Overview" contains a diagram displaying the hierarchy of the EDM metadata.

To help you get started, here are some of the critical parts of the hierarchy:

`CurrentValues.DataRecordInfo.FieldMetadata`
: This is an array of `FieldMetadata` objects for each scalar property (this includes complex types) in the entity. Each item in the `Metadata` array is a `Metadata.Edm.MetadataProperty`.

`CurrentValues.DataRecordInfo.RecordType.EdmType`
: This contains the property settings of the entity; for example, `Name`, `Abstract`, and `NamespaceName`.

`CurrentValues.DataRecordInfo.RecordType.EdmType.EntityType`
: In addition to the same properties that are exposed directly from `EdmType`, in here you can find the full metadata for each of the entity's "members," which means not only the scalar properties, but also the navigation properties.

  Each member is detailed either as an `EdmProperty` or as a navigation property. Opening these will display the details of each property—the property's name, its facets, and its `TypeUsage`, which contains information regarding its type (`String`, `DateTime`, etc.).

  The `KeyMembers` property shows only those members that comprise the `EntityKey`. The `Members` property lists all of the members.

As you begin to investigate the `EntityType`, it starts to become clear that everything you did to define the entity, its properties, and its relationships is available here.

Additionally, the `DataRecordInfo` provides a variety of views. For example, `FieldMetaData` is a subset of `RecordType.EdmType.EntityType.Members`.

So, you really can get at the metadata you are seeking in a variety of ways. You'll get a chance to take advantage of this in the next example.

Leveraging the ObjectStateManager During Saves

One of the most useful places to take advantage of the `ObjectStateManager` is when saving changes, either by overriding the `ObjectContext.SaveChanges` method or in the `ObjectContext.SavingChanges` event handler. You saw some examples of using the `SavingChanges` event in Chapter 10, where you used `GetObjectStateEntries` to find `Modified` and `Added` entries, to do some last-minute work on particular types.

The other events, `PropertyChanged/Changing` and `AssociationChanged`, do not have access to the `ObjectContext` or its `ObjectStateManager`, so you won't include this type of functionality in those event handlers.

Now that you have some additional tools at your disposal, you can create validators that will generically work with entities, without knowing their type. Example 21-12 locates any Added or Modified entries that have a ModifiedDate property and then updates that property with the current date and time.

This example handles two gotchas that you need to watch out for, but only if you are using independent associations. The first is that if the entry is a RelationshipEntry, an exception will be thrown when you try to read the metadata. Although you could use IsRelationship to test this, another method will kill two birds with one stone: by testing to see whether the ObjectStateEntry has an Entity value, you not only filter out relationships, but also filter out the "stub" entries that exist only to provide an end for EntityReferences when the entity is not in the context. This filter is used in the first query that returns the entries variable. If all of your associations are defined with foreign keys, this extra where operator will be unnecessary.

The second gotcha is that it's possible that a field named ModifiedDate is not a DateTime field. Never assume!

The LINQ query in the example drills into the CurrentValues of each entry. Then, using the Where method, it looks at the names of each FieldMetaData item for that entry, picking up only those whose name is ModifiedDate. You saw code similar to this when building the visualizer earlier in this chapter. Next, the If statement verifies that the ModifiedDate property is a DateTime field; then it updates the field using CurrentValues.SetDateTime.

Example 21-12. Updating ModifiedDate fields during SavingChanges

```
internal void FixupModifiedDates()
{
  var entries =
    from ose in this.ObjectStateManager.GetObjectStateEntries
      (EntityState.Added | EntityState.Modified)
    where ose.Entity != null
    select ose;

  foreach (var entry in entries)
  {
    var fieldMetaData = entry.CurrentValues.DataRecordInfo.FieldMetadata;
    FieldMetadata modifiedField = fieldMetaData
      .Where(f => f.FieldType.Name == "ModifiedDate")
      .FirstOrDefault();
    if (modifiedField.FieldType != null)
    {
      string fieldTypeName = modifiedField.FieldType.TypeUsage.EdmType.Name;

      if (fieldTypeName == PrimitiveTypeKind.DateTime.ToString())
      {
        entry.CurrentValues.SetDateTime(modifiedField.Ordinal,
                                        DateTime.Now);
      }
    }
 }}
```

You can call this method from within the `SavingChanges` event to be sure that any `ModifiedDate` field is automatically updated.

Importing the `System.Data.Metadata.Edm` namespace gives you access to the `PrimitiveTypeKind` class.

This code takes advantage of a lot of the details exposed in the metadata. The `foreach` has filtered down to any entity that has a `ModifiedDate` property, but you still need to know which property that is in order to call the `SetValue`/`SetDateTime` method. This is why you see the line of code that finds the exact property and returns the ordinal that can be found in the metadata.

Using ObjectStateManager to Build an EntityState Visualizer

Now let's look at the tool for visualizing an `ObjectStateEntry`, which you saw briefly in Chapter 10. This tool reads information from the `ObjectStateEntry` and displays it on a Windows form. I have found it to be a handy tool to use when debugging Entity Framework applications.

Building this tool will also provide you with hands-on experience in interacting with the entries and entities in a variety of ways. In the end you will have not only a useful tool for your application development, but also a much better understanding of how to work directly with `ObjectStateEntry` objects.

The visualizer is an extension method of `ObjectContext`, which takes as a parameter the entity you would like to inspect. This allows it to be used for `EntityObject` or POCO entities.

For those who are familiar with debugger visualizers, introduced in Visual Studio 2005, the `ObjectStateEntry` visualizer is not a debugger visualizer. Debugger visualizers require the target object to be serializable so that it can be moved to the debugger process. However, like `ObjectStateManager`, `ObjectStateEntry` classes are not serializable. In fact, if you do want to serialize them, you will need to deconstruct them and reconstruct them using the tools you are learning about in this chapter. Instead, this visualizer will be wrapped into an extension method with an attribute that makes it available only during debugging.

Although the tool is handy to have, the lessons you will learn by writing this code will be valuable. The code provides a practical demonstration of inspecting and extracting details of an `ObjectStateEntry` using its properties and methods.

You can download the code for the visualizer from the book's website. If you want to build it while walking through the explanation in this chapter, you'll need to create a new class library project with a reference to `System.Data.Entity`. In the primary code file, add `Imports` or `using` statements for the following namespaces:

- `System.Runtime.CompilerServices`
- `System.Data.Objects`
- `System.Data`
- `System.Data.Common`
- `System.Windows.Forms`

Add a Windows form to the project. You'll work on this after you have created the extension method. Name the form `debuggerForm`.

Example 21-13 shows the method stub for the `VisualEntityState` method of the `Visualizer` class you will be building.

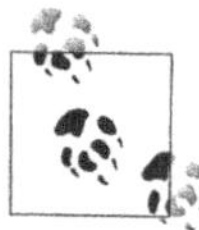

Remember that the VB extension will be in a method whereas the C# is a method of a static class.

Example 21-13. Base module and method for the Visualizer class

```
namespace EFExtensionMethods
{
  public static class Visualizer
  {
    public static void VisualizeEntityState
    (this ObjectContext context,object entity)
    {
      //code will go here
    }
  }
}
```

The entire code listing is displayed in Example 21-23 after the various parts have been explained.

Retrieving an ObjectStateEntry Using an EntityKey

`VisualizeEntityState`'s first task is to retrieve the `ObjectStateEntry` from the context. If the entity is detached, there will be no entry in the context, so you should use `TryGetObjectStateEntry` to be safe. The code in Example 21-14 goes in the new method.

The visualizer displays its results in a Windows form; therefore, you should already be in the correct environment for displaying a `MessageBox`.

Example 21-14. Getting the ObjectStateEntry

```
ObjectStateEntry ose = null;
/If object is Detached, there will be no Entry in the ObjectStateManager
  if (!context.ObjectStateManager.TryGetObjectStateEntry(entity, out ose))
  MessageBox.Show
    ("Object is not currently being change tracked " +
     "and no ObjectStateEntry exists.", "ObjectState Visualizer",
     MessageBoxButtons.OK, MessageBoxIcon.Warning);
else
{ ...
```

Reading the OriginalValues and CurrentValues of an ObjectStateEntry

If the entry exists, the next step is to retrieve the current and original values from the entry. However, there's a potential problem with `OriginalValues`. As noted earlier, entities in the "Added" state do not have original values and the property will throw an exception. Therefore, you'll declare a variable to contain the `OriginalValues` and populate it only if the state is not `Added` (see Example 21-15).

Example 21-15. Getting the CurrentValues and OriginalValues

```
var currentValues = ose.CurrentValues;
DbDataRecord originalValues = null;
if (ose.State != EntityState.Added)
  originalValues = ose.OriginalValues;
```

Next, create an array to store the data you'll be collecting for each property. The visualizer will need to not only display the current and original values, but also retrieve the property name by drilling into the metadata.

Iterate through the items in `CurrentValues`, picking up the value and the property as well as its related item value in the `OriginalValues` array. The values are captured in a number of variables and at the end will be pushed into the new array. Example 21-16 shows how `DataRecordInfo` is used to drill into the metadata to get the field names. For added records, you'll use a default of "n/a" in place of the nonexistent original value.

Example 21-16. Reading through the value arrays

```
//walk through arrays to get the values
var valueArray = new System.Collections.ArrayList();
for (var i = 0; i < currentValues.FieldCount; i++)
{
  //metadata provides field names
  var sName = currentValues.DataRecordInfo.FieldMetadata[i].FieldType.Name;
  var sCurrVal = currentValues[i];
```

```
object sOrigVal = null;
if (originalValues == null)
  sOrigVal = "n/a"; //this will be for Added entities
else
  sOrigVal = originalValues[i];
```

Determining Whether a Property Has Been Modified

Although you could just compare original to current values to determine whether the property has been modified, `ObjectStateEntry` has a method called `GetModifiedProperties` that returns an array of strings listing the names of any properties that have changed. Example 21-17 uses a LINQ to Objects query to check whether the current property is in that list.

Example 21-17. Determining whether the value has changed

```
string changedProp = (from prop in ose.GetModifiedProperties()
                      where prop == sName
                      select prop).FirstOrDefault();
string propModified;
if(changedProp == null)
  {propModified= "";}
else
  {propModified="X";}
```

Finally, gather all of the information you just collected regarding that item and place it into the array you created at the start (see Example 21-18).

Example 21-18. Pushing the property information into the array

```
valueArray.Add(new { _Index = i.ToString(), _Property = sName,
                     Current = sCurrVal, Original = sOrigVal,
                     ValueModified = propModified });
} //this closes the for loop opened in Example 21-16
```

Displaying the State and Entity Type

When this is complete, the array is passed into a Windows form and is displayed in a grid.

Two more pieces of data are sent along as well: the `ObjectStateEntry.State` and `ObjectStateEntry.Entity.ToString` properties. `ObjectStateEntry.Entity.ToString` returns the fully qualified name of the entity's type (see Example 21-19). You can see the results in Figure 21-5.

Example 21-19 assumes you have added the appropriate labels and a `DataGridView` to the form. To access the controls from the class, you will need to set their `Modifiers` property to `Friend` in Visual Basic and to `Internal` in C#.

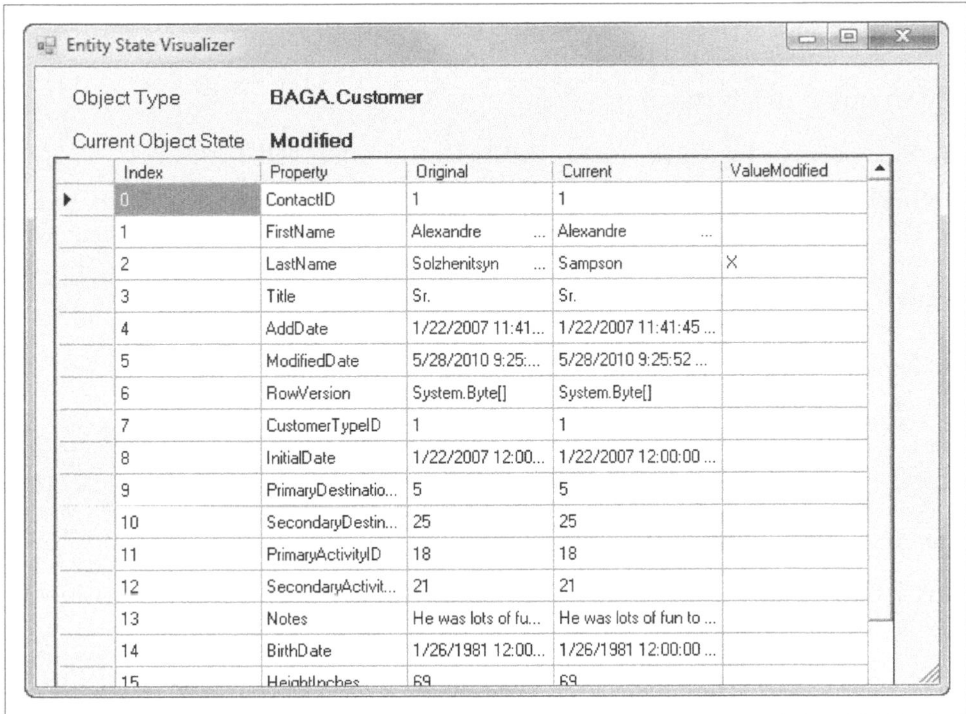

Figure 21-5. The visualizer populated with ObjectStateEntry information

Example 21-19. Pushing the values into the form

```
debuggerForm frm = new debuggerForm();
frm.dataGridView1.DataSource = valueArray;
frm.lblState.Text = ose.State.ToString();
frm.lblType.Text = ose.Entity.ToString();
frm.ShowDialog();
```

Getting ComplexType Properties Out of ObjectStateEntry

There's one more twist that the preceding code doesn't take into account: the possibility of a complex type in your properties.

If the entity contains a complex type, the value of that item will be a `DbDataRecord`, not a normal scalar value. Using the preceding solution, this will display in the grid as `System.Data.Objects.ObjectStateEntryDbUpdatableDataRecord`. Instead, you'll need to read the array values of the complex type.

Your first step is to determine whether the property is a complex type. The simple way to do this is to look for a `DbDataRecord` type using a type comparison, as shown in Example 21-20.

Example 21-20. Testing to see whether a property is a complex type

VB
```
If TypeOf (currentValues(i)) Is DbDataRecord Then
```

C#
```
if (currentValues[i] is DbDataRecord)
```

No other property types will render a `DbDataRecord`, so this will do the trick.

Although it is not practical for this example, it is possible, as shown in Example 21-21, to get much more granular by drilling even deeper into the entry where you can use the metadata to identify the complex type, or any other entity type, for that matter.

You can compare the `BuiltInTypeKind` property to the `BuiltInTypeKind` enumerator. You can use `BuiltInTypeKind` to identify any one of 40 schema types in an EDM, beginning alphabetically with `AssociationEndMember`.

Example 21-21. An alternative way to check for a complex type

```
if (currentValues.DataRecordInfo.FieldMetadata[i].FieldType
      .TypeUsage.EdmType.BuiltInTypeKind ==
      System.Data.Metadata.Edm.BuiltInTypeKind.ComplexType)
```

Your code can then return the scalar item or, if it is a complex type, further process the item to extract its values. The visualizer uses a separate function, `ComplexTypeString`, for that task.

`ComplexTypeString` takes the `DbDataRecord` and returns a string with the internal values of the complex value, as shown in Example 21-22.

Example 21-22. Finding a value in the complex type

```
private string ComplexTypeString(DbDataRecord record)
{
  var stringBuilder = new StringBuilder();
  for (var i = 0; i < record.FieldCount; i++)
  {
    if (record[i] == DBNull.Value)
    {
      stringBuilder.AppendLine("");
    }
    else
    {
      stringBuilder.AppendLine((String)(record[i]));
    }
  }
  return stringBuilder.ToString();
}
```

You could take this a step further and find the property names of the complex type. You probably don't want to attempt to find these from within the `DataRecordInfo`. It would be much simpler to use the `MetadataWorkspace` API directly to read the CSDL and determine the property name of the complex type—in this case, `AddressDetail`. You can discover that name through the same `TypeUsage` property you used earlier to identify that this was a `ComplexType`:

```
currentValues.DataRecordInfo.FieldMetadata[i]
          .FieldType.TypeUsage.EdmType.Name
```

Shortly, you'll see how to perform the next steps with the `MetaDataWorkspace` API.

Figure 21-6 displays the results (without the additional property names of the complex type).

Download the visualizer's complete code from the book's website, *http://www.learnentityframework.com*.

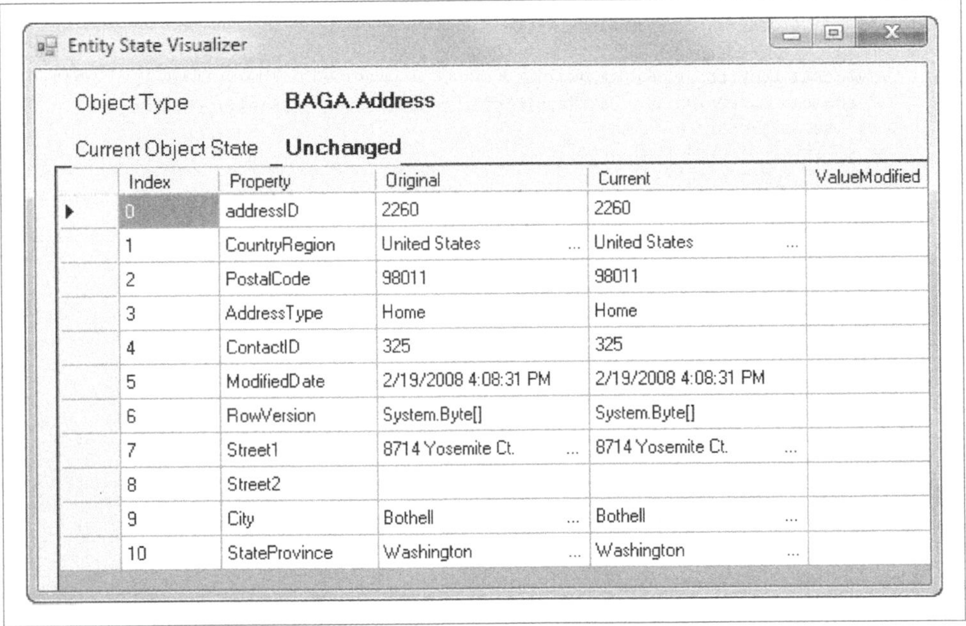

Figure 21-6. An Address entity with a ComplexType property displayed in the visualizer by reading the ObjectStateEntry

Example 21-23 displays the complete code listing of the `VisualizeEntityState` method along with the `ComplexTypeString` method.

Example 21-23. The VisualizeEntityState and ComplexTypeString methods

```
public static void VisualizeEntityState(this ObjectContext context,object entity)
{
  ObjectStateEntry ose = null;
  //If object is Detached, then there will be no Entry in the ObjectStateManager
  //new entities that are not attached will not even have an entitykey
  if (!context.ObjectStateManager.TryGetObjectStateEntry(entity, out ose))
    MessageBox.Show("Object is not currently being change tracked " +
      " and no ObjectStateEntry exists.",
      "ObjectState Visualizer", MessageBoxButtons.OK, MessageBoxIcon.Warning);
  else  {
    var currentValues = ose.CurrentValues;
    //If Object is Added, there will be no Original values
   //and it will throw an exception
    DbDataRecord originalValues = null;
    if (ose.State != EntityState.Added)
      originalValues = ose.OriginalValues;

    //walk through arrays to get the values
    var valueArray = new System.Collections.ArrayList();
    for (var i = 0; i < currentValues.FieldCount; i++)
    {
      //metadata provides field names
      var sName = currentValues.DataRecordInfo.FieldMetadata[i].FieldType.Name;
      bool isdbDataRecord = false;
      var sCurrVal = currentValues[i];
      object sOrigVal = null;

      //test for complex type
      if (currentValues[i] is DbDataRecord)
        isdbDataRecord = true;

      if (isdbDataRecord == false)
      {//normal scalar data
        sCurrVal = currentValues[i];
      }
      else
      {
        //complex type, anything else?
        sCurrVal = ComplexTypeString((DbDataRecord)currentValues[i]);
      }

      if (ose.State == EntityState.Added)
        sOrigVal = "n/a"; //this will be for Added entities
      else
        if (isdbDataRecord == false)
        {//normal scalar data
          sOrigVal = originalValues[i];
        }
        else
        {
          //complex type
          sOrigVal = ComplexTypeString((DbDataRecord)originalValues[i]);
        }
      string changedProp = (
```

```
            from prop in ose.GetModifiedProperties()
            where prop == sName
            select prop).FirstOrDefault();

      string propModified;

      if (changedProp == null)
        propModified = "";
      else
        propModified = "X";
      valueArray.Add(new {Index = i.ToString(), Property = sName,
        Original = sOrigVal, Current = sCurrVal,ValueModified = propModified });
    }
    var form = new VisualizerForm();
    form.dataGridView1.DataSource = valueArray;
    form.lblState.Text = ose.State.ToString();
    form.lblType.Text = ose.Entity.ToString();
    form.ShowDialog();
  }
}
private static string ComplexTypeString(DbDataRecord item)
{
  var dbRecString = new StringBuilder();
  for (var i = 0; i < item.FieldCount; i++)
  {
    if (item[i] == DBNull.Value)
    {
      dbRecString.AppendLine("");
    }
    else
    {
      dbRecString.AppendLine((String)(item[i]));
    }
  }
  return dbRecString.ToString();
}
```

Modifying Values with ObjectStateManager

Because the `CurrentValues` property returns an updatable `DbDataRecord`, it is possible to modify the values directly through the `ObjectStateManager`.

Like the various accessors for a `DbDataReader` and a `DbDataRecord`, `CurrentValues` allows you to change a value using `SetValue` or one of the type-specific setters such as `SetString`, `SetInt32`, or even `SetDBNull`.

The signature for these methods is to pass in the value to be used for updating and the index of the item in the array. Again, remember that you can do this directly only with the scalar values. If you need to change relationships, more work is involved.

Example 21-24 shows the signature for `CurrentValueRecord.SetBoolean`.

Example 21-24. Changing a Boolean property with SetBoolean

```
ObjectStateEntry.CurrentValues.SetBoolean(3,false)
```

The plural `SetValues` lets you pass in an array to update all of the values, as shown in Example 21-25. `SetValues` requires that you know the order and types of the properties. There are two fields that you don't want to change, however: the `ContactID` and `TimeStamp` values. Those fields will just have their current values passed back in.

Example 21-25. Changing all of the values with SetValues

```
currentValues.SetValues(currentValues[0],"Pablo","Castro","Sr.",
                        DateTime.Now,DateTime.Now, currentValues[6]);
```

Working with Relationships in ObjectStateManager

If you are using independent associations in your model and do not have direct access to foreign key scalar properties, you may find yourself needing to work explicitly with `ObjectStateEntry` types that have been instantiated to represent relationships.

Because this is outside the norm in Visual Studio 2010 and you are more likely to have access to the foreign keys, the extended discussion of this topic that existed in the first edition of this book is not repeated here. You can download the relevant portion of the first edition chapter (Chapter 17) from the downloads page of the book's website, at *http://www.learnentityframework.com*.

With models that use foreign key associations, you can work directly with a foreign key scalar when you want to interact with a foreign key relationship. However, if you want to write dynamic code that handles related collections or instantiated foreign key objects, you can use the `RelationshipManager`.

Building graphs directly with the RelationshipManager

It is possible to get your hands on an instance of the `RelationshipManager` to build graphs on the fly, creating relationships directly in your code.

The `RelationshipManager`'s entry point is through an `ObjectStateEntry`. `EntityObject` implements the `IEntityWithRelationships` interface, and any custom objects that you build will need to implement it as well if you want to have relationships managed by Object Services.

The entity does not need to be attached to an `ObjectContext` to get the `RelationshipManager`.

To get the `IEntityWithRelationships` view of an existing entity, cast the entity to `IEntityWithRelationships`. From there, you can get a `RelationshipManager` associated specifically with your entity.

Example 21-26 shows two ways to get the `RelationshipManager`. The first code line casts an `EntityObject`, `customer`, to `IEntityWithRelationships` and then gets its `RelationshipManager`. The second, which will also work for POCO entities, uses an `ObjectStateEntry`.

Example 21-26. Two ways to get a RelationshipManager

```
var pmtRelMgr=((IEntityWithRelationships) myPayment).RelationshipManager;
//or
var pmtRelMgr = pmtObjectStateEntry.RelationshipManager;
```

Once you have the `RelationshipManager`, the next step is to get a reference to the other end of the relationship that you want to add. To do this, you need to identify which association and which end of the association you want to work with. Unfortunately, you won't be able to do this in a strongly typed way. You'll have to use a string to specify the association's name.

In Example 21-27, the goal is to add a `Reservation` to the `Payment` used in Example 21-26, so you'll need to work with the `FK_Payments_Reservations` association and add it to the "Reservations" end.

Some of the tricks that `RelationshipManager` performs do not require the `ObjectContext`. This is handy to know if you are building generic code without the aid of the `ObjectContext`. Check out the MSDN Entity Framework forum post titled "Remove Associations from Entity," which shows how to use `IRelatedEnd` with reflection to strip related data from an entity. (When reading this forum thread, which I started, you'll also see that I learned this lesson the hard way, too.)

`RelatedEnd` has an `Add` method, which is the final call you'll need to make. Example 21-27 shows how you can add the existing `Reservation` entity to the `RelatedEnd`. This will create a new relationship between the `Payment` entity and the `Reservation` entity.

Example 21-27. Creating a relationship on the fly using the RelationshipManager created in Example 21-26

```
IRelatedEnd resRelEnd =
  pmtRelMgr.GetRelatedEnd("FK_Reservations_Customers", "Reservations");
resRelEnd.Add(myReservation);
```

This method of building graphs works exactly the same as if you had called `pmt.Reservation=myReservation`. That is because the navigation properties inherit from `IRelatedEnd` as does the `RelatedEnd` type.

If neither object is attached to the context, you will still get a graph; however, no `RelationshipEntry` will be created in the context. If only one of the entities is attached to the context, the other one will be pulled in and given the appropriate EntityState (Attached or Added).

Like navigation properties, RelatedEnd also has Attach, Remove, and other methods that you have already been working with.

Using the MetadataWorkspace

At this point, you have interacted with the metadata—the raw XML that describes the CSDL, MSL, and SSDL for your model—through the ObjectStateManager. You can also work directly with the metadata through the MetadataWorkspace, which is in the System.Data.Metadata.Edm namespace.

The MetadataWorkspace API is used internally throughout the Entity Framework. It is the mechanism that reads the EDM. It can also read the generated classes, as you've seen in this chapter's examples thus far. In addition to being able to get metadata about the entity types and other model objects, the EntityClient uses the metadata during query processing. After the LINQ to Entities or Entity SQL queries are turned into command trees using the conceptual model, these command trees are then transformed into a command tree using the store schema. The conceptual, store, and mapping layers of the model are read in order to perform this task.

You can use the MetadataWorkspace API to read and dissect each of the three layers, as well as the entity classes that are based on the model. The power of the MetadataWorkspace lies in its ability to let you not only write generic code, but also write code that can create objects on the fly. You could write utilities or entire applications that have no knowledge in advance of the conceptual model.

Loading the MetadataWorkspace

In Chapter 20, you learned that if the metadata has not already been loaded into the application memory, an EntityConnection will load the metadata when the connection is opened. Typically, it does this by loading the actual files (CSDL, MSL, and SSDL) that the metadata attribute of the connection string points to. It is also possible to load these files into a memory stream and pass that memory stream in when you are instantiating an EntityConnection.

The MetadataWorkspace can work only with metadata that has already been loaded, which happens when an EntityConnection is created directly or as a result of an ObjectContext being instantiated.

Example 21-28 demonstrates loading the MetadataWorkspace from an EntityConnection and then from an ObjectContext.

Example 21-28. Accessing the MetadataWorkspace from an EntityConnection and an ObjectContext

```
var connection = new EntityConnection("name=BAEntities");
var metadataWorskpace = connection.GetMetadataWorkspace();

BAEntities context = new BAEntities();
var metadataWorskpace = context.MetadataWorkspace;
```

Creating a MetadataWorkspace without an EntityConnection

You can also instantiate a `MetadataWorkspace` if you don't need to make a connection, by using the overload of the `MetadataWorkspace` constructor, which takes file paths and assemblies.

You can point directly to the files or instantiate a `System.Reflection.Assembly` to use this constructor. One enumerable that contains file paths and another enumerable that contains assemblies are required; however, you can leave the enumerables empty.

Example 21-29 loads the conceptual and store metadata directly from files using syntax to create an array on the fly. Because no assembly is needed in this example, an empty array is created for the second parameter.

Example 21-29. Creating a MetadataWorkspace using EDM files

```
var mdw = new MetadataWorkspace
   (new string[] { "C:\\EFModels\\BAModel.csdl",
                   "C:\\EFModels\\BAModel.ssdl" },
    new Assembly[]{});
```

If the model is embedded in an assembly, you can use syntax similar to the metadata property of an `EntityConnection` string to point to the files and then provide an assembly that is a type loaded in through `System.Reflection`. This enables the Entity Framework to inspect the assembly and find the embedded files. Example 21-30 shows one of many ways to load an assembly.

Example 21-30. Creating a MetadataWorkspace from EDM files embedded in an assembly file

```
Assembly assembly = Assembly.LoadFile("C:\\myapp\\BreakAwayModel.dll");
var metadataWorkspace = new MetadataWorkspace
   (new string[] { "res://*/BAModel.csdl", "res://*/BAModel.ssdl" },
    new Assembly[] { assembly });
```

If you need to use the `MetadataWorkspace` only to read the models, this is a nice option to leverage.

Clearing the MetadataWorkspace from Memory

Remember that loading the metadata into memory is expensive, so you should leave it in an application cache for the lifetime of the application. It is possible, however, to clear it out and force it to be reloaded if you require it again, by calling `MetadataWorkspace.ClearCache`.

Understanding the MetadataWorkspace ItemCollections

At runtime, the metadata can be found either as resources that are compiled into the model's assembly or in individual *.csdl*, *.msl*, and *.ssdl* files. The `MetadataWorkspace` contains five separate item collections, one for each of these different resources. Once you have the `MetadataWorkspace`, you can start to drill into the metadata, but you always need to specify which item collection to access by using a `DataSpace` enum: `CSpace` for the conceptual model, `SSpace` for the storage model, `OSpace` for the object model, `CSSpace` for the mapping layer, and finally, `OCSpace` for a mapping between the conceptual layer and the object model.

When you're reading about the Entity Framework, you will find that developers who have been working with the Entity Framework for a while sometimes use the words *C-Space* and *O-Space*, among other similar terms, to refer to the `DataSpace`. This is how they differentiate between the classes and the various parts of the model, since so many of the terms cross over into all of these areas. Saying "the contact in the *O-Space*" makes it clear that you are talking about the object. "The contact in the *C-Space*" means the contact specified in the conceptual model, as opposed to "the contact in the *S-Space*," which refers to the `Contact` table from the database as it is described in the model's store layer.

These terms also appear in messages when the model can't be validated because of an error somewhere in the schema.

Although the compiler will allow you to combine the `DataSpace` enums using operators such as `And` and `Or`, the enums are integers, not expressions, and they are not meant to be combined in this way. You won't get an exception, but the returned values will be incorrect. Instead, perform the methods on one `DataSpace` at a time and then combine the results. You can use LINQ's `Union` operator for this purpose.

When the `MetadataWorkspace` is created as the result of an `EntityCollection` being instantiated, not all of the item collections are loaded right away. For example, the metadata from the store layer isn't loaded until the first time something is done that requires the store layer—a query execution, for instance, or a call to the `ToTraceString` method.

If you attempt to extract metadata from an item collection that has not yet been loaded, an exception will be thrown. Therefore, most of the methods for extracting metadata (e.g., `GetItem`, `GetFunctions`) come paired with a method using the Try pattern (`TryGetItem`, `TryGetFunctions`), which returns Booleans rather than risking an exception being thrown if no data is returned.

When you use the MetadataWorkspace constructor with the file paths overload as shown earlier, all of the designated models are loaded immediately.

Determining whether an ItemCollection has been loaded

You can also test to see whether an ItemCollection has been loaded prior to attempting to get information from it, by using GetItemCollection and TryGetItemCollection. It makes more sense to use the latter so that you don't get an exception.

The code in Example 21-31 tests to see whether the SSpace is loaded.

Example 21-31. Testing to see whether a DataSpace, specifically the SSpace, is loaded

```
ItemCollection collection = null;
if (metadataWorkspace.TryGetItemCollection(DataSpace.SSpace, out collection))
```

Other than triggering the model to load through query generation, as explained earlier, there's no other way to force a model to load to an existing MetadataWorkspace.

You'll need to add the System.Data.Metadata.Edm namespace to your using or Imports statements to get at these Edm members.

Retrieving Metadata from the MetadataWorkspace

You can pull information from these collections using a variety of methods.

Retrieving sets of items from the metadata with GetItems and TryGetItem

You can use GetItems or TryGetItems to find all items or items of a specific type in a model. Example 21-32 will return a .NET generic collection type, ReadOnlyCollection, of every item defined in the model. The common base type for the items is GlobalItem.

Example 21-32. Requesting an array of every item defined in the CSDL

```
ReadOnlyCollection<GlobalItem> items =
  metadataWorkspace.GetItems(DataSpace.CSpace);
```

You'll find in here not only the EntityType and AssociationType items that are defined in your model, but also all of the PrimitiveTypes and FunctionTypes that the model needs to be aware of. PrimitiveTypes are .NET, EDM, and store types. FunctionTypes are built-in functions from the provider as well as the functions that are created from stored procedures in the database. Most likely you will not need access to all of these items; therefore, the GetItems overload shown in Example 21-33, which lets you specify which types to return, might be more useful and efficient.

Example 21-33. Requesting an array of all EntityTypes in the CSDL

```
ReadOnlyCollection<EntityType> items =
  metadataWorkspace.GetItems<EntityType>(DataSpace.CSpace);
```

The common base type for these items is `EntityType` and the method returns an array of `EntityType` objects. Figure 21-7 expands the first of these, `BAModel.Activity`.

The details shown in Figure 21-7 may look familiar to you. `CurrentValues.DataRecordInfo.RecordType.EdmType.EntityType` returns the same `Edm.EntityTypes`. In there, you can find out anything you might want or need to know about the structure of an entity. The Visual Basic debugger view is shown in Figure 21-7 because it displays the interesting information more succinctly. With C#'s debugger you'll have to dig around a lot more to discover all of these properties.

As with the other Try alternatives you have seen already, `TryGetItems` follows the .NET Try pattern to avoid an exception if no matching items are returned.

(0)_	{BAModel.Activity}	System.Data.Metadata.Edm.EntityType
Abstract	False	Boolean
BaseType	Nothing	System.Data.Metadata.Edm.EdmType
BuiltInTypeKind	EntityType {14}	System.Data.Metadata.Edm.BuiltInTypeKind
CacheIdentity	"BAModel.Activity"	String
ClrType	Nothing	System.Type
CollectionKindFacetDescription	{CollectionKind}	System.Data.Metadata.Edm.FacetDescription
DataSpace	CSpace {1}	System.Data.Metadata.Edm.DataSpace
DefaultValueFacetDescription	{DefaultValue}	System.Data.Metadata.Edm.FacetDescription
Documentation	Nothing	System.Data.Metadata.Edm.Documentation
EdmProviderManifest	{System.Data.Metadata.Edm.EdmProviderN	System.Data.Metadata.Edm.EdmProviderManifest
FullName	"BAModel.Activity"	String
Identity	"BAModel.Activity"	String
IsReadOnly	True	Boolean
KeyMemberNames	{Length=1}	String()
KeyMembers	Count = 1	System.Data.Metadata.Edm.ReadOnlyMetadataColle
Members	Count = 8	System.Data.Metadata.Edm.ReadOnlyMetadataColle
MetadataProperties	Count = 9	System.Data.Metadata.Edm.ReadOnlyMetadataColle
Name	"Activity"	String
NamespaceName	"BAModel"	String
NavigationProperties	Count = 4	System.Data.Metadata.Edm.ReadOnlyMetadataColle
NullableFacetDescription	{Nullable}	System.Data.Metadata.Edm.FacetDescription
NullType	EdmType={NullType}, Facets.Count=2	System.Data.Metadata.Edm.TypeUsage
Properties	Count = 4	System.Data.Metadata.Edm.ReadOnlyMetadataColle
RawMetadataProperties	{System.Data.Metadata.Edm.MetadataProp	System.Data.Metadata.Edm.MetadataCollection(Of
(1)	{BAModel.Contact}	System.Data.Metadata.Edm.EntityType
(2)	{BAModel.CustomerType}	System.Data.Metadata.Edm.EntityType

Figure 21-7. The VB debugger view of EntityType items returned from MetadataWorkspace.GetItems

Notice again how the entity's properties are grouped in a few different ways to make it easier to access what you are looking for:

- `KeyMembers` returns only the properties that are used to build the `EntityKey`.
- `Members` returns all of the properties.
- `NavigationProperties` returns a subset of members.
- `Properties` returns only the scalar properties (including `ComplexTypes`).

The biggest benefit of being able to get at this information is the ability to write dynamic functionality in your application. Not only can you instantiate objects, as you'll see in a bit, but also this metadata is an optimal source for report design tools, just as other schemas, such as the DataSet XSD files, are used for report design.

Retrieving specific items from the metadata with GetItem and TryGetItem

GetItem and TryGetItem allow you to pass in a string to specify the name of the item you would like to get from the model, rather than returning an array. The name must be fully qualified, not just the string used for the entity's name property. Example 21-34 shows how to call GetItem.

Example 21-34. Getting EntityTypes that are Contacts from the CSDL

```
metadataWorkspace.GetItem<EntityType>("BAModel.Contact", DataSpace.CSpace);
```

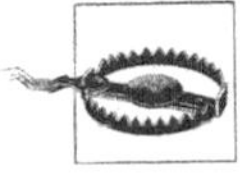

If you pass multiple DataSpace enums into this method and one or more of them do not contain this particular item, an exception will be thrown. Use TryGetItem as a precaution. In Example 21-34, you can assume that the model to search is obvious, but if you are building generic methods where you always have a number of models in the parameter, it is possible to run into this problem.

Retrieving functions from the metadata with GetFunctions and TryGetFunctions

GetFunctions and TryGetFunctions will return only functions, but they are different from just calling GetItems<EdmFunction>. Instead, you need to specify the name and the namespace of the function separately (as opposed to the fully qualified name requirement in GetItem), as well as the DataSpace.

The code in Example 21-35 returns the EdmFunction whose public properties are displayed in Figure 21-8.

Example 21-35. Getting a specific function from the SSDL

```
metadataWorkspace.GetFunctions("UpdateContact", "BreakAwayModel.Store", DataSpace.SSpace);
```

Compare this to the function's description in the SSDL, shown in Example 21-36.

Example 21-36. The UpdateContact function listing in the SSDL

```
<Function Name="UpdateContact" Aggregate="false" BuiltIn="false"
          NiladicFunction="false" IsComposable="false"
         ParameterTypeSemantics="AllowImplicitConversion" Schema="dbo">
   <Parameter Name="ContactID" Type="int" Mode="In" />
   <Parameter Name="FirstName" Type="nchar" Mode="In" />
   <Parameter Name="LastName" Type="nchar" Mode="In" />
   <Parameter Name="Title" Type="nchar" Mode="In" />
</Function>
```

Everything you see in the schema is available through the MetadataWorkspace.

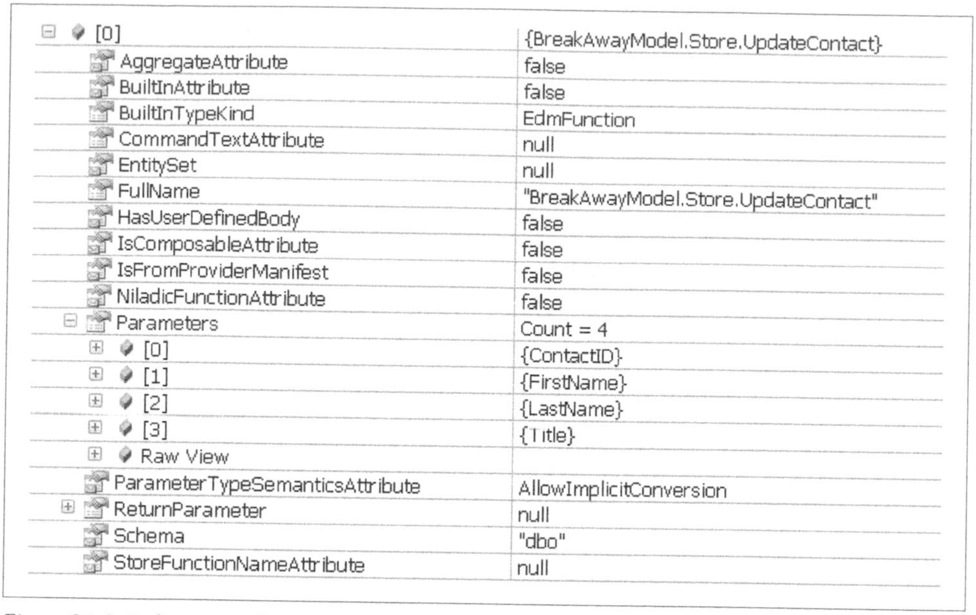

[0]	{BreakAwayModel.Store.UpdateContact}
AggregateAttribute	false
BuiltInAttribute	false
BuiltInTypeKind	EdmFunction
CommandTextAttribute	null
EntitySet	null
FullName	"BreakAwayModel.Store.UpdateContact"
HasUserDefinedBody	false
IsComposableAttribute	false
IsFromProviderManifest	false
NiladicFunctionAttribute	false
Parameters	Count = 4
[0]	{ContactID}
[1]	{FirstName}
[2]	{LastName}
[3]	{Title}
Raw View	
ParameterTypeSemanticsAttribute	AllowImplicitConversion
ReturnParameter	null
Schema	"dbo"
StoreFunctionNameAttribute	null

Figure 21-8. Debugging a function's metadata

Querying the Metadata with LINQ to Objects

It's also possible to perform standard LINQ queries (i.e., LINQ to Objects) against item collections. As an example, the method query in Example 21-37 searches the store model's `ItemCollection` to find any item that has *Contact* in the name.

Example 21-37. Querying the items of the model with LINQ

```
mdw.GetItems<EdmType>(DataSpace.SSpace)
    .Where(i => i.Name.Contains("Contact")).ToList();
```

From the BreakAway model, this query returns 10 items that represent the database schema:

- `Contact` and `ContactPersonalInfo EntityTypes` (tables)
- `FK_Address_Contact`, `FK_Lodging_Contact`, and `FK_Customers_Contact AssociationTypes`
- Five different functions (stored procedures) with *Contact* in the title

If you want to search across models, you can use LINQ's `Union` query method, which follows the pattern ***`query1`***`.Union(`***`query2`***`).`***`otherMethods`***, as shown in Example 21-38.

Example 21-38. Combining items from the CSDL and SSDL in one request

```
mdw.GetItems<EdmType>(DataSpace.CSpace)
 .Union(mdw.GetItems<EdmType>(DataSpace.SSpace))
 .Where(i => i.Name.Contains("Contact")).ToList();
```

This returns all of the items with the word *Contact* in both the conceptual and store models.

Building Dynamic Queries and Reading Results

Now that you have had a good look at the `ObjectStateManager` and the `MetadataWorkspace`, you might be interested in what types of problems you can solve with these tools.

The following example will show you how to build queries dynamically, first using the metadata and then using Entity Framework 4's new `CreateObjectSet` method. While the latter method is much simpler, you'll see that the metadata scenario will give you the flexibility to build more complex queries.

After these two samples, you'll use the `ObjectStateManager` to read through the results of the query even though at design time you won't know what types are being returned.

Building Entity SQL Queries Dynamically Using Metadata

You can also use the metadata to build Entity SQL queries thanks to the fact that an Entity SQL expression is simply a string.

The example in this section proposes what may seem to be an edge case, but in doing so it will give you a much better understanding of interacting with the `MetadataWorkspace`. There are also opportunities to achieve this more simply thanks to the introduction of Entity Framework's `ObjectSet` in .NET 4.0. Look for additional examples that combine an `ObjectSet` feature with query builder methods in the next section of this chapter.

Imagine that you have a query that returns data from every navigation property (`EntityCollections` or `EntityReferences`):

```
Select contact, contact.Addresses,contact.Orders from MyEntities.Contacts ....
```

When the application is first written, `Addresses` and `Orders` comprise the only child data for the contact. But perhaps another navigation property is introduced with additional child data, such as `PhoneNumbers`. By writing the query dynamically using the metadata, you'll never have to modify the query manually. The application will always be able to follow the rule of returning a contact with all of its child data without having to know what the definition of "all of its child data" is.

Building the query dynamically will also mean you won't know exactly what is contained in the results, and therefore you may also need to use the metadata to handle the results.

It's a good idea to establish patterns in your model naming for many reasons. Being able to construct generic code in this way is one of those reasons.

The `SingleEntityEsql` method described on the next few pages will build the query dynamically. Example 21-39 shows the signature of the method, which uses the generic `<TEntity>` to specify what entity type the query will be based on a generic type. The method parameters are the entity's key value and a reference to the context that will be used to execute the query.

Example 21-39. The SingleEntityEsql signature

```
private static string SingleEntityEsql<TEntity>
  (Int32 entityID, ObjectContext context)
```

Next, you're going to need the `EntityContainer` so that you can find the entity's `EntitySet` name further on in the method, as well as the `NamespaceName` so that you can use the `GetItem` method. You can find the `NamespaceName` within various types, but not directly from the `MetadataWorkspace`, so the code in Example 21-40 grabs a random `EntityType` from the `CSpace` and gets the `NamespaceName` from there.

Example 21-40. Finding the Container and Namespace names using the MetadataWorkspace

```
{
  var metadataWorkspace = context.MetadataWorkspace;
  var container = metadataWorkspace.GetItems<EntityContainer>
     (DataSpace.CSpace).First();
  var namespaceName = metadataWorkspace.GetItems<EntityType>(DataSpace.CSpace)
                     .First().NamespaceName;
```

Next, using the entity's `Name`, you can find the name of its `EntitySet` as well as its `EntityType`. From the `EntityType`, you can find its navigation properties and then iterate through the navigation properties, adding each name to a `List` (see Example 21-41).

Example 21-41. Creating a list of navigation property names

```
var entityName = typeof(TEntity).Name;
var setName = container.BaseEntitySets
   .First(set => set.ElementType.Name == entityName).Name;
var entityType = metadataWorkspace.GetItem<EntityType>
   (namespaceName + "." + entityName, DataSpace.CSpace);
var propertyNames = entityType.NavigationProperties.Select(np => np.Name).ToList();
```

The `KeyMembers` property discussed in "Getting started with the FieldMetadata hierarchy" on page 610 will provide the name of the property or properties that contain the key field. The code in Example 21-42 assumes that only one property is used for the `EntityKey` and only one key value has been passed in (`EntityID`).

Example 21-42. Getting the name of an entity's key property

```
var propertyName = entityType.KeyMembers[0].Name;
```

For Reservation, this will return the string, ReservationID.

Now you can finally build the string using the names in propertyNames and the other variables you have collected along the way (see Example 21-43).

Example 21-43. Building the Entity SQL expression and closing the method

```
var stringBuilder = new StringBuilder().Append("SELECT entity ");
foreach (var name in propertyNames)
{
  stringBuilder.Append(",ent." + name);
}
stringBuilder.Append(" FROM " + container.Name.Trim() + "."
                     + setName + " AS entity ");
stringBuilder.Append(" WHERE entity." + propertyName + " = " + entityId);
return stringBuilder.ToString();
} //end of the method
```

Example 21-44 displays a method that calls the SingleEntityEsql method you've just built. Note that the query is explicitly executed so that you can work with the results, not the actual query, and so that you don't have to worry about inadvertently executing the query again.

Example 21-44. Testing the SingleEntityEsql method

```
private static void DynamicESQLTest()
{
  using (BAEntities context = new BAEntities())
  {
    var eSql = SingleEntityEsql <Reservation>(90, context);
    var query = context.CreateQuery<DbDataRecord>(eSql);
    var results = query.Execute(MergeOption.AppendOnly);
    //PLACEHOLDER: iterate through the results (Example 21-47)
}
```

Example 21-45 shows the Entity SQL expression created by the SingleEntityEsql method.

Example 21-45. The Entity SQL expression that results

```
SELECT entity,entity.Customer,entity.Trip,entity.Payments,entity.UnpaidReservation
FROM BAEntities.Reservations  AS entity
WHERE entity.ReservationID = 90
```

Creating Queries on the Fly with CreateObjectSet and Query Builder Methods

The previous section went through a lot of steps to build an Entity SQL expression on the fly. It also gave you an example that helped to deepen your understanding of working with the metadata. However, you can take advantage of the Entity SQL query builder methods to simplify some of the steps performed in that example.

If you recall working with query builder methods as early as Chapter 3 in this book, you'll remember that these methods require a minimal amount of Entity SQL syntax and will build the Entity SQL in the background for you as well as create an `ObjectQuery` that you must then execute.

Creating the queries in this manner does require an instantiated `ObjectContext`, whereas building the Entity SQL using the example provided in the previous section could have been built without an `ObjectContext`, although that method did use the context in order to leverage the simplest way to get access to the `MetadataWorkspace`.

Much of the work with the `MetadataWorkspace` in the previous example is focused on discovering the navigation properties, and you can't avoid using the `MetadataWorkspace` for that purpose.

But in a scenario where the discovery is unnecessary—perhaps the method does not need to do projections—or if the required properties are passed in for projection or even for another purpose, such as filtering or ordering, you can the skip the `MetadataWorkspace` completely. Following are a few examples.

The first is a common scenario where you might want to return a set of entities with a particular sort order.

Example 21-46 encapsulates logic in a method that can be called from an external method that is unaware of the `ObjectContext`. Notice that the method uses a variable called `localContext`. That refers to a local property that either returns an already existing instance of an `ObjectContext` or instantiates a new one if needed. The `SortedEntityList` method doesn't care where the context comes from.

Example 21-46. A generic method to return a sorted list of objects

```
private static List<TEntity> SortedEntityList<TEntity>(string sortProperty)
  where TEntity : class
{
  var query = (ObjectQuery<TEntity>)localContext.CreateObjectSet<TEntity>();
  if (!string.IsNullOrWhiteSpace(sortProperty))
  {
    query = query.OrderBy("it." + sortProperty);
  }
  return query.ToList();
}
```

You can then call, for example, SortedEntityList<Customer>("LastName") from another layer in the application without it needing to know about the ObjectContext. This works well for separation concerns whether you are working with POCOs or EntityObject types.

The method uses CreateObjectSet to enable you to generically define the entity to query for. This is cast to an ObjectQuery in order to allow the OrderBy composition. Notice that OrderBy uses an Entity SQL predicate, indicating that it is a query builder method, not a LINQ query. The method executes the query and returns the results in a List<T>. If the method were to return the query, it would force the calling code to have access to the context in order to execute the query—exactly what we are trying to avoid.

While the EntitySet name was not needed in this example, you can easily get the EntitySet name by calling ObjectSet.EntitySet.Name as opposed to the means of extracting it from the metadata that was used in the previous example.

There are a few scenarios you should consider for this type of method. If you want to do a projection in your query, you'll be returning DbDataRecord types; therefore, the calling code would pass in <DbDataRecord> as the generic type to be used and returned by the method.

In Chapter 15, you learned how to build model-defined functions. You can use these functions as well in a dynamic method; however, because the Entity SQL syntax is different, you'll need to account for that.

An expression that sorts with the FullNameReverse model-defined function could look like this:

```
localContext.CreateObjectSet<Customer>().OrderBy("BAModel.FullNameReverse(it)")
```

It would be a little trickier to write something that can handle this and a simple scalar property at the same time. You'd have to either require the caller to pass in the model namespace or go dig it out of the metadata, and you would need an indication that this is a function so that your code will know to express the OrderBy differently.

Leveraging CreateObjectSet to return Entity SQL, not just a query

The method creates and executes a query, then returns results. What if you really want the Entity SQL expression? As an example, you might be using EntityClient, which requires Entity SQL.

You can still benefit from the simpler means of building the query.

Once the query has been created, rather than executing it, you can grab its `CommandText` property using `query.CommandText`. The `CommandText` of the query created in `SortedEntityList<Customer>("LastName")` is:

```
"SELECT VALUE it FROM ([BAEntities].[Contacts]) AS it ORDER BY it.LastName"
```

Reading the Results of a Dynamically Created Query

Iterating through the data without knowing what is in there might be a little tricky. However, since this was an `ObjectQuery`, all of the data is in the `ObjectContext`. So, as you iterate through the data, you can access `ObjectStateEntries` and use the tricks you learned earlier in this chapter to find out about the entities using generic code.

You can replace the empty iteration used earlier with a new bit of code that will do the following for each `DbDataRecord` returned by the query:

1. Cast the row to an `IExtendedDataRecord`, which will turn the `DbDataRecord` into a record containing a `DataRecordInfo` object, a `FieldCount` property, and a list of items representing the fields of the row.

   Based on the query executed in Example 21-44, you should expect the row to contain the following:

   - Field(0): A `Reservation` entity
   - Field(1): A `Customer` entity
   - Field(2): A `Trip` entity
   - Field(3): `EntityCollection<Payment>`
2. Iterate through each field in the row.
3. Identify whether the field is an `EntityType`.
4. Pass the `EntityKey` of the entity to another method that will find the `ObjectStateEntry` in the `ObjectStateManager` and list the name and value of each field.
5. Identify whether the field is an `EntityCollectionType`.
6. Cast the field to an `IEnumerable`, and then iterate through the entities in that collection and perform the same method on the `EntityKey` of each entity.

Casting to the `IEnumerable` is not a random act of coding. You need to cast the field to something in order to access it, but the `EntityCollection` surfaces as a generic `List<Payment>`, which causes a problem. Because this code is dynamic, you can't specify the type. It would be nice to cast it to a `List<EntityObject>`, but you cannot cast a generic `List<T>` to another generic `List<T>`. Therefore, casting to a standard list type, such as `ICollection` or `IEnumerable`, does the trick. Internally, there are advantages to using `IEnumerable`, so this was the winning target of the cast.

In Example 21-44, a line of code indicated a placeholder for iterating through the data. Replace that placeholder with the code in Example 21-47, which drills deep into the `FieldMetadata` hierarchy. The routine calls out to another method, `DisplayFields`, shown in Example 21-48.

Example 21-47. Iterating through the results and determining whether the navigation properties are entities or EntityCollections

```
foreach (IExtendedDataRecord record in results)
{
  var fieldMetadata = record.DataRecordInfo.FieldMetadata;
  for (int i = 0; i < record.FieldCount; i++)
  {
    //If the navigation property is an Entity, list its fields.
    switch (fieldMetadata[i].FieldType.TypeUsage.
      EdmType.BuiltInTypeKind)
    {
      case BuiltInTypeKind.EntityType:
        DisplayFields(((EntityObject)(record[i])).EntityKey, context);
        break;
      case BuiltInTypeKind.CollectionType:
        {
          var entities = (System.Collections.ICollection)(record[i]);
          foreach (EntityObject entity in entities )
            DisplayFields(entity.EntityKey, context);
        }
        break;
    }
  }
  Console.ReadKey();
}
```

The `DisplayFields` method takes the `EntityKey` and the context, and then digs into the `ObjectStateManager` to get the information it needs regarding the entity. Like the visualizer, this method takes into account the possibility of complex types, as shown in Example 21-48.

Example 21-48. The DisplayFields method getting the field names and values from metadata

```
private static void DisplayFields(EntityKey key, ObjectContext context)
{
  var entry = context.ObjectStateManager.GetObjectStateEntry(ekey);
  var fieldcount = entry.CurrentValues.FieldCount;
  var metadata = entry.CurrentValues.DataRecordInfo.FieldMetadata;
  Console.WriteLine(entry.CurrentValues.DataRecordInfo
                          .RecordType.EdmType.Name);
  for (var i = 0; i < fieldcount; i++)
  {
    switch (metadata[i].FieldType.TypeUsage.EdmType.BuiltInTypeKind)
    {
      case BuiltInTypeKind.PrimitiveType:
        Console.WriteLine(" " + metadata[i].FieldType.Name + ": " +
                          entEntry.CurrentValues[i].ToString());
        break;
```

```
        case BuiltInTypeKind.ComplexType:
          var complexType = entEntry.CurrentValues.GetDataRecord(i);
          for (var j = 0; j <= complexType.FieldCount; j++)
            Console.WriteLine("  " + cType.GetName(i) + ": " +
                              complexType[j].ToString());
          break;
      }
    }
    Console.WriteLine();
  }
```

Example 21-49 shows the final output of the sample, using the dynamically built Entity SQL query from Example 21-44 and the dynamically evaluated results.

Example 21-49. The results of the generic query displayed using generic code

```
Reservation
 ReservationID: 90
 ReservationDate: 12/4/2005 12:00:00 AM
 ContactID: 569
 TripID: 32
 RowVersion: System.Byte[]

Customer
 ContactID: 569
 FirstName: Cecil
 LastName: Allison
 Title: Mr.
 AddDate: 1/10/2004 5:46:14 PM
 ModifiedDate: 8/7/2008 8:27:07 AM
 RowVersion: System.Byte[]
 CustomerTypeID: 3
 InitialDate: 10/21/2003 6:19:27 AM
 PrimaryDestinationID: 48
 SecondaryDestinationID: 51
 PrimaryActivityID: 28
 SecondaryActivityID: 4
 Notes:
 BirthDate: 4/13/1988 12:00:00 AM
 HeightInches: 63
 WeightPounds: 152
 DietaryRestrictions:
 CustRowVersion: System.Byte[]

Trip
 TripID: 32
 DestinationID: 34
 LodgingID: 224
 StartDate: 3/4/2006 12:00:00 AM
 EndDate: 3/11/2006 12:00:00 AM
 TripCostUSD: 1500

Payment
 PaymentID: 8
 PaymentDate: 4/1/2005 12:00:00 AM
```

```
 ReservationID: 90
 Amount: 300.0000
 ModifiedDate: 4/1/2005 12:00:00 AM
 RowVersion: System.Byte[]

Payment
 PaymentID: 9
 PaymentDate: 5/2/2005 12:00:00 AM
 ReservationID: 90
 Amount: 1200.0000
 ModifiedDate: 5/2/2005 12:00:00 AM
 RowVersion: System.Byte[]
```

This demonstrates the power you can access by combining the `MetadataWorkspace` and the `ObjectStateManager`.

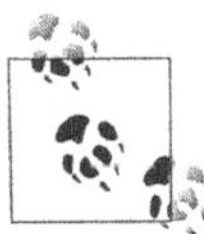

Zlatko Michailov's blog post titled "How to Parse an EntityDataReader" will give you the tools you need to iterate through the shaped results of an `EntityClient` query, identifying whether the items contain scalar values, a single entity object, an `EntityCollection`, and more. The post is at *http://blogs.msdn.com/esql/* in the November 2007 archive.

Creating and Manipulating Entities Dynamically

Now, you will combine what you have learned in this chapter in these last two examples, which will let you use the `MetadataWorkspace` and `ObjectStateManager` along with .NET's Reflection API to create entities on the fly without previous knowledge of their types. The second example will show you how to build not just an entity, but an entity graph dynamically and then persist modifications back to the database.

If you need to build reusable, generic code, there are a lot of important lessons embedded into these examples. If you do not anticipate building code like this, it is likely that you will find the capabilities exposed in these samples to be very educational with respect to how much control the Entity Framework runtime can put in your hands.

Creating EntityObjects Without Entity Classes

Much of the metadata work done in the previous examples used metadata to inspect existing classes that were created through an `ObjectContext`. What if you want to create classes without the benefit of the generated entity classes? For example, you could have an application that works with any Entity Framework EDM passed to it that has no previous knowledge of the classes.

You can do this by combining the `MetadataWorkspace` API with `System.Reflection`.

Although many people are familiar with using `System.Reflection` for inspecting .NET objects, you also can use it to instantiate objects using type information. You can generate that type information through the MetadataWorkspace API and then let reflection create object instances for you.

> **For System.Reflection Newbies**
>
> Although System.Reflection sounds like a daunting topic (it certainly did to me at one point), once you've used it a few times it's not so scary. Types in .NET have classes that you can instantiate—for example, you just saw some code where an assembly object was instantiated using an assembly file.
>
> In the same way you have been investigating the metadata with the MetadataWorkspace API, System.Reflection allows you to open assemblies and read information about modules, classes, parameters, events, and so forth. For example, Assembly has a method called GetTypes, which returns all of the types defined in the assembly.
>
> Also, Assembly has a CreateInstance method, which allows you to create an instance of an object. Assembly.CreateInstance calls System.Activator.CreateInstance, which you can also use directly.
>
> You can do a lot of amazing things with System.Reflection. Look for the MSDN documentation topic titled "Reflection Overview" for more information.

Creating a new entity with CreateInstance

You can instantiate a new class using the CreateInstance method of either System.Activator or System.Reflection.Assembly. Using Assembly.CreateInstance requires that you have a type instance of an assembly. Internally, Assembly.CreateInstance will eventually call Activator.CreateInstance.

There are reasons for choosing one over the other, but Assembly.CreateInstance suits the needs of these examples since the sample will do some other things with the assembly.

> **ObjectStateManager and MetadataWorkspace Versus Reflection**
>
> You can see how similar reflection is to the MetadataWorkspace API by calling Assembly.GetTypes:
>
> ```
> Dim someTypes = myAssembly.GetTypes _
> .Where(Function(t) t.BaseType.Name = "EntityObject")
> ```
>
> So, why use one over the other?
>
> Each API offers functionality that is not available in the other. For example, reflection lets you create new instances of objects, whereas the ObjectStateManager doesn't. Furthermore, the ObjectStateManager has methods and properties that are specific to entities, such as GetKeyMembers. However, some of the functionality overlaps, most notably the ability to set values. Although doing this with reflection takes fewer steps, setting values on EntityObjects using the CurrentValueRecord.SetValue and related

SetString, SetDateTime, and similar methods performs much better. So, it will not be uncommon to mix the two APIs in a solution.

Getting a reference to an assembly. You can load an assembly into an Assembly type in a number of ways. One way is to use an existing object that comes from that assembly.

For example, if you have created a Customer object from the BreakAway model's assembly, you can use that object to get a handle to the assembly using the static method Assembly.GetAssembly, as shown in Example 21-50.

Example 21-50. Loading an assembly programmatically

```
var customer=context.Customers.First();
var assembly=Assembly.GetAssembly(customer.GetType);
```

Creating an entity from the assembly. Now you can use this assembly object to instantiate any class within the assembly. You can do this by passing in the strongly typed name of the class, as shown in Example 21-51.

Example 21-51. Instantiating a class in the assembly

```
var payment = assembly.CreateInstance("BAGA.Payment");
```

This will create a new Payment object instance.

You can see how using reflection can let you build dynamic code. You can create objects just by passing in a string.

Notice that the strong name of the type does not use the model name, as you are required to do when working with the metadata. Instead, it needs the strongly typed name of the class as it is known to the assembly, and in this example, the assembly's namespace is BAGA.

Using System.Type to inspect the EntityType

The object in the preceding section is a Payment entity, which has only the methods and properties of a Payment entity. That hasn't gotten you very far with dynamic programming.

However, you can additionally create a Type object, either directly from the assembly or from the Payment instance. (See Example 21-52.)

Example 21-52. Creating a Type object to be used with reflection

```
var typeInfo=assembly.GetType("BAGA.Payment");
```

A Type object allows you to do the same type of detective work on the Payment type that you did on the metadata.

System.Type also lets you set values. Although setting scalar values using an Entity Framework CurrentValueRecord provides better performance, you cannot modify any other properties. System.Type will allow you to access and modify all of the properties of the object, including navigation properties. You'll do this in the next example.

Creating Entities and Graphs Dynamically

Now it's time to try out some of these tricks. The following example is a culmination of many of the techniques explained in this chapter, from using the MetadataWorkspace to dynamically creating relationships on the fly using the RelationshipManager. The code enables you to create entities, build a graph, and save the graph data—all with generic code that has no knowledge of the entity classes that it will work with. The example in this section will do the following:

1. Receive information about an existing parent entity and the child to be created dynamically. An array of KeyValuePairs will be used to provide field names and values for populating the new object.
2. Query the model to retrieve the parent entity.
3. Create a new instance of the child.
4. Populate the child with the data.
5. Attach the child to the parent using the RelationshipManager shown earlier in this chapter.
6. Save the new child to the database.

You will do all of this without any references to the actual entity types so that you can use any parent and child with the method.

The method shown in Example 21-53 takes advantage of a few custom extension methods that are listed in the following example. The extension methods are handy for a lot of MetadataWorkspace and ObjectStateManager scenarios.

Comments throughout the code explain what's happening in detail.

Example 21-53. Building an entity graph dynamically with database interaction

```
private static bool AddChildToParentObject<TEntity, TChildEntity>
 (ObjectContext context,
  KeyValuePair<string, int> parentId,
  KeyValuePair<string, object>[] fieldValues)
    where TEntity : class
    where TChildEntity : class
{
  var metadataWorkspace = context.MetadataWorkspace;
  string childSetName = context.CreateObjectSet<TChildEntity>().EntitySet.Name;
  string parentSetName = context.CreateObjectSet<TEntity>().EntitySet.Name;


  ObjectQuery<TEntity> parentQuery =
```

```
        context.CreateObjectSet<TEntity>()
               .Where("it." + parentId.Key + "=" + parentId.Value.ToString());

  TEntity parentObject = parentQuery.FirstOrDefault();
  if (parentObject == null)
  {
    return false;
  }

  var assembly = Assembly.GetAssembly(parentObject.GetType());
  //System.Type of the child entity for type inspection
  Type childType = assembly.GetTypes()
                                .First(t => t.Name == typeof(TChildEntity).Name);
  var childEntity = Activator.CreateInstance(childType);

  //association name to get the related end
  //GetAssociationName is a custom extension method
  var associationName = metadataWorkspace.GetAssociationName
                      (childSetName, parentSetName);

  //this works for EntityObjects and POCOs, too
  var parentRelMgr =
    context.ObjectStateManager.GetObjectStateEntry(parentObject).RelationshipManager;

  var parentRelatedEnd = parentRelMgr.GetRelatedEnd(associationName, childSetName);

  parentRelatedEnd.Add(childEntity);

  //modify child properties through ObjectStateEntry, _
  //provides better performance in this case than with reflection
  var childEntry = context.ObjectStateManager.GetObjectStateEntry(childEntity);

  //iterate through FieldValues passed in to assign the properties
  foreach (var item in fieldValues)
  {
    childEntry.CurrentValues.SetValue
      (childEntry.GetOrdinalforProperty(item.Key), item.Value);
  }
  return true;
}
```

A lot is going on in this example, but you learned most of it earlier in the chapter. The example serves two purposes. First, it demonstrates how to use reflection to create entities dynamically, as well as how to build graphs dynamically. Second, it demonstrates the combined power of the `ObjectStateManager`, the `MetadataWorkspace`, and reflection to build dynamic code, whether it is an entire application that is purely dynamic or part of an application that needs to be dynamic.

Custom extension methods used by AddChildToParentObject

The `AddChildToParentObject` method leverages two custom methods. One is an extension method for `MetadataWorkspace` and the other is for `ObjectStateEntry`. Example 21-54 lists these two methods.

Example 21-54. The GetAssociationName extension method

```
public static string GetAssociationName
  (this MetadataWorkspace metadataWorkspace, string endA, string endB)
{
  return (from a in metadataWorkspace.GetItems<AssociationType>(DataSpace.CSpace)
          where a.AssociationEndMembers.Any(ae => ae.Name == endA)
          where a.AssociationEndMembers.Any(ae => ae.Name == endB)
          select a.Name).FirstOrDefault();
}
public static int GetOrdinalByPropertyName
 (this ObjectStateEntry ose, string propertyName)
{
  var property = ose.CurrentValues.DataRecordInfo.FieldMetadata
               .Where(f => f.FieldType.Name == propertyName).FirstOrDefault();
  if (property.FieldType != null)
  {
    return property.Ordinal;
  }
  else {
    throw new ArgumentOutOfRangeException("propertyName",
         "No such property found: " + propertyName);
  }
}
```

Calling the AddChildToParentObject method

The `AddChildToParentObject` method takes its parent and child types as generic types and requires a number of values to be passed in as parameters, as listed here and shown in Example 21-55, where the method is called:

- The key field name and value for the parent, which are bundled in a `KeyValuePair`. This allows the method to query the database for the parent record. The method assumes that only a single value is required for the key, which will suffice for most cases.
- An array of `KeyValuePairs`, which take a string and an object. Each key/value pair represents the field name and value of the fields that will be populated for the new child entity.

Example 21-55. Calling the dynamic method

```
Reservation res;
using (var context = new BAPOCOs())
{
  var kvpParent = new KeyValuePair<string, int>("ReservationID", res.10);
  KeyValuePair<string, object>[] kvpChildValues = {
        new KeyValuePair<string, object>("PaymentDate", DateTime.Now),
        new KeyValuePair<string, object>("Amount", (Decimal) 400)};
  if (
    AddChildToParentObject<Reservation, Payment>
     (context, kvpParent, kvpChildValues))
  {
    context.SaveChanges();
```

```
    }
}
```

Out of context, this looks like a lot of work—even more work than just using classic ADO.NET. But if you need to create dynamic functionality in your applications that can handle any entity types you throw at it, this is definitely the way to go.

Summary

In this chapter, you investigated `ObjectStateManager` and `MetadataWorkspace`—the two APIs that provide most of the internal functionality of the Entity Framework—and you put them to work. Using the same classes and features that Object Services and `EntityClient` use to parse queries and materialize objects, you learned how to create a variety of dynamic functionality and explored some useful scenarios for taking advantage of these features.

In addition to your new knowledge, you now have at your disposal a slew of methods and utilities that you can use in your applications, such as:

- A set of handy overloads to extract `ObjectStateEntries` from the `ObjectStateManager`
- A method to allow you to explore objects that are being managed by the context
- A number of methods for working with entities without knowing in advance what their types will be

Although you might not be able to overcome some of the more sophisticated challenges in your applications with a simple method that is already available in the Entity Framework, access to these low-level tools enables you to build your own tools and functionality. And keep in mind that you have the entire .NET framework at your disposal to solve your application challenges. Don't always expect to lean on the Entity Framework runtime just because you are using entities.

CHAPTER 22

Handling Exceptions

Things can go awry in many ways when you're querying or updating entities. You might attempt to save entities to the database that are missing related data—a reservation without a trip, perhaps, or a reservation without a customer. The database might have a constraint that is not reflected in the model; if a user saves data that breaks the rule of the constraint, the database will throw an error. Or someone may have modified or even deleted a record while another user was editing it.

The Entity Framework includes a specialized set of exceptions for capturing problems like these that arise during query compilation and command execution.

In your application, you should embed each query execution or call you make to `SaveChanges` in some sort of mechanism for catching these. When one of these exceptions is raised, it is up to your code to handle it.

In this chapter, we'll look at exceptions that are unique to the Entity Framework and how to handle them. Some exceptions are Entity Framework-specific exceptions, and others are .NET exceptions caused by faulty operations when using the Entity Framework.

You should strongly consider exception handling for any application you write. If this is a new topic for you, plenty of resources are available on the Web, in the MSDN documentation, and in a variety of books to teach you accepted patterns and practices for implementing exception handling in .NET.

Preparing for Exceptions

In Object Services, you can get exceptions from the moment you try to instantiate an `ObjectContext` to the time you call `SaveChanges`. Use `try/catch` blocks around this functionality to capture exceptions.

In these examples, I show the catch clause calling imaginary methods such as MyExceptionHandler.

For instance, you can dispose the context in the finally clause in case it was instantiated before the error occurred, as shown in Example 22-1.

Example 22-1. Catching an exception and disposing the ObjectContext in finally

```
BAEntities context = null;
try
{
  context = new BAEntities();
  var res = context.Reservations.First();
  return res;
}
catch (Exception ex)
{
  MyExceptionHandler(ex);
}
finally
{

  if (context != null){
    context.Dispose();
  }
}
```

When you employ the using block in the context's instantiation, as shown in Example 22-2, the context and any resources that it controls will be disposed at the end of the block. The using block is wrapped in a try/catch so that an exception can be handled—for example, with an imaginary MyExceptionHandler method.

When it sees a using block, the compiler actually creates a try/finally block with a call to dispose in the finally.

Example 22-2. Catching an exception when ObjectContext is automatically disposed

```
try
{
  using (BAEntities context = new BAEntities())
  {
    var res = context.Reservations.First();
  }
}
catch (Exception ex)
{
```

```
  MyExceptionHandler(ex);
}
```

Exceptions can occur when you're creating connections and executing commands with `EntityClient`. It's equally important to capture those exceptions and be sure the connections and `DataReaders` are properly disposed. Example 22-3 shows a `using` block being employed to ensure that these objects are disposed. The `using` block is wrapped by a `try/catch` block so that exceptions thrown from inside the `using` block can be caught and reported—for example, by the same imaginary `MyExceptionHandler` method used in Example 22-2.

Example 22-3. Catching an exception when using EntityClient

```
var eSql = "SELECT VALUE r FROM BAEntities.Reservations AS r";
try
{
  using (var connection =  new EntityConnection("Name = BAEntities"))
  {
    var command = connection.CreateCommand();
    EntityDataReader dataReader = null;
    command.CommandText = eSql;
    connection.Open();
    dataReader = command.ExecuteReader
     (CommandBehavior.SequentialAccess | CommandBehavior.CloseConnection);
    while (dataReader.Read())
    {
      //process results
    }
    connection.Close();
  }
}
catch (Exception ex)
{
  MyExceptionHandler(ex);
}
```

The variables that were instantiated inside the `using` block—`eConn`, `eComm`, and `eReader`—will all be disposed at the end of the block even if an exception is thrown from within that block. Therefore, you don't need to explicitly dispose them.

As an example, if there was a problem with the Entity SQL string, a `System.Data.EntitySqlException` will be thrown from the `using` block and caught in the `catch` block.

Handling EntityConnectionString Exceptions

A number of problems are the result of a missing, misinformed, or even malformed `EntityConnectionString`. Let's first look at what exceptions you might encounter and then how to handle them.

Connection String Can't Be Found or Is Improperly Configured: System.ArgumentException

When you instantiate an `ObjectContext`, the context requires an `EntityConnection`, which in turn depends on the `EntityConnectionString`.

If the default or specified connection string cannot be found either in the application's *.config* file or in other locations that you've designated, a `System.ArgumentException` will be thrown that reads as follows:

```
The specified named connection is either not found in the configuration,
 not intended to be used with the EntityClient provider, or not valid.
```

You will get this error if you are creating the `EntityConnection` directly and are passing in a connection string name with the same problem.

This is easier to deal with during debug mode than at runtime. In debug mode, check your entity connection string. If you are relying on the default in the *.config* file, make sure its name matches the `EntityContainer` name of your model. In our examples, the `EntityContainer` is `BAEntities` and the connection string should have the same name:

```
<connectionStrings>
<add name="BAEntities"  .... />
```

If that's not the problem, check that the string doesn't contain some type of invalid formatting.

Metadata Files Cannot Be Found: System.Data.MetadataException

This is a problem that developers encounter frequently.

The metadata attribute of the connection string has the names and paths of the model files (e.g., *BAModel.csdl*, *BAModel.msl*, *BAModel.ssdl*) hardcoded into it. The path could be a file path:

```
res:C:/BAModel.csdl|C:/BAModel.ssdl|C:/BAModel.msl
```

or a notation that indicates the files are embedded in an assembly:

```
res://*/BAModel.csdl|res://*/BAModel.ssdl|res://*/BAModel.msl
```

Many times in the `ObjectContext` life cycle these files need to be read. When you instantiate the context, it looks for the files. If the files specified in the metadata tag cannot be found in the designated file path or in one of the referenced assemblies, a `System.Data.MetadataException` will be thrown.

If you have changed the name of the EDMX file in your solution, this can cause problems with the metadata attribute.

Handling Connection String Exceptions

Example 22-4 shows how to prepare for possible exceptions the aforementioned problems can throw. It looks for the message related to a missing or invalid `ConnectionString` as well as the `MetadataException`. You can handle the errors right in the code or throw them to the calling code.

Example 22-4. Catching a connection string problem in an ArgumentException

```
catch (ArgumentException ex)
{
  if (ex.Message.Contains("specified named connection is either not found"))
  {
    MyBadConnectionNameExceptionHandler(ex);
  }
  else
  {  MyArgumentExceptionHandler(ex);
  }
}
catch (MetadataException ex)
{
    MyMetadataExceptionHandler(ex);
}
catch (Exception ex)
{
  MyExceptionHandler(ex);
}
```

It's not easy to resolve these types of problems in your code, and your best resolution in your exception handler is to exit out of the method elegantly, provide the end user with some information, and log the error in such a way that an administrator or support person can assist with the issue. The `System.Data.MetadataException` or `System.ArgumentException` contains no special information other than the message itself. You will benefit by using standard exception-handling methods, such as reporting the message along with the connection string and where the message came from.

Handling Query Compilation Exceptions

If the connection succeeds, the next thing you will probably do that involves an Entity Framework-related exception is to create and execute a query. Again, let's first look at the possible exceptions and then how to handle them, where possible.

Invalid LINQ to Entities Query Expressions: System.NotSupportedException

LINQ's syntax has the benefit of IntelliSense and compile-time checking, so it is less prone to runtime errors. However, certain syntax will be valid to the compiler, but not when it comes time to process the query.

A good example of this is the use of the .NET method `ToShortDateString()`. The following LINQ query passes through the compiler's checks because `ToShortDateString` is a valid method for a `Date` type:

```
from r in context.Reservations select r.ReservationDate.ToShortDateString()
```

But at runtime, when it attempts to compile the query into a native store command, it will discover that `ToShortDateString` has no direct mapping to any function in the store. Thus, the store command cannot be created, which results in a `System.NotSupportedException` with the following message:

```
LINQ to Entities does not recognize the method 'System.String ToShortDateString()'
method, and this method cannot be translated into a store expression.
```

You should be able to catch these during debug mode.

Invalid Entity SQL Query Expressions: EntitySqlException

`EntitySqlException` will probably be the most common exception you will encounter as you are learning Entity SQL and debugging your applications. So, you might as well make friends with it straightaway. Also, remember that the query builder methods can help you with a good portion of your Entity SQL queries, even though they provide only a subset of the operators and functions you can use when you write Entity SQL directly.

`EntitySqlException` is thrown when your Entity SQL expression cannot be parsed or processed. You should be testing every one of the Entity SQL expressions you write so that you don't have any runtime surprises. However, if you are building dynamic queries, chances are greater that bad syntax will sneak in. And there are always the "what if" scenarios that you can't even imagine until they occur, but that you might lie awake worrying about at night. So, rather than lose sleep, you can hedge your bets by making sure you catch any of the exceptions properly.

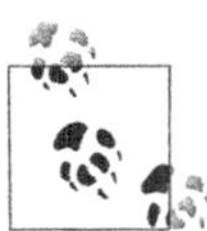

Don't forget about using LINQPad to test your LINQ to Entities and Entity SQL query expressions, which you were introduced to in early chapters of this book. It's a great help for testing queries and expressions without having to constantly debug your code to do so.

Here's an example of a malformed expression where the `AS` operator is missing (a common mistake). The expression should be using `AS con` after `contacts`; but with that missing, the variable `con` used elsewhere in the expression has no meaning.

```
SELECT VALUE con FROM BAEntities.contacts WHERE left(con.Lastname,1)='S'
```

The exception passes back some very helpful information contained in its properties.

The exception details are as follows:

`Column= 61`

In the preceding code, column `61` is where `con.Lastname` begins.

`ErrorContext= multipart identifier`

`multipart identifier` refers to the fact that multiple items (`con` and `Lastname`) exist and the parser has an issue with one (or more) of them. If the expression had selected a single value (`SELECT VALUE con`), the `ErrorContext` would be a single-part identifier.

`ErrorDescription = "'con.Lastname' could not be resolved in the current scope or context. Make sure that all referenced variables are in scope, that required schemas are loaded, and that namespaces are referenced correctly."`

Again, this is saying that the parser just can't figure out what `con.Lastname` is, and is listing all of the possible causes.

Another example occurs when you use incorrect functions or operators. Even the provider-specific functions and operators will be checked here. For instance, the following expression will throw an error because it incorrectly uses `SqlServer.AVERAGE` instead of the correct function, `SqlServer.AVG`:

```
SELECT VALUE SqlServer.AVERAGE(p.amount)
FROM BAEntities.Payments  AS p
```

The exception's message will read as follows:

```
'SqlServer.AVERAGE' cannot be resolved into a valid type constructor or function,
near function, method or type constructor, line 1, column 30."
```

The line break is not accounted for in the message. In addition, the parsing occurs long before any attempts to touch the database are made.

Handling an EntitySqlException

Example 22-5 shows the newly added `catch` block to trap an `EntitySqlException`.

Example 22-5. Adding a check for an Entity SQL problem

```
catch (EntitySqlException ex)
{
   MyESqlExceptionHandler(ex);
}
catch (ArgumentException ex)
{
  if (ex.Message.Contains("specified named connection is either not found"))
  {
    MyBadConnectionNameExceptionHandler(ex);
  }
  else
  {
    MyArgumentExceptionHandler(ex);
  }
}
catch (MetadataException ex)
```

```
{
  MyMetadataExceptionHandler(ex);
}
catch (Exception ex)
{
  MyExceptionHandler(ex);
}
```

EntityCommandCompilationException Thrown by the Store Provider

Command compilation occurs when the Entity Framework creates the command tree to represent a store query. It's possible that the provider compiling the query is causing a problem. In this case, an `EntityCommandCompilationException` will be thrown with the following message, and no additional details:

```
An error occurred while preparing the command definition.
```

This is another tricky one to solve, although you won't be able to solve it in your code. The best you can do is to log the exception, inform the user if necessary, and gracefully exit the method. In a more layered application you may desire different behavior in response to the exception.

Creating a Common Wrapper to Handle Query Execution Exceptions

If you have a defined system for handling or perhaps logging errors, you wouldn't want to rewrite that handling code for every query. Instead, you could build a set of wrappers to execute queries and handle particular exceptions. Each wrapper method would take either an `ObjectQuery` or a LINQ to Entities query as an argument and return either a single object or some type of enumerable collection of objects. If the query execution fails, the method could provide code to handle the different types of exceptions.

Here are the signatures of two methods, each with the two overloads for `ObjectQuery` or LINQ to Entities queries. The first method returns a single entity and the second returns a `List` of entities:

```
public TEntity GetFirstorDefault<TEntity>(ObjectQuery<TEntity> objectQuery)
public TEntity GetFirstorDefault<TEntity>(IQueryable<TEntity> L2EQuery)

public List<TEntity> GetList<TEntity>(ObjectQuery<TEntity> objectQuery)
public List<TEntity> GetList<TEntity>(IQueryable <TEntity> L2EQuery)
```

Each method executes the given query and returns the requested result. For example, the first method would call `return objectQuery.FirstOrDefault()` to execute the query. The two methods that take `ObjectQuery` parameters can take an `ObjectQuery` whether it was created using `context.CreateQuery`, a new `ObjectQuery`, or a `QueryBuilder` method. The methods that accept LINQ to Entities queries can take straight LINQ to Entities queries or those that were created by invoking a `CompiledQuery`.

Example 22-6 shows the first of these methods with all of its `Exceptions` stubbed out. Remember that the `ObjectQuery` queries can throw `EntitySqlExceptions`, while the LINQ to Entities queries can throw `InvalidOperationExceptions`.

Example 22-6. The GetFirstOrDefault wrapper method for executing ObjectQuery queries

```
public TEntity GetFirstOrDefault<TEntity>(ObjectQuery<TEntity> objectQuery)
{
  try
  {
    return objectQuery.FirstOrDefault();
  }
  catch (EntitySqlException ex)
  {
    MyESqlExceptionHandler(ex);
  }
  catch (ArgumentException ex)
  {
    if (ex.Message.Contains("specified named connection is either not found"))
    {
      MyBadConnectionNameExceptionHandler(ex);
    }
    else
    {
      MyArgumentExceptionHandler(ex);
    }
  }
   catch (MetadataException ex)
  {
    MyMetadataExceptionHandler(ex);
  }
  catch (Exception ex)
  {
    MyExceptionHandler(ex);
    throw(ex); //a single example of throwing
               // the exception back to the calling code
  }
}
```

Example 22-7 shows code that calls the `GetList` method overload to execute a LINQ query.

Example 22-7. Executing a LINQ to Entities query with the GetList method

```
var query = context.Contacts.OfType<Customer>()
                   .Include("Reservations")
                   .Where(c => c.Reservations.Any());
var custList = dal.GetList<Customer>(query);
```

If you want error handling in the calling code to handle particular scenarios, you will need to throw the exceptions after handling them, demonstrated in the final `catch` block of Example 22-6. But these query helper methods allow you to avoid repeating exception-handling code that you may want to repeat for every query. Note that you don't necessarily need to return defined entities from the queries. You could return a DbDataRecord, a List<DbDataRecord>, or any other predefined class. The only thing that you can't return would be an anonymous type that results from a LINQ to Entities projection because anonymous types are designed only to work within the method that creates them.

Handling Exceptions Thrown During SaveChanges Command Execution

When it's time to save changes back to the database you have another set of problems to be aware of. The connection issues raised earlier in this chapter will come into play if you are instantiating a new ObjectContext or EntityConnection to perform the update. But the data itself causes other problems. The Entity Framework will catch some of the problems and prevent the data from going to the database. The database will detect others and will return an error to the application.

UpdateException: Thrown When Independent Association Mapping Constraints Are Broken

This type of UpdateException is particular to independent associations where foreign keys are not present. If you have violated a relationship constraint built into the model, an UpdateException will be thrown.

In a relationship without foreign keys, relationships are mapping constraints. If an association defines a 1:* (One to Many) relationship between two entities, any child in that relationship that is being saved needs to have some evidence of a parent. Even if the parent entity is not attached to the child, the EntityReference must have an EntityKey. Example 22-8 shows a new reservation being created in memory and added to the context, which then calls SaveChanges. But no Customer is associated with the context, not even an EntityKey for the CustomerReference. As a result, this call to SaveChanges will fail.

Example 22-8. A SaveChanges call that will fail because the new reservation has no Customer identified

```
var res = new Reservation();
res.Trip = myTrip; //this Trip instance exists in memory
res.ReservationDate = DateTime.Today;
using (var context = new BAEntities())
{
  context.Reservations.AddObject(res);
  context.SaveChanges(); //fails
}
```

With the independent association, SaveChanges throws an UpdateException with the following message:

```
Entities in 'BAEntities.Reservations' participate in the FK_Reservations_Customers'
relationship.
0 related 'Customers' were found. 1 'Customers' is expected.
```

The ObjectContext doesn't do this type of validation when you add the reservation to the context, because you might attach a Customer; set its CustomerID; or in the case of entities that inherit from EntityObject, assign the CustomerReference.EntityKey, later. Therefore, the only time it's confident that you have no intention of identifying a Customer is when you are calling SavingChanges, and that's when it does its check.

You should detect this type of problem before your code goes into production. You can also employ your own business rules to perform these types of checks before it's time to call SaveChanges. You'll find validation code being executed as part of a SaveChanges command in later chapters of this book.

For example, you could have specific rules in the Reservation class that test to see whether a Customer is defined by checking for the presence of the CustomerReference.EntityKey or by checking that the Customer property is not null. The code behind SaveChanges uses the MetadataWorkspace to read the model, identify the constraints, and then check the entities in the cache to see whether they pass or fail the constraints. You could write similar generic code to perform this type of function as well, if it makes sense for you to do so.

UpdateException: Thrown by Broken Constraints in the Database

Unsatisfied relationships that are defined by foreign keys will also throw an UpdateException, but the exception will most likely be the result of an error returned by the database. I discussed this problem earlier in Chapter 19 in the section "Understanding Referential Integrity and Constraints" on page 539. Other constraints may not be defined in the mappings or handled by any business logic. If Example 22-8 were run against our current model where the relationship between reservation and customer is defined using the Reservation.CustomerID, the UpdateException's error will be different than in the previous case. The error message will be:

```
An error occurred while updating the entries. See the inner exception
for details.
```

The inner exception comes from the database provider—for example, a System.Data.SqlClientException with the message:

```
The INSERT statement conflicted with the FOREIGN KEY constraint
"FK_Reservations_Customers". The conflict occurred in database
"BreakAway", table "dbo.Customers", column 'ContactID'. The statement
has been terminated.
```

Another common problem with a foreign key constraint occurs when the database does not define a cascading delete. Such is the case with the BreakAway database, which will not automatically delete all payments related to a reservation if that reservation is being deleted. Therefore, if an attempt is made to delete a reservation that would leave orphaned `Payment` records, the database will throw an error and will not execute the delete command. That error is passed back to the client. If the client is the Entity Framework and the error was a result of a `SaveChanges` call, an `UpdateException` will be thrown with the following message:

```
The DELETE statement conflicted with the REFERENCE constraint
"FK_Payments_Reservations".

The conflict occurred in database "BreakAway", table "dbo.Payments",
column 'ReservationID'.
```

Relying on Entity Framework to Automatically Roll Back When an UpdateException Occurs

In Chapter 20, you learned that `SaveChanges` is wrapped in an implicit transaction. If an `UpdateException` is thrown during the call to `SaveChanges`, this halts the entire `SaveChanges` method and causes any previously executed commands to be rolled back. Entity Framework will not commit changes to the in-memory entities until the entire transaction has succeeded.

Gleaning Details from UpdateException

`UpdateException` is part of the `System.Data.Entity` API and is an Object Services exception. It inherits from .NET's `DataException` class and adds to it a valuable piece of information: the `ObjectStateEntry` of the entity being processed when the error occurred.

Figure 22-1 shows the `UpdateException` thrown by `SaveChanges` in Example 22-8, where the `Reservation` has no `Customer`.

Name	Value
⊟ ex	{"An error occurred while updating the entries. See the i
⊟ [System.Data.UpdateException]	{"An error occurred while updating the entries. See the i
⊞ base	{"An error occurred while updating the entries. See the i
⊟ StateEntries	Count = 1
⊟ [0]	{System.Data.Objects.EntityEntry}
⊞ [System.Data.Objects.EntityEntr	{System.Data.Objects.EntityEntry}
⊞ Entity	{BAGA.Reservation}
⊞ EntityKey	"EntitySet=Reservations"
⊞ EntitySet	{Reservations}
IsRelationship	false
⊞ ObjectStateManager	{System.Data.Objects.ObjectStateManager}
⊞ RelationshipManager	{System.Data.Objects.DataClasses.RelationshipManager}
State	Added

Figure 22-1. Exceptions from Object Services containing an ObjectStateEntry

In the exception, you can see the `StateEntries` property. Multiple entries can appear in this property; for example, if you have relationships to other entities being managed by the context, the `RelationshipEntry` objects will be in this collection. But only the primary entry will be displayed in the debug window. And in this window you can see the `ObjectStateEntry` that is related to the `Reservation`, and that the entry has a pointer back to the entity.

If you want to you can log this information or present it to the user.

Because the context might be tracking a number of entities, it's not always going to be obvious which entity caused the problem. By having this information returned in the exception, you can handle the exception intelligently.

Planning for Other Exceptions Related to the Entity Framework

A number of other exceptions derive from the generic `System.Data.EntityException`. Although some of these exceptions are internal, some may be raised simply as an `EntityException`.

For example, if there is a problem with the database server during command execution, an `EntityException` with the following message could be thrown:

```
"An error occurred while starting a transaction on the provider connection.
See the inner exception for details."
```

The `InnerException` will contain the actual error from the database, such as the following error in which, for dramatic effect, the SQL Server service was paused on the server:

```
"SQL Server service has been paused. No new connections will be allowed.
To resume the service, use SQL Computer Manager or the Services application
in Control Panel. Login failed for user 'domain\julie'. A severe error occurred
on the current command.  The results, if any, should be discarded."
```

Although these are the exceptions you will most likely encounter, check the documentation of the `EntityException` base class to learn about some of the other exceptions that can occur during query and command execution.

Not all exceptions that occur when working with entities occur during query or command execution. One example you may encounter is the `System.InvalidOperationException`. This will be thrown when, for instance, you try to detach an entity that is not attached to the context.

`InvalidOperationException` is another exception you may want to plan for when working with entities.

Handling Concurrency Exceptions

Another important exception in the Entity Framework is the `OptimisticConcurrencyException`, which can be thrown when there are conflicts during database updates. The next chapter is devoted to understanding how concurrency works in the Entity Framework, how you can impact Entity Framework's behavior, and how to handle the conflicts when they occur.

Summary

In this chapter, you saw that there are many opportunities for exceptions to be thrown when querying or updating entities. You'll need to catch these exceptions and do something about them, or you will have some very unhappy end users.

The various examples of handling these exceptions showed the handler within the code where the exception occurred. Another common pattern is to raise exceptions to a common `ExceptionHandler` that you can use throughout your application. This is not specific to the Entity Framework, and you can find plenty of guidance on .NET exception handling in the documentation, articles, and other books that focus on handling exceptions.

Now let's learn about concurrency and how to handle exceptions that are specific to problems related to database concurrency.

CHAPTER 23

Planning for Concurrency Problems

Concurrency issues are the bane of data access developers. In any sizable organization, it is not uncommon for multiple users or services to be processing the same sets of information. Not infrequently, different users may be updating the same piece of data concurrently, and a conflict occurs. For instance, a salesperson could be modifying a payment at the same time an accounting system is processing it. Or a scheduler might delete a calendar item while another person in a different department was in the middle of editing the same item.

These are two very different types of concurrency problems. In the first problem, you need to consider whose changes are saved. Does the accounting system rule over the salesperson, or vice versa? Do you simply take the last changes that were sent to the database, overriding the changes that were just saved moments ago? In some organizations, the focus is on a single record, whereas other organizations might get as granular as worrying about which fields in the record were updated by whom.

Another common type of concurrency problem occurs when a user tries to save changes to data that no longer exists in the database. What do you do then? You might minimally want to inform the user about the problem and give her an opportunity to take further action, if she has the proper permissions.

It is a tangled web of conundrums and decision making on the part of the application designer. Once your organization has devised the rules, it is up to the developer to implement them.

In this chapter you'll learn how to set up your model so that the Entity Framework will alert you to conflicts when persisting data to the database, and then you'll learn how to capture and handle `OptimisticConcurrencyExceptions`.

Understanding Database Concurrency Conflicts

In the database world, there are two ways to deal with concurrency conflicts. One involves pessimistic concurrency, where you expect the worst; the other is optimistic concurrency, where you hope for the best.

With pessimistic concurrency the database row is locked when a user retrieves that data and is then released when the user is finished working with that row. Nobody else can touch that data until the row is unlocked. It greatly reduces the potential of conflicts, but it comes at a price. Pessimistic concurrency is not scalable, because it maintains open connections and it can cause excessive locking, long waits, or even deadlocks.

A number of data access technologies do not support pessimistic concurrency because of the overhead involved. ADO.NET does not support it naturally (although it can be simulated), nor does the ADO.NET Entity Framework. Therefore, this chapter will not cover pessimistic concurrency, but will focus instead on optimistic concurrency.

Optimistic concurrency does not lock the database rows, and relies on you, the developer, to provide logic in your application to handle potential update conflicts.

Concurrency is an age-old problem for anybody who designs line-of-business applications, and there is no silver bullet solution. You need to understand your business rules, be aware that these scenarios will need to be considered, and build your business logic to follow the rules you desire.

The Entity Framework does not magically solve the problem for you, either; however, it does provide tools for you to implement your business logic.

Understanding Optimistic Concurrency Options in the Entity Framework

With Entity Framework, what are your options when multiple people (or processes) are concurrently editing data? First we'll survey the lay of the land, and then we'll dig into implementation.

A few solutions are commonly used; however, a narrower field of applications will process concurrency conflicts in a very granular way, which is not as common.

We'll look at these options as they are generally used in software and then focus on how the Entity Framework addresses them.

Ignoring Concurrency Conflicts

Many small systems don't even worry about these conflicts. When a user saves her changes, they are written to the database regardless of what anybody else is doing or has done.

The Entity Framework's default commands play an interesting role here. Because an Entity Framework update will update only the fields the user edited, it's possible that concurrent editing won't even cause a problem. Imagine that User A retrieves a `Customer` record, and while she is editing that record User B edits the same `Customer`, changing the `BirthDate` property. User B saves his changes. User A modifies the `Customer`'s `Notes` field and saves. The Entity Framework will write a command to update the `Notes` field for that `Customer`. It won't touch the `BirthDate`, so all of the edits by both users are safe.

When using stored procedures to update, however, this scenario won't be so rosy. Typically, a procedure will update every field regardless of its status. So, in that case, the original `BirthDate` value will be saved back to the database, and User B's changes will simply disappear.

Forcing the User's Data to the Server (ClientWins)

In a system designed to alert you of conflicts, the system would alert you when User A attempts to save her data, indicating that the record has been modified since the time she initially retrieved it. In the Entity Framework, one possible response in this case is to force the current user's updates to the database. This is also referred to as *client wins*. It's different from ignoring the conflict, however, because it will update all of the values in the entity, even those that have not been edited. The impact in the scenario described in the preceding section is that the `BirthDate` field and every other field in the database record will be changed to reflect the user's version of the data. It would have the same effect as a stored procedure update.

Refreshing the User's Data with Server Data (StoreWins)

In this second possible resolution, when the conflict is detected the user's data is refreshed from the server. The entity that she has just modified in her application will be updated to reflect the server's current version of the data. Any edits she made will be lost. That may sound malicious, but if this is the expected behavior of the application, it shouldn't be a problem. The application can alert the user and she can apply her edits to the `Notes` field again (or the application can do that for her if, for example, the changes still exist in memory, or even in the `Text` value of a user control), and then she can save again. If a process that doesn't involve a user is making the updates, you should apply logic that doesn't require the user interface.

Determining the Scope of Changes

You can discover whether data has changed on the server while a user is in the process of editing the same data in a number of ways:

Check for any change at all to the record
: To do this, you would need to compare every field in the row to see whether that row was edited. The Entity Framework supports this using a `ConcurrencyMode` property that can be set to `Fixed` for any property that you want to check. Another mechanism that developers use is a database function called `checksum` that computes a hash value from all of the data in a particular row. The Entity Framework doesn't have direct support for `checksum`, but you can access it using Entity SQL, because of the way Entity SQL allows you to use database functions.

Check for particular field changes
: Here you need to focus on only one or more specific fields that would indicate a change has been made. Database `rowversion` (a.k.a. timestamp) fields are great for this, although not every database supports this data type. But you may really be interested in a few specific properties. For example, with an employee record, you may determine that the only piece of data in which a conflict would create a problem is the Social Security number. Rather than using `rowversion`, which indicates that something changed with no regard to which field that may have been, you could specifically watch only the Social Security number field. If it was updated during a concurrent operation, it's time to raise a flag.

Check to see whether the fields you are updating have changed
: While the Entity Framework does this by checking the original and current values of its entities, it will not build commands that will do this comparison in the database. You would have to do additional queries to check in this way.

Using rowversion (a.k.a. timestamp) for Concurrency Checks

The simplest mechanism for detecting that anything in a database row has changed is to use a *rowversion* field. A `rowversion` is a binary field that is automatically updated whenever changes are made to any columns in the row. Many databases have a specific data type that is used for this. As noted earlier, SQL Server's `timestamp` is actually an alias for the `rowversion` field and does not contain a date time. (See the sidebar "The Designer View of SQL Server 2008's rowversion Data Type" on page 665.) With databases that do not have an explicit `rowversion` type, patterns are available for creating triggers to update fields in your database.

If you use `rowversion` fields in your database and they are surfaced as properties in your entities, the Entity Framework will need to cause that single field to be checked to detect whether a change was made to the data in the data store.

The Designer View of SQL Server 2008's rowversion Data Type

Because the BreakAway database is a SQL Server database and uses the `timestamp` data type, I will use that term frequently in this discussion. Microsoft will eventually deprecate the use of `timestamp` as an alias for `rowversion`. The database design tools in Visual Studio 2010 and SQL Server Management Studio still use the `timestamp` type and do not appear to know about `rowversion`. The EDM Wizard will identify the store types as `timestamp` which is still common for a number of databases. In SSDL, `rowversion` is valid, but you would have to type that in manually and this change would be overwritten by the Designer anytime you update the model from the database.

A number of entities in the BreakAway model have `RowVersion` properties, which map to `timestamp` types in the database. Because the designers do not support the new type's name, `rowversion`, you will still see the name `timestamp` used for these fields' type.

In the conceptual model, the `RowVersion` properties are non-nullable binary fields. In the store schema in the EDMX, the field is also non-nullable (`Nullable=false`) and its `StoreGeneratedPattern` is `Computed`, so the Entity Framework does not need to worry about managing this field:

```
CSDL
<Property Name="RowVersion" Type="Binary" Nullable="false" MaxLength="8"
          FixedLength="true" />
SSDL
<Property Name=" RowVersion " Type="timestamp" Nullable="false"
          StoreGeneratedPattern="Computed" />
```

When working with disconnected data, a `rowversion` field—whether your database inherently supports it or you have to use a binary field with triggers—is one of the most important tools you have in your arsenal for dealing with concurrent systems. Otherwise, if you want to identify that a change has been made to a table row, you may have to consider a less efficient method of concurrency checking, such as checking every single field in the row.

Implementing Optimistic Concurrency with the Entity Framework

In the Entity Framework, there are two ways to enable optimistic concurrency. You were introduced to the first in Chapter 7 when mapping stored procedures to entities. The `Update` function allows you to flag fields to check for concurrency using any fields that were marked with "Use Original Value" and then checking the returned Rows Affected property.

See the section in Chapter 7 titled "Concurrency checking with Use Original Value and Rows Affected Parameter options" on page 150 for a refresher on that feature as well as an explanation of how the database is involved in concurrency checking.

The second way to leverage concurrency checks with Entity Framework is done when you are not using stored procedures for your updates. Using this feature requires two steps:

1. Define which property or properties will be used to perform the concurrency check.
2. Handle the `OptimisticConcurrencyException` that is thrown when the check fails.

First we'll look at the various methods and effects of identifying the properties for the concurrency checks, and after that we'll dig into the exception handling.

Flagging a Property for Concurrency Checking

Because concurrency is defined on a property-by-property basis in the Entity Framework, the first step is to identify the property or properties that you will use for concurrency checking. We'll use the `Contact` entity's `RowVersion` property.

`ConcurrencyMode` is used to flag a property for concurrency checking and can be found in the Properties window. Its options are `None`, which is the default, and `Fixed`, as shown in Figure 23-1.

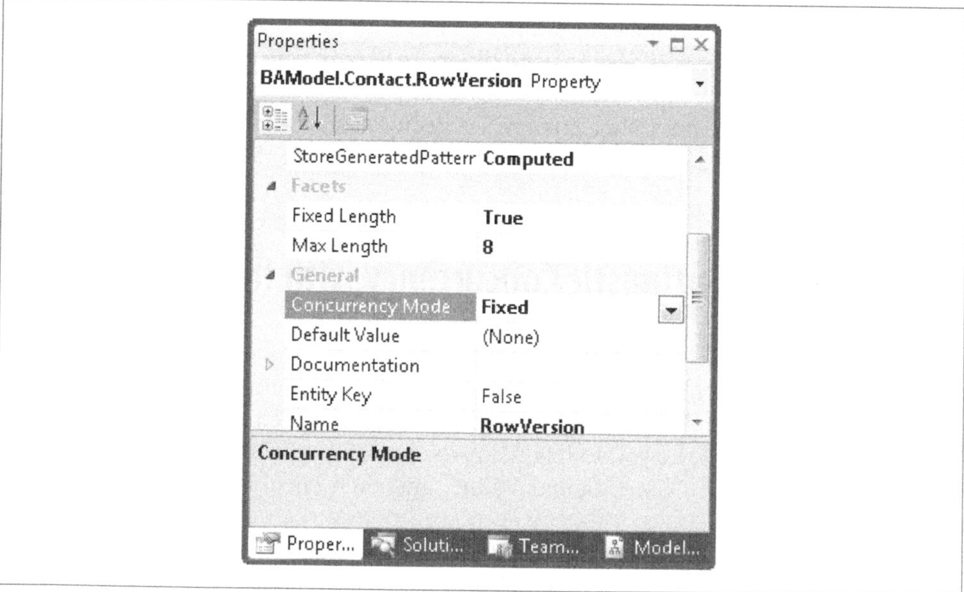

Figure 23-1. Setting a property's concurrency mode

By setting Concurrency Mode to Fixed, you ensure that the property value is included in the where predicate when an entity is updated or deleted during a call to SaveChanges.

How the Entity Framework Uses the ConcurrencyMode Property

Following is a closer look at the inner workings of ConcurrencyMode than you learned in Chapter 10. When Object Services prepares an Update or Delete command, it uses any properties marked for concurrency checking as a filter in the command along with the identity key(s).

With the ConcurrencyMode of Contact.RowVersion set to Fixed, anytime a Contact is updated, the Update command will look for the Contact using its EntityKey and its RowVersion property.

For example, if Charles Petzold is knighted, as many of us think he should be, his Title property will change from Mr. to Sir, as shown in Example 23-1.

Example 23-1. Changing a property of an entity with a concurrency-checking property

```
using (BAEntities context = new BAEntities())
{
  var contact = context.Contacts
          .FirstOrDefault(c => c.LastName == "Petzold"
                          && c.FirstName == "Charles");
  contact.Title = "Sir";
  context.SaveChanges();
}
```

When SaveChanges is called, the command shown in Example 23-2 will be sent to the database.

Example 23-2. The T-SQL Update command when using a rowversion field for concurrency checking

```
exec sp_executesql N'update [dbo].[Contact]
set [Title] = @0
where (([ContactID] = @1) and ([RowVersion] = @2))
select [RowVersion]
from [dbo].[Contact]
where @@ROWCOUNT > 0 and [ContactID] = @1',N'@0 nchar(3),@1 int,@2
binary(8)',@0=N'Sir',@1=850,@2=0x000000000000791A
```

That last value in Example 23-2 is the binary RowVersion field. The command is attempting to update a Contact record where ContactID=1 and RowVersion=0x000000000000791A, the original value of RowVersion when the contact was first retrieved.

Notice that the command is designed to return the updated RowVersion value so that the entity will get the new value.

If that RowVersion value had changed since the first query, due to someone else editing that record, the Update command will not find a matching record and will return an error to the client. The Entity Framework will report this as an `OptimisticConcurrencyException`.

This same type of concurrency check will also happen if the user is attempting to delete the contact. It will add the `RowVersion` to the `WHERE` clause of the command. Every property that is marked as `ConcurrencyMode=Fixed` in your entity will be incorporated into the `WHERE` clause of `Update` and `Delete` commands in this way.

You'll read more about `OptimisticConcurrencyException` after reviewing some other options.

Concurrency Checking Without a rowversion Field

Although the `rowversion` concurrency checks are the most common methods developers use, you may not have that data type available as an option.

In that case, you can use the `ModifiedDate DateTime` properties in place of a `rowversion` field, marking their `ConcurrencyMode` as `Fixed`, but you need to be sure they are being updated. Although the `SavingChanges` customization example in Chapter 11 ensures that a particular model's `ObjectContext` always updates the `ModifiedDate` fields, this does not give you full coverage. You need to be sure that any application, process, or even user accessing the database directly updates that field every time, or the concurrency check will not detect a change.

Another method is to mark every property in the entity as `FIXED`. Although this does the trick, it makes your commands less efficient because all of the properties' original values will become part of every `WHERE` clause.

Concurrency Checking on a Checksum in the Data Store

With the assumption that you are thinking about `CheckSum` because you are unable to modify the database to use `rowversion` fields, a last resort is to use a `QueryView` or a SSDL function, and to write store function queries (store queries written directly in the SSDL, as you saw in Chapter 16) directly into your model.

If you have checksum functions in the data store or you are implementing them in the SSDL, you still need to consider the actual act of performing the update so that you can get a concurrency check. If the `CheckSum` value is directly in the data table, it is represented in your entity as a binary property. It can be marked as a `Fixed` field and used for concurrency checks in the same way you use the `RowVersion` or any other property in an entity.

If you have used `QueryView` or a store function to query data that includes a checksum value, you will need to use stored procedures for the update and delete operations, and these stored procedures will need to perform the concurrency checking.

SqlServer.CHECKSUM Won't Cut It for Concurrency Checks

SQL Server's `CHECKSUM` function is included in the `SqlClient` and you can use it in Entity SQL. However, because you can use only provider-specific functions with Entity SQL, you cannot use this, or the checksum functions that other providers offer, with LINQ. If you were to use `CHECKSUM` directly in T-SQL, you could write `CHECKSUM(*)`, but the Entity SQL version requires that the individual expressions be listed—in this case, properties of an entity.

`SqlServer.CHECKSUM` has a few limitations that prevent it from being useful in Entity SQL as a way to do a concurrency check when you don't have access to the server. The first limitation is that it will take up to only three parameters, so you can't pass in an entire list of properties. The second is that all of the values must be of the same type.

Concurrency Checks for EntityReference Navigation Properties

If an entity that contains a concurrency field is part of an independent association (no foreign key) and the navigation property for that association points to a parent or "One" side of a relationship, the concurrency check will still take place if that relationship changes. In the database, a foreign key value represents the relationship. So, as long as something changes that value and causes the `RowVersion` field to change, when your application attempts to update the same row the change will be detected.

Concurrency Checks and Inherited Types

The Entity Framework does not support concurrency checks in derived types, period. You will see this quickly if you attempt to change the `ConcurrencyMode` property of any property in a derived type.

With inherited types, however, you may only use properties from the base type for concurrency checks. If you set the `ConcurrencyMode` of any property in a derived type to `Fixed`, you will get a validation error on the model that says that new concurrency requirements are not allowed for subtypes of base `EntitySet` types.

Given that you can't perform concurrency checks on derived types, it's important to see what behavior you can expect if the base type has any concurrency properties.

When you edit an inherited type that has a concurrency check in its base type, concurrency checking will happen, but only on the base type itself. Let's take a closer look at this.

In the BreakAway model, `Customer` inherits from `Contact` and `Contact` has a `RowVersion` field that is now being used for concurrency checks. What happens when a `Customer` entity is being edited and a field that is specific to `Customer` has been modified? (See Example 23-3.)

Example 23-3. Modifying a derived entity whose base entity has a concurrency-checking property

```
var customer = context.Contacts.OfType<Customer>.First();
customer.InitialDate = customer.InitialDate.Value.AddDays(1);
context.SaveChanges();
```

In this case, two commands will be sent to the database. The first will test to see whether anything in the `Contact` has changed. It is an update command that first declares a new variable (`@p`) and then attempts to update it using the `ContactID` and `RowVersion` filter, as shown in Example 23-4.

Example 23-4. T-SQL checking for a change in the table related to the base entity before updating the derived entity

```
exec sp_executesql N'declare @p int
update [dbo].[Contact]
set @p = 0
where (([ContactID] = @0) and ([RowVersion] = @1))
select [RowVersion]
from [dbo].[Contact]
where @@ROWCOUNT > 0 and [ContactID] = @0',N'@0 int,@1
binary(8)',@0=1,@1=0x00000000000016B9
```

If `Contact` is not found, the command will throw an error back to the `ObjectContext`, which will in turn throw an `OptimisticConcurrencyException`. However, if the first command succeeds, the context will send the next command, which is the one to update the `InitialDate` field in the `Customer` table, to be executed in the database.

There is a problem that you need to keep an eye on here. This mechanism assumes that all updates are being made through this model and that anytime something in the `Customer` table is changed, the `RowVersion` field of the `Contact` table will be modified.

However, other applications may be using the same data, or even other EDMs that map to this data where the `Customer` is not a derived type. If one of the `Customer` table fields in the database is modified, the concurrency check will not detect it.

In this case, if you do need the check to be performed, you may want to rely on stored procedures for your DML commands.

Concurrency Checks and Stored Procedures

If you have mapped stored procedures to the insert, update, and delete functions of an entity, any properties marked as `Fixed` in that entity will not automatically be used in concurrency checks. However, you can define concurrency checking in the function mappings; the stored procedure that the functions are based on needs to be designed correctly.

Defining a stored procedure to perform concurrency checking

If your stored procedure has one or more parameters that take in values to be used for concurrency checking, when mapping to these parameters you can force the original value to be sent to that parameter with the Use Original Value checkbox.

There is one other important requirement for the stored procedure and the mapping. The database needs to return the new `timestamp` value to the entity. That way, if you need to use the original value again, it will be the correct version.

Adding an additional `SELECT` statement after the `UPDATE` command will impact the procedure's ability to return an error, because the `SELECT` statement will most likely succeed. Therefore, between the `UPDATE` command and the `SELECT` command, you will need to test to see whether the update was successful. If it was, continue with the `SELECT`; otherwise, the procedure will be finished and the error will be returned to your application.

The `UpdatePayment` stored procedure you already mapped to the `Payment` entity is written for you to use in this way. Example 23-5 displays the stored procedure.

Example 23-5. The UpdatePayment stored procedure

```
ALTER PROCEDURE [dbo].[UpdatePayment]
@PaymentID INT,
@date DATETIME,
@reservationID INT,
@amount MONEY,
@modifiedDate DATETIME,
@rowversion timestamp

AS

UPDATE payments
SET paymentdate=@date,reservationID=@reservationID,amount=@amount
WHERE
paymentid=@paymentid AND RowVersion=@rowversion

IF @@ROWCOUNT>0
     SELECT RowVersion AS newRowVersion
     FROM payments WHERE paymentid=@paymentid
```

In Chapter 8, when you mapped the `UpdatePayment` function, you selected Use Original Value next to the `RowVersion` property and you instructed the function to capture the `RowVersion` value that the stored procedure returned.

If you want to see this in action, now you can test the concurrency checking with Example 23-6, a short routine you can use to test the `UpdatePayment` procedure.

Example 23-6. Testing for update conflicts with function mappings

```
using (var context = new BAEntities())
{
  var payment = context.Payments.First();
  if (payment.PaymentDate != null)
  {
    payment.PaymentDate = payment.PaymentDate.Value.AddDays(1);
  }
  var origRowVersion = payment.RowVersion;
  try
  {
    context.SaveChanges();
    var newRowVersion = payment.RowVersion;
    if (newRowVersion == origRowVersion)
    {
      Console.WriteLine("RowVersion not updated");
    }
    else
    {
      Console.WriteLine("RowVersion updated");
    }
  }
  catch (OptimisticConcurrencyException)
  {
    Console.WriteLine("Concurrency Exception was thrown");
  }
}
```

You'll see that the `Payment` entity's `RowVersion` property is updated when the update is successful. If you test the collision by editing the database manually at the suggested breakpoint, an `OptimisticConcurrencyException` will be thrown.

Handling OptimisticConcurrencyExceptions

Now it's time to look at the other piece of the concurrency puzzle: handling the exception that is thrown when a concurrency check fails.

When a check fails and a `System.Data.OptimisticConcurrencyException` is thrown, this is where you can inject your business logic to determine how to deal with the issue.

The most common resolutions, as described earlier, are to force the client-side data to the server, or to pull the server-side data to the client and lose the client's edits. You can perform either of these actions using `ObjectContext.Refresh`. While many applications handle concurrency conflicts, it is more common to have a sweeping rule rather than to have logic handle very narrow cases. We'll look at both scenarios, but we'll spend more time on the more commonly used patterns.

Using ObjectContext.Refresh

`ObjectContext.Refresh` allows you to refresh entities in the context from the database. You can also use it in other places in your application. Here we'll focus on using it to handle `OptimisticConcurrencyExceptions`.

You can use `Refresh` to force either a `ClientWins` scenario or a `StoreWins` scenario with your updates.

`Refresh` takes two parameters. The first is `RefreshMode`, which has the options `RefreshMode.ClientWins` and `RefreshMode.StoreWins`. The second parameter is either a single entity or an `IEnumerable` of entities. The `IEnumerable` can be something such as a `List` or an `Array`, or even an `IQueryable` (LINQ to Entities query) or `ObjectQuery`:

```
context.Refresh(RefreshMode.ClientWins, aTrip)
```

If the `RefreshMode` is `ClientWins`, a query will be executed against the database to get the current server values for the entity. Then it will push those values into the original values of the entity. That will make the entity think it started out with those server values and it will build the update commands accordingly when `SaveChanges` is called again.

`StoreWins` will replace all of the current and original values of the entity with the data from the server. The user will lose her edits, and instead the cached data will be in sync with the database. Entities that are refreshed with `StoreWins` will have an `Unchanged` state and will be ignored by `SaveChanges` until they are edited again.

To get your first look at this, let's focus on a single entity and see what `Refresh` looks like in a basic scenario.

Using Refresh with ClientWins

In Example 23-7, a simple query returns a single entity. If a conflict arises during a call to `SaveChanges`, that same entity is passed into the `Refresh` method.

Example 23-7. A ClientWins refresh on a single entity

```
using (var context = new BAEntities())
{
  var con = context.Contacts
          .FirstOrDefault(c => c.LastName == "Petzold"
                          && c.FirstName == "Charles");
  con.Title = "Sir";
  try
  {
    context.SaveChanges();
  }
  catch (OptimisticConcurrencyException)
  {
    //Refresh the contact entity,using ClientWins;
    context.Refresh(RefreshMode.ClientWins, con);
```

```
        //SaveChanges again;
        context.SaveChanges();
    }
}
```

Before SaveChanges is called, another user has edited the same contact, causing the RowVersion field to be updated. An OptimisticConcurrencyException will be thrown when SaveChanges is called.

To test the OptimisticConcurrencyException, you'll need to emulate an edit being made by another user or process. To do this, place a breakpoint on context.SaveChanges. When the breakpoint is hit, open the Contact table in the Solution Explorer and edit the matching record.

Figure 23-2 shows the state of that contact using the Entity State Visualizer (which you built in Chapter 21) before the Refresh is executed.

Entity State Visualizer

Object Type **BAGA.Customer**

Current Object State **Modified**

_Index	_Property	Original	Current	ValueModified
0	ContactID	22	22	
1	FirstName	Charles	Charles	
2	LastName	Petzold	Petzold	
3	Title	Mr.	Sir	X
4	AddDate	8/20/2005 5:09:...	8/20/2005 5:09:...	
5	ModifiedDate	8/7/2008 8:27:0...	5/19/2010 2:11:...	X
6	RowVersion	System.Byte[]	System.Byte[]	
7	CustomerTypeID	1	1	

Figure 23-2. The state of the Contact entity before calling ObjectContext.Refresh

The only changed fields are Title, with the current value of Sir and original value of Mr., and the ModifiedDate field, which was altered in the SavingChanges event handler.

Next, Refresh(ClientWins) is called, which executes a query to retrieve the current values of this entity in the database, including the new timestamp. Figure 23-3 shows the contact after Refresh has been called.

All of the *original* fields have been updated to reflect the latest server values, and you can see that on the server side some naughty person changed Mr. Petzold's first name to Chuck, causing the RowVersion field to be updated.

Because every property was modified in this entity, each property's EntityState was changed to Modified. That means when SaveChanges is called again, every value will be

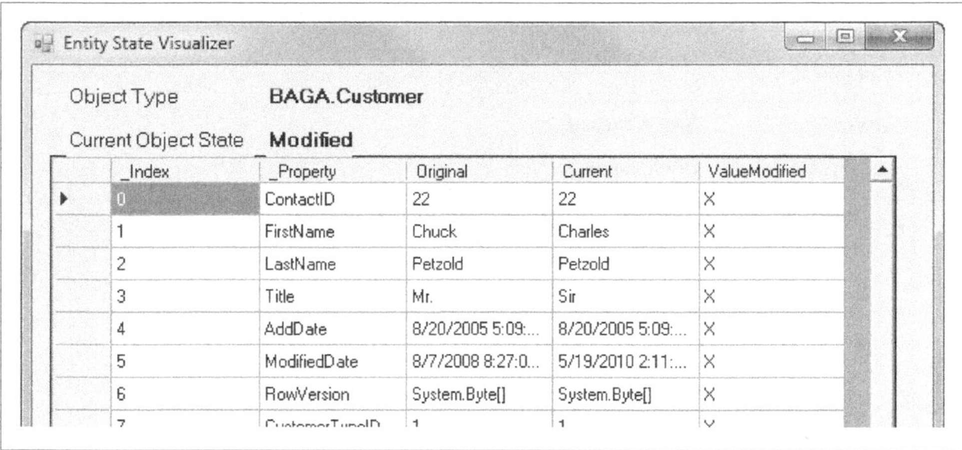

Figure 23-3. ObjectContext.Refresh with ClientWins refreshing all of the original values of the designated entities, even those that have not changed, leaving every property modified

sent to the server for updating. This time the record will be found because you have the new value of the `RowVersion` for the `WHERE` clause. The update succeeds and we now have Sir Charles Petzold, which has quite a nice ring to it.

Using Refresh with StoreWins

Let's take the same scenario and see what happens when you choose the `StoreWins` option.

Figure 23-4 shows the state of the `Contact` entity after `Refresh(StoreWins, con)` has been called. The entity's state is `Unchanged` and the `Current` and `Original` values have been replaced with the server-side values. The local entity has lost its nice title of Sir and has acquired the nickname Chuck. When `SaveChanges` is called again, it will do nothing because this entity is now `Unchanged`.

In this case, there is no need to call `SaveChanges` again, because you have done a `StoreWins` refresh on a single entity, which happens also to be the only entity in the `ObjectContext`. However, if you are building a generic routine, it's safer to call `SaveChanges` anyway, as you may have other entities in the `ObjectContext` that you need to deal with. It doesn't waste any resources if there is nothing to change.

Refreshing Collections of Entities

You also can use `Refresh` with a collection of entities. The easiest scenario with which to use this overload is when you already have a set of entities encapsulated in a collection. For example, if you are working with a list of `Contact` entities, you can refresh the entire list at once. This makes an assumption that your business rules don't require any

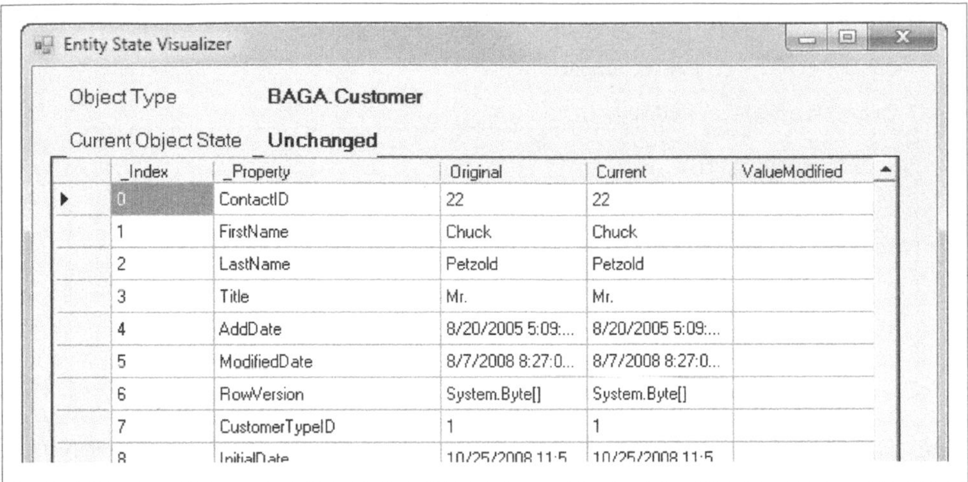

Figure 23-4. ObjectContext.Refresh with StoreWins refreshing the entities by completely synchronizing them with the database

granular decision making to determine whether this type of update is appropriate for every entity in that collection.

Example 23-8 shows a simple query that changes any contact with a `FirstName` of `Chuck` to `Charles`. Then, if there is a concurrency exception, it uses the brute force of a `ClientWins` refresh to ensure that this change is made to the database.

Example 23-8. Doing a ClientWins refresh on a set of entities

```
using (var context = new BAEntities())
{
  var contacts = context.Contacts.Where(c=>c.FirstName =="Chuck").ToList();
  foreach (var contact in contacts)
    contact.FirstName = "Charles";
  try
  {
    context.SaveChanges();
  }
  catch (OptimisticConcurrencyException ex)
  {
    context.Refresh(RefreshMode.ClientWins, contacts);
    context.SaveChanges();
  }
}
```

In this case, we are passing the entire list of `Contact` entities to the `Refresh` method.

As I explained earlier in the book, I recommend that you not work directly with the query unless you want to execute it again, and instead that you create a set of results, such as a `List`. This is to avoid accidental query execution. However, I did test to see what would happen if I passed an `ObjectQuery` and a LINQ `IQueryable` directly into a `Refresh` command. Did it wreak havoc? No. It made no attempt to execute the query again. The behavior was no different from passing in the `List`, as in Example 23-8.

`Refresh` builds a query to retrieve the current store contact data by placing the `EntityKeys` into one big `WHERE` clause so that it is a single query:

```
WHERE [Extent1].[ContactID] IN (218,219,222,228)
```

This is an improvement over the query that was built in Entity Framework in .NET 3.5, which put the predicates into a series of `OR`s—for example, `WHERE ([Extent1].[ContactID] = 218) OR ([Extent1].[ContactID] = 219)`, and so on.

This way, it is able to refresh all of the items in the collection at once.

Refreshing Related Entities in a Graph

If a modified entity is within a graph and it causes a concurrency exception, be cautious about which entities you pass into the `Refresh` method.

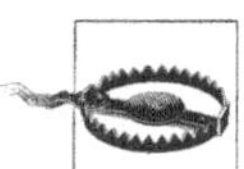

Beware! `Refresh` does not impact graphs. It will only refresh the root (parent) node of the graph.

For instance, in Example 23-9, `addressGraph` is a graph whose main entity is an address that contains a contact. If the contact's update throws a concurrency exception when `SaveChanges` is called, you might want to solve that by calling `Refresh` on the `addressGraph`.

Example 23-9. Refreshing a graph—not the results you might expect

```
var addressGraph = context.Addresses.Include("Contact").First();
addressGraph.Contact.Title = "Dr.";
try
{
  context.SaveChanges();
}
catch (OptimisticConcurrencyException)
{
  context.Refresh(RefreshMode.StoreWins, addressGraph);
  context.SaveChanges();
}
```

But only the parent entity of the graph, the Address entity, will be refreshed. The contact will continue to cause the exception every time you save changes.

There is a way to attack this problem, however. Remember that the exception returns ObjectStateEntry objects for the entity that was causing the problem.

This means that in the exception, you will have the ObjectStateEntry for the contact, which contains a reference to the entity. You can extract that entry's entity and call Refresh on the contact, and then call SaveChanges again if necessary. Example 23-10 shows the code for this. Note that I've added the ex variable to the catch clause so that I can use it.

Example 23-10. Getting a graph child to refresh

```
catch (OptimisticConcurrencyException ex)
{
  var contact = ex.StateEntries[0].Entity;
  context.Refresh(RefreshMode.ClientWins, contact);
  context.SaveAllChanges();
}
```

Rewinding and Starting Again, and Maybe Again After That

It's important to realize that when handling these exceptions, SaveChanges won't just continue on its merry way, updating the next entity in the context. If you hit the exception, the SaveChanges method rolls back whatever it has already done and then halts.

In the exception handler you can call SaveChanges again. However, if that call fails, you need to catch it again. If you are pushing a lot of changes in one SaveChanges call and a number of exceptions are in there, each time you call SaveChanges you may have fixed the last problem but you will then hit the next one.

So again, you need to trap that error, handle it, and call SaveChanges again. You may end up with code that looks like the code in Example 23-11.

Example 23-11. Catching a number of concurrency exceptions

```
try
{
  context.SaveChanges();
}
catch (OptimisticConcurrencyException ex)
{
 //do some work, then try again
  try
  {
    context.SaveChanges();
  }
  catch (OptimisticConcurrencyException ex)
  {
   //do some work, then try again
    try
```

```
    {
      context.SaveChanges();
      }
      catch (OptimisticConcurrencyException ex)
      {
       //do some work, then try again
        try
        {
          context.SaveChanges();
        }
        catch (OptimisticConcurrencyException ex)
        {
          //and so on and so forth....
        }
    }
  }
}
```

You will be better off taking advantage of the virtual SaveChanges method, overriding it to apply your own exception-handling code. Then you can call the method recursively as needed. Example 23-12 shows the overridden SaveChanges method, which I've added to the partial class for BAEntities.

Example 23-12. Handling concurrency exceptions recursively in the overridden SaveChanges method

```
public override int SaveChanges(System.Data.Objects.SaveOptions options)
{
  //TODO: perform any validations
  try
  {
    return base.SaveChanges(options);
  }
  catch (OptimisticConcurrencyException ex)
  {
    //handle concurrency exception, e.g. with ClientWins, here then try again
    Refresh(RefreshMode.ClientWins, ex.StateEntries[0].Entity);
    return SaveChanges(options);
  }
  catch (Exception ex)
  {
    MyEventHandler(ex);
    throw ex;
  }
}
```

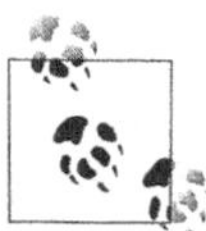

You can find other ways to recursively call SaveChanges in the MSDN documentation. One example, which is combined with a System.Transaction.TransactionScope (more on transactions and exceptions later in this chapter), is in the topic titled "How to: Manage Object Services Transactions (Entity Framework)."

Reporting an Exception

Using the details from the exception, you can create a log error or even a message to a user that describes the conflict in detail. The client-side data is readily available to create this report. If you need even more details from the server, you'll have to hit the server to get details about what actually changed there, although this is not a common scenario.

Don't forget about the EF Tracing and Caching Provider Wrappers by EF team member Jarek Kowalski that I've pointed to earlier in this book. They could be very helpful if you want to log the exceptions. You can find the sample at *http://code.msdn.com/EFProviderWrappers*.

Reporting the exception could be as simple as alerting the user that there was a conflict when updating this payment.

You can use the techniques you learned in Chapter 21 to access the property names and values in the `ObjectStateEntry` provided by the `StateEntries` property and then build a string to report a message to the user or store that message in a logging system.

If a user modified a variety of data, knowing which specific piece of data was causing the problem could be useful in letting the user decide whether her edits should be sent to the server or whether she would rather have the latest data from the server.

The level of information to access is up to you. Do you want the exception handler to retrieve the current store values as well? Should the user know who made that last change and when? These are common decisions that have to be made for handling concurrent data access, and again, they are not new to the Entity Framework.

Handling Concurrency Exceptions at a Lower Level

Although the generic `ClientWins` and `StoreWins` will suffice for many applications, in some applications more granular exception handling is required. It's difficult to come up with rules for automating intricate exception handling, but because of the information in the exception, if you do need to go to this level, many possibilities are open to you. The rest of this chapter will explore some more heavy-duty exception handling.

Handling Exceptions in a Granular Way Without User Intervention

You may have your own concurrency rules that don't require a user to get involved. Perhaps for `Payment` entities, your rule is that if the client is editing the amount, the client's data should win; otherwise, refresh the payment information from the server. You may decide that the client should update all contact data. You may not even place a concurrency check on the contact for this reason, but you may have a best practice that requires concurrency checks on every entity.

Because the last suggested rule is that all contacts should get a ClientWins, it doesn't make sense to hit them one at a time. So, on the first occurrence of a conflict with a contact, the code will refresh all contacts in the ObjectContext. The ManagedEntities extension method that you created in Example 21-7 in Chapter 21 will come in handy in this scenario.

Let's see what the exception code looks like for these different scenarios. First, you can separate the logic for the various types into their own methods, as shown in Example 23-13. The methods are designed to be in the BAEntities context class.

Example 23-13. Subroutines for handling exceptions differently for payments than for contacts

```
private void RefreshPayment(ref ObjectStateEntry entry)
{
 //rule - if amount was changed locally, then clientwins, otherwise, storewins
  if (entry.GetModifiedProperties().Contains("Amount"))
  {
    Refresh(RefreshMode.ClientWins, entry.Entity);
  }
  else
  {
    Refresh(RefreshMode.StoreWins, entry.Entity);
  }
}

private void RefreshContacts()
{
 //Contacts will always have a ClientWins refresh
 //Refresh all of the contacts when the first Contact conflict occurs
  var managedContacts = ManagedEntities<Contact>();
  Refresh(RefreshMode.ClientWins, managedContacts);
}
```

If during the course of the call to SaveChanges another concurrency conflict arises with a contact, all of the contacts will be refreshed again. However, this will refresh even those contacts that have not been modified. When your entities inherit from EntityObject, you can filter the managedContext variable using the entity's EntityS tate property:

```
var managedContacts = ManagedEntities<Contact>()
                              .Where(c=>c.EntityState==EntityState.Modified);
```

For POCOs, however, you'll need to provide a version of the ManagedEntities method to do the job in ObjectStateManager.

Example 23-14 shows an overload of a ManagedEntities extension method for ObjectContext, which filters by EntityState.

Example 23-14. OverloadedManagedEntities extension, which filters by EntityState

```
public static IEnumerable<T> ManagedEntities<T>
 (this ObjectContext context, EntityState entityState)
{
```

```
  var oses = context.ObjectStateManager.GetObjectStateEntries();
  return oses
      .Where(entry => entry.Entity is T)
      .Where(entry=>entry.State==entityState)
      .Select(entry => (T)entry.Entity);
}
```

Then you can populate the `managedContacts` variable as follows:

```
var managedContacts = ManagedEntities<Contact>(EntityState.Modified)
```

The updated exception code inside `SaveChanges` now farms out the `Refresh` call to the appropriate method after it tests to be sure the entry is not a relationship, as shown in Example 23-15.

Example 23-15. Updated exception handling for calling subroutines

```
var conflictEntry = ex.StateEntries[0];
if (! conflictEntry.IsRelationship)
{
  var entity = conflictEntry.Entity;
  if (entity is Contact) //this will refresh customers, too
  {
    RefreshContacts(ref conflictEntry);
  }
  else if (entity is Payment)
  {
    RefreshPayment(ref conflictEntry);
  }
  else
  {
    Refresh(RefreshMode.ClientWins, conflictEntry);
  }
}
```

You can use many variations of this once you've gotten into the exception and you know how to drill into the details to make some decisions based on what you've found.

Handling Multiple Conflicts

The default method of conflict resolution in the Entity Framework has a few downsides. The first is that none of the data in the context will be saved until every conflict has been resolved. If you are updating a lot of records at once in a highly concurrent system, your `SaveChanges` operation may go through many loops before all of the commands execute successfully. The user may or may not notice the delay, but the delay could cause other conflicts.

Another downside is that you can't easily gather a list of all of the conflicts to present to the user at a later time for resolution. You might want to give the user a list of the conflicts, rather than giving the user one conflict at a time, with no indication of how many more there might be. This is because you have to resolve the first conflict encountered before you can get a report of the next conflict; otherwise, that first conflict will keep coming back.

Separating the good from the bad and the ugly

One way to set the conflicting entities aside is to remove them from the context and save all of the entities that don't pose any conflicts. Then, as soon as the save is complete, pull them back into the context in such a way that you can reconstruct their state. This is not a simple task, but you have already learned the necessary steps to pull it off.

When all of the conflicting entries have been removed from the context, `SaveChanges` will succeed and the other data changes will be applied to the data store. On the book's website, you can find a `PersistedStateEntry` class in both VB and C# that achieves this pattern. This class takes advantage of many of the things you learned regarding `MetadataWorkspace` and `ObjectStateManager`. It also uses reflection because the `ObjectContext` (and therefore the `ObjectStateManager`) are not available for setting properties.

There are two principal functions. The first is to store the state entry information. This is done by storing the main `ObjectStateEntry`'s `EntityKey`, original values, and entity in the constructor and then adding the information for each `RelationshipEntry` that also came back in the `StateEntries`. The second main function is performed by the `NewEntityfromOrig` method, which reconstructs the object with its state and the `EntityReferences` that were defined by the `RelationshipEntries` in the exception's `StateEntries`.

Along with the code for the `PersistedEntry` class on the book's website, you will find an example of a `Save` routine that uses the class. Essentially, the routine instantiates a list of `PersistedEntry` objects, and anytime an `OptimisticConcurrencyException` is encountered, a new `PersistedEntry` is created from the `ObjectStateEntry` that caused the problem. Its `Entity` is detached from the context and added into the list. The method repeats this process until all of the exceptions are encountered, and then on a final call to `SaveChanges`, the valid updates are persisted to the database. The entities that were persisted are reconstructed and reattached to the context along with their relationship information. All of the information about the entity along with the exception's message and any inner exception information is available from the `PersistedEntry` class for building an informational UI for the end user, for logging the problems, or for any other task you may want to perform as part of your exception handling.

This is one pattern for separating conflicting data from good data that not only allows you to get the good data into the database more quickly, but also provides you an opportunity to present all of the conflicts to a user at once.

Handling Exceptions When Transactions Are Your Own

When you allow the Entity Framework to provide its default transactions, rollbacks and commits will occur automatically. In addition, `ObjectContext.AcceptChanges` will be called at the end of a successful `SaveChanges` so that the state of the entities becomes `Unchanged`.

If, however, you are using your own transactions as described in Chapter 20, you will need to roll back and commit the transactions yourself depending on the success or failure of the call to `SaveChanges`.

Depending on your application architecture and business rules, you may even choose to commit changes that have already been sent to the database, rather than rolling them back. You will also need to call `AcceptAllChanges` manually when the commands are completed successfully. Example 23-16 shows a basic pattern for using your own transaction with an `OptimisticConcurrencyException`.

Example 23-16. Handling an exception in a manual transaction

```
using (var tran = new System.Transactions.TransactionScope())
{
  try
  {
    context.SaveChanges(SaveOptions.None);
    //for snapshot POCOs, use SaveOptions.DetectChangesBeforeSave
    tran.Complete();
    context.AcceptAllChanges();
  }
  catch (OptimisticConcurrencyException ex)
  {
    //TODO: add code for handling exception
    context.SaveChanges(SaveOptions.None);
    tran.Complete();
    context.AcceptAllChanges();
  }
}
```

Although `Complete` and `AcceptAllChanges` won't be executed anytime an exception is thrown, you still may want to separate those calls from the `SaveChanges` loop.

Example 23-17 shows a pattern that allows you to shift the location of some of the logic.

Example 23-17. Moving the transaction completion into a finally clause

```
bool success = false;
using (var tran = new System.Transactions.TransactionScope())
{
  try
  {
    context.SaveChanges(SaveOptions.None);
    success = true;
  }
  catch (OptimisticConcurrencyException ex)
```

```
    {
      //TODO: add code for handling exception
      context.SaveChanges();
      success = true;
    }
    finally
    {
      if (success)
      {
        tran.Complete();
        context.AcceptAllChanges();
      }
    }
  }
```

Summary

In this chapter, you learned how to prepare for concurrency conflicts and a variety of ways to handle them when they occur.

Rules for handling concurrency problems vary among enterprises and applications. Because it is difficult to even come up with rules for resolving these issues at a granular level, you'll find that most commonly, the three sweeping solutions—client always wins with no concurrency checks, client wins with a complete replacement of the server data, and server wins with a complete replacement of the client data—are the ones chosen.

But you do have some options for handling exceptions in a more detailed way, and hopefully you'll find the patterns that I laid out in the final pages of the chapter both interesting and useful.

CHAPTER 24

Building Persistent Ignorant, Testable Applications

One of the significant additions to Entity Framework in .NET 4 is its support for separating concerns in your application architecture, which not only leads to cleaner architecture and more maintainable code but also enables better testing practices. Entity Framework now allows you to benefit from the Entity Framework without forcing every part of your application to be aware of the Entity Framework, separating entities from the infrastructure. You can create classes that can focus on their business rules without regard to how they are persisted (where the data is stored and how the data gets back and forth between your objects). You can also create unit tests for your applications that don't force you to interact with the `ObjectContext` and data store.

The POCO support that you learned about earlier in this book provides the foundation for these capabilities. Together with this POCO support, the `IObjectSet` interface that was introduced in .NET 4 enables you to separate the concerns of your various application layers. You've already worked frequently with `ObjectSet`, which is the Entity Framework's concrete implementation of `IObjectSet`.

This chapter has two separate goals. The first is to provide information for developers who are already designing applications in this way and are interested in bringing the Entity Framework into the sphere of their development practices. The second is to ensure that developers who are unfamiliar with testing and other agile coding practices get to come along for the ride and receive an introduction to these methods while learning more about the Entity Framework. For those of you who are new to this world, it will be important to keep in mind that this is only a narrow slice of agile programming, and there are many wonderful, expert resources where you can learn so much more.

Testing the BreakAway Application Components

Software testing is often lumped into a single category called *unit testing*, although unit testing is just one type of software test. The three most common types of tests are:

Unit test
: Tests a single piece of code in isolation from any external dependency

Integration test
: Tests code that hits external resources such as a database or a web service

Interaction test
: Tests the interaction between your own classes and other classes or APIs that they collaborate with

We'll be using Visual Studio's testing tools, which refer to all of these as unit tests. All of the tests and other code you build in this chapter will use the POCO classes that you created in Chapter 13 and then modified in Chapter 18 when using them in WCF Services.

We'll begin with simple tests that you could write against `EntityObjects` as well, and then isolate our logic using some of the new Entity Framework 4 features to build tests that will not engage Entity Framework's data access or change-tracking functionality.

These first tests will verify that your POCO classes interact properly with the `ObjectContext`. Rather than testing the functionality of a single independent class, these tests check how different classes and APIs work together.

Interaction testing is used to verify that your own classes interact with their collaborators. *Integration testing* involves external resources such as a database. The tests you will be writing at the beginning of this chapter combine interaction testing with integration testing.

Later in the chapter, you will create a new solution and organize it in a way that allows you to test your entities and the objects that manipulate them without having to interact with the database or depend on the `ObjectContext`. You will evolve the solution over a number of steps in order to understand how all of the pieces work together. In the end, not only will you have testable classes, but also you will discover a greater benefit. Application layers such as the user interface will be able to exist with no dependency at all on the Entity Framework. These become very reusable and easier to modify as needed, and they and can then interact with any backend data provider with minimal modification.

Throughout this book, we have used console apps for the purpose of understanding how Entity Framework behaves. Tests are not for the type of discovery that you have been doing with the console applications, but to verify that *your* code behaves as expected. You would normally create tests against methods that you have written. This is quite different from using tests to explore, for example, if or how the Entity Framework is doing its job.

As an example, writing a test to verify that the contact class fixes up the relationship with the address class is a unit test. You are only testing your own code. Testing to see if `ObjectContext.DetectChanges` does its job with your classes is an integration test because you are testing the behavior of the `ObjectContext` class that Microsoft wrote. Writing tests to just see how Entity Framework works is a handy way to avoid all of the little console applications, but you can test so much more!

Getting Started with Testing

If you've never created a Visual Studio test before, the following example will walk you through the simplest way to create and run unit tests in Visual Studio. It's a great habit to get into, and many developers will not program at all without these tests.

Writing an Integration Test That Hits the Database

This first small test will be an integration test, to verify that the `ObjectContext` is recognizing your POCO classes. It will mimic the first console application you built for the same purpose.

In this particular case, you want to test the actual interaction with the database to demonstrate that the POCOs really do work. In more typical tests, you would "fake" the database interaction by creating representative objects in memory, and we'll do that later in this chapter. If you do need to test the database interaction, you should use a local sample database and also consider patterns that will allow you to set the database back to its original state. Such guidance is beyond the scope of what we're doing in this example, so let's just move forward with a simple test that impacts our test database directly.

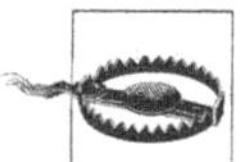

The Unit Testing tools are available in Visual Studio Professional and later versions. You will not find this feature built into Visual Studio Express or Visual Studio Basic. There are third-party tools such as NUnit (*http://www.nunit.org*) that integrate into Visual Studio. Otherwise, you may prefer to continue to use console apps to test your POCO classes using the code in the following test examples.

Start by opening the *Entities.cs* code file. Then right-click on the declaration for the `Contacts` property, and from the context menu, select Create Unit Tests.

Expand the current project in the list of types and select Contacts inside the Entities class. This is the `Contacts` property that returns an `ObjectSet` of `Contact` types.

Be sure that the Output project says "Create a new Visual C# test project..." or "Create a new Visual Basic project" depending on the language you are using. Click OK.

Enter POCOTestProject as the project name and click Create. If you get a warning message saying that your type is marked as Friend or Internal, select "No" in answer to the question about changing the visibility of your type.

A new project will be created that has the appropriate references necessary to test your Entities class. The project will create a new class file that contains your first test. The default name for this test is ContactsTest. Since the test will check that you can properly retrieve a contact and eager-load its addresses, rename it to Can_Get_A_Contact_With_Addresses_EagerLoad.

The test will be instantiating an ObjectContext and executing queries; therefore, it will need access to the EntityConnection string. So, copy the *app.config* file from the main project into this unit test project, and then add the System.Linq namespace to the declarations (using/Imports) at the top of the code file. You'll need System.Linq because you'll be executing LINQ queries in your test.

The default test will return the entire Contacts ObjectSet. Modify the test to perform a similar test to what you did in the console application earlier. Note that the variable named target is an instance of your Entities ObjectContext, which we have commonly named "context". There's no need to change it if you don't want to.

The core task of a test is to check the results of your operation. This is performed with the Assert method. The modified Assert tests to validate that the contacts were indeed returned and that addresses did in fact come along with those contacts.

Modify the default tests as shown in Example 24-1.

Example 24-1. Simple test to ensure that you are getting graph data from the database

```
[TestMethod()]
public void Can_A_Contact_With_An_Address_EagerLoad()
{
  var context = new BAEntities();
  context.ContextOptions.LazyLoadingEnabled = false;
  var contact = context.Contacts.Include("Addresses")
                        .Where(c=>c.Addresses.Any()).FirstOrDefault();
  Assert.IsNotNull(contact);
  Assert.IsTrue(contact.Addresses.Count>0);
}
```

Much of the code in this test is the same as the code you used in the console application routine. However, I have disabled lazy loading to ensure that the addresses were retrieved because of the Include method.

Now it's time to run the test. Unit tests can be run or debugged. First you will run it. So, right-click on the Can_A_Contact_With_An_Address_EagerLoad declaration, and from the context menu, select Run Tests.

The Test Results window should be automatically displayed, and if all went well, you should see that the test passed, as shown in Figure 24-1.

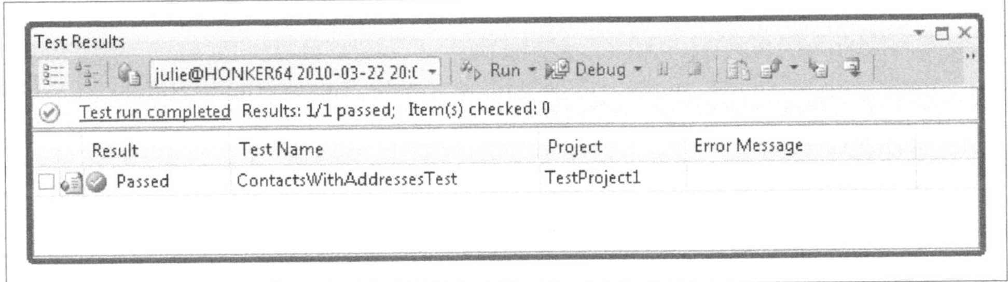

Figure 24-1. Visual Studio's Unit Testing Test Results window displaying a successful test

Inspecting a Failed Test

A test failure could result from a failure in the method you are testing or from a bug in your actual testing code.

It's also possible to have a test incorrectly pass simply because the test wasn't written correctly. Therefore, it is common to initially design a test so that it will fail and then modify it so that it passes, helping to ensure that the test is actually testing what you intended.

There are a few ways to determine what caused your test to fail. An error message will display any exception that caused your test to fail. For example, you may have forgotten to include the *app.config* in your project or mistyped the `Addresses` string in the `Include` path. These will result in an exception. If the test failed because no addresses were returned, meaning that there is probably something wrong in your entities, the error message will tell you that `Assert.IsTrue` failed.

When a test fails, the hyperlink that says "Test run completed" in Figure 24-1 will say "Test run failed." You can also click on that hyperlink for more details. Finally, you can debug the test. In this same figure, notice the Debug All Tests in Test Results toolbar item. That's one of a number of ways you can debug the test rather than just running it. You can put breakpoints in the test just as you would in regular code.

Writing a Unit Test That Focuses on Custom Logic

Another test you could write that has no dependency on the context or the database is a simple unit test that tests only logic in the entity classes. You could write a test like this for `EntityObject` classes for logic that does not require an `ObjectContext` or database interaction just as easily as for POCOs.

A typical unit test might verify that validation logic in your classes is working correctly. For example, you could add logic to the `Contact` class to ensure that it does not allow the `LastName` property to comprise more than 50 characters, as seen in Example 24-2.

If you are using the template customization from Chapter 13, which added in MaxLength validation, this code will already be part of your `Contact` class.

Example 24-2. Validating the length of the LastName property

```
public string LastName
{
  get { return _lastName; }
  set
  {
    if (value.Length > 50)
    {
      throw new ArgumentException
               ("Last Name field is too long. Max length is 50.");
    }
    else
      _lastName = value;
  }
}
```

A test to verify that the `ArgumentException` is getting thrown when it should be would look like that shown in Example 24-3, where the test leverages the `ExpectedException` attribute rather than an `Assert`.

Example 24-3. A test method to ensure that the length validation throws an exception when it should

```
[TestMethod()]
[ExpectedException (typeof(ArgumentException),
                    "Last Name field is too long. Max length is 50.")]
 public void Setting_LastName_To_Greater_Than_50_Chars_Throws()
{
  new Customer {LastName = "x".PadLeft(51, '.')};
}
```

When you run this test, the `LastName` property will throw the `ArgumentException`. The test will pass because the method threw the expected exception. You could have a second test, such as the one displayed in Example 24-4, that ensures that you can assign a `LastName` property that is no longer than 50 characters.

Example 24-4. A test method to ensure that the LastName property accepts valid data

```
[TestMethod()]
public void Can_Set_LastName_to_50_Chars_or_Less()
{
  var expected = "x".PadLeft(40, '.');  //total length will be 40
  var item = new Customer { LastName = expected };
  Assert.AreEqual(expected, item.LastName);
}
```

These tests are not specific to the fact that you are working with Entity Framework, but it is important to understand the difference between unit tests against your classes and those that involve more complex operations.

Another method that would be convenient in an application for the BreakAway company would be one that lets you know if a reservation has been paid or not. Customers are allowed to make installment payments for a reservation, and therefore a reservation can have one of four statuses: Unpaid, Partially Paid, Paid in Full, or Overpaid. An application might display the status in a UI or use the status to trigger other actions.

Rather than walking through this in its entirety, let's contemplate the method and test(s) for this.

Example 24-5 shows what the method that returns the payment status might look like.

Example 24-5. Calculating the status of payments for a reservation

```
public PaymentStatus GetPaymentStatus()
{
  int tripCost = Trip.TripCostUSD.Value;
  decimal? paymentSum = Payments.Sum(p => p.Amount);
  if (paymentSum == 0)
  {
    return PaymentStatus.UnPaid;
  }
  if (tripCost > paymentSum)
  {
    return PaymentStatus.PartiallyPaid;
  }
  if (tripCost == paymentSum)
  {
    return PaymentStatus.PaidInFull;
  }
  return PaymentStatus.OverPaid;
}
```

The reservation first identifies the cost of the trip. If the trip has not been loaded, the method relies on lazy loading to get the trip information. Then the method gets the sum of all of the payments that have been made. Again, lazy loading will be relied upon in case the payments are not yet in memory.

Lazy Loading and Its Triggers

When you count on lazy loading to get related data for you, be sure you know when it will and won't do its job. Lazy loading is not persistent ignorant. It depends on the underlying infrastructure.

With Entity Framework, lazy loading must be enabled, and with new models, it will be by default. But even when it is enabled, it doesn't trigger a database call anytime you ask for the related data. If you have already loaded the navigation property, either by eager loading (`include`), lazy loading, or explicit loading (`Load` or `LoadProperty`), the context will consider the navigation loaded. The next time you make a reference to the navigation, the context will only read from memory. If, however, you have brought the related data in through a separate query or in a projection, the context will not consider the data loaded and will hit the database for lazy loading.

One important factor to consider when you are depending on lazy loading is that if the navigation has been loaded and additional data has been added to the database, you won't be aware of it. For example, the PaymentStatus method could miss a new payment that was entered and you might want to force the Payments property to load explicitly before performing the calculation.

Finally, don't ignore the fact that your class may not be connected to the context at the time that the lazy loading is being requested. If you know it will be, it's safe to depend on it, but otherwise it's best not to.

So, what would you want to test here? Retrieving the reservation? Lazy loading the trip and payments? No, what you want to test is that given the data (trip cost and payments), the method returns the correct status. It doesn't matter where the data comes from or when it's loaded. This is where a practice referred to as using *test fakes* (or *test doubles*) becomes a convenient pattern in testing, and you'll see this in action shortly.

Creating a test from the method using the Visual Studio Create Unit Test Wizard that you used before would result in the test shown in Example 24-6.

Example 24-6. Default test that Visual Studio creates from the GetPaymentStatus method

```
[TestMethod()]
public void GetPaymentStatusTest()
{
  Reservation target = new Reservation.PaymentStatus();
  Reservation.PaymentStatus expected = new Reservation.PaymentStatus();
  Reservation.PaymentStatus actual;
  actual = target.GetPaymentStatus();
  Assert.AreEqual(expected, actual);
  Assert.Inconclusive("Verify the correctness of this test method.");
}
```

If the PaymentStatus method took parameters, you could just set the payment total and trip cost values in the test. Unfortunately, it's not quite that simple. The method depends on the Reservation having access to the Trip and the Payments collection. So, you will have to provide that. There are a few ways you could do this. You could just call into the BAGAContext and grab data from the database.

But the goal is to avoid simply hitting the database during your tests. One reason is because it's much faster to run tests when you are not interacting with the database. Another reason is that removing dependencies on external resources or APIs allows your tests to focus solely on your classes. You could also just create the data on the fly in the test—instantiating a new reservation, a new trip, and some payments and attaching them all without involving the context. This makes the most sense for this method. You would want to have one test for each status. Let's create two of them here.

The first will be easy. We'll verify that the method properly returns the Unpaid status. That means we'll need a reservation and a trip but no payments. You can satisfy that by instantiating a new Reservation with a new Trip that costs $1,000. Then you should check the status without adding any payments. Example 24-7 displays the `PaymentStatus_Returns_UnPaid_When_No_Payments` method that performs this test.

Example 24-7. Test to ensure that the PaymentStatus method correctly calculates an Unpaid reservation

```
[TestMethod()]
public void PaymentStatus_Returns_UnPaid_When_No_Payments()
{
  var reservation = new Reservation();
  reservation.Trip = new Trip { TripCostUSD = 1000 };
  Assert.AreEqual(reservation.GetPaymentStatus(),
                  Reservation.PaymentStatus.UnPaid);
}
```

Next, you can add in a single payment that does not fulfill the trip cost. This should result in a `PartiallyPaid` status, as shown in Example 24-8.

Example 24-8. Test to ensure that the PaymentStatus method correctly calculates a partially paid reservation

```
public void PaymentStatus_Returns_PartiallyPaid_When_Insufficient_Payments()
{
  var reservation = new Reservation();
  reservation.Trip = new Trip { TripCostUSD = 1000 };
  reservation.Payments.Add(new Payment {Amount = 500});
  Assert.AreEqual(reservation.GetPaymentStatus(),
                  Reservation.PaymentStatus.PartiallyPaid);
}
```

These are scenarios where you would be able to test the POCO without involving the context or the database.

In a real application, it is possible that the method calls to `reservation.Trip` and `reservation.Payments` may trigger a database query, thanks to lazy loading, but the method doesn't actually care how the related data is provided. That is a mechanism of the infrastructure concerns and the method doesn't need to worry about how it's implemented. That is why it was OK to build the fake graph of `Reservation` with a `Trip` and some `Payments` for the method to work with.

Creating Persistent Ignorant Entities

The preceding paragraph described a method that has no intimate knowledge of the source of the data it consumes. This highlights the essence of persistence ignorance—which is when your classes and many of our application layers around them don't care how the data is stored. In the .NET 3.5 version of Entity Framework, if you wanted to use preexisting classes, you were required to modify them by forcing them to derive from `EntityObject`. In .NET 4 this is no longer necessary. You don't have to modify your entities in order for them to participate in Entity Framework operations. This allows us to build applications that embrace loose coupling and *separation of concerns*. With these coding patterns, your classes are only concerned with their own jobs and many layers of your application, including the UI, have no dependencies on external logic, such as the Entity Framework APIs, yet those external APIs are able to interact with our entities.

For a great read on separation of concerns, check out the article "Separation of Concerns: A Brownfield Development Series" from *MSDN Magazine* at *http://msdn.microsoft.com/en-us/magazine/ee210417.aspx*.

Attempting to build unit tests with entities quickly highlights some of the dependencies as described earlier. For example, what if you built a method that contains a query plus some additional logic, and it is the additional logic, not the query, that you wanted to test?

A common example concerns validating incoming parameters, such as an ID that is to be used for a query. You'll want to test that the validation is doing its job, but you don't want to execute the query. The current `BAEntities ObjectContext` won't allow you to separate the query from the query execution. The result is that in order to test that the method is properly validating the incoming ID parameter, the method will run all of its logic, including the query execution and hitting the database.

If `BAEntities` were persistent ignorant, we could separate query execution from database interaction. Let's see how to do that.

You will have many methods in your applications that involve a query. Unless you want to test the query itself, there's no reason to work with real data when testing; however, you still have to have a mechanism for allowing the method to execute its query. This is referred to as *faking* the data. The classes used for providing fake data and even fake methods such as `SaveChanges` are called *fakes* or *test doubles*.

Remember, these will be baby steps for unit testing, but hopefully that will be enough to get testing pros the information they need regarding how to test within Entity Framework, and at the same time enough to get newbies started and, hopefully, encouraged to learn more.

On the following pages, you will restructure the example to make it flexible enough to use test doubles. At the same time, you will invest in a much more agile architecture for your application. You'll start with the reorganization, and then, step by step, you'll evolve the solution into one that is testable. Then you'll build a new context that returns fake data and use that for your testing.

The method you will use as the basis for testing will simply return a customer given its ID. The method must first check that the ID is valid before executing the query, and it is this check that you will be testing, not the query itself.

While we're on the topic of persistence ignorance, you might be interested in this great article by Jeremy D. Miller in the April 2009 issue of *MSDN Magazine*, "Persistence Patterns," *http://msdn.microsoft.com/en-us/magazine/dd569757.aspx*.

Planning the Project Structure

When you first created POCO classes in Chapter 13, you created all of the puzzle pieces in a single project—the model, the POCO classes, the `Entities` class that provided an `ObjectContext`, and even a little console app to bang on the classes a bit.

For this example, you'll build a more realistic solution that separates the classes to provide flexibility and reuse. There are a lot of working parts in this solution, so I will introduce them bit by bit.

An important design pattern for building agile software is called the *Repository Pattern*. A repository is a wrapper that lets us work with our entities as though they are part of a collection. The repository lets us add, update, and delete entities in the collection rather than being concerned with how to get those entities into and out of a database or how to send and retrieve the entities from a web service. You don't have to call a stored procedure or, in the case of the Entity Framework, create an `ObjectContext` and execute queries.

There are a few ways to implement repositories. Some solutions will build a separate repository for each "root" entity while others will build repositories that focus on a particular group of concerns. In the following set of examples, we'll build repositories for each entity, although in some cases, an entity, such as a `Customer`, will bring back related data, such as `Reservations`, as part of a graph making Customer the root of the graph or *aggregate root*.

The Repository Pattern

You'll find definitions of the Repository Pattern described in many resources. Eric Evans, author of *Domain-Driven Design: Tackling Complexity in the Heart of Software* (Addison-Wesley Professional), the canonical book on domain-driven design, defines a repository as:

> ...a mechanism for encapsulating storage, retrieval, and search behavior which emulates a collection of objects.

Source: *http://domaindrivendesign.org/node/123*

The model and the `ObjectContext` should be separate from your *own* queries that rely on the model and `ObjectContext` (e.g., `GetReservationsForCustomer`), and these will be in the repositories. Once you have tackled the basic concept, you can fine-tune the architecture even further.

A basic pattern to begin splitting up the logical pieces would be:

Classes: Entity Classes (Class Library)
: Your POCO classes go in here. No reference to `System.Data.Entity` is necessary.

Model: Entity Data Model and `ObjectContext` *(Class Library)*
: This project would have the EDMX and the class that inherits from `ObjectContext`. The project will have a reference to `System.Data.Entity` and to the project that contains the POCO classes.

Repositories (Class Library)
: For each entity class, you'll build another wrapper class called a repository that will be our means of interacting with the entities. Repository is a known programming pattern that you'll be leveraging. The repositories implement an `IRepository` interface which is also in this project. See the sidebar "The Repository Pattern" on page 697.

Interfaces (Class Library)
: This project will contain an important interface that will be for context classes.

User Interface
: In the case of a client-side application (e.g., console app, Windows form, or WPF), you'll need a reference to both the repository project and the classes project. The UI will call into the repository and receive the classes. As you build larger applications, you will create more separation between your UI and the repository, but for this sample, calling into the repository from the UI will be sufficient.

Testing Project
: Although the UI is necessary for the real application, it is the testing project that will provide the interaction with the supporting layers as you validate them.

You will build this pattern in small steps. Note that test-driven developers design the tests based on their domain needs first and then build the code to fulfill the tests. This walkthrough is aimed at developers who are new to testing. Therefore, we will build the application pieces first and then create tests to validate them.

The first stage of these tests will hit the database. Then you will implement the fake entities and enable tests that do not hit the database.

The following pages where you restructure the framework for testing and then build the necessary classes for the purpose of building the test doubles will cover a lot of ground. They will not make you an expert in testing, but if you are new to testing and agile development, they should provide a helpful start. However, you will need to be patient as you work through the examples and explanations of new concepts. There are a lot of pieces to this puzzle. But remember to follow up with further resources to learn good practices in agile development.

If you are a seasoned agile developer and are looking for guidance on what you need to do within the context of Entity Framework, you should find what you need in the following examples. You can then incorporate them into your own existing patterns.

Starting with the Model and Its POCO Entities

The goal for step 1 is to create the model, a model context, and the entity classes for your solution. The entity classes must be in their own project, which has no references to `System.Data.Entity`.

You've already done all of these things in previous chapters of the book. In fact, in Chapter 18, you used a modified POCO template that removed all of the `virtual` keywords from the properties and forced each entity class to inherit from the `ObjectState` class. While you won't be leveraging the `ObjectState` class in this walkthrough, you can use these classes and the model for this walkthrough. This will require an additional reference to the `ObjectState`'s project any time you reference the entities.

You'll need to make two important (and very minor) changes to the template that builds the `ObjectContext`. This is the *BreakAway.Context.tt* file that is in the same project as the model. We want the context methods to return `IObjectSet` rather than `ObjectSet`. Using the more generalized interface is critical as we plan ahead for building in the ability to switch from the real context to a fake context.

There are two places early on in the T4 template where you need to add the `I`.

Somewhere near line 92, you'll find this code, which is a single line:

```
<#=Accessibility.ForReadOnlyProperty(entitySet)#>
  ObjectSet<<#=code.Escape(entitySet.ElementType)#>>
  <#=code.Escape(entitySet)#>
```

Change that `ObjectSet` to `IObjectSet`.

Make the same change to this next line of code, which should be only a few lines below the first:

```
private ObjectSet<<#=code.Escape(entitySet.ElementType)#>>
 <#=code.FieldName(entitySet)#>;
```

Building an Interface to Represent a Context

Previously in this book, you have always used an `ObjectContext` to do your entity bidding for you. Now that you are going to create persistence ignorance, you want to have a more generic context that might be an `ObjectContext` in some scenarios and might be some other type of context in other scenarios. Whichever context you use, it does need to be particular to your domain. It will need to be able to expose your data (`Customers`, `Reservations`, etc.) and allow you to perform critical tasks such as saving.

This will be best represented by an interface that the `BAEntities` context can implement. Therefore, you'll build the interface, `IContext`, with similar members as `BAEntities`.

First you need a new project. Create a Class Library project. I've named mine Interfaces and the namespace of the assembly is `BAGA.Repository.Interfaces`.

The project needs the following references:

`System.Data.Entity`
: This is so that the interface you're building will have access to the `IObjectSet` interface.

`BreakAwayEntities`
: This is the project that contains the entity classes generated from the model along with their T4 template.

`POCOState`
: This is another project you created in Chapter 18. The entities above each inherit from the `StateObject` class.

Now you can create the `IContext` interface, shown in Example 24-9, inside this project.

For the sake of brevity, this example interface does not expose every `EntitySet` in the model.

Example 24-9. The IContext interface

```
using System.Collections.Generic;
using System.Data.Objects;
using OBAGA;

namespace POCOBAGA.Repository.Interfaces
{
  public interface IContext
  {
    IObjectSet<Contact> Contacts { get; }
    IQueryable<Customer> Customers { get; }
    IObjectSet<Trip> Trips { get; }
    IObjectSet<Reservation> Reservations { get; }
    IObjectSet<Payment> Payments { get; }
```

```
        string Save();
        IEnumerable<T> ManagedEntities<T>();
        bool ValidateBeforeSave(out string validationErrors);
    }
}
```

The interface contains the IObjectSet properties for five of the EntitySets in your model. The fact that you can use IObjectSet rather than being limited to the ObjectSet class will become an essential ingredient in your recipe for building testable code. As you get further on in the sample, this will become clearer.

Notice that Customers returns an IQueryable, not an IObjectSet. That's because there is no Customers EntitySet in the model. Customer inherits from Contact and is part of the Contacts EntitySet. But it's a drag to always have to query for Contacts.OfType<Customer>. The interface will let you simplify querying for the developers and uses an interface that, like IObjectSet, allows you to enumerate customers. As you build the repository later on for Customer, you'll revert to the Contacts IObjectSet to add and remove items.

In addition to these and the Save method, there are two other members: a generic ManagedEntities property and a method for performing validation before saving. The ManagedEntities is similar to the extension method that you saw in Chapter 21. However, that method was an extension to the ObjectContext class and depended on other Entity Framework features. Now, we need it to be more generic in this solution, and therefore you will create a special interface member that you can implement however you want in classes that derive from it. This will be very useful when working with the repositories.

You'll see more about the validation method as you get further into this example.

Modifying the BAEntities ObjectContext Class to Implement the New Interface

Now that you have an interface, the existing context, BAEntities, will need to implement it. At this point, you have the option to modify the T4 that generates it or create your own independent class. In this case, I'm going to choose the latter and get rid of the *BreakAwayContext.tt* file. It already has most of what I need thanks to the T4, but I want to make some changes and would rather make them directly in code than in the template. Read the sidebar "T4 Templates and an Evolving Interface" for more details.

T4 Templates and an Evolving Interface

I plan to make more modifications to the IContext interface in Example 24-9 throughout this chapter and don't want to have to continuously modify the T4 template for the BAEntities ObjectContext class. It will be simpler for me to work directly with the class, which is why I'm breaking the code generation. At some point, you will have a solid interface and then it will make sense to go back to using the T4 template. A more interesting solution, but too complex for our purposes here, would be to enable the T4 template to ensure that the class it is generating automatically implements the interface members.

Disconnecting the context class from the T4 template

You'll find that you can't just move the generated class that is attached to the T4 template in the Solution Explorer. Instead, you'll need to perform the following steps:

1. Create a new class file, *BAEntitiesContext.cs.*
2. Open the *BreakAwayContext.cs* file.
3. Copy and paste its contents into the new file in the same solution.
4. Delete the *BreakAwayContext.tt* file. The generated class file will automatically be deleted along with the template file.

Implementing the IContext interface

Currently, the `BAEntities` class inherits from `ObjectContext`. This will not change. However, in addition to this, it should also implement the `IContext` interface.

1. Add a reference to the Interfaces project.
2. Modify the class declaration as follows:

VB
```
Public Partial Class BAEntities
  Inherits ObjectContext
  Implements IContext
```

C#
```
public partial class BAEntities : ObjectContext, IContext
```

While the context already implements many of the members of `IContext` (e.g., `Activities` and `Contacts`), there are some members that it still must implement. In fact, you'll get a compiler error that informs you of this.

Implementing the remaining interface members

One way to do this in C# is by right-clicking `IContext` in the class declaration and selecting Implement Interface, and then from its submenu, Implement Interface. In Visual Basic, pressing the Enter key after `IContext` will automatically implement the remaining members.

The new members will be placed at the bottom of the code file, as shown in Example 24-10.

Example 24-10. IContext member implementation

```
#region IContext Members

public IQueryable <Customer> Customers
{
```

```
    get { throw new NotImplementedException(); }
  }

  public string Save()
  {
    throw new NotImplementedException();
  }

  public System.Collections.Generic.IEnumerable<T> ManagedEntities<T>()
  {
    throw new NotImplementedException();
  }

  public bool ValidateBeforeSave(out string validationErrors)
  {
    throw new NotImplementedException();
  }

  #endregion
```

Fill out the logic for `Customers`, `Save`, and `ManagedEntities`, as shown in Example 24-11.

Example 24-11. Providing code for IContext members in the BAEntities implementation

```
public IQueryable<Customer> Customers
{
  get { return _customers ?? (_customers =
        CreateObjectSet<Contact>("Contacts").OfType<Customer>()); }
}
private IQueryable<Customer> _customers;

public string Save()
{
  string validationErrors;
  if (ValidateBeforeSave(out validationErrors))
  {
    SaveChanges();
    return "";
  }
  return "Data Not Saved due to Validation Errors: " + validationErrors;
}

public System.Collections.Generic.IEnumerable<T> ManagedEntities<T>()
{
  var oses = ObjectStateManager.GetObjectStateEntries();
  return oses.Where(entry => entry.Entity is T)
             .Select(entry => (T)entry.Entity);
}
```

`Customers` now prefilters the `Contacts` entities for you. `ManagedEntities` does its job as defined previously in Chapter 21, and leverages the `GetObjectStateEntries` overload from that chapter as well. `Save` will make a call to the `ValidateBeforeSave` method before `SaveChanges` is called. You'll provide the validations in the class repositories and then flesh out the `ValidateBeforeSave` method after that.

`BAEntities` is only the first class to derive from `IContext`. You'll be creating some more a bit later in this chapter, but unlike `BAEntities`, these will be classes that have no knowledge at all about the Entity Framework.

Creating the IEntityRepository Interface

Before you can build the repositories, you'll need to build the `IEntityRepository` interface that they will all implement. The interface will go into a new project along with the repository classes, which you will build after the interface is set up.

Remember that this is just one way to build the architecture. And I am building it very explicitly so that you are able to see all of the working parts. As more developers learn how to use these features of Entity Framework, you will find a greater variety of patterns to learn from. Jarod Ferguson is one such developer who is able to apply his architecture expertise and existing patterns to build advanced architectures with Entity Framework. Check out his December 2009 post "Unity Extension for Entity Framework POCO Configuration, Repository and Unit of Work (*http://elegantcode.com/2009/12/15/building-a-unity-extension-for-entity-framework-poco-configuration-repository-and-unit-of-work/*), and keep an eye on his blog for updates.

Create a new Class Library project called Repositories. The repositories themselves need not be ignorant of the persistence layer and will have references to the model project.

The project needs references to the following:

- `BreakAwayEntities`
- `BreakAwayModel`
- `Interfaces`
- `POCOState`

Create a new interface project item called `IEntityRepository`. The interface will let you map out expectations for the repository classes as described earlier.

Example 24-12 lists the code for the generic `IEntityRepository<TEntity>`.

Example 24-12. The IEntityRepository class

```
using System.Collections.Generic;

namespace BAGA.Repository.Interfaces
{
  public interface IEntityRepository<TEntity>
  {
    TEntity GetById(int id);
    void Add(TEntity entity);
```

```
    void Delete(TEntity entity);
    IList<TEntity> All();
  }
}
```

In addition to the methods and properties described earlier in the chapter (`GetByID`, `Add`, `Delete`, and `All`), the repository has the ability to return an `IContext` with the read-only `Context` property. We'll use a constructor to set a context in each repository class, allowing us to force the repository to use a particular context as a *unit of work*. With Entity Framework this is important because we will frequently be working with various types but want them to be managed by the same context.

Creating the Repository Classes

Create a new class named `ReservationRepository`. Force the class to implement from `IEntityRepository` using `Reservation` as the generic type. You will want to add a `using`/`Imports` declaration to `BAGA.Repository.Interfaces` so that you don't have to fully qualify the interface.

Be sure to change the class declaration of the new classes to `public` in C#, as by default they will be `internal`.

After implementing the interface, the `ReservationRepository` class file should look like the code in Example 24-13.

Example 24-13. The ReservationRepository with IEntityRepository members

```
using System;
using System.Collections.Generic;
using BAGA;
using BAGA.Repository.Interfaces;

namespace BAGA.Repository.Repositories
{
  public class ReservationRepository: IEntityRepository<Reservation>
  {
    #region IEntityRepository<Reservation> Members

    public Reservation GetById(int id)
    {
      throw new NotImplementedException();
    }

    public void Add(Reservation entity)
    {
      throw new NotImplementedException();
    }
```

```
    public void Delete(Reservation entity)
    {
      throw new NotImplementedException();
    }

    public IList<Reservation> All()
    {
      throw new NotImplementedException();
    }
    #endregion
  }
}
```

Before filling out the logic for the interface members, we'll add a constructor to allow the developer to pass in an existing `IContext` when instantiating the `ReservationRepository`.

You could additionally add a parameterless constructor that presumes that the class should instantiate a `BAEntities ObjectContext` if no context is passed in. This will require a reference to `System.Data.Entity`. Since it is the entity classes that are being designed to be persistent ignorant, not the repositories, it's not a problem to have this reference.

You'll also need a local variable to which to assign the context, shown along with the constructor and the rest of the implementation in Example 24-14.

Example 24-14. ReservationRepository

```
using System.Collections.Generic;
using System.Linq;
using BAGA.Repository.Interfaces;

namespace BAGA.Repository.Repositories
{
  public class ReservationRepository: IEntityRepository<Reservation>
  {

    private readonly IContext _context;

    public ReservationRepository(IContext context)
    {
      _context = context;
    }

    public Reservation GetById(int id)
    {
     return _context.Reservations
             .FirstOrDefault(r => r.ReservationID == id);
    }

    public void Add(Reservation entity)
    {
```

```
            _context.Reservations.AddObject(entity);
        }

        public void Delete(Reservation entity)
        {
            _context.Reservations.DeleteObject(entity);
        }

        public IList<Reservation> All()
        {
            return _context.Reservations.ToList();
        }

    }
}
```

The ReservationRepository needs an additional method that is not part of the interface. GetReservationsForCustomer, shown in Example 24-15, is an example of a method described earlier in the chapter. It validates the customerId passed in before executing the query. You'll be writing a unit test for this shortly but will want to test this method without hitting the database.

In a more advanced repository pattern, you might have an architecture that would allow you to put logic that is not defined by the IRepository interface in separate classes.

Example 24-15. The ReservationRepository.GetReservationsForCustomer method

```
public IList<Reservation> GetReservationsForCustomer(int customerId)
{
  if (customerId < 1)
  {
    throw new ArgumentOutOfRangeException();
  }
  return _context.Reservations
         .Where(r => r.ContactID == customerId).ToList();
}
```

Most of the other repositories will look similar to the ReservationRepository. However, the CustomerRepository implementation differs from the other repositories because the Customer class inherits from Contact. In the model, this means that Customer is served up not by a Customers EntitySet, but by the Contacts EntitySet. As a result, there is no ObjectSet for Customers. Instead, you retrieve customer entities by filtering the Contacts ObjectSet.

Let's see how to implement a repository for a derived entity.

The Add and Delete methods leverage the Contacts IObjectSet (of which Customer is a part).

Remember the special IEnumerable<Customer> property that you created in IContext and then implemented in the BAEntities class? You can now see the benefit of that special property when implementing the All and GetById methods in CustomerRepository. Both of these methods retrieve their results by using the Customers property.

The CustomerRespository is listed in Example 24-16.

Example 24-16. CustomerRepository with logic added

```
using System.Collections.Generic;
using System.Linq;
using BAGA.Repository.Interfaces;

namespace BAGA.Repository.Repositories
{
  public class CustomerRepository: IEntityRepository<Customer>
  {
    private readonly IContext _context;

    public Customer GetById(int id)
    {
      return _context.Customers
             .FirstOrDefault(c => c.ContactID == id);
    }

    public void Add(Customer entity)
    {
      _context.Contacts.Add(entity);
    }

    public void Delete(Customer entity)
    {
      _context.Contacts.Remove(entity);
    }

    public IList<Customer> All()
    {
      return _context.Customers.ToList();
    }
  }
}
```

Now that you have these repositories, you can build some tests against them, although at this point these tests will test both interaction (with the Entity Framework) and integration (with the database).

Testing GetReservationsForCustomer Against the Database

Before moving on with the classes and repositories, this is a good time to build a test to verify the behavior of your GetReservationsForCustomer method. The test is not concerned with the results of the query, but whether the method allows the query to be executed. Since you haven't built any fakes yet for testing, understand that if the customerId is valid, you are going to hit the database. The purpose for testing at this point is for the benefit of those of you who are new to building tests. Building and testing with the fakes will make more sense once you have something to compare them to.

1. Open the ReservationRepository class.
2. Right-click on the GetReservationsForCustomer method and choose Create Unit Tests.

   The Create Unit Tests Wizard should show this method checked with the Output project as "Create a new Visual C# test project..." (or Visual Basic depending on your code base).
3. Click OK.
4. In the New Test Project window, change the project name to POCOEFTests and click Create.

If a dialog pops up asking if you want to add the InternalsVisibleTo attribute to your classes, it means the classes are private. Be sure to change them to public.

   Because you are still testing the repository that hits the database, the test needs access to the EntityConnection string.
5. Copy the *app.config* file from the Model project into the new test project.

   You won't simply test the method (as the automatically created unit tests will specify), but instead you'll verify that the validation works. You'll create one test to make sure the method properly responds to bad IDs and another to correctly respond to good IDs.
6. In the new test class, find the GetReservationsForCustomerTest and rename it to Passing_ID_of_Zero_To_GetReservationsForCustomer_Throws.
7. Modify the test method (or just delete it and start from scratch) and then make and modify a copy of it so that you end up with the two tests shown in Example 24-17.

Example 24-17. Tests to verify that GetReservationsForCustomer checks the incoming ID

```
[TestMethod()]
[ExpectedException(typeof(ArgumentOutOfRangeException),
                   "GetReservations for Customer allowed an ID<1")]
public void Passing_ID_of_Zero_To_GetReservationsForCustomer_Throws()
{
  var repository = new ReservationRepository(new BAEntities());
  repository.GetReservationsForCustomer(0);
}

[TestMethod()]
public void Can_Pass_ID_Greater_Than_Zero_To_GetReservationsForCustomer()
```

```
{
  var repository = new ReservationRepository(new BAEntities());
  Assert.IsNotNull(repository.GetReservationsForCustomer(1));
}
```

8. Right-click in the code window (but not on a test name) and choose Run Tests. This will run all of the tests in the test class.

The first test expects an exception and does not bother with an `Assert`. The second needs to verify that something is returned from the method call. Rather than checking for the count of `Reservations` in the returned list, the test only asks if the list exists. It's possible that we queried a customer that had no reservations, which would return a list with no items.

Creating a Fake Context

Now that you see how the test works, let's go to the next step of testing: creating a fake context that will not hit the database.

Only the tests will need the fake context, so you can create it inside the test project.

In projects that have a lot of tests, you might split the tests and various components, such as the fakes, into different projects. For this example, we will keep everything in one project.

The new fake context will implement the `IContext`, and in place of hitting the database, the fake will create some test data on the fly. When you execute queries, this test data will be returned in place of database data.

In the test project add a new class, `FakeContext`. At the top of the class, add the following namespaces to the `using`/`Imports` declarations:

```
using System.Data.Objects;
using BAGA
using BAGA.Repository.Interface;
```

Force the class to implement `IContext` and its members. After implementing the interface, the class should look like Example 24-18.

Example 24-18. FakeContext with the IContext members

```
class FakeContext:IContext
{
  #region IContext Members
  public IObjectSet<Contact> Contacts
  {
    get { throw new NotImplementedException(); }
  }
  public IQueryable<Customer> Customers
  {
```

```
    get { throw new NotImplementedException(); }
  }
  public IObjectSet<Trip> Trips
  {
    get { throw new NotImplementedException(); }
  }
  public IObjectSet<Reservation> Reservations
  {
    get { throw new NotImplementedException(); }
  }
  public IObjectSet<Payment> Payments
  {
    get { throw new NotImplementedException(); }
  }
  public string Save()
  {
    throw new NotImplementedException();
  }
  public IEnumerable<T> ManagedEntities<T>()
  {
    throw new NotImplementedException();
  }
  public bool ValidateBeforeSave(out string validationErrors)
  {
    throw new NotImplementedException();
  }
  #endregion
}
```

In `BAEntities`, you have a constructor that enables lazy loading, which is a feature of Entity Framework's `ObjectContext`. Your fake context won't be depending on lazy loading. The fake repository is free to provide the related data any way that it pleases. The classes that request the data don't care how the repository acquires the data, just as long as it passes that data along.

Keep that in mind; but for now, the next step is to force the `Reservations` property to return some data.

Add a class scoped variable for the `Reservations`:

```
private IObjectSet<Reservation> _reservations;
```

Then add a new method, `CreateReservations`, which will build some new `Reservation` objects for your test on the fly (see Example 24-19).

Example 24-19. The CreateReservations fake data method

```
private void CreateReservations()
{
  if (_reservations == null)
  {
    _reservations = new FakeObjectSet<Reservation>();
    _reservations.AddObject(new Reservation
                         { ReservationID = 1, TripID = 1, ContactID = 2 });
    _reservations.AddObject(new Reservation
```

```
                            { ReservationID = 2, TripID = 2, ContactID = 2 });
    _reservations.AddObject(new Reservation
                            { ReservationID = 3, TripID = 1, ContactID = 3 });
  }
}
```

We've created two reservations for one customer (ContactID 2) and one reservation for another customer (ContactID 3).

Notice that you are instantiating a FakeObjectSet, not IObjectSet. You cannot instantiate an interface. But you don't want to instantiate an ObjectSet class. ObjectSet implements ObjectQuery and you would then be back to being completely bound to the Entity Framework's querying mechanism. The goal here is to be lightweight and not tangled up with someone else's framework; no matter how much you may like that framework.

> **Build It Yourself or Use a Mocking Framework**
>
> A number of third-party mocking frameworks, such as Moq, TypeMock Isolator, and RhinoMocks, simplify the task of building fake contexts for your tests. Rather than force you to depend on a particular third-party tool and to give you the benefit of seeing all of the pieces of this puzzle, we will take the longer route of creating our own classes so that you can see how it works.

Creating a FakeObjectSet Class

For the tests, you'll need a class that, like ObjectSet, implements the IObjectSet interface but, unlike ObjectSet, does not inherit from ObjectQuery. This is an important piece of the puzzle and the reason the ObjectSet and IObjectSet were created for the second version of Entity Framework. They provide a means for developers to write more agile, testable code.

IObjectSet has only a handful of methods that need to be implemented: AddObject, Attach, DeleteObject, and Detach. IObjectSet also implements interfaces that make it possible to query—IEnumerable and IQueryable, along with their generic counterparts.

Here is the signature of IObjectSet:

```
public interface IObjectSet<TEntity>
  : IQueryable<TEntity>, IEnumerable<TEntity>,
    IQueryable, IEnumerable
    where TEntity : class
```

The FakeObjectSet must also implement anything that is required by the additional interfaces that IObjectSet implements. Finally, you'll need to enforce the same constraint that the generic type passed in as a class. In the IObjectSet, this is defined by where TEntity : class.

Create a new class in the test project and name it `FakeObjectSet`. Then add `System.Data.Objects` to the namespaces declared at the top of the class.

Force the class to accept a generic type with the constraint described earlier and inherit from `IObjectSet`.

VB
```
Public Class FakeObjectSet (Of T As Class)
Implements IObjectSet(Of T)
```

C#
```
class FakeObjectSet<T> : IObjectSet<T> where T : class
```

When you implement the interface, you will get the four methods listed earlier as well as `ElementType`, `Expression`, `Provider`, and two `GetEnumerator` methods. These last five methods come from the `IEnumerable` and `IQueryable` interfaces.

The `FakeObjectSet` needs a container to hold the classes in the set. You'll use an `IList` (using the same generic type that is passed into the `FakeObjectSet`) for this. Then the `Add`, `Attach`, `Delete`, and `Detach` methods will move objects in and out of that `IList`.

The other methods will contain standard code that is common to classes that implement those interfaces.

Example 24-20 shows what the `FakeObjectSet` should look like when it is fleshed out.

Example 24-20. The FakeObjectSet class

```
class FakeObjectSet<T> : IObjectSet<T> where T : class
{
  readonly IList<T> _container = new List<T>();

    public void AddObject(T entity)
  {
    _container.Add(entity);
  }

  public void Attach(T entity)
  {
    _container.Add(entity);
  }

  public void DeleteObject(T entity)
  {
    _container.Remove(entity);
  }

  public void Detach(T entity)
  {
    _container.Remove(entity);
  }

  public IEnumerator<T> GetEnumerator()
  {
    return _container.GetEnumerator();
  }
```

```
    IEnumerator IEnumerable.GetEnumerator()
    {
      return _container.GetEnumerator();
    }

    public Type ElementType
    {
      get{return typeof(T);}
    }

    public System.Linq.Expressions.Expression Expression
    {
      get { return _container.AsQueryable<T>().Expression; }
    }

    public IQueryProvider Provider
    {
      get { return _container.AsQueryable<T>().Provider; }
    }
  }
```

Now you have something that you can instantiate that implements `IObjectSet` but does not tie you to an `ObjectQuery`.

Completing the Fake Context

The method you built in Example 24-19, `CreateReservations`, will instantiate this new class.

The `GetReservationsForCustomer` method really only requires that you provide some reservations in your fake context. But we'll add some customers also in case you want to do some additional testing.

Even though `Customer` inherits from `Contact` and does not have its own `EntitySet`, we can still use an `IObjectSet` to contain the `Customer` objects in the `FakeContext`. Because `IObjectSet` implements `IQueryable`, it will resolve properly when `IContext.Customers` expects an `IQueryable`.

1. Add class-level field variables for a few other properties:

```
private IObjectSet <Customer> _customers;
private IObjectSet<Trip> _trips;
private IObjectSet<Reservation> _reservations;
private IObjectSet<Payment> _payments;
```

2. Add the additional create methods shown in Example 24-21. Notice that the values of the various methods are defined so that the objects will be related.

Example 24-21. FakeContext methods

```
private void CreateCustomers()
{
  if (_customers == null)
  {
```

```
        _customers = new FakeObjectSet<Customer>();
        _customers.AddObject(new Customer
          { ContactID = 1, FirstName = "Matthieu", LastName = "Mezil" });
        _customers.AddObject(new Customer
          { ContactID = 2, FirstName = "Kristofer", LastName = "Anderson" });
        _customers.AddObject(new Customer
          { ContactID = 3, FirstName = "Bobby", LastName = "Johnson" });
    }
    private void CreatePayments()
    {
      if (_payments == null)
      {
        _payments = new FakeObjectSet<Payment>();
        //create an incomplete payment for reservation 1 (a $1000 trip)
        _payments.AddObject(new Payment { PaymentID = 1,
                                          ReservationID = 1, Amount = 500 });
        //create a full payment for reservation 2
        _payments.AddObject(new Payment { PaymentID = 2,
                                          ReservationID = 2, Amount = 1200 });
      }
    }
    private void CreateTrips()
    {
      if (_trips == null)
      {
        _trips = new FakeObjectSet<Trip>();
        //one customer has two reservations, the other only has one
        _trips.AddObject(new Trip
                          { TripID = 1, DestinationID = 1,TripCostUSD=1000 });
        _trips.AddObject(new Trip
                          { TripID = 2, DestinationID = 2, TripCostUSD=1200 });
      }
    }
```

3. Modify the properties so that they call the creation methods if necessary and return the local fields, as shown in Example 24-22.

Example 24-22. The MockContext Customers properties

```
public IObjectSet<Customer> Customers
{
  get
  {        CreateCustomers();
           return _customers;      }
}
```

4. Do the same for the `Trips`, `Reservations`, and `Payments` properties.

Modify the tests to use the fake repository

Now that you have a fake repository to work with you can change the two tests to use the fake, rather than the actual context that hits the database.

In each of the two tests, modify the code that instantiates a new context so that it uses the `FakeRepository` class instead of `BAGAContext`.

```
IBAGARepository context = new FakeRepository();
```

Rerun the tests

Go ahead and run the tests again. They should pass. You might want to debug the tests so that you can watch what happens as the code steps through the `FakeRepository` and `FakeObjectSet`.

Keep in mind that since our tests are designed to test the method validation and not the functionality of Entity Framework, providing fake data does not affect the feasibility of the tests.

Building Tests That Do Not Hit the Database

In this next phase of the example, you will refactor the solution even more. The goal here will test validation logic that is part of a save method without hitting the database. You will introduce some class validation that needs to be performed prior to saving changes back to the database. Then you will write tests to ensure that the validation is doing its job correctly. You'll tweak the repository in order to enable this, and in doing so, create even better separation between the various tasks in your application.

Adding Validation Logic to the POCO Class

The first task here is to add a class validation to the `Reservation` class—not to the generated class but to a partial class that extends `Reservation`. This allows the class to be responsible for validating itself. In order for a reservation to be saved to the database, it must have a `ReservationDate`, a `Contact` (or `ContactID`), and a `Trip` (or `TripID`).

> **Partial Classes for POCOs?**
>
> For those of you with more experience with persistence ignorance, repositories, and designing for separation of concerns, you may be thinking "code smell" at this point. Adding a partial class for a POCO seems to be outside the bounds of a POCO class. But because we are using code generation for the POCOs, we'll be stuck with having to lean on the partial classes. A more advanced approach might use an `IValidator<T>` interface. Take a look at the Validation Application Block in Microsoft's Enterprise Library for more information and ideas (*http://msdn.microsoft.com/en-us/library/ff664356(v=PandP.50).aspx*).
>
> For a completely different approach, take a look at the code-first implementation that is introduced in the next chapter. With code first, there is no model and no code generation. You can define your classes by hand and structure them as you wish.

If any of this critical data does not exist, the method will throw a `System.ArgumentNullException` along with the name of the invalid property.

Validating that the `Reservation` has a `Customer` and a `Trip` is a little tricky. `TripID` is nullable, so it would be null if it hasn't been assigned. However, the `Trip` property might have been assigned instead, so `TripID` can be null and valid at the same time. `ContactID` is non-nullable and will always be at least 0, so testing for 0 is useless for that reason and also in the case that the `Customer/Contact` is new and does not yet have an ID. Therefore, we test that one or the other (foreign key value or entity reference) has been assigned.

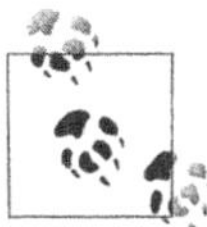

The problem I have just described with validating that there is a `Trip` attached to the reservation is the same problem that Entity Framework runtime has when attempting to validate the foreign key constraint. See the section "Checking for missing entity references with and without foreign keys" on page 540 for a discussion of the runtime validation.

Example 24-23 lists the `Validate` method added to the `Reservation` class. It uses a parameter to notify the calling method which properties were invalid. You can see that being constructed throughout the method.

Example 24-23. The Reservation class's Validate method

```
public bool Validate(out string validationError)
{
 bool isvalid = true;
 validationError = "";
 if (TripID == null & Trip==null)
 {
   isvalid = false;
   validationError = "Trip";
 }
 if (ContactID == 0 & Customer == null)
 {
   isvalid = false;
   validationError += ",Contact";
 }
 if (ReservationDate == DateTime.MinValue)
 {
   isvalid = false;
   validationError += ",Date";
 }
 if (validationError != "")
   validationError = string.Format
      ("[ReservationID {0}: {1}]", ReservationID, validationError);
 return isvalid;
}
```

This method will be called from the context's `ValidateBeforeSave` method anytime the application wants to save data back to the database.

Adding Validation Logic to the Context

Now that you have some validation logic, you can call it from the ValidateBefore Save methods along with validations that you might create in any other classes. Example 24-24 shows the code for the BAEntities.ValidateBeforeSave method. If there are multiple reservations with validation errors, those are combined in the validationEr rors string, which is passed out to whatever method calls ValidateBeforeSave.

Example 24-24. Validation in the context classes

```
public bool ValidateBeforeSave(out string validationErrors)
{
  bool isvalid = true;
  validationErrors = "";

  foreach (var res in ManagedEntities<Reservation>())
  {
    string validationError;
    bool isResValid = res.Validate(out validationError);
    if (!isResValid)
    {
      isvalid = false;
      validationErrors += validationError;
    }
  }
  return isvalid;
}
```

Here you can also see the ManagedEntities<TEntity> property come into play. Validation is being done on only those reservations that are currently being change-tracked (i.e., managed).

The FakeContext would have the same exact logic in its ValidateBeforeSave method, giving you a way to test the context's logic without hitting the database.

Providing ManagedEntities in the FakeContext

The FakeContext can create a fake collection of Reservations to represent what might be currently managed by the context. This method, shown in Example 24-25, creates only a single reservation to place in the returned data.

Example 24-25. Building the fake reservation data for ManagedEntities

```
public IEnumerable<T> ManagedEntities<T>()
{
  if (typeof(T) == typeof(Reservation))
  {
    var newRes = new Reservation
                 {
                   ReservationID = 1,
                   ContactID = 1,
                   TripID = 1,
```

```
                    ReservationDate = new DateTime(2009, 08, 01)
                  };

    var managedRes = new List<Reservation>{newRes};
    return (IEnumerable<T>) managedRes.AsEnumerable();
  }
  return null;
}
```

But for testing purposes, something is missing. This is a valid reservation. The tests will need to verify that the validation correctly identifies valid reservations. However, they also need to verify that the validation responds properly to invalid reservations.

How can you coerce the `ManagedReservations` property to provide data to test both scenarios? This is where a mocking framework will alleviate a bunch of work, but again, I want to work through all of the necessary parts in order to have a good understanding of what's necessary. One answer is to create another fake repository, one whose job is to return bad data for testing purposes.

Another tactic rather than forcing various contexts to be responsible for creating data is to create it in the test. I prefer not to do that because it's redundant code. By placing the data in the contexts, I have dependable data. In an edge case, I can create the data on the fly in the test code.

Copy the *FakeContext* file to a new file called *FakeContextBadData*. I will only focus on the new method for returning bad data.

Change the name of the class in the new file to `FakeContextBadData`. Then modify the `ManagedEntities` method by removing the code to assign the `ContactID` and `TripID`. It should look like Example 24-26.

Example 24-26. Fake data to return invalid managed reservations for testing

```
public IEnumerable<T> ManagedEntities<T>()
{
  if (typeof(T) == typeof(Reservation))
  {
    var newRes = new Reservation
                  {
                    ReservationID = 1,
                    ReservationDate = new DateTime(2009, 08, 01)
                  };

    var managedRes = new List<Reservation>{newRes};
    return (IEnumerable<T>) managedRes.AsEnumerable();
  }
  return null;
}
```

You now have three classes that implement the `IContext` interface, which demonstrates the additional value provided by using an interface. You can use the different contexts interchangeably thanks to the interface.

Now you can build two tests to ensure that the validation all the way down inside the `Reservation` class is working properly (see Example 24-27).

Example 24-27. Tests to verify the validation method

```
[TestMethod()]
public void Validators_Return_True_and_Empty_ErrorString_With_Good_Data()
{
  var context = new FakeContext();
  string validationErrors = "";
  bool valid = context.ValidateBeforeSave(out validationErrors);
  Assert.IsTrue(valid);
  Assert.AreEqual(validationErrors, "");
}

[TestMethod()]
public void Validators_Return_False_and_NotEmpty_ErrorString_With_Bad_Data()
{
  var context = new FakeContextBadData();
  string validationErrors = "";
  bool valid = context.ValidateBeforeSave(out validationErrors);
  Assert.IsFalse(valid);
  Assert.AreNotEqual(validationErrors, "");
}
```

The first test uses the `FakeRepository` to provide fake data. We know that it will give us a valid reservation, so the expectation of this test is that the return from the `ValidateBeforeSave` method will be `true`. There is an extra `Assert` in there to ensure that the `validationErrors` string is empty, which it should be if there are no problems with the data.

The second test uses the repository that returns an invalid reservation. The expectation, therefore, is that the `valid` variable will be `false` and there will be some text in the `validationErrors`. A more fine-grained set of tests would ensure that the `validationErrors` string is also correct in different scenarios.

Hiding the Context from the Lower Layers with Unit of Work

In the tests involving the repository thus far, the test methods have instantiated a context and passed it into the repository's constructor. This is convenient in the tests because it allows you to pick and choose which repository to pass in. If this were a UI, or another layer close to the UI, it means the UI would also need to instantiate the context after all the work that you've done to create separation in your application. The UI should not be aware of the context. The repositories are there to protect the UI from interacting directly with the context. You may even want another layer in between the UI and the context, but let's focus on this simpler scenario for now.

How can you have your cake and eat it too? You want to control which context gets used when testing, but you do not want the UI layer to be calling code to instantiate a context.

One approach would be to allow the default constructor of each repository to instantiate a `BAEntities` context. You could even then retrieve that context instance and share it with other repositories thanks to the constructor that takes a context instance.

The repositories would then own the saving mechanism via:

```
ReservationRepository.Context.Save();
```

The problem with this is that you would be using the `ReservationRepository` to trigger a save that might reverberate through different types—`CustomerRepository`, `PaymentRepository`, and so forth—if they are all using the same context. Having the `Save` be accessed from inside a repository, therefore, would be misleading since it appears that the call would only be saving the reservation data, which is not always the case.

A solution is to create a class that represents a unit of work and would own the context while providing a separation between the context and the UI layer.

The Unit of Work Pattern

Unit of Work is a recognized software development pattern. It is described in Martin Fowler's *Patterns of Enterprise Application Architecture (P of EAA)* (*http://www.martinfowler.com/eaaCatalog/unitOfWork.html*) as follows:

> Maintains a list of objects affected by a business transaction and coordinates the writing out of changes and the resolution of concurrency problems.

An `ObjectContext` is a Unit of Work for the Entity Framework. The `UnitOfWork` class that you are building in this section is a wrapper for the `IContext` interface.

The new class could then instantiate a default `BAEntities` context if none were passed in. When would you pass a context in? When calling the Unit of Work from a unit test.

Since this is a simple example, I'll put my `UnitOfWork` class inside my Repositories project rather than creating another project to contain it. Example 24-28 shows the `UnitOfWork` class.

Example 24-28. The UnitOfWork class

```
using BAGA.Repository.Interfaces;

namespace BAGA.Repository.Repositories
{
  public class UnitOfWork
  {
     private readonly IContext _context;
```

```
        public UnitOfWork()
          {
              _context = new BAEntities();
          }

          public UnitOfWork(IContext context)
          {
              _context = context;
          }
      public string Save()
      {
        return _context.Save();
      }
     internal IContext Context
      {
        get { return _context; }
      }
  }
}
```

Like the repositories, this class lets you pass in the context instance; otherwise, it will instantiate one. It exposes a `Save` method that will call its context's `Save` method.

Now your business layer or UI that needs to be able to retrieve and update entities can do so only through the `UnitOfWork`.

But this means you'll need to make a change to each of the repositories, which also need to be aware of the `UnitOfWork` so that they can get access to its context for the various methods that use the context.

Add a new constructor to each repository. The new constructor will take a `UnitOfWork` class as a parameter and then set the local to that of the `UnitOfWork.Context`. The internal `UnitOfWork.Context` is accessible to the repositories because they are in the same assembly (see Example 24-29).

Example 24-29. UnitOfWork overload for a repository constructor

```
public ReservationRepository(UnitOfWork uow)
{
  _context = uow.Context;
}
```

Testing UnitOfWork Against the Database

The following test, shown in Example 24-30, validates a few behaviors of `UnitOfWork` and does so with true database interaction.

The test checks that the `UnitOfWork` does, indeed, create the default context, `BAEntities`. Next, it verifies that queries against the database are being performed as expected using the single `UnitOfWork`. After this, it performs a database update and an insert which depend on the `UnitOfWork` managing the various entities and their changes via its internal context. Finally, a new UnitOfWork is created to requery the key data from the database and verify that it reflects the expected updates.

Example 24-30. Testing UnitOfWork with the BAEntities context

```
[TestMethod()]
public void UoW_with_Default_Context_Saves_To_and_Retrieves_from_Database()
{
  //let UOW create a default BAEntities context
  var uow = new UnitOfWork();
  var cRep = new CustomerRepository(uow);
  var rRep = new ReservationRepository(uow);
  var customer = cRep.GetById(20);
  string newNotes = DateTime.Now.ToString();
  customer.Notes = newNotes;
  var resCount = rRep.GetReservationsForCustomer(20).Count;
  var newRes = new Reservation
               {
                 Customer = customer, TripID = 3,
                 ReservationDate = DateTime.Now
               };
  customer.Reservations.Add(newRes);
  //single UOW manages all entities and updates
  string result = uow.Save();
  //use a new UOW to retrieve and verify db changes
  uow = new UnitOfWork();
  cRep = new CustomerRepository(uow);
  rRep = new ReservationRepository(uow);
  customer = cRep.GetById(20);
  Assert.IsTrue(customer.Notes == newNotes);
  Assert.IsTrue(rRep.GetReservationsForCustomer(20).Count == resCount + 1);
}
```

Enabling Eager Loading in IContext

Eager loading is an important feature of the Entity Framework's querying capabilities, but the method that enables it, Include, is a method of ObjectQuery. ObjectSet has an Include method only because it inherits from ObjectQuery.

Now that you are generically using IObjectSet directly, you have lost access to Include and definitely need it back.

The easiest way to provide Include to IObjectSet is through an extension method. But the extension will be for IQueryable, not IObjectSet. This allows not only the IObjectSet to benefit, but also the IQueryable that you are using for Customers. Add the extension method listed in Example 24-31 to the EFExtensionMethods class in the model project.

Example 24-31. Providing an Include method that will work with IContext

```
public static IQueryable<TSource> Include<TSource>
  (this IQueryable<TSource> source, string path)
{
```

```
    var objectQuery = source as ObjectQuery<TSource>;
    if (objectQuery != null)
    {
      return objectQuery.Include(path);
    }
    return source;
  }
```

This will allow the true `ObjectQuery`s to continue to use `Include`; however, it will simply strip the `Include` from queries using the fake contexts. The benefit is that your queries won't completely fail in your tests, but you have to be very careful about tests that depend on the eager-loaded related data since it won't be there as a result of this include.

Eager loading with a fake context

To test methods that contain eager-loading queries using `Include`, you should consider creating a special fake context that returns shaped results—for example, a `Customer` object with the `Reservations` populated since the `Include` method will simply be ignored.

Leveraging Precompiled Queries in Your Repositories

In Chapter 20, you learned about precompiling LINQ queries for a major query performance improvement. You can continue to get this advantage even in your repository, but you'll have to write some extra code to do so. Not every query will need to be precompiled. As mentioned in the earlier chapter, if the query is not reused, you will end up paying an unnecessary price for the precompilation/invoke which is a bit more expensive than simply executing a query.

The pattern I recommend is to have a separate set of repositories that are specifically designed to maintain and invoke compiled queries. As an example, alongside the `CustomerRepository`, you would have another class, `CustomerPreCompiledRepository`, which would contain the static `CompiledQuery` functions and methods that would return data as a result of invoking these various precompiled queries.

You can learn more about implementing this pattern from my December 2009 blog post titled "Agile EF 4 Repositories Part 4: Compiled LINQ Queries" (*http://thedatafarm.com/blog/data-access/agile-ef-4-repositories-part-4-compiled-linq-queries*).

Pay attention to the blog post's explanation of additions to `IContext`, which allow you to easily differentiate between `IContext` implementers that support precompiling and those that don't.

Using the New Infrastructure in Your Application

All of the database and `ObjectContext` interaction required by your application—performing queries, inspecting objects in the `ObjectStateManager`, persisting data to the database, and so on—will be encapsulated in various repositories, whether that is a single class or a set of classes. In a more highly architected application, you will likely be breaking this logic up even further. For now we'll stick with our simpler solution.

To see how this works, you'll create a UI layer in the solution and have it retrieve and save some data through the `UnitOfWork` and various repositories. This isn't too different from what you've already done in the test from Example 24-30, since that test used `BAEntities` and hit the database. The only real difference is that rather than performing asserts, you would be displaying the data.

The reason for this last exercise is to highlight the fact that the UI will be completely separated from Entity Framework thanks to the repositories and the persistent ignorant classes.

Note that I've added a new method, displayed in Example 24-32, to the `CustomerRepository`.

Example 24-32. A new method for CustomerRepository

```
public Customer CustomerAndReservations(int id)
{
  return _context.Customers.Include("Reservations")
                 .FirstOrDefault(c => c.ContactID == id);
}
```

We'll call this method from our console app.

Adding a UI Layer That Calls the Repository

Start by creating a new Console Application project in the solution. Then, create a reference to the following projects:

- BreakAwayEntities (the POCO classes)
- Repositories
- POCOState
- Interfaces

In the file that contains the `Main` method (*program.cs* or *Module.vb*) add a method to query the model, modify some data, and save it back to the database. This method, shown in Example 24-33, is similar to the test against the `UnitOfWork` test from Example 24-30.

Example 24-33. A simple console app using the new architecture

```
using System;
using BAGA;
using BAGA.Repository.Repositories;

namespace RepositoryUI
{
  class Program
  {
    static void Main(string[] args)
    {
      RetrieveAndModifySomeData();
    }

    private static void RetrieveAndModifySomeData()
    {
      var uow = new UnitOfWork(); //defaults to BAEntities context
      var cCust = new CustomerRepository(uow);
      var customer = cCust.CustomerAndReservations(20);
      Console.WriteLine(customer.LastName.Trim() + customer.FirstName);
      foreach (var res in customer.Reservations)
      {
        Console.WriteLine("    Res. Date: {0}", res.ReservationDate);
      }
      string newNotes = DateTime.Now.ToString();
      customer.Notes = newNotes;
      var resCount = customer.Reservations.Count;
      var newRes = new Reservation
      {
        Customer = customer,
        TripID = 4,
        ReservationDate = DateTime.Now
      };
      customer.Reservations.Add(newRes);
      string result = uow.Save();
      Console.WriteLine("ReservationID from DB: {0}", newRes.ReservationID);
      Console.ReadKey();
    }
  }
}
```

Application Architecture Benefits from Designing Testable Code

There are three notable points to make about this final example.

First, the UI project has no reference to the project that contains the model project (which contains the model and `ObjectContext`), nor to `System.Data.Entity`. This means your UI has no need to know anything about `System.Data.Entity`. Your UI and other layers that consume the `UnitOfWork` and repositories are now completely independent of a backend framework. The classes are totally unconcerned with how their data is stored and retrieved.

Second, the method works without having to instantiate the context. That means the repositories are doing their job.

Finally, thanks to the tests, most of the kinks in the backend of this application have already been worked out. Putting it together meant, in my case, that everything worked perfectly the first time I tried it.

Considering Mocking Frameworks?

You can do so much more with testing as your applications grow with your architecture, but this should certainly get you started.

Don't forget the earlier mention of third-party mocking frameworks. These will take away some of the pain of creating the mock repository manually.

As mentioned in an earlier sidebar in this chapter, I have seen mocking frameworks such as Moq, RhinoMocks, and TypeMock Isolator used successfully with the Entity Framework. You can learn more about mocking frameworks from myriad resources.

Summary

If you have never built repositories or unit tests before now, congratulations on completing this chapter! But remember, this is just the beginning of properly testing and designing your applications. Testing is an important part of application development, and being able to build tests that can easily and continuously verify your application is a great benefit to software development.

You've learned how the new POCO support and the `IObjectSet` enable you to create persistent ignorant classes and use repository classes to take charge of all of the interaction with the `ObjectContext`. You've built a very loosely coupled and maintainable architecture and implemented unit tests against methods that provide interaction with the persistence layer without being forced to hit the database.

The goal of the chapter was to demonstrate how the Entity Framework can be used in this type of development. The Entity Framework team put a great deal of effort into providing support for POCOs, persistence ignorance, and testability in the .NET 4.0 version of Entity Framework. As you have seen, targeting this style of development forces you to think carefully about your application architecture and can encourage you to build more sustainable and loosely coupled applications.

CHAPTER 25

Domain-Centric Modeling

Visual Studio 2010 brought new approaches to modeling for Entity Framework. The Sample and BreakAway models you have created and worked with thus far were reverse-engineered from existing databases. We call this type of modeling *database first.*

While basing an application on an existing corporate database is often necessary, many developers are able to design the database behind their model, completely from scratch. Other developers, such as those who follow Domain-Driven Development (DDD) patterns, prefer not to begin with the database, but rather with a conceptual model of their domain or simply with their own domain classes.

Beginning with Visual Studio 2010, the Entity Data Model Designer supports both of these development styles in addition to database first.

You can begin by describing your application domain as an Entity Data Model and then use that model to define a database. This is referred to as *model first*.

Alternatively, you can eliminate the EDMX model completely and focus on describing your application domain through your classes. This feature is called *code first* and is a future feature that Microsoft is currently building for the Entity Framework.

While this is the only chapter in which I discuss these other approaches, I do not mean to imply that they are less significant than database-first design. They are, in fact, very significant and if you are used to beginning with a database, you may find enlightenment as you explore these approaches, here in this introductory chapter and beyond, in various other resources.

In this chapter, you will learn three new ways to build applications that do not begin with the database. You'll learn first how to use the new model-first feature. A side benefit of designing a model from scratch is that you will learn about interacting with the design tools. Then you'll get a look at code first, which is included with Microsoft's Entity Framework Feature Community Technical Preview (CTP). Finally, you'll get a short introduction to another future technology, SQL Server Modeling and its modeling language, currently code-named "M." Because these last two technologies are still in development, I will limit discussion of them to a high level and point you to resources where you can keep up with them as they evolve.

Creating a Model and Database Using Model First

While the Entity Data Model Designer has always allowed you to build a model from scratch, there was never an easy way to create a database or the store and mapping metadata from that model. Even if a database already existed, creating the metadata between a model of your own design and a database was a very difficult task.

Now the design tools have been enhanced so that you can successfully begin by designing your model in the Designer and then let the tools build the appropriate metadata and a database from your model.

The Entity Data Model Designer supports creating entities, relationships, and inheritance hierarchies directly on the design surface. You have had some interaction with these features already, but you will do a lot more designing in this chapter.

The code generation will continue to perform its job of creating classes based on the model. But the conceptual model still needs a backing database along with the additional metadata—store schema and mappings—in order for the Entity Framework runtime to do its job.

The Designer's context menu has a Generate Database from Model option. But this is a bit of a misnomer. This feature will create the necessary SQL to define tables and constraints for a database. This is called the Database Definition Language, or DDL. But it will not create a database and it will not automatically execute this SQL. It will only build the DDL for you; it will be up to you to execute the DDL.

Additionally, the feature will create the model's store schema (SSDL) and mappings (MSL) based on the objects defined in the DDL.

There is a Visual Studio extension built by the Entity Framework team that allows you to take some additional control over how the DDL and metadata generation is created. You'll get a look at that shortly.

Let's start with a walkthrough to familiarize you with the basics and then follow up with a look at some more advanced features.

Creating a Conceptual Model in the Designer

Since by now you might be a little tired of the BreakAway Geek Adventure application and its data, you'll create a new application designed to track information about a developer conference. We can call it the ConferenceManager.

The ConferenceManager model will need conference tracks, speakers, and sessions, which provides us with a variety of relationships to work with. Also, some sessions may be workshops, which gives us an opportunity to build in an inheritance hierarchy.

On paper the model looks like Figure 25-1. Now you can build it in the Designer.

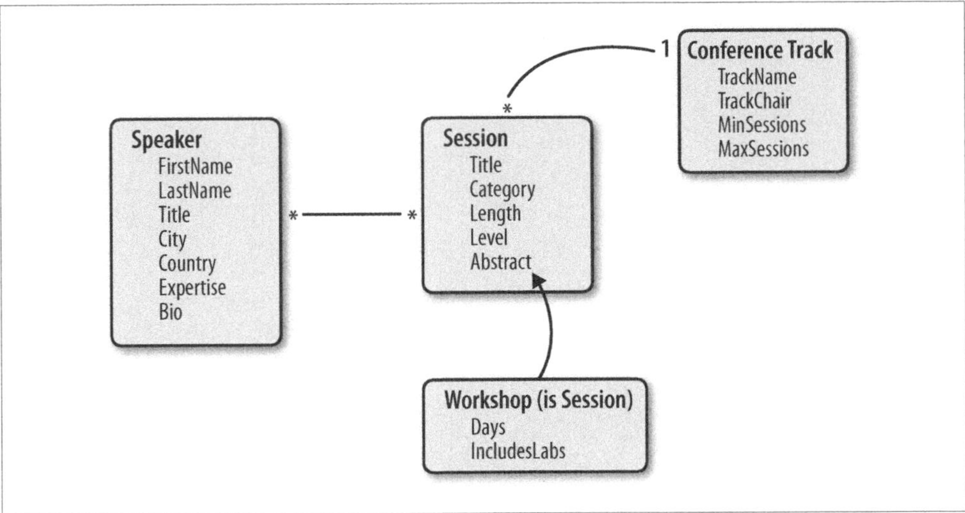

Figure 25-1. The ConferenceManager model to be built in the Designer

1. Create a new class library project for your model.
2. Add an ADO.NET Entity Data Model item into the project.
3. On the Choose Model Contents page of the wizard, select Empty Model and then click Finish.

And now you have a completely empty design surface.

> The Empty Model option was available in Visual Studio 2008 SP1 also. But unlike the Visual Studio 2010 Designer, there was no tooling to generate a database schema from the model or the additional metadata. I once tried to build a model from scratch and then create the metadata to connect to a database, and finally just gave up in frustration. I have never met anyone who managed to succeed at it.

There are two ways you can add items to the model's design surface: from the Designer's Toolbox, shown in Figure 25-2, or from the Add item of the Designer's context menu, shown in Figure 25-3.

In Figure 25-3, the Association and Inheritance items are inactive because this menu is being displayed in a brand-new, empty model. Once there are entities on the surface, then it will be logical to add these items.

Adding items from the Toolbox simply places the item on the surface using defaults, whereas adding items from the context menu opens a dialog for you to define the critical attributes of that item.

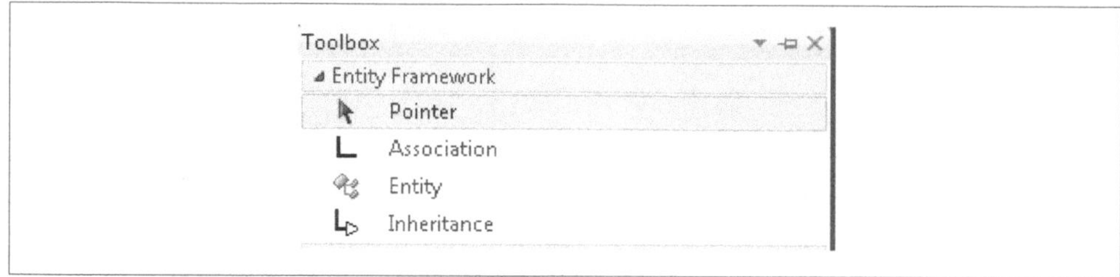

Figure 25-2. The Toolbox for the Entity Data Model Designer

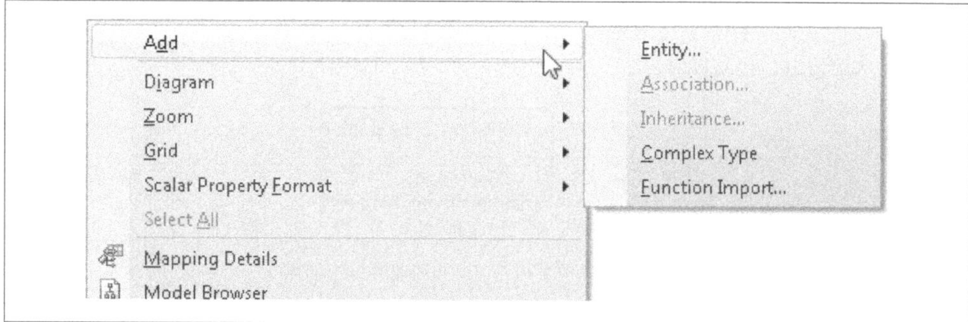

Figure 25-3. Adding items to the model from the Designer's context menu

For example, if you drag an entity from the Toolbox, the result will be a new entity with a default name and a default property that is identified as an `EntityKey`, as shown in Figure 25-4.

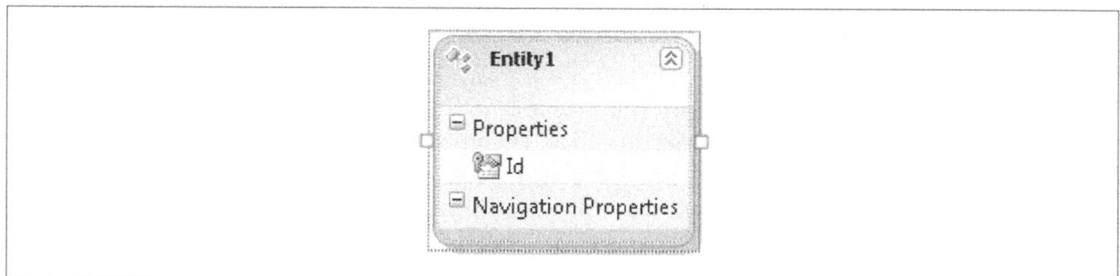

Figure 25-4. A default entity created from the Toolbox

If you add a new entity from the context menu, you'll get the Add Entity dialog, shown in Figure 25-5, which allows you to have more granular control over how the new entity will be defined. The default settings match the defaults that are used when you create an entity from the Toolbox.

Creating the Entities

For this walkthrough, I recommend using the context menu so that you can get the dialogs. You'll begin by creating a `Speaker` entity for your ConferenceManager model.

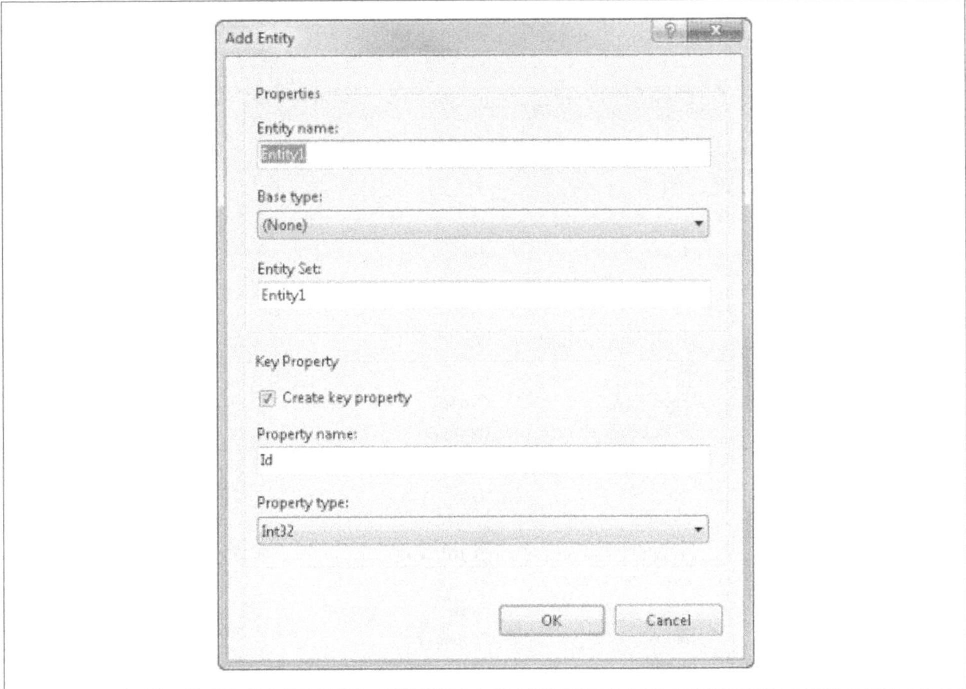

Figure 25-5. The Add Entity dialog from the Designer's context menu

You will not be using this model for any further examples in the book, so it is not critical that you create every property exactly as defined. However, many of the steps are here to specifically point out particular behaviors.

Start by creating a new entity from the context menu. In the Add Entity dialog, change the name to `Speaker`. Notice that, by default, the Entity Set name automatically changes itself to the plural form of the entity name.

You do want a key property, so leave that checked, but change the name from `Id` to `SpeakerId`. The type, `Int32`, is correct.

Click OK and you'll see the new entity on the Designer.

Now create some scalar properties. All of the properties for `Speaker` happen to be strings, which will make creating new properties a quick process, since string is the default type.

You can add new properties in three ways: either from the entity's context menu or by pressing the Insert or Enter key on your keyboard. The Insert/Enter keys will work only when a property or the Properties header is already highlighted.

New properties will be created with a default name of `Property`.

Pay attention to the attributes of a newly created property, as shown in Figure 25-6.

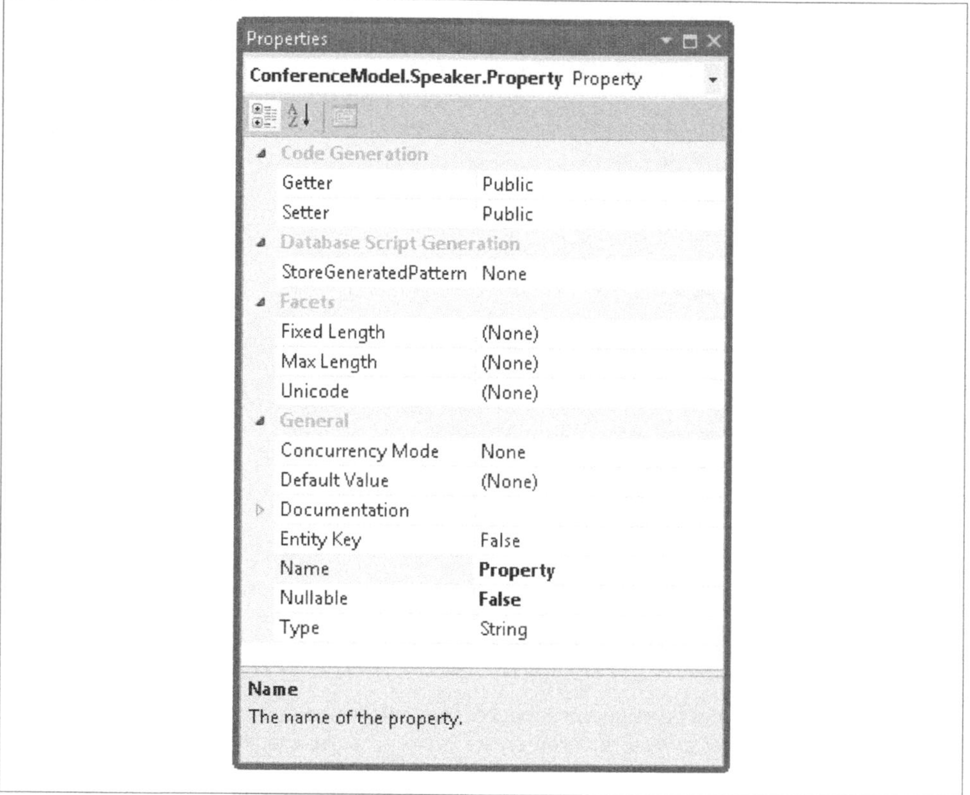

Figure 25-6. Default attributes of a newly created property

New scalar properties begin as non-nullable `String` types. Because we are building a model-first model, the `Database Script Generation` and `Facet` attributes will be important when it comes to generating the DDL for the database.

In fact, if you look at the properties for the `SpeakerID` you already created, you'll see that because it was set up as an identity key, its `StoreGeneratedPattern` was automatically set to `Identity`.

Setting attributes of the entity's properties

Now walk through the process of setting attributes of the entity's properties. First, change the name of the first property to `FirstName`. Then change the `Max Length` value to `50`.

Recall from earlier chapters that `Max Length` does not affect the length of the entity property. Instead, it describes what the `Max Length` attribute of the database column should be. In our previous models, the EDM Designer wizards read that information from the database and provided it here. Now that you are doing model-first design, this value will be used when creating the schema of the database.

Add the rest of the properties to the `Speaker` entity, as shown earlier in Figure 25-1.

In order to inspect some differences between `Max Length` and `Fixed Length`, be sure to include the following attributes on these scalar properties:

- Title: Be sure to leave Max Length = (None)
- Bio: Max Length = Max and Nullable = True
- Country: Fixed Length = True and Max Length = 50

When you generate the DDL, you'll get a look at how these settings affect the database schema.

Add the `Session` and `Track` entities as shown in Figure 25-1 along with the identity keys that the dialog box settings will have you create. Feel free to change their names.

Add the scalar properties for the new entities, and for now just use the default attributes. We'll tweak some of these attributes after the fact to better understand their effect on the model, your classes, and the generated database schema.

You can set the default value of the `Session.Length` property to `60`, as in 60-minute sessions, but with the understanding that this is only for the benefit of the `Session` class, not the database table that will be created.

See the sidebar "Understanding Entity Property Defaults Versus Database Defaults and Model First" on page 745 to learn more about the impact of setting defaults on entity properties.

Recall that by default, all new scalar properties are non-nullable `String` types. Not all of our properties are meant to be `Strings`, such as the `Session.Length` property.

So, change the `Session.Length` to `Int32`, and change `ConferenceTrack.MinSessions` and `MaxSessions` to `Int32`.

If you want to explore how some of the other types are translated to database types, feel free to set other properties to those types.

Because you won't be using this model going forward, I have not focused on additional attributes of the entity properties.

Creating Association and Inheritance Hierarchies

Now you'll define how the entities relate to one another. You'll be defining a one-to-many relationship and a many-to-many relationship in this small model, as well as creating an inheritance between `Session` and the new entity.

Creating a one-to-many relationship

Begin with the simplest relationship, a one-to-many relationship between `Session` and `ConferenceTrack`. Each track can have many sessions, but a session can belong in only one conference track.

Again, you have the option to use the Toolbox (with default settings) or create the relationship from the Designer's context menu and apply the settings explicitly. The latter approach is much more educational and preferable if you like to have more control over how things are defined, so I'll have you use that.

You can start from the Designer background or an entity. If you begin with an entity, the dialog will use that entity as the first end of the relationship. You can easily modify this.

Right-click the `ConferenceTrack` entity; select Add and then Association.

By default, the dialog will begin with `ConferenceTrack` as one end of the relationship, and as you can see in Figure 25-7, it has automatically chosen `Speaker` as the other end. A default 1:* relationship is defined.

Using the drop-down list, change the `End Entity` to `Session`. Notice that the Association name gets automatically updated to reflect the new pair of ends.

The multiplicity on both ends is correct, since you want to define a one-to-many relationship between `ConferenceTrack` and `Session`.

By default, the dialog will create navigation properties in the entities. `ConferenceTrack` will get a property named `Sessions`, which will act as a wrapper to the collection of `Sessions` related to the `ConferenceTrack`. `Session` will get a new property to point to the related `ConferenceTrack`.

Finally, the dialog box defaults to create any necessary foreign key properties in the "child" entity, `Session`.

Figure 25-8 shows the effect of this new association on the entities.

As the image shows, there is a new scalar property in `Session` that is the foreign key property to the conference entity. You might want to change the default name. The association is in place along with the new navigation properties, `ConferenceTrack` and `Session`.

What does this mean for the code generation? In addition to the new scalar property becoming a column in the `Session` table, the referential constraint created for the

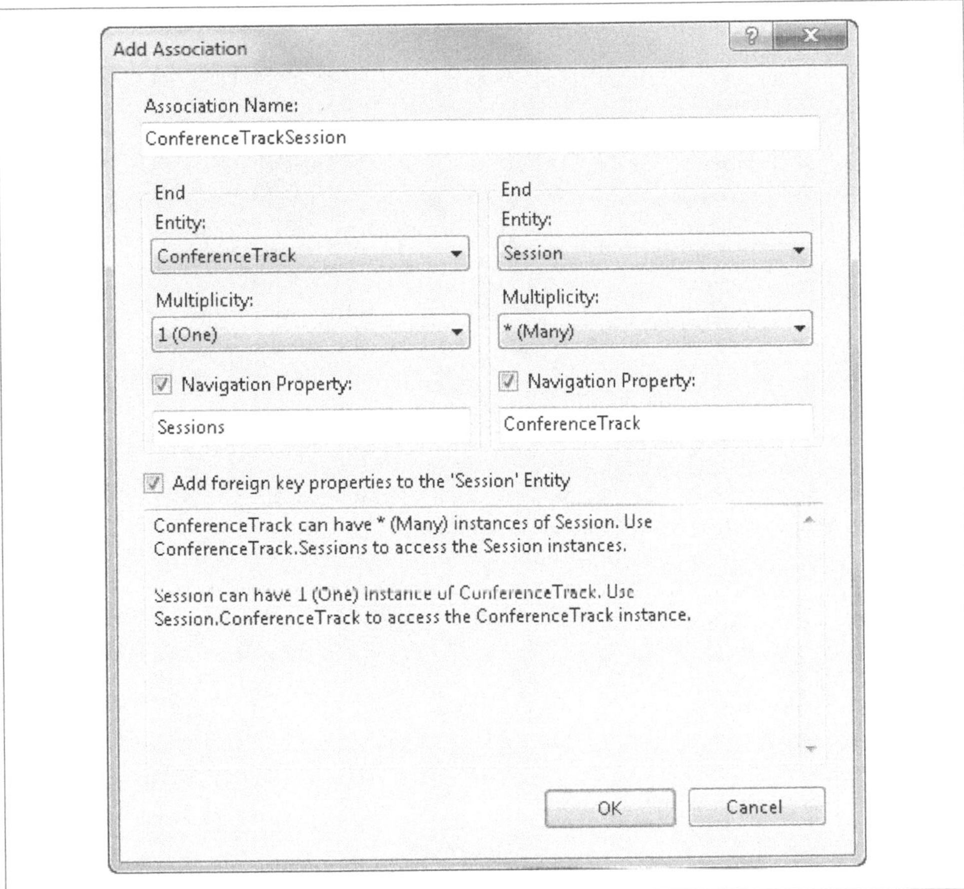

Figure 25-7. Defining a new association

association (shown in Figure 25-9) will be translated into a primary key/foreign key constraint in the database.

You'll make one more change to this association's properties and then follow up in a bit to see the impact on the generated DDL. Here, you will define a cascade delete in the model so that if a `ConferenceTrack` object is deleted in your application, all of the associated `Session` objects will automatically be deleted. This is probably not something you would want to happen in a real conference model, but the goal is to see how this affects the DDL.

In this association, `End1` is the `ConferenceTrack`. Change `End1 OnDelete` from `None` to `Cascade` to ensure that all of a `ConferenceTrack`'s `Sessions` get deleted when the `ConferenceTrack` is deleted.

Recall that in Chapter 19, you first worked with the model's `OnDelete` setting. Now you are able to see that this setting serves two purposes. The first is that it defines a cascade

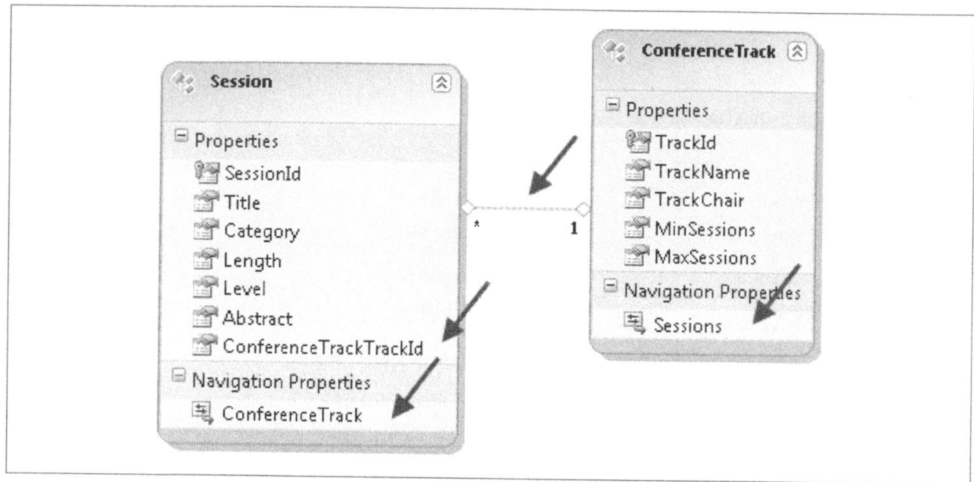

Figure 25-8. New properties created with the association

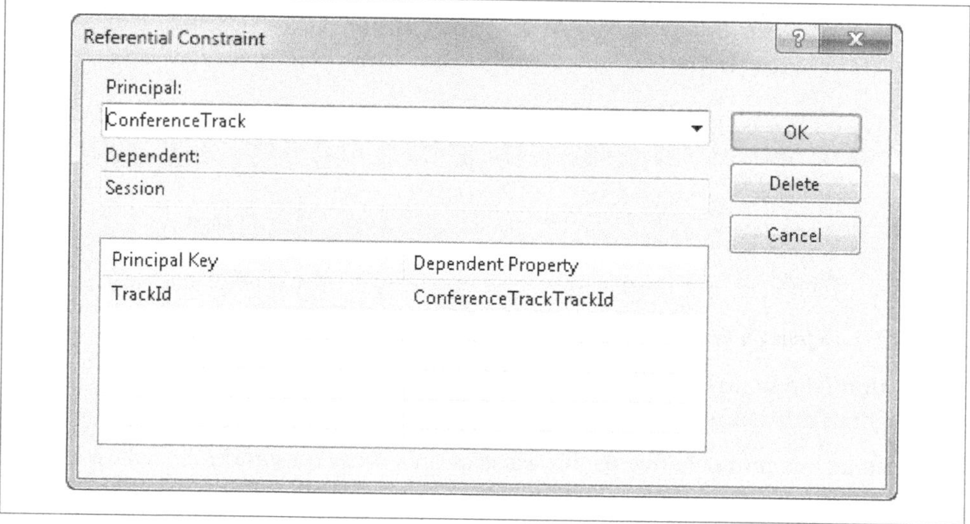

Figure 25-9. The automatically created referential constraint

delete operation for in-memory objects. The second is that when generating DDL from the model, it additionally instructs the DDL generator to define the database constraint as a cascade delete.

Unfortunately, the model property designer is inconsistent in defining model and database schema at the same time. In the case of `OnDelete`, you are defining behavior for the model and for the generated database. However, with other properties, such as `Default`, you are only defining the model setting, and with still others, such as `MaxLength`, you are only defining a database setting. This can be very confusing, and your only recourse is to pay close attention and be aware of what you are impacting with these settings.

Creating a many-to-many relationship

Here, you'll create a many-to-many relationship between `Speaker` and `Session`, as it's possible for a session to have more than one speaker.

1. Right-click on an entity or the Designer background.
2. Select Add, then Association.
3. Define the association as shown in Figure 25-10.

   Since both ends of this relationship are Many, there is no need for any foreign keys, which is why the "Add foreign key" option is inactive.
4. Click OK and you'll see the representation of the many-to-many association drawn between the `Speaker` and `Session` entities.

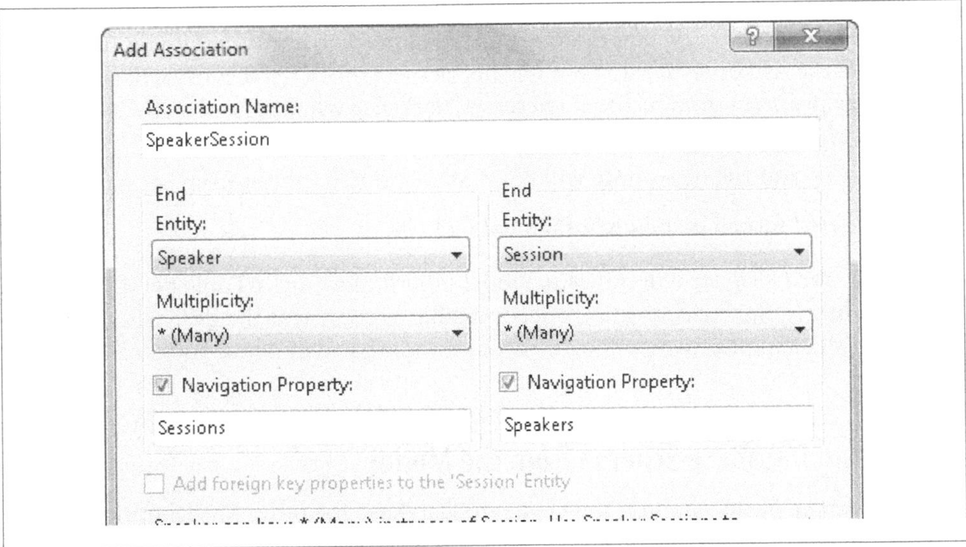

Figure 25-10. Association properties for a many-to-many relationship

Entities with a many-to-many relationship rely on a join table in the database. When you created many-to-many relationships from the BreakAway database, you learned that if the join table has more than just the foreign keys of the tables to be joined, the model must create a separate entity to map to that table. In that case, rather than having a many-to-many association between the two entities, those entities would be related to the join entity.

That rule still applies, just in reverse. The association you just created defines a *:* directly between the entities. Therefore, the DDL will define a join table that only contains `SpeakerId` and `SessionId` columns. If you need more information in that join table, you cannot use the *:* association. Instead, you should create another entity in between the two target entities.

Creating an inheritance hierarchy

The last entity in this model will be a `Workshop` entity. In Figure 25-1, shown earlier, displaying the model, you can see that `Workshop` is defined as a special type of `Session`. You'll create the entity and force it to inherit from `Session`.

In Chapter 14, you created an inheritance between two existing entities. Here, you'll define the inheritance at the same time we define the new `Workshop` entity.

1. Add a new entity to the model.
2. Name the entity `Workshop`.
3. Under Base Type, select Session.

   Notice that as a result of selecting a Base Type, the EntitySet and Key Property items of the dialog box become inactive. The new `Workshop` entity will be part of the Sessions entity set, and therefore does not need an entity set. If you recall from your earlier experience with defining inheritance, the derived entity will also inherit the key property from its base. Therefore, `Workshop` will not need its own key property either.
4. Click OK and the new entity will be created and will inherit from `Session`.

The completed model is shown in Figure 25-11.

By default, the Designer will translate model inheritance into a Table per Type (TPT) hierarchy in the database, creating a second table to represent the derived entity. Further on in this chapter, you will learn about a tool that will allow you to change this default.

Generating Database Schema from the Model

As I said earlier in the chapter, the Generate Database from the Model option is a bit misleading in its name. The database itself must exist before the Designer can generate the DDL.

The database needs to exist in advance for two reasons. The first is that the DDL Generation Wizard will also create an entity connection string, which, as you know, includes a database connection string. Therefore, the wizard will ask you to select the target database. The wizard, which is based on the same database selection wizard used

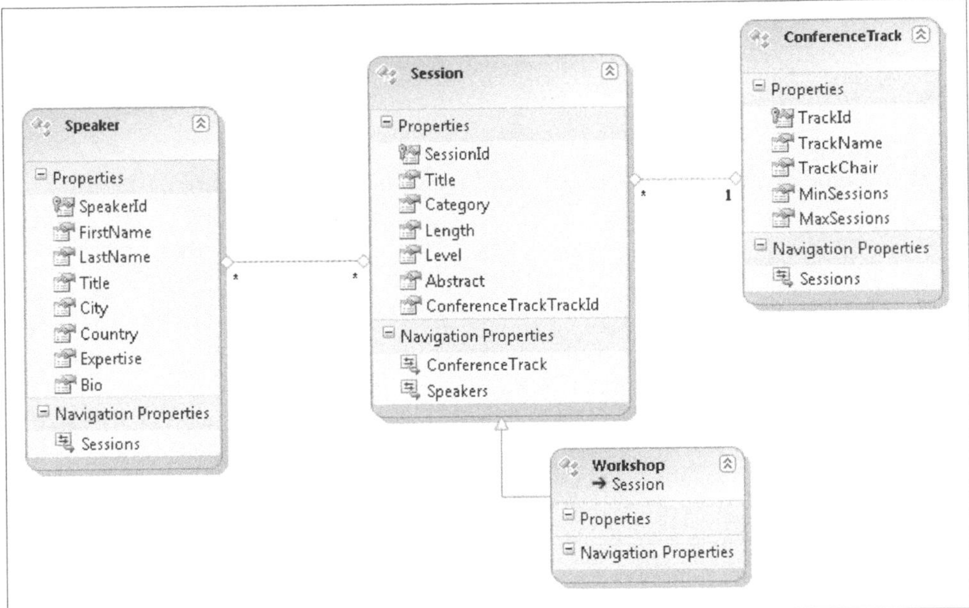

Figure 25-11. The final model

by many other database connection features in Visual Studio, provides an opportunity to create a new database on the fly. The second reason is that the generated DDL will not include script to create a database. The DDL script will only know how to create schema.

If you don't already have a database to work with, now is the time to create it. The specific instructions for creating a new database differ depending on what type of database server you are using. I am using SQL Server; therefore, when I right-click on Data Connections, there is a menu option to Create a New SQL Server Database. In its wizard I can select my server and then provide the name for the new database, which is Conferences.

As an alternative, you can select any available database when you generate the DDL. I have a dummy database for this purpose. Just be sure your application has the correct database string at runtime.

Right-click on the Entity Data Model design surface and choose Generate Database from the Model.

The wizard will first ask you to select a database so that it can create the connection string. Select the appropriate database connection and click OK.

If you already have an available `EntityConnection` string for this model (e.g., in a *.config* file in your project), the wizard will skip this step.

Next you'll be presented with the generated DDL, as shown in Figure 25-12.

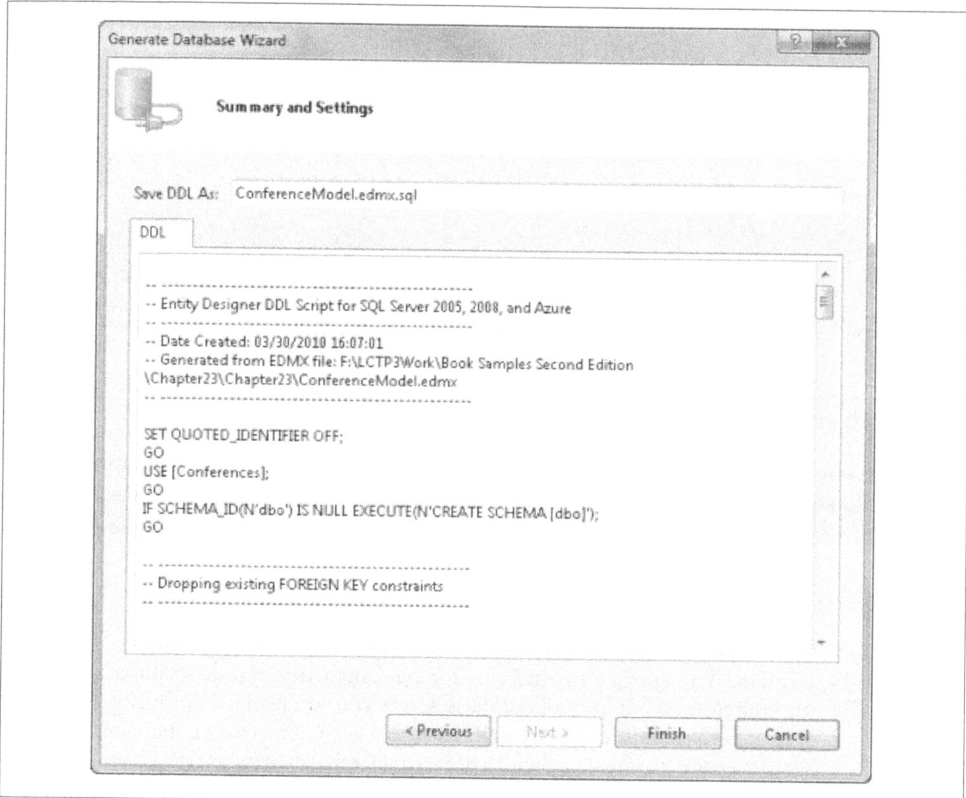

Figure 25-12. The generated DDL script

Exploring the generated DDL

I'm using SQL Server as my database, so my DDL is T-SQL. You'll notice that at the top there's a comment specifying that the script is for SQL Server 2005, SQL Server 2008, and SQL Azure.

Because model first is a new feature in Entity Framework 4, the third-party providers that were written to support Entity Framework in .NET 3.5 are being updated by their creators to support this new feature. See the Resources page on the book's website where I try to keep an up-to-date list of Entity Framework providers.

As you scroll down the script, you'll first see SQL for dropping existing constraints and tables. If you are regenerating an existing database, be aware that your data will be lost. Later in this chapter I'll point to a tool which will allow you to do incremental database updates from the model which you should consider using especially if your model is already in production. Otherwise, you will want to back up your data before running the script. I find Visual Studio's Database Publishing Wizard helpful for making a snapshot of the data that can be imported into a newly created database.

As with code generation, the DDL generation is dependent on a T4 template. When we look at more advanced features later in this chapter, you'll see how it is possible to impact the DDL generation.

See the sidebar, "Extra! Extra! Entity Designer Database Generation Power Pack" on page 749, to learn about an external toolkit that will allow you to customize the DDL generation.

Next you'll find the SQL for creating the tables. The `Speakers` table SQL is shown in Example 25-1.

Example 25-1. Generated T-SQL to create the Speakers table

```
CREATE TABLE [dbo].[Speakers] (
    [SpeakerId] int IDENTITY(1,1) NOT NULL,
    [FirstName] nvarchar(max)  NOT NULL,
    [LastName] nvarchar(max)  NOT NULL,
    [Title] nvarchar(max)  NOT NULL,
    [City] nvarchar(max)  NOT NULL,
    [Country] nchar(50)  NOT NULL,
    [Expertise] nvarchar(max)  NOT NULL,
    [Bio] nvarchar(max)  NULL
);
```

The first thing to notice is that the table name is plural. It comes not from the name of the `Entity`, but from the name of the `EntitySet`. `SpeakerId` is being defined as an auto-incrementing `IDENTITY` field. This is thanks to the combination of the property's `EntityKey` flag and the `StoreGeneratedPattern` set to `Identity`.

Remember setting the `Bio`'s max length to `Max` and leaving most of the other attributes at `None`? `Nvarchar(max)` is the default, which is why the types are all the same except for `Country`.

`Country` is an `nchar` rather than an `nvarchar`. That's because you set its `Fixed Length` property to `True`.

SQL Server Data Types Versus Entity Framework Types

Here is a list of how the Entity Data Model Wizard interprets SQL Server data types when it is creating entities. Note that Entity Framework has no way to represent some of the types introduced in SQL Server 2008—**`geography`**, **`geometry`**, **`hierarchyid`**, and **`sqlvariant`**.

This chart is equally helpful when you are building a model that will be used to generate DDL for SQL Server.

SQL Server type	Entity type	SQL Server type (cont.)	Entity type (cont.)
`bigint`	`Int64`	`numeric`	`Decimal`
`binary`	`Binary`	`nvarchar`	`String`
`bit`	`Boolean`	`nvarcharmax`	`String`
`char`	`String`	`real`	`Single`
`date` (2008)	`DateTime`	`smalldatetime`	`DateTime`
`datetime`	`DateTime`	`smallint`	`Int16`
`datetime2` (2008)	`DateTime`	`smallmoney`	`Decimal`
`datetimeoffset`	`DateTimeOffset`	`sqlvariant` (2008)	`N/A`
`decimal`	`Decimal`	`text`	`String`
`float`	`Double`	`time` (2008)	`Time`
`geography` (2008)	`N/A`	`timestamp/rowversion`	`Binary`
`geometry` (2008)	`N/A`	`tinyint`	`Byte`
`hierarchyid` (2008)	`N/A`	`uniqueidentifier`	`Guid`
`image`	`Binary`	`varbinary`	`Binary`
`int`	`Int32`	`varbinarymax`	`Binary`
`money`	`Decimal`	`varchar`	`String`
`nchar`	`String`	`varcharmax`	`String`
`ntext`	`String`	`xml`	`String`

These comparisons give you an idea of the type of impact you can have on the generated database schema.

Looking at the result of the inheritance

Scrolling farther down you'll see that a table named `Sessions_Workshop` was created using the combination names of the base and derived entities from the inheritance you defined. Because a separate table is used for the derived type, this is a TPT inheritance. TPT is the default inheritance type supported by model first.

The table has `SessionId` as its property. This was defined thanks to the inheritance from `Session`. Since you didn't add any other properties to the `Workshop` entity, there are no additional fields.

Noting the result of the many-to-many relationship

There's one more table, `SpeakerSession`. This is the join table created to support the many-to-many relationship we defined in the model. Notice that rather than naming the fields `SpeakerId` and `SessionID`, it includes the name of the tables that those fields point to.

Exploring the constraints

Below the table definitions you will find all of the constraints. This is where the primary keys and foreign keys are defined.

Notice that on the constraint for the relationship between `ConferenceTrack` and `Session`, you can see `ON DELETE CASCADE`, which we defined in the association's properties. The cascade delete will happen in memory as well as in the database. If you recall from Chapter 19, it is recommended that you have cascade delete in both places or not at all; otherwise, you can create conflicts.

> **Understanding Entity Property Defaults Versus Database Defaults and Model First**
>
> Entity properties have default values, and you interacted with them earlier in this book. But it's important to understand the difference between the default values that you can set in the conceptual model and the database defaults. They are completely unrelated.
>
> If you reverse-engineer a database that has default values set on columns, that default will not get picked up in the store schema or by the entity itself.
>
> If you define a default value for a property of an entity, the default `EntityObject` T4 code generation template and the default POCO Entities template will both set that property's default value in the generated class.
>
> However, now that we are focused on building a model that will be used to generate a database schema, it's important to be aware that none of the default values you define for an entity's property will get pushed to the database.

Completing the generation of the DDL

When you click the wizard's Finish button, a few events occur:

- The DDL is saved in a file and added to your project.
- An *app.config* file is created if it doesn't already exist in your project.
- An `EntityConnection` string, including the database connection string, is added to the *.config* file.
- The SSDL and MSL portions of your EDMX metadata file are created.

This last point is notable. While you worked on your model, all you were building in the metadata was the CSDL. There was no database for which to provide a store schema, and therefore no mappings, either. Now that we have a store schema described (in the DDL) that same information was used to define the SSDL and the mappings between your model and that SSDL.

Feel free to open the model in the XML Editor to take a look.

Creating the Database and Its Schema

The last step in this walkthrough is to execute the script.

It is safe to run the script on your local machine against a sample test database, but otherwise, tread carefully. See the sidebar "Run Database Scripts from Visual Studio? Are You Kidding Me?" for more information.

> **Run Database Scripts from Visual Studio? Are You Kidding Me?**
>
> Giving developers to the ability to execute database scripts from Visual Studio is a touchy subject in many enterprises. If you are in an enterprise, it's likely that you have specific practices in place and security on the databases so that no unwanted accidents occur. In a development environment, you wouldn't (shouldn't) dream of touching your production database anyway. But messing with a local, test database isn't such a cause for alarm.

Double-click the new *.sql* file in the Solution Explorer. The file will open in Visual Studio's Transact-SQL Editor window.

Learn more about the Transact-SQL Editor in the MSDN Library topic "Editing Database Scripts and Objects with the Transact-SQL Editor," at *http://msdn.microsoft.com/en-us/library/dd380721(v=VS.100).aspx*.

The Transact-SQL Editor has its own set of commands. You can access them either from the Data menu or from the window's context menu.

Right-click in the editor to open the context menu for SQL, part of which is shown in Figure 25-13.

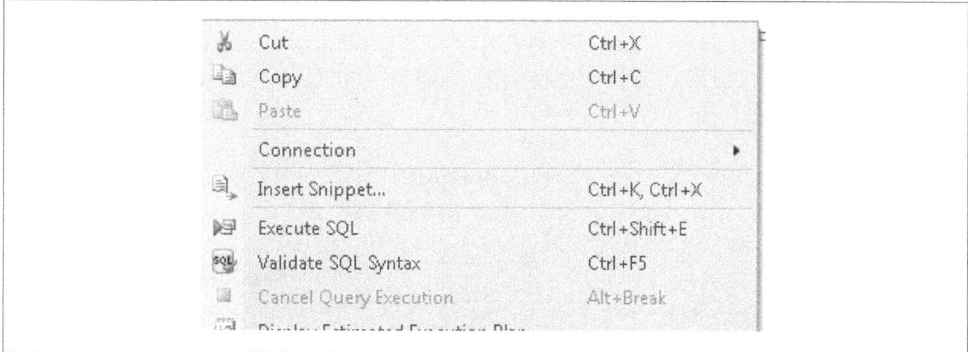

Figure 25-13. Part of the Transact-SQL Editor menu

The Transact-SQL Editor does not rely on the connection string in the *app.config* file to determine on which database server you'll be executing the script. The database name itself (e.g., *Conferences*) is part of the script (`USE [Conferences];`). If the connection has not yet been set for this script file, Execute SQL will first prompt you to set the connection. Otherwise, you can change it explicitly from the `Connection` command.

This connection can work only with server databases, whether that's SQL Server or SQL Server Express. You won't be able to connect to database files directly as you are able to in many of the other "Add Connection" dialogs in Visual Studio.

Once you have provided the connection information, the script will then execute. Visual Studio's Messages window should open with the message "Command(s) completed successfully." Figure 25-14 shows the diagram of the newly generated database.

Now, working with this model will be no different from working with a model that was created using the database-first method.

Overriding the DDL Generation

As mentioned earlier, the DDL is created using a T4 template that, like the T4 code generation, reads the model's XML and spits out T-SQL based on the template's instructions. This means you have an opportunity to control the output.

If you look at the model's properties, you'll see a section called Database Script Generation. In there are properties related to Workflow, a Template, and Schema Name (see Figure 25-15).

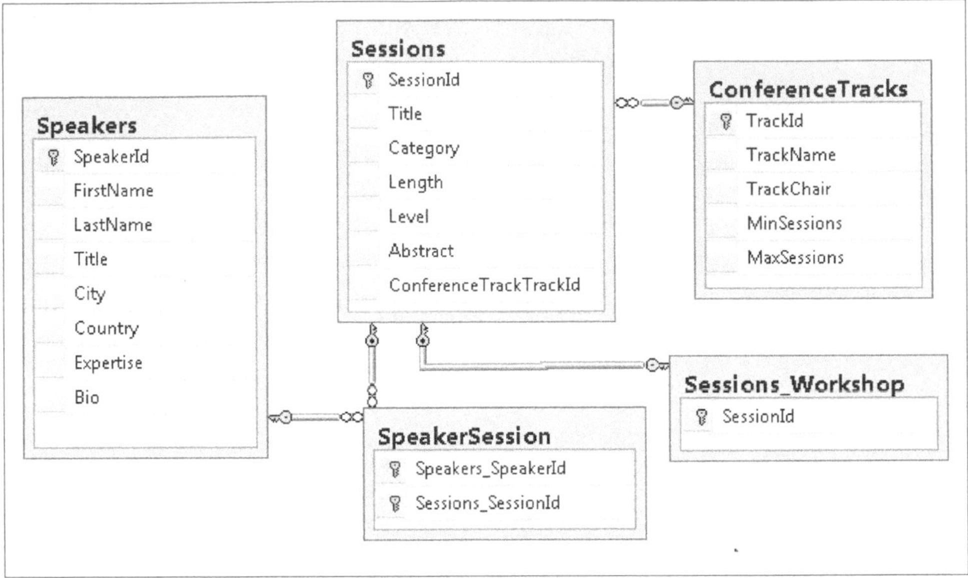

Figure 25-14. Diagram of the tables created from the DDL

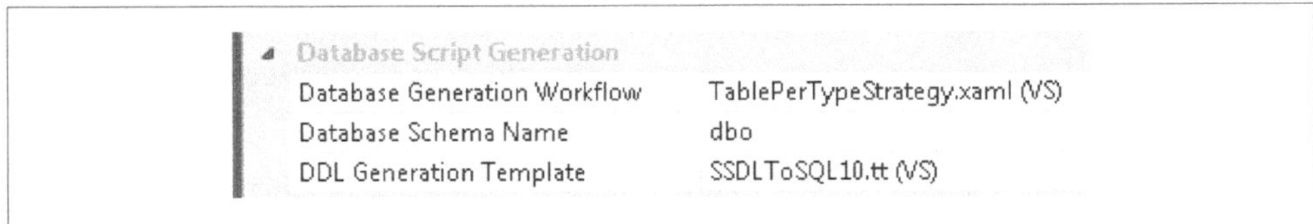

Figure 25-15. Properties to change how the DDL is generated

You can easily change the schema name used for the database objects by changing the `Database Schema Name` property.

`Database Generation Workflow` refers to the .NET's Workflow Foundation item that is used when the generation is executed. If you are familiar with using WF, this allows you to modify the steps that occur when you generate the DDL. Running the T4 template is just one of those steps. The `TablePerTypeStrategy` workflow is the only one included in Visual Studio 2010.

`DDL Generation Template` refers to the template being used. By default, `SSDLToSQL10` is the only template in Visual Studio 2010. It's not as easy to customize as it was to customize the model's code generation. You'll have to manually copy that file in Windows File Explorer in order to use and modify another version.

You can find the template in *<Program Files>\Microsoft Visual Studio 10.0\Common7\IDE\Extensions\Microsoft\Entity Framework Tools\DBGen*. You can make a new copy.

I've simply copied and pasted the file (in Windows File Explorer, not in Visual Studio) and left its default name. Now when I drop down the `DDL Generation Template` property, the new file is an available option (see Figure 25-16).

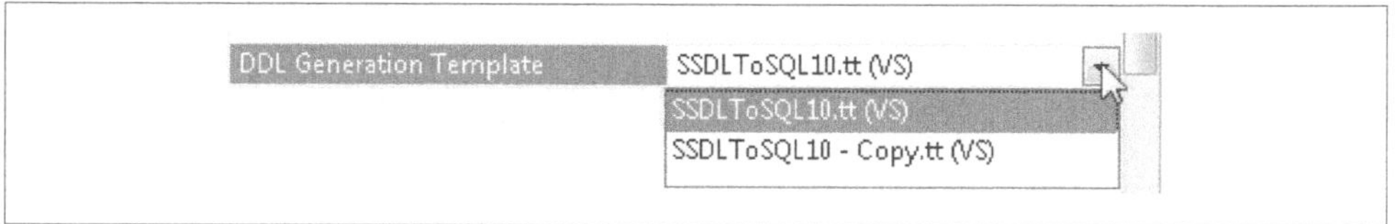

Figure 25-16. Selecting a new T4 template

Therefore, it's possible to modify the template and customize how the DDL is built.

Extra! Extra! Entity Designer Database Generation Power Pack

Microsoft has already created a few additional templates and workflows as part of a great toolkit that it is releasing on its Code Gallery site, called the Entity Designer Database Generation Power Pack. You can find this toolkit in the Online Gallery of the Visual Studio Extensions and install it through the Extension Manager.

The Power Pack includes additional templates such as one to force Table per Hierarchy (TPH) for inheritance (i.e., a condition field for filtering will be included in the `Sessions` table rather than a separate table).

The Power Pack also provides the capability to migrate an existing database when you have made changes to your model, rather than completely overwriting the existing database schema (and data).

Most importantly, this tool is a starting point for creating your own workflows and strategies around database generation from your model.

Once the Power Pack is installed, anytime you select Generate Database from Model you will be presented with the Power Packs UI, shown in Figure 25-17.

You can learn more about many features of the Power Pack on its Visual Studio Gallery page at *http://visualstudiogallery.msdn.microsoft.com/en-us/df3541c3-d833-4b65-b942-989e7ec74c87*.

Using the Feature CTP Code-First Add-On

So far, you've created models using database-first and model-first features of Visual Studio. There is yet another way to use Entity Framework, and that is with a feature called *code first*. With code first, you avoid working with a visual model completely. You build your own POCO classes and continue to benefit from Entity Framework's querying, change tracking, and database update features.

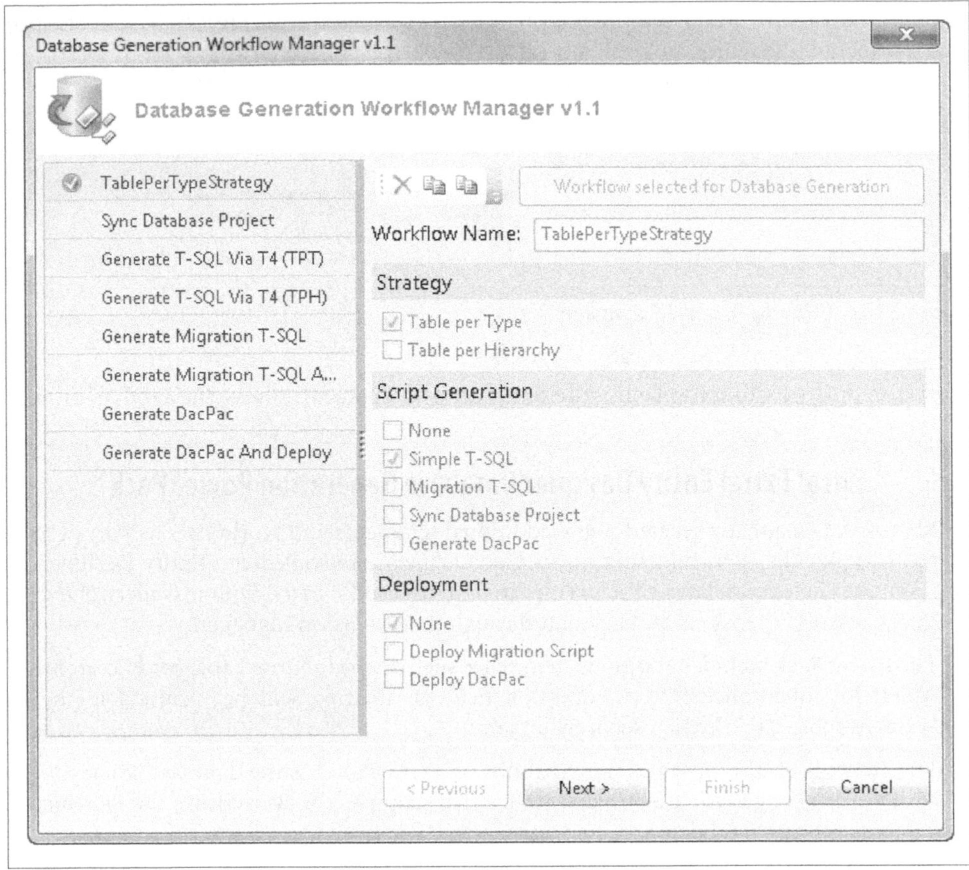

Figure 25-17. The Power Pack's database generation wizard

When Entity Framework was first released, its core support was for database-first modeling. This was great for a huge swath of developers who work from the perspective of the database and have legacy databases against which they must create software. However, this approach left out developers who do not develop applications beginning with the database. Developers who follow the path of Domain-Driven Design (DDD) principles prefer to begin by coding their classes first and then generating the database required to persist their data. The Entity Framework team sought the counsel of several major players in the DDD field—including Jimmy Nilsson, Eric Evans, and Martin Fowler—to help them better understand what DDD developers needed in an object relational modeling tool and how to make Entity Framework more useful to them. You can learn more about this Data Programmability Advisory Council in a blog posted by Danny Simmons at *http://blogs.msdn.com/dsimmons/archive/2008/06/03/dp-advisory-council.aspx*.

Entity Framework's runtime relies heavily on the metadata from the Entity Data Model in order to do so much of its work—most importantly, the transformation of Entity

Framework queries into store queries and then the transformation of database-generated data into our entities.

The code-first runtime API will create that necessary metadata on the fly based on a combination of what it finds in the classes you have designed and additional configuration information that you provide. Code first follows the *convention over configuration* approach described in Chapter 12 when discussing Dynamic Data websites. It will infer a runtime model based on the assumption that your classes follow specific rules, or conventions. Then, in any case where your classes divert from those rules, you can use additional configurations to describe how Entity Framework should infer the metadata.

Like model first, code first also has the ability to generate a database for you as needed. But unlike model first, code first can literally create the database, not just a file containing DDL script. You have control over whether this will happen.

Code first is still only in preview at the time of this writing. As it is not part of.NET 4, be aware that anything in this section can change. The goal of this discussion of code first is to provide you with a basic understanding of the concepts.

Entity Framework's code-first feature is currently not supported directly in Visual Studio 2010 and .NET 4.0. It is an additional feature created by the Entity Framework team that was not synchronized with .NET 4's schedule. You will need to download and install the Entity Framework Feature CTP from the MSDN Download Center. Because the CTP will continue to evolve until it is part of the core .NET Framework, the download link is difficult to provide in print. You can look on the team's blog (*http://blogs.msdn.com/efdesign*), where they discuss future features, or on the Resources page of this book's website for a current link.

Understanding Code-First Design

It's helpful to understand that you can think of your classes as a model, often referred to as a domain model. It's just not a model with the same type of metadata as the model we've been working with until now. It is not visual and it is not described in XML, but it is still a model.

However, because Entity Framework's APIs were designed around the XML metadata defined by the CSDL, MSL, and SSDL schemas, Entity Framework needs to "translate" the domain model into metadata, which it knows how to use. At runtime, it reads the definition of the classes, and then combines that with the knowledge that you provide in the additional configurations (which can be code or declarative); then it creates an in-memory representation of CSDL, MSL, and SSDL, as shown in Figure 25-18. The in-memory metadata is not the XML, but the objects from `System.Data.Edm`. In Chapter 21, you did a lot of work with the `MetadataWorkspace` that read the XML metadata

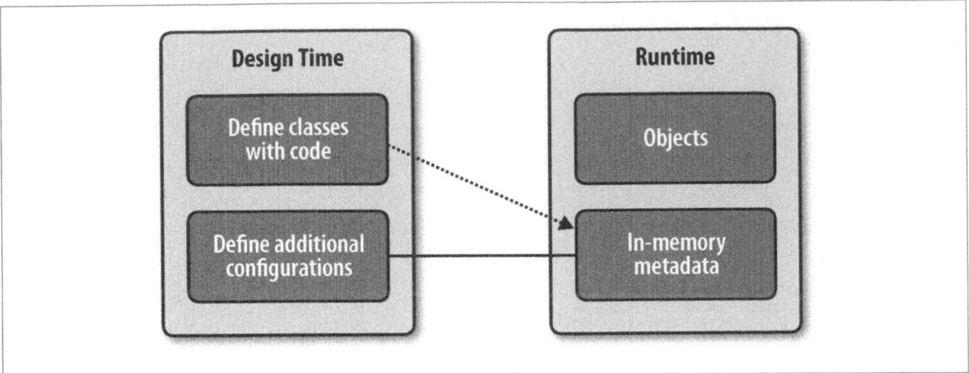

Figure 25-18. How code first creates metadata for the Entity Framework runtime

and created metadata objects such as an `EntityType`. Code first creates these metadata objects from the domain classes and works with them just as you did that chapter.

The configurations not only provide additional attribute details for the CSDL (e.g., default property values) and SSDL (e.g., `StoreGeneratedPattern=Identity`), but can also help to determine if, for example, an inheritance defined in some classes should be translated to TPT or TPH in the store schema. If your application includes the CTP code for creating a database on the fly, the SSDL will be used as the basis for doing this.

As this feature is still evolving, this chapter will not go too deeply into its details, but will provide a small walkthrough to clarify some of the high-level concepts. While some of the implementation details are likely to change, the overall process by which code first uses either declaritive attributes or a fluent configuration on top of specific patterns to infer a runtime model is highly unlikely to change.

Does This Make Entity Framework Truly Ready for Domain-Driven Development?

Many domain-driven developers are quite excited about what they can now achieve using Entity Framework and code first. Others are still skeptical and awaiting the continued evolution. My goal here is to provide you with the information you need to help you to come to your own conclusion.

Like the POCO entities you have worked with, classes used with code first depend on a separate context class to enable and execute queries, manage their state, and persist data back to the data store.

What's different is that the code first API provides a `ModelBuilder` class, which is where the configurations can be defined and the metadata is created at runtime. Alternatively, configurations can be defined with data annotations on the domain classes and their properties. Data annotations are described using attributes as you'll see in following examples. However, using the ModelBuilder configuration allows you to keep all of the entity framework logic out of your domain classes.

The new API also takes advantage of new classes in the CTP that provide lighter weight versions of the ObjectContext and ObjectSet classes. These are called DbContext and DbSet. You have the option of using either pair. In Example 25-2, I'll use the new classes. So, for example, your context class (in its simplest form) would be similar to Example 25-2.

Example 25-2. A context created for code first

```
using CodeFirstClasses;
using System.Data.Entity;
using System.Data.Entity.ModelConfiguration;

namespace CodeFirst.Persistence
{
  public class ConferenceModel : DbContext
  {
    public DbSet<Speaker> Speakers { get; set; }
    public DbSet<Session> Sessions { get; set; }
    public DbSet<ConferenceTrack> ConferenceTracks { get; set; }

    protected override void OnModelCreating(ModelBuilder modelBuilder)
    {
      modelBuilder.Entity<Session>().Property(s => s.Title)
                  .HasMaxLength(100).IsRequired();
      modelBuilder.Entity<ConferenceTrack>().HasKey(ct => ct.TrackId);
    }
  }
}
```

Installing the Feature CTP

If you are interested in installing the CTP, the CTP is an MSI installer file that you execute in Windows as you would any other installer. Once you have installed the latest version of the CTP, you won't see a difference in the Visual Studio IDE. Code-first support is provided by a single assembly, *Microsoft.Data.Entity.Ctp.Dll*, which gets installed into *<Program Files>\Microsoft ADO.NET Entity Framework Feature CTPX \Binaries* (where *X* is the version number of the CTP you have installed).

Now it's only a matter of referencing this assembly in your projects where you are using code first and using it with the System.Data.Entity namespace.

Exploring Some Configuration Examples

You are not bound to the assumptions that code first will make about your classes when it attempts to infer the metadata at runtime. Here are some examples of how you can provide additional configurations to further describe the metadata.

The ConferenceTrack class has a property named TrackId that should be its key. The convention of code first is that any field called Id or any field with a name that is the combination of the class plus Id (e.g., ConferenceTrackId) will become a primary key in the store schema and an EntityKey in the conceptual schema. TrackId does not fit either convention, so you need to override that. Notice in Example 25-2 that this was done in the OnModelCreating method using the following configuration code:

```
modelBuilder.Entity<ConferenceTrack>().HasKey(ct => ct.TrackId);
```

The ModelBuilder.Entity method allows you to add configurations to entities and their properties.

The HasKey method allows you to identify which property should be used in the entity's EntityKey. This information is important for the conceptual model, not the database. This will also result in the database field that is based on this property being set as a auto-incrementing primary key.

As mentioned, you can alternatively use data annotations. Example 25-3 shows the ConferenceTrack class using the [Key] attribute on the TrackId property.

Example 25-3. Using a data annotation to specify that TrackId is the key for the ConferenceTrack class

```
using System.Collections.Generic;
using System.ComponentModel.DataAnnotations;

namespace CodeFirstClasses
{

  public class ConferenceTrack
  {
    [Key]
    public int TrackId { get; set; }
    public string TrackName { get; set;}
    public string TrackChair { get; set; }
    public int MinSessions { get; set; }
    public int MaxSessions { get; set; }
    public ICollection<Session> Sessions  { get; set; }
  }
}
```

Speaker and Session both have identity names that fit the convention, so it is not necessary to use the HasKey method.

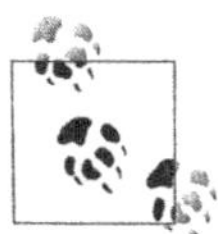

Having seen these configurations, NHibernate users may agree with other NHibernate users who compare this to Fluent NHibernate.

Example 25-4 shows the other domain model classes. Notice there is no additional configuration for these. Shortly, you'll see how code first is able to build a database using nothing more than the class definitions and the two additional configurations defined earlier.

Example 25-4. Additional domain model classes

```
namespace CodeFirstClasses
{
  public class Session
  {
    public  int SessionId{ get; set; }

    public  string Title{ get; set; }
    public string Category { get; set; }
    public string Length
    {
      get { return _length; }
      set { _length = value; }
    }
    private string _length = "60";

    public string Level { get; set; }
    public string Abstract { get; set; }
    public ConferenceTrack ConferenceTrack { get; set; }
    public ICollection<Speaker> Speakers { get; set; }
  }

  public  class Workshop : Session
  {
  }

  public  class Speaker
  {
    public int SpeakerId { get; set; }
    public   string FirstName { get; set;}
    public   string LastName { get; set;}
    public string Name
    {
      get { return FirstName.TrimEnd() + " " + LastName; }
    }
    public   string Title { get; set;}
    public   string City { get; set;}
    public   string Country { get; set;}
    public   string Expertise { get; set;}
    public   string Bio { get; set;}
    public   ICollection<Session> Sessions { get; set;}

  }
```

Testing the Code-First Application and Database

With all of this in place, Example 25-5 shows a method that runs the code-first classes, configuration, and context through its paces. But in fact, there's not much in there that's any different than typical .NET code. The only special code in there is that which creates a new database from the model. In this particular example, the code completely deletes any existing database before creating the new one because it's for testing, not for production. Once the database has been built, the code then instantiates a number of objects, builds relationships between them, saves the data to the database, and then reads it back out again.

Example 25-5. Putting the code-first features through their paces

```
private static void runCodeFirst()
{
using (var context=new ConferenceModel())
  {
    context.Database.DeleteIfExists();
    context.Database.Create();

    var speaker = new Speaker {FirstName = "Julie", LastName = "Lerman"};
    var session = new Session
                    {
                      Title = "Code First Design",
                      ConferenceTrack =
                        new ConferenceTrack {
                            TrackName = "Data",
                            TrackChair = "Rowan Miller",
                            MinSessions = 5},
                      Abstract = "tbd",
                    };
    var session2 = new Session
                     {
                       Title = "From Sap to Syrup",
                       ConferenceTrack =
                         new ConferenceTrack {
                             TrackName = "Vermont",
                             TrackChair = "Ethan Allen"},
                       Abstract = "How maple syrup is made",
                     };
    var speaker2 = new Speaker
                 { FirstName = "Suzanne",
                   LastName = "Shushereba" };
    context.Speakers.Add(speaker);
    context.Speakers.Add(speaker2);
    speaker.Sessions = new List<Session>();
    speaker.Sessions.Add(session);
    speaker.Sessions.Add(session2);
    speaker2.Sessions = new List<Session>();
    speaker2.Sessions.Add(session2);
    context.SaveChanges();
    Speaker dbSpeaker = context.Speakers.FirstOrDefault();
    Console.WriteLine(dbSpeaker.Name);
    foreach (var dbSession in dbSpeaker.Sessions   )
    {
      Console.WriteLine(dbSession.Title);
      foreach (var speakers in
         dbSession.Speakers.Where(s=>s.SpeakerId!=dbSpeaker.SpeakerId))
      {
```

```
            Console.WriteLine("Addtl Speaker: {0}", speakers.Name);
        }

      }
      Console.ReadKey();
    }
}
```

The database that is created is similar to the one we created in the model-first example, except for an important difference. While model first defaults to TPT inheritance, code first defaults to TPH inheritance. The `Sessions` table created in the earlier example has a column called `Discriminator` that is used to identify the `Workshop` types in our application. Code first figured out all of the relationships based on the class properties that point to each other, e.g., `ConferenceTrack.Sessions`. You can use configurations to override this as well.

There are many other features of code first, such as the ability to generate an EDMX file based on the in-memory metadata, that I am not covering here because of the volatile nature of the early version of code first. This section has given you an overview of what to expect from code first and only a subset of the available configurations. What you've seen here is based on the CTP4 that was released in July 2010. The syntax and implementation details are very likely to change as the CTP moves toward inclusion in Visual Studio at a later date. I recommend following the Entity Framework team's design blog (*http://blogs.msdn.com/efdesign*) for updated information, walkthroughs, and guidance as the CTP evolves.

Using SQL Server Modeling's "M" Language

In late 2009, Microsoft formalized work it was doing on a project formerly called Oslo as SQL Server Modeling. SQL Server Modeling is made of three core components:

- A modeling language that is currently identified by its code name, "M"
- A visual tool, Quadrant, for interacting with relational data
- A set of services targeted at creating and managing large, enterprise-scale databases

Using SQL Server Modeling's language, code-named "M," you can define a model using a simple syntax that you can add to dynamically. In the previous section, I hinted that a model does not need to be specified in XML or viewed in a designer, such as the Entity Framework metadata that includes a conceptual model. In code first, your model was the set of domain classes you defined in .NET code.

With M, you can define a model using an even simpler syntax than one of the .NET languages. SQL Server Modeling's runtime can generate a SQL Server database directly from what you describe using M. It can also generate an EDMX.

Because SQL Server Modeling is still a future technology, I will show only a very small example of what a model might look like using M.

I'll be basing this explanation on the November 2009 Release 2 of SQL Server Modeling.

SQL Server Modeling has design tools that integrate with Visual Studio 2010. After you install the SQL Server Model CTP, a new project item, the "Oslo" Modeling Class Library, is available in Visual Studio. The version I am working with still has the original code name, Oslo, attached to the template, rather than "SQL Server Modeling."

A new *.m* file is created as part of an Oslo Modeling Class Library project. The default *.m* file that the template creates for you is shown in Example 25-6.

Example 25-6. The default .m file created by the template

```
module SqlModelingClassLibrary
{
  type Model
  {
    Id : Integer32 => AutoNumber();
    Field : Integer32;
  }
  Modelsamples : {Model*} where identity Id;
}
```

While the braces and semicolons may suggest C++ or C#, keep in mind that this is a completely new language. It is a Domain-Specific Language (DSL). This means that, unlike the .NET runtime, which has thousands of classes and rules, this language has a small set of keywords, functions, and operators from which you can build a more streamlined set of functionality specific to your domain.

Check out the SQL Server Modeling CTP Terminology page on MSDN to get a better understanding of many of the terms, such as *DSL* and *extent*, which may be new to you (*http://msdn.microsoft.com/en-us/library/dd819894(VS.85).aspx*).

It defines a module, and within that a type (temporarily named `Model`), and specifies what's called an *extent* (`Modelsamples`) that describes the storage attributes for the model, including, for example, the types. In the model definition, the `Id` is defined as an `Integer32` which will auto-increment. The `Field` property is another `Integer32`.

Additionally, the extent instructs M's compiler to make the `Id` property of the `Model` type its identity property.

Example 25-7 modifies the default to define one of the types you've already used in this chapter, `Speaker`.

Example 25-7. An M specification for a Speaker type and its extent, Speakers

```
type Speaker
{
    SpeakerId : Integer32 => AutoNumber();
    FirstName : Text;
    LastName : Text;
}
Speakers : {Speaker*} where identity SpeakerId;
```

Once you've designated the (existing) database to inject this model into using the project properties for M Deployment, as shown in Figure 25-19, I can deploy the project.

Deploy will only create the database schema. You'll do more with Build shortly.

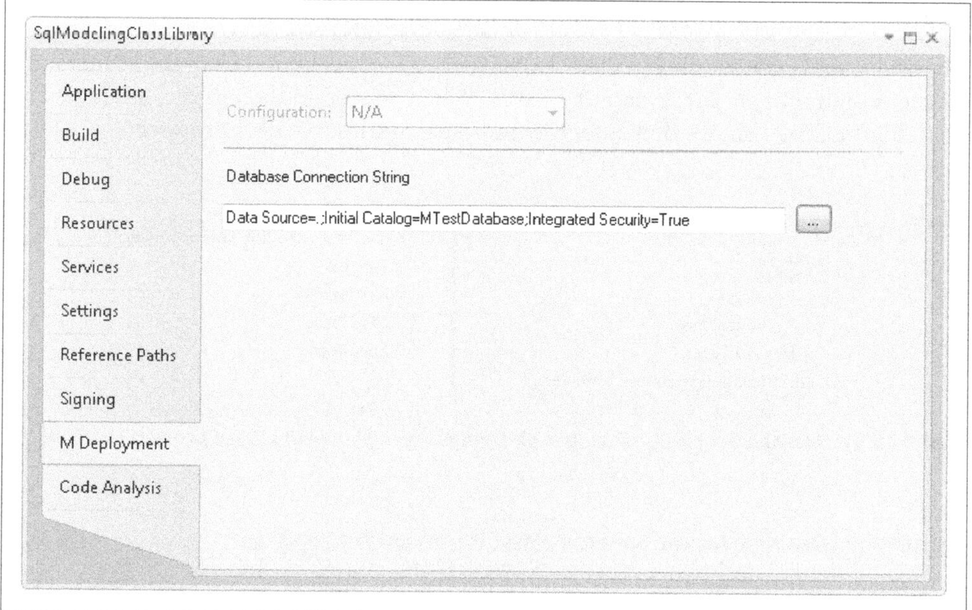

Figure 25-19. Specifying the database in which to create tables

As a result, a new table is created in the database, called `Speakers` (see Figure 25-20).

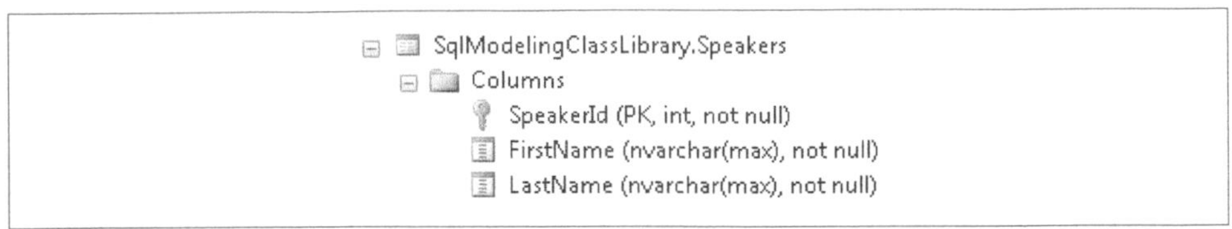

Figure 25-20. The Speakers SQL Server table created from M

What is shown in Example 25-7 is metadata. It looks a lot different from the XML-style metadata of an EDMX file.

Interestingly, when you continuc cvolving your M application, you will be coding against this metadata. This is called *Model-Driven Development* (see "Understanding Model-Driven Development" at *http://msdn.microsoft.com/library/dd129514.aspx*) and may take a bit of work to wrap your head around, which is out of the scope of this book.

Using M Metadata in Entity Framework Applications

Then why am I even showing you M? Because the types generated from the M metadata by the design tool are `EntityObject` classes. When you build the project, a DLL is created. Figure 25-21 shows that assembly in Visual Studio's Object Browser.

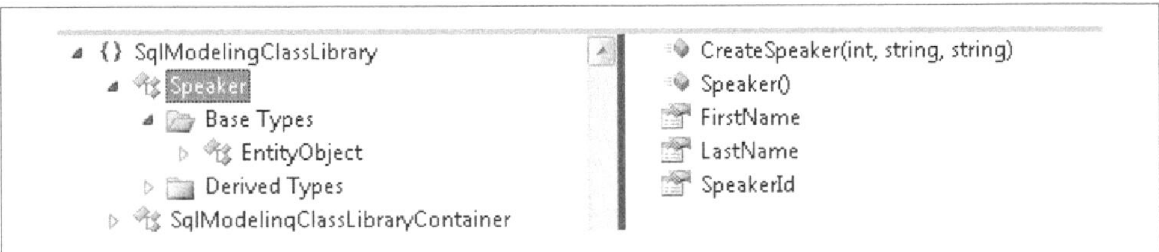

Figure 25-21. The Speaker class, deriving from EntityObject, shown in Object Browser

Notice the base type for the `Speaker` class. It's an `EntityObject`.

When you use this library in your applications, you will write Entity Framework code.

Building the project also created a file with the extension *.mx* in the *bin* folder.

You can generate an EDMX file directly from the model using SQL Server Modeling's command-line tool, *mex.exe*, against that *.mx* file:

```
mex "F:\Chapter23\OsloWebApplication1\bin\OsloWebApplication1.mx"
    /target:Edmx
```

This creates an EDMX file with the `Speaker` entity already in place, as shown in Figure 25-22. The store schema and mappings are also included in the EDMX.

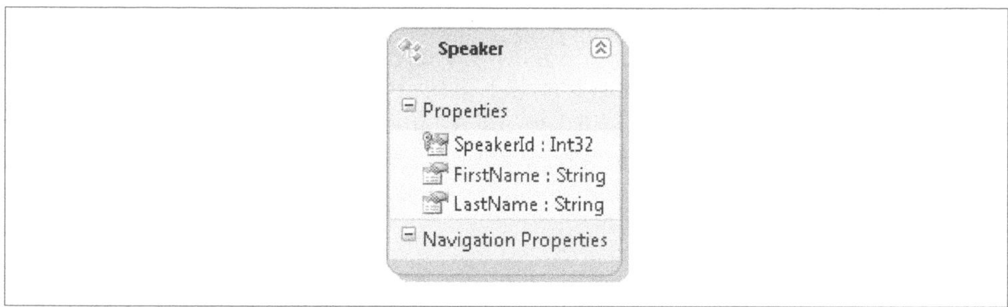

Figure 25-22. The Speaker entity of the newly generated EDMX

You don't need to generate an EDMX file to use your M metadata and classes in an application, but I've shown you this step to help demonstrate the tight integration between SQL Server Modeling and Entity Framework.

Because it is a future technology with many iterations to go before it is released, I will end the discussion of SQL Server Modeling here.

Summary

Throughout this book, we've worked mostly with a model that was generated from a database. But in this chapter, you learned that there are other ways to create the model. In fact, a very important concept of this chapter was that a model isn't necessarily an EDMX file. Entity Framework depends on the CSDL + MSL + SSDL metadata to do its job. But you can create other types of models (e.g., classes or M models). As long as there's a way to coerce those models into Entity Framework's required metadata, those models are perfectly acceptable for the task. In fact, the CSDL is the only piece of the metadata that is a model. It's the conceptual model, and it, too, is only part of the complete metadata required by Entity Framework.

Model first lets you create a model from scratch, and then a database from the model is fully supported by Visual Studio 2010. While learning about model first, you also learned a lot of new tricks with the Designer, such as the difference between creating objects from the Toolbox versus creating them from the Designer's context menu.

For developers who want only to design their classes and not to build and maintain a visual model, there is the upcoming code-first feature. Code first lets you take advantage of Entity Framework's querying, change tracking, and database update features by creating runtime metadata on your behalf. It will eventually become a first-class feature of .NET 4.0, but until then, it will be developed and released "out of band." Perhaps we'll see it become fully integrated in a Visual Studio 2010 Service Pack (in the same way that Entity Framework version 1 was first wrapped into Visual Studio 2008 with Service Pack 1) rather than waiting for the next version of Visual Studio. In the meantime, watch the ADO.NET team blog for new releases of the CTP and the impact on code first.

Finally, we took a quick look at SQL Server Modeling's M language and how it extends the modeling capabilities for Entity Framework. SQL Server Modeling's Visual Studio design tools can build an Entity Data Model and `EntityObjects` from a model defined with M. SQL Server Modeling is still a future technology, but not so far in the future that you shouldn't start looking at it now if it's of interest. M is only one part of SQL Server Modeling. You can learn more about it on the MSDN Data Developer Center at *http://msdn.microsoft.com/data*.

CHAPTER 26

Using Entities in Layered Client-Side Applications

In previous chapters, you have built client applications whose controls were bound directly to `EntityObjects` managed by an `ObjectContext`, an approach favored in Rapid Application Design (RAD). While this may be a reasonable approach for small applications, when it's time to architect enterprise applications this tightly bound design falls apart fairly quickly.

When you build large applications, it is prudent to separate your logic so that the UI is responsible for UI tasks (e.g., responding to user actions), business logic is handled by business classes, and data access is handled by classes designed specifically for data access.

A client-side application such as Windows Forms or WPF does come with the benefit of letting you use a long-running context to manage the entities while the user is working on them. This is different from disconnected client applications that consume services, whether that it a Silverlight application or even a disconnected Windows Forms or WPF application. The client-side applications this chapter focuses on are those which are not running in a disconnected environment.

In Chapter 24, you learned how to create persistent ignorant entities and use a repository to allow the UI to be completely ignorant of the Entity Framework. You could certainly use these repositories in client applications, but in this chapter I won't be concerned with keeping Entity Framework out of the client. Instead, we'll explore ways in which you can disentangle the UI of a layered client application from its business and data access logic while retaining certain key benefits of the Entity Framework. You'll learn how to take advantage of the repositories in the next chapter.

An important lesson in this chapter is that of keeping the data persistence code out of the user interface even though it's so easy to just slap an `ObjectContext` into your form's code-behind. There are many ways to implement the separation, whether you use simple layers (similar to what I did in the first edition of this book) or engage patterns such as Presentation View Model or Model View ViewModel (MVVM).

In Chapter 9, you built a Windows Forms application and a WPF application, both of which put every bit of application logic (with the exception of the model and its generated classes) in the code-behind of the user interface. In fact, you began with the UI and wrote code to populate it.

In a layered application, the UI can be the last bit of code you might write in your application. Think back to the chapter where you built the repository classes. The user interface was almost an afterthought once you had the business logic worked out. This lets you focus on building application logic based on your domain needs, not based on the needs of a particular user interface.

In order to gain a clear understanding of which code does and does not belong in the UI, most of this chapter will demonstrate restructuring the WPF application from Chapter 9. A side benefit is that you will get to leverage the UI that you've already created rather than building a new one.

In the end, your application will have three logical tiers:

- User Interface
- DataBridge, which uses Entity Framework to retrieve data, track changes, and persist to the database
- TripBridge, which provides Entity Framework-specific business logic for `Trip` entities

You'll work with `EntityObject` entities and then take a look at how using POCOs might impact the design.

Isolating the ObjectContext

As a first look at structuring a layered client app, you'll move all of the code that is not related to the UI out of the code-behind of the WPF application from Chapter 9. Most of this is code that interacts directly or indirectly with the `ObjectContext`.

Where you can move it to is a class in a new project that you'll call DataBridge. It will compound some data access and some business logic all into a single class. After this, you'll break this logic apart into more logical tiers, but for now the process of cleaning up the UI logic will be job number one.

You might be happiest creating copies of the folders that contain the previously used projects to use in a new solution. The existing projects that you'll need in this new solution are the project that contains the Chapter 9 WPF application and the project which contains the latest version of your model with the default `EntityObject` classes. There is no reason you can't use the projects that you created with the POCO classes, but this walkthrough will use the `EntityObjects`.

1. Create a new solution with these two projects.
2. Add a new Class Library project to the solution, named BAGABridge.
3. To this new project, add references to `System.Data.Entity` and the model project. If you are using the POCO projects where the classes are in a separate project, make a reference to that as well.
4. Delete the default class (`Class1`).
5. Create a new class called `DataBridge` and set its namespace to `BAGA.Bridge`.

   The first chunk of code you'll deal with is the initializers in the WPF form's `Window_Loaded` event shown in Example 26-1.

   Example 26-1. Initializers in original WPF example

```
_context = new BAEntities();
_activities = context.Activities.OrderBy(a => a.Name).ToList();
_destinations = context.Destinations.OrderBy(d => d.Name).ToList();
_lodgings = context.Lodgings.OrderBy(l => l.LodgingName).ToList();
_trips = new ObservableCollection<Trip>(
          context.Trips.Include("Activities")
             .OrderBy("it.Destination.Name"));
```

6. Delete these five lines of code as well as the class declaration for the `_context` variable.

   The WPF window will only be concerned with UI elements and user actions. You do not want it to work directly with the context at all.
7. In the `DataBridge` class, add declarations for the context and the four variables, as shown in Example 26-2.

   Example 26-2. Initializers in the new class

```
private BAEntities _context = new BAEntities();
private List<Activity> _activities;
private List<Destination> _destinations;
private List<Lodging> _lodgings;
private List<Trip> _trips;
```

Notice that here the `_trips` variable is a `List<Trip>`, not an `ObservableCollection<Trip>`, as in the UI. The WPF layer needs to work with an `ObservableCollection<Trip>`, but there might be other consumers of the `DataBridge` class that want a `List`. So, you can use a `List` for all of these local variables. See the sidebar "Making Generic Lists More Flexible" on page 766 for an example of how to provide a means to expose them as `List<T>` as well as `ObservableCollection<T>`.

Freeing Entities from Change Tracking

In previous chapters, you saw different ways to write generic code to create lists of entities. In this example, you'll get a chance to ramp that up a notch in a few ways.

First, you will ensure that the lists are not change-tracked. Users won't be editing the values of entities in the lists, so there is no need to force the context to waste resources creating and maintaining `ObjectStateEntries` for them. Second, you should avoid re-querying lists that already exist. To satisfy this goal, you will store lists in the variables declared in Example 26-2. You could make these static for the entire application, but since this is just a single windowed application, they'll simply be local.

While you can create a generic method to return lists, you'll need specialized getters and setters to interact with the `List` variables.

Let's first look at the generic method that can return a `List` of the requested type, shown in Example 26-3.

Example 26-3. A method to return untracked generic lists

```
public List<T> GetUnTrackedList<T>(Expression<Func<T, object>> sortExpression)
  where T : class
{
  {
    var storedList = GetStoredList<T>();
    if (storedList == null)
    {
      var query = _context.CreateObjectSet<T>();
      query.MergeOption = System.Data.Objects.MergeOption.NoTracking;
      storedList = query.OrderBy(sortExpression).ToList();
      SetStoredList<T>(storedList);
    }
    return storedList;
  }
}
```

This method takes a function that will allow you to use a lambda expression to specify a sort property. It also constrains the generic type to be a class. You don't want to constrain it to an `EntityObject` in case you're using POCO entities.

The method calls `GetStoredList<T>`. If it's null, a `NoTracking` query is executed and the variable is set with `SetStoredList<T>`.

Making Generic Lists More Flexible

To enable this class to be flexible enough to return plain `Lists` or to return `Observable Collections`, you can add a wrapper to `GetUntrackedList` that returns an `Observable Collection`:

```
public ObservableCollection<T>
 GetUntrackedObservableCollection<T>
 (Expression<Func<T, object>> sortExpression)where T : class
```

```
    {
      return new ObservableCollection<T>
    (GetUntrackedList(sortExpression));
    }
```

This overload calls the method in Example 26-3 but then casts the results to an `ObservableCollection`. You won't use the method in the chapter's example but might benefit from it in your own applications.

Example 26-4 shows the `SetStoredList` and `GetStoredList` methods, two generic methods that I can use internally in my class to do the job.

Example 26-4. SetStoredList and GetStoredList methods

```
private void SetStoredList<T>(List<T> newList)
{
  string typeName = typeof(T).Name;

  switch (typeName)
  {
    case "Activity":
      _activities = newList as List<Activity>;
      break;
    case "Destination":
      _destinations = newList as List<Destination>;
      break;
    case "Lodging":
      _lodgings = newList as List<Lodging>;
      break;
     default:
       throw new NotSupportedException
        ("You cannot make an UntrackedList from this type");
  }
}
private List<T> GetStoredList<T>()
{
  string typeName = typeof(T).Name;
  List<T> _list = null;
  switch (typeName)
  {
    case "Activity":
      _list = _activities as List<T>;
      break;
    case "Destination":
      _list = _destinations as List<T>;
      break;
    case "Lodging":
      _list = _lodgings as List<T>;
      break;
    default:
      throw new NotSupportedException
        ("You cannot make an UntrackedList from this type");;
  }
  return _list;
}
```

SetStoredList will take a List that was created elsewhere—for example, in GetUntrackedList—and set it to the appropriate variable once the method has determined which entity type it's working with. GetStoredList will return the appropriate list.

Trips are special since, as you experienced in the earlier WPF application, the Trip entity relies on the Destination.Name to make it useful. The ObservableTrips property, shown in Example 26-5, eager-loads Destination along with Trip as needed.

Example 26-5. Returning graphs of trips in an ObservableCollection

```
public ObservableCollection<Trip> ObservableTrips
{
  get
  {
    if (_trips == null)
    {
      var query = _context.Trips.Include("Destination");
      query.MergeOption = MergeOption.NoTracking;
      _trips = query.OrderBy(t=>t.Destination.Name).ToList();
    }
    return new ObservableCollection<Trip>(_trips);
  }
}
```

This method also ensures that the trips are not change-tracked by using a NoTracking query. This will be a benefit to resource usage. When it's time to edit a Trip, just attach it to the context. You'll see this shortly.

Now you have a mechanism for getting data into the WPF window without the UI code Stouching the context.

The WPF form can simply instantiate the DataBridge class and then use the GetUntrackedList methods to get generic lists and call the ObservableTrips property as needed:

```
_bridge.GetUntrackedList<Destination>(d => d.Name);
_bridge.GetUnTrackedList<Activity>(a => a.Name);
_bridge.GetUnTrackedList<Lodging>(l => l.LodgingName);
```

Enabling Change Tracking Across Tiers

As a result of actions taken in the previous section, none of the data returned to the UI is being change-tracked. This is OK for the drop-down lists, but you may recall that this WPF app allows users to edit existing Trips and create new ones.

You need to attach the untracked entity to the context so that the context will keep track of edits.

When the user decides it's time to edit one of the trips in the list, you could signal the DataBridge to attach that trip to the current ObjectContext (_context). Here's a method you might add to the DataBridge to do this:

```
public void TrackChanges(Trip trip)
{
  _context.Trips.Attach(trip);
}
```

But that's too easy, and of course, there's a catch—in fact, two. Once you've attached a trip to the context, if you attempt to attach it a second time, the context will throw an exception since it already has an `ObjectStateEntry` with the same `EntityKey`. You can avoid this by wrapping an `if` statement around the `Attach`, like this:

```
if (trip.EntityState == System.Data.EntityState.Detached)
{
   context.Trips.Attach(trip);
}
```

That was the first catch. The second is due to the fact that you eager-loaded the `Destination` for each `Trip`. Therefore, the `Trip` is really a graph, and when you attach it, you'll also be attaching its `Destination`.

BreakAway frequently repeats trips; therefore, you'll find that many trips contain the same `Destination`, and you have the ability to attach the same `Destination` to the context that was attached along with a different trip graph. Since the `Destination` instances are unique, you can't test for `EntityState.Detached` as with the trip. Instead, you'll need to look inside the `ObjectStateManager` for a matching `ObjectStateEntry`.

If that `Destination` is already being tracked, remove it from the trip graph before attaching it to the context. Example 26-6 shows the complete `TrackChanges` method.

Example 26-6. Attaching a Trip graph to the context

```
public void TrackChanges(Trip trip)
{
if (trip.EntityState==System.Data.EntityState.Detached)
  {
    //if attached destination is already managed,
    //delete it from trip graph
    ObjectStateEntry existingOse;
    var currentDest = trip.Destination;
    if (_context.ObjectStateManager.TryGetObjectStateEntry
          (trip.Destination.EntityKey, out existingOse))
    {
      trip.Destination = null;
    }
    _context.Trips.Attach(trip);
  }
}
```

Because this code is using `EntityObjects`, the trip still has an `EntityReference` for that `Destination` and will be automatically related to the `Destination` that is already being tracked. When using POCOs, you'll need to write a little extra code to ensure that the relationship remains intact.

Moving Other ObjectContext-Dependent Logic to the DataBridge

In the WPF app, the user is allowed to set various properties of the trip being edited. The start and end dates are scalar properties. When those are edited in the UI, it impacts the `Trip` directly. There's no explicit code for doing that, so this doesn't pose a concern. However, there is explicit code for setting navigation properties and it needs to be moved out of the UI.

In the `btnAddActivity`'s `Click` event, the line of code that adds the selected activity to the trip's collection of activities should be moved and enhanced because the `Activities` are no longer attached to the context by default. Example 26-7 shows the `AddTripActivity` method in the `DataBridge` class.

Example 26-7. Attaching an activity to a Trip

```
public void AddTripActivity(Trip trip, Activity activity)
{
  if (activity.EntityState == EntityState.Detached)
  {
    //necessary because it's a Notracking entity
    _context.Activities.Attach(activity);
  }
  trip.Activities.Add(activity);
}
```

There is a business rule that a `Trip` must be attached to the context before the user can begin modifying it. Therefore, in this method, you can presume that the `Trip` is already attached. However, the `Activity` may not be. Normally, you could simply add the activity to the attached `Trip` and relationship span would pull the `Activity` into the context. But, because the activities were queried using `NoTracking`, relationship span won't work. That's why you see the extra code for explicitly attaching the `Activity`.

There are three more chunks of non-UI logic in the WPF window. These are the features that allow users to create new trips and to save trips.

You can create a new method in `DataBridge`, `GetNewTrip`, shown in Example 26-8, to move the "new trip" logic into. This will also return the newly created trip to the consumer.

Example 26-8. Generating a new trip

```
public Trip GetNewTrip()
{
  var newTrip = new Trip { StartDate = DateTime.Today, EndDate = DateTime.Today };
  //add to context for change tracking
  _context.Trips.AddObject(newTrip);
  //add to observable collection of trips
  _trips.Add(newTrip);
  return newTrip;
}
```

Now you can replace those lines of code in the WPF window's `btnNewTrip_Click` event with the call to `GetNewTrip`, as shown in Example 26-9. Because the `ObservableCollection<Trip>` is not a locally stored variable, you'll need to refresh the `tripViewSource`, which populates the listbox. This does not reexecute the query for trips, but simply uses the existing list of trips. Therefore, the trips that have been attached to the context are still attached along with any changes that have been tracked.

Example 26-9. The UI's trigger for creating a new trip

```
private void btnNewTrip_Click(object sender, RoutedEventArgs e)
{
  Trip newTrip = _bridge.GetNewTrip();
  ViewSource(ViewSources.tripViewSource).Source =_bridge.ObservableTrips;
  tripListBox.SelectedItem = newTrip;
}
```

Finally, move the call to `context.SaveChanges` out of the UI and into the `DataBridge`, as shown in Example 26-10. Along with this move, you can add some validation code for any new trips that were created before calling `SaveChanges`. This is similar to how the `IContext` classes' `SaveChanges` method performed validation logic in Chapter 24.

Example 26-10. SaveChanges moving out of the UI

```
public bool SaveChanges(out string messages)
{

  if (!PreSavingValidate(out messages))
  {return false;}
  _context.SaveChanges();
  return true;
}
```

In Chapter 22, you added a `Validate` method to the `Reservation` class. Example 26-11 shows a similar method as in Chapter 22 that I've added to `DataBridge`, except that it calls a (not yet defined) `Validate` method for the `Trip` entity.

Example 26-11. Adding in some validation

```
private bool PreSavingValidate(out string validationErrors)
{
  bool isvalid = true;
  validationErrors = "";

  foreach (var trip in ManagedEntities<Trip>())
  {
    string validationError;
    bool isTripValid = trip.Validate(out validationError);
    if (!isTripValid)
    {
      isvalid = false;
      validationErrors += validationError;
    }
  }
```

```
  return isvalid;
}
```

What's left in the UI's code-behind is only the code that interacts with the user interface elements and calls to the `DataBridge` to perform any business or data access interaction. Example 26-12 shows the trimmed down code.

Example 26-12. The full listing of the UI after removing non-UI code

```
public partial class MainWindow : Window
{
  private Trip _currentTrip;
  private readonly DataBridge _bridge = new DataBridge();
  private IEnumerable<Activity> _activities;
  private IEnumerable<Destination> _destinations;
  private IEnumerable<Lodging> _lodgings;

  public MainWindow()
  {
    InitializeComponent();
  }

  private void Window_Loaded(object sender, RoutedEventArgs e)
  {

    ViewSource(ViewSources.tripViewSource).Source = _bridge.ObservableTrips;

    _destinations = _bridge.GetUntrackedList<Destination>(d => d.Name);
    ViewSource(ViewSources.destinationViewSource).Source = _destinations;

    _lodgings = _bridge.GetUntrackedList<Lodging>(l => l.LodgingName);
    ViewSource(ViewSources.lodgingViewSource).Source = _lodgings;

    _activities = _bridge.GetUntrackedList<Activity>(a => a.Name);
    activityComboBox.ItemsSource = _activities;

    EditSortDescriptions(SortAction.Add);
  }

  private void button1_Click(object sender, RoutedEventArgs e)
  {
    string saveMessages;
    if (!_bridge.SaveChanges(out saveMessages))
    {
      MessageBox.Show(saveMessages);
    }
  }
  private void btnAddActivity_Click(object sender, RoutedEventArgs e)
  {
    var selectedActivity = activityComboBox.SelectedItem as Activity;
    if (selectedActivity != null)
    {
      _bridge.AddTripActivity(_currentTrip, selectedActivity);
     activitiesListBox.ItemsSource = _currentTrip.Activities;
    }
```

```
    }

    private void btnNewTrip_Click(object sender, RoutedEventArgs e)
    {
      Trip newTrip = _bridge.GetNewTrip();
      ViewSource(ViewSources.tripViewSource).Source = _bridge.ObservableTrips;
      tripListBox.SelectedItem = newTrip;
    }

    private void tripListBox_SelectionChanged
     (object sender, System.Windows.Controls.SelectionChangedEventArgs e)
    {
      _currentTrip = (Trip) e.AddedItems[0];
      _bridge.TrackChanges(_currentTrip);
       activitiesListBox.ItemsSource = _currentTrip.Activities;
    }
  }
```

Note the code to set the `activitiesListBox.ItemsSource` in the `tripListBox_SelectionChanged` and `btnAddActivity_Click` events. You'll find an explanation for this at the end of this section.

There are some additional helper methods, such as the `ViewSource` method and enums which encapsulate the code for finding the `CollectionViewSource` XAML elements in the window. These are displayed in Example 26-13.

Example 26-13. Helper method and enums for CollectionViewSources

```
    private CollectionViewSource ViewSource(ViewSources source)
    {
      return FindResource(source.ToString()) as CollectionViewSource;
    }


    private enum ViewSources
    {
      //enums are lower case to match control names
      tripViewSource,
      destinationViewSource,
      lodgingViewSource
    }
```

And finally, the WPF mechanism which we added into the previous WPF window to apply UI-controlled sorting to the `tripListBox` and the destination combo is shown in Example 26-14.

Example 26-14. Providing sort capability in the UI

```
  enum SortAction
  {
    Add = 1,
    Delete = 2
  }
  private void destinationComboBox_DropDownClosed
```

```
  (object sender, EventArgs e)
{
  EditSortDescriptions(SortAction.Delete);
  EditSortDescriptions(SortAction.Add);
}

private void EditSortDescriptions(SortAction sortAction)
{
  var sortDestination = (new SortDescription
    ("TripDetails", ListSortDirection.Ascending));
  var sortDate = (new SortDescription("StartDate",
   ListSortDirection.Descending));

  switch (sortAction)
  {
    case SortAction.Add:
      tripListBox.Items.SortDescriptions.Add(sortDestination);
      tripListBox.Items.SortDescriptions.Add(sortDate);
      break;
    case SortAction.Delete:
      if (tripListBox.Items.SortDescriptions.Contains(sortDate))
      {
        tripListBox.Items.SortDescriptions.Remove(sortDestination);
        tripListBox.Items.SortDescriptions.Remove(sortDate);
      }
      break;
    default:
      break;
  }
}
```

Now you have achieved the goal of pulling all of the data access and business logic out of the UI as a first look at building a layered application using the Entity Framework.

Unlike the repositories you built in Chapter 24, this example is not ignorant of how the data is persisted. The Entity Framework is involved in every layer, even though there is no Entity Framework-specific code in the UI. The objects returned from the `DataBridge` to the UI are `EntityObjects`, and in some cases they are bound to the active context.

Ensuring That Lazy Loading Doesn't Negatively Impact the Layered Application

As users select trips to work with in the UI, the context's lazy loading will automatically hit the database to retrieve the `Trip`'s `Activities`. This happens thanks to the binding defined on the `Activities ListBox`.

You may recall that in the earlier chapter you created a `CollectionViewSource` that was bound to the `tripViewSource` and provided access to the `Activities` property of the `Trips`:

```
<CollectionViewSource x:Key="tripActivitiesViewSource"
 Source="{Binding Path=Activities,
         Source={StaticResource tripViewSource}}" />
```

Then the `ListBox` itself was bound to that source:

```
<ListBox DisplayMemberPath="Name" Height="100" HorizontalAlignment="Left"
 ItemsSource="{Binding Source={StaticResource tripActivitiesViewSource}}"
 Margin="51,315,0,0" Name="activitiesListBox" SelectedValuePath="ActivityID"
 VerticalAlignment="Top" Width="227" />
```

The binding triggers a request for the selected `Trip`'s `Activities`. Entity Framework's lazy loading feature, in turn, triggers a request to the database to retrieve those `Activities` if they haven't already been loaded. This is a good example of Entity Framework still being very much involved at the UI level.

This worked nicely in Chapter 9, but because these entities are now `NoTracking` entities, this can create a conflict when adding an activity to a trip.

This is why I removed the `ItemsSource` parameter from the `ListBox` and set the `ItemsSource` programmatically in the code-behind which you saw in code listed in Example 26-12.

This is not to say that you shouldn't have lazy loading in a layered client application. This action was due to particular behavior of Entity Framework that you want to avoid. In fact, there is still one more place where your UI is benefiting from lazy loading. Lazy loading is triggered by the UI's `EditSortDescriptions` method, which forces the `tripListBox` to sort by the `TripDetails` property. The `TripDetails` property requires its `Destination` navigation property. Although you have eager-loaded the `Destination` with each `Trip`, the lazy loading will be used in certain cases involving trips that the user creates on the fly.

The context is also keeping track of property changes made in the UI—for example, if the user edits one of the dates, or selects a new `Destination` (`DestinationID` is bound) or `Lodging` (`LodgingID` is bound).

Noting Additional Benefits of the Layered Application

While focusing on moving code around, you may not have noticed that in this whole process, you never modified the XAML of the window, except for removing the ListBox's ItemsSource. The WPF app still works as it did in the earlier chapter, even with all of the changes you've made to the code in this chapter.

However, in addition to making this application layered, you also applied a number of other beneficial features thanks to many of the things you learned in the chapters between. You've reduced the memory usage and increased performance by executing most of the queries as `NoTracking` queries. Because of this, it was unnecessary to create all of the extra change tracking infrastructure for retrieved data. Additionally, the context only needs to keep track of the few entities attached to it, rather than all of the

Trips, Activities, Destinations, and Lodgings that were used to populate the various lists.

Separating Entity-Specific Logic from ObjectContext Logic

Moving the logic out of the UI is a great start to building layered applications, but it is really only a start. If you want your application to be organized, you probably don't want to pile all of your various data access and business logic into one class, as with the DataBridge. But you don't necessarily have to go to the other extreme (and I'm not using the term *extreme* in a negative way here) of the repositories and interfaces that you built in Chapter 24. There are a lot of ways that you can break your logic apart. Most of them are not specific to Entity Framework, but because of Entity Framework's behaviors, there are nuances that you need to address when breaking up your logic.

I am looking forward to the future that Microsoft's Nikhil Kothari envisions in his April 2010 tweet: "My goal – making MVVM mainstream, in other words simple, common and there by default for the average developer." (Source: *http://twitter.com/nikhilk/status/11763201393*)

Considering the MVVM Pattern

One pattern that is very useful in WPF and Silverlight applications in the Model View ViewModel (MVVM) pattern. There is a lot to learn in order to build MVVM, and unfortunately, that would take us too far out of the scope of this book.

MVVM simplifies data binding to controls while maintaining a good separation of concerns when architecting your applications. Essentially, with MVVM you create new ViewModels (i.e., classes) that are designed specifically for use in the user interface. These ViewModels are separate from your entities, but you populate them with values from your entities. Be aware that there are many variations on the MVVM pattern.

The *MSDN Magazine* article, "WPF Apps With the Model-View-ViewModel Design Pattern," by Josh Smith (*http://msdn.microsoft.com/en-us/magazine/dd419663.aspx*), is frequently referenced as the ultimate resource for getting started with MVVM. Josh is a recognized MVVM guru and blogs at *http://joshsmithonwpf.wordpress.com*.

This Channel 9 video from Microsoft's Karl Schifflet is another great resource: *http://channel9.msdn.com/shows/Continuum/MVVM/*.

Microsoft's Jesse Liberty offers his perspective on MVVM here, which I like because it's easier to grasp if you are totally new to the topic: "MVVM – It's Not Kool-Aid*" (*http://jesseliberty.com/2010/05/08/mvvm-its-not-kool-aid-3*).

This section will take the DataBridge one step further and extract logic where the code interacts with the Trip class in a way that can't be written generically for any entity. It helps to encapsulate some of the Trip-related logic that the DataBridge is now performing. You could do the same for other entity types as well.

In order to create this separation, you'll need to constantly consider which layer is interacting with which classes. It also requires making some additional changes to the XAML window code-behind.

As you walk through this code, keep in mind that the focus is to highlight the specific Entity Framework challenges that you will encounter as you continue to break apart your logic. I am not suggesting that this code is the perfectly architected application that you should copy and paste into your enterprise applications.

The logic I will target for removing from the DataBridge is:

- TrackChanges which is designed specifically for a Trip
- ValidateTrips
- AddTripActivity
- GetNewTrip
- AddLodging
- AddDestination
- SetCurrentDestination

Because the current trip will be encapsulated in this wrapper, you will also have to expose a few additional properties. The TripBridge class is shown in Example 26-15.

Example 26-15. The TripBridge class designed for EntityObjects

```
using System;
using System.Collections.Generic;
using System.Data;
using System.Data.Objects;
using System.Linq;
using EFExtensionMethods;

namespace BAGA.DataLayer
{
  public class TripBridge
  {
    private Trip _currentTrip;
    private readonly BAEntities _context;

    public TripBridge(BAEntities context)
    {
      _context = context;
    }

    public List<Activity> CurrentActivities
    {
```

```
    get { return _currentTrip.Activities.ToList(); }
  }

  internal Trip GetNewTrip()
  {
    var newTrip = new Trip
                  {
                    StartDate = DateTime.Today,
                    EndDate = DateTime.Today
                  };
    //add to context for change tracking
    _context.Trips.AddObject(newTrip);
    _currentTrip = newTrip;
    return newTrip;
  }

  public void TrackCurrent(Trip trip)
  {
    _currentTrip = trip;
    if (_currentTrip.EntityState == EntityState.Detached)
    {
      //if attached destination is already managed, delete it from trip graph
      ObjectStateEntry existingOse;
      if (_context.ObjectStateManager
           .TryGetObjectStateEntry(_currentTrip.Destination, out existingOse))
      {
        _currentTrip.Destination = null;
      }
      _context.Trips.Attach(_currentTrip);
    }
  }

  public void AddActivity(Activity activity)
  {
    if (activity.EntityState == EntityState.Detached)
    {
      //if already another instance in context, use that instead
      ObjectStateEntry existingOse;
      if (_context.ObjectStateManager
                .TryGetObjectStateEntry(activity, out existingOse))
      {
        activity = existingOse.Entity as Activity;
      }
      else //otherwise attach the untracked activity
      {
        _context.Activities.Attach(activity);
      }
    }
    _currentTrip.Activities.Add(activity);
  }

  public bool ValidateBeforeSave(out string validationError)
  {
    bool isvalid = true;
    validationError = "";
```

```
        foreach (var trip in _context.ManagedEntities<Trip>())
        {
          isvalid = trip.ValidateBeforeSave(out validationError);
        }
        return isvalid;
      }

      public void AddLodging(Trip trip, Lodging lodging)
      {
        _currentTrip.LodgingID = lodging.LodgingID;
      }

      public void AddDestination(Destination dest)
      {
        ObjectStateEntry existingOse;
        //create entity key on the fly in case we're using POCOs
        var destinationEntityKey = _context.CreateEntityKey
         (_context.CreateObjectSet<Destination>().Name, dest);

        if (!_context.ObjectStateManager
              .TryGetObjectStateEntry(destinationEntityKey, out existingOse))
        {
          _context.Destinations.AddObject(dest);
        }
        _currentTrip.DestinationID = dest.DestinationID;
      }


      public void SetCurrentDestination(Destination dest)
      {
        _currentTrip.Destination = dest;
      }

    }
  }
```

The `TripBridge` constructor requires that you inject the current context when the `TripBridge` is instantiated. That allows you to keep logic related to attaching related entities in this layer.

One context-related function that stays in the `DataBridge` is the query and execution to retrieve the trips. I chose to keep all of the context-specific tasks in the `DataBridge`. There is a subtle difference between these direct calls to the context and the use of the context in the `TripBridge`, and I chose to keep the explicit queries in the `DataBridge`.

There are some other minor changes, such as renaming a few of the methods so that they make more sense within the context of the wrapper (e.g., `TrackCurrent` and `AddActivity`).

If you are following more specific design patterns, you might approach this very differently. The preceding examples should highlight some particular Entity Framework problems that you are likely to encounter along with the details you need to solve those problems.

The DataBridge now exposes a TripBridge property:

```
private readonly TripBridge _tripBridge;
public TripBridge TripBridge
{
  get
  {
   return _tripBridge;
  }
}
```

The DataBridge constructor instantiates the context and the TripBridge, passing the new context into the TripBridge's constructor:

```
public DataBridge2()
{
  _context = new BAPOCOs();
  _tripBridge = new TripBridge(_context);
}
```

The UI now must call some of the methods that were originally in the DataBridge, through the DataBridge's TripBridge property.

For example, in the Click event for btnAddActivity, you'll rely on the TripBridge to add the activity to the current trip and to return the entire list of current activities. Here's the updated method:

```
private void btnAddActivity_Click(object sender, RoutedEventArgs e)
{
  var selectedActivity = activityComboBox.SelectedItem as Activity;
  if (selectedActivity != null)
  {
    _bridge.TripBridge.AddActivity(selectedActivity);
    activitiesListBox.ItemsSource = _bridge.TripBridge.CurrentActivities;
  }
}
```

You can download the entire modified solution from the book's website at *http://www.learnentityframework.com*.

Working with POCO Entities

The code you have used so far in this chapter leverages EntityObjects. You can also use POCOs, whether they are POCOs that are tied to dynamic proxies or POCOs that are truly independent of the Entity Framework APIs.

I'll highlight a few important differences in the DataBridge and TripBridge if you are using snapshot POCOs rather than EntityObjects. The POCOs that use dynamic proxies will, for the most part, behave the same as the EntityObjects. But the simpler POCOs need some additional attention.

Providing EntityState

There are a few methods in the bridge layer that depend on an entity's EntityState property. EntityObject.EntityState exposes the EntityState of the entity's ObjectStateEntry managed by the context. A POCO entity won't have access to this, so you'll have to make accommodate for it.

In Chapter 18, where you used RIA Services with POCO entities, you encountered the same problem. The Domain Service has some methods that depend on EntityObject.EntityState. You can use the same solution here (as in Example 18-13) by replacing the use of the EntityState property with a method that retrieves the EntityState directly from the context.

For example, in the method where you attach a Trip to the context so that you can edit it (TripBridge.TrackCurrent and DataBridge.TrackChanges in the first iteration of the solution), you first test to be sure that the trip is not already attached:

```
if (_currentTrip.EntityState == EntityState.Detached)
```

The snapshot POCO entity will not have the EntityState property which gets the state from the context. Example 26-16 displays the GetEntityState method we created in the previous chapter.

Example 26-16. Getting at EntityState without an EntityObject

```
private EntityState GetEntityState(object entity)
{
  ObjectStateEntry ose;
  if (_context.ObjectStateManager.TryGetObjectStateEntry
          (entity, out ose))
  {
    return ose.State;
  }
  return EntityState.Detached;
}
```

With this method available, you can change calls such as the preceding one to:

```
if (GetEntityState(_currentTrip) == EntityState.Detached)
```

You might prefer this to be an extension method of the context. Example 26-17 shows the method rewritten as an extension method.

Example 26-17. An alternative GetEntityState extension method

```
public static EntityState GetEntityState(this ObjectContext context,object entity)
{
  ObjectStateEntry ose;
  if (context.ObjectStateManager.TryGetObjectStateEntry(entity, out ose))
  {
    return ose.State;
  }
  return EntityState.Detached;
}
```

Another problem you'll run into concerns the code that checks to ensure that `Destinations` you are about to attach to the context as part of a `Trip` graph aren't already represented in the context. Normally, you can use a POCO entity as a parameter just as you would with an `EntityObject`.

Here is the line of code that will cause a problem:

```
if (_context.ObjectStateManager.TryGetObjectStateEntry
     (_currentTrip.Destination, out existingOse))
```

`GetObjectStateEntry` and `TryGetObjectStateEntry` first look for an `EntityKey` in the object. If they find an `EntityKey`, they can easily check to see if there's a matching `ObjectStateEntry`. If there is no `EntityKey`, internally it will look through the existing `ObjectStateEntry` objects, and then at the entities tied to those entries for the same instance that was passed in.

And wherein lies the problem. Remember that you used eager loading to query the trips and related destinations. When there are two trips that go to Nepal, you'll have two separate instances of the Nepal `Destination` object. So, when Entity Framework tries to find "the matching instance" it will find none. The logic will fail. Seeing that the destination is not already in the context, the code will attempt to attach the `Trip` graph and will be greeted by an exception because, yes, that `Destination` is already there.

The solution to this is simpler than the explanation. Construct an `EntityKey` and let `TryGetObjectStateEntry` perform its check using the `EntityKey`, as shown in Example 26-18.

Example 26-18. Creating an EntityKey to check for an ObjectStateEntry

```
var destKey = new EntityKey
 ("BAPOCOs.Destinations", "DestinationID", _currentTrip.DestinationID);
if (_context.ObjectStateManager
       .TryGetObjectStateEntry(destKey, out existingOse))
```

With so many strings, this code is not very flexible. Example 26-19 shows another extension method for the context. This one has you identify the type using generics which lets you get the `EntitySet`. It also takes a lambda expression in place of the property name string. Then it builds up the entity key and checks for the `ObjectStateEntry`.

Example 26-19. An extension method to check for an ObjectStateEntry when no object is available

```
public static bool IsTracked<TEntity>(this ObjectContext context,
  Expression<Func<TEntity, object>> keyProperty, int keyId) where TEntity : class
{
  var keyPropertyName = ((keyProperty.Body as UnaryExpression).Operand as MemberExpression).
  Member.Name;
  var os = context.CreateObjectSet<TEntity>();
  var entitySetName = os.EntitySet.EntityContainer.Name + "." + os.EntitySet.Name;
  var key = new EntityKey(entitySetName, keyPropertyName, keyId);
  ObjectStateEntry ose;
  if (context.ObjectStateManager.TryGetObjectStateEntry(key, out ose))
```

```
  {
    return true;
  }
  return false;
}
```

Now, rather than include those two clunky lines of code, you can check for the ObjectStateEntry with this simpler code:

```
if (_context.IsTracked<Destination>(d => d.DestinationID,
     _currentTrip.DestinationID))
```

Providing Logic in Place of Other EntityObject Behavior

Remember that with snapshot POCO entities there is no lazy loading. In the TrackCurrent method (or TrackChanges in the first version of the DataBridge), you'll need to explicitly load Activities after you've attached the trip to the context. You can do this using ObjectContext's LoadProperty method:

```
_context.LoadProperty<Trip>(_currentTrip, t => t.Activities);
```

Finally, you also need to make up for the fact that, unless you have logic in your POCO object to do fix-ups, assigning the foreign key IDs (e.g., Trip.DestinationID) won't automatically link the related object. When you create a new Trip, the UI presumes that you will be providing a Destination name along with the Trip. When a user selects a destination for a new trip, the UI automatically updates Trip.DestinationID thanks to data binding. If you were using an EntityObject, it will synchronize with the Destination object if it's in memory. But you can't build this into the POCO entity's logic, as the POCO won't have the ability to automatically find the Destination.

So, how can you achieve the same goal when using POCOs? One plan of attack would be as follows.

1. First, check to be sure that the wiring is even necessary. If the Trip already has a Destination and its ID matches Trip.DestinationID, there's no need to go further.
2. Next, get the Destination from the context if it already exists. We'll build an EntityKey to do this as we did in the previous section, and then grab the Entity property of the returned ObjectStateEntry.
3. Finally, if the entity is not found, we want to get it from the List<Destination> that we created earlier.

This is a complicated path. I've listed it so that you can see what's involved and understand why I'm going to select an easier route. Another possibility is to change the binding attributes for the DropDown list, but I don't want to deal with any possible repercussions from that. What I will do instead is expose a method in the DataBridge that will allow the UI to pass in the selected Destination to be attached to the current Trip:

```
public void SetCurrentDestination(Destination dest)
{
  _currentTrip.Destination = dest;
}
```

Now in the `Destination` `DropDown`'s `SelectionChanged` event, I can easily call this method, as shown in Example 26-20.

Example 26-20. Letting the UI set the selected Destination

```
private void destinationComboBox_SelectionChanged(object sender,
 System.Windows.Controls.SelectionChangedEventArgs e)
{
  if (e.AddedItems.Count > 0)
  {
    _bridge.TripBridge.SetCurrentDestination(e.AddedItems[0] as Destination);
  }
}
```

These were the two barriers I encountered when replacing my `EntityObject` entities with the snapshot POCO entities. After making these changes, everything continues to work as expected.

Summary

In many client applications, you may want to leverage the benefits of the Entity Framework throughout the layers of the application. In this chapter, you learned a number of ways to benefit from the Entity Framework's features, while at the same time, create an application that also benefits from a logically tiered architecture. The chapter provided examples for building these applications. As a first step, you ensured that the only logic in the UI was that related to user interface activity. You isolated data access and specific business logic into a separate class (the `DataBridge`). Then you took a second pass and separated entity-specific logic from the more generalized logic, moving methods from the `DataBridge` class into a `TripBridge` class. Of equal importance, you learned various strategies that you can benefit from no matter how your application is architected.

Earlier in this book you learned a few ways to provide data to a client without the client having any knowledge of the Entity Framework. In Chapters 17 and 18, you supplied data through various services. In Chapter 24, you learned how to create persistence ignorant entities that could be consumed by a client that requires no references to `System.Data.Entity`. These scenarios lend themselves easily to layered applications.

CHAPTER 27

Building Layered Web Applications

In Chapter 12, you learned how to create websites using Entity Framework's ASP.NET `EntityDataSource` control. While this approach is fast, it uses data access code that is tied directly to the user interface. You've since learned a lot more about working with the Entity Framework, so we'll finish this book with a look at some better ways to use entities in better architected web applications. Several of these techniques are new to Entity Framework in .NET 4. The introduction of POCO support enables many new possibilities, such as the use of the repositories you built in Chapter 24. Foreign keys and the new state modification methods (e.g., `ObjectStateManager.ChangeState`) provide more control when working with `EntityObject` or POCO entities.

In this chapter, you'll first learn about the life cycle of web pages in a web application and how that impacts some of the choices you will have to make when planning to use the Entity Framework as your data access layer in a tiered application. Then you will build two very different types of web applications, though both will take advantage of the repositories from Chapter 24.

The first will be an ASP.NET Web Forms application where you can take advantage of ASP.NET's Session and ViewState features to retain object data across postbacks.

The second will use classes in a simple ASP.NET Model-View-Controller (MVC) application. Many introductory demos of MVC using Entity Framework place the `ObjectContext` directly in the model classes. You'll see how to separate the logic out using similar methods as in the previous chapter. You'll also learn a few tricks that are specific to entities in MVC applications.

Understanding How ObjectContext Fits into the Web Page Life Cycle

Before you can put Entity Framework to work in a web application, it's helpful to first review the life cycle of an ASP.NET web page in order to grasp why it creates a problem for the `ObjectContext`. This will provide you with the ability not only to understand some of the guidance put forth in this chapter, but also to aid you in making decisions when building your own web applications that use Entity Framework for their data access.

The `Page` object itself exists only for as long as it takes ASP.NET to render the HTML. Once the HTML has been created, the `Page` object is disposed along with any objects that it contained (see Figure 27-1).

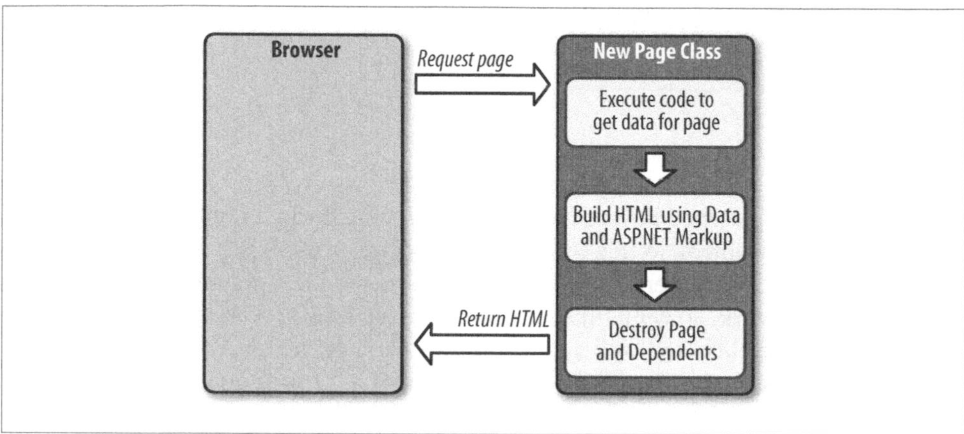

Figure 27-1. ASP.NET page life cycle

Even if you did all of your work with the `ObjectContext` in the page's code-behind, that context, which the page instantiates, will be destroyed when the page is disposed. Any objects, including entities, that were created in the page will be destroyed as well, which is why web pages are considered stateless by nature (see Figure 27-2).

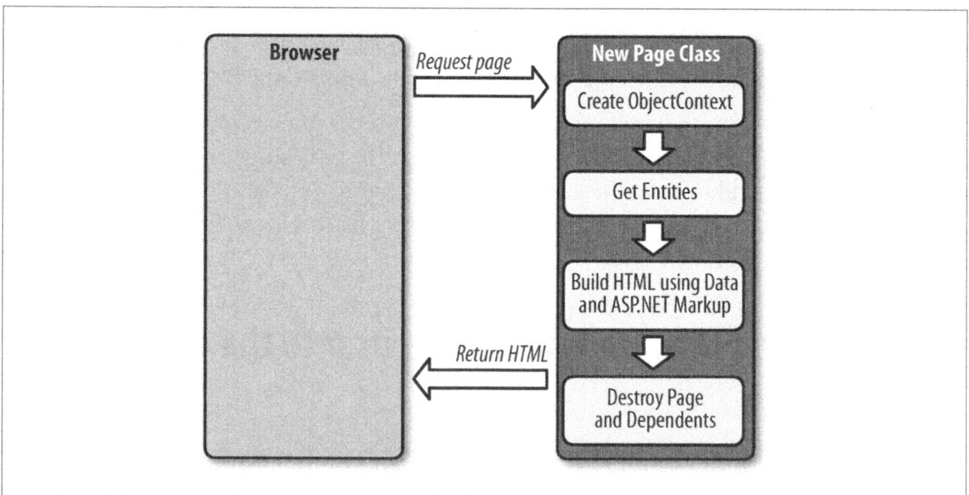

Figure 27-2. ASP.NET page using an ObjectContext

Introducing a new layer into the mix continues to pose the problem of the disappearing context. Consider a class similar to the DataBridge class from Chapter 26 that instantiates an ObjectContext and retrieves or updates data on behalf of the UI using it.

Now the web page's .NET code can instantiate a new DataBridge class, which creates an ObjectContext and some entities. When the page completes its life cycle, it is disposed along with any objects that it owns, including the DataBridge object. When that object is disposed, so is the ObjectContext that it owns, and finally, the entities are also destroyed (see Figure 27-3).

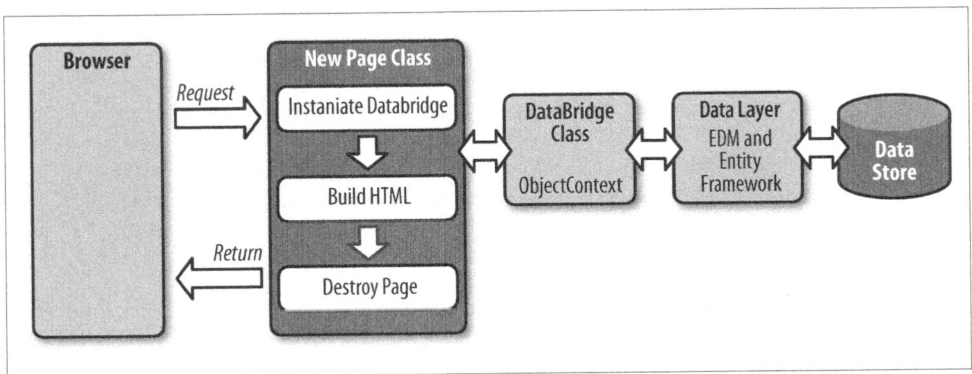

Figure 27-3. Moving the ObjectContext out of the ASP.NET page and into a DataBridge class in the middle tier

All of this means that you can't merely instantiate an ObjectContext, query for entities, modify those entities, and then call SaveChanges after a postback occurs. You will never be coming back to the same ObjectContext, and therefore change tracking will never be performed and no changes will be persisted to the database.

In the following pages, you'll find some basic guidance that will help prepare you for overcoming these problems as you build the websites in this chapter.

Return Results, Not Queries, from the DataBridge Class

Although you can get away with binding a query when working directly in the code-behind of an ASP.NET page, remember that the query's job is to be executed and return results. Query execution requires an ObjectContext. If you return the query itself from a business class, it will be detached from the context as soon as the business object is disposed (which in turn disposes the context).

Here's an example of a method within a business class that returns an IQueryable of customer objects:

```
public IQueryable<Customer> GetCustomer(int custID)
{
  return _ctx.Customer.Where(c => c.CustomerID == custID);
}
```

In a web app, you might set the data source of a control to the results. Because you are returning an `IEnumerable`, this will be allowed even though it contains only a single item:

```
ListView1.DataSource=dal.GetCustomer(570);
```

The query will not be executed until the page begins to render the `ListView` control. By then it's quite possible that the business object will be long gone and the execution will fail.

So, in the business class, be sure to return results, not queries. That way, you don't have to worry about how the methods are used from the UI.

Many of the repositories I have seen developers build with the Entity Framework contain methods that return `IQueryables`. The repositories you built in Chapter 24 do not do this in order to avoid this same problem of returning a query that becomes disconnected from an `ObjectContext`. If it is simply a LINQ to Objects query and not a LINQ to Entities query, you won't encounter the problem of a query that needs to be executed against a context and database, and you should be safe.

An additional benefit is that by executing the query and forcing the results to be iterated through using something such as `First`, `ToList`, or `Execute`, when the iteration is complete the `EntityConnection` and its database connection are disposed. Therefore, you won't have to think twice about the database connection, which is an unmanaged resource.

Using Entities in Read-Only Web Pages

The big challenges for working with objects in ASP.NET occur mostly in scenarios where you need the user to update data, especially with a graph of entities, such as a master/detail page.

If you are building pages that merely need to display data, things are much simpler. You can return data of any shape to the page and use the page's code-behind to populate controls or bind data.

You could have a method that returns a full graph of information for a customer along with her reservation information, payments for those reservations, and details regarding the trips for which she made the reservations. You can grab all of this information in a single query, as shown in Example 27-1.

Example 27-1. Creating a deep graph to return to a web page for display

```
public Customer GetCustomerWithRelatedData(Int32 ContactID)
{
  var custs = _commonContext.Contacts.OfType<Customer>()
                        .Include("Addresses")
                        .Include("Reservations.Trip.Destination")
                        .Include("PrimaryActivity")
                        .Include("SecondaryActivity")
                        .Include("PrimaryDestination")
                        .Include("SecondaryDestination")
                        .Where("it.Contactid=" + ContactID);
   //important return the customer object, not the custs query;
   return custs.FirstOrDefault();}
```

A web page could then instantiate the class, call `GetCustomerWithRelatedData`, and then populate controls using the returned data, as shown in Example 27-2.

Example 27-2. Retrieving entities from a separate class

```
protected void Page_Load(object sender, System.EventArgs e)
{
  if (!IsPostBack)
  {
    var dal = new DataBridge();
    var customer = dal.GetCustomerWithRelatedData(_custID);
    populateTextBoxes(customer);
    gridView_Addresses.DataSource = customer.Addresses;
    gridView_Addresses.DataBind();
    gridView_Reservations.DataSource = customer.Reservations;
    gridView_Reservations.DataBind();
  }
}
```

Because the default behavior of the controls is to save their display values in view state, it is not necessary to retrieve the data each time the page posts back.

Keep in mind that Example 27-2 is showing a query that will be expensive from the perspective of the database because of the numerous `Include`s. The purpose of this example is only to demonstrate the simplicity of displaying data that is not being edited. In that case, you should also consider turning off ASP.NET's viewstate as there's no need to cache the read-only data.

A class similar to the one you created for the WPF application that provides methods for retrieving data can do the trick. The web page can instantiate that class, request data, and then dispose the class.

As long as the user will not be editing any data, things are pretty straightforward.

Exploring Options for Updating Entities in an ASP.NET Web Forms Application

The need to update data is where the complexities lie—especially if you want to use `ObjectContext` to track and save changes.

Single or batch updates?

It would be pragmatic to first determine whether you need to be able to update one entity (or graph) at a time, or more than one. This can make a big difference in how you approach the updates.

In web applications, it is common for a user to work with one object at a time and perform a save to the database before moving on to another object. This is the simplest scenario to implement and all of the ASP.NET data source controls use it, including `EntityDataSource`.

In some applications, having batch edits and update scenarios is desired. An example of this is editing a number of rows in a grid, and then performing an update when the user has completed all of his edits. This also introduces more potential concurrency conflicts if a user is holding onto modifications for a longer period of time. Implementing this scenario has always been a challenge, and the problems regarding persisting large amounts of data to enable batch updates in ASP.NET are not new. The Entity Framework merely adds a few more irons to the fire.

Persist entities or use independent values?

It's easiest to make a call to `SaveChanges` when you have a long-running `ObjectContext`. But that is not a feasible option in the web scenario.

What about *Global.asax*? Although it is technically possible to spin up an `ObjectContext` in *Global.asax* when the web application starts up on the server and to use that as a global cache for entities, this would wreak havoc on your web server. That single context will attempt to coordinate every user's queries and updates.

Without the long-running context, there are a few possible paths to take:

1. The first involves persisting the entities in memory on the server—most likely in the user's session. When the user wants to update you can attach those entities to a new context and update them using the new values coming from the controls on the page, then call `SaveChanges`. As long as you don't have a lot of concurrent sessions, this is a reasonable solution. Although you will run into trouble if you are spreading your app across a server farm where a user can't count on returning to the same server which is retaining the user's session information.

2. A potential compromise to storing the full graph is to store only the entity values, but you would need to store the relationships as well, and since the entities don't have much more information in them than their values, you won't reduce the amount of data that is being persisted. At the same time, walking through a graph and extracting the properties, as well as those of all of the related entities, and then rebuilding them will be quite an intensive process.
3. Another path for allowing `SaveChanges` to do its job would entail performing the query again prior to saving. You can then update the newly queried entities with the values coming from the client.
4. Finally, you can leverage the new state management methods just as you did in the WCF Services examples earlier in this book.

In the Web Forms example later in this chapter, I'll use the first pattern which will allow me to minimize hits to the database and reduce the amount of data that I'm sending.

Before you consider whether to persist the data in memory, you will need to understand ASP.NET's mechanisms for storing data in memory and how those mechanisms are impacted when using entities.

Comparing ASP.NET's State Solutions to the Needs of the Entity Framework

ASP.NET provides a number of mechanisms for maintaining the state of objects after a `Page` object is destroyed. Let's take a look at three of them—view state, application cache, and session state—and see how they work for the entities.

View state

View state creates an encrypted binary stream of data representing objects or other data that it adds to the HTML of the page. Many ASP.NET controls use view state as a way to retain the contents of the control even if the page is posted back. For example, the text in a `Label` or the values in a `GridView` can automatically be stored in view state. When the page posts back, ASP.NET reads the view state and uses what it finds to help render the new HTML.

View state is a user interface mechanism and not something you would use outside the ASP.NET `Page` class. If you don't have a lot of experience with ASP.NET, there are things about view state with respect to the Entity Framework that you should be aware of.

You can actually see the view state data if you view the source of an ASP.NET page in your web browser. The contents of view state can easily bloat the HTML and create performance problems if you use it without care. The biggest abuser of view state is generally a `GridView`, which could contain many rows and many columns' worth of data that it is trying to save across postbacks.

Although many of ASP.NET's controls and features can automatically read and write to view state, it is also possible for a developer to explicitly store objects into view state and retrieve them again when needed using a key to identify the data being stored (see Example 27-3). You'll need to cast the view state data back to its correct type when you retrieve it.

View state is a good place to persist small bits of data such as entity key information or `TimeStamp` values, but it is not advisable to use view state to persist entire entity objects, graphs, or even collections of entities. And keep in mind that viewstate can store only items that are serializable. You'll see shortly that `ObjectContext` fails this rule.

Example 27-3. Explicitly storing and retrieving a small piece of data in view state

```
Page.ViewState["myKey"] = myCustomer.EntityKey;
custkey = (EntityKey)(ViewState["custKey"]);
```

The `EntityDataSource` control uses view state behind the scenes to retain entity values; most importantly, the original values of the entity being edited so that when it's time to call `SaveChanges`, the context has access to `Original` and `Current` values and is able to build update commands based on them.

Although the focus of this chapter is on pulling the `ObjectContext` out of the UI layer, you may be curious about pushing entities into view state. `ObjectContext` is thankfully not an option, because it is not serializable.

Figure 27-4 shows the source for a simple page where a single `Customer` entity is being retrieved and put into view state. The only control on the page is a `TextBox` to serve as a basis for measuring view state and a button to provide a way to force a postback on the page. The figure shows a screenshot of only half of the source of the page. The other half is filled with the view state as well.

When the customer is not being stored in view state, the size of the page is about 1,000 bytes. With the single customer stored in view state the size of the page grows to nearly 11,400 bytes. That is a pretty significant amount of data. And you can see in Table 27-1 how it could easily grow even larger. You need to watch out for this with any objects that you persist in view state, such as data sets, not just entities.

Table 27-1. Impact of Customer entities on view state

Customer entities in view state	Size of page (bytes)
0	1,038
1	11,380
20	44,588
50	97,676

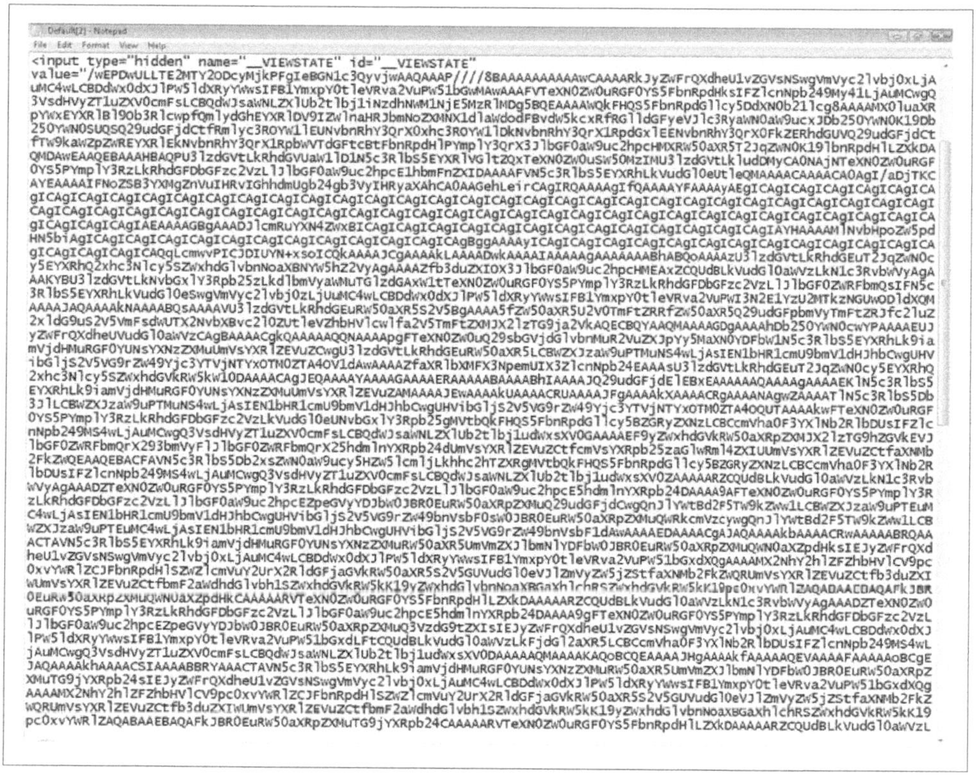

<input type="hidden" name="__VIEWSTATE" id="__VIEWSTATE"

Figure 27-4. *Half of the view state for a page that contains only a single Customer entity*

This gives you a good idea of the potential impact of storing entities in view state. As the view state increases, the time it takes to deliver the page to the browser also increases. The first entity stored in view state has additional data included in it. After that, the additional `Customer` entities are only about 1,750 bytes each. You may not want to incur this additional cost in your applications.

Application cache and session state

The most common alternative to retaining objects in memory is to store them in the server's memory using either the application cache or ASP.NET session state.

Application cache is used to retain data that is accessed frequently but does not change frequently. More importantly, application cache is shared across all active sessions of a web application. It does not provide unique storage of memory for each user. Instead, every user would be working with the same set of data. You could use application cache for read-only data that you want to share among users, and you'll see a pattern for doing this further on in this chapter. However, if that data needs to participate in relationships with data that the users are editing, which would require them to be managed by the same `ObjectContext`, this wouldn't be feasible. Finally, you probably do not want to consider editing data that is being retained in the application cache unless you have a very specific need and are confident that you will have precise control over the interaction.

With session state, however, ASP.NET preserves a cache of memory on the server for every user currently accessing your website using a class called `Session`. Not only is session state a great way to retain information in memory, but as a user moves from page to page in your web application, the session state remains available. When the user ends her session with your website, that chunk of memory is disposed after the configured session timeout, which is 20 minutes by default. Session state is most commonly accessed through a `Page` class, but you can also use it from a business layer.

Like view state, session state can only store objects that are serializable, and like view state it can grow out of control if you are not paying attention, but in a way that can be worse than an individual user's view state.

Although view state offloads this information to the browser, session state puts all of the stored information for every user hitting the website on the server. If 10 people are using your website, the server needs to store the session state for those 10 people in memory. If 1,000 people are using your website, imagine how much of the server's memory you might need to store all of their session state information. If you are concerned with scalability, you should use session state wisely.

For websites that scale out dramatically, to the extent that multiple servers are used, session state can become problematic as a user may not hit the same server after a postback, unless you are employing logic to ensure what's called *sticky sessions*. In this case, where you aren't using sticky sessions to ensure that the user returns to the same web server, your options will be to hit the database (using a `ClientWins Refresh` or requery) or to use one of the other session state solutions available for ASP.NET. The latter is a topic to be researched in the many resources and books that are dedicated to ASP.NET and website performance.

Another important thing to realize regarding session state is that a lot of effort is required for ASP.NET to move objects in and out of `Session`.

In the long run, session state is a very tempting place to store data, but you should use it for storing only small amounts of information as it comes with a lot of baggage.

ASP.NET provides another option which is a reasonable balance between achieving a high-end *n*-tier architecture and getting the job done without a huge amount of complexity: the `ObjectDataSource` control.

> **Why Not Use the ObjectDataSource Control?**
>
> In the previous edition of this book, I used EntityObjects with a series of ASP.NET ObjectDataSource controls. Although this remains a perfectly viable choice, I will not be repeating that in this chapter. However, I want to point out that the new foreign key support reduces the amount of code—and confusion—caused by the HTML markup's need to access foreign keys in a variety of scenarios. Look on the Downloads page of the book's website for a sample Visual Studio 2010 project that uses EntityDataSource controls.

In the long run, your best bet is to approach a web application from the perspective of a disconnected application using short-lived contexts and performing simple updates rather than worrying about change tracking and trying to send large amounts of data or sets of graphs to the server from the client. The repository you built in Chapter 22 sets you up very nicely to achieve this. Like the EntityDataSource, the ObjectDataSource works with a single record at a time when updates are performed, and doesn't depend on Entity Framework to provide change tracking information from the client. The new state management methods such as ChangeObjectState which you used in the WCF services will enable you to use entities in applications that use Web Forms in their front end.

Let's take a look at how you might construct a simple Web Forms application using many of the tools we've learned about in previous chapters. Because the real challenge is generally encountered with master-details forms, the example will add that into the mix but sticking with EntityObjects. The MVC example that follows uses POCOs and the repositories from Chapter 24.

Building an N-Tier Web Forms Application

The bridge layers you built in the previous chapter were not designed for general-purpose use, regardless of the style of application. Those classes were built with a dependency on a long-running ObjectContext to track changes made to objects in the UI. This tactic will not work in a web application which will require a short-lived context. Some of the concepts you applied in the WCF Service will work well for a web application, except for the ability to receive graphs from the client.

The user interface can populate its controls using data that is presented in graphs, but once the page is rendered those objects no longer exist unless you start wrestling with the session. All the UI has are values in the HTML. The code-behind of the UI should not be in the business of constructing objects to pass back to the data tier.

There are a variety of alternatives in ASP.NET Web Forms when allowing users to edit data and then persisting that data back to the database.

You could simply read the values from the various controls on the page and pass those values to a method which will then handle the object creation and updates.

As discussed previously, using session or view state comes with its price. If you are not a fan of this price, you will probably prefer to work with ASP.NET MVC and will be happier with the example in the latter portion of this chapter.

You'll take advantage of session state for this Web Forms solution so that you can see how the additional layers differ from those used in the client app, and at the same time, how they resonate with the WCF Services. If your web application ends up distributed across many servers you will have to replace the session state with a different caching mechanism. See the sidebar "Caching in Scaled-Out Web Applications" for pointers to information on this advanced topic.

Caching in Scaled-Out Web Applications

Session state is a reasonable choice for applications that do not need to scale. However, if you have lots of users/usage and need to push your apps onto multiple web servers, you will quickly run into problems as users post back, expecting to find their session data, but arrive at a different server. At this point, you should consider using a more advanced form of caching. One solution to this would be to use ASP.NET's State Server Mode (*http://msdn.microsoft.com/en-us/library/ms178586.aspx*). Additionally, you could use a caching solution. A common caching solution for web applications is the popular open source (and free) Memcached (*http://memcached.org/*). Microsoft's Windows Server AppFabric (*http://msdn.microsoft.com/en-us/windowsserver/ee695849.aspx*) includes advanced caching capabilities. AppFabric was originally known by its code name, Velocity. It also has the option of being integrated with Windows Azure which is part of the Windows Azure Platform (*http://www.microsoft.com/windowsazure/appfabric*).

Another route is to build the caching into Entity Framework using a custom provider. Jarek Kowalski, from the Entity Framework team, has created a sample implementation of tracing and caching providers for Entity Framework which you can find at *http://code.msdn.microsoft.com/EFProviderWrappers*.

Designing the Application

You'll base this example on a web app that allows customers to log in and manage their profile. In addition, they can see a list of their trips along with balance due information. Figure 27-5 displays a mock-up of this application.

Notice that the customer information is editable and contains drop-down lists. Additionally, addresses can be edited, deleted, or modified. The form presents a variety of challenges thanks to the desires of BreakAway's consumer relations department.

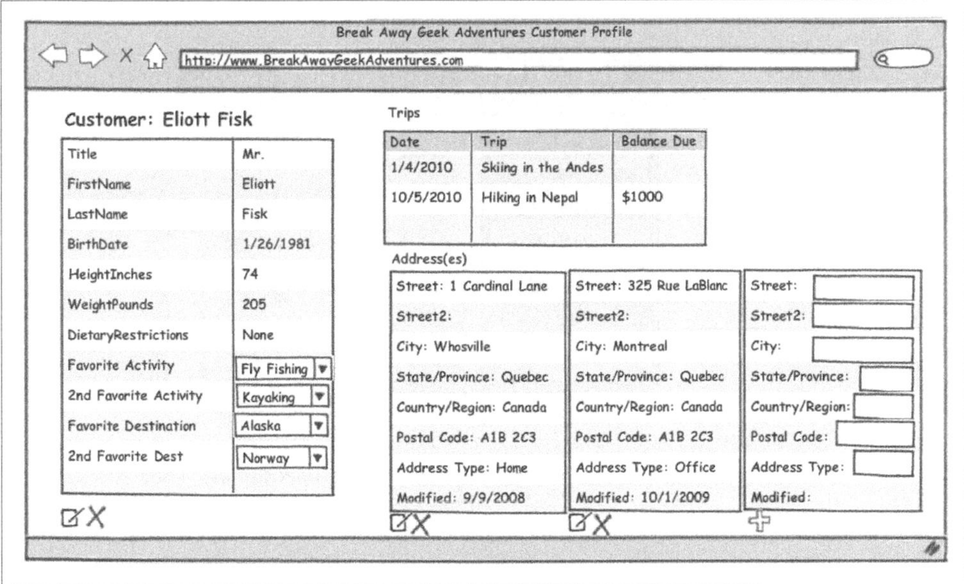

Figure 27-5. The consumer profile management web page

Using the Existing Repositories

Because you already have your nice repositories from Chapter 24, you can easily leverage these for your web application. If you want to use `EntityObjects` you can build a similar repository architecture with a unit of work and individual repositories. You will only be missing the persistence ignorance and the ability to run unit tests without hitting the database.

But the web page will not talk directly to the repositories. That would put too much logic in the hands of the web page. Instead, as you did with the WPF application, you'll build a class that will go between the UI and, in this case, the repositories and unit of work, as shown in the diagram in Figure 27-6.

I've added some new repositories to the mix, as you'll see in the next pages.

Building an Entity Manager to Act As a DataBridge

In order for your web application to interact with the unit of work and repositories, you can add a server-side class into your solution that will be responsible for managing the entities. Then the code-behind of your web pages can work with that class, just as the WPF window code in the previous chapter worked directly with the `DataBridge` class. In both cases, your UI will be sheltered from the context.

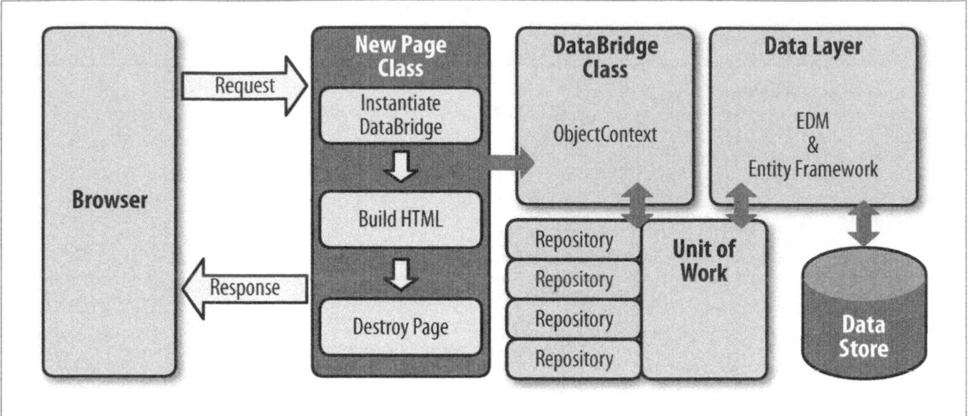

Figure 27-6. Adding the repositories and unit of work into the web application architecture

Here are the goals of the entity manager:

1. Retrieve data from the database.
2. Store the original entities in the session cache.
3. Capture updated data sent from the user interface.
4. Retrieve original data from the session cache.
5. Attach original data to a new context.
6. Apply changed values from the client.
7. Save the data to the database.

For operations that retrieve data to be displayed in Web Forms, you can instantiate your repository and return the necessary data. But before the data is returned to the form, you can store it away in your caching mechanism. Again, you'll be using ASP.NET session state for caching.

Because the manager will rely on the current session to cache data, you'll create this class in the same project as the web form.

Example 27-4 shows the shell for the class along with the declarations for the `UnitOfWork` and `CustomerRepository` that the class will use frequently.

Example 27-4. The shell of the EntityManager class

```
using System;
using System.Collections.Generic;
using System.Linq;
using System.Web;
using BAGA.Repository.Repositories;
using BAGA;

namespace Ch27WebForm
```

```
{
  public class EntityManager
  {
    readonly UnitOfWork _uow = new UnitOfWork();
    CustomerRepository _cRep ;
  }
}
```

Retrieving Data for Display and for Future Updates

The data needed for display is different from that needed for performing updates, and therefore you will handle them separately. Considering the main profile section, you would need to query the customer but also include the four references to the favorite activities and destinations. Because you can't lazy-load once you are in the UI, this means you would have to eager-load the related data. Thanks to the improvements in .NET 4, the query generated from multiple `Includes` is not so bad. However, this approach would require you to deal with shaped data in the UI or to build some type of wrapper in the manager.

Instead, I've chosen to add a `QueryView` to the model to return flattened data. The new entity, `ProjectedCustomer`, is shown in Figure 27-7.

The `QueryView` that maps data to this entity is shown in Example 27-5.

Example 27-5. A QueryView to provide flattened data

```
<EntitySetMapping Name="ProjectedCustomers">
  <QueryView>
    SELECT VALUE BAModel.ProjectedCustomer(
    c.ContactID, c.FirstName,c.LastName,c.Title,
    cu.PrimaryDesintation,cu.SecondaryDestination,
    cu.PrimaryActivity,cu.SecondaryActivity,
    cu.Notes,cp.BirthDate,cp.HeightInches,cp.WeightPounds,
    cp.DietaryRestrictions,
    D1.LocationName,D2.LocationName,A1.Activity,A2.Activity)
    FROM BreakAwayModelStoreContainer.Contact  AS c
    JOIN BreakAwayModelStoreContainer.Customers as cu ON c.ContactID=cu.ContactID
    JOIN BreakAwayModelStoreContainer.ContactPersonalInfo as cp
         ON c.ContactID=cp.ContactID
    INNER JOIN BreakAwayModelStoreContainer.Locations as D1
          ON cu.PrimaryDesintation=D1.LocationID
    INNER JOIN BreakAwayModelStoreContainer.Locations as D2
          ON cu.SecondaryDestination=D2.LocationID
    INNER JOIN BreakAwayModelStoreContainer.Activities as A1
          ON cu.PrimaryActivity=A1.ActivityID
    INNER JOIN BreakAwayModelStoreContainer.Activities as A2
          ON cu.SecondaryActivity=A2.ActivityID
  </QueryView>
</EntitySetMapping>
```

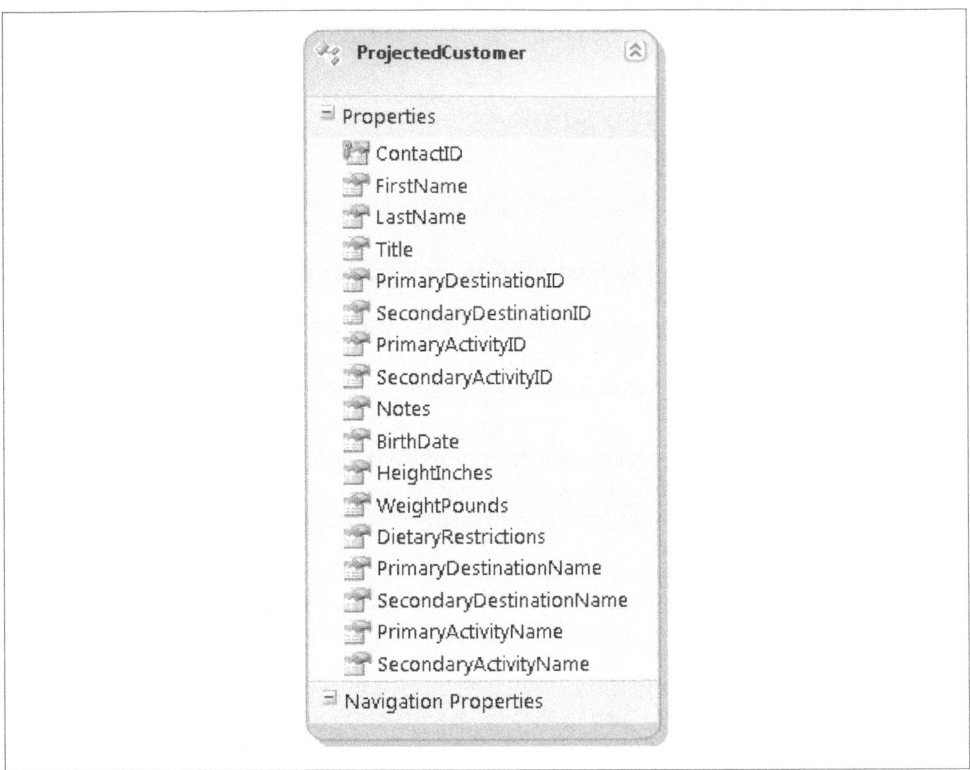

Figure 27-7. The ProjectCustomer entity supplied by a QueryView

I've added the method shown in Example 27-6 to the `CustomerRepository` which will return this entity.

Example 27-6. CustomerRepository.ProjectedCustomer method

```
public ProjectedCustomer ProjectedCustomer(int id)
{
  return _context.ProjectedCustomers.FirstOrDefault(c => c.ContactID == id);
}
```

That satisfies the data for displaying. You'll also pull back a true `Customer` entity to use for any modifications that need to be saved to the database.

You may recall that if an entity is mapped with a `QueryView`, any related entities must be as well. Therefore, the `ProjectedCustomer` is isolated. However, the form also needs reservations and addresses for the customer. You can return those along with the customer entity. That means in addition to the existing `GetById` method, you'll need a specialized method in my repository to bring back the graph.

Finally, this example calls for storing the data in a cache so that on postbacks, the app won't have to return to the database again, as it would if you were using an

EntityDataSource. Example 27-7 shows the method which does this retrieval and caching along with the public method that the UI will call to trigger the data retrieval and return the necessary data to the UI.

Example 27-7. Manager methods to get customer data from the database, into the cache, and back to the client

```
internal ProjectedCustomer GetProjectedCustomer(int contactId)
{
  var cust = HttpContext.Current.Session
             ["ProjectedCust" + contactId] as ProjectedCustomer;
  if (cust==null)
  {
    RetrieveAndStoreCustomerGraph(contactId);
    cust = HttpContext.Current.Session
          ["ProjectedCust" + contactId] as ProjectedCustomer;
  }
  return cust;
}

private void RetrieveAndStoreCustomerGraph(int contactId)
{
  _cRep = new CustomerRepository(_uow);
  var cust = _cRep.CustomerAndReservationsAndAddresses(contactId);
  HttpContext.Current.Session["Cust" + contactId] = cust;
  HttpContext.Current.Session["CustAddresses" + contactId] =
    cust.Addresses.ToList();
  HttpContext.Current.Session["CustReservations" + contactId] =
    cust.Reservations.ToList();
  var projectedCust = _cRep.GetProjectedCustomerById(contactId);
  HttpContext.Current.Session["ProjectedCust" + contactId] = projectedCust;
}
```

Notice that I'm using the contactId as part of the key for each session item. This sets me up for a future time when I need to move to a more scalable means of caching data and I might need to distinguish which customer's data to retrieve from the cache.

So far all of the data is coming from the Customer repository. It is providing me with a customer, with a special view of a customer, and with some related data, addresses, and reservations. We'll shake things up a bit when it's time to save data from the client side.

Making the Related Data Accessible to the Client

I'll also provide methods to retrieve the address and reservation collections from the cache. If for some reason they have not been stored yet, the method fires off the RetrieveAndStoreCustomerGraph. If the customer simply had no addresses or reservations, the list will exist with no data as opposed to being null (see Example 27-8).

Example 27-8. EntityManager methods to return addresses and reservations to client

```
internal List<Address> GetCustomerAddresses(int contactId)
{
  var addList = HttpContext.Current.Session["CustAddresses" + contactId];
  if (addList == null)
  {
    RetrieveAndStoreCustomerGraph(contactId);
    addList = HttpContext.Current.Session["CustAddresses" + contactId];
  }
  return addList as List<Address>;
}

internal List<Reservation> GetCustomerReservations(int contactId)
{
  var resList = HttpContext.Current.Session["CustReservations" + contactId];
  if (resList == null)
  {
    RetrieveAndStoreCustomerGraph(contactId);
    resList = HttpContext.Current.Session["CustReservations" + contactId];
  }
  return resList as List<Reservation>;
}
```

Getting Data from the Manager to the Client

At this point the manager has everything needed for the client to display the data.

My UI code can instantiate the `EntityManager` class and call the exposed methods, as shown in Example 27-9.

Example 27-9. Web form code-behind retrieving data from the EntityManager

```
public partial class _Default : System.Web.UI.Page
{
  private readonly EntityManager mgr = new EntityManager();
  protected void Page_Load(object sender, EventArgs e)
  {
    if (!IsDataBound)
    {
      BindCustomer();
      BindAddressesAndReservations();
    }
  }

  public bool IsDataBound
  {
    get
    {
      object o = ViewState["IsDataBound"];
      if (o == null) return false;
      else return (bool) o;
    }
    set
    {
```

```
            ViewState["IsDataBound"] = value;
        }
    }

    private void BindCustomer()
    {
        var cust = mgr.GetProjectedCustomer(currentId);
        //returns customer and addresses and reservations
        CustomerDetailsView.DataSource = new List<ProjectedCustomer> { cust };
        CustomerDetailsView.DataBind();
        IsDataBound = true;
    }

    private void BindAddressesAndReservations()
    {
        ReservationsListView.DataSource = mgr.GetCustomerReservations(currentId);
        ReservationsListView.DataBind();
        AddressesListView.DataSource = mgr.GetCustomerAddresses(currentId);
        AddressesListView.DataBind();
        IsDataBound = true;
    }
}
```

The form will allow users to edit customers and addresses. Additionally, they will be able to add and delete addresses. The `EntityManager` will use the `CustomerRepository` to send updates for the customer and the new `AddressRepository` to enact inserts, updates, and deletes on the addresses.

The manager will also be in charge of the `UnitOfWork`. Notice that the `UnitOfWork` is instantiated every time the `EntityManager` is instantiated. And the `EntityManager` will be instantiated every time the `Page` class is instantiated. So, each `UnitOfWork` will be short-lived. You won't attempt to track changes across postbacks, but thanks to the cached entities, you'll still be able to perform efficient updates without extra trips to the database.

For updating customers, the `EntityManager` class has a method called `UpdateCustomerProfile`. Its signature is shown in Example 27-10.

Example 27-10. EntityManager.UpdateCustomerProfile signature

```
internal void UpdateCustomerProfile(int contactId, string title, string lastName,
  string firstName, DateTime birthday, int height, int weight,
  string restrictions, int primaryDestinationId, int primaryActivityId,
  int secondaryDestinationId, int secondaryActivityId)
```

By designing the `UpdateCustomerProfile` method to receive values rather than an object, you won't force the UI developer to worry about building an object to send back.

Within the method, the manager will retrieve the original customer object from the cache, and attach it to the repository. Once it's attached, the context will track any changes made to the object, so next you can apply the changed property values. With this pattern, the update command sent to the database will only contain changed properties, rather than every property regardless of whether the user has edited it, as you've done in previous chapters. The method is shown in Example 27-11.

Example 27-11. UpdateCustomerProfile in the EntityManager

```
internal void UpdateCustomerProfile(int contactId, string title, string lastName,
  string firstName, DateTime birthday, int height, int weight,
  string restrictions, int primaryDestinationId, int primaryActivityId,
  int secondaryDestinationId, int secondaryActivityId)
    {
      _cRep = new CustomerRepository(_uow);
      var origCust = HttpContext.Current.Session["Cust" + contactId] as Customer;
      _cRep.Attach(origCust);

      //TODO: test for origCust==null and handle if necessary

      //update only fields changed by client
      if (title != origCust.Title)
        origCust.Title = title;
      if (lastName.Trim() != origCust.LastName)
        origCust.LastName = lastName.Trim();
      if (firstName != origCust.FirstName)
        origCust.FirstName = firstName;
      if (birthday != origCust.BirthDate)
        origCust.BirthDate = birthday;
      if (weight != origCust.WeightPounds)
        origCust.WeightPounds = weight;
      if (height != origCust.HeightInches)
        origCust.HeightInches = height;
      if (restrictions != origCust.DietaryRestrictions)
        origCust.DietaryRestrictions = restrictions;
      if (primaryDestinationId != origCust.PrimaryDestinationID)
        origCust.PrimaryDestinationID = primaryDestinationId;
      if (primaryActivityId != origCust.PrimaryActivityID)
        origCust.PrimaryActivityID = primaryActivityId;
      if (secondaryDestinationId != origCust.SecondaryDestinationID)
        origCust.SecondaryDestinationID = secondaryDestinationId;
      if (secondaryActivityId != origCust.SecondaryActivityID)
        origCust.SecondaryActivityID = secondaryActivityId;

      _uow.Save();
      RetrieveAndStoreCustomerGraph(origCust.ContactID);
    }
```

After the changes have been made, call the `UnitOfWork`'s `Save` method and then completely refresh all of the cached data from the database.

When the web page refreshes, it will call the `GetCustomer` method and update the display.

Adding Lists for User Selection Controls

When the user edits the customer profiler, the UI will need access to the `Destination` and `Activity` lists.

These lists will change infrequently, so there's no need for each customer to cause a hit to the database. Therefore, you can place them in the application cache for efficiency.

I've leveraged some code that you've seen earlier in this book to build a class, shown in Example 27-12, for providing cached drop-down lists. These lists are queried using the `NoTracking MergeOption`. Thanks to the foreign key support in Entity Framework, the consuming application can simply use the keys to identify the related entity without attaching these references and having to deal with the related entities' state. See the sidebar, "Forcing Consumers to Set Foreign Keys" on page 808.

Although its methods are generic, the `Lists` class gives you explicit control over what types of lists are allowed. Each list is a static variable so that it will get reused. If it does not yet exist, a query will be executed to create the list. This class currently supports lists of `Activity` types and `Destination` types.

Example 27-12. A class for providing static lists

```
using System;
using System.Collections.Generic;
using System.Data.Objects;
using System.Linq;
using System.Linq.Expressions;

namespace BAGA.Repository.Repositories
{
  public static class Lists
  {
    private static List<Destination> _destinations;
    private static List<Activity> _activities;

    public static List<T> UntrackedList<T>
        (Expression<Func<T, object>> sortProperty) where T : class
    {
      var uow = new UnitOfWork();
      var storedList = GetStoredList<T>();
      if (storedList == null)
      {
        var query = ((BAEntities)uow.Context).CreateObjectSet<T>();
        query.MergeOption = MergeOption.NoTracking;
        storedList = query.OrderBy(sortProperty).ToList();
        SetStoredList(storedList);
      }
      return storedList;
      //TODO: exception handling
    }

    private static List<T> GetStoredList<T>()
    {
```

```
        string typeName = typeof(T).Name;
        List<T> list;
        switch (typeName)
        {
          case "Activity":
            list = _activities as List<T>;
            break;
          case "Destination":
            list = _destinations as List<T>;
            break;
          default:
            throw new NotSupportedException
             ("You cannot make an UntrackedList from this type");
        }
        return list;
      }

      private static void SetStoredList<T>(IEnumerable<T> newList)
      {
        string typeName = typeof(T).Name;
        switch (typeName)
        {
          case "Activity":
            _activities = newList as List<Activity>;
            break;
          case "Destination":
            _destinations = newList as List<Destination>;
            break;
          default:
            throw new NotSupportedException
              ("You cannot make an UntrackedList from this type");
        }
      }
    }
  }
```

Now the `EntityManager` class can easily expose these lists for the consuming application, as shown in Example 27-13.

Example 27-13. Providing access to drop-down lists in the EntityManager

```
internal List<Activity> GetActivities()
{
  return Lists.GetUntrackedList<Activity>(a => a.Name);
}

internal List<Destination> GetDestinations()
{
  return Lists.GetUntrackedList<Destination>(d => d.Name);
}
```

And the consuming application can use these to bind to drop downs when customers edit their profile, allowing them to modify their choices for preferred activities and destinations.

Allowing a User to Modify Related Data

As mentioned earlier, customers will have the ability to edit their addresses. The addresses are originally provided for display as part of a graph supplied by the CustomerRepository. Editing, however, will be done using the AddressRepository. Like the UpdateCustomer method, the method signatures for modifying, inserting, and deleting Addresses will accept scalar values, rather than an object, as its parameters. These three methods are shown in Example 27-14.

Example 27-14. Methods to update, insert, and delete Address entities

```
internal void UpdateAddress(int id, string street1, string street2, string city,
                            string state, string country, string postal,
                            string type, int contactId)
{
  var aRep = new AddressRepository(_uow);
  var addresses = GetCustomerAddresses(contactId);
  var origAddress = addresses.First(a => a.addressID == id);
  aRep.Attach(origAddress);
  if (origAddress == null) return;
  //update only changed fields
  if (street1 != origAddress.Street1)
    origAddress.Street1 = street1;
  if (origAddress.Street2 != street2)
    origAddress.Street2 = street2;
  if (country != origAddress.CountryRegion)
    origAddress.CountryRegion = country;
  if (state != origAddress.StateProvince)
    origAddress.StateProvince = state;
  _uow.Save();
}

internal void InsertAddress(string street1, string street2, string city,
                            string state, string country, string postal,
                            string type, int contactId)
{
  var aRep = new AddressRepository(_uow);
  var address = new Address
                {
                  Street1 = street1,
                  Street2 = street2,
                  City = city,
                  StateProvince = state,
                  CountryRegion = country,
                  ContactID = contactId,
                  PostalCode = postal,
                  AddressType = type
                };
  aRep.Add(address);
  _uow.Save();
  RetrieveAndStoreCustomerGraph(contactId);
}

internal void DeleteAddress(int id, int contactId)
```

```
{
  var aRep = new AddressRepository(_uow);
  var addresses = GetCustomerAddresses(contactId);
  var origAddress = addresses.First(a => a.addressID == id);
  aRep.Delete(origAddress);
  _uow.Save();
  RetrieveAndStoreCustomerGraph(contactId);
}
```

Now you have all of the methods that the EntityManager needs for not only retrieving and displaying data, but also updating various types within a relationship hierarchy.

A single repository is responsible for providing the display data, while explicit type repositories handle updates.

There are many ways to define repositories, and the important lesson here was not the repository architecture, but the use of the EntityManager to keep the concerns of the user interface completely separate from the concerns of the business objects and their persistence in a Web Forms application.

Forcing Consumers to Set Foreign Keys

Don't forget about the Getter and Setter properties in the Entity Data Model Designer. You can use these to avoid complications that result from developers assigning entities as references (such as those entities being marked as Added if they are attached to new entities). Set the Setter Code Generation attribute of the navigation property (e.g., Customer.PrimaryActivity) to something other than the default, Public. Choose Internal/Friend, Private, or Protected based on your application's needs. This way, the developer will not be able to set the reference, but will be forced to use the foreign key instead.

Building an ASP.NET MVC Application

ASP.NET MVC is an alternative to using ASP.NET Web Forms to develop web applications. While Web Forms attempts to work around the lack of state in web applications by providing features such as view state, ASP.NET MVC embraces the statelessness. MVC depends only on whatever data is available in the markup (e.g., the current value of the Text or Label control) combined with specific methods defined in the application to carry values across postbacks or use them for database updates or elsewhere. MVC does not change what you have learned so far in this chapter about using the ObjectContext in web applications. You will continue to work with a short-lived context. But because MVC is designed with no expectations of state (your own or that maintained by the ObjectContext) across postbacks, you won't be tempted to depend on the ObjectContext for change tracking.

ASP.NET MVC will not be every developer's cup of tea since there is more to learn and more coding involved. But in the end, those who love MVC are extremely passionate about the advantages it gives them at the cost of more explicitly coding an architecture than is necessary with some Web Forms applications.

MVC? What About Web Forms?

While MVC is the "hot new kid" in ASP.NET development, it is not replacing Web Forms. Rather, MVC provides an alternative style of ASP.NET development for developers who were frustrated with the complexities introduced as Web Forms attempts to make web applications stateful, even though is not in their inherent nature. See the excellent article by Dino Esposito, "Comparing Web Forms and ASP.NET MVC," from the July 2009 issue of *MSDN Magazine* (*http://msdn.microsoft.com/en-us/magazine/dd942833.aspx*).

Now comes the challenge of describing MVC briefly for those who have no experience with it. I do highly recommend that if you are new to MVC, you follow up with some more dedicated MVC resources. You can start with *http://www.asp.net/mvc/*. In fact, you might want to look at some of those introductory materials before reading this section as I will not be providing a thorough introduction to MVC.

MVC stands for Model View Controller. MVC is a pattern that has been around for a while and has been adopted recently by Microsoft for ASP.NET development. The goal of MVC is to enable separation of the various types of logic in your web applications. As you have seen in earlier chapters, a model is not necessarily this XML metadata that we have been using in our Entity Data Model. A model can also be a description of a class. We looked at models like this in Chapter 25 that discussed code first and SQL Server Modeling's M. In MVC, the *M* refers to whatever provides schema of the data to be used in the user interface. It does not explicitly refer to our Entity Data Model. Similar to the way that the `DataBridge` and `TripWrapper` classes exposed our Entity Data Model classes to the WPF UI in the previous chapters, the MVC model will act as a part of the bridge between our Entity Data Model and our UI.

And this is where I want to deviate from the typical MVC introduction. ASP.NET MVC doesn't care what your model is. There are many types of models. MVC's model could be an Entity Data Model and its context. It could be a business object, or something else yet.

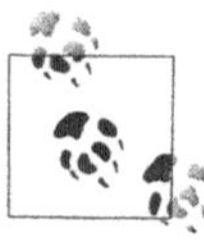

See K. Scott Allen's blog post series, "Putting the M in MVC." Here is a link to the third post which has links to the earlier ones: *http://odetocode.com/Blogs/scott/archive/2009/04/06/putting-the-m-in-mvc-part-iii.aspx*. Because of this blog series, I was thrilled to introduce Scott to Trygve Reenskaug, the originator of the MVC pattern, when we were all at the same conference in late 2009.

But that's only one part of MVC. What about the *V* (View) and *C* (Controller)? The view is the UI. And contrary to what you might presume here, the view does not talk directly to the model. This is where the controller comes in. The controller matches up the models and the views at runtime. A controller is associated with a particular view. By default, MVC associates views and controllers that have matching names.

Here you can take a quick look at the default for creating an MVC app using an EDM as the model.

Start by creating a new MVC2 Web Application project. After adding a reference to the BreakAway model project, which contains the generated `EntityObject` classes, you can add a new `Controller` for working with `Contact` entities into the project. The Add Controller Wizard, shown in Figure 27-8, allows you to create a `Controller` that exposes methods for adding, updating, and deleting `Contacts`.

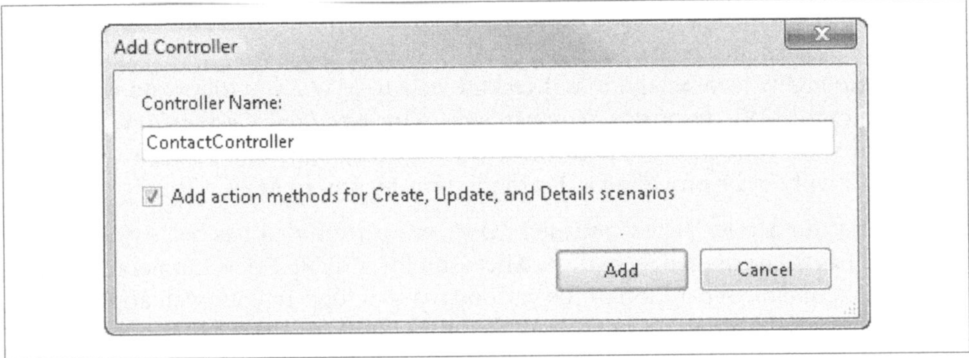

Figure 27-8. The Add Controller Wizard

The controller is simply a class. From within the class Visual Studio lets you create the views you need for each action: one for viewing `Contact` details, another for editing a contact, and another for creating a contact. There's also an Index view and you can use this one to display a list of `Contacts` from which to perform any of the other actions. Right-click the `Index` method declaration (`public ActionResult Index()`) and you'll see Add View from the context menu. Choose this to add a new Index view of `Contact`.

The wizard, shown in Figure 27-9, lets you create a view from the `Contact` class. I've indicated that I want a List of Contact types displayed in the View content drop down.

This, in turn, generates a new *Contact* folder in the *Views* folder of the MVC project and an *Index.aspx* page, as shown in Figure 27-10.

The *.aspx* page has markup for displaying the list and explicitly populating it from the controller's methods. A lot of dynamic activity occurs behind the scenes in MVC, which I won't be explaining here. Much of that is dependent on the naming of views, controllers, methods, and actions by default.

Looking back at the `Index` method in the `Controller` class, nothing has changed. If you run the app and navigate to this page, you'll get an error. When a user requests the `Contact/Index`, the controller responds by returning a view. By default, it looks for the

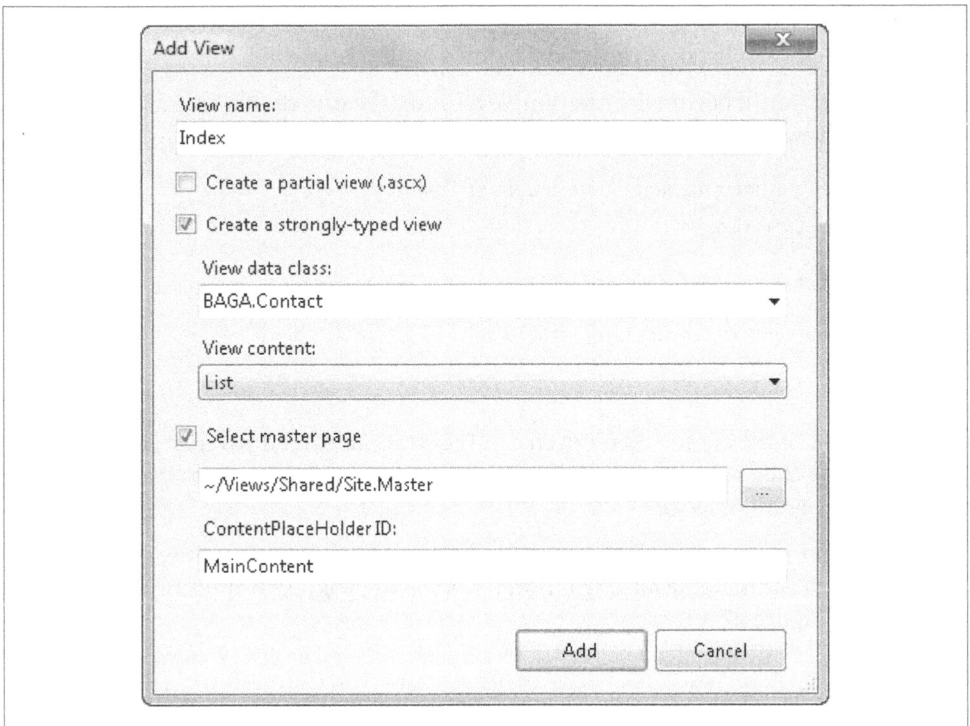

Figure 27-9. MVC's Add View Wizard

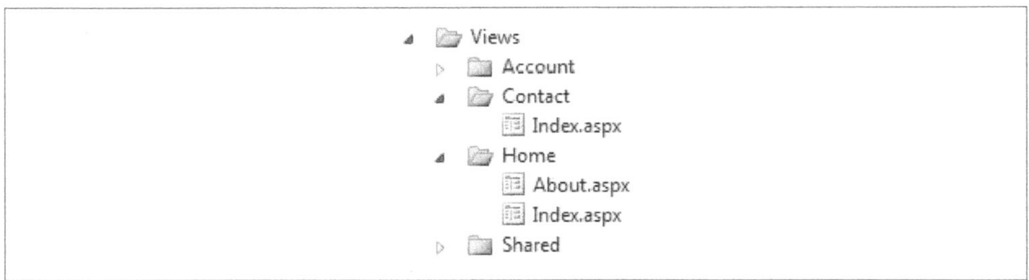

Figure 27-10. Folders created for each controller in the MVC app solution

view matching the method name. The method is `Index`, and therefore it will look for the *Index.aspx* page, but the code is incomplete:

```
public ActionResult Index()
{
  return View();
}
```

Since the *Index.aspx* page expects data to be passed into it, you need to supply data to this `View`. You can do that by returning the data as a parameter of the `View` method. Where does the data come from? It comes from the model.

The View itself is not aware of the model. The view simply takes whatever the controller provides. The controller uses the model to provide the data which the view will display.

Here is where you'll begin with the simplest route, the one that is commonly demonstrated, as shown in Example 27-15, using the context directly.

Example 27-15. An Index method to return a list of Contacts

```
public ActionResult Index()
{
  using (context = new BAGA.BAEntities())
  {
    return View(context.Contacts.ToList());
  }
}
```

Frankly, most of the demos won't even call ToList, and instead will just send back the query, forcing the view to execute the query. You know by now that even if it works, it's not a very good practice.

With no additional work in the code or the markup, the Index page now displays a list (and a long one at that, because you haven't done any paging or filtering) of Contacts, as shown in Figure 27-11.

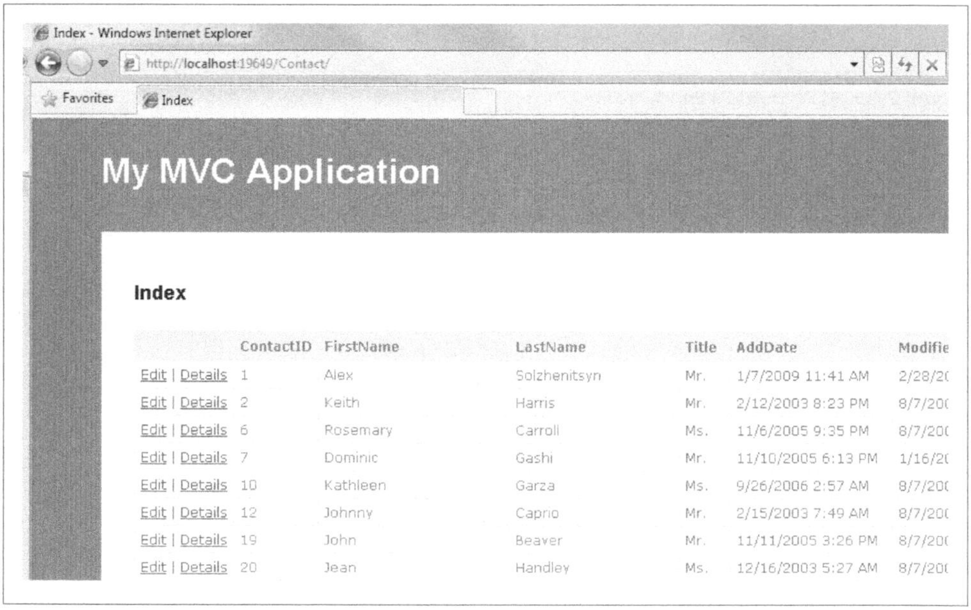

Figure 27-11. An unadorned Index view of Contact entities

Next, you can provide some data to be returned in the Details view. The controller has a method that will be called when the user clicks on Details, shown in Example 27-16.

Example 27-16. The default code in a Details action

```
public ActionResult Details(int id)
{
  return View();
}
```

The Index page will have MVC call the `Controller's Details` method when you click on the Details link.

Right-click on the method and add a new Details view. Then give the method some code to return the selected `Contact`, as in Example 27-17.

Example 27-17. The Details action fleshed out with logic

```
public ActionResult Details(int id)
{
  using (context = new BAGA.BAEntities)
  {
    var contact = context.Contacts.SingleOrDefault(c => c.ContactID == id);
    return View(contact);
  }
}
```

Notice that this method instantiates the context again. This is a web application and the context will not stick around across postbacks. You have to create a new one on each call. This is important to keep in mind when dealing with inserts and updates, which you'll see when we switch to the more layered implementation.

And, with the default formatting, you can click on Details from the Index view and return a Details view of the selected contact, shown in Figure 27-12.

This works nicely and simply has logic separation thanks to the MVC pattern. There is no reliance on all of the mechanisms that Web Forms uses to emulate a stateful client application. But I find it deeply unsatisfying. The `Controller` interacts directly with the context, and as your solutions get more complex, this tight binding to the context and the entire set of classes exposed by it will make your life more difficult. Also, you have seen how much you can do directly with the Entity Framework to exert more control over its behavior. Do you really want to have to do all of that work directly in the controllers? That is not really the job of the controller.

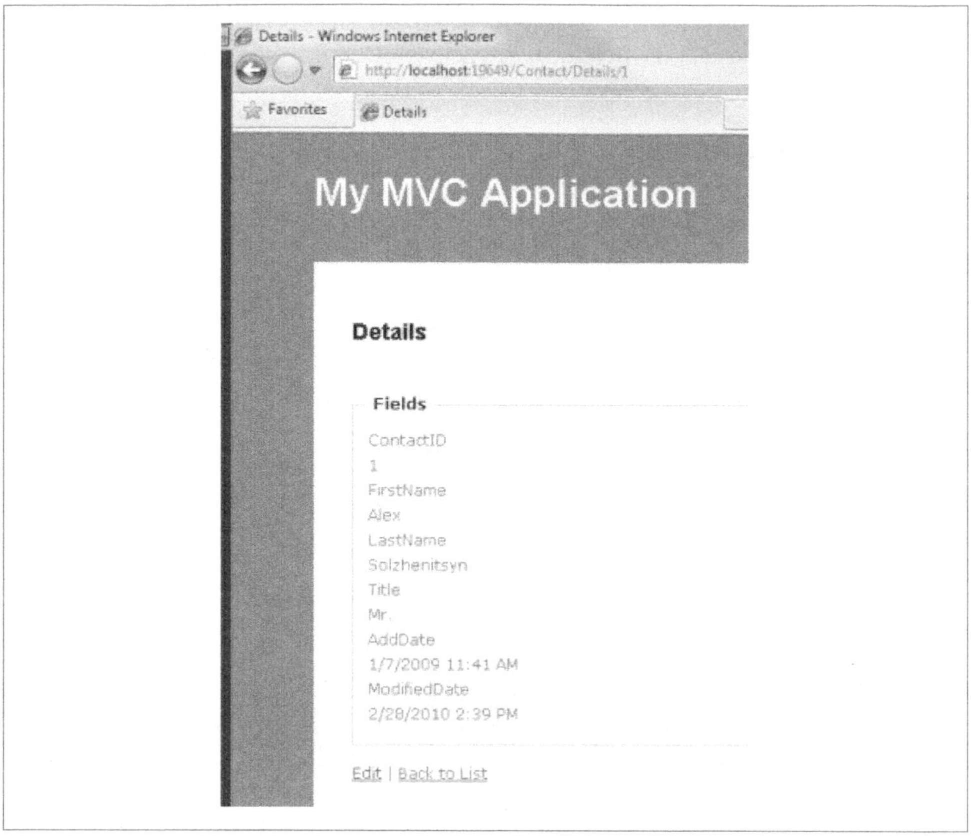

Figure 27-12. A simple Details view

> For those of you who are brand-new to MVC there are other controller actions and views. For example, you can create a view for editing, and then one controller method will return the view with the entity to be modified, and another controller method will capture a postback from that view and save data back to the database. Similarly, you can have a pair of methods to create an insert view and then capture the insert view's postback to save to the database. You can easily find many examples of all of this functionality, so I won't repeat it here.

You'll be much better off if you do not use the EDM and context directly as the MVC model. Instead, create models that are more focused on the needs of each domain. That way, the interaction between the controllers and those models can be simple and the complexities of interacting with the context and entities can be behind the models.

In Chapter 26, you built a layer that was suited for client applications, but it was not focused on being a one-layer-fits-all to be used in various architectures. That layer was designed to leverage a long-running context.

You could absolutely build one or more layers for your MVC model using `EntityObjects`, but I'm going to go down a different path here.The repository you used earlier in the Web Forms application is very well suited for use in an MVC application. You can bring the repository into this solution so that you can see the repository in action in MVC.

Replacing the Context with Repositories

There's not much to do to make the switch, which highlights the beauty of MVC. Remove the references to the BreakAway model and add references to the various projects created in Chapter 24, including:

- BreakAwayEntities
- Interfaces
- POCOState
- Repositories

Be sure to clean the solution and rebuild to make sure there are no references remaining to the previous model project.

You can also remove the reference to `System.Data.Entity` from the MvcApplication project since it is no longer bound to the Entity Framework.

With the references in place, it's simply a matter of modifying the code to use the repositories.

Note that I have added a `Contact` repository to my repositories:

```
public class ContactController : Controller
{
  private UnitOfWork uow = new UnitOfWork();
  private ContactRepository cRepository;

  public ActionResult Index()
  {
    cRepository = new ContactRepository(uow);
    return View(cRepository.All());
  }

  public ActionResult Details(int id)
  {
    cRepository = new ContactRepository(uow);
    return View(cRepository.GetById(id));
  }
```

`UnitOfWork` gets instantiated in the class declarations so that you don't have to repeat that call in each method.

You should consider making your repository classes implement `IDisposable`, which would allow you to not only dispose them but use them in a construct as you've done with the context in previous examples.

If you run your app again, the Index and Details pages work just as they did earlier.

Editing Entities and Graphs on an MVC Application

So far this MVC application is pretty simplistic. It is reading and displaying entities directly out of the store. Let's add some editing and graphs as well.

You should have not one, but two, `Edit ActionResult` methods in the controller. The first is similar to the `Details ActionResult`. It returns an `Edit` view of the selected contact.

Add a `View` to this controller method. Be sure to bind it to the `BAGA.Contact` and select Edit from the View content drop down so that the wizard will build an edit form for you. You can fill out the method so that it looks like Example 27-18.

Example 27-18. The Edit action method which returns an Edit View for Contact

```
public ActionResult Edit(int id)
{
  cRepository = new ContactRepository(uow);
  return View(cRepository.GetById(id));
}
```

One pattern you should pay attention to is that we are not storing the contact data across postbacks. Every method returns to the repository to get data. In this case, because the repository then goes to the database, it is hitting the database over and over to get the same record as the application performs various actions on the data. If you wanted to add in some type of caching mechanism, it would be the responsibility of the repository (or an additional layer behind the repository) to manage that, not the MVC application.

The second is marked with an `HttpPost` attribute. This handles the postback when the user submits the Edit view. This method takes the ID of the current entity and a `FormCollection` which will contain the values of the entity. You can also change the parameter to receive the data as the target entity and MVC will automatically create the new entity from the collection data. However, you can't do that with `Contact` because in the BreakAway model, `Contact` is an abstract class. You can create an overload to handle each of the derived types.

By default, the view will send those values back to the controller. It's your job to add in the logic to perform the update.

The initial method takes an MVC `FormCollection` as its parameter:

```
[HttpPost]
public ActionResult Edit(int id, FormCollection collection)
{
  try
  {
    returnRedirectToAction("Index");
  }
  catch
  {
    returnView();
  }
}
```

You can dig into the `FormCollection` to extract the values you need for updating the entity, or you can change the signature to accept the entity as an object. MVC will create the object for you.

Now there's a little hiccup to deal with. As mentioned earlier, you won't be able to instantiate the abstract `Contact` class. Since I'm unconcerned with the properties of the `Customer` derivative of `Contact`, I'll just use the `NonCustomer` type instead in the method displayed in Example 27-19.

Example 27-19. The Edit action which responds to a postback from the Edit view

```
[HttpPost]
public ActionResult Edit(int id, NonCustomer contact)
{
  try
  {
    _cRepository = new ContactRepository(_uow);
    _cRepository.Attach(contact);
    _uow.Save();
    return RedirectToAction("Index");
  }
  catch
  {
      return View(contact);
  }
}
```

This code uses the repository `Attach` method which, if you recall from Chapter 24, will `Attach` and then fix the state of the entity to be `Modified` so that `SaveChanges` will properly create the update command.

Now you can edit the contacts from your MVC application.

So far, all of this has been pretty simple thanks to the fact that the repository has been built already. The nice thing about the repositories is that not only do they not care about what the backend is, but they also don't care what the front end is.

As you learn more about working with MVC, you may leverage tricks such as creating master detail forms whether they are for data entry or not.

You won't find lots of master detail examples for MVC. The reason is that it's not a typical MVC pattern. Because of its stateless nature, MVC is generally used for working with explicit types per transaction. So in MVC, a more common master–detail scenario would have the master object on one page (e.g., reservations for a customer), then the user would click a link ("see payments for this reservation") to bring her to a separate page with the child details (payments for a single reservation).

But your clients don't necessarily think in the MVC pattern, and you may find yourself in a scenario where you need to not only display master details on a single page, but enable editing as well.

In addressing this, I will focus more on the controller interaction with the repositories than the views which involve a few tricks that use AJAX. You can download a full example from the book's website to see how all of the pieces fit together.

This app begins with a view that lists customers. Upon selecting a customer, you get to the view page displayed in Figure 27-13 which lists the customer's reservations. For each reservation, there is a link to display payments. Clicking the Payments link engages ASP.NET AJAX to display the payments in an MVC view control. As you will see in the code example to follow, ASP.NET AJAX provides the benefit of executing logic and rendering only a portion of a form while leaving the rest of the form's markup intact. This means that you don't have to worry about re-retrieving data displayed in other portions of the form.

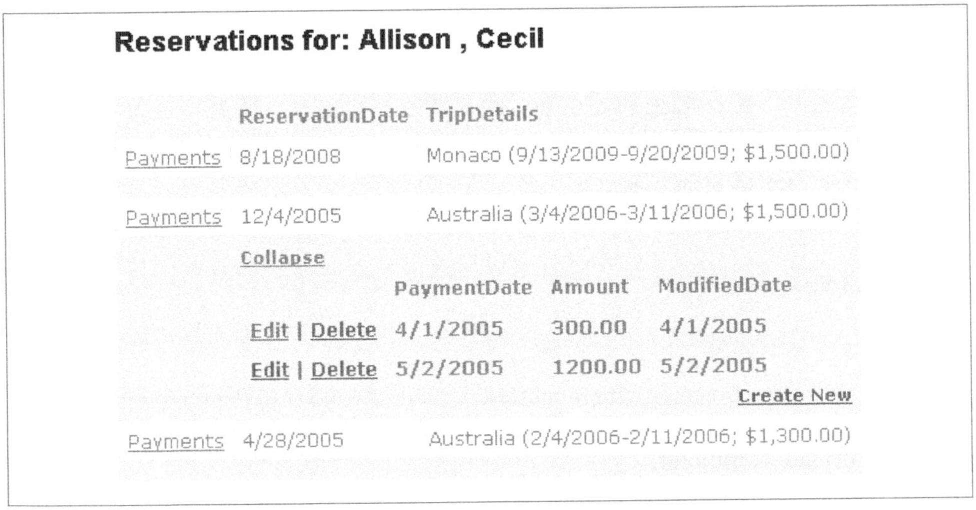

Reservations for: Allison , Cecil

	ReservationDate	TripDetails
Payments	8/18/2008	Monaco (9/13/2009-9/20/2009; $1,500.00)
Payments	12/4/2005	Australia (3/4/2006-3/11/2006; $1,500.00)

Collapse

	PaymentDate	Amount	ModifiedDate
Edit | Delete	4/1/2005	300.00	4/1/2005
Edit | Delete	5/2/2005	1200.00	5/2/2005

Create New

Payments	4/28/2005	Australia (2/4/2006-2/11/2006; $1,300.00)

Figure 27-13. A details view that uses AJAX to display and edit hierarchical data

Creating a Repository for Payments

The original set of repositories you created in Chapter 24 did not include a repository for payments. I've added a new `PaymentRepository` class which is similar to the others. It has one additional method to return the payments for a particular reservation. This method, shown in Example 27-20, mimics the `GetReservationsForCustomer` method of the `ReservationRepository`.

Example 27-20. The GetPaymentsForReservation method of PaymentRepository

```
public IList<Payment> GetPaymentsForReservation(int reservationId)
{
  if (reservationId.Value < 1)
  {
    throw new ArgumentOutOfRangeException();
  }
  return _context.Payments
        .Where(r => r.ReservationID == reservationId).ToList();
}
```

Interacting with the ReservationController

The application also has a controller for `Customers` and another for interacting with `Reservations` and `Payments`.

When the user selects the link to display the reservations for a particular customer, the link routes the request to an action in the `ReservationController`, passing in the identity key of the customer and the customer's name so that it can be displayed in the next page. The `ActionLink` is displayed in Example 27-21.

Example 27-21. Markup in the Customer view calling a view in a different controller

```
<%= Html.ActionLink("Reservations",
    "../Reservation/Index",
    new {customerId=item.ContactID,name=item.LastName + ", " +item.FirstName})
%>
```

The `ReservationController.Index` action shown in Example 27-22 uses the ID to query for the customer's reservations, places the list of reservations along with the customer name into a controller's `ViewData`, and returns the `Reservation`'s `View`. Because there is no incoming parameter, this `ViewData` will be used to construct the view.

Example 27-22. The Reservations index action retrieving multiple parameters

```
public ActionResult Index(int customerId,string name)
{
    _rRepository = new ReservationRepository(_uow);
    ViewData.Add("Model", _rRepository.GetReservationsForCustomer(customerId));
    ViewData.Add("custname", name);
    return View();
}
```

The ReservationController is also responsible for returning the reservation's payments through an action named ReservationPayments (see Example 27-23), which uses the PaymentRepository to provide its results.

Example 27-23. The ReservationPayments action of the ReservationRepository

```
public ActionResult ReservationPayments(int reservationId)
{
  _pRespository = new PaymentRepository(_uow);
  return View(_pRespository.GetPaymentsForReservation(reservationId));
}
```

In the Reservation View page, the AJAX method which responds to the user's request to see payments calls this action method and returns the results in the Payments view which is an *.ascx* control rather than an *.aspx* page. That way, the control can be used within the Reservation page.

The critical piece of the AJAX function calls the ReservationPayments, passing in the ID of the selected Reservation, and loads those results into an element defined elsewhere in the markup:

```
[element to display payments].load
 ('<%= Url.Action("ReservationPayments") %>',
   { ReservationId: this.id })
```

Because the action is named ReservationPayments, by default MVC will look for a view named ReservationPayments to return from the action. The *.ascx* control for displaying payments is named ReservationPayments, so that's what will be used.

You can also wire up the Edit, Delete, and New links to actions which let the user edit the payments. This might be done by routing to a PaymentController which returns explicit payment views and works further with the PaymentRepository.

There's so much more to learn about working with MVC, but you have now seen how you can ensure that the context is not part of the UI in this setup, whether you are working with one type at a time or multiple types as in the master–detail scenario.

Summary

In this chapter, you were able to put to use many of the lessons you learned in this book to see how Entity Framework can be used in more advanced enterprise web applications. While we didn't combine every feature of Entity Framework that you learned about in one example, the samples in this chapter deal with scenarios that provide numerous challenges. Thanks to the many enhancements in Entity Framework in .NET 4.0, such as POCO support, IObjectSet, and state management methods, we are able to design *n*-tier applications that use entities without too much difficulty.

While it would be much easier to design a Web Forms application with the `ObjectDataSource` controls, you will be constrained by the requirements of `ObjectDataSource`. Both the Web Forms example in the first half of this chapter and the ASP.NET MVC example in the second half took approaches that involve more manual labor, but give you more control over the design of your classes and application architecture. Both examples demonstrate solutions to the many problems you will encounter when building web applications with entities.

While I chose to use the previously built POCO repositories in both examples, this does not mean you can't do the same with `EntityObjects`. You have the tools you need to do this as well.

Don't forget the variety of additional functionality you learned about, such as measures to improve performance, capture exceptions, control transactions, and more.

APPENDIX A

Entity Framework Assemblies and Namespaces

This appendix will provide you with a high-level overview of the assemblies and namespaces of the Entity Framework. You will learn about the files that are used for the Entity Framework and the namespaces of the Entity Framework and their purpose.

Unpacking the Entity Framework Files

You'll find the physical DLL files that contain the Entity Framework APIs in the following directory:

- *<system drive>:\Program Files\Reference Assemblies\Microsoft\Framework\.NET-Framework\v4.0*, which contains:
  - —*System.Data.Entity.Design.dll*

    This file contains functionality related to the design tools, such as the Designer, the mapping details, and the model viewer.
  - —*System.Data.Entity.dll*

    This file is the root of the Entity Framework. It contains all of the namespaces and classes for programming against the Entity Data Model (EDM).

Exploring the Namespaces

The Entity Framework lives within the `System.Data` namespace of the .NET Framework. New functionality (classes, properties, and methods) has been added to existing namespaces in the `System.Data` hierarchy, along with a number of new namespaces that begin with the term *System.Data.Entity*. The *System.Data.Entity.dll* assembly provides all of the namespaces, as shown in Figure A-1.

Figure A-1. Namespaces provided in System.Data.Entity.dll

Existing Namespaces That Include Entity Framework Classes and Functionality

A number of existing namespaces have classes and functionality added to them to support the Entity Framework:

`System.Data`
: `System.Data` is the namespace in the .NET Framework that provides all of .NET's data access functionality. Some functionality is contained directly in `System.Data`, and much more exists in its subnamespaces.

  The Entity Framework adds `Exception` classes directly to this namespace, as well as `EntityKey`, which provides a durable reference to an entity.

`System.Data.Common`
: `System.Data.Common` provides base classes that are common to all of the data providers written for .NET. For example, `DbDataReader` is the base of `SqlDataReader`, `OleDbDataReader`, `OracleDataReader`, and more. The Entity Framework adds a few high-level `DbProvider` members into this namespace, along with `DataRecordInfo` to expose query results in the form of a `DbDataRecord` and `EntityRecordInfo` which provides access to the metadata of an entity.

`System.Data.SqlClient`
: The provider information that allows the ADO.NET Entity Framework to communicate with Microsoft SQL Server is added into the `System.Data.SqlClient` class through additional classes added into the `System.Data.Entity` assembly.

`System.Linq.Expressions`
: `System.Linq.Expressions` adds LINQ to Entities query functionality to the `System.Linq.Expressions` namespace.

Entity Framework-Specific Namespaces

All of the functionality that you will use directly or indirectly when working in the Entity Framework lives in the following namespaces:

`System.Data.Common.CommandTrees`
: `System.Data.Common.CommandTrees` adds logic for building Entity Framework command trees from LINQ to Entities and Entity SQL expressions. Each provider that is written to work with the Entity Framework will have the ability to turn these command trees into store queries.

`System.Data.Entity`
: `System.Data.Entity` does not contain any classes or methods; it is the base for a hierarchy of other namespaces—namely, `System.Data.Entity.Design` and `System.Data.Entity.Design.ASP.NET` (discussed shortly).

`System.Data.EntityClient`
: `System.Data.EntityClient` is a standard ADO.NET managed provider supporting access to the data described in the EDM. This namespace is comparable to `System.Data.SqlClient` or `System.Data.OracleClient` and provides classes such as `EntityConnection`, `EntityCommand`, and `EntityDataReader`.

`System.Data.Mapping`
: `System.Data.Mapping` provides logic for performing view generation from query expressions.

`System.Data.Metadata.Edm`
: `System.Data.Metadata.Edm` contains the types that are represented in the conceptual, mapping, and store schemas that define and support the EDM. Using these types directly, it is possible to programmatically work with the metadata of the model.

`System.Data.Objects`
: `System.Data.Objects` is the most important namespace in the Entity Framework. It provides the classes for querying, change tracking, relationship management, and updating the data store through the EDM. The functionality provided by `System.Data.Objects` and its child namespace, `DataClasses`, is referred to as "Object Services."

`System.Data.Objects.DataClasses`
: `System.Data.Objects.DataClasses` contains the classes and interfaces that allow types described in the EDM to be instantiated as objects. With these classes you can programmatically interact with the data that is provided as a result of querying the EDM.

`System.Linq.Expressions`
: `System.Linq.Expressions` adds the necessary expressions for performing LINQ to Entities queries.

`System.Data.Entity.Design`
: `System.Data.Entity.Design` provides functionality for generating an EDM as well as performing the code generation to create classes from the EDM.

`System.Data.Entity.Design.ASP.NET`
: `System.Data.Entity.Design.ASP.NET` provides the build providers used in the build environment for ASP.NET.

`System.Data.Query.InternalTrees`
: `System.Data.Query.InternalTrees` provides the tools for converting query expressions to command trees that are executed against the Entity Framework. This is very low-level and all of the members in this namespace are sealed.

`System.Data.Query.PlanCompiler`
: `System.Data.Query.PlanCompiler` is another namespace filled with low-level functionality for processing queries.

`System.Data.QueryResultAssembly`
: `System.Data.QueryResultAssembly`, the third subnamespace in `System.Data.Query`, is also low-level and sealed. When data is returned from the data store, it needs to be transformed into objects. This namespace contains the tools that are used internally to perform this transformation.

APPENDIX B

Data-Binding with Complex Types

In Chapter 14, you learned how to create complex types and use them to encapsulate properties in an entity. As an example, you temporarily encapsulated a number of properties (`Street1`, `Street2`, `City`, and `StateProvince`) of the `Address` entity into a complex type called `Mail`, as shown in Figure B-1.

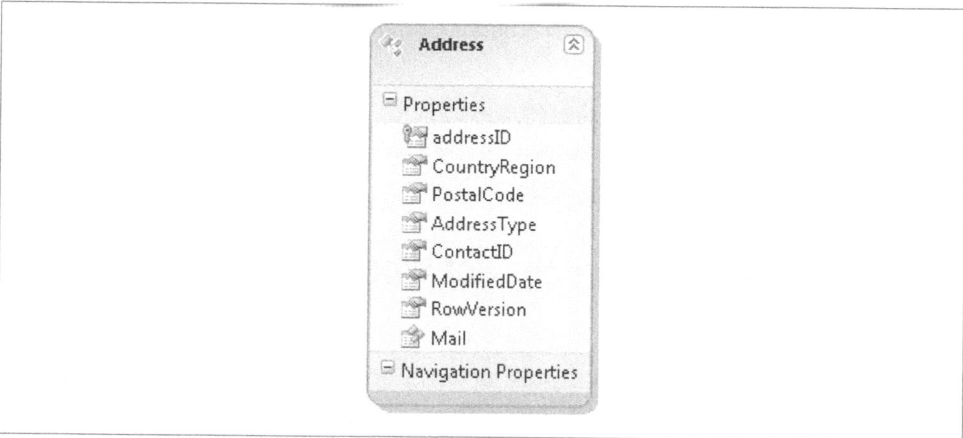

Figure B-1. The Address entity with its Mail complex property

The chapter looked briefly at data binding when an entity contains a complex type. Complex types may not behave the way you would expect them to in data binding. Therefore, this appendix will take a look at a number of specific data-binding scenarios that you may encounter in your applications.

Using Complex Types with ASP.NET EntityDataSource

When you use complex types with the `EntityDataSource`, the `EntityDataSource` "flattens" the properties within the complex type to make them easily accessible. When configuring the `EntityDataSource`, you will see the type, but not the properties.

However, when binding controls to the data source, the properties of the complex type appear as though they were simply properties of the parent type. You can see this in the screenshot in Figure B-2.

ModifiedDate	TimeStamp	Mail	Mail.Street1	Mail.Street2	Mail.City	Mail.StateProvince	Contact
12/3/2009 12:00:00 AM	abc	abc	abc	abc	abc	abc	abc
12/3/2009 12:00:00 AM	abc	abc	abc	abc	abc	abc	abc
12/3/2009 12:00:00 AM	abc	abc	abc	abc	abc	abc	abc

Figure B-2. The complex type properties automatically flattened

This flattening of the properties is a feature of the `EntityDataSource`, though it will occur only under specific conditions. For details, see the blog post "EntityDataSource: To wrap or not to wrap" by Diego Vega, EntityDataSource program manager at Microsoft (*http://blogs.msdn.com/b/diego/archive/2008/05/13/entitydatasource-to-wrap-or-not-to-wrap.aspx*).

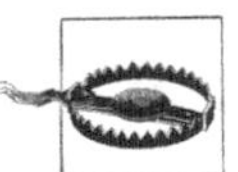

Be aware that Dynamic Data templates do not recognize complex types. Therefore, you will not be able to use complex types in a web application built with the Dynamic Data controls.

Identifying Unexpected Behavior When Binding Complex Types

Whether in ASP.NET, Windows Forms, or other applications, when you attempt to perform data binding against query results where complex types are involved without the aid of `DataSource` controls, you won't have such easy access to the properties.

For example, the following code in an ASP.NET page will fail, with a message saying that `Address` does not contain a property with the name `Mail.City`:

```
var addresses = context.Addresses.ToList();
dropDownList1.DataTextField = "Mail.City";
dropDownList1.DataValueField = "addressID";
dropDownList1.DataSource = addresses;
dropDownList1.DataBind();
```

Attempting a similar binding to a `ComboBox` in a Windows form will have a different effect. In the following code, the `addressID` will be displayed in the drop-down list, rather than the `ComplexType` property that is used for `DisplayMember`:

```
var addresses = context.Addresses.ToList();
comboBox1.DataSource = addresses;
```

```
comboBox1.DisplayMember = "Mail.City";
comboBox1.ValueMember = "addressID";
```

Yet, if you were to debug into the results of the query and request the properties from the complex type, you would see that they are definitely available, just not for these data-binding scenarios.

In a Windows form, if you bound the results of a query programmatically, such as in the following code:

```
dataGridView1.DataSource = context.Addresses.ToList();
```

the `Mail` property would be represented incorrectly as a single column.

You'll get the same effect even if you create a Windows Forms `DataSource` and bind to that.

Even if you explicitly bind properties to the columns in this way:

```
DataGridView1.Columns[1].DataPropertyName = "Mail.Street1";
```

the binding will fail, with the columns that result being empty.

So, how can you get at these properties in these scenarios? The following sections will provide some patterns.

Successfully Using Binding to Complex Types in ASP.NET Without Data Source Controls

With ASP.NET, you have three paths to follow: list controls, data-bound controls, and templated controls. With each, you will need to take a different route for using a complex type.

List controls

`DropDownList` is not actually a data-bound control. It is a list web server control. Other controls in the category are `ListBox`, `CheckBoxList`, `RadioButtonList`, and `BulletedList`.

Instead of returning the objects that contain complex types (which can't be displayed), your best bet is to use projections to flatten the properties yourself. As an example, here is a LINQ query that returns a list of distinct cities. You can bind this to a drop-down list and, upon selection, query for contacts from the selected city:

```
var uniqueCities =
   (from a in context.Addresses select a.Mail.City)
   .Distinct().ToList();
DropDownList1.DataSource = uniqueCities;
DropDownList1.DataBind();
```

Data-bound controls

GridView and FormView are bound controls and have the same limitation as list controls. If you are not able to use the EntityDataSource, you will need to do projection to flatten the ComplexType properties. With projection, you lose your ability to do updating, so you may want to consider the EntityDataSource for this scenario.

Templated controls

With templated controls, such as ListView, you can access the ComplexType properties using inline script.

Reverting back to the query:

```
context.Addresses.ToList()
```

you can bind directly to the results with the following markup in a ListView (see Example B-1).

Example B-1. Formatting the markup of a ListView to display complex type properties

```
<asp:ListView runat="server" ID="ListView1">
  <LayoutTemplate>
    <table runat="server" id="table1" >
      <tr runat="server" id="itemPlaceholder" ></tr>
    </table>
  </LayoutTemplate>
  <ItemTemplate>
    <tr runat="server">
      <td id="Td1" runat="server">
        <%-- Data-bound content. --%>
        <asp:Label ID="NameLabel" runat="server"
          Text='<%#Eval("Mail.Street1") %>' />
      </td>
      <td id="Td2" runat="server">
        <%-- Data-bound content. --%>
        <asp:Label ID="Label1" runat="server"
          Text='<%#Eval("Mail.City") %>' />
      </td>
    </tr>
  </ItemTemplate>
</asp:ListView>
```

Windows Forms DataSource and Complex Types

Like the EntityDataSource, data sources in Windows Forms let you work fairly easily with entities and their properties that are complex types.

Figure B-3 shows an Object data source created from the revised Address entity.

You can use the complex type in a Windows form, which is displayed and updated along with the rest of the entity. You can see in the simple form shown in Figure B-4 that the complex type properties blend in as though they were scalar properties of

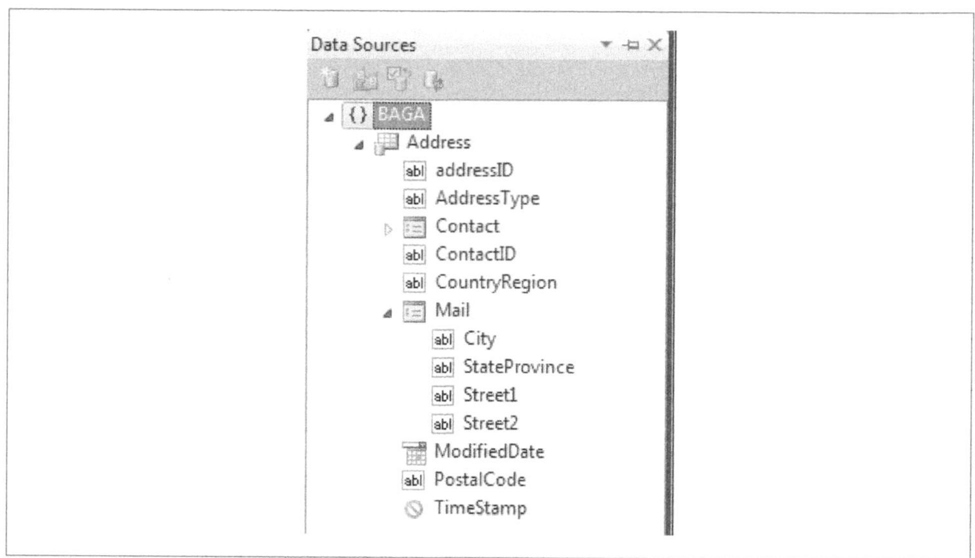

Figure B-3. Windows Forms data source reading complex type properties such as the Mail property of Address

`Address`. The fields displayed are the result of dragging the Address data source onto the form prior to doing any UI clean-up.

Example B-2 demonstrates that with the binding source, you won't need to make any special accommodations to work with the complex type.

Example B-2. Querying for entities with a complex type—which is no different from entities without a complex type

```
public partial class Form1 : Form
{
  BAEntities _context;
  public Form1()
  {
    InitializeComponent();
  }

  private void Form1_Load(object sender, EventArgs e)
  {
  _context = new BAEntities();
  var query = from a in _context.Addresses select a;
  addressBindingSource.DataSource = query;
  }

  private void addressBindingNavigatorSaveItem_Click
   (object sender, EventArgs e)
  {
    _context.SaveChanges();
  }
}
```

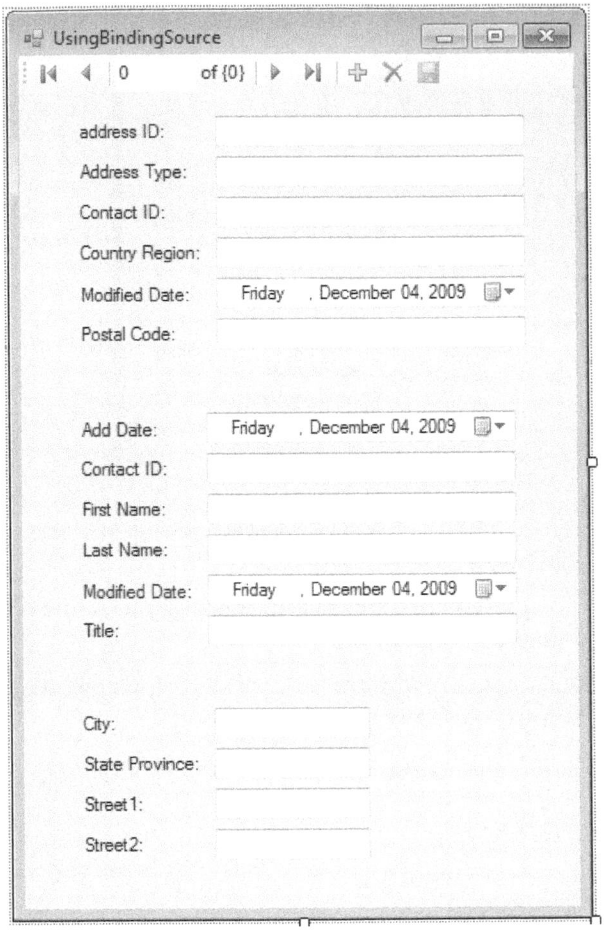

Figure B-4. The Mail complex type provided among the default fields of the Address data source

APPENDIX C

Additional Details About Entity Data Model Metadata

In Chapter 2, you created your first Entity Data Model and inspected it in the Entity Data Model Designer as well as looking at the raw XML.

There are some portions of the metadata that you might never need to work with and they were not included in that chapter. Those details are listed in this appendix in case you have a need for them.

Seeing EDMX Schema Validation in Action

The EDMX file leverages schema files for validation. To see a schema's rules in action, try editing the XML manually. For example, start entering a new `<Property>` element inside the `Address EntityType`. IntelliSense will provide a list of options within the property. Alternatively, you can intentionally break something! For example, change the spelling of an element name—perhaps change `EntityType` to `ElephantType`. The XML will provide visual clues to indicate that something is amiss, and the Errors List will list warnings regarding any invalid elements. Don't forget to undo these changes!

Additional Conceptual Model Details

Schema

The outer element, `Schema`, defines the name of the entire model's namespace, which in this case is `SampleModel`. The namespace is defined by default to have the name of the database from which the model is derived, plus the word *Model*. The schema also defines an `Alias`, which by default is `Self`. This is just a nickname for the model and you can name it anything you like. There is also an `xmlns` namespace URI, which defines the origin of Microsoft's schema file.

You can also see and modify the model's namespace in the model's Properties window when the model is open in Design view.

XML Representation of an Association

Example C-1 shows the XML for the model's `FK_Address_Contact` association, which provides the same elements as you see in the Properties window displayed in Figure 2-13 in Chapter 2. The only difference is that in the XML, the `Contact` and `Address` types are strongly typed—for example, `SampleModel.Address`.

Example C-1. The association between Contact and Address

```
<Association Name="FK_Address_Contact">
  <End Role="Contact" Type="SampleModel.Contact" Multiplicity="1">
    <OnDelete Action="Cascade" />
  </End>
  <End Role="Address" Type="SampleModel.Address" Multiplicity="*" />
  <ReferentialConstraint>
    <Principal Role="Contact">
      <PropertyRef Name="ContactID" />
    </Principal>
    <Dependent Role="Address">
      <PropertyRef Name="ContactID" />
    </Dependent>
  </ReferentialConstraint>
</Association>
```

AssociationSet

Along with `EntitySets`, the `EntityContainer` contains `AssociationSets`. Just as the `EntitySet` is a container for entity types, the `AssociationSet` is a container for an association. Therefore, it should not surprise you to see that the association in the following code snippet is a container for the `FK_Address_Contact` association:

```
<AssociationSet Name="FK_Address_Contact"
                Association="SampleModel.FK_Address_Contact">
  <End EntitySet="Contacts" Role="Contact" />
  <End EntitySet="Addresses" Role="Address" />
</AssociationSet>
```

Although it makes sense to have a container for an entity because you could have many contact entities to work with, how would there be a collection of associations? If you have a single contact with multiple addresses in memory, there would be one `FK_Address_Contact` association object for each relationship. How the associations are realized depends on whether you have foreign keys in your entities. Figure C-1 shows two association objects that are used to define relationships between a single contact and two addresses.

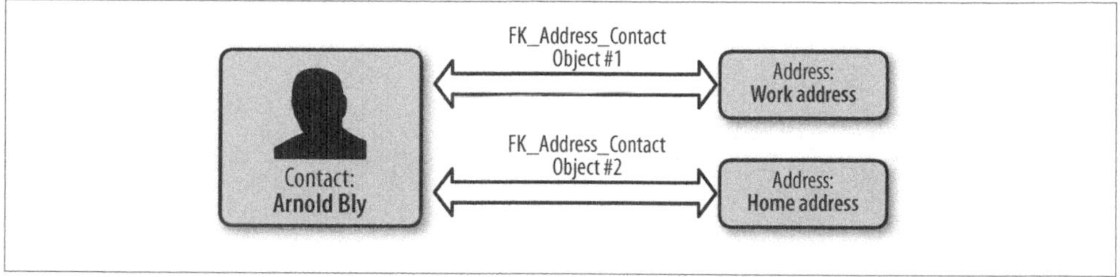

Figure C-1. Two association objects defining relationships between a single contact and two addresses

Notice that the XML description of the `AssociationSet` binds each endpoint of the association (by referencing the role) to the `EntitySet`. This now creates a thread through the model so that the APIs will be able to move through an `EntitySet` and discover various entities that are related to each other.

When I first realized how the role was being used in the `AssociationSet` metadata, something finally clicked for me and I was able to see the big picture of the model. It was almost as though the last piece of the puzzle had just been put into place and I could see the clear image for the first time.

Additional SSDL Metadata Details

SSDL Association and AssociationSet Elements

You've seen the `Association` and `AssociationSet` elements in the CSDL, but they exist in the SSDL as well.

In Example C-2, the SSDL `Association` and `AssociationSet` have been expanded and you can see a pattern that is similar to that of their CSDL counterparts. The `Association` description displays how the database defines the primary key/foreign key relationship between `Contact` and `Address`.

Example C-2. SSDL Association and AssociationSet

```
<Association Name="FK_Address_Contact">
  <End Role="Contact" Type="SampleModel.Store.Contact"
       Multiplicity="1">
    <OnDelete Action="Cascade" />
  </End>
  <End Role="Address" Type="SampleModel.Store.Address"
       Multiplicity="*" />
  <ReferentialConstraint>
    <Principal Role="Contact">
      <PropertyRef Name="ContactID" />
    </Principal>
    <Dependent Role="Address">
      <PropertyRef Name="ContactID" />
```

```
    </Dependent>
  </ReferentialConstraint>
</Association>

<AssociationSet Name="FK_Address_Contact"
         Association="SampleModel.Store.FK_Address_Contact">
  <End Role="Contact" EntitySet="Contact" />
  <End Role="Address" EntitySet="Address" />
</AssociationSet>
```

The generic term *Association* in the SSDL is referring to the relationship defined in the database. Figure C-2 shows the origin of this in the database's `Address` table.

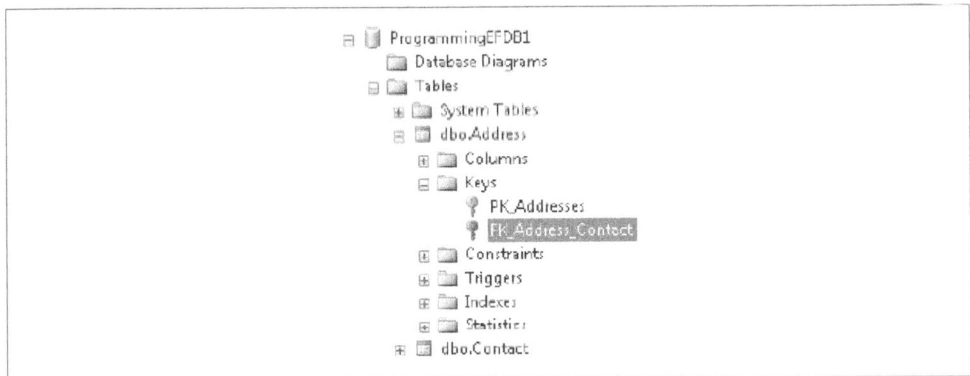

Figure C-2. The primary key/foreign key relationship between Address and Contact in the database

The Entity Data Model Wizard infers an `AssociationSet` for each SSDL `Association`. Each SSDL `AssociationSet`, like its CSDL counterpart, acts as a wrapper for an `Association`.

The first version of Entity Framework did not support building associations using foreign key scalar properties in an entity. Instead, you built independent associations with mappings that depended on the SSDL `AssociationSets`. Although foreign key associations are the default in Visual Studio 2010, it is still possible to define independent associations or use ones that are brought forward from an application built with Visual Studio 2008 SP1.

ReferentialConstraint

The `ReferentialConstraint` element is similar to its CSDL counterpart. It specifies the direction of the relationship between the tables in the database using the `Principal` and `Dependent` role elements. In the example, `Address` is dependent upon `Contact`. This also translates to defining the primary key/foreign key relationship. If you have chosen to build a model that does not incorporate foreign keys, the SSDL `ReferentialConstraint` plays a critical role in defining the associations at the model level. You learned more about this alternative in Chapter 19. Finally, we see the foreign key in the `Address` table identified: it is the `ContactID`.

The last purpose of the `ReferentialConstraint` element is to stipulate that a row in the `Address` table cannot exist without a reference to a row in the `Contact` table. This rule exists in the database, but because of the `ReferentialConstraint`, the Entity Framework will also check this rule. The Entity Framework APIs will check to see whether the data passes this rule before any attempt is made to send the data to the database. If your code creates an address without associating it with a person and then tries to save this change to the database, the data will fail the constraint check. The check happens when the code attempts to save changes back to the database.

Other rules and constraints in the database can be described in the store schema, such as noting whether the database will perform a cascading delete. Don't confuse this with the `CascadeDelete` which you can define in the conceptual model to affect in-memory objects.

Additional MSL Metadata Details

To explore the XML representation of the `Contact` entity mappings described in Chapter 2, open the `SampleModel` in the XML Editor again and expand the `<edmx:Mappings>` section; you'll see that there is one big difference in how the mapping is described under the covers. The mapping, as shown in Example C-3, is being made from the `Entity Set`, not the actual entity. When you add inherited types into the mix, you may also be mapping `Customer` entities which are a type of `Contact`. When you map the `EntitySet` you cover all of the entity types in an inheritance hierarchy. Therefore, the mapping needs to be done to the `EntitySet`, not a specific entity.

Example C-3. The XML view of the Contact entity mapping to the Contact table

```
<edmx:Mappings>
  <Mapping Space="C-S" xmlns="http://schemas.microsoft.com/ado/2008/09/mapping/cs">
    <EntityContainerMapping
      StorageEntityContainer="ProgrammingEFDB1ModelStoreContainer"
      CdmEntityContainer="SampleEntities">
      <EntitySetMapping Name="Contacts">
        <EntityTypeMapping TypeName="SampleModel.Contact">
          <MappingFragment StoreEntitySet="Contact">
            <ScalarProperty Name="ContactID" ColumnName="ContactID" />
            <ScalarProperty Name="FirstName" ColumnName="FirstName" />
            <ScalarProperty Name="LastName" ColumnName="LastName" />
            <ScalarProperty Name="Title" ColumnName="Title" />
            <ScalarProperty Name="AddDate" ColumnName="AddDate" />
            <ScalarProperty Name="ModifiedDate" ColumnName="ModifiedDate" />
          </MappingFragment>
        </EntityTypeMapping>
      </EntitySetMapping>
      ... additional EntitySetMapping elements
    </EntityContainerMapping>
  </Mapping>
</edmx:Mappings>
```

The MSL Elements

Let's back up a bit and take a look at the `Mappings` section before drilling deeper into the mapping for the `Contact` entity.

We've inspected the CSDL and SSDL already, so you'll notice that the MSL has elements that look familiar, though they are specific to mapping.

Mapping

The first thing to notice in Example C-3 is that the parent element isn't a `Schema` but a `Mapping`, with its own `xml` namespace and a `Space` attribute of `C-S`, telling you that it is mapping from C (the conceptual layer) to S (the store layer).

You'll find that when discussing mapping, authors and presenters will sometimes use the terms *C-side* and *S-side*. They are referring to the conceptual end of the mapping and the store end of the mapping, respectively.

EntityContainerMapping

All of the mappings are within the `EntityContainerMapping` element. This element describes which SSDL and CSDL will be used for the mapping by identifying the same container names that the SSDL and CSDL listed previously: `SampleModelStoreContainer` and `SampleEntities`.

Next, the mappings are grouped by `EntitySet`. Because this is a very simple model, the mappings are easy to read.

EntitySetMapping

You had a look at the `EntitySetMapping` already. Its elements are described as follows.

EntityTypeMapping. The mapping for each `EntityType` is defined in an `EntityTypeMapping` element that defines which `EntityType` is being mapped. There is an additional attribute not seen in this example, `IsTypeOf()`, which takes the fully qualified name of the type. `IsTypeOf` is a .NET Framework method. In this particular example, `IsTypeOf` is not required. Chapter 14 provided examples of entity inheritance and showed how `IsTypeOf` can impact the meaning of mappings.

MappingFragment. The `EntityType` mapping element contains a `MappingFragment`. This doesn't seem logical with our example, but as you saw in Chapter 12, it is possible to do something called *entity splitting* whereby one entity is composed of properties that map to columns in multiple tables. In that case, each table that you are mapping to will be represented within a single `MappingFragment`. The `StoreEntitySet` refers to the `EntitySet` for the table listed in the SSDL.

ScalarProperty. The `ScalarProperty` mappings map the property name of the entity type in the CSDL to the column name of the table. In the case of our simple model, the property names and the field names are identical, which makes this particular mapping pretty straightforward.

AssociationSetMapping

This model does not have `AssociationSetMapping` elements. These are used in models which do not include foreign keys. When the foreign key is not available in the entity, the model needs a way to define how one entity is connected to another. To enable backward compatibility with models from the first version of Entity Framework, you can choose between association mappings or model-level referential constraints when the relationship defines a primary-key-to-primary-key relationship.

Index

A

We'd like to hear your suggestions for improving our indexes. Send email to *index@oreilly.com*.

D

E

F

G

H

I

J

K

L

M

N

O

P

Q

R

S

T

U

V

W

X

About the Author

Julia Lerman is the leading independent authority on the Entity Framework and has been using and teaching the technology since its inception in 2006. She is well known in the .NET community as a Microsoft MVP, ASPInsider, and INETA Speaker. Julie is a frequent presenter at technical conferences around the world and writes articles for many well-known technical publications, including the Data Points column in *MSDN Magazine*.

Julie lives in Vermont with her husband, Rich, and gigantic dog, Sampson, where she runs the Vermont.NET User Group. You can read her blog at *http://thedatafarm.com/blog/* and follow her on Twitter @julielerman.

Colophon

The animal on the cover of *Programming Entity Framework* is a Seychelles blue pigeon (*Alectroenas pulcherrima*). Also known as a Seychelles blue fruit dove, this medium-size pigeon is approximately 10 inches long and inhabits the woodlands of the Seychelles archipelago. Its wings, underbody, and tail are dark blue, while its head and breast are a silvery-gray or a pale blue. It has a characteristic patch of crimson skin that runs from its forehead to its crown. Its diet consists mostly of fruit.

The cover image is from *Riverside Natural History* vol. IV. The cover font is Adobe ITC Garamond. The text font is Linotype Birka; the heading font is Adobe Myriad Condensed; and the code font is LucasFont's TheSansMonoCondensed.

CPSIA information can be obtained at www.ICGtesting.com
Printed in the USA
BVOW101155040313

314658BV00008B/75/P